Gott loben, segnen, verkündigen

Gott loben, segnen, verkündigen

75 Jahre Dominikanerprovinz des hl. Albert in Süddeutschland und Österreich

Herausgegeben von Wolfram Hoyer OP

HERDER

FREIBURG · BASEL · WIEN

Gedruckt mit Unterstützung durch die Capa –
Gemeinnützige Gesellschaft zur Förderung dominikanischer Ordenstätigkeit mbH.

FSC www.fsc.org
MIX
Papier aus verantwortungsvollen Quellen
FSC® C106847

Originalausgabe

www.herder.de

Umschlaggestaltung: Christian Langohr, Freiburg
Umschlagmotiv: Gotischer Doppelfensterbogen aus dem 13. Jh., Dominikanerkloster Wien
(Foto: Adam Rokosz, Wien)

Satz: Barbara Herrmann, Freiburg
Herstellung: fgb · freiburger graphische betriebe
www.fgb.de

Printed in Germany
ISBN 978-3-451-33336-1

Inhalt

RÜCKBLICK

Grußwort des Meisters des Ordens der Predigerbrüder

P. Fr. Bruno Cadoré OP

Seit dem Advent 2005 bereitet die Dominikanische Familie weltweit den 800. Jahrestag der päpstlichen Bestätigung des Predigerordens vor, der 2016 stattfinden wird. Tatsächlich war die Gründung unseres Ordens kein einzelner Akt, sondern ein über ein Jahrzehnt dauernder Prozess, beginnend mit der Übernahme einer Predigtmission durch Bischof Diego von Osma und seinen Begleiter Dominikus 1206 in Montpellier. Im selben Jahr schufen sie in Prouilhe bei Carcassonne in Südfrankreich das erste Frauenkloster ihrer Gemeinschaft. 1215 legte Petrus Seilhan die Profess in die Hände von Dominikus ab, als erster eigentlicher Predigerbruder. Im Sommer 1216 stellte Bischof Fulko von Toulouse den Brüdern die Kirche St. Romanus in der Stadt als erste Klosterkirche zur Verfügung. Am 22. Dezember 1216 erkannte Papst Honorius III. mit der Bulle „Religiosam Vitam" die Gemeinschaft als Orden der Kirche an.

Diesem Rechnung tragend, hat der Orden beschlossen, sich ein ganzes Jahrzehnt lang über seine Ursprünge Gedanken zu machen. Als Leitmotiv oder Überschrift dazu haben wir eine Aussage des hl. Paulus gewählt, von der wir glauben, dass sie die Absichten und Ereignisse einfängt, durch die unsere Ordensgemeinschaft begründet wurde: „Weh mir, wenn ich das Evangelium nicht verkünde!" (1 Kor 9, 16).

Für Euch, liebe Schwestern und Brüder in Süddeutschland und Österreich, steht 2014 die Erinnerung an die Errichtung eurer Provinz vor 75 Jahren an. Im Vergleich zu den bald acht Jahrhunderten, die unser Orden alt ist, scheint ein dreiviertel Jahrhundert unbedeutend zu sein. Dafür liegt uns Menschen so ein kurzer Zeitraum näher; manche unserer Zeitgenossen können sich daran sogar noch erinnern. Ganz gleich, ob es sich um das Jubiläum des Ordens oder um euer Jubiläum handelt: Bedeutung erlangt es nur, wenn wir es zum Anlass einer echten Rückbesinnung nützen, wenn wir also die Impulse der Gründungszeit als Anfragen an uns selber und unsere konkrete Gemeinschaft nehmen, wenn wir erkennen, was Dominikus oder die ersten eurer Brüder antrieb, wie sie ihr Ordensideal in ihrer Zeit umsetzten, die Fragen ihrer Zukunft beantworteten und die Schwierigkeiten meisterten, die sich ihnen in den Weg legten. Gerade hier

zeigt sich die Berechtigung des Jubiläumsmottos: Wehe uns, wenn wir die frohe Botschaft Jesu Christi nicht verkündigen! So, wie Dominikus zu seiner Zeit diesem Aufruf folgte, so, wie 1939 die Mitbrüder in Süddeutschland und Österreich versuchten, ihn in die Tat umzusetzen, so seid auch ihr gerufen, in unserem 21. Jahrhundert das Evangelium zu verkünden. Lasst mich hinzufügen: Wehe euch, wenn ihr es nicht tut!

Der Titel der Festschrift zu eurem Jubiläum lautet „Gott loben, segnen, verkündigen“. Das ist nichts anderes, als die Übersetzung des alten Ordensmottos „Laudare, Benedicere, Prædicare“. In ihm sind die drei wesentlichen Elemente unseres gemeinsamen Ideales gefasst: Wir wollen Gott im gemeinsamen und persönlichen Gebet und im Gottesdienst loben. Wir wollen uns dem Heil der Seele unserer Nächsten widmen – dafür wurde unser Orden als erster Seelsorgeorden der Kirche gegründet, wie es „Religiosam Vitam“ schon bestätigte – und zum Segen für die Menschen werden. Wir wollen die Wahrheit Gottes verstehen und sie durch unsere Verkündigung in die Welt tragen. Wehe uns, wenn wir das nicht tun!

Einer, der es sicher getan hat, ist euer Provinzpatron, der hl. Albert. Er wird zu Recht „der Große“ genannt, denn er war Beter, Philosoph, Theologe, Bischof, Friedensstifter, Lehrer und Prediger. Was ihn besonders auszeichnete, war, dass er die Wissenschaft seiner Zeit und den Glauben in Einklang zu bringen vermochte. Es ist kaum notwendig, ausdrücklich zu sagen, dass dies genau die Herausforderung ist, die wir als Orden heute zu bewältigen haben. So schließe ich mit den Worten des Tagesgebetes zum Fest des hl. Albert: „Gott, du Quell aller Weisheit, gib uns die Weite des Geistes des hl. Albert, damit der Fortschritt der Wissenschaft uns hilft, dich tiefer zu erkennen und dir näher zu kommen.“ Dies scheint mir ein unabdingbares Element unseres Verkündigungsauftrages heute zu sein: nicht nur zu belehren, sondern im gemeinsamen Gespräch mit denen, an die wir uns wenden, die Wirklichkeit Gottes zu erarbeiten. Wehe uns, wenn wir dies nicht tun!

Rom, am Tag des hl. Alberts des Großen, den 15. November 2013
fr. Bruno Cadoré OP
Ordensmeister

Grußwort des Provinzials der Ordensprovinz Teutonia

P. Fr. Johannes Bunnenberg

Mit 75 Jahren ist die süddeutsch-österreichische Provinz angesichts einer fast 800-jährigen Geschichte des Dominikanerordens eine recht junge Provinz. Aber sie hat alte Wurzeln. Zu ihr gehört mit Wien einer der wenigen Konvente weltweit, die seit dem Mittelalter eine durchgehende historische und bauliche Kontinuität aufweisen können. Sie erstreckt sich auf Orte und Regionen, in denen sehr früh (seit 1221) Gründungen des Ordens entstanden. Und auf ihrem heutigen Gebiet lebten bedeutende Heilige und Selige des Ordens wie der Mystiker Heinrich Seuse, der Glasmaler Jakob von Ulm und der Universalgelehrte Albertus Magnus.

Vom hl. Albert dem Großen, den die Provinz als Patron wählte, findet sich in der Wiener Konventsbibliothek ein Autograph. Und es existiert noch eine zweite „materielle Brücke" zwischen Albert und Wien: ein gotisches Doppelbogenfenster im Kreuzgang, das das Umschlagmotiv für den vorliegenden Band liefert. Es gehört zur Ausstattung des Kreuzgangs seit der Renovierung, die unter Albert als Provinzial (1254–1257) vorgenommen wurde, und ist eines der ältesten Zeugnisse gotischer Kunst in Ostösterreich. Insofern steht es für die innovativen Impulse, die Albert insgesamt auszeichnen. Eine seiner großen Leistungen ist ja die Aufnahme der Philosophie des Aristoteles in die theologische Reflexion, und nicht zufällig sprechen manche Wissenschaftler von einer ersten Aufklärung, die dadurch eingeleitet wurde. Das gotische Fenster ist dafür ein sprechendes Symbol: Es lässt das Licht der Schöpfung in den Raum des Klosters einfallen, und – andersherum betrachtet – ermöglicht es den Blick aus dem Innenraum in die Außenwelt. Zur gotischen Baukunst gehört, dass sie mit dem Licht spielt, dass sie Räume für eine zunehmende Individualisierung der Frömmigkeit schafft und dass sie mit ihren Gewölben in die Höhe strebt. Darin lassen sich zentrale Anliegen des hl. Albert wiedererkennen: den Glauben mit dem Licht der Vernunft zu durchdringen, eine „Kathedrale" zu bauen, in der Philosophie und Theologie zur Synthese kommen, Schöpfung und Heilsgeschichte gegenseitig zu beleuchten, profane und sakrale Wirklichkeit in Beziehung zu setzen. Ein Fenster ist eine Schnittstelle, dort berühren sich innen und außen. Vielfach war der hl. Albert genau an den Schnittstellen von Kirche und Gesellschaft,

von Theologie und anderen Wissenschaften tätig: Ihm lag an einer angemessenen Eigenständigkeit weltlicher Bereiche, an einer Ethik, die die konkreten Umstände und individuellen Situationen berücksichtigt, und er wirkte in seinen Vermittlungen zwischen geistlichen und weltlichen Instanzen, zwischen Bischöfen und Städten darauf hin, dass die Anliegen von Städten und Bürgern zu ihrem Recht kamen.

Dass der hl. Albert als Patron der süddeutsch-österreichischen Provinz gewählt wurde, hat sicher auch mit geographischer und historischer Nähe zu tun: Sein Geburtsort Lauingen und eine Reihe seiner späteren Wirkungsstätten (z. B. Regensburg und Würzburg) liegen auf dem Gebiet der Provinz; im früheren Kapitelssaal im Kreuzgang des ehemaligen Dominikanerklosters in Regensburg erinnert eine alte „Kathedra" an das dortige Wirken Alberts als Lektor.

Der hl. Albert ist zudem eine Gestalt, an der beide deutschsprachigen Provinzen Anteil haben. Sein Grab befindet sich in der St. Andreas-Kirche in Köln, die die Dominikaner betreuen; in Köln hat Albert ab 1248 das „Studium generale" aufgebaut, dort hat er seinen Lebensabend verbracht. Nicht nur sein Horizont, auch sein Wirkungsradius waren weit, und so kann er gut für das stehen, was die Dominikaner zwischen Hamburg und Wien, zwischen Berlin und Freiburg über Provinzgrenzen hinaus verbindet. Diese Gemeinsamkeit hat sich in den zurückliegenden 75 Jahren in vielfältiger Weise Ausdruck verschafft: Über Jahrzehnte hinweg schickte die Südprovinz ihre Novizen in den Noviziatskonvent der Teutonia ins westfälische Warburg; von Beginn an war die Philosophisch-Theologische Hochschule in Walberberg gemeinsamer Studienort, an dem auch Dozenten aus dem Süden tätig waren; die Provinz des hl. Albert beteiligte sich an der Mission auf Taiwan, und es gab immer Brüder, die im Bereich der jeweils anderen Provinz arbeiteten und lebten, manche wurden auch zu Oberen gewählt.

Indessen herrscht unter Brüdern nicht nur und nicht immer eitel Sonnenschein – weder in einer Familie noch im Orden. Es gab Streitpunkte, unterschiedliche Stile und Profile, Konkurrenzdenken. Manches ist zurückzuführen auf die Unterschiede in der Mentalität zwischen Nord und Süd, die Deutschland insgesamt kennzeichnen und sich von kulturellen Eigenheiten bis in die religiöse Praxis bemerkbar machen.

In den letzten Jahrzehnten hat sich eine wachsende Zusammenarbeit auf verschiedenen Ebenen entwickelt. Vor allem in der Aus- und Fortbildung gab und gibt es vielfache Berührungspunkte: Jedes Jahr findet eine

gemeinsame Studienwoche der Studenten statt; seit 2001 befindet sich in Worms der gemeinsame Noviziatskonvent; in Augsburg treffen sich einmal im Jahr Dominikanerinnen und Dominikaner aus dem deutschsprachigen Raum zum Arbeitskreis „Theologie und Verkündigung“; wissenschaftliche Arbeit in Instituten und in Veröffentlichungen übergreift die Provinzgrenzen; ebenso treten die Provinzen bei Katholikentagen und anderen Großveranstaltungen gemeinsam auf. Darüber hinaus ist es selbstverständlich, dass man Praktika und Studien in der anderen Provinz absolvieren kann, dass man sich besucht, dass man an wichtigen Ereignissen gegenseitig teilnimmt – von Professfeiern und Priesterweihen bis hin zu Jubiläen und Beerdigungen. So werden wir im Rahmen des 800-jährigen Ordensjubiläums auch überlegen, wie wir gemeinsam als Dominikaner in Deutschland in Erscheinung treten können.

Die Gründung der Provinz erfolgte 1939 unter schwierigsten politischen Bedingungen; das nationalsozialistische Regime bedrohte die Existenz der Orden. Heute sind die Herausforderungen anderer Art, und sie unterscheiden sich im Norden und Süden Deutschlands nur unwesentlich. Uns ist gemeinsam die Aufgabe gestellt, in einer säkular geprägten Umwelt nach Wegen zu einer überzeugenden Verkündigung des Evangeliums zu suchen, in Kultur und Gesellschaft als Denkende, Betende und Handelnde präsent zu sein und junge Menschen für unsere Lebensform zu gewinnen.

Zum Jubiläum wünsche ich der Provinz des hl. Albert in Süddeutschland und Österreich Kraft und Mut aus dem Glauben und aus dem reichen dominikanischen Erbe, das ihr gegeben ist und das Potential für die Zukunft enthält. Ich hoffe, dass wir in brüderlicher Nachbarschaft unsere Zusammenarbeit fortentwickeln und dass es uns gelingt, den Predigerorden im deutschsprachigen Raum in einladender Weise zu präsentieren.

fr. Johannes Bunnenberg OP
Provinzial der Dominikanerprovinz Teutonia

Grußwort des Provinzials der Ordensprovinz des hl. Albertus Magnus in Süddeutschland und Österreich

P. Fr. Christophe Holzer OP

Unsere Ordensprovinz wird 75 Jahre alt. In meiner Aufgabe als Provinzial bin ich recht häufig in unserem Provinzgebiet unterwegs, oft von einer unserer Niederlassungen zur nächsten. Und meistens nehme ich den Zug. Da fällt mir auf, wie gut die Zahl 75 zu unserer Provinz passt. Wenn ich die Eisenbahnkarte ausbreite und darauf die Orte mit den Konventen unserer Provinz suche, dann stelle ich fest: Von Wien nach München sind es mit dem Zug rund 6 mal 75 Kilometer. Und wenn ich nach Augsburg weiterfahre, kommen noch einmal knapp 75 Kilometer dazu. Von dort nach Freiburg im Breisgau sind es noch einmal ungefähr 5 mal 75 Kilometer. Sogar beim Blick nach Süden gilt dies, denn von Wien zu unserem erst neulich aufgelassenen Konvent in Graz sind es mit dem Zug, wie könnte es anders sein, nicht ganz 3 mal 75 Kilometer.

Der Orden der Predigerbrüder setzt sich aus den Provinzen zusammen, so sagt es uns die Nr. 252 unserer Satzungen. Und die Provinzen bestehen aus den Konventen und Häusern. Das steht dort im zweiten Satz. Die Provinz, gebildet aus den Konventen und Häusern, ist also der Lebensraum, in dem wir als Predigerbrüder unser dominikanisches Leben gestalten. Am greifbarsten in unserem Leben ist wohl der konkrete Konvent oder das Haus, in welchem wir leben. Da spielt sich der Alltag unseres Ordenslebens ab. Hier findet unser Gemeinschaftsleben seinen Ausdruck: das gemeinsame Beten, die Feier der Eucharistie, aber auch die Zeit im Refektorium, im Beichtstuhl oder hinter dem Schreibtisch. Das alles hat mit unserer Sendung als Ordensgemeinschaft für die Kirche und die Menschen zu tun. Gerade auch dann, wenn wir oft Dinge, die wir als Gemeinschaft tun, auch als Einzelne, von der Gemeinschaft Gesendete tun. So habe ich ganz bewusst unsere Arbeit im Beichtstuhl erwähnt. Hierzu gehören auch andere Formen von Gesprächsseelsorge, der Begleitung von Menschen in unterschiedlichen Situationen. Ein anderes Beispiel dafür ist die wissenschaftliche Arbeit in Lehre und Forschung. Als Predigerbrüder wissen wir um unseren gemeinsamen Auftrag für die Kirche, aber wir wollen ihn nicht in romantisierender Weise verklären.

Unser Lebensraum geht aber über die einzelne Niederlassung hinaus. Es soll einem nicht nur am Herzen liegen, was der Bruder in der gleichen Stadt, im gleichen Konvent tut und wie es ihm geht. Wir sind als Ordensprovinz in einen größeren Zusammenhang gestellt. Das ist eine Herausforderung, die uns gut tut und die wichtig ist. Natürlich ist der Weg von unserem Konvent in Wien zur nächsten Niederlassung der Gesellschaft Jesu kürzer als zu unserem Konvent in Freiburg im Breisgau, nämlich nur über die Straße und um eine Ecke, aber dennoch sind wir als Brüder in der gleichen Ordensprovinz ungleich stärker miteinander verbunden. Das Singen der Dominikus-Antiphon beim Abendgebet kann Ausdruck davon sein. Auch das Wissen, dass der nächste Einsatzort München, Augsburg, Freiburg oder Wien heißt, hilft uns, über den einzelnen Konvent hinaus miteinander verbunden zu sein und über den einzelnen Konvent hinaus zu denken. Die Provinz ist für unsere tägliche Erfahrung klar eine abstraktere Größe als der Konvent, aber die Tatsache, dass wir in einer Ordensprovinz zusammengehören, lehrt uns, über den Horizont hinauszuschauen.

Der Segen Gottes hat unsere Provinz des heiligen Albert in Süddeutschland und Österreich 75 Jahre hindurch begleitet und geleitet. Sicher, es mag Momente gegeben haben, in denen wir mehr Mitbrüder zählten und auch mehr Niederlassungen unser Eigen nennen durften, als wir es gegenwärtig tun. Wenn ich aber den Altersdurchschnitt unserer Provinz betrachte, der zum Beginn des Jahres 2014 weniger als 59 Jahre beträgt, dann erfüllt mich das mit Zuversicht und Freude.

Der Auftrag unseres Ordens, das Wort Gottes im persönlichen Gebet zu betrachten und das Betrachtete an die Menschen zu verkünden, gilt weiter. So hoffen wir gerne, dass wir noch lange die Kraft haben, das Wort Gottes aufrichtig zu den Menschen zu tragen.

Und übrigens, die Eisenbahndistanzen zwischen den Konventen ließen sich auch in Abschnitten von jeweils 150 Kilometern messen.

Augsburg, am Fest unseres Provinzpatrons,
des heiligen Albert des Großen 2013,
P. Christophe Holzer OP, Provinzial

DOMINIKANISCHE THEOLOGIE
UND PHILOSOPHIE

The Raison D'être of Oath

Michael Carragher OP

Recently there have been two monographs published in English on Oath, namely, one an Italian translation of Giorgio Agamben *The Sacrament of Language. An Archaeology of the Oath* (Homo Sacer 11,3)[1] and the other, Steve Sheppard *I do Solemnly Swear. The Moral Obligations of Legal Officials.*[2] Obviously bibliography and references to other literature would be of interest to those wishing to pursue an analysis of this topic. However, both books were found to be of limited value because of the stance taken by the respective authors. The Italian book focussed on the philosophy of language (as the back cover states) and the bibliography reflects that interest. Sheppard provides an overview of what his book is about in the Introduction: Seven Questions about What is Fit for an Official to Do. An apt quotation will demonstrate his perspective. "Officials see the law as a set of rules arising from an archive created by earlier acts of officials, interpreted and applied according to the culture of contemporary legal officials. Subjects see a host of signs in the law that are to an extent amorphous and to an extent the result of individuals acts, whether by identified individuals or by anonymous actors working through a corporate body."[3]

John Finnis confronts this quotation quite openly. He states that "no one ever can rationally treat a *fact alone* as giving reason for anything, let alone something as demanding and choice-restricting as law".[4] So much then for an archive! Indeed it is not the best chosen or illuminating metaphor. Archives are usually off-limits and require special permission to access them in addition to the supervision required to ensure that nothing is

1 Cambridge: Polity Press, 2011.

2 Cambridge: Cambridge University Press, 2009. However other books published around this time may contain sections or even chapters dedicated to this topic. For example, David Ibbetson *A Historical Introduction to the Law of Obligations* Oxford: Oxford University Press, 1999. However, it is not the intention of this article to review contemporary literature.

3 Ibidem page 4.

4 John Finnis *Philosophy of Law Collected Essays: Volume IV* Oxford: Oxford University Press, 2011, page 4. Italics in the original.

stolen or tampered with. This procedure contrasts sharply with the concept and reality of promulgation where everything is on public view and there are no restrictions on admission. However Finnis continues by posing and answering a relevant question bearing on this issue of law and officials.

> "What reason do I have as a citizen or judge for identifying certain utterances as now legally directive (for me or for anyone else), utterances made on some past occasion by an assembly styling itself constituent or legislative or a tribunal styling itself a superior court of record? The answer must, to make sense, refer to some basic good or goods (human need or needs) that will be promoted if I make the identification or prejudiced if I do not. And second, in no legal system responsive to human needs do citizens, judges, or other officials look to the bare social fact of a past legislative act or act of adjudication. Always that reference is to such acts in their intra-systemic context."[5]

Ibbetson provides a useful summary capturing the main contours of oath taking.[6]

> "This [oath-taking] would normally involve the recitation of words in a set form accompanied by some form of ritual gesture – for example placing one's (right) hand on a weapon, on a cross, on the bible, on a reliquary or on the bones of an ancestor, or simply holding the right hand with the thumb and the first two fingers extended (note omitted). ...In its typical form, it presupposed an external power, normally a god, by whom the swearer swore the oath; should the oath be broken, the god was called upon to impose punishment ... it followed from the fact that the oath created a relationship between the swearer and the god by whose name it was sworn, obliging the swearer to perform that it could be used not merely to strengthen undertakings of beneficence but also to strengthen maledictions."

Incidentally, this author Ibbetson uses the smaller case 'g' to denote god not the usual capital. Nicholas Thomas Wright explains his reason why he prefers god with a small 'g'. "It is to remind myself, as well as the reader, that in the first century, as increasingly in the twenty-first, the question is not whether we believe in 'God' (with it being assumed that we all know who or what that word refers to), but rather to wonder which god, out of then many available candidates, we might be talking about."[7]

---

5 Ibidem page 4. On page 5 Finnis elaborates this second reason.

6 Supra note 4 page 4 passim.

7 N. T. Wright *The Resurrection of the Son of God* London: SPCK, 2003, page xviii.

But as we are discussing canon 1199 of the Latin Code of Canon Law[8] the wider context is Christian revelation. In the Code itself the immediate context is Book Four which treats of the sanctifying function of the Church. There are two main and public ways in which we express our filial relationship with God one of which is the sacred liturgy which means primordially the sacraments especially participation in the Eucharist. Our chosen state of life will determine what other sacraments one wishes to receive. Sacraments are covered in Part One while Part Two covers the other acts of divine worship and the second way in which we express our filial relationship with God, for example, is in personal prayer either recited in the Divine Office (either publicly or privately) or private prayer carried out in a manner proper to each person's temper and disposition as night vigils are not suited for all and sundry. Those expressions of our devotion we can and should make use of as much as the other duties of our state in life will permit, e. g. weekly Mass, frequent use of the sacrament of reconciliation and daily prayer. There is no restriction on their use arising from the nature of the actions themselves.

There are, however, some other religious gestures which while also expressing our reverence for God are only to be used in certain conditions, so that outside those conditions they would cease to express that reverence. Two examples typical of such gestures are a vow and an oath. Both serve special purposes beside the general purpose of showing reverence for God, purposes that manifest themselves on singular occasions even though some may involve long term commitments such as joining the order of virgins, installation in an ecclesiastical office, while others treat of temporary undertakings, e. g. pilgrimages, daily Mass during the month of November for the holy souls or abstaining from alcohol beverages during the season of lent. Because of those determined purposes vows and oaths will occur much less frequently in our life.

A vow very briefly may be described as follows. It is a promise made to God in his honour regarding a possible and better good. We shall examine each of these elements singly. We express to another person our wish or intention of having something done for us by that person who is subject to our authority or direction – by a command – or who is not subject to our

8 *Code of Canon Law Latin-English Edition New English Translation* Prepared under the auspices of the Canon Law Society of America. Washington, DC, Canon Law Society of America, 1999.

authority – through a request or petition. We, on the other hand, intimate to another person our resolve of doing something for that person – through a promise. A promise involves an intention of doing something for another with the determination to carry out that intention, the committing of ourselves to it as well as the communication of that fact to the interested person. We give our word or pledge.

In the case of a command the obligation to execute our intention is placed on another; in a promise we impose the obligation on ourselves, we bind ourselves to do it. The fulfilment of a command is an exercise of the virtue of obedience; whereas the fulfilment of a promise is an exercise of the virtue of fidelity. Accordingly, if one makes a sincere promise but afterwards changes one's mind and does not carry it out, one is guilty of a sin against fidelity. But if the promise is insincere from the start it is in the same category as a lie or falsehood. Both insincere and broken promises may also involve a sin against injustice by reason of the harm done or loss the person to whom it was given suffers. The presumed beneficiary may have been put to a great deal of inconvenience, lose much time, even involve breaking commitments with other people as the result of the chain reaction of having relied upon the fulfilment of the initial promise. It is as if the beneficiary had been cheated out of something. For that reason if we do not intend to keep our promise or would think little of breaking it, it is obviously better not to make it at all, even though it might seem a very friendly gesture at the time.[9]

In human relations the outward expression of our intention is necessary in order to make known to the person whom it concerns. Otherwise he could not come to know of it. But the inner determination of our will to carry our intention is the more essential element and it is there that the

---

9 Robert Rowthorn "Marriage and Trust: some lessons from economics" *Cambridge Journal of Economics* 23 (1999) 661–691. "This paper examines the role of marriage as an institution for providing couples with the confidence to make long-term investments in their relationship. No-fault divorce has undermined the notion of marriage as a contract, thereby reducing the security offered by marriage and promoting opportunism by men. This has weakened the bargaining power of wives, both within marriage and when divorce occurs. Current legal reforms will improve the economic position of all divorced wives, including those who are primarily responsible for the breakdown of their marriage. The latter feature will encourage opportunism by women and make men less prepared to invest in their marriage. The paper argues that the only way to achieve parity between men and women, and deter opportunism by either sex, is to return to fault based divorce. Both divorce settlements and the custody of children should depend on preceding marital conduct."

value of the action lies. Besides making the interested party aware of our intention a promise would normally give it added force and stability in that we have now pledged ourselves, that is, given our word to another. And if our intention is good that fuller commitment of ourselves increases its goodness; for it is normally an indication of a firm and definite intention to express it to another. It is almost like entering a contract with that person to do what one promises. James Gordley[10] in his book *The Philosophical Origins of Modern Contract Doctrine* develops this issue exploiting the doctrine of St. Thomas.

A vow is a special sort of promise in that it is made to God alone about a possible and better good, even though in making it we may invoke Our Lady and the saints, or although we often make it to one who is God's representative. What Heuston states, writing about religious vows, is applicable to other types of vows.

> "All must love God and keep his commandments. The counsels of themselves do not make anyone good, but their observance makes it easier to keep the commandments. They are a means or a way to keep what is commanded. But they are not the only way; if they were they would no longer be of counsel but of strict precept. Indeed, for many they are not the best means, and for some they may even be a pitfall and a snare. For those to whom they are suited they cut at the root of the three great impediments to goodness – the concupiscence of the eyes, the concupiscence of the flesh, and the pride of life. The renunciation of possessions, the profession of chastity, the voluntary submission to others, prevent the consequences from getting out of hand – so long as they are practised."[11]

Just as in other religious gestures we do not express our intention outwardly in order to make God aware of it but because:

1) it is our natural or reasonable way of acting as human beings;
2) it strengthens our will's resolve by the extra force of our pledge;
3) it gives honour to God in that it expresses our earnestness and devotedness to him in his service, for not only do we give him the present deed but we also pledge to him to some extent our future deeds as well.

10 Oxford: Clarendon Press, 1991, page 11. See also Alain Supiot *Homo Juridicus. On the Anthropological Function of the Law.* Translated by Saskia Brown London: Verso, 2007, especially chapter 3, The Binding Force of the Word: *pacta sunt servanda*.

11 John M. Hueston OP "The Book of the Month. Follow me. The Three Vows of Religion Ascetically Canonically Considered" *The Irish Rosary* March 1942, pages 229–234 at 231.

Although those deeds are still to be carried out we already put them in his hands by our promise. As Heuston continues to say:

> "Vows are made to counteract man's fickleness. What today seems to us the only thing worthwhile tomorrow is dung. The vow makes one's decision irrevocable. What before was quite optional becomes obligatory so soon as it is promised to God. To this obligation the religious man can cling in the bad times when he is not himself; when he feels inclined to change he can remember that his mind was made up once for all long ago."[12]

To do something is his honour means that the content of the promise must be pleasing and acceptable to God. For that requirement to be realized a promise must be possible as far as one can humanly ascertain. It would be irreverent to promise God something we had no hope of being able to accomplish. We should not promise God that we will sponsor someone at university if we lack the financial resources to do so. If, through no fault of our own, the promised action or deed does turn out to be impossible then we are released from our obligation, e. g. we become unemployed or money becomes devalued. When what has been promised is only partially possible our obligation to do what we can depends on whether the content is divisible or not; e. g. a vow to give a hundred Euro to some charitable cause is divisible, a vow to go to Rome is not.

In addition, the promised content must be good either in itself (nourishment, alms, education, religious practice) or by reason of our good intention (participating in secular events to meet young people in order to share our faith). Normally something better or more than usual rather than something we are already bound to do or are in the habit of doing, e. g. a priest to say morning and evening prayer. Likewise, the promised deed should not be trivial but of some consequence, involving a considerable amount of sacrifice, e. g. to abstain from addictive substances rather than travelling by luxury coach to a well organized sanctuary. It is that eagerness to do more that is characteristic of a vow. It demonstrates our generosity to God's service and gives him honour. Finally the deed should be performed from free choice, i. e. not something we have to do naturally, e. g. eating or sleeping, nor something we have to do by external factors, e. g. relinquish the use of alcohol for health reasons because of its incompatibility with medicine prescribed by a medical doctor.

---

12 Ibidem page 231.

What are the advantages of making a promise or professing a vow? The general benefit of a promise or a vow is as a psychological means of strengthening one's will or resolve in the right direction by pledging ourselves to carry out some definite task or follow a definite course of action. By making our aim more definite and realistic it safeguards us from being too vague and abstract in our approach to others and even to God. That practice has the fortunate consequence that our commitments will be less rash and imprudent. The obligation is freely self-imposed.

In addition, the specific benefits of vows is they have religious overtones as one expresses devotedness to God and generosity to others for as Gordley says, when St. Thomas discusses the requirements for a promise to be binding "a party could perform either an act of liberality or an act of commutative justice".[13]

Having briefly discussed promise one should now analyse oaths.

What is the difference between promises (and vows) and oaths? John Finnis[14] describes what a promise is.

> "A certain set of facts affords an opportunity of answering to a standing need of the common good, the need for individuals to be able to make reliable arrangements with others for the determinate and lasting but flexible solution of co-ordination problems and more generally, for the realizing of the goods of individual self-constitution and of community. (Mutual trustworthiness is not merely a means to further distinct ends; it is it itself a valuable component of any common life)."

In harmony with this statement Elizabeth Anscombe writes:[15]

> "But if the procedure has the role of an instrument in people's attainment of so many of the goods of common life, the necessity that people should both actually adopt the procedure, i. e. often give undertakings; and also go along with the procedure, i. e. tend to accept the necessity expressed in that reaction also treat this as a *rule* – this necessity is a necessity of a quite different sort: it is the necessity that Aristotle spoke of, by which something is called necessary if without it good cannot be attained."

---

13 Ibidem page 10.

14 John Finnis *Natural Law and Natural Rights* Oxford: Clarendon Law Series, 2nd Edition 2011, page 306.

15 G. E. M. Anscombe *Ethics, Religion and Politics. Collected Philosophical Papers* Volume III Oxford: Basil Blackwell, 1981 especially chapter 2 "On Promising and it Justice, and whether it Need be Respected in the *Foro Interno*" pages 10–21 at pages 18–9.

It has already been stated that a vow is defined as a promise made to God for a better and possible good. An oath, on the contrary, is the invocation of the Divine Name as a witness when one asserts something as true or confirms that one will faithfully fulfil what one has promised. Thus there are two kinds of oath: assertory and promissory.

Although St Thomas Aquinas[16] treats of oaths comprehensively in ten articles our present interest lies only in examining the rationale of oath. He describes an oath as an external act of religion, whereby something Divine is appropriated by a human being and this is either a sacrament or the name of God. Sacraments enjoy their own philosophical, anthropological and theological integrity. A vast literature, past and present, is available. It is otherwise with oath. The name of God is taken by human beings in three ways.

1) by way of oath in order to confirm one's own assertion:
2) to adjure (to invoke the divine name in order to command or beseech another).
   a. Romans 12:1 "Think of God's mercy, my brothers, and worship him, *I beg you,* in a way that is worthy of thinking beings".
   b. Matthew 26:63. "And the high priest said to Jesus, 'I put you on oath by the living God to tell us if you are the Christ, the Son of God'".
3) by way of invocation for the purpose of prayer or praise.

Numbers 1 and 2 are relevant to our discussion. An oath is to swear, is to call God to witness either to confirm what has already happened or to strengthen one's promise by the invocation of a self curse.[17]

---

16 *Summa Theologiae* II-II, q. 89. Much of the following is indebted to that question.

17 David Ibbetson *A Historical Introduction to the Law of Obligations* Oxford: Oxford University Press, 1999, page 4: "In early medieval Europe, an individual who wished to take on a solemn obligation as to future behaviour would do so by means of an oath (note omitted). This would normally involve the recitation of words in a set form accompanied by some form of ritual gesture – for example placing one's (right) hand on a weapon, on a cross, on the bible, on a reliquary or on the bones of an ancestor, or simply holding up the right hand with the thumb and first two fingers extended (note omitted). The overtones of these symbolic acts were complex and wide-ranging, but the essential core of oath taking was relatively stable. In its typical form, it presupposed an external power, normally a god, by whom the swearer swore the oath; should the oath be broken, the god was called upon to impose punishment. Though oath ranked alongside murder in the hierarchy of wrongdoing (note omitted) it attracted no human sanction. Nor was there any sense in which the beneficiary of an oath was entitled to take steps to secure its performance. It followed from the fact that the oath created a relationship between the swearer and the god by whose name it was sworn, obliging the swearer to perform, but also to strengthen maledictions. In this context there was no difference between threats and prom-

Canon 1199: "An oath is the invocation of the divine name as witness to the truth. It cannot be taken except in truth, judgment, and justice".

1) Sometimes God is called to witness when we assert present or past events, and this is termed a "declaratory or assertive oath"; oaths are taken for the purpose of confirmation. An example can be found in canon 1532: "Unless a grave reason suggests otherwise, in cases in which the public good is at stake the judge is to administer to the parties an oath that they will tell the truth or at least that what they have said is the truth".

2) While sometimes God is called to witness in confirmation of something future, and this is termed a "promissory oath". Canon 1283 § 1° "Before administrators undertake their duties they must take an oath in the presence of the ordinary or his delegate, that they will well and truly perform their office".

Human witness does not suffice to confirm particular contingent facts for two reasons:

(a) human beings may be inclined to lie for reasons of expediency, fear or affection.

(b) on account of ignorance since humans can know neither the future, nor secret thoughts, nor distant events or places: and yet they presume to speak about such matters.

Indeed at times, our everyday life requires that we should have some certitude about the predictable behaviour of others. Hence the need to have recourse to a divine witness, for neither can God deceive (for that action would be incompatible with his holiness), nor is there anything hidden from him (for that would compromise his omnipotence). Now to call God to witness is termed *jurare* [to swear] because it is established as though it were a principle of law [*jure*] that what a human being asserts under the invocation of God as his witness should be accepted as true.[18]

---

ises: in neither was there any room for second thoughts if the swearer came to regret the oath." Note 12 refers to the following literature. "For the oath, see in general R. Verdier (ed.) *Le Serment* Paris, 1991. For its use in medieval Europe, centering on Germany, see L. Kolmer *Promissorische Eide im Mittelalter.* Kallmünz, 1989, esp. chapters 3 and 4."

18 R. H. Helmholz *The Oxford History of the Laws of England. Volume One: The Canon Law and Ecclesiastical Jurisdiction from 597 to the 1640s* Oxford: Oxford University Press, 2004, pp. 334–5. "Despite biblical injunctions that seemed to forbid the taking of oaths (e.g. Matt. 5:34), oaths became fixtures in the *ius comune.* In canon law, they became a source of contractual obligation, a basis for disciplining lawyers, and a protection against deceit by parties and witnesses. Oaths were relied upon, despite the evident dangers of

Canon 1199 states that there are three accompanying conditions of an oath as the prophet Jeremiah wrote (4:2):

justice,
judgment, (discretion, prudence)
and truth.

What is a reasonable use of oath? Two conditions are required for the sound employment of an oath, namely, firstly, that one would swear, not for trivial, but for substantial reasons (e. g. in a tribunal where someone is on trial), and with discretion (the assumption of an office) and this requires judgment or discretion on the part of the person who swears that he possesses the appropriate capacities and the intention to carry out his duties in conformity with the law.

Secondly, that the point of the oath to be confirmed by oath be neither false nor unlawful. This requirement demands one to employ an oath to confirm what is true and just so that what one confirms to be lawful. Evil deeds should have no place in the context of an oath or vow. Thus an impetuous oath lacks thought and consequently judgment whereas a false oath lacks truth and a wicked or unlawful oath lacks justice. After all, justice is the reason for swearing. Reading St. Mark's Gospel chapter 6 verses 14–29 provides a salutary warning about pronouncing vows and oaths without aforethought.

Whether it is lawful to swear?

It is a commonplace to state that if society is to function properly human beings need to be able to trust each other. An oath is a mechanism or instrument forged through experience to further that common enterprise of maintaining rapport with friends and strangers alike. If people believe in God then that belief is put to good use by uniting a person's relationship with the divinity, with others and with themselves. In other words personal integrity, civic friendship[19], and religious orthopraxis are inextricably entwined. Any change or compromise in one relationship will have repercus-

perjury they entailed, because the canonists concluded that without them it would be impossible to discover the truth (X 2.19.2). The English ecclesiastical courts followed that lead."

19 John M. Cooper *Reason and Emotion Essays on Ancient Moral Psychology and Ethical Theory* Princeton: Princeton University Press, 1999, Chapter Sixteen, Political Animals and Civic Friendship.

sions for the others. That is why something that is praiseworthy in itself may become a source of evil for one who misuses it as exemplified in the case of the reception of the Eucharist as St Paul writes: one who receives Holy Communion "unworthily, eats and drinks judgment to himself" (1 Cor. 11:29). St. Paul here was not so much concerned about ritual purity or liturgical rubrics as how one Christian was treating another even through the force of bad example. If there is no sharing of basic amenities such as nourishment then spiritual exhortation is empty. The Acts of the Apostles dramatizes this inconsistency so graphically in chapter 6 verse 1: "Now in these days when the disciples were increasing in number, the Hellenists murmured against the Hebrews because their widows were neglected in the daily distribution".

Self-knowledge coupled with the ability to cooperate with others are prerequisites for the invocation of an oath. Learning a language can only take place in society.[20] But the acquisition of a language is not a neutral activity but rather it is closely associated with communication which entails moral criteria.

An oath is in itself lawful and commendable. This is verified from its genesis and its purpose. From its origin, because swearing owes its introduction to the faith whereby a human being believes that God possesses unerring truth and universal knowledge and foresight of all things: and from its end, since oaths are employed in order to justify human beings, and to put an end to controversy (Heb. 6:16, "Men, of course, swear an oath by something greater than themselves, and between men, confirmation by an oath puts an end to all dispute").

Yet an oath becomes a source of evil to those that misuse it, that is, those who employ it without necessity and due caution. For if a human being calls God as witness, for some trivial reason, it would seemingly show him to have but little reverence for God, since he would not treat even a good person in this manner. St. Augustine states (*De Mendacio* xv), "that the Apostle Paul swore only when writing, because thought brings caution and avoids hasty words." Galatians 1:20, "And I swear before God that what I have written is the literal truth".

20 Deborah Levine Gera *Ancient Greek Ideas on Speech, Language and Civilization* Oxford: Oxford University Press, 2003. See also William A. Wallace OP *The Elements of Philosophy. A Compendium for Philosophers and Theologians* New York: Alba House St. Pauls, 1977, page 179.

There is great danger in swearing, both on account of the greatness of God who is called upon to bear witness, and on account of the frailty of the human tongue, the words of which are confirmed by oath. Whatsoever we do, we should do it in honour of God: wherefore there is no hindrance, if by intending to assure a human being, we show reverence to God.

Whether oaths are desirable and to be used frequently as something useful and good?

Augustine says (*De Mendacio* xv) that "the Lord forbade swearing, in order that for your own part you might not be fond of it, and take pleasure in seeking occasions of swearing, as though it were a good thing."

Whatever is required merely as a remedy for an infirmity or a defect, is not reckoned among those things that are desirable for their own sake, but among those that are necessary: this is clear in the case of medicine which is required as a remedy for sickness. Now an oath is required as a remedy to a defect, namely, some human being's lack of belief in another human being.[21] Even as a medicine is useful for healing, and yet, the stronger it is, the greater harm it does if it be taken unduly, so too an oath is useful indeed as a means of confirmation, yet the greater the reverence it demands the more dangerous it is, unless it be employed aright.

Whether an oath has a binding force?

It is written (Matt: 5:33): "You must not break your oaths, but you must fulfil your oaths to the Lord." Exodus 20:7 ("You shall not take the name of the Lord your God in vain; for the Lord will not hold him guiltless who takes his name in vain".)

An obligation implies something to be done or omitted. In the oath that is made about something to be done by us, the obligation focuses on the content of the oath that has been guaranteed by the action of the one who is swearing. For a human being is bound to make true what he/her has sworn, else his/her oath lacks truth.

---

21 John Finnis, "Natural Law and the Ethics of Discourse" *American Journal of Jurisprudence* 43 (1998) 53–73 at 56 note 17, "so we must read with due reserve Aquinas' (Aristotle's) generous-minded praise of his opponents in discourse; it is due only on the assumption of their goodwill, an assumption often falsified in other contexts. *Sententia super Metaphysicam* XII lect. 9 n. 14: Since, in choosing what to believe and what to reject we ought to be guided more by groundedness than by affection towards those who hold an opinion so we should love those whose opinion we follow and those opinion we reject – for they each were seeking to inquire after truth, and each assisted us to do this."

Now if this proposed act be such as not to be in his/her power, his / her oath is lacking in judgment of discretion.

If it be something that he/she can do, but ought not to, either because it is essentially evil, or because it is a hindrance to a good, then his/her oath is lacking in justice: wherefore an oath must not be kept when it involves a sin or a hindrance to good.

Sometimes a person is compelled against his/her will to promise something under oath.

There is a twofold obligation in the oath which a person takes under compulsion: one, whereby he is beholden to the person to whom he promises something; and this obligation is cancelled by the compulsion, because he that uses force deserves that the promise made to him should not be kept.

The other is an obligation whereby a person is beholden to God, in virtue of which he is bound to fulfil what he has promised in his name. This obligation is not removed in the tribunal of conscience, because that person ought rather to suffer temporal loss, than violate his oath. He can, however, seek in a court of justice to recover what he has paid, or present the matter to his superior even if he has sworn to the contrary, because such an oath would lead to evil results since it would be contrary to public justice. The Roman Pontiffs, in absolving people from oaths of this kind, did not pronounce such oaths to be unbinding, but relaxed the obligation for some just cause.

If someone does not believe that there is a divine being or that it would be difficult to know anything certain about its nature then the taking of the oath becomes problematic. It might seem that the best way to approach the contentious issue would be to begin with a theory that contained only what is common to all generally recognized ethical theories. Such a theory would be acceptable to everybody even those without religious beliefs. In that way everybody would be in agreement about the need to observe certain rules of human conduct and to fulfil certain duties, especially those that promote peace and harmony in the community. Each person could then complete that basic theory in his or her own way by including those elements that he regards as essential for a good moral and civil life. A person with religious beliefs could add his relationship with God, while an unbeliever would not be discouraged from living a moral life by what he regards as a serious stumbling block.

While a commendable agreement on a number of specific moral requirements, especially those affecting the social order, could undoubtedly

be secured in that way, for they can be justified by standards other than God, that approach has some serious defects. Our duties to God, while acknowledged as important, tend to be treated like those other duties that are to be fulfilled only on particular occasions, or in specific situations rather than a constant attitude or spirit underlying and expressing itself in all our activities. Moreover, our duties to God tend to be regarded as independent duties to be carried out separately rather than as requirements to be fulfilled in the accomplishment of every other duty, if it is to be performed properly. In other words, our relationship with God is not seen as the animating spirit not only of every specific moral and civic duty but of our whole human life. The question of the ultimate objective standard and governing motive becomes secondary. All that matters is that certain rules are observed or duties fulfilled. But only a personal attachment to an ultimate objective standard such as God can ensure a disinterested attitude that is universal and effective enough to prevent self-interest from becoming regulative at some point. But how that requirement can be fulfilled by those without belief in God raises the question of their good faith, for in proposing an ethical position no concessions can be made to those in bad faith. The basic requirement consists of:

> The acceptance of an objective moral standard and motive
> in a sincere and disinterested manner.

What is vital here is the sincere and disinterested attitude, for that is the basic moral disposition. If whatever is adopted as the ultimate objective standard in a person's life, i. e. provides the ultimate justification for his conduct, however vague and indefinite it may be in his consciousness, ensures a sufficiently sincere and disinterested attitude, then that vital requirement would be fulfilled. But this rather abstract observation needs to be tested. Christian revelation supplies the creed and the commandments which are further elaborated in many documents issued by the *magisterium*. Theological and philosophical comment is not lacking. Outside that context how does one advance what is meant by 'disinterested attitude' or objective standard? Finnis puts forward certain requisites that one must assimilate in order to attain truth and reasonable opinion.[22]

---

22 John Finnis *Reasons In Action. Collected Essays Volume* 1 Oxford: Oxford University Press, 2011, essay 18, Freedom of Speech, pages 202–3. See also The Collected Works of Eric Voegelin Volume 27 *The Nature of Law and Related legal Writings* Edited by Robert A. Pascal James Lee Babin and John W. Corrington Baton Rouge: Louisiana State Univer-

"One is not likely to attain truth and reasonable beliefs unless one understands something of one's psychical make-up and the snares to which it leads for fully rational thinking; unless one is willing to impose on oneself the necessary disciplines of learning, reflecting, testing, and rejecting parti pris and amour propre; unless one can engage in rational discussion with one's fellows, or has experienced the exigencies of oral discussion and can reproduce them in one's private debate; unless the economic, social, and political conditions in which one works permit one leisure for sound judgment about human nature and society; and (but this list will scarcely have exhausted the preconditions) unless one is equipped with the linguistic conceptual skills necessary to conceive, let alone complete the project of reaching truth and reasonable opinion about human life in political society."

We should understand, however, that in excusing a person on grounds of good faith we are not thereby admitting that his moral views are correct. Good faith means that the person is in error, sometimes even without blame. To be free from blame is not the same thing as to be free from error. Though one should bear in mind the caveat of Burtchaell.[23]

"The most terrible thing about Harlem is that it tends to smother the integrity of its people, it tends to make them evil people. Harlem's makers are those who kill the soul as well as the body, and this is why Harlem is Hell. It is never radical enough to admit that an evil situation has made the poor woman act wrongly, while leaving her blameless; it has wreaked a far more tragic evil upon her by drawing her to absorb its evil values. The same, of course, might be said of Grosse Pointe or San Sebastián or Rome."

Finnis is even more incisive.[24]

"But if one is going to recall that truth, one had better recall its companion: if one reaches such a judgment one had made a grievous moral error, is entangled in ethical incoherence and corruption, has wandered away from God's law and therefore from God's wisdom and from the terms of the divine

---

sity Press, 1991, page 67. "In a very small community under cramped economic conditions, with little relation with the outside world, and no appreciable means for personal education and development, even the best order possible under such conditions will give little opportunity for unfolding the potentialities of human nature". André F. Cournand and Harriet Zuckerman "The Code of Science Analysis and Some Reflections on Its Future" *Studium Generale* 23(1970) 941–962.

23 James Tunstead Burtchaell *Philemon's Problem a theology of grace* Cambridge U.K.: William B. Eerdmans Publishing Company 1998, pages 133–4.

24 John Finnis *Religion and Public Reason Collected Essays: Volume V* Oxford University Press, 2011, essay 10 "Faith, Morals, and Thomas More" page 171.

> offer of friendship and adoptive sonship; and, if one has heard the gospel, preached in its integrity, such an error is scarcely possible without a sinful failure of faith, hope, and love, threatening salvation at its root. For to repeat, in forming one's conscience one is not so much seeking to form oneself, or to secure one's personal integrity and authenticity, as to discern the truth about the meaning and worth which human existence is meant by its divine author to have, and does in each human life have, for good or ill, for heaven- haven or shipwreck."

Accordingly, a correct ethical theory does not have to exclude those elements which people do not understand or do not admit, even though they themselves are not at fault in doing so. Nor is the fact that we cannot persuade them to accept our ethical theory as it stands sufficient justification for modifying it to suit their erroneous views. We respect their sincerity and good faith without admitting either that their views are correct or that a satisfactory ethical theory must exclude everything that is not acceptable to them. We propose a theory that is correct on objective grounds and then excuse on grounds of good faith but aware also of the sometimes dire personal consequences of those who cannot accept all that it contains. There is no reason why a person's relationship with God should not only be included in an acceptable ethical theory but even made the basis for it.

In order to accomplish that commitment ethics has to borrow data from other branches of philosophy particularly from psychology (and related sciences such as anthropology, sociology) from which we learn about the potentialities and distinctive functions of the human person. In 1958 Anscombe had written the following comment about the study of moral philosophy: "The first is that it is not profitable for us at present to do moral philosophy; that should be laid aside at any rate until we have an adequate philosophy of psychology in which we are conspicuously lacking."[25] Happily that situation is now changing.[26] But we should take on board what Finnis[27] writes: "And, as Aquinas never tires of reminding us, it is by understanding objects of action that we understand action, and only by

25 G. E. M. Anscombe *Ethics, Religion and Politics Collected Philosophical Papers* Volume III Oxford: Basil Blackwell, 1981 especially chapter 4, "Modern Moral Philosophy" pages 26–42 at 26.
26 See Sabina Alkire *Valuing Freedoms: Sen's Capability Approach and Poverty Reduction* Oxford: Oxford University Press, 2002 for further information and bibliography.
27 John Finnis *Religion and Public Reason Collected Essays Volume* V Oxford University Press, 2011, essay 3 Secular's Practical Meaning page 61.

understanding a being's action can we understand its capacities, and only by understanding its capacities can we understand its nature."

In addition to psychology natural or civic theology, from which we learn about the distinctive characteristics of God,[28] should also be studied as the ancients did but bearing in mind the caveat of St. Augustine.[29] Finnis articulates this caution in his own inimitable way. He takes his cue from Plato.[30]

> "In his last great work, Laws, he [Plato] sketches a cluster of dispositions which shape up around one or another of three propositions: there is no God; no God has any concern with human affairs; or any such divine concern with the human is easily appeased by a superficial piety and requires no demanding reform of human vice (note omitted). And the three propositions – no God, God absent; and God soft-spirited – match closely modern secularism characteristic forms: atheism; a deistic assumption that human history knows no divine intervention, (note omitted) no revelation of God's intentions for us; and a liberal religiosity which presumes upon divine benevolence, and has no time for warnings of the alienation from God inherent in immorality and potentially final (as Plato too warns in his prophetic meditation on wrongdoing's retribution, the Republic's myth of Er." (note omitted)

---

28 See, for example, among this vast literature Robert Mayhew *Plato Laws 10* Translated with an Introduction and Commentary Oxford: Clarendon Plato Series. 2008. Germain Grisez *God? A Philosophical Preface to Faith* Indiana, South Bend: St. Augustine's Press, 2005.

29 See Miriam T. Griffin *Seneca on Society. A Guide to De Beneficiis* Oxford University Press, 2013; Eric Voegelin *The New Science of Politics An Introduction* Chicago: The University of Chicago Press, 1952. Gerard O'Daly *Augustine's City of God. A Reader's Guide* Oxford: Oxford University Press, 1999, page 107. "The principal focus of Book 6 has been discourse about civic religion, or '*theologia civilis*'. In Book 7 Augustine turns to Varro's 'select gods' ('*di selecti*') the twenty most important gods enumerated by him including the major gods of the Roman pantheon (7.1–2)."

30 John Finnis supra 23, page 57 passim.

Theologie der Geschichte bei Thomas von Aquin?

Eine thomistische Debatte aus der zweiten Hälfte des 20. Jahrhunderts

Paul D. Hellmeier OP

0. Vorbemerkung

Als die „Oberdeutsche Provinz“ im Februar des Jahres 1939 gegründet wurde, stand die Welt am Vorabend eines mit äußerster Menschenverachtung geführten globalen Krieges. Viele ihrer Gründungsmitglieder hatten bereits den Ersten Weltkrieg und dessen katastrophalen Folgen erlebt. Nach 1945 fanden sich die Überlebenden in einer anderen Welt wieder. Es war die Welt nach Auschwitz und Hiroshima. Europa war für Jahrzehnte durch den „Eisernen Vorhang“ in zwei Hälften geteilt. Es war aber auch die Welt des Wiederaufbaus und im Westen die des Wirtschaftswunders und des zunehmenden Konsumismus. Was war geschehen? Warum war es geschehen? Warum geschah überhaupt so etwas? Wie war das Geschehene in die Heilsgeschichte einzuordnen? Konnte man das überhaupt? Was sollte Heilsgeschichte angesichts des Geschehenen noch bedeuten? Solche und ähnliche Fragen stellten sich wohl auch die Mitglieder der Oberdeutschen Provinz in den Jahrzehnten nach dem 2. Weltkrieg. Über ihre möglichen Antworten können wir nur spekulieren. Aufgrund ihrer Ausbildung im Dominikanerorden ist aber anzunehmen, dass sich viele von ihnen für eine in der zweiten Hälfte des 20. Jahrhunderts geführte innerthomistische Debatte interessierten. Darin ging es nicht zuletzt um die menschliche Geschichte und ihre theologische Deutung bei Thomas von Aquin. Diese Debatte soll im Folgenden nachgezeichnet werden. Unter den vielen Stellungnahmen war freilich eine Auswahl zu treffen. Zunächst werden die Positionen von drei der bedeutendsten Dominikanertheologen des 20. Jahrhunderts in Erinnerung gerufen. Begonnen wird mit M.-Dominique Chenus zyklischem Modell der Heilsgeschichte. Hierauf werden die beiden linearen Modelle von Yves Congar und Edward Schillebeeckx vorgestellt. Zu erwägen ist anschließend die Position des Tübinger Fundamentaltheologen Max Seckler, der erneut an Chenu anknüpfte und ihn zugleich korrigierte. Zuletzt sollen die Überlegungen des Ex-Dominikaners Otto Hermann Pesch betrachtet werden.

1. Der Ort der Suche

Philosophia perennis, Theologia perennis – kein anderes Denken wurde mehr mit diesen Schlagworten in Verbindung gebracht als das des Thomas von Aquin. Es erscheint daher müßig, bei ihm nach Ansätzen einer „Theologie der Geschichte" oder einer „geschichtlichen Theologie" zu fahnden. Und tatsächlich: Verglichen mit den Werken Augustins, Joachims von Fiore oder Bonaventuras finden sich in seinem Opus relativ wenig Reflexionen über die christliche Heilsgeschichte. Diese Zurückhaltung blieb in der Forschung nicht unbeachtet:

> „(...) so ist Thomas gerade darin kühn und originell, dass er über Weltalter, Geschichtsmorphologie und errechenbaren Geschichtsverlauf kaum ein Wort verliert. Die Kühnheit seiner Konzeption liegt in bestimmter Hinsicht nicht in positiven Aussagen und Deutungen, sondern in Weglassungen und Lücken, die für den, der die Hochscholastik kennt, als schlichter Mangel oder als unerhörte Neuerung erscheinen müssen."[1]

Die von Max Seckler vorgeschlagenen Alternativen zur Bewertung des Sachverhalts sind in der Tat diskussionswürdig. Soll man die thomasische Zurückhaltung in Sachen Heilsgeschichte als unverzeihliche Geschichtsvergessenheit oder als fruchtbare Neuerung interpretieren? Und falls Letzteres zutrifft: Welche Bedeutung könnte diese Neuerung *des Mittelalters* für die heute offensichtlich in der Krise befindliche Geschichtstheologie haben?

Auf den ersten Blick scheint die erste Alternative, die bei Thomas einen nicht zu behebenden Mangel an Geschichtsbewusstsein vermutet, näher zu liegen. Denn die wenigen und knappen Stellen, an denen Thomas von der Geschichte an sich oder von der Heilsgeschichte spricht, sind fast unauffindbar im Meer seiner größtenteils metaphysisch-spekulativen Gedankengänge. Erschwerend kommt hinzu, dass er sich an den meisten dieser Stellen in negativer Weise über geschichtstheologische Versuche äußert. Die Vorschläge anderer Theologen, die einem geschichtlichen Denken gegenüber aufgeschlossener sind als er selbst, verwirft er schlichtweg. Das beste und bekannteste Beispiel hierfür ist die sichtlich emotionale Zurückweisung der Ideen Joachims von Fiore, die in jüngster Zeit wieder ihre Verteidiger gefunden haben (z. B. Bruno Forte). Thomas, der keinen Hehl aus seiner fundamentalen Ablehnung macht, nimmt dagegen kein Blatt vor

---

1 Max Seckler, Das Heil in der Geschichte. Geschichtstheologisches Denken bei Thomas von Aquin, München 1964, 24.

den Mund: „Istae vanitates“, „stultissimum est dicere.“[2] In Anbetracht dieser rein negativen Aussagen scheint es ein unmögliches Unterfangen zu sein, eine thomasische Theologie der Geschichte konstruieren zu wollen. Andererseits steht für Thomas fest, dass man ohne eigenen positiven Standpunkt auch keine negativen Aussagen treffen kann:

> „Et praeterea intellectus negationis semper fundatur in aliqua affirmatione; quod ex hoc patet quia omnis negativa per affirmationem probatur; (...).“[3]

Wo aber lässt sich eine solche positive Position, ein veritables heilsgeschichtliches Konzept bei Thomas finden? Wie bereits gesagt: Abgesehen von zu vernachlässigenden Einzelheiten findet sich hierzu nichts im *Inhalt* seines Opus. Für die Suche bleibt daher nur die *formale* Seite seiner Werke, d. h. ihr Plan. Besonderes Augenmerk verdient dabei natürlich der Plan des Hauptwerkes, der Summa Theologiae. Fände man darin ein heilsgeschichtliches Konzept, dann gewännen auch die erwähnten kurzen historischen Betrachtungen und die Ablehnungen anderer Positionen an Bedeutung und Tiefe.

2. Die Summa Theologiae: Zyklische Struktur?

2.1. Die Entdeckung M.-D. Chenus: Exitus und reditus als interne Struktur

Im Schicksalsjahr 1939 veröffentlichte Chenu einen Aufsatz, in dem er zum ersten Mal auf die Bedeutung der Architektur und der internen Struktur der Summa Theologiae für das Verständnis der Intention dieses Werkes hinwies.[4] Die Diskussion über seine Thesen setzte jedoch erst ein, als er sie – diesmal in erweiterter Form – erneut im Jahre 1950 in seiner berühmten Thomas-Einführung präsentierte.[5] Von diesem Moment an begann

---

2 Sth I–II, q. 106 a. 4 ad 2 et ad 4. Zwar wird Joachim von Fiore an dieser Stelle nicht namentlich genannt, doch handelt es sich zweifellos um sein Gedankengut, das in der Thomas vorliegenden Form möglicherweise bereits von anderen Theologen der Spiritualen modifiziert worden war.

3 De Pot. Q. 7 a. 5.

4 M.-D. Chenu, Le plan de la Somme théologique de S. Thomas, in: Revue Thomiste 45 (1939), 93–107.

5 Ders., Introduction à l'étude de Saint Thomas d'Aquin, Paris 1950. Dt. Übersetzung: Das Werk des Hl. Thomas von Aquin, Graz 1960. Die verzögerte Rezeption der Thesen war wohl dem Krieg geschuldet.

eine rege Diskussion über die Richtigkeit und den Erkenntniswert dieser Thesen, an der sich viele bedeutende Theologen über einen Zeitraum von zwanzig Jahren hin beteiligten.[6] Vor allem zwei Entdeckungen Chenus riefen die Diskussion hervor: Erstens seine Ansicht, die interne Struktur sei als – freilich „getauftes", d. h. christlich umgewandeltes – neuplatonisches *exitus-reditus*-Schema zu bestimmen. Mehr noch als diese Bestimmung gab die zweite Grundidee Chenus der Debatte Nahrung, nämlich die Applikation der inneren Struktur auf den äußeren Plan der Summa, d. h. auf die Reihenfolge der Bücher I, II und III.[7]

Beginnen wir zunächst mit der internen Struktur. Obwohl die Worte *exitus* und *reditus* in den verschiedenen Prologen und Zwischenprologen der Summa Theologiae nicht auftauchen, kann man sie der Bedeutung nach dennoch dort finden. Beispielsweise schreibt Thomas an einer dieser Stellen:

> „Quia igitur principalis intentio huius sacrae doctrinae est Dei cognitionem tradere, et non solum secundum quod in se est, sed etiam secundum quod est principium rerum et finis earum, et specialiter rationalis creaturae (…)."[8]

Chenu war vor allem deshalb davon überzeugt, dass diese Weise von Gott zu sprechen, d. h. nicht nur gemäß seines Seins in sich, sondern auch insofern als er Ursprung und Ziel aller Dinge ist, das Schema *exitus-reditus* widerspiegelt, weil Thomas dieses Schema bereits in seinem Sentenzenkommentar ausdrücklich erwähnt:

---

6 Eine sehr negative Einschätzung der Thesen Chenus gab übrigens Jahrzehnte später Wilhelm Metz, Die Architektonik der Summa Theologiae des Thomas von Aquin. Zur Gesamtsicht des thomasischen Gedankens, Hamburg 1998, 200–204. Sein eigener Vorschlag zur Architektonik kann jedoch nicht überzeugen. Vgl. allein die hochkomplexe Zeichnung zur Prima Pars (ebd. 206).

7 An dieser Stelle ist eine Klärung der Begriffe unausweichlich. Denn ohne Präzisierung der *termini technici* läuft man schnell Gefahr, bei diesem komplizierten Thema, zu dem sich viele Autoren mit ihrer jeweiligen Terminologie in unterschiedlicher Weise geäußert haben, den Überblick zu verlieren. Aus diesem Grund seien nun drei Begriffe definiert. Sie müssen stets voneinander unterschieden werden, auch wenn dies nicht alle der in diesem Aufsatz zitierten Autoren getan haben. Zu unterscheiden sind also: 1. Die *innere Struktur* (wir benützen den Begriff in gleicher Weise wie Chenu): es handelt sich um die grundsätzliche, leitende Idee der Summa Theologiae. 2. Der *Plan*: Damit ist die Abfolge der drei Bücher der Summa Theologiae gemeint (Chenu benützt diesen Begriff einerseits wie wir, andererseits versteht er darunter aber auch die *innere Struktur*. Wir werden später sehen, warum er das tut). 3. Der *Verlauf*: Hiermit ist die reale Abfolge der Ereignisse in der Heilsgeschichte gemeint.

8 Sth I q. 2 prol.; s. auch q. 1 a. 7.

> „Cum enim (…) sacrae doctrinae intentio sit circa divina; divinum autem sumitur secundum relationem ad Deum, vel ut principium, vel ut finem, (…); consideratio huius doctrinae erit de rebus, secundum quod exeunt a Deo ut a principio, et secundum quod referuntur in ipsum ut in finem. Unde in prima parte determinat de rebus divinis secundum exitum a principio, in secunda secundum reditum in finem.“[9]

Es sticht ins Auge, dass sich hier nicht nur das Schema *exitus-reditus* findet, sondern auch die Stichworte *principium* und *finis*, die später in der Summa Theologiae im gleichen Sinn noch immer verwendet werden. Thomas hätte dort also nur auf den Gebrauch der Begriffe *exitus* und *reditus* verzichtet, nicht aber auf das damit bezeichnete Konzept selbst.

Aus welchen Gründen griff Thomas schon zu Beginn seiner Karriere auf dieses Konzept zurück? Gemäß Chenu spielte hierbei die aristotelische Wissenschaftslehre eine wichtige Rolle. Aristoteles fordert von einer echten Wissenschaft unter anderem, dass sie ein einziges wohldefiniertes Subjekt (i. S. eines Hauptgegenstandes) haben müsse. Für eine Wissenschaft des christlichen Glaubens entsteht damit aber ein gravierendes Problem. Offensichtlich behandelt sie eine Vielzahl von Einzelwesen und -fakten: Gott, die Schöpfung, Christus, die Morallehre, die Kirche, die Heilige Schrift, usw. Als Antwort auf dieses Problem erwählte Thomas Gott selbst als einziges Subjekt der Theologie, jedoch insofern als er Ursprung und Ziel aller Dinge ist. Chenu beschrieb diese Lösung in folgender Weise:

> „Thomas nimmt jenseits des wissenschaftlichen Universums des Aristoteles seine Zuflucht zu dem platonischen Thema von Ausgang [Emanation] und Rückkehr. Da die Theologie die Wissenschaft von Gott ist, hat man alle Dinge zu untersuchen gemäß ihrer Beziehung zu Gott, sei es in ihrer Hervorbringung, sei es in ihrem Zielstreben: *exitus* und *reditus*. Eine großartige Quelle des Verstehens! Jedes Ding, jedes Seiende, jede Handlung, jedes Schicksal wird von dieser obersten Ursächlichkeit her eingeordnet, erkannt und beurteilt, in der der Grund seines Seins sich im Lichte Gottes selbst völlig enthüllt.“[10]

Nach Chenu fand Thomas also unter dem Einfluss des aristotelischen Wissenschaftsbegriffs und mit Hilfe einer neuplatonischen Idee eine Quelle der theologischen Erkenntnis. Zugleich fand er aber auch eine Struktur, anhand der sich die gesamte Materie der Theologie schlüssig anordnen lässt:

9 I Sent. d. 2.

10 Chenu, Das Werk, 343 f. (in der frz. Originalausgabe S. 260 f.).

einen *ordo disciplinae*, der vollständig mit dem *ordo rerum* korrespondiert.[11] Alle Dinge werden hinsichtlich ihrer Herkunft von Gott und ihrem Weg zu ihm behandelt. Aus diesem Grund steht das *exitus-reditus*-Schema auch einer historischen Betrachtung des Heils von sich aus offen:

> „Ebenso aber ist dieses Schema der Geschichte geöffnet, jener Heilsgeschichte, auf deren erster Seite sich gerade die Beschreibung des Ausgangs der Welt findet, deren ganzer Verlauf die göttliche Leitung der Kreaturen beinhaltet und deren Geschick sich durch die aus dem Glückseligkeitsstreben geborenen Werke der Menschen gestaltet in eine Rückkehr zu Gott. Auf dieser Linie können die Tatsachen und Ereignisse der Heilsgeschichte ihren Ort finden – mit all ihrer göttlichen und menschlichen Kontingenz (das freilich ist das Eigengut des *christlichen* Neuplatonismus!)."[12]

Die positive Wertschätzung der kontingenten und auf freie Entschlüsse zurückgehenden Tatsachen, die sich in ihrem Zusammenhang als *Geschichte* präsentieren, ist der entscheidende Unterschied zu den im eigentlichen Sinne neuplatonischen Systemen, die sich allesamt auf den Gedanken einer aus Notwendigkeit erfolgenden Emanation gründen. Diese Wertschätzung geht sogar so weit, dass der in Freiheit gesetzte Akt der Selbstoffenbarung Gottes den Ausgangspunkt des ganzen theologischen Systems bildet. Damit ist aber der originäre neuplatonische Charakter des *exitus-reditus*-Schemas bei Thomas stark abgeschwächt. Befreit von allen emanatistischen Spekulationen benützt er dieses Schema nur noch als „eine Ordnung des Wissens, die das Offenbarungsgut von innen her verstehen lässt".[13] Zugleich ist dieses Schema zutiefst biblisch, bezeichnet sich doch Gott selbst in seiner Offenbarung als „den Anfang und das Ende" (Offb 21, 6).

2.2. Der Plan der Summa Theologiae nach M.-D. Chenu

Der zweite Teil des Kapitels, in dem Chenu die Summa Theologiae behandelte, widmet sich ihrer „Konstruktion".[14] Wie bereits gesagt ist unserer Ansicht nach stets die „innere Struktur" der Summa Theologiae von ihrem „Plan", d. h. von der Abfolge ihrer drei Bücher, zu unterscheiden. Schon bei Chenu selbst gibt es ein unübersehbares Zeichen dafür, dass auch er eine

---

11 Vgl. ebd. 342.
12 Ebd. 344 (261).
13 Vgl. ebd. 347 (263).
14 Ebd. 351 (266).

gewisse Differenz ahnte, nämlich die Zweiteilung des Kapitels, in dem er die Summa Theologiae behandelt. Wie wir gezeigt haben, fand er die „innere Struktur“ in der zyklischen Bewegung *exitus-reditus*, d. h. in der „inneren Bewegung“, die dieses Werk „belebt“.[15] Im Laufe des zweiten Kapitels seiner Darstellung versuchte er, diese innere Struktur auf den Plan der Summa Theologiae, den er auch als deren „Konstruktion“ oder „Architektur“ bezeichnet, anzuwenden.

Ausgangspunkt für Chenu war das Problem, „eine Heilsgeschichte in eine organisierte Wissenschaft überzuführen“.[16] Als Lösung des Thomas verstand er dessen Wahl des Subjektes der Theologie, d. h. Gott, insofern dieser Wirk- und Zielursache aller Dinge ist. Innerhalb dieses Kreises – hierbei handelt es sich natürlich um ein bloßes Bild – glaubte Chenu, eine gewisse Versöhnung zwischen einer Theologie, die sich auf historische Fakten stützt, und einer aristotelischen Wissenschaft im strikten Sinne erreichen zu können. Die kreisförmige Bewegung hat nämlich an sich bereits einen gewissen Notwendigkeitscharakter. Es beruht ja nicht auf einem Zufall oder auf einem neuen zweiten Entschluss des göttlichen Willens, dass sich der Kreis wieder schließt. Die höchste Wirkursache zielt vielmehr von Anfang an auf die Vollendung ihrer Schöpfung in sich selbst. Oder anders gesagt: Die höchste Zielursache zieht bereits von Beginn an ihre Schöpfung wieder an sich.

> „Besser noch: Die Hervorbringung der seienden Dinge, ihr ‚Hervorgang‘, der sich in beständig-wirklichen Dingen, in ‚Naturen‘ vollendet, ist selbst auch Grund der Rückkehr und fundiert ontologisch deren Quellgründe und Vollzug. Denn das hervorgebrachte Seiende wendet sich *naturnotwendig* am Zielpunkt der Bewegung, die es hervorgebracht hat, in einer gegenläufigen Bewegung zurück, in einer ‚Be-kehrung‘ zum Grund seiner Hervorbringung.“[17]

Die Applikation dieser einzigartigen Bewegung auf den Plan der Summa Theologiae verstand sich für Chenu fast von selbst. Die *Prima Pars* repräsentiert den *exitus*, die Emanation der Wirkursache, während die Secunda Pars den *reditus* bildet.[18] Wie und wo aber soll man Christus einordnen, den vollkommensten Ausdruck von Gottes freigeschenkter Liebe? Das Anfangsproblem, das Problem des kontingenten Charakters des Heils,

15 Ebd. 340 (258).
16 Ebd. 340 f. (258).
17 Ebd. 252 (267).
18 Vgl. ebd. 244 (261).

scheint nach wie vor zu bestehen. Und in der Tat war Chenu der Meinung, dass Christus gemäß der thomasischen Konzeption nicht in den abstrakten Kreis von *exitus* und *reditus* eingehe. Vielmehr sei er lediglich das Instrument bzw. der kontingente Weg, durch das bzw. auf dem die Rückkehr möglich gemacht wird. Entsprechend ist sein Platz im Plan, bzw. in der Architektur der *Summa* die *Tertia Pars*. Diese spielt folglich nur die Rolle „eines nachträglich hinzugefügten Abschnittes“.[19] Chenu selbst beschrieb die Beziehung der Tertia zu den vorausgehenden Teilen der Summa in folgender Weise:

> „Der Übergang von der II^a^ zu III^a^ Pars stellt den Übergang von der notwendigen Ordnung zu den geschichtlichen Verwirklichungen, vom Gebiet der Strukturen zur konkreten Geschichte der Gaben Gottes dar.“[20]

Fassen wir Chenus Aussagen über die Beziehung von innerer Struktur und Plan der Summa zusammen! Prima und Secunda Pars behandeln *exitus* und *reditus* in *abstrakter Weise*. Die Tertia Pars dagegen hat den kontingenten und freien Weg, auf dem sich der *reditus* ereignet, zum Inhalt.

An dieser Stelle ist kritisch zu fragen: Was wurde mit diesem Modell eigentlich für die Entwicklung einer Theologie der Geschichte bei Thomas erreicht? – Wie es scheint, nicht viel. Die Grundidee, die zu Beginn von Chenus Darlegungen Erfolg versprach, hat sich am Ende als wenig ergiebig für unser Anliegen erwiesen. Zu Beginn schien das *exitus-reditus*-Schema dazu geeignet, die Strukturen der Heilsgeschichte erklären zu können. Es war die Rede von einem Schema, das „offen für die Heilsgeschichte“ ist. Doch am Ende blieb nur ein abstrakter Kreislauf, ein dürres „Schema“ (Prima und Secunda Pars), von dem der Inhalt der Heilsgeschichte (Tertia Pars) selbst völlig abgeschnitten ist. Erschwerend kommt hinzu, dass dieser Inhalt immer nur *a posteriori* und ohne jede historische Spekulation behandelt wird. Die Suche nach einer im Plan der Summa verborgenen Theologie der Geschichte bei Thomas scheint sich damit als aussichtslos erwiesen zu haben.

---

19 Ebd. 351 (266).
20 Ebd. 357 (270).

3. Lineare Struktur der Summa Theologiae?

3.1. Der Plan der Summa Theologiae gemäß Yves Congar

Die Weise, in der Yves Congar die Struktur und den Plan der Summa Theologiae versteht, unterscheidet sich gänzlich von den Ideen Chenus. Trotzdem übte Congar nirgends offene Kritik an diesen Ideen. Ein Grund für die fehlende Kritik liegt wohl darin, dass das Problem der Struktur bzw. des Plans der Summa in seinem Denken niemals die Bedeutung erlangte, die es für Chenu hatte. Dennoch behandelte Congar es mehrere Male.[21] So z. B. in seinem Buch *Le mystère du Temple*. Dort beschrieb er die verschiedenen Weisen der göttlichen Anwesenheit in der Welt. Genauer gesagt handelt es sich dabei nicht um je für sich bestehende und untereinander unverbundene Weisen, sondern um Grade. Congar selbst sprach von „façons (…) en profondeur et en intimité croissantes“.[22] In einer erklärenden Bemerkung versuchte er, diese drei Weisen auf den Plan der Summa Theologiae anzuwenden.

> « Sans doute ne serait-il pas exagéré à l'intention de S. Thomas de retrouver les trois modes ou degrès d'union à Dieu et de présence, respectivement dans les trois parties de la Somme: I, présence par la puissance créatrice, selon la similitude; II, présence par la grâce, selon l'union à Dieu comme objet connu, aimé et possédé; III, présence par l'union hypostatique, selon l'être. Ou encore: immanence générale de Dieu à sa création, immanence à sa création raisonnable et libre, immanence singulière et suprême en Jésus-Christ. »[23]

Congars Idee ist klar und bedarf keiner weiteren Erklärung. Einleuchtend erscheint v. a. die Darstellung der drei Grade göttlicher Immanenz. Tatsächlich spricht auch Thomas von ihnen in der Summa Theologiae und in anderen Werken.[24] Aber lassen sie sich wirklich strikt chronologisch anordnen? Und kann man sie wirklich in dieser exakten Weise den verschiedenen Teilen der Summa Theologiae zuordnen? Wie steht es bspw. mit den Engeln und den Menschen in der Prima Pars: Ist hier etwa noch nicht da-

---

21 Yves Congar, Le sens de l'économie salutaire dans ‚théologie' de S. Thomas d'Aquin (Somme théologique), in: Glaube und Geschichte, Baden-Baden 1958, Bd. II, 76–85; Le mystère du Temple ou l'économie de la présence de Dieu à sa créature de la Genèse à l'Apocalypse, Paris 1958, 282–286.

22 Ebd. 282.

23 Ebd.

24 I Sent. d. 37 q. 1 a. 2; Comp. theol. I, 7; Sth I q.43 a. 1 ad 1; III q. 1 a. 1.

von die Rede, dass Gott von diesen Wesen erkannt und geliebt wird? Oder man denke an die Rolle Christi in den Quaestiones über das Gesetz in der Prima Secundae.

Congars Sicht unterscheidet sich von derjenigen seines dominikanischen Mitbruders Chenu besonders darin, dass er die Struktur der Summa nicht als zyklisch, sondern als *linear* begreift. Doch was gewinnt man mit dieser linearen Perspektive für unsere Suche nach einer thomasischen Theologie der Geschichte? Struktur und Plan der Summa koinzidieren nun mit der realen Abfolge der Heilsgeschichte. Auch dieses Ergebnis erscheint eher dürftig zu sein.

3.2. Die „Pyramide" von Edward Schillebeeckx

Edward Schillebeeckx' These zur Struktur der Summa Theologiae ähnelt besonders in einem Punkt derjenigen Congars, denn auch er vertrat ein lineares Konzept. Zugleich setzte er sich intensiv mit Chenus Grundidee auseinander. Seine These verdankt sich daher in vielerlei Hinsicht der Diskussion mit diesem. Ausgangspunkt seiner Kritik an Chenu war die Aufteilung in eine notwendige Struktur (Prima und Secunda Pars) und in einen christologischen Zusatz mit kontingent-konkretem Charakter (Tertia Pars). Für Schillebeeckx war diese Aufteilung falsch, da bereits die Schöpfung, ebenso wie die in Christus erfolgte Versöhnung, einen freien und kontingenten Akt darstellt.[25] Es gebe nur *eine* Geschichte des Heils in der Summa Theologiae, da Thomas eine einheitliche Konzeption des Heilswerkes habe. In einer solchen Sicht sei die rationale Kreatur, gleich ob Engel oder Mensch, von Anfang an auf die Vergöttlichung hingeordnet.[26] An dieser Stelle ist freilich kritisch zu fragen, ob Chenu im ersten Teil seines Kapitels über die Summa Theologiae nicht dasselbe sagte, als er von Gott als Wirk- *und* Zielursache sprach. Doch selbst wenn Chenu und Schillebeeckx in diesem Punkt weniger trennt, als es zunächst scheint, sind ihre Analysen des Plans der Summa doch grundverschieden. Für Schillebeeckx sind Prima, Secunda und Tertia Pars lediglich Aspekte der *einen* weiten und kontingenten Bewegung der rationalen Kreatur zu Gott hin (*motus*

25 H. Schillebeeckx, De sacramentele heilseconomie. Theologische bezinning op S. Thomas' sacramentenleer in het licht van de traditie en van de hedendaagse sacramentsproblematiek, Anvers 1952, 3.
26 Vgl. ebd. 3–5.

rationalis in Deum).[27] Wenn Thomas bspw. von der Gnade spreche, dann meine er damit in allen Teilen der Summa die Gnade Christi.[28] Die Struktur der Summa sei daher eindeutig *christologisch*. Man könnte sagen, dass Christus als Weg für Schillebeeckx nicht so sehr *Inhalt*, als vielmehr *Form* der Summa ist. Vom Beginn der Summa an beseele Christus als Weg die Bewegung des Heils. Wohl aufgrund seiner Auseinandersetzung mit Chenus Konzept verstand Schillebeeckx diese Bewegung aber nicht als kreisförmig, sondern als linear-progressiv bzw. linear aufsteigend.[29] Mit einem anderen Bild sprach er auch von einer „Pyramide", deren Spitze Christus als das fleischgewordene Wort Gottes bilde. Ebenso sei Christus die christlich-sakramentale Spitze der Summa Theologiae, d. h. er sei Inhalt der Tertia Pars, während Prima und Secunda die natürlichen und übernatürlichen Fundamente der Pyramide legten.[30]

Verglichen mit den in die gleiche Richtung weisenden Äußerungen Congars wirkt Schillebeeckx' lineares Konzept weiter ausgearbeitet. Zustimmung verdient besonders sein Insistieren auf einer einheitlichen Konzeption des Heils bei Thomas. Leider widersteht aber auch er nicht der Versuchung, die Bewegung des Heils in Christus in direkter Weise auf den Plan der Summa zu übertragen, indem er die verschiedenen Etappen dieser Bewegung auf deren drei Bücher verteilt. Mit dieser unmittelbaren Verbindung des Verlaufs der Heilsgeschichte und des Plans ihrer Darstellung führt er aber „durch die Hintertür" die von ihm selbst so vehement bekämpfte „Stockwerkstheologie" mit ihrer strikten Trennung von Natur und Übernatur wieder ein.

> „Schillebeeckx setzt sich damit, obwohl er die Einheit betont, der Gefahr aus, dass die von ihm selbst abgelehnte ‚Stockwerkstheologie' unter der Hand wieder auftaucht, insofern sie ins Lineare transponiert wird."[31]

Congar und Schillebeeckx versuchten auf je eigene Weise, eine lineare Deutung der Struktur der Summa Theologiae zu geben.[32] Auf den ersten Blick

---

27 Vgl. ebd. 12.

28 Vgl. ebd. 5.

29 Vgl. ebd. 5–6.

30 Vgl. ebd. 6; 8–9.

31 Seckler, 41.

32 Es wurden noch mindestens zwei andere lineare Modelle entwickelt. Vgl. Per Eric Person, Le plan de la Somme théologique et le rapport ‚ratio-revelatio, in Revue philosophique de Louvain 56 (1958), 545–575; Albert Patfoort, L'unité de la I^a Pars et le mouvement in-

scheinen ihre Modelle bei der Suche nach einer Theologie der Geschichte bei Thomas mehr Erfolg zu verheißen und mit modernen Vorstellungen über Geschichte besser zu harmonieren.[33] Bei Lichte betrachtet fällt die Bilanz aber auch hier eher ernüchternd aus. Denn selbst wenn die lineare Deutung im Hinblick auf den Text der Summa Theologiae gerechtfertigt sein sollte (zu den Zweifeln im Falle von Congars Modell s. o.) – was hätte man gewonnen? Eine „Historiosophie minimalsten Inhalts (…), die dann mit Recht gegenüber den heilsgeschichtlichen Aufrissen der Zeitgenossen des Aquinaten als äußerst verarmt empfunden würde“.[34] Und so wäre es doch sehr vermessen, einen Plan oder eine Struktur, die nichts anderes sagten, als dass die gesamte Geschichte vor Christus auf Christus hinzielte, als hinreichendes Kriterium für eine veritable Theologie der Geschichte zu bezeichnen.

4. Versuch einer Präzisierung der These Chenus

4.1. Die klare Unterscheidung von innerer Struktur, Plan und Verlauf bei Max Seckler

In seinem Buch „Das Heil in der Geschichte“ griff Max Seckler Chenus Spekulationen über das *exitus-reditus*-Schema wieder auf und verteidigte das zyklische Modell gegen die linearen Deutungen.[35] Zugleich sah er sehr wohl ein, dass Chenus Modell einiger Korrekturen bedurfte. Wie vor ihm Schillebeeckx kritisierte er die scharfe Trennung von notwendigen Strukturen (Prima und Secunda Pars) und kontingenter Geschichte (Tertia Pars).[36] Auch er äußerte sich dahingehend, dass eine präzise Aufteilung der *einen* Bewegung des Heils unmöglich ist:

---

terne de la Somme théologique de S. Thomas d'Aquin, in Revue des sciences philosophiques et théologiques 47 (1963), 513–544. Die beiden Versuche kommen der These Congars ziemlich nahe. Besonders Patfoorts Theorie ist sehr elaboriert, versteigt sich am Ende aber immer mehr, wenn er eine Zuordnung der drei Bücher der Summa zu den drei göttlichen Personen versucht (vgl. 540).

33 Selbst wenn spätestens seit Walter Benjamins „Engel der Geschichte“ starke Zweifel am Fortschrittsmodell aufgetreten sind.

34 Otto Hermann Pesch, Um den Plan der Summa Theologiae des hl. Thomas von Aquin, in: Thomas von Aquin, Bd. 1, hrsg. von K. Bernath, Darmstadt 1978, 412 (erstmals erschienen in Münchener Theologische Zeitschrift 16 (1965), 128–137).

35 Vgl. v. a. Seckler, 33–47.

36 Vgl. ebd. 45.

> „Im theologischen Entwurf des Aquinaten mischen sich abstrakte und konkrete, notwendige und kontingente, strukturelle und faktische Elemente einer der Sache nach ‚angemessenen', das heißt *sinnvollen* Geschichte, die erkennend nachvollzogen wird, aber diese Elemente lassen sich nicht so scheiden, dass man sie auf die verschiedenen Bücher dieses Werkes aufteilen könnte."[37]

Seckler ging in seiner konstruktiven Kritik an Chenus Position aber noch weiter, denn er versuchte, die Gründe aufzuzeigen, die Chenu zu seiner These bewogen hatten. Anders gesagt: Er wollte den Kerngedanken freilegen, der der Ungenauigkeit von Chenus These zugrunde liegt. Für ihn stand fest, dass Chenu das Problem der Wissenschaftlichkeit der theologischen Erkenntnis zu sehr ins Zentrum gerückt hatte.[38] Tatsächlich betrachtete Chenu die Überführung einer kontingenten Geschichte in eine echte Wissenschaft, die von notwendigen Zusammenhängen handelt, als *die* große Frage, die Thomas bei der Abfassung der Summa Theologiae bewegte. Auf der Suche nach einem Vehikel zur Durchführung dieser Transformation entdeckte Chenu die Kreisbewegung von *exitus* und *reditus*. Ein Problem blieb aber immer noch ungelöst: Die in radikaler Weise kontingente und sich *in* und *aus* Freiheit ereignende Geschichte Jesu Christi. Angesichts dieses Problems suchte Thomas, so Chenu, seine Zuflucht bei einem speziellen Hilfsmittel: dem Konvenienzargument, das seiner Meinung nach vor allem für die Tertia Pars Bedeutung hat.[39] Dieses Argument der „Angemessenheit" des göttlichen Handelns sei Ausdruck eines defizienten Erkenntnismodus und schwächer als ein mit Notwendigkeit zwingendes Argument. Dafür rette es die Freiheit des Ereignisses. Chenu selbst fasste seine Lösung wie folgt zusammen:

> „Es ist das paradoxe Geglücktsein einer Theologie, die im Bewusstsein der Transzendenz Gottes die Wissenschaft vom Notwendigen und die Ehrfurcht vor den Fügungen einer stets freien Liebe zu verbinden weiß. Die III[a] Pars ist der Ausdruck dieses Geglücktseins."[40]

---

37 Ebd. 46.

38 Vgl. ebd. 37; 45. Dass Chenu dieses Thema überbewertete, erscheint wenig verwunderlich, da er sich lebenslang mit der Frage nach der Wissenschaftlichkeit der Theologie in der Scholastik beschäftigte.

39 Freilich ist sich Chenu selbst bewusst, dass das Konvenienzargument die *ganze* Summa Theologiae durchzieht. Vgl. Chenu, 347 (in der frz. Originalausgabe S. 263).

40 Ebd. 358 (271).

Vor allem am Ende seines Kapitels über die Summa Theologiae schloss Chenu den Begriff „kontingent“ aus der Struktur *exitus-reditus* aus. Als kontingent erschien nun allein die Tertia Pars. Und im Hinblick auf ihren Inhalt galt es, Argumente der Angemessenheit zu finden, um der wissenschaftlichen Vorgehensweise Genüge zu tun. Offensichtlich verstand er diese Konvenienzargumente als *Ersatz*. Hier setzte Secklers Kritik ein. Überzeugend legte er dar, dass es zwei verschiedene Arten von Konvenienzargumenten gibt.[41] Bei der einen Art geht es um Angemessenheit im weiteren Sinne. Hier wird z. B. erklärt, warum Gott zu diesem Zeitpunkt oder unter diesen Umständen Mensch wurde. Zur anderen, wichtigeren Art gehören die Konvenienzargumente im engeren Sinne. Hier wird bspw. die Frage beantwortet, warum es überhaupt zu einer Inkarnation Gottes kam. Diese Frage hat mit Fragen der ersten Art, also bspw. nach dem Wann und dem Wo der Inkarnation, offensichtlich nichts zu tun:

> „Die Frage des Zeitpunktes, der historischen Entwicklung und der innergeschichtlich ‚angemessenen‘ Verlaufsform spielt dabei überhaupt keine Rolle. Thomas nennt vielmehr zwei Argumente, die mit dem Wesen der Sache und der Struktur des Geschehens zu tun haben: es entspricht dem Wesen des höchsten Gutes, dass es sich auf unüberbietbare Weise der Kreatur mitteilt (*ad rationem summi boni pertinet quod summo modo se creaturae communicet*), und: es ist höchst angemessen, dass das Unsichtbare Gottes sich im Sichtbaren zeigt (*videtur esse convenientissimum, ut per visibilia monstrentur invisibilia Dei*).“[42]

Dies bedeutet, dass in der Tertia Pars nicht nur historische Fakten dargestellt und bedacht werden. Vielmehr enthält sie auch *strukturelle* Spekulationen von großer Tiefe. Dennoch handelt es sich dabei, wie im angeführten Beispiel, um *nicht-notwendige* Konvenienzargumente. Seckler schloss daraus:

> „(…) mit der ‚Angemessenheit‘ ist nicht ein defizienter Erkenntnismodus ausgesagt, sondern das logisch notwendige Apriori freien geschichtlichen Geschehens.“[43]

Die Begriffe „Struktur der Geschichte“ und „kontingent“ sind also keineswegs Gegensätze. Im Gegenteil, es gehört notwendig zu dieser Struktur, frei und damit kontingent zu sein.

41 Vgl. ebd. 45.
42 Ebd. (Verweise auf Sth III q. 1 a.1 c. et s.c.).
43 Ebd.

Gemäß Max Seckler beging Chenu aufgrund seiner Sorge um die wissenschaftliche Erkenntnisweise einen weiteren folgenschweren Fehler: Er vermischte zumindest teilweise die ontologische Struktur des Werdens der Welt, d. h. das Fundament der Geschichte, mit dieser Geschichte selbst:

> „Auch Chenu entgeht der allerdings naheliegenden Gefahr einer Vermischung von Struktur und Realität bzw. Abfolge der Ereignisse nicht völlig, wenn er von Thomas sagt, er entwickle innerhalb einer Reihe kontingenter Ereignisse die Gründe ihres Eintreffens und ihrer Abfolge, um so eine heilige Geschichte in eine organisierte Wissenschaft zu übertragen."[44]

Seckler kritisierte Chenu dafür, dass er die Struktur *exitus-reditus* vollständig mit der großen realen Bewegung des Von-Gott-wieder-zu-Gott-zurück identifizierte. Ein Zeichen hierfür ist seine Gleichsetzung der Prima Pars mit dem *exitus* und der Secunda Pars mit dem *reditus*. Diese notwendige Struktur wird dann mit dem kontingenten *Inhalt* der Tertia sozusagen „aufgefüllt". Dadurch wird die Struktur aber zur realen Geschichte und umgekehrt. Dagegen wandte Seckler ein, dass sich die reale Bewegung zwar tatsächlich gemäß dieser Struktur ereignet. Die Struktur selbst sei aber etwas anderes, denn ihre Bedeutung sei weiter. Sie sei nämlich nicht nur Struktur der realen Geschichte und der Geschichte in ihrer Totalität. Vielmehr sei sie auch Struktur einer jeden sich in und aus Freiheit vollziehenden Bewegung.[45]

Offensichtlich unterscheiden sich die Theorien Chenus und Secklers also durch ihre andersgeartete Einschätzung der zirkulären *exitus-reditus*-Struktur. Doch wie begründete Seckler sein Verständnis derselben als Struktur eines jeden freien Ereignisses? Hierzu vertiefte er einen Gedanken, der sich bereits bei Chenu fand. Wie dieser machte auch Seckler den Ursprung des zyklischen Denkens bei Thomas in der aristotelischen Ursachenlehre aus. Diese kann erklären, was auf den ersten Blick wie ein präphilosophisches, vielleicht sogar wie ein mythologisches Axiom anmutet:

> „Tunc enim effectus maxime perfectus est quando in suum redit principium: unde et circulus inter omnes figuras, et motus circularis inter omnes motus, est maxime perfectus, quia in eis ad principium reditur. Ad hoc igitur quod universum creaturarum ultimam perfectionem consequatur, oportet creaturas ad suum redire principium."[46]

44 Seckler, 44.
45 Vgl. ebd. 30–33; 50.
46 ScG II, 46.

Die Erklärung für diese Vollendung der kreisförmigen Bewegung ist folgende: die Wirkursache und die Zielursache sind lediglich zwei verschiedene Aspekte eines einzigen Aktes. Beide haben daher ihren Ursprung im Urheber dieses Aktes. Das bedeutet aber, dass die Wirkursache vom Beginn des Aktes an ihr Ziel verfolgt; oder umgekehrt gesagt, dass die Zielursache von Anfang an die sich entwickelnde Sache an sich zieht. Im direkten Anschluss an die eben zitierte Stelle aus dem zweiten Buch der Summa contra Gentiles gibt Thomas das Beispiel eines Hausbaues. Das Haus ist vollendet, wenn es in Wirklichkeit dem Plan des Erbauers gleicht. Das geistige Konzept dieses Urhebers ist dann gleichzeitig Wirk- und Zielursache. Der Kreis hat sich geschlossen, wenn das Haus gemäß dem Plan errichtet ist. Im Falle des Menschen, dessen Natur es ist, vernunftbegabt und frei zu sein, hat sich der Kreis geschlossen, wenn er seinen Urheber Gott erkennt und in freier Zustimmung liebt, wodurch er in dynamischer Weise zu einem wahren Abbild seines Schöpfers wird.[47] Seckler wies darauf hin, dass sich in analoger Weise in Gott selbst eine solche kreisförmige Bewegung ereignet. Auch hier gibt es einen freien Hervorgang, nämlich die Zeugung des Sohnes, und eine Rückkehr oder Wiederaufnahme in der Hauchung der gemeinsamen Liebe, des Heiligen Geistes. Diese Bewegung der Dreifaltigkeit ist das Fundament oder die „Grammatik“ der Schöpfung.[48] Auf diesem Hintergrund wird der tiefere Sinn der thomasischen Rede von der „Rückkehr aller Dinge zu ihrem Ursprung“ deutlich:

> „Erst wo die analogische Ordnung der Wirklichkeit betrachtet wird, differenziert sich die Rückkehr der Dinge gemäß ihrer Natur, ihrem Wesen und ihrer geschichtlichen Verfasstheit. Aber sie hat ihr Fundament in der einen Liebe, in der der dreifaltige Gott sich selbst liebt und darin das Geschöpf nach Maßgabe seiner Fassungskraft. Die Struktur des Geschehens, gemäß welcher der Auskehr eine vermittelte Rückkehr ins Heil zugeordnet ist, ist kein äußerlich dekretiertes Gesetz, sondern die reale Ordnung der Liebe, in der Gott die Rückkehr oder ‚Bekehrung‘ wirkt. Die Ordnung der Rückkehr selbst aber entspricht der Ordnung des Hervorgangs im Akt der Schöpfung.“[49]

---

47 Vgl. hierzu ausführlich Seckler, 56 f.

48 Vgl. ebd. 30; 51. Aus diesem Grund kann Thomas sagen, dass die Kenntnis der Dreifaltigkeit eine wichtige, vielleicht sogar eine notwendige Rolle spielt, um die Schöpfung wirklich zu verstehen (vgl. Sth I q. 32 a. 1 ad 3).

49 Ebd. 51. An dieser Stelle dürfte klar geworden sein, dass es sich bei Thomas mitnichten um ein mythologisches zyklisches Denken handelt, sondern um „eine besondere Art zyklischen Denkens“ (ebd. 52).

Diese Struktur, die jedem Ereignis, jedem freien Akt, der gesamten Geschichte und in analoger Weise sogar dem dreifaltigen Gott zugrunde liegt, ist zugleich die Struktur der Summa Theologiae. Aufgrund ihrer Komplexität lassen sich die verschiedenen Aspekte dieser Struktur aber nicht in präziser Weise auf den Plan der Summa, d. h. auf die Abfolge ihrer drei Bücher, beziehen:

> „Im theologischen Entwurf des Aquinaten mischen sich abstrakte und konkrete, notwendige und kontingente, strukturelle und faktische Elemente einer der Sache nach ‚angemessenen', das heißt *sinnvollen* Geschichte, die erkennend nachvollzogen wird, aber diese Elemente lassen sich nicht so scheiden, dass man sie auf die verschiedenen Bücher dieses Werkes aufteilen könnte. Vielmehr durchdringen sie sich wie die Struktur das Ereignis und der Sinn das Geschehen. Das Egreß-Regreß-Schema aber, der Bau-Plan der theologischen Summe, spiegelt das fundamentalste Gesetz allen Seins wider, das auch (...) für das trinitarische Leben Gottes gilt: Auskehr und vermittelte Rückkehr."[50]

4.2. Theologie der Geschichtlichkeit

Als Zwischenresultat ist festzuhalten, dass der Plan der Summa Theologiae keine *Theologie der Geschichte* in sich birgt. Was sich jedoch darin findet, ist die die Summe durchdringende Struktur *exitus-reditus*, die zugleich Struktur der Geschichte selbst ist. Über sie nachzudenken heißt deshalb, auf die Bedingungen und Seinsgründe der Geschichte selbst zu reflektieren. Den *Verlauf* der Geschichte beschreibt sie aber ebenso wenig wie das der Plan der Summa Theologiae tut. Die Theologie des Thomas von Aquin ist deshalb keine Theologie der Geschichte im Sinne einer Reflexion über deren Verlauf, also keine Geschichts*verlaufs*theologie, sondern „nur" eine *Theologie der Geschichtlichkeit*. Ihr zufolge bedeutet die geschichtliche Existenz des Menschen schlicht und einfach: „Von Gott durch die Welt zu Gott."[51]

Natürlich könnte man einwenden, diese Formel sei trivial. Bedenkt man jedoch ihren Hintergrund, d. h. die gedanklichen Schritte, die Seckler zu ihr geführt haben, dann werden ihre gewichtigen Folgen sichtbar. Die erste ist: Welt und Zeit, und damit auch die Geschichte, sind nicht das Resultat eines Sündenfalls oder Abfalls vom Einen, sondern *processio Dei ad*

50 Ebd. 46.
51 Ebd. 29.

extra.[52] Sie sind *vestigium* und *imitatio Dei.*[53] Die Theologie des heiligen Thomas ist daher von sich aus offen für die Geschichte und erkennt die Positivität des zeitlichen Geschehens an. Entscheidend ist, dass sie diese Positivität spekulativ zu begründen vermag.[54]

Als zweite wichtige Folge ergibt sich: Christus hat in dieser Theologie zentrale Bedeutung. Er hat uns in sich selbst den neuen Weg eröffnet (*initiavit nobis viam novam*[55]). Er ist der Wendepunkt der Geschichte, der Punkt, an dem die Rückkehr des Menschen zu Gott bereits real und unwiderruflich begonnen hat. Die Zeit nach Christus ist deshalb schon *ultima aetas*, das letzte Zeitalter, das unmittelbar auf die Vollendung zugeht. Dieses Zeitalter Christi, das zugleich dasjenige seiner Kirche ist,[56] ist nicht bloß eine Zwischenperiode, die einem erst noch zu erwartenden „Himmel auf Erden" vorausgeht, in dem die gesamte Geschichte dann ihren Sinn und ihre Erfüllung finden wird. Einer solchen Vorstellung kann Thomas nicht zustimmen. Für ihn wird das Heil vielmehr *jetzt* gewirkt, für ihn geschieht das Entscheidende *jetzt, in unserer Zeit.* Die mit der Zeitlichkeit notwendig einhergehende Offenheit gilt dann aber auch für die in Christus erschlossene *via nova* selbst: Der Weg des Heiles ist radikal offen. Es ist uns nicht möglich, im Vorhinein die Abfolge seiner Ereignisse zu konstruieren oder Einzelheiten seines Verlaufs zu wissen.[57] Auf diesem Hintergrund wird Thomas' scharfe Ablehnung der Thesen des Joachim von Fiore verständlich: Thomas verwirft ein Konzept, das Christus darauf reduziert, Prinzip einer Zwischenzeit zu sein, und das vorgibt, alle Einzelheiten der Zukunft schon zu kennen.[58]

4.3. Warum die Tertia Pars? – Eine Antwort von Otto Hermann Pesch

Unsere Ausgangsfrage war: Birgt der Plan der Summa Theologiae eine „Theologie der Geschichte" in sich? Der Gang durch die Positionen verschiedener Thomisten des 20. Jahrhunderts hat eine negative Antwort ergeben. Nein, der Plan der Summa enthält keine „Theologie der Geschichte", wenn man darunter eine Geschichtstheologie im geläufigen Sinne

---

52 Ebd. 181.
53 Vgl. ebd. 182.
54 Vgl. ebd.
55 Sth I–II q. 106 a.4 c. (Thomas zitiert hier Hebr 10, 19).
56 S. hierzu ausführlich Seckler, 217–260.
57 Vgl. ebd. 193 f.
58 Vgl. ebd. 190 f.

versteht, d. h. eine Theologie, die etwas über den Verlauf der Heilsgeschichte aussagen will. Neben diesem negativen Resultat steht aber auch ein positives, denn die Untersuchung der inneren Struktur der Summa gibt eine „Theologie der Geschichtlichkeit" preis. Diese innere Struktur verrät nichts über den realen Verlauf der Geschichte. Ebenso wenig lassen sich ihre Teilaspekte in präziser Weise auf die Abfolge der Bücher der Summa übertragen. Denn die *eine* Bewegung *exitus-reditus* erstreckt sich auf alle drei Bücher. Vor allem lässt sich die Tertia Pars nicht als „Appendix des Kontingenten" verstehen, bzw. als „konkreter Inhalt", mit dem die abstrakte Struktur der beiden vorausgehenden Bücher „gefüllt" wird. Ferner ist Christus schon ab der Prima Pars präsent, wenn auch oft in verborgener Weise.[59] Die Aufteilung des theologischen Stoffes scheint daher lediglich formale oder didaktische Gründe zu haben. Doch um welche Gründe handelt es sich? Lässt sich die innere Struktur wenigstens auf der formalen oder didaktischen Ebene auf die Reihenfolge der Bücher beziehen? Vor allem stellt sich die Frage, was die Abtrennung des größten Teils der christologischen Materie und seine geschlossene Darstellung in der Tertia Pars zu bedeuten hat.[60] Otto Hermann Pesch versuchte, hierauf eine Antwort zu formulieren. Obwohl sie nicht alle Probleme löst, macht sie doch auf einen wichtigen Sachverhalt aufmerksam.

Trotz vieler Übereinstimmungen mit Seckler greift Pesch Chenus zentrale Idee, nämlich die Unterscheidung von Struktur (Prima und Secunda Pars) und „*concretissimum*" (Tertia Pars) wieder auf. Aber bereits das Wort „*concretissimum*", das er selbst in die Debatte einführte, weist darauf hin, dass er Chenus Idee modifizierte. Denn obgleich Prima und Secunda Pars vor allem die Strukturen behandeln, stehen sie stets unter christologischer Perspektive. Ferner untersucht die Prima Pars nicht allein den *exitus*, vielmehr behandelt sie auch schon die Voraussetzungen für den *reditus* des Menschen – und ebenso den bereits vollzogenen *reditus* der Engel.[61] Die Tertia Pars betrachtet die Rückkehr des Menschen, doch in anderer Weise, als die Secunda Pars dies tut. Für Pesch besteht der Unterschied im Kreuzes-

---

59 Pesch, Um den Plan, 417: „Am Beginn der theologischen Synthese wird Christus ausdrücklich eingeführt als der ‚Weg', auf dem der *reditus* der Kreatur verläuft – das ist eine deutliche Anweisung, bei der Lektüre der I[a] und der II[a] den Inhalt der III[a] stets mitzudenken."

60 Vor dieser Frage scheint Seckler kapituliert zu haben. Vgl. Pesch, Thomas von Aquin. Grenze und Größe mittelalterlicher Theologie, Mainz 1988, 392.

61 Vgl. Pesch, Um den Plan, 416.

geschehen, welches er das „*concretissimum*“ der Heilsgeschichte nennt, und in dem er die endgültige Antwort Gottes auf die Sünde des Menschen erblickt.[62] Gemäß dieser Idee behandeln die Prima und die Secunda Pars den *exitus* und den *reditus* tatsächlich bereits unter christologischer Perspektive, wobei jedoch (fast! s. u.) jeder Aspekt der Sünde ferngehalten wird. Christus spielt demzufolge in den beiden ersten Büchern die Rolle eines kosmologischen und eschatologischen Mittlers in einer hypothetisch sündenlosen Schöpfung.[63] Natürlich stellt sich hier erneut die alte, von Thomisten und Skotisten seit jeher diskutierte Frage, ob Christus auch ohne den Sündenfall Mensch geworden wäre. Sie klingt auch bei Pesch an, obwohl er das Problem der Sonderstellung der Tertia Pars primär auf der Ebene der formalen, bzw. der didaktischen Stoffeinteilung betrachtet. Seine Lösung stimmt mit Seckler darin überein, dass er der *exitus-reditus*-Struktur eine grundsätzliche Bedeutung zuerkennt. Ferner ist auch er davon überzeugt, dass die drei Bücher der Summa *von Anfang an* aufeinander bezogen sind. Trotzdem billigt er der Tertia, die das „*conretissimum*“ enthalte, einen gewissen Sonderstatus zu:

> „Der Plan der beiden ersten Bücher formuliert also die Richtung der Grundbewegung aller Heilsgeschichte überhaupt, die immer eine christusbezogene Bewegung ist, welchen besonderen konkreten Verlauf sie auch haben mag. In diesem Sinne sind die beiden ersten Bücher der STh heilsgeschichtlich und auf das *concretissimum* der faktischen Heilsgeschichte zugleich bezogen und dagegen abgegrenzt.“[64]

Auf der Basis dieser Lösung versucht Pesch, die grundlegende Perspektive der thomasischen Theologie herauszuarbeiten. Diese sei vom Thema der Schöpfung, bzw. des Schöpfers bestimmt. Ganz richtig sieht er, dass allein dieser Theozentrismus die Möglichkeit gibt, die Einheit von Erlösungs- und Schöpfungswerk zu wahren.[65]

Dennoch entdeckt Pesch selbst eine letzte Inkonsequenz in dieser von hypothetischen Überlegungen bestimmten Aufteilung von „immer schon konkreter Struktur“ und „*concretissimum*“. Hierbei handelt es sich um die Stellung des alttestamentarischen Gesetzes. Dieses ist gemäß Thomas nur aufgrund der Sünde erlassen worden. Dennoch behandelt er es bereits in der Prima Secundae!

---

62 Vgl. ebd. 421; Pesch, Thomas, 394.
63 Pesch, Um den Plan, 421.
64 Pesch, Thomas, 395.
65 Vgl. hierzu ausführlich ebd. 395–400.

> „Thomas gibt denn auch deutlich zu erkennen, dass das Alte Gesetz hauptsächlich der Sünde wegen gegeben wurde und nicht gewissermaßen aus ‚Systemzwang' des geschichtlichen Heilshandelns Gottes selber. Und trotzdem hat er, optisch systemwidrig, gerade an dieser Stelle die Lehre vom Alten Gesetz stehenlassen und damit stillschweigend eingestanden, dass jeder systematisch-theologische Ansatz seine Grenze findet am Reichtum des Geheimnisses, dem er zu dienen hat und das ihm gegenüber den Mehrwert des uneinholbaren letzten Wortes behalten muss."[66]

Fassen wir zusammen: Falls Pesch richtig liegt,[67] dann hätte Thomas Christus als Gekreuzigten als Gottes „konkreteste" Antwort auf die Sünde von der übrigen theologischen Materie gewissermaßen abgetrennt. Diese Antwort wäre für ihn – sehr menschlich gesprochen – nicht Teil des göttlichen Systems gewesen. Die Tertia Pars wäre damit ein Zeichen für die reine Gnadenhaftigkeit der Erlösung. Zugleich durchbräche die Stellung des alttestamentarischen Gesetzes diese „saubere", von hypothetischen Überlegungen bestimmte Stoffeinteilung. Obwohl Formulierungen wie „Hätte der Mensch nicht ...", „Hätte Gott gewollt, dass ..." in der Theologie nützlich und sogar notwendig sind, vermag der Mensch auch mit ihrer Hilfe das Ganze seiner (Heils-)Geschichte nicht zu ergründen.

Hieran anknüpfend sei zum Schluss noch ein Wort gesagt zur Frage der Theodizee, die in den geschichtstheologischen Versuchen der letzten Jahrzehnte eine wichtige Rolle spielte (Jüngel, Moltmann u. a.): Sicherlich hatte diese Frage für den mittelalterlichen Theologen Thomas von Aquin nicht die gleiche dramatische Bedeutung wie für die Theologen des 20. Jahrhunderts.[68] Dennoch: Die von der Sünde verursachten Brüche und Verwundungen hinterließen in seiner Theologie sogar auf der didaktischen Ebene der Stoffeinteilung unübersehbare Spuren. Und Thomas versuchte nicht, sie zu bemänteln oder zu verschleiern.

---

66 Ebd. 399.

67 Die Sachlage scheint komplizierter zu sein, denn Pesch vergisst bspw. den Sündenfall der Engel, den Thomas bereits in der Prima Pars behandelt.

68 Obwohl auch er sich ausführlich mit der Frage nach dem *malum* beschäftigte.

Wozu und wie Philosophie im Dominikanerorden?

Philippe-André Holzer OP

Der Orden wurde für die Predigt gegründet. Wozu also Philosophie? Es scheint völlig abwegig zu sein, Prediger in Philosophie auszubilden. Prediger sprechen über Gott oder mit Gott. Mehr als Theologie scheint dazu nicht vonnöten zu sein.

Dieser Eindruck trügt. Tatsache ist, dass die Theologie selbst auf die Philosophie angewiesen ist und bleibt – so wie die Gnade Gottes seine Schöpfung und damit geschaffene Natur voraussetzt. Denn ebenso wenig wie die Bibel ist die Theologie nicht ohne Einbezug von Menschen einfach vom Himmel gefallen. Menschliches Nachdenken über Gott ist immer das Nachdenken von konkreten Menschen über Gott. Es ist klar, dass diesem Nachdenken des Menschen das Denken Gottes über Gott vorangeht. Auch wenn wir durch Schöpfung und Offenbarung an diesem Denken teilnehmen dürfen, wird das Nachdenken des Menschen nicht durch Gottes eigenes Denken ersetzt; da wir Menschen nicht Gott sind, bleibt uns letzteres zunächst einmal verborgen.

Das Denken von Menschen ist fehlbar; wir irren uns immer wieder. Daran ist positiv, dass wir bemerken, dass wir uns irren. Aus diesem Grund verzweifeln wir nicht, gerade weil wir uns irren und dies wissen. Deswegen versuchen wir vielmehr, einander das Ergebnis unserer Denk-Anstrengungen mitzuteilen. So entstehen menschliche Fertigkeiten und Künste, die von Generation zu Generation weitergegeben und günstigenfalls vermehrt und verbessert werden. Das ist kein einfacher Vorgang, denn die Einsicht in die eigenen Fehler und in unsere Angewiesenheit auf andere braucht Zeit und Energie. Es bleibt uns immer die Versuchung, das Eigene, das wir uns zusammengebaut haben, dem Gemeinsamen vorzuziehen, denn da können wir uns doch profilieren.

Philippe-André Holzer OP

Vom Generalkapitel 1980 zur Reform des Philosophiestudiums 2011

Das Generalkapitel von Walberberg 1980 hat eindrücklich über das Studium gesprochen: Es muss unserem Willen zur Predigt der Wahrheit und dem Gebet entspringen, sonst werden auch die schönsten Ermahnungen dazu nichts nützen.[1] Dieses Studium soll theologisch und systematisch sein; was das aber konkret heißt, scheint heute unklar geworden zu sein. Diese Unklarheit darf nicht zur Flucht in die biblische Theologie verleiten,[2] – letztere fordert vielmehr zum systematischen theologischen Denken heraus. Wo liegt die Lösung zur Klärung und Vertiefung der systematischen Theologie? Nach den Kapitelsvätern von Walberberg in einer guten philosophischen Bildung; diese darf sich nicht auf museumsmäßige Informationen über einige wichtige Philosophen beschränken, sondern muss die Studenten befähigen, selbständig philosophische Urteile zu fällen.[3] Das ist ein hoher Anspruch, und ich habe nicht den Eindruck, dass man ihm überall gerecht wird. Die angesprochene Krise von Theologie und Philosophie ist nicht auf den Orden beschränkt; sie hat die ganze Kirche erfasst.

Warum sollen Gläubige intelligent sein und Fragen stellen? Warum sollen sie denken – genügt der Glaube nicht? Dass der Glaube nach dem Denken verlangt (und dass in letzter Betrachtung in dieser Welt auch das Denken nach dem Glauben verlangt), wurde in der Enzyklika «Fides et Ra-

---

1 Siehe Acta capituli generalis provincialium ordinis Praedicatorum apud Walberberg in conventu s. Alberti Magni a die 3. usque ad diem 27. Septembris 1980 [celebratum]. Romae 1980, Nummer 103.2.

2 Ebd., Nummer 103.4: «multi fratres nostris diebus (…) ad theologiam biblicam confugiunt»; Nummer 103.5: «Theologia biblica non est alternativa theologiae systematicae nec refugium ab ea, nec ad meram et immediatam utilitatem pastoralem reduci potest. Habet exigentias scientificas et technicas sine quibus sensus verbi Dei (…) ex sacris libris fideliter erui non potest.» Leider kann man heute nicht mehr von einer Flucht zur Bibel sprechen; ich bin mehreren (in den biblischen Wissenschaften) gut ausgebildeten Brüdern begegnet, die es vorziehen, in die Pastoral zurückzukehren, als ihre Kompetenz der Kirche als Dozenten und Forscher fruchtbar zu machen. Es scheint mir, dass es dem Orden nach dem Konzil nicht mehr gelungen ist, dem Nachwuchs Lehre und Forschung als gültige Verwirklichungen der dominikanischen Lebensform darzustellen.

3 Ebd., Nummer 103.3: «Nobis videtur quod ratio principalis huius incertitudinis est carentia bonae formationis philosophicae. Nec ex parte iuvenum novas definitiones et methodos theologiae systematicae expectare possumus quamdiu, ut saepe in Ordine accidit, formatio philosophica eorum exigua est, vel in sola informatione historica de aliquibus philosophis, sine criteriis pro iudicio personali consistit. Urget gravis necessitas de hac formatione philosophica in Ordine providendi.»

tio» dargestellt – diese Überzeugung liegt auch anderen neuen Enzykliken zugrunde. Dass die gegenseitige Verwiesenheit von Theologie und Philosophie vermehrt in der Ausbildung von Priestern berücksichtigt werden soll, zeigt das «Dekret zur Reform der kirchlichen Studien der Philosophie» der Kongregation für das katholische Bildungswesen vom 28. Januar 2011. Nach diesem Dekret sollen die grundlegenden Pflichtfächer der Philosophie mindestens 60 Prozent der Kreditpunkte der ersten zwei Jahre im Theologiestudium ausmachen.[4] Unter diesen Pflichtfächern findet man die Philosophiegeschichte vom Altertum bis zur Gegenwart sowie die systematischen Fächer Metaphysik, Naturphilosophie, Logik, Erkenntnislehre sowie philosophische Anthropologie, Ethik und Politik.

Die Theologie braucht die Philosophie, damit sie den Boden unter den Füßen nicht verliert.[5] Konkrete Konsequenz dieser Gebrauchs-Konzeption der Philosophie ist die Tatsache, dass der Dekan der Theologischen Fakultät entscheidende Befugnis über Philosophiestudien im Rahmen der Priesterausbildung erhält – auch da, wo diese Studien in einer kirchlichen philosophischen Fakultät durchgeführt werden. Offensichtlich misstraut man in diesem Bereich dem eigenständigen Urteilsvermögen der kirchlich ausgebildeten Lehrer der Philosophie.

Ziel des kirchlichen Studiums der Philosophie ist die Heranbildung einer philosophischen Haltung, die es erlaubt, selbständig «stringent zu denken, zu erkennen und zu begründen und auch auf wirksame Weise und ohne Angst mit jedermann in einen Dialog einzutreten».[6] Damit sind auch gewisse Inhalte verknüpft, denn nicht jeder philosophische Inhalt ist gleichermaßen geeignet, durch die Theologie gebraucht zu werden. In Nummer 11 der Präambel des Dekretes werden folgende Wahrheiten aufgezählt, die als besonders wichtig und aktuell zu untersuchen und zu verteidigen sind:

---

4 Das ergibt ein Minimum von 72 ETCS-credits für Studien unter dem System von Bologna. Siehe Artikel 51, 1°a) der Verordnungen [Ordinationes] zu besagtem Dekret. Dieser Artikel bezieht sich auf die entsprechende Verordnung für den Studiengang einer kirchlichen Fakultät für Philosophie in Artikel 60, 1 a). Der Text des Dekrets ist auf vatican.va unter «Kongregationen», «Kongregation für das Katholische Bildungswesen» unter dem Datum 28. Januar 2011 in verschiedenen Sprachen zugänglich. – Alternative zur Integration der philosophischen Fächer ins Theologiestudium ist ein unabhängiges zweijähriges Studium an einer kirchlichen philosophischen Fakultät.

5 Vgl. Dekret, Präambel, Nummer 9 besonders das Zitat von Joseph Ratzinger.

6 Dekret, Präambel, Nummer 11.

a) Der Mensch ist fähig, objektive allgemeine Wahrheiten zu erkennen.
b) Er kann metaphysisch gültige Erkenntnisse erwerben.
c) Der Mensch ist eine Einheit aus Seele und Leib.
d) Jeder Mensch hat eine persönliche Würde.
e) Die Natur und die Freiheit des Menschen stehen in Beziehung zueinander.
f) Das Naturgesetz und der Gegenstand einer Handlung gehören zu den wichtigsten Quellen des moralischen Handelns des Menschen.
g) Staatliche Gesetze sollten den moralischen Gesetzen angeglichen werden.

Im Dekret werden diese weithin anthropozentrischen und ethikorientierten Thesen genannt; der Hauptakzent aber scheint auf den ersten beiden Thesen zu liegen. Was kann der Mensch wissen? Mit der Lehre der Kirche ist weder die Ansicht kompatibel, nach welcher er nichts wissen kann, noch diejenige, dass er alles wissen kann. Denn nach der ersten Sicht gibt es auch keinen Platz für das Wissen und damit auch nicht für eine menschliche Theologie, nach der zweiten gibt es kaum mehr einen Platz für den Glauben. Es ist der Kirche durchaus nicht selbstverständlich und daher hoch anzurechnen, dass sie sich für die Philosophie starkmacht – sie hätte der Versuchung erliegen können, mit dem Glauben all das ersetzen zu wollen, was wir wissen können. Das ist eine Versuchung, der nicht nur die Kirche erliegen könnte; mehrere Teilbereiche der Naturwissenschaften, aber auch philosophisch verankerte Ideologien haben immer wieder ähnliche Ansprüche auf ein derartiges Gesamtwissen gemacht.

Nimmt man für den Menschen einen Mittelweg zwischen völligem Nichtwissen und Allwissen an, hat das konkrete Konsequenzen. Dazu gehört die schon erwähnte Einsicht, dass Wissen schwer zu erwerben und oft mit Irrtum behaftet ist; es gehört aber auch eine positive Einstellung dazu, dass es in der Tat mehrere Wissenschaften gibt. Diese Wissenschaften haben verschiedene Gegenstände und benützen jeweils ihren Gegenständen entsprechende Methoden. Das Feld des Wissbaren ist nicht einförmig und kann nicht mit einem einzigen Akt vom Menschen umfangen werden. Diese Tatsachen sind nicht zu bedauern und nicht zu unterdrücken – oft genug wurde dies versucht, und oft genug haben solche Versuche unheilvolle Wirkungen gehabt.

Metaphysik

Diesem Bereich der Philosophie wird im Dekret eine große Wertschätzung zuteil. Denn die Vielzahl der Wissenschaften steht nicht wahllos nebeneinander, sondern wie ihre Gegenstandsbereiche zueinander in Beziehung stehen, so auch die entsprechenden Wissenschaften. Eine beschränkte Einsicht in die Abhängigkeiten zwischen Wissenschaften findet man auch in den Wissenschaften selbst; Aufgabe der Metaphysik ist es, diese Einsicht zu vertiefen und den Blick auf das Ganze zu weiten.

Die Zahl der Wissenschaften ist erheblich, und im Laufe der Geschichte haben mehrere davon den Anspruch erhoben, die erste oder letzte, die grundlegendste zu sein. Ein plausibler Kandidat für diese Rolle war und ist die Wissenschaft von der Natur – die Physik. Aristoteles hat sich in fruchtbarer Weise mit diesem Anspruch auseinandergesetzt und damit die Grundlagen für eine systematische Metaphysik gelegt. Er hat gezeigt, wie die Physik zur Erklärung natürlicher Vorgänge und Entitäten auf deren Ursache Bezug nimmt. Die Physik wäre nur dann die erste Wissenschaft, wenn gezeigt werden könnte, dass der Bereich der Natur selbst nicht verursacht wäre. Gerade dieser Nachweis kann der Physik selbst nicht gelingen, da der Versuch dazu den Zuständigkeitsbereich dieser Wissenschaft überschreitet.

So öffnet sich ein Feld systematischer metaphysischer Forschung und Lehre, welche eine Reflexion über die Kausalität (und ihre verschiedenen Arten), die seienden Dinge und das Sein (den allgemeinsten denkbaren Gegenstandsbereich), das Wesen menschlichen Wissens und menschlicher Wissenschaften (ihre Vielzahl, ihre unterschiedlichen Methoden und Ausgangspunkte, ihre Gegenstandsbereiche, die Beziehungen untereinander) einschließt.

Da der Gegenstandsbereich der Metaphysik der denkbar allgemeinste ist, es sich also um eine grundlegendste oder letzte menschliche Denkanstrengung handelt, welche die ersten und letzten Ursachen mit einbezieht, handelt es sich nicht mehr um eine Einzelwissenschaft; die Metaphysik nimmt vielmehr eine Sonderstellung gegenüber allen Künsten und Wissenschaften ein. Indem er den alltäglichen Sprachgebrauch seiner Zeitgenossen erhebt, ihn reflektiert und schließlich systematisiert, kommt Aristoteles dazu, die Metaphysik als «Weisheit» zu bezeichnen. Das oben genannte Dekret zur Reform der kirchlichen Studien der Philosophie von 2011 betont gerade diesen weisheitlichen Charakter und die Wichtigkeit der Ausrichtung der Metaphysik auf das Sein.

Es mag sein, dass die Metaphysik im Lager der «kontinentalen Philosophie» derzeit wenig beachtet wird; oft wird auf die verschiedenen Überwindungsversuche seit dem 18. Jahrhundert hingewiesen. Im Bereich der analytischen Philosophie dagegen sind insbesondere ontologische Diskussionen seit etwa fünfzig Jahren an der Tagesordnung. Auch wenn die Diskussion um den Nominalismus dabei eine wichtige Stellung einnimmt, kann auf ein wiedererwachtes Interesse an Aristoteles hingewiesen werden. Wo Aristoteles Gehör findet, wäre es schade, wenn der Beitrag des Thomas von Aquin übergangen würde. Ich denke, dass Dominikaner, die einen lebendigen Bezug zum Denken des Thomas haben, einen wertvollen Beitrag zur Wiederentdeckung der Metaphysik nicht nur als wissenschaftliche Ontologie, sondern darüber hinaus auch als Weisheit leisten könnten, wenn sie sich – gut informiert über die zeitgenössische Diskussion – vermehrt auf dieses für sie ungewohnte Feld wagen würden. Das könnte ihnen auch helfen, gewissen Verengungen des Gesichtsfeldes, die es in der thomistischen Überlieferung auch gibt, zu entgehen.

Wie Philosophie treiben und lehren?

Wenn es wahr ist, dass das Studium der Philosophie zunächst zur Ausbildung einer philosophischen Haltung und zur Befähigung zum philosophischen Urteilen führen soll, denke ich, dass es sich in erster Linie auf philosophische Texte stützen sollte. Das Lesen und Verstehen von Texten wird manchmal als selbstverständlich angesehen; aus Erfahrung kann ich sagen, dass man das auch bei Abiturienten nicht einfach voraussetzen kann.

Da ist Logik sehr hilfreich. Die Fähigkeit, zu argumentieren und Texte logisch zu analysieren und zu strukturieren, halte ich für jeden, der sich mit Wissenschaft beschäftigt, aber auch für jeden Prediger für unabdingbar. So begrüße ich, dass Logik wieder an den Anfang des Studiums gesetzt werden kann – zu meiner Zeit wurden wir erst in Predigtseminarien damit konfrontiert. Selbstverständlich gibt es auch einen theoretischen Teil der Logik; ich würde der Praxis aber die größte Priorität zumessen. Nur die konkrete praktische Kenntnis satzübergreifender Strukturen gibt uns die Möglichkeit, zielgerichtet und einigermaßen konzis zu sprechen und zu schreiben.

Die ältesten überlieferten philosophischen Texte weisen ganz verschiedene literarische Ausrichtungen und Strukturen auf; auch das Problem der Textkritik stellt sich ganz klar (gerade bei Aristoteles). Die Aus-

einandersetzung mit diesen Dingen kann helfen, Methoden des Textverstehens zu erlernen, ohne dass gleich die Fragen nach Inspiration und Offenbarung dazukommen und die Gefahr besteht, dass die Frageebenen vermischt werden. So kann sich ein Gespür für die Chancen und Grenzen verschiedener Methoden entspannter heranbilden.

Systematische Philosophie und Philosophiegeschichte sollten aporetisch gelehrt werden, das heißt mit einem Blick auf das Fragen in Situationen, in denen keine der vorgelegten oder vorgegebenen Antworten überzeugt. Nur wer Fragen ernst nimmt, wird eine ernstzunehmende Antwort geben können. Philosophie und ihre Tradition ist keine Maschine zur Produktion von Antworten, zu denen niemand die Frage formuliert hat, oder zu denen die Fragen schon lange vergessen sind. Nur in der Entsprechung zur Frage wird die Antwort wirklich adäquat sein können. In der Metaphysik von Aristoteles findet man mehr als ein ganzes Buch voller ungelöster Fragen (mit jeweils mehreren möglichen Antworten), und es ist ein durchaus ernstzunehmender Gemeinplatz, dass wichtige Werke von Thomas von Aquin durch Fragen und Unter-Fragen gegliedert sind, und nicht etwa (wie vielleicht bei einigen neueren Philosophen) durch Antworten.[7]

Ein text- und fragenzentriertes Arbeiten in der Philosophie stellt für viele eine Herausforderung dar und ist nicht leicht zu vermitteln. Ich denke aber, dass sich gerade zukünftige Theologen und Prediger dieser Herausforderung möglichst früh stellen sollten, damit sie in ihrem eigenen Gebiet wachsen können. Hier sehe ich auch die Wichtigkeit der Auseinandersetzung mit zeitgenössischen Strömungen in der Philosophie, welche gerade Ordensleuten und Seminaristen schwer zu vermitteln ist, denn oft denken sie, das Denken heutiger Philosophen sei atheistisch oder zumindest antikirchlich und könne ihnen daher bei der Erarbeitung einer eigenen philosophischen Position, die für die Offenbarung offen ist, in keiner Weise behilflich sein. Allerdings müssen sie sich sagen lassen, dass die Leute, zu denen sie gesandt sind, oft so denken, und sie wissen müssen, mit welchen Vorurteilen und Urteilen sie zu rechnen haben. Auch ist es keineswegs so, dass ich nur von Leuten lernen könnte, deren Meinung ich mehr oder weniger teile; Aristoteles hat festgehalten, dass wir auch denen dankbar sein müssen, die geirrt

7 Vgl. Aristoteles, *Metaphysica* B, sowie das empfehlenswerte Buch von P. Michael Booth OP, *Aristotelian Aporetic Ontology in Islamic and Christian Thinkers*, «Cambridge Studies in Medieval Life and Thought», third series, volume 20, Cambridge: Cambridge University Press, 1983, reprint 2008.

haben – nicht nur weil sich niemand vollständig irren kann, sondern auch weil die Einsicht in einen Irrtum den Weg zur Wahrheit vertieft.

Manchmal treffe ich allerdings Theologen, die so begeistert sind von der Methode, die sie praktizieren, dass sie nicht glauben, dass irgendeine andere Methode auch gerechtfertigt sein könnte. Mit solchen Denkschemata stehen diese Theologen allerdings nicht allein. Nur allzu oft findet man ein analoges Phänomen bei Naturwissenschaftlern, etwa bei Physikern.[8] Sie glauben, es könne nur *eine* Methode geben, die uns zum Wissen bringen kann. Dass es in der Tat mehrere Wissenschaften gibt und mit den verschiedenen Wissenschaften auch verschiedene Methoden, die ganz verschiedenartige Kenntnisse liefern können, scheint ihnen nur ein vorläufiges und zufälliges Ergebnis der Geschichte zu sein, das in nächster Zeit zu überwinden ist. Sie scheuen sich nicht, die Ergebnisse der einzig wahren Wissenschaft der Zukunft vorauszusagen – mit welcher Berechtigung (und Methode) sie dies tun, reflektieren sie meist nicht.

Ich glaube nicht, dass die Vielzahl der Wissenschaften und der Methoden ein Unfall der Geschichte ist, sondern dass sie die Stellung des Menschen zum Wissen widerspiegelt. Ja, etwas zu wissen braucht Anstrengung, in der Regel nicht nur eines Einzelnen, sondern einer Gemeinschaft von Leuten, die untereinander kommunizieren – auch über die Jahrhunderte hinweg. Dass die Wissenschaften viele sind, bezeugt unsere Fähigkeit, etwas zu wissen über die verschiedensten Aspekte der Wirklichkeit. Es fordert gleichzeitig unsere Anstrengung heraus, die Ergebnisse über die Fächergrenzen hinaus zu kommunizieren, und die verschiedenen Wissenschaften ordnend zu verbinden. Die Offenheit und Klarheit, die dazu notwendig ist, ist nicht leicht zu erwerben; letztlich übersteigt sie die Wissenschaft und erfordert Weisheit.

Es ist diese philosophische oder irdische Weisheit, die es dem Prediger und dem Theologen ermöglicht, in Dialog zu treten mit der Welt, mit den Wissenschaften, mit anderen Konfessionen und anderen Religionen. Wie jeder Philosoph die wichtigsten Grundbegriffe in eigentümlicher Weise benützt, gilt Ähnliches von den verschiedenen wissenschaftlichen und religiösen Traditionen.

8 Im 19. und 20. Jahrhundert haben Vertreter verschiedener Wissenschaften beansprucht, letztgültiges Wissen zu besitzen, welches alle anderen Wissenschaften erklären und gründen könnte: Ich nenne hier nur die Geschichte, die Soziologie und die Psychologie.

Von der Kraft des Wortes

Thomas von Aquin und Meister Eckhart zur Frage: Wie und von woher empfängt die menschliche Vernunft ihr Wort?

Rupert Johannes Mayer OP

Die Provinz der Dominikaner in Süddeutschland und Österreich feiert im Jahr 2014 ihren 75. Geburtstag. Sie ist Teil eines Ordens, der im Jahr 2016 auf 800 Jahre dominikanischer Predigt zurückblickt. Der Orden stellt sich mit seiner Predigt in die Reihe derer, die die Aufgabe übernommen haben, den Glauben an den einen und dreieinigen Gott zu verkünden. Die ursprünglichen Dokumente dieses Glaubens sind mehrere tausend Jahre alt, die dominikanische Reflexion des Glaubens beginnt im 13. Jahrhundert. Dennoch findet diese Überlieferung bis heute Hörer, die ihr Glauben schenken. So deutet sich an, dass sich in dieser Botschaft etwas Bleibendes äußert. Die Worte des Glaubens sind nicht wie Blätter im Wind, die heute hierhin und morgen dahin geweht werden. Vielleicht können Thomas von Aquin und Meister Eckhart, zwei Dominikaner und Autoren aus der Anfangszeit des Ordens, die heute noch gelesen werden, uns an die Quelle führen, der das bleibende Wort entspringt. Fragen wir sie, warum ein Wort, das vor langer Zeit gesprochen wurde, auch heute noch verstanden werden und die Herzen der Menschen bewegen kann, warum das Wort uralt und doch völlig neu ist. Dieses Fragen führt uns zuerst in die Philosophie, die den Ursprung des menschlichen Sprechens bedenkt. In einem zweiten Schritt ist zu erhellen, wie das Wort der göttlichen Offenbarung – oder Gottes Wort im Menschenwort – aus dem Boden der menschlichen Worte hervor wächst und sich durch menschliche Worte kundtut. Denn die Gnade setzt die Natur voraus und vollendet sie.[1]

---

1 Vgl. z. B. Reden der Unterscheidung: 22. Wie man Gott nachfolgen soll und von guter Weise, Quint 93, 14–26 (= DW V, 288, 10–289, 10), De veritate q14 a9 ad8, a10 ad9, Summa Theologiae I q1 a8 ad2, q60 a1 ad3. Die Werke Eckharts werden zitiert nach Meister Eckhart, Die deutschen und lateinischen Werke. Josef Koch, Josef Quint et al. (Hgg.), Stuttgart 1936 ff. (DW = Deutsche Werke, LW = Lateinische Werke), sowie Meister Eckhart, Deutsche Predigten und Traktate. Josef Quint (Hg.), Zürich 1979 (Quint). Die Werke des Thomas werden folgenden Ausgaben entnommen: Sancti Thomae Aqui-

1. Philosophische Bemerkungen zum Ursprung der Sprache

Thomas geht davon aus, dass jedes Verständnis oder innere Wort, das in der Vernunft empfangen und durch ein gesprochenes Wort ausgedrückt und bezeichnet wird, sich vom ewigen Wort Gottes herleitet.[2] Gott ist auf diese Weise der erste Ursprung des menschlichen Wortes, doch nicht der unmittelbare Ursprung. Unmittelbar geht das Wort aus der Erfahrung der Wirklichkeit hervor. Die erkannten Dinge selbst sind der Ursprung des menschlichen Verständnisses oder Wortes.[3] Dennoch kommt die Kraft des Wortes letztlich von Gottes ewigem Wort.

Ähnlich kann Meister Eckhart sagen: „Alle Worte haben Kraft vom ersten Wort."[4] Dieses göttliche und erste Wort liegt in der Seele. Doch ist es so verborgen, dass der Mensch, der auf andere Stimmen hört, nichts davon vernimmt, es sei denn, er sammelt sich in einem Stillschweigen, worin dem Wort in der Tiefe Gehör verschafft wird.[5] Eckhart fügt also hinzu, dass das verborgene Sprechen Gottes und damit die Kraft aller Worte im Menschen weilt. Der gesammelte Mensch vermag sein Sprechen aus diesem Wort zu empfangen. Eckhart deutet damit an, wie das menschliche Wort aus dem göttlichen Wort entspringt. Im Folgenden ist also der zweifache

---

natis Opera omnia iussu Leonis XIII. P.M. edita, cura et studio fratrum praedicatorum. Rom 1882 ff. (Ed. Leonina). Darin noch nicht herausgegebene Texte folgen der Ed. Marietti, Turin 1948 ff., dem Sentenzenkommentar der Ausgabe S. TOMMASO D'AQUINO, Commento alle Sentenze di Pietro Lombardo, Bologna 2001. Die lateinischen Texte von Thomas und Augustinus finden sich auf http://www.corpusthomisticum.org/iopera.html und http://www.augustinus.it/latino.

2 „Verbum enim Dei ab aeterno conceptum, in paterno intellectu est verbum primordiale, de quo Eccli. I, 5 dicitur: Fons sapientiae verbum Dei in excelsis. Et quia est primordiale, ideo ab ipso derivantur omnia alia verba, quae nihil aliud sunt quam quaedam conceptiones expressae in mente angeli, vel nostra. Unde illud verbum est expressio omnium verborum, quasi fons quidam. Et illa, quae dicuntur de illo verbo, quodammodo aptantur ad alia verba, secundum suum modum" (Super epistolam ad Hebraeos IV 2, n. 217).

3 Vgl. z. B. Compendium Theologiae I 38.

4 Predigt 18, Quint 235, 30–31 (= DW I, Predigt 18, 306, 6–7).

5 „Der himmlische Vater spricht ein Wort und spricht es ewiglich, ... und er spricht in diesem Worte seine ganze göttliche Natur und alle Kreaturen aus. Das Wort liegt in der Seele verborgen, so dass man es nicht weiß noch hört, dafern ihm nicht in der Tiefe Gehör verschafft wird; vorher wird es nicht gehört; vielmehr müssen alle Stimmen und alle Laute hinweg, und es muss eine lautere Stille da sein, ein Stillschweigen" (Predigt 19, Quint 237, 3–10 = DW I, Predigt 19, 312, 3–9).

Ursprung des Wortes, aus der Erfahrung der Wirklichkeit und aus dem Wort Gottes, in den Blick zu nehmen.

1.1. Inneres Wort und Erfahrung der Wirklichkeit durch die Sinne

1.1.1. Bei Thomas von Aquin

Zunächst beschreibt Thomas das menschliche Erkennen im Ausgang von Aristoteles und somit analog zur sinnlichen Wahrnehmung. Wenn ein Mensch etwas wahrnimmt, steht er in der Gegenwart des Wahrnehmbaren, z. B. erscheint die weiße Wand in ihrem Weißsein für das Auge. Wir nehmen nicht immer dasselbe wahr und die äußeren Sinne können Wahrnehmungen nicht aktiv hervorbringen, da sie für ihr Wirken auf die Gegenwart des Wahrgenommenen angewiesen sind. Deshalb muss die Gegenwart eines Wahrnehmbaren so auf den Sinn einwirken, dass dieser das Sinnfällige vernimmt. Die Gegenwart des Wahrnehmbaren für den Betrachter wird deshalb auf ein Abbild des Sinnfälligen zurückgeführt, das die Sinne vom Sinnfälligen empfangen.[6] Dieses Empfangen geschieht nicht direkt. Das Auge sieht z. B. nur, wenn ein durchsichtiges Medium zwischen ihm und seinem Gegenstand liegt, wenn das Licht die Farbe dieses Gegenstands aufscheinen lässt und an das Auge vermittelt.[7] Über Aristoteles hinausgehend verdeutlicht Thomas, dass der Mensch auf diese Weise nicht die Abbilder der Dinge wahrnimmt, sondern die Dinge selbst durch die Abbilder. Das Abbild vergegenwärtigt nicht sich selbst, sondern das Abgebildete erscheint für den Betrachter und bietet ihm den Anblick des wirklichen Dinges, das er in den Blick nimmt.[8]

Die Vernunft gleicht den Sinnen insofern, als sie ohne Erfahrung ihrer Gegenstände nichts von ihnen weiß. Vor der Erfahrung steht sie in der

---

6 Vgl. Sentencia Libri De Anima II 10–12, 24, Summa Theologiae I q78 a3, sowie Brennan, Robert E., Thomistische Psychologie. Eine philosophische Analyse der menschlichen Natur, Graz 1957, 95–123 und 142–168, Pickavé, Martin, Human Knowledge. In: B. Davies und E. Stump (Hgg.), The Oxford Handbook of Aquinas, New York 2012, 311–326.

7 Vgl. Sentencia Libri De Anima II 14–15.

8 Vgl. Summa Theologiae I q85 a2, sowie Mayer, Rupert J., De veritate: Quid est? Vom Wesen der Wahrheit. Ein Gespräch mit Thomas von Aquin, Freiburg/Schweiz 2002, 279–283, Imbach Rüedi, DEUS EST INTELLIGERE. Das Verhältnis von Sein und Denken in seiner Bedeutung für das Gottesverständnis bei Thomas von Aquin und in den Pariser Quaestionen Meister Eckharts, Freiburg/Schweiz 1976, 78–79, 179.

Möglichkeit, etwas zu wissen. Durch Erfahrung gewinnt sie ein Wissen von den Dingen. Deshalb kann sich ein Blinder kein genaues Bild von Farben machen, selbst wenn wir ihm von Farben erzählen. So muss auch die Vernunft ein Vermögen sein, das von seinem Gegenstand ein Abbild empfängt.[9] Doch dieses Abbild vergegenwärtigt nichts Sinnfälliges, sondern das Wesen oder Sein eines Dinges. Während die Sinne oder die Einbildungskraft das Äußere eines Dinges wahrnehmen, z. B. seine Größe und Gestalt, seine Farbe und seine Bewegung oder Ruhe, dringt die Vernunft durch diese Eigenschaften durch zum inneren Wesen und Sein der Dinge.[10] Sie sieht nicht auf etwas in seinem Weiß- oder Grausein, in seiner Größe oder seiner Gestalt hier und jetzt, sondern vernimmt es in seinem Menschsein oder Eselsein, unabhängig von Zeit und Raum oder von diesem oder jenem Individuum.[11] Ein Esel ist immer ein Esel und hat dies mit allen anderen Eseln gemein. Dieses Durchdringen zum Sein und Wesen der Dinge wäre der Vernunft nicht möglich, wenn ihr nicht ein geistiges Licht geschenkt wäre, in dem das innere Wesen der Dinge für sie aufstrahlt, wenn die Einbildungskraft das Äußere der Dinge betrachtet. Nur in diesem Licht, dem *intellectus agens*, vermag die Vernunft dieses und jenes in seinem je eigenen Wesen zu vergleichen, d. h. Selbiges zu identifizieren und Verschiedenes auseinanderzuhalten, um so das Allgemeine und Eine in den vielen Dingen selbigen Wesens zu verstehen.[12]

Diese Beschreibung der Vernunft, die ein Abbild des Wesens der Dinge empfängt und durch dieses Abbild die Dinge in ihrem Wesen und nicht nur die eigenen Gedanken versteht, stimmt mit einem Teil unserer Erfahrung überein. Denn wir vernehmen die Gegenwart des Wesens der wirklichen Dinge, die uns umgeben, ähnlich wie das Äußere der Dinge für die Sinne gegenwärtig ist. Doch die Sinne stehen nur in der unmittelbaren

---

9 Vgl. Summa Theologiae I q79 a2, q84 a7, q85 a2.

10 „[N]omen intellectus quandam intimam cognitionem importat: dicitur enim intelligere quasi intus legere. Et hoc manifeste patet considerantibus differentiam intellectus et sensus: nam cognitio sensitiva occupatur circa qualitates sensibiles exteriores; cognitio autem intellectiva penetrat usque ad essentiam rei, obiectum enim intellectus est quod quid est“ (Summa Theologiae II–II q8 a1).

11 Vgl. Summa Theologiae I q1 a3, q85 a1, q87 a3 ad1, Super Boetium De Trinitate q5 a2.

12 Summa Theologiae I q79 a3 bis a5, q84 a5, q85 a1 ad3 und ad4, besonders Expositio Libri Posteriorum II 20, sowie Mayer, Rupert J., Abstraction: Apriori or Aporia? A Remark Concerning the Question of the Beginning of Thought in Aquinas, Aristotle, and Kant, Angelicum 87 (2010) 709–746, hier: 714–715.

Gegenwart des Sinnfälligen, ohne diese Gegenwart in einem Wort auszudrücken oder verschiedene Wahrnehmungen in Gedanken schlussfolgernd zu verbinden. Die Vernunft unterscheidet sich also von den Sinnen, indem sie nicht nur in der vernommenen Gegenwart des Wesens der wirklichen Dinge steht, sondern diese Gegenwart auch in Gedanken ausdrückt. Thomas nennt diese Gedanken ein inneres Wort, das durch das gesprochene Wort bezeichnet wird. Das gesprochene Wort verweist als nur vermittels des inneren Wortes auf die benannte Wirklichkeit.[13]

Während das Abbild des Wesens uns unmittelbar an das erkannte Ding in seiner Gegenwart verweist, vermittelt der von der Vernunft hervorgebrachte Gedanke zwischen uns und den Dingen, d. h. er hält sie in einer gewissen Distanz und befähigt uns, von den Dingen zu denken und zu sprechen, wann immer wir wollen, ohne auf ihre unmittelbare Gegenwart angewiesen zu sein. Denn das innere Wort vom Wesen der Dinge ist primär selbst ein Erkanntes und nur sekundär ein Spiegel der Dinge, die durch das innere Wort vernommen werden.[14]

Das Denken hat also zwei Aspekte: Es blickt auf das wirkliche Wesen der Dinge und drückt gleichzeitig das so erblickte Wesen aus. In diesem Sinn spricht Thomas von einem *cogitando intueri*, das durch das Schauen des Denkens das Wort empfängt.[15] Dennoch ist menschliches Denken nicht nur empfänglich. Wenn das Wesensbild der Dinge aufgenommen ist,

---

13 Vgl. Klima, Gyula, Theory of Language. In: B. Davies und E. Stump (Hgg.), The Oxford Handbook of Aquinas, 371–397, hier: 372–376.

14 Summa contra Gentiles I 53, IV 11, De veritate q3 a2, q4 a2 ad3, De potentia q9 a5. Zum inneren Wort bei Thomas vgl. Paissac, Hyacinthe, Théologie du Verbe. Saint Augustin et saint Thomas, Paris 1951, Floucat, Yves, L'intellection et son verbe selon saint Thomas d'Aquin, Revue Thomiste 97 (1997) 443–484 und 640–693, Emery, Gilles, The Trinitarian Theology of St Thomas Aquinas, New York 2010, 180–192, Mayer, Rupert J., De veritate: Quid est?, 267–279.

15 Summa Theologiae I q34 a2 ad2. Ähnlich kann Thomas von der Vernunft eines Architekten, die durch ein Wesensbild als *principium intelligendi* zur Erkenntnis gelangt ist, sagen: „artifex intelligendo excogitat formam domus; et cum illa forma sit excogitata per actum intelligendi, et quasi per actum effecta, non potest esse principium actus intelligendi, ut sit primum quo intelligatur; sed magis se habet ut intellectum quo intelligens aliquid operatur" (De veritate q3 a2). Diese Unterscheidung von *principium* und *terminus intelligendi* oder *forma excogitata* wiederholt, dass die Vernunft, die durch das Wesensbild auf die wirkliche Sache blickt, sich in einem erdachten Wort ausdrückt. Letzteres ist zunächst selbst ein Erkanntes, wie z. B. der Plan eines Hauses, den sich der Architekt ausdenkt. Dennoch wird durch diesen Plan das Haus erkannt. Doch ist diese Erkenntnis mittelbar, nicht unmittelbar wie durch das Wesensbild.

drückt die Vernunft dieses Wesen in einem inneren Wort oder Verständnis aus, bedenkt es in einer Definition, zieht gewisse Schlüsse daraus.[16]

In einem gewissen Sinn verbindet Thomas hier Aristoteles und Augustinus miteinander. Der griechische Philosoph kannte nur das Wesensbild der Dinge und war noch nicht fähig, zwischen der unmittelbaren Gegenwart durch das Wesensbild und der mittelbaren Gegenwart in einem Verständnis zu unterscheiden. Auch der Aspekt der aktiven Hervorbringung des Verständnisses wurde von Aristoteles nicht bedacht. Auf der anderen Seite ersetzte Augustinus die abstrahierende Aufnahme eines Wesensbildes durch die Einstrahlung des göttlichen Ideenlichts, die es dem Menschen gestattet, ein geistiges Wort hervorzubringen. Seine sprachphilosophischen Erwägungen waren vom Prolog des Johannesevangeliums angestoßen und gründeten im Glauben, weniger in einer philosophischen Betrachtung der Vernunft und ihres inneren Wortes.

1.1.2. Bei Meister Eckhart

Es mag überraschen, dass auch Eckhart die aristotelische Beschreibung der Vernunft übernimmt: Die menschliche Vernunft ist grundlegend empfänglich für ein Wesensbild, wodurch die erkannte Sache gegenwärtig wird und nicht etwa das Bild selbst.[17] Ebenso hat jedwede menschliche Erkenntnis ihren Ursprung in der Erfahrung durch die Sinne.[18] Diese abstrahierende Erkenntnis wird durch das Licht der Vernunft ermöglicht, d. h. durch den *intellectus agens*, die wirkende Vernunft.[19] Wie bei Thomas empfängt die

---

16 De veritate q4 a2.

17 Vgl. LW V, Quaestio Parisiensis I, n. 7, Quaestio Parisiensis II, nn. 4–6, LW III, n. 194, sowie Imbach, Rüedi, DEUS EST INTELLIGERE, 179, Mayer, Rupert J., Meister Eckharts erste *Quaestio Parisiensis* oder: Wie kann Gottes Vernehmen das *fundamentum* seines Seins sein?, Freiburger Zeitschrift für Philosophie und Theologie 54 (2007) 430–463, hier: 450–454. Eckhart charakterisiert die *species* als *principium operationis sensitivae vel intellectivae*, wodurch die Dinge erkannt werden.

18 „[O]mnis cognitio nostra ortum habet a sensibus" (LW II, Expositio libri Exodi, n. 57, vgl. hier und im folgenden Manstetten, Rainer, Esse est Deus. Meister Eckharts christologische Versöhnung von Philosophie und Religion und ihre Ursprünge in der Tradition des Abendlandes, Freiburg/Breisgau 1993, 357–406).

19 „Wieder in einem andern Sinne wollen wir nun von den »zwei Söhnen« der Vernunft sprechen. Der eine ist die »Möglichkeit«, der andere ist die »Wirklichkeit«. Nun spricht ein heidnischer Meister: Die Seele hat in dieser Kraft (d. h. in der »möglichen« Vernunft) das Vermögen, geistig zu allen Dingen zu werden. In der wirkenden Kraft gleicht sie dem Vater und wirkt alle Dinge zu einem neuen Sein" (Predigt 51, Quint 394, 9–15 = DW II, Predigt 37, 220, 1–221, 1, vgl. LW II, Expositio libri Sapientiae, n. 93, LW III, n. 94).

Vernunft nicht nur ein Wesensbild, sondern sie hat auch einen *conceptus mentis*, der die Wesensdefinition ausdrückt. Ein solches inneres Wort wird durch das Vernehmen geformt (*intelligendo formatur*).[20] Das geistige Sprechen bedingt die Zeugung eines Sprosses, der das im Herzen gezeugte Wort ist, das durch ein äußeres Wort bezeichnet wird.[21] Dieses Wort ist wie bei Thomas eine *conceptio actualis*.[22] Mit anderen Worten: Die Vernunft bringt ihr Wort nur im Vollzug des Erkennens hervor. Im Gedächtnis bewahrt sie nur die Wesensbilder der Dinge auf, nicht die inneren Worte.

Trotz dieser Übereinstimmung mit Thomas dem Wortlaut nach kann man daran zweifeln, ob Eckhart sagen möchte, dass die Vernunft durch das empfangene Wesensbild auf ein Ding blickt und entsprechend ein inneres Wort formt, das der vernommenen Sache entspricht. Denn er nennt das Wesensbild wie Thomas ein *principium intelligendi*, hebt davon aber nicht das innere Wort als *terminus intelligendi* ab. Nach Thomas wird nur das Wort von der Vernunft geboren. Eckhart kann jedoch sagen, dass auch die *species*, d. h. das Wesensbild, im Erkenntnisvermögen gezeugt wird, freilich nicht vom Vermögen selbst, sondern von seinem Gegenstand.[23] Dies ist jedoch kein Widerspruch zu Thomas, insoweit letzterer schreibt, dass der Gegenstand vermittels der *species* gleichwie der Vater des Wortes ist, sodass die Vernunft das Empfangene passiv gebiert.[24] Doch entsteht der Eindruck, als würde Eckhart nicht zwischen empfangenem Wesensbild und hervorgebrachtem Wort unterscheiden. Eckhart zerstreut diese Zweifel, wenn er auf mittelhochdeutsch sagt:

> „Wir hân dâ vor gesprochen von einer würkender vernunft und von einer lîdender vernunft. Diu würkende vernunft houwet diu bilde abe von den ûzern dingen und entkleidet sie von materie und zuovalle und setzet sie in die lîdende vernunft, und die gebirt ir geistlichiu bilde in sie. Und sô diu

---

20 Vgl. LW III, n. 9, n. 31, n. 38.

21 „[E]t in nobis dicere est generare prolem: verbum scilicet genitum nobis in corde" (LW III, n. 642, vgl. n. 132).

22 LW III, n. 6, vgl. De veritate q4 a2 c und ad2.

23 „[I]n omni potentia sensitiva vel rationali nostra primo omnium necesse est gigni speciem, prolem obiecti, ita quod visus actu est alius, non aliud quam visibile actu, sed sunt unum" (LW III, n. 57, vgl. n. 193 und n. 486). Eckhart benützt also die Sprache des Augustinus, ohne dabei das aristotelische Verständnis der Sinneswahrnehmung aufzugeben. Denn nach Augustinus formt die Seele selbst, nicht aber der wahrgenommene Gegenstand, die *species* in den Sinnen: „Neque enim corpus sentit, sed anima per corpus, quo velut nuntio utitur ad formandum in seipsa quod extrinsecus nuntiatur" (De Genesi ad litteram XII 24. 51).

24 Compendium Theologiae I 39.

> lîdende vernunft von der würkenden swanger worden ist, sô behebet und bekennet sie diu dinc mit helfe der würkenden vernunft."[25]

Die wirkende Vernunft, d. h. das Licht der Vernunft, trennt die Bilder (wörtlich: schlägt die Bilder ab, *houwet diu bilde abe*) von den äußeren Dingen und entkleidet sie von stofflichen Bedingungen und Zufall. Die Bilder sind also nicht mehr an dieses oder jenes Ding gebunden, erscheinen nicht in dieser oder jener Materie, nicht in Raum und Zeit. So wird das Bild zum Bild des Wesens, das frei ist von allem Zufall. Dann setzt die wirkende Vernunft diese Bilder in die leidende oder mögliche Vernunft, die wiederum ihr geistliches Bild in diese Bilder hinein gebiert. Denn durch das Bild, das die wirkende Vernunft in die mögliche Vernunft hinein schrieb, wurde letztere schwanger und gebar das Wort. Nur im beständigen Lichtschein der wirkenden Vernunft ist die mögliche Vernunft so zur Erkenntnis fähig.

Beide Dominikaner sehen also, dass die Vernunft nicht nur ein Bild von den Dingen empfängt, sondern auch ein Wort von der Wirklichkeit spricht. Doch gemäß dieser ersten Beschreibung des Verstehens wird kaum sichtbar, wie das göttliche Wort der erste Ursprung jedes menschlichen Wortes ist. Denn über die Gabe der Vernunft und des vernünftigen Lichtes hinaus spricht Gott nur durch die Erschaffung der Dinge oder durch das Sein der Dinge zur Vernunft, wenn wir der obigen Beschreibung folgen.[26] Die Dinge erzeugen im Licht der Vernunft ihr Wesensbild in der möglichen Vernunft, die darauf das Wort hervorbringt. Doch diese Beschreibung ist durch ein weiteres Element zu ergänzen:

1.2. Der Ursprung aller menschlichen Worte

1.2.1. Bei Thomas von Aquin

In einer wenig beachteten Bemerkung seines Kommentars zu Aristoteles' *De Interpretatione* schreibt Thomas, dass das Wort ‚das Seiende' der Ursprung und Quell aller Worte ist.[27] Demgemäß entstehen die Verständ-

25 DW IV, 1, Predigt 104 A, ZZ. 222–232.

26 „[V]eritas procedit et oritur ab esse rerum. Nam ab eo quod ‹est›, est verum quod dicitur, et res sic se habent in veritate sicut se habent in entitate … . Spiritus autem, utpote deus, … est causa omnis esse. Ergo est causa omnis veritatis et verae doctrinae" (LW III, n. 619).

27 „fons et origo <omnium uerborum, scilicet> ipsum ens" (Expositio Libri Peryerme-

nisse des Menschen nicht nur als Antwort auf die Abstraktion eines Wesensbildes, sondern entspringen auch aus dem einen Verständnis, das alles andere Verstehen aus sich entlässt. Der erste Artikel der *Quaestiones disputatae de veritate* hatte ‚das Seiende' deshalb das erste Prinzip einer jeden Wesensdefinition genannt. Dieses Verständnis ist in sich so weit, dass es alle andere Erkenntnis umfängt, da der Mensch über das Seiende hinaus nur dessen verschiedene Weisen vernimmt. Das Wahrsein und das Einssein sind ebenso weite Weisen des Seins wie das Seiende selbst. Das Substanzsein, das Menschsein oder das Eselsein schränken das Sein dagegen auf eine bestimmte Seinsweise ein. Diese Weisen des Seins sind alle im ‚Seienden' schon enthalten, werden aber nicht durch den Namen ‚das Seiende' benannt.[28]

Wenn Thomas gefragt wird, wie ein solches erstes Prinzip zu definieren sei, antwortet er: Im strikten Sinn ist es nicht definierbar. Als erstes Prinzip jedweder Definition steht es über allen Definitionen, Gattungen oder Differenzen und kann nicht in ihnen verortet werden. Doch können wir versuchen, das Prinzip aus seiner Wirkweise zu erkennen, d. h. wir müssen die Frage stellen: Was tut das Sein?[29] Die Antwort ist nicht schwer:

---

nias I 5, ll. 315 f. gemäß Ed. Leonina, vgl. Mayer, Rupert J., De veritate: Quid est?, 284–292).

28 „Dicendum quod sicut in demonstrabilibus oportet fieri reductionem in aliqua principia per se intellectui nota, ita investigando quid est unumquodque, alias utrobique in infinitum iretur, et sic periret omnino scientia et cognitio rerum; illud autem quod primo intellectus concipit quasi notissimum, et in quod conceptiones omnes resolvit, est ens, ut Avicenna dicit in principio suae Metaphysicae; unde oportet quod omnes aliae conceptiones intellectus accipiantur ex additione ad ens. Sed enti non possunt addi aliqua quasi extranea per modum quo differentia additur generi, vel accidens subiecto, quia quaelibet natura est essentialiter ens; unde probat etiam Philosophus in III Metaphysicae quod ens non potest esse genus, sed secundum hoc aliqua dicuntur addere super ens, in quantum exprimunt modum ipsius entis qui nomine entis non exprimitur, quod dupliciter contingit. Uno modo ut modus expressus sit aliquis specialis modus entis; sunt enim diversi gradus entitatis, secundum quos accipiuntur diversi modi essendi, et iuxta hos modos accipiuntur diversa rerum genera: substantia enim non addit super ens aliquam differentiam, quae designet aliquam naturam superadditam enti, sed nomine substantiae exprimitur specialis quidam modus essendi, scilicet per se ens; et ita est in aliis generibus. – Alio modo ita quod modus expressus sit modus generalis consequens omne ens" (De veritate q1 a1).

29 „Circa quod considerandum est, quod bonum numeratur inter prima: adeo quod secundum Platonicos, bonum est prius ente. Sed secundum rei veritatem bonum cum ente convertitur. Prima autem non possunt notificari per aliqua priora, sed notificantur per posteriora, sicut causae per proprios effectus. Cum autem bonum proprie sit

Das Sein verleiht allen Dingen das Dasein. Jedes Ding, jedwedes Wesen und alle Eigenschaften sind nur durch das Dasein, das sie verwirklicht.[30] So verschiedene Dinge wie ein Stein oder ein Mensch werden so vom Dasein verwirklicht. Wir verstehen dadurch, dass ‚Seiendes' sich in verschiedenen Seinsgraden zeigt. Denn im menschlichen Sein finden wir Leben und Erkennen, im Sein des Steins nur das nackte Dasein. In dem Wort ‚das Seiende' verbirgt sich also eine unendliche Vielfalt an Seinsweisen. Thomas nennt diesen Reichtum das Wirklichsein allen Wirklichseins.[31]

Von hier aus beantwortet sich die Frage, wie das allgemeine Verständnis des Seienden jedes andere Verständnis in sich enthält. Gewöhnlich gehen wir davon aus, dass die Allgemeinheit eines Verständnisses so weit ist, dass anderes darin inbegriffen ist, wie z. B. eine Gattung die unter ihr versammelten Arten umgreift. Diese Arten finden sich jedoch nur als mögliche Fortbestimmungen in der Gattung. Denn die Abstraktion, die von der Art zur Gattung führt, lässt die Unterschiede zurück, die eine Gattung in verschiedene Arten aufteilen. Insofern liegt die artspezifische Differenz außerhalb der Gattung. Wenn sie zur Gattung hinzukommt, wird die Gattung kontrahiert und die Art zeigt sich. Das Seiende trägt dagegen alle Gattungen, Differenzen und Arten in sich. Es kann unter keiner Hinsicht bestimmt werden, da es alles andere in sich enthält.[32] Dennoch geht Thomas von einer Bestimmung des Seins durch die einzelnen Seinsweisen aus. Denn die letztere ziehen das Wirklichsein allen Wirklichseins zusammen, so dass sich in einem Ding nur seine eigene Seinsweise findet, nicht aber die aller anderen Dinge. Diese Beschränkung des Seins geschieht durch die begrenzte Aufnahmefähigkeit des Dinges und seines Wesens. Denn im Stein findet sich nur Steinsein, nicht aber das Sein eines Pferdes. Entspre-

---

motivum appetitus, describitur bonum per motum appetitus, sicut solet manifestari vis motiva per motum. Et ideo dicit, quod philosophi bene enunciaverunt, bonum esse id quod omnia appetunt" (Sentencia Libri Ethicorum I 1, ll. 149 ff.). Bei der Definition eines Wesens ist ebenso auf das Wirken zu achten, weil das Wesen aus seiner Wirkung erscheint, nicht weil es durch etwas Späteres definiert würde. Z. B. erkennt man den Menschen nur an seinem Sprechen als vernünftig.

30 Summa Theologiae I q3 a4, q4 a1 ad3, q5 a1.

31 Die Expositio Libri Peryermenias I 5, ll. 394–399 sagt dies explizit: Das Wort *ist* „significat enim id quod primo cadit in intellectu per modum actualitatis absolute; nam ‚est' simpliciter dictum significat esse actu, et ideo significat per modum uerbi. Quia uero actualitas, quam principaliter significat hoc uerbum ‚est', est communiter actualitas omnis forme uel actus … ." Vgl. die *actualitas omnium actuum* in De potentia q7 a2 ad9.

32 De veritate q21 a1.

chend wird das Sein nicht bestimmt wie die Gattung, die durch eine Differenz in einer Art verwirklicht wird. Das Sein verwirklicht anderes und wird nicht von ihm verwirklicht. Doch wird das Sein durch das begrenzte Aufnahmevermögen der Dinge für das Sein bestimmt.[33] Denn die Begrenztheit des Wesens lässt in den Dingen nicht mehr Sein zu, als sie empfangen können. Das Verständnis des ‚Seienden' spiegelt diesen natürlichen Sachverhalt, da jedwedes Verständnis von begrenzten Dingen ähnlich aus ‚dem Seienden' hervorgeht, wie das eingeschränkte So-Sein aus dem Sein selbst. Es ist also zu zeigen, wie die Vernunft versteht, dass ein bestimmtes Verständnis sich auf ein begrenztes Sein bezieht. Thomas beschreibt das Definieren eines begrenzten Wesens wie folgt:

> „Ähnlich sind in der Vernunft auf natürliche Weise gewisse Verständnisse [sc. *conceptiones*], die allen bekannt sind, wie das [Verständnis] des Seienden, des Einen, des Guten und dergleichen. Von ihnen geht die Vernunft auf dieselbe Weise aus, das Wesen eines jeden Dinges zu erkennen, wie sie auch von durch sich selbst bekannten Prinzipien ausgeht, um daraus Folgerungen zu erkennen. Dies geschieht entweder durch das, was einer durch die Sinne wahrnimmt, wie wenn ich durch die sinnfälligen Eigenschaften irgendeines Dinges dessen Wesen vernehme; oder es geschieht durch das, was einer von einem anderen hört, wie wenn ein musikalischer Laie, der nicht weiß, was Musik ist, wenn er hört, dass es eine Kunst sei, durch die man sich auf das Singen und Psallieren versteht, das Wesen der Musik vernimmt, wenn er selbst vorher darum weiß, was Kunst ist und was Singen ist; oder es geschieht auch durch das, was aus der Offenbarung aufgewiesen wird, wie in den Dingen, die zum Glauben gehören: Wenn wir nämlich glauben, dass etwas in uns ist, was von Gott gegeben worden ist, wodurch unser Wille Gott geeint wird, vernehmen wir das Wesen der Liebe, indem wir verstehen, dass die Liebe eine Gabe Gottes ist, durch die der Wille mit Gott vereint wird. Dennoch müssen wir zuvor darum wissen, was Gabe ist und was Wille ist und was Vereinigung ist. Auch von diesen können wir nicht wissen, was sie sind, wenn wir sie nicht bis auf zuvor Bekanntes zurückverfolgen, bis wir so zu den ersten Verständnissen der menschlichen Vernunft gelangen, die allen von Natur aus bekannt sind. Und weil die natürliche Erkenntnis ein gewisses Gleichnis der göttlichen Wahrheit ist, das unserem Geist aufgeprägt wurde, gemäß jenem Psalmwort: ‚Wir sind besiegelt mit dem Licht deines Ange-

33 De potentia q7 a2 ad9, De ente et essentia c. 5, vgl. Wippel, John F., Thomas Aquinas and the Axiom that Unreceived Act Is Unlimited. In: ders., Metaphysical Themes in Thomas Aquinas II (Studies in Philosophy and the History of Philosophy Vol. 47), Washington 2007, 123–51.

> sichts, o Herr', deshalb sagt Augustinus in De Trinitate X, dass dergleichen Habitus in der ersten Wahrheit erkannt werden."[34]

Nach Thomas liegen die ersten Prinzipien des Definierens, wie z. B. das Verständnis des Seienden und des Einen, naturhaft in der menschlichen Vernunft vor. Von diesen Verständnissen geht die Vernunft bei jeder Definition aus und auf sie führt sie jede Definition zurück, ähnlich wie im schlussfolgernden Erkennen, das den Nicht-Widerspruch in allen Urteilen voraussetzt. Dabei geht der Nicht-Widerspruch nicht wie ein Ober- oder Untersatz in das Denken ein, aus dem sich etwas ableiten ließe. Doch ist jede Aussage an die Form der Widerspruchslosigkeit gebunden. D. h.: Jede bejahende Aussage, die ein Subjekt mit einem Prädikat verbindet, hat die Form ‚S ist P.' Denn auch Sätze wie ‚Platon lacht' sind als Seinsaussagen zu verstehen, die eine bestimmte Seinsweise ins Wort heben: Platon *ist* lachend. Der Nicht-Widerspruch besagt, dass etwas nicht zugleich sein und nicht sein kann, logisch gesprochen, dass dasselbe nicht zugleich bejaht und verneint werden kann. Deshalb wird in jedem Satz der Form ‚S ist P' unausgesprochen ein ‚und ist nicht zugleich Nicht-P' mitgedacht, auch wenn damit nicht mehr gesagt ist als in dem einfachen Satz ‚S ist P'.[35]

---

34 Quodlibet VIII q2 a2 (eigene Übersetzung). Der lateinische Text lautet: „Et similiter etiam in intellectu insunt nobis naturaliter quedam conceptiones ab omnibus note, ut entis, unius, boni et huiusmodi, a quibus eodem modo procedit intellectus ad cognoscendum quidditatem uniuscuiusque rei per quem procedit a principiis per se notis ad cognoscendas conclusiones. Et hoc uel per ea que quis sensu percipit, sicut cum per sensibiles proprietates alicuius rei concipio illius rei quidditatem; uel per ea que ab aliis quis audit, ut cum laicus qui nescit quid sit musica, cum audit aliquam artem esse per quam scit canere uel psallere, concipit quidditatem musice, cum ipse presciat quid sit ars et quid sit canere; aut etiam per ea que ex reuelatione habentur, ut est in his que fidei sunt: cum enim credimus aliquid esse in nobis diuinitus datum quo affectus noster Deo unitur, concipimus caritatis quidditatem, intelligentes caritatem esse donum Dei quo affectus Deo unitur, precognoscentes tamen quid sit donum et quid affectus et quid unio, de quibus etiam quid sint scire non possumus nisi resoluendo in aliqua prius nota, et sic quo usque perueniamus ad primas conceptiones humani intellectus, que sunt omnibus naturaliter note. Et quia naturalis cognitio est quedam similitudo diuine ueritatis menti nostre impressa, secundum illud Psalmi: *Signatum est super nos lumen uultus tui, Domine*, ideo dicit Augustinus, X de Trinitate, quod huiusmodi habitus cognoscuntur in prima ueritate." Vgl. hierzu Mayer, Rupert J., De veritate: Quid est?, 479–490.

35 Thomas verneint zunächst nur, dass der Nicht-Widerspruch als Prinzip in eine Beweisführung eingeht, indem wir sagen: S ist P und nicht zugleich Nicht-P. Denn der Zusatz fügt keinen Inhalt hinzu. Doch gibt Thomas zu, dass das Prinzip die Aussagen der Beweisführung durch die Unterscheidung von P und Nicht-P prägt. Denn die ganze

Nur eine tiefer gehende Reflexion bringt diese ursprüngliche oder naturgegebene Nicht-Widersprüchlichkeit ans Licht und führt das Denken in Aussagen und Schlüssen explizit auf den Nicht-Widerspruch zurück. So wenig die Formulierung ‚und ist nicht zugleich Nicht-P' einer Beweisführung nützt, so viel sagt sie über das Denken des Menschen aus. Denn der Mensch bedenkt nicht nur dieses eine Prädikat, das er einem Subjekt zuweist. Vielmehr scheint in der Aussage das Sein des Subjekts unter einer bestimmten Hinsicht auf, die von allen anderen Hinsichten auf das Sein geschieden ist. Das Seinsganze wird im Bedenken von diesem und jenem immer mitgedacht, obwohl es nicht explizit in eine Beweisführung eingeht. Thomas stellt deshalb gegen Aristoteles fest, dass jedwede Definition implizit immer die ganze Welt mit bedenkt.[36]

Wie den Aussagen der Nicht-Widerspruch zugrunde liegt, so bauen Definitionen auf das Verständnis des Seienden auf. ‚Das Seiende' fällt zuerst in der Vernunft oder in ihrem Vernehmen, so dass das Verständnis des Seienden in allem enthalten ist, was jemand vernimmt.[37] Das Enthaltensein meint, dass alles *als seiend* vernommen wird, ohne dies zunächst explizit auszusprechen. Denn ‚das Seiende' ist der formale Gegenstand der Vernunft, die nur das Seiende und die unendliche Fülle seiner Weisen versteht. Formaler Gegenstand bedeutet hier soviel wie die Hinsicht, unter der jedweder Gegenstand für die Vernunft erscheint.[38]

Wahrheit der Prämissen hängt daran, dass nicht zugleich ihr Widerspruch angenommen wird: „nulla *demonstratio* accipit hoc principium quod non contingit *simul affirmare et negare*: si enim aliqua demonstratio eo uteretur ad ostendendum aliquam conclusionem, oporteret ut *sic* eo uteretur quod acciperet *primum*, id est maiorem extremitatem, affirmari *de medio* et non negari, quia, si acciperet affirmationem et negationem ex parte medii, *nichil* differret utrum sic uel sic esset; et eadem ratio est de tercio, id est de minori extremitate, per comparationem ad medium. … Cum autem accipitur affirmatio uel negatio ex parte maioris extremitatis, differt quidem quantum ad conclusionem, immo etiam quantum ad veritatem premissarum: si enim homo esset non animal, non esset verum quod homo est animal neque sequeretur quod Callias esset animal. Tamen nichil plus certificatur cum dicitur: «Homo est animal et non est non animal», quam cum dicitur solum: «Homo est animal»: idem enim intelligitur per utrumque" (Expositio Libri Posteriorum I 20, ll. 23–63).

36 Expositio Libri Posteriorum II 16, ll. 110 ff. Entsprechend erklärt Thomas, dass in den Prinzipien implizit die ganze Welt vorhererkannt ist (vgl. De veritate q18 a4).

37 „[I]llud quod primo cadit in apprehensione, est ens, cuius intellectus includitur in omnibus quaecumque quis apprehendit" (Summa Theologiae I–II q94 a2, vgl. hier und im folgenden Mayer, Rupert J., Abstraction: Apriori or Aporia?, 716–733).

38 Summa Theologiae I q5 a2, q78 a1, q79 a2.

Insofern der Mensch ohne sinnliche Erfahrung nichts erkennen kann, wird ‚das Seiende' zuerst in diesem oder jenem vernommen. Wir erkennen dieses oder jenes Seiende, d. h. dieses oder jenes als seiend oder in seinem Sein. Im Ausgang vom Nicht-Widerspruch erscheint damit auch, dass dieses Seiende nicht jenes ist, sehr wohl aber es selbst. Das bedeutet, dass mehrere Individuen vorliegen, die ein je verschiedenes Sein haben.[39] Dieses Sein kann jedoch unter einer gewissen Hinsicht auch selbig sein, wie z. B. zwei Menschen dasselbe Menschsein zukommt, obwohl jeder sein je eigenes und individuelles Sein hat.[40]

Das Seinsverständnis des Menschen bedingt, dass wir zunächst verschiedene Seinsweisen implizit vernehmen, sie unterscheiden oder auch identifizieren. Worte drücken nur diese vielfältigen Weisen des Seins aus, ohne dass wir explizit Menschsein, Tiersein, Bananensein oder Steinsein sagen. Die sinnliche Erfahrung erlaubt uns, ‚das Seiende' in unendlichen Variationen zu erfahren und den Reichtum des Seins ins Wort zu heben. Die Abstraktion dringt dabei nur deshalb zum Sein durch, das unter sinnfälligen Eigenschaften verborgen ist, weil die Vernunft das Seiende schon immer natürlich vernommen hat. Thomas nennt deshalb die ersten Prinzipien Instrumente der wirkenden Vernunft zur Ermöglichung der Abstraktion.[41]

---

39 De potentia q9 a7 ad15, Super Boetium De Trinitate q4 a1.

40 De veritate q2 a11.

41 „Si enim loquamur de intellectu in actu qui est in ipso addiscente, contingit quod intellectus possibilis alicuius sit in potentia quantum ad aliquid, et quantum ad aliquid in actu. Et per id quod est in actu potest reduci, etiam quantum ad id quod est in potentia, in actum: sicut per id quod est actu cognoscens principia fit actu cognoscens conclusiones, quas prius cognoscebat in potentia. Set tamen actualem cognitionem principiorum habere non potest intellectus possibilis nisi per intellectum agentem. Cognitio enim principiorum a sensibilibus accipitur, ut dicitur in fine Posteriorum. A sensibilibus autem non possunt intelligibilia accipi nisi per abstractionem intellectus agentis. Et ita patet quod intellectus in actu principiorum non sufficit ad reducendum intellectum possibilem de potentia in actu sine intellectu agente. Set in hac reductione intellectus agens se habet sicut artifex, et principia demonstrationis sicut instrumenta" (De anima q4 ad6, vgl. De veritate q11 a3). Thomas spricht nicht nur von den Prinzipien als Instrumenten der Abstraktion. Er klärt auch die Schwierigkeit des doppelten Ursprungs der Prinzipien, die sowohl von Gott eingeprägt als auch durch Abstraktion erkannt sind. Die Frage lautet: Wie kann das Instrument der Abstraktion, ohne das Abstraktion unmöglich ist, einer Abstraktion entnommen werden, bei der es schon als Instrument gegeben sein müsste? Grundsätzlich gilt, dass die Vernunft schon immer die ersten Prinzipien *in actu* haben muss. Denn nur wenn sie unter einer gewissen Hinsicht schon versteht, kann sie das, was sie nicht kennt, auf das schon Gewusste zurückführen. Aristoteles meint, dass es ge-

Wenn wir das Seiende in diesem oder jenem Seienden verstehen, oder in dieser oder jener Seinsweise, ist also mitbedacht oder mitoffenbar, dass dieses oder jenes nicht die Fülle des Seins in sich trägt, sondern nur eine der unendlich vielen Seinsweisen. Dem eingeschränkten Sein der Dinge entspricht im Denken das Verständnis, dass diesem oder jenem nicht die Fülle des Seins eignet, obwohl ihm Sein in einer bestimmten Weise zukommt, die sich von allen anderen Weisen unterscheidet. Wenn das Seiende nicht von jeher vernommen wäre, gäbe es für die Vernunft nichts zu unterscheiden. Dass Denken »Unterscheiden des Seins« ist, zeigt Thomas, wenn er vom Verstehen des Menschen analog auf Gottes Erkenntnis von der Welt schließt:

> „Das Wesen Gottes aber begreift die Vorzüge alles Seienden in sich, freilich nicht auf die Weise der Zusammensetzung, sondern nach Art einer Vollkommenheit, (...). Jede Form, sowohl die spezifische als auch die allgemeine, ist eine Vollkommenheit, insofern sie etwas setzt. Sie schließt jedoch keine Unvollkommenheit ein, es sei denn, insofern sie gegenüber dem wahren Sein abfällt. Die Vernunft Gottes kann also das Spezifische eines jeden im göttlichen Wesen selbst erfassen, indem sie vernimmt, worin ein jedes das Wesen Gottes nachahmt, und worin es von dessen Vollkommenheit abfällt."[42]

Die Einfachheit dieser Beschreibung ist erstaunlich: Gott selbst ist das reine Sein, das alle Vollkommenheiten in seiner Einheit umfängt. Er erkennt alles andere durch sich selbst, indem er sieht, wie das Geschöpf mit dem reinen Sein identisch ist und wie es sich davon unterscheidet.[43] Entsprechend sieht Gott, wie eine Pflanze das bloße Dasein und das Leben Gottes nachahmt, ohne jedoch etwas von Gottes Erkennen in sich zu tragen. Dieser Schluss auf Gottes Wissen von dieser Welt spiegelt Thomas' Seinsverständnis: Auch

---

nügt, alles Wissen der Vernunft auf sinnliche Wahrnehmung und damit nicht auf Wissen zu gründen (vgl. Analytica Posteriora II 19). Thomas sagt, dass eine solche Rückführung zu kurz greift. Vernünftig Erkennbares kann nur aus vernünftig Erkennbarem hervorgehen, nicht aber aus einer sinnlichen Wahrnehmung, die vom Sein nichts versteht. Trotzdem vermag die Vernunft, die schon an den Prinzipien teilhat, diese nicht ohne Abstraktion *aktuell* zu erkennen. Deshalb kann auch die Vernunft ihre Folgerungen nicht aus den Prinzipien ableiten, wenn sie das Licht des *intellectus agens* nicht hat. Denn die Vernunft erkennt die Prinzipien unmittelbar in diesem oder jenem (vgl. De veritate q17 a2). Entsprechend ist es notwendig, die Allgemeinheit der Prinzipien durch Abstraktion zurück zu gewinnen.

42 Summa contra Gentiles I 54, in: Albert, Karl, und Engelhardt, Paulus (Hgg.), Thomas von Aquin. Summe gegen die Heiden. Darmstadt ^{2}1987, 205.

43 Vgl. De veritate q2 a3 ad16, Summa Theologiae I q14 a2, a5 und a6.

der Mensch vernimmt nur, indem er dieses Seiende in seiner Identität und Differenz mit dem Seienden selbst, das alle Seinsweisen in sich birgt, erkennt.

Das Wirklichsein allen Wirklichseins begabt den Menschen mit einem Übermaß an Intelligibilität, das die Menschheit niemals erschöpfend bedenken kann. Unausgesprochen durchspielt die Fülle des Seins alles Denken des Menschen. Thomas hält deshalb, dass alles univoke Aussagen auf ein Erstes zurückgeht, das analog ausgesagt wird: das Seiende.[44] Die Schwierigkeit, das Seinsverständnis ausdrücklich werden zu lassen, liegt daran, dass das Seiende, wenn es mit einem Namen angesprochen wird, wie ein Gegenstand unter vielen anderen erscheint. Das vergegenständlichende Vorstellen kann den einen Ursprung, der jedes andere Verständnis aus sich entlässt und alle Verständnisse in der Einheit des Seins zusammenhält und verbindet, nicht auf der Höhe bedenken, auf der ihm das Seiende begegnet. Selbst die Reflexion auf das Seinsverständnis zeigt sich uns notwendig als seiend. Auch das Nichts, das nicht ein Seiendes unter anderen ist, ist für unser Denken gegenwärtig. Thomas nennt es deshalb ein *ens rationis*, ein Seiendes, das durch die Betrachtungsweise der Vernunft entsteht oder für uns gegenwärtig ist, obwohl ihm in der Wirklichkeit nichts entspricht. *Seiend* heißt also alles für die Vernunft offenbar Seiende oder Gegenwärtige, selbst dann, wenn es in sich nicht ist. Thomas nennt diese ganze Gegenstandsweite der Vernunft deshalb *ens intelligibile*, Offenbarseiendes, das alle Gattungen und Arten des Seienden in sich trägt.[45] Das wirkliche Sein der Dinge in sich selbst hat den Namen *esse naturae* oder *naturale*.[46] Entsprechend ist das wirkliche Sein der Dinge durch ihr Offenbarsein in der Vernunft für den Menschen gegenwärtig, aber ebenso sind Gedanken gegenwärtig und selbst «Dinge» die nicht sind, wie das Nichts.

Wenn das vergegenständlichende Vorstellen zu kurz greift, um das Seiende zu bedenken, muss ihm eine andere Weise des Denkens entsprechen. Thomas verdeutlicht dies durch Gegenüberstellung von Sinnen und

---

44 „[L]icet in praedicationibus oporteat aequivoca ad univoca reduci, tamen in actionibus agens non univocum ex necessitate praecedit agens univocum. Agens enim non univocum est causa universalis totius speciei, ut sol est causa generationis omnium hominum. … Hoc autem agens universale, licet non sit univocum, non tamen est omnino aequivocum, quia sic non faceret sibi simile; sed potest dici agens analogicum, sicut in praedicationibus omnia univoca reducuntur ad unum primum, non univocum, sed analogicum, quod est ens" (Summa Theologiae I q13 a5 ad1).

45 Summa contra Gentiles II 98.

46 Vgl. z. B. Summa Theologiae I q13 a7.

Vernunft. Wenn die menschliche Vernunft Dinge aus der Erfahrung erkennt, dann vergleicht sie vieles, das sie willentlich vorstellt, abstrahiert das vielen Gemeinsame und zieht Schlüsse. Die Sinne dagegen nehmen nicht wahr, indem sie vergleichen. Das geöffnete Auge erblickt die Farbe unmittelbar. Ähnlich verhält sich die Vernunft zu den Prinzipien, die durch sich selbst vernommen werden oder durch sich selbst offenbar sind. Diese Prinzipien werden gesehen, nicht willentlich vorgestellt. Sie eignen der Vernunft von Natur aus.[47] Die Natur ist eine Gabe des Schöpfers.[48] Deshalb zeigt sich das natürliche Vernehmen als Gleichnis der göttlichen Wahrheit, mit dem Gott die Vernunft besiegelt.[49] Thomas möchte damit nicht ausschließen, dass die Prinzipien durch Abstraktion erkannt werden.[50] Doch der Inhalt der Prinzipien entstammt keiner Abstraktion. Durch die Abstraktion werden wir fähig, die Prinzipien zu unterscheiden und ihre Allgemeinheit zu erkennen.[51]

---

47 „Ad cuius evidentiam sciendum est, quod inter intellectum et corporalem visum haec est differentia quod visui corporali omnia sua obiecta aequaliter sunt propinqua ad cognoscendum: sensus enim non est vis collativa, ut ex uno obiectorum suorum necesse habeat pervenire in aliud; sed intellectui non omnia intelligibilia aequaliter vicina sunt ad cognoscendum, sed quaedam statim conspicere potest, quaedam vero non conspicit nisi ex aliis prius inspectis. Sic igitur homo ignotorum cognitionem per duo accipit: scilicet per lumen intellectuale, et per primas conceptiones per se notas quae comparantur ad istud lumen quod est intellectus agentis, sicut instrumenta ad artificem. – Quantum igitur ad utrumque, Deus hominis scientiae causa est excellentissimo modo quia et ipsam animam intellectuali lumine insignivit et notitiam primorum principiorum ei impressit, quae sunt quasi seminaria scientiarum, sicut et aliis rebus naturalibus impressit seminales rationes omnium effectuum producendorum“ (De veritate q11 a3).

48 Vgl. Summa contra Gentiles I 7.

49 Quodlibet VIII q2 a2 (vgl. Anmerkung 34).

50 Vgl. Super Boetium De Trinitate q1 a3 ad3 und ad6, q6 a4, De veritate q11 a1, Summa Theologiae I–II q51 a1. Die genaueren Texte sprechen von einer Bestimmung der angeborenen Prinzipienerkenntnis durch sinnliche Erfahrung. Die *synderesis* ist ein *habitus* „qui est quodammodo innatus menti nostrae ex ipso lumine intellectus agentis, sicut et habitus principiorum speculativorum, ut, omne totum est majus sua parte, et hujusmodi; licet ad determinationem cognitionis eorum sensu et memoria indigeamus“ (Super II Sententiarum d24 q2 a3).

51 „[H]abitus infusus similis est habitui innato: quia sicut naturalis habitus datur in creatione, ita infusus in reparatione. Naturalis autem habitus, sicut intellectus principiorum, indiget ut cognitio determinetur per sensum, quo acquisitus non indiget: quia dum acquiritur, per actum determinationem recipit. (…) habitus principiorum dicitur acquiri per sensum quantum ad distinctionem principiorum, non quantum ad lumen quo principia cognoscuntur“ (Super III Sententiarum d23 q3 a2 ad1).

Entsprechend richtet sich das Sehen des Seienden als ersten Prinzips auf etwas, das der Vernunft durch sich selbst bekannt ist und nicht durch anderes. Alles Denken von diesem und jenem Wesen kommt erst dann zur Ruhe, wenn es eine Sache in ihrem Sein berührt, d. h., wenn die bedachte Sache in ihrer Identität und Differenz mit dem ersten Prinzip vernommen und ins Wort gehoben wurde, so dass ein Einblick in das, was ist, besteht. Dann kann die Vernunft von sich sagen, dass sie ein Wort geboren hat. Letztere Redewendung möchte Thomas durchaus wörtlich verstanden wissen:

> „Das, was in der Vernunft wie ein inneres Wort enthalten ist, wird nach allgemeinem Sprachgebrauch Empfängnis [sc. *conceptio*] der Vernunft genannt. Denn etwas heißt leiblich empfangen, wenn es im Schoß eines lebendigen Sinnenwesens durch eine Leben verleihende Kraft gebildet wird, wobei das Männliche wirkt, und das Weibliche, in dem sich die Empfängnis vollzieht, etwas aufnimmt. … Was aber die Vernunft erfasst, wird in der Vernunft gebildet, wobei das Vernehmbare in einem gewissen Sinn wirkt und die Vernunft etwas aufnimmt. Und das, was die Vernunft erfasst und was in der Vernunft existiert, ist der Wesensform nach dem bewegenden Vernehmbaren ähnlich, dessen Wesensbild es ist. Es ähnelt aber auch der aufnehmenden Vernunft, insoweit es ein Offenbarsein hat [und kein natürliches Sein]. Deshalb heißt das, was von der Vernunft erfasst wird, nicht grundlos Empfängnis der Vernunft.“[52]

Das Wort ist also eine Empfängnis, die von der Vernunft, die das Wesensbild eines Dinges in sich aufgenommen hat, hervorzubringen ist. Eine solche Geburt vollzieht sich nicht ohne Mühe. Denn das Wesensbild wird nur empfangen, wenn der Mensch über vieles nachdenkt, es erwägt, mit anderem vergleicht und dadurch zu einer bleibenden Einsicht in das gelangt, was ist. Solange sich das Denken nicht in einem bleibenden Wort verfestigt, kann man es Nachdenken nennen. Doch vernommen hat es in diesem Zustand des Überlegens noch nichts.[53]

Thomas hatte gesagt, dass diese Empfängnis sich letztlich vom göttlichen Wort herleitet. Das Gemeinte ist nun klarer geworden: Gott schenkt

---

52 Compendium Theologiae I 38, in: Tannhof, Rudolf (Hg.), Compendium Theologiae. Grundriss der Glaubenslehre, Heidelberg 1962, 54–55.

53 „Ipsum enim intelligere non perficitur nisi aliquid in mente intelligentis concipiatur, quod dicitur verbum; non enim dicimur intelligere, sed cogitare ad intelligendum, antequam conceptio aliqua in mente nostra stabiliatur“ (De potentia q9 a9, vgl. Super evangelium S. Ioannis I 1, n. 26).

dem Menschen das Grundverständnis des Seienden, aus dem jedes menschliche Wort hervor fließt, wenn der Mensch durch sinnliche Erfahrung mit der Wirklichkeit in Berührung kommt. Denn es ist der Quell und Ursprung aller Worte und damit die Kraft des Wortes. In seinem frühen Sentenzenkommentar findet Thomas noch den Namen *scintilla rationis* für dieses Grundverständnis, das nicht nur das Seiende betrifft, sondern auch das Gute, also nicht nur die spekulative Vernunft, sondern auch die praktische. Das Fünklein der Vernunft lenkt alles Denken und hält es von jedwedem Irrtum fern, solange sich der Mensch an die Einsicht in das Seiende hält. Im Bereich des praktischen Wissens um das Gute heißt das Grundverständnis *synderesis* und bildet den Kern des menschlichen Gewissens. Spekulatives Denken geht auf den *habitus principiorum* zurück, der ebenso im Bild des Fünkleins enthalten ist wie die *synderesis.*[54]

Das Seinsverständnis und seine Prinzipien prägen auf natürliche Weise unser Denken: Das Seiende ist das *obiectum naturale*, von den Prinzipien haben wir eine *conceptio naturalis* und einen *habitus naturalis*, sowie eine *cognitio naturalis.*[55] »Natürlich« bedeutet hier: ein Vernehmen, das nicht durch einen Willensakt befohlen werden kann.[56] Das Seiende ist also nicht willentlich vorstellbar. Denn die Natur ist an ein einziges Ziel gebunden und liegt vor allem, was der Wille befehlen kann.[57] Ein Apfelbaum bringt einen Apfelbaum hervor, der Mensch zeugt einen Menschen, und die Vernunft vernimmt allein das Seiende auf natürliche Weise, d. h. der *conceptus entis* und die ersten Prinzipien gehen natürlich aus ihr hervor.[58]

54 „[U]nde et talis virtus intellectus vocatur, secundum quod est in speculativis, quae etiam secundum quod in operativis est, synderesis dicitur: et haec virtus scintilla convenienter dicitur, quod sicut scintilla est modicum ex igne evolans; ita haec virtus est quaedam modica participatio intellectualitatis, respectu ejus quod de intellectualitate in angelo est: et propter hoc etiam superior pars rationis scintilla dicitur quia in natura rationali supremum est“ (Super II Sententiarum d39 q3 a1). Eine genauere Unterscheidung findet nur Prinzipien des Urteilens im *habitus intellectus* oder der *synderesis*: Man kann nicht dasselbe zugleich bejahen und verneinen. Gutes ist zu tun, Böses ist zu lassen. Das Seiende selbst ist dagegen das erste Prinzip des Definierens, das der Weisheit zugerechnet wird (vgl. Summa Theologiae I–II q66 a5 ad4, q57 a2).

55 Vgl. Super IV Sententiarum d33 q1 a1, Summa contra Gentiles II 83, Summa Theologiae I–II q10 a1, q51 a1, De veritate q8 a7 ad13.

56 Wenn Thomas die Frage stellt, ob jedwedes Denken auf einen willentlichen Befehl zurückgeht, antwortet er: „unde oportet ponere statum in actu intellectus qui naturaliter intellectum consequitur, ita quod a voluntate non imperatur“ (De potentia q2 a3 ad3).

57 Vgl. Summa Theologiae I q60 a1 und a2, De veritate q22 a5.

58 Vgl. Summa contra Gentiles IV 11.

Bezüglich eines *obiectum naturale* gibt es also keine Wahl. Doch wird dieses Grundverständnis von allen Gedanken, von Vorstellungen der Einbildungskraft und von der Gebundenheit an Raum und Zeit überschattet. Die hin und her überlegende Vernunft (*ratio*) ist ein *intellectus obumbratus*.[59] Durch diese Überschattung und die Unmöglichkeit, das Seiende willentlich vorzustellen, kann der Mensch schnell das Seiende vergessen. Er verdunkelt dann das, womit Gott seine Vernunft besiegelt hat – die Sprache Gottes. Wer so handelt, setzt seine Hoffnung auf menschliche Weisheit und übersieht den Lehrer, der ihm die Prinzipien gegeben hat, vermittels derer er die Welt beurteilen kann. Denn insofern die *cognitio naturalis* ein Gleichnis der göttlichen Wahrheit ist, erkennt der Mensch die Prinzipien in Gott.[60] Thomas verleugnet also die augustinische Verankerung des menschlichen Denkens in der göttlichen Wahrheit nicht ganz. Doch reduziert er es auf die ersten Prinzipien und dreht die Erkenntnisweise um. Denn nach Augustinus werden die Ideen oder *rationes ideales* in der göttlichen Wahrheit erkannt. Thomas erklärt ebenso, dass die Prinzipien in Gott vernommen werden. Doch legt er dies so aus, dass die Prinzipien als Gleichnis Gottes erkannt sind. Gott selbst bleibt somit hinter seiner Sprache verborgen.

1.2.2. Bei Meister Eckhart

Wenn Eckhart in seinen deutschen Predigten vom Fünklein der Vernunft oder der Seele spricht, nennt er es Synteresis. Letztere ist wie bei Thomas ein Licht oder natürliches Licht, das der Vernunft oder der Seele von oben,

---

59 „Ratiocinatur homo discurrendo et inquirendo lumine intellectuali per continuum et tempus obumbrato, ex hoc quod cognitionem a sensu et imagine accipit“ (Super II Sententiarum d3 q1 a2, vgl. d16 q1 a3, Super I Sententiarum d3 q4 a1 ad4, De veritate q8 a3 ad3, Super Boetium De Trinitate q1 a1 ad4).

60 „Prohibemur enim hoc modo hominem vocare magistrum, ut ei principalitatem magisterii attribuamus quae Deo competit; quasi in hominum sapientia spem ponentes, et non magis de his quae ab homine audivimus divinam veritatem consulentes quae in nobis loquitur per suae similitudinis impressionem qua de omnibus possumus iudicare“ (De veritate q11 a1 ad1). Diese *similitudo*, durch die wir alles beurteilen können, sind die ersten Prinzipien: „Sicut enim a veritate intellectus divini effluunt in intellectum angelicum species rerum innatae secundum quas omnia cognoscit, ita a veritate intellectus divini exemplariter procedit in intellectum nostrum veritas primorum principiorum secundum quam de omnibus iudicamus. Et quia per eam iudicare non possumus nisi secundum quod est similitudo primae veritatis, ideo secundum primam veritatem de omnibus dicimur iudicare“ (De veritate q1 a4 ad5).

d. h. von Gott, eingedrückt ist.[61] Die lateinischen Schriftkommentare Eckharts sprechen nie von einer *scintilla rationis*, erwähnen jedoch den *habitus principiorum* und die *synderesis*:

> „Samen und Wurzel der Tugenden ist die Synderesis (...) Denn immer beharrt die Synderesis auf ihrem Widerspruch gegen das Böse und macht auch in den Verdammten noch zum Guten geneigt. (...) Same der Wissenschaft aber ist der Habitus der Prinzipien, die allen von Natur bekannt sind und durch die der Mensch befugt und fähig ist, über Wahr und Falsch zu urteilen – das im Hinblick auf seine spekulative Vernunft – und zwischen Gut und Böse zu unterscheiden – das im Hinblick auf seine praktische Vernunft. Das Licht der Vernunft in uns, das Teilhabe an dem obersten, göttlichen Licht ist, ist also ebenso der Same für die Tugenden wie für die Wissenschaften. Auf sie lässt sich das Wort: ‚viele fragen: wer zeigt uns das Gute?' und die Antwort des Psalms: ‚aufgeprägt ist uns das Licht deines Antlitzes, o Herr' beziehen. Dieses Licht bleibt immer und sein Urheber ist Gott."[62]

Diese kurze Charakterisierung scheint Wort für Wort auf Thomas zurückzugehen, der auch dasselbe Psalmenzitat benützt, um auf die Übereinstimmung von Offenbarung und natürlicher Vernunft hinzuweisen.[63] Auch

61 Vgl. DW I, Predigt 20 a, 332, 3–334, 4; Predigt 20 b, 348, 1–12; DW II, Predigt 48, 418, 1–420, 10, sowie Super II Sententiarum d39 q3 a1 ad1, De veritate q16 a3 ad1 zum *lumen synderesis* bei Thomas. Eine Zusammenfassung der Texte zum Fünklein bei Eckhart gibt Wéber, Edouard-Henri, La petite Etincelle et le Fond de l'âme. In: E. zum Brunn (Hg.), Voici Maître Eckhart, Grenoble 1998, 105–118.

62 LW I, Liber parabolarum Genesis, nn. 199–200: „Semen autem et radix virtutum synderesis est ... . Semper enim synderesis manet malo remurmurans, ad bonum inclinans, etiam in damnatis. ... Semen autem scientiarum habitus est principiorum, quae naturaliter nota sunt omnibus, per quae habet et potest iudicare homo de veritate et falsitate, quantum ad intellectum speculativum, et inter bonum et malum, quantum ad intellectum practicum. Lumen ergo rationis in nobis, quod est participatio divini et supremi luminis, semen est tam virtutum quam scientiarum, de qua exponi potest illud: ‚multi dicunt: quis ostendit nobis bona?' et respondet Psalmus: ‚signatum est super nos lumen vultus tui, domine'. Hoc lumen semper manet et eius auctor est deus."

63 „Et talis participatio legis aeternae in rationali creatura lex naturalis dicitur. Unde cum Psalmista dixisset, sacrificate sacrificium iustitiae, quasi quibusdam quaerentibus quae sunt iustitiae opera, subiungit, multi dicunt, quis ostendit nobis bona? Cui quaestioni respondens, dicit, signatum est super nos lumen vultus tui, domine, quasi lumen rationis naturalis, quo discernimus quid sit bonum et malum, quod pertinet ad naturalem legem, nihil aliud sit quam impressio divini luminis in nobis. Unde patet quod lex naturalis nihil aliud est quam participatio legis aeternae in rationali creatura" (Summa Theologiae I–II q91 a2). Die Unterscheidung zwischen spekulativer und praktischer Vernunft findet sich im nächsten Artikel: „ratio humana non potest participare ad plenum dicta-

nach Eckhart sind die Prinzipien natürlich und durch sich selbst erkannt.[64] Ebenso warnt Eckhart davor, dass das Fünklein als Bild Gottes in uns von Vorstellungen überschattet (*obumbratur*) wird.[65] Es ist für Eckhart genauso entscheidend wie für Thomas, dass das Seiende der Gegenstand der Vernunft ist.[66] In einer deutschen Predigt erklärt Eckhart:

> „Die Seele hat zwei Augen, ein inneres und ein äußeres. Das innere Auge der Seele ist jenes, das in das Sein schaut und sein Sein ganz unmittelbar von Gott empfängt: dies ist sein ihm eigenes Werk. Das äußere Auge der Seele ist jenes, das da allen Kreaturen zugewendet ist und sie in bildhafter Weise und der Wirkweise einer Kraft wahrnimmt."[67]

Das äußere Auge wirkt nach Weise einer Kraft, die der Mensch einsetzt wie er will. Demgegenüber kann sich das innere Auge samt seinem Blick ins Sein nur von Gott her empfangen, da es als natürliche Erkenntnis eine Gabe des Schöpfers ist. Der Blick ins Sein ist für den Menschen nicht machbar. Nur das Daseinlassen des Seins führt die Vernunft in ihre natürliche Erkenntnis zurück. Andernorts heißt es entsprechend, der »vürwurf« (*ob-iectum:* das Entgegengeworfene, der Gegenwurf) der Vernunft ist das bloße, lautere Sein in ihm selbst, ohne jedweden Zufall.[68] Manche meinen, dieses Sein mit Gott identifizieren zu müssen, da Eckhart selbst sagt: *Esse deus est.*[69] Diese Identifikation von Seins- und Gotteserkenntnis vergisst

---

men rationis divinae, sed suo modo et imperfecte. Et ideo sicut ex parte rationis speculativae, per naturalem participationem divinae sapientiae, inest nobis cognitio quorundam communium principiorum, non autem cuiuslibet veritatis propria cognitio, sicut in divina sapientia continetur; ita etiam ex parte rationis practicae naturaliter homo participat legem aeternam secundum quaedam communia principia, non autem secundum particulares directiones singulorum, quae tamen in aeterna lege continentur" (Summa Theologiae I–II q91 a3 ad1, vgl. corpus articuli). Summa Theologiae I–II q90 a4 ad1 spricht vom Naturrecht, das Gott in den Geist des Menschen säte, damit er es auf natürliche Weise erkenne. Die *prima principia* als *semina scientiarum* finden sich in dem oben angeführten De veritate q11 a3. Die *synderesis* in ihrem *remurmurare* gegen das Böse und ihrem *instigare* zum Guten wird in Summa Theologiae I q79 a12 beschrieben.

64 Vgl. LW II, Expositio libri Exodi, n. 280 zu den *prima principia* als *per se nota*.

65 Vgl. LW I, Expositio libri Genesis, n. 301, DW III, Predigt 76, 315, 6–317, 2.

66 „Obiectum autem intellectus proprie est ens nudum simpliciter et absolute" (LW III, n. 677).

67 Predigt 11, Quint 203, 17–22 (= DW I, Predigt 10, 165, 4–8).

68 DW IV, 1, Predigt 104 A, ZZ. 295–298.

69 Vgl., LW I, Prologus in opus propositionum, n. 1, sowie Schönberger, Rolf, Predigt 10: ‚In diebus suis placuit deo'. In: G. Steer and L. Sturlese (Hgg.), Lectura Eckhardi II. Predigten Meister Eckharts von Fachgelehrten gelesen und gedeutet, Stuttgart 2003,

Eckharts Mahnung: „Unde dicit auctor De causis: »prima rerum creatarum est esse«. Unde statim cum venimus ad esse, venimus ad creaturam. Esse ergo habet primum rationem creabilis.“[70] Wer das Sein erkennt, kommt zum Geschöpf, weil das Sein der formale Gegenstand (*ratio*) der Schöpfung ist. Deshalb gilt:

> „Grobsinnige Meister sagen, Gott sei ein lauteres Sein; er ist so hoch über dem Sein, wie es der oberste Engel über einer Mücke ist. Ich würde etwas ebenso Unrichtiges sagen, wenn ich Gott ein Sein nennte, wie wenn ich die Sonne bleich oder schwarz nennen wollte. Gott ist weder dies noch das. (...) Wenn ich aber gesagt habe, Gott sei kein Sein und sei über dem Sein, so habe ich ihm damit nicht das Sein abgesprochen, vielmehr habe ich es in ihm erhöht.“[71]

Eckharts Negativtheologie will nicht leugnen, dass Gott das Sein ist. Sie will sagen, dass das unerkennbare Sein Gottes weit über dem geschöpflichen Sein steht. Denn der Mensch erkennt transzendentale Vollkommenheiten wie das Sein oder das Eine aus den Geschöpfen. Deshalb ist ein Satz wie: »Das Sein ist Gott«, zweifach zu betrachten. Einerseits sagt er die reine Wahrheit. Denn wir wissen, dass der Schöpfer allen Seins diese Vollkommenheit selbst im Übermaß in sich tragen muss. Andererseits erkennt der Mensch das Sein nur, wie es in Geschöpfen ist. Deshalb bezeichnet das menschliche Verständnis das Sein so, wie es den Geschöpfen eignet. Diese Bezeichnungsweise ist bezüglich Gott unwahr und muss deshalb verneint werden. Auch dies ist Wort für Wort eine Wiederholung von Kernaussagen der Analogielehre des Thomas.[72]

53–88, hier: 78, und Albert, Karl, Eckharts intellektuelle Mystik. In: A. Speer (Hg.), Meister Eckhart in Erfurt, Berlin 2005, 231–238, hier: 235–237. Schönberger weist darauf hin, dass schon Avicenna (De anima I 5) von zwei Augen der Seele spricht (ibid.). Nur beschreibt Avicenna, wie auch Augustinus, das innere Auge nicht als Auge, das ins Sein oder auf erste Prinzipien blickt. Der Unterschied zwischen innerem und äußerem Auge liegt im Blick auf Gott oder auf die Geschöpfe. Thomas dagegen kennt eine innere Vernunft (*ratio interior*), die auf die ersten Prinzipien schaut und nicht auf vorstellbare Dinge, wie die äußere Vernunft (vgl. Expositio Libri Posteriorum I 19, Sentencia Libri Metaphysicae XI 5, n. 2212, De veritate q10 a12 sed contra 2).

70 LW V, Quaestio Parisiensis I, n. 4.

71 Predigt 10, Quint, 196, 18–27 (= DW I, Predigt 9, 145, 7–146, 6).

72 „Quod autem Dionysius dicit 2. c. Caelestis hierarchiae, quod »negationes de deo sunt verae, affirmationes vero incompactae«, non obstat. Hoc enim verum est quantum ad modum significandi in talibus. Intellectus enim noster perfectiones quae ad esse pertinent, apprehendit ex creaturis, ubi huiusmodi perfectiones imperfectae sunt et divisae sparsim, et secundum illum modum significat. In his enim propositionibus est duo con-

Damit stellt sich die Frage: Was erkennt das innere Auge, wenn es das Sein vernimmt? Zunächst beschreibt Eckhart das Sein wie auch schon Thomas als *actualitas formalis omnis formae universaliter et essentiae.*[73] Insoweit nach Eckhart Gott nur das virtuelle Sein der Dinge ist, nicht aber das ihnen formal eignende Sein, kann diese Beschreibung nicht Gott selbst bezeichnen. Denn in der Sprechweise Eckharts liegen Formen auf formale Weise in den Dingen, obwohl sie sich virtuell oder als Ideen im göttlichen Geist finden.[74] Andererseits eignet keinem Ding das Wirklichsein einer jeden Wesenheit, sondern nur das Sein der je eigenen Wesenheit. Somit liegt das Sein als *actualitas formalis omnis essentiae* weder in den Dingen noch in Gott. Gibt es noch eine dritte Möglichkeit? Eckhart schreibt:

> „[W]ie das ganze Weltall zuerst beabsichtigt ist von der ersten Ursache, so auch das eine Sein des Weltalls selbst, aber jeder Teil und sein Sein ist (nur) an zweiter Stelle beabsichtigt. Er empfängt Sein von der Ursache des Weltalls nur vermittels des einen Seins selbst des Weltalls, in ihm, durch es und um seinetwillen, und zwar gleichermaßen notwendig, weil im Einen keine

---

siderare, scilicet ipsas perfectiones significatas, puta bonitatem, veritatem, vitam, intelligere et huiusmodi; et sic sunt compactae et verae. Est etiam considerare in talibus modum significandi; et sic incompactae sunt" (LW II, Expositio libri Exodi, n. 78, vgl. n. 58, LW I, Expositio libri Genesis, n. 270, LW III, n. 86, und Summa Theologiae I q13 a3, Super I Sententiarum d22 q1 a2, Summa contra Gentiles I 30, De potentia q7 a5, sowie Rocca, Gregory P., The Distinction between *Res Significata* and *Modus Significandi* in Aquinas's Theological Epistemology, The Thomist 55 (1991) 173–197). Eckhart kopiert nahezu die Texte des Thomas bezüglich der Transzendentalien, die in ihrem eigentlichen Sinn Gottes Wesen beschreiben. Trotz dieser Nähe der Transzendentalien zu Gott eignet ihnen in der menschlichen Erkenntnis eine geschöpfliche Bezeichnungsweise, insoweit alle menschliche Erkenntnis von den Geschöpfen und ihren Vollkommenheiten ausgeht. Wer die Transzendentalien als Gottesnamen benützt, muss deshalb diese Bezeichnungsweise verneinen. Die Behauptung, Thomas sähe die Transzendentalien ausschließlich als von Gott verursacht, während Eckhart in ihnen nur das göttliche Wesen erkennt, ist also höchst fraglich (vgl. zu dieser Behauptung Kobusch, Theo, Transzendenz und Transzendentalien, Meister-Eckhart-Jahrbuch 5 (2011) 41–54, hier: 46–49). Ebenso fraglich ist die Behauptung, dass Thomas zu erklären versuche, wie die Transzendentalien, die wir in Geschöpfen finden, von Gott auszusagen seien, während Eckhart diese Frage auf den Kopf stellt, d. h. davon spricht, wie die Transzendentalien als Gottes Wesen von Geschöpfen ausgesagt werden können (so Aertsen, Jan A., Die Bedeutung der Transzendentalbegriffe für das Denken Meister Eckharts, Meister-Eckhart-Jahrbuch 5 (2011) 27–39, hier: 38–39). Der genannte Text Eckharts spricht gegen diese Behauptungen.

73 LW I, Prologus in opus propositionum, n. 14.

74 LW I, Expositio libri Genesis, n. 77, Liber parabolarum Genesis, n. 35, LW II, Expositio libri Exodi, n. 121.

> Ungleichheit ist. (…) Denn obgleich die einzelnen Seienden untereinander ungleich und mehr oder weniger vollkommen sind, empfangen, erhalten oder nehmen sie doch ihr Sein unter der Hinsicht des einen Seins auf, das durch sich selbst und zuerst unter die Ursächlichkeit und den Blick der ersten Ursache allen Seins fällt.“[75]

An dieser und anderen Stellen seines Kommentars zum Buch der Weisheit[76] wiederholt Eckhart, dass das Sein der formale Gegenstand der Schöpfung ist, d. h. die Hinsicht des Schöpfers auf die Schöpfung. Unter dieser Hinsicht wird die Welt auch von Gott verursacht, der selbst das Sein ist. Entsprechend hat Gott das Gesamt der Schöpfung vor Augen, doch nicht irgendwie, sondern unter der Hinsicht des Seins, da er die gesamte Welt aus dem Nichtsein ins Dasein ruft.[77] Dennoch unterdrückt das eine und einzige Sein des Alls, vermittels dessen Gott die Dinge schafft, nicht deren Seinsvielfalt. Die einzelnen Seienden sind verschieden und besitzen mehr oder weniger vollkommenes Sein, d. h. es gibt verschiedene Seinsgrade. Wie ist es möglich, dass Gott das Sein des Alls in den einzelnen Dingen schafft und diese doch nur ihr je eigenes Sein haben und nicht das Sein des ganzen Alls? Wir dürfen nicht vergessen, dass die Dinge ihr je eigenes Wesen und dessen innere Ursachen, Form und Stoff, haben, die durch das Sein als *actualitas essentiae* verwirklicht werden. Insofern ein Ding durch das Zusammenkommen von Form und Stoff wird, gilt, dass die Form das Sein gibt. Doch Eckhart insistiert: *formae dent esse hoc aut hoc, in quantum hoc aut hoc, non autem in quantum esse.*[78] Allein Gott gibt das Sein als Sein, d. h. als Sein des ganzen Alls oder *actualitas formalis omnis formae universaliter et essentiae*. Doch die innere Ursache lässt das Sein des Alls zum Dies-und-Das-Sein der einzelnen Dinge werden. In diesem oder jenem ist das Sein auf eine bestimmte Natur des Seienden eingeschränkt. Entsprechend ist ganz anders zu sprechen vom Sein selbst, d. h.

---

75 LW II, Expositio libri Sapientiae, n. 72: „[S]icut totum universum est primo intentum a causa prima, et esse ipsius universi unum, partes autem quaelibet et ipsarum esse secundario, accipiunt esse a causa universi mediante ipso uno esse universi, in ipso, per ipsum et propter ipsum, et aequaliter necessario, eo quod in uno non sit inaequalitas. … Singula enim entia, quamvis inter se inaequalia, plus minusque perfecta, [accipiunt esse] sub ratione unius esse, quod per se et primo cadit sub causalitate et aspectu primae causae omnis esse, accipiunt et excipiunt sive suscipiunt suum esse.“

76 Vgl. ibid., nn. 23–24.

77 Vgl. ibid., n. 25.

78 LW I, Prologus in opus propositionum, n. 21.

vom Sein des Alls, und von diesem oder jenem Seienden, in dem sich nur dieses Sein findet, das jedwedes andere Sein von sich ausschließt.[79]

Auch hier zeigt sich, dass Eckhart die Lehre des Thomas vom Sein oder Seienden als formalem Gegenstand der Schöpfung wiederholt.[80] Denn nach Thomas ist das Sein nicht nur die Hinsicht, unter der die ganze Schöpfung von Gott ausfließt, sondern auch das, was Gott in einem jeden Ding erschafft. Trotzdem ist das Sein des Alls nicht das Sein, wodurch ein jedes Ding ist, da die Wesenheiten das Sein in diesem oder jenem Ding begrenzen.[81]

Für die Frage nach dem *vürwurf* des inneren Auges ist damit folgendes gewonnen: Das Auge, das ins Sein blickt, teilt Gottes Blick auf seine Schöpfung. Obwohl die Vernunft an Gottes Seinsverständnis teilhat, gilt: *potentiae immateriales abstractione ascendunt. Stat autem abstractio in esse, supra quod deus est, utpote causa esse.*[82] Obwohl die ersten Prinzipien von Gott eingeprägt sind, muss die Vernunft abstrahieren, sich von diesem und jenem Seienden freimachen, um zum Sein selbst vorzustoßen. Doch damit erreicht sie nur das Sein selbst, nicht aber die göttliche Ursache des Seins, die über dem Sein ist. Das Gebet als Aufstieg der Vernunft zu Gott muss

---

79 LW I, Tabula prologorum in opus tripartitum, n. 1. Vladimir Lossky hat die genannten Charakteristika des Seins und der Schöpfung bei Meister Eckhart deutlich nachgezeichnet (vgl. Lossky, Vladimir, Théologie négative et connaissance de Dieu chez Maître Eckhart, Paris 1973, 44–56, 77–84, 137–157, 195, 298–312). Obwohl Eckhart sagt, dass Sein und Wesen *der Dinge* unterschieden sind wie *quo est* und *quod est*, sowie dass beide Prinzipien, d. h. Sein und Wesen, geschaffen sind (vgl. LW I, Liber parabolarum Genesis, n. 34), verneint Lossky, dass dies auf einen wirklichen Unterschied von Sein und Wesen in den Dingen schließen lässt. Auch die Beschreibung des Seins als *actus essentiae* soll demnach nicht auf einen Unterschied in den Dingen bezogen werden. Wenn Eckhart erklärt, die Dinge hätten ihr So-Sein von der Wesensform, das absolute Sein jedoch von Gott, dann soll damit gemeint sein: Das absolute Sein ist Gott, der das Wesen wirklich sein lässt. Die Unterscheidung von *quo est* und *quod est* wäre folglich der Unterschied zwischen Gott und wirklichem Wesen der Dinge. Diese Auslegung widerspricht nicht nur dem Wortsinn, sondern auch dem Denken Eckharts, der schreibt: Das allgemeine Sein, das durch Abstraktion vernommen wird, ist nicht die göttliche Ursache des Seins, die weit über dem Sein steht (vgl. LW IV, Sermo XXII, n. 212, Sermo XXIV, 2, n. 247).

80 Vgl. Summa Theologiae I q45 a1, a4 ad1, De potentia q3 a16 ad4.

81 Gott erschafft das *esse universale*, d. h. die *actualitas omnium* in den Dingen, obwohl die verschiedenen Naturen, in denen das Sein aufgenommen wird, dieses Sein von jenem Sein unterscheiden (vgl. Summa Theologiae I q105 a5, De Potentia q7 a2 corpus, ad6 und ad9).

82 LW IV, Sermo XXII, n. 212.

deshalb nicht nur alle Vorstellungen der Einbildungskraft hinter sich lassen, sondern auch alles Verstehbare. Selbst wenn die Vernunft alles in das Sein auflöst oder alles auf es zurückführt (*resolvit ad esse*), muss sie auch das Sein noch übersteigen, um zu Gott zu gelangen. Denn das Sein ist nicht die Ursache des Seins, sondern etwas weit Höheres, zu dem es aufzusteigen gilt.[83] Wer zu Gott aufsteigen will, muss also das Sein als Ersterkanntes zurücklassen. Insofern das Seiende selbst als Ersterkanntes dasjenige ist, wodurch alles andere verstehbar wird, heißt dies, alles Verstehbare zu übersteigen und Gott im Reich des Nicht-Verstehbaren zu suchen.

Eckhart verfolgt immer einen Weg, der sein Denken in die Ursache allen Seins zurückgehen lässt. Dies zeigt sich besonders, wenn er das göttliche Sein als Ursache jedes Namens betrachtet, die über jedem Namen und jedem Seienden steht. Denn als Ursache jedes Seienden muss Gott das allen gemeinsame Sein auf ununterschiedene Weise in sich tragen, d. h. das je eigene Wesen der Dinge, z. B. das Menschsein oder Tigersein, ist nicht Gottes eigenes Wesen, doch das Sein selbst muss ihm als sein Eigenes gehören und deshalb sein eigener Name sein. Sonst wäre Gott nicht die Ursache allen Seins und seiner Verschiedenheit in den Dingen.[84]

Doch Eckhart sagt an dieser Stelle, dass das Sein nicht nur allen Seienden, sondern auch allen Namen gemeinsam ist. Denn was nicht am Sein teilhat, ist weder ein Seiendes noch ein Name. Eckhart möchte damit weniger sagen, dass ein Name ein Seiendes ist, als dass er Seiendes bezeichnet: Jeder Name verweist auf Seiendes. Denn für gewöhnlich ist ein gesprochenes oder geschriebenes Wort oder ein Name ein Zeichen für einen *conceptus*, durch den ein Name ein Seiendes oder Ding bezeichnet.[85] Insofern das Seiende zuerst in der Vernunft fällt, kann die Vernunft nur Seiendes bedenken und benennen, da alles Erkennbare im Seienden gründet und es enthält. Ebenso trägt das So-und-so-Sein als Fortbestimmung

---

83 „[O]ratio est »intellectus in deum ascensus«. Igitur intellectus ‹deum› in se non attingit, nisi ascendat. Ascensus autem ad superius est. Transcendere igitur oportet non solum imaginabilia, sed etiam intelligibilia. Item cum intellectus resolvat ad esse, oportet et hoc transire. Esse namque non est causa esse, sicut nec ignis est causa ignis, sed aliquid longe altius, in quod oportet ascendere“ (LW IV, Sermo XXIV, 2, n. 247).

84 LW II, Expositio libri Exodi, n. 166.

85 „[O]rationes sive propositiones respondent primo et per se non rebus, sed rerum conceptionibus. Sunt enim voces signa et »notae earum quae sunt in anima passionum«. Propter quod ipsam conceptionem notant et indicant et significant“ (LW II, Expositio libri Exodi, n. 55, vgl. n. 167, LW III, n. 132).

des Seins das Sein selbst in sich.[86] Auch die Rede vom »Nichts« ist auf das Seiende gegründet, ohne das das Nichts nicht erkannt wird. In diesem Sinn nennt Eckhart das Nichts nicht nur »niht«, sondern auch »unwesene«.[87] Thomas nennt das Nichts deshalb ein *ens rationis*, das durch unsere Weise des Erkennens entsteht. Jeder Name bezeichnet also »Seiendes«, zumeist etwas, das in Wirklichkeit ist, manchmal auch ein Gedankengebilde. In sich Widersprüchliches ist dabei kein »Name«, da es nicht sein kann und nur Abwesenheit des Seienden bedeutet.[88] Solche Namen sind deshalb in sich leer und erdichtet.[89] Eckhart schließt diesen Gedankengang wie folgt ab:

> „Außerdem ‚ist das Seiende das erste, was in der Vernunft fällt‘, nach Avicenna, und [was] generell in der Vernehmung [fällt]. Daher setzt der Metaphysiker, der von den ersten Seienden und den ersten Prinzipien der Dinge handelt, das Seiende voraus. Das Seiende ist und heißt deshalb sein Gegenstand [sc. *subiectum*], weil es einem jeden zugrunde liegt [sc. *subicitur*] und in allem vorausgesetzt ist, auch in der ersten Erkenntnis und Vernehmung. Aber jeder Name oder jedes Wort ist ein Merkmal oder ein Zeichen einer vorangehenden Vernehmung. Daher ist der Sinn [des Schriftwortes Lukas 1, 37]: ‚alles‘, ‚bei Gott Unmögliche‘, d. h. was unmöglich sein kann, ‚wird weder sein‘ ‚ein Wort‘, noch ist es ein Wort.“[90]

---

86 „[D]e non ente autem non formatur verbum, sed nec formari potest in quantum huiusmodi. Ratio est quia ens est primum, quod in intellectu cadit, ut ait Avicenna. Quomodo enim scibile esset, quod non esset? … Praeterea verum, scibile et universaliter comprehensibile fundantur omnia in esse et ipsum includunt, sicut duo unum et sicut esse tale esse simpliciter“ (LW II, Expositio libri Exodi, n. 29).

87 DW I, Predigt 9, 151, 12, vgl. Schürmann, Reiner, Meister Eckhart's ‚Verbal‘ Understanding of Being as a Ground for Destruction of Practical Teleology. In: Kluxen, Wolfgang, et al. (Hgg.), Sprache und Erkenntnis im Mittelalter, Berlin 1981, 803–809, hier: 803, sowie Mayer, Rupert J., Meister Eckharts erste *Quaestio Parisiensis*, 459–460.

88 „[D]icimus deum non posse omnia, quae implicant contradictionem. Si enim contradictoria ponantur simul esse, sequitur neutrum eorum esse“ (LW II, Expositio libri Exodi, n. 32). Eckhart diskutiert an dieser Stelle sowohl das, was nicht erschaffbar ist, als auch das, was nicht nennbar ist, unter dem Titel des Widersprüchlichen.

89 „Quod enim sine esse est, nec est nec nomen est, sed falsum, vanum et fictum nomen est. Sed nec nomen est, quia non notificat“ (LW II, Expositio libri Exodi, n. 167).

90 LW II, Expositio libri Exodi, n. 169 (eigene Übersetzung): „Adhuc autem »primum, quod cadit in intellectu«, secundum Avicennam, et universaliter in apprehensione, »est ens«. Propter quod etiam primus philosophus tractans de primis entibus et primis rerum principiis praesupponit ens. Et ipsum ob hoc est et dicitur eius subiectum, eo quod subicitur et praesupponitur omni, etiam primae cognitioni et apprehensioni. Nomen autem sive verbum omne nota est et signum praecedentis apprehensionis. Unde sensus est,

Eckhart kommt noch einmal darauf zurück, dass das Seiende in allem und jedem zuerst vernommen wird. Menschliches Nennen und Sprechen, d. h. menschliche Sprache kann sich deshalb nur auf Seiendes beziehen und es bezeichnen. Denn menschliches Sprechen entgegnet dem Seienden, das sich dem Menschen schon immer gezeigt hat. Das Ersterkannte wird vom Denken in allem vorausgesetzt, sogar beim ersten Vernehmen von etwas. Das Seiende wird natürlich und *universaliter* vernommen, d. h. in allem. Auch in der zeitlich ersten Erkenntnis eines bestimmten Gegenstands, d. h. von diesem oder jenem Seienden, das ganz allgemein *als Seiendes* betrachtet wird, fällt das Seiende zuerst in den Blick. Vor der ersten Erkenntnis dieses Menschen ist die Seinserkenntnis schon vorausgesetzt, die der menschlichen Vernunftnatur als solcher eignet.

Vor diesem Hintergrund sagt Eckhart: Jedes Wort oder jeder Name ist das Zeichen eines vorausgehenden Vernehmens. Das Vernehmen, auf das das Wort und der Name »das Seiende« Bezug nehmen, kann nur das göttliche Vernehmen sein, an dem der Mensch teilhat. Nur Gottes Vernehmen besteht vor jedem menschlichen Erkennen und gibt letzterem seine eigene Natur als Verständnis des Seienden. Der Name »das Seiende« ist deshalb ein Name über allen Namen, der den anderen Namen gemeinsam ist. Denn alle Namen bezeichnen eine bestimmte Seinsweise, nicht aber das Seiende selbst. Einzig der Widerspruch zum Seienden, das was nicht sein kann, kann nicht sinnvoll benannt werden. Sein und Sprache sind im Menschen untrennbar verbunden. Diese Gründung des Denkens kann Eckhart wie folgt ins Wort fassen:

> „Vernünfticheit nimet wol von lîplîchen dingen: in dem stücke ist wille edeler; aber ez ist an einem teile der vernünfticheit in einem nidersehenne und in einem nidervalle, dâ diz verstantnisse bilde nimet von lîplîchen dingen. Aber in dem obersten würket diu vernünfticheit âne zuonemunge von lîplîchen dingen. Ez sprichet ein grôz meister: allez, daz îngetragen wirt ze den sinnen, daz enkumet nit ze der sêle noch in die oberste kraft der sêle. Sant Augustînus sprichet und sprichet ouch Plâtô, ein heidenischer meister, daz diu sêle in ir hat natiurlîche alle kunst; dar umbe enbedarf si niht von ûzen die kunst in sich ziehen, sunder von der üebunge ûzer kunst sô wirt diu kunst offenbâr, diu in der sêle ist natiurlîche verborgen. (…) Alsô engibet niht der sêle lieht allez, daz îngetragen wirt ze den sinnen von bilden und von

quod ‚omne' ‚impossibile apud deum', id est impossibile esse, ‚non erit' ‚verbum' nec est verbum."

> formen, mêr: ez bereitet und liutert aleine die sêle, daz si blôz nemen mac in irm obersten des engels lieht und mit im götlich lieht."[91]

Eckhart setzt an dieser Stelle die platonische Sprache ein, obwohl er nicht wie Platon oder Augustinus denkt. Der Mensch hat in den natürlich vernommenen Prinzipien nur den Samen aller Kunst und Wissenschaft in sich, nicht aber alle Künste.[92] Das Oberste der Seele oder der Vernunft liegt in dieser Prinzipienerkenntnis. Doch nimmt sie ebenso durch die Sinne die Bilder der Dinge in sich auf. In diesem Aufnehmen wird vor allem das offenbar, was schon in der Seele ist, das Verständnis des Seienden und aller damit gegebenen Prinzipien. Denn die Seele entfaltet ihr natürliches Wissen durch Erfahrung. In diesem Sinn entspringt der Erfahrung der Dinge kein Licht, obwohl die Dinge uns diese und jene Seinsweise vergegenwärtigen. Vielmehr sind die Prinzipien das Licht, das menschliche Erfahrung ermöglicht. Das Seiende wird durch die Erfahrung der Dinge in allen seinen Weisen vernommen, die jedoch zuvor schon im Seienden enthalten sind. Dazu läutert die Erfahrung die Seele und befähigt sie, die Prinzipienerkenntnis, die sie mit den Engeln teilt, als solche Teilnahme zu erkennen, die letztlich Teilhabe an Gottes Licht ist. Trotz der Höhe dieser Teilhabe muss menschliche Erkenntnis zu den Sinnen niederfallen und hinunterschauen, um sich zu bewähren und das Seiende in diesem oder jenem wahrzunehmen:

> „Nû merket dise berihtunge! Der vernunft vürwurf und ir enthalt ist wesen und niht zuoval, sondern daz blôz lûter wesen in im selber. Swenne diu vernunft bekennet ein wârheit eines wesens, zehant sô neiget si sich dar ûf und lât sich dâ in ein ruowe, und dâ sprichet si ir wort vernünfticlîche von den vürwurfe, den si dâ hât. Mêr: alsô lange diu vernunft des wesens wârheit

---

91 DW II, Predigt 36b, 201, 17–203, 5.

92 Vgl. LW I, Liber parabolarum Genesis, nn. 199–200, LW III, n. 662. Der Heilige Geist prägt der Seele nur die ersten Prinzipien der Erkenntnis ein, d. h. die Transzendentalien, das Vernehmen des Nicht-Widerspruchs, etc. Alles andere Erkennen ist durch die Dinge vermittelt. Vladimir Lossky meint dagegen wegen obiger Predigt (vgl. Anmerkung 91), dass Eckhart die Gattungen und Arten der Dinge mit den Prinzipien identifiziert, also wie Platon oder Augustinus denkt. Entsprechend müsste die Vernunft nichts von den Dingen empfangen, da sie bereits alle Erkenntnis besitzt. Nur wegen Erbschuld muss die Vernunft sich zu den Dingen kehren, um von ihnen ein Bild zu empfangen (Lossky, Vladimir, Théologie négative et connaissance de Dieu chez Maître Eckhart, 232–242). Dagegen steht, dass Eckhart die Erkenntnis des Fünkleins nicht auf viele Prinzipien aufteilt, sondern es als Bild Gottes versteht, in dem alle Dinge eins sind (vgl. DW III, Predigt 76, 315, 6–317, 2).

> eigenlîche niht envindet, noch daz si den grunt niht enrüeret, alsô daz si müge sprechen: diz ist diz und ist alsô und anders niht, alsô lange stât si alles in einem suochenne und in einem beitenne und enneiget sich niht noch enruowet niht, mêr: si arbeitet noch alles und leget abe alles suochende in einem beitenne. Und alsô ist si ein jâr oder mê in einem arbeitenne in einer natiurlîchen wârheit, swâz ez sî, jâ, si muoz noch lange arbeiten in einem abelegenne, waz ez niht ensî. Und als lange stât si âne allen enthalt und ensprichet ouch kein wort von keinen dingen, die wîle si den grunt der wârheit niht vunden enhât mit wârem bekantnisse."[93]

Eckhart bittet uns, dieser Unterweisung Gehör zu schenken. Der Gegenstand der Vernunft, ihr Aufenthalt oder Stillstand (*enthalt*), ist das reine, lautere Sein oder Wesen an ihm selbst, wenn wir es – durch Abstraktion – ohne all das betrachten, was ihm hier und jetzt, in diesem oder jenem zufällt. Eckhart nimmt uns damit die Vorstellbarkeit des Seins weg. Es ist kein willentlich vorstellbarer Gegenstand (*vürwurf*), sondern der Ort, an dem sich die Vernunft aufhält, und die Ruhe, von der jede Denkbewegung ausgeht und zu der sie zurückkehrt. Denn die suchende Vernunft muss im Sehen des Seins Ruhe finden.[94] Wenn die Vernunft die Wahrheit eines Dinges, d. h. sein vernehmbares Wesen oder Sein, erkennt, neigt sie sich dieser Wahrheit sofort zu und ruht in ihr, indem sie ihr inneres Wort von dem erkannten Ding spricht. Solange die Vernunft jedoch sucht und die Wahrheit des Seins nicht findet, d. h. solange sie die Wahrheit des Dinges nicht

93 DW IV, 1, Predigt 104 A, ZZ. 295–319.

94 Vgl. hierzu bei Thomas: „Intelligere enim est simpliciter veritatem intelligibilem apprehendere. Ratiocinari autem est procedere de uno intellecto ad aliud, ad veritatem intelligibilem cognoscendam. Et ideo angeli, qui perfecte possident, secundum modum suae naturae, cognitionem intelligibilis veritatis, non habent necesse procedere de uno ad aliud; sed simpliciter et absque discursu veritatem rerum apprehendunt, ut Dionysius dicit, VII cap. de Divinis Nominibus. Homines autem ad intelligibilem veritatem cognoscendam perveniunt, procedendo de uno ad aliud, ut ibidem dicitur, et ideo rationales dicuntur. Patet ergo quod ratiocinari comparatur ad intelligere sicut moveri ad quiescere, vel acquirere ad habere: quorum unum est perfecti, aliud autem imperfecti. Et quia motus semper ab immobili procedit, et ad aliquid quietum terminatur; inde est quod ratiocinatio humana, secundum viam inquisitionis vel inventionis, procedit a quibusdam simpliciter intellectis, quae sunt prima principia; et rursus, in via iudicii, resolvendo redit ad prima principia, ad quae inventa examinat" (Summa Theologiae I q79 a8). Eckhart spricht ebenso von einer suchenden Vernunft, die in seinen lateinischen Werken *ratio* genannt wird im Gegensatz zum *intellectus*: „Ratio enim discursus est inter multa et quasi negotiatio trahens ad extra" (LW III, n. 267, vgl. DW III, Predigt 71, 215, 7–11, sowie Manstetten, Reiner, Esse est Deus, 367–370).

in den ersten Prinzipien oder dem »grunt der wârheit« der Dinge vernimmt, solange spricht sie kein inneres Wort und steht wortlos da. Denn die Dinge leuchten nur, wenn sie im Sein, d. h. im Aufenthalt der Vernunft, betrachtet werden. Denn das Sein als erstes Prinzip des Vernehmens ist ein Licht, das die Dunkelheit der oder Nicht-Offenbarkeit der Dinge für die Vernunft erhellt. So werden die Dinge selbst zu einem Licht, das in seinem Prinzip leuchtet.[95]

Das Sein eines bestimmten Dinges ist berührt, wenn die Vernunft sprechen kann: Dies ist dies und es ist so und nicht anders. Ein Ding muss in seinem Selbigsein mit sich selbst und seinem Verschiedensein von allem anderen erkannt werden. Die Vernunft sucht in den Blick zu nehmen, was etwas ist, und muss deshalb alles verneinen, was der Gegenstand nicht ist. Nur durch die Erkenntnis dessen, was etwas nicht ist, kann sich die Vernunft zu dem vorarbeiten, was das Ding ist. Denn es geht darum, eine Seinsweise in ihrer Geschiedenheit oder ihrem Anderssein gegenüber anderen Seinsweisen hervorzuheben. In diesem Zustand ist die Vernunft ruhelos. Sie sucht und harrt (*beitet*) darauf, dass sich ihr der Anblick des Wesens in den Prinzipien zeigt. Mit großer Anstrengung arbeitet und müht sich das Denken ab, die Dinge so in den Blick zu bekommen, dass alles Zufällige abfällt und das Wesen in seinem Eigenen erscheinen kann. Dieser Zustand des Harrens und der Suche kann oft ein Jahr oder länger dauern, bis das Wesen sich zeigt und die Vernunft ihr inneres Wort sprechen kann. Denn schon um einer natürlichen Wahrheit willen muss die Vernunft sich so anstrengen. Insoweit sich die natürliche Wahrheit von der übernatürlichen Wahrheit Gottes abhebt,[96] ist nun in einem zweiten Schritt zu fragen, ob und wie der Mensch ein Wort von der übernatürlichen Wahrheit aussprechen kann.

95 „Et hoc est proprium hominis et rationis cognoscere res in suis principiis. … Unumquodque enim lux est et lucet in suis principiis. Omnis enim cognitio rerum est per sua principia et in suis principiis; et quousque resolvatur in sua principia, semper obscura, tenebrosa et opaca est, quia cum formidine partis alterius. Demonstratio autem, idest syllogismus, faciens scire sine formidine et opinione, est ex propriis principiis. Et … homo accipit cognitionem suam a posterioribus, procedens ad principia ratiocinando. … Ideo lux in tenebris est cognitio a posteriori, cognitio in phantasmate er per phantasmata“ (LW III, n. 18 und n. 20).

96 „Dar umbe gerüeret diu vernunft niemer in disem lebene den grunt der übernatiurlîchen wârheit, diu got ist“ (DW IV, 1, Predigt 104 A, ZZ. 319–322).

2. Gottes Wort im Menschenwort

2.1 *Das fehlende Wort von Gott oder die Abwesenheit Gottes*

2.1.1. Bei Thomas von Aquin

Im *Quodlibet VIII q2 a2* deutet Thomas an, dass alle Worte, auch die der Offenbarung, auf ihren Ursprung im Seienden zurückgehen.[97] Denn Gott spricht nicht direkt zu uns, sondern durch menschliche Worte. Insoweit die Offenbarung menschliche Worte in ihren Dienst nimmt, haben diese Worte denselben Ursprung wie alle anderen Worte, die Menschen sprechen: das Seiende. Dennoch übersteigt Gottes Sprechen alles, was ein Mensch verstehen kann.[98] Deshalb kann die Wahrheit der Offenbarung nicht ganz im Seienden enthalten sein. Thomas merkt an, dass die Offenbarung nur insoweit in den ersten Prinzipien liegt, als sie diesen Prinzipien nicht widerspricht. Der Nicht-Widerspruch gilt auch im Bereich des offenbarten Wortes.[99] Ansonsten muss die Vernunft anerkennen, dass die Wahrheit Gottes alles Verstehen übersteigt. So ist zu fragen, wie sich dieser Überstieg in unserem Denken äußert und wie der Glaubende vernimmt, dass ein Wort Gottes Wort ist und nicht Menschenwort.

Wenn wir von der Gegenwart einer Sache für die Vernunft sprechen, ist zu klären, was »Gegenwart« bedeutet. Denn bezüglich der Sinne liegt die Gegenwart von etwas im Hier und Jetzt. Für die Vernunft, die das Wesen der Dinge durch Abstraktion von Zeit und Raum erkennt oder eine Wahrheit erschließt, ist Gegenwart nicht an das Hier und Jetzt gebunden.[100] Gegenwart heißt für die Vernunft soviel wie Aufleuchten des

---

97 Vgl. Anmerkung 34.

98 Vgl. De veritate q14 a8.

99 „Insunt enim nobis naturaliter quedam prima principia complexa omnibus nota, ex quibus ratio procedit ad cognoscendum in actu conclusiones que in predictis principiis potencialiter cognoscuntur, siue per inuentionem propriam siue per doctrinam alienam siue per reuelationem diuinam. In quibus omnibus modis cognoscendi homo iuuatur ex principiis naturaliter cognitis, uel ita quod ipsa principia cognita ad cognitionem acquirendam sufficiant, adminiculantibus sensu et ymaginatione, sicut cum aliquam cognitionem acquirimus per inuentionem uel doctrinam; uel ita quod principia predicta ad cognitionem acquirendam non sufficiant, nichilominus tamen in huiusmodi cognoscendis principia dirigunt in quantum inueniuntur non repugnare principiis naturaliter cognitis, quod si esset, intellectus nullo modo eis assentiret, sicut non potest dissentire principiis" (Quodlibet VIII q2 a2).

100 „[S]ecundum Augustinum (…) «creduntur illa quae absunt a sensibus nostris si

Erkennbaren, wenn etwas in den ersten Prinzipien der Vernunft vernommen wird. Denn diese Prinzipien sind für die Vernunft durch sich selbst gegenwärtig, gleichwie ein gegenwärtiges »Ding«. Sie führt alles auf diese Prinzipien zurück. Doch die Offenbarung, zumindest in ihren tiefsten Geheimnissen, der Menschwerdung und der Dreifaltigkeit Gottes, lässt sich nicht auf die Prinzipien zurückführen. Der sich offenbarende Gott ist deshalb für die Vernunft ein Abwesender, d. h. die Vernunft kann ihn nicht verstehen. Denn nach dem Zeugnis des Hebräerbriefs ist der Glaube auf das bezogen, was nicht gesehen wird.[101] Thomas legt dieses Schriftwort so aus, dass die Kenntnis Gottes das übersteigt, was durch die ersten Prinzipien erkennbar ist.

Diese Abwesenheit Gottes ist zweifach zu beschreiben. Denn die Vernunft blickt einerseits auf das Wesen der Dinge und versucht andererseits, etwas von ihnen zu erschließen. Die Wesenserkenntnis erfolgt durch Abstraktion, wenn uns etwas durch die sinnliche Erfahrung begegnet. Insofern Gott nicht sinnlich erfahrbar ist, kann der Mensch Gottes Wesen nicht durch Abstraktion erkennen. Dieselbe Abwesenheit für die Wesenskenntnis zeigt sich im Vergleich zum Gegenstand der Vernunft, dem Seienden. Im strengen Sinn ist Seiendes oder das, was ist, solches, das am Sein teilhat.[102] Gott aber ist nicht durch Teilhabe am Sein. Er übersteigt deshalb den for-

videtur idoneum testimonium quod eis perhibetur, videntur autem quae praesto sunt vel animi vel corporis sensibus»; quae quidem differentia evidens est in his quae praesto sunt corporis sensibus in quibus manifestum est quid praesto sit sensibus et quid non sit praesto, sed in sensibus animi quid praesto esse dicatur magis latet“ (De veritate q14 a9).

101 „Illa tamen praesto esse dicuntur intellectui quae capacitatem eius non excedunt ut intuitus intellectus in eis figatur: talibus enim aliquis assentit non propter testimonium alienum sed propter testimonium proprii intellectus; illa vero quae facultatem intellectus excedunt absentia esse dicuntur a sensibus animi, unde intellectus in eis figi non potest, unde eis non possumus assentire propter proprium testimonium sed propter testimonium alienum; et haec proprie credita esse dicuntur. – Unde fidei obiectum proprie est id quod est absens ab intellectu – «creduntur enim absentia sed videntur praesentia», (…) vel etiam res non apparens, id est res non visa quia, ut dicitur Hebr. XI, «fides est argumentum non apparentum». Quandocumque autem deficit ratio proprii obiecti, oportet quod et actus deficiat; unde quam cito incipit aliquid esse praesens vel apparens, non potest ut obiectum subesse actui fidei; quaecumque autem sciuntur proprie accepta scientia, cognoscuntur per resolutionem in prima principia quae per se praesto sunt intellectui, et sic omnis scientia in visione rei praesentis perficitur“ (De veritate q14 a9, vgl. Mayer, Rupert J., De veritate: Quid est?, 117–120).

102 Vgl. Expositio Libri De ebdomadibus II.

malen Gegenstand der Vernunft und kann nicht darauf zurückgeführt werden: Gott ist der Gott jenseits des Seienden.[103]

Die Vernunft kann also Gott nicht im Seienden, dem Quell aller Worte, erkennen. Wo der Quell versagt, fehlt das Wort. Deshalb macht Thomas die Erfahrung: *obiectum fidei, idest Deus, formationem intellectus nostri subterfugit.*[104] Mit *formatio* bezeichnet Thomas die Wesenserkenntnis, die in eine Definition des erkannten Was mündet. Gott flieht davor, sich in eine Wesensdefinition fassen zu lassen. In diesem Leben bleibt er unsichtbar für den Wesensblick einer Vernunft, die sich auf Seiendes richtet. Er ist nicht nur unsichtbar, weil er uns keine sinnliche Erfahrung seines geistigen Wesens geben kann. Er ist vielmehr unsichtbar, weil wir uns kein Verständnis von seinem Wesen bilden können. Wir haben kein inneres Wort von Gott, nicht nur keine sinnliche Anschauung. Denn Gott flieht vor jeder Vernunft, die ihn in einem Wort umfassen möchte.

Obwohl Gottes Wesen unerkennbar ist, erschließt die Vernunft, dass er ist, dass er Schöpfer ist, und dass ihm als Schöpfer notwendig die transzendentalen Vollkommenheiten Sein, Einssein, Gutsein und Wahrsein eignen, nicht aber dass Gott dreifaltig ist.[105] Denn Gott wirkt in der Schöpfung als der eine Gott, so dass die Personen als solche nicht aus der Schöpfung erkannt werden können.[106] Das aussagende oder urteilende Denken spricht also von Gott, obwohl die tiefsten Geheimnisse auch im aussagenden Denken für den Menschen verborgen bleiben. Doch von wem spricht das aussagende Denken, wenn es von Gott kein Wort gibt,

---

103 „Deus dicitur invisibilis, quia excedit capacitatem visionis cuiuscumque intellectus creati, ita quod nullus intellectus creatus naturali cognitione potest pertingere ad eius essentiam. … Ratio huius assignatur a Dionysio, quia omnis cognitio terminatur ad existens, id est ad aliquam naturam participantem esse. Deus autem est ipsum esse non participans sed participatum, ergo est incognitus" (Super epistolam ad Colossenses I 4, n. 30, vgl. Summa Theologiae I q12 a4 corpus und ad3).

104 Super III Sententiarum d24 q1 a2 sol1. Noch deutlicher spricht Thomas das Fehlen des Wortes in diesem Zitat aus: „in cor ascendit quod per operationem cordis formari potest; et hoc est quod videtur: et per istum modum quae praeparavit deus diligentibus se, in cor hominis non ascendunt" (Super III Sententiarum d24 q1 a2 sol3 ad2).

105 „Quaedam namque vera sunt de Deo quae omnem facultatem humanae rationis excedunt, ut Deum esse trinum et unum. Quaedam vero sunt ad quae etiam ratio naturalis pertingere potest, sicut est Deum esse, Deum esse unum, et alia huiusmodi; quae etiam philosophi demonstrative de Deo probaverunt, ducti naturalis luminis rationis" (Summa contra Gentiles I 3).

106 Vgl. Summa Theologiae I q32 a1.

das sein Wesen ausspricht? Es spricht von dem, den alle Gott nennen, wenn sie von einer höchsten Ursache dieser Welt sprechen oder versuchen zu beweisen, dass eine solche Ursache ist.[107] In einem solchen Beweis wird vorausgesetzt, dass der Name »Gott« die höchste Ursache bezeichnet. Doch wissen wir nicht, was sie ist. Deshalb werden die Wirkungen dieser Ursache betrachtet und Gott wird aus diesen Wirkungen als Ursache erkannt und benannt, obwohl sein Wesen verborgen bleibt.[108] Denn der Name »Ursache« offenbart Gottes Bezug zu uns, nicht sein Wesen.[109]

Was die Verborgenheit Gottes für das menschliche Seinsverständnis bedeutet, klärt Thomas durch den Hinweis, dass das Wort »Sein« mehrfach verstanden wird. Zum einen ist das Seiende der Ursprung der Wesensdefinition und offenbart das wesenhafte Sein der Dinge, das Sein als *actus essendi* oder *actus essentiae*, das durch Abstraktion von allem Zufall vernommen wird, also nicht an das Hier und Jetzt, Dies und Das gebunden ist. Das Sein als *actus essendi* vernehmen wir in der *simplex intelligentia*. Andererseits können wir auch sagen: Ich weiß, dass Gott ist. Oder: Der Baum ist da. Dann sprechen wir nicht vom wesenhaften Sein der Dinge. Vielmehr wollen wir mit einem solchen Urteil sagen, dass dies oder das ist, sich so oder so verhält. Das »ist« bezeichnet dann die Wahrheit eines Satzes. Denn hier und jetzt vergleicht sich unsere Vernunft mit dem Gegenstand, der ist, und weiß, dass er jetzt ist. Das Urteil spricht also von einem Sein im Jetzt, nicht von einem Sein, das von der Zeit abstrahiert. Während die Wesenskenntnis die Zeit zurücklässt, verortet das Urteil das Denken wieder in der Zeit.[110]

Wenn wir von Gott sagen, dass er ist, wissen wir, dass dieser Satz wahr ist. Von Gottes Wesen wissen wir durch diesen Satz jedoch nichts. Denn dieser Satz gründet in der Wahrnehmung von Gottes Wirkungen, nicht

---

107 Vgl. Summa Theologiae I q2 a3.

108 „[L]icet de Deo non possimus scire quid est, utimur tamen eius effectu in hac doctrina, vel naturae vel gratiae, loco definitionis ad ea quae de Deo in hac doctrina considerantur: sicut et in aliquibus scientiis philosophicis demonstratur aliquid de causa per effectum, accipiendo effectum loco definitionis causae“ (Summa Theologiae I q1 a7 ad1, vgl. q2 a2 ad2, sowie Pickavé, Martin, Human Knowledge, 321–322).

109 Summa Theologiae I q13 a7 ad1. Zwar ist Gottes schöpferisches Wirken sein Wesen, doch bedingt dieses Wirken ein Verhältnis, das durch den Namen »Schöpfer« bezeichnet wird.

110 „Nam ens quod significat compositionem propositionis est praedicatum accidentale, quia compositio fit per intellectum secundum determinatum tempus. Esse autem in hoc tempore vel in illo, est accidentale praedicatum. Sed ens quod dividitur per decem praedicamenta, significat ipsas naturas decem generum secundum quod sunt actu vel potentia“ (Sentencia Libri Metaphysicae X 3, n. 1982, vgl. Summa contra Gentiles II 96).

im Vernehmen der Wahrheit seines Wesens.[111] Ganz anders verhält es sich bei dem Satz: Der Baum ist da. Denn hier steht das Wesen des Baumes im Blick der Vernunft und ihr Ist-Sagen bezieht sich auf das wesenhafte Sein des Baumes, das sich dem Betrachter schon vor jedem Aussagen gezeigt hat, nicht aber auf eine Wirkung des Baumes.[112] D. h.: Das aussagende Denken vergleicht sich mit der Wirklichkeit des Baumes, die zunächst in der *simplex intelligentia* vernommen ist.[113] Da Gott für die *simplex intelligentia* abwest, ist dieser Vergleich im Sprechen von Gott nicht möglich. Die Wahrheit des Sprechens von Gott gründet deshalb im Vergleich der Aussage mit der geschöpflichen Wirklichkeit.

Das Denken von Gott darf deshalb nie vergessen, dass es ohne Verständnis von Gottes Wesen bleibt: Es ist nicht wortlos, insofern es von Gott in beweisbaren Aussagen spricht, doch wortlos, insofern es von seinem Wesen nichts weiß und seine tiefsten Geheimnisse nicht ergründen kann. Es benützt nur einen Namen, der auf eine höchste Ursache verweist. Dies gilt für Theologie und Philosophie, für Denken und Glauben.[114] Die Vernunft, die weiß, dass Gott ist, trägt deshalb die Sehnsucht in sich zu verstehen, was Gott ist, d. h. sie sehnt sich danach, Gottes Antlitz zu schauen, obwohl dies in dieser Welt nicht möglich ist.[115]

---

111 „*[E]sse* dupliciter dicitur: uno modo, significat actum essendi; alio modo, significat compositionem propositionis, quam anima adinvenit coniungens praedicatum subiecto. Primo igitur modo accipiendo *esse*, non possumus scire esse Dei, sicut nec eius essentiam: sed solum secundo modo. Scimus enim quod haec propositio quam formamus de Deo, cum dicimus *Deus est*, vera est. Et hoc scimus ex eius effectibus" (Summa Theologiae I q3 a4 ad2, vgl. Super I Sententiarum d33 q1 a1 ad1).

112 „Tertio modo dicitur esse quod significat veritatem compositionis in propositionibus, secundum quod «est» dicitur copula: et secundum hoc est in intellectu componente et dividente quantum ad sui complementum; sed fundatur in esse rei, quod est actus essentiae" (Super I Sententiarum d33 q1 a1 ad1, vgl. d19 q5 a1). Nach Thomas gilt also: Das Sein wird sowohl in der *simplex intelligentia* als auch im Urteil erkannt. Das Urteil ist jedoch auf die reine Faktizität, dass etwas hier und jetzt ist, beschränkt. Den bleibenden *actus essendi* oder *actus essentiae* ohne Zeit und Raum (vgl. Summa Theologiae I q75 a6) kann der Mensch im Urteil nicht vernehmen, obwohl das Urteil auf den *actus essendi* Bezug nimmt oder in ihm gründet. Etienne Gilson legte das Denken dagegen darauf fest, das Sein nur im Urteil zu verstehen (vgl. zu diesem Problemkreis Wippel, John F., The Metaphysical Thought of Thomas Aquinas. From Finite Being to Uncreated Being, Washington 2000, 23–44).

113 Vgl. Summa Theologiae I q16 a2, De veritate q1 a3.

114 Vgl. Summa Theologiae I q1 a7 ad1, II–II q2 a1.

115 Vgl. Summa Theologiae I–II q3 a8.

Der Name »Gott« steht also für das, worauf sich die tiefste Sehnsucht der Vernunft richtet. Dieses Worauf muss seltsam leer bleiben, weil es kein inneres Wort gibt, das das Wesen Gottes ausdrücken könnte. An die Stelle dieses inneren Wortes treten viele Aussagen, die uns sagen, was Gott nicht ist. Das Denken von Gott beschreitet also seine gewohnten Wege, um so weit als möglich auf Gott zuzugehen. Denn um ein Wesen zu erkennen, muss es in einer Gattung verankert werden, die durch spezifische Differenzen unterschieden wird. Von Gott können wir keine Gattung angeben, weil er jede Gattung übersteigt. Auch können wir keine positive Differenz finden, die ihn von anderen unterscheidet, wie den Menschen seine Vernünftigkeit aus allen anderen Sinnenwesen heraushebt. Doch können wir die Unterschiedenheit Gottes von allem anderen durch verneinende Aussagen ans Licht bringen: Gott ist nicht zeitlich, nicht stofflich, nicht zusammengesetzt, hat keine sinnliche Wahrnehmung, denkt nicht in Sätzen, etc. Je mehr wir Gott so von allem anderen unterscheiden, umso mehr zeigt sich das eigene Sein Gottes, ohne dass wir sagen könnten, *was* er *in sich* ist. Denn die negativen Unterschiede zeigen nur, dass Gott von anderem verschieden ist.[116] Dennoch ist dieses Nicht-Wissen für die Vernunft von höchstem Wert, da ihre ganze Sehnsucht darauf abzielt, Gott zu erkennen.

116 „Tantoque eius notitiae magis appropinquamus, quanto plura per intellectum nostrum ab eo poterimus removere. Tanto enim unumquodque perfectius cognoscimus, quanto differentias eius ad alia plenius intuemur: habet enim res unaquaeque in seipsa esse proprium ab omnibus aliis rebus distinctum. Unde et in rebus quarum definitiones cognoscimus, primo eas in genere collocamus, per quod scimus in communi quid est; et postmodum differentias addimus, quibus a rebus aliis distinguatur; et sic perficitur substantiae rei completa notitia. – Sed quia in consideratione substantiae divinae non possumus accipere quid, quasi genus; nec distinctionem eius ab aliis rebus per affirmativas differentias accipere possumus, oportet eam accipere per differentias negativas. Sicut autem in affirmativis differentiis una aliam contrahit, et magis ad completam designationem rei appropinquat secundum quod a pluribus differre facit; ita una differentia negativa per aliam contrahitur, quae a pluribus differre facit. Sicut, si dicamus Deum non esse accidens, per hoc ab omnibus accidentibus distinguitur; deinde si addamus ipsum non esse corpus, distinguemus ipsum etiam ab aliquibus substantiis; et sic per ordinem ab omni eo quod est praeter ipsum, per negationes huiusmodi distinguetur; et tunc de substantia eius erit propria consideratio cum cognoscetur ut ab omnibus distinctus. Non tamen erit perfecta: quia non cognoscetur quid in se sit“ (Summa contra Gentiles I 14, vgl. Super Boetium De Trinitate q6 a3).

2.1.2. Bei Meister Eckhart

Auch Eckhart ist überzeugt, dass wir uns von der übernatürlichen Wahrheit Gottes kein Verständnis bilden können:

> „Dar umbe gerüeret diu vernunft niemer in disem lebene den grunt der übernatiurlîchen wârheit, diu got ist. Und dar umbe sô stât si alles in einem beitenne und in einem arbeitenne. Und daz muoz mê heizen ein unwizzen dan ein wizzen alles, daz si hie haben mac von gote. Got offenbâret sich niemer sô sêre in disem lebene, ez ensî nochdenne ein niht gegen dem, daz er ist. Wie daz diu wârheit sî in dem grunde, si ist aber bedecket und verborgen der vernunft. Und alle die wîle sô daz ist, sô enwirt diu vernunft niht enthalten, daz si niht ruowe enhabe als in einem unwandellîchen vürwurfe. Si enruowet noch niht, mêr: si beitet und bereitet sich noch ze einem, daz noch bekannt sol werden und noch verborgen ist. Alsô enmac der mensche zemâle niht wizzen, waz got ist, mêr: etwaz weiz er wol, waz got niht enist. Und daz selbe scheidet der vernünftic mensche allez abe. Die wîle enwirt diu vernunft niht enthalten in keinem wesenlîchen vürwurfe.“[117]

Die übernatürliche Wahrheit Gottes in ihrem eigenen Grund erreicht die Vernunft in diesem Leben nie. Sein Wesen bleibt ihr verborgen. Deshalb harrt sie der Gotteserkenntnis immer entgegen und müht sich ab, alles von ihm wegzunehmen, was er nicht ist. Doch ein inneres Wort von Gott kann sie nicht sprechen. Mit der Unmöglichkeit, ein Wort von der übernatürlichen Wahrheit zu sprechen, verweist uns Eckhart in den Bereich des Glaubens. Doch wie soll der Glaubende ein Wort von Gott sagen, wenn er keines hat?

Die Wortlosigkeit der Vernunft in Bezug auf Gott bedeutet zunächst: Wir verstehen das Wesen Gottes nicht und können es nicht definieren. Doch wo ein Wesensverständnis fehlt und wir keine *forma cognita* von Gott haben, kann der Mensch auch nichts durch Schlussfolgerungen aus diesem Verständnis ableiten. Alles Beweisen von Gott ist auf Gottes Wirkungen in der Schöpfung angewiesen,[118] so dass die menschliche Rede von Gott im Geschöpf gründet. Gott wird deshalb am meisten dadurch erkannt, dass wir ihm geschöpfliche Seinsweisen absprechen.[119]

---

117 DW IV, 1, Predigt 104 A, ZZ. 319–341.

118 „[N]on contingit nos de deo aliquid scire nisi per effectus“ (LW V, Sermo die beati Augustini Parisius habitus, n. 11).

119 „Et cum demonstratio de re cognoscibili fiat ad sensum vel ad intellectum, de deo autem cognoscendo non potest fieri demonstratio ad sensum, quia est incorporeus, nec ad intellectum, quia forma nobis cognita caret, sed per solam alterius formam remotio-

Ebenso erklärt Eckhart, dass Gott als Ursache des Seins jenseits des Seins zu suchen sei, jenseits alles Erkennbaren.[120] Durch sich erkennbar ist nur das lautere Sein, das als Fünklein der Vernunft vernommen wird.[121] Insofern Eckhart alles Denken auf das Sein zurückführt, besser: auf das Seiende, wird er es in ein Jenseits des Seins führen müssen, wenn Gott im Reich des Nicht-Erkennbaren wohnt. Deshalb schreibt er:

> „Wenn sich der Mensch abkehrt von sich selbst und von allen geschaffenen Dingen – so weit du das tust, so weit wirst du geeint und beseligt in dem Fünklein in der Seele, das weder Zeit noch Raum je berührte. Dieser Funke widersagt allen Kreaturen und will nichts als Gott, unverhüllt, wie er in sich selbst ist. Ihm genügt's weder am Vater noch am Sohne noch am Heiligen Geist noch an den drei Personen, sofern eine jede in ihrer Eigenheit besteht. Ich sage fürwahr, dass es diesem Lichte auch nicht genügt an der Einheitlichkeit des fruchtträchtigen Schoßes göttlicher Natur. Ja, ich will noch mehr sagen, was noch erstaunlicher klingt: Ich sage bei der ewigen und bei der immerwährenden Wahrheit, dass es diesem Lichte nicht genügt an dem einfaltigen, stillstehenden göttlichen Sein, das weder gibt noch nimmt: es will wissen, woher dieses Sein kommt, es will in den einfaltigen Grund, in die stille Wüste, in die nie Unterschiedenheit hineinlugte, weder Vater noch Sohn noch Heiliger Geist. In dem Innersten, wo niemand daheim ist, dort genügt es diesem Licht, und darin ist es innerlicher als in sich selbst. Denn dieser Grund ist eine einfaltige Stille, die in sich selbst unbeweglich ist; von dieser Unbeweglichkeit aber werden alle Dinge bewegt und werden alle diejenigen ‚Leben' empfangen, die vernunftbegabt in sich selbst leben."[122]

Der Funke der Vernunft, der von jedem anderen Verständnis oder Namen verdeckt oder verhüllt wird, sucht den unverhüllten Gott, d. h. den Gott,

---

nem" (LW V, Sermo die beati Augustini Parisius habitus, n. 4). Eckhart ergänzt, dass Gott nicht nur durch Verneinung (*ablatio*, *remotio*) erkannt wird, sondern ebenso durch Ursächlichkeit und durch die Annahme, dass er in allen Seinsvollkommenheiten seine Geschöpfe unendlich übertrifft (*eminentia*). Vgl. hierzu z. B. Summa Theologiae I q12 a12.

120 Vgl. Anmerkung 82.

121 Eckhart schreibt deshalb, dass mit der ersten Kraft, der Vernunft, die reine Erkennbarkeit, das Sein, aus dem Grund der Seele ausfließt: „Diu aller êrste kraft, diu dâ entspringet ûz dem lûtern grunde, daz ist blôziu bekantlicheit: komet diu blôz ûf den market, sô wirt si aldâ gekleidet, si wirt behülset. Aleine si dâ inne sî, si vellet ûf lûter wesen, aber zehant ziuhet si eine hülsen umbe sich, daz ist wârheit; si bekennet ein wâr wesen" (DW IV, 1, Predigt 94, ZZ. 66–69). Damit ist wieder angedeutet, dass jedes normale Verständnis eines bestimmten Wesens das grundlegende Seinsverständnis verdeckt, d. h. das mit dem äußeren Auge Erkannte verdeckt das, was vor dem inneren Auge steht.

122 Predigt 34, Quint 315, 35–316, 20 (= DW II, Predigt 48, 419, 1–421, 3).

der nicht von einer Vorstellung von Gott verdeckt wird. Selbst Namen wie Vater, Sohn und Heiliger Geist sind Vorstellungen, die den Gott verbergen, den der Funke sucht. Die Vorstellung von drei Personen verdeckt die Einheit Gottes. Aber selbst wenn wir die *eine* göttliche Natur bedenken, durch die der Vater den Sohn gebiert und die ganze Welt erschafft, ist dies eine Vorstellung von Gott. Der Funke sucht keine solche Vorstellung. Denn der Funke ist ein inneres Verständnis oder Licht, das auf natürliche Weise und durch sich selbst gegenwärtig ist, ohne dass es durch einen Namen gerufen werden müsste. Deshalb sucht dieses Licht Gott im Namenlosen. Doch Eckhart steigt noch höher. Wir können versuchen, durch die reine und stille Gegenwärtigkeit des Seins im Fünklein das einfaltige, stillstehende göttliche Sein zu bedenken. Doch dann verstehen wir das Sein immer noch so, wie Menschen es im Ausgang von den Geschöpfen erkennen. Die göttliche Seinsweise bleibt verborgen. Denn wer das Sein bedenkt, kommt sofort zum Geschöpf. Gott ist als das verborgene Sein die Ursache geschöpflichen Seins. Deswegen sucht das Fünklein Gott nicht als das Sein. Es sucht das Woher des Seins über dem Sein. An dieser Stelle überschreitet Eckhart das, was erkennbar ist, und gelangt in eine stille Wüste, wo kein Name erklingt.[123] In demselben Sinn kann Eckhart sagen:

> „Gott wird, wo alle Kreaturen Gott aussprechen: da wird ‚Gott'. (…) So also reden alle Kreaturen von ‚Gott'. Und warum reden sie nicht von der Gottheit? Alles das, was in der Gottheit ist, das ist Eins, und davon kann man nicht reden. Gott wirkt, die Gottheit wirkt nicht, sie hat auch nichts zu wirken, in ihr ist kein Werk. (…) Gott und Gottheit sind unterschieden durch Wirken und Nichtwirken."[124]

---

123 Vgl. den folgenden Text des Thomas, der durch ähnliche Verneinungen zum Gott jenseits des Seins in der Dunkelheit der Wolke vorstößt: „alia omnia nomina dicunt esse determinatum et particulatum; sicut sapiens dicit aliquid esse; sed hoc nomen *qui est* dicit esse absolutum et indeterminatum per aliquid additum; et ideo dicit Damascenus quod non significat quid est Deus, sed significat quoddam pelagus substantiae infinitum, quasi non determinatum. Unde quando in deum procedimus per viam remotionis, primo negamus ab eo corporalia; et secundo etiam intellectualia, secundum quod inveniuntur in creaturis, ut bonitas et sapientia; et tunc remanet tantum in intellectu nostro, quia est, et nihil amplius: unde est sicut in quadam confusione. Ad ultimum autem etiam hoc ipsum esse, secundum quod est in creaturis, ab ipso removemus; et tunc remanet in quadam tenebra ignorantiae, secundum quam ignorantiam, quantum ad statum viae pertinet, optime deo coniungimur, ut dicit Dionysius, et haec est quaedam caligo, in qua Deus habitare dicitur" (I Sent d8 q1 a1 ad4).

124 Predigt 26, Quint 273, 10–21 (= DW IV, 2, Predigt 109, ZZ. 56–64).

Die Gottheit ist das Wesen Gottes, von dem kein Mensch in dieser Welt ein inneres Wort hat. Doch alle Geschöpfe sprechen von Gott, da sie von ihm »gewirkt« werden. Gott ist also nur »Gott«, d. h. der von den Geschöpfen geoffenbarte Gott, insofern er alles aus dem Nichts ins Dasein ruft. Doch Gottes Wirkungen offenbaren sein Wesen nicht. Denn in Gott sind alle geschöpflichen Vollkommenheiten eins, während jedes Geschöpf nur seine je eigene Vollkommenheit besitzt. Insofern menschliches Sprechen den vielen Dingen dieser Welt entspricht, kann die eine Gottheit, die alles in sich umfasst, nicht durch ein menschliches Wort ausgedrückt werden. Doch sprechen wir von Gott als der einen Ursache des vielen, die sich in allem zeigt und verbirgt. Deshalb sind „Gott und Gottheit … so weit voneinander verschieden wie Himmel und Erde",[125] d. h. wie der Gott, der sich durch die Geschöpfe in seinem Wirken auf der Erde zeigt, und die Gottheit, die in sich im Himmel ist und keine Geschöpfe wirkt. Diese Gottheit ist die stille, unerkannte Wüste. Kein Mensch würde versuchen, in diese stille Wüste einzugehen, wenn Gott ihn nicht durch das Licht der Gnade, d. h. durch den Glauben und die Liebe, dahin brächte, das natürliche Licht, an dem die Natur sich freut, zu verlassen. Denn die Vernunftnatur wird durch die Gnade über sich selbst hinaus gerückt und sucht Gott jenseits des Fünkleins, d. h. jenseits ihres eigenen Lichts.[126]

---

125 Predigt 26, Quint 272, 13–15 (= DW IV, 2, Predigt 109, ZZ. 34–35).

126 „Die zweite Liebe Gottes, die da ‹gnadenhaft oder› geistig ist, damit fließt er in die Seele und in den Engel, wie ich vorhin sagte, dass die vernunftbegabte Kreatur aus ihr selbst gerückt werden muss mit einem Lichte, das oberhalb alles naturhaften Lichtes liegt. Da alle Kreaturen in ihrem naturhaften Lichte soviel Lust empfinden, so muss es ein Höheres sein, dass ein Gnadenlicht sie daraus emporzieht. Denn in dem naturhaften Licht hat der Mensch Lust in sich selbst; das Licht der Gnade aber, das unaussprechlich größer ist, das nimmt dem Menschen die Eigenlust und zieht ihn in sich ‹ = das Gnadenlicht› selbst hinein. (…) Nun kann man Gott nicht lieben, man müsse ihn denn vorher erkennen, denn der wesenhafte Punkt der Gott ist, der da in der Mitte steht, gleich fern und nah allen Kreaturen, soll ich dem angenähert werden, so muss meine naturhafte Vernunft hinausgerückt werden mit einem Lichte, das oberhalb ihrer ist. So wie wenn mein Auge ein Licht und so stark wäre, dass es das Licht der Sonne in seiner Kraft aufnähme und damit eins würde, so sähe es nicht allein mit seiner Kraft, sondern es sähe mit dem Licht der Sonne ‹so stark›, wie sie in sich selbst ist. So ‹auch› ist es mit meiner Vernunft. Kehre ich die Vernunft, die ein Licht ist, von allen Dingen weg geradeswegs auf Gott hin, so wird diese meine Vernunft, da Gott ja doch ohne Unterlaß mit Gnaden ausfließt, erleuchtet und mit dieser ‹Gnaden-›Liebe vereint und darin Gott erkennend und liebend so, wie er in sich selber ist. Hierdurch werden wir ‹darüber› unterwiesen, wie Gott mit dem Lichte der Gnade ausfließt in die vernunftbegabten Kreaturen und wie wir mit un-

Wegen dieser Suche jenseits des Verstehbaren, die den Glauben von der natürlichen Vernunft unterscheidet, arbeitet sich die Vernunft daran ab, Gott zu verstehen. Sie kann dies nur tun, indem sie alles, was Gott nicht ist, von ihm verneint. Und je mehr dieser Verneinungen sie ihm zuspricht, umso näher kommt sie der Gotteserkenntnis. Wir können dies an einem Gleichnis verdeutlichen. Würden wir einem Menschen, der nie ein Schiff gesehen hat, sagen, was ein Schiff sei, dann sähe der Mensch, dass alles, was er sieht, kein Schiff ist. Sähe er einen Stein, er sähe, dass ein Stein kein Schiff ist. Je mehr er von dem sähe, was nicht als Schiff geschaffen ist, umso näher käme er der Erkenntnis eines Schiffes. So ist es auch mit Gott. Je mehr die Seele zur Erkenntnis kommt, dass Gott allen Naturen ungleich ist, so gerät sie in ein Staunen und wird zurückgetrieben und kommt in ein Schweigen. Mit der Stille senkt sich Gott in die Seele und sie wird mit Gnade begossen. So soll sie wurzeln im Glauben und wachsen in der Liebe.[127] Insofern ist das gott-lose Erkennen, das ohne ein inneres Wort von Gott auskommen muss und deshalb alles von ihm verneint, von größtem Nutzen für die Seele, die im liebenden Glauben wachsen soll. Denn das Verneinen führt ins schweigende Staunen, das den Raum der Seele für Gott öffnet. Die Seele schweigt, weil Gott alles Verstehen übersteigt, aber auch, weil die Liebe keinen Grund hat, etwas zu benennen. Sie kennt Gott aus Erfahrung.[128]

---

serer Vernunft diesem gnadenhaften Licht uns nähern und uns selbst entzogen werden und emporsteigen sollen in ein Licht, das Gott selber ist“ (DW III, Predigt 75, 297, 1–298, 13, Übersetzung 560). Zum Licht des Glaubens in Eckharts Predigten vgl. z. B. DW II, Predigt 32, 142, 1–5.

127 „Ie man sîn mê lougent, ie man in mê lobet. Ie man im mê unglîches zuoleget, ie man sînem bekantnisse næher kumet, als ich ein glîchnisse sagen wil. Wolte ich einem menschen sagen, waz ein schif wære, der nie keinez gesehen enhæte, swaz der mensche sæhe, er sæhe daz wol, daz ez niht ein schif enwære. Sæhe er einen stein, er sæhe daz wol, daz ein stein ein schif niht enwære. Ie er des mê sæhe, daz ez niht geschaffen wære als ein schif, ie er des schiffes bekantnisse næher kæme. Alsô ist es umbe got. Ie man im mê unglîches zuoleget, ie man sînem bekantnisse næher kumet. ... Als diu sêle in daz bekantnisse kumet, daz got alsô unglîch ist allen natûren, sô kumet si in ein wunder und wirt wider getriben und kumet in ein swîgen. Mit der stille senket sich got in die sêle, und mit der gnâde wirt si begozzen. (...) Daz sterben der sêle daz sol sîn an dem bekantnisse gotes, daz si von ir selber vliehen sol und daz ir alliu dinc âsmec und stinkende suln werden, daz got niht enist. Si sol wurzeln an dem glouben und wahsen an der liebe“ (DW IV, 1, Predigt 95 B, ZZ. 220–256).

128 „Sponsa omnibus dimissis ab ipsomet verbo quaerit experiri dicens: *indica mihi*, id est intus dicas, quia secundum Augustinum »intus in domicilio cogitationis« etc. ... *In-*

2.2. Die Anwesenheit Gottes durch den liebenden Glauben

2.2.1. Bei Thomas von Aquin

Thomas geht davon aus, dass Gott durch die Offenbarung zum Menschen spricht, d. h. durch menschliche Worte hindurch, die in der heiligen Schrift aufgezeichnet sind. Die Frage ist, wie der Mensch die Schrift als Wort Gottes verstehen kann. Begegnete uns die Schrift wie ein Seiendes durch den natürlichen Gegenstand der Vernunft, würden wir sie wie ein Buch unter anderen Büchern lesen. Alle Worte der Schrift sprächen vom Seienden und könnten uns auf den Gott hinweisen, von dem alles Seiende kommt. So verstanden wäre die Schrift ein frommes Buch, das von Gott spricht und von Menschen verfasst ist. Aber sie wäre nicht die Offenbarung des lebendigen Gottes, der durch die Worte der Schrift unmittelbar zu uns spricht und nicht durch geschöpfliche Vermittlung. Das natürliche Licht der Vernunft reicht nicht hin, die Schrift als Wort Gottes zu hören. Sie braucht ein höheres Licht, indem sie die menschlichen Worte der Schrift als das erkennt, was sie wahrhaft sind: als Wort Gottes.[129] Das Licht des Glaubens gibt der Vernunft dazu einen höheren formalen Gegenstand, den Thomas die erste oder göttliche Wahrheit nennt oder das göttlich Offenbarte. Denn der Mensch, der von Gott mit dem Licht des Glaubens besiegelt ist, glaubt die Worte Gottes, weil sie von Gott gesprochen sind.[130] Im Glauben werden die Worte nicht nur auf das Seiende zurückgeführt, sondern primär auf Gott selbst.[131]

---

dica, quia verba exteriora deficiunt. Tertio *indica*, ne illud indicatissimum in voces exteriores transfusum decipiat obumbratum. … Non nominat, quia scit ipsum omne nomen excedere. Secundo, quia more amantis omnis, de quo loquitur, putat scire. Tertio, quia amor non habet rationem nominandi“ (LW II, Expositio Cantici Canticorum, nn. 1–2, vgl. Wilde, Mauritius, Das neue Bild vom Gottesbild. Bild und Theologie bei Meister Eckhart, Freiburg/Schweiz, 2000, 228).

129 Vgl. 1 Thessalonicher 2, 13.

130 Vgl. z. B. Summa Theologiae II–II q1 a1, I q1 a3, De veritate q14 a8, Super Boetium De Trinitate q2 a2, sowie Donneaud, Henry, Objet formel et objet matériel de la foi. Genèse d’un instrument philosophique chez saint Thomas et quelques autres, Revue Thomiste 100 (2000) 5–44, Mayer, Rupert J., De veritate: Quid est?, 387–392.

131 „[P]erceptio divinae veritatis quae fit per rationem naturalem, tendit, sicut in id cui innititur, in intellectum principiorum; sed perceptio divinae veritatis quae est articulus, tendit in primam veritatem non solum sicut in finem, vel obiectum, sed sicut in id in quod resolvitur sicut in causam suae credulitatis“ (Super III Sententiarum d25 q1 a1sol1 ad4).

Durch den Glauben geschieht demnach ein Wechsel des ersten Prinzips: Gott selbst macht sich durch das Licht des Glaubens zum ersten Prinzip des Glaubens, doch so, dass er und sein Sich-Offenbaren für die Vernunft unsichtbar bleiben. Dennoch erscheint im Licht des Glaubens, dass die Offenbarung als Wort Gottes glaubhaft ist, ohne dass die Vernunft durch die Offenbarkeit Gottes zum Glauben gezwungen würde.[132] Sie bleibt von sich her unentschieden und hat kein Wesenswort von Gott. Die Offenbarung sagt ihr z. B. nur, dass Gott dreifaltig ist, ohne ihr einen Einblick in das dreifaltige Wesen zu schenken oder ihr einen Beweis dafür zu geben, dass Gott dreifaltig ist. In dieser Unentschiedenheit der Vernunft eilt ihr der Wille zu Hilfe. Denn im Licht des Glaubens erscheint es als gut, dem Wort Gottes Glauben zu schenken. Letztlich bewegt also der Wille die Vernunft, die aus sich kein Wort von Gott hat und auch keinen Grund, aus dem sie die Wahrheit der Offenbarung ableiten könnte, zur Zustimmung des Glaubens. Entsprechend gesteht Thomas dem Willen eine leitende Rolle im Glauben zu, obwohl der Glaube seinen Sitz in der Vernunft hat.[133]

Einerseits bedeutet dies, dass der Mensch mit Hilfe des einladenden Gottes wählen muss zu glauben.[134] Doch wenn der Glaube von der Liebe durchformt ist, d. h. wenn der Mensch Gott um Gottes willen glaubt, ist die Zustimmung nicht nur eine Wahl zwischen beliebigen Möglichkeiten. Denn die Liebe verleiht dem Menschen eine Wesensverwandtschaft mit Gott und stimmt sein Gemüt auf Gott hin. Thomas spricht in diesem Fall von einer *praesentia in affectu*, einer Gegenwart Gottes im Gemüt oder im liebenden Willen, die die Abwesenheit Gottes von der Vernunft ausgleicht.[135] Wer Gott liebt, lebt in der Gegenwart des geliebten Gottes. Er stimmt mit größter Sicherheit dem zu, was Gott sagt, und verneint das, was Gott fremd ist.[136] Denn die Vernunft übersetzt die Zuneigung des Wil-

---

132 Vgl. Summa Theologiae II–II q1 a4 ad3, a5 ad1, Super Boetium De Trinitate q3 a1 ad4.

133 Vgl. Summa Theologiae II–II q1 a4, De veritate q14 a1 und a2, Summa contra Gentiles III 40.

134 Vgl. Summa Theologiae II–II q2 a9 ad3.

135 „Per cognitionem autem fidei non fit res credita intellectui praesens perfecte: quia fides de absentibus est, non de praesentibus. (…) Fit tamen per fidem Deus praesens affectui, cum voluntarie credens Deo assentiat: secundum quod dicitur Ephes. III, ‚habitare Christum per fidem in cordibus nostris'" (Summa contra Gentiles III 40).

136 Zum konnaturalen Urteil vgl. Summa Theologiae I q1 a6 ad3, II–II q2 a3 ad2, q45 a2.

lens in eine Bejahung, die Abneigung des Willens in eine Verneinung.[137] Obwohl diese Erkenntnisweise vermittels der Gegenwart im Willen ein Urteil der Vernunft ermöglicht, kann Thomas es auch ein Sehen im Licht des Glaubens nennen.[138]

Wo das Wort fehlt, das die Gegenwart Gottes für die Vernunft ausspricht, ersetzt die Liebe zu Gott die fehlende Einsicht und vergegenwärtigt Gott für den Glauben. Die Kraft des Offenbarungswortes im Menschen hängt also am Licht des Glaubens und an der Liebe. Denn das Licht des Glaubens ermöglicht, dass wir Gottes Wort als Gottes Wort empfangen. Die Liebe zeigt uns, dass wir hier nicht nur einem Gott glauben, der alles Verstehen übersteigt, sondern einem Gott, der in seinen Worten und in uns gegenwärtig ist, so dass wir dem zustimmen, den wir durch die Liebe kennen, und der durch die Liebe oder den liebenden Glauben in uns wohnt. Denn Glaube bedeutet, dass wir in Gott wohnen und er oder seine Wahrheit in uns.[139] Wenn die Gegenwart Gottes für die Vernunft fehlt, weil sie weder sein Wesen vernimmt, noch seine tiefsten Geheimnisse erschließen kann, kann ein festes Wort des Glaubens nur auf dem Boden der Gegenwart Gottes im Gemüt stehen. Die Liebe berührt den gegenwärtigen Gott und ersetzt so die fehlende Einsicht, für die Gott ein Abwesender bleibt.

2.2.2. Bei Meister Eckhart

Auch für Eckhart gilt, dass dem einen Gott um seiner selbst willen zu glauben ist, weil er die Wahrheit von allem und durch sich selbst wahr ist, so dass man nach keinem Grund über ihm suchen kann, um ihn zu verstehen.[140] Die Vernunft muss deshalb von Gott erleuchtet werden, damit sie

---

137 Sentencia Libri Ethicorum VI 2.

138 „[L]umen fidei facit videre ea quae creduntur. Sicut enim per alios habitus virtutum homo videt illud quod est sibi conveniens secundum habitum illum, ita etiam per habitum fidei inclinatur mens hominis ad assentiendum his quae conveniunt rectae fidei et non aliis" (Summa Theologiae II–II q1 a4 ad3, vgl. Mayer, Rupert J., De veritate: Quid est?, 393–420, sowie zur Erkenntnis aus Wesensverwandtschaft: d'Avenia, Marco, La conoscenza per connaturalità in S. Tommaso d'Aquino, Bologna 1992).

139 Vgl. Summa Theologiae II-II q4 a1, Super epistolam ad Ephesios III 4, n. 172, Super epistolam ad Hebraeos XI 1, n. 557.

140 „Tertio notandum quod, quia ipsa divina seipsis sunt vera, fixa et stabilia, quaerere istorum causam et probationem sive rationem – cum sit ipsa veritas et ratio omnium, Ioh. 1: ‚in principio erat verbum' sive ratio – dementiae est et ignorantis veritatem dei. Oportet ergo credere in talibus et ipsis propter seipsa fidem adhibere" (LW I, Expositio libri Genesis, n. 275, vgl. Haas, Alois M., Aktualität und Normativität Meister Eckharts.

durch den Glauben zu dem erhoben wird, wohin sie durch ihre Natur nicht gelangen kann.[141] Dieser Glaube, d. h. die *fides formata caritate*, ist eine Einwohnung Christi und damit des lebendigen Gottes. Denn der liebende Glaube vollendet nicht nur die Vernunft, sondern auch den Willen und damit das Gemüt. Entsprechend streckt sich der Mensch nur dann nach dem Geglaubten, d. h. nach Christus, aus, wenn er ihn liebt. So ist Christus zweifach in uns. Verstehen wir den Glauben als Glauben, bewohnt Christus durch den Glauben die Vernunft. Durch die Liebe, die den Glauben durchformt und zu Gott hinneigt, ist Christus im Willen. Der Mensch, der so mit Gott verbunden ist, hat das ewige Leben zumindest in der Hoffnung.[142]

Die Verbundenheit mit Gott durch den Glauben gleicht also einer Totenerweckung. Eckhart versucht, dies anhand der Totenerweckung des Jünglings von Naïn zu verdeutlichen. Er beschreibt, wie die Seele dabei von Gott berührt wird. Denn der Jüngling kommt nur durch das Wort Gottes, durch das alles erschaffen ist und getragen wird, ins Leben zurück. Dieses Wort prägt der Seele in ihrem Grund seine eigene Form und sein Gleichnis auf, damit die Seele etwas dem göttlichen Wort Ähnliches wirke. Aber das erste Wort gleicht den Menschen nicht nur sich selbst an, es prägt ihm auch Worte ein.[143] Denn im eigentlichen Sinn spricht die Seele und formt ihr Wort innen, wenn sie sich im Bereich des Fünkleins oder ihres eigenen geistigen Lichts aufhält. Dann steht sie auch im Bereich des Lichtes der Engel und Gottes. Im Licht des Fünkleins »tagt« jedes Geschöpf, das im Licht des Seins geschaffen ist und in seinem ersten Prinzip leuchtet, so dass

---

In: R. Imbach and H. Stirnimann (Hgg.), Eckardus Theutonicus, homo doctus et sanctus. Nachweise und Berichte zum Prozeß gegen Meister Eckhart, Freiburg/Schweiz 1992, 205–268, hier: 245–259).

141 „Secundo cognoscitur in via per speculum et in lumine, quando scilicet lux divina per effectum suum aliquem specialem irradiat super potentias cognoscentes et super medium in cognitione, elevans intellectum ipsum ad id quod naturaliter non potest. »Mentis enim humanae acies invalida in tam excellenti lumine non figitur, nisi per iustitiam fidei prius purius emundetur«, secundum Augustinum libro De trinitate" (LW V, Sermo die beati Augustini Parisius habitus, n. 5, vgl. LW III, n. 650, LW II, Expositio libri Exodi, n. 13).

142 Vgl. LW IV, Sermo V, 2, n. 38.

143 „Verbo enim dei, quo creata sunt et portantur omnia, rediit ad vitam. (…) Unde hoc verbum ipsi animae impresserat formam et similitudinem suam, ut abinde primo operaretur sibi simile. (…) Si enim herbae et gemmae miranda agunt, impressa a caelo et stellis, quanto magis verba in quantum huiusmodi, impressa ab ‹et› in primo verbo" (LW IV, Sermo XXXVI, 1, n. 369).

die Seele ein inneres Wort von ihm sprechen kann.[144] Auch die Worte des Glaubens werden in diesem Bereich gesprochen. Wenn diese Worte unser natürliches Verstehen übersteigen, da das Sein nur alle Geschöpfe in ihr »Tagen« bringt, hat die Vernunft kein eigentliches inneres Verständnis.[145] Entsprechend kommentiert Eckhart das Wort des Paulus, „Niemand kann sagen: Jesus ist Herr, es sei denn im Heiligen Geist“:[146]

> „Viele haben von alters her mit diesem Wort gerungen und ringen heute noch damit; spricht doch der Erlöser: ‚nicht jeder, der zu mir sagt: Herr, Herr, wird in das Himmelreich eingehen‘ (Matth. 7, 21). Daraus erhellt, dass einer, der die Liebe und folglich den Heiligen Geist nicht hat, durch den die Liebe in die Herzen ausgegossen wird, auch nicht sagen kann: ‚Herr, Herr‘, oder: Herr ist Jesus. Es kann zwar einer der Materie nach, insofern er die äußerlichen Worte [sc. *vox*] ausspricht, sagen: Herr ist Jesus, aber nicht der Form nach, gemäß der Bedeutung der Worte [sc. insofern sie ein inneres Wort bezeichnen]. Er kann es sagen mit dem Mund, aber er kann es nicht sagen und fühlen mit dem Herzen, nach jenem Wort Jesajas: ‚Dieses Volk ehrt mich mit den Lippen, ihr Herz aber [ergänze: ist fern von mir].‘“[147]

Eckhart verdeutlicht, dass die Liebe zu Gott das fehlende innere Wort, das durch ein gesprochenes Wort bezeichnet wird, ersetzt. Denn der Gott liebende Mensch fühlt die Gegenwart dessen, der in seinem Herzen wohnt. Das Wort »Herr« bezeichnet dann eine vernommene oder offenbare Gegenwart und nicht nichts. Fehlt die Liebe, ist Gott, von dem die Vernunft kein Wort hat, nicht durch den Willen für die Vernunft gegenwärtig. Der Name »Herr« ist dann in diesem Menschen leer und kraftlos, da er weder Gottes Gegenwart bezeichnet, noch den Menschen in ein Verhältnis zu

144 „Dic quomodo proprie anima loquitur et verbum format intus in concursu trium luminum sive dierum. Nam lumen sive dies proprie est, cum omne acceptum ab anima accipitur et reducitur sub lumine intellectus. Diescit enim omnis creatura huius mundi, cum cadit super ipsam radius splendoris intellectualis. Haec est prima dies. – Secunda est, cum sub illo lumine stans cum ipso lumine perfunditur radio splendoris angelici. … Tertia dies est, cum sic unita ratio splendori intellectuali perfunditur pari modo lumnine divino unito lumine sive luminibus, de quo iam supra. Et haec dies perfecta est“ (LW IV, Sermo XXXVI, 1, nn. 370–371, vgl. Löser, Freimut, Predigt 19: ‚Sta in porta domus domini‘. In: G. Steer and L. Sturlese (Hgg.), Lectura Eckhardi I. Predigten Meister Eckharts von Fachgelehrten gelesen und gedeutet, Stuttgart 1998, 117–149, hier: 137–140).

145 „Oportet enim captivare intellectivum sive rationem naturalem, faciem scilicet propriam, volentem videre secretiora et profundiora dei in lumine gratiae, in spiritu scilicet, propter quod et supernaturalia dicta sunt“ (LW II, Expositio libri Exodi, n. 13).

146 1 Korinther 12, 3.

147 LW IV, Sermo XXIII, n. 217.

Gott setzt, das das Aussprechen des Namens »Herr« rechtfertigt. In Eckharts Werk künden nahezu alle Worte von der geliebten Gegenwart Gottes, besonders die Reden der Unterscheidung:

> „War ane liget nû diz wâre haben gotes, daz man in wærlîche habe? – Diz wærlîche haben gotes liget an dem gemüete und an einem inniclîchen vernünftigen zuokêrenne und meinenne gotes, niht an einem stæten anegedenkenne in einer glîchen wîse, wan daz wære unmügelich der natûre in der meinunge ze habenne und sêre swære und ouch daz aller beste niht. Der mensche ensol niht haben noch im lâzen genüegen mit einem gedâhten gote, wan, swenne der gedank vergât, sô vergât ouch der got. Mêr: man sol haben einen gewesenden got, der verre ist obe den gedenken des menschen und aller crêatûre. Dér got envergât niht, der mensche enkêre denne williclîche abe. – Der got alsô in wesenne hât, der nimet got götlîchen, und dem liuhtet er in allen dingen; wan alliu dinc smeckent im götlîchen, und got erbildet sich im ûz allen dingen. In im blicket got alle zît, in im ist ein abegescheiden abekêren und ein înbilden sînes geminneten gegenwertigen gotes. Glîcher wîs, als den dâ hitziclîchen dürstet in rehtem durste, der tæte wol anders dan trinken und mac ouch wol ander dinc gedenken; mêr: aber swaz er tuo oder bî swem er sî, in swelher meinunge oder swaz er gedenke oder swaz er würke, im envergât doch daz bilde des trankes niht, die wîle der durst wert; und als vil grœzer der durst ist, als vil mêr und inwendiger und gegenwertiger und stæter ist daz bilde des trankes. Oder der dâ hitziclîchen ein dinc minnet mit ganzer kraft alsô, daz im niht anders ensmecket und ze herzen gât dan daz, und meinet daz aleine und anders zemâle nihtes: entriuwen, swâ der mensche ist oder bî swem er ist oder swes er beginnet oder swaz er tuot, sô erlischet niemer in im, daz er alsô minnet, und in allen dingen vindet er des dinges bilde und ist im als gegenwertic, als vil der minne mêrer und mêrer ist.“[148]

Noch einmal erläutert Eckhart, dass die Gegenwart Gottes für den Glauben an der Liebe zu ihm hängt. Je stärker die Liebe zu Gott ist, desto gegenwärtiger wird Gott für den Menschen. Denn was der Mensch liebt, dessen Bild findet er in allen Dingen, auch wenn er nicht unmittelbar an den Geliebten denkt. Aber er findet den Geliebten nicht nur in allen Dingen, vor allem im Grund der eigenen Seele, sondern besonders in seinem Wort. Insoweit gibt die Liebe durch die Hoffnung dem Menschen nicht nur ein echtes Gottvertrauen, „sondern sie besitzt auch ein wahres Wissen und eine zweifelsfreie

148 DW V, Reden der Unterscheidung: 6. Von der Abgeschiedenheit und vom Besitzen Gottes, 205, 1–206, 13. Zur Erkenntnis auf Grund einer Wesensverwandtschaft bei Eckhart vgl. Schönberger, Rolf, Wer sind „grobe liute“? Eckharts Reflexion des Verstehens. In: K. Jacobi (Hg.), Meister Eckhart: Lebensstationen – Redesituationen, Berlin 1997, 239–259, hier: 253–258.

Sicherheit."[149] Der so gegenwärtige Gott ist kein gedachter oder vorgestellter Gott, sondern der wirklich anwesende Gott, dem sich der Mensch zukehrt, von dem er alle Inspiration zu Wort und Werk erfährt. Das Wort des Glaubens ist also nicht auf Sand gebaut. Durch die Liebe ruht es in Gott selbst und tritt aus Gottes Gegenwart im Menschen hervor. Denn der Glaube ist die Gegenwart des Abwesenden.[150]

3. Die Kraft des Wortes

Dieser kurze Blick auf die Geburt des Wortes im Menschen zeigt, dass wir nur das wahrhaft verstehen und in ein Wort heben können, was uns gegenwärtig ist. Diese Gegenwart meint nicht die Gegenwart für die Sinne hier und jetzt, obwohl wir ohne sinnliche Wahrnehmung nichts verstehen können. Im natürlichen Bereich sprechen Thomas und Eckhart von einer Gegenwart für die Vernunft, die alles Seiende oder alle Dinge umfasst. Innerhalb dieses Seinsverständnisses wird ein Ding dann und nur dann gegenwärtig, wenn seine eigene Seinsweise im Unterschied zu anderen Seinsweisen und ohne alles Zufällige vernommen wird. Entsprechend kann das äußere Wort des Menschen leicht darüber hinweg täuschen, dass es nicht aus einer inneren Gegenwart entspringt. Oft spiegelt das äußere Wort den Zustand einer Vernunft, die noch überlegt und meint, dass etwas so oder anders sein könnte.

Obwohl wir das vom äußeren Wort bezeichnete Verständnis »inneres« Wort nennen, ist es kein inneres Verstehen. Denn wir empfangen das Verständnis oder innere Wort einerseits von den Dingen. Solches Verstehen verdeckt das Fünklein des Seinsvernehmens, d. h. jene innere Erkenntnis, die mit der Vernunft aus dem Grund und Sein der Seele hervor fließt, genauso wie die Liebe, die von Gott in die Seele gegossen wird und uns befähigt, uns als seine Kinder zu erkennen und in seiner Gegenwart zu leben.[151] Wer von dieser inneren Gegenwart nichts weiß, der kann letztlich

149 DW V, Reden der Unterscheidung: 14. Von der wahren Zuversicht und von der Hoffnung, 239, 8–9, vgl. Quint, 74, 15–16.

150 So sagt Eckhart mit Augustinus: „Idem De trinitate XIII c. 5: »rerum absentium praesens est fides, rerum quae foris sunt intus est fides, rerum quae non videntur videtur fides«" (LW IV, Sermo XXXII, n. 331).

151 „Die Seele hat etwas in sich, ein Fünklein der Vernünftigkeit, das nimmer erlischt, und in dieses Bild als in das oberste Teil des Gemütes verlegt man das »Bild« der Seele.

auch kein eigentliches Wort sprechen, das dieser Gegenwart zu entnehmen ist. Wie Eckhart sagt:

> „Was im eigentlichen Sinne in Worten geäußert werden kann, das muss von innen heraus kommen und sich durch die innere Form bewegen, nicht dagegen von außen herein kommen, sondern: von innen muss es heraus kommen. Es lebt recht eigentlich im Innersten der Seele. Dort sind dir alle Dinge gegenwärtig und im Innern lebend und suchend und sind (dort) im Besten und im Höchsten. Weshalb merkst du nichts davon? Weil du dort nicht daheim bist. Je edler etwas ist, um so allgemeiner ist es. Den Sinn habe ich mit den Tieren gemein und das Leben mit den Bäumen. Das Sein ist mir noch innerlicher, das habe ich gemein mit allen Kreaturen."[152]

Die innere Form der Erkenntnis ist ihr Seinsverstehen, in dem alle Dinge eins sind. Wer ein echtes Wort sprechen will, das in der wesenhaften Gegenwart des vernommenen Dinges gründet, muss deshalb im Innersten seiner Seele beheimatet sein. Er muss manchmal auch Jahre warten, harren und sich abmühen, um die Wahrheit eines Wesens in den Blick nehmen und ins Wort heben zu können. Denn alle Kraft der natürlichen Worte kommt aus der Gegenwart des Seienden, d. h. des Fünkleins der Vernünftigkeit. Ähnlich ist es auch im Glauben, der seine Worte nur durch die Liebe der Gegenwart Gottes entnehmen kann. Ohne Liebe ist der Glaube hohl und fußt nicht in der Gegenwart Gottes. Der Intellekt kann dann immer noch durch das Glaubenslicht die Worte Gottes als Worte Gottes annehmen. Aber wenn die Liebe fehlt, bleibt Gott ein Abwesender. Die Worte eines solchen Glaubens sind einerseits kräftig, weil sie für Worte Gottes gehalten werden. Andererseits sind sie schwach und leer, weil sie nicht aus der Gegenwart Gottes hervorquellen. Deshalb ist ein solcher Glaube auch nicht rettend. Denn er vermag Gott nicht die Antwort zu geben, die er hören will:

Nun gibt es aber in unseren Seelen auch ein auf äußere Dinge gerichtetes Erkennen, nämlich das sinnliche und verstandesmäßige Erkennen, das ein Erkennen in Vorstellungsbildern und Begriffen ist und das uns jenes (Erkennen) verbirgt. – Wie (aber nun) sind wir »Söhne Gottes«? Dadurch, dass wir ein Sein mit ihm haben. Dass wir indessen etwas davon erkennen, dass wir der Sohn Gottes sind, dazu muss man inneres und äußeres Erkennen zu unterscheiden wissen. Das innere Erkennen ist jenes, das sich als vernunftartig im Sein der Seele fundiert. Indessen ist es nicht der Seele Sein, vielmehr wurzelt es darin und ist etwas vom Leben der Seele. … Und dieses Erkennen ist ohne Zeit, ohne Raum und ohne Hier und Nun. In diesem Leben sind alle Dinge eins und alle Dinge miteinander alles in allem und alles in allem geeint" (Predigt 35, Quint 318, 5–23, = DW III, Predigt 76, 315, 6–317, 2).

152 Predigt 4, Quint 170, 4–14 (= DW I, Predigt 4, 66, 3–67, 2).

> „[D]arum soll sich die Seele in ihrem natürlichen Lichte in das Höchste und in das Lauterste erheben und so eintreten in das Engelslicht und mit dem Engelslicht in das göttliche Licht gelangen und so stehen zwischen den drei Lichtern in der Wegscheide, in der Höhe, wo die Lichter zusammenstoßen. Dort spricht ihr das Wort das Leben ein; dort wird die Seele lebendig und antwortend in dem Worte."[153]

Das natürliche Licht oder Fünklein hat die Vernunft mit den Engeln gemein, auch wenn das Licht in ihr schwächer ist als in einem Engel. Deshalb versteht Eckhart den Eintritt in das Seinsverstehen immer als einen Aufstieg in das Licht der Engel. Insofern das Seinsverständnis ebenso ein Bild Gottes ist, gelangt die Vernunft durch dieses Bild vor den Allerhöchsten. Dieser Aufstieg ist ihr ohne den Glauben verwehrt, da die Vernunft nicht über ihr eigenes Licht hinaussteigen möchte. Zu sehr freut sie sich natürlicherweise an ihrem eigenen Licht. Deshalb entführt der Heilige Geist das Fünklein in den Ursprung, der Gott ist.[154] In dieser Höhe spricht ihr das göttliche Wort das Leben des Glaubens ein. Wenn die Seele durch den liebenden Glauben antwortet, der in Gottes Gegenwart zu stehen kommt, ist sie lebendig. Sie antwortet Gott in Gottes Wort. Insofern hat das liebende Sprechen des Glaubens eine unendliche Kraft. Wo Worte nach langer Zeit des Harrens aus solchen Tiefen geschöpft sind, sind sie ewig alt und ewig neu, frisch gehört und doch bleibend wahr.

Von Meistern des Wortes wie Thomas oder Eckhart kann man lernen, nicht oberflächlich und ohne verstandene Gegenwart dahinzureden, sondern die Worte aus einer inneren Quelle zu schöpfen, die unaussprechlich reich ist. Wo Menschen mit ihrem Sprechen in diese Quelle zurückgehen, gibt es keine Sprachverwirrung mehr, sondern echtes Verstehen des anderen. Denn alle Menschen stehen an diesem inneren Quell. Ob sie schöpfen, hängt daran, ob sie zuhause sind. Die dominikanische Botschaft möchte die Menschen dahin zurückführen, wo die geistigen Wasser und alle wahren Worte fließen. Menschen wie Meister Eckhart oder Thomas von Aquin schrieben deshalb nicht Worte, die nur informieren, wie die sinnliche

153 Predigt 18, Quint 235, 33–236, 3 (= DW I, Predigt 18, 306, 9–307, 4).

154 „Ebenso eigentlich nimmt die Kraft des Heiligen Geistes das Lauterste und das Feinste und das Höchste, das Fünklein der Seele, und trägt es ganz empor im Brande, in der Liebe. … Ganz so wird auf alle Weise das Fünklein in der Seele emporgetragen in dem Lichte und in dem Heiligen Geiste und auf solche Weise hinaufgetragen in den ersten Ursprung und wird so ganz eins mit Gott" (Predigt 21, Quint 247, 11–19 = DW I, Predigt 20 b, 344, 9–345, 3).

Wahrnehmung uns Auskunft gibt, dass dies hier und jetzt ist. Bei ihren Worten geht es um ein inneres Verstehen, nicht um ein äußerliches Hören. Der Weg zum Verstehen ist nicht immer leicht. Aber ein liebendes Herz findet mit Gottes Hilfe seinen Weg zur Quelle.

Thomas und die Frage nach dem Islam – oder inwieweit kann die Studie des Heiligen als Vorgabe für den aktuellen Dialog Christentum / Islam dienen?

Wolfgang Müller OP

„Im Mittelalter begegnen sich die christlichen Völker Europas und der Islam. Diese Begegnung hatte Auswirkungen auf fast alle Bereiche des Lebens. Sie zeigten sich besonders deutlich an europäisch besiedelten Ländern, die lange Zeit hindurch unter muslimischer Herrschaft standen. Auch in den Kreuzzügen trafen die Völker mit ihren unterschiedlichen Religionen und Lebensformen aufeinander. Die Folgen machten sich nicht nur in den unmittelbar betroffenen Regionen bemerkbar. Die islamischen Völker erwiesen sich als Träger einer vielseitigen und erstaunlich hochentwickelten Kultur, die in Europa natürlich Bewunderung fand und zur Nachahmung anregte. Nicht zuletzt auf dem Gebiet der Wissenschaften lernten die Europäer sehr viel Neues kennen und übernahmen es mit Eifer. Manches wiederum wurde mit Skepsis betrachtet. Das galt vor allem von der islamischen Religion selbst und von deren Auswirkungen auf die Lebensgestaltung der Muslime.“[1]

Der interreligiöse Kontext stellt heute eine besondere Herausforderung theologischer Reflexion dar, wie sie an staatlichen Universitäten betreiben wird. Auf die weitere wachsende Pluralität religiöser Bekenntnisse muss Kirche und Theologie in den offenen pluralen Gesellschaften reagieren. Gegenwartsbezogenenen interreligiösen Fragestellungen kommt dabei ein großer Stellenwert zu. Religionen erweisen sich als Konzentration der jeweiligen kulturellen Besonderheiten. Als ‚way of life‘ ist Religion kein isolierbarer, individualisierbarer Gegenstand, sondern stets auf Gesellschaft, Kultur und Geschichte bezogen. Für das gesellschaftliche Miteinander ist der Dialog der Religionen ein Gebot der Stunde.[2]

---

1 Albert Zimmermann / Ingrid Craemer-Ruegensberg (Hg.): Orientalische Kultur und europäisches Mittelalter. Berlin/N.Y. 1985, Vorwort S. V.

2 Für den europäischen Kontext siehe das Programm der Charta Oecumenica (www.unilu.ch/files/charta_oecumenica.pdf, abgerufen 2. April 2012), exemplarisch für die Frage Christentum/Islam siehe beispielsweise: Chrétiens du monde arabe. Dirigé par

Angesichts der heute aktuellen Debatte um Islam und europäische Gesellschaft(en), Christentum und Islam ist es angebracht, nach theologischen Reflexionen über den Islam bei Meistern der theologischen Wissenschaft vergangener Zeiten Ausschau zu halten. Vorliegendem Beitrag geht es darum, die Fragestellung bei Thomas von Aquin in einer systematischen Sicht zu betrachten, um mögliche Impulse für den heute postulierten Dialog beider Religionen in dem Werk des theologischen Altmeister zu suchen. Dabei soll jedoch nicht das gesamte Spektrum der Fragestellung ‚Thomas von Aquin und seine Sichtweise und Behandlung des Islam' anschnitten werden, sondern nur einzelne Aspekte aus den vielfältigen Bezügen seines Werkes im Blick auf den Islam hervorgehoben und reflektiert werden. Damit wird eine Reihe von Fragen nicht eingehend besprochen und reflektiert werden wie zum Beispiel:

– Kenntnis und Einfluss arabischer Philosophie im Werk des Aquinaten: Es stellt sich die Frage, welche muslimische Autoren der Aquinate kannte. Hier sind beispielsweise zu nennen: Avicenna (Ibn Sina, gest. 1037), al-Gazzali (gest. 1111), Averroes (Ibn Rusd, gest. 1198). Werke dieser Autoren wurden ins Lateinische übersetzt und hatten damit einen großen Einfluss auf die Intellektuellenszene der Pariser Universität wie auf das intellektuelle Leben Italiens. Thomas unterrichtete Papst Alexander IV. über diesen Sachverhalt. Der Papst beauftragte Albertus Magnus, sich der Frage nach der Einheit des Intellektes anzunehmen. Die damalige Lektüre von Aristoteles war vielschichtig, d. h. es gab Lesearten, die in einem Gegensatz zum christlichen Denken standen, hier wäre an Person und Werk von Siger von Brabant zu denken. Die Arbeit, die der Papst einforderte, ging also darum, eine Antwort aus christlicher Sicht auf die erkenntnistheoretischen Fragestellungen der damaligen Zeit zu erarbeiten. Dieser kurze Problemaufriss soll hier genügen. Es sei noch erwähnt, dass das intellektuelle Zentrum dieser Übersetzungsarbeiten in Andalusien lag; hier sind besonders Toledo und Sevilla zu nennen. Dieses zeitgenössische intellektuelle Abenteuer wird durch Kaiser Fried-

Bernard Heyberger. Paris, 2003, Martin Tamcke: Christen in der islamischen Welt. München, 2008, Christian W. Troll: Unterscheiden um zu klären. Freiburg i.Br. 2008, Wolfgang W. Müller (Hg.): Christentum und Islam. Plädoyer für den Dialog. Edition NZN bei ZVZ, Zürich, 2009. Der interreligiöse Dialog als Aufgabe des Ordens unterstreicht der ehemalige Ordensmeister fr. Carlos A. Azpiroz Costa op in seinem Brief an den Orden vom 7. November 2002 (siehe: www.dominicains.ca/documents/maitre_ordre/Costa/annonce-evangile.htm, abgerufen 2. April 2012)

rich II. fortgeführt, der in Neapel eine Universität gegründet hatte. Toledo, Neapel Paris hießen die intellektuellen Zentren, in denen die heißen Fragen der damaligen Intelligentia und akademischen Jugend debattiert wurden. Die zeitgenössischen Debatten umfassten dabei sowohl philosophische als auch theologische Fragestellungen. Der französische Mediävist Jacques Le Goff nennt die geduldige Suche nach dem schwierigen Gleichgewicht zwischen Glauben und Vernunft das aristotelische Abenteuer im 13. Jahrhundert. Bekanntermaßen gab es bzgl. dieser Thematik zwei große Bewegungen: hie ein christlicher ‚Aristotelismus', wie ihn Albertus, Thomas vertraten, da ein ‚Averrroismus' eines Siger von Brabant.[3]

- Kenntnisse und Reflexionen über den Islam im Werk des Aquinaten. Thomas von Aquin konnte in einer lateinischen Übersetzung des Korans lesen. Petrus Venerabilis, Abt von Cluny, ist die Initiative zu verdanken, eine lateinische Übersetzung des Korans anfertigen zu lassen (notabene in Toledo). Dieser Theologe war von einer inhaltlichen Auseinandersetzung mit dem Islam beseelt und wollte damit folgende Ziele erreichen: a) Abbau des Informationsdefizits, b) Kritik an militärischen Aktionen, Wahrung der Priorität der Apologie des Glaubens. Das Projekt einer lateinischen Koranübersetzung, die im Juli 1143 vollendet war, war für die damalige Zeit zweifellos ein Schritt nach vorne und diente einer inhaltlichen Auseinandersetzung mit dem Islam und seiner heiligen Schrift.[4]
- In einem weiteren Umfeld der Fragestellung müsste dann ebenfalls die Frage nach Judentum und jüdischen Denkern im Werk des Aquinaten bedacht und thematisiert werden.[5]

---

3 Jacques Le Goff: Die Intellektuellen im Mittelalter. 4. durchggesehene und um ein Nachwort erw. Aufl., Stuttgart 2001; Alain de Libera: Denken im Mittelalter. München 2003; Volker Leppin: Theologie im Mittelalter. Leipzig: Evangelische Verlagsanstalt, 2007, S. 96–127.

4 Ludwig Hagemann: Die erste lateinische Koranübersetzung – Mittel zur Verständigung zwischen Christen und Muslimen im Mittelalter?: In: Albert Zimmermann / Ingrid Craemer-Ruegenberg (Hg.): Orientalische Kultur und europäisches Mittelalter. Berlin/ N.Y. 1985, S. 45–58, 55.

5 Vgl. dazu etwa: Dieter Berg: Servitus Judaeorum. Zum Verhältnis des Thomas von Aquin und seines Ordens zu den Juden Europas im 13. Jahrhundert. In: Orientalische Kultur und europäisches Mittelalter, aaO., S. 439–458.

Im Folgenden soll nur auf eine kleine Schrift unseres Heiligen eingegangen werden, die in der Debatte ‚Thomas und die Frage nach dem Islam' bis auf den heutigen Tag oft übergangen wird: gemeint ist die Gelegenheitsschrift des Aquinaten ‚De rationibus fidei'.[6]

Um sich über den Sitz im Leben dieser Schrift zu verständigen, muss man die Missionspraxis zu Beginn des 13. Jahrhunderts rekapitulieren. Franziskaner wie Dominikaner begannen zu dieser Zeit mit ihren Missionen unter Muslimen in Europa, vor allem auf der iberischen Halbinsel, und im Orient. Damit setzte eine neue Phase der Auseinandersetzung des Christentums mit dem Islam ein. War zuvor in einer polemischen Zuspitzung von der Schrift des Korans und dem Propheten die Rede, so installierte sich jetzt eine apologetische Tendenz. Es galt, Missionierungen in diesen Ländern zu erreichen, nachdem der erhoffte Missionserfolg durch die Kreuzzüge ausgeblieben war. Es begann nun eine inhaltliche Auseinandersetzung, die bei den Franziskanern mittels ihres Lebensbeispiels konzipiert wurde. Das exemplarische Leben, das die Mitglieder des neuen Ordens führten, sollte als Beispiel und Ansporn für die Mission unter Muslimen gelten. Hierbei wäre beispielsweise an das Gespräch Franz von Assisis mit Sultan Melek el-Kamil zu erinnern, das der Ordensgründer im Jahr 1291 in Ägypten führte. Sultan Melek el-Kamil, ein Neffen des Sultans Saladin, gilt bis heute als einer der bedeutendsten mittelalterlichen islamischen Herrscher des Orients.[7] Das Treffen beider wird geschichtlich eher eine marginalere Bedeutung zukommen, als es die franziskanische Hagiographie in-

6 Thomas von Aquin: De rationibus fidei, eingeleitet und editiert von H.-F. Dondaine. Rom 1968. Ludwig B. Hagemann: Thomas von Aquin: De rationibus fidei. Kommentierte lat.-deutsche Textausgabe. Altenberge 1987; ders.: Missionstheoretische Ansätze bei Thomas von Aquin in seiner Schrift De rationibus fidei. In: Albert Zimmermann: Thomas von Aquin. Werk und Wirkung im Licht neuerer Forschungen. Berlin/N.Y. 1988, S. 459–483.

7 Bonaventura schildert diese Begegnung in der Legenda maior. Kap. IX. wie folgt: „Er predigte dem Sultan mit solcher Unerschrockenheit, Geisteskraft und Glut den einen, dreifaltigen Gott und den Erlöser aller Menschen Jesus Christus, dass in Wahrheit in ihm das Wort des Evangeliums erfüllt schien: , Ich selbst werde euch eine Sprache und Weisheit geben, der alle eure Gegner nicht widerstehen und widersprechen können.'" (Bonaventura von Bagnoregio. Legenda Maior – das große Franziskusleben. Auf der Grundlage der Überarbeitung von Sophrinus Clasen OFM (+) neu bearbeitet von M. Schlosser und von Paul Zahner OFM. In: Dieter Berg / Leonhard Lehmann (Hg.): Franziskus-Quellen. Die Schriften des heiligen Franziskus, Lebensbeschreibung, Chronik und Zeugnisse über ihn und seinen Orden. Kevelaer: Butzon & Bercker 2009, S. 686–844, 745) Zur Reise des Franziskus siehe allgemein: Franco Cardini: Europa und der Islam.

terpretierend deutet, denn die Heere der Sarazenen und Christen standen zu gleicher Zeit in heftigem Kampf gegeneinander.

Die Frage der Mission unter den Muslimen stellte sich auch für den Dominikanerorden. In ihren missionarischen Bemühungen trat bei den Predigerbrüdern neben die Thematik eines exemplarischen Lebens zugleich das Postulat einer intellektuellen Auseinandersetzung mit Religion und Kultur des Islams. Für diesen Missionsauftrag wurden im Predigerorden spezielle Arbeitsinstrumente geschaffen. Das anvisierte Ziel einer inhaltlichen Auseinandersetzung wurde erreicht, indem einerseits Handbücher für die Missionstätigkeit geschrieben wurden, andererseits die Predigerbrüder eigene Sprachschulen für das Arabische einrichteten. Dank dieser Maßnahmen konnte die christlich-muslimische Kontroverse auf ein höheres Niveau als bis anhin gehoben werden. Raimund von Penafort, die Ordenstradition nennt ihn „Vater der (bekehrten) Sarazenen", und Humbertus de Romanis plädierten für eine solche Ausbildung und vertraten gegenüber ihrem Orden die Idee der Errichtung eines „studium arabicum": Solche Initiativen unterstützen im Orden das Provinzkapitel von Saragossa 1256 oder das Generalkapitel 1259 in Valenciennes, nachdem Humbertus bereits im Jahr 1256 einen Brief in diesem Anliegen an den Generalmeister des Ordens geschrieben hatte.[8]

Auf dem genannten Hintergrund ist das Entstehen der vorzustellenden Schrift ‚De rationibus fidei' zu sehen. Die kleine theologische Studie des Aquinaten bildet ein Antwortschreiben auf eine Frage eines Mitbruders.[9] Über Cantor Antiochenus, so heißt der Mitbruder, der bei Thomas anfragte, kennt man keine genaueren Einzelheiten. Er kennt sich in der Religion des Islams aus und möchte die christlichen Positionen seinen muslimischen Gesprächspartner näher bringen. Mit anderen Worten: Die Schrift soll Fragen im Rahmen der Missionierung arabischer Staaten behandeln. Muslime sollten durch intellektuelle Argumente zum christlichen Glauben gebracht werden. Man kann annehmen, dass der genannte Fragesteller ein

---

München, 2000, S. 131–135, J. Tolan: Le saint chez le Sultan. La rencontre de François d'Assise et de l'Islam. Huit siècles d'interprétation, Paris 2007.

8 Siehe dazu: Marie-Dominique Chenu: Das Werk des Hl. Thomas von Aquin. Heidelberg/Graz 1960, S. 333f.

9 In der Sekundärliteratur finden immer wieder Stimmen, die die Schrift des Aquinaten strikt als apologetische bewerten, indem sie den ideologischen Überbau der Missionierung lieferte, z. B. Franco Cardini: Europa und der Islam, aaO., 120f.

Predigerbruder in der Islammission war und sich mit seinem Anliegen an seinen renommierten Mitbruder wandte.

Auch die Frage der Abfassungszeit der Schrift wird in der Forschung kontrovers diskutiert, dies soll hier nicht referiert werden.[10] Sicher steht jedenfalls fest, dass die Schrift ‚De rationibus fidei' nach der Abfassung der Schrift ‚Summa contra Gentiles' des Aquinaten anzusetzen ist, d. h. man hat mit einer Abfassungszeit nach 1267 (= Jahr des Abschlusses der Redaktion der ‚Summa contra Gentiles'), also etwa mit dem Jahr 1268 als Erscheinungsjahr der Schrift zu rechnen. Mit der großen philosophischen Summe hat diese kleine Gelegenheitsschrift den religionsphilosophischen Ansatz gemeinsam, das Depositium fidei mittels der Vernunft nachzuweisen und so Juden und Muslimen Plausibilitätsstrukturen christlichen Glaubens argumentativ zu vermitteln.[11] Heuristisch bleibt jedoch zu bedenken, dass Thomas auch in dieser Schrift, selbst wenn sie als Antwortschreiben eine Gelegenheitsschrift des Aquinaten darstellt, die ihm gestellten Fragen in (s)einer bekannten grundsätzlichen Art und Weise behandelt. Thomas wurde von seinem Mitbruder mit der Bitte um Beantwortung bestimmter Fragen angegangen. Thomas wiederum möchte seinem Mitbruder eine intellektuelle Hilfestellung für seine pastorale Aufgabe geben, damit dieser theologisch vor Ort auf die Einwände der Muslime bzgl. einiger christlicher Glaubenssätze eingehen und sie begründen kann.

Als hermeneutische Prämisse gibt Thomas seinem Mitbruder die Weisung mit auf den Weg, in seiner Auseinandersetzung mit Muslimen nicht den Glauben beweisen zu wollen und die Rationalität des im Glauben Vorgegebenen demonstrieren zu wollen, sondern in seinem solchen Gespräch gelte es, die Vernünftigkeit des Glaubens, also seine Rationalität aufzuzeigen. Thomas rekurriert deswegen zu Beginn seiner Schrift auf das Schriftwort aus dem Ersten Petrusbrief: „Seid stets bereit zur Verantwortung jedem gegenüber, der von euch Rechenschaft fordert über das, was an Hoffnung und Glauben in euch ist." (1 Petr 3,15) Thomas benennt die

10 Siehe dazu etwa: Thomas von Aquin: De rationibus fidei, aaO., S. 15–17.

11 So urteilt Volker Leppin über den methodischen Ansatz der Schrift ‚Summa contra gentiles', dass es sich bei dieser Schrift um « eine grossangelegte Apologie" handelt, „in der der Theologe Thomas die Denkbarkeit des christlichen Glaubens gegen tatsächliche und mögliche Einwände aus dem Hintergrund paganer Philosophie verteidigt, wobei der konkrete Kontext auch durch die Auseinandersetzungen um den konsequenten Aristotelismus bestimmt gewesen zu scheint." (Volker Leppin: Thomas von Aquin. Münster, 2009, S. 95.

Grundsätze seiner theologischen Methode im Gegenüber zu Nichtchristen wie folgt: Der von Gott geoffenbarte Glaube kann nicht falsch sein, da Gott selbst Garant dieses Glaubens ist. Die göttlich verbürgte Wahrheit kann demnach auch nicht in einem unlösbaren Widerspruch zur Vernunftwahrheit stehen. Denn das, was nicht falsch ist, weil es nicht falsch sein kann, kann auch nicht durch zwingende Vernunftgründe widerlegt werden. Aus dieser Annahme wird folgendes Fazit gezogen: Christlicher Glaube ist nicht zu beweisen, sondern das Ziel der theologischen Diskussion muss darauf ausgerichtet sein, den christlichen Glauben zu verteidigen resp. zu bezeugen. Bei dieser erkenntnistheoretischen Grundlegung bei Thomas soll das Augenmerk auf zwei Dinge gerichtet werden:

a) Zunächst ist auf die methodologische Grundlage des Gesprächs zu achten. Thomas benutzt in seiner Auseinandersetzung mit Nichtchristen keinen Verweis auf die Bibel als normierende Schrift christlichen Glaubens, da dieser Tatbestand bei seinem Gegenüber nicht vorausgesetzt werden kann. Denn es ist einsichtig, dass in einer Auseinandersetzung mit anderen Religionen nicht auf die eigene normierende Schrift rekurriert werden kann, da diese von den Andersgläubigen in dieser Eigenschaft und Dignität nicht anerkannt ist. Als gemeinsame Basis eines Gesprächs mit Andersgläubigen bleibt also nur die natürliche Vernunft. „Zuerst will ich dich doch daran erinnern, dass du in Disputationen gegen Ungläubige über Glaubensartikel nicht darauf aus sein darfst, den Glauben durch zwingende Gründe zu beweisen; dies würde nämlich der Erhabenheit des Glaubens Abbruch tun, dessen Wahrheit nicht nur den menschlichen Geist, sondern sogar den der Engel überschreitet; wir halten die Glaubensinhalte vielmehr für gleichsam von Gott selbst geoffenbart. Weil aber das, was aus der höchsten Wahrheit hervorgeht, nicht falsch sein kann, und nichts mit zwingenden Gründen widerlegt werden kann, was nicht falsch ist, so kann unser Glaube, ebenso wie er nicht mit zwingenden Gründen bewiesen werden kann, weil der den menschlichen Glauben überschreitet, wegen seiner Wahrheit auch nicht mit zwingenden Gründen widerlegt werden.“[12] Eine Ausnahme dieses hermeneutischen Axioms theologischer Erkenntnislehre gilt es allerdings in dieser Schrift des Aquinaten zu bedenken: Werden in dieser Schrift Themen erörtert, die ebenfalls das Gespräch mit den Juden berührt, dann kann Thomas verständlicherweise auf das Alte Testament verwei-

12 Thomas von Aquin: De rationibus fidei, aaO., S. 65.

sen. In der zu untersuchenden Schrift gibt es noch eine weitere Ausnahme von dieser Regel. Im 9. Kapitel wird die Frage nach der theologischen Begründung des Purgatoriums behandelt; diese Thematik sieht Thomas im Kontext der damaligen Unionsbemühungen mit Griechen und Armeniern.

b) In seiner Gotteslehre spricht Thomas als höchste Form menschlicher Gotteserkenntnis von der Unerkennbarkeit Gottes. Die klassische Formulierung dieses theologischen Axioms hat Thomas in seinem Kommentar zur Schrift ‚De causis' vorgelegt. Im Kontext der thomasischen Seinslehre schreibt er: „Aber in Wahrheit liegt die erste Ursache über dem Seienden (ens) insofern, als sie das unendliche Sein (esse) selbst ist. ‚Seiendes' wird nämlich das genannt, was am Sein auf endliche Weise teilnimmt. Und das ist unserer Vernunft angemessen, deren Gegenstand die Washeit ist. Nur das ist von unserer Vernunft erfassbar, was eine am Sein teilnehmende Washeit hat. Gottes Washeit jedoch ist das Sein selbst. Deshalb liegt sie jenseits der Vernunft."[13] Thomas lehrt mit aller Dringlichkeit, dass Gott nicht das Ersterkannte ist, ens ist das Ersterkannte. Während die Existenz eines ens unmittelbar erfassbar ist, kann die Existenz Gottes nur am Ende eines Denkprozesses stehen.[14]

Die vorzustellende Schrift möchte weder Kompendium noch Kurzfassung christlichen Glaubens sein, sondern befasst sich (als eine ‚Gelegenheitsschrift') mit bestimmten, an den Theologen Thomas gestellten Fragen, die sich aus der Missionstätigkeit der Predigerbrüder in arabischen und muslimischen Ländern ergeben haben. Dabei handelt es sich um Themenkomplexe, die auch für den heutigen Dialog mit dem Islam in einer inhaltlichen wie systematischen Perspektive relevant sind:

1) Christologie: Die Schrift setzt sich mit dem Vorwurf auseinander, Muslime spotteten über die Bezeichnung Christi als Sohn Gottes. Die christozentrische Basis des Glaubens widerspreche, so lautet der Vorwurf von islamischer Seite, der Lehre von der exklusiven Einheit und Einzigkeit Gottes. Damit geht ein weiterer Vorwurf einher:

13 Thomas von Aquin: De causis, lect. 6.

14 Die zentrale Stelle bei Thomas lautet dazu: „Das, was ich Sein nenne, ist die Aktualität aller Akte, und deshalb ist es die Perfektion aller Perfektionen./Hoc quod dico est actualis omnium actuum, et propter hoc est perfectio omnium perfectionum." (De pot. Q. 7, a. 2, ad 9)

2) Die Trinitätstheologie wird in apologetischer Absicht als die Lehre eines Tritheismus verstanden.
3) Der Kreuzestod Christi wird geleugnet, weil Gott aufgrund seiner Allmacht die Menschheit auch anders hätte erlösen können.
4) Der eucharistischen Praxis und Lehre der Eucharistie werden ein Unverständnis entgegengebracht, insofern es als abstrus erscheint davon zu sprechen, dass die Christen den ‚Leib Christi' konsumieren.
5) Das Verhältnis von Handlungsfreiheit und Determinismus wird in der Anthropologie und Theologie des Islams anders erörtert und verhandelt als in der christlichen Theologie.

Die einzelnen Kapiteln der Schrift ‚De rationibus fidei' wollen auf die verschiedenen Einwände der muslimischen Theologie eine Antwort bieten. Thomas greift in seiner Gelegenheitsschrift auf Aussagen und Reflexionen, die er an anderer Stelle bereits ausführlicher formulierte. So schreibt er seinem Mitbruder in der Einleitung der Schrift: „Weil ich also deiner Bitte Genüge leisten will, die aus deinem frommen Wunsch hervorzugehen scheint, gemäß der apostolischen Lehre bereit zur Verantwortung jedem gegenüber zu sein, der von dir Rechenschaft verlangt, werde ich dir über die oben genannten Probleme, wenn es die Stofffülle erlaubte, einige leicht einsehbare Dinge darlegen, die ich anderswo doch recht zerstreut untersucht habe."[15] Wie geht Thomas in seiner Argumentation vor?

Die Inkarnation ist nicht als Verwandlung eines Menschen zu verstehen. Thomas setzt in seiner Begründung bei der altkirchlichen Christologie an. „Wenn wir sagen, Gott werde Mensch, sollte niemand meinen, dies sei so aufzufassen, dass Gott sich in einen Menschen verwandle, wie etwa Luft zu Feuer wird, indem sie sich darein verwandeln."[16] Der christologischen Aussage des Konzils von Chalcedon geht es vielmehr um eine Vereinigung der göttlichen mit der menschlichen Natur. Die logische Begründung für den Aufweis geht, gemäß dem methodologischen Postulat der thomasischen Gelegenheitsschrift, nicht mittels eines offenbarungstheologischen Beweisganges vor, sondern argumentiert mit Gründen der menschlichen Vernunft. Es kann nämlich eine gewisse Parallelität zur Vereinigung der geistigen mit der körperlichen Natur des Menschen gesehen werden.

15 Thomas von Aquin: De rationibus fidei, aaO., S. 63. Der Verweis ‚an anderer Stelle' bezieht sich auf die Schrift Summa contra gentiles.
16 Thomas von Aquin: De rationibus fidei, aaO., S. 87.

„Wenn man das Geheimnis der göttlichen Fleischwerdung in irgendeiner Weise betrachtet, muss man beachten, dass jedes Wesen, das verstandesmäßig tätig ist, durch einen Begriff des Verstandes, Wort genannt, wirkt, so wie es offenbar bei einem Baumeister oder einem beliebigen Künstler der Fall ist, der gemäß der Form, die er im Geist entwirft, nach außen hin tätig wird; weil also der Sohn Gottes das Wort Gottes selbst ist, folgt, dass Gott durch seinen Sohn alles geschaffen hat."[17] Wobei jedoch ein Unterschied zu beachten ist: Seele und Leib vereinigen sich nämlich so, dass es zu einer neuen Natur kommt, wobei die Seele den dominierenden Teil darstellt und den Leib gleichsam beherrscht; ähnlich dominiert in Christus die göttliche Natur. Hier endet die Analogie, denn es besteht in Christus keine neue Natur. Göttliche und menschliche Natur bestehen nebeneinander. Man kann sagen, dass die göttliche Natur die menschliche als die vorzüglichere besitzt. Christus ist kraft der menschlichen Natur auch Person der göttlichen, weil die menschliche Natur Christi ihre Vollendung in der göttlichen findet. Über Christus kann man deswegen nicht sagen, er sei ‚zwei Personen'. Die göttliche Person ist mit ihm identisch. So kann man die göttliche Natur von Christus auch abstrakt aussagen, d. h. er ist göttliche Natur, während die menschliche Natur von ihm nur in konkreter Weise ausgesagt werden kann, d. h. er hat eine menschliche Natur. Aussagen über Christus werden deshalb entweder seiner göttlichen Natur oder seiner menschlichen Natur nach gemacht. Auch die Idiomenlehre der hypostatischen Natur erklärt Thomas in einem ‚argumentum ad hominem': „Bei den verschiedenen Aussagen, die man über Christus macht, muss man jeweils genau unterscheiden, in welcher Hinsicht man etwas über Christus aussagt: Gewisse Dinge werden nämlich gemäß der menschlichen Natur, andere gemäß der göttlichen Natur ausgesagt; wenn man aber bedenkt, von wem sie ausgesagt werden, werden sie ununterschieden vorgebracht, weil es dieselbe Hypostase ist, von der Göttliches und Menschliches ausgesagt wird. Ebenso verhielte es sich, wenn ich sagte, es sei derselbe Mensch, der sieht und hört, aber nicht aufgrund desselben, denn er sieht mit den Augen, hört aber mit den Ohren; dasselbe Obst ist es auch, das man sieht und riecht, aber das eine durch die Farbe, das andere durch den Duft: In Rücksicht darauf können wir sagen, dass der Sehende hört und der Hörende sieht und dass das Gesehene gerochen und das Gerochene gesehen wird. In ähnlicher Weise", so folgert Thomas in seiner Argu-

17 Thomas von Aquin: De rationibus fidei, aaO., S. 79.

mentation, „können wir sagen, dass Gott aufgrund seiner menschlichen Natur von der Jungfrau geboren wird und als Mensch aufgrund seiner göttlichen Natur einzig ist.“[18]

Um einen argumentativen Zugang zur Lehre der Trinität zu gewinnen, geht Thomas bei seinen Überlegungen vom Gedanken der Zeugung aus. Zeugung kann verschieden vonstatten gehen, bei Pflanzen anders als bei Tieren. „Jeder verständige Mensch“, so setzt Thomas seine Begründung der Zeugung an, „vermag aber doch einzusehen, dass die Art und Weise der Zeugung nicht bei allen Dingen die gleiche ist, sondern dass man bei jedem einzelnen eine Zeugung gemäß der Eigentümlichkeit seiner eigenen Natur findet: Bei einigen Tieren geschieht sie nämlich durch eine Gemeinschaft von Männchen und Weibchen, bei den Pflanzen aber durch das Treiben und Hervorsprossen, und bei anderen auf andere Weise.“[19] So zeugt Gott gemäß seiner göttlichen Natur; die Art dieser Zeugung kann in Analogie zur Zeugung des menschlichen Verstandes erklärt werden. Ist der Verstand tätig, zeugt er Gedanken. Wird dieser mit einem Laut versehen, entsteht ein Wort. Wird von der Zeugung des göttlichen Wortes gesprochen, so heißt dies Folgendes: Weil Gottes Sein mit der Tätigkeit seines Verstandes identisch ist, ist das Wort, das sein Verstand zeugt, von derselben Wesenheit wie Gott. Gebraucht man die menschliche Analogie der Zeugung für diesen Sachverhalt, dann kann man sagen: Gott sei der Vater, das Wort der Sohn und die Erzeugung des Wortes die Zeugung des Sohnes. Ist beim Menschen die Zeugung vergänglich, so ist dies bei Gott nicht der Fall. Das Wort, das Gott zeugt, ist ihm gleich ewig, wesensgleich und vollkommen. Der Geist versteht Thomas in diesem Kontext wie folgt: Jedem Erkenntnisgegenstand folgt eine ‚strebende Tätigkeit‘, so kann die Liebe verstanden werden als Prinzip der appetitiven Struktur des menschlichen wie göttlichen Erkenntnisprozesses. Geht das Wort aus der erkennenden Verstandestätigkeit hervor, so geht die Liebe aus der strebenden Tätigkeit des Verstandes hervor.

Da also Wort und Liebe mit Gott wesensgleich sind, können die drei Personen oder Hypostasen nicht nach ihrer Wesenheit verschieden sein, sondern nur nach der Beziehung ihres Hervorgehens aus der göttlichen Wesenheit. Vater, Sohn sind ergo nur bezüglich der Vaterschaft und Sohnschaft unterschieden, nicht aber ihrer Wesenheit nach. Alle anderen Bezeichnungen wie ‚gleich ewig‘, ‚einzig‘, ‚vollkommen‘ werden unterschieds-

---

18 Thomas von Aquin: De ratione fidei, aaO., S. 101.
19 Thomas von Aquin: De ratione fidei, aaO., S. 65.

los von Vater, Sohn (und Geist) ausgesagt. Die drei göttlichen Personen sind also keineswegs drei Götter, wie es die muslimische Polemik meint, sondern bezeichnen den einen und wahren und vollkommenen Gott. Drei menschliche Personen sind immer als verschiedene Menschen zu betrachten, da die menschliche Natur bei allen unterschiedlich ist. Alle drei sind jedoch dem Wesen nach menschliche Personen.[20]

Nach dem Motiv der Inkarnation befragt, leugnet Thomas nicht, dass Gott hätte anders handeln können. Er möchte jedoch zeigen, dass der Kreuzestod die angemessenste Form war, um die Menschen zu erlösen. Thomas setzt dazu bei der anselmschen Satisfaktionstheorie an. Sinn und Ziel der Menschwerdung Jesu bestand darin, die Menschen zur Umkehr zu bringen und ihr Leben auf Gott auszurichten. Das Leben Jesu zeigt in seinem Beispielcharakter eine Verachtung menschlicher Güter (z. B. Reichtum, Ehre, Ruhm, …). Der Kreuzestod ist eine letzte Konsequenz dieser Sichtweise. Die freiwillige Übernahme der Strafe für die Sünden der Menschen manifestiert nochmals die unbegreifliche Güte Gottes. Ein bloßer Mensch wäre dazu nicht in der Lage gewesen. „Die Weisheit Gottes zeigte sich also besonders darin, dass er sowohl die Ordnung der Gerechtigkeit als auch die der Natur bewahrte, und dass er dennoch in seiner Barmherzigkeit durch die Fleischwerdung und den Tod seines Sohnes dem Menschen ein Heilmittel zu seiner Erlösung verschafft hat."[21] Im Anschluss an die Überlegungen zum Leiden Christi geht Thomas zur Erörterung der Eucharistie (Transsubstantiation!) über. Wie geht hierbei seine Argumentation? Das Messopfer feiert die Kirche im Andenken an Leiden und Sterben Jesu Christi. Der Leib Christ wird weder zerstückelt und verzehrt, wenn das

---

20 Die drei göttlichen Personen bezeichnen demnach das eine göttliche Wesen, den wahren und vollommenen Gott. „Bei den Menschen hingegen werden drei Personen als drei Menschen bezeichnet und nicht als ein einziger Mensch, weil die Natur der menschlichen Wesenheit, die den dreien gemeinsam ist, wegen ihres materiellen Getrenntseins in verschiedener Weise auf sie zutrifft. Davon kann bei Gott überhaupt keine Rede sein. Weil es daher bei drei Menschen drei der Zahl nach verschiedene menschliche Wesenheiten gibt, ist ihnen nur der Begriff der menschlichen Wesenheit gemeinsam. In den drei göttlichen Personen hingegen gibt es nicht drei der Zahl nach verschiedene göttliche Wesenheiten, sondern es muss eine einzige einfache göttliche Wesenheit sein, weil es kein vom Wesen Gottes verschiedene Wesen des Wortes und der Liebe in Gott gibt; so bekennen wir wegen der einzigen und einfachen göttlichen Wesenheit in drei Personen nicht drei Götter, sondern nur einen einzigen Gott." (Thomas von Aquin: De rationibus fidei, aaO., S. 77/79)

21 Thomas von Aquin: De rationibus fidei, aaO., S. 113.

Brot in ihn verwandelt wird. Denn es vollzieht sich für die Sinne keine Wandlung und die Christen essen weder echtes Fleisch noch trinken sie echtes Blut. Gott belässt den in ihrer Substanz zu Christi Leib und Blut verwandelten Gaben Brot und Wein ihre sichtbaren Akzidenzien. Thomas erläutert diesen Vorgang mittels des aristotelischen Begriffspaares ‚Substanz und Akzidenz', das auch der muslimischen Philosophie bekannt ist. „Wir behaupten jedoch nicht, dass die Gestalten, die den Sinnen im Sakrament des Altares erscheinen, allein in der Phantasie der Sehenden existieren, so wie es gewöhnlich in den Gaukeleien der magischen Künste ist – denn das Sakrament der Wahrheit verbietet jede Gaukelei: Gott, der Schöpfer von Substanz und Akzidenz, kann sichtbare Akzidenzien im Sein bewahren, während die Substanzen in etwas anderes verwandelt werden."[22] Gott, so folgert Thomas, kann nämlich die Wirkungen von sekundären Ursachen durch seine Allmacht ohne die sekundären Ursachen selbst hervorrufen und im Sein bewahren.[23] Da die Muslime ebenfalls an die Allmacht Gottes glauben, sollte dieser Gedankengang für sie ebenfalls nachvollziehbar sein. Es ist interessant, dass Thomas im Sinne der altkirchlichen Arkandisziplin in diesem Kontext keine weiteren Aussagen der kirchlichen Eucharistielehre und deren Praxis referiert und erläutert.[24]

Im Schlusskapitel seiner Schrift geht Thomas der spekulativ hoch brisanten Frage nach, wie sich göttliches Vorauswissen und menschliche Willensfreiheit verhalten. Zu dieser Frage gibt Thomas zwei Dinge zu bedenken. Zum einen, dass die menschlichen Handlungen dem göttlichen Vorauswissen unterliegen, zum anderen aber, dass die Willensfreiheit als ein unverzichtbares Postulat der praktischen Vernunft angesehen werden muss. Als Basissatz der thomasischen Reflexion hat zu gelten: Gottes Wissen ist, anders als das Wissen der Menschen, ewig. Das Verhältnis von Zeit und Ewigkeit entspricht etwa dem von etwas Unteilbarem, etwa einem Punkt, zu einem zusammengesetzten Ganzen. Die Ewigkeit gleicht nun einem Punkt, der außerhalb einer Linie liegt und die aufeinanderfolgenden Punkte einer Linie ‚gleichzeitig' betrachtet. Oder in einem weiteren geometrischen Vergleich spricht Thomas von der Ewigkeit als einem Mittel-

---

22 Thomas von Aquin: De rationibus fidei, aaO., S. 117.

23 Vgl. Thomas von Aquin: De rationibus fidei, aaO., S. 117.

24 Vgl. dazu: „Andere Geheimnisse dieses Sakramentes sind hier nicht näher zu diskutieren, weil ‚vor Ungläubigen die Geheimnisse des Glaubens nicht ausgebreitet werden dürfen'" (Thomas von Aquin: De rationibus fidei, aaO., S. 117).

punkt, von dem alle Punkte der Peripherie gleichweit entfernt sind. Gott betrachtet also von seinem Standpunkt aus den gesamten Ablauf der Zeit als gegenwärtig. Mit diesem Bild veranschaulicht Thomas das göttliche Vorauswissen Gottes und sein Verhältnis zur menschlichen Freiheit. Das göttliche Wissen um die Zukunft legt demnach dem menschlichen Willen keinen Zwang auf. Der Mensch in seiner Pilgerschaft sieht nur das Gegenwärtige und teilweise das Vergangene, das Zukünftige entzieht sich seiner Sicht. Gott dagegen sieht von seiner erhöhten Warte aus alles als zugleich gegenwärtig.

Das sind die Grundlinien der thomasischen Schrift ‚De rationibus fidei', deren gedankliche Mitte eine Apologie des christlichen Glaubens darstellt. Dieser Darstellung ist jedoch jede Polemik fremd. „Nüchtern und sachbezogen", so urteilt Ludwig Hagemann, „tritt Thomas den ihm von Cantor Antiochenus vorgelegten muslimischen Objektionen gegen den christlichen Glauben entgegen."[25] Anders als Zeiten vor und nach ihm bezeichnet Thomas die Muslime weder als (christliche) Häretiker noch als Apostaten, sondern er bezeichnet sie als infideles. Damit möchte Thomas die Differenz beider Religionen betonen.

Eingangs wurde auf die Nähe dieser kleinen theologischen Schrift zum großen Werk ‚Summa contra Gentiles' hingewiesen. Diese Nähe gilt es sowohl in einer werkgenetischen als auch systematischen Perspektive zu bedenken. Der ursprüngliche Titel dieses Werkes hieß „Liber de veritate theologiae catholicae fidei contra errores infidelium": Buch von der katholischen Wahrheit gegen die Irrtümer der Ungläubigen. Den heute üblichen Titel erhielt das Buch erst im 16. oder 17. Jahrhundert (in Verbindung mit der damaligen Jesuitenmission!). Der Gedanke, den man damit verband, war, Thomas habe ein Handbuch für die Mission seiner Mitbrüder geschrieben. Allerdings wird diese These in der heutigen Forschung nicht mehr vertreten. Eher handelt es sich um eine groß angelegte Apologie christlichen Glaubens gegen reale oder imaginierte Einwände aus dem Kontext paganer Philosophie, wie sie das bereits genannte intellektuelle Milieu Europas zur Zeit von Thomas kannte.[26] Beide Schriften wollen auf der Basis eines vernünftigen Zugangs zu Gott zum einen Glaubensinhalte darstellen, zum anderen zumindest begründen, warum zu bestimmten Glaubensinhalten eine Offenbarung nötig sei (z. B. Trinität). Der pragmatische Handbuchcharakter ist

25 Ludwig B. Hagemann: Missionstheoretische Ansätze, aaO., S. 480.
26 Volker Leppin: Thomas von Aquin. Münster 2009, S. 95.

eher der kleinen Schrift als der großen Summe zu eigen. Das zeigt die Größe und Grenze dieses Werkes auf. Positiv lässt sich vermerken, dass Thomas das Anliegen einer intellektuellen Auseinandersetzung mit dem Islam ernst nimmt und ihm unpolemisch begegnet. Thomas kennt und bearbeitet aber weder die Quellen noch Theologien des Islams aus historischer Sicht, sondern vertritt in dieser Schrift eine strikt rationale Argumentation. Dass die thomasische Theologie, ausgehend von den großen Summen unseres Heiligen, Differenzen wie Gemeinsamkeiten anders benennen kann, zeigt seine systematische Betrachtung im dogmatischen Traktat ‚De Deo uno', der die Theozentrik jeglicher christlicher wie islamischer Theologie bedenken lässt. Der Ansatz von Thomas kann erkenntnistheoretisch nicht als interreligiöser Dialog avant la lettre verstanden werden, sondern als ein Suchen und Ringen nach Wahrheit und Heil. Der interreligiöse Dialog bei Thomas, so urteilt Jaroslav Vokoun, ist „kein Ziel an sich, das eigentliche Ziel ist vielmehr das Finden und Formulieren der ‚Wahrheit der geoffenbarten Dinge', und diesem Ziel dient der Dialog. Derjenige, der die Wahrheit sucht, kann bei anderen dazulernen – dank ihrer wird man die eigene Position besser verstehen. Gegenüber den Herausforderungen, die ihrerseits begegnen, ist man offen im lebendigen Vertrauen auf die Wahrheit der eigenen Überlieferung."[27]

Erkenntnistheoretische wie theozentrische Momente der theologischen Reflexion des Aquinaten zu den beiden Offenbarungsreligionen Christentum und Islam können im aktuellen Dialog eine zentrale Rolle spielen, insofern sie neben den außertheologischen Motiven der Begegnung das theologische Moment mit in die Diskussion einbringen. Daneben gilt es noch, die ethische Dimension eines jeden interreligiösen Gesprächs zu bedenken. Das Postulat, eine gemeinsame Basis im Handeln in der Welt zu haben, lässt sich aus dem Motiv der Liebe als Grund der Inkarnation wie Versöhnung ableiten. Predigerbrüder wie Riccoldo da Monte di Croce, weitere italienische Predigerbrüder im Orient zwischen dem 13. und 14. Jh., die dominikanische Mission im Iran, in Ägypten, in der Türkei, in Pakistan bis in unsere Tage, Pater Georges Anawati und andere haben von diesen theozentrischen Reflexionen einer thomasischen Theologie ihre systematische Inspiration für einen Dialog mit dem Islam gezogen.[28]

---

27 Jaroslav Vokoun: Die ‚ökumenische Hermeneutik' des Thomas von Aquin. In: Cath 65(2011), S. 211–229, 216.

28 Für die genannten Personen und Institutionen siehe das Themenheft „Les Dominicains et les mondes muselmans" (Mémoire dominicaine, No. 15, Paris 2001). Zu Georges

Die theozentrischen Ansätze der thomasischen Studie können heute methodisch im Sinne einer ‚komparativen Theologie' aufgegriffen werden.[29] Programm und Profil dieser theologischen Methode besteht darin, Theologie in einer religionsvergleichenden Perspektive zu betreiben. Man setzt sich dabei konstruktiv mit anderen religiösen Traditionen auseinander, führt mit ihnen Gespräche, um so das Selbstverständnis der Anderen ins eigene theologische Denken einzubeziehen. Alterität und Identität stehen dabei in einem Wechselbezug, indem das Andere in die eigene Theologie einbezogen, der Glaube der Anderen in den je eigene Glaubensreflexionen mitbedacht wird.

Anawati siehe: Jean-Jacques Pérennès: Georges Anawati (1905–1994). Ein ägyptischer Christ und das Geheimnis des Islam, Freiburg 2010.

29 Zum Paradigma der komparativen Theologie siehe etwa: Francis X. Clooney: Comparative Theology. In: John Webster/Kathryn Tanner/Iain Torrance (Ed.): The Oxford Handbook of Systematic Theology. Oxford 2007, 653–669; Robert C. Nelville: On the Scope and Truth of theology. Theology as Symbolic Engagement, N.Y. 2006; Klaus von Stosch: Komparative Theologie als Wegweiser in der Welt der Religionen. Paderborn, 2012.

Fremdkörper oder Wurzel – Christentum in Europa

Rede zum Michaelsempfang am 12. September 2012 in Berlin

Kardinal Dr. Christoph Schönborn

Sehr geehrte Frau Bundeskanzlerin und Vertreter der Bundesregierung!
Hochwürdigster Herr Apostolischer Nuntius!
Lieber Erzbischof Zollitsch! Lieber Kardinal Woelki!
Liebe Mitbrüder im bischöflichen und priesterlichen Dienst!
Geschätzte Vertreter der Ökumene!
Sehr geehrte Damen und Herren!

Es ehrt mich, heute hier in Berlin Gast sein zu dürfen und beim Michaelsempfang einige Worte an Sie richten zu können. Wien und Berlin haben vieles gemeinsam, in der Geschichte, in der Kultur, in der Sprache, auch wenn Karl Kraus, der große Wiener Literat gesagt hat: „Was Deutschland von Österreich trennt, ist die gemeinsame Sprache". Auch anderes trennt uns: Berlin ist die wiedergewonnene Hauptstadt eines wiedervereinigten Deutschland; Wien ist der Wasserkopf eines kleinen Landes, der einmal die Hauptstadt eines großen Reiches war. Wie sagte doch der eben schon zitierte Karl Kraus über unser kleingewordenes Österreich? „Wir haben eine große Zukunft – hinter uns!"

Doch Spaß beiseite. Haben wir eine große Zukunft vor uns? Wir, die Europäer, die Europäische Union? Wir, die Nettozahler dieses großen Zukunftsprojektes der europäischen Integration? Oder liegt diese Zukunft bereits hinter uns? Sind die Zeichen nicht auf Sturm, auf Krise? Stehen wir vor großen Zusammenbrüchen? Passen auf unsere Tage die Worte, die Karl Kraus, um ihn ein drittes und letztes Mal zu zitieren, in einem berühmten Aufsatz zu Beginn des Ersten Weltkrieges geschrieben hat, als alle bombastisch von „dieser großen Zeit" sprachen? „In dieser großen Zeit, die ich kannte, als sie noch klein war, und die wieder klein werden wird, wenn ihr noch Zeit bleibt".

Bleibt uns noch Zeit angesichts des rasanten Anwachsens der Schulden? Wird das europäische Integrationsprojekt den Spannungen standhalten, denen es schon jetzt ausgesetzt ist und die wohl noch stärker werden? Sie werden von mir sicher keine Antwort auf die Fragen erwarten, die sich zurzeit den politisch Verantwortlichen in Europa stellen. Dazu bin ich we-

der kompetent, noch ist es meine Aufgabe. Es ist aber auch für Politiker kein Zeichen der Schwäche, wenn sie ihre Ratlosigkeit eingestehen.

Ich versuche vielmehr, Ihnen einige Gedanken zum Verhältnis zwischen dem Christentum und dem europäischen Projekt vorzulegen.

Ich beginne mit einer kleinen Episode, die mir stark in Erinnerung geblieben ist. Im Oktober 2007 trafen sich die Vorsitzenden der europäischen römisch-katholischen Bischofskonferenzen zur jährlichen Vollversammlung im portugiesischen Marienwallfahrtsort Fatima. Thema war die Familie in Europa. Einer von uns brachte die von ihm und von anderen als dramatisch eingeschätzte Lage folgendermaßen auf den Punkt: Könnte nicht schon bald der Zeitpunkt kommen, da die europäische Gesellschaft in ihrer Mehrheit den Christen sagt: Ihr seid ein Fremdkörper unter uns! Eure Werte sind nicht unsere. Die „europäischen Werte“ sind anders als die christlichen. Ihr gehört nicht zu uns!

Ist das übertrieben, wehleidig? Ist das Christentum im säkularen Europa inzwischen zum Fremdkörper geworden? Jenes Christentum, das doch offensichtlich eine der tragenden Wurzeln der europäischen Identität war – oder noch immer ist? Zunehmend empfinden sich Christen, die ihr Christentum ernstnehmen, marginalisiert. Ja zum Teil sogar diskriminiert. Die OSZE mit Sitz in Wien hat eine eigene Stelle errichtet, die in den Ländern der OSZE Diskriminierung von Christen beobachtet und registriert. Sie hat zu tun!

In immer mehr Bereichen geht der „mainstream“ in eine andere Richtung als das Christentum. Überblicken wir die letzten 40 Jahre, dann erscheint mir die Feststellung unausweichlich: das Christentum wird immer marginaler. Ich sage das nüchtern diagnostisch. Als in Österreich 1974 die sozialistische Alleinregierung unter Bruno Kreisky daranging, die Abtreibung weitgehend straffrei zu stellen, gab es intensive Debatten, die auch zu einer Abstimmung im Parlament und einem Volksbegehren führten. Ich erinnere mich an ein Fernsehinterview mit Bundeskanzler Kreisky. Auf die Frage eines Journalisten, ob er sich nicht vorstellen könnte, dass es in Österreich Menschen geben, die mit der sogenannten „Fristenlösung“ Schwierigkeiten haben werden, antwortete er: „Ich kann mir vorstellen, dass sehr, sehr religiöse Menschen damit Schwierigkeiten haben könnten.“ Das klang so, als wären diese Menschen „sehr, sehr“ seltsam. Religiös, das ist auf jeden Fall rückständig, nicht auf der Höhe der Zeit, und sicher eine Minderheit. Es muss nicht sein, dass Kreisky das damals verächtlich meinte. Es war es dennoch allemal.

Die Abstimmung ging extrem knapp aus: 93 zu 88 Stimmen für die Fristenregelung. Ein Volksbegehren zum „Schutz des Lebens" erhielt große Unterstützung, blieb aber wirkungslos. Und bis heute hat es keine österreichische Regierung zustande gebracht, alle damals versprochenen „flankierenden Maßnahmen" zu beschließen, die den Lebensschutz verbessern sollten.

Viel tragischer aber ist meines Erachtens, dass für Kreisky der Widerstand gegen die Fristenregelung vor allem bei „sehr, sehr religiösen Menschen" geortet wurde. Der vor allem kirchliche, christliche Widerstand, angeführt von Kardinal Franz König, war aber nicht primär religiös begründet, auch wenn er stark religiös motiviert war. Es ging vielmehr um die Anerkennung und den gesetzlichen Schutz des menschlichen Lebens, also um elementares Menschenrecht. Die Kirche verteidigte hier nicht konfessionelles Sonderrecht, sondern vernunftbegründetes Menschenrecht. Papst Benedikt XVI. hat in seiner Rede vor dem deutschen Bundestag (22. September 2011) genau darauf hingewiesen. Woran liegt es, dass sich, wie der Papst sagte, „im letzten halben Jahrhundert eine dramatische Veränderung der Situation zugetragen" hat? „Der Gedanke des Naturrechts gilt heute", so sagte er weiter, „als eine katholische Sonderlehre, über die außerhalb des katholischen Raumes zu diskutieren nicht lohnen würde, sodass man sich schon beinahe schämt, das Wort überhaupt zu erwähnen."

Seit den Siebzigerjahren ist die Entwicklung konsequent in dieselbe Richtung weitergegangen. Nach der rechtlichen „Freigabe" des Lebensanfangs kam unausweichlich die des Lebensendes. Die Euthanasiedebatte erfasst mit unerbittlicher Konsequenz immer mehr Länder Europas. Österreich ist (noch?) in der glücklichen Lage, dass es einen Allparteienkonsens gegen die Euthanasie und für die Hospizbewegung zur Sterbebegleitung gibt. Hier verdanken wir viel dem kräftigen Zeugnis von Kardinal König, der wenige Wochen vor seinem Tod (im 99. Lebensjahr) in einem unvergesslichen Brief an den österreichischen Verfassungskonvent den Satz geprägt hat: „Menschen sollen an der Hand eines anderen Menschen sterben, und nicht durch die Hand eines anderen Menschen." Wie lange wird dieser Konsens in Österreich dem Druck des europäischen Mainstreams standhalten? Ich enthalte mich des Kommentars zur innerdeutschen Entwicklung in dieser Frage. Es sei nur darauf hingewiesen, dass Präsident Horst Köhler das Wort von Kardinal König öfters zitiert hat.

Ein drittes Beispiel sei genannt, wo von kirchlicher Seite mit dem Naturrecht, der unveräußerlichen Menschenwürde, und gerade nicht reli-

giös argumentiert wird, und wo dennoch die kirchliche Position eindeutig auf der Verliererseite ist: die verbrauchende Embryonenforschung. Einige Jahre lang hat eine Sperrminorität von EU-Ländern verhindern können, dass EU-Gelder in die embryonen-verbrauchende, d. h. embryonentötende Forschung, vor allem im Stammzellenbereich, fließen: Deutschland, gemeinsam mit Polen, Italien, Irland, Österreich und Portugal haben hier blockiert. Diese Front hat nicht lange gehalten. Wie auch jene andere, die sich gegen eine gesetzliche Gleichstellung von gleichgeschlechtlichen Partnerschaften mit der Ehe wehrte.

„Ich kann mir vorstellen, dass sehr, sehr religiöse Menschen damit Schwierigkeiten haben", meinte Bruno Kreisky 1974. Ist in dieser seither scheinbar unaufhaltbaren, unumkehrbaren Entwicklung das Christentum in Europa, von einem Nachhutgefecht zum anderen, auf unaufhaltsamen Rückzug? Sind seine Werte längst nicht mehr die so oft beschworenen „europäischen Werte"? Immer mehr erleben sich engagierte Christen als Minderheit. In den diversen Ethikkommissionen figurieren sie mit ihren Positionen meist „unter ferner liefen". Das hat die Stammzellendebatte gezeigt, das zeigt sich jetzt bei den Diskussionen um Bluttests zur frühzeitigen Feststellung von Behinderung, oder bei der Frage der Präimplantationsdiagnostik.

Manche katholische Mitglieder in den diversen Ethikkommissionen klagen darüber, dass stets nur ihr Nein zu neuen Entwicklungen gehört wird, und nicht das Ja, das ihre Position motiviert: das Ja zum Leben, zum Lebensschutz, zum unbedingten Respekt vor der Würde des Menschen von der Empfängnis bis zum natürlichen Tod.

Ich glaube, wir haben noch zu wenig reflektiert, was diese Marginalisierung für die christliche Identität im heutigen säkularen Europa bedeutet. Wie sich mit den „christlichen Werten" in einem Europa positionieren, das mehr und mehr den Christen sagt: „Eure Werte" sind nicht „unsere Werte"? Ich denke, viele von uns, ob Gläubige oder Amtsträger, schwanken zwischen Anpassung und Abgrenzung. Beides hat Grenzen. Wie weit kann der politische Kompromiss gehen, der sich bei der Gesetzgebung der parlamentarischen Mehrheit beugt? Sicher sind viele Gesetzesmaterien kompromissfähig. Papst Benedikt hat im Bundestag aber darauf hingewiesen – ähnlich wie in seiner beeindruckenden Rede in Whitehall, im Parlament in London –, „dass in den Grundfragen des Rechts, in denen es um die Würde des Menschen und der Menschheit geht, das Mehrheitsprinzip nicht ausreicht".

Was aber, wenn dank des Mehrheitsprinzips die Gesetzgebung und der durch sie abgebildete und zugleich auch mitgeprägte gesellschaftliche Konsens sich von den „christlichen Werten" weg entwickelt und damit die Christen nicht nur in eine Minderheitsposition, sondern auch in Gewissenskonflikte bringen?

Dann ist die Versuchung naheliegend, sich, wie Paulus warnend sagt, „dieser Welt anzugleichen" (Röm 12,2). Dann fehlt die Kraft zum Widerstand, der Mut zur Alternative. Am letzten Tag seines Deutschlandbesuches, bei seiner Rede in Freiburg (25. September 2011), hat Papst Benedikt auf die Gefahr der „Verweltlichung" der Kirche hingewiesen, auf die „Tendenz, dass die Kirche zufrieden wird mit sich selbst, sich in dieser Welt einrichtet, selbstgenügsam ist und sich den Maßstäben der Welt angleicht". Der Versuch, den „christlichen Werten" im Kanon der säkularen Gesellschaft Raum zu geben, scheitert meist schon daran, dass vieles in der Kirche schon soweit säkularisiert ist, dass es profillos und kaum zu unterscheiden ist. Dann hat die Kirche in die säkulare Gesellschaft nichts mehr einzubringen. „Wenn das Salz schal wird, taugt es zu nichts mehr", hat Jesus gesagt (Mt 5,13). Das vieldiskutierte Wort Papst Benedikts von der „Entweltlichung" ist das Gegenstück zur „Verweltlichung" der Kirche.

Wie bei vielen anderen Gelegenheiten ermutigt Papst Benedikt die Christen heute, zur säkularen Gesellschaft ein positives Verhältnis zu gewinnen, nicht im Sinne der Anpassung. Vielmehr sollen die Christen in aller Freiheit in einer pluralistischen Gesellschaft das Eigene einbringen. Gerade in Staaten, die ein stark kooperatives Verhältnis zu den Kirchen haben wie Deutschland oder Österreich, ist die Versuchung groß, mehr auf die eigene kirchliche Institution und Organisation zu schauen, als auf die ursprüngliche Berufung des Christen in der Welt. Gerade in einer säkularen Gesellschaft ist ein „verweltlichtes" Christentum uninteressant, denn „weltlich" sein, das können die Säkularen meist besser als die Kirchlichen. Papst Benedikts Aufruf zu einer „Entweltlichung" der Kirche zielt, so sehe ich es, genau auf diese Situation eines „verweltlichten" kirchlichen Lebens. Paradoxerweise ist eine „entweltlichte" Kirche besser geeignet, weltoffen zu sein, wie es das Konzil wollte: „Sie öffnet sich der Welt, nicht um die Menschen für eine Institution mit eigenen Machtansprüchen zu gewinnen, sondern um sie zu sich selber zu führen", indem sie sie zu Gott führt.

Mich beeindruckt immer wieder, wie sehr Papst Benedikt die Kirche dazu auffordert, zur säkularen Gesellschaft, zum „secular age" (Charles Taylor) ein positives Verhältnis zu gewinnen. In Freiburg sagte er, durchaus

überraschend: „Die Geschichte kommt der Kirche in gewisser Weise durch die verschiedenen Epochen der Säkularisierung zur Hilfe, die zu ihrer Läuterung und inneren Reform wesentlich beigetragen haben."

Diese „Entweltlichung" meint sicher nicht den Rückzug aus allen institutionellen, rechtlichen, gesellschaftlichen Vernetzungen der Kirche mit der zivilen Gesellschaft und dem Staat, wohl aber ein Freierwerden für das Eigentliche des Christentums, das Evangelium und seine Bezeugung. So kann der kontinuierliche Rückgang an Einfluss- und Bestimmungsmöglichkeit der Kirche auf die Gesellschaft, die Gesetzgebung, den Staat, durchaus nicht nur als Verlust gesehen werden. Papst Benedikt zeigt den müden und resignierten Christen unermüdlich, dass sie nicht zu verzagen brauchen, wenn sie auf die argumentative Kraft von Vernunft und Glauben und auf die Leuchtkraft der gelebten Christusnachfolge setzen. Gerade in der säkularen Gesellschaft hat der Gläubige die Freiheit, seine Überzeugung ins Spiel zu bringen. Er darf nur nicht wehleidig sein, und auch nicht prätentiös.

Die Beschneidungsdebatte ist ein spannender Fall für das Thema Religion in der säkularen Gesellschaft. Es fehlt an der Zeit, ausführlicher darauf einzugehen. Das Menschenrecht auf körperliche Integrität wird gegen das Menschenrecht auf Religionsfreiheit ausgespielt. In der säkularen Gesellschaft hat ersteres eine größere Plausibilität als letzteres. Man wünschte sich, dass das Recht auf körperliche Integrität des zur Abtreibung freigegebenen Ungeborenen mit ebensolcher Vehemenz verteidigt würde wie das Recht, über das Haben oder Nichthaben des Praeputiums (für Nichtlateiner: der Vorhaut) selber entscheiden zu können. Jan Ross hat in der „Zeit" meines Erachtens die Sache auf den Punkt gebracht, wenn er seinen Artikel zum Beschneidungsurteil betitelt: „Hilfe, die glauben". Ja, da gibt es Menschen, die Teil unserer Gesellschaft sind, die ernsthaft glauben, dass die Beschneidung das Bundeszeichen der Treue Gottes zu seinem erwählten Volk ist, und die daher lieber aus Deutschland auswandern würden, als dass sie sich vom Gesetzgeber die Beschneidung verbieten lassen.

Welchen Platz hat der Glauben von Menschen in der säkularen Gesellschaft? Hat sie dafür Toleranz übrig? „Sehr, sehr religiöse Menschen", wie Kreisky sie nannte, haben sie (noch) Platz in einem Reservat für eine aussterbende Spezies? Oder werden sie als Mitbürger in ihrer eigenen religiösen Überzeugung ernst genommen?

Lange Zeit galt als Argumentationsfigur für den Platz der Religion in der säkularen Gesellschaft der Hinweis auf ihren pragmatischen Nutzen;

etwa: Religion ist nützlich für die Moral. Sie fördert kulturelle Werte. Sie stärkt soziales Verhalten. Das mag alles stimmen. Aber es ist nicht das Herz der Religion, es ist nicht der Grund für das Gläubigsein. Gläubig sind Menschen nicht, weil es nützlich ist, sondern weil sie an Gott glauben. Weil Gott für sie „die alles bestimmende Wirklichkeit" ist, wie Rudolf Bultmann sagte.

Ganz einfach bringt das eine junge Muslima auf den Punkt. Sie antwortete in Österreich einem Journalisten auf die Frage, ob sie das Kreuz im öffentlichen Raum nicht störe, es tue ihr gut, dadurch zu wissen, dass sie in einem Land lebt, in dem Menschen an Gott glauben.

Jürgen Habermas spricht von „unabgegoltenen religiösen Bedeutungspotentialen", die im liberalen Staat nicht übersehen oder verdrängt werden dürfen. Religiöse Mitbürger können sie einbringen.

Dazu müssten sie aber als Personen ernst genommen werden. Umgekehrt wird den religiösen Menschen im säkularen Kontext zugemutet, dass sie sich bemühen, ihre Inhalte in die Sprache der säkularen Welt zu übersetzen. Wenige können Letzteres so meisterhaft wie Papst Benedikt. Nicht umsonst wird er von nichtreligiösen Menschen wie kaum ein anderer christlicher Autor gelesen.

In seinen Reden und Schriften kommen die großen Worte des Glaubens zu neuem Leuchten, wirken unverbraucht frisch, wie neu. Und sie lassen etwas von der unerschöpflichen Quelle spüren, aus der sie kommen, Worte wie Glaube, Hoffnung, Liebe. Ein Wort wie Barmherzigkeit meint mehr als niemandem weh tun zu wollen, als Solidarität, ja mehr als Gutsein. Gnade wäre zu nennen und Heil – das so missbrauchte Wort. Martin Walser hat in einem großartigen Buch das Wort Rechtfertigung (durch den Glauben) hervorgeholt und wieder neu zur Geltung gebracht. Es steht im Kontrast zum heute allgegenwärtigen Rechthaben. Das sind einige große Worte des Glaubens, auf die zu verzichten ein zu großer Verlust wäre.

Doch mehr als alle Worte spricht die Tat. Vielleicht müssen wir Christen mehr darauf vertrauen, dass die selbstlose, interessensfreie Tat des Glaubens oft mehr bewirkt als alle noch so wichtigen gesetzgeberischen Maßnahmen. Kaum jemand hat in den letzten Jahrzehnten mehr überzeugt als Mutter Teresa von Kalkutta. In der so schmerzlichen Auseinandersetzung um den Lebensschutz hat sie die einzig überzeugende Antwort gefunden: die direkt helfende Tat, indem sie sagte: „Tötet sie nicht! Gebt sie mir!"

Fremdkörper oder Wurzel Europas: das Christentum: Es hat dem Christentum gut getan, dass es durch das Feuer der Kritik von Aufklärung

und Säkularismus gehen musste. Es ist die Chance der Läuterung. Es ist die Frage nach seiner Glaubwürdigkeit. Ist nicht in so mancher säkularen Kritik am Christentum auch ein Stück Sehnsucht verborgen, es möge doch so etwas wie ein authentisches, gelebtes Christentum geben? Insgeheim wissen wir wohl, ob säkular oder gläubig, dass hier die tragfähigen Wurzeln Europas liegen. Nahe kommen wir dem fremdgewordenen Christentum freilich nur um einen Preis: die eigene Bekehrung. Und die ist ein lebenslanger Prozess, und er beginnt bei uns selbst.

Ich danke für Ihre Aufmerksamkeit.

Kulturelles Gedächtnis und kulturelle Identität

Franz Gero Thimm OP und Jochen Wolffgramm

A. Einleitung

Kollektives Gedächtnis

Das individuelle Gedächtnis befasst sich mit der Speicherung von Information durch ein Individuum, das es diesem ermöglicht, besser auf seine Umwelt eingestellt zu sein. Neben dem Eigenerwerb von Gedächtnisinhalten durch einen Menschen oder ein Tier gibt es auch generationsübergreifend Gedächtnisinhalte, die weiter übermittelt werden können. Der Verhaltensbiologe spricht von tradiertem Gedächtnis oder kurz von Tradition. Tradiertes Gedächtnis ermöglicht es einem Individuum vom Wissen früherer Generationen zu profitieren und nicht alles aufgrund eigener Erfahrung neu erlernen zu müssen.

Im Gegensatz zum individuellen Gedächtnis ist das kollektive Gedächtnis nicht an ein Einzelwesen gebunden, sondern stellt ein Allgemeingut dar, welches von der Gemeinschaft häufig auch als kulturelle, soziale und rechtliche Norm übernommen wird. Basis dieses kollektiven Gedächtnisses ist wiederum die biologische Kommunikation zwischen Individuen und des darauf basierenden tradierten Gedächtnisses, weitergegeben von Generation zu Generation. In seiner einfachsten Form finden wir ein solches kollektives Gedächtnis bereits bei vielen sozial lebenden Tieren. Ein solcher Fall existiert z. B. bei den Dialekten von Singvogelarten. Singvögel lernen in vielen Fällen die Motive ihres Gesangs von ihren Eltern, bzw., wenn nur Männchen singen, von ihrem Vater und den benachbarten Vögeln der gleichen Art. Bei den sogenannten Spöttern können auch Motive aus anderer Quelle bis hin zu Pfeiftönen des Menschen gelernt werden. Damit bildet sich durch rein tradiertes Lernen in einer Region eine Art gemeinsames Muster aus, der sogenannte Dialekt. Das ist gar nicht so viel anders als bei Dialekten menschlicher Sprache. Auch hier entsteht ein verbindendes Moment auf der Basis einer tradierten Gedächtnisbildung.

B. Kulturelles Gedächtnis

1. Dialekte

Man sollte die Bedeutung solcher Traditionscluster keinesfalls unterschätzen. Auch bei den Vögeln haben solche Dialekte nicht nur eine verbindende Wirkung, sondern auch eine ausgrenzende gegenüber allen, die andere Dialekte aufweisen. Bei Singvögeln kann das zu einer Ausbildung regionaler Rassen führen und im Extremfall sogar zu neuen Arten. Die Weibchen aus der einen Dialektgruppe verstehen die Männchen aus der anderen Dialektgruppe nicht mehr richtig, sie sind ihnen fremd. Dadurch entstehen sogenannte Fortpflanzungsgemeinschaften. Ein Genaustausch zwischen den Dialektgruppen findet nicht mehr statt und beide können sich in verschiedene Richtungen entwickeln. Dieses Prinzip der Separation, dem wir eine Vielzahl neu entstandener Arten verdanken, fördert also die kollektive Gedächtnisbildung und ermöglicht sie überhaupt erst.

2. Sprache in der Diaspora

Kollektiv-kulturelle Gedächtnisse beim Menschen gehen aber über die vergleichsweise einfache Form, wie wir sie bei Dialekten, z. B. bei Vögeln, finden, deutlich hinaus. Eindrucksvolle Beispiele dafür sind kulturelle Identifikationen, die nicht regional gebunden sind, sondern sich über lange Zeiträume etwa unter Diasporabedingungen fortsetzen. Eine jüdische Identität hat zwei Jahrtausende der Zersprengung einer nationalen Identität überdauert. Eine rein individuelle Weitergabe von Gedächtnisinhalten könnte diese unglaubliche Stabilität kaum erklären. Denn es würde im Laufe der Zeit zu immer mehr Aufsplitterungen und damit zu zunehmenden Ungenauigkeiten kommen. Auch die menschliche Sprache allein reicht zur Erklärung der Unterschiede nicht aus. Sie ist zwar in viel höherem Maße dazu geeignet, Informationen generationsübergreifend weiterzugeben als alle tierischen Kommunikationsmittel. Das liegt daran, dass die Informationsdichte weitaus höher und vielgestaltiger ist als bei fast allen tierischen Kommunikationsformen, von wenigen Ausnahmen z. B. bei Papagei und vielleicht Walen einmal abgesehen. Trotzdem bleibt das Prinzip der Informationsübertragung von einem zum nächsten Individuum erhalten. Beim Kinder- und Gesellschaftsspiel „Stille Post“ zum Beispiel wird ein geflüstertes Wort von Person zu Person weitergegeben, bis es schließlich

zur Unkenntlichkeit verändert ist. Auch bei verbal tradierter Kommunikation ist der Effekt auf Dauer schwer vermeidbar. Von Schritt zu Schritt verändern sich die Inhalte, es entsteht eher eine kollektiv-kulturelle Variabilität als eine Identität.

3. Schrift

Der wahrscheinlich entscheidende Schritt zur Bildung kollektiver Gedächtnisinhalte ist die geschriebene Sprache. Im Gegensatz zur Sprache ermöglicht sie Traditionsbildung über mehrere Generationen hinweg. Vom informationstheoretischen Standpunkt aus, hat dies eine stabilisierende Wirkung. Abweichende Überlieferungen werden gleichsam wieder eingefangen. Die schriftliche Überlieferung ist die verbindliche Norm geworden. Wir stellen fest, dass Kulturen, die ein kollektives Gedächtnis entwickelt haben, alle über ausgeprägte schriftliche Überlieferungen verfügen.

4. Geschichtsschreibung und Gesetzgebung

Von Anfang an dienten schon die ersten schriftlichen Überlieferungen, ob sie nun aus Ägypten oder Mesopotamien stammten, zweierlei Zwecken: 1. Der Übermittlung von Wissensinhalten: König X hat im yten Jahr seiner Regierung einen neuen Tempel bauen lassen; oder König Z vernichtend geschlagen. Das war der Beginn der Geschichtsschreibung, zunächst noch sporadisch, später systematisch durchgeführt. Der 2. fast parallel dazu auftretende Zweck schriftlicher Überlieferung war der herrschaftliche Imperativ, also Anweisungen an die Bewohner: Gebote, Verbote, kurz: der Beginn einer Rechtsschaffung und Gesetzgebung. Das Alte Testament entspricht sehr gut diesen ursprünglichen Formen der schriftlichen Überlieferung. Es vereint Funktionen der Geschichtsschreibung und der Setzung gesellschaftlicher und religiöser Normen. Dadurch, dass diese Bücher Generationen ohne nennenswerte Änderungen überdauern konnten, war es ihnen möglich, jene kulturellen Werte zu übermitteln, die bei rein mündlicher Überlieferung mit der Zeit immer verwaschener und variabler geworden wären.

Kulturelle Identifikation eines Kollektivs setzt also die verbindliche schriftliche Fixierung sowohl von Wissen (selbst wenn es oft um geschöntes, manchmal vages und fehlinterpretiertes Wissen handelte) als auch von Werten voraus. Diese Werte sind keine freien, variabel angebotenen, sondern verbindliche Normen. Wie man auch im Alten Testament sehen kann,

sind Wissen, also Geschichtsschreibung, und Werte, also Gebote, Verbote und Normen, nicht streng voneinander getrennt, sondern werden als harmonische Einheit gesehen.

5. Wir-Gefühl

a. Gemeinsames Handeln
Beide Arten der schriftlichen Überlieferung sind unabdingbare Voraussetzungen für ein kollektives kulturelles Gedächtnis, sind aber für sich allein noch nicht vollständig effektiv. Grund dafür ist ihr noch weitgehend abstrakter Charakter. Wissensvermittlung soll nicht nur geschichtliches Wissen übertragen, sondern auch einen moralischen Nährwert haben. Wir sollen aus den erzählten Geschichten etwas lernen, entweder um etwas richtig zu machen, also einem Vorbild zu folgen, oder bestimmte Fehler eines Protagonisten zu vermeiden. Daraus entstehen im Kollektiv verbindendes Wissen und verbindende Normen und Werte, aber noch kein verbindendes Wollen und kein verbindendes Tun. Für eine Bildung eines kollektiven Wir-Gefühls ist dagegen ein gemeinsames Handeln unumgänglich. Dies können ein gemeinsamer Tanz, ein Treffen der Dorfgemeinschaft ebenso wie eine religiöse Zeremonie sein. Die 3. Komponente in der Entwicklung einer kulturellen Identität ist die Entwicklung gemeinsamer Riten.

b. Riten
Profane Riten erfüllen diese Aufgabe in gewissem Umfang, ohne aber eine ähnliche verbindende Funktion ausüben zu können, wie es für religiöse Riten charakteristisch ist. Erst mit ihnen entwickelt sich aus einem kollektiven Gedächtnis mit Wissen und Werten eine kulturelle Identität mit ausgeprägtem Wir-Gefühl.

c. Normen
Dieses Gefühl entsteht aus dem gemeinsamen Handeln und der verbindlichen Norm, auf welcher das gemeinsame Handeln beruht. Normen, gerade auch gesellschaftliche Normen sind ja eigentliche Zwänge. Sie schreiben vor, engen ein und schließen diejenigen aus, die ihnen nicht genügen. Dennoch sehnen sich die Menschen nach ihnen. Die Mehrzahl fühlt sich unglücklich, wenn sie in einer normarmen, freien Gesellschaft leben sollen. Warum ist das so? Norm vermittelt einschließlich der mit ihnen verbundenen Riten kulturelle Identität in einem Kollektiv, dem man sich zugehörig

fühlen kann. Sie vermitteln damit Sicherheit. Es ist ja keineswegs so, dass Normen voll und ganz verbindlich sind. Normverstöße sind gewissermaßen Teil jeder kulturellen Identität und damit auch jeder Religion. Gerade der Widerspruch zwischen den vorgegebenen Regeln, die einem Sicherheit und Orientierung geben, und gelegentlichen Regelverstößen sind charakteristisch für ein kulturelles und religiöses Wir-Gefühl.

d. Religion

Halten wir fest: kulturelle Identität setzt voraus, dass sowohl Wissen und Werte als auch Riten und Gebräuche mit eingeschlossen sind. Sie basiert auf einer gemeinsamen Sprache und auf einer gemeinsamen Religion. Wer sich in diesem Wir-Gefühl geborgen fühlt, der wird wenig Probleme haben. Gelegentliche Regelverstöße werden, sofern sie das Gesamtgefüge nicht gefährden, in der Regel verziehen. Schwieriger wird es für die, welche aus dieser heilen Welt ausbrechen wollen als sogenannte Rebellen. Aber auch darauf ist das Kollektiv gut vorbereitet. Außenseiter und Rebellen gelten als re-integrationsfähig, solange ihre Rebellion in jungen Jahren erfolgt. Ältere Rebellen kann die Gesellschaft in der Regel als eine Art „bunter Vögel" einschließen. Echte Rebellion wird dagegen weniger geduldet und führt zur Ächtung des Betroffenen.

6. Verschiedene kulturelle Kollektive auf engem Raum

a. Minderheiten und Migranten

Solange ein derart zusammengehaltenes Kollektiv auch kompakt zusammenlebt, gibt es demnach nur begrenzte Probleme mit ein paar Außenseitern. Viel schwieriger wird es, wenn verschiedene kulturelle Kollektive auf vergleichsweise engem Raum miteinander existieren müssen. Jedes dieser Kollektive hat seine eigene Tradition, seine eigenen Normen und seine eigenen Riten. Nur stimmen sie nicht mit denen des anderen Kollektivs überein. Das war schon immer der Fall bei Juden im christlichen Umfeld, bei Sinti und Roma und auch bei vielen nationalen Minderheiten. Ganz drastisch ist das Nebeneinander bis heute in manchen Gebieten des Balkans, wo Kroaten, Serben, Albaner, Bosnier etc. jeweils ihre eigene kulturelle Identität entwickelt haben, die sich von der ihrer unmittelbaren Nachbarn abgrenzt. In Westeuropa hat sich die Problemlage nach dem 2. Weltkrieg zunächst fast unmerklich, dann aber deutlich verändert, als Migranten aus islamischen Ländern, insbesondere der Türkei, eine eigene kulturelle Identität mitgebracht und etabliert haben.

b. Staatliches und religiöses Rechtssystem

Dadurch ist ein neues, echtes Problem entstanden, welches mit dem einfachen Gegenkonzept der Toleranz leider gar nicht so einfach in den Griff zu bekommen ist. Im Falle der Jahrtausende alten jüdischen Identität, die mit der christlichen mehr oder weniger gut koexistierte, wäre Toleranz ein äußerst akzeptables Rezept gewesen, und war es zum Teil auch. (Die jüdische moralische Religion erhebt keinen missionarischen Anspruch und kollidiert mit ihren Werten und Normen auch nicht fundamental mit christlichen Wertvorstellungen. Judenverfolgung machte sich typischerweise u. a. an den unterschiedlichen Riten beider Glaubensgemeinschaften fest). Genau so, könnte man meinen, ließe sich auch durch Toleranz mit islamisch orientierten Kollektiven umgehen und diese vice versa mit christlich geprägten. Bei vielen Spielarten des Islams ist das aber nur begrenzt möglich. Während in Westeuropa christlich geprägte Kollektive fast überall vom Säkularismus der französischen Revolution und ihrer Nachfolger beeinflusst sind und daher das Kirchenrecht nur eine untergeordnete Rolle spielt, hat im Islam eine solche Säkularisierung nur selten stattgefunden. Als rechtsverbindlich gilt das an den Koran gebundene religiöse Rechtssystem der Scharia. Damit haben wir zwischen zwei zusammenlebenden Kollektiven nicht nur Unterschiede in den Riten, sondern auch im Norm- und Rechtsempfinden.

c. Konzepte des Zusammenlebens

Der Umgang damit trennt die Gemüter quer durch politische Rechts- und Linkslager hindurch. Das traditionelle linksalternative Konzept ist das einer multikulturellen Gesellschaft mit einem friedlichen Zusammenleben verschiedener kultureller Identitäten. Ausdruck dieser gesellschaftlichen Utopie ist etwa der Berliner Karneval der Kulturen. Dem Multi-Kulti-Konzept entgegen steht das von völkisch Rechten vertretene Konzept der Wagenburg, einem Begriff aus dem Burenkrieg, wo sich die Gemeinschaft der Buren hinter einem Ring von Wagen verteidigten. Die ideologische Botschaft lautet: Wir müssen gegen äußere Feinde zusammenhalten. In der Bundesrepublik Deutschland gilt ausgesprochen oder unausgesprochen das Prinzip der christlich-abendländischen Wertegemeinschaft. Das ist zunächst einmal eine Art eines völkischen Wagenburgkonzepts, allerdings mit dem Zusatz, dass Außenseiter nicht mehr generell draußen bleiben müssen, sondern unter bestimmten Voraussetzungen in die Wagenburg, also in unsere Wir-Identität hineingelassen werden können. Voraussetzung ist, dass man

sein Ursprungskollektiv abschwächt und sich assimiliert. Gegenüber der Rassenideologie der Faschisten und Nationalsozialisten ist dies sicherlich ein Fortschritt, aber er verlangt die Aufgabe der kulturellen Identität. Rigoros wurden solche Programme durchgezogen in Ländern, in denen weiße Einwanderer die Ureinwohner beherrschten, wie in den USA und Australien. Während die USA ihr Verhältnis zu den Ureinwohnern nicht aufgearbeitet hat, hat sich die australische Regierung erst kürzlich bei den Aborigines für die gewaltsame Zerstörung ihrer kulturellen Identität entschuldigt.

7. Unveräußerlichkeit der Menschenrechte

a. Keine Scharia-Rechtsprechung

In Deutschland sind z. B. die Einbürgerungstests eher eine milde Variante, gehen aber in die gleiche Richtung. Wenn wir bedenken, welches Unheil Ausgrenzung und Rassismus gerade in Deutschland, aber auch anderswo in der Welt angerichtet haben, sollte man für einen toleranteren Umgang der kulturellen Kollektive miteinander plädieren. Also doch Multi-Kulti? Ganz so einfach ist das leider doch nicht. Wir haben in den letzten 100 bis 200 Jahren Wertvorstellungen entwickelt, die wir mit Grund als übergreifend ansehen. Im Wesentlichen handelt es sich um das, was wir als fundamentale Menschenrechte ansehen. Dazu gehört das Recht auf freie Meinungsäußerung, die Gleichberechtigung der Frau, die unantastbare Würde des Menschen und vieles mehr. Dürfen wir diese Rechte grundsätzlich aufgeben, wenn der Betreffende sich einer anderen kulturellen Identität zugehörig fühlt? Dürfen wir die Steinigung von Ehebrecherinnen zulassen? Die bedingungslose Unterordnung der Frau unter den Mann, die Zwangsehe von Kindern oder sogenannte Ehrenmorde? Hier befinden wir uns in einem Dilemma. Gerade manche Konservative auch aus christlichen Kirchen plädieren hier für eine Freiheit der kulturell-religiösen Identität und wollen bei Muslimen eine scharia-konforme Rechtsprechung zulassen, während Liberale eine stärkere Reglementierung orientiert an der Menschenrechts-Deklaration durchsetzen wollen. Solange die Kulturen – frei nach Goethe „fern in der Türkei die Feinde auf einander schlagen" – weit auseinander liegen, mischt man sich besser nicht ein und überlässt die Kulturen der eigenen Geschichtsentwicklung. Ein Export unserer eigenen Wertvorstellungen hat sich meist als wenig hilfreich erwiesen. Ob im Falle Afghanistans eine solche moralisch legitimierte Intervention erfolgreich sein wird, ist

mehr als ungewiss. Menschenrechte sind schwer exportierbar, es sei denn, man benutzte als Transportartikel eine mindestens über Jahrhunderte entstandene kulturelle Tradition, die sich langsam weiterentwickelt.

b. Die staatliche Zuständigkeit der Rechtsprechung

Wie aber geht man mit einer fremden z. B. islamischen Kultur im eigenen Land um? Einerseits führt Abschottung zur Abgrenzung und fördert Rassismus, andererseits sind bei uns manche Menschenrechtsverletzungen nicht tolerierbar. Wahrscheinlich müssen wir, wie es schon vor 200 Jahren in Westeuropa geschah, Rechtsnormen, welche die Menschenrechte betreffen, generell aus dem religiösen Kultur- und Norm-Umfeld ausgrenzen und säkularisieren. Moralische, aber damit nicht rechtsverbindliche Normen können und müssen wohl auch einer kulturell-religiösen Gemeinschaft zugestanden werden. Die Gemeinschaft aber muss sich damit abfinden, und unsere Kirchen haben das schließlich auch gemacht, dass der Umgang mit Rechtsverstößen ebenso wie die Definition des Rechts selber Sache des Staates ist, in dem wir leben. Sonderrechte, welche die Menschenwürde verletzen, darf es nicht geben. Keines der denkbaren religiösen oder nichtreligiösen Kollektive darf sich auf solche Sonderrechte als Teil der tradierten Überlieferung berufen.

C. Kulturell-christliches Gedächtnis und christliche Identifikation

1. Die christliche Überlieferung

a. Die Begründung der christlichen Tradition

Die christliche Religion glaubt, dass sie als Gemeinde in dem Wirken Gottes begründet ist. So heißt es in 2 Kor 18. „Aber das alles ist von Gott, der uns mit sich selbst versöhnt hat durch Christus und uns das Amt gegeben hat, das die Versöhnung predigt". Diese Geschichte begründet sie. Die Gemeinde bewahrt und vergegenwärtigt sie. Das ist ihre Tradition. In ihr wird die Verkündigung der christlichen Gemeinde (vor allem der Urgemeinde) bewahrt. Diese Verkündigung geht auf die Verkündigung, auf Jesu Wort und Tat zurück. Es gibt darin einen geschichtlichen und einen eschatologischen Bezug, d. h. Christus wird gleichzeitig als das Ende und die Vollendung der Geschichte gedacht. Wenn man so will, ist das paradox: Geschichte und bereits Ende oder auch Aufhebung der Geschichte. In der

Welt leben und als Fremde in dieser Welt leben, Verantwortung für die Welt übernehmen und doch schon aus dieser Welt genommen, in der Welt, aber nicht von dieser Welt sein. Auf der einen Seite stellt Lukas in seinem Evangelium und in der Apostelgeschichte die Heilsgeschichte als eine Weltgeschichte dar. Das Ende der Geschichte ist in weite Ferne gerückt. Auf der anderen Seite würde nur die Verkündigung stehen, die auf das historische Geschehen verzichtet. Der Gegenpol zu Lukas wäre Johannes. Aber er bekennt auch Jesus als das „Wort, das Fleisch geworden ist und unter uns gewohnt hat". Johannes arbeitet aber nicht das Leben Jesu heraus, sondern den Sinn seines Lebens: dass Gott sich im Menschen Jesus offenbart. Gottes Wort wurde also von einem Menschen gesprochen und bleibt gegenwärtig. In der Kraft des Geistes wird dieses Wort von Jesus verkündigt, gegenwärtig gesetzt. Die Tradition ist hier die Predigt der Gemeinde, in der Jesus im Geiste gegenwärtig ist. Der Evangelist Markus hält eine andere, etwa – wenn man das so sagen kann – mittlere Position ein. Er betont die Wunder und Ereignisse wie Taufe und Verklärung Jesu. In ihnen wird der historische Jesus als Sohn Gottes geoffenbart, allerdings nur für den, der glaubt. Das Leben Jesu ist ein wunderbares, wenn auch für viele ein verborgenes Auftreten des Mannes aus Nazareth, der im Auftrag und mit der Vollmacht Gottes handelt. In der Taufe Jesu und im Abendmahl wird erzählt und geoffenbart: „auf ihn sollt ihr hören" und „Nehmet, das ist mein Leib". Das Leben Jesu ist Dasein des Gottessohnes, Erscheinen des Gottessohnes, gesehen und geglaubt von der Auferstehung Jesu her.

Diese Traditionen des Neuen Testamentes erfordern Kontinuität und Übertragung durch Nachfolge und Sukzession. Sie sind in unserer Kirche institutionell und sakramental überliefert. Zunächst waren es die Apostel, die tradierten. So heißt es in der Apostelgeschichte bei der Hinzuwahl eines vakanten Apostelsitzes: „Es muss nun einer von den Männern sein, die mit uns gezogen sind in der ganzen Zeit, in welcher der Herr Jesus bei uns ein- und ausging, von Anfang an seit der Taufe des Johannes bis zu dem Tage, da er emporgehoben ward von uns fort – es muss einer von diesen Zeugen seiner Auferstehung werden." (Apg 1,21f). Das Evangelium erzählt dann von der Aussendung und Mission der Zwölf und der Jünger („Wanderprediger").

Im Evangelium haben wir es mit einem kollektiven religiösen, sprich hier christlichen Gedächtnis zu tun. Es wird im Neuen Testament vom gemeinsamen Handeln und von kollektiven Riten, z. B. der Feier der Eucharistie als Gedächtnis des Herrn, berichtet und es werden appellative Nor-

men aufgestellt, z. B. die der Bergpredigt, aber auch Normen, um die Kontinuität mit der Geschichte Jesu aufrechtzuerhalten, nämlich Normen der Verkündigung, genauer der Mission, der Sendung und Durchführung der Verkündigung. Sie sollen die Echtheit der Verkündigung sicherstellen. Normen setzen voraus, dass ihnen Feststellungen um einen Sachverhalt zugrunde liegen. Die Sache, um die es geht, ist das Wort und die Tat Jesu. Jesus sendet im Markusevangelium die Zwölf zur Predigt und zur Heilung aus. Stichworte sind: Umkehrpredigt (das Gottesreich ist nahe) und die begleitenden Zeichen der heilenden Macht (Dämonenaustreibung und Krankenheilung). Jesus (bzw. die Urgemeinde) gibt ihnen Regeln vor, wie sie ausgerüstet und wie sie sich verhalten sollen. Auf ihren Wanderpredigten sollen sie nichts mitnehmen, „außer einem Stab allein, keinen Ranzen, kein Geld im Gürtel, nur Sandalen untergebunden und zieht nicht zwei Leibröcke an“ (Mk 6, 8f). Die Verhaltensregeln betreffen die Aufnahme der Wanderprediger in Häuser oder Ortschaften oder deren Ablehnung. Es soll eine Mission der Friedfertigkeit und der Friedensbereitschaft sein. Sie ist wehrlos und arm. Es herrschen ein tiefer Ernst und eine eschatologische Spannung, denn das Himmelreich ist nahe. Sicher verlief die christliche Mission im Lauf der Geschichte auch in anderen Maßstäben und Normenvorgaben, die wir hier nicht weiter behandeln können. Die Besinnung auf die Mission in der Urgemeinde sollte einen Hinweis auf einen heutigen Dialog innerhalb und zwischen den Religionen in Toleranz und Friedfertigkeit geben. Des Weiteren tut sich neben dem kulturell-christlichen Gedächtnis ein weites Gesprächsfeld zwischen säkularer Wissenschaft und Religion im Hinblick auf christliche Identifikation und persönlichem Glauben auf. Denn das Gedächtnis, Erinnern und Gedenken sowohl als individuelles als auch als kollektives Gedächtnis, Erinnern und Gedenken geschieht in einer sich wandelnden Weltzeit und braucht Zeit, um eine individuelle wie kollektive, kulturelle wie religiöse, Identifikation zu tradieren, aber auch zu erneuern und anzupassen.

Rudolf Bultmann and a Specifically Dominican Approach to Holy Scripture

Benedict Thomas Viviano OP

The question, what is a specifically Dominican approach to the interpretation of Scripture, cannot easily be answered in isolation. An answer becomes easier to formulate when it is structured as a contrast between an alternative approach and a Dominican one. Bultmann does not represent all non-Dominican exegesis and not all Dominican exegetes will sympathize with my approach. Thus my answer will be personal and for some controversial.

I have chosen Bultmann for a simple reason. His approach is well known internationally and especially in Germany. It is perhaps exaggeratedly clear and extreme. This makes the work of comparison and contrast easier. In the last months the thorough biography of Bultmann by Konrad Hammann has been translated into English and I read it with fascination, not to mention occasional horror and dismay.[1] It is important to add that younger Protestant New Testament scholars in Germany almost all claim to be most influenced by Bultmann, so his influence is enduring.[2]

I. Bultmann's Methods and Approach to the Interpretation of Scripture

1. On 21 April 1941 Bultmann gave his famous demythologizing lecture in Alpirsbach (Baden-Württemberg) and then in several other places. This program includes eight denials of classical pre-modern theological belief. These are: (a) the ascension of Christ to heaven; (b) belief in spirits and demons; (c) miracles as actual happenings; (d) mythical eschatology; (e)

1 Konrad Hammann, *Rudolf Bultmann* (Tübingen: Mohr Siebeck, 2009); English translation by Philip E. Devenish (Salem Oregon: Polebridge Press, 2013).

2 Eve-Marie Becker, ed., *Neutestamentliche Wissenschaft: Autobiographische Essays aus der Evangelischen Theologie* (Tübingen und Basel: A. Francke Verlag, 2003.) From Midwestern Dominicans, see T.F. O'Meara and D.M. Weisser, eds., *Rudolf Bultmann in Catholic Thought* (New York: Herder & Herder, 1968).

the idea of a supernatural agency of the Spirit and the sacraments; (f) the conception of death as punishment for sin; (g) the doctrine of satisfaction; (h) the understanding of the resurrection as a physical occurrence.[3] We can say that the conviction that the New Testament must be demythologized is Bultmann's first presupposition.

2. Bultmann's second presupposition is voluntarism, the preeminence of the will, in theological thinking. This can lead to weepy sentimentality and to irrationality. This voluntarism partly reflects the Lutheran reception of St Francis and St Bernard of Clairvaux, partly some forms of nominalism.

3. Bultmann grew up in the heyday of neo-Kantianism. Kant, in his main works, was agnostic on the three big questions: Does God exist? Is the soul immortal? Is our will free to produce moral actions? On these three points, Bultmann also remains agnostic. In addition to this third, Kantian, presupposition, Bultmann decided to use the existential analysis of the human predicament developed by his Marburg colleague, Martin Heidegger, to express the anthropology at the heart of the New Testament. [Since the Heideggerian jargon is not easy for many listeners to understand, the joke became that when repeatedly questioned, for example, on the bodily resurrection of Jesus Christ, Bultmann would simply repeat his answer in variations of the Heideggerian jargon. The questioner understood no better than before, but began to get used to it.][4]

4. Bultmann studied systematic theology with Wilhelm Hermann at Marburg and always acknowledged his influence later in life. Concretely this means that there can be no objectifying talk about God or Christ. Our views must therefore remain quite subjective.[5] Hermann's strong neo-

---

3 Hammann, pp. 325–326. R.E. Bultmann, *Neues Testament und Mythologie* (BevTh 96; Munich: Kaiser, 1941); translated as The New Testanent and Mythology in H.W. Bartsch, ed., *Kerygma and Myth: A Theological Debate* (New York: Harper & Row, 1961), pp. 1–44. This essay contains a condensed presentation of Bultmann's whole theology of the New Testament. In this essay Bultmann is trying to meet the challenge thrown down by Wilhelm Kamlah, one of his former students, who was turning "brown," and on the other hand a pure repristination of orthodox formulas, such as that attempted by Hans Asmussen, which Bultmann regarded as inadequate to face the challenges of modernity.

4 Hammann, p. 115.

5 Falk Wagner, "Theologische Neukantianismus: Wilhelm Hermann,' in *Profile des neu-*

Kantianism caused him to retreat from Ritschl's moderately substantial concept of the Kingdom of God. It is said that Hermann replaced Ritschl's idea of the Kingdom as the highest good with the idea or the ideal of the ethical personality. That is, he replaced the social world with anthropology, individualism, psychology. Even if this is not fair to Hermann, it reflects Bultmann's accents which he claims he received from Hermann.

5. Bultmann represents a type of religious thought which emphasizes the inward values of faith. This thought remains unconnected with politics, it remains resolutely non-partisan. [Hammann tries to show that Bultmann belonged to the *Deutsche Demokratische Partei* during the Weimar republic, the party founded by Max Weber and Ernst Troeltsch as a Protestant alternative to the Socialists, to the Center party and to the right wing militarist parties, a party that could collaborate with the Socialists and the Catholic Center party to form genuinely democratic parliamentary governing coalitions during Weimar. As these two noble founders died young from overwork, and as the National Socialists rose in importance, and as the collaboration between Center and the Socialists was made impossible by the encyclical *Quadragesimo Anno* (1931), the younger leaders of the DDP tragically supported the Nazis before desolving the party. Hammann rejects efforts to show that Bultmann was ever a member of the Socialist Party.] Thus Bultmann could remain a full professor during the Brown Years without much trouble. And his students could be named professors after the war because they had not been tainted with a too ardent support of the Nazi regime.

This element of inwardness means that his form of religion is also highly individualistic. There is hardly any ecclesiology in Bultmann and that includes a very weak view of sacraments. These things are rejected or suspected as Hellenistic religiosity or else as "early Catholic," a fall from eschatological purity and fervor.

6. Bultmann was also deeply marked by the History of Religions school associated especially with Göttingen University before the First World War. From the point of view of the present essay, this is rather a positive element in Bultmann's formation. It means a stricly historical reading of the New

---

zeitlichen Protestantismus, ed. F.W. Graf, Band 2, Teil 2 (Gutersloh: Mohn, 1993), pp. 250–278.

Testament, on which are brought to bear very great learning, especially in the collecting and analysis of pagan and Jewish parallels to the Scriptures. One of Bultmann's professors at Göttingen was Johannes Weiss. His commentary on 1 Corinthians is still in print and considered the model of a commentary in this spirit. Bultmann always felt a special appreciation for this epistle and its sequel; he tried to write a commentary on 2 Corinthians but this was never completed. Besides Weiss, Hermann Gunkel, Wilhelm Bousset, William Wrede, Hans Lietzmann and Hans Windisch belonged to this rather liberal school. This school made the immense ecumenical contribution of understanding Paul as he really was, before the later period of Augustine, when Augustine was misled by his polemical ardor to distort Paul in his struggle with the Pelagians. This was done by Wrede's little book on Paul, and by Lietzmann's commentaries on the four main epistles of Paul. Johannes Weiss, in his little classic of 1897, *The Kingdom of God in the Proclamation of Jesus*, shattered the Kantian cultural Protestantism which identified the Kingdom of God with the Prussian state and with a purely formal ethics. Weiss recaptured the Jewish apocalyptic eschatological sense of this theme in the preaching of Jesus and Paul. This historically correct understanding, which can easily be rejected as crude mythology, nevertheless contains a revolutionary social dynamic (the kingdom of God includes justice, peace and joy in the Holy Spirit, Rom 14:17; Matt 6:33). Later on Ernst Bloch, Jürgen Moltmann and Johann B. Metz were able to integrate and develop these insights.

This is however a negative element in this History of Religions school. The members of this school presupposed the work of the immediately preceding generation, especially the history of dogma of Adolf Harnack. Harnack's bold thesis was that the very idea of dogma was a Hellenistic idea foreign to the Bible and that this idea which had been so dominant in Christian theology up to the Reformation, came to an end with Luther.[6] Bultmann embraces this non-dogmatic form of Christian faith. What remains is only the bare fact of revelation in Jesus' death on the cross, *nur das dass der Offenbarung*, and behind it the guiding principle of justification by faith alone. This represents a drastic reduction in content.

6 Karl Heinz Neufeld, *Adolf von Harnack: Theologie als Suche nach der Kirche, "Tertium genus ecclesiae,"* (Konfessionskundliche und Kontroverstheologische Studien 41: Paderborn: Bonifacius Verlag, 1977); *A. Harnacks Konflikt mit der Kirche* (Innsbruck: Tyrolia, 1979). Cf. my review of these books in *Revue Biblique* 94 (1987) 473–475.

7. Somewhat oddly, there is a strong element of Stoicism in Bultmann. This means among other things that no matter what happens outwardly, military, political or ethical disasters, one continues to be happy quietly in one's bourgeois academic way. One remains in Stoic *ataraxia*, unshakeability or imperturbability. One of Bultmann's favorite texts is 1 Cor 7:29–31, "I mean, brethren, the appointed time has grown very short; from now on, let those who have wives live as though (*hos me*) they had none, and those who mourn as though they were not mourning, and those who rejoice as though they were not rejoicing, and those who buy as though they had no goods, and those who deal with the world as though they had no dealings with it. For the form of this world is passing away." Although this text seems strange for someone who was relatively happily married his whole adult life, it does express a certain Stoic detachment or distance from or indifference to the world. It seems to have been a guiding principle in Bultmann's life.

II. A Modern Dominican Midwestern Thomistic Approach to Scripture

Although this section will be rather autobiographical, the life in question has been marked from the beginning by central Dominican values and personalities, so that its experience is representative of many Dominicans, let us hope, once the idiosyncrasies have been removed.

I was baptized Thomas Aquinas by my parents who were young American Catholics of some university education, and were of pure South Italian ancestry and conscious of their cultural heritage. They chose the name Thomas because they knew he was the patron of Catholic schools and a great doctor of the church. As a child I learned about my patron saint and the order of which he was a member from the *Encyclopedia Britannica*. I bought my first anthology of Thomas when I was twelve. In my Catholic boys high school (gymnasium) and early university, I learned modern science, especially biology and chemistry, Latin and Greek, and also religion. In biology, Darwinian evolution was taught and presupposed as true. The Fifties were a period of high religious practice, sustained in the US by the television preaching of Fulton Sheen and by the best-selling books of the monk Thomas Merton.

My family was Catholic and practicing on both sides, but my maternal grandfather was a sort of Garibaldian Italian nationalist anti-clerical,

that is, as a young man still in Italy he did not not accept the church prohibition to vote in Italian elections. He was proud of a unified Italy and so he voted, even though this meant a kind of excommunication, a consequence which he accepted until the excommunication was lifted. This model of my grandfather meant that I learned early to maintain a critical distance from the positions of the Holy See, at least politically. On this darker side, I must add that in the days before television, that is, before 1952, people went to the cinema often. There were two films, not one. Between the two films there was a news reel. Already as a five or six year old I thus saw the filmed reports of the discovery of the deathcamps, like Buchenwald and Auschwitz. These sights seared my soul and gave me my first idea of the human capacity for grave evil. Later this meant that I chose a form of religion which would enable me to denounce these evils in the name of God.

At fifteen, in a course on the life of Christ through the four gospels, I first heard the story of pere Marie-Joseph Lagrange, O.P., and his unmerited suffering during and after the anti-Modernist witchhunt. My passionate little Sicilian heart was on fire with sympathy for him, for his desire to develop modern historical-critical scholarship in the Church, and for his school in Jerusalem. The mid-fifties were also the time of the craze for the Dead Sea Scrolls discoveries and of the publication of the *Jerusalem Bible*, first in French (1956). Roland de Vaux, the editor and excavator, was a household name, promoted by William Foxwell Albright, the American archaeological hero of the time. I could follow these issues through TIME magazine at first. I also discovered a fresh translation of the New Testament into beautiful modern English, by Monsignor Ronald Knox. By the end of my high school years I had read the entire New Testament. I had to decide whether or not God existed. Here both Thomas and nature helped me to make the decision for God. Since I was basically happy, my question to God was: What do you want me to do? I found the answer in the Sermon on the Mount. For me this represents wisdom about life. Jesus is thus the Teacher/Master par excellence. (Of course his teaching presupposes the whole Old Testament, especially the Pentateuch.) To complete the picture of my adolescence, we must add that I grew up in a country where parliamentary representative democracy was presupposed. The Dominican tradition of government, as rediscovered by Lacordaire, easily fits with this political tradition. Indeed, the Dominican constitutions contributed to the shaping of this tradition.

The Catholic Church in the USA in the Fifties was also marked by a controversy over the need for more Catholic contributions to the intellec-

tual life and culture. This was provoked by the essay of Monsignor John Tracy Ellis of 1955.[7] This essay gave young people like me the sense that we could contribute to the life of the Church by becoming scholars and writers. This essay in large measure explains my decision to become a Dominican, a biblical scholar, and to choose a dissertation topic on the biblical basis for a strong engagement in the intellectual life.

1. The Chicago Dominican province I entered in 1959 had a good spirit of study, inspired by Walter Farrell, Benedict Ashley (d. 23 February 2013) and especially by James Athanasius Weisheipl. These and others founded the River Forest School of Thomism, which emphasized Thomas' commentaries on Aristotle as containing his true philosophy. (This was against Etienne Gilson who found Thomas's philosophy in his theological works). This school was fiercely philosophical and was interested in the dialogue with modern science, especially with biology. The works of Raymond Jude Nogar represent this point of view, especially his works *The Wisdom of Evolution* and *The Lord of the Absurd*. The study of theology, after three years of philosophy, meant primarily the study of the *Summa* of St Thomas. In the study of Scripture, the works of Pere Lagrange, de Vaux and Benoit were considered normative. Of course by 1963 the new winds of thought emerging from the Council began to have their effect. Our formation was balanced by a strict observance of the rules of Dominican life, especially the divine office, silence and total poverty (no money in your pocket).

From this background what needs to be retained for a study of the Scriptures is a minimum dogmatic framework. It presupposes the Nicene Creed, for example, and specific ethical precepts: the Ten Commandments, the two great Commandments of love of God and of neighbor, the lists of virtues such as one finds in Wisdom 8:7 (=Plato and Aristotle), and in Paul, for example 1 Cor 13:13. This framework already distinguishes us from Bultmann who accepts no dogmatic framework, in the spirit of Harnack. Bultmann grew up in a church where the creed was not recited on Sunday, due to the influence of Harnack in the Apostolikum Streit. When it was proposed after 1945 to return to the Creed, Bultmann was against this. (German Protestant Church believers had begun to return to reciting the Creed during the Nazi period as a badge of identity.)

---

7 J.T. Ellis, *American Catholics and the Intellectual Life* (Chicago: Heritage, 1956).

Modern critical study, especially the quest for the historical Jesus, would however lead the Dominican biblical scholar of today to shift the accent in the study of the gospels from John (the favorite of medieval Dominicans like Thomas and Meister Eckhardt) to the Synoptics. Here again there is a difference from Bultmann. He accepted the view set forth by Wellhausen, that Jesus was a Jew and that his teaching belongs to the theology of Judaism, not of Christianity (identified with Paul reduced to justification by faith alone and its anthropological consequences). That is why Bultmann accords so little place to Jesus in his *Theology of the New Testament*.[8]

We would also accept the two-source hypothesis, which means beginning with Mark and with Q. John is accepted and studied as a great inspired commentary on the Synoptics, a commentary which is indispensible for understanding the later doctrinal traditions of theology, but which is only to a small degree an independent source of historical information.

A more delicate issue concerns apocalyptic eschatology. It would be very hard to speak even for all Thomists here. I personally accept as a matter of faith a full, crude, primitive, early Christian hope or expectation of the second coming of Christ to earth in glory, bringing the Kingdom of God in its fullness. Christ will reign on earth for a long period, as a way of fulfilling the biblical promises that God's plans for a history of salvation will be realized in a future which is both in this world and in the next, yet in this world as in some way transformed. One can easily accuse this view or hope or expectation of being some form of millenarianism, which some think is a condemned heresy. (That it is a heresy is in fact not so clear.) But strictly speaking, it is not millenarianism, because this hope does not speak of a literal thousand years. Rev 20:1–10 speaks of a thousand years, six times in the text, but the wider Christian and Jewish tradition does not insist on the thousand years. The phrase in Jewish tradition can mean a long time.

From the 18th century (e. g., Reimarus) this early Christian hope has been rejected as primitive mythology. What has enabled serious Christian systematic theology to take this element of biblical revelation seriously as meaningful even today is the philosophy of hope of Ernst Bloch, incorporated into the theologies of Jürgen Moltmann and J. B. Metz. This message gives hope to humanity, a hope which includes both this world and the

8 H.D. Betz, "Wellhausen's Dictum Jesus was not a Christian, but a Jew, in light of Present Scholarship," *Studia Theologica* (Copenhagen) 45 (1991) 83–110.

next. This hope is not Pelagian, the illusion that we build the Kingdom of God on earth ourselves. This Pelagian error has been tried before (e. g., Third Reich, Soviet empire) and is a monstrous distortion. But this hope includes a human, ethical contribution: like John the Baptist we are called to prepare the way of the Lord, to remove obstacles, but not directly to build the Kingdom. That remains the endtime gift of God, a free grace which he gives when he decides. Nevertheless contemporary Dominican biblical scholarship includes a strong liberationist tendency, including some political involvement, even if avoiding identifying the Kingdom of God with some particular political project.

In his 1941 essay, Bultmann gives a little history of earlier ways of dealing with the difficult passages of Scripture before he insists on his own existentialist solution of demythologizing.[9] He lists four previous solutions: patristic allegory, liberal-modernist reinterpretation and interiorization, neo-Orthodox (Karl Barth) uncritical acceptance of the Easter kerygma, History of Religions conversion of the myths into truths of liturgy and spirituality, the experience of mystical union with Christ. The first of these, allegory, is abundantly present in the Dominican tradition, beginning with Hugh of St Cher. Thomas is free to use it but he prefers to base doctrinal interpretations on the literal sense. Modern Dominicans will generally share Thomas' preference, but we can learn from all four of these approaches.

Modern Dominican biblically based spirituality can share Bultmann's affection for the Stoicism of 1 Cor 7:29–31, insofar as it expresses eschatological urgency and an indifference to personal comfort or even a positive free embrace of poverty and simplicity of life and detachment from worldly honors. Nevertheless Dominicans will not have a purely other-worldly idea of salvation. Dominic resisted the Manichaeans. Dominicans must take this world seriously as the object of God's care and concern. Matter is capable of bearing grace. Grace sanctifies both this world and the next.

2. Dominican exegesis should strive to be as objective as possible. This means sharing the ideals of the historical positivity of the second half of the 19th century (von Ranke), even though today these ideals are often rejected as impossible or useless. Besides the works of Lagrange, for us a good example is Johannes Weiss' commentary on 1 Corinthians (1910).

9 Bartsch, *Kerygma and Myth*, pp. 12–15.

Behind this desire for objectivity stands a classical Greek epistemological confidence that the human mind is made to know truth, that we can know physical reality and can also arrive at minimal metaphysical conclusions such as that God is, and that the soul is immaterial and thus immortal, and that there is a certain moral responsibility and freedom of the will, even though hampered by original sin and subconscious and external socio-political pressures. In this sense Dominican exegesis should remain pre-Kantian and anti-Kantian. This does not mean that we cannot learn from and share certain of Kant's other contributions: the goal of universal peace through something like the UN, human enlightenment, the centrality of the Kingdom of God to religious faith, the view that theology should properly and primarily be an interpretation of Sacred Scripture.

Dominican exegesis should also include a discriminating embrace of Hegel's philosophy of history (or Schlegel's) insofar as this includes a belief in the activity of the Spirit of God as present and active in both the world and the Church. In this sense St Thomas (and other mainstream medieval theologians) needs a theology of history, a Hegelian supplement. (I have written on this but this is not the right place to develop this point.)

Dominican exegesis will continue to wrestle with the phenomenon of miracles. It will not be able to dismiss all miracles out of hand. Besides the distinction made by Hume between healing miracles and nature miracles, we will have to weigh the intentions of the sacred author and the truths of physics. We do not want to repeat the mistakes some of us made in the Galileo case. We do not want to set artificial or dogmatic limits to God's power or to discourage prayer for divine help. We want to learn from the discretion of Psalm 77:19. We will want to avoid the uncritical embrace of all miracles as exhibited by Rene Latourelle.[10]

If we return to Bultmann's 1941 essay for a moment, we can see that the program of what needs to be demythologized occurs in the first eight pages, his description of the problem to be solved. In these eight pages there are two parts: first, problems arising from modern science and its understanding of nature, which includes a problem with the nature miracles, especially the resurrection; second, problems arising from modern man's understanding of himself (pp. 6–8). The first set of problems is real for every thoughtful person, already in antiquity (cf. Acts 17: 32), even

10 Rene Latourelle, *The Miracles of Jesus and the Theology of Miracles* (New York: Paulist, 1988).

more so today. The second set of problems is less impressive. They are not necessarily urgent problems to someone who is not a Lutheran Kantian. The description of modern man's psychology as totally unified, closed to outside influences especially from above; that modern man has total moral and personal responsibility; that modern man cannot imagine atonement through another person's sacrifice; that sin cannot have a juridical character to a certain extent, these assertions are not at all necessary. It only takes a little *Einfühlen,* historical empathy and imagination to overcome these conceptual difficulties, and this is not hard to achieve. One needs a less rigid understanding of man and nature than the Kantian model of Bultmann.[11]

When Bultmann asks why salvation must take this particular form, and why this revelation is the fulfillment of human life and the realization of our true being, we must reflect. There is no necessity to it. It lies within God's free choice. He could have done it in many other ways. Indeed, the New Testament itself offers several models of redemption. Incarnation is only one of them. A culture which is more used to freedom and to variety than was nineteenth century Prussia has less difficulty with these ways God has freely chosen to speak and to redeem.

3. Dominicans will want to share St Thomas' moderate intellectualism, in contrast with Duns Scotus' voluntarism. We want to avoid voluntarism in politics of state and church ("sit pro ratione voluntas"), to favor an intelligent, truthful obedience to lawful authority. In the controversy between Dominicans and Franciscans over the primacy of intellect or will in beatitude, we will remain loyal to St Thomas insofar as this old debate cannot be overcome by redefining beatitude as life in the Kingdom of God (on earth as well as in heaven), a social goal, rather than the Augustinian-Johannine individualistic goal of the beatific vision. Because, when the debate depends upon this vision as the goal of beatitude, we cannot help winning. For us the will must be guided and controlled by a graced reason.

We seek in the Bible a sober, moral piety. Therefore we can be ethically philo-Semitic. We will no longer try to burn the Talmud. We will learn from it too. And we will respect the great accumulation of insight and wisdom to be found in Jewish literature, including rabbinic literature. This is part of our tradition but it has not always been held in honor.

---

11 On the imagination (even Harry Potter), see Justin Taylor, *The Treatment of Reality in the Gospels* (Cahiers de la Revue Biblique 78; Paris/Pende: Gabalda, 2011)

4. Although this will depend on individual personality and gifts, I would personally like to see Dominicans as both socially extravert and politically committed to a real democratic, socially just politics. The political model I recommend is the constitution of Belgium which includes a Catholic monarchy subject to control by parliament. In German terms, either CDU or SPD but not CSU or FPD. In academic life, socially extravert means concretely participating in scholarly meetings like the Catholic Biblical Association or the Society of Biblical Literature., presenting papers, serving on committees, editorial boards and the like.

5. Our vows commit us to taking seriously and literally the conditions of discipleship as taught by Jesus in both Q and Mark, as well as Matthew and Luke (Luke 14:25–27; 17:33; 9:23–24; Mark 8:34–35; 10:29–30; Matt 10:37–39; 16:24–25; John 12:25). It is true that nowadays all committed Christians want to regard themselves as disciples, literally lifelong *learners* from Jesus and as his companions along the road of salvation history to the Kingdom. We want to encourage them in this path. But we can claim a more literal, original form of discipleship, present in the earliest layers of the gospel tradition, before the concept gets watered down, or broadened out.

6. We are not to be afraid of sacramental objectivity, a great difference from Bultmann. We do not need to force the texts to say more than they do, but I think we should admit the sacramental teaching of the gospel of John, even though his way of speaking does not make this totally evident. But we do not need to fall into crude Berengarius views or to ignore the major conclusions of the modern liturgical movement as received by the Second Vatican Council and the post-conciliar official reforms. (These continue.) Our role will be especially important in helping people to use well the wonderful lectionaries of 1970.

7. Newer methods and approaches. Since the Second Vatican Council there has been in the biblical field a swarm of new methods and approaches. To help students who may be confused by this overdose, the Pontifical Biblical Commission in 1993 produced a useful 130 page document called *The Interpretation of the Bible in the Church.*[12] On the whole this document has

12 Pontifical Biblical Commission, *The Interpretation of the Bible in the Church* (Rome: Vatican, 1993).

been widely and well received. It repeatedly and firmly affirms the normativity of the historical-critical method. Among the newer literary methods it lists: rhetorical analysis, narrative analysis, and semiotic analysis. Younger Dominicans are usually well trained in these methods. Semiotics is probably only a passing intellectual fad and of little importance. The other two have been of some utility in paying attention to neglected features of the composition of the text, for example, noting the narrative flow. Since many biblical books are not narratives, e. g., epistles, they can be analyzed by rhetorical categories. If these methods are wholly separated from historical inquiry, they become quickly sterile and trivial. Other approaches, based on tradition, include the canonical, the use of Jewish traditions, and the issue of history of the influence of the text (*Wirkungsgeschichte*). This last issue comes close to the field of history of interpretation of the texts. This has become a growth industry, in connection with patristics and the study of the Septuagint.

Still other approaches are the sociological, the cultural anthropological, the psychological and psychoanalytic. Then there are the liberationist and the feminist approaches, the charismatic and even the fundamentalist readings. In reality there are Dominicans active in all of these approaches, whether we rejoice in this fact or not. The document is reserved about fundamentalist approaches and has offended Evangelicals in this section. Close to the liberationist model is one not mentioned in the PBC document: the post-colonial. Some of these methods have been accused of "advocacy scholarship." At their best however they can help us to see things that are really in the biblical texts but which we have neglected in the past, such as the biblical stories of violence toward women, e. g., Jephthah's daughter. This is genuine helpful honest biblical scholarship and represents real progress.[13]

My experience is that most of these approaches can be sterile or boring if they are too far separated from ancient history and classical philological learning. In America the canonical approach has proven fruitful both in its more liberal (J. A. Sanders) and in its more conservative (Brevard Childs) versions. Childs' commentary on Exodus is a miracle of richness, no matter what one's theological position. The Commission document, to which several Dominicans contributed (Loza and Barthelemy), then

13 A positive example of feminist exegesis is Phyllis Trible's *Texts of Terror* (Philadelphia: Fortress, 1984). This work has been translated into German.

goes on to address vast hermeneutical issues. The document is too short to treat these issues adequately. Subsequent documents of the Commission have tried to improve their treatment of some of these issues.

8. In contrast with Bultmann's individualism, we will want to emphasize the role of community in our exegesis of the biblical texts. So we can help nourish the life of families, the Dominican order and other groups of vowed religious, the wider Church, and the civil community. At our best we achieve such professional success and recognition that we are called upon by the episcopal and Roman magisteriums to help draft documents, including the best encyclicals. So we try to help the magisterium, as did St Dominic in his day. (Examples: Zigliara with *Rerum Novarum*, Voste with *Divino Afflante Spiritu*). By resisting quietly and politely mistaken policies and decisions of the Church authorities, we can help to prepare the way for better policies, as in ecumenism, biblical studies, ecclesiology, educational or social policies. In this regard our more recent heroes, Lacordaire, Lagrange, Congar and Chenu are good models.[14] Another example, from among the German Dominicans, is the delayed victory of Dominikus Koster over Emile Mersch in the conflict over the biblical ecclesiological models "People of God" versus "Body of Christ." Mersch "won" in the encyclical *Mystici Corporis* of 1943; Koster "won" in the Constitution on the Church *Lumen Gentium* in 1964. The work *in* the Church *for* the Church requires great patience and great tact. But we stand in a great tradition, we have great models, and we can wait.

14 B.T. Viviano, "The Church in the Modern World and the French Dominicans," *Freiburger Zeitschrift fuer Philosophie und Theologie*," 50 (2003) 512–521; Viviano, "The Renewal of Biblical Studies in France 1934–1954 as an Element in Theological Ressourcement," in *Ressourcement,* ed. Gabriel Flynn and P.D Murray (Oxford: Oxford University Press, 2012), pp. 305–317.

SEELSORGE

Haltung annehmen oder einüben?

Manfred Entrich OP

Offen faszinierend

„Immer wieder wird es darum gehen, dass bei der menschlichen Initiative der innerste Grund und Antrieb die Fügsamkeit zu Gott ist, und immer wird sie, plötzlich, wie aus heiterem Himmel, neu gefordert und eingeübt werden.“[1]

Schmerzlich sind die Erfahrungen vieler Seelsorger, wenn sie ihre Mühe und ihren Einsatz nicht mit einem von ihnen erhofften Erfolg gekrönt sehen. Die vorgeschriebenen Kirchenzählungen zeigen jedes Jahr – meist in unbestechlicher Weise – wie es um den Kirchenbesuch steht. Es ist der Augenblick, wo nicht selten dumpfe Mutlosigkeit nach uns greift und wir spüren, wie Kirchenmitgliedschaft und Kirchenbesuch in eine kaum noch einzuholende Spannung geraten. Darüber hinaus dann auch noch das Wissen um nicht wenige, die die Kirche ganz verlassen.

Es scheint schwerer geworden zu sein, Menschen über längere Zeit hinaus für eine Aufgabe zu interessieren und sie auch bleibend an eine Gemeinde zu binden. Auswählen und selbstbestimmt unverbindlich bleiben, gilt für viele als eine besondere Qualität des Lebens.[2] Dahinter steht die Haltung des ‚Offen-Bleibens‘ für das noch nicht Geplante, aber vielleicht Mögliche, selbst das Moment der Überraschung, es könnte ja auf mich noch etwas Förderlicheres zukommen, das ich verpassen würde, legte ich mich zu früh auf anderes fest. Diese Haltung des immer ‚Offen-Bleibens‘ auf Zukunft hin hat für viele eine besondere Faszination, aber sie führt auch sehr viele in eine – fast möchte man sagen – flatterhafte Orientierungslosigkeit.

Kirche und Gesellschaft in ihren Organisationen sind von diesem Grundgefühl vieler Menschen schmerzlich berührt. Sie machen nicht selten die Erfahrung, dass es an kontinuierlicher Mitarbeit fehlt, an verlässlicher Bereitschaft, auch einmal lange Wege mitzugehen.

---

1 M. Kehl, U. W. Löser, In der Fülle des Glaubens, Hans Urs von Balthasar-Lesebuch. Freiburg/Breisgau[2] 1980, 121.

2 Vgl. K. Müller, Homiletik. Ein Handbuch für kritische Zeiten. Regensburg 1994, 35–41.

Manfred Entrich OP

Stop and Go

Auf einem Kundenstopper in New York vor einer anglikanischen Kirche sah ich das Plakat: „Willst Du kurze Wege gehen, dann geh allein, wenn Du lange Wege gehen willst, dann nimm jemanden mit.“ Es war das Zitat eines indianischen Sprichwortes und mir scheint, dass wir damit auch etwas von unserer Pastoral skizziert haben. Den kurzen Weg, wo Anfang und Ende eines Einsatzes überschaubar und im Kräftepotential berechenbar sind, den können sowohl die, die haupt- und nebenamtlich Dienst tun, aber auch die, die sich ehrenamtlich engagieren, allein gehen. Einen längeren Weg zu gehen bedeutet, einen langen Atem zu haben, eine präzise Zielvorstellung und die nüchterne Einschätzung der Möglichkeiten des eigenen Kräftehaushaltes. Hier ist das Mitgehen, das zu zweit unterwegs sein, eine uns stärkende Notwendigkeit, damit wir auf dem Weg nicht ins Abseits geraten, weil wir das Ziel aus den Augen verlieren. Die Produktpalette an Informationen, Unterhaltungsangeboten und Sinnentwürfen liegen für jeden Menschen zum Greifen nahe am Wegrand. Es fordert zunehmend mehr Kraft und Phantasie, eine Wahl zu treffen für sich selbst, sich damit zu platzieren, einen Ort zu finden und ein Ziel auszumachen. Dies gilt allemal dann für den Weg, den wir mit den Menschen gehen, nicht abseits ihrer Straßen, sondern mitten in ihren Lebenswegen.

Im Mix der unterschiedlichen Lebensentwürfe und Sinnorientierungen ist es nicht einfach, in christlicher Gelassenheit die Botschaft der Bibel in die Öffentlichkeit zu tragen. Die Erfahrungen der Menschen mit Gott im Alten Testament, die Sendung Jesu, die sich in den Schriften des Neuen Testamentes ausdrückt, unverkrampft, ungeschönt, aber auch mit angemessener Bescheidenheit in die realen Lebenskontexte der Menschen hineinzusagen, das braucht schon etwas. Das braucht vor allem die eigene Option, sich auf diesen Weg verbindlich einzulassen.

Die rechte Weise, die Botschaft des Evangeliums zu verkünden – auch außerhalb des eigentlichen Kirchraumes – stellt unsere Verkündigung vor neue Herausforderungen. Das betrifft vor allem auch die Frage, wie im ‚ungeschützten und offenen Raum‘ der Gesellschaft eine Verkündigung geschehen kann, die Menschen erreicht, die nicht mehr oder noch nicht vom Christentum berührt worden sind. Aber auch innerhalb der Kirche muss die Verkündigung härter um ihre Legitimation ringen.[3] In diesen

3 Welche unverzichtbare Aufgabe die Gemeinden hier erwartet, ist kaum im Blick. Si-

Schwierigkeiten fühlen wir uns häufig überfordert, die wachsende Zahl von sehr unterschiedlichen Aufgaben lässt oft den schalen Geschmack der Überforderung in uns spüren. Hinzu kommt die Melancholie und Traurigkeit über den geringen Erfolg des Engagements, kurz: Wir stehen nicht selten kurz vor einer spirituellen Lähmung.

Glaubwürdig unterbrechen

Vielleicht braucht es wirklich die Kraft zur Unterbrechung, den von Zeit zu Zeit radikalen Schnitt, um nicht im Wald der Aufgaben die Orientierung zu verlieren. Es ist sicher nicht leicht zu sagen, das mache ich jetzt einmal nicht. Es ist sicher genauso schwer zu sagen, das will ich jetzt einmal tun, aber Priorisierungen, Durchforsten des Dickichts, in dem wir uns bewegen, werden helfen die Agenda unseres Dienstes zu ordnen, den Blick freizubekommen, die Entscheidungen mit vorzubereiten und vor allem der eigenen Lebenskultur wieder auf die Füße zu helfen. Damit ist das Stichwort gegeben: Kultur. Von Papst Johannes Paul II. kennen wir das Wort von der Kultur des Lebens und der Kultur des Todes. Die Bipolarität, die ausgedrückt ist, spannt den Entscheidungshorizont auf, vor dem wir stehen und mit Recht vermerkt Hans-Joachim Höhn die Spannung, in die Seelsorgepastoral und Verkündigung geraten, wenn er schreibt: „Eine Theologie, die den Zeitkolorit der Kultur und der Religion in gleicher Weise ernst nimmt, muss sich zum einen Gedanken machen, die bloß in der Zeit sind. Sie muss die dominanten geistigen Strömungen erfassen … Sie wird jedoch zum bloßen Notar des Zeitgeistes, wenn sie nicht auch jene Gedanken aufnimmt, die an der Zeit sind und doch über sie hinaus weisen."[4] Da ist das Stichwort gesetzt von der Kultur, ein Kulturbezug, der nicht in einer Sonderwelt eigenartige Blüten kreiert, sondern eine Kultur, die mitten in der Realität des Lebens steht, meiner Stadt, meines Landkreises, meiner Gemeinde, politisch und kirchlich, wo

---

cher gilt es, Gemeinden nicht zu überfordern und vor allem nicht den Blick auf den immer auch weiteren Raum des mit dem Wort bezeichneten Großraums zu verlieren. Die Gemeinde ist aber auch immer einer der Orte, an denen der Glaube real werden kann. Zur Diskussion hierzu: M. N. Ebertz, Kirche im Gegenwind. Zum Umbruch der religiösen Landschaft. Freiburg i. Breisgau[2] 1998.

4 H.-J. Höhn (Hrsg.), Theologie, die an der Zeit ist. Entwicklungen – Positionen – Konsequenzen, dort: Ders., Distanz und Dissens. Theologie zwischen Moderne und Postmoderne. Paderborn 1992, 11–15 und 12.

auch immer, nicht zum Notar des Zeitgeistes werden, sondern die Gedanken der Zeit aufnehmen und die doch über diese Zeit hinaus weisen.

Noch einmal: Wenn Du lange Wege gehen willst, nimm jemanden mit – miteinander sprechen, das Zeitkolorit erfassen, die theologische Perspektive abtasten und behutsam machbare Prioritäten setzen.

Unsere Zeit bietet in allem, was sie in ihrer oft verwirrenden kulturellen Vielfalt so aufregend macht, auch eine Fülle versteckter Botschaften. Vor allem im Bereich von Kunst, Kultur, in den vielfältigsten Ausdrucksformen werden wir von Gedanken berührt, die auf Zeitströmungen hinweisen. Zeitströmungen, die zutiefst auch mit dem verbunden sind, was in seinem lebensbestimmenden Kräftepotential über den Augenblick hinausweist. Wir berühren mit unserer Botschaft die Botschaften der Zeit. Wir tasten einander gegenseitig ab und es entsteht nicht selten ein Lichtbogen zwischen beiden, der uns verstehen lässt, in welcher Zeit wir leben und aus welcher Hoffnung wir unsere Kraft schöpfen. Das nahende und sich ausbreitende Gottesreich zeigt sich in einem ersten Anleuchten und gibt uns die notwendige Sicherheit, den Weg zu gehen.

Der Film „Von Göttern und Menschen" erzählt die Geschichte des Suchens, der Liebe und des Todes einer kleinen Kommunität von Trappisten im Norden Afrikas. Sie geraten in die politischen Auseinandersetzungen Algeriens. Ihrem Leben wird die Alltäglichkeit einer beständigen Ordnung genommen. Sie müssen sich entscheiden zu bleiben oder zu gehen. In der Stunde der Entscheidung werden die einzelnen Charaktereigenschaften der Brüder deutlich. Der noch junge Abt, dessen Leitungsstil sich noch am gewachsenen Charakter der Mitbrüder abschleifen muss oder der schlichte Spirituelle, der Zögerliche und Nachdenkliche, der Praktische und Ängstliche, sie alle zeigen, wie Individualität und Kommunität unverwechselbar klar kontrastiert unter einem Sinnhorizont stehen. Sie fällen die Entscheidung zu bleiben und sie feiern ihr Leben wie die Zelebration des Abendmahles. Zeitströmungen und Nachrichten, die weit über den Augenblick hinausweisen, werden zur Entscheidung vorgelegt. Sie müssen entscheiden. So legt der Film den Schleier diskreter Zurückhaltung über die Szenen und öffnet damit den Blick für die Tiefe. Es geht nicht um brutale Nacktheit in diesem Film, sondern um reale und damit poetische Schönheit. Der Film gibt den Blick frei für das alles Verbindende, nämlich das Geheimnis von Tod und Leben, von Liebe und Hoffnung.

Die recht verstandene Glaubwürdigkeit der Christen besteht darin, dass ihre Lebensweise Nichtglaubende zu der Frage provoziert, woher sie

den Mut und die Kraft für ein Verhalten schöpfen, das angesichts des drohenden Nicht-mehr-Seins von der Angst geleiteten Sorge um das eigene Dasein bestimmt ist. Hans-Joachim Höhn schiebt hier den Vorhang beiseite und macht dadurch den Blick frei für alles, was wir mit dem Wort Hoffnung berühren und all der Angst, dass diese Hoffnung in ein Nichts zerfällt. Christliche Botschaft provoziert zur Nachdenklichkeit und lädt ein auf den langen Weg, den man nur zu zweit gehen kann.

Zukunft berühren

Nach der Zukunft des Glaubens zu fragen, heißt aber auch, nach dem Kern des Glaubens zu fragen.[5] Trauen wir denn der Wahrheit wirklich zu, dass sie den Menschen erreicht und trauen wir es uns zu, dass wir die Nähe zur Wahrheit tatsächlich suchen und ihren Anspruch nach Ausschließlichkeit ertragen können und damit auch in einer gewissen Vorbehaltlosigkeit die Tür des eigenen Lebens öffnen und so zur Einladung werden für andere? Das ist nicht wenig, das ist sehr viel. Weggemeinschaft, das bedeutet auch Lebensbeziehung, Begegnung wird zur Bewegung, Bewegungen berühren. Wir geraten in ein Feld hoher Nähe und Dichte unserer Lebensbeziehungen, aber eben auch mit dem auferstandenen Herrn selbst. Es gilt, sich vom Angstschatten nicht ergreifen zu lassen, zu kurz zu kommen oder zu nah zu sein, die Angst, sich zu verlieren oder einfach Verlierer zu sein.

Verkündigung, Seelsorge und pastorales Engagement werden unter dieser Perspektive von einem hohen Anspruch geleitet, der unverzichtbar ist, wenn wir vom Glauben sprechen und den Glauben weitergeben wollen.[6] Die ‚Bühnensprache der Zeit' zu lesen, das kulturelle Leben in seinen vielfältigen Formen wahr- und aufzunehmen, wird zu einer gleichgewichtigen Voraussetzung für die theologische Arbeit, das täglich ‚seelsorglich-pastorale Handeln', damit der Geschmack am Reich Gottes nicht verloren geht.

---

5 G. Lohfink, Gottes Volksbegehren. Biblische Herausforderungen. München, Zürich, Wien 1998, bringt in seinen biblischen Meditationen auf einfühlsame und konturierte Weise die Vielschichtigkeit der biblischen Gottesbilder zur Sprache und regt somit zu einem dem benannten Anspruch entsprechenden Handeln an.

6 M. Entrich, Ins Wort genommen. Ein Leitfaden für den Prediger. Graz-Wien-Köln 1997, 139–141.

Sichtbar/berührbar werden – das ist für nicht wenige eine wirklich vertrauensbildende Maßnahme. Was macht unser Pfarrer, wo ist er gerade, warum ist er nicht da, wenn ich ihn brauche? Solche und ähnliche Fragen werden oft genug in einem Pfarrbüro gestellt. Es hilft sicher, wenn in immer unüberschaubareren pastoralen Räumen nicht nur die Dienstzeit des Pfarrers angegeben ist, die Zeit, wann er zu sprechen ist, sondern darüber hinaus auch die Hinweise, welche Aufgabe er wo und wann zu bewältigen hat. Zu schnell schleicht sich eine Unsicherheit, manchmal sogar ein Verdacht bei den Gläubigen ein, dass der Pfarrer sich ihnen entzieht, obwohl er doch an anderem Ort im pastoralen Raum seinen Dienst versieht. Sich sichtbar und berührbar zu machen, hat viel mit der Spiritualität eines priesterlichen Lebens zu tun, weil damit den Menschen jene Nähe und Zuwendung angezeigt wird, die sie von der Kirche und damit auch von uns erwarten. Obwohl vielfach schon an einer guten Organisation der Pfarrbüros gearbeitet wird, kommt es eben noch allzu oft vor, dass bei einem Telefonanruf auf die Frage, ob der Pfarrer da sei, nur die lakonische Antwort erfolgt: Er ist weg. Diese Auskunft ist für unser pastorales Mühen eine wirkliche Wunde. Der Pfarrer ist nicht *real präsent*, sondern *real weg*. Das ist die Botschaft! Die pastorale Herausforderung, vor der wir stehen, ist die, einen deutlichen Eindruck davon zu vermitteln, dass die Priester und auch die Seelsorgeteams real *präsent* sind in ihrem pastoralen Raum. Man kann nachvollziehen, wo sie sich befinden, man sieht ihre Spuren und man versteht die Zeichen.

Eine Verkündigung also, die sich als einfache Botschaft versteht, ist nicht zu verwechseln mit den Trivialaussagen billig am Sinnmarkt zu erwerbender Sprüche. Einfachheit in der Verkündigung meint im Ergebnis jenes Bemühen der Verkündenden, sich durch das Dickicht der komplizierten und verwirrenden Lebensfragen hindurch zu kämpfen, um die Grundfragen des Lebens aufzuspüren. In einem Interview mit dem Direktor des McKinsey-Institutes Peter Barrenstein sagt dieser über die Chancen und Probleme bei der Übertragung von Unternehmensstrategien auf die Kirche: „Eine Werbekampagne steht immer erst am Ende einer erfolgreichen Unternehmensstrategie. Zuerst geht es darum, seine Kunden zu verstehen, die eigene Aufmarschstellung zu verbessern, die Zielsetzung zu überarbeiten, das Angebotskonzept weiter zu entwickeln. Erst dann kann ich werben.“[7] Barren-

7 Stärkere Orientierung am Kunden, Interview mit P. Barrenstein (McKinsey-Institut), in: Herder Korrespondenz 52 (1998), 342–347, 343.

stein betont in dem Interview, die Notwendigkeit, die eigene Ziel-Orientierung zu schärfen und so die Bedürfnisse der Kunden präziser in den Blick zu nehmen. Er betont, dass eine Werbung ohne diese Verbesserung der eigenen Angebotskonzepte nur dazu führt, dass diejenigen, die geworben werden konnten, sich dann doch nur enttäuscht wieder abwenden.

Spuren ertasten

In der Lebensspur Jesu die eigene Spur zu finden, ist die grundlegende Option aller pastoralen Arbeit und geht jeder durchaus nüchternen und kritischen Hinterfragung vielfältiger pastoraler Ansätze voraus. Oft können wir den schlichten Satz hören: Er versucht zu leben, was er sagt! Damit ist alles gesagt. Was immer sonst in schwierigen Situationen konfliktreich gelöst wird, das Grundvertrauen in den Lebensentwurf dessen, der für die anderen da sein soll, ist nicht gebrochen. Berührbarkeit verlangt zunächst Transparenz von denen, die zum seelsorglichen Dienst beauftragt sind.

Der Text „Zeit zur Aussaat – Missionarisch Kirche sein“[8] der Deutschen Bischofskonferenz fand eine erstaunlich offene Aufnahme in unserem Land. In angemessener Selbstbescheidenheit darf man wohl sagen, dass der Text eigentlich nichts Neues bietet. Alles, was dort an Hinweisen zur Zeitanalyse und zu möglichen Reaktionen auf die neuen Herausforderungen beschrieben ist, konnte man schon vorher anderenorts lesen. Die vielfältigen Rückmeldungen auf diesen Text und eine Reihe größerer Veranstaltungen, wie z. B. im Bereich der Citypastoral, haben gezeigt, dass es weniger die einzelnen Konkretionen sind, die haben aufhorchen und zum Nachdenken bzw. zum Handeln haben anleiten lassen, sondern dass es die „Botschaft in der Botschaft ist“, die etwas angesprochen hat, was an der „Zeit“ war. Der Text der Deutschen Bischofskonferenz ist eine Ermutigung, unter den konkreten Bedingungen unserer Gesellschaft und im Blick auf die organisatorischen Veränderungen in unserer Kirche einen neuen Aufbruch zu wagen, den der Text als „Zeit zur Aussaat“ formuliert.[9] Es geht nicht um eine neue Aktion neben anderen, die hier vorgeschlagen wird und keinesfalls sollen zusätzliche pastorale Pflichtübungen in den Katalog des pastoral zu Bearbeitenden aufgenommen werden. Wie die anschlie-

8 Die deutschen Bischöfe, Nr. 68.
9 Ebd.

ßende Arbeitshilfe zu „Zeit zur Aussaat“ ausweist, geht es darum, die vielfältigen Aktivitäten aus einer veränderten Perspektive wahrzunehmen und sie auf dem Hintergrund einer evangelisierenden Pastoral und missionarischen Seelsorge neu verstehen zu lernen bzw. ihnen auf diese Weise eine neue Zielführung zu geben.

Um Haltung geht es

In dem Buch „Gottes Wahl“, das in ausführlichen Interviews mit Kardinal Jean-Marie Lustiger dessen Leben und Werdegang sowie seine Perspektiven und Grundeinstellungen darlegt, wird Kardinal Lustiger vom Interviewer über die Situation der Studentenunruhen 1968 befragt. U. a. berichtet er davon, dass sie in der Studentengemeinde inmitten der revolutionären Bewegungen und des gesellschaftlichen Chaos sich darum bemühten „eine Art Anlaufstelle für die Jugendlichen zu sein“, mit denen sie Umgang hatten. „Wir haben weiterhin Gottesdienste abgehalten, immer wieder gebetet und auch den Studenten die Möglichkeit gegeben, zu beten und zu beichten. Im Gegensatz zu früher jedoch, wo die Liturgie gesungen wurde, herrschte nun während der Messen tiefes Schweigen. Diese Besinnung und Andacht war nötig, um die christlichen Grundwahrheiten des Evangeliums in Erinnerung zu rufen: Achtung vor dem Mitmenschen, Liebe zu dem Nächsten, Ablehnung von Gewalt als erlaubtem Mittel, es sei denn, man befindet sich in einer Notwehrsituation.“[10] In ungemein schwieriger Zeit prägte sich in der Studentengemeinde eine bemerkenswerte Haltung aus.

Inmitten der gesellschaftlichen Umbrüche der stunden- und tagelangen Diskussionen über die Zukunftsorientierung der Gesellschaft setzte das Studentenzentrum in einem Kernbereich auf Kontinuität. Kontinuität bedeutet in diesem Zusammenhang, sich auf das zurückzubesinnen, was Kern der eigentlichen Sendung ist, nämlich „die christlichen Grundwahrheiten des Evangeliums in Erinnerung zu rufen“.[11] Dies geschieht nicht durch Angleichung an die Diskussionen und Demonstrationen, sondern dadurch, dass man inmitten der Wortinflation in die Einfachheit des Schweigens zu-

10 Lustiger, Gottes Wahl. Jüdische Herkunft, Übertritt zum Katholizismus, Zukunft von Kirche und Gesellschaft. Gespräche mit Jean-Louis Misika und Dominique Woltern, Paris 1987, S. 254.
11 Ebd.

rückfindet. Genannt wurden Gebet und Beichte als zwei wesentliche Vollzüge, die das Besondere der christlichen Botschaft enthalten und ihre prophetische Kraft ermöglichen. Der Gottesdienst wird zu einem Raum des Schweigens, in dem das Wort des Evangeliums seine besondere Bedeutung bekommt. In einer Zeit der intensivsten Kommunikationsmöglichkeiten ist das Schweigen eine massive Provokation, die wir in das Stimmen-Wirrwarr klärend einbringen.

Der Rosenkranz: Ja oder Nein?

Paul M. Schäferskküpper OP

In seiner Enzyklika „Rosarium Virginis Mariae" aus dem Jahre 2002 stellt Papst Johannes Paul II. eine interessante These auf, die er mit einer Frage verbindet: „Die Geschichte des Rosenkranzes zeigt uns, wie gerade dieses Gebet in schwierigen Zeiten besonders von den Dominikanern benutzt wurde, um die Kirche vor den sich verbreitenden Häresien zu schützen. Heute stehen wir vor neuen Herausforderungen. Warum nehmen wir den Rosenkranz nicht mit dem Glauben unserer Vorfahren in die Hände?"[1]

Gesellschaftlich suchen die Menschen Westeuropas Orientierung für ihr Leben und laufen auf der Sehnsucht nach einem sinnerfüllten Leben vielen quasi religiösen Angeboten nach, ohne darauf zu achten, auf was sie sich einlassen. Gleichzeitig ist unserer Gesellschaft die Muße abhandengekommen. Die Menschen können sich nicht mehr die Zeit nehmen, um sich auf einen geistigen Prozess einzulassen. Auch das müssen sie wieder lernen. Kann der Rosenkranz das leisten?

Wer die Kirche vor Häresien schützen will, muss ihren Gläubigen das richtige Glaubenswissen, vor allem aber die Wahrheit vermitteln, und die ist für uns Jesus Christus. Neuevangelisierung ist das Gebot der Stunde; denn erst muss die Kirche ihren eigenen Gliedern das rechte Glaubenswissen vermitteln, ehe sie sich der Frage zuwenden kann, wie sie für Außenstehende attraktiv wird. Und auch hier stellt sich die Frage, ob der Rosenkranz das leisten kann.

Neu ist die These von Johannes Paul II. nicht. Zum Teil kann man sie in der Geisteshaltung des heiligen Albertus Magnus wiederfinden, von dem eine Aussage überliefert wird, die Eingang in das Offizium des Heiligen gefunden hat: „Mehr durch Gebet und Frömmigkeit als durch den Eifer des Studierens wird diese heilige Lehre erworben."[2] Es ist schon erstaunlich,

1 Johannes Paul II.: Rosarium virginis Mariae. Apostolisches Schreiben vom 16. Oktober 2002. Hg. von der Deutschen Bischofskonverenz. Verlautbarungen des Apostolischen Stuhls 156. Bonn 2002.

2 Proprium des Predigerordens. III: Feier des Stundengebetes. Proprium der Heiligen. Ausgabe in deutscher Sprache. Köln 1991, S. 734–756; Zitat S. 748.

dass ausgerechnet Albert, der wegen seiner universellen Bildung den Ehrentitel Magnus, der Große, erhalten hat, die Ansicht vertritt, dass Gebet und Frömmigkeit für den Erwerb des Glaubensgutes wichtiger seien als das Studium. Das hängt wohl damit zusammen, dass das Glaubensgut mehr als bloßes Wissen ist. Wenn es uns nicht dazu führt, Gott selbst anzunehmen, dann bleibt uns das Wesentliche des Glaubensgutes verborgen. Anders ausgedrückt: Wenn der Tod Jesu Christi uns nicht an seine Auferstehung glauben lässt, verfehlen wir das Ziel des Glaubens, unsere Erlösung.

Seit seiner Entstehung im 15. Jahrhundert hat sich der Rosenkranz zum erfolgreichsten Gebet der sogenannten Volksfrömmigkeit entwickelt. Bis heute wird er Tag für Tag auf unserem Provinzgebiet von abertausenden Menschen gebetet. Trotzdem oder gerade deshalb ist er nicht unumstritten. Für die meisten Päpste seit Leo XIII. waren das Rosenkranzgebet und seine Verbreitung ein wichtiges, persönliches Anliegen. Papst Franziskus reihte sich allerdings in die Schar der Gegner ein, als er sich öffentlich über eine Gruppe lustig machte, die für ihn den Rosenkranz betete, und diese Menschen „die, die die Gebete zählen"[3] nannte. Es setzt also auch innerhalb der Kirche einigen Mut voraus, den Rosenkranz zu beten und dazu zu stehen, dass man es tut.

Dabei sollte man eigentlich glauben, dass der Rosenkranz für Katholiken besonders wichtig ist, weil ihm mit dem 7. Oktober ein eigenes Fest gewidmet ist. Das soll uns daran erinnern, dass in der Seeschlacht von Lepanto an diesem Tag des Jahres 1571 die jahrhundertelange Auseinandersetzung zwischen dem Christentum und dem Islam durch den Sieg der hl. Liga ein vorläufiges Ende fand. Papst Pius V., so wird berichtet, hatte in einer Vision gesehen, dass die Gottesmutter den Christen zum Siege verholfen hat, und deshalb diesen Tag zu einem Marienfest gemacht, das dem Gedächtnis Unserer Lieben Frau vom Siege geweiht ist, und das kurz Rosenkranzfest genannt wird. In den Wirren der Reformation und am Beginn der Neuzeit hat Pius V. mit der Fokussierung auf die Mutter Gottes ein polarisierendes Zeichen gesetzt, das die Protestanten als Affront werteten und den Rosenkranz in ihren Augen zum „verbreitetsten katholischen meditativen Volksgebet"[4] werden ließ.

---

3 Zitiert nach einem offenen Brief von Lucrecia Rego de la Planas an Papst Franziskus geschrieben am 21.10.2013, in www.katholisches.info.

4 Siehe die Artikel zum Rosenkranz in: Die Religion in Geschichte und Gegenwart. Tübingen 1998ff. und Theologische Realenzyklopädie 1977ff.

Seither wird der Rosenkranz von vielen Katholiken als Siegeszeichen angesehen, das uns durch die Fürbitte Mariens geschenkt ist und mit dessen Hilfe wir in Gefahr geschützt sind, auf unserem Weg Orientierung finden und sogar die Schrecken des Todes überwinden. Die Logik dahinter ist, dass die Rosenkranzgeheimnisse auch vom Sieg Jesu Christi über den Tod erzählen. Wer diese Geheimnisse einmal begriffen hat, fragt mit dem hl. Paulus: „Tod, wo ist dein Sieg, Tod, wo ist dein Stachel?" (1 Kor 15,55). Er hat begriffen, dass es im Rosenkranzgebet nicht um Maria, die Mutter Jesu geht, sondern um das Erlösungswerk, den Kern des Auftrages, mit dem Jesus Christus in die Welt gekommen ist. Daran hat neben unserem Herrn Jesus Christus auch Maria, seine Mutter, einen entscheidenden Anteil. Überlegungen zum Rosenkranz haben deshalb auch die Beziehung zwischen diesen beiden Personen zu beachten.

Doch in seinem Entstehen ist der Rosenkranz als eine Devotion an die Gottesmutter Maria anzusehen, zum mindesten dann, wenn man die Entwicklung des marianischen Psalters als seine Wurzel ansieht. In ihm werden, der Anzahl der Psalmen entsprechend, 150 Ave Maria – der Legende nach – als geistiger Kranz von Rosen aufgeopfert, den ein Zisterzienser der Muttergottes darbrachte, weil er nicht dazu gekommen war, ihr aus echten Rosen einen Kranz zu binden. Daher auch der Name Rosenkranz. Ähnliches wird von Heinrich Seuse berichtet. Er pflegte als Andachtsübung die Bekrönung eines Marienbildwerkes mit einem Kranz aus echten Blumen. „Wenn der schöne Sommer kam und die zarten Blümlein zuerst entsprangen, so brach er die Blumen mit manchen minniglichen Gedanken und trug sie in die Zelle und machte einen Kranz daraus und ging hin in den Chor oder in unserer Frauen Kapelle und kniete demütiglich vor die liebe Frau und setzte ihrem Bilde den minniglichen Kranz auf."[5] In dieser Schilderung fällt die kindlich innige Selbstvergessenheit auf, die dieses liebevolle Handeln auszeichnet. Ich glaube, auch damals hat man Heinrich Seuse dafür belächelt, um es vorsichtig auszudrücken; aber im Prinzip geht es beim Rosenkranz durchaus um das Hineinwachsen in eine Haltung, die aus der Freude über das Erlöstsein „Verrücktes" für Gott tut und dasselbe von ihm auch erwartet.

Auf den marianischen Psalter aufbauend verband sich mit dem Mariengruß im 15. Jahrhundert – wohl ausgehend von den Kartäusern – eine systematische Betrachtung von Szenen aus dem Leben Jesu, wie sie in den

---

5 Keller, Nikolaus: Des Mystikers Heinrich Seuse O.Pr. deutsche Schriften. Regensburg 1926, S. 104.

Evangelien geschildert werden. Hier beginnt der Rosenkranz, wie wir ihn heute kennen. Dieser jesuanische Bezug ist von Anfang an vorhanden. Er wird aber mit der Zeit von der starken Betonung der Bedeutung Mariens in Zuge der Gegenreformation, durch die oben erwähnte Zuschreibung durch Papst Pius V. und den neuen Schub der Marienfrömmigkeit, die im ausgehenden neunzehnten Jahrhundert entstand und bis zum zweiten Vaticanum dauerte, überlagert. Damals entstand die Legio Mariae, die sich in ihrem Apostolat stark auf das Rosenkranzgebet der Mitglieder stützt, um selbst im Glauben gefestigt zu werden und aus der Betrachtung der Rosenkranzgeheimnisse Argumente für den Glauben zu finden.

Das Vertrauen der Menschen in die besondere Schutzkraft Mariens kommt u. a. in einem Lied zum Ausdruck, das in Mehrerau um 1916 entstand. Die letzte Strophe des Liedes lautet:

> „Siegesjubel folgt den Pfaden,
> Die der Rosenkranz betritt –
> Und der Feind kann nimmer schaden,
> Weichen muss er Schritt für Schritt.
> Im Triumph der Rosenkranz
> siegt beim grausen Waffentanz.“[6]

Die Sichtweise Papst Pius V. ist, wie man sieht, hier zur vollen Blüte herangereift. Dazu hat sicherlich beigetragen, dass Papst Leo XIII. um die Jahrhundertwende den Gläubigen das tägliche Rosenkranzgebet dringend empfohlen hat.

Auf die rettende Hand Mariens weist auch Bertignol in seinem Artikel über den Rosenkranz hin, der in demselben Heft erschienen ist. Er begründet das mit der engen Beziehung zwischen Maria und dem Beter; denn der Rosenkranz, so schreibt der Autor, „schlingt ein Band der innigsten Zusammengehörigkeit um Maria und jenen Christen, die der Rosenkranzbruderschaft angehören oder wenigstens den Rosenkranz bei sich tragen und ihn eifrig beten“[7]. Etwas salopp formuliert vertraut der Beter darauf, dass

---

6 Theiler, Plazidus 1916 Der Triumph des Rosenkranzes, in: Klotz, Leander M., 1216–1916 Zum Jubiläum des Prediger-Ordens, Graz 1916, S. 201–202; Zitat S. 202.

7 Bertignol, Benedikt 1916 Die Segnungen des Rosenkranzes, in: Klotz, Leander M., 1216–1916 Zum Jubiläum des Prediger-Ordens, Moser’s Buchhandlung Graz 1916, S. 211–212; Zitat S. 211.

er durch Marias Intervention von Gott alles erhält, was er will, entsprechend dem Schriftwort: „Wenn ihr in mir bleibt, (…) dann bittet, um was ihr wollt, ihr werdet es erhalten" (Joh 15,7). Die Mittlerschaft Mariens wird dadurch unterstrichen.

In den Unruhen des zweiten Weltkrieges schreibt Guardini seine Abhandlung über den Rosenkranz. „Darin geht es (…) um ein Verweilen vor Gott, (…) ein inneres Sich-finden und Ruhig-werden – jedoch so, dass das Wort gleichsam zum Strombett wird, in welchem das Gebet läuft, und zur Kraft, die es in Bewegung hält."[8] In der Unruhe der Kriegszeit öffnet der Rosenkranz dem Menschen einen Raum der Stille, so die These Guardinis, und er begründet auch, warum wir diesen Raum brauchen: „Wir bedürfen dieses Raumes; stets, besonders aber dann, wenn die Erschütterung der Zeiten etwas deutlich macht, (…) nämlich die Heimatlosigkeit des Daseins. Dann wird vom Menschen eine besondere Tapferkeit verlangt; nicht nur die Bereitschaft mehr zu entbehren und Größeres zu leisten als sonst, sondern in einer Ortlosigkeit auszuharren, die unter anderen Umständen nicht fühlbar wird."[9]

Aus der Haltung des Vertrauens in die Hilfe Mariens sind auch die Erscheinungen von Fatima zu sehen, in denen die Muttergottes zum täglichen Rosenkranzgebet aufruft, um verstockte Sünder und die Armen Seelen vor der Hölle zu bewahren. Eindringlich wirbt Maria auch darum, für die Bekehrung Russlands zu beten. Bei ihren Forderungen beruft sich Maria auf die Autorität ihres Sohnes Jesus Christus. In der zweiten Erscheinung von Fatima soll sie den Seherkindern gesagt haben: „Jesus will sich deiner bedienen, damit mich die Menschen kennen und lieben lernen."[10] Aus den Erscheinungen von Fatima hat sich unter dem Eindruck der Schrecken des zweiten Weltkrieges 1947 der so genannte Rosenkranzsühnekreuzzug entwickelt, der damit begründet wird, dass sie „die würdige Mutter Gottes", „die wahre und wirkliche Königin der Schöpfung" und „unsere wahre und wirkliche Mutter" ist. „Sie hat darum ein unvergleichlich höheres Recht auf Ehrfurcht, Liebe und Gehorsam, als jede irdische Mutter. In Wahrheit aber wird Maria von den allermeisten Menschen nicht gekannt, geehrt und geliebt."[11] Der Rosenkranzsühnekreuzzug, eine Devotion an das unbefleckte

8 Guardini, Romano: Der Rosenkranz unserer lieben Frau. Würzburg 1940, S. 14.
9 Ebd., S. 28.
10 Sühne-Rosenkranz zu Ehren des unbefleckten Herzens Mariä. Neumarkt 1947, S. 4.
11 Ebd., S. 1.

Herz Mariens, soll der Mutter Gottes dafür und für die Sünden der Welt Sühne leisten, und Gott durch Maria bitten, Russland zu bekehren und die Welt zu befrieden. Dabei wird die Kraft des Rosenkranzgebetes sehr hoch eingestuft. Menschen, die ihn beten, „werden von Gott bevorzugt, werden wie Blumen, die ich (Maria) vor seinen Thron bringe“[12].

Die Liste der Gruppen, die sich im Kampf mit dem Bösen der Hilfe Mariens versichern und sie quasi zum Garanten dafür machen, dass der Beter den Sieg davon trägt, ließe sich beliebig weit fortführen, und bis heute entstehen solche Gruppen immer wieder. Dagegen wendet sich das zweite vatikanische Konzil, das sich um eine positive, achtsame Einstellung der Welt, dem Mitmenschen und dem Fremden gegenüber bemüht. Devotionen an Maria, die den Beter in Auseinandersetzung mit der Welt und dem Bösen sehen, treten so in den Hintergrund der katholischen Frömmigkeitsformen. Der Rosenkranz, einst quasi als katholisches Fanal hochgehalten, wird im Zuge der Liturgiereform zurückgedrängt und der Tagzeitenliturgie nachgeordnet.

Auch die Gottesmutter Maria wird in ihrer Bedeutung für Glaube und Frömmigkeit auf Jesus Christus, den Sohn Gottes, hin- und ihm nachgeordnet. Dem entsprechend treten auch im Rosenkranz sein betrachtender Charakter und seine Christuszentrierung deutlicher hervor. Schon Guardini hatte darauf hingewiesen und eine theologische Deutung gegeben, die heute noch bestechend ist. Nachdem er festgestellt hat, dass „in dem Raum, den das heilige Wort (d. i. der Text des Rosenkranzgebetes) bildet, die Gestalt Marias als unmittelbarer Inhalt des Rosenkranzgebetes erscheint“[13], geht er der Frage nach, wer Maria eigentlich ist. Sie ist die Mutter Gottes, „jene, für welche Jesus Christus, Gottes Sohn und unser Erlöser, zum Inhalt ihres Frauenlebens wurde“. Über den Rosenkranz sagt Guardini dann: „Dieses Gebet bedeutet das Verweilen in der Lebenssphäre Mariens, deren Inhalt Christus war. So ist der Rosenkranz im Tiefsten ein Christusgebet.“[14]

Seine Geheimnisse werden bei der klassischen Form in drei Gruppen zu je 5 Geheimnissen aufgeteilt. Die ersten führen dem Beter die Erniedrigung des Gottessohnes in unsere Menschengestalt vor Augen. Sie haben ihren Namen, die freudenreichen Geheimnisse, davon, dass dieses Geschehen als Weg unserer Erlösung für uns Menschen eine froh machende Bot-

12 Ebd., S. 4.
13 Guardini, Der Rosenkranz, S. 21.
14 Ebd., S. 25.

schaft und voll Freude ist, weil Gottes unendliche Liebe zu uns Menschen darin zum Ausdruck. Der schmerzhafte Rosenkranz zeigt uns das Leiden des Menschensohnes, der den Weg der leidenden Kreatur geht und unser Schicksal bis in den Tod hinein teil. Dabei hat er nie die Hoffnung verloren, dass Gott ihn aus dem Tode errettet. Er hatte keine andere Hoffnung als Gott, aber diese Hoffnung hatte er ganz. Den glorreichen Rosenkranz bildet das Geheimnis unseres Glaubens, dass Jesus als erster der Entschlafenen von den Toten auferstanden ist und auch uns aus dem Tod heraus ins ewige Leben führt, wie er es mit Maria gemacht hat.

Die mystagogische Effektivität der 15 Geheimnisse benennt Papst Paul VI. in seiner Enzyklika sehr klar. „Es ist weiterhin bemerkt worden, dass die dreifache Aufteilung der Geheimnisse des Rosenkranzes nicht nur streng der zeitlichen Ordnung der Geschehnisse folgt, sondern vor allem das Schema der frühchristlichen Glaubensverkündigung und das Geheimnis Christi auf dieselbe Weise vorstellt, wie es vom heiligen Paulus im berühmten ‚Hymnus' des Briefes an die Philipper gesehen wird: Erniedrigung, Tod, Verherrlichung (Phil 2,6–11)."[15] Demnach eignet sich der Rosenkranz in seiner heutigen, klassischen Form sehr gut für die Verkündigung, weil er das Wesentliche des Evangeliums von Jesus Christus, unsere Erlösung, nicht nur klar, sondern auch sehr knapp darstellt.

„Um den christologischen Gehalt dieses Gebetes deutlicher zu machen, halte ich es für angebracht, eine angemessene Ergänzung vorzunehmen, die auch die *Geheimnisse des öffentlichen Lebens zwischen der Taufe und dem Leidensweg Christi* einbezieht, wobei ich es dem einzelnen und den Gemeinschaften überlasse, davon Gebrauch zu machen."[16] Ausgerechnet Papst Johannes Paul II., der als großer Marienverehrer gilt, beharrt ausdrücklich auf dem christologischen Gehalt des Rosenkranzes und erweitert ihn sogar um fünf Geheimnisse, in denen Szenen aus dem öffentlichen Wirken Jesu erinnert werden. Er nennt diese Gruppe die lichtreichen Geheimnisse, weil Jesus in ihnen als das Licht erscheint, das die Dunkelheit des Erdendaseins erleuchten soll. Im Kontext mit den schmerzhaften Geheimnissen lässt sich allerdings mit dem Johannesevangelium kommentieren: „Das Licht leuchtet in der Finsternis, und die Finsternis hat es nicht erfasst" (Joh 1,5).

---

15 Paul VI.: Marialis cultus. Die rechte Pflege und Entfaltung der Marienverehrung. 3. Teil: Hinweis auf zwei religiöse Üungen. Apostolisches Schreiben vom 2. Februar 1974. Wien 1974, S. 53.

16 Johannes Paul II.: Rosarium virginis Mariae, S. 21.

Der Erfolg des Rosenkranzes mag darauf zurückzuführen sein, dass er die enge Verbundenheit zwischen der Gottesmutter Maria und Jesus Christus, ihrem Sohn, so deutlich herausarbeitet und diese Spannung ganz bewusst aufrechterhält. Denn bei aller Christusbezogenheit darf nicht übersehen werden, dass im freudenreichen Rosenkranz und später bei der Verherrlichung Maria direkt angesprochen wird: „den Du … empfangen, zu Elisabeth getragen, geboren, im Tempel aufgeopfert und dort wiedergefunden hast.“ Später heißt es dann, „der dich in den Himmel aufgenommen und gekrönt hat“. Bewusst wird hier Maria als der Mensch angesprochen, der Heilsgeschichte ermöglicht und dem Heil widerfährt. Die mystagogische Botschaft dieser Geheimnisse ist klar: Du, Mensch, tue dein Möglichstes, um dem Herrn den Weg zu bereiten, und lass Gott das Gute, das er in Dir begonnen hat, zur Vollendung führen.

Mehr noch: Es ist die Verbindung der Betrachtung des Heilsgeschehens aus der Perspektive Mariens, die dem Rosenkranz bis heute seine Aktualität gibt. Er leitet uns dazu an, die Geheimnisse der Entäußerung des Wortes Gottes, seines Handelns und heilbringenden Leidens, sowie seiner und unserer Erhöhung mit den Augen der Mutter Gottes zu betrachten. Sie war vom Beginn bis zum Ende seines Lebens seine treueste Weggefährtin und hat schon jetzt den vollen Anteil an seiner Herrlichkeit. Papst Johannes Paul II. stimmt mit Trémeau[17] darin überein, dass jenseits der fünfzehn oder zwanzig Geheimnisse darin das Geheimnis Mariens und des Rosenkranzes selbst liegt.

Durch das Jawort Mariens ist uns der Weg zum Heil geöffnet worden. Den Rosenkranz zu beten, soll deshalb immer auch ein Ausdruck unserer besonderen Verehrung für Maria sein, wie das Symbol eines Kranzes aus echten Rosen ja auch besagen würde. Es nimmt dem Sohn Gottes nichts von seiner Größe, Einmaligkeit und Einzigartigkeit, wenn wir seine Mutter in besonderer Weise verehren und auf sie all die Ehrentitel anwenden, die er hat, und die sie auch haben kann. Ganz im Gegenteil, möchte man sagen. Es ist im Interesse Jesu, wenn seine Mutter vor allen anderen Menschen herausgestellt wird, denn sie ist ja keine Konkurrenz für ihn, sondern in ihr ehren wir ihn.

Am Beginn dieses Textes stehen zwei Fragen: Bringt der Rosenkranz, den Bedürfnissen unserer Zeit entsprechend, das Wesentliche unseres Glaubens knapp und klar zur Sprache, und vermittelt er Glaubenswissen, dass sich auch – sozusagen – für den internen Gebrauch eignet? Ich würde beide Fragen mit „Ja!“ beantworten. Aber urteilen Sie selbst.

17 Trémeau, Marc: Das Geheimnis des Rosenkranzes. Pottendorf 1982.

Was heißt und zu welchem Ende betreiben Dominikaner Hochschulseelsorge?

Martin Staszak OP

1. Kurzer historischer Abriss der Hochschul- und Studierendenseelsorge auf dem Gebiet der Ordensprovinz

Nimmt man an, dass, noch bevor es eine eigentliche Hochschulseelsorge gab, Theologieprofessoren an ihrem akademischen Wirkungsort pastorale Aufgaben gleichsam „nebenbei" wahrnahmen, dann hat diese Studentenseelsorge an der theologischen Fakultät der Freiburger Universität, die hier als Beispiel genannt sei, schon in deren frühen Geschichte auch durch Predigerbrüder stattgefunden. Neben Vertretern der Mendikantenorden der Franziskaner und Augustiner-Eremiten lehrten zwischen 1480 und 1536 insgesamt acht Dominikaner als Theologieprofessoren in Freiburg, am weitesten gereist war Johannes von Mera, der dem Nijmegener Konvent angehörte.[1]

1620 setzte Erzherzog Leopold von Österreich allerdings die Einführung der Jesuiten an der Freiburger Albertina durch. Die Societas Jesu bekam die Theologische und die Artistenfakultät übertragen, nur zwei Theologieprofessuren blieben dem Diözesanklerus vorbehalten.[2] Doch wurden 1773 die Jesuiten im Breisgau aufgehoben, am 9. Oktober dieses Jahres erging die Anordnung, dass die theologischen Lehrstühle, wenn von Religiosen, dann nur noch von Dominikanern, Augustinern und Franziskanern besetzt werden sollten, doch konnten die Dominikaner – entgegen ihren Hoffnungen – kaum noch neue Professoren stellen.[3]

1 Bauer, Johannes Joseph SCJ, Zur Frühgeschichte der theologischen Fakultät der Universität Freiburg i.Br. (1460–1620), Freiburg 1957, 181–185. Ab 1540 änderte sich die Situation: Ambrosius Pelargus OP erhielt eine Absage, u. a. deshalb, weil sich die Fakulät nicht auf einen Religiosen verlassen wollte, der zu leicht von seinem Oberen versetzt werden konnte (ebd., 84).

2 Haumann, Heiko und Schadek, Hans (Hg.), Geschichte der Stadt Freiburg im Breisgau, Band 2: Vom Bauernkrieg bis zum Ende der habsburgischen Herrschaft, Stuttgart ^{2}2001, 501.

3 Ebd., 442.

Wenn wir nun einen größeren zeitlichen Sprung machen und auf die Zwischenkriegszeit schauen, treffen wir auf dem Provinzgebiet auf Dominikaner, die die Seelsorge in Studentenverbindungen wahrnahmen. Hier sind zu nennen:[4]

Ambrosius Blattmann, der 1921 in Aussig Präses der Sektion „Militiae Angelicae“ war.

Ludwig Bertrand Broglie wirkte 1927–1933 in Wien als Präses der Studenten-Kongregation „Reginæ sacratissimi Rosarii“ und Jordan Ganshorn in Retz 1927–1933 als ordentlicher Beichtvater der Studenten im Seminar Oberhollabrunn

Während des Zweiten Weltkriegs und danach wirkte Lucius Simeon von 1939 bis mindestens 1952 im schweizerischen Fribourg als Universitätsseelsorger der deutschsprachigen Studenten. Es ist möglich, dass er das noch länger war, doch sind Angaben dazu für die süddeutsch-österreichische Provinz nicht mehr zugänglich, da Simeon als Schweizer 1953 in die neu gegründete Schweizer Provinz des Ordens übertrat.

Zu einer eigentlichen dominikanischen Hochschulseelsorge in der 1939 gegründeten süddeutsch-österreichischen Provinz des Predigerordens kam es dann durch Ambrosius Karl Ruf, der 1983 den Orden verließ. Er war 1959–1967 als Kurat bzw. Pfarrer der Studierenden in Freiburg tätig, von 1960–1965 auch Bundesseelsorger der Hochschulgemeinschaft der Pfadfinderschaft D.P.S.G. Er war zudem seit 1962 Gründungsdirektor des Studentenwohnheims „Thomas-Morus-Burse“ in Freiburg-Littenweiler, das in Trägerschaft der Erzdiözese ist, in dem er auch 1964–1967 wohnte. Er prägte dabei die Statuten dieses Wohnheims mit, die z. B. einen Anteil von 20 % ausländischer Studierender vorsehen.

Ihm folgte Anselm Henssler, der 1967–1971 in Freiburg Studentenpfarrer an der pädagogischen Hochschule war und in dem anderen großen Studentenwohnheim der Diözese wohnte, dem Alban-Stolz-Haus. A. Henssler könnte dieses Amt länger gehabt haben, doch gibt es bei den Provinzkatalogen eine Lücke von mehreren Jahren; 1977 ist er jedenfalls nicht mehr Studentenseelsorger.

In Augsburg wirkten Dominikaner teilweise wiederum als Kuraten von Studentenverbindungen, so Eckehart Mayer in den Jahren 1962 und 1963, von 1965 bis 1971 Sturmius (Christoph) Nowowiejski.

4 Für die folgenden umfangreichen Angaben danke ich P. Dr. Wolfram Hoyer OP (Augsburg), der sie aus den Katalogen (Personalverzeichnissen) der Provinz erhoben hat.

An der katholischen Hochschulgemeinde arbeiteten Paul Dominikus Hellmeier (2005–2008) und Sebastian Tönnesen (2009–2011).

In München war die Wirksamkeit von dominikanischer Seite nie stark ausgeprägt, da die Hochschulseelsorge dort traditionell von den Jesuiten versehen wird. Zu nennen ist jedoch Stephan Unger, der 1963–1964 Kaplan des Studentinnenheims „Unserer Lieben Frau am Anger" und 1965–1966 Hilfskaplan der Studenten der Universität München war.

Vor ihm war Franz Martin Schmölz in den Jahren 1960/61 Kaplan katholischer Studentenverbindungen.

Anders verhält es sich mit den österreichischen Konventen. Hier konnte eine über längere Jahre andauernde, vielfältige Tätigkeit im Bereich der Hochschulen entwickelt werden. So gab es in Graz von 1965 bis 1991 eine Wirksamkeit von Dominikanern in den Bereichen der Betreuung von Studentenverbindungen (durch Jordan Gebhard von 1965–1982, der auch als Seelsorger der Studierenden der Grazer Universität arbeitete) und der Hochschulseelsorge durch Wolfgang Keil (1967 bis mindestens 1969), Christoph von Schönborn (1973–1974), Manfred Kellner (1976–1980), Hilarius Barth (1984–1987) und Dominikus Jakob (1988–1991).

In Wien war von 1969–1980 Fulko Hilgefort Kurat der Universitätsstudiernden, mit ihm arbeitete Helmut Oberguggenberger bis 1971 zusammen. Von 1994–1997 war Rupert Johannes Mayer Studentenseelsorger an der Wiener Universität, während Max Svoboda zehn Jahre lang (1991–2001) Verbindungsseelsorger war (KÖHV Nordgau).

Seit 1987 haben Dominikaner den Posten des Kirchenrektors der Kirche St. Ursula in Wien inne. Es handelt sich dabei um die Kirche des Instituts für kirchenmusikalische Werkpraxis der seinerzeitigen Wiener Hochschule (jetzt Universität) für Musik und Darstellende Kunst. Mit diesem Posten war immer die Seelsorge der Studierenden dieses Instituts und dieser Hochschule verbunden. Tätig waren dort 1987–1989 Hilarius Barth, 1989–1997 Innozenz Varga, 1997–2000 Wolfram Hoyer, 2000–2012 Rupert Johannes Mayer, seit 2012 Jörg Wegscheider, der neben dem Kirchenrektorat jetzt auch ein reguläres Deputat als Studentenseelsorger erhalten hat.

Außerhalb der Konvente der Provinz arbeitete von 1969 bis mindestens 1973 Chrysostomus Reif als Hochschulseelsorger an der Universität in Heidelberg (er gehörte zum Wiener Konvent und wurde 1981 in die Erzdiözese Freiburg inkardiniert).

In Regensburg war Mirko Šarič in der Zeit von 1981–1982 Seelsorger der Studentenkongregation.

Dieser Durchgang durch die verschiedenen Facetten der Seelsorge mit Studierenden durch Dominikaner der süddeutsch-österreichischen Ordensprovinz kann also eine beachtliche Tätigkeit auf diesem Gebiet aufzeigen. Er belegt, dass die Mitbrüder sich ihrer Sendung zu den Hochschulangehörigen bewusst waren und sind. Diese Sendung wird von ihnen und dem Orden als Teil der dominikanischen Pastoral ebenso wie als Teil des dominikanischen Programms verstanden, Glauben und Wissen in einer jeden Epoche miteinander zu verbinden.

Wenn wir zum geografischen Ausgangspunkt dieses kurzen historischen Abrisses zurückkehren, kommt nochmals Freiburg im Breisgau in den Blick, wo es ab 2003 wieder zu einer verstärkten Präsenz im Bereich der Hochschulseelsorge (die als Pastoral an einer offiziell errichteten Hochschulgemeinde eine diözesane Beauftragung darstellt) kam. Mit dem 1. Dezember nahm ich selber meine Tätigkeit als priesterlicher Mitarbeiter in der Seelsorge an der Katholischen Hochschule, der Pädagogischen Hochschule und in den großen katholischen Wohnheimen in Freiburg auf. Seit dem Wintersemester 2010/11 bin ich nun Hochschulpfarrer der Katholischen Hochschulgemeinde Edith Stein, die für die Universität und die Musikhochschule zuständig ist. An meinem früheren Arbeitsplatz war 2010–2011 Johannes Weise und ist jetzt Sebastian Tönnesen tätig, der zuvor (2009–2011) an der Augsburger Hochschulgemeinde gearbeitet hatte. Davor noch hatte er ab dem Wintersemester 2007/08 zusammen mit Johannes Weise die Hochschulgemeinde an den Standorten Offenburg und Kehl gegründet, mithin Pionierarbeit geleistet, die sich an der technisch orientierten Offenburger Hochschule, die eine kirchliche Präsenz bis dahin nicht gewohnt war, nicht einfach gestaltete. Ein davon verschiedenes pastorales Feld war die Verwaltungshochschule in Kehl, in der die Arbeit der Mitbrüder vom Interesse und Einsatz einer Professorin profitieren konnte, die ehrenamtlich in der Diözese engagiert ist. Die Hochschulgemeinde Offenburg-Kehl wird mittlerweile von einem Seelsorger der Erzdiözese Freiburg geleitet.

Zum gegenwärtigen Zeitpunkt betreuen mithin Mitbrüder auf dem Provinzgebiet insgesamt vier Hochschulgemeinden an den Standorten Freiburg und Wien. Es zeichnet somit gegenwärtig den Freiburger, und in etwas schwächerem Maß den Wiener Konvent aus, dass die beiden Tätigkeitsfelder der Innenstadt- und Hochschulpastoral Schwerpunkte ihrer Arbeit und Ausstrahlung sind (an beiden Standorten gibt es eine Innenstadt- und Pfarrkirche, die gleichzeitig die Konventskirche ist). Diese Schwer-

punktsetzung wurde auf dem Provinzkapitel 2006 als pastorales Profil der Provinz beschlossen.

2. Dominikanische Hochschulseelsorge im heutigen Wissenschaftsbetrieb

Hier entsteht nun die Notwendigkeit, sich kurz darüber Rechenschaft abzugeben, warum Hochschulpastoral ein dominikanisches Aufgabenfeld ist und was der Predigerorden damit eigentlich bezweckt, zu welchem Ende er sie also betreibt. Diese Reflexion findet auf dem Hintergrund der heutigen Bedingungen und Anforderungen statt, die sich von denen früherer Epochen deutlich unterscheiden. Das Verhältnis von Kirche und Hochschule und auch das von Glauben und Wissen ist ja nicht unabhängig von dem Stellenwert, den Religion im Allgemeinen, das Christentum im Besonderen und mit ihm die Kirchen als Institutionen in der Gesellschaft einnehmen. Die Wandlungsprozesse auf diesem Gebiet sind evident; somit sind auch die folgenden Überlegungen letztlich nur eine Momentaufnahme und unterliegen der Notwendigkeit zur Revision.

Warum also sind Predigerbrüder an den Hochschulen und in deren Seelsorge zu finden? Es ließe sich jetzt schnell antworten, und es wird auch geantwortet, dass auch die Hochschule die Gottesfrage als umfassenden Sinnhorizont ihres Arbeitens brauche, um in den Verästelungen des Alltagsbetriebs und der fortschreitenden Ausdifferenzierung der Wissenschaften das Eigentliche nicht aus dem Blick zu verlieren, als Beispiel seien nur die inzwischen modularisierten Studiengänge genannt. Ja, doch könnte der Studienbetrieb an jeder Hochschule letztlich ohne diesen Gesamthorizont funktionieren, Bestrebungen dazu sind inzwischen keine Einzelfälle mehr; der Hochschulbetrieb ist heute ein Unternehmen, das Selbstläufer zu sein vermag. Wenn also die Gottesfrage, wenn das Evangelium an einer Hochschule eingebracht wird, dann – vom akademischen Betrieb her gesehen – als etwas Dazukommendes, das heute erst einmal nicht im System Hochschule als solchem angelegt ist und sich aus ihm wie von selber entwickeln würde, mithin der Begründung bedarf – der Glaube ist heute in der Tat eine Option.[5] Denn Effizienz steigernd ist eine Hochschulgemeinde

5 Joas, Hans, Glaube als Option. Zukunftsmöglichkeiten des Christentums, Freiburg, Basel, Wien 2012.

nicht, das kostbare Gut Zeit mehrt sie auch nicht, eher im Gegenteil. Es lässt sich feststellen, dass es zwar den Hochschulgemeinden und ihren Seelsorgern und Seelsorgerinnen nicht an Verständnis für ihre Hochschulen und deren Sachzwänge mangelt, wohl aber, dass umgekehrt die Hochschulgemeinden immer wieder einseitig nutzenorientiert eingeschätzt werden. Nicht selten nämlich sind sie in der Wahrnehmung einer Hochschulleitung lediglich das Auffangbecken für diejenigen Studierenden, die sich schwer tun und erfolglos bleiben, im Studium wie auch in ihrer menschlichen Entwicklung. Zwar sind Hochschulgemeinden wie alle Seelsorgestellen gerade auch für solche Menschen da, die Randständigen sollen und dürfen niemals aus dem Blick geraten – bei aller Effizienz und hochkarätigen Leistung, doch erschöpft sich der hochschulpastorale Anspruch nicht in dieser akademischen *Diakonia* und empfängt nicht allein aus dieser seine Existenzberechtigung.

Die Hochschulgemeinden führen als kirchliche Institution vor Ort den Dialog mit den verschiedenen Wissenschaften. Sie tun dies nicht einfach aus intellektueller Neugier heraus, sondern weil sie sich unter den heutigen Bedingungen nur so verorten können. Wenn sie denn von Gott und seiner Selbstmitteilung an die Menschen sprechen, wenn sie diese ihren Adressaten verkünden wollen, müssen sie wissen, wovon eben diese Adressaten sonst sprechen, wie sie denken, wie ihr Weltverständnis und ihre Weltgestaltung heute aussehen. Es gehört zu meinen festen Gewohnheiten, mindestens einmal im Semester an die technische Fakultät der Freiburger Universität zu fahren (auf dem Gelände eines außerhalb der Stadt liegenden ehemaligen französischen Militärflughafens), mich dort mit Studenten zu treffen und mir ihren Arbeitsplatz, ihr Labor oder ihre neueste Softwareentwicklung zeigen zu lassen. Nebenbei verfolge ich die Entwicklung der Neubauten dieses Areals, das wie kein anderes der Universität expandiert. Dabei zeigt sich ein Weiteres: Verkündigung findet heute nicht mehr als Einbahnstraße statt, auch der Prediger kann an solchen Orten staunen und lernen, seine Predigt aus dem Theologenjargon befreien und sie weiten. Die Umsetzung findet während der Semester durch entsprechende Vortrags- und Dialogveranstaltungen der Hochschulgemeinden z. B. zu den Themenkomplexen „Kirche und Humanwissenschaften“ oder „Glaube und Naturwissenschaft“ statt, Letzteres für mich vorzugsweise in den Räumen der Naturwissenschaften, nicht der Hochschulgemeinde. Blickt man auf die äußerst universitätsfreundliche Stimmung in der Frühzeit unseres Ordens, wird deutlich, dass dieser

Wissenschaftsdialog ein genuin dominikanisches Tätigkeitsfeld sein kann. Nur auf dem Weg dieser Verortung und des Dialogs, der gegenseitigen Lernbereitschaft und der intellektuellen „Demut" des Theologen kann die Gottesfrage tatsächlich in den universitären Wissensbetrieb eingebracht und dort vermittelt werden, ohne als „Fremdkörper" marginalisiert oder gar abgestoßen zu werden. Unschwer lassen sich hier die Veränderungen und heute höheren Anforderungen ablesen, die sich im Lauf von nur wenigen Jahrzehnten ergeben haben.

Neben diesen nur beispielhaft vorgestellten Dialog zwischen christlicher Gemeinde und Universität tritt das, was die deutschen Bischöfe letzthin die „Mitverantwortung für einen universitären Wertekanon" nannten.[6] Gemeint ist damit, dass „die Kirche offensiv zur akademischen Gewissensbildung beitragen" muss, damit die Ziele, die sich aus der europäischen Universitätsgeschichte stellen, erhalten bleiben: „Humanität, geistige Avantgarde und Knotenpunkt des Netzwerks der Intellektualität im Interesse des Gemeinwohls". Es geht den Bischöfen ebenso wie jeder Hochschulgemeinde, die sich ihrer Sendung bewusst ist, um die ethische Vertretbarkeit der Forschung und des Handelns. Diese von den „Leitungen, Lehrkörpern und hochschulpolitischen Akteuren … immer wieder … einzufordern", wie es die Bischöfe den Hochschulgemeinden zur Aufgabe machen, bedarf einer umfassenden Kenntnis des akademischen Betriebs, seiner Möglichkeiten und Grenzen, um qualifiziert mitreden zu können. Es ist leicht zu erkennen, dass es sich hier um ein von der oben beschriebenen *Diakonia* unterschiedenes Feld handelt, andererseits in eben diesem Bemühen um „Weltkenntnis" wiederum ein gut dominikanisches Moment der Reflexion und Wirksamkeit steckt. Die kirchliche und gesellschaftliche Relevanz einer solchen Hochschulseelsorge liegt in unserer Bildungsgesellschaft auf der Hand. Hinzu kommt ebenfalls, dass die zunehmende Spezialisierung der Wissenschaften dazu führt, dass der einzelne Wissenschaftler das Ganze mitsamt den Folgen seines Tuns fast zwangsläufig aus den Augen verlieren muss. Eben dieses Ganze und eine Ethik der Folgen sind auch Thema der Kirche und ihrer Hochschulpastoral.

6 Die deutschen Bischöfe, Kommission für Wissenschaft und Kultur (Nr. 36), Hochschulpastoral als Dienst der Kirche im öffentlichen Leben Deutschlands, Status quo und Zukunftsperspektiven, Bonn 2013, 16. Die weiteren Zitate dieses Abschnitts ebd.

3. Lebendiges Geben und Nehmen

Will man die verschiedenen Aspekte der Hochschulseelsorge auf einen Begriff bringen, dann ließe sie sich am besten als Begleitpastoral charakterisieren. Sie begleitet sowohl den Wissenschaftsbetrieb unserer Hochschulen, um dort die ihr eigene Gottes- und Menschenfrage einzubringen; sie begleitet aber auch die einzelnen Menschen, die als Hochschulangehörige mit ihr im Kontakt sind. Für die Studierenden ist die Zeit des Studiums ein prägender Abschnitt ihres Lebens, verbunden mit der „Ablösung von der Familie, Schritt in die Eigenständigkeit, Partnersuche, erste Schritte ins Berufsleben".[7] Gelingt es, in dieser wichtigen Lebensphase den christlichen Glauben und die christliche Praxis als Orientierung des Lebens lebendig zu halten bzw. dem studentischen Lebensabschnitt gemäß weiter zu entwickeln oder gar zuerst zu entdecken, hat dies weit reichende Auswirkungen auf die Lebensgestaltung der betreffenden Menschen. Und auch auf die Zukunft der Kirche; denn in den Hochschulgemeinden werden auch Modelle für ein zukunftsfähiges Gemeindeleben entworfen und ausprobiert, die von einer weit reichenden Mitbestimmung der Gemeindemitglieder bei Entscheidungsfindungen bis zur lebens- und gemeindenahen Liturgiegestaltung reichen. Vieles, was in den Pfarrgemeinden heute selbstverständlich ist, wurde in den Hochschulgemeinden gleichsam vorentworfen.

Neben dem Rückkoppelungseffekt für die Kirche als ganze gibt es auch einen für die in der Hochschulpastoral tätigen Dominikaner und ihre Konvente. Nicht nur, dass die Arbeit mit den jungen Menschen an die Gegenwartsfragen der ganzen Gesellschaft heranführt, nicht nur, dass „das passagere Moment von Hochschulpastoral als ‚Gemeinde auf Zeit'"[8] dabei ein hohes Maß an Flexibilität erfordert, die auch auf die Konvente ausstrahlen kann. Der konventuale Austausch über die verschiedenen Wirkungsfelder wird, wenn sich eine ernsthaft betriebene Hochschulseelsorge darunter findet, dem Axiom einer Zusammenschau (nicht Identifizierung) von Kirche und Gesellschaft, Glaube und Wissen gerecht werden können. Dominikanische Pastoral und Verkündigung kann durch die Hochschulpastoral Impulse für eine zukunftsfähige und adressatenorientierte Verkündigung erhalten, die sich im 21. Jahrhundert insofern als nochmals schwieriger erweist, als die Predigt des Evangeliums nicht mehr einfachhin

7 Kirche im Leben der Hochschule, Leitbild der Erzdiözese Freiburg, 2007, 9.

8 Die deutschen Bischöfe, Hochschulpastoral als Dienst der Kirche, 15.

abgelehnt wird, sondern selber zuerst Vorbedingungen schaffen muss, um überhaupt verstanden zu werden. Nebenbei sei noch angemerkt, dass Hochschulpastoral, die als Vollzeitaufgabe an einem großen Universitätsstandort betrieben wird, nur noch in Vernetzung der Hochschulseelsorger untereinander bewältigt werden kann, wenn sie die nötigen Qualitätsstandards erfüllen soll. Will sie sich in der heutigen akademischen Landschaft zurechtfinden und dort den ihr eigenen Auftrag erfüllen, ist sie auf Informationen, Fortbildungen und den kollegialen Austausch angewiesen, die sich ein einzelner Seelsorger heute nicht mehr selber beschaffen kann.

„Was heißt und zu welchem Ende?" Der Titel dieses Beitrags ist der Jenaer Antrittsvorlesung des Professors Friedrich Schiller entlehnt, die er im Revolutionsjahr 1789 in Bezug auf das Studium der Universalgeschichte hielt.[9] Er verstand Geschichte als Fortschrittsgeschichte, die sich auch gegen den negativen Willen des Menschen als Fortschritt durchsetzt, und meinte: „daß der selbstsüchtige Mensch niedrige Zwecke zwar verfolgen kann, aber unbewußt vortrefliche (sic!) befördert."[10] Man kann daran zweifeln, ob der Poet der Freiheit das 150 Jahre später, also 1939, auch noch so gesehen hätte. Solche optimistischen Universalkonzepte sind nicht mehr möglich, und auch unsere heutigen Ideen und Überzeugungen haben sich der Tatsache ihrer Geschichtlichkeit zu stellen. Deshalb sollten sie kirchlicherseits auch nicht wiederholt werden. Wenn eine Hochschulgemeinde die Gottesfrage als Horizont des Lebens und Arbeitens im akademischen Umfeld offenhalten will, dann versteht sie sich selber eben auch immer als eine Suchende, die in ihrer historischen Bedingtheit – ebenso wie der Wissenschaftsbetrieb – eine Suchende und gerade deshalb irrtumsanfällig ist, dennoch aber einen unverzichtbaren Beitrag leisten kann und will. In dieser Bescheidenheit, aber in ihr unabdingbar wollen Hochschulgemeinden ihren Teil dazu beitragen, dass die Hochschulen ihrer eigenen Sendung treu bleiben. Als Teil der Kirche schöpfen sie dabei aus der Selbstmitteilung Gottes an uns Menschen und aus einer langen und wechselhaften Tradition, um jedoch gerade im Bewusstsein des Reichtums und der Relativität ihrer Geschichtlichkeit nach vorn zu denken und die Zukunft der Hochschullandschaft mit zu gestalten. Noch einmal Schiller:

---

9 „Was heißt und zu welchem Ende studiert man Universalgeschichte? Eine akademische Antrittsrede", in: Schillers Werke, Nationalausgabe, Bd. 17, Historische Schriften, erster Teil, herausgegeben von Karl-Heinz Hahn, Weimar 1970, 359–376.

10 Ebd., 375.

„Sie (die Geschichte, M.St.) heilt uns von der übertriebenen Bewunderung des Alterthums, und von der kindischen Sehnsucht nach vergangenen Zeiten; ...“[11] Eine jede Gesellschaft und mit ihr die Hochschulen müssen die Gefahr der Nostalgie wie auch die des Traditionsverlusts im Auge behalten; denn beide haben nur zu schnell auch einen Verlust an Ethik im Schlepptau. Im Interesse ihrer eigenen Sendung wird aber auch die Kirche und wird der Predigerorden (wie alle, die an der kirchlichen Sendung teilhaben) dieser Gefahr konsequent ausweichen, wenn denn ihre Verkündigung und Seelsorge sprachfähig sein und die jeweilige Gegenwart auf Zukunft hin gestalten wollen.

11 Ebd.

SCHWESTERN, NONNEN UND LAIENGEMEINSCHAFTEN

„In deinem Licht schauen wir das Licht!" (Ps 36,10)

Von der kontemplativen Dimension des Lebens, vom Weg zum Glück und von der Vollendung der Kontemplation im ewigen Leben

Dominika Geyder OP

Der Predigerorden wurde „uneingeschränkt einzig zur Verkündigung des Wortes Gottes bestellt".[1] Dass er mit dieser Zielsetzung auch 800 Jahre nach seiner Bestätigung im Jahre 1216 durch Papst Honorius III. nach wie vor nicht nur zeitgemäß ist, sondern sich ungebrochener Aktualität erfreut, zeigt die Tatsache, dass die Ordentliche Vollversammlung der Bischofssynode im Oktober 2012 dem Thema „Die neue Evangelisierung für die Weitergabe des christlichen Glaubens" gewidmet war. Die Evangelisierung, die Verkündigung, auf die das dominikanische Leben ausgerichtet ist, soll „aus der Fülle der Kontemplation"[2] entspringen. Das bekräftigte der Ordensmeister, P. Bruno Cadoré, in seiner Wortmeldung am 15. Oktober 2012 während der genannten Bischofssynode, als er sagte, der Einsatz für die Evangelisierung gründe in der Kontemplation, in der daraus geschöpften Freude und Kraft.[3] Weitere Bestätigung für die Überzeugung, dass die Vitalität des Ordens in der Kontemplation seiner Mitglieder gründet, ist die Tatsache, dass im Rahmen der Jahresnovene zur Vorbereitung auf das 800-jährige Gründungsjubiläum für das Jahr 2013 folgendes Thema gewählt wurde: *„Mir geschehe, wie du gesagt hast"* (Lk 1,38): Maria: Kontemplation und Verkündigung des Wortes. Dieses Motiv stellte der Ordensmeister in den Mittelpunkt seines Briefes, den er im Februar dieses Jahres an den Orden gerichtet hat.

---

1 Liber Constitutionum et Ordinationum Fratrum Ordinis Praedicatorum (im Folgenden abgekürzt mit LCO) 1 § III zitiert: Honorius III, S. Dominico, die 18.1.1221.

2 LCO 1 § IV.

3 http://www.vatican.va/news_services/press/sinodo/documents/bollettino_25_xiii-ordinaria-2012/03_francese/b17_03.html (gelesen am 22.01.2013).

Kontemplation – Ursprung und Quelle dominikanischen Lebens

Das Generalkapitel von Providence 2001, zu dessen Anliegen die Rückbesinnung auf die kontemplative Tradition des Ordens gehörte, um dadurch den Boden zu bereiten für die Wiedergewinnung der kontemplativen Dimension des dominikanischen Lebens, beschreibt Kontemplation mit Blick auf die dominikanische Tradition als dynamische Haltung der Offenheit für Gottes kreative und erlösende Gegenwart im gegenwärtigen Augenblick, die unser ganzes Leben durchdringen soll.[4]

Was damit gemeint ist, zeigt uns der Blick auf Dominikus, dessen Leben und Wirken ganz in der Kontemplation verwurzelt war. Die achte ihm zugeschriebene Gebetsweise beschreibt, wie er sich zurückzieht, um in Stille und Einsamkeit in der Heiligen Schrift zu lesen, wie er sich in die Gegenwart Christi begibt und mit ihm Zwiesprache hält. Es entwickelt sich eine persönliche Freundschaftsbeziehung mit dem Herrn, der seinen Freunden mitteilt, was er, der am Herzen des Vaters ruht, von ihm empfangen hat (vgl. Joh 1,18):

> „(…) Et sedebat quietus (…) et legebat et afficiebatur mente dulciter ac si audiret dominum loquentum, sicut dicitur in psalmo: ‚Audia quit loquitur in me dominus deus‘ (…) Et quasi cum socio disputabat uocibus et mente (…)“[5]

Ein ganz wesentliches Element der Freundschaft besteht im vertrauten Umgang mit dem Freunde, der vertraute Umgang des Menschen mit Gott erfolgt in der Kontemplation, dazu befähigt ihn der Heilige Geist. Durch ihn erlangt er Anteil an der Weisheit Gottes *im Glauben*. Darin werden die Erkenntnis und Glückseligkeit vorweggenommen, die in der ewigen Heimat in vollkommener Weise *im Schauen* erlangt werden (vgl. Joh 17,3). Darauf wird noch näher einzugehen sein.

---

4 Vgl. Acta capituli generalis electivi ordinis Praedicatorum Provicentiae … celebrati. Romae 2001, 207.

5 Zitiert nach der Transkription der Handschrift im Codex Rossianus 3 von Leonard Boyle in: Cod. Ross. 3 (1) Modi orandi Sancti Dominici. Die Gebets- und Andachtsgesten des heiligen Dominikus. Eine Bilderhandschrift. Kommentarband zur Faksimile-Ausgabe, Zürich 1995, S. 61. Vladimir Koudelka, Dominikus – Gotteserfahrung und Weg in die Welt, Olten 1983, S. 123f. bietet folgende Übersetzung: „(…) Da saß er dann ruhig (…) so las er und ließ sein Gemüt vom Gelesenen sanft bewegen, als könnte er den Herrn selber zu sich reden hören. Wie es im Psalm heißt: „Lauschen will ich auf das, was der Herr, mein Gott in mir spricht …“ (Ps 84, 9). Es war, als würde er mit einem Gefährten ein bewegtes Gespräch führen (…)“.

In der neunten Gebetsweise wird beschrieben, wie die Kontemplation bei Dominikus zum Habitus geworden ist, so dass auch unterwegs die Verbundenheit, ja die freundschaftliche Gefährtenschaft mit Gott nicht abriss, sondern ihm daraus die Fähigkeit zu mutiger und glühender Predigt erwuchs.[6]

Der Ausgangspunkt ist die Heilige Schrift, Gegenstand der Kontemplation ist das Wort, das Gott zu uns gesprochen hat durch seinen Sohn, der in die Welt gekommen ist, um für die Wahrheit Zeugnis abzulegen (vgl. Joh 18,37), für die Wahrheit, die in ihm Person ist. Das Wort ist das wahre Licht, das jeden Menschen erleuchtet (vgl. Joh 1). Es gilt, in der Stille darauf zu hören und nachzusinnen über die Glaubensgeheimnisse.

Der vertraute Umgang mit dem Wort Gottes führt aber auch zur Erkenntnis der eigenen Erlösungsbedürftigkeit sowie zum Erkennen der eigenen Berufung. Das Wort Gottes wird zum Licht auf dem Weg der Nachfolge, es gibt Orientierung für die persönliche Lebensgestaltung und die Bewältigung des Alltags. Die Betrachtung des Lebens Christi wird zur Belehrung für den, der ihm nachfolgen und ihm im Geiste der Seligpreisungen gleichförmig werden will.

Es geht also nicht um Weltflucht, sondern allenfalls um Rückzug, um sich dann der Welt mit geläutertem Blick zuwenden zu können – gewissermaßen mit den Augen Gottes und in der Gesinnung Jesu. Der Blick des Kontemplativen richtet sich auf die Schöpfung, wo er in liebendem und staunendem Wahrnehmen des Seienden, des Schönen und des Guten die Spuren der Gegenwart Gottes erkennt und dadurch zu Lobpreis, Dank und Anbetung bewegt wird.

Der Kontemplative erkennt im Nächsten das Ebenbild Gottes; und die Kontemplation der Barmherzigkeit Christi, dessen Heilswille sich auf alle erstreckt, wird sich auf die Wahrnehmung und die Begegnung mit den Mitmenschen auswirken: Er wird ihre Existenz bejahen, ihr Daseinsrecht anerkennen, sie achten und wertschätzen, so dass ein konstruktives Miteinander zum Wohle aller gelingen kann. Die Kontemplation ist Grundvoraussetzung für gedeihliches Gemeinschaftsleben, in dem sich in einer Spiritualität der Gemeinschaft die Freundschaft mit Gott weitet zur geistlichen Freundschaft mit den Brüdern und Schwestern in Jesus Christus, so dass die Gemeinschaft zum „Sakrament“ der Freundschaft Gottes mit der Welt wird.[7] Das Zeugnis

6 Siehe Fußnote 5: Leonard Boyle S. 62f. und Vladimir Koudelka S. 125.

7 Vgl. Bruno Cadoré a. a. O. (Fußnote 3).

für diese Freundschaft und Liebe Gottes zu den Menschen entspringt dem kontemplativen Leben.

So ist Dominikus aus seiner kastilischen Heimat aufgebrochen und hat das zurückgezogene Leben als Kanoniker hinter sich gelassen. Die geistliche Not der Menschen in Südfrankreich, die der katharischen Irrlehre anhängen, rührt in zutiefst an. Er macht sich ihr Armutsideal zu eigen, nimmt ihr Verlangen nach spiritueller und geistig-moralischer Erneuerung ernst und sucht die Begegnung auf gleicher Augenhöhe. Zusammen mit den Gefährten, die sich um ihn scharen, verschreibt er sich dem Werk der „sacra praedicatio", um den Menschen, um deren Heil er sich sorgt, durch Predigt, Disputation und Dialog auf den Weg des wahren Glaubens zurückzuführen.

Seine Bemühungen zeitigen erste Erfolge, als sich einige Frauen bekehren. Er sorgt für ihre Eingliederung in das Sozialgefüge der damaligen Gesellschaft und für die Institutionalisierung der entstehenden Gemeinschaft. Er gibt ihnen eine Regel und führt sie durch seine Unterweisung ins Ordensleben ein, so dass sie, die allein für Gott da sein wollten, ihr bisheriges asketisches Leben in neuer Beheimatung fortsetzen können. So entsteht 1206 als erste Frucht der „sacra praedicatio" das Nonnenkloster in Prouilhe, die „Wiege des Ordens", der zehn Jahre später durch den Papst bestätigt werden sollte. Von den ersten Anfängen an nehmen die Nonnen im Orden als integraler Teil einen festen Platz ein und partizipieren durch ihr Mitwirken auf geistlicher Ebene an dessen Sendung.[8] Dem kontemplativen Leben kommt also eine wesentlich missionarische Dimension zu.

Das kontemplative Leben der Nonnen

Während die Brüder sich vom Evangelium prägen lassen[9] und besonders zur Predigt berufen sind, durchforschen die Nonnen mit brennendem Herzen die Heilige Schrift[10] und verkünden das Evangelium Gottes durch das Beispiel ihres Lebens[11], indem sie ihr Kloster zur Wohnstätte für das Wort Gottes machen, um nach dem Beispiel des Vorläufers dem Herrn in der

8 Vgl. Liber Constitutionum Monialium Ordinis Praedicatorum (im Folgenden abgekürzt mit LCM) 1.I.
9 Vgl. LCO 1 § II.
10 Vgl. LCM 1.V.
11 Vgl. LCM 96.I.

Wüste den Weg zu bereiten[12], „so dass das Wort, das aus dem Munde Gottes hervorgeht, nicht leer zu ihm zurückkehrt, sondern all das erreicht, wozu er es gesandt hat (vgl. Jes 55,11)"[13].

Die Nonnen trachten danach, das Wort Gottes immer mehr zur Mitte ihres Lebens zu machen, auf dass es in ihnen und unter ihnen wohne und so Gemeinschaft unter ihnen stifte. Indem sie an ihm festhalten, in ihm wohnen und in ihm bleiben in der Weise reziproker Immanenz, dienen sie der Sendung des Ordens, nämlich der Verkündigung des Wortes. Ihr Leben stellt gewissermaßen ein Mahnzeichen dar. In diesem Sinne richteten die Kapitulare, die 2007 zum Generalkapitel in Bogotá versammelt waren, einen Brief an die Nonnen,[14] in dem sie sie darum ersuchen, alle Zweige der Dominikanischen Familie an ihre kontemplative Berufung und an die kontemplative Dimension ihres Lebens zu erinnern sowie daran, dass die Predigt ihre Fruchtbarkeit aus der Stille empfängt und dass es deshalb gilt, sich vor Aktivismus in Acht zu nehmen.

Darüber hinaus ist das Leben der Nonnen, da Religiosität wesentlich zur menschlichen Natur gehört und dem menschlichen Leben eine kontemplative Dimension zukommt, ein prophetisches Zeichen für alle, die die Frage nach dem Sinn des Lebens, in dem es eben nicht allein um Machen und Haben gehen kann, nach der Wahrheit, nach Gott stellen: „Durch ihr verborgenes Leben verkünden sie auf prophetische Weise: Christus ist das einzige Glück im gegenwärtigen Leben durch die Gnade, im zukünftigen durch die Herrlichkeit."[15] Angesichts des postmodernen Nihilismus und weit verbreiteter Gottvergessenheit einer Welt, in der Zeit und Raum für Gott fehlen und in der es im Denken, Fühlen und Wollen des Menschen keinen Platz für Gott gibt[16], weist das kontemplative Leben hin auf die Existenz und Gegenwart Gottes sowie auf die transzendente Bestimmung des Menschen. In exemplarischer Vorwegnahme der endzeitlichen Existenz unterstreicht es den Primat des Spirituellen über das Irdische und erinnert daran, dass die innerweltlichen Güter dem Menschen niemals genügen

12 Vgl. LCM 96.II.

13 LCM 1.II.

14 Acta capituli generalis priorum provincialium ordinis Praedicatorum Bogotae celebrati … Romae 2007, 45.

15 LCM 1.V.

16 Vgl. Predigt Papst Benedikts XVI. in der Christmette am 24.12.2012: http://www.vatican.va/holy_father/benedict_xvi/homilies/2012/documents/hf_ben-xvi_hom_20121224_christmas_ge.html (gelesen am 22.01.2013).

können, da er nicht vom Brot allein lebt, sondern von jedem Wort, das aus dem Munde Gottes kommt (vgl. Mt 4,4). Das Wort Gottes ist in Jesus Christus Mensch geworden, weil Gott die Welt so sehr geliebt hat, dass er seinen einzigen Sohn in die Welt gesandt hat, damit alle, die an ihn glauben, das ewige Leben haben (vgl. Joh 3,16–17). Gott ist Mensch geworden, weil er der Freund aller sein will. Für seine Freunde hat Jesus Christus sein Leben hingegeben. Dieser Freundschaft Gottes mit seinem Volk wollen die Nonnen durch ihre Fürbitte dienen und – wie Dominikus – sich im Gebet für das Heil aller Menschen einsetzen.

Da somit kontemplatives Leben nicht auf innerweltliche Ziele ausgerichtet ist, entzieht es sich jeder Nützlichkeitserwägung; nach utilitaristischen Maßstäben ist es nutzlos, so nutzlos etwa wie die Salbung Jesu zu Bethanien, die Judas Iskariot für Verschwendung hielt (vgl. Joh 12,1–11). In ähnlicher Weise würde er kontemplatives Leben für nutzlos halten und nicht verstehen, dass das Wort Gottes zu einer Antwort herausfordert, dass die Leidenschaft für den lebendigen Gott, durch dessen Wort alles geworden ist, zur exklusiven Hingabe an den Herrn drängt, die jedoch nicht unfruchtbar bleibt, sondern auf unsichtbare Weise beiträgt zur Ausbreitung des Reiches Gottes in dieser Welt.

Ziel und Vollendung des kontemplativen Lebens – eschatologischer Ausblick

Zu den menschlichen Grunderfahrungen gehört die Sehnsucht nach Glück, nach Erfüllung. Die Glückseligkeit und höchste Erfüllung des Menschen als geistiges, vernunftbegabtes Geschöpf besteht in der Verstandestätigkeit, die sich auf das edelste Erkennbare bezieht. Das kontemplative Leben entspricht diesem natürlichen Verlangen nach der Erkenntnis der höchsten und tiefsten, ersten und letzten Wahrheit, nämlich Gott. Die Beschäftigung mit der Wirklichkeit Gottes, die Freude an der Wahrheit, ist die Quelle der Glückseligkeit. Die Betrachtung der göttlichen Wahrheit beginnt in diesem Leben. Die Wahrheit erkennt, wer am Wort Gottes festhält (vgl. Joh 8,31–32). Zu Betrachtern Gottes werden wir durch den Heiligen Geist, den Geist der Wahrheit, der uns die Worte Jesu in Erinnerung ruft (vgl. Joh 14,26). Aufgrund der Freundschaft mit Gott offenbart er die göttlichen Geheimnisse, denn zur Freundschaft gehört, dass die Freunde sich ihre Geheimnisse mitteilen, so wie Jesus seinen Jüngern alles mitteilt, was er vom

Vater gehört hat (vgl. Joh 15,15). Kontemplative Erkenntnis Gottes erfolgt unter dem Einfluss der Gnade. Es ist eine erfahrungsmäßige Erkenntnis Gottes im Glauben im Sinne eines intuitives Erfassens und intellektueller Intuition wie in einem Spiegel (vgl. 1 Kor 13,12) aufgrund der Gabe der Weisheit.

Im kontemplativen Akt gelangt das kontemplative Leben zur Vollendung. Er ist der höchste Akt des menschlichen Verstandes. Auf größtmögliche Weise macht er Gott ähnlich und verbindet mit Gott. Diese anfanghafte Gotteserkenntnis im jetzigen Leben gelangt im zukünftigen zur Vollendung in der immerwährenden Anschauung Gottes von Angesicht zu Angesicht, wenn wir ihm ähnlich sein werden und ihn sehen werden, wie er ist (vgl. 1 Joh 3,2). Darin besteht die Fülle des ewigen Lebens in der Lebens-, Liebens- und Seinseinheit mit Gott, die denen zuteil wird, die das Wort Gottes hören und daran festhalten (vgl. Joh 5,24; Joh 8,51). Sie erfahren endgültig die Wahrheit des Psalmverses: „Bei dir ist die Quelle des Lebens, in deinem Licht schauen wir das Licht".

An den Wächtern vorbei

Maria von Magdala als Modell dominikanerischer Verkündigung

Benedikta Hintersberger OP · Aurelia Spendel OP

Patronin des Ordens

Maria von Magdala ist die Patronin des Ordens der Predigerschwestern und -brüder. Ihr galt als erstem Menschen der Auftrag Jesu, seine Auferstehung zu verkünden. Damit war und ist sie eine der wegweisenden Gestalten des Predigerordens, an der es Maß zu nehmen gilt, wenn die Botschaft des Evangeliums authentisch gesagt werden soll.

Der Auftrag Jesu, „den Brüdern" Nachricht zu geben vom Geschehen im Garten, bedarf der immer neuen geistlichen Betrachtung und einer je zeitgemäßen Interpretation. Die Reflexion der Gestalt der Maria von Magdala eröffnet somit wichtige Perspektiven für die Grundlagen dominikanischer Predigt. Von daher gilt dieser Frauengestalt unser besonderes Interesse: Wie ist Maria von Magdala, bzw. das, was wir von ihr aus biblischen Quellen erfahren, zu verstehen und wie ist ihr Auftrag heute zu deuten?

Ein fragwürdiges Magdalenenbild

Maria aus Magdala war die Frau, die Jesus als erwachsenem Mann wohl am nächsten stand. Sie begleitete ihn nach ihrer ersten Begegnung und Heilung als seine Jüngerin bis unter das Kreuz. Sie war die erste Botin des Auferstandenen und wurde deshalb in der frühen Kirche als „Apostolin der Apostel" verstanden und verehrt.[1] Leider kennen viele Christinnen und Christen sie nur als „Maria, die Hetäre, Maria Magdalena, also Mirjam vom Westufer des Kinnereth-Sees, der Jesus sieben böse Geister ausgetrie-

1 Papst Johannes Paul II. bezeichnetet Maria von Magdala in seinem am 15. August 1988 gegebenen Apostolischen Schreiben *Mulieris Dignitatem* (17) zwar als „Apostel (sic!) der Apostel" (apostola apostolorum), dies wird jedoch leider in einer eindeutig falschen, weil männlichen deutschen Übersetzung wiedergegeben.

ben haben soll, die man später gern mit den sieben Todsünden in Verbindung brachte, (…) Urbild der Sünderin, die Jesus in seinen Kreis aufnimmt".[2]

Wie konnte dieses fragwürdige Magdalenenbild entstehen? Vermutlich begann unter Bischof Ambrosius von Mailand, einem großen Marienverehrer, die Vermischung der verschiedenen Salbungsgeschichten bei Matthäus (26,6–13), Markus (14,3–9), Lukas (7,36–50) und Johannes (12,1–11). Auch die Interpretation der „sieben bösen Geister" als sexuelle Verstrickung reicht bis in diese Zeit zurück. Aus der „Gesamtschau" dreier biblischer Frauengestalten – die der stadtbekannten Prostituierten, von der nur Lukas erzählt (Lk 7,37), der Maria von Bethanien, der Schwester des Lazarus und der Martha, und der Maria aus Magdala wurde eine „Großgestalt" gewonnen, die die biblischen Stränge verwebte und als mehr und mehr zum religiösen Archetyp einer „guten", bußfertigen Christin wurde.

So zeigen die Magdalenenhomilien Gregors des Großen drei Jahrhunderte später Maria von Magdala als asketische, reuige Sünderin. Sie büßt ihre Verfehlungen und wird neben der ganz und gar geistlichen Idealgestalt weiblichen Christentums, der allzeit jungfräulichen Mutter des Gottessohnes, die schon vor ihrer Geburt geheiligt wurde, zur seiner weltlich verhafteten Idealgestalt, die ihre Heiligung auf dem Weg lebenslanger Buße findet.

Die Charakteristik dieser Kompilationsfigur prägte jahrhundertelang das kirchliche Frauenbild, weil sie es Frauen erlaubte, durch Buße für die fleischliche Lust und radikale sexuelle Entsagung die naturale Gebundenheit an Sexualität, Fruchtbarkeit und Mutterschaft zu übersteigen und in die Sphäre geistlicher Existenz aufzusteigen.

Neben der Büßerin verschwinden in der Folge die Vorbildfiguren der selbstlos Dienenden und der treu liebenden Jüngerin fast vollständig. Damit gerät auch Maria von Magdala als biblisch bezeugte Verkünderin der Auferstehung mehr und mehr in Vergessenheit und mit ihr der apostolische Gesichtspunkt, der sie als erste, vom auferstandenen Jesus selbst autorisierte „Predigerin" versteht.

---

2 Vgl. Elisabeth Moltmann-Wendel, Ein eigener Mensch werden. Frauen um Jesus, Gütersloh 1984, Ss. 66–95, hier S. 69. Moltmann-Wendel zitiert hier sinngemäß Shalom Ben Chorin. Ihr Buch und die Publikation von Ingrid Maisch, Maria Magdalena. Zwischen Verachtung und Verehrung. Das Bild eine Frau im Spiegel der Jahrhunderte, Fr-B-W 1996 gehören neben der Arbeit von Andrea Taschl-Erber, Maria von Magdala – erste Apostolin? Joh 20,1–18: Tradition und Relecture (Herders Biblische Studien 51; Fr-B-W 2007) noch immer zu den fundiertesten Untersuchungen zu Maria von Magdala.

Die mittelalterliche Renaissance einer biblisch orientierten Magdalenen-Verehrung, wie sie sich in der predigenden Magdalena französischer und deutscher Kathedralen-Glasfenstern niederschlägt, dauert nur kurz und war nicht nachhaltig. Erst heute wird Maria von Magdala als Urapostolin wieder entdeckt.

Die biblische Maria aus Magdala

Eigentlich heißt sie nur Maria, Mirjam. Ihren Beiname erhältt sie von ihrem Heimatort Magdala, einer geschäftigen Stadt am See Genezareth.[3] Mirjam hat nicht viel vom Reichtum ihrer Stadt und ihrem eigenen. Sie lebt ein Leben unter schwarzen Schleiern, leidet wohl unter Schwermut und Depressionen. In der Begegnung mit Jesus von Nazareth findet sie sich selber und findet den Weg heraus aus der Dunkelheit ihrer Seele, weg von den sieben Dämonen, die sie quälen. Die Evangelien berichten nichts Näheres über diese Heilung.

Nach ihrer ersten Jesusbegegnung kehrt sie nicht in die alten Verhältnisse zurück. Sie wird eine seiner Jüngerinnen, bleibt bei ihm und teilt ihren Wohlstand mit der Jesusgruppe. Da im Unterschied zu der miterwähnten Johanna, der Frau des Chuzas, Maria nicht als verheiratet vorgestellt wird, ist davon auszugehen, dass sie als selbständige Frau unverheiratet lebte. Sicher ist, dass sie in der Frauengruppe um Jesus eine wichtige Rolle spielte. Ihr Name wird stets als erster Name aus der Gruppe der Jüngerinnen genannt.

Über die gemeinsame Zeit der Wanderschaft der Magdalena mit Jesus wissen wir nichts. Die Evangelien berichten jedoch übereinstimmend, dass sie mit den Frauen, die ihm folgten, unter dem Kreuz stand, beim Begräbnis anwesend war und am Ostermorgen als erste zum Grab kam.

Maria aber stand draußen vor dem Grab und weinte. Während sie weinte, beugte sie sich in die Grabkammer hinein. Da sah sie zwei Engel in weißen Gewändern sitzen, den einen dort, wo der Kopf, den anderen dort, wo die Füße des Leichnams Jesu gelegen hatten. Die Engel sagten zu ihr: Frau,

3 Ausgrabungen in Magdala haben 2009 u. a. eine sehr frühe Synagoge, den biblischen Marktplatz, Häuserreste und die Ruinen einer Wasserleitung freigelegt. Vgl. http://www.welt.de/wissenschaft/article4532087/Synagoge-aus-der-Zeit-Jesu-entdeckt.html (14.09.2009).

warum weinst du? Sie antwortete ihnen: Man hat meinen Herrn weggenommen, und ich weiß nicht, wohin man ihn gelegt hat. Als sie das gesagt hatte, wandte sie sich um und sah Jesus dastehen, wusste aber nicht, dass es Jesus war. Jesus sagte zu ihr: Frau, warum weinst du? Wen suchst du? Sie meinte, es sei der Gärtner, und sagte zu ihm: Herr, wenn du ihn weggebracht hast, sag mir, wohin du ihn gelegt hast. Dann will ich ihn holen. Jesus sagte zu ihr: Maria! Da wandte sie sich ihm zu und sagte auf Hebräisch zu ihm: Rabbuni!, das heißt: Meister. Jesus sagte zu ihr: Halte mich nicht fest; denn ich bin noch nicht zum Vater hinaufgegangen. Geh aber zu meinen Brüdern, und sag ihnen: Ich gehe hinauf zu meinem Vater und zu eurem Vater, zu meinem Gott und zu eurem Gott. Maria von Magdala ging zu den Jüngern und verkündete ihnen: Ich habe den Herrn gesehen. Und sie richtete aus, was er ihr gesagt hatte. (Joh 20,11–18)

Predigerin der Auferstehung

Diese Szene begründet die Sonderrolle der Maria von Magdala in der jungen Kirche: Ihr wird als erstem Menschen deutlich, dass der Leib des Gekreuzigten sich nicht festhalten und nicht zurückholen lässt. Es ist der Gleiche und doch ein anderer, der sich den Menschen vor bzw. nach Ostern zeigt und der sie anredet um einer Beziehung und um eines Auftrages willen.

Der Schock, den das harsche und ablehnende Wort Jeus bei Maria von Magdala auslöst, darf nicht geleugnet werden. Der Auferstandene ist nicht mehr der ihr nahe und vertraute Jesus. Nur seine Stimme und die Fähigkeit, sie bei ihrem Namen zu nennen und sie damit in der Tiefe ihrer Existenz zu erkennen, sind noch nah und vertraut. Mit dieser Stimme gibt Jesus ihr seinen Auftrag: „Geh und sag von mir: Ich gehe zu dem zurück, der mein und euer Vater ist, mein und euer Gott.“

Geht man die inneren Stationen Marias in dieser Perikope sorgfältig nach, findet sich die gleiche Dynamik, die sich in den vorösterlichen Gesprächen Jesu mit Frauen und mit Nikodemus als dem einzig vergleichbar Interessierten feststellen lässt.[4] Es geht – neben anderen Gemeinsamkeiten – um die mehrfache innere „Kehre“, um jene existentielle Öffnung und Ver-

4 Hier sind gemeint die Gespräche Jesu mit Marta bei der Erweckung des Lazarus (Joh 11,20–27), mit der Samariterin am Jakobsbrunnen (Joh 4,5–30) und mit Nikodemus in der Nacht (Joh 3,1–13).

wandlung, in der sich das zentrale Moment menschlicher Existenz, aktiv und passiv zugleich, ansprechen lässt von der Erfahrung einer gegenwärtigen transzendentalen Wirklichkeit. Maria von Magdala durchlebt diese österliche „Wendung“ in drei Phasen: Sie wendet sich vom Grab weg, als sie erkennt, dass sie im Gespräch mit den Engeln keine Antwort auf ihre Frage nach dem Verbleib Jesu findet. Sie wendet sich dem Menschen zu, der sie nicht wie die Engel nach ihrer innerlichen Befindlichkeit fragt, sondern nach ihrer Beziehung, die sich nach außen auf ein Du hin orientiert, das sie verloren hat. Sie wendet sich in die Richtung – ohne dass dieser Begriff im biblischen Text benutzt würde –, in der sie auf ihre Brüder und Schwestern[5] stoßen wird, wenn sie den Auftrag Jesu zur Verkündigung annimmt. Also: vom leeren Grab hin zum Garten als dem Ort des Lebens; vom Garten hin zum Gärtner, der sich ihr in diesem Garten zeigt; vom Gärtner, den sie (wieder-)erkennt als ihren Meister, zu den Brüdern und Schwestern, zu denen er sie sendet.

Die Bewegungen, die notwendig sind, um verwandelt zu werden von einer trauernden Lernenden, die keine Hoffnung mehr hat, zur predigenden Lehrerin der Nachfolgegemeinschaft der Brüder und Schwestern, sind vielfältig. Maria muss zuerst lange genug hinschauen, um zu verstehen, was es mit dem Grab auf sich hat. Es genügt kein flüchtiger Blick in die Dunkelheit hinein, um zu sehen: Hier geht es nicht mehr weiter. Erst als sie genug gesehen hat, ist sie bereit, den Blick vom Ort des Todes abzuwenden und ihn neu zu fokussieren auf den Ort des Lebens hin. Es muss etwas Anziehenderes als der Anblick des Grabes und der Engel in diesem Grab geben, um wahrnehmen zu können, dass es außerhalb des Grabes noch etwas und noch jemand anderes gibt, etwas Wichtigeres als das Vertraute und als die eigene Person. Hätte Maria den Gärtner mit einem gleichgültigen oder in sich gekehrten Blick gestreift – er kann mir auch nichts anders sagen als die Engel! –, hätte sie nicht wahrnehmen können, wer sich ihr als Gegenüber zeigt. Schließlich geht der Weg vom Wahrnehmen zum Erkennen: Rabbuni! Endlich sieht Maria mit den äußeren und mit den inneren Augen den, den sie liebt. Erst jetzt ist sie frei, um schließlich die in den Blick zu nehmen, zu denen er sie senden wird.

---

5 Siehe zur Bedeutung des Begriffs „Brüder“ den Aufsatz von Luzia Sutter Rehmann, Warum finden sich keine ‚Männer‘ um Jesus?, in: Bibel heute (3/2013), 10–13.

An den Wächtern vorbei

Bei aufmerksamer Betrachtung wird hinter der johanneischen Osterperikope und dem dort geschilderten inneren Weg der Maria von Magdala das Hohelied des Ersten Testaments sichtbar.

Des Nachts auf meinem Lager suchte ich ihn, den meine Seele liebt. Ich suchte ihn und fand ihn nicht. Aufstehen will ich, die Stadt durchstreifen, die Gassen und Plätze, ihn suchen, den meine Seele liebt. Ich suchte ihn und fand ihn nicht. Mich fanden die Wächter bei ihrer Runde durch die Stadt. Habt ihr ihn gesehen, den meine Seele liebt? Kaum war ich an ihnen vorüber, fand ich ihn, den meine Seele liebt. Ich packte ihn, ließ ihn nicht mehr los, bis ich ihn ins Haus meiner Mutter brachte, in die Kammer derer, die mich geboren hat. (Hld 3,1–4)

Maria sucht wie die Braut, die den Bräutigam ersehnt, in der Nacht – der Nacht des Todes – den, den ihre Seele liebt. Sie sucht ihn und findet ihn nicht – nicht in der Erinnerung an gute Zeiten, nicht im Nachsinnen über die entsetzlichen letzten Tage, nicht in ihrem Innern. Sie steht auf und streift in der Dunkelheit der Nacht durch die Gassen Jerusalems, über seine Plätze, um den zu suchen, den ihre Seele liebt. Die Wächter, auf die sie stößt, als sie den Garten aufsucht, um nicht ganz die Verbindung zu ihrem Geliebten zu verlieren, sind ihre Verlusterfahrung, ihre Trauer, das Nichtwahrhabenwollen und der seelische Schmerz. Sie wachen über die Stadt ihrer Seele und dulden keine anderen Mächte als die, die sie jetzt so machtvoll und umfassend beherrschen. Diese Wächter können nicht antworten auf Marias Frage: *Habt ihr ihn gesehen, den meine Seele liebt?* Diese Wächter sind blind und taub.

Erst als Maria an ihnen vorbei ist, findet sie den, den ihre Seele liebt. Zeichen dieses „vorbei an den Wächtern“ ist die Akzeptanz des harschen Wortes Jesu: *Halte mich nicht fest.* Es ist vorbei, was einmal war; es lässt sich nicht festhalten, was gewesen ist. Es kommt das Neue; nur dieses Neue hat Lebensqualität in sich, die dem Reich Gottes entspricht, das der vorösterliche Jesus angekündigt hat. Erst als der Predigtauftrag Jesu Maria von Magdala „gepackt“ hat, braucht sie ihn nicht mehr festzuhalten in seiner vergangenen, gestorbenen Gestalt, sondern kann ihn „packen“, muss ihn nie wieder loslassen, bis sie ihn für immer „besitzt“ in der Kammer ihrer Gebärerin. In der allegorischen Auslegung steht hier die Kirche. Sie ist die Mutter der Glaubenden, die immer neu fruchtbare Gemeinschaft, durch die das Leben in und aus der Taufe ständig neu Gestalt annimmt und Fleisch wird.

Um dominikanisch zu predigen muss die Predigerin/der Prediger immer wieder neu die dreifache Kehre der Maria von Magdala im eigenen Leben vollziehen. Er/sie muss sich selber immer besser kennenlernen, sich selber studieren, um nicht gefesselt zu sein an die leblosen Räume der eigenen Person oder an die unerforschten Düsternisse der eigenen Biographie. Die zweite Kehre führt weg von jeder Unglücksprophetie, die nicht mit der je neuen lebensspendenden Kraft Gottes rechnet, die er in Treue gerade auch in verfahren und unhaltbaren Situationen von Kirche und Welt durch seinem Geist einströmen lassen will. Die Predigerin/der Prediger hat als Hoffnungswort „den verborgenen Plan der göttlichen Vorsehung“[6] zu studieren, muss also aus der eigenen Erfahrung vom Wort des Lebens reden können (1 Joh 1,1). Deshalb sind, um diese Kehre vollziehen zu können, das Studium der Bibel und das der Zeichen der Zeit unabdingbar. Die dritte Kehre schließlich ist die in die unbekannte Situation der Menschen hinein, die an den Rändern von Gesellschaft und Kirche zu finden sind.[7]

Nochmals: Patronin des Ordens

Die Bedeutung der Frau aus Magdala für heute ist augenscheinlich, ist doch der christliche Glaube solange unvollständig, wie er mit Maria von Magdala seine weibliche Seite verdrängt und die jesuanische Ermächtigung von Frauen zur Glaubensverkündigung verleugnet. Die Anerkennung die-

---

6 „In der gegenwärtigen Entwicklung der menschlichen Ereignisse, durch welche die Menschheit in eine Ordnung einzutreten scheint, muss man (...) einen verborgenen Plan der göttlichen Vorsehung anerkennen. Dieser verfolgt mit dem Ablauf der Zeiten, durch die Werke der Menschen und meistens über ihre Erwartungen hinaus sein eigenes Ziel, und alles, auch die entgegengesetzten menschlichen Interessen, lenkt er weise zum Heil der Kirche.“ Johannes XXIII., Eröffnungsrede zum II. Vatikanischen Konzil *Gaudet Mater Ecclesiae*, 11. Oktober 1962.

7 1986 formulierte das Generalkapitel der Dominikaner in Avila die dominikanische Mission bzw. die Sendung des Ordens als Mission „an den Rändern“ bzw. als Sendung zu den „Menschen an Grenzen“. Diese Grenzen werden bezeichnet durch die Konfrontation von Leben/Tod; menschlich/unmenschlich; christliche Erfahrungen/universalistische Religionen; religiöse Erfahrungen/weltliche Ideologien; Kirche/nicht-katholische Konfessionen und Sekten. Vgl. Thomas Eggensperger, Die „fünf Grenzen“. Relecture zu einer Theorie der Sendung in der Gegenwart (Von Avila 1986 zu Rom 2010). Vortrag auf der XIII. Studienwoche OP in Dubrovnik 2010 (unveröffentlicht).

ser weiblichen Dimension in ihrer ganzen Fülle ist Voraussetzung für die Lösung der Frauenfrage in der Kirche.

Romanos der Melode lässt Maria in einem Hymnus zum Ostersonntag sprechen: „Ich zögere nicht, es zu sagen: Mir wurde derselbe Ruhm zuteil wie Mose; ich habe gesehen, ja, ich habe nicht auf dem Berg, sondern beim Grab den Meister und Herrn der himmlischen Heere gesehen."[8] Diese Gleichsetzung der Bedeutung der Maria vom Magdala mit der des Mose für die Offenbarung Gottes unter den Menschen ist atemberaubend. Damit die Kirche ungeteilte Erinnerungsgemeinschaft dieser Offenbarung sein kann, ist ihre radikale Identifizierung mit der Gestalt der Maria von Magdala unabdingbar. So muss z. B. die Frage gestellt werden, ob es ohne Maria aus Magdala überhaupt eine Osterbotschaft gegeben hätte? Hätten die Jüngerinnen und Jünger ohne Maria je von der Auferstehung Jesu erfahren? Die Antwort darauf ist nicht eindeutig, aber die Vorliebe Jesu für die Frauen besonders am Ostermorgen unübersehbar.

Weil die Theologie der Maria von Magdala noch nicht geschrieben ist, ist auch das zutiefst jesuanisch inspirierte und fundierte Ziel einer geschwisterlichen Kirche, eines geschwisterlich-partnerschaftlichen Ordens, einer geschwisterlichen Verkündigung noch kaum realisiert. Unsere Kirche und unser Orden sähen sicher anders aus, wenn sie die Glaubenserfahrung und die Predigtsendung der Maria von Magdala – und die ihrer Schwestern – genauso ernst genommen hätten und ernst nehmen würden wie die der Jünger. Wir haben als Dominikanerinnen und Dominikaner das *ganze* Vermächtnis Jesu weiterzugeben und danach zu leben. Wir sind nicht nur eine Petrus-Kirche, sondern auch eine Magdalenen-Kirche. Schwestern und Brüder – im jesuanischen Sinn gemeint – sind berufen, als Predigerinnen und Prediger Zeugnis vom Auferstandenen zu geben. Wir werden uns jede/jeder für sich und gemeinsam überlegen müssen, wie wir diesen Auftrag Jesu unter den Augen und mit der Hilfe unsere Patronin Maria von Magdala gerecht werden können.

---

8 Proprium des Predigerordens, III Feier des Stundengebetes. Proprium der Heiligen, Köln 1991, 456.

Stilfragen

Einige Reflexionen (nicht nur) über die Laien im Predigerorden

Gabriele Neu-Yilik

Unser Empfehlungsschreiben seid ihr; es ist eingeschrieben in unser Herz, und alle Menschen können es lesen und verstehen. Unverkennbar seid ihr ein Brief Christi, ausgefertigt durch unseren Dienst, geschrieben nicht mit Tinte, sondern mit dem Geist des lebendigen Gottes, nicht auf Tafeln aus Stein, sondern – wie auf Tafeln – in Herzen von Fleisch. (2 Kor 3,2–3)

Der Orden der Prediger verfügt über einen Laienzweig. Das ist in sich schon überraschend, denn wer heute mit dem Stichwort „Dominikaner" überhaupt noch etwas anzufangen weiß, denkt im Allgemeinen an Männer (zumeist Priester) und Frauen im schwarzweißen Habit, die in Klöstern leben. Noch erstaunlicher aber ist die Tatsache, dass ein Teil dieser Dominikanischen Laien mit den Brüdern, den Schwestern und den Moniales den inneren Kern der weitverzweigten Dominikanischen Familie bildet. Obwohl innerhalb der *Familia dominicana* am wenigsten klar definiert, gehören die Dominikanischen Laien überdies zu den ältesten Zweigen des Ordens. Ihr Ursprung ist bisher wenig erforscht und lässt sich möglicherweise nicht mehr vollständig klären, doch sind begründete Vermutungen durchaus möglich. Am wahrscheinlichsten ist die Herkunft nicht aus einer, sondern aus mehreren Wurzeln.[1] Von Anfang an gab es Wohltäter und Donaten, Laien, die in der Nähe der Klöster der Bettelorden lebten und ihnen ihr Vermögen ganz oder teilweise zur Verfügung stellten. Im Gegenzug konnten sie Versorgungsprivilegien und Anteil an den geistlichen Gnadenmitteln und Verdiensten des Ordens erhalten.[2] Als eine zweite Wurzel wird häufig die „Militia Jesu Christi" genannt, die zeitweise als die eigentliche Vorgängerin des „Dritten Ordens des hl. Dominikus" angesehen wurde, jedoch vermutlich selbst heterogenen Ursprungs ist. Gruppierungen mit der

1 Richard Weber: History of the Dominican Laity http://www.southerndominicanlaity.org/HISTORY%20OF%20THE%20DOMINICAN%20LAITY.pdf.

2 Hilarius Barth, Der vergessene Ursprung der Dominikanischen Gemeinschaft. Bisher unveröffentlicht.

Bezeichnung Militia Christi gab es zwischen dem 11. bis zum frühen 14. Jahrhundert etliche, sowohl vor als auch nach der Zeit des hl. Dominikus de Guzmán. Solche Bruderschaften hatten die Verteidigung der Kirche, der Kirchengüter und des Glaubens gegen Häretiker zum Ziel und setzten sich im 11. und 12. Jahrhundert für die innerkirchlichen Reformbewegungen und die *libertas ecclesiae*, die Freiheit der Kirche von weltlicher Gewalt, ein. Die Anbindung einer solchen Militia an den Predigerorden wird durch eine Bulle Gregors IX von 1235 bezeugt. Sie wurde wohl von Bischof Fulco von Toulouse und vielleicht Simon de Montfort zur Zeit des Albingenserkreuzzugs zur Unterstützung des Kampfes gegen die Häretiker gegründet. Eine Beteiligung des hl. Dominikus an ihrer Gründung wird zwar von Raimund von Capua in der „Legenda major" berichtet, ist aber nicht belegt. Eine zweite der geistlichen Leitung durch den Dominikanerorden unterstellte „Militia Jesu Christi" scheint außerdem 1233 durch den Dominikanerbischof Bartholomäus von Vincenza in Parma gegründet worden zu sein und erlosch schon nach wenigen Jahrzehnten wieder. Außerdem schlossen sich schon früh aus den großen geistlichen Aufbrüchen oder als Wiederbekehrte aus den Häresiebewegungen des 13. Jahrhunderts stammende Laien dem hl. Dominikus an, die innerhalb der Kirche evangeliumsgemäß leben wollten und vom Predigerorden geistliche Orientierung erhofften, umgekehrt jedoch auch die Brüder in vielfältiger Weise mit ihren weltlichen Gütern unterstützten. 1285, nur wenige Jahrzehnte nach seiner Gründung, institutionalisierte der Orden unter dem 7. Generalmagister Muñio von Zamora seine Verpflichtung gegenüber diesen Gruppen und gab ihnen eine Regel (*Regula Fratrum et Sororum Ordinis de Paenitentiae Beati Dominici*), die nicht nur die Bindung an den Orden stärkte, sondern auch die Partizipation am apostolischen Auftrag des Ordens einschloss, wenn auch eher nicht in einem heutigen Verständnis von Laienapostolat. Sie sollten „auf ihre Art erfüllt sein vom äußersten, brennenden Eifer für die Wahrheit des katholischen Glaubens".[3] William Hinnebusch hat betont, dass die Promulgation dieser bis 1923 unverändert gültigen Regel durch den ansonsten als Ordensmeister eher glücklosen Muñio de Zamora dessen wichtigste Handlung gewesen sei, da er dadurch ein Instrument schuf, den

3 Zaida Rocha Ferreira, Eine kurze Geschichte des Europäischen Rates der Dominikanischen Laiengemeinschaften. In: Johannes H. Weise (Hrsg), Jeder ist ein Wort Gottes für den anderen. Grundlagentexte der Dominikanischen Laiengemeinschaft. St. Benno-Verlag, Leipzig, 2009. S. 19ff.

Wirkungskreis des Ordens auszudehnen.[4] Besonders hervorzuheben ist in diesem Zusammenhang der damals beispiellose Vorgang, dass Muñio Laien seiner direkten Jurisdiktion unterstellte; diese nach einer Regel lebenden „inkorporierten" Laien waren damit und sind seither ein integraler Bestandteil des Predigerordens. Fortan trugen die unter der Regel geeinten Laien die Bezeichnung „Brüder und Schwestern des Ordens von der Buße des hl. Dominikus"; die später und bis weit ins 20. Jahrhundert verwendete Bezeichnung „Dritter Orden von der Buße des hl. Dominikus" entstand erst im 15. Jahrhundert.

Schon vor aber auch nach der heute als Gründungsdatum des Laienzweiges des Dominikanerordens angesehenen Promulgation der Regel existierten neben diesen inkorporierten Laien ein ganzer Strauß von dem Predigerorden verbundenen Gruppen, Vereinigungen und Einzelpersonen, die in unterschiedlicher Weise und Intensität an seinem geistlichen (und auch praktischen) Leben und seinem Charisma Anteil hatten und in direkter Bindung an ein Kloster oder auch innerhalb eines Klosters lebten, ein Phänomen, das wir auch heute noch beobachten, wenn auch vielleicht nicht mehr in der gleichen Vielfalt wie in der Entstehungszeit des Ordens. Dazu gehörten Rosenkranz- und andere Bruderschaften und fromme Frauengemeinschaften wie u. a. die Beginen, die oft von Dominikanern seelsorglich betreut wurden und – manchmal nur auf Zeit – die dominikanische Regel annahmen.[5]

Die dem Orden verbundenen Laien schenkten ihm nicht wenige Heilige und Selige. Zu ihnen zählen Katharina von Siena, Rosa von Lima, Zdislava von Lemberk, Albert von Bergamo, Bartholomäus Longo, Laurentius Ruiz von Manila, der erste Heilige der philippinischen Kirche, Dominikus Pham Trong Kham und zahlreiche andere Terziaren, die in Japan, China und Vietnam das Martyrium erlitten, sowie mit dem ersten seliggesprochenen Roma Zephyrinus Giménez Malla, den Märtyrern des spanischen Bür-

---

4 William Hinnebusch, Kleine Geschichte des Dominikanerordens. St. Benno Verlag Leipzig, 2004. S. 70.

5 Siehe Hilarius Barth, Der vergessene Ursprung … Einen aktuellen Prozess der Entstehung eines Laienzweiges innerhalb eines Ordens bzw. einer Ordensfamilie kann man anschaulich bei den noch recht neuen Gemeinschaften von Jerusalem beobachten. Aber auch der Baum des hl. Dominikus treibt noch heute neue Zweige, wie beispielsweise die „Gemeinschaft vom Lamm", die weltweit und auch in unserer Provinz in Wien gleichzeitig klösterliche Gemeinschaften von Brüdern und Schwestern und eine eigene Familienstruktur mit Freundeskreisen von Laien entwickelt.

gerkriegs Antero Mateo García und Miguel Peiró Victori und mit Pietro Giorgio Frassati, dem Schutzpatron des Weltjugendtags 2008 in Sidney und „Mann der Seligpreisungen",[6] etliche Selige des 20. Jahrhunderts. Aber auch andere Persönlichkeiten des öffentlichen Lebens gehörten als Laien dem Orden des hl. Dominikus an, schöpften aus ihrer Ordenszugehörigkeit Kraft und Orientierung und schenkten dem Orden ihr Leben und Werk. Unter ihnen sind zu nennen die norwegische Literaturnobelpreisträgerin Sigrid Unseld; der 1978 von den Roten Brigaden ermordete ehemalige italienische Ministerpräsident Aldo Moro; die 2012 verstorbene Mitbegründerin der Freien Universität Berlin, langjährige rheinland-pfälzische Kultusministerin, Berliner Schulsenatorin und Bundestagsabgeordnete Hanna-Renate Laurien;[7] der Florenzer Bürgermeister und unermüdliche „Friedensarbeiter" Giorgio La Pira und nicht zuletzt und natürlich von besonderer Bedeutung für die süddeutsch-österreichische Provinz: Kaiserin Claudia Felicitas, die zweite Gemahlin von Kaiser Leopold I., die in der Dominikanergruft unter der Kirche Maria Rotunda zu Wien bestattet liegt.[8] Die Nennung dieser „Celebrities" schmälert jedoch in keiner Weise den unmessbaren Verdienst all der vielen Ungenannten und Unbekannten, die als Laien ihr Leben mit dem Orden verbanden und ihm und seinem Auftrag in vielfacher Weise dienten und dienen.

Je nach Zeitgeschmack wurde mal die eine, mal die andere der Wurzeln der Dominikanischen Laien in den Vordergrund gerückt. So wird in einem „Lehr- und Regelbuch für die Brüder und Schwestern des dritten Ordens von der Buße des hl. Vaters Dominicus" von 1864 nahezu ausschließlich die „Militia Jesu Christi" als Ursprung des Dritten Ordens erwähnt und ihre Bereitschaft des Kampfes für Christus und die Kirche als erstrebenswertes Ideal vorgestellt.[9] Wir Heutigen identifizieren uns leichter mit unseren „Vorfahren" in den Büßer-, also den *Umkehr*bewegungen des

---

6 Provinzzeitung Nr. 2/2007.

7 Provinzzeitung Nr. 03/10.

8 Quelle: http://www.erzdioezese-wien.at/content/schwerpunkte/habsburg/0/articles/2011/07/12/a26272/. Viele dieser Informationen verdanke ich Heidemarie Barratta, Einzelmitglied in Wien.

9 Lehr- und Regelbuch für die Brüder und Schwestern des Dritten Ordens von der Buße des heiligen Vaters Dominicus. Nach dem Handbuche des hochwürdigsten P. Alexander Vincentius Jandel und einem alten französischen Ordenshandbuche übersetzt und bearbeitet von P. Fr. Albertus Maria Trapp. Dritte Auflage Laumann'sche Buchhandlung, Dülmen 1894.

12. und 13. Jahrhunderts. Möglicherweise liegt der Grund lediglich darin, dass sie uns aus der Ferne friedlicher erscheinen als die anfangs sogar bewaffnete „Militia Jesu Christi". Dennoch mag diese vielleicht eher unreflektierte Sympathie einer Nachkriegs- und Nachpazifismusgeneration berechtigt sein, denn in mancher Hinsicht sind die Zeiten vergleichbar. Wie das 12. und 13. Jahrhundert ist auch die Gegenwart des 20. und 21. Jahrhunderts gezeichnet durch Gewalt, massive gesellschaftliche und kulturelle Umbrüche und den rapiden Verlust von geistigen, geistlichen, moralischen und materiellen Sicherheiten. Wie damals ist die Kirche auch heute erschüttert von Skandalen und Skandalisierung. Auch heute ist der Glaube bedrängt von innen und von außen. Auch heute kämpfen Amts- und Funktionsträger der Kirche (nicht nur die geweihten) mit einem enormen Vertrauensverlust. Glaubenslehre und Glaubenswahrheit erleiden nicht nur einen Glaubwürdigkeitsverlust, sondern sind weitgehend schlicht nicht mehr bekannt, selbst innerhalb der Kirche. Ebenso wie im Jahrhundert des Ordensgründers stellt die Neu-Evangelisierung ein drängendes Problem dar. Gleichzeitig existiert vielfach eine große Sehnsucht nach Einfachheit und evangeliumsgemäßem Lebensstil; und damals wie heute gibt es lautstarke – orthodoxe wie heterodoxe – Forderungen von Laienseite nach kirchlichen Reformen.

Historisches Laienapostolat?

Hatte der hl. Dominikus für die mit seiner Bewegung und seinen Gründungen verbundenen Laien, und hatte Muñio de Zamora für die Brüder und Schwestern von der Buße des hl. Dominikus ein „Laienapostolat" im Sinn? Obwohl gelegentlich bezweifelt, kann das jedoch auch nicht letztgültig ausgeschlossen werden.[10] Die Büßer-, „Armuts"- und Reformbewegungen und letztlich auch die Häretikerbewegungen waren ja eigentlich nichts anderes als bewusst gelebtes Laienchristentum und -apostolat.[11] Zwar suchten die Laien, die sich Dominikus de Guzmán und seinen Brüdern anschlossen, eine geistliche Führung, doch ist schwer vorstellbar, dass zumindest diejenigen von ihnen, die an den laikal-religiösen Reformbestrebungen

10 Richard Weber, History of the Dominican Laity.

11 Dass Laien in dieser Hinsicht aktiv waren, zeigt nicht zuletzt das Beispiel des hl. Franz von Assisi, eines Zeitgenossen des hl. Dominikus.

einer unruhigen Zeit beteiligt waren, sich dann mit einer geistlichen „Versorgung“ zufrieden gegeben hätten. Vielmehr ist wahrscheinlich, dass sie sich von dem jungen und attraktiven Bettelorden angezogen fühlten, weil sie mit seinen Zielen und seinem Charisma übereinstimmten und darin ihre eigenen Anliegen wiedererkannten. Besonders noch in der Zeit vor der offiziellen Gründung des Predigerordens scheint Dominikus Versprechen von Laien entgegengenommen zu haben, die sich und ihren Besitz seinem „Erstlingswerk“, der *Sancta Praedicatio*, der Heiligen Verkündigung, zur Verfügung stellen wollten.[12] Die detaillierte Erforschung einer Beteiligung von Laien an den apostolischen Aufgaben des Dominikanerordens in diesen frühen Zeiten, aber auch deren Wandel im Lauf der Jahrhunderte ist ein Desiderat, dem sich idealerweise Dominikanische Laien widmen würden. Nicht zu bezweifeln ist aber, dass Dominikus sich die Strategien der Laienbewegungen seiner Zeit und ihr Streben nach einem evangeliumsgemäßen Leben zu eigen und zunutze gemacht hat. Man kann also sogar mit einer gewissen Berechtigung behaupten, dass nicht nur der Dritte Orden, sondern der ganze Orden Wurzeln in den mittelalterlichen Laienbewegungen hat.

Dritter Orden?

Lange Zeit wurden die Dominikanischen Laien ordensintern kurz als der *Dritte Orden* bezeichnet, später, als im Zusammenhang mit dem Siegeszug der „political correctness“ das „Dritte“ anstelle eines Zeichens der Vielfalt oder der Möglichkeit eines „Dritten Weges“ innerhalb des Ordens[13] nurmehr noch als herabsetzende „Nachordnung“ (miss)verstanden wurde, entweder als *Dominikanische Laien* oder als *Laiendominikaner*. Allerdings enthalten auch diese beiden letzteren Bezeichnungen eine gewisse Unschärfe, auf die weiter unten eingegangen werden wird.

Schon bald nach seiner Entstehung begann der Begriff des Dritten Ordens (bzw. des Ordens von der Buße des hl. Dominikus) mehrdeutig zu werden. Das liegt darin begründet, dass manche dominikanische Laiengruppierungen mit der Zeit Lebens- und Gütergemeinschaften bildeten,

12 Hilarius Barth, Der vergessene Ursprung …

13 Richard Weber, A History and Theology of Sharing Responsibility for the Church, 1985; http://www.spiritualitytoday.org/spir2day/853721weber.html.

sich eine klösterliche Regel gaben und Gelübde ablegten und dass es schon seit dem 13. Jahrhundert zu Gründungen von Schwesterngemeinschaften kam, die sich von vorneherein als Ordensfrauen betrachteten, jedoch nicht dem zweiten Orden angehörten. Deshalb wurde es notwendig, zwischen dem regulierten und dem weltlichen Dritten Orden zu differenzieren, eine Unterscheidung, die aus Dokumenten, Berichten und wissenschaftlichen Publikationen nicht immer klar hervorgeht. Andererseits entspricht diese begriffliche Unschärfe vermutlich in vielen Fällen der Realität, denn auch manche nicht regulierten Gemeinschaften lebten einen klösterlichen Lebensstil, und auch die weltlichen Fraternitäten trugen lange Zeit immer oder zumindest bei manchen Gelegenheiten einen Habit und übernahmen für ihre Organisationsstrukturen Begriffe aus dem Klosterleben. Gefördert wurde dies auch durch die Terminologie in allen Varianten der Regel für den weltlichen Dritten Orden, bis dies schließlich bei ihrer letzten Reform von 1985 geändert wurde.

Auch bei den Heiligen wird deutlich, dass manchmal nicht scharf zwischen den Angehörigen des regulierten und denen des säkularen Dritten Ordens zu unterscheiden ist. Die sel. Zdislava von Lemberk wird im gegenwärtigen Proprium des Predigerordens (das zwischen den weltlichen und regulierten Mitgliedern des Dritten Ordens nicht klar erkennbar unterscheidet) als „Terziarin“ geführt, obwohl sie 1252 starb, also zu einem Zeitpunkt, als es den „Orden der Brüder und Schwestern von der Buße des Hl. Dominikus“ noch nicht gab, geschweige denn den „Dritten Orden“. Zdislava war verheiratet und Mutter von vier Kindern, wurde jedoch unter Johannes von Wildeshausen „den Brüdern gleich“ in die volle Teilhabe an den geistlichen Gnadenmitteln des Predigerordens aufgenommen, eine Formulierung, die bald darauf für die Ordenslaien nicht mehr möglich war.[14] Die hl. Katharina von Siena ist schon in der Ikonographie nicht von einer Ordensfrau zu unterscheiden, da sie stets im Habit dargestellt ist; in ihrem religiösen und asketischen Leben stand sie einer solchen ohnehin in nichts nach. Trotzdem hat sie ein Leben außerhalb des Klosters vorgezogen. Auf diese Weise konnte sie Lebensbereiche ihrer Zeitgenossen erreichen, die den Brüdern und klausurierten Schwestern verschlossen blieben, und sie konnte mit großer Selbständigkeit und Unabhängigkeit agieren. Mit welch kompromissloser und furchtloser Hingabe sie das tat, muss für alle Zweige des Ordens, besonders aber für seine Laien, Vorbild,

14 Hilarius Barth, Der vergessene Ursprung …

Ermutigung und Herausforderung bleiben. Andere, wie die sel. Maria Mancini, wechselten nach einiger Zeit vom Dritten in den Zweiten Orden. Die Richtung dieses Wechsels ist kein Zufall, denn lange Zeit war es für die Mitglieder des Dritten Ordens nicht möglich, wieder in den Laienstand außerhalb des Ordens oder in einen anderen Dritten Orden zu wechseln;[15] das mag uns heute restriktiv erscheinen, kann aber auch als ein Zeichen dafür gesehen werden, dass einst der Ordensmitgliedschaft der Laien und somit der gegenseitig eingegangenen Verpflichtung als eine *Lebensentscheidung* eine sehr ernste Bedeutung beigemessen wurde.

Dominikanische Laien – Laiendominikaner?

Heute gibt es die in den Orden inkorporierten Laien, die in Gruppen oder Fraternitäten organisiert sind und einen mehrjährigen Ausbildungs- und Eingliederungsprozess durchlaufen, an dessen Ende sie ein Versprechen auf Lebenszeit ablegen, nach der Regel der Dominikanischen Laiengemeinschaften zu leben, und sich damit der Jurisdiktion des Ordensmeisters unterstellen. Darüber hinaus kennt die Dominikanische Familie sogenannte assoziierte Gemeinschaften, die keine oder nur zeitlich begrenzte Versprechen ablegen, die jedoch vom Charisma des hl. Dominikus inspiriert einer apostolischen Berufung in Anbindung an den Orden oder an einzelne dominikanische Klöster folgen wollen.[16]

Eine Besonderheit des Dominikanerordens und in ihm seines Laienzweiges stellen die sogenannten Einzelmitglieder dar. Schon immer, aber infolge hoher Mobilität und tiefgreifender gesellschaftlicher Veränderungen heute wieder zunehmend, interessieren sich auch Einzelpersonen für die Nachfolge des hl. Dominikus als Laien. Auch wenn nicht alle von ihnen alleine leben, repräsentieren sie in gewisser Weise eine zumindest in unserem Teil der Welt ständig wachsende Bevölkerungsgruppe, in deren Leben sie Einblick haben und für die und deren Probleme sie ein besonderes Verständnis mitbringen. Dies ist als ein Zeichen der Zeit zu werten und stellt für den Orden in Zeiten zunehmender Vereinzelung eine noch nicht voll ausgelotete Chance dar. Personen, die sich aus persönlichen oder berufli-

15 Richard Weber, History of the Dominican Laity.
16 Von überregionaler Bedeutung sind das „International Dominican Youth Movement“ (IDYM) und die „Dominican Volunteers International“ (DVI).

chen Gründen nicht einer Fraternität anschließen können oder wollen oder fern einer Fraternität oder eines Konvents leben, können deshalb nach Abwägung der Umstände zur Einzelmitgliedschaft zugelassen werden.

Ebenso wie der merkwürdig oszillierende Begriff des Dritten Ordens zwischen regulierten und säkularen Mitgliedern nicht genau unterschied, ist auch heute die korrekte Bezeichnung und Selbstbezeichnung der Laien im Orden nicht geklärt. Dürfen, ja sollen sie sich Dominikaner nennen? Kürzlich hörte ich bei einer Podiumsdiskussion den bekannten Heidelberger Theologen Klaus Berger sich selbst als Zisterzienser bezeichnen. Professor Berger ist verheiratet und lebt „in der Welt". Er ist Familiar des Zisterzienser-Ordens und scheint kein Problem damit zu haben, in der Öffentlichkeit keinerlei sprachlichen Unterschied zwischen sich und den Mönchen des Ordens zu machen. Nur wenige Dominikanische Laien würden mit ähnlichem Selbstbewusstsein, und ohne wenigstens ein paar Erläuterungen abzugeben, als Dominikaner auftreten. Ausdruck dieser Unsicherheit über ihren Status innerhalb des Ordens ist die Tatsache, dass nach der Ablösung des „Dritten Ordens" mindestens zwei Begriffe im Umlauf sind, nämlich „Laiendominikaner" und „Dominikanische Laien". Beide haben einiges für sich.[17] „Dominikanische Laien" bringt mehr das Charakteristische, nämlich den *Laien*status dieses Zweigs der Dominikanischen Familie zum Ausdruck und somit die Tatsache, dass *Laien* eine dominikanische Berufung und einen Platz im Auftrag des Ordens haben. „Laien*dominikaner*" betont hingegen, dass Laien vollwertige Glieder des Ordens und somit Dominikaner und Dominikanerinnen sein können. Vielleicht könnte man aber auch für mehr pragmatische Zwecke „Dominikanische Laien" als einen Oberbegriff ansehen, der sowohl die inkorporierten Laien als auch die loser assoziierten Gemeinschaften umfasst. Laiendominikaner wären dann die inkorporierten Laien, die ein Versprechen auf Regel und Ordensmeister ablegen und dessen Jurisdiktion unterstellt sind. Sie sind authentische Mitglieder des Ordens und bilden mit den Brüdern, den Schwestern und den Moniales den Orden der Prediger. Trotzdem findet seit Langem innerhalb des Ordens eine intensive Diskussion über Stellung, Rezeption, Anerkennung und Selbstbild seiner Laien statt, die u. a. ihren Ausdruck in der Frage findet, ob die dominikanischen Laien be-

---

17 S. u. a.: Richard Weber, History of the Dominican Laity; und Charles R. Malatesta, The Purpose of the Dominican Laity http://www.southerndominicanlaity.org/THE%20PURPOSE%20OF%20THE%20DOMINICAN%20LAITY.pdf.

rechtigt sind, das Ordenskürzel OP (*Ordo Praedicatorum*) im Namen zu führen. Diese Frage wurde vor Kurzem geklärt: Die inkorporierten Laien dürfen das Kürzel ihrem Namen anfügen, allerdings nur im Rahmen einer Tätigkeit für den Orden. Zur eindeutigen Kennzeichnung als Laien müssen sie zudem ihrem Namen die Bezeichnung Herr oder Frau voranstellen. Das hinterlässt einen etwas schalen Beigeschmack. Erstens dürfen die Mitglieder der vom Ordensmeister unabhängigen apostolischen Schwesternkongregationen das OP ohne Einschränkung führen. Zweitens wirkt es unnatürlich und verkrampft, wenn man ein Dokument beispielsweise mit *Frau* Lieschen Müller OP unterschreibt, eine Wendung, die im normalen Schriftverkehr völlig unüblich ist. Vermutlich gibt noch nicht einmal jeder kulturelle Kontext diese Möglichkeit her. Drittens ist eine ordensinterne Verwendung eigentlich gerade *nicht* nötig.[18] Die vom Orden approbierte Regel für die Dominikanischen Gemeinschaften sagt ausdrücklich, dass die Dominikanischen Laien Mitglieder des Ordens sind und gemeinsam mit den Ordensbrüdern und -schwestern das Apostolat des Ordens tragen (I.9) und dass sie „wie jedes Mitglied des Dominikanerordens fähig [sein] müssen, das Wort Gottes zu verkündigen" (I.12). Wenn dem so ist, wie ist dann zu begründen, dass ich nur in wenigen Situationen (und nicht auf eigene Initiative) als Mitglied des Ordens erkennbar sein soll? Entweder ich bin „Dominikanerin in der Welt" und somit beides – in der Welt und Dominikanerin – oder ich bin Letzteres eben doch nicht. Hinzu kommt, dass es auch für die christlichen Laien immer schwieriger wird, ihre Stimme in der säkularisierten Welt hörbar zu machen. Die durch einen sorgsam verwendeten Namenszusatz diskret erkennbare Mitgliedschaft als Laie in einem alten Orden erregt oft Erstaunen, Neugier und Respekt und erleichtert gerade in vollkommen glaubensfernen Lebensbereichen den Einstieg ins Gespräch über Glaubensfragen – und somit ins Apostolat. Wenn man sich (noch?) nicht dazu durchringen kann, wenigstens die inkorporierten dominikanischen Laien als volle und mit den „klösterlichen" Zweigen der Familie gleichwertige Mitglieder des Ordens zu sehen, hätte man ihnen besser das eine Zeitlang übliche, seit Inkrafttreten der neuen Regelung aber nicht mehr erlaubte Kürzel OPL zur Unterscheidung von

18 Noch schwieriger wird diese Regelung dadurch, dass das „Frau" oder „Herr" bei Laien mit akademischen Titel durch „Dr." ersetzt werden kann. Das bringt nun die Mitglieder des Ersten und Zweiten Ordens in die Verlegenheit, sich als „P. Dr." oder „Sr. Dr." eindeutig identifizieren zu müssen.

den regulierten Ordensleuten, aber ohne die oben genannten Einschränkungen, zuerkannt. Das würde außerdem gleich zwei Fliegen mit einer Klappe schlagen: einerseits die Mitgliedschaft im Dominikanerorden und andererseits den ausdrücklich (und erwünscht) säkularen Charakter der Dominikanischen Laien erkennbar zu machen.

Wozu Laien in einem Orden?

Gleichgültig wie der Laienzweig des Predigerordens genannt wird oder sich selbst bezeichnet, stellt sich die Frage, was eine solche Einrichtung soll. Wozu hat ein Orden einen Laienzweig? Und wozu schließen sich Laien einem Orden an? Können Laien wirklich genuine Mitglieder eines Ordens sein?[19]

Im Gespräch mit Außenstehenden kommt häufig zuerst die Frage auf, ob man als Laiendominikaner zum Zölibat verpflichtet sei und sein Einkommen an den Orden abgeben müsse. Von innerhalb der Kirche dagegen wird häufig argumentiert, man sei eben doch kein „richtiger" Ordenschrist, denn dann hätte man ja das Leben im Kloster gewählt. Diese teils amüsanten, teils ernsthaften Anfragen spiegeln natürlich die Annahme wider, die Mitglieder der weltlichen Zweige mancher Orden seien so eine Art Mini-Religiose, die das klösterliche Leben imitieren, für den eigentlichen Schritt aber doch nicht den Mut aufgebracht haben. Über lange Zeiträume mag dieses Unbehagen berechtigt gewesen sein, und solche Anfragen an und Zweifel über die Identität des Dritten Ordens respektive der Dominikanischen Laiengemeinschaften sind auch heute nicht immer unbegründet.

P. Edward Schillebeeckx beschäftigte sich mit dieser Frage in seinem 1960 erschienenen kritischen Artikel „The Dominican Third Order: Old and New Style", einige Jahre bevor eine schrittweise Revision der Regel für die dominikanischen Laien begann.[20] Er schrieb: „Niemand kann leugnen,

---

19 S. hierzu auch: Burkhard Conrad, Die anderen Prediger. Die Dominikanische Gemeinschaft als Teil des *Ordo Praedicatorum.* Ordenskorrespondenz – Zeitschrift für Fragen des Ordenslebens, Jg. 52/2011, Nr. 2, S. 133–142.

20 Veröffentlicht in dem niederländischen Terziarenmagazin „Zwarp of Wit" in der Ausgabe von August/September 1960. Vor der Publikation als Vortrag vor den regionalen Oberen des Dritten Ordens in Leuwen am 6. Juni 1960 und in Utrecht am 29. Juni 1960; Quelle dieser Angaben und englische Übersetzung des Artikels von E. Schillebeeckx: http://www.dominicanwitness.com/?page_id=1031.

dass der Dritte Orden heute ein Problem darstellt. Dass es sich nicht nur um ein regionales, sondern vielmehr ein universales Problem handelt, wird offenkundig aus den Formulierungen des Generalkapitels von Caleruega im Jahr 1958: „Während die Notwendigkeit für zahlreiche Änderungen in der Regel der Terziaren aus den Berichten der Promotoren ersichtlich ist, ersuchen wir dringend unseren hochwürdigen Generalmeister eine Kommission einzurichten, die eine gründliche Studie *über die Natur des Dritten Ordens* durchzuführen hat.'" (Übersetzung aus dem Englischen und Hervorhebung GNY). Laut P. Schillebeeckx brachte das Generalkapitel somit nicht nur Zweifel an gewissen Varianten und Ausformungen laiendominikanischer Existenz zum Ausdruck, sondern eine fundamentale Unsicherheit in Bezug auf den Dritten Orden überhaupt und forderte auf zu prüfen, ob der Laienzweig entweder als Ganzes obsolet sei oder einer grundlegenden Erneuerung bedürfe. Er führt weiter aus, dass der Dritte Orden zu einer devotionalen Gebetsgemeinschaft von zumeist älteren Leuten geworden sei, die sich aus dem einen oder anderen Grund einem dominikanischen Kloster verbunden fühlten. Wann immer jedoch die Brüder für ihre apostolischen Aufgaben Rat und Unterstützung von Laien brauchten, wendeten sie sich ohne Ausnahme (!) an andere moderne katholische Laienorganisationen, während die eigenen Ordenslaien lediglich für Hilfsdienste wie das Adressieren von Briefen und Unterstützung bei Pfarrfesten herangezogen würden. Den Grund sieht er darin, dass der Dritte Orden sich als eine Art Anhängsel des Ersten Ordens (der Brüder also) im monastischen, nicht aber im apostolischen Sinn präsentiere und im Gegensatz zu anderen Laienbewegungen die Chance verpasst habe, eine reife, auf das Apostolat ausgerichtete Laienspiritualität zu entwickeln. Die sich in der (damaligen) Regel, der Terminologie und den Gruppenstrukturen spiegelnde Imitation des Monastischen sieht Schillebeeckx zu Recht als unnatürlich und der Laienspiritualität fremd an und verortet darin die mangelnde Attraktivität des Dritten Ordens insbesondere für junge Leute in der Mitte des 20. Jahrhunderts, das doch zugleich schon *vor* dem II. Vatikanischen Konzil und erst recht danach ein zunehmendes Bewusstsein der Laien für ihre Rolle und Verantwortung in der und für die Kirche erlebte. Nach dieser bitteren Bestandsaufnahme schlägt Schillebeeckx eine Neuorientierung des Dritten Ordens vor. Zwar gehörten die Laien, wie alle Glieder der Kirche zu den *separata a mundo*, den aus der Welt für Gott Herausgerufenen, die nicht in dieser Welt, sondern im himmlischen Königreich zu Hause sind. Doch sind sie das auf andere Weise als die Priester und die

Ordensleute, die ein klösterliches Leben gewählt haben. Wie jene müssen sie aus dem Gebet leben und die „Häresie der Aktion", also einen leeren Aktivismus meiden. Doch sollte ein erneuerter Geist des Dritten Ordens, der zu einem bewussten geistlichen Leben im Sinne der Bergpredigt führt, sich in jeder Hinsicht, auch im Gebet, nicht in monastischen, sondern in eigenen (laikalen) Formen ausdrücken. Vor diesem gedanklichen Hintergrund wäre der Dritte Orden *new style* als eine apostolische Laienbewegung und als *Dominikanische* Laienbewegung dann tatsächlich als eine Erweiterung und Ergänzung des Ersten Ordens anzusehen. Als Vorbild könnten die neuen apostolischen Laienbewegungen (damals z. B. die katholische Aktion) dienen, die eigentlich bereits das verkörpern, was Dominikus für seinen Laienzweig im Sinn gehabt haben mag. Was wäre dann aber das unterscheidend Dominikanische an einem solchen Dritten Orden *new style*? Ein solcher *Dominikanischer* Dritter Orden wären nach Schillebeeckx genuine Laien, die im vollen Einklang mit den Nöten und Bedürfnissen der Zeit am Apostolat des Ersten Ordens Anteil haben, dessen priesterliche Aufgaben häufig durch die apostolische (und heutzutage auch administrative) Beanspruchung in den Hintergrund gedrängt werden. Das Laienapostolat wäre komplementär zum Apostolat des priesterlichen Dienstes womit der apostolische Radius des Ordens erheblich in Bereiche ausgedehnt werden könnte, die für die Ordensleute nicht oder nur schwer erreichbar sind.

Manches von dem, was P. Schillebeeckx in diesem Artikel im Jahr 1960, also noch vor dem II. Vatikanum, vorschlug, ist inzwischen umgesetzt worden. Ab 1964 wurde die Regel einer mehrjährigen Phase der experimentellen Weiterentwicklung unterzogen,[21] bis sie 1985[22] zur derzeit gültigen Form fand, in der weitestgehend auf monastische Implikationen verzichtet und das Laienapostolat stark betont wird.[23]

21 Jean Bernard Dousse, Die Dominikanischen Laiengemeinschaften vor und nach dem Zweiten Vatikanischen Konzil. In Johannes H. Weise, Jeder ist ein Wort Gottes für den andern. S. 34 ff.

22 Approbation durch den hl. Stuhl 1987.

23 Zumindest im deutschen Sprachraum ist längere Zeit in den Übersetzungen der Regel und in den Direktorien der Dominikanischen Laien auf monastische Begriffe verzichtet worden. In Anpassung an den internationalen Sprachgebrauch ist im neuen Direktorium unserer Nachbarprovinz Teutonia wieder von Fraternitäten, Novizen, Novizenmeistern u.ä. die Rede, eine Terminologie, die aus demselben Grund voraussichtlich auch im zukünftigen Direktorium der süddeutsch-österreichischen Provinz Verwendung finden wird. Das ist eine Entwicklung, die ich für unglücklich halte und von der ich annehme, dass sie über kurz oder lang revidiert werden wird.

Die Entwicklung der Dominikanischen Laiengemeinschaften fand in den Generalkapiteln des Ordens seit den Achtziger Jahren stets große Beachtung. Viele der dort gefassten Beschlüsse und Vorschläge wurden zielstrebig und mit großem Engagement umgesetzt, was den Berichten der Ordensmeister und der Generalpromotoren für die Laien bzw. für die Dominikanische Familie und den jeweiligen Kapitelsakten entnommen werden kann.[24] Beispielsweise fand in den letzten Jahren eine zunehmende Vernetzung der dominikanischen Laien auf internationaler Ebene statt, die in der Gründung von kontinentalen Räten wie des European Council of Lay Dominican Fraternities (ECLDF) und eines internationalen Rats der Dominikanischen Laiengemeinschaften (International Council of Lay Dominican Fraternities, ICLDF) eine wichtige Institutionalisierung erreichte. Das hatte zur Folge, dass die Dominikanischen Laien seit der Beklagung des *status quo* in den Kapitelsakten von 1958 wesentlich selbständiger geworden sind und viele ihrer Angelegenheiten in Kooperation mit den Generalpromotoren für die Laien inzwischen selbst regeln. Seinen Ausdruck fand dies u. a. darin, dass die aktuelle Regel 1985 auf dem ersten Weltkongress der Dominikanischen Laiengemeinschaften in Montréal formuliert wurde. Dieser Umstand ist deshalb bemerkenswert, weil erstmals Laiendominikaner an der Formulierung ihrer eigenen Regel beteiligt waren,[25] und somit eine der wesentlichen Forderungen von P. Schillebeeckx nach mehr Autonomie für den „Dritten Orden *new style*" verwirklicht wurde.

Anders als von P. Schillebeeckx vorgeschlagen wurde auch in der neuen Regel auf eigene Gebetsformen verzichtet; vielmehr wird die Pflege der traditionellen dominikanischen Gebetsformen, des Stundengebets und des Rosenkranzes ausdrücklich empfohlen. Das ist kein Rückfall in quasimonastische Gepflogenheiten des Dritten Ordens. Das Insistieren auf *ausschließlich* eigenen Gebetsweisen würde eine Parallelwelt der Laien innerhalb des Ordens befördern. Vor allem das Stundengebet ist ein starkes verbindendes Element zwischen allen Zweigen der Dominikanischen Familie und sollte nicht leichtfertig aufgegeben werden, auch wenn die Einhaltung wenigstens der großen Horen im Trubel des Alltags „in der Welt" oftmals nicht leicht ist. Das schließt natürlich nicht aus, dass die einzelnen Fraternitäten oder auch Provinzen zusätzlich eigene Gebetstraditionen entwickeln.

---

24 S. z. B. Johannes H. Weise, Jeder ist ein Wort Gottes für den anderen. S. 246 ff.
25 Ebd., S. 22 f.

P. Schillebeeckx mag 1960 übersehen haben, was inzwischen andernorts konstatiert wurde: dass es gute und schlechte, fruchtbare und unfruchtbare Zeiten im Dritten Orden gibt, die getreulich die Höhen und Tiefen des Ersten Ordens widerspiegeln und dass jeder erfolgreichen Reform des Ersten eine Erneuerung des Dritten Ordens folgte; dass beide also, wie es der amerikanische Dominikaner Richard Weber († 1995) formuliert hat, in einem symbiotischen Verhältnis zu stehen scheinen.[26] Dennoch und trotz der positiven Entwicklungen können wir nicht ignorieren, dass einige der von Schillebeeckx mit schonungsloser Deutlichkeit geäußerten Kritikpunkte immer noch valide sind. Die Entwicklung des Dritten Ordens, seit 1974 Dominikanische Laiengemeinschaft (DLG) genannt, zu einer Dominikanischen Laien*bewegung* ist ein Traum geblieben. Noch immer gelingt es uns zumindest in den westlichen Ländern zumeist nicht, junge Leute in nennenswerter Zahl anzuziehen oder als aktive und apostolische Gemeinschaften erkennbar zu sein.[27]

Natürlich ist dies teilweise auch in allgemeinen Trends der Zeit begründet, beispielsweise einem weit verbreiteten Unwillen, sich langfristig zu binden, Vorbehalte gegen Lehren im weitesten Sinne und die kirchliche im Besonderen und eine tiefe Krise des Vertrauens in alle Institutionen. Das Individuum in den westlichen Gesellschaften vertraut nur noch sich selbst und seinen persönlichen Erfahrungen. Mehr als alle anderen trifft dieses Misstrauen die Institution, die sich auf zwei Quellen beruft, die das Gegenteil individueller Erfahrung zu sein scheinen: die Heilige Schrift und die Tradition. Innerkirchlich mangelt es an einer erwachsenen katholischen Laienspiritualität; statt ein genuin laikales Bewusstsein und eine ausgereifte Laienspiritualität und -ekklesiologie zu entwickeln, scheinen zumindest hierzulande viele Laien mit dem Wunsch nach Weihen, Ordinationen und Ämtern eher einen Hang zu einer gewissen „Klerikalisierung“ zu haben, die eigentlich einer echten Laikalität ebenso fremd sein sollte wie monastische Lebensformen; diese und andere strukturelle Themen scheinen viele katholische Laien (zumindest im Vordergrund) mehr zu bewegen als Fragen des

---

26 Richard Weber, History of the Dominican Laity.

27 Das Bild der Dominikanischen Laien präsentiert sich weltweit sehr unterschiedlich. Während sie in Teilen Asiens und der USA florieren und dort eigenständige und selbstbewusste Zweige des Ordens darstellen (allein in Vietnam soll es etwa 100 000 Dominikanische Laien geben), stagnieren sie im „Alten Europa“. Hier sind Aufbrüche in der Kirche eher mit den neuen geistlichen Bewegungen als mit den alten Dritten Orden bzw. den Dominikanischen Laien verbunden.

geistlichen Lebens, einer tiefen Freundschaft mit Christus und einer engagierten, freudigen und überzeugenden Weitergabe des Glaubens. Genau dafür könnten jedoch die Spiritualität des Dominikanerordens ebenso wie seine flexible und demokratische Struktur ein hervorragendes Modell bieten. Diese organische Spiritualität, die sich im Lauf der 800-jährigen Ordensgeschichte in vielfältigen Facetten manifestiert hat und den ganzen Menschen fordert und anspricht – die Einheit von Gemeinschaft, Gebet, Studium und Zeugnis-Geben, Kontemplation und Aktion, Verwurzelung im Reichtum der Tradition und Ausgreifen nach Gegenwart und Zukunft – ist eigentlich kein Spezifikum des Predigerordens, sondern nichts anderes als eine Blaupause für eine aus dem Vollen schöpfende, eine „ganzheitliche" christliche Existenz. Es ist allerdings hervorzuheben, dass die explizite Integration des Studiums das spezifisch dominikanische Kennzeichen eines solchen Programms christlichen Lebens darstellt, ein Programmpunkt, der heute in Zeiten rapide schwindender Kenntnisse aller Aspekte des Christlichen und Katholischen mehr Not tut denn je.

Daher kann man die Frage, ob Laien sinnvoll Mitglieder eines Ordens sein können und ob es sinnvoll für einen Orden ist, einen integrierten Laienzweig zu haben, für den Dominikanerorden zumindest theoretisch mit Ja beantworten. Die Berufung der Ordenslaien ist nicht die Berufung zu einem Lebensstil, wie es die der Brüder und Schwestern zumindest *auch* sein mag oder wie es eine Berufung zum Eheleben darstellt; vielmehr teilen alle Zweige des Ordens die Berufung zu einem Charisma,[28] das gut durch die Motti des Ordens – [Streben nach der Erkenntnis der] Wahrheit, Loben, Segnen, Verkünden – und in pragmatischer Hinsicht durch die vier Säulen dominikanischen Lebens – Gemeinschaft, Gebet, Studium und Verkündigung – beschrieben werden kann.

Dieses dominikanische Ideal ist attraktiv und anspruchsvoll, wird aber in seiner Gänze nur selten gelebt. Die meisten Gruppen treffen sich zwar regelmäßig zum gemeinsamen Gebet und sorgen auch für eine gewisse Weiterbildung durch gemeinsame Lektüre, Vorträge oder die Organisation von Studientagen. Viele ihrer Mitglieder wirken im Stillen in ihrer privaten und beruflichen Umgebung im apostolischen Sinn, eine Form von Verkündigung, die gerade wegen ihres diskreten Auftretens unersetzlich ist. Aber trotz der im und durch den Orden reichhaltig vorhandenen

---

28 Vivian Gilbreth, Can Dominicans Really Be Lay People? 1985, http://www.spiritualitytoday.org/spir2day/853725gilbreth.html.

Ressourcen und Erfahrungen ist es uns, den dominikanischen Laien, immer noch nicht gelungen, zu einer lebendigen und sich ständig erneuernden apostolischen Bewegung zu werden. Häufig unterscheidet unsere Fraternitäten nicht viel von anderen Laiengruppen, die sich im Umfeld von Klöstern auch von Orden ansiedeln, die über keinen Laienzweig verfügen. Der Orden hat seit dem Generalkapitel von Bologna 1998 zwar auch lose assoziierte Gruppen und neue Initiativen, die vom dominikanischen Charisma inspiriert werden, ausdrücklich begrüßt und ermutigt, aber auch von solchen gelegentlich entstehenden Gruppierungen ist bisher keine grundlegende Änderung dieser Situation ausgegangen. Woran liegt das?

Einige Gründe sind vermutlich in der allgemein-kirchlichen Realität in den deutschsprachigen Ländern zu finden. Wie bereits oben angesprochen ist auch 50 Jahre nach dem Konzil das Bewusstsein der Laien, des Gottesvolkes also, für ihre Verantwortung für die Ausbreitung des Wortes noch nicht sehr entwickelt. Gleichzeitig ist trotz der heute im Vergleich zur ersten Hälfte des 20. Jahrhunderts so viel größeren Möglichkeiten der Information und Selbstbildung der Wissensstand in Sachen Glaube und Kirche auf ein beklagenswertes Niveau gesunken. Ich wage zu behaupten, dass dieser Wissensstand bei jedem durchschnittlichen Katholiken nur durch die Katechese vonseiten der Familie als „Hauskirche" und die Pfarrei in Deutschland vor dem Konzil wesentlich höher war als heute, so dass das Projekt der Neu-Evangelisierung eigentlich zunächst im Innern der Kirche ansetzen muss. In Gemeindekreisen weiß man, dass inzwischen viele Eltern fast genauso in den Erstkommunionunterricht einbezogen werden müssen wie ihre Kinder. Das belegt jedoch eindrücklich, wie sehr heute ein echtes Laienapostolat nottut, nachdem die traditionellen Quellen der Glaubensvermittlung mehr und mehr wegfallen. Hinzu kommt eine allgemeine Ratlosigkeit über die Möglichkeit religiöser Rede, des Sprechens von Gott in einer Welt, die so radikal säkularisiert ist, dass diese Rede sehr schnell zu Befremden und oft schon fast reflexartigen Abwehrreaktionen führt. Für viele von uns ist daher ein Verkündigungsauftrag eine große Herausforderung – in mehrfacher Hinsicht. Auf der anderen Seite bringen die Laien des Ordens aus ihren Berufen und außerberuflichen Tätigkeiten sehr viele Fach- und Spezialkenntnisse ebenso mit, wie Erfahrungen aus ihren vielfältigen persönlichen Lebensumständen, die für die Brüder und Schwestern nicht oder nur schwer erschließbar sind. Diese beiden Aspekte zusammenzubringen, nämlich einerseits die Laienmitglieder des Dominikanerordens für ihren Verkündigungsauftrag zu stärken und zu schulen

und andererseits ihre fachlichen, intellektuellen, spirituellen und persönlichen Ressourcen in Zusammenarbeit mit den anderen Ordenszweigen für den ganzen Orden nutzbar zu machen, ist eine drängende Aufgabe, der sich der Orden zum eigenen Nutzen mehr als bisher stellen muss. Genau das ist eins um andere Mal von Generalkapiteln[29] ebenso wie den Kapiteln der Provinz des hl. Albert gefordert worden. Stellvertretend sollen hier zwei Ausschnitte aus dem Bericht des Ordensmeisters für das Generalkapitel in Providence 2001 zitiert werden, die in wesentlichen Teilen auch Eingang in die offiziellen Kapitelsakten gefunden haben:

> „Es gibt einen wachsenden Sinn für die Freundschaft innerhalb der Dominikanischen Familie, aber dennoch gibt es oft wenig Fortschritt hinsichtlich einer gemeinsamen Mission. Oft sind die Brüder und Schwestern so überausgelastet, dass keine Zeit bleibt für die Entwicklung neuer gemeinsamer Projekte. … Manchmal unterschätzen die Brüder die Begabungen der Schwestern und Laien gewaltig, indem sie in Bezug auf die Dominikanische Familie eher an eine weitere Verpflichtung als an eine immense Ressource für die Verkündigung des Evangeliums denken … Manche Regionen wie Nordamerika und Europa müssen Strukturen entwickeln, die alle Zweige der Dominikanischen Familie zusammenbringen.“[30]

> „Die Vitalität der [Dominikanischen] Laiengemeinschaften hängt weitgehend davon ab, ob wir sie als aktive Mitarbeiter in der Mission des Ordens verstehen, die aufgrund ihrer Erfahrung als Laien und ihrer Fachkenntnis einen einzigartigen Beitrag zu leisten haben. Manchmal sehen die Brüder sie als fromme Jünger, deren Rolle lediglich darin besteht, uns zuzuhören. Einige Laiendominikaner bringen akademische Kenntnisse in Bereichen wie Wirtschaft, Wissenschaft, Ökologie, Soziologie usw. mit, die dem Orden helfen können, an den gesellschaftlichen Debatten teilzunehmen. Andere haben Erfahrungen mit der Industrie und mit den Künsten. Manche helfen uns, Gruppen zu erreichen, die vielleicht weg sind von der Kirche, wie junge Leute oder Arme. Zum Zweiten bedeutet die Vorbereitung auf diesen Auftrag eine tiefgründige Ausbildung in unserer theologischen Tradition. Das ist mehr als nur ein Lernen über das Leben des hl. Dominikus und der hl. Katharina. Es ist eine Initiation hinein in unsere Art Theologie zu treiben, ob nun akademisch oder nicht.“[31]

Wie können diese „Träume“ Wirklichkeit werden? Die beiden Zitate lassen zwei Schwerpunkte erkennen: Kooperation und Ausbildung. An beidem

29 Johannes H. Weise, Jeder ist ein Wort Gottes für den andern. S. 246 ff.
30 Ebd., S. 299.
31 Ebd., S. 300.

mangelt es erheblich. Die einzelnen Zweige der dominikanischen Familie, ja sogar die der Kernfamilie – Brüder, Schwestern, Moniales und inkorporierte Laien – führen hierzulande oft eine Art Parallelexistenz, die ihre Berührungspunkte nur durch die Arbeit der Promotoren, durch einzelne persönliche Kontakte oder gelegentlich bei lokalen oder provinzweiten „Tagen der Dominkanischen Familie“ finden. Das mag zu Zeiten großer Mitgliederzahlen durchaus seine Berechtigung gehabt haben. Es ist auch nicht von der Hand zu weisen, dass die seelsorgerliche Arbeit der Brüder für Schwestern und Laien und manchmal auch die von Schwesterngemeinschaften für Laiengruppen eine zusätzliche Belastung in einem sowieso schon übervollen Programm darstellt. Das ist aber nur solange so, wie das jeweilige Potenzial für die gemeinsamen Ziele nicht aktiviert und ausgeschöpft wird. Hier kommt dann der zweite Punkt ins Spiel. Wenn der Laienzweig des Dominikanerordens ein fruchttragender Zweig werden soll, muss er besser ausgebildet werden, als das bisher der Fall war und derzeit der Fall ist. Damit sind natürlich zuerst die Laien selbst, ihre Ordensassistenten, ihre Räte und Promotoren angesprochen. Darüber hinaus sollte der Orden jedoch erwägen (und mehr als nur erwägen), seine Institutionen für die Ausbildung (z. B. auf Provinzebene) zumindest bei geeigneten Themen für alle Zweige zu öffnen und entsprechend zu planen. Das könnte auch neue Wege beinhalten, wie die gezielte Entwicklung von einzelnen Unterrichtseinheiten mindestens für alle deutschsprachigen Entitäten (in Deutschland, Österreich und der Schweiz), vielleicht aber auch darüber hinaus, die gegebenenfalls auch virtuell, also über das Internet zugänglich gemacht werden können. Eine gute Kenntnis der bei den Laien vorhandenen Qualifikationen (z. B. Wirtschaft, Medizin, Kunst, Soziologie, Psychologie, Naturwissenschaften, alle Sozialberufe und vieles mehr) kann darüber hinaus für alle, auch für die Novizen der klösterlichen Zweige, Zugang zu Ausbildungsinhalten erleichtern, die man sich sonst woanders zusammensuchen muss. Gleichzeitig muss auch bei den Laien ein Bewusstseinswandel eintreten. Es ist heute eine enorme Herausforderung, „Prediger des Wortes“ zu sein. Wir können auf fast nichts mehr bauen. Wir brauchen eine Ausbildung, die weit über ein paar grundlegende Kenntnisse über den hl. Dominikus, die Ordensgeschichte und die Spiritualität des Ordens hinausgeht. Nur so können wir über ein Nischendasein innerhalb und außerhalb des Ordens hinauskommen und fruchtbarer in den Dienst des Evangeliums treten. Dafür brauchen wir unsere Brüder und Schwestern, mit denen gemeinsam wir neue Konzepte entwickeln müssen. In anderen Ländern, wie

in Vietnam, den Philippinen, aber auch in Osteuropa und in den USA, ist man in beiden Punkten – Kooperation und gemeinsame bzw. gegenseitige Ausbildung – schon weiter.[32] Das ist eine gute Nachricht, denn das bedeutet, dass es Orte gibt, wo wir uns Rat und Inspiration holen können.

Die dominikanischen Laien in der Provinz des heiligen Albert in Süddeutschland und Österreich

In der Provinz des hl. Albert gibt es wie fast überall Dominikanische Laien mit unterschiedlichen „Lebensformen". Unter ihnen finden sich Sozialarbeiter und Ärzte, Behördenmitarbeiter, Gemeindereferenten und Künstler, Wissenschaftler und Juristen, Studenten und Hausfrauen, Alte und Junge, Männer und Frauen, Väter, Mütter und Singles. Sie arbeiten freischaffend und in Firmen, an Universitäten und in Pfarrgemeinden, an Behörden und ehrenamtlich. Gruppen im Sinne der Dominikanischen Laiengemeinschaften, deren Mitglieder Versprechen ablegen, existieren in München, Graz, Freiburg, Regensburg, Preying, Blitzenreute und Bamberg. Einzelmitglieder leben in Wien, Innsbruck, Heidelberg, Bad Wörishofen und Bronnbach. Assoziierte Gruppen ohne Versprechen gibt es in Wien und Konstanz. Bis vor Kurzem waren die Gruppen und Einzelmitglieder recht isoliert voneinander, und es gab keine provinzweiten Strukturen, wie sie das Direktorium aus dem Jahr 1992 vorsieht. Das hat sich grundlegend geändert und ist der engagierten und beharrlichen Aufbauarbeit zu danken, die P. Johannes H. Weise in den letzten Jahren zunächst als Assistent des Provinzpromotors für die Dominikanischen Laien und ab 2011 als Provinzpromotor geleistet hat und die seither Früchte in Gestalt von Neuaufnahmen, zeitlichen und endgültigen Versprechen, der Gründung der Freiburger Gruppe und einer neuen Gemeinschaft in München, einer zunehmenden Vernetzung und der Installation überregionaler Strukturen getragen hat.

32 Johannes H. Weise (Hrsg), Jeder ist ein Wort Gottes für den anderen. S. 287f.; außerdem: http://vietcatholic.net/News/Html/73012.htm und http://www.ordopraedicatorum.org/tag/vietnamese-martyrs/.

Die inkorporierten Laiengruppen und Einzelmitglieder in der Provinz

Mit Schreiben des damaligen Provinzials P. Dietmar Schon wurde im November 2007 in *Bamberg* eine neue Dominikanische Laiengemeinschaft errichtet und die Priorin des Dominikanerinnenklosters Heilig Grab Sr. Berthilla Heil zur Ordensassistentin mit dem Auftrag ernannt, die Entfaltung der Gruppe zu begleiten, Impulse aus der geistlichen Tradition des Ordens zu vermitteln und für die Verbindung der Laiengemeinschaft zum Gesamtorden zu sorgen.[33] Die Gruppe ist dem Kloster und seiner Spiritualität eng verbunden. Nachdem sich in den vergangenen Jahren einige Mitglieder auf den Weg in die fester umrissene Bindung als Dominikanische Laien gemacht haben und auch schon erste Versprechen abgelegt wurden, steht die Gruppe nun vor der Herausforderung, die demokratischen Leitungsstrukturen auszubilden, von denen die Dominikanischen Laiengemeinschaften wie der ganze Orden gekennzeichnet sind. Im November 2011 war die Gruppe Gastgeber des provinzweiten Studientags zum Thema „Abendmahl und Eucharistie in ökumenischer Perspektive“.[34]

Die Dominikanische Laiengemeinschaft St. Raphael in *Blitzenreute* wurde 1989 am Fest des hl. Dominikus im ehemaligen Kloster Heiligkreuzthal unter der Assistenz von P. Dr. Michael Marsch gegründet. Sie besteht heute aus fünf Mitgliedern, die sich an jedem ersten Sonntag im Monat mit weiteren Interessierten zu einem Studientag treffen. Ein solcher Studientag beginnt mit Rosenkranz und hl. Messe in der Dominikuskapelle in Vorsee und wird mit einem Vortrag und einem gemeinsamen Mittagessen fortgesetzt.[35]

Im Januar 2010 entstand mit P. Johannes H. Weise als Ordensassistenten an der von Dominikanern betreuten Pfarrei St. Martin eine Gruppe der Dominikanischen Laiengemeinschaften in *Freiburg im Breisgau*, die sich unter das Patronat Jordans von Sachsen stellte. Drittordensgemeinschaften sind in Freiburg schon für das 15. Jahrhundert belegt[36] – eine Tradition, die nach langer Pause jetzt also wieder aufgenommen wird. Die Gruppe star-

33 Provinzzeitung Nr. 12/2007.

34 http://downloads.eo-bamberg.de/2/124/1/29863973190842599661.pdf.

35 P. Johannes H. Weise, persönliche Mitteilung.

36 William Hinnebusch: Kleine Geschichte des Dominikanerordens. St. Benno Verlag Leipzig, 2004. S. 118.

tete mit sechs Männern und Frauen ins Noviziat,[37] von denen vier ein Jahr später im Januar 2011 ihr einjähriges Versprechen ablegten. Im selben Jahr mussten allerdings zwei der Mitglieder aus beruflichen Gründen Freiburg verlassen. Dennoch legten drei Mitglieder im Januar 2012 im Rahmen eines Studientages im Kloster Heilig Kreuz in Augsburg das dreijährige Versprechen ab, und das vierte Mitglied erneuerte das einjährige Versprechen um ein weiteres Jahr. Melanie Maria Immaculata Delpech, die Präsidentin der Gruppe, wurde ebenfalls im Januar 2012 zur ersten Provinzpräsidentin der Dominikanischen Laiengemeinschaften gewählt. Im Dezember 2012 konnte ein neues Mitglied ins Postulat aufgenommen werden. Seit dem Weggang von P. Johannes nach München ist P. Martin R. Grandinger der Ordensassistent der Gruppe, die sich einmal im Monat zum gemeinsamen Studium und Gebet trifft. Außerdem finden seit Sommer 2011 im etwa achtwöchigen Turnus mit einem eigenen Programm abwechselnd in Freiburg und Heidelberg Treffen mit den beiden Heidelberger Einzelmitgliedern statt. Das Apostolat der Gruppe gestaltet sich nach den individuellen Möglichkeiten im Beruf und in Zusammenarbeit mit den Dominikanern in der Pfarrei. Alle bisherigen Mitglieder verfügen mit ihrer beruflichen und ehrenamtlichen Ausbildung (Theologiestudium, Ausbildung in seelsorglicher Gesprächsbegleitung) und ihrer langjährigen Erfahrung in der Gemeindearbeit über außerordentlich gute Qualifikationen für den Dienst in der Verkündigung.[38]

In *Graz* gab es schon vor 1938 zwei Gruppen, damals noch Dritter Orden und in Männer- und Frauengruppe getrennt. Einen Hinweis darauf gibt die Inschrift an einem Grab des Dritten Ordens, das 1938 als erste Jahreszahl trägt. Diese Geschlechtertrennung wurde bis in die jüngere Vergangenheit aufrecht erhalten, bis der 2012 verstorbene P. Max Svoboda die beiden Gruppen schließlich zusammenführte. Als deren Ordensassistent gelang es ihm außerdem, neues Interesse für die Dominikanische Laiengemeinschaft zu wecken.[39] Nach dem tragischen Tod von P. Max und der kurz danach angekündigten Auflösung des dominikanischen Standorts in Graz ging die Gruppe durch eine Zeit der Krise und Neuorientierung. Nach einem schweren Jahr legten jedoch im Februar 2013 vier der neuen

37 Provinzzeitung Nr. 02/10.

38 Melanie Maria Immaculata Delpech, persönliche Mitteilung.

39 Provinzzeitung Nr. 12/2008.

Mitglieder ihre dreijährigen Versprechen ab.[40] Neuer Ordensassistent ist P. Thomas Gabriel Brogl, der die Fraternität etwa alle zwei Monate von Wien aus besucht. Es ist bemerkenswert, dass also heute in Graz die seit 1466 bestehende traditionsreiche dominikanische Präsenz[41] allein von den Dominikanischen Laien weitergeführt wird. Zurzeit besteht die Gruppe aus zwölf Mitgliedern mit Versprechen und überschreitet somit als einzige in der Provinz die für eine Fraternität vorgeschriebene Mindestzahl von sechs Mitgliedern.

In *München* gab es schon vor dem ersten Dominikanerkonvent eine dominikanische Drittordensgemeinschaft, die sich um die vorletzte Jahrhundertwende gründete, nach einiger Zeit wieder unterging und in den 1950er Jahren, nachdem die Theatinerkirche den Dominikanern anvertraut worden war, neu gegründet wurde. Die Fraternität trifft sich einmal im Monat zu Gebet und Vortrag mit P. Klaus Obermeyer. Gegenwärtig befindet sich außerdem an der Theatinerkirche eine zweite Gemeinschaft im Aufbau, die an einer stark apostolischen Ausrichtung interessiert ist. Die neue werdende Fraternität trifft sich seit Februar 2013 einmal im Monat, um sich in das Leben als Dominikanische Laiengemeinschaft einzuüben, sich den reichen Schatz dominikanischer Quellen und Tradition und die dominikanische Spiritualität anzueignen und sich auf ihren apostolischen Auftrag vorzubereiten.[42]

Eine in *Preying* schon länger bestehende Gruppe wurde im Juni 2012 durch ein Dekret des Provinzials als Dominikanische Laiengemeinschaft „im Aufbau" errichtet und im Juli 2012 vom Provinzpromotor für die Laien in der Pfarrkirche von Preying offiziell eingeführt. Als Moderator wurde Diakon Dr. Stephan Laurentius Rank, früher Mitglied der Regensburger Laiengemeinschaft, bestimmt. Der Gemeinschaft gehören neun Personen an, von denen die meisten aus dem heimatlichen Pfarrverband stammen. Die Gemeinschaft kommt einmal im Monat zu einem Treffen zusammen, das mit der eucharistischen Anbetung in der Pfarrkirche beginnt. Dabei steht neben dem persönlichen Austausch und der gegenseitigen Stärkung im Glauben die katechetische Fortbildung in Form von Schriftauslegung, Auseinandersetzung mit Ordensgeschichte und Glaubenslehre sowie mit Fragen des täglichen Lebens in Familie, Beruf und Gemeinde im Mittelpunkt. Einige der Mitglieder sind als Grund- und Haupt-

40 Wolfgang Habith, persönliche Mitteilung.
41 Die Geschichte der Dominikaner in Graz. Provinzzeitung Nr. 07–08/2008.
42 Dr. W. Antonia Genovich und P. Johannes Weise, persönliche Mitteilung.

schullehrerinnen katechetisch tätig und können in der Gemeinschaft Anregungen für ihre berufliche Tätigkeit gewinnen, während andere in der Pfarrseelsorge oder im Beruf in der Auseinandersetzung mit der sozialen und gesellschaftlichen Realität stehen.[43]

Die Idee der Gründung einer Dominikanischen Laiengemeinschaft in *Regensburg*[44] kam 1992 im Anschluss an eine der damals sehr populären Kirchenführungen von Sr. M. Johanna Geßner in der Dominikanerinnenkirche Heilig Kreuz auf. Gefördert durch die Bereitschaft der Schwestern und die Unterstützung durch P. Hilarius Barth, der zu dieser Zeit gute Kontakte zum Kloster pflegte und später auch die ersten Versprechen abnahm, konnte bereits ein Jahr später durch Sr. Margarete Reisinger eine kleine Gruppe sowohl in Regensburg als auch in Altenthann gegründet werden. Sr. Johanna wurde die erste geistliche Assistentin der Regensburger Gruppe. Derzeit umfasst die Gruppe vier Mitglieder mit Versprechen. An den monatlichen Treffen nehmen stets auch einige Gäste teil, die sich zwar nicht oder noch nicht durch ein Versprechen binden möchten, aber bei den Aktionen der Gruppe wie Wallfahrten, Begegnungstagen, Teilnahme an diözesanen Treffen bzw. bei Besuchen anderer Gruppen der Ordensfamilie dabei sind und im November 2012 halfen, einen provinzweiten Studientag zu dem Thema: „Wie heute von Gott sprechen?“ mit etwa 30 Teilnehmern im Dominikanischen Zentrum Regensburg zu organisieren.

Die monatlichen Treffen beginnen mit Gebet und gemeinsamer Schriftlesung mit anschließender Aussprache, die von einem Mitglied vorbereitet wird. Um selbst von Gott sprechen zu können, legt die Gruppe bei ihren Zusammenkünften großen Wert auf die von der Ordensassistentin (derzeit Sr. M. Marina Dirks) geleitete Katechese und die Erarbeitung eines fundierten Glaubenswissens. Die Treffen schließen mit dem Angelus und dem Gedenken für die Verstorbenen. Für die Mitglieder ist die gegenseitige Unterstützung vor allem durch das Gebet und die Verbundenheit mit dem Orden eine Kraftquelle für das apostolische Wirken in Familie, Beruf und Gemeinde.[45]

In *Wien* liegt eine besondere Situation vor. Die inkorporierten dominikanischen Laien werden durch drei Einzelmitglieder mit Versprechen

43 Dr. Stefan Laurentius Rank, persönliche Mitteilung.

44 Sr. M. Marina Dirks, Die Dominikanische Laiengemeinschaft in Regensburg. http://www.dominikaner.org/Dominikusheft/dominikus2007.pdf.

45 Dr. A. Therese Treiber, persönliche Mitteilung.

und einen Novizen für die Einzelmitgliedschaft repräsentiert. Außerdem gibt es je eine assoziierte Gruppe am Dominikanerkloster in der Postgasse und am Konvent der Dominikanerinnen in Wien-Hacking (s. u.). Derzeit wird die Gründung einer inkorporierten Laiengemeinschaft angestrebt.

Außer in *Wien* gibt es Einzelmitglieder mit Versprechen in *Bronnbach, Heidelberg, Innsbruck* und *Bad Wörishofen*.

Assoziierte Gruppen

Im April 2010 gründete sich am Dominikanerinnenkloster Zoffingen in *Konstanz* eine assoziierte Laiengemeinschaft, die sich zum Ziel gesetzt hat, ein Bindeglied zwischen Kloster und Welt zu sein. Die Initiative möchte Kontakte und Informationen ermöglichen, das Konstanzer Kloster auf seinem Weg begleiten, auch ungewohnte Wege christlicher Lebensgemeinschaft gehen und zur Nachfolge Jesu in Ordensgemeinschaften ermutigen. Die Gruppe veranstaltet offene Gesprächsabende zu dominikanischen und anderen Themen, die mit der gemeinsamen Vesper in der Klosterkirche beginnen.[46]

In *Wien* gibt es zwei assoziierte Gruppen. Die „Gemeinschaft St. Dominikus Wien" existiert seit 1990 und besteht aus Frauen und Männern unterschiedlicher Herkunft, Bildung und Alters. Bei ihren Treffen stehen Bibellektüre, spirituelle Weiterbildung und Gemeinschaft im Glauben im Mittelpunkt. Die Gruppe trifft sich meist am zweiten Samstagnachmittag im Monat und wird von P. Clemens Wehrle geistlich begleitet. Eine gewisse Verbindlichkeit in Form von Bereitschaft zur Bindung an die Gruppe und an den Konvent wird erwartet, damit Gemeinschaft wachsen kann, Versprechen werden jedoch nicht abgelegt.[47]

Eine etwa fünfzehnköpfige Gruppe in *Wien-Hacking* besteht schon seit mehr als zehn Jahren und wird von Sr. Katharina Deifel geistlich begleitet. Die Gruppe trifft sich in etwa monatlichen Abständen meist an einem Sonntagvormittag zu Gottesdienst, Gebet und Gespräch zu biblischen, glaubensrelevanten oder gesellschaftlichen Themen.[48]

---

46 http//www.freunde-kloster-zoffigen.de und http://www.dominikaner.org/Dominikusheft/dominikus2008.pdf.

47 http://dominikaner-wien.at/page4/page4.html.

48 Sr. Katharina Deifel, persönliche Mitteilung.

Neue Entwicklungen auf Provinzebene

Im Juli 2011 trat erstmals in der Geschichte der Provinz des hl. Albert ein Provinzkapitel der Laien, bestehend aus Delegierten der Gruppen und Einzelmitglieder, zusammen, das dann am 22. Januar 2012 den Provinzrat der Dominikanischen Laiengemeinschaften wählte – ein wichtiger Schritt in eine größere Unabhängigkeit. Der Provinzrat besteht aus Mitgliedern von Amts wegen, nämlich den Delegierten der Gruppen und dem Provinzpromotor, und aus gewählten Mitgliedern, nämlich aus der Provinzpräsidentin, ihrem Stellvertreter, der Schriftführerin, und Kassiererin, der Beisitzenden für Öffentlichkeitsarbeit, Ausbildung und Kontakt zur Nachbarprovinz Teutonia und der Beisitzenden für den Kontakt zu den Einzelmitgliedern sowie zu ECDLF und ICDLF. Der Provinzrat vertritt alle inkorporierten Laien, die nach der Regel leben, und ist Ansprechpartner des Ordensmeisters und seiner Stellvertreter. Er gibt ein Votum zur Ernennung des Provinzpromotors an das Provinzkapitel der Brüder ab, stellt Anträge an das Generalkapitel bzw. das Provinzkapitel des Ordens und hat den Auftrag, die Arbeit der Gruppen zu fördern und zu koordinieren. Seine ersten Aufgaben bestanden darin, das Direktorium für die Dominikanischen Laiengemeinschaften unserer Provinz zu überarbeiten und eine Ausbildungsordnung zu erstellen. Er entsendet außerdem Delegierte zu den europäischen und internationalen Treffen der dominikanischen Laien. Zu den Versammlungen des Provinzrats sollen nach einer ersten Konsolidierungsphase Vertreter der assoziierten Gruppen eingeladen werden.

Nicht nur die Installation eines Provinzrats ist von Bedeutung für eine zunehmende Vernetzung und Entwicklung der dominikanischen Laien der Provinz. Die schon seit 2007 zweimal jährlich stattfindenden Dominikanischen Studientage haben bereits davor eine wachsende Verbindung auf überregionaler Ebene und ein vorher so nicht dagewesenes Bewusstsein der Dominikanischen Laien unserer Provinz für den Orden und ihre Stellung darin geschaffen. Die Studientage haben bisher stets jeweils an den Wochenenden am oder nach dem Gedenktag der Übertragung der Gebeine des hl. Vaters Dominikus (24. Mai) und dem Fest des hl. Albertus magnus (15. November) stattgefunden und hatten so unterschiedliche Themen wie Wirtschaftsethik, Meister Eckhart, Individualismus, Willensfreiheit, Zukunft der Kirche, Eucharistie und die Möglichkeiten heute von Gott zu sprechen. Die Studientage sind öffentlich, doch fand sich bisher unter den Teilnehmern stets eine große Zahl von Mitgliedern der Domini-

kanischen Laiengemeinschaften. Mit der Zeit wurde deutlich, dass neben den Studientagen auch andere Wünsche für gemeinsame Aktivitäten bestehen. Im Januar 2012 fanden deshalb im Kloster Heilig Kreuz in Augsburg erstmals Einkehrtage für Mitglieder der Dominikanischen Laiengemeinschaften statt, die auf ein überraschend starkes Interesse stießen und deshalb auf einhelligen Wunsch zu einem jährlichen Fixpunkt werden sollen. Ebenfalls erstmals machte sich im Oktober 2012 eine Gruppe von Laiendominikanern aus allen Teilen der Provinz zusammen mit dem Provinzpromotor zu einer Wallfahrt nach Rom auf. Inzwischen wurde außerdem der Wunsch erkennbar, die schwierige Aufgabe des Apostolats einzuüben. Aus diesen Initiativen hat sich ein Geflecht gemeinsamer Aktivitäten der Dominikanischen Laien in unserer Provinz entwickelt, das bei näherem Hinsehen die Grundausrichtung dominikanischer Spiritualität widerspiegelt: Einkehrtage in der Fastenzeit (Gebet), ein Studientag im Mai (Studium), ein Apostolatstag bevorzugt im November, der aber je nach der sich bietenden Gelegenheit auch zu einem anderen Termin sein kann (Verkündigung), und eine Wallfahrt im Spätsommer oder Herbst (Gemeinschaft).

„I have a dream“

2014 ist nicht nur das Jahr, in dem die Provinz des hl. Albert ihres 75-jährigen Bestehens gedenkt. Im Jahr 2016 feiert der Orden den 800. Jahrestag seiner Bestätigung durch Papst Honorius III. Innerhalb der Jahresnovene, während derer sich alle Zweige der Dominikanischen Familie auf dieses große Jubiläum des Gesamtordens vorbereiten und die 2006 in Fanjeaux begann, ist 2014 das Jahr der Laien, das unter dem Motto steht: „*Eure Söhne und eure Töchter werden Propheten sein, eure Alten werden Träume haben und eure jungen Männer Visionen* (Joel 3,1) – *Die dominikanischen Laien und die Verkündigung*“. In einem Brief an die Moniales schrieb das Generalkapitel von Bologna: „Diese neun Jahre stellen eine Pilgerfahrt zu unseren Wurzeln dar; sie dient der Wiederentdeckung der ursprünglichen Absichten des hl. Dominikus, um diese in Kirche und Gesellschaft und in der Welt von heute wieder zu beleben, indem wir gemeinsam neue Wege nach vorn auftun.“[49]

Was sind diese ursprünglichen Absichten und was könnten diese neuen Wege sein?

49 Quelle: http://www.dominikaner.de/ordenjubilaeum1.php.

Vielleicht kann die Erinnerung an die Herangehensweise des Ordensgründers seinen zeitgenössischen Söhnen und Töchtern zum Vorbild dienen. Er wandte sich denen zu, die am Rand der Kirche standen. Die Art, wie Dominikus das tat, wie er sich an die Menschen am Rand der Kirche wandte, nämlich an die großen Häresiebewegungen des 12. Jahrhunderts, ist überraschend: zunächst machte er sich nämlich zu eigen, was *sie* vom Evangelium besser verstanden und v. a. besser verwirklichten als die, die in der Mitte der Kirche standen. *Er* übernahm von *ihnen* die evangelische Armut und die Leidenschaft für das Evangelium.

An Menschen, die am Rand der Kirche stehen, gibt es auch heute keinen Mangel – genau genommen sind das in unserer säkularisierten post-christlichen Gesellschaft die meisten. Viele, die am Rand der Kirche stehen und von draußen hereinschauen, so mancher, der sich ganz abgewandt hat, hat vielleicht mehr vom Evangelium verstanden, als wir glauben, und kann uns helfen zu erkennen, warum wir, die *in* der Kirche sind, manchmal nicht überzeugen oder Gottes Wort verdunkeln, statt es zu erhellen. Deshalb ist es für uns zunächst notwendig, uns zu fragen, ob *wir* ein evangeliumsgemäßes Leben führen, ob wir das leben, wovon wir Zeugnis ablegen wollen. „Predigen" bedeutet deshalb für uns nicht, durchzusetzen, dass wir in der Messe predigen dürfen, es bedeutet auch nicht in erster Linie spektakuläre Aktionen auf der Straße, Reden halten im Park, noch nicht einmal die traditionelle Gemeindearbeit, sondern es bedeutet, auf die zu achten, die am Rand der Gemeinden stehen und im Verborgenen nach dem Herrn Ausschau halten. Nur wenn Er sie beim Namen ruft, werden sie hereinkommen. Wir müssen dem Herrn dafür unsere Stimme leihen.

Wie geht das? In Ländern mit starken evangelikalen und charismatischen Bewegungen wäre die Situation des 13. Jahrhundert vielleicht übertragbar: „Prüft alles und behaltet das Gute" lehrt uns der Apostel Paulus. Dort könnte man von den Evangelikalen mit ihrer ausgeprägten Laienspiritualität lernen und sich im Sinne des Ordensgründers manche ihrer Ansätze zu eigen machen, um die Menschen für Christus und die Kirche (zurück) zu gewinnen. Mit dem von einem Dominikanerpater und einer Laiendominikanerin, einer konvertierten Evangelikalen, gegründeten Catherine of Siena Institute gibt es ein Projekt der Western Dominican Province in den USA, das das versucht.[50] Im stark säkularisierten westeuro-

50 http://www.siena.org.

päischen Umfeld stellt sich die Situation anders dar. Im Gegensatz zu den (wenn auch heterogen) religiösen Gesellschaften Nord- und Südamerikas treffen wir hier im besten Fall auf Gleichgültigkeit, oft aber auch auf Befremden, Ablehnung, Verspottung und Verdächtigung. Trotzdem gibt es auch hier bei den meisten noch eine gewisse, wenn auch stark verarmte christliche Sozialisation, auf der wir aufbauen können. Dazu ist es vor allem nötig, dass wir lernen, die ernsten Anfragen von der Polemik zu trennen und Antworten auf sie zu finden.

Die flexible und demokratische Struktur dominikanischen Lebens und die Ganzheitlichkeit der dominikanischen Spiritualität können richtungsweisend für ein echtes Laienapostolat sein. Es wäre wünschenswert, dass nicht nur die Laien, sondern auch die Brüder und Schwestern das zunehmend realisieren und unter diesem Aspekt versuchen, neue Mitglieder für die Dominikanischen Laiengemeinschaften zu werben und an einer Entwicklung der Dominikanischen Laiengemeinschaften in unserer Provinz hin zu einer Dominikanischen Laien*bewegung* mitzuarbeiten. Ein schwacher Laienzweig ist die zusätzliche Belastung, als die die Dominikanischen Laien vor allem von den Brüdern oft gesehen werden. Ein starker und gut ausgebildeter Laienzweig ist das Gegenteil.

Die althergebrachte Flexibilität dominikanischen Lebens kann uns aber auch in anderer Hinsicht inspirieren. In Zeiten der Auflösung der gewohnten Pfarrstrukturen kann man sich diese Tradition der Flexibilität zunutze machen und neue Wege jenseits der Grenzen von lokalen Gemeinschaften, Pfarreien und Diözesen, aber auch von Ordenszweigen und Ordensprovinzen suchen. Wenn wir auf die Ursprünge zurückschauen, werden wir finden, dass diese Vorstellung so neu gar nicht ist und nur wiederbelebt werden muss. Damian Byrne hat darauf hingewiesen, dass „das Gründungsprojekt der Bettelorden ein Konzept von Kirche jenseits dieser Grenzen [von Pfarreien und Diözesen] war".[51] Die Vorstellung von der *ganzen* Kirche als dem pilgernden Volk Gottes ist alt; die wachsende Globalisierung, die weltweite Vernetzung durch die modernen Kommunikationsmittel, die verschwimmenden Grenzen zwischen Nationalitäten und Ethnien sind jedoch eine Chance, dieses alte Bild mit neuem Leben zu füllen, das aus Erfahrungsbereichen schöpft, die heute zum Alltag auch noch der Kirchenfernsten gehört.

---

51 Damian Byrne, „Mögen sie wachsen!" Die Laien und die Sendung des Ordens. In Johannes H. Weise. Jeder ist ein Wort Gottes, S. 71.

Ich habe einen Traum. Ich träume davon, dass die Umbruchsituation der Dominikanischen Laien in unserer Provinz, die, wie könnte es anders sein, für manche auch schmerzlich und irritierend ist, zu einem echten Aufbruch wird, der auch die anderen Ordenszweige nicht unbeteiligt lässt.

Ich träume davon, dass die Brüder und Schwestern uns lehren, von Gott zu sprechen. Von Männern und Frauen im Ordensgewand erwartet man, dass sie das tun. In unseren stark säkularisierten Lebensbereichen außerhalb der Gemeinden erwartet man von uns anderen oft das Gegenteil. Die religiöse Rede ist verstummt. Wir müssen sie wiederfinden und dafür brauchen wir die Hilfe der „Profis", die ja keine anderen als unsere Brüder und Schwestern im Orden sind.

Ich träume davon, dass sich die Zweige unseres Ordens besser kennenlernen und dadurch im Anschluss an die lange Tradition der Freundschaft im Orden ein Netz von Freundschaften wächst, das die gemeinsame Identität und den Sinn für unsere gemeinsamen Wurzeln und Anliegen stärkt und die Zusammenarbeit zu einer Selbstverständlichkeit werden lässt.

Ich träume davon, dass neben den etablierten Gruppen und Fraternitäten neue Interaktionsformen und Organisationsformen entstehen, die eventuell nur temporär sind. Unter solchen neuen Formen könnte man sich beispielsweise die gemeinsame Arbeit an apostolischen Projekten vorstellen, an denen sich nicht nur Mitglieder verschiedener Fraternitäten, sondern auch der anderen Ordenszweige beteiligen, und in die auch Einzelmitglieder problemlos integriert werden können. Die Glieder eines solchen dynamischen Netzwerkes könnten sich flexibel zusammenfinden, voneinander lernen, einander unterstützen und die Zusammenarbeit wieder beenden, wenn das Projekt beendet ist. Das kann jedoch nur dann gelingen, wenn alle Mitglieder des Ordens voneinander wissen und die Interessengebiete, Kompetenzen, Fähigkeiten und Charismen zumindest von denen, die an einer solchen Art der Zusammenarbeit interessiert sind, bekannt sind.

Ich träume von einer „Dominikanischen Denkschmiede" oder einem „virtuellen Studienhaus", die zwar in sich feste Einrichtungen wären, die man sich aber durchaus mit wechselnder Besetzung aus allen Zweigen des Ordens denken kann. Eine solche Denkschmiede würde unter Zuhilfenahme der vielfältigen Kenntnisse und Erfahrungen ihrer Mitglieder neue Wege der Evangelisierung erkunden und erproben. Ein virtuelles Studienhaus würde dieselben Kenntnisse und Ressourcen bündeln und sie allen Zweigen der Dominikanischen Familie zugänglich machen. Auch hierfür

ist die Grundvoraussetzung, dass die Potentiale der Provinz bekannt sind. Wir brauchen ein „Who is Who" der Provinz für alle Zweige des Ordens.

Ich träume davon, dass wir Dominikanische Laien ein wachsendes Gespür für unsere Identität als Dominikaner und Dominikanerinnen entwickeln und in sie hineinwachsen. Dass wir immer mehr unsere Mitverantwortung für den Orden und für die Kirche erkennen und in die Tat umsetzen. Der Apostel Petrus hat uns dazu aufgefordert, stets bereit zu sein, über die Hoffnung Auskunft zu geben, die uns erfüllt. Aber er hat nicht gesagt, dass wir das Rad neu erfinden müssen. Manche werden – wie die Regel es ausdrückt – vom Geist Gottes bewegt, die Forderung des Apostels in den Fußstapfen des hl. Dominikus und seiner Brüder und Schwestern zu erfüllen. Die Gemeinschaft des Ordens in Vergangenheit und Gegenwart mit seinen Missionaren, Bekennern, Gelehrten und Mystikern beiderlei Geschlechts und aus allen Zweigen der Dominikanischen Familie auch mit den Suchenden, Irrenden und Gescheiterten gibt uns die Kraft und das Instrumentarium an die Hand, um an der nun schon 800 Jahre alten dominikanischen Familiengeschichte weiter zu schreiben und den „goldenen Faden"[52] weiter zu weben, den jetzt auch wir in Händen halten. Dann wird auch irgendwann der Tag kommen, an dem wir in freier Verantwortung und mit Stolz unseren Namen das OP anfügen werden.

52 Edward Schillebeeckx, Dominikanische Spiritualität. In Ulrich Engel (Hrsg), Dominikanische Spiritualität, St. Benno-Verlag, 2000, S. 43 ff.

PORTRÄTS

„Nur das wird aus jedem, was er selber aus sich macht“

Interview mit P. Donatus Leicher

Hermann Leicher wurde 1921 als ältestes von sechs Kindern in Emmendingen geboren und wuchs in Heimbach auf. Bald nach einer Malerlehre, die er mit der Gesellenprüfung abschloss, wurde er zum Kriegsdienst eingezogen, bei dem er sich in Russland schwere Verwundungen zuzog. Nach zwei Jahren in französischer Kriegsgefangenschaft trat er 1947 in den Predigerorden ein; bei seiner Einkleidung erhielt er den Ordensnamen Fr. Donatus. 1948 legte er seine Ordensprofess ab und holte dann das Abitur nach. Vom Wintersemester 1950/51 bis zum Sommersemester 1957 studierte er Philosophie und Theologie an der Hochschule des Ordens in Walberberg bei Bonn. 1955 wurde er zum Priester geweiht. 1957 wurde er in den Konvent St. Albert in Freiburg im Breisgau versetzt, dem er seither angehört. In den folgenden Jahrzehnten nahm er verschiedene klosterinterne Aufgaben wahr; so diente er seiner Gemeinschaft von 1960 bis 1969 als Prior und danach bis 1982 als Subprior. Neben Predigt- und Beichtdienst, der seelsorglichen Betreuung von Schwesterngemeinschaften und der Leitung der Drittordensgemeinschaften in Karlsruhe, Ettlingen und Stuttgart wirkte P. Donatus auch als Religionslehrer an der Gewerbeschule Freiburg im Fachbereich des Steinmetz-, Stein- und Holzbildhauerhandwerks. Er war Mitglied des Kulturausschusses im Zentralverband des deutschen Handwerks in Bonn als Fachberater des wissenschaftlichen Beirats des Bundesinnungsverbandes des deutschen Steinmetz-, Stein- und Holzbildhauerhandwerks und geistlicher Betreuer der Jungmeistergruppen desselben Verbandes, sowie Beiratsmitglied der Arbeitsgemeinschaft Friedhof und Denkmal in Kassel (AFD). Zusammen mit zweien seiner Schüler, Steinmetzmeister Wilhelm Brenner (Augsburg) und Steinmetzmeister Gerhard Schröder (Türkheim), besuchte ihn P. Wolfram Hoyer am 16. Juli 2013 in Freiburg im Breisgau und konnte das folgende Gespräch mit ihm führen.

Hoyer: Warum sind Sie gerade Dominikaner geworden?

Leicher: Ich komme aus einer Familie, in der sowohl von der Seite der Mutter wie von der Seite des Vaters viele Verwandte in den verschiedensten Or-

den Gott dienen. Schon in jungen Jahren fühlte auch ich mich dazu berufen, doch ich habe zu niemand davon gesprochen, auch nicht mit meinen Eltern. Die Zeit (1933–1945) hatte dafür kein Verständnis. Im Jahre 1936 starb mein Vater an einem durchbrochenen Blinddarm. Ich bin das älteste von sechs Kindern. Wir waren arm und ich konnte aus Geldmangel nicht auf eine höhere Schule gehen. So erlernte ich das Malerhandwerk. 1934 begegnete ich als Ministrant dem Dominikaner P. Augustinus Gierlich, dem ich mein Geheimnis offenbarte. Inzwischen brach der Krieg aus. Im Januar 1941 wurde ich als Soldat eingezogen und an der Ostfront dreimal schwer verwundet. Am Ende des Krieges begegnete ich als Verwundeter im Lazarett in Konstanz dem Novizenmeister P. Theophil Tschipke, mit dem ich dann während meiner Gefangenschaft brieflich in Verbindung blieb.

Abb. 1: Dominikanerkloster St. Albert in Freiburg: Textilcollage mit dem Antlitz des dornengekrönten Christus (Foto: Wolfram Hoyer).

Nach viereinhalb Jahren Krieg und zwei Jahren in französischer Gefangenschaft – davon ein Jahr als Holzfäller und ein Jahr im Theologengefangenenlager in Chartres – trat ich im August 1947 in München ins Noviziat ein. Auf die Frage meines Novizenmeisters, wie ich mir das Leben im Dominikanerorden vorstellte, gab ich zur Antwort: Ich bin während des Krieges mit vielen Kunstschaffenden zusammengekommen und erfuhr von ihnen, dass die offizielle Kirche und ihre Vertreter ihnen gegenüber kein Verständnis für ihr Schaffen hätten. In vielen Gesprächen begegnete

ich der existenziellen und seelischen Not, in der diese Menschen leben, und da kam mir der Gedanke, mich dieser Menschengruppe als Seelsorger anzunehmen, also Seelsorger für die Künstler zu werden. Die Antwort, die man mir darauf gegeben hat, war: Die Kunst kommt bei uns an zweiter Stelle. An erster Stelle steht der Orden und die Arbeit im Orden und für den Orden. Ich habe diese Antwort akzeptiert und bis heute dem Inhalt nach gehalten.

Nach dem Noviziat schickte man mich im September 1948 nach Freiburg, um in zwei Jahren die für das Studium notwendigen Kenntnisse nachzuholen. Im September 1950 fuhr ich nach Walberberg. In dieser Zeit verzichtete ich fast ganz auf das Schaffen von künstlerischen Dingen, um alle Kraft für das philosophische und theologische Studium bereit zu halten.

Nach dem Studium wurde ich 1957 nach Freiburg versetzt, um im Auftrag von P. Provinzial Marianus Vetter das dortige Juvenat aufzulösen. Es war eine unangenehme und harte Arbeit, die gegen den Willen von P. Ulrich Kaiser, der Prior war und das Juvenat gegründet hatte, ausgeführt werden musste.

Hoyer: Und wie ging es weiter?

Leicher: Neben der Auflösung des Juvenates habe ich alle im Konvent anfallenden Arbeiten übernommen, wie Aushilfen in der Umgebung von Freiburg, Beichthören, Vorträge für Kolpingsöhne, freie Krankenschwestern und Ordensschwestern, Männereinkehrtage, Vorträge für Meisterschüler im Bildhauer- und Steinmetzhandwerk auf Bundesebene im Fach Symbolik, Mitarbeit bei den Jungmeistertreffen im Steinmetz- und Bildhauerhandwerk im Hinblick auf den Friedhof als Feld der Verkündigung der Frohen Botschaft vom Leben.

Da in der Freiburger Münsterbauhütte mein Bruder Ludwig als Steinmetz arbeitete, den ich oft besuchte, regte sich bald auch in mir das Steinhauerblut meiner Ahnen, und ich versuchte unter Anleitung des Hüttenmeisters Sepp Jakob den rohen Sandsteinblock fachgerecht zu bearbeiten. Denken im Stein war für mich eine große Überraschung und eine wunderbare Sache. Leider konnte ich mich dafür nur einen halben Tag in der Woche freihalten und das auch nur für einige Monate. Damit legte ich aber die notwendige Grundlage für alle späteren Arbeiten am Stein.

Nach drei arbeitsreichen Jahren im Freiburger Konvent erbat ich von P. Provinzial die Erlaubnis, wenigstens zwei Jahre die Kunstgewerbeschule

in Graz besuchen zu dürfen, denn nach dem 40. Lebensjahr war es schwer, dort noch aufgenommen zu werden. Er erteilte mir die Erlaubnis unter der Bedingung, dass ich bereit war, die Volksmission in München und Umgebung als Vorbereitung auf den Eucharistischen Kongress 1960 noch mitzupredigen, was ich getan habe. Zum Schulbeginn September 1960 fuhr ich nach Graz und wohnte in unserem Konvent in der Münzgrabenstraße. Professor Rudolf Szyszkowitz, dem ich einige Zeichnungen vorgelegt habe, nahm mich sofort in seine Klasse für figurale Malerei auf. Da in Freiburg die Priorwahl anstand, musste ich Anfang Oktober nach Freiburg zurück und wurde am 8. Oktober, an meinem 39. Geburtstag, zum Prior von Freiburg gewählt. Da niemand damit gerechnet hatte – ich auch nicht – habe ich auf das Drängen zweier jüngerer Mitbrüder auf das Studium in Graz verzichtet, um ihnen als Prior Windschatten zu gewähren gegen die älteren Mitbrüder, die unsere fortschrittlichen Gedanken nicht akzeptierten. So zerplatzte der Traum vom Studium der Kunst. Noch bevor ich nach Graz ging, schuf ich das Grabmal für meine Mitbrüder auf dem Freiburger Friedhof. Das war im Sommer 1960 und es war meine erste große Steinmetzarbeit.

Abb. 2: Friedhof in Freiburg im Breisgau: Grabmal der Dominikaner (Vorderseite); die Inschrift am Fuß lautet: „Hier erwarten die Predigerbrüder den Tag der Auferstehung."
(Foto: Sebastian Tönnesen).

Hoyer: Wie kamen Sie auf die Internationale Sommerakademie für bildende Kunst in Salzburg?

Leicher: Der Maler Oskar Kokoschka hat zusammen mit dem Galeristen Friedrich Welz die Akademie als Schule des Sehens 1953 gegründet und bis 1963 geleitet. Als er 1963 die Leitung an Professor Hermann Stuppäck übergab, schlug er Professor Szyszkowitz als Leiter der Klasse für figurale Malerei vor, die er selber elf Jahre geleitet hatte. Szyszkowitz nahm diese Berufung durch Kokoschka an. Nach 1963 bekam ich von ihm die Einladung, im folgenden Jahr zur Sommerakademie nach Salzburg zu kommen, um dort weiterzumachen, wo ich in Graz bei ihm hatte aufhören müssen.

Meine Teilnahme war aber erst im Jahr 1968 möglich, wo ich in meinen Ferien für vier Wochen die Sommerakademie besuchen konnte. Dieser Einstieg war erfolgreich, und so verbrachte ich über zehn Jahre meine Ferien dort, in den Klassen der figuralen Malerei, der Radierklasse und ein Jahr in der Bildhauerklasse. Ich wohnte während dieser Zeit bei den Salzburger Dominikanerinnen und übernahm dort die Seelsorge. Mit diesen Studien habe ich mir die Grundkenntnisse für meine weiteren Arbeiten auf künstlerischem Gebiet erworben.

Hoyer: Wie war Ihre Begegnung als Ordensmann mit den Mitstudenten in Salzburg, da Sie ja sicher einer der ältesten waren?

Leicher: Außer mir waren noch zwei Ordensfrauen in der Klasse der figuralen Malerei, eine Benediktinerin, die später Äbtissin wurde, und eine Franziskanerin. Die Atmosphäre war ausgezeichnet, gemischt mit Juden und Christen, Gläubigen und Ungläubigen, Suchenden und Zweiflern. Meine Anwesenheit führte zu fruchtbaren Gesprächen und wertvollen menschlichen Begegnungen. Mein alter Wunsch, in der Künstlerseelsorge zu arbeiten, fand hier seine Bestätigung.

Hoyer: Sie haben im Jahre 1971 ein Mahnmal für den Frieden in Ihrem Heimatdorf Heimbach geschaffen. Dieses Werk fand damals viel Beachtung und wurde auch in einer angesehenen Fachzeitschrift für Steinmetze und Bildhauer 1972 veröffentlicht.[1]

---

1 Donatus Leicher: Das Mahnmal für den Frieden in Heimbach, in: Steinmetz + Bildhauer.

Abb. 3: Heimbach: Mahnmal für den Frieden: Außenansicht des Eingangsbereichs (Foto: Wolfram Hoyer).

Leicher: Das habe ich nicht alleine gemacht, sondern in Zusammenarbeit mit dem Münsterbaumeister Sepp Jakob und meinem Bruder, dem Steinmetz Ludwig Leicher. Es steht gegenüber der Kirche von Heimbach. Dabei handelt es sich um einen Raum von 12 auf 8,5 Metern, der von einer 170 Zentimeter hohen Bruchsteinmauer umgeben wird. Es ging uns darum, aller Toten, und nicht nur der Toten der Weltkriege, zu gedenken, auch derer, die in den sogenannten Religionskriegen ihr Leben verloren haben, deshalb steht am Eingang folgende Inschrift: „Wir gedenken der Toten, die durch Kämpfe jeder Art ihr Leben verloren haben, weil der Hass in der Welt mächtiger war als die Liebe.“ Auf der anderen Seite des Eingangs fällt der Blick auf einen Engelskopf mit einer Totenleuchte, der über die Höhe der Mauer hinausragt. Die Idee, die hinter diesem Engel stand, war, dass Unterschiede, Spalten und Klüfte zwischen Freund und Feind, hoch und niedrig, arm und reich, im privaten wie im gesellschaftlichen Leben, sich nicht von einem rein materiellen Denken aus schließen oder überbrücken lassen, sondern nur durch eine große geistige Anstrengung, die immer über das rein Materielle, sowohl im Denken als auch im Tun, hinausragt. Der Engel

---

Handwerk, Technik, Industrie. November 1972, 88. Jahrgang. München (Callwey), S. 620–624.

Abb. 4: Heimbach: Mahnmal für den Frieden: Inschrift rechts vom Eingang: „Wir gedenken der Toten ..." (Foto: Wolfram Hoyer).

Abb. 5: Heimbach: Mahnmal für den Frieden: Engelskopf mit Totenleuchte links vom Eingang (Foto: Wolfram Hoyer).

dient als Sinnbild für das Geistige, das Licht. Ursprünglich wollte ich nur den Engelskopf machen; der war in mir drin. Aber am Schluss blieb mir die Gesamtplanung des Mahnmals und seine Gestaltung mir. Auch die Texte der Inschriften habe ich verfasst. Die Schriftgestaltung hat Sepp Jakob entworfen und mein Bruder und ein befreundeter Kollege haben die Inschriften dann in Stein geschlagen.

Hoyer: An der Innenseite der Mauer befindet sich Ihr Reliefzyklus, der aus zwei Teilen besteht.

Leicher: Zum einen ein verkürzter Kreuzweg mit vier Stationen: Verrat, Unrecht, Leid in den verschiedenen Formen und Tod. Der Verrat hat am wenigsten Raum. Unrecht: Ein Alter bricht den Stab, die Jungen schauen zu. Leid: Last; dort ist Mitleid, sie tragen mit. Und der Tod: Erstarrung. Vor diesen Reliefs ist als zweites ein liegendes Kreuz, geformt aus den Namenstafeln des alten Ehrenmals, mit den Namen der Kriegstoten des Dorfes. Wo

die beiden Balken sich kreuzen, ist ein Symbol, eine abstrakte Knospe, als Zeichen: Die Erde bricht auf, etwas Neues kommt hervor.

Abb. 6: Heimbach: Mahnmal für den Frieden: Reliefzyklus: links „Verrat", in der Mitte: „Unrecht" (Foto Wolfram Hoyer).

Abb. 7: Heimbach: Mahnmal für den Frieden: Reliefzyklus: „Leid – Last" (Foto: Wolfram Hoyer).

Hoyer: Dieses Mahnmal wurde 1971 geschaffen, ist aber immer noch aktuell.

Abb. 8: Heimbach: Mahnmal für den Frieden: Reliefzyklus: „Leid – Mitleid" (Foto: Wolfram Hoyer).

Abb. 9: Heimbach: Mahnmal für den Frieden: Reliefzyklus: „Tod – Erstarrung" (Foto: Wolfram Hoyer).

Abb. 10: Heimbach: Mahnmal für den Frieden: Detail des aus den Tafeln mit den Namen der Kriegstoten des Ortes geformten liegenden Kreuzes; am Kreuzungspunkt der Balken eine abstrakte Knospe als Symbol für neu aufbrechendes Leben (Foto: Wolfram Hoyer).

Leicher: Denn gegenüber der Reliefs habe ich einen Chronikstein gesetzt und darauf geschrieben: „Diese Stätte will ein Protest sein gegen den Krieg und ein Aufruf zu Versöhnung und Frieden. Heute, im Jahre 1971, herrschen in der Welt Rassenhass, Klassenkampf, Hunger, Angst, Unsicherheit, trotz Wohlstand und weltweiter Hilfe!" Und das könnte man auch heute noch so sagen.

Ebenso ist auch die Gesamtaussage des Werkes noch aktuell: die des christlichen Glaubens, dass im Tod nicht alles aus ist, sondern dass das eigentliche Leben im Tod erst beginnt. Deshalb ist am Ausgang des Mahnmals zu lesen: „Uns, den noch Lebenden, gilt die Mahnung, den Frieden zu schaffen. Doch Friede wird nur, wenn zur Versöhnung jeder bereit ist." Und daher wird auch das ganze Mahnmal von einem Barockkreuz aus dem Jahre 1739 überragt, das ursprünglich vom Kirchhof stammte, das wir hierhin aufgestellt haben und dessen Sockel noch seine alte Inschrift trägt: „Ich bin die Auferstehung und das Leben."

Bei dem bundesweiten Wettbewerb ‚Unser Dorf soll schöner werden' wurde Heimbach unter anderem wegen des Mahnmals für den Frieden mit der Goldmedaille ausgezeichnet.

Hoyer: Ich bin kein Künstler, daher interessiert mich eine Frage innerlich sehr – die Frage nach der Umsetzung einer Idee, die man aus einem Steinblock herausschlägt oder auf eine Leinwand überträgt.

Leicher: Als Antwort auf Ihre Frage habe ich eine Erzählung. Im alten China hat der Kaiser dem bedeutendsten Maler seines Reiches den Auftrag erteilt, ihm ein Pferd zu malen. Der Kaiser musste jahrelang darauf warten. Bei einem Spaziergang sieht er dann den Maler im Gras liegen, wie er den Wolken nachschaut. Der Kaiser fährt in an: Du Faulpelz! Jahrelang warte ich auf mein Pferd und du liegst hier im Gras und träumst! Die Antwort des Malers war: Jetzt male ich und wenn ich nach Hause komme, dann beschäftige ich mich damit. Und der Kaiser fragt: Wann bekomme ich mein Bild? Die Antwort des Malers: Majestät, kommen Sie mit. Er holt einen Bogen Papier, Tusche und Pinsel und malt in Gegenwart des Kaisers das gewünschte Pferd. Die Reaktion des Kaisers: Und darauf musste ich jahrelang warten? Der Maler nimmt den Kaiser mit in das Nebenzimmer, das angefüllt ist mit hunderten Studienblättern von Pferden. Diese Arbeit hielt der Maler für notwendig, um in wenigen Minuten das vollkommenste Pferd zu malen.

Die künstlerische Veranlagung ist ein Geschenk, das mühsam entfaltet werden muss. Erst dann kann eine Idee realisiert werden. Das wachsame und geschulte Auge eines künstlerisch Begabten sieht in den Dingen, im Baumstamm, im Steinblock Möglichkeiten, seine Ideen zu verwirklichen.

Hoyer: Nehmen wir als Beispiel die von Ihnen geschaffene Albertus-Magnus-Stele.

Leicher: Eine neunzig bis hundert Jahre alte Thuja stand im Eingangsbereich unseres Klosters und war von oben her dürr geworden. Von unten her hatte sie einen Pilzbefall. Eines Morgens war das Gartenamt da, um den Baum zu fällen. Den Baumfällern sagte ich: Die unteren fünf Meter gehören mir. Man fragte mich: Warum? Meine Antwort: Ich möchte aus dem noch stehenden Stamm etwas machen. Es kam die Frage: Und was? Ich weiß es noch nicht, war meine Antwort. Ich hatte noch keine Idee. Ich ging um den Stamm herum, betrachtete ihn von der Straße her. Wie sieht er aus, wenn ich vom Schlossberg herabkomme? Wie, wenn ich ihn von unten her betrachte? Diese Eindrücke gingen mit mir tagelang um. Dann wurde mir klar: Ich darf die Rundung des Stamms nicht zerstören.

Abb. 11: auf dem Weg zum fertigen Werk: P. Donatus Leicher bei der Arbeit an der Albertusstele (Foto: Donatus Leicher).

Ich fing an die Rinde zu entfernen, und bei diesem Tun kam mir die Idee, aus dem Stamm die Gestalt des hl. Albertus Magnus, des Patrons unseres Klosters, herauszuholen. Ich machte einige Skizzen im Maßstab 1:10, um die richtige Proportion für die Höhe des Stammes zu finden, und es wurde mir beim Skizzieren bewusst, dass die ganze Gestalt im Stamm drin bleiben musste. Ein zweites wurde mir klar: Um die Rundung des Stammes zu erhalten, brauchte ich drei Seiten. Die eine war für die Gestalt des Albertus und die zweite, da er Bischof von Regensburg war, für die Insignien eines Bischofs, Mitra und Stab, und für eine kurze Biographie. Und die dritte Seite könnte die Requisiten einer Studierstube aufweisen.

Nachdem ein Baugerüst um den Stamm errichtet war, fing ich an, die Figur des Albert 1:1 auf den Stamm zu übertragen. Ursprünglich wollte ich mir mit Hilfe einer Elektrosäge die Arbeit erleichtern, aber die war mir dann zu schnell und ich blieb beim Hammer und beim Meißel, beim Knüpfel und beim Stecheisen. Bei den ersten Schlägen spürte ich, dass ein Anderer mir die Hand führt und dass das aus dem Stamm herausgeholte

Abb. 12 (links): Dominikanerkloster St. Albert in Freiburg: Albertus-Magnus-Stele: Detail: die Gestalt des hl. Albert (Foto: Wolfram Hoyer).

Abb. 13 (oben): Dominikanerkloster St. Albert in Freiburg: Albertus-Magnus-Stele: Detail: Albert mit seinen Bischofsinsignien, Mitra und Stab, dazwischen Efeuranken (Foto: Wolfram Hoyer).

Abb. 14: Dominikanerkloster St. Albert in Freiburg: Albertus-Magnus-Stele: Detail: die „Studierstube" des hl. Albert mit Büchern, Totenschädel, Tintenfass, Pflanzen und Mörser, sowie einer verschlossenen Schublade (Foto: Wolfram Hoyer).

Gesicht mich anspricht. Und wenn meine Hände ruhen mussten, gingen meine Gedanken weiter. Herz, Seele und Geist durchströmen das handwerkliche Schaffen.

Die dritte Seite mit der Studierstube wird oben abgeschlossen mit einer abgelaufenen Sanduhr inmitten von Alpha und Omega; darunter sind ein Raum mit Büchern, die Albert geschrieben hat, ein Tintenfass mit Schreibfeder und ein Totenschädel, denn Albert war auch Anatom. Im Raum darunter steht ein Mörser zum Zerreiben der Pflanzen, die als Heilmittel verwendet wurden, weil zu Alberts Wissensbereich auch die Botanik gehörte. Den Abschluss nach unten bildet eine Schublade.

Hoyer: Warum die Schublade? Die Schublade ist ja kein klassisches Symbol.

Leicher: In dieser Schublade sind die ganzen naturwissenschaftlichen Experimente seiner Forschung drin, an die niemand herankommen soll, denn Albert galt zu seiner Zeit als Magier. Weil er mehr wusste, als viele Gelehrte seiner Zeit, traute man ihm nicht. Er musste bis 1934 warten, um heiliggesprochen zu werden.

Da Albert auch als Friedensstifter galt, setzte ich über ihn das Symbol der Friedenstaube. Ich saß oben auf dem Baugerüst und rief mir die Geschichte um Noah ins Gedächtnis: Zuerst schickte Noah den Raben zur Erkundung der Lage hinaus. Der kam bald schreiend zurück, weil er keinen Platz zum Ausruhen gefunden hatte. Dann kam die Taube an der Reihe. Noah hatte immer zwei von jeder Tierart mitgenommen. Es war sicherlich das Weibchen, das er zuerst geschickt hat. Der Täuberich blieb in der Arche. Und siehe, die Taube kam mit einem kleinen Blättchen zurück. Das hat Noah in Freude versetzt: Das Wasser ist gefallen; neues Leben ersteht. Und er sagt zum Täuberich: So, jetzt gehst du auch hinaus und schaust, was draußen los ist. Der Täuberich fliegt hinaus und denkt bei sich: Wenn Noah sich über ein so kleines Blättchen gefreut hat, dann bringe ich ihm einen großen Zweig. Er bricht also einen großen Zweig ab, fliegt mit letzter Kraft bis zur Arche und stellt fest: Das Flugloch ist zu klein. Er wollte angeben, aber alles Gezerre hilft nichts. Der Zweig fällt ins Wasser. Was nun? Hineingehen? Sich blamieren? Da er das nicht will, haut er einfach ab. Er verschwindet und kommt nicht wieder. Also: typisch Mann! Das waren so meine Gedanken um die Friedenstaube mit dem großen Zweig.

Ein Ast am oberen Ende des Stammes bot sich an, um an dieser Stelle eine Eule hinzusetzen, als Zeichen der Wissenschaft. Eine kleine Eule kam

Abb. 15: Dominikanerkloster St. Albert in Freiburg: Albertus-Magnus-Stele: Detail: das Symbol des „Friedens-täuberichs" über der Gestalt des hl. Albert (Foto: Wolfram Hoyer).

Abb. 16: Dominikanerkloster St. Albert in Freiburg: Albertus-Magnus-Stele: Detail: zwei Eulen als Symbole der Weisheit des hl. Alberts (Foto: Wolfram Hoyer).

im Hintergrund dazu, weil ein zweiter Ast sich dazu anbot. Die zwei großen Flächen werden eingerahmt von Efeuranken, denn der Efeu war mit Schuld am Absterben des Baumes. Und nun diente er mir als Schmuck. Damit man sieht, aus welchem Geist das Ganze geschaffen wurde, steht darüber weithin sichtbar der Spruch: *Soli Deo Gloria* – Gott allein die Ehre.

Abb. 17: P. Donatus Leicher bei der Segnung der vollendeten Albertus-Magnus-Stele (Foto: Donatus Leicher).

Hoyer: War die Stele des Albertus Magnus Ihre einzige große Arbeit aus Holz?

Leicher: Einige Jahre früher musste wegen einer Platzgestaltung im früheren Pfarrgarten von Heimbach ein alter Nussbaum gefällt werden, der von oben herab dürr geworden war. Als Kinder haben wir die Nüsse, die er über die Mauer auf die Straße hin abgeworfen hat, gesammelt. Irgendwie fühlte ich mich mit ihm verbunden, sodass ich bei seiner Fällung mit dabei sein wollte. Als die ersten Äste fielen, rief ich dem Baumfäller zu, er solle die unteren Äste etwa einen Meter stehen lassen. Auf die Frage: Warum? gab ich zur Antwort: Da steckt einer im Stamm, der schreit; den will ich herausholen. Der neben mir stehende Ortsvorsteher, der das hörte, sagte zornig: Ich hör nix!

Ich bat darum, den Stamm nicht zu zersägen. Aber damit hatte ich ein Problem geschaffen, denn man wusste nicht, wohin man ihn bringen sollte. Es schien, als gäbe es im ganzen Dorf keinen Platz. Als ich ihn nach

Abb. 18: P. Donatus Leicher bei der Arbeit an der Gallus-Statue für Heimbach (Foto: Donatus Leicher).

Wochen suchte, fand ich ihn schließlich auf einem Abfallhaufen, mit Brennnesseln zugewachsen, am äußersten Rand des Ortes. Auf meinen Protest hin transportierte man ihn auf den Platz einer Zimmerei und bockte ihn auf, damit er trockenen konnte. Nach einigen Wochen ließ man mich wissen, dass man den Platz bräuchte. Ich ließ den Stamm aufstellen und am vorspringenden Dach eines Schuppens befestigen. Als ein Gerüst um den Stamm gebaut war, begann ich, ihn von der Rinde zu befreien. Bei dieser mühsamen Arbeit haben mir Freunde geholfen.

Es war inzwischen Sommer geworden und die Tage waren ungewöhnlich heiß. Den Durst stillte ich mit dem guten Wasser des Dorfbrunnens, den Hunger mit dem mitgebrachten trockenen Brot. Bis gegen Mittag konnte ich im Schatten arbeiten. Auf einem Brett im Schatten, ein Stück Holz im Nacken, so hielt ich meinen Mittagsschlaf. Erst gegen Abend konnte ich weiterarbeiten. Es waren meine Ferien, in denen ich den schreienden Gallus aus dem Stamm befreien konnte. Der aufgerichtete Baum sah wie ein Gabelkreuz aus, sodass es geeignet schien, auf die Fläche eines abgesägten Astes das INRI anzubringen. Das Ende des senkrechten Stammes schmückt eine Dornenkrone. Die Gestalt des rufenden Gallus steckt noch halb im Stamm und zeigt die Verbundenheit mit dem an, der einst am Kreuz hing.

Das Dorf Heimbach gehörte ursprünglich zum Kloster Sankt Gallen und wurde um 759 zum ersten Mal erwähnt. Im Jahr 2009 feierte die Gemeinde ihr 1250-jähriges Jubiläum. Zu diesem Ereignis wollte ich der Gemeinde das 4,50 Meter hohe Kreuz mit der Figur des hl. Gallus schenken. Die Probleme, die mit diesem Geschenk und dem Aufstellen an dem von mir vorgesehenen Platz verbunden waren, möchte ich verschweigen.

Hoyer: Sie sind Dominikaner und Sie sind schon länger im Orden, als ich auf der Welt bin. Ich gehe davon aus, dass Sie Ihre künstlerische Arbeit als Verkündigung betrachten?

Leicher: Nur!

Hoyer: Verkündigung durch Kunst – wie hat sich das bei Ihnen entwickelt?

Leicher: Von Entwicklung kann man eigentlich nicht sprechen, weil die Neigung zur Verkündigung durch Kunst bei mir immer vorhanden war und weil die Erkenntnis, dass ein Kunstwerk, das vom Geist des Christentums erfüllt und formal gut gestaltet ist, länger predigt als der Prediger auf

Abb. 19: Statue des Orpheus und der Eurydike (Foto: Donatus Leicher).

der Kanzel – diese Erkenntnis war schon früh in mir lebendig, wie auch das Bemühen, den Steinmetzen klar zu machen, dass ihre Arbeit am Grabmal auf dem Friedhof nicht nur eine kulturelle Arbeit ist, sondern auch eine religiöse, weil der Friedhof ein Feld der Verkündigung der Frohen Botschaft vom Leben sein soll, eine immerwährende Verkündigung. Das Gleiche gilt auch für die vielen Gestaltungsseminare, die ich über ein halbes Jahrhundert lang gehalten habe. Gestaltung ist nicht nur auf die Kunst hin gemeint, sondern gilt auch für das ganze Leben eines Menschen. Das uns von Gott geschenkte Leben soll von uns durch unsere Begabungen gestaltet und geformt werden, um da zu sein für den Dienst am Menschen und für den Dienst für Gott.

Hoyer: Wenn ich mich umsehe und Ihre Werke betrachte, so scheint es, dass hinter jedem eine eigene Entstehungsgeschichte steckt. Stimmt das?

Leicher: Sie haben recht. Und vielleicht wundert Sie auch, dass neben einer Kreuzabnahme und einer Pietà, neben einem Engel und einem Geschundenen, also einem Schmerzensmann, auch eine Arbeit aus der griechischen Mythologie zu finden ist. Dazu Folgendes: Die Geschichte von Orpheus und Eurydike hat mich seit meiner frühesten Jugend fasziniert. In vielen Skizzen habe ich versucht, diesem Thema eine mir eigene Form zu geben. Es vergingen Jahrzehnte, bis ich diese Form fand.

In der Nachbarschaft unseres Klosters wurde wegen eines Neubaus eine alte Linde gefällt. Man bot mir an, Holz, das für mich geeignet schien, zu holen. Da ich weiß, wie schwer es ist, mit ganzen Baumstämmen umzugehen, wählte ich kleinere Stücke, die ein Mann bewegen kann. Um dieses geschenkte Holz kreisten dann meine Gedanken. Mit Skizzen 1:10 versuchte ich eine Lösung zu finden, und mir war bewusst, dass die Rundung des Stammes berücksichtigt werden musste. Es sollten aber beide Gestalten, Orpheus und Eurydike, in Erscheinung treten.

Hier zur Erinnerung die Geschichte: Orpheus war ein berühmter Sänger, der mit seinem Gesang die wildesten Tiere beruhigte. Er bildete mit Eurydike ein Paar. Beim Spielen im Gras wurde sie von einer Giftschlange gebissen und starb. Als Tote kam sie in den Hades. Orpheus trauerte um sie und er erwirkte mit seinem Gesang beim Herrscher der Unterwelt die Erlaubnis, Eurydike aus dem Hades wieder herauszuholen, unter der Bedingung, dass er sich bei diesem Gang nicht umdrehen würde, um zu sehen, ob Eurydike ihm auf wirklich folgte. In seiner Ungeduld drehte Orpheus sich aber um und verlor Eurydike damit für immer. Hier soll gezeigt werden, was die Ungeduld in unserem Leben bewirken kann.

Hoyer: Und was für eine Geschichte steht hinter Ihrer eigenwilligen Kreuzabnahme?

Leicher: Bei einem Spaziergang in meinem Heimatdorf sah ich einen scheckigen Eichenbalken in der Erde vor einem Neubau liegen, auf den man einen Blumentopf gestellt hatte. Ich fand es schade, dass der Stamm dort vermodern musste, und erkundigte mich, ob ich ihn bekommen könne, um etwas daraus zu machen. Er hatte eine Länge von fast drei Metern und einen Durchmesser von 32 Zentimetern. Der Besitzer hatte ihn von einem Zimmermann bekommen, dem er versprechen musste, dass er ihn nicht zersägte. So legte er ihn also vor sein Haus, als Unterlage für seine Blumentöpfe. Mein Verhandeln mit dem Besitzer hatte Erfolg und ich konnte den Balken nach Freiburg transportieren. In der Werkstatt eines befreundeten Bildhauers konnte ich ihn deponieren.

Da der Stamm einige Jahre in der feuchten Erde gelegen hatte, hatten sich auf seiner unteren Seite Risse gebildet, in die man die flache Hand hineinstecken konnte. Die obere Seite war noch heil. Als ich den Stamm von der Erde gereinigt hatte und die tiefen und breiten Risse sah, hörte ich in mir eine Stimme sagen: Zeige, was du kannst, und mach daraus eine Kreuzabnahme. Dieser Gedanke erschreckte und faszinierte mich zugleich.

Ich fing an, mit Skizzen nach einer Lösung zu suchen, und mir war klar, dass irgendwie das Achteck des Stammes sichtbar bleiben musste. In meinen Skizzen erschien die Form eines angedeuteten Kreuzes und einer angenagelten Hand. Der Arm, in die Länge gezogen, hält einen schweren, toten Körper. An diese wenigen Entwurfsstriche hielt ich mich bei den ersten Schlägen ins harte Eichenholz. Das untere Ende des Stammes hatte morsche Stellen, doch ich konnte mit etwas Geschick noch einen Toten-

Abb. 20: Pfarrkirche St. Gallus in Heimbach: Kreuzabnahme (Foto: Donatus Leicher).

Abb. 21 rechts oben: Pfarrkirche St. Gallus in Heimbach: Kreuzabnahme: Detail: Profil des Gekreuzigten (Foto: Wolfram Hoyer).

Abb. 22 rechts unten: Pfarrkirche St. Gallus in Heimbach: Kreuzabnahme: Detail der noch angenagelten rechten Hand des Gekreuzigten, INRI-Inschrift und stilisierte Dornenkrone (Foto: Wolfram Hoyer).

schädel ausformen, als Hinweis auf die Schädelstätte. In das am oberen Ende des Stammes stehengebliebene Achteck schlug ich eine Dornenkrone. Aus den tiefen Spalten auf der Rückseite ließ ich Blätter wachsen, als Zeichen von neuem Leben, und schlug mit großen, tief gehauenen Buchstaben: SED RESURREXIT TERTIA DIE – aber am dritten Tage auferstanden. Statt der Dornenkrone sieht man auf der Vorderseite einen Kranz von Blüten, als Zeichen des Lebens.

Hoyer: Wenn ich Ihren Posaunenengel näher betrachte, scheint mir, dass im Holz Spuren von Fäulnis zu sehen sind?

Leicher: Sie sehen leider richtig. Das Holz stammt von derselben Linde, aus der auch der Orpheus gemacht wurde. Auch dieses Holz, in dem der Engel noch verborgen war, wurde in der Werkstatt eines mit mir befreundeten Bildhauers deponiert. Irgend jemand, dem es im Weg war, stellte es an die Außenwand der Werkstatt, direkt unter die Dachtraufe. Fast drei Jahre stand es dort, bei Wind und Wetter. Als ich endlich den Engel befreien wollte, stellte ich fest, dass der Stamm 15 Zentimeter von unten her total verfault war. Mein Freund, der Bildhauer, sah mein Gesicht und sagte nur: Donatus, Brennholz! Aber ich sah immer noch meinen Engel drin stecken. Wir sägten das faule Holz am unteren Ende des Stammes ab. Ich entfernte die Rinde und auch das verfaulte und stockig gewordene Holz. Aus dem Rest, der noch gesund schien, schuf ich dann meinen Engel, mit verbissener Miene, der seine Posaune unter sein Kinn drückt. Einige Spuren vom verfaulten Holz blieben leider zurück.

Hoyer: Herr Brenner hat uns gestern im Auto erzählt, dass Sie in den Gestaltungsseminaren für Steinmetze bei einer Betrachtung zwei Jahre über einen Kieselstein sprechen könnten, wenn man Sie ließe. Wie bereiten Sie sich auf so etwas vor?

Leicher: Zunächst: Zwei Jahre, das ist sicherlich eine Übertreibung. Aber je länger man einen Gegenstand betrachtet, umso mehr sieht und fühlt man, was drinnen steckt.

Um kurz auf Ihre Frage zu antworten, folgendes: Der Kieselstein ruht vor mir oder ruht in meiner Hand. Ich habe ihn vielleicht auf dem Weg, den ich ging, gefunden. Es war Winter, und er war eisig kalt. Und nun beginnt meine Beobachtung. Er nimmt die Wärme meiner Hand an. Die

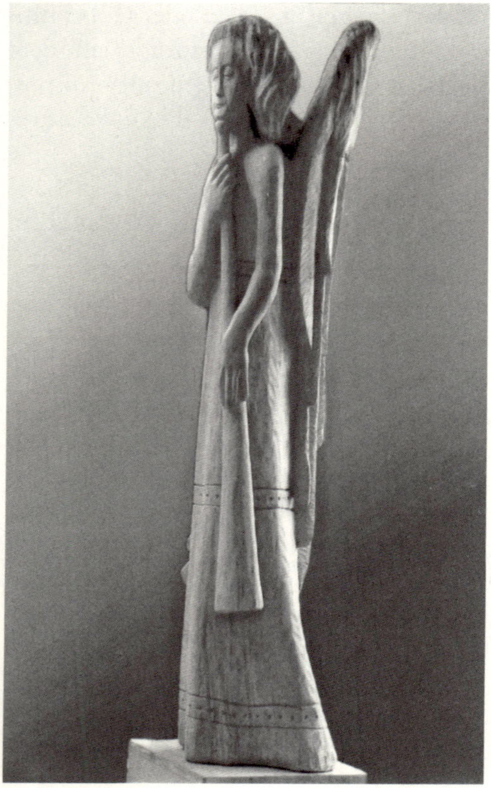

Abb. 23: Posaunenengel (Foto: Donatus Leicher).

Kälte schwindet. Seine Rundung und Glätte schmeichelt meiner Hand. Und die Frage taucht auf: Wo kommt der Stein her? Von welchem Felsen wurde er gebrochen? War es ein Granit, ein Gneis, ein Kalk- oder ein Sandstein? Wie weit war der Weg bis zu meiner Hand? Alle diese Fragen könnte man auch auf die Menschen übertragen, die mir täglich begegnen. Und wenn man bei diesem Betrachten des Steins wach bleibt, kommen immer weitere Fragen und auch Antworten auf einen zu. Der ganze Reichtum an Gedanken, den uns der Kieselstein offenbart, wird uns beim geduldigen Schauen und Hören geschenkt. Bei einem solchen Betrachten üben wir uns in Geduld, ohne die kein menschliches Leben gelebt werden kann.

Hoyer: Überträgt sich eine solche meditative Denkweise auch auf das Schaffen eines Bildhauers?

Leicher: Das ist wechselseitig. Denn das Schaffen am Stein oder Holz formt auch unser Denken. Als ich den Grabstein für meine Mitbrüder auf dem Friedhof in Freiburg geschaffen habe, sind meine Predigten oder Ansprachen, die ich in jener Zeit gehalten habe, viel prägnanter und kürzer gewesen. Das Schaffen im Stein formte auch meine Sprache.

Hoyer: Das heißt also: Jeder, der predigt, sollte sich zuerst am Stein abmühen?

Leicher: Das wäre bestimmt kein Nachteil für die Predigt.

Abb. 24: Pietà: Gesamtansicht (Foto: Wolfram Hoyer).

Hoyer: Unter Ihren Werken befinden sich auch eine Pietà und ein Schmerzensmann oder, wie Sie sagen, ein Geschundener. Warum haben Sie gerade diese Themen gestaltet?

Leicher: Das Leid vieler Mütter, die ihre Söhne im Krieg verloren haben, hat mich nie losgelassen. Diesen Frauen zum Trost wollte ich eine Pietà schaffen, um zu zeigen, dass es vor ihnen eine Frau gab, die Mutter des Herrn, die das gleiche Schicksal zu erleiden hatte wie sie.

Da vor unserem Kloster in Freiburg zwei Bäume gefällt werden mussten, weil eine Garage gebaut werden sollte, kam ich unverhofft zu einem dafür geeigneten Material. Beide Bäume waren sogenannte Exoten, Blauglockenbäume, also Zierbäume mit dem botanischen Namen Paulownia, benannt nach der russischen Zarentochter Anna Pawlowna. Ihre Blüten waren blau, ihre Blätter sehr groß, im Durchschnitt 30 bis 40 Zentimeter; die Jahresringe waren ein bis zwei Zentimeter breit, was auf ein rasches Wachstum hinweist. Das Holz war also vorhanden, doch es

Abb. 25: Pietà: Detail der Gesichter von Maria und Jesus (Foto: Wolfram Hoyer).

dauerte über drei Jahre, bis in mir die Gestalten von Mutter und Sohn ausgereift waren. Ein Bildhauer bot mir zum Arbeiten seine Werkstatt an.

Ich begann mit dem Gesicht der Mutter, die ihren Sohn, der auf ihrem Schoß sitzt, an ihr Herz drückt. Beide Gestalten habe ich in den aufrecht stehenden Stamm eingebunden. Die Stelle eines vor vielen Jahren abgesägten Astes bot sich für das Gesicht des toten Sohnes an. Da sich der ganze Schmutz der Umwelt durch den jahrelang darauf fallenden Regen in das offene Holz eingefressen hatte, wurde das ansonsten sehr helle Paulowniaholz an dieser Stelle dunkel gefärbt. Die Mutter hält ihren toten Sohn, der über sie hinausragt, aufrecht, als lebe er noch. Ein Rest der Rinde des abgesägten Astes bot sich als Dornenkrone an. Die halboffenen Augen des Toten schauen in abgrundtiefe Ferne.

Der zweite Stamm, etwas schmaler in seiner Form und kürzer, musste lange warten, bis der in ihm verborgene Geschundene herausgearbeitet werden konnte. Irgendwann musste ich die abgemagerten und ausgemergelten Gestalten meiner Mitkriegsgefangenen aus meiner Erinnerung loswerden. Im Rücken des Geschundenen steckt der Pfahl, an den er mit einem Strick um den Hals und an den Füßen angebunden ist. Seine Hände aber sind frei. Ursprünglich sollte in seiner linken Hand ein Stock, anstelle eines Schilfrohrs, seinen Platz finden. Ich verzichtete schließlich darauf, um die Geschlossenheit der Figur nicht zu zerstören. Ein Mitbruder, der meine Arbeit kritisch betrachtete, machte mich darauf aufmerksam, dass die linke Hand in ihrer jetzigen Form eine Mudra des Buddha sei, eine symbolische Geste der Handhaltung, die bedeute: Ich, Sohn der Erde. So bekam das Ganze einen anderen Sinn, an den ich nie gedacht hätte. Der kahle Schädel drückt die ganze Ausweglosigkeit und Hoffnungslosigkeit eines gequälten Menschen aus. Eine Dornenkrone, losgelöst vom Schädel, schwebt wie ein Strahlenkranz über dem Ganzen und weist auf eine andere Welt hin.

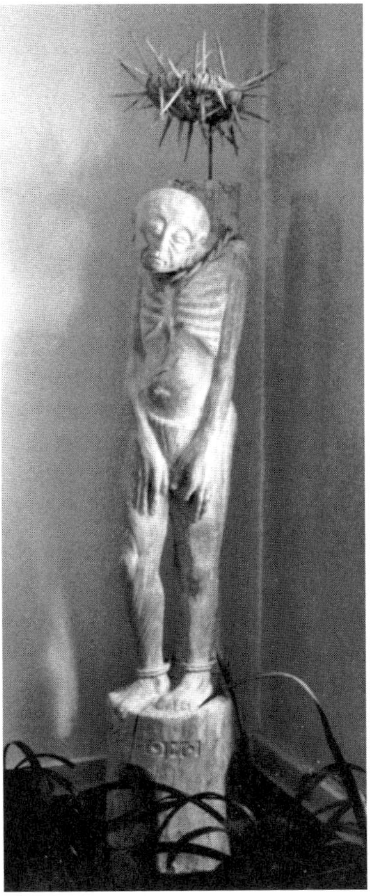

Abb. 26 (links): Der Geschundene: Gesamtansicht; zu seinen Füssen die Inschrift: „Ecce Homo" (Foto: Donatus Leicher).

Abb. 27 oben): Der Geschundene: Detailansicht des Oberkörpers, Gesichts und der Strahlenkranz-Dornenkrone (Foto: Donatus Leicher).

Hoyer: Beim Gang durch Ihr Kloster in Freiburg entdeckte ich ein Kreuz, das einem sogenannten Triumphkreuz gleicht, wie man es in romanischen Kirchen findet. Es ist wohl auch von Ihnen? Und warum hängt es im Treppenhaus, wo es keine eigentliche Funktion hat?

Leicher: Ich spreche nicht gerne über dieses Kreuz, obwohl es eine meiner besten Arbeiten ist und mein einziger Auftrag. Ich habe es im Auftrag eines Frauenklosters für deren neuromanische Kirche mit Herzblut und vielem Beten so gestaltet, wie meine Seele, also mein Inneres, empfunden hat: Der Herr ist gekreuzigt und er ist auferstanden. – Beides sollte sichtbar in Erscheinung treten. Bei der Arbeit hat ein Anderer meine Hand geführt.

Das ganze in Holz geschaffene Kreuz wurde mit einer Aluminiumfolie überzogen und mit einer Lasur getönt. An den Balkenenden leuchten auf orangefarbenem Grund die Symbole der vier Evangelisten, und der Corpus ruht auf blauem Grund.

Dieses Kreuz hing ungefähr zwei Jahre vor einem romanischen Bogen, der die ansonsten bildlose Apsis der Klosterkirche abschloss. Ohne mein Wissen hat man dann das Kreuz aus der Apsis entfernt und auf den Kirchenspeicher gelegt, weil die Apsis mit einem Mosaik eines namhaften Künstlers, mit dem ich befreundet war, geschmückt werden sollte. Nach schwierigen Verhandlungen konnte ich das Kreuz wieder zurückkaufen. Und nun hängt es hier und wartet darauf, dass man es holt, um anderswo die Botschaft von Tod und Auferstehung unseres Herrn verkünden zu dürfen.

Abb. 28: Dominikanerkloster St. Albert in Freiburg: Triumphkreuz (Foto: Wolfram Hoyer).

Abb. 29: Dominikanerkloster St. Albert in Freiburg: Triumphkreuz: Detailansicht mit dem Antlitz des Gekreuzigten, darüber das Symbol des Evangelisten Matthäus (Foto: Wolfram Hoyer).

Abb. 30: Aquarell: Portrait der Bildhauerin Gisela Heim (Foto: Donatus Leicher).

Hoyer: Über Ihre zahlreichen Aquarelle und Zeichnungen haben wir noch gar nicht gesprochen. Was machen Sie damit?

Leicher: Darf ich Sie an die Geschichte mit dem chinesischen Maler erinnern? Dort haben Sie die Antwort. Es sind mir einige ausgezeichnete Portraitzeichnungen gelungen. Dazu gehört auch eine Zeichnung von meiner Mutter. Die entstand allerdings noch vor meiner Ausbildung auf der Sommerakademie in Salzburg. Ölbilder, vor allem Portraits, gibt es wenige. Dazu gehört auch jenes, das ich vom früheren Provinzial P. Innozenz Varga gemacht habe, der dieser Tage seinen 100. Geburtstag feiern konnte. Leider ist es unvollendet geblieben.

Abb. 31: Ölbild: Portrait von Provinzial P. Innozenz Varga (unvollendet; Foto: Wolfram Hoyer).

Hoyer: Abschließend möchte ich Sie noch fragen: Gibt es etwas, womit Sie dieses Interview beenden möchten?

Leicher: Ich möchte eigentlich nur das sagen, was P. Alexander Siemer zu einer Gruppe von uns Studenten damals in Walberberg gesagt hat: „Merkt euch eines: In unserem Orden wird man nur das, was jeder selbst aus sich macht!"

Hoyer: Ich bedanke mich für das Gespräch.

Abb. 32: Bildhauerzeichen von P. Donatus Leicher auf der Rückseite der Gallus-Statue in Heimbach (Foto: Wolfram Hoyer).

In der Schule Jesu

Wie P. Christoph Schönborn seine Ordensberufung entdeckte

Erich Leitenberger

In Wien ist vielen Leuten – nicht nur den regelmäßigen Kirchgängern – bewusst, dass Kardinal Christoph Schönborn aus dem Dominikanerorden kommt. Und der Kardinal verbirgt es auch nicht: Wenn es die Umstände gestatten, legt er den Habit der Dominikaner an. Gelegentlich kann das auch Schlagzeilen machen: So etwa, als er am 25. April 2007 auf der Bühne des Wiener Burgtheaters im Rahmen der Veranstaltungsreihe „Shakespeare – eine Republik von Fehlern" über die „Kraft des Verzeihens" sprach. Der Wiener Erzbischof sorgte mit seinem Vortrag für die theologische „Einbegleitung" von Shakespeares Tragikomödie „Maß für Maß", die dann am 28. April in der „Burg" Premiere hatte. Die Ausführungen des Kardinals auf der Bühne gipfelten in einem Zitat aus der Bergpredigt Jesu: „Richtet nicht, damit ihr nicht gerichtet werdet! Denn wie ihr richtet, so werdet ihr gerichtet werden, und nach dem Maß, mit dem ihr messt und zuteilt, wird auch euch zugeteilt werden". Und er fügte hinzu: „Gnade ist das Maß, mit dem wir von Gott gemessen werden." Eindrucksvoll machte Christoph Schönborn klar, dass es in diesem Shakespeare-Stück um Vergebung, Barmherzigkeit und Gnade geht.

Die Ausführungen des Kardinals im Habit der Dominikaner stießen auf großes Interesse. Die „Frankfurter Allgemeine Zeitung" (FAZ), die internationale katholische Nachrichtenagentur „Zenit" und andere druckten seine Darlegungen im Wortlaut ab. Der Wiener Erzbischof hatte sichtlich einen Nerv getroffen; die Leute spürten, wie sehr die drei Begriffe Vergebung, Barmherzigkeit, Gnade für ihn selbst „Worte des Lebens" sind. Worte, die auch seine Entscheidung zum Eintritt in die Gemeinschaft des Heiligen Dominikus mitbestimmt haben mögen.

Diesen Schritt in das Noviziat der Dominikaner machte Christoph Schönborn vor 50 Jahren knapp nach der Matura 1963. Die Entscheidung für das Priestertum, für den Eintritt in die lebenslange Schule Jesu, hatte er schon früher getroffen. Er schildert diesen Weg so:

Abb. 1: das Geburtshaus in Skalken (Skalka) in Böhmen (Foto: privat).

„Schon früh hat mich der Gedanke an die Priesterberufung bewegt. Seit meinem 11. Lebensjahr dachte ich fest daran. Mit 14 Jahren lernte ich einen Dominikanerpater kennen, P. Paulus Gunz (gestorben 1968). Er hat mich für den Orden begeistert. Was war es? Ich glaube, die ganz besondere Mischung von Studium und Apostolat, von Gemeinschaft und Christusnachfolge, die Begeisterung für die Theologie des Heiligen Thomas von Aquin und die schlichte Volksfrömmigkeit des Rosenkranzes. Nach manchem Auf und Ab in meiner Gewissheit, ob der Weg zum Orden und Priestertum wirklich der meine ist, haben Einkehrtage vor der Matura schließlich die Klärung gebracht. So trat ich mit 18 Jahren, nach der Matura, ins Noviziat der Dominikaner in Warburg ein. In diesen bewegten Jahren des Konzils und der Nachkonzilszeit gab es manche Stürme im Orden, die wieder große Krisen, Erschütterungen und Zweifel auslösten."

Abb. 2: auf einem Motorrad, 1959 in Frankreich (Foto: privat).

Vielleicht war es biographischer Zufall, dass er das Noviziat im Kloster Warburg begann, ein Kloster, das von den Dominikanern nach Umstrukturierungen der Ordensprovinz Teutonia 1993 abgegeben wurde. 1996 wurde es von der syrisch-orthodoxen Kirche gekauft und ist jetzt das Kloster des Heiligen Jakob von Sarug. Aber was ist im geistlichen Leben schon Zufall? Es ist jedenfalls bemerkenswert, dass Christoph Schönborns Noviziatskloster heute einer Ostkirche dient, einer jener Kirchen, mit denen der Kardinal – auch in seiner Funktion als Vorsitzender des Kuratoriums der Wiener Stiftung „Pro Oriente" – ständig im Dialog steht. Und wie die Dominikaner Nachfolger gefunden haben, die im Kloster weiter die Botschaft der Barmherzigkeit des Evangeliums verkünden und die Heilige Eucharistie feiern, so ist es auch das Bestreben des Kardinals, Gotteshäuser in der Großstadt Wien, die auf Grund der demographischen und sozialen Veränderungen nicht mehr für die katholische Seelsorge benötigt werden, an befreundete „Schwesterkirchen" zu übergeben.

Warburg hat eine lange dominikanische Geschichte, die bis ins Jahr 1281 zurückreicht. Wie in vielen Städten Mitteleuropas bedeutete die Säkularisation von 1810 zunächst das Aus für die Dominikaner, aber an der Wende vom 19. zum 20. Jahrhundert kehrten sie zurück und bauten neu – wie man damals baute, historisierend, aber durchaus imposant. In diesem Kloster erlebte Christoph Schönborn seine Noviziatsjahre, die Jahre des Konzils und der heftigen Diskussionen über den Weg der Kirche zu den Menschen von heute.

In einem Interview aus Anlass seines 50-jährigen Jubiläums als Dominikaner erinnerte Kardinal Schönborn daran, dass Lebensentscheidungen „Tag für Tag durchgehalten und immer wieder erneuert werden müssen". Und er wies auch darauf hin, dass solche Entscheidungen fürs ganze Leben immer wieder auch von Krisen, Durststrecken und dunklen Phasen begleitet werden, „wo alles zu zerbrechen droht, wo nichts mehr sicher scheint".

Als am 1. Juli des heurigen Jahres in der Wiener Dominikanerkirche Maria Rotunda der 100. Geburtstag von P. Innozenz Varga (er sollte am 8. September, dem Fest Mariä Geburt, dann in die ewige Heimat gehen) gefeiert wurde, erinnerte der Kardinal daran, was er dem langjährigen Prior zu verdanken habe. In seiner Predigt sagte der Wiener Erzbischof, er würde heute nicht am Altar stehen „ohne die entscheidende Hilfe von P. Innozenz". Und wörtlich fügte er hinzu: „P. Innozenz hat meine Berufung gerettet und mir den Weg zum Priestertum eröffnet." Im Verhalten des damaligen Priors habe er gleichsam „eine Seite des Evangeliums" gelesen, so der Wiener Erzbischof.

Abb. 3: am Tag der Einkleidung, 29. September 1963, im Ordensgewand (Foto: privat).

Abb. 4: am Tag der Priesterweihe, 27. Dezember 1970, im Gespräch mit Kardinal König (Foto: privat).

Christoph Schönborn, der mit 18 Jahren bei den Dominikanern eingetreten ist, gehört zu den „Arbeitern der ersten Stunde". Am 27. Dezember 1970 (ein ungewöhnlicher, aber wieder „zufälliger" Termin) wurde er in Wien von Kardinal Franz König zum Priester geweiht. Ab 1971 absolvierte er am Institut Catholique in Paris ein Promotionsstudium, das er 1974 mit einer Dissertation mit dem Titel „L'Icône du Christ. Fondements théologiques" („Die Christus-Ikone. Theologische Grundlagen") abschloss. In diesem Buch wird deutlich, wie sehr ihn seit jeher die Tatsache fasziniert, dass Gott in Jesus Christus Mensch geworden, ganz nahe gekommen ist, als „einer von uns". Dem Buch über die Christus-Ikone und seiner Vertrautheit mit dem Denken der Kirchenväter ist die Beliebtheit Kardinal Schönborns in der orthodoxen Welt zu verdanken; man empfindet ihn dort als einen Bischof, „der uns versteht, der weiß, wie wir denken und fühlen".

In seiner Noviziats- und Studienzeit lernte Christoph Schönborn nicht nur die großen Vordenker des Konzils unter den französischen Dominikanern wie Marie-Dominique Chenu kennen, er wurde auch mit dramatischen Spannungen im Orden konfrontiert. Aber im Rückblick sagt er heute: „Ich bin voller Dankbarkeit, dass der Herr mich durch alle diese Klippen sicher geführt hat, ohne mein Verdienst, allein, weil Er so gut ist".

Abb. 5: als Weihbischof im Gespräch mit Mutter Eleonore, nach 1991 (Foto: privat).

Es freut ihn, dass – als neuester Trend – wieder Maturanten ins Priesterseminar eintreten. Was rät er – eingedenk seiner eigenen Erfahrungen – heute jungen Menschen? Sie sollen nicht zu lang zögern, wenn sie eine Berufung zum Ordensleben spüren: „Es ist schön, schon früh am Morgen des Lebens in den Weinberg des Herrn zu gehen." Kardinal Schönborn ist sich bewusst, dass viele meinen, die beste Lebensschule auch für einen angehenden Priester oder Ordenschristen sei es, sich zunächst einmal „in der Welt" zu bewähren. Aber er ist überzeugt, dass das Ordensleben eine „große Schule der Menschlichkeit und des persönlichen Reifens" ist. Deshalb sein Appell an die Jugendlichen, nicht zu „zögern", wenn sie in die „Schule Jesu" eintreten wollen.

Wer als Dominikaner in die Schule Jesu eintreten will, muss bereit sein, sich an die Seite der Armen, der an den Rand Gedrängten, der Ausgeschlossenen zu stellen. Schließlich sind die Dominikaner als Bettelorden entstanden; dieses ursprüngliche Charisma tritt heute wieder in den Vordergrund. So war es auch konsequent, dass Kardinal Schönborn nicht nur auf der Bühne des Burgtheaters im Dominikanerhabit in Erscheinung trat, sondern z. B. auch am 28. September 2013, als er an einer Buswallfahrt der

Abb. 6: bei der Diakonenweihe eines Ordensmitbruders in der Wiener Dominikanerkirche am 8. November 2008 (Foto: Sebastian Tönnesen).

„Essens-Gäste“ der Wiener Franziskaner nach Frauenkirchen teilnahm. Die „Gäste“, die bei den Franziskanern regelmäßig verköstigt werden, staunten nicht schlecht, als wenige Minuten vor Abfahrt der Kardinal im Dominikanerhabit den Bus bestieg, alle freundlich begrüßte, sich einen freien Platz suchte und bald mit den Nachbarn ins Gespräch vertieft war. Es wurde eine besinnliche und zugleich fröhliche Wallfahrt, die in Frauenkirchen in kreative Arbeitsgruppen, einen feierlichen Gottesdienst und ein festliches Mahl mündete. Der Kardinal im Dominikanerhabit wirkte daran mit, in das oft gleichförmige Dasein der „Gäste“ ein Licht der Hoffnung und der Freude zu bringen.

Politik und Gemeinwohl

Die Beiträge von Arthur F. Utz OP und Franz-Martin Schmölz OP zum Aufbau einer sozial gerechten Nachkriegsordnung in Europa

Wolfgang Hariolf Spindler OP

Von den 75 Jahren, die seit der Gründung der Süddeutsch-Österreichischen Dominikanerprovinz des hl. Albertus des Großen vergangen sind, waren die letzten 69 Jahre von einem Frieden in Mitteleuropa geprägt. Für die jüngere Generation von Österreichern, Deutschen und auch Schweizern, die in diesen Jahrzehnten zum Orden und in die Provinz gefunden hat, stellte der *zwischenstaatliche* Friede eine Selbstverständlichkeit dar. Mit ihm ging ein von Bürgerkrieg und längeren gewalttätigen Auseinandersetzungen freier *gesellschaftlicher* Friede einher. Von daher mag Frieden als Normalzustand angesehen werden, zu dessen Entstehung und Erhaltung man nichts zu tun habe. Wer freilich den Blick an die Ränder Europas oder in andere Regionen der Erde schweifen lässt, wird schnell eines Besseren belehrt. Blutige Konflikte sind vielerorts an der Tagesordnung. Kriege – auch solche, die nicht mehr so genannt, aber mit gleicher Vernichtungskraft geführt werden – rauben Abertausenden von Menschen das Leben. Sie zerstören die materiellen Lebensgrundlagen und, nicht weniger schlimm, das gegenseitige Vertrauen. Die Ältesten von uns wissen dies noch aus eigenem Erleben. Die beiden durch Unruhen und Umbrüche miteinander verketteten Weltkriege haben es auf schreckliche Weise gelehrt. 2014 liegt der Ausbruch dieses „dreißigjährigen Krieges“ ein ganzes Säkulum zurück. In ungezählten Büchern, Filmen, Erlebnisberichten, Dokumentationen, Mahn- und Gedenkveranstaltungen wird einmal mehr an die schrecklichen Ereignisse erinnert. Zugleich werden die Wiederaufbauleistungen der Nachkriegsjahre und die Eingliederung der beiden Nachfolgestaaten auf dem Gebiet des untergangenen Deutschen Reiches in die internationale Staatengemeinschaft – die Sonderrolle der DDR bedarf einer eigenen Betrachtung – gewürdigt.

Keineswegs waren es nur Politiker, die den Weg der Völkerversöhnung, der Verständigung, der multilateralen Zusammenarbeit und der staatlichen Erneuerung eingeschlagen haben. Die Nachkriegsordnung in

der 1945 wiedererrichteten Republik Österreich, im 1949 (in den drei Westzonen) als „Bundesrepublik" ausgerufenen Deutschland und auch in den vom Krieg betroffenen Nachbarstaaten verdankt sich auch einer Riege von Staatsdenkern, Sozialphilosophen, Juristen und Nationalökonomen, die eine genaue Vorstellung von freien, rechtsstaatlich-demokratisch geordneten und ökonomisch überlebensfähigen Gemeinwesen in Europa hatten. Auf ihren Ideen, Vorschlägen und praktischen Interventionen beruht der Wohlstand, der seitdem – trotz unvermeidlicher sozial- und rechtspolitischer Defizite – diese Länder prägt. Wirtschaftlich setzte sich in Deutschland wie in Österreich die Soziale Marktwirtschaft durch. An ihrer Fundierung und praktischen Verwirklichung hatten Männer beider Länder wie Walter Eucken, Franz Böhm, Alexander Rüstow, Friedrich August von Hayek, Wilhelm Röpke und Alfred Müller-Armack erheblichen Anteil. Dass dabei unter den Ökonomen, insbesondere zwischen der „paläoliberalen" (v. Hayek in der Nachfolge seines Lehrers Ludwig von Mises) und der „neoliberalen" (vor allem Röpke und Rüstow) Schule, erhebliche Spannungen ausgetragen wurden, kann angesichts der Übereinstimmung in den *Grundsätzen* unter „ordnungspolitisches Waffengetöse" subsumiert werden.[1] Ihr auf freiem Markt und individueller wie kollektiver Verantwortung beruhendes Konzept hat beiden Ländern jahrzehntelang Wohlfahrt und sozialen Frieden beschert.

Weniger in das allgemeine Bewusstsein gedrungen ist, welche maßgebliche Rolle Dominikaner bei dieser positiven Entwicklung im deutschsprachigen Raum gespielt haben. Es war vor allem ein aus dem Kloster Walberberg hervorgegangener Kreis von Patres, der erheblichen Einfluss auf die politisch-sozialen Geschicke in den Jahren und Jahrzehnten nach 1945 genommen hat.

---

1 Joachim Starbatty, Soziale Marktwirtschaft als Konzeption, in: Nils Goldschmidt / Michael Wohlgemuth, Die Zukunft der Sozialen Marktwirtschaft, Tübingen: Mohr Siebeck, 2004, 136. Angemerkt sei, dass die „Neoliberalen" von damals mit den heute so Genannten wenig gemein haben; der Begriff hat eine problematische Wandlung ins Pejorative, Polemische erfahren.

I. Der Walberberger Kreis

Der 1925 gegründete Konvent St. Albert in Walberberg, gelegen in Bornheim, einem Dorf zwischen Köln und Bonn, war von 1934 an das Studienhaus der Dominikaner der Provinz *Teutonia*; später wurde die „Albertus-Magnus-Akademie“ zur Philosophisch-Theologischen Hochschule ausgebaut, bis diese 1974 infolge der Identitätskrise, die das Zweite Vatikanische Konzil (1962–1965) und die revolutionären Umtriebe von 1968 in Kirche und Orden ausgelöst hatten, geschlossen wurde. Auch die Klerikerstudenten aus dem süddeutschen und österreichischen Raum erhielten hier ihre akademische Grundausbildung. In den dreißiger Jahren und dann wieder nach dem Zweiten Weltkrieg erlangte das Kloster eine überregionale öffentliche Bedeutung. Über das typisch dominikanische Engagement in Predigt, Seelsorge und Theologie hinaus wurde Walberberg zu einem geistigen Zentrum, das mit seiner auf der Katholischen Soziallehre (vor allem der Päpste Pius XI. und Pius XII.) beruhenden antitotalitären Ausrichtung und zahlreichen sozialethischen und sozialpolitischen Impulsen den christlichen Widerstand gegen das NS-Regime stärkte und nach 1945 eine demokratische Staats- und Gesellschaftsordnung aufbauen half.[2] Hier wurden gerade nur zwei Monate nach Kriegsende die „Kölner Leitsätze“ formuliert[3], auf deren Grundlage die (rheinische) CDU entstanden ist.[4] Hier

---

2 Vgl. dazu Wolfgang Ockenfels, Der Walberberger Kreis. Zur sozialethischen Bedeutung der Dominikaner in Deutschland, in: Die Neue Ordnung, 65. Jg., Sonderheft November 2011, insbes. 2–13; ders., Arthur F. Utz (1908–2001), in: Zeitgeschichte in Lebensbildern. Aus dem deutschen Katholizismus des 19. und 20. Jahrhunderts, hrsg. von Jürgen Aretz, Rudolf Morsey und Anton Rauscher, Bd. 12, Münster: Aschendorff Verlag, 2007, 143–154, 144 f.; Rainer Maria Groothuis, Im Dienste einer überstaatlichen Macht – Die deutschen Dominikaner unter der NS-Diktatur, Münster: Verlag Regensberg, 2002, insbes. 153–176.

3 http://www.grundsatzprogramm.cdu.de/doc/1945_2_Koelner-Leitsaetze.pdf [gelesen am 8.10.2013].

4 Bei der offiziellen Gründung am 19. August 1945 hieß sie zunächst „Christlich-Demokratische Partei“ (CDP); die Übernahme des in Berlin geprägten Namens „Christliche-Demokratische Union“ Deutschlands (CDU) erfolgte im Dezember desselben Jahres. Vgl. Leo Schwering, Die Entstehung der CDU, Köln: Troschel, 1946; ders., Vorgeschichte und Entstehung der CDU, 2., neu bearbeitete und erweiterte Ausgabe, Köln: Verlag Deutsche Glocke, 1952; ders., Frühgeschichte der Christlich-Demokratischen Union, Recklinghausen: Kommunal-Verlag, 1963; ders., Weltweite Wirkung: P. Welty: Mann des Widerstandes, Baumeister neuer Zeit, Echo der Zeit, 13. Juni 1965, 8; Hans Georg Wieck, Die Entstehung der CDU und die Wiedergründung des Zentrums im Jahre 1945 (= Bei-

gründeten Laurentius Siemer OP (1888–1956),[5] resoluter Provinzial (1932–1946) in schwieriger Zeit, und Eberhard Welty OP (1902–1965), Sozialphilosoph und „Seele der Verhandlungen“ (Leo Schwering) bei der Gründung der CDU, 1946 die Zeitschrift „Die Neue Ordnung“ als Ideenplattform und Diskussionsforum für ein neues, anderes Deutschland.[6] Hier tagten kirchliche, gewerkschaftliche und politische Gruppierungen, um eine freiheitlich-demokratische Verfassung und eine neue Gesellschaftsordnung vorzubereiten. Hier stellte Welty gleich 1945 ein Erwachsenenbildungswerk auf die Beine, das sozialethische Kurse und Fortbildungen für Entscheidungsträger anbot. Hier hob er 1951 zusammen mit christlichen Politikern, Verbandsvertretern und Unternehmern das „Institut für Gesellschaftswissenschaften Walberberg“ aus der Taufe.[7] Letzteres wurde zwar 1984 von politisch nach links abgedrifteten Brüdern aus dem Kloster verdrängt, erfreut sich aber, aus Ordensstrukturen herausgelöst und in Bonn angesiedelt, bis heute eines blühenden Lebens mit zahlreichen Veranstaltungen und Publikationen. Es firmiert nunmehr als einzige Einrichtung mit dem einst klangvollen Namen Walberberg, während der Konvent selbst nach einem beispiellosen Auflösungsprozess 2007 untergegangen ist.

Neben den genannten Namen sind weitere Persönlichkeiten zu erwähnen. Auch sie sind aus dem Walberberger Kreis heraus mit zahlreichen Einrichtungen, Initiativen, Veröffentlichungen, Kongressen, Diskussionsforen und Gesprächskreisen hervorgetreten: Edgar Nawroth OP (1912–2010), enger Mitarbeiter Weltys, 1961 promoviert bei Arthur F. Utz OP (1908–2001) in Freiburg im Uechtland (Schweiz), 1965–1984 Chefredakteur der „Neuen Ordnung“, 1963–1985 Professor für Christliche Sozialwissenschaften in

träge zur Geschichte des Parlamentarismus und der politischen Parteien, Bd. 2), Düsseldorf: Droste, 1953.

5 Zu seiner Vita vgl. die CD „Pater Laurentius Siemer OP 1888–1956“. Idee, Redaktion und Kommentierung: Angelika Ditscheid (Copyright). Hrsg. vom Institut für Gesellschaftswissenschaften Walberberg, Bonn 2009; Groothuis (wie Anm. 2), 361–405.

6 Programmatisch vor allem Eberhard Welty, Was nun? Grundsätze und Hinweise zur Neuordnung im deutschen Lebensraum, Brühl-Köln: Becher, o. J. [1946]; ders., Die Entscheidung in die Zukunft. Grundsätze und Hinweise zur Neuordnung im deutschen Lebensraum, Heidelberg: Kerle, 1946. Zur Geschichte der sozialethischen Zweimonatsschrift vgl. Wolfgang Hariolf Spindler, „Die Neue Ordnung“ – ein sozialethischer Kompass. 65 Jahre Orientierungen für das gesellschaftliche Leben, in: Kontakt. Freundesgabe der Dominikanerprovinz Teutonia 39/2011, 64–65.

7 Ockenfels, Der Walberberger Kreis (wie Anm. 2), 14.

Trier;[8] Heinrich Basilius Streithofen OP (1925–2006), erst Geschäftsführer (ab 1967), dann Vorsitzender (1993–2006) des „Instituts für Gesellschaftswissenschaften Walberberg", 1967 bei Utz promoviert, einflussreicher und medienwirksamer Organisator, Publizist und CDU-Berater;[9] schließlich – als letzter Spross der „Walberberger" – Wolfgang Ockenfels OP (geb. 1947), 1978 auch er bei Utz in Freiburg promoviert, 1984 bei Anton Rauscher SJ (geb. 1928) in Augsburg habilitiert, seit 1985 Ordinarius für Christliche Sozialwissenschaften an der Theologischen Fakultät Trier, seit 1992 Chefredakteur der „Neuen Ordnung", seit 2003 Consultor des Päpstlichen Rates „Justitia et Pax", seit 2007 Vorsitzender des „Instituts für Gesellschaftswissenschaften Walberberg", daneben in vielen anderen Gremien und Institutionen leitend oder beratend tätig sowie als wortgewaltiger Vortragender, Redner, TV-Gast und Publizist ebenso geachtet wie gefürchtet.

Rückblickend betont Ockenfels die heterogene Zusammensetzung des Walberberger Kreises, den offenkundig fehlenden Willen zur Herausbildung einer Schule, aber auch die gemeinsame Basis, die im Festhalten an der „thomasischen Tradition" des Dominikanerordens bestanden habe. Zu dieser Tradition gehört, wie zu ergänzen ist, die Treue gegenüber dem Lehr- und Hirtenamt der Päpste und der Bischöfe in Glaubens- und Moraldingen – eine Tugend, deren Vernachlässigung in den letzten fünf Jahrzehnten (nicht allein) im Predigerorden zu Verfallserscheinungen und allgemeinem Ansehensverlust geführt hat. Die Anteile an diesem Gemeinschaftswerk von Individualisten sieht Ockenfels wie folgt verteilt: „Die ‚Walberberger' fanden in Siemer ihren tatkräftigen Initiator, in Welty den programmatischen Kopf, in Utz einen überragenden Systematiker, in Nawroth ihren ideologiekritischen Geist und in Streithofen einen öffentlichkeitswirksamen Politikberater."[10] Er selbst kann in Anlehnung an einen päpstlichen Ehrentitel als prononciert katholischer *Defensor rationis* bezeichnet werden.

8 Zu Nawroth vgl. ebd., 23–26.

9 Vgl. ebd., 26 f.

10 Ebd., 3; ders., Arthur F. Utz (wie Anm. 2), 144.

II. Zwei dominikanische Anwälte der sozialen und politischen Ethik

Von den bisher Genannten gehörte allein Utz der Süddeutsch-Österreichischen Ordensprovinz an. Eingetreten ist er noch in die niederdeutsche Provinz *Teutonia*. Erst im Jahre 1939, bei Gründung der oberdeutschen Provinz, trat Utz über – was vor allem mit seiner landsmannschaftlichen Herkunft zu tun hatte.

Der Name des zehn Jahre später in die *Germania superior* eingetretenen Franz-Martin Schmölz OP ist bisher noch nicht gefallen. Auch dieser steht mit Walberberg in Verbindung. Was Utz und Schmölz – ungeachtet unterschiedlicher Charaktere – miteinander teilen, ist freilich nicht allein die Provinzzugehörigkeit, sondern zuvörderst die Tatsache, dass beide als bedeutende Anwälte der sozialen und politischen Ethik im 20. Jahrhundert in die Geschichte eingegangen sind und durch ihr Denken und Handeln am Aufbau einer auf soziale Gerechtigkeit bedachten europäischen Nachkriegsordnung entscheidend mitgewirkt haben.

Im Folgenden soll ihr Werdegang im Orden und in der Welt der Wissenschaften mit kurzen Strichen nachgezeichnet und gewürdigt werden.

1. Arthur F. Utz OP

Arthur Utz[11] wurde als Sohn eines Angestellten der badischen Bahn am 15. April 1908 in Basel geboren. Die Mutter stammte von einem Lörracher Sandsteinbruchbesitzer ab. Utz legte 1928 in Freiburg im Breisgau das Abitur ab und trat danach in den Predigerorden ein, wo er den ungeliebten und später nur mehr selten ausgeschriebenen Ordensnamen Fridolin Maria erhielt. Nach dem Noviziat in Venlo (Holland) legte er am 4. Juni 1929 die

11 Zu Biographie und Werk vgl. ausführlich Bernd Kettern, Sozialethik und Gemeinwohl. Die Begründung einer realistischen Sozialethik bei Arthur F. Utz (= Sozialwissenschaftliche Schriften, H. 22), Berlin: Duncker & Humblot, 1992; Wolfgang Ockenfels, Arthur F. Utz (wie Anm. 2); Anita Zocchi Fischer, Arthur Fridolin Utz (1908–2001), in: Schweizer Ethiker im 20. Jahrhundert. Der Beitrag theologischer Denker, hrsg. von Wolfgang Lienemann und Frank Mathwig, Zürich: Theologischer Verlag, 2005, 133–148; Wolfgang Hariolf Spindler, Art. Utz, Arthur F., in: Thomistenlexikon, hrsg. v. David Berger / Jörgen Vijgen, Bonn: nova & vetera, 2006, Sp. 677–684, 677 ff.; ders., Art. Utz, Arthur F., in: Neue Deutsche Biographie (NDB), Bd. 26, für die Historische Kommission bei der Bayerischen Akademie der Wissenschaften, hrsg. von Maximilian Lanzinner, Berlin: Duncker & Humblot, [voraussichtlich] 2014. Weitere Informationen zu Utz unter http://www.stiftung-utz.org.

(erste) Profess ab,[12] bevor er die philosophischen und theologischen Studien in Walberberg absolvierte und am 27. Juli 1934 in Köln zum Priester geweiht wurde. Mit einer lateinisch verfassten Arbeit über den inneren Zusammenhang der moralischen Tugenden nach Thomas von Aquin wurde er 1937 nach einem nur einjährigen Doktoratsstudium in Freiburg i. Ue. bei Santiago Ramírez OP (1891–1967) promoviert, den er bis zuletzt für den größten Denker seit Thomas von Aquin hielt. Anschließend war Utz bis zur Enteignung des Klosters 1942 als Ontologie-Dozent in Walberberg tätig und lebte danach, verborgen vor der Geheimen Staatspolizei, die sich im Kloster eingenistet hatte, als Kirchenrektor in Lüttershausen im Bergischen Land, bevor er 1946 von Provinzial Marianus Vetter (1892–1968) in Wien assigniert wurde, wo er an der Katholischen Akademie lehren, die Übersetzungen der „Deutschen Thomasausgabe" der *Summa Theologiae* leiten[13] und sich in Moraltheologie habilitieren sollte.

Es kam anders. Denn die sowjetische Besatzungsbehörde in Wien verweigerte ihm die Einreise. Doch wurde just zu dieser Zeit an der Philosophischen Fakultät der Universität Freiburg i. Ue. eine außerordentliche Professur für Ethik und Sozialphilosophie eingerichtet. Auf Bitten des Ordensgenerals wurde die Professur mit Utz besetzt, weil Welty, Studienregens in Walberberg, von der *Teutonia* nicht freigegeben worden war.[14] Anfang Januar 1946 kehrte Utz also an den Ort seiner Promotion zurück und trat schon am 7. Januar die Vorlesungen in diesem ihm bis zu diesem Zeitpunkt nicht vertrauten Fach an. Assigniert wurde er im *Albertinum*, dem Professorenkonvent der vom Orden getragenen Universität.[15] Mit Wintersemester 1951/52[16] erfolgte die Umwandlung in einen Lehrstuhl mit ordentlicher Professur. 1954–1955 fungierte Utz außerdem als Dekan der Fakultät, danach für ein Jahr als Vizedekan.[17] Anfang der 1950er Jahre ließ er sich in die Schweiz einbürgern. Sein Wohnsitz blieb über Jahrzehnte hinweg Freiburg. Als Leiter des von ihm und den Freiburger Professorenkollegen Joseph Piller (1890–1954) und Eugène Bongras (1905–1981) ge-

12 PK 1939, 33. Abkürzungen wie im Beitrag von Wolfram Hoyer in diesem Band.

13 PK 1946, 9.

14 Vgl. Arthur F. Utz, Die Lehre, die ich aus meinem Curriculum ziehe, in: Rundbrief der Dominikanerprovinz des Hl. Albert in Süddeutschland und Österreich, o. O., 2/1998, 12–14, 13.

15 PK 1948, 23.

16 Zocchi Fischer (wie Anm. 11), 137; vgl. auch PK 1953, 25.

17 PK 1955, 24; PK 1956, 24.

gründeten, transfakultären „Internationalen Instituts für Sozialwissenschaften und Politik“ (École internationale des sciences sociales et politiques)[18] setzte er sich 1946–1978 dafür ein, die Katholische Soziallehre auszulegen, weiterzuentwickeln und für die politisch-sozioökonomische Praxis fruchtbar zu machen. Dazu diente auch die von ihm herausgegebene institutseigene Zeitschrift „Politeia“, die 1949–1953 existierte. Begünstigt wurde die Arbeit damals durch zwei in Madrid und Regensburg errichtete Zweigniederlassungen. Die Firma Krauss-Maffei sponserte sogar einen Omnibus für „Propaganda“-Zwecke, allerdings kam dieser in der Schweiz nie zum Einsatz.[19]

Nach der Emeritierung im Jahre 1978 verfolgte Utz seine Ziele mit Hilfe der „Union de Fribourg – Internationales Institut für Sozial- und Politikwissenschaften“,[20] einer Nachbildung der 1885 von Gaspard Kardinal Mermillod (1824–1892) gegründeten „Union catholique d’études sociales et économiques“, die an der Vorbereitung der berühmten Enzyklika *Rerum Novarum* (1891) mitgewirkt hatte. Eine beträchtliche Zahl von Kongressen und Veröffentlichungen zeugt von der regen Aktivität des Institutes. 1976–1998 präsidierte Utz der „Internationalen Stiftung Humanum“ (Bern, heute Lugano), die im Sinne des Vatikanum II den Dialog zwischen Kirche und Welt fördert und dazu den hochdotierten Augustin-Bea-Preis verleiht; Preisträger waren bisher u. a. Willem A. Visser ’t Hooft, Johannes Messner, Josef Kardinal Frings, Erzbischof Isidore de Souza, Joseph Kardinal Ratzinger und Paul Kirchhof. Das mit der Stiftung verbundene „Scientia-Humana-Institut“ in Bonn leitete Utz ebenso, wie er 1966–1993 als Vorsitzender des „Instituts für Gesellschaftswissenschaften Walberberg“ wirkte. Ein Lehrauftrag für Sozialethik führte Utz nach seiner Emeritierung fünf Jahre lang regelmäßig nach Roermond (Holland), wo er am Priesterseminar unterrichtete.

---

18 Die Gründung war mit anderen Organisationen und Interessen, vor allem der „*Pax Romana*“, verflochten; vgl. dazu Bernhard Salzmann, Europa als Thema katholischer Eliten: das katholische Europa-Netzwerk der Schweiz von 1945 bis Mitte der 1950er Jahre, Freiburg: Academic Press / Paulusverlag Freiburg Schweiz, 2006, 89 ff.

19 Arthur F. Utz, Gründung und Entwicklung des Internationalen Instituts für Sozial- und Politikwissenschaften (sic!) an der Univ. Fribourg (Bericht für Prof. Fleck im Hinblick auf die Jubiläumsschrift der Universität), Manuskript [masch.], Juli 1989, 3 S. [unveröffentlicht].

20 Utz wohnte auch von da an am Sitz des Instituts, einem alten Bauernhaus in Pensier nahe Freiburg.

Utz war darüber hinaus in zahlreichen Institutionen und Gremien in leitender Funktion oder als Berater tätig. So wurde er gleich nach dem Krieg in das Kuratorium der „Internationalen Vereinigung für Rechts- und Sozialphilosophie" gewählt. Später wurde er ihr Präsident und trug zur weltweiten Verbreitung der Vereinigung bei; 1979 ernannte sie ihn zum Ehrenpräsidenten. Von 1984 an war er für einige Jahre Mitglied der an der Päpstlichen Universität der Dominikaner *Angelicum* in Rom angesiedelten Kommission für Sozialwissenschaften.[21] Hochstehende Repräsentanten der Kirche, Politiker, Arbeitnehmer- und Arbeitgeberverbände, auch die deutsche Bundesregierung[22] schätzten seinen Rat.

So konnten hohe Ehrungen und Auszeichnungen nicht ausbleiben. Der Ordensmeister ehrte Utz 1965 mit der Ernennung zum „Magister in Sacra Theologia".[23] Das Großkreuz des Verdienstordens der Bundesrepublik Deutschland wurde ihm 1968 verliehen. Die Philosophische Fakultät der Universität Basel promovierte ihn 1985 zum Dr. phil. *honoris causa.* 1990 erhielt er in Wien den angesehenen Leopold-Kunschak-Preis.[24] 1991 nahm Utz das Große Goldene Ehrenzeichen für Verdienste um die Republik Österreich in Empfang. Nachdem Utz sich maßgeblich für die Gründung der Päpstlichen Akademie der Sozialwissenschaften eingesetzt hatte,[25] berief ihn Papst Johannes Paul II. (1920–2005) am 19. Januar 1994 als einen der ersten in dieses honorige Gremium.[26]

In jenen Jahren intervenierte Utz mitunter bei der römischen Glaubenskongregation. Zum Beispiel monierte er an den Abschnitten 73–74 der Enzyklika *Evangelium vitae* (1995) von Johannes Paul II., dass darin Zugeständnisse an naturrechtswidrige Konzepte enthalten seien.[27] Leider ist der Schriftwechsel mit Joseph Kardinal Ratzinger (geb. 1927), dem spä-

21 PK 1984, 16; PK 1987, 16.

22 Vgl. Brief von Utz an Streithofen, Ostersonntag 1984, 3 S. [masch., unveröffentlicht].

23 PK 1966, 26.

24 PR2, 10. 3. 1990, Nr. 13.

25 Hans F. Zacher, Päpstliche Akademie für Sozialwissenschaften. Ein neuer institutioneller Ansatz der katholischen Soziallehre, in: Stimmen der Zeit, Bd. 130 (2005) 736–748, 740.

26 http://www.pass.va/content/scienzesociali/en/academicians/deceased.html [gelesen am 7.10.2013].

27 Vgl. Arthur F. Utz, Die „Enzyklika ‚Evangelium vitae' und die Lehre vom ‚voluntarium indirectum', Theologisches 27 (1997) 182–184; ders., Das „Voluntarium indirectum" in der Enzyklika Evangelium Vitae. Versuch einer Verdeutlichung im Hinblick auf die Abänderung der gesetzlichen Indikation der Abtreibung, Theologisches 28 (1998) 131–138; ders., Das Unheil der Nr. 73/74 der Enzyklika Evangelium vitae, Theologisches

teren Papst Benedikt XVI. (2005–2013), nicht erhalten geblieben. Utz, in persönlichen Dingen übervorsichtig, verbrannte im hohen Alter seine Korrespondenz. Die (aus seiner Sicht) sich häufenden Fehler und Defizite in lehramtlichen Dokumenten führte der Gelehrte übrigens auf mangelhafte Latein- und Thomas-Kenntnisse von Kurienmitarbeitern zurück.

In seinen letzten Lebensjahren trieben Utz vermehrt derartige moraltheologische und auch kirchenpolitische Fragen um. Das letzte Buch, an dem er bis kurz vor dem Tode schrieb, bedeutete für ihn eine Rückkehr zu seiner „ersten Liebe", der Moraltheologie.[28] Leider war es ihm nicht vergönnt, das Manuskript zu vollenden. 2011 ist das Werk postum erschienen.[29] Es trägt den Titel „Der Weg des Menschen zu dauerhaftem Glück und innerem Frieden. Ein Resümee der Ethik und der Moraltheologie des Thomas von Aquin". Utz verbrachte die letzten Lebensjahre im „Foyer Jean-Paul II", einem Alters- und Pflegeheim für Priester[30] in Villars-sur-Glâne bei Freiburg i. Ue., wo er täglich die hl. Messe las.[31] Dort ist er am 18. Oktober 2001 verstorben. Bestattet wurde Utz in der Krypta des *Albertinum.*

Wie in der oben zitierten Einschätzung Ockenfels' angeklungen, ist Arthur F. Utz als vorerst letzter großer Systematiker einer (nicht phänomenologischen und nicht transzendentalphilosophischen) *realistischen* Sozialethik anzusehen. Wie wohl kein Zweiter hat er dazu die Katholische Soziallehre spekulativ durchdrungen, ohne auf diese festgelegt werden zu können. Zwar war er mit dem Gesamtwerk des hl. Thomas bestens vertraut und er kommentierte davon – nicht zuletzt aus seelsorglichen Gründen – die Traktate der *Summa Theologiae* über den Glauben,[32] die Hoff-

---

28 (1998) 307–310; ders., Die Ethik der Schadensbegrenzung und die Politik, Die Neue Ordnung 54 (2000) 44–49.

28 Wolfgang Hariolf Spindler, Wahrheit und Glück – Arthur F. Utz als Moraltheologe, in: Arthur F. Utz, Der Weg des Menschen zu dauerhaftem Glück und innerem Frieden. Ein Resümee der Ethik und der Moraltheologie des Thomas von Aquin. Im Auftrag des Instituts für Gesellschaftswissenschaften Walberberg und der Stiftung Prof. Dr. A. F. Utz hrsg. und mit einem Vorwort versehen von Wolfgang Hariolf Spindler, Bonn: nova & vetera, 2011, 5–9.

29 Vgl. vorige Anm.

30 Seit 2006 in ein für alle offenstehendes „Foyer La Rose d'Automne" umgewandelt.

31 Über die Mess-Stipendien führte er stets genau Buch und rechnete sie mit der Ordensprovinz ab.

32 Thomas von Aquin, Summa theologica II–II 1–16: Glaube als Tugend. Anmerkungen und Kommentar von Arthur F. Utz (= Deutsche Thomasausgabe, Bd. 15), Heidelberg-München: Kerle, 1950.

nung[33] und das geistliche Leben;[34] den Schwerpunkt seines Interesses an Thomas bildete aber dessen Ethik. In der aristotelisch-thomasischen Handlungs-, Tugend- und Gerechtigkeitslehre fand Utz den „ganzheitlichen" Ansatz, mit dem sich eine von den Seinswirklichkeiten ausgehende Ethik wissenschaftlich normativ begründen ließ. Ihm war daran gelegen, eine echte, sämtliche Bereiche des gesellschaftlichen, politischen und wirtschaftlichen Lebens erfassende *Sozial*ethik[35] zu entwerfen, die nicht als bloßes Anhängsel der *Individual*ethik wie noch bei Victor Cathrein SJ (1845–1931) oder als überholte „Standesethik" erscheinen konnte. Die Gesellschaft (zum Beispiel eines Staates) müsse mit Thomas als *wirkliche* (und nicht nur gedachte) *Einheit* und nicht lediglich als Summe von Individuen aufgefasst werden. Ein christlicher Personalismus im engeren Sinn, wie etwa von Gustav Gundlach SJ (1892–1963) und Oswald v. Nell-Breuning SJ (1890–1991) vertreten, könne nicht erklären, wie aus einem Nebeneinander von Personenrechten ein soziales Ganzes entstehen soll. Wie das Individuum in seiner Ausrichtung auf Gott als die „universale Quelle jeglichen Gutseins"[36] wahres Glück (als Erfahrung des Guten) anstrebe, so sei im sozialen Bereich das Objekt der sittlichen Entscheidung das Gemeinwohl (*bonum commune*), das *vor* der Formulierung sozialer Handlungsprinzipien wie Solidarität, Subsidiarität, „goldene Regel" und so weiter bestimmt werden müsse. Das Gemeinwohl – die zentrale Kategorie der Utzschen Ethik – sei zwar den Einzelnen vorgeordnet, seine Definition erfordere aber die Berücksichtigung der Interessen aller ihre persönliche Vervollkommnung anstrebenden Individuen. Sonst „werden sich diejenigen mit Protestaktionen melden, die in ihren Daseinserwartungen zu kurz gekommen sind".[37]

---

33 Thomas von Aquin, Die Hoffnung. Theologische Summe II–II 17–22. Anmerkungen und Kommentar von Arthur F. Utz, Freiburg i. Br.: Herder, 1988.

34 Thomas von Aquin, Religion – Opfer – Gebet – Gelübde: lateinischer Text [der Summa theologica II–II 80–88] mit Übersetzung [von Josef Groner], Anmerkungen und Kommentar von Arthur F. Utz, Paderborn: Bonifatius, 1998. Der Kommentar zu den Fragen 89–100 blieb unvollendet.

35 Zu Begriff und Genese des Begriffs „Sozialethik" vgl. Wilhelm Korff, „Work in progress", in: Christliche Sozialethik – Architektur einer jungen Disziplin. Akademischer Festakt zum 85. Geburtstag von Wilhelm Korff, hrsg. von Markus Vogt (= LMUniversum, Bd. 12), München: Archiv der LMU München, 2012, 61–93, 63 ff.

36 Thomas von Aquin, *Summa Theologiae*, I–II 2, 8 ad 1.

37 Peter Paul Müller-Schmid, Politische Ethik – Prüfstein der Gesellschaftsethik. Zum 5. Band des Standardwerks von Arthur F. Utz, Die Neue Ordnung 55 (2001) 298–308, 299.

Die Gesetze, die dem Gemeinwohl dienen sollen, dürfen sich nach Utz nicht nur an den „Tugendhaften" orientieren; sie können nicht mehr als das ethische Minimum sichern. Daher interpretiert Utz die thomasische Ethik des Sozialen strikt (seins-)*philosophisch* und nicht als Ausfluss einer sozialen (Offenbarungs-)*Theologie*. Über die Annahme eines Schöpfergottes, der – auch nach katholischem Dogma[38] – auf der Basis einer natürlichen Theologie rational erkannt werden kann,[39] hinaus bedarf es keiner theologischen oder Glaubensvoraussetzungen, um „spontan" zu erkennen, dass das (jeweils) Böse zu meiden und das (jeweils) Gute zu tun ist. Die Utzsche Sozialethik wendet sich damit dezidiert auch an Nichtchristen und Nichtreligiöse, wodurch sie gerade in Ländern wie Japan und China eine bis heute anhaltende Resonanz erfahren hat und für die Situation in weithin säkularisierten, postchristlichen Gesellschaften geeigneter erscheint als (offenbarungs-)theologische Ethiken. Normen werden gemäß Utz aus ganzheitlicher metaphysischer *Real*abstraktion unter Einbeziehung der „vorwissenschaftlichen" inneren Erfahrung sittlicher Verantwortung schöpferisch gewonnen; ihre jeweilige Formulierung weist freilich einen strikt *analogen* Charakter auf[40] und nimmt die äußere Erfahrung im Kontext des gesellschaftlichen Diskurses mit auf.

Neben Johannes Messner (1891–1984), Robert Spaemann (geb. 1927) und Wolfgang Waldstein (geb. 1928) gehört Utz damit zu der Minderheit von deutschsprachigen Philosophen und Theologen des 20. und 21. Jahrhunderts, die noch uneingeschränkt, freilich hochreflexiv naturrechtlich argumentiert. Utz scheute sich nicht, die in der Spätmoderne tonangebenden philosophischen Richtungen wie etwa den (Neu-)Kantianismus, den „kritischen Rationalismus" (Karl Popper), den (Rechts-)Positivismus (Hans Kelsen), den Utilitarismus (Jeremy Bentham), den Neomarxismus (Ota Šik), die „Kritische Theorie" (Jürgen Habermas), den Pragmatismus

38 Vgl. Vatikanum I, in: Heinrich Denzinger, Enchiridion symbolorum, definitionum et declarationum de rebus fidei et morum, hrsg. von Peter Hünermann, 39. Aufl., Freiburg u. a.: Herder, 2001, Nr. 3004.

39 Vgl. dazu Wolfgang Spindler, „Humanistisches Appeasement"? Hans Barions Kritik an der Staats- und Soziallehre des Zweiten Vatikanischen Konzils, Berlin: Duncker & Humblot, 2011, 29 f. Anm. 54.

40 Vgl. Santiago Ramírez, De analogia, in: ders., Opera omnia, Editio praeparata a Facultate Theologica Sancti Stephani Salmantini sub directione Victorini Rodríguez, Teil 1 (Bd. 2,1), Teil 2 (Bd. 2,2), Teil 3 (Bd. 2,3) und Teil 4 (Bd. 2,4), Madrid: Instituto de Filosofía „Luis Vives", 1970–1972.

(Charles Sanders Peirce, William James) – nicht zuletzt wegen ihrer Erkenntnistheorien – in Frage zu stellen und an der *Metaphysik* auch gegen die „banale Einschüchterungsphrase", man könne so „heute nicht mehr" argumentieren,[41] festzuhalten.

Trotz – oder vielleicht gerade wegen – seiner nüchternen Art und seiner „trockenen", den teilweise hohen Abstraktionsgrad der philosophischen Sozialethik in Kauf nehmenden Sprache hatte Utz die Gabe, politische, wirtschaftliche und gesellschaftliche Fragen aufzugreifen und, für Laien und Multiplikatoren verständlich, auf die dahinter steckenden sozialen Probleme und Normen zurückzuführen. Bereits der 1950 im Auftrag des Apostolischen Stuhls von Utzens Freiburger Institut organisierte Kongress für Sozialwissenschaft, auf dem Pius XII. seine bekannte Ansprache zur betrieblichen Mitbestimmung hielt,[42] wies ihn als einen praxisbezogenen Wissenschaftler aus. Zahlreiche weitere internationale, vorbildlich dokumentierte Kongresse, unter anderem 1958 in Madrid über mittelständische Unternehmen, 1976 über die „Christliche Konzeption der pluralistischen Unternehmen", brachten nicht nur Wissenschaftler und Praktiker der katholisch-sozialen Bewegung zusammen, sondern übten auch Einfluss auf politische Entscheidungsprozesse aus, etwa in der deutschen Mittelstandspolitik oder bei der Entstehung der parlamentarischen Demokratie in Spanien nach dem Ende des Franquismus (1936–1975). Utz, der außer auf englisch in den romanischen Sprachen fließend dozieren konnte, war davon überzeugt, dass die Katholische Soziallehre nur dann prägend wirken könne, wenn ihre Vertreter international denken, handeln und zusammenarbeiten. Eine Vielzahl seiner Veröffentlichungen, zum Beispiel die elfbändige „Bibliographie der Sozialethik",[43] erschien deshalb in mehreren Sprachen. Teile seines systematisches Hauptwerks, der fünfbändigen „Sozialethik",[44] sind auf Spanisch, Italienisch und Japanisch erschienen; die

41 Robert Spaemann, Einleitung, in: ders., Philosophische Essays. Erweiterte Ausgabe, Stuttgart: Philipp Reclam jun., 1994, 3–18, 8.

42 Pius XII., Ansprache *Nous vous adressons Notre salut de bienvenue* an die Teilnehmer des internationalen Kongresses für Sozialwissenschaft, 3.6.1950, in: Acta Apostolicae Sedis 42 (1950) 485–488.

43 Arthur F. Utz, Bibliographie der Sozialethik. Grundsatzfragen des öffentlichen Lebens. Recht, Gesellschaft, Wirtschaft, Staat, hrsg. von A. F. Utz, 11 Bde., Freiburg i. Br.-Barcelona-Basel u. a.: Herder [ab Bd. 10 Fribourg: Valores], 1960–1980.

44 Arthur F. Utz, Sozialethik, mit internationaler Bibliographie, I. Teil: Die Prinzipien der Gesellschaftslehre, Heidelberg: Kerle, 1958, 2. Aufl. 1964; II. Teil: Rechtsphilosophie,

laufende Übertragung des letzten Bandes, der „Politischen Ethik", ins Japanische wird 2014 abgeschlossen sein. Überhaupt kann die „Politische Ethik" als das reifste Werk von Utz betrachtet werden. Darin enthalten ist eine hochinteressante Auseinandersetzung mit dem vieldiskutierten Staatsrechtslehrer Carl Schmitt (1888–1985), mit dem zu diskutieren Utz schon als junger Mann die Gelegenheit hatte, als nämlich Schmitt Ende der 1940er, Anfang der 1950er Jahre tage- und wochenweise in Walberberg zu Gast war.[45]

Utz erkannte den Pluralismus der Anschauungen als eine zentrale Herausforderung unserer Zeit. Er warb, seinem Bild vom sozial konditionierten Menschen entsprechend, trotz aller Mühen für *gemeinsam* anzustrebende Lösungen. Sein Ansatz „ist kein Katalog von fertigen Rezepten, aber er gibt realitätsnahe Grundnormen menschlichen Zusammenlebens an. Da er diese Grundnormen aus dem Mensch-Sein zu erkennen versucht, haben sie die Potenz, universal einsichtig zu sein."[46] Dass dieser Ansatz „Ausgangsbasis für gegenseitiges Verständigung werden"[47] kann, hat sich schon zu Lebzeiten in der hohen Anerkennung erwiesen, die Utz in verschiedensten Kreisen fand. Die seinem Werk verpflichtete „Stiftung Professor Dr. Arthur F. Utz", 1976 von Brigitta Gräfin von Galen (1920–2008) errichtet, ist darum bemüht, dieses Ethos auch weiterhin in die Gesellschaft zu tragen.

2. Franz-Martin Schmölz OP

Um eine Generation jünger als Utz war Martin Schmölz. Seine frühesten wissenschaftlichen Wurzeln sind ebenfalls in Walberberg zu suchen. Dennoch ist Schmölz nicht im engeren Sinn dem „Walberberger Kreis" zuzurechnen, weil ihn sein persönlicher Werdegang örtlich wie geistig bald in andere Einfluss- und Aktionsbereiche führte und die Anbindung nach

Heidelberg-Löwen: Kerle / E. Nauwelaerts, 1963; III. Teil: Die soziale Ordnung, Bonn: IfG Verlagsgesellschaft mbH, 1986; IV. Teil: Wirtschaftsethik, Bonn: Scientia-Humana-Institut, 1994; V. Teil: Politische Ethik, Bonn: Scientia-Humana-Institut, 2000.

45 Vgl. dazu Briefwechsel Eberhard Welty / Carl Schmitt [unveröffentlicht]; Reinhard Mehring, Carl Schmitt. Aufstieg und Fall, München: Verlag C. H. Beck, 2009, 470 ff., ferner die Hinweise etwa in Carl Schmitt, Glossarium. Aufzeichnungen der Jahre 1947–1951, hrsg. von Eberhard Freiherr von Medem, Berlin: Duncker & Humblot, 1991.

46 Zocchi Fischer (wie Anm. 11), 145.

47 Ebd.

Walberberg, etwa über die ordenseigene Zeitschrift „Die Neue Ordnung“, nach einigen Jahren verlorenging.[48]

Schmölz wurde am 16. Dezember 1927 in Fischen im Allgäu, einem bis zur bayerischen Gebietsreform von 1972 im Landkreis Sonthofen (heute Landkreis Oberallgäu) gelegenen Kurort im Oberen Illertal, geboren. Nachdem er 1944 im Alter von 17 Jahren noch für ein Jahr zum Kriegsdienst eingezogen worden war, legte er zwei Jahre nach Kriegsende an der Oberrealschule mit Gymnasium Kaufbeuren das Abitur ab. Im selben Jahr nahm er an der Philosophisch-Theologischen Hochschule Dillingen (Donau), einer bis 1971 existenten Ausbildungsstätte für angehende Geistliche des Bistums Augsburg, das Studium der Philosophie auf. 1948 trat er dem Predigerorden bei, erhielt den Ordensnamen Franz Maria und legte nach dem Noviziat in München-Freimann am 2. Mai 1949 die Profess ab. Er zog ins Studienhaus nach Walberberg, wo er bis 1952 Philosophie und dann bis 1954 Theologie studierte. Am 25. Juli 1954 wurde Schmölz zum Priester geweiht. Seine theologische Ausbildung vollendete er in den folgenden Jahren am ordenseigenen *Pontificium Athenaeum Angelicum* in Rom, wo er 1955 das Bakkalaureat, ein Jahr später das Lektorat und das Lizentiat, schließlich 1957 das Doktorat erwarb. Zum 30. September desselben Jahres wurde er zu Ergänzungsstudien und seelsorglichen Aufgaben nach Augsburg assigniert. Ab 8. Januar 1959 war Schmölz in München-Freimann assigniert. Im Wintersemester 1959/60 schrieb er sich als Student an der Staatswissenschaftlichen Fakultät der Ludwig-Maximilians-Universität München (LMU) ein. Am Ende des Semesters wurde er in die in der Münchner Innenstadt gelegene, universitätsnahe *Domus* an St. Kajetan („Theatinerkirche“) assigniert, die 1954 errichtet[49] worden war. Neben dem Ergänzungsstudium betätigte er sich als Schwesternbeichtvater und geistlicher Assistent des Heliand-Bundes. Ab Wintersemester 1960/61 fungierte Schmölz als wissenschaftlicher Assistent am „Institut für Politische Wissenschaft“ der LMU,[50] dessen Vorstand der bekannte Remigrant Eric

48 Die Mitgliedschaft als auswärtiges Redaktionsmitglied der Zeitschrift währte von 1964 bis 1979 (vgl. PK 1964, 11; PK 1979, 11), sein letzter Beitrag erschien 1982.

49 Vgl. Wolfgang Müller OP, Stadt ohne Gott? Der Verkündigungsauftrag der Dominikaner, in: „50 Jahre Dominikaner in München-St. Kajetan“, hrsg. von der Katholischen Kirchenstiftung St. Kajetan (Theatinerkirche), München 2004, 1–17, 2, 9 f.

50 PK 1961, 22. Nicht nur in diesem Punkt weichen die zeitnahen Angaben der Provinzkataloge vom Jahrzehnte später geschriebenen, im Rückblick auf die universitäre Laufbahn wohl auch etwas geglätteten *Curriculum vitae* ab. Laut Lebenslauf, in: Politik

Voegelin (1901–1985) war. Noch im selben Semester wurde er zum Hilfskaplan in der katholischen Hochschulseelsorge bestellt.[51]

Im Bestreben, die 1810 geschlossene Salzburger Universität wiederzubeleben, segnete am 5. August 1961 der Salzburger Bischof Andreas Rohracher (1892–1976) das von dem Maria Laacher Konventualen Thomas Michels OSB (1892–1979) gegründete „Internationale Forschungszentrum für Grundfragen der Wissenschaften Salzburg“ (IFZ)[52] auf dem dortigen Mönchsberg; 1964 erfolgte die kanonische Errichtung durch die Österreichische Bischofskonferenz und die staatliche Anerkennung durch das zuständige Bundesministerium für Unterricht. Schmölz arbeitete von Anfang an als Dozent und Vorstand des „Instituts für Politische Wissenschaft“ in diesem Zentrum mit. Am 9. Oktober 1962[53] wurde er zum a. o. Professor (Privatdozent) der Philosophischen Fakultät an der im selben Jahr neubegründeten Salzburger Universität ernannt. Für seine Habilitationsarbeit über „Zerstörung und Rekonstruktion der politischen Ethik“[54] im Fach Philosophische Gesellschaftslehre und Rechtsphilosophie erhielt er am 9. Dezember 1963 den Kardinal-Innitzer-Preis. Ein halbes Jahr zuvor, am 13. Juni 1963, war er von München in den Wiener Konvent umassigniert worden, doch lebte er fortan *extra conventum* in Salzburg, seiner wissenschaftlichen Wirkungsstätte, wo er sich nach Aussagen von Mitbrüdern lange Zeit eine dominikanische Niederlassung erhoffte. Am 14. Mai 1965 wurde Schmölz zum Extraordinarius für Philosophische Gesellschaftslehre und Politische Theorie an der Universität Salzburg ernannt und stand von da an dem „Institut für Philosophische Gesellschaftslehre und Politische Theorie“ vor. Zu diesem Zeitpunkt war er bereits seit ein paar Monaten korrespondierendes Redaktionsmitglied der Zeitschriften „Die Neue Ord-

---

und christliche Verantwortung. Festschrift für Franz-Martin Schmölz, hrsg. von Gertraud Putz / Herbert Dachs / Franz Horner / Ferdinand Reisinger (= Veröffentlichungen des Internationalen Forschungszentrums für Grundfragen der Wissenschaften, Salzburg, N. F., Bd. 53), Innsbruck-Wien: Tyrolia-Verlag, 1992, 355 f., war Schmölz bereits 1959 Assistent bei Voegelin, was unwahrscheinlich ist.

51 PK 1961, 22.

52 Anfang 2009 wurde es in ein „Internationales Forschungszentrum für soziale und ethische Fragen. Wissenschaft für Menschen“ umgewidmet und konzentriert sich seither zeitgeistgemäß auf „angewandte Ethik“.

53 PR1, p. 150, 9. 10. 1962, Nr. 254. Laut Lebenslauf (wie Anm. 50) erfolgte die Ernennung bereits am 2. Oktober 1962.

54 Franz Martin Schmölz, Zerstörung und Rekonstruktion der politischen Ethik (= Münchener Studien zur Politik, 2), München: Beck, 1963.

nung“ (Walberberg) und „Der Seelsorger“ (Wien) sowie Beichtvater bei den Dominikanerinnen in Salzburg-Parsch. Die ersehnte Ernennung zum Ordentlichen Universitätsprofessor für Christliche Gesellschaftslehre erfolgte am 11. April 1967. Wenige Jahre später wurde er mehrmals Dekan beziehungsweise Prodekan der Theologischen Fakultät, 1972–1974 zudem Vorstand des „Interfakultären Instituts für Politische Wissenschaft“ an der Salzburger Universität. Am 1. Januar 1987 wurde er vom Salzburger Erzbischof Karl Berg (1908–1997), bei dessen Ehrenpromotion am 20. Januar 1989 Schmölz die Laudatio halten sollte, zum Präsidenten des IFZ ernannt. Diese Funktion übte er nach erneuter Ernennung am 1. Januar 1988 für insgesamt neun weitere Jahre aus. Emeritiert wurde er zum 1. November 1990. Der Erzbischöfliche Konsistorialrat Schmölz, der trotz eines chronischen Rückenleidens leidenschaftlicher Skifahrer und – wie Utz – nicht minder leidenschaftlicher Zigarrenraucher war, starb am 12. Februar 2003 in Salzburg. Begraben wurde er eine Woche später in seiner Allgäuer Heimat in Pfronten.

Franz-Martin Schmölz war – auch nach eigenem Selbstverständnis – weniger ein Interpret der Katholischen Soziallehre als ein philosophischer Grundleger der (erst nach dem Zweiten Weltkrieg aus den USA importierten) Wissenschaft von der Politik.[55] Sein Politikverständnis ist stark ordnungs- und institutionenethisch geprägt.[56] Danach besteht die Gesellschaft nicht aus einer Summe von Individuen, die als Einzelne „Welt“ und „Polis“ gegenüberstehen und darin agieren. Vielmehr sind alle Menschen in eine je vorgegebene, freilich geschichtlich gewachsene „ontische“ Ordnung eingebunden und über eine Vielgestalt von Institutionen zusammengeschlossen, die zur Verwirklichung menschlicher Daseinszwecke vonnöten sind. Politik ist nach einer 1965 formulierten Definition von Schmölz der „Gesamtkomplex der Ordnung innerhalb einer gesellschaftlichen Organisation“.[57] Im Zentrum stehen nicht Staat, Parteien, „Pressure Groups“ und so weiter; es geht vielmehr um „die Existenz des Menschen

---

55 Vgl. Franz-Martin Schmölz, Gesammelte Werke, Band1–3, hrsg. von Gertraud Putz, Salzburg [Eigenverlag] Dezember 1993.

56 Vgl. vor allem Franz-Martin Schmölz, Societas civilis sive Respublica sive Populus, in: Der Mensch in der politischen Institution. Hrsg. von dems., Wien: Springer, 1964, 28–50.

57 Zit. nach Josef Klaus, In der Spur des Franz-Martin Schmölz, in: Politik und christliche Verantwortung (wie Anm. 50), 21–27, 23.

in der Gesellschaft".[58] Dementsprechend versteht Schmölz, wie er oft wiederholte, unter Politischer Wissenschaft „die Wissenschaft vom rationalen Handeln des Menschen in Gesellschaft".[59] Dieser nicht auf die politische Einzelhandlung abhebende, vielmehr ganzheitliche und ideologiekritische[60] Ansatz lässt deutlich sein Vorbild erkennen: die Politische Wissenschaft von Schmölzens bedeutendem Lehrer Eric Voegelin.[61]

Weiterer Referenzautor des Schmölzschen Ordungsdenkens ist – angesichts des Walberberger Ausbildungsweges kaum verwunderlich – der große Dominikaner und Kirchenlehrer Thomas von Aquin. Vor allem dessen Anthropologie und den Tugendtraktat der *Summa Theologiae* hat Schmölz in immer neuen Anläufen auf die moderne demokratische Gesellschaft angewendet und für eine Politik aus christlicher Verantwortung fruchtbar zu machen versucht. Schmölz kann zwar – entgegen Putz[62] – nicht (wie Utz) zu den herausragenden Kennern oder Interpreten des thomasischen Werkes des letzten Jahrhunderts gezählt werden – nach seiner Dissertation über „Das Naturrecht und seine dynamische Kraft" (1959), in der er dem damals üblichen Vorwurf eines „statischen" Naturrechtsverständnisses des (Neu-)Thomismus entgegentrat, hat Schmölz keine Monographien oder Kommentare zu Werken des Thomas mehr vorgelegt, und seine Applikationen auf die politisch-ethischen Verhältnisse seiner Zeit bewegen sich in einem für Dominikanergelehrte konventionellen Rahmen. Dennoch gab ihm Thomas einen Leitfaden in die Hand, um politisch ak-

---

58 Franz-Martin Schmölz, Theoretische Grundlagen einer politischen Ethik, Die Neue Ordnung 15 (1961) 81–88, 87.

59 Ebd., 88.

60 Franz-Martin Schmölz, Ideologie und Ordnung in „Mater et Magistra", Die Neue Ordnung 16 (1962) 91–97; ders., Politik zwischen Ordnung und Ideologie, in: Steirische Akademie 1965. Der Humanitätsbegriff als Gegenstand ideologiekritischer Auseinandersetzung, hrsg. vom Kulturreferat der Steiermärkischen Landesregierung, 76–85; Claus Heimes, Antipositivistische Staatslehre: Eric Voegelin und Carl Schmitt zwischen Wissenschaft und Ideologie: Eric-Voegelin-Archiv an der Ludwig-Maximilians-Universität, 2004.

61 Vgl. vor allem Eric Voegelin, Die neue Wissenschaft der Politik. Eine Einführung, hrsg. von Peter J. Opitz, München: Wilhelm Fink Verlag, 2004 [in dt. Sprache zuerst 1959]; ders., Ordnung und Geschichte, hrsg. von Peter J. Opitz und Dietmar Herz, Bd. 10: Auf der Suche nach Ordnung, München: Wilhelm Fink Verlag, 2004; Henning Ottmann, Geschichte des politischen Denkens, Bd. 4/1: Das 20. Jahrhundert. Der Totalitarismus und seine Überwindung, Stuttgart-Weimar: Verlag J. B. Metzler, 2010, 454–469.

62 Gertraud Putz, Art. Schmölz, Franz-Martin, in: Biographisch-Bibliographisches Kirchenlexikon, begründet und hrsg. von Friedrich Wilhelm Bautz, fortgeführt von Traugott Bautz, Bd. 23, Sp. 1296–1306, Hamm: Bautz 2004.

tuelle Fragen wie die der globalen Friedenssicherung, des Pluralismus, der Demokratie und der Menschenrechte, des Verhältnisses von Kirche und Staat, von Recht und Moral einordnen und behandeln zu können. Die Vorliebe für Max Weber (1864–1920), den wohl wichtigsten Wirtschafts- und Herrschaftssoziologen seiner Zeit und berühmten Vorläufer auf Voegelins Münchner Lehrstuhl, sowie ein den politischen Realitätssinn schärfendes Interesse für Niccolò Machiavelli (1469–1527) ergänzten das theoretische Instrumentarium, mit dem Schmölz seine Wissenschaft betrieb.

Die größte Wirkung entfaltete Franz-Martin Schmölz da, wo sich Politikwissenschaft und Christliche Gesellschaftslehre im Ernstfall zu bewähren haben: in der Praxis. Schmölz avancierte gleich nach seiner Umzug von München nach Salzburg zu einem gefragten Politikerberater, und zwar auf hoher Ebene. Beredtes Zeugnis dafür ist der biographisch-dokumentarisch bemerkenswerte Festschrift-Beitrag des früheren österreichischen Bundeskanzlers Josef Klaus (1910–2001). Der Bäckermeisterssohn und langjährige Landeshauptmann (1949–1961) des Bundeslandes Salzburg von der Österreichischen Volkspartei (ÖVP) führte 1964–1970 die erste Alleinregierung nach dem Zweiten Krieg. Wie Klaus in seinen Erinnerungen zu erkennen gibt, ist seine heute noch anerkannte „Politik der Sachlichkeit“ zu einem beträchtlichen Teil auf die theoretische Grundlage und die philosophische Inspiration von Pater Schmölz zurückzuführen, den er Anfang 1963 beim Skifahren auf der Tauernpasshöhe kennengelernt hatte. Klaus zitiert den Ausspruch des Schriftstellers Alexander Lernet Holenia (1897–1976), der nach der Kanzlerschaft des gebürtigen Kärtners resümierte: „Der Dr. Klaus hatte ja geradezu mittelalterliche Ideen!“[63] Klaus stimmt mit Hinweis auf Schmölzens Vermittlung der überkommenen Lehren von Aristoteles, Cicero, Augustinus und vor allem Thomas von Aquin vorbehaltlos zu. Auch sein Lehr- und Schreibstil scheint Klaus und anderen Politikern zupassgekommen zu sein. Schmölzens Sätze sind meist einfach gebaut, inhaltlich komplexitätsreduziert, um knappe Definitionen und Zusammenfassungen bemüht, kurz: leicht zugänglich.

Bekannt ist auch Schmölzens beratende Tätigkeit für Wilfried Haslauer (1926–1992),[64] ebenfalls ÖVP, der 1977–1989 Salzburger Landeshauptmann war. In dessen Amtszeit war Schmölz geschäftsführender Vorsitzender der

---

63 Josef Klaus, In der Spur des Franz-Martin Schmölz (wie Anm. 50), 26.

64 Vgl. Herbert Batliner, Peter Kaiser – Gestern und heute, in: Politik und christliche Verantwortung (wie Anm. 50), 29–36, 29.

„Salzburg-Kommission",[65] einer offiziösen Beraterkommission der Landesregierung. Ob ihm Schmölz jedoch geraten hat, am gesetzlichen Feiertag der *Immaculata Conceptio* des 8. Dezember 1984, einem Samstag, Salzburger Einzelhandelsgeschäften per Verordnung zu erlauben, ihre Läden zu öffnen, um das Vorweihnachtsgeschäft finanziell voll ausschöpfen zu können, wird man mit Fug und Recht bezweifeln dürfen. Der Fall ging damals durch die Presse und führte zur Feststellung einer Rechtsverletzung von Seiten des christdemokratischen Landeshauptmanns durch den Österreichischen Verfassungsgerichtshofs. Haslauer hatte die Weisung des zuständigen Bundesministers für soziale Verwaltung, Alfred Dallinger (1926–1989) von der SPÖ, die erlassene Arbeitsruhe-Ausnahmeverordnung abzuändern oder aufzuheben, schlichtweg ignoriert.[66]

Das zweite praktische Betätigungsfeld war das der Wissenschafts- und Hochschulpolitik. Allein seine Mitgliedschaften sprechen eine deutliche Sprache.[67] Ab den frühen 1960er Jahren schloss er sich nach und nach folgenden Organisationen an: der „Österreichischen Edmund Burke-Gesellschaft", der „Deutschen Gesellschaft für Politische Wissenschaft", der deutschen „Görres-Gesellschaft zur Pflege der Wissenschaft", der „Gottfried-Wilhelm-Leibnitz-Gesellschaft", der „Philosophischen Gesellschaft in Salzburg", der „Katholischen Sozialakademie Österreichs", dem „Katholischen Akademikerverband Österreichs", der „Vereinigung Deutscher Wissenschaftler", der „Arbeitsgemeinschaft für Friedens- und Konfliktforschung e. V.". Darüber hinaus gehörte er 1971–1973 dem wissenschaftlichen Beirat des Katholischen Büros in Bonn und dem „Zentralkomitee der Deutschen Katholiken" in Bad Godesberg, ferner ab 1990 der „International Academy of Science" in München an. Schmölz war nicht nur ein gefragter Berater und fähiger Organisator von Kongressen und Diskussionsforen. Er ermunterte auch andere, Forschungsprojekte zu initiieren, und unterstützte Schüler und Kollegen mit Rat und Tat. Die berühmten Salzburger Hochschulwochen würde es ohne sein Engagement heute wohl nicht mehr geben,[68] und auch die Ottobeurer Hochschulwochen

65 PK 1979, 11; PK 1989, 11.

66 Spruch des Österreichischen Verfassungsgerichtshofs vom 28. Juni 1985, in: www.ris2.bka.gv.at/Dokumente/Vfgh/JFT_10149372_84E00002_00.pdf [gelesen am 27.9.2013].

67 PK 1961, 22 bis PK 2000, 20.

68 Gertraud Putz, Ein ehrlicher Ratgeber für Salzburger Politiker, Rupertusblatt, Nr. 16/2013, 21. April 2013.

konnten auf ihn zählen.[69] All das war in den Anfangsjahren der neubegründeten Salzburger Universität und zumal für die kleine (Katholisch-)Theologische Fakultät, an der er beispielsweise 1966–1981 die „Österreichische Arbeitsgemeinschaft für Atheismusforschung" maßgeblich vertrat,[70] von großem Wert.[71]

Nicht von ungefähr wurden Schmölz hochklassige Auszeichnungen zuteil: 1978 das Große Silberne Ehrenzeichen für Verdienste um die Republik Österreich, 1988 das Silberne Ehrenzeichen des Landes Salzburg, 1989 das Ehrenkreuz für Wissenschaft und Kunst 1. Klasse. Nicht nur seine Lehre, auch seine menschlichen Fähigkeiten, vor allem die zur Freundschaft, wirken nach. So gibt es dank der Liechtensteiner „Peter Kaiser-Stiftung", in deren Stiftungsrat Schmölz von ihrer Gründung an 1985–1997 mitgewirkt hat, seit wenigen Jahren eine „Gastprofessur P. Franz-Martin Schmölz OP im Fachbereich Philosophie der Theologischen Fakultät" der Salzburger Paris-Lodron-Universität. Deren Inhaber ist seit 2010 Clemens Sedmak. Schmölz bleibt dort bis heute unvergessen. An sein vielfältiges Wirken in Wissenschaft und Politik erinnerte zuletzt ein Symposium, das zum 10. Todestag am 2. April 2013 – naturgemäß in Salzburg – abgehalten wurde.[72]

III. Abschließende Würdigung

Die Dominikanerprovinz des hl. Albert des Großen in Süddeutschland und Österreich kann in ihrer 75 Jahre jungen Geschichte mit Arthur F. Utz und Franz-Martin Schmölz zwei bedeutende Gelehrte verzeichnen, die sich um das Gemeinwesen in beiden Ländern – und weit darüber hinaus! – verdient gemacht haben. Beide hatten in Walberberg ein thomistisch geprägtes Bildungsprogramm durchlaufen, mit dem sie sie sich auf vergleichbarem Parkett in Wissenschaft und Praxis bewegen konnten und das sie im Hinblick auf sozial-, wirtschafts- und politisch-ethische Fragen ihrer Zeit und ihres Lebensumfeldes ausbauten und verfeinerten.

69 PK 1967, 11; PK 1971, 12.
70 PK 1967, 11 bis PK 1981, 11.
71 Vgl. dazu auch Wolfgang Beilner, „Gebt allen, was ihnen geschuldet ist" (Röm 13,7), in: Politik und christliche Verantwortung (wie Anm. 50), 51–65, 51 f.
72 Vgl. Gertraud Putz, Ein ehrlicher Ratgeber für Salzburger Politiker (wie Anm. 67).

In den großen Umbrüchen nach den verheerenden Weltkriegen des 20. Jahrhunderts wiesen sie mit ihrer Begabung, ihrer Charakterstärke und ihrer dominikanisch-priesterlichen Integrität den Weg in eine demokratische, um sozialen Ausgleich bemühte Gesellschaftsordnung in Europa. Politik und Gemeinwohl vermochten sie in Lehre und Leben in Einklang zu bringen. Den nachfolgenden Generationen im Orden mögen sie Vorbild und Ansporn sein, über den Tellerrand selbstgenügsamer Theologie- und Lebensauffassungen zu schauen und sich mit Glaube und Vernunft für die Gemeinschaft einzusetzen!

Bibelwissenschaftler im Gebiet der süddeutsch-österreichischen Provinz: Persönliche Erinnerungen und geschichtliche Vergewisserung

Hans Ulrich Steymans OP

Liber prohibitus – durch den Index der verbotenen Bücher katholischer Leserschaft entzogenes Buch – prangt als Stempel auf der Titelseite einer Hebräischen Bibel in der Bibliothek der Wiener Dominikaner. Es handelt sich um die Ausgabe der hebräischen Bibel durch Rudolph Kittel, die 1913 in Leipzig in zweiter Auflage erschien. 2013 begaben sich die Studenten der süddeutsch-österreichischen Provinz, deren Mehrzahl im Dominikanerkonvent zu Wien lebt, auf eine Wallfahrt ins Heilige Land. Dort erlebten sie einen Hebräisch sprechenden jüdischen Staat und besuchten zu Beginn des Sabbats die Reformsynagoge *Kehilat Har-El*, wo ihnen ein hebräisch-deutsches Gebetsbuch ausgehändigt wurde. Krasser kann man die Entwicklung kaum auf den Punkt bringen, die sich in den letzten hundert Jahren in der Bibelwissenschaft und im Verhältnis zwischen Kirche und Israel vollzogen hat. Ökumene ist entstanden. 1913 waren hebräische Bibeln gebannt, weil sie von protestantischen Herausgebern stammten. 2013 feiern Katholiken den Gottesdienst Israels mit. Die Kommission für die religiösen Beziehungen mit dem Judentum ist im Vatikan eine Unterabteilung des Päpstlichen Rats zur Förderung der Einheit der Christen. Die katholische Kirche betrachtet das Judentum also nicht als eine fremde Religion, sondern als eine Bekenntnisform zu dem Gott Israels, an den auch die Christen glauben.

Die hier folgenden Lebensbeschreibungen spiegeln den Blickwinkel des Verfassers, der, geleitet von Erinnerungen, auf die Mitbrüder blickt, die sich intensiv mit der Bibel beschäftigt haben. Diese Dominikaner haben zumindest zeitweilig in Wien oder Freiburg im Breisgau gewohnt. Von 1985 bis 1998 gehörte der Verfasser dem Konvent in Wien an, heute dem in Freiburg i. Br. Wer den Vorzug genießt, im Wiener Konvent in den dritten Stock der Klausur steigen zu dürfen, wo die Konventsbibliothek hinter braunen Flügeltüren ihre Schätze bewahrt, stößt neben der Bibliothekstür auf die Plastik eines Charakterkopfes. Es handelt sich um die Gesichtszüge des Neutestamentlers Benno Riedele, der von 1925 bis 1940 Bibliothekar des Wiener Dominikanerklosters war. Er hat der Bibliothek sprachwissenschaftliche Werke

von forschungsgeschichtlicher Bedeutung hinterlassen, die er vor der späteren Eingliederung in die Bibliothek mit einem lila Stempelabdruck seines Doktortitels und Namens gekennzeichnet hatte. Für mich, den Studenten und jungen Pater, der von 1989 bis 1994 ein Doktoratsstudium im AT und ein Zusatzstudium in Altorientalistik absolvierte und zeitweise als Konventsbibliothekar waltete, waren die Bücher meines Vorgängers in diesem Amt eine Fundgrube. Als die Dominikaner Anfang der 90er Jahre die Wochentagsmessen für die Dominikanerinnen in Wien-Hacking zelebrierten, war es mir gestattet, im Gästehaus der Schwestern zu übernachten. Man quartierte mich in ein Zimmer mit hohen Wänden ein, in dem alte Bücher in hölzernen Schränken standen, die mit Glastüren verschlossen waren. In diesem Zimmer hat der emeritierte Professor für Altes Testament an der Universität Freiburg im Uechtland, Vincenz Zapletal, seinen Lebensabend verbracht. Unvergessen ist allen, die ihn kannten, Pater Maximilian Göbel, der sich durch nichts davon abbringen ließ, täglich im Refektorium zu Wien den Tischdienst zu versehen. Auch in seinem Zimmer gab es durch Glastüren geschützte bibelwissenschaftliche Bücher, war er doch in Jerusalem zum Alttestamentler ausgebildet worden. Im Konvent zu Wien lebten auch der Judaistikexperte Manfred Kniewasser und Augustine Agwulonu, der aus Nigeria stammende Doktorand im Neuen Testament. Der Neutestamentler Benedict Viviano ist seit 2011 dort ansässig. Die Alttestamentler Josef Schumpp und Martin Staszak sowie der Neutestamentler Odilo Kaiser sind mit Freiburg i. Br. verbunden. Die Ausnahme von Wien und Freiburg i. Br. als Lebensfeld von Bibelwissenschaftlern stellte der Inder Dominic Mendonca dar, der sich ebenfalls für das NT spezialisiert und, wie der Verfasser, zeitweilig im Konvent zu Augsburg gewohnt hat.

Die meisten Bibelwissenschaftler der süddeutsch-österreichischen Provinz haben das AT erforscht. Welche Gründe mögen dazu geführt haben? Meine These ist, dass die Ausbildung und die Liturgie im Dominikanerorden die Novizen und Studenten im 19. Jahrhundert dem Alten Testament nahe brachten. Die Entwicklung der Geschichtswissenschaft damals mag dazu beigetragen haben, sich mit der Geschichte Israels zu beschäftigen. Außerdem wird dieser Aufsatz zeigen, dass die Haltung der katholischen Kirche zur Bibelwissenschaft davon bestimmt ist, wie das kirchliche Lehramt Offenbarung versteht.[1] Sah man in der Offenbarung, wie vom

1 Der Begriff „Offenbarung" entsteht erst im christlichen Mittelalter. Zur Forschung über Offenbarung vgl. Bongardt 2005.

Abb. 1: Büste von Benno Riedele OP im Bibliotheksgang des Dominikanerklosters zu Wien (Foto: privat).

Ersten Vatikanischen Konzil festgeschrieben, eine göttliche Lehre, welche die Inspiration der Bibel einschrieb, so betrachtete man alles, was in der Bibel stand, als Information von Seiten Gottes. Deshalb befürwortete das kirchliche Lehramt nicht nur den Monogenismus, nach dem alle Menschen auf einen gemeinsamen Stammvater (Adam) zurückgehen, sondern lehnte auch den Versuch von Marie-Joseph Lagrange ab, die Genesis als Werk verschiedener Verfasser zu lesen. Erst als das Zweite Vatikanische Konzil die Offenbarung als Selbstmitteilung Gottes in der Geschichte und in der Person Jesu darlegte, wurde es in der katholischen Bibelwissenschaft statthaft, die Bibel als Werk von Menschen auszulegen, die, vom Heiligen Geist geleitet, geschichtliche Ereignisse als Sichtbarwerden Gottes gedeutet haben.

Die Zusammenführung von persönlichen Begegnungen mit Bibelwissenschaftlern einerseits und der Theologie- und Geistesgeschichte der letzten zwei Jahrhunderte andererseits kann dieser Aufsatz nur in Stichpunkten leisten. Als Hilfsmittel dienen die Arbeiten des Ordensgeschichtlers Angelus Walz, Biographien über Lagrange und Zapletal sowie zwei Sammelbände zur jüngeren Theologiegeschichte, zum einen *Ressourcement*,

das die Entwicklung der *Nouvelle Théologie* und die dominikanische Beteilung daran nachzeichnet, zum anderen *Erinnerung an die Zukunft*, das 50 Jahre Wirkungsgeschichte des Zweiten Vatikanischen Konzils beschreibt. Die mir als Geburtsjahrgang 1961 fremde Geisteswelt der katholischen Kirche vor 1965 eröffnen Artikel der beiden Ausgaben des Lexikons für Theologie und Kirche von 1930ff und 1957ff.

Die Lebensgeschichten der biblisch arbeitenden Dominikaner, die sich im 19. und 20. Jahrhundert im Gebiet der süddeutsch-österreichischen Provinz aufgehalten haben, werden zwischen dem Ersten und Zweiten Vatikanischen Konzil nach den Regierungszeiten der Päpste gegliedert, deren bibelwissenschaftliche Lehrschreiben Erwähnung finden. Davor und danach ist auf die geisteswissenschaftlichen Strömungen hinzuweisen, welche die Bibelwissenschaften zu Beginn des 19. Jahrhunderts und gegen Ende des 20. Jahrhunderts beeinflusst haben. Das sind die so genannten Wenden zur Geschichtswissenschaft, zur Sprachwissenschaft und zur Kulturwissenschaft. Ein weiterer roter Faden ist das Verhältnis der Dominikaner zum Judentum, angefangen mit dem jüdischstämmigen Pater Ludwig Adler im 19. Jahrhundert bis zur Hinwendung zu den Studienfeldern Judaistik und Frühjudentum nach dem Zweiten Weltkrieg. Doch als erstes gilt es, sich der Geschichte der Dominikaner in Deutschland und Österreich zu vergewissern. Die Konvente, in denen die zu nennenden Dominikaner lebten (Wien, Graz und Freiburg i. Br.), gehörten zu Jahresbeginn 2012 zur süddeutsch-österreichischen Provinz,[2] doch auf dem Provinzgebiet bestanden zwischen 1800 und 1938 vier Provinzen.

Provinzen und Generalstudien des Dominikanerordens

Zur Vorgeschichte der süddeutschen bzw. oberdeutschen Provinz heißt es bei Walz:

> „Unter dem Generalat des Ordensmeisters Antonin Cloche (1682–1720) sind mehrere Provinzänderungen vorgenommen worden. Einige betreffen gerade das Gebiet des deutschen Sprachraums. Im Südwesten wurde 1690 eine Gruppe von Konventen und Schwesternklöstern aus der Teutonia ausge-

2 Der Konvent in Graz ist inzwischen geschlossen, der Konvent St. Albert (Ludwigstraße 35) in Freiburg im Breisgau zum Filialhaus des 2012 gegründeten Konvents St. Martin (Rathausplatz 3) umgewandelt.

> schieden und zur elsässischen Kongregation vereinigt. Im Südosten schlossen sich die österreichischen Klöster mit den ungarischen zusammen. Der Name dieser Provinz wechselte von Hungaria zu Imperii (Reichsprovinz 1865–1905 mit Einschluß der böhmischen Konvente) und Austro-Hungarica (1905–1938). Auf dem Generalkapitel zu Bologna 1706 wurde über die Bildung einer süddeutschen Provinz verhandelt. (…) Der Ordensgeneral (…) trennte die Germania Superior von der Teutonia. Das geschah am 1. Juni 1709. Die neue oberdeutsche Provinz erhielt den Platz und die Privilegien der früheren sächsischen Provinz. In der Amtssprache kommt bald die Bezeichnung oberdeutsche, bald sächsische Provinz vor, wenn die Provinz in Süddeutschland genannt wird."[3]

Zu Beginn des 19. Jahrhunderts erfolgte die Auflösung der Oberdeutschen Provinz. 1797 wurde der Konvent zu Freiburg i. Br. aufgehoben. Die Klostergüter und Einkünfte erhielt die Universität als Entschädigung für den Verlust ihrer Besitzungen im Elsass. 1804 kam das Klosterareal zur Versteigerung, die Kirche zerstörte 1944 ein Bombenangriff.[4] 1801 säkularisierte der Kurfürst von Pfalz-Bayern den Konvent in Heidelberg, im selben Jahr wurde der Konvent von Landshut samt seinen Einkünften der Universität Landshut als Stiftung einverleibt. 1805 mussten die Dominikaner den Augsburger Konvent verlassen. In Bamberg wohnten mehrere Patres bis 1819 im Habit beisammen.[5]

Die Überschreibung von Einkünften und Besitz der Dominikanerkonvente an Universitäten ist ein Zeichen für die Verbundenheit der Dominikaner mit der universitären Lehre. Mitglieder der Oberdeutschen Provinz waren Professoren an den theologischen Fakultäten zu Mergentheim und Freiburg i. Br. gewesen.[6] Als 1889 die *Université cantonale et catholique de Fribourg* gegründet wurde, in einer Stadt des schweizerischen Mittellandes, die auf Deutsch Freiburg im Uechtland heißt und eine mittelalterliche Gründung der Zähringer aus Freiburg im Breisgau ist, sollten Dominikaner wieder an die Universitätskatheder treten. Die Gründer der Universität,

---

3 Walz, 1967, 96. „Die elsässischen Dominikaner und Dominikanerinnen hätten sich gern der oberdeutschen Provinz angeschlossen." Ebd., 97. Da das Königreich Frankreich zwischen 1633 und 1681 nach und nach im Elsass die Landesherrschaft übernommen hatte und ab 1697 und 1714 die politische Gewalt in den annektierten Gebieten ausübte, wurde der Anschluss der elsässischen Kongregation an die Oberdeutsche Provinz nicht erlaubt.

4 Vgl. Mayr, 2002, 123.

5 Vgl. Walz, 1967, 110.

6 Vgl. Walz, 1967, 97.

Georges Python und Kaspar Decurtins waren überzeugte Katholiken und wandten sich zur Gründung der theologischen Fakultät an den Dominikanerorden. Am 24. Dezember 1889 unterzeichneten Decurtins, und der Ordensmeister José Maria Larroca (1879–1891) eine Konvention, in der sich der Orden verpflichtete, Professoren für die theologischen und drei philosophischen Lehrstühle zu schicken. Im Jahre 1890 trat die kantonale Regierung der Konvention bei und man erhielt die päpstliche Approbation. Die drei ersten Dominikanerprofessoren kamen Ostern 1890 in Freiburg i. Ue. an. Joachim Berthier OP wurde Gründer der theologischen Fakultät und erster Rektor der Universität.[7]

Während der Säkularisation im 19. Jahrhundert überlebten Dominikanerkonvente in West- und Mitteleuropa nur im Kaiserreich Österreich-Ungarn, das 1855 ein Konkordat mit dem Heiligen Stuhl abschloss. In Graz erhielten die Dominikaner durch Kaiser Franz I. 1807 das ehemalige Augustinerkloster im Münzgraben als freies Eigentum. Also übernahmen die Dominikaner die Pfarre Münzgraben mit der Annakirche.[8] Am 1. August 1857 bestimmte der Ordensgeneral Alexandre Vincent Jandel (1850–1872) den Grazer Konvent zum Haus der strengen Ordenszucht mit Noviziat für die am 20. April 1857 errichtete Provinz des habsburgischen Reiches (*Imperii* genannt), welche Böhmen, Mähren, Österreich und Ungarn umfasste. Der Italiener Thomas Anselmi war 1856 nach Graz gekommen und begann den Aufbau eines Generalstudiums der Dominikaner, indem er Vorlesungen der Philosophie hielt.[9] Er beherrschte kein Deutsch und konnte nicht in der Seelsorge wirken. Für seinen auf Latein gehaltenen Unterricht stand ihm aber das lateinische Lehrbuch der Philosophie von Antoine Goudin († 1695) zur Verfügung, das 1859 in Orvieto neu aufgelegt worden war.[10]

---

7 Vgl. Petráček, 2007, 13f.

8 1832 war die Dominikanergemeinschaft stark geschrumpft und wurde kurzzeitig aufgehoben; das Kloster wurde den Jesuiten übergeben und später als Militärkonvaleszentenhaus genutzt. 1857 kehren die Dominikaner nach Münzgraben zurück, die Pfarre wurde jedoch von Weltpriestern geleitet. 1908 übertrug man den Dominikanern die Pfarrleitung. Nach der Jahrtausendwende schloss das Bistum die Pfarrseelsorge mit der Nachbarpfarre zusammen. 2012 wurde die Aufhebung des Grazer Konvents beschlossen, weil die Leitung eines Pfarrverbandes im Dienst des Bistums nicht dem Ordensziel entspricht.

9 Thomas Anselmi OP stammte aus Montegrazia bei Genua, war in S. Maria della Quercia bei Viterbo in den Dominkanerorden eingetreten und hatte dort und in Santa Sabina in Rom studiert. Vgl. Walz, 1950, 34.

10 Vgl. Walz 1950, 32–35, 47.

Mit dem Neuen Testament waren die Dominikanerstudenten vertraut, schrieb doch das Buch *L'instruction des novices* des späteren Ordensmeisters Hyacinthe-Marie Cormier (1832–1916) vor, dass der Novize täglich eine Viertelstunde kniend aus dem Neuen Testament zu lesen hatte. In demselben Werk forderte Cormier, dass die Dominikaner sich ihr ganzes Leben lang dem Studium der Heiligen Schrift widmen sollten. Dem damaligen Offenbarungsverständnis entsprechend, sah er die Bibel als göttlichen Brief, den der Heilige Geist geheiligten Schriftstellern diktiert habe.[11] Wenn man täglich drei Kapitel der Bibel lese, habe man am Ende des Noviziatsjahres die Heilige Schrift durchgelesen.[12]

Die Novizen erhielten sicher eine Einführung in den lateinischen Psalter. Das dominikanische Brevier bestand vor der Reform der Tagzeitenliturgie durch Pius X. aus zwei Bänden, die jeweils mit dem *Psalterium David* begannen.[13] Das enthielt nach dem *Venite* (Psalm 95) zum Invitatorium den gesamten Psalter von Psalm 1, dem ersten Psalm der Matutin am Sonntag früh, bis zum Psalm 147, dem letzten Psalm der Vesper am Samstag, gefolgt von den für die täglichen Laudes bestimmten Psalmen 148–150 und von alttestamentlichen Cantica.[14] Die Psalmen waren in der kanonischen Abfolge des biblischen Buchs gedruckt. Über Psalmen, die für bestimmte Tagzeiten reserviert waren, stand ein N (wohl für *non dicitur*), um anzuzeigen, dass man diesen Psalm in der Matutin oder Vesper zu überspringen hatte.[15] Die Psalmen waren also nicht wie heute über das Brevier verteilt. Der Psalter wurde vielmehr in der Form des biblischen Buches wahrgenommen. Ausführliche Beschäftigung mit dem Alten Testament forderten den Novizen und Studenten die Schriftlesungen der Matutin ab, die von diesen im Chorgebet laut vorzulesen waren. Für den Vortrag

11 ‚Il faut s'adonner à l'étude de l'Écriture sainte pendant toute sa vie, soit pour sa propre utilité, soit pour l'utilité du prochain. Les Livres saints sont notre consolation, comme ils étaient celle des Juifs, pendant le temps de leurs afflictions. (…) L'Écriture (…) est une Lettre divine que l'Esprit-Saint lui même a dictée aux écrivains sacrés, afin de nous parler d'une patrie d'où nous sommes exilés pour un temps." Cormier, 1905, 342f.

12 Vgl. Cormier, 1905, 144, 342–344.

13 Breviarium, 1893.

14 Sonntags Dan 3 (Gesang der Jünglinge im Feuerofen); montags Jes 12 (Hymnus); dienstags Jes 38 (Gebet des Königs Hisjika); mittwochs 1Sam 2 (Lied der Hanna); donnerstags Ex 15 (Schilfmeerlied); freitags Hab 3 (klagend hymnischer Psalm); samstags Dtn 32 (Moselied).

15 Das war erstmals bei Psalm 4 der Fall, der täglich in der Komplet gebetet wurde.

musste der lateinische Bibeltext vorbereitet werden. Auch das dominikanische Messbuch war keineswegs frei von alttestamentlichen Lesungen. Im Gegenteil, an den Quatembertagen viermal im Jahr,[16] zu zahlreichen Heiligenfesten und vor allem zu den Vigilien (das waren Messformulare für die Vortage von großen Festen) gab es Lesungen aus dem Alten Testament. Die Ausbildung der Dominikaner bot vielfältige Begegnungsmöglichkeiten mit dem Alten Testament.

> „Durch Erlaß vom 3. Oktober 1870 errichtete der Ordensmeister P. Jandel (...) im Grazer Konvent ein Formalstudium (...) [*Collegium Graecensis*], in dem von nun an die Dozenten für Theologie und Philosophie ausgebildet werden und für den (...) Unterricht des Ordens die Vollmacht erhalten konnten, das kirchliche Lehramt auszuüben."[17]

Professor für Exegese und Hebräisch war damals Ludwig Adler. Die Studenten hatten offensichtlich biblisches Hebräisch zu lernen. Griechischkenntnisse brachten sie aus den Gymnasien mit.

Ludwig Bertrand Adler OP wurde am 28. Februar 1837 in Aschaffenburg als Sohn des jüdischen Handelsmanns Moses Adler und der Margarita Fulda geboren und von seinen Eltern Isidor genannt, Taufname Franz, gestorben 2. Januar 1907 in Graz. Auf dem Gymnasium wurde Franz Brentano (1832–1917) Isidors Freund. Mit 18 Jahren ließ sich Isidor Adler 1855 taufen und nahm den Vornamen seines Taufpaten Franz Brentano an.[18] Nach erfolglosen Versuchen, Benediktiner zu werden, studierte Franz

16 Quatember war ein Fasten, viermal im Jahr (*quatuor tempora*) am Mittwoch, Freitag und Samstag nach dem ersten Sonntag der Fastenzeit, in der Pfingstwoche, in der Woche nach Kreuzerhöhung (14. September) und nach dem dritten Adventssonntag. In den Quatembermessen gedachte man besonders der Verstorbenen.

17 Walz, 1957, 80.

18 Vorbereitet war der Wunsch zur Konversion nicht nur durch die Freundschaft mit Brentano. Vielleicht war sie auch durch gesellschaftliche Bedingungen gefördert, die das jüdische Leben in Bayern einschränkten. Die Hep-Hep! Unruhen in Franken gehörten dazu. Das waren antisemitische Ausschreitungen im Jahre 1819. Nach der Eingliederung in das Königreich Bayern kam 1813 in Franken für Juden das bayerische Toleranzedikt in Geltung, das ihnen das Recht gab, sich niederzulassen und ein Gewerbe auszuüben. 1816 erlaubte das Judenedikt Juden in Bayern, Grundbesitz zu erwerben, und öffnete ihnen den Zugang zu den Universitäten. Doch das Edikt enthielt Familiengesetze, die für jeden Ort eine Höchstzahl jüdischer Familien festlegte und Familiengründungen erschwerte. Anfang August 1819 genehmigte der bayerische König eine von der Ständeversammlung vorbereitete Verbesserung der Rechte der Juden. Das löste zwischen dem 9. und 15. August vom Schlachtruf „Hep-Hep!" begleitete antisemitische Ausschreitungen und An-

Abb. 2: Ludwig Adler OP, aufgenommen um 1880
(Foto: Archiv des Wiener Dominikanerkonvents).

Adler ab 1856 an der Universität Würzburg Theologie, wurde 1857 in das Priesterseminar aufgenommen und 1860 zum Priester geweiht. Nach einer kurzen seelsorglichen Tätigkeit in deutschsprachigen katholischen Gemeinde in London trat er 1863 in das Noviziat in Graz ein, wo sein Freund Franz Brentano 1862 Novize gewesen, aber im selben Jahr wieder ausgetreten war. Franz (Isidor) Adler bekam den Ordensnamen Ludwig Bertrand. Seine jüdische Herkunft war in der Provinz bekannt. Die Oberen werden ihn deshalb dazu angehalten haben, ab 1870 in Graz Hebräisch und Bibel

griffe in fränkischen Ortschaften aus, die sich später auf den ganzen Deutschen Bund ausbreiteten. 1828 kam es zu ähnlichen Unruhen mit dem Ausruf „Achhie!". Mitte der dreißiger Jahre des 19. Jahrhunderts wurde auch die Höchstzahl der jüdischen Familien pro Ort zu einem Problem. Denn es durfte nur heiraten, wer eine Familiennummer besaß. Diese wurde an den ältesten Sohn weitergegeben. Unter Teilen der jüdischen Bevölkerung verstärkte all das den Drang zur Assimilation bis hin zur Konversion. Vgl. Avneri, 1978, 343f.; Kestenberg-Gladstein, 1978, 1163, Meyer, 2011, 165.

zu lehren. 1872 versetzte man Pater Ludwig nach Wien. Dort wurde er 1880 für mehrere Amtszeiten Prior, hatte weitere Leitungsämter wie das des Novizenmeisters inne und unterrichtete ab 1881 dort am Generalstudium. Vom 29. Mai bis 4. Juni 1898 durfte Pater Ludwig Adler als Hausoberer Gastgeber des Generalkapitels der Dominikaner sein, das im Wiener Konvent tagte. Der spätere General Andreas Frühwirth war sein Noviziatskollege und betrachtete ihn als seinen Freund.[19]

Das Kloster in Graz und dessen Studienbetrieb unterstand direkt dem Ordensmeister in Rom, weil es ein Vorzeigekonvent für die Observanzreform sein sollte. Im Laufe der Jahrhunderte hatte sich das Leben der Dominikaner in den Klöstern Böhmens und Mährens, Österreichs und Ungarns dem von Großbürgern angeglichen.[20] Klosterzucht herrschte dagegen in Graz und sollte nach Plan des Ordensmeisters die anderen Klöster der Reichsprovinz anstecken. In der Fastenzeit, die vom 14. September, dem Fest der Kreuzerhöhung, bis Ostern dauerte, aß man überhaupt kein Fleisch und eine vollständige Mahlzeit gab es nur mittags. Im Noviziatskonvent hielt man den Nachtchor.[21] Wer mehr über den Tagesablauf in einem Kloster der Reformbewegung erfahren will, lese *L'instruction des novices*. Da Hyacinthe-Marie Cormier darin neben der scholastischen Dogmatik auch die Kirchengeschichte den Novizen zum Studium empfahl, mag die Entstehung der Geschichtswissenschaft im 19. Jahrhundert bei diesen Interesse für die biblischen Quellen der Geschichte Israels und des Judentums geweckt haben.

Julius Wellhausen und seine Geschichte des Judentums

Die Bibelwissenschaft entstand im 17. Jahrhundert im französischen Katholizismus und im holländischen Judentum. An beiden Stellen wurde sie bald unterdrückt. Sie lebte dann in protestantischen Bereichen weiter erst in England, dann im 19. Jahrhundert vor allem im evangelischen Deutsch-

---

19 Vgl. Walz, 1957, 37, 80, 112, 117, 137, 139; Hoyer, im Druck.

20 Die Konvente hatten Grundbesitz und den Patres wurden Geldbeträge für ihren Beitrag zum Klosterleben und zur Seelsorge gezahlt. Die Laienbrüder umsorgten die Patres wie Hausdiener, Prioren setzten Klostergut beim Kartenspiel, außerhalb des Klosters trugen manche Frack und Zylinder.

21 Vgl. Walz, 1957, 43.

land.[22] Wenn hier Julius Wellhausen erwähnt wird, dann deshalb, weil sich zum einem an ihm die Problematik der historisch-kritischen Methode für die Theologie aufzeigen lässt und weil er zum anderem in Briefverkehr mit Vincenz Zapletal stand. Für letzteren war er „der grösßte deutsche Exeget, der zugleich Arabist ist".[23] Weil sie in der Theologie ewige Wahrheiten suchten, empfanden manche Katholiken im 19. Jahrhundert schon die Vorstellung einer geschichtlichen Entwicklung in Glaubensdingen als bedrohlich. Vincenz Zapletal dagegen lieferte mit *Der Totemismus und die Religion Israels* wohl die erste Religionsgeschichte zum Alten Testament aus katholischer Feder. Wellhausen schrieb ihm am 24. April 1901 aus Göttingen: „Hochverehrter Herr College! Vielen Dank für die gütige Übersendung Ihres Totemismus. Ich habe die sorgfältige und gelehrte Abhandlung mit Vergnügung gelesen und finde die Polemik größtenteils berechtigt, wenngleich ich der Bibel gegenüber im Allgemeinen auf einem profaneren Standpunkt stehe. Hochachtungsvoll Ihr ergebener Wellhausen."[24] Pater Vincenz war von diesem Schreiben so beglückt, dass er darüber gleich an den Staatsrat Georges Python schrieb und über Wellhausen hinzufügte: „Der betreffende hat nämlich keinen Glauben".[25]

Und da liegt das Problem: Julius Wellhausen (1844–1918) wollte gar kein Theologe sein, sondern Historiker und Semitist. Sein Vater war orthodoxer Lutheraner und Stadtpfarrer in Hameln gewesen.

> „Nach lustlos absolvierten Gymnasialjahren in Hannover (...) ging er 1862 nach Göttingen, um Theologie zu studieren. Er wollte in die Fußstapfen seines Vaters treten, zudem liebte er die Erzählungen des Alten Testaments (...). Doch schon im ersten Semester mußte er merken, dass das für ein Theologiestudium nicht ausreichte. (...) In der theologischen Fakultät hielt ihn ein Buch, das ihm in den Osterferien 1863 zufällig in die Hände fiel, Heinrich Ewalds Geschichte des Volkes Israel. (...) Ewald (1803–1875) war eine besondere (...) Erscheinung. (...) Wellhausen war der letzte in einer Reihe seiner Schüler. (...) Doch schon bald wurde er gegenüber dem Lehrer

22 Vgl. Lohfink, 2013.

23 Schreiben von Vincenz Zapletal an Georges Python, zitiert nach Petráček, 2007, 36, Anm. 127. Die Hochschätzung für Wellhausen kommt weiter mit folgenden Worten zum Ausdruck: „Auf sein Urteil kam mir viel an, weil er als die erste Autorität gilt."

24 Ebd.

25 Ebd. Der Satz geht weiter: „er selbst ist in meinem Buche selber vielfach angegriffen, obgleich ich ihn immer mit Glacéhandschuhen angeführt habe." Die berechtigte Polemik, die Wellhausen erwähnt, mag sich auf diese Angriffe beziehen, eher aber auf die Art, wie Zapletal die Thesen von William Robertson Smith widerlegte.

> selbständig. (...) Im Winter 1872/73 untersucht Wellhausen die Genesis, im Winter 1874/75 den übrigen Pentateuch, das Ergebnis veröffentlicht er 1876/77 unter dem Titel „Die Composition des Hexateuchs“. (...) Das Neue an der ‚Composition‘ war, die Literarkritik (...) zu betreiben, (um) mit ihrer Hilfe die Geschichte des alten Israel zu rekonstruieren; die Schichten der Historiographie repräsentieren nämlich Stadien dieser Geschichte. Das zu zeigen, ist die Hauptaufgabe von Wellhausens berühmtestem Werk, der ‚Geschichte Israels I‘ von 1878, von der 2. Auflage an (1883) ‚Prolegomena zur Geschichte Israels‘ genannt.“[26]

Zweck der historisch-kritischen Exegese nach Wellhausen war nicht, den religiös-theologischen Gehalt der Bibel wahrzunehmen, sondern sie als geschichtliche Quelle auszuschlachten.[27] Die Motive und Maßstäbe der Geschichtsschreibung Wellhausens waren vorgezeichnet durch „Carlyle, Mommsen und Buckhardt“.[28] Um Lagrange und Zapletal zu verstehen, muss man etwas über die Geschichtswissenschaft ihrer Zeit wissen. Im 19. Jahrhundert kann man drei historische Erklärungsmuster unterscheiden:

1) Der *formalistische* Ansatz legt auf die Individualität der Einzelereignisse Wert, entwirft das Bild einer bunten Welt jenseits verallgemeinernder Strukturen. Ein Beispiel für solch eine literarisch-essayistische Geschichtsschreibung ist Thomas Carlyle (1795–1881) mit seinen Biographien über Oliver Cromwell, Friedrich II. und John Sterling.
2) Die *organizistische* Erklärung geht von gemeinsamen Ideen und Entwicklungen aus und verbindet Einzelerlebnisse zu Synthesen. Ein Beispiel dafür ist Theodor Mommsen (1817–1903) mit seinen Werken zur römischen Geschichte.

---

26 Smend, 1989, 100–106. 1881 veröffentlichte Wellhausen in der Encylopaedia Britannica einen ausführlichen Artikel über die gesamte israelitische Geschichte. Daraus wurde 1894 seine „Israelitische und jüdische Geschichte“. Vgl. ebd., 110f.

27 „Wellhausen (...) glaubte sich in der theologischen Fakultät nicht am richtigen Platz, (...). Der Grund lag (...) in der notwendigen Beziehung der Theologie auf die Kirche. Wellhausen hatte als Theologieprofessor die Studenten auf den Dienst in der evangelischen Kirche vorzubereiten, aber er fühlte sich dieser Kirche nur noch äußerlich angehörig. So kam ihm die Ausübung seines Amtes wie eine Lüge vor. [Dieses] Gewissensproblem bestimmte ihn, dem preußischen Kultusminister 1880 mündlich die Bitte um Versetzung in die philosophische Fakultät vorzutragen (...). Der Minister machte ihn (...) zum außerordentlichen Professor an der philosophischen Fakultät in Halle.“ Smend, 1989, 108.

28 Smend, 1998, 107.

3) Der *Kontextualismus* verfolgt die Vorfälle in ihren Kontexten und spinnt Fäden von Wechselbeziehungen. Der Kontextualist beansprucht nicht, das gesamte historische Feld auszuleuchten. Der Kunsthistoriker Jakob Christoph Burckhard (1818–1879) zeigte Kontexte und Wechselbeziehungen bereits in seinem 1853 veröffentlichten ersten Hauptwerk *Die Zeit Constantins des Großen*, insofern er diese Epoche als Übergang von der Antike zum Christentum und als Grundlage der mittelalterlichen Kultur beschieb.[29] Mehr noch kommt das Bemühen, die Summe aller sozialpsychologischen Faktoren als Einheit darzustellen, in seinem Buch *Kultur der Renaissance in Italien* von 1859 zum Vorschein.[30]

Jakob Burckhard gilt als Gewährsmann für eine Kulturgeschichte, die im Gegensatz zur politischen Geschichte, als der Geschichtsschreibung über den Staat und die Regierenden, das kollektive historische Gattungswesen Mensch hervorhob. Eine Schlüsselrolle kam in der Kulturgeschichte des 19. Jahrhunderts dem historischen Roman zu.[31]

Das Erste Vatikanische Konzil (1869–70) und die Offenbarung als Belehrung

Das Erste Vatikanische Konzil hat den Offenbarungscharakter der christlichen Wahrheit in einer Fortentwicklung in der neuscholastischen Schultheologie begründet. Es äußerte sich über den katholischen Glauben im Verhältnis zur Vernunft in der dogmatischen Konstitution *Dei filius,* die am 24. April 1870 verabschiedet wurde. In dieser Konstitution wird ein Offenbarungsdenken sichtbar, das die Autorität einer übernatürlichen Offenbarung argumentativ entwickelt und dem kirchlichen Lehramt überantwortet.[32] Damit wird ein in der mittelalterlichen Theologie angebahntes Offenbarungsverständnis verfestigt, in dem das offenbarende Sprechen Got-

29 Vgl. Schößler, 2006: 103.
30 Vgl. Böhme, Matussek, Müller, 2007, 52.
31 Vgl. Böhme, Matussek, Müller, 2007, 49f.
32 Das Konzil sprach von der „Lehre Christi" als der Geschichte enthobener Heilsdoktrin (*Depositum fidei*) und ihrer unverfälschten Überlieferung. Das Judentum kennt eine gleichartige Vorstellung von Offenbarung als Lehre in seinem Konzept der Tora. Die Tora ist Unterweisung. Auch die Offenbarung des Koran an Muhammad ist Mitteilung von Text.

tes unterweisenden Charakter hat. Die Belehrung durch Gott erstreckt sich auf Wahrheiten der Heilsbestimmung des Menschen, die sich einer Überprüfung durch die Vernunft entziehen. Den Konzilsvätern galt der Glaube als

> „eine übernatürliche Tugend, durch die wir mit Anregung und Unterstützung der Gnade Gottes glauben, daß das von ihm Geoffenbarte wahr ist, und zwar nicht wegen der mit dem natürlichen Licht der Vernunft durchschauten inneren Wahrheit der Dinge, sondern wegen der Autorität des ... offenbarenden Gottes, der sich täuschen noch andere täuschen kann."[33]

Papst Leo XIII. (1878–1903) und die Gründungen in Jerusalem und Fribourg

Leo XIII. erhob 1879 in seinem Schreiben *Aeterni Patris* die Philosophie des Thomas von Aquin und die Neuscholastik zur offiziellen Philosophie und Theologie der katholischen Kirche und der Ausbildung in den Seminaren.[34] Schon 1856 hatte der Erzbischof von Wien Joseph Othmar Ritter von Rauscher (1797–1875) mit dem Generalmeister Alexandre Vincent Jandel über die Erneuerung thomistischer Studien an der Universität Wien gesprochen. Er würde den Kaiser bitten, Dominikanern eine entsprechende Lehrkanzel zu verleihen, hatten Dominikaner doch schon vom Ende des 14. bis zum Ende des 18. Jahrhunderts ununterbrochen wenigstens einen Lehrstuhl der Theologie an der Universität inne. Also unterrichteten von 1857 bis 1863 Filippo Maria Guidi OP (1815–1879) und ab 1863 Hyazinth Pellegrinetti OP an der Wiener theologischen Fakultät.[35] 1880 verfügte das Provinzkapitel, dass die Brüder aus Böhmen, die im 1878 zum Noviziatskonvent erhobenen Kloster in Olmütz die einfachen Gelübde abgelegt hätten, in Wien studieren

33 Dei Filius III, Wohlmuth 2002, 807, Zeile 6–9.

34 Vgl. Conway 2012, 76f.

35 Walz, 1950, 46. „Die theologische Fakultät der Wiener Hochschule hatte sich 1886 bei der Besetzung des neuen Lehrstuhls für Apologetik um P. Weiß oder P. Esser bemüht. Leider waren beide schon anderswo in Verwendung." Ebd., 139. Es handelt sich um Albert Maria Weiß OP, der aus dem Weltklerus in den Dominikanerorden eingetreten war und 1877 in Graz die einfachen Gelübde abgelegt hatte. Er unterrichtete im Grazer Studienhaus Moral, Exegese und Hebräisch und wird später in Freiburg i. Ue. als Gegenspieler Zapletals von Bedeutung sein. Der andere ist der aus Aachen stammende Thomas (Herman Joseph) Esser OP, der 1873 zum Priester des Erzbistums Köln geweiht worden war und mit einem 1875 erworbenen römischen Doktorat 1878 ins Noviziat nach Graz kam. Vgl. Ebd. 103–105.

sollten. Den philosophischen Teil ihrer Studien, welcher der eigentlichen Theologie vorausging, konnten sie durch Vorlesungen an der Universität abdecken. Ab 1885 gab es in Wien wieder ein dominikanisches Hausstudium.[36] Wien als Ausbildungsstätte junger Dominikaner und die Verbindungen zur Universität mögen dazu beigetragen haben, dass der bedeutendste Bibelwissenschaftler des Dominikanerordens, Marie-Joseph Lagrange, drei Semester lang im Wiener Konvent lebte.

Marie-Joseph Lagrange OP (Taufname Albert Marie-Henri, 1855–1938) trat nach dem Studium der Rechtswissenschaften 1879 in das Noviziat der Provinz von Toulouse ein, wo er das Ordensgewand vom damaligen Provinzial Hyacinthe-Marie Cormier erhielt. Im selben Jahr mussten die Dominikaner auf staatlichen Druck den Konvent Saint Maximin in Südfrankreich verlassen und nach Salamanca ausweichen. Lagrange verfolgte thomistische Studien in Salamanca. Als ihn 1881 die Oberen bestimmten, die Heilige Schrift zu unterrichten, belegte er den Hebräischkurs an der Universität. 1886 kehrten die Dominikaner nach Toulouse zurück und Lagrange unterrichtet dort bis 1888 die Bibel. Im September 1888 entschied das Provinzkonsil, Lagrange nach Paris zum Studium der orientalischen Sprachen zu schicken. Dort gab es den aus Lothringen stammenden Orientalisten Vinzent (Jean) Scheil OP (1858–1940), bewandert im Ägyptischen und einer der Gründerväter der Assyriologie.[37] Doch da die Dominikaner in Paris Pater Marie-Joseph nicht aufnehmen konnten, erwirkte der aus Metz stammende Provinzial von Toulouse, Réginald Colchen, vom Ordensmeister die Erlaubnis, dass sich Lagrange an der Universität Wien einschreiben dürfe. Von 1888 bis 1890 studierte Marie-Joseph Lagrange an der Universität Wien orientalische Sprachen: Ägyptisch bei Leo Simon Reinisch, dem Begründer der Ägyptologie und Afrikanistik in Österreich, und Assyrisch und Arabisch bei David-Heinrich Müller, dem Professor für semitische Sprachen. Letzterer führte ihn auch in die Mischna und die rabbinische Schriftauslegung ein. Zusätzlich besuchte er noch einen Arabischkurs an der Handelsschule. Mit dem Prior und späteren Ordensmeister Andreas Frühwirth entwickelte sich eine Freundschaft, die bei kommenden Anfeindungen gegen den Gründer der *École biblique de Jérusalem* hilfreich werden sollten.[38]

---

36 Vgl. Walz, 1950, 100–102, 122f, 138–140.

37 Seine Berufung auf den Lehrstuhl für Assyriologie am College de France sollte 1905 scheitern, da er katholischer Geistlicher war.

38 Vgl. Montagnes, 2004, 35–41, 61 Anm. 5.

In Jerusalem hatte Matthieu Lecomte OP (1831–1887) den Konvent *Saint-Étienne* gegründet. Pater Matthieu war Mitglied der Provinz von Lyon, die sich von der von Dominique (Jean Baptiste Henri) Lacordaire (1802–1861) gegründeten Provinz *Francia* abgespalten hatte, um strenger zu leben. Erschöpft von der seelsorglichen Arbeit, wollte er sich in einen Konvent seiner Reformprovinz zurückziehen, doch die nächtlichen Gebetszeiten, die strengen Fasten und die mit religiösen und gemeinschaftlichen Verrichtungen vollgestopfte Tagesordnung entzogen ihm so viel Kraft, dass er nicht geistig arbeiten konnte. Als ihn die Assumptionisten 1882 baten, die von ihnen organisierte Pilgerreise ins Heilige Land durch Predigten zu begleiten, kam ihm in Jerusalem die Idee, im Land der Bibel eine dominikanische Niederlassung zu gründen. Der Ordensmeister gab die Erlaubnis und Matthieu Lecomte kaufte ein Gelände, an dem man die Steinigung des heiligen Stephanus erinnerte und wo Kaiserin Eudokia eine Basilika hatte errichten lassen. Sein plötzlicher Tod im Jahre 1887 stürzte die junge Gemeinschaft in *Saint-Étienne* in Not. Um dem Konvent Dominikaner zuzuführen, fasste der Orden 1888 den Plan, dort Bibelstudien einzurichten. Vom Interesse des Ordens geleitet, schrieb Provinzial Colchen am 2. Februar 1889 sowohl nach Jerusalem als auch nach Wien, um Pater Lagrange mitzueilen, dass er ihn dem Prior von Jerusalem zur Verfügung stelle. Der Empfänger des Schreibens in Wien war geschockt. Ein Leben in Jerusalem würde ihn von der akademischen Welt abschneiden. Doch im Gehorsam nahm er die Herausforderung an, vor allem als ihm eine Studienreise in den Orient erlaubt wurde.[39]

Der Aufenthalt in Jerusalem begeisterte ihn: Eine *École pratique des hautes études bibliques* kann keinen besseren Ort finden als Jerusalem, schreibt er dem Ordensmeister, von dem er ein *Praeceptum formale*, einen Befehl im Gehorsam, zur Übersiedlung nach *Saint-Étienne* verlangt, um die Gründung der Bibelschule nicht seiner Initiative, sondern dem Gehorsam zuzuschreiben.

39 „Les dernières hésitations du P. Lagrange allaient être levées, après un troisième semestre à Vienne, par le voyage d'études que le prieur provincial Colchen demande au maitre de l'Ordre d'autoriser. ‚Le P. Joseph Lagrange, écrit-il à Rome le 18 janvier 1890, terminera à Vienne, au commencement du mois de février, les études de langues orientales qu'il y est allé faire. Je vous demande la permission de les lui faire compléter par un voyage en Orient, qui comprendra l'Egypte, la Palestine et le Liban.' Le P. Lagrange (...) s'embarque à Trieste le 14 février, débarque à Alexandrie le mercredi des cendres (19 février), visite le Caire (...), arrive à Jaffa le troisième dimanche de carême (9 mars). (...) Le lendemain, il arrive à Jérusalem, où il va rester plus de quatre mois. Il n'en partira qu'à mi-juillet et il sera de retour à Saint-Maximin au début d'août." Montagnes, 2004, 63f.

Ein römisches Schreiben vom 29. September 1890 setzt Pater Lagrange im *Studium* zu *Saint-Étienne* als Leiter ein und erklärt damit gleichzeitig den Konvent zum Studienhaus. Noch in Wien hatte Marie-Joseph Lagrange ein akademisches[40] und geistliches Programm für die Lehre in der École biblique erstellt, das als katholischer Gegenentwurf zum historisch-kritischen Vorgehen im Stile Wellhausens gelten darf: Die Bibelstudien sollten getränkt sein von liturgischem Gebet, allerdings um den Nachtchor erleichtert, geführt vom Geist des Ordens und den Segnungen Gottes, genährt von übernatürlichem Glauben, um keine gefährlichen Apostaten hervorzubringen, und Wirkung auf die religiöse Bevölkerung des Orients zeitigen.[41]

‚Geist des Dominikanerordens' meint neben der klösterlichen Lebensform wohl das Vertrauen auf die Vereinbarkeit von Glaube und Vernunft im aristotelisch geprägten Weltbild des Thomas von Aquin.[42] Der Gottesdienst, besonders die Teilnahme am Stundengebet der Klostergemeinschaft, sollten Forschende und Studierende davor bewahren, im Bibelstudium beim Zusammenprall von liebgewordenen Glaubensvorstellungen (Adam wurde am sechsten Tag erschaffen) und geschichtlichen Unwahrscheinlichkeiten (Millionen Jahre alte Dinosaurierknochen widersprechen dem biblischen Schöpfungsbericht) den Glauben zu verlieren.[43]

---

40 „Écriture sainte et hébreu: 1 professeur, 5 classes ; arabe et archéologie: 1 professeur, 5 classes ; grec: 1 professeur, 4 classes ; assyrien et égyptien: 1 professeur, 4 classes ; araméen, 1 professeur." Montagnes, 2004, 62 Anm. 3, zitiert aus dem *Journal spirituel* von Lagrange, Eintrag vom 8. Februar 1889. Mit *classe* meinte Lagrange die für das jeweilige Fach zu absolvierenden Studienjahre.

41 Vgl. Montagnes, 2004, 63.

42 Diese Denkhaltung sollte auch jene französischen Dominikaner beeinflussen, die sich um die Jahrhundertwende in Le Saulchoir zu den Quellen der Theologie (Ressourcement) wandten: „Dort (...) in der Interferenz des natürlichen Vernunftgebrauchs und des übernatürlichen Glaubensvollzugs, fand Le Saulchoir, dominikanischer Tradition und der weitsichtigen Mahnung Leos XIII. folgend, im heiligen Thomas die sicherste Grundlage für seine Arbeit. Wenn es nämlich einen Haupt- und Zentralpunkt in der Lehre des Thomas gibt, dann die Konzeption einer rationalen Ordnung, die, ohne deshalb eine in sich geschlossene Welt zu bilden, über ein autonomes Methodeninstrumentar verfügt und sich durch ein intelligibles Verfahren auszeichnet." Chenu, 2003, 99.

43 Die Gefahr, vom Glauben abzufallen und Apostat zu werden, ging nicht nur von der wissenschaftlichen Exegese aus, welche die überkommene Lehre der Kirche fragwürdig machte, sondern auch vom römischen Lehramt, das die Exegeten schikanierte. 1903 verbot man fünf Bücher des Franzosen Alfred Loisy (1857–1940), 1908 exkommunizierte man ihn, weil er die Möglichkeit leugnete, einen definitiven Glaubenskern zu finden, der einmal festgeschrieben für alle Zeiten gültig wäre, und Offenbarung und Glaube

Mit der Enzyklika *Providentissimus Deus* (1893) von Leo XIII. begann die Kirche ermutigend über die Bibel zu sprechen, obwohl sie den inspirierten und irrtumsfreien Status der Heiligen Schrift betonte.[44] Lagrange nahm die Enzyklika positiv auf, war allerdings überzeugt, dass die dogmatische Tradition der Kirche in keiner Weise verpflichtete, zu glauben, dass die Bücher der Bibel das Werk der Personen seien, deren Namen in den Überschriften aufscheinen.[45] Lagrange hatte das Wohlwollen von Leo XIII. sowohl für die von ihm gegründete Schule als auch für die *Revue Biblique*, deren erstes Heft 1882 erschien. Bis 1909 war sie das offizielle Mitteilungsorgan für die Entscheidungen der 1902 vom Papst eingesetzten Bibelkommission (*Commissio de re biblica*), für die Lagrange ein Berater war.[46] Lebenslang strebte Lagrange danach, die Bibel sowohl als Wort Gottes anzunehmen als auch sie historisch-kritisch durchzuarbeiten. Um dasselbe bemühte sich sein Schüler Vincenz Zapletal.

Vincenz Zapletal OP (Taufname Adolph, geboren 1867 in Vilémov in Zentralmähren als Kind tschechisch sprechender Eltern, gestorben 1938 in Wien Hacking, XIV. Gemeindebezirk) besuchte das K. u. K. Slawische Gymnasium in Olmütz, wo er Latein und Griechisch sowie gut Deutsch lernte, sodass er später in Freiburg i. Ue. als deutschsprachiger Professor wirken würde.[47] Die Vorlesungen wurden freilich auf Latein gehalten. In Olmütz machte er die Bekanntschaft der Dominikaner und trat 1883 im Alter von 16 Jahren dort ins böhmische Noviziat der Reichsprovinz ein. Von 1884 bis 1891 studierte Vincenz Zapletal am Studium der Dominikaner in Wien. Er begegnete also Marie-Joseph Lagrange während dessen Wienaufenthalt. Da die Oberen seine Sprachbegabung und seinen Geschmack an der Exegese erkannten, sandten sie Zapletal noch 1891 nach einem kurzen Einsatz als Kaplan der Wiener Dominikanerpfarre, der auf die Priesterweihe 1890

---

eher in demjenigen fand, der sieht, als in dem, was gesehen wird. Vgl. Loughlin, 2012, 39, 42. 1905 wurde Vincent Rose OP, Inhaber des Lehrstuhls für NT in Freiburg i. Ue., aus dem Lehrkörper entfernt, weil er die historisch-kritische Methode angewandt und zu häufig protestantische Kollegen zitiert hatte. Er hat daraufhin den Orden verlassen, geheiratet – was für einen Priester automatisch die Exkommunikation nach sich zieht – und in Nizza als Gymnasiallehrer gearbeitet. Vgl. Petráček, 2007, 30f, 67 Anm. 244.

44 Vgl. Loughlin, 2012, 41; Viviano, 2012, 306.

45 Vgl. Montagnes, 2004, 85f.

46 Vgl. Montagnes, 2004, 86; Hildebrand Höpfl, Art. „Bibelkommission", LThK[1], Zweiter Band, 1931, 286.

47 Er hat sich seine Bücher durch Dominikaner deutscher Muttersprache Korrektur lesen lassen. Vgl. Petráček, 2007, 96, 119f. Anm. 470.

folgte, nach Jerusalem, wo er bis 1893 blieb. Er gab dort schließlich eine Vorlesung über das Buch Jesaja am hebräischen Text, bevor ihn sein zum Ordensgeneral gewählter früherer Prior von Wien, Andreas Frühwirth (im Amt von 1891 bis 1904), im Februar 1893 als Ablösung des aus Lyon stammenden Paters Albert Fritsch (1840–1920) zum Professor für Exegese des Alten Testaments an der Universität Freiburg i. Ue. ernannte. 1888 wählte die Fakultät Zapletal zum Dekan, ein damals nur ein Jahr dauerndes Ehrenamt. 1902 bat er über den Ordensmeister Andreas Frühwirth um die Erlaubnis, „seinen Hörern die Lectüre von protestantischen Büchern gestatten zu können".[48] Im selben Jahr erschien sein erstes Buch über die Genesis, das die Quellen J und P von Wellhausen übernahm und den Schöpfungsbericht in ägyptische, phönizische und babylonische Traditionen einordnete. Die Studie erhielt Lob von katholischer und protestantischer Seite, erweckte aber den Widerspruch der *Revue de l'Institut catholique de Paris* und des Rabbiners von Luzern, der am 13. Juni 1905 an Zapletal schrieb: „Wer in der Genesis Quellen (vermutet?), verstößt (…) gegen den Glauben (…) [n]ach jüdische[r] Auffassung (…)! Bis jetzt glaubte ich, dass auch die streng christliche Auffassung so ist. Nur protestantische Bibelkritiker (…) dürfen das Messer an die Pergamentrollen legen."[49] Die folgenden Päpste sollten die „streng christliche Auffassung" festschreiben und die katholische Bibelwissenschaft in einen Dornröschenschlaf versetzen.

Pius X. (1903–1914) und die Modernismuskrise

Das erste Jahrzehnt des 20. Jahrhunderts brachte neue Führungsgestalten: Papst Pius X. an der Spitze der Kirche und den 72 Jahre alten Hyacinthe-Marie Cormier OP an der Spitze des Ordens (im Amt von 1904 bis 1916). 1905 gliederte man die böhmische Provinz aus der Reichsprovinz aus, und schuf aus deren Rest die österreichisch-ungarische Provinz. Zwischen 1905 und 1910 veröffentlichte die Päpstliche Bibelkommission fünf Dokumente, welche die Auslegung des Alten Testaments regeln sollten. Gemäß dem vom 23. Juni 1905 waren alle Bücher des AT streng als glaubwürdige geschichtliche Zeugnisse zu betrachten. Am 25. Juni 1906 ging es gegen das Buch von Marie-Joseph Lagrange über die Genesis, das nie veröffentlicht

48 Brief Zapletals an Frühwirth, zitiert aus Petráček, 2007, 27f. Anm. 95.
49 Petráček, 2007, 55 Anm. 199; vgl. ebd. 52, 56.

werden durfte. Im Schreiben vom 19. Juni 1908 ging es gegen die Annahme, Jesaja 40–55 stamme nicht vom Propheten aus dem 8. Jahrhundert v. Chr. Die geschichtliche Korrektheit wurde am 30. Juni 1909 noch besonders für die ersten drei Kapitel der Genesis, also Schöpfungs- und Sündenfallerzählung betont.[50] Es dürfe im Pentateuch keine Quellenscheidung[51] gemacht werden. Am 3. Juli 1907 verwarf das Heilige Offizium[52] im Dekret *Lamentabili sane exitu* 65 Irrtümer, die neben Dogmatischem vor allem Exegese und Lehramt, Inspiration und Irrtumslosigkeit der Bibel betrafen.[53] Am 8. September 1907 erließ Pius X. die *Enzyklika Pascendi Domini Gregis*, die Irrlehren unter dem Etikett „Modernismus" brandmarkte. 1909 wurde das päpstliche Bibelinstitut durch das apostolische Schreiben *Vinea*

---

50 Damit wollte man dogmatisch die Lehre von der Erbsünde sichern. Woher sollte die kommen, wenn es geschichtlich Adam und Eva nie gegeben hat? Der biblische Text selbst gibt Antwort: In üblichen Bibelausgaben endet die Urgeschichte in Genesis 11. Mit Genesis 12 beginnt die Erzelterngeschichte. Nun haben Bibelwissenschaftler aber gezeigt, dass die Urgeschichte in Genesis 9 endet, während Kapitel 10, die Völkertafel, und Kapitel 11, der Turm zu Babel, ein Pufferstück zur Erzelterngeschichte bilden. Die so abgegrenzte Urgeschichte liegt räumlich und zeitlich außerhalb von Geographie und Geschichte. Räumlich kann kein Ort, den Genesis 1–9 nennt (Eden, die von Kain gegründete Stadt, Noahs Weinberg), aufgesucht werden, auch nicht die vermeintlichen Ausnahmen Ararat und Kanaan. Die Gegend um den Ararat, wo die Arche strandet, war von den Sintflutgeschichten Vorderasiens vorgegeben: Im Gilgamesch-Epos landete die Arche am Berg Nimusch im irakischen Kurdistan, Berossos nannte Gordiene, eine Bergregion um den Van-See. Kanaan ist ein Personenname für den Enkels Noahs. Zeitlich startet nach Genesis 2,4a und dem Ende des siebten Schöpfungstags nicht eine neue Woche, sondern die Erschaffung der Erde beginnt in Genesis 2,4b von vorn. Menschen werden mehrere hundert Jahre alt. Die Urgeschichte spielt in einer Anderswelt. Diese Anderswelt ist nicht vergangen, sondern spiegelt immer die konkrete Lebenswelt, die ist, wie sie ist, weil Menschen Gottes Gebot übertreten, wie Adam und Eva, weil Brüder einander umbringen, wie Kain den Abel. Erst mit der Völkertafel und dem Turmbau zu Babel erscheinen Länder, in die man reisen kann. Erst mit Abrahams Familie beginnt die fortlaufende Erzählung von Geschichte.

51 „Willhelm Vatke (...) arbeitete (...) Beobachtungen zu einer ersten kritischen Geschichte der altisraelitischen Religion aus (...), die (...) Mißtrauen erweckte, (...) weil die Arbeit an den Quellen, d. h. vor allem am Pentateuch, noch nicht weit genug war. (...) In den Jahrzehnten nach Vatke (...) gelangte man zur Unterscheidung von vier Pentateuchquellen: drei durchlaufende Erzählungen, von denen zwei den Gottesnamen Elohim und eine den Gottesnamen Jahwe gebrauchten, dazu das Deuteronomium." Smend, 1989, 103f.

52 Das Heilige Officium hieß eigentlich Sacra Congregatio Sancti Officii und war die höchste Kurialbehörde. Vgl. Klaus Mörsdorf, Art. „Kardinalskongregationen", LThK^2, Fünfter Band, 1960, 1344–1349, 1347.

53 Vgl. Johannes Beumer, Art. „Lamentabili", LThK^2, Sechster Band, 1961, 765.

Electa aus einem Kurs an der römischen Jesuitenhochschule *Gregoriana* heraus gegründet. Deshalb war die Lehre dort der Gesellschaft Jesu übertragen, mit der Aufgabe, die kritische Bibelwissenschaft zu widerlegen. Im Motuproprio *Sacrorum Antistitum* vom 1.9.1910 führte Pius X. für den gesamten Klerus den Antimodernisteneid ein, der von allen Priestern und Lehrern von Priestern geschworen werden musste und in dem in Form eines Glaubensbekenntnisses die in *Pascendi* und *Lamentabili* dargestellten Irrtümer des Modernismus zusammengefasst und verworfen wurden.[54] Er blieb bis 1967 in Kraft. Dieser Eid schuf eine Kultur des Verfolgungswahns und der Anpassung, indem er es erlaubte, jede theologische Abweichung als Modernismus anzuschwärzen.[55] Das Interesse der Modernisten an der Geschichte, ihre Wahrnehmung der Weise, wie der kulturelle und gesellschaftliche Zusammenhang jede geistige Vorstellung festlegt und wie die Zeit beides wandelt, führte zum Vorwurf des Relativismus. Die unwandelbare Kirche der Neuscholastiker versprach Sicherheit im 19. und 20. Jahrhundert, als die Kirche zunehmenden Verlust an politischer Macht erlitt.[56]

Stimmen aus Freiburg i. Ue., wohl auch der zum treuen Verfechter römischer Rechtgläubigkeit gewordene Caspar Decurtins, schwärzten Zapletal beim Heiligen Offizium an. So verbot Papst Piux X. 1910 in einem Brief an den Ordensmeister Cormier, dass Zapletal sich als Kandidat für das Amt des Rektors der Universität aufstellen lasse. Der Angefeindete reiste nach Rom und verfasste mit Cormier eine Eingabe an den Papst, in dem der Ordensmeister seinen Rücktritt androhte, da er Vincenz Zapletal als seinen Vikar im Abertinum, dem Haus der Dominikaner zu Freiburg i. Ue., eingesetzt habe und damit ebenfalls untragbar sei, wenn der Papst Zapletal als Rektor der Universität für unannehmbar halte.[57] Obwohl Pius X. es ablehnte, Zaple-

54 Vgl. Johannes Chr. Pilz, Art. „Antimodernisteneid", LThK^2, Erster Band, 1957, 640f.

55 Vgl. Loughlin, 2012, 38. Die Verfolgung startete nicht mit dem Verbrennen, aber mit dem Verbieten von Büchern. 1903 verbot man fünf Bücher des Franzosen Alfred Loisy (1857–1940), 1908 exkommunizierte man ihn. Der Ire George Tyrrell (1861–1909) war 1891 Jesuit geworden und einer der fähigsten und bekanntesten Lehrer und Schriftsteller unter den Jesuiten. Man zwang ihn 1905, den Jesuitenorden zu verlassen. Als er 1907 gegen *Pascendi* veröffentlichte, wurde er exkommuniziert, so dass ihm bei seinem Tod 1909 ein katholisches Begräbnis verwehrt war. Vgl. Ebd. 39.

56 Vgl. Loughlin, 2012, 48f.

57 Da die Bundesverfassung der Schweiz von 1874 jede neue Klostergründung untersagt hatte, war das Albertinum kein Konvent, sondern ein Wohnheim für Dominikanerpatres und ein Seminar. Der Ordensmeister setzte den Oberen ein, vier Amtszeiten lang, von 1906 bis 1918 übte Zapletal dieses Amt aus. Vgl. Petráček, 2007, 14, 70, 74, 83–85. Cor-

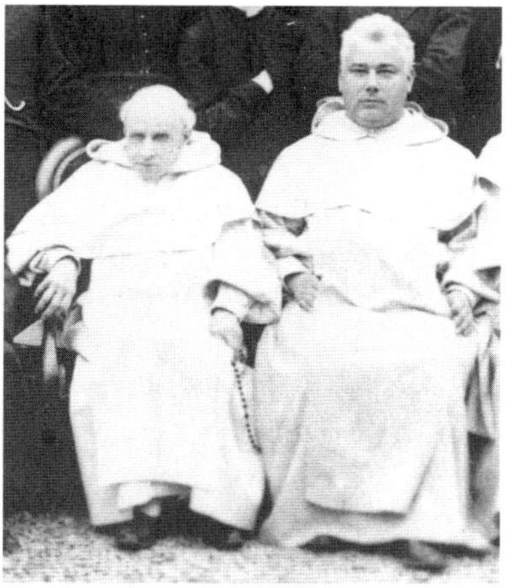

Abb. 3: Ordensmeister Hyacinthe-Marie Cormier (links) und Vincenz Zapletal OP, anlässlich eines Besuchs Cormiers 1914 im Albertinum in Freiburg im Uechtland (Foto: Archiv des Albertinums, Freiburg i. Ue.).

tal zu empfangen, schwand sein Widerstand gegen die Rektorswahl, bei der Zapletal am 15. Juli 1910 mit 42 von 44 Stimmen gewählt wurde. Am *Dies Academicus*, dem Fest des Heiligen Albertus Magnus am 15. November 1910, hielt Rektor Zapletal eine Rede über die Aufgaben der katholischen Exegese.[58] Da die Veröffentlichungen der Päpstlichen Bibelkommission nicht unfehlbar sind, allerdings das Gewissen der Katholiken binden und bei Zuwiderhandlung die Sünde des Ungehorsams drohte, war es möglich, aber auch mutig, in der Rede zu betonen, dass die Quellenscheidung im Pentateuch keine Irrlehre sei. Trotz des Aufschreis in kirchenamtlich orientierter Presse, gab es keinen offiziellen Tadel. Die Rektoratsrede von 1910, dem Jahr des Antimodernisteneids, ist ein Zeitdokument und als Anhang am Ende dieses Aufsatzes abgedruckt. Ihre Bedeutung als Aufruf zum Durchhalten wird in den Übersetzungen und der Neuauflage 1911 deutlich.[59]

---

mier wurde 1994 selig, Pius X. 1954 heilig gesprochen. Wie beide ihre Konflikte um Zapletal und Lagrange wohl im Himmel betrachten? Der Seligsprechungsprozess für Marie-Joseph Lagrange läuft noch.

58 Über einige Aufgaben der katholischen alttestamentlichen Exegese: Rektoratsrede gehalten am 15. November 1910 zur feierlichen Eröffnung des Studienjahres 1910–1911, Universität Freiburg Schweiz, Freiburg (Schweiz): St. Paulus-Druckerei, 1910, 39 Seiten = L'exégèse catholique de l'Ancien testament: discours prononcé le 15 nov. 1910, Fribourg [etc.]: O. Gschwend [etc.], 1911.

59 Die Rede wurde ins Tschechische, Französische, Englische, Spanische, Ungarische und Rumänische übersetzt. Vgl. Petráček, 2007, 86f.

Benedikt XV. (1914–1922) und die Enzyklika *Spiritus Paraclitus* (1920)

Unter Benedikt XV., der als Seminarist von Cormier in den Dritten Orden der Dominikaner aufgenommen worden war, kam die katholische Bibelwissenschaft zu einem Stillstand, der bis 1943 dauern sollte. Zwischen 1915 und 1938 gab die Päpstliche Bibelkommission nur drei Erlasse heraus.[60] In seiner Enzyklika über die Bibelstudien *Spiritus Paraclitus* vom 15. Dezember 1920 anlässlich des 1500. Geburtstags des heiligen Hieronymus, dem Bibelübersetzer unter den Kirchenvätern, wurden die letzten Freiräume für die moderne Bibelforschung geschlossen.[61]

Das kirchliche Lehramt war in der Sackgasse seines Offenbarungsverständnisses gefangen. Wenn Offenbarung Information von Seiten Gottes war, dann muss diese Information doch stimmen! Wenn die Bibel ein Brief Gottes an die Menschheit ist, dann kann der göttliche Verfasser doch nichts Unwahres hineingeschrieben haben. Im Zeitraum biblischen Stillstands unter den Katholiken während der Zwischenkriegszeit geschah jedoch in jüdischen, reformierten und katholischen Kreisen ein Aufbruch im Verständnis dessen, was Offenbarung ist. Martin Buber (1878–1965) gehört zusammen mit Franz Rosenzweig und dem Katholiken Ferdinand Ebner zu den Vertretern einer Geistesströmung, die sich das „neue dialogische Denken" nannte. Der Mensch ist in Beziehung. Die zwischenmenschliche Begegnung ist offen für Gott, das ewige Du.[62] Für Buber ist der sich offenbarende Gott kein Gegenstand, sondern ein Du, dass im Offenbarungsmoment mit dem ihm begegnenden Menschen verschmilzt. Die Bibel ist das Wort, in dem sich der Glaube Israels über die Situationen und Begegnungen der Offenbarung ausdrückt. Ferdinand Ebner (1882–1931), ein österreichischer Katholik und Volksschullehrer, vertrat einen ähnlichen Personalismus. Sein Hauptwerk *Das Wort und die geistigen Realitäten* von 1921 beeinflusste den Gesprächspartner Karl Barths, Emil Brunner. In der Beziehung zum menschlichen Du ist die Beziehung des Ich zum absoluten Du Gottes erfahrbar, welches das menschliche Du durch sein Wort erschaffen und zur Erwiderung aufgerufen hat.[63] Karl Barth (1886–1968) war mütterlicherseits mit dem Kunst- und Kulturgeschichtler Jakob Burckhardt verwandt.

60 Vgl. Petráček, 2007, 95, 111.
61 Vgl. Petráček, 2007, 109.
62 Vgl. Christian Schütz, Art. „Martin Buber", TRE VII, 1981, 253–258. 254f.
63 Vgl. Markus Mühling-Schlapkohl, Art. „Ebner, Ferdinand", RGG 2, 1999, 1044f.

Er begründete den gegen die liberale Theologie des 19. Jahrhunderts gerichteten „dialektischen Weg" der Theologie. Offenbarung ist christologisch. Das Wort Gottes ist voraussetzungslos und offenbart sich in Jesus Christus als erwählendem Gott und erwähltem Menschen.[64]

Von diesen Entwicklungen in der Theologie bekam Vincenz Zapletal wahrscheinlich wenig mit.[65] Wohl aber vollzog er eine Wende zur Kulturgeschichte. Zuerst veröffentlichte er eine Studie über den Wein in der Bibel. Das Manuskript war 1918 fertig. Im selben Jahr erreichte eine fünfköpfige Universitätskommission, bei der Zapletal Mitglied war, dass die Kantonsregierung für Professoren eine Rentenkasse einführte.[66] Das Buch erschien 1920. Dann schrieb er Erzählungen über biblische Gestalten. Alle diese Bücher tragen die Stichwörter „Kulturbilder" „kulturgeschichtliche" oder „kulturhistorische" Erzählung im Untertitel.[67] Zapletal schrieb 1925 an den Ordensmeister, den Niederländer Ludwig Theissling (im Amt

---

64 Vgl. Eberhard Jüngel, Art. „Karl Barth", TRE V, 1980, 251–268, 252, 257, 263f.

65 Nach 1920 gibt es von ihm keine wissenschaftlich exegetischen Bücher mehr. Das Manuskript des Richterkommentars, der 1923 erschien, war Weihnachten 1915 fertig. Die wichtigsten Werke Zapletals sind: Hermeneutica biblica, Friburgi Helvetiorum: B. Veith, 1897; Ed. altera, emendata 1908; Grammatica linguae hebraicae cum exercitiis et glossario: studiis academicis accomodata, Paderbornae, 1902; Das Buch Ḳohelet kritisch und metrisch untersucht, übersetzt und erklärt (Collectanea Friburgensia. N.S. fasc. 7), Freiburg (Schweiz): Kommissionsverl. der Universitäts-Buchhandlung, 1905, 2., verb. Aufl.: Freiburg i.B.: Herdersche Verlagshandlung, 1911; Die Metrik des Buches Koheleth, Freiburg, 1904; Das Deboralied, Freiburg, 1905; Liber Ecclesiastae: textum Hebraicum critice et metrice, Halis Saxonum: Haupt, 1906; Das Hohelied kritisch und metrisch untersucht Freiburg, 1907; Der Schöpfungsbericht der Genesis (1, 1–2, 3), m. Berücks. d. neuesten Entdeckungen u. Forschungen, Freiburg: B. Veith, 1902 = Le récit de la création dans la Genèse / V. Zapletal ; trad. de l'allemand par P. Meyer Boggio de Stadelhofen, Genève: H. Kündig ; Paris: F. Alcan, 1904; Nachdruck der deutschen Auflage: Regensburg: Manz, 1911; Das Buch der Richter (Exegetisches Handbuch zum Alten Testament Bd. 7, Teil 1), Münster in Westf.: Aschendorff Verl., 1923.

66 Vgl. Petráček, 2007, 108.

67 Joseph und seine Brüder: kulturhistorische Erzählung aus biblischer Zeit, Paderborn: F. Schöningh, 1931; Mose, der Volksführer: kulturgeschichtliche Erzählung aus biblischer Zeit, Paderborn: Schöningh, 1926; Mose, der Gottsucher: kulturgeschichtliche Erzählung aus dem alten Ägypten, Paderborn: Schöningh, 1925; Jephtas Tochter: Kulturbilder aus der Frühzeit des jüdischen Volkes, Paderborn: F. Schöningh, 1924; David und Bethsabe: Kulturgeschichtliche Erzählung aus biblischer Zeit, Paderborn: Schöningh, 1923; David und Saul: kulturgeschichtliche Erzählung aus biblischer Zeit, Paderborn: Schöningh, 1921; Der Wein in der Bibel: kulturgeschichtliche und exegetische Studie, Paderborn: Schöningh, [1920].

1916–1925) auf Deutsch: „Für eine kulturgeschichtliche Darstellung Israels sammle ich das Material seit 15 Jahren und habe bereits viele Notizen. (…) Ich hoffe (…), dass ich in einigen Jahren (…) mit einem Verleger einig werde über (…) den Charakter (…) einer israelitischen Kulturgeschichte."[68] Bis es soweit sein würde, malte er mit seinen Erzählungen das Bild einer bunten Welt, wie es die Lebensgeschichten eines Thomas Carlyle zeichneten, und spannte in Kontexten versponnene Fäden im Stil eines Jacob Burckhardt. Das sind Wurzeln der Kulturwissenschaft und des *cultural turn*, der Jahrzehnte später von der Bibelwissenschaft aufgenommen werden sollte.[69] Für den *linguistic turn*, die Wende zur Sprachwissenschaft, war die Untersuchung von Karl Bühler (1879–1963) *Sprachtheorie. Die Darstellungsfunktion der Sprache* aus dem Jahre 1934 grundlegend, die sich mit dem Stempel „Dr. Benno Riedele O. Pr." versehen in der Konventsbibliothek zu Wien befindet.

Abb. 4: Benno Riedele OP in jungen Jahren
(Foto: Archiv des Wiener Dominikanerkonvents).

68 Petráček, 2007, 123 Anm. 475.
69 Vgl. Böhme, Matussek, Müller, 2007, 44–56; Schößler, 2006, 79f, 101–108.

Benno Riedele OP (Taufname Martin, geboren am 28. Februar 1885 in Schwabmünchen, gestorben am 20. Juni 1942 in Graz) wurde am 23. September 1904 im Noviziat zu Graz eingekleidet. Dort legte er am 23. September 1905 die einfache Profess ab. Von 1905 bis 1939 gehörte er zur Provinz *Austro-Hungaricae*, ab 1939 zur *Germania Superioris*, die ab 1962 süddeutsch-österreichische Provinz heißen sollte. Ab 1913 gehörte er zum Konvent in Wien, gab 1918 auch Religionsunterricht in der Schule der Dominikanerinnen in Hacking und wurde 1921 an der Universität Wien mit der Arbeit *Die Wiederkunft Christi nach den katholischen Briefen* zum Dr. theol. promoviert.[70] Er war demnach Neutestamentler, hat aber auch alttestamentliche und altorientalische Literatur besessen, darunter eine Textsammlung zum Erlernen der babylonischen und assyrischen Keilschrift. Pater Benno interessierte sich für das neu entstehende Fach der Altorientalistik zu einem Zeitpunkt, als Benno Landsberger (1890–1968) mit seinem Artikel *Die Eigenbegrifflichkeit der babylonischen Welt* in der Zeitschrift *Islamica* (1926, 335–371) für die Trennung von altorientalischer und alttestamentlicher Forschung eintrat. Von 1925 bis 1939 war er Bibliothekar im Konvent zu Wien. 1941 wurde er nach Graz versetzt und starb dort mit nur 57 Jahren.

Pius XI. (1922–1939): Ende des Generalstudiums in Graz, Gründung der süddeutschen Provinz

Im Juni 1925 starb der Ordensmeister Ludwig Theissling und ein Spanier namens Serapius Tamayo, der als Mitglied der Rosenkranzprovinz Provinzial der Dominikaner in den Philippinen war, wurde Generalvikar des Ordens, bis ein Generalkapitel einberufen und ein neuer General gewählt werden konnte.[71]

---

70 398. Riedele, Martin Benno: Die Wiederkunft Christi nach den katholischen Briefen. (1921) XVII, 180 Bl. Diss.1020. https: // fedora.phaidra.univie.ac.at /fedora /get /o:15315 /bdef .../ download, Zugriff am 27.11.2013.

71 Newspaper Archive of Southern Cross, The Bulletin of the Catholic Layman's Association of Georgia, Savanna Georga, June 13, 1925, 4: „Washington – Official announcement was received at the Dominican College here that the Very Rev. Serapius Tamayo, O. P., S. T. L., Pr. D., J. C. D., Superior of the Dominican Order in the Philippines, will succeed the Most Rev. Louis Theissling, who died recently, as head of the Order. Father Tamayo's title will be Vicar-General, and he will administer the order until a General Chapter selects a Master-General. It is expected that the general gathering will be held in 1926.

In diese Zwischenzeit fielen Ereignisse, die für Vincenz Zapletal schmerzhaft sein würden. Am 25. Juni 1925 wählte ihn die Theologische Fakultät der Unversität Prag aus vier in Erwägung gezogenen Kandidaten *unico loco*, d. h. als einzigen ans Ministerium übermittelten Namen, zum Ordentlichen Professor für Altes Testament. Zapletal wäre gerne in seine Heimat aufgebrochen, wollte aber nichts ohne Zustimmung der Oberen in Rom tun. Nun war der für Freiburg i. Ue. zuständige Sozius des Ordensmeisters, Léonard Lehu (1867–1939) aus der Observanzprovinz Lyon, auch Berater des Heiligen Offiziums. Er betrachtete Zapletal als Störenfried. Georges Python wollte Zapletal in Freiburg behalten und übte Druck auf die Ordensleitung aus. Also legte der Generalvikar Serapius Tamayo in einem Schreiben vom 16. Oktober sein Veto gegen den Wechsel nach Prag ein, und zwar auch wegen Zapletals mangelhafter Treue zur kirchlichen Lehre. Dagegen erhob der Beschuldigte in einem vierseitigen Schreiben an Tamayo Einspruch. Aus diesem Schreiben erfährt man, dass 1922 die Theologische Fakultät der Universität Wien erwogen haben muss, Vincenz Zapletal zu berufen, doch dann sei der Lehrstuhl nicht frei geworden. Nach einigem Hin und Her lehnte Serapius Tamayo Ende November 1925 die Annahme des Rufs an die Universität Prag endgültig ab, auch wegen der antikatholischen Haltung der tschechischen Regierung zu dieser Zeit.[72]

Von dieser Enttäuschung erholte sich Vincenz Zapletal nicht mehr. 1928 wollte er seine Lehrtätigkeit beenden. Er schrieb am 28. Juli: „Es tut mir sehr leid, aber ich muss Sie doch um Enthebung vom Lehramt bitten, weil ich sehe, dass meine Gesundheit sehr erschüttert ist. (…) Dazu kommt, dass mein Lehrfach nicht geeignet ist, meine Gesundheit zu fördern. Seit 20 Jahren muss ich als Exeget Krieg führen, wenn auch nur Defensionkrieg. Kriegsjahre aber zählen überall doppelt, weil sie die Kräfte

---

Father Tamayo was born of Spanish parents at Espinosa de Cerrato, Castille, Spain, Nov. 8, 1866. He received his early education in Castille and made his simple profession in the Dominican Order Sept. 8, 1883, at the Convent of St. Dominic, Ocaña, Toledo, Spain. He pursued his higher studies in the Dominican convents of Spain, displaying unusual ability, and was in course of time successively awarded the degrees of Lector of Sacred Theology, Doctor of Philosophy and Doctor of Canon Law. In 1921 he was reelected Provincial of his Province, the post which he held at the time of his call to Rome to assume the duties of head of the order.“ Serapio Tamayo war von 1914–1917 und von 1926–1936 Rektor der University of Santo Tomas in Manila.

72 Vgl. Petráček, 2007, 125–133.

mehr abnutzen."[73] Der Staatsrat wollte ihn halten und wandelte seinen Rentenantrag mit Zustimmung des Ordensmeisters am 15. September 1928 in unbefristeten Urlaub um. Zapletal zog sich nach Wien zu den Dominikanerinnen in Hacking zurück.[74] Da sich seine Gesundheit nicht besserte, nahm der Staatsrat am 20. Juli 1929 seinen Rücktritt von den Funktionen als Professor für Exegese des Alten Testaments an der Theologischen Fakultät und als Professor für Alte Sprachen an der Philosophischen Fakultät an, in der Hoffnung, dass Zapletal ab und zu als Lehrbeauftragter zu Vorlesungen nach Freiburg i. Ue. kommen möge.[75] Am 26. Januar 1934 ernannte ihn der Staatsrat zum Honorarprofessor. Am 21. Januar 1938 hörte das Herz von Pater Vincenz auf zu schlagen, während er den Schwestern in Hacking den sakramentalen Segen erteilte.[76] Seine Lebensgeschichte nimmt in diesem Artikel viel Raum ein, weil ihn der Konvent in Wien, die Dominikanerinnen in Hacking und die theologische Fakultät von Freiburg i. Ue. mit dem Verfasser verbinden.[77]

Im Schreiben *Deus scientiarum Dominus* wurde der Antimodernisteneid 1931 von Pius XI. für die Professoren der Theologie und Philosophie an

---

73 Petráček, 2007, 139 Anm. 521.

74 „Depuis son séjour à Vienne, Zapletal était resté fort attaché au monastère des dominicains de Hacking, dans la banlieue: il aimait à passer les vacances d'été, de Noël et de Pâques. En 1895, il se voyait confirmé comme confesseur extraordinaire de la communauté par l'archevêque de Vienne (...) ." Petráček, 2007, 20.

75 Vgl. Barthélemy, 1991, 151. Nachdem Zapletal den Hebräischunterricht nach dem Weggang des deutschen Professors an der philosophischen Fakultät schon zwei Jahre unentgeltlich gesichert hatte, sprach der Staatsrat ihm am 5. Oktober 1912 den Lehrstuhl für Semitische Sprache und Literatur zu. Die Exegese wurde zum Teil an den Iren Vincent Rowan OP (1880–1996) übertragen, der 1912 Privatdozent, 1913 außerordentlicher und 1918 ordentlicher Professor wurde.

76 Vgl. Petráček, 2007, 142.

77 Nachdem die beiden ersten Dominikaner Albert Fritsch 1890/91 und Joachim Berthier (1848–1924) 1891/92–1893 *Scriptura sacra*, also Altes und Neues Testament unterrichtet hatten, wurde die Lehre 1893 aufgeteilt. Fritsch übernahm bis zum WS 1896/97 *Introductio in Scripturam Sacram*, Vincent Rose OP (1866–1944) unterrichtete bis 1905 NT, und Zapletal unterrichtete AT, *Archaeologia biblica* und *Introductio specialis in scripturam* bis 1912, ab dann Exegesevorlesungen und Seminare am hebräischen Text, während Vincent Rowan OP ab 1912/13 *Scriptura Sacra in V.T.* am lateinischen Text der *Vulgata* unterrichtete. Die Abfolge der Professoren für Altes Testament ist somit: Vincenz Zapletal 1893–1929 (ab 1912 zusammen mit Vincent Rowan), Vincent Rowan (1912–)1930, Marc Antoine Van den Oudenrijn OP 1930–1957, Dominique Barthélemy OP 1957–1989, ab 1973 in französischer Sprache, Othmar Keel in deutscher Sprache 1973–2003, Hans Ulrich Steymans OP ab 2004.

kirchlichen Lehranstalten und bei Beförderung zu kirchlichen akademischen Graden verpflichtend.[78] „Nach eingehender amtlicher Prüfung durch die Rituskongregation schritt Pius XI. mit der Bulle ‚In thesauris sapientiae' vom 16. Dezember 1931 zur Heiligsprechung Alberts des Großen unter gleichzeitiger Erhebung zum Kirchenlehrer."[79] Mit Albert (1193–1280) wurde ein süddeutscher Dominikaner geehrt, der Exeget war. Die Auslegung der Heiligen Schrift war der Gipfel der Aufgaben des mittelalterlichen Theologieprofessors. An der Universität Paris hat Albert biblische Vorlesungen gehalten und von ihm stammen mehrere Bibelkommentare, darunter der zu Jeremia, in dem er die Lehre von der Heiligung im Mutterleib für Jeremia, Johannes den Täufer und Maria entwickelt: dominikanische Alternative zur Unbefleckten Empfängnis.[80]

In Deutschland hatte die 1895 wiedererrichtete Ordensprovinz *Teutonia* 1924 die mittelalterliche Rheindorfer Burg aus dem Jahre 1140 oberhalb des Ortes Walberberg bei Brühl gekauft und umgebaut. Das Leben im Kloster begann 1925. Drei Jahrzehnte zuvor, im September 1894, war das Ordensstudium vom niederländischen Venlo nach Düsseldorf verlegt worden. Am 13. Dezember 1897 hatte man das Düsseldorfer Studienhaus zum *Studium generale* erhoben, d. h. zur vollberechtigten akademischen Ausbildungsstätte innerhalb des Ordens. 1934 wurde das Generalstudium nach Walberberg überführt. Nach einer Unterbrechung in den Kriegsjahren nahm die Albertus-Magnus-Akademie in Walberberg 1949 ihren Lehrbetrieb wieder auf, 1974 endete er. Nahezu alle deutschen Dominikaner absolvierten dort in dieser Zeit einen Teil ihres Studiums. Das Dominikanerkloster zu Walberberg bestand von 1925 bis 2007.

Anfang der dreißiger Jahre gründete die Provinz *Teutonia* Konvente in Süddeutschland. In Augsburg übertrug man ihr am 7. März 1932 die Seelsorge an

> „der Wallfahrtskirche Heilig-Kreuz. (…) 1939 wurde das Augsburger Kloster zum Konvent erhoben. (…) Wohnten die Dominikaner zunächst im Ottmarsgäßchen, so wurde am 14. Juli 1956 der Grundstein zu einem neuen Gebäude gelegt. Es konnte 1957 bezogen werden."[81]

78 Vgl. Johannes Pilz, Art. „Antimodernisteneid", in: LThK², Erster Band, 1957, 640f.
79 Walz, 1967, 130.
80 Opera omnia T. 21, pars 1, Super Matthaeum, T. 21, pars 2, Super Matthaeum, T. 19, Postilla super Isaiam ; Postilla super Ieremiam et Postilla super Ezechielem fragmenta.
81 Walz, 1967, 130f.

> „Am Fuß des Schloßbergs in Freiburg im Breisgau befand sich ein Studentenheim mit angebauter Kapelle. Erzbischof Göber wollte es abgeben. (...) Die dominikanische Gründung wurde vereinbart. Am Rosenkranzfest, den 7. Oktober 1934, wurde das Haus feierlich bezogen."[82]

Das Haus sollte Mitgliedern des Ordens die Möglichkeit geben, an der Universität Feiburg Ergänzungsstudien zu machen. Ab 1939 gehörte Pater Meinrad Schumpp der Klostergemeinschaft an.

Meinrad Schumpp OP (Taufname Joseph, geboren am 17. November 1882 in Neustadt Bistum Freiburg i. Br., gestorben ebendort am 15. Juli 1951) legte am 4. August 1900 im Noviziat der Provinz *Teutonia* zu Venlo das Ordenskleid der Dominikaner an und wurde am 10. August 1907 zum Priester geweiht. Da er schon im Besitz des Grades des Lektors der Theologie war, studierte er von 1908 bis 1910 zusätzlich an der *Ecole Biblique* in Jerusalem. Im Jahre 1910 begann er, Exegese am Generalstudium in Düsseldorf zu unterrichten, eine Tätigkeit, die er auch nach dem Ersten Weltkrieg wieder aufnahm, nachdem er als Militärkaplan gedient hatte. Er war Regens des Generalstudiums (1926–1939), zuerst in Düsseldorf und dann, ab dem Jahre 1934, in Walberberg, wofür er im Jahr 1932 den Titel *Magister in Sacra Theologia* erhielt. Er wirkte mündlich und schriftlich als Exeget.[83] Als im Jahre 1939 die süddeutsche Provinz wiedererrichtet wurde, begab er sich in den Konvent von Freiburg i. Br. Am 4. August 1939 und am 24. August 1942 wurde er als Prior des Freiburger Dominikanerkonvents bestätigt. Da das Freiburger Kloster während des Zweiten Weltkriegs schwer zerstört worden und zum Teil unbewohnbar war, wurde der Konvent zu einer *Domus formata* hinuntergestuft. Provinzial Marianus Vetter setzte Pater Meinrad Schumpp nach Ablauf seiner ordentlichen Amtszeit als Prior am 10. November 1946 zum Superior der verkleinerten Niederlassung ein. Die Kriegsbeschädigungen des Freiburger Hauses ließ er emsig reparieren. Doch dieser Sprung in die Nachkriegszeit eilt den kirchlichen Ereignissen voraus.

---

82 Walz, 1967, 132.

83 Zu seinen bibelwissenschaftlichen Arbeiten gehören: *Das Buch Tobias übersetzt und erklärt* (Exeget. Handbuch zum AT hg. von A. Schulz, 11. Bd.) Münster, Aschendorff 1933. *Das Buch Ezechiel* (Herders Bibelkommentar Bd. X-1, hg. von E. Kalt und W. Lauck) Freiburg i. Br., Herder, 1942. *Das Buch der zwölf Propheten.* (Herders Bibelkommentar Bd. X-2) Freiburg i. Br., Herder, 1950.

Während Papst Pius XI. den Nationalsozialismus ablehnte,[84] feierten katholische Kreise die Ratifizierung des Konkordats zwischen Nazi-Deutschland und dem Vatikan am 10. September 1933 in Berlin mit einem Dankgottesdienst in der St.-Hedwigs-Kathedrale. Domprediger Pater Marianus Vetter OP (1892 in Windheim, Diözese Bamberg geboren, gestorben in Augsburg 1968) predigte über „den Geist des Konkordats“ und dankte nachdrücklich für die Vereinbarung zwischen dem Heiligen Vater und dem Führer, der allgemein bekannt sei für seine Hingabe zu Gott und seine Sorge um das deutsche Volk. Die Begeisterung legte sich bald. Das mit der Enzyklika *Quas Primas* vom 11. Dezember 1925 durch Pius XI. eingeführte Christkönigsfest wurde zum Bekenntnistag der katholischen Jugend gegen die Ideologie der Nazis.[85] Marianus Vetter übernahm mehrmals Predigten zur Christkönigs-Woche im Dom zu Bamberg.[86] Weil er bei einer dieser Predigten sagte, der Titel des Buches von Alfred Rosenberg *Der Mythus des 20. Jahrhunderts* verrate, dass dieser Mythos im 21. Jahrhundert nicht mehr gelten werde, legte die Gestapo eine Akte über ihn an.[87] Das Landesarchiv Baden-Württemberg bezeugt ein Predigtverbot im Jahre 1942.[88]

> „Nachdem Österreich im Jahre 1938 durch Hitler ans Reich angeschlossen worden war, trennten sich die ungarischen Häuser von den österreichischen, mit denen sie zusammen eine Provinz gebildet hatten. So lebte 1938 die Hungaria wieder auf und Österreich blieb ein Vikariat unter P. Alfons Well, Prior von Wien, als Vikar. Es entstand der Gedanke, die Konvente Österreichs

84 Die Ablehnung kommt später in seiner Enzyklika *Mit brennender Sorge* zum Ausdruck, die 1937 auf den Bruch des Reichskonkordats durch die nationalsozialistische Regierung reagierte, und in dem Entwurf zur „verborgenen Enzyklika“ *Humani Generis Unitas*, welche die Rassenideologie der Nazis verurteilen sollte.

85 Ab dem 23. Juli 1935 war den katholischen Jugendverbänden durch Polizeiverordnung jede Betätigung außer der rein-religiösen verboten. Der jährliche Bekenntnissonntag bekam von daher einen neuen Stellenwert. 1935 verlegten die Nationalsozialisten das Reichssportfest auf den Dreifaltigkeitssonntag und nahmen damit den katholischen Jugendverbänden die Möglichkeit, sich weiterhin an diesem Tag zu treffen. Als Ausweichtermin wurde Christkönigssonntag, damals der letzte Sonntag im Oktober, gewählt.

86 Vgl. Marianus Vetter; Jacobus von Hauck, Katholisches Apostolat: Eine Christkönigs-Woche im Kaiserdom zu Bamberg, Bamberg: St. Otto-Verl., 1935.

87 Der *Mythus des 20. Jahrhunderts* war am 7. Februar 1934 vom Vatikan auf den Index der für Katholiken verbotenen Bücher gesetzt worden.

88 „Einzelfälle, Hektographierte Rundschreiben und Fahndungsbriefe. 1942; 10) Redeverbot für den Domprediger und Dominikaner-Ordensprovinzial Dr. Johann Vetter (genannt Pater Marianus) in Wien.“ Landesarchiv Baden-Württemberg, Staatsarchiv Ludwigsburg. Bestand K 100: Staatspolizeileitstelle Stuttgart.

> mit den süddeutschen Häusern zusammenzuschließen in einer Provinz. Als vorbereitender Generalvikar wurde P. Marianus Vetter, Prior von Köln, ausersehen. Die Bitten, der Provinz den rechtlichen und geschichtlichen Platz der Germania superior von 1709 zu gewähren, wurden von P. General und seinem Konsil nicht berücksichtigt. Die Provinzgründungsfeier fand an Mariä Lichtmess 1939 in Wien statt. (...) Im Kapitelsaal des Wiener Konvents wurde vor der versammelten Gemeinschaft und den geladenen Gästen durch P. Well (...) die Urkunde verlesen, durch die der Ordensmeister P. Martin Stanislaus Gillet die oberdeutsche Provinz errichtete und als ihr erster Provinzial P. Marianus Vetter ernannt wurde. (...) Neunzehn lange und zum Teil besonders schwere Jahre leitete P. Marianus Vetter die Geschicke der neuen Provinz. Drückend war zumal die Zeit des Krieges, der schon am 1. September 1939 einsetzte."[89]

Dieser Krieg sollte die alttestamentliche Lehrtätigkeit von Pater Maximilian Göbel beenden.

Maximilian Göbel OP (Taufname Leonhard, geboren am 2. Oktober 1903 in Augsburg, gestorben am 13. März 1996 in Hinterbrühl bei Wien) studierte nach seiner einfachen Profess am 23. Mai 1923 in Graz im Studienhaus der österreichisch-ungarischen Provinz, deren Mitglied er von 1923 bis 1939 war. Ab 1931 befand er sich zu Ergänzungsstudien in Wien. Nachdem er im selben Jahre *Sacrae theologiae Lector* geworden war, übernahm er 1932 die Aufgabe eines Professors für Biblische Einleitung und Hebräische Sprache am Studienhaus der Provinz in Graz. Von dort wurde er zur Weiterbildung an die *Ecole Biblique* nach Jerusalem geschickt, wo er 1934 den Titel eines *Sacrae Scripturae Prolytha* erwarb. Von 1935 bis 1938 lehrte er wieder in Graz. Das Generalstudium der österreichisch-ungarischen Provinz in Graz lief mit den Gründungen der ungarischen der süddeutschen Provinzen aus. Mit Dekret vom 8. Mai 1938 wurde die ungarische Provinz wiederhergestellt. Daraufhin waren zum Wintersemester 1938/39 die ungarischen Studenten alle in Ungarn und die deutschösterreichischen wurden nach Walberberg geschickt.[90] Ab 1939 lehrte Maximilian Göbel in Walber-

---

89 Walz, 1967, 132f.

90 Zwischen 8. Mai 1938 (Abteilung der ungarischen Provinz) und 2. Februar 1939 (Errichtung der *Provincia Germania Superoris*) waren die Österreicher ein eigenes Generalsvikariat unter Generalsvikar Marianus Vetter. Im Errichtungsdekret der süddeutschen Provinz von Ordensmeister Gillet vom 19. Dezember 1938 steht: „Novitii huius provinciae [sc. Germaniae superioris] primis in annis novitiatum peragent in novitiatu provinciae Teutoniae et in eiusdem provinciae studio generali post professionem studiis incumbent, usquedum provincia sibi ipsi providere poterit." (Abdruck des Dekrets im Volltext

Abb. 5: Maximilian Göbel OP in arabischer Kleidung während seines Aufenthalts in Jerusalem im Jahre 1934 (Foto: Archiv des Wiener Dominikanerkonvents).

berg biblische Einleitung. Ebenfalls 1939 erwarb er den akademischen Grad eines *Licentiatus sacrae Scripturae* vor der Päpstlichen Bibelkommission in Rom. 1940 wurde er nach Augsburg und 1941 nach Freiburg im Breisgau versetzt, weil die Klosteranlage in Walberberg während des Krieges als Lazarett genutzt, 1941 zugunsten des „Großdeutschen Reiches" beschlagnahmt und erst 1945 dem Orden zurückgegeben wurde.

Von 1942 bis 1946 war Pater Maximilian Prior in Wien. Von 1950 bis 1952 war er Novizenmeister in Wien, von 1952 bis 1958 und von 1966 bis 1969 wieder Prior. An der Bibelwissenschaft hat er angesichts der seelsorglichen und administrativen Aufgaben in Wien nicht mehr gearbeitet. Stolz

in: Acta capituli provincialis provinciae Germaniae superioris (s. Alberti Magni) ordinis fratrum Praedicatorum Viennae in conventu ad basilicam ss. Rosarii diebus 3.–6. Maii 1939 celebrati. Viennae 1939, p. 3–5; Zitat p. 5)

zeigte er mir einmal sein Diplom des Bibellizentiats aus Rom. Pater Maximilian verkörperte den Bibelwissenschaftler, den sich Cormier und Pius X. gewünscht haben, die Bibel betrachtend und nie Lehramtliches in Frage stellend. Er bleibt mit seiner Dienstbereitschaft im Refektorium und als Beichtvater unvergessen.

Pius XII. (1939–1958): Ressourcement und zwei Enzykliken

Im Laufe der Jahrzehnte hatte das Päpstliche Bibelinstitut in Rom seine Linie geändert. Als sein Rektor der spätere Kardinal Bea war, übte man dort kritische Bibelwissenschaft – also wurde das Institut bekämpft. Augustin Bea SJ (1881–1968) war von 1939 bis 1949 Rektor des Päpstlichen Bibelinstituts.[91] In seiner Amtszeit hat Pius XII. versucht, durch eine Enzyklika die Auseinandersetzungen um die Bibel und das Päpstliche Bibelinstitut zu beenden.

Mitten im Zweiten Weltkrieg erließ Papst Pius XII am 30. September 1943 die Enzyklika *Divinu Afflante Spiritu*, in der die Annahme von literarischen Gattungen in der Bibel erlaubt wurde. Damit erkannte das kirchliche Lehramt an, dass nicht alles in der Bibel wörtlich wahr und geschichtlich gewesen ist. Die Bibel ist eben kein göttlicher Brief, sondern enthält neben Geschichtsschreibung auch Gesetze, Prophetie, Weisheitssprüche und Lob. Es gibt sogar erbauliche Novellen wie die Jonaschrift und das Aufgreifen mythologischer Themen und Motive. Damit war aber noch nicht zugestanden, dass die Bibel in für das menschliche Heil unbedeutenden Punkten wie Geographie und Kosmologie irren könne. Daher blieb für Katholiken die Schwierigkeit, naturwissenschaftliche Auffassungen wie die Evolutionstheorie und das große Alter der Erde mit den biblischen Erzählungen in Genesis 1–3 in Einklang zu bringen. Am 16. Januar 1948 gestattete ein Brief des Sekretärs der Päpstlichen Bibelkommission, Jacques Vosté OP, der selbst ein Student von Lagrange gewesen war, an den Erzbischof von Paris, Emmanuel Kardinal Suhard, bei der Auslegung von Genesis

---

91 Augustin Bea hat bis 1902 vor dem Eintritt in den Jesuitenorden in Freiburg im Breisgau studiert, wurde 1917 Professor für Altes Testament im Ignatiushaus der Jesuiten zu Valkenburg, 1924 Professor für Biblische Einleitungswissenschaft und alttestamentliche Exegese an der Päpstlichen Universität Gregoriana in Rom. Er war Ehrendoktor und Ehrensenator der Universität Freiburg i. Ue.

1–3 alle Quellen moderner Naturwissenschaft und alle Hilfsmittel historisch-kritischer Forschung zu berücksichtigen.[92]

Die anti-klerikale Politik Frankreichs zu Anfang des 20. Jahrhunderts hatte die Dominikaner der Pariser Provinz nach Belgien getrieben, wo sie in Le Saulchoir bei Tournai ihr Studienhaus gründete. Erst in der zweiten Hälfte der dreißiger Jahre verlegte man es nach Paris, etwa ein Jahrzehnt, nachdem die französischen Jesuiten aus Hastings in England nach Lyon-Fourvièvre umgesiedelt waren. Die Studienhäuser Le Saulchoir in Paris und Fourvièvre in Lyon waren die Keimzellen einer Ablösung von der scholastischen Handbuchtheologie durch eine Bewegung, die man *Ressourcement* (Rückbesinnung auf die Quellen) nennt. Ihre Gegner etikettierten sie als *novelle théologie*. Für die Dominikaner Yves Congar, Marie-Dominique Chenu and Henri-Marie Féret, die das Gedankengut von Marie-Josephe Lagrange aufnahmen, war die vorrangige Quelle, auf die sie sich in ihrer Schaffensperiode von 1935 bis 1942 besannen, Thomas von Aquin. Statt Kommentare zu Thomas aus dem 16. und 17. Jh. zu lesen, überwanden sie mit dem Thomas aus dem 13. Jh. das neuscholastische System. Von 1944 bis 1947 traten dann die Jesuiten Henri Bouillard, Jean Danielou und Henri de Lubac in den Vordergrund. Sie integrierten noch stärker als die Dominikaner die geschichtlichen Entwicklungen in die Theologie, indem sie auf alte Quellen, sei es Thomas, seien es die Kirchenväter, sei es die Bibel zurückgriffen.[93]

Im Jahre 1950 verkündete Papst Pius XII in der Enzyklika *Humani Generis* die Neuscholastik als vorschriftsmäßigen Rahmen für rechtgläubige Theologie, wobei er „neue" Tendenzen zurückwies, was das Etikett *Nouvelle Théologie* anklingen lässt. Doch das *Ressourcement* hatte die Grenzen Frankreichs schon überschritten und den flämischen Dominikaner Edward Schillebeeckx angesteckt.[94] Im Studienhaus der deutschen Dominikaner zu Walberberg war bereits 1940 von Mannes Dominikus Koster eine Volk-Gottes-Theologie entwickelt worden, die das Zweite Vatikanische Konzil beeinflussen sollte.[95] In Walberberg wirkte zeitweilig Augustinus Maria Gierlich.

Augustinus Maria Gierlich OP (Taufname Friedrich, 1904–1984, *filius*

92 Vgl. Viviano, 2012, 307–310.
93 Vgl. Mettepenningen, 2012, 174–181; Flynn, 2012, 220–231.
94 Vgl. Barwasser, 2007, 232–241.
95 Vgl. Viviano, 2013, 308; Pesch, 2007, 191–228.

provinciae Teutoniae) hat zwischen der einfachen Profess am 27. Dezember 1927 und seiner Priesterweihe am 29. Juli 1932 am Generalstudium der Dominikaner an der Herzogstraße in Düsseldorf studiert. P. Augustinus hat auch in Walberberg gelebt und sich als *Sanctae theolologiae lector et doctor* im Alten Testament spezialisiert. Seine 1940 an der Universität Freiburg i. Br. eingereichte Doktorarbeit, *Der Lichtgedanke in den Psalmen: Eine terminologisch-exegetische Studie*, wurde noch 1940 als Band 56 der Reihe *Freiburger theologische Studien* bei Herder veröffentlicht. Von ihm fand sich unter den nicht eingeordneten Bücherstapeln an der Rückwand der Bibliothek des Wiener Konvents ein Exemplar des Hebräischen und Aramäischen Handwörterbuchs von Wilhelm Gesenius (17. Auflage, unveränderter Nachdruck 1921), das handschriftlich auf dem Blatt vor der Titelseite die Bleistifteintragung trägt *fr. Aug. M. Gierlich O.P. Walberberg*. Es handelt sich wohl um sein hebräisches Wörterbuch aus Studientagen, das er nach Wien mitgenommen hatte. „Als nach dem Krieg Österreich seine politische Selbständigkeit wiedergewann, blieb die Provinz geeint, aber wie von Beginn an, mit getrennter Verwaltung. Von 1958 bis 1966 stand P. Dr. Augustinus Gierlich der Provinz vor.“[96]

Zweites Vatikanisches Konzil (1962–1965): Nostra Aetate und Dei Verbum

1959 wurde Augustinus Bea zum Kardinal ernannt und Mitglied der Kommission für Bibelstudien. Aus dieser Arbeit ging die Erklärung *Nostra Aetate* des Zweiten Vatikanischen Konzils hervor. Es war der Wunsch von Papst Johannes XXIII., die Beteiligung der katholischen Kirche an der ökumenischen Bewegung zu einem Hauptanliegen des Konzils zu machen.[97]

---

96 Walz, 1967, 132. Der süddeutsche und österreichische Provinzteil werden zwar aufgrund der verschiedenen Ländergesetze weiterhin getrennt verwaltet, doch der Beitritt Österreichs zur Europäischen Union und die Einführung des Euro sowie die Ausbildung des Nachwuchses in Wien seit 1982 haben die Provinzteile zusammenwachsen lassen. Inzwischen konnte die Organisationsstruktur, was die Stellung als juristische Person und die Altersvorsorge anbelangt, in Süddeutschland und Österreich aneinander angeglichen werden.

97 „1959 hatte Johannes XXIII. der Karfreitagsfürbitte für die Juden ein neues Gesicht gegeben. Aus der Aufforderung ‚Oremus pro perfidis Iudaeis – Lasset uns beten für die nicht [an Christus] gläubigen Juden‘ hatte er das Eigenschaftswort perfidus und aus dem Text perfidia Iudaica ausmerzen lassen.“ Oesterreicher, 1967, 407.

Daher schuf er am 5. Juni 1960 ein „Sekretariat zur Förderung der Einheit der Christen“ als eine der vorbereitenden Konzilskommissionen und ernannte Kardinal Augustin Bea zu dessen Präsidenten. 1960 erhielt dieser von Papst Johannes XXIII. den Auftrag, eine Erklärung über die Beziehung der Kirche zum Judentum vorzubereiten.

Das römische Bibelinstitut unterbreitete am 24. April 1960 der Kommission, welche die Erklärung zur Beziehung mit Israel vorbereitete, eine Eingabe, die bat,

> „das Konzil möge unter den den Ökumenismus betreffenden Fragen auch (…) Israel behandeln. (…) Nie dürfe man (…) behaupten, das jüdische Volk als solches sei ‚verworfen‘. (…) Das Ersuchen betont dann besonders, alle Christgläubigen mögen ermahnt werden, (…) jene Sprechweisen aufs peinlichste zu vermeiden, die (…) aufgrund einer fehlerhaften Exegese die ‚Verfluchung‘, ‚Verwerfung‘ wie die ‚Kollektivschuld‘ des jüdischen Volkes lehren.“[98]

1961 wurde ein Entwurf eines *Decretum de Iudaeis* ausgearbeitet. Am Vorabend der Konzilseröffnung richtete der Oberrabbiner von Rom eine Botschaft an die Konzilsväter. Eine überarbeitete Fassung des Dekrets wurde dem Konzil am 8. November 1963 während der zweiten Sitzungsperiode ausgehändigt. Es sollte Kapitel 4 eines Dekrets über die Ökumene werden.[99] Darin war neben dem Verhältnis von Kirche und Synagoge auch die Religionsfreiheit Thema, was manchen Konzilsvätern nicht gefiel. So kam der Vorschlag auf, die Verhältnisbestimmung zum Judentum zu kürzen und dem Schema über die Kirche einzuverleiben. Doch Papst Paul VI. wollte keine Kürzung, und *Lumen Gentium* war schon zu weit gediehen, um einen die Synagoge betreffenden Absatz noch harmonisch einzufügen. Außerdem hatten sich Bischöfe aus Kanada, Türkei, Japan, Kamerun, Vietnam und

98 Oesterreicher, 1967, 410.

99 „Der ökumenische Theologe, der meines Wissens als erster ‚Israel als ökumenisches Problem‘ ausführlich behandelt hat, ist Bernard Lambert OP: ‚Das Judentum bleibt außerhalb der Kirche und wirkt doch unaufhörlich auf sie und in ihr. Es wirkt in ihr durch die jüdischen Ursprünge des Christentums. (…) Wir können also an (…) Israel nicht herangehen, als ob es sich ganz einfach um eine missionarische Frage handelte, ähnlich denen, wie man sie in nichtchristlichen Gebieten antrifft, denn zwischen Israeliten und Gottlosen liegt der Abstand der Auserwählung. Diese Auserwählung ist unwiderruflich. (…) Ein Ökumenismus, der sich nur auf die Beziehungen zwischen den Christen beschränkte, wäre von vornherein zur Aussichtslosigkeit verurteilt, weil er sich auf eine zu enge Grundlage stellte.“ Lambert 1964/1962 zitiert nach Oesterreicher, 1967, 432f.

Indien dafür stark gemacht, im Geist der Neubegegnung über alle Nichtchristen zu sprechen. So wurden die Worte des Konzils zum jüdischen Volk am 28. November 1965 als Teil der Erklärung über das Verhältnis der Kirche zu den nichtchristlichen Religionen angenommen.[100] Zum ersten Mal wird durch ein Konzil ausdrücklich festgehalten: Auch wenn die Juden das Evangelium nicht angenommen haben, „bleiben die Juden gemäß dem Apostel Gott, dessen Gaben und Berufung ohne Reue sind, immer noch äußerst lieb wegen der Väter" (Röm 11,28–29).

In der Konstitution *Dei Verbum* entwickelte das Zweite Vatikanische Konzil ein neues Verständnis der Offenbarung, in dem es die Geschichte als Raum der Selbstmitteilung Gottes ernst nahm und kirchliches Reden von Offenbarung nicht mehr als Instruktion über Lehrinhalte, sondern als Gottkünden auffasst. Doch bis dahin war es ein mühsamer Weg. Denn als die Bischöfe der Welt 1962 in Rom zum Konzil zusammenkamen, gab es viele, die weder vom Streit um die Bibelwissenschaft noch von der liturgischen und biblischen Bewegung eine Ahnung hatten. Aber die ersten Wochen des Konzils waren eine bewegte Zeit. Die Bischöfe lernten einander kennen und sie lernten voneinander – und zwar gerade in diesen Dingen. Denn das erste Thema, das auf den Tisch kam, war die Liturgie, und dann folgte sofort die Bibel. Für die Bibel war ein Entwurf vorbereitet worden mit dem Titel „Die Quellen der Offenbarung". Wenn dieser durchgekommen wäre, hätte das Konzil eine katholische Bibelwissenschaft definitiv verboten.[101] In Fortführung der scholastischen Theologie machte der Entwurf die Offenbarung zum Datensatz.[102] Bei den Bischöfen breitete sich Unmut über den am 14.

---

100 Oesterreicher, 1967, 449f., 470.

101 Vgl. Lohfink, 2013. „In der Vorbereitenden theologischen Kommission (…) entstand (…) ein in fünf Kapiteln aufgebautes Schema Constitutionis dogmaticae de fontibus Revelationis (…) . Alle anstehenden Fragen waren im rein defensiven Sinn entschieden: größere inhaltliche Ausdehnung der Tradition gegenüber der Schrift, reichlich verbalistische Fassung des Inspirationsbegriffs, engste Form von Auslegung der Irrtumslosigkeit (‚in qualibet re religiosa et profana'), problemlose Fassung des Begriffs der Historizität der Evangelien usw. In dem Ringen, das die katholische Theologie in allen diesen Fragen bewegte, wären damit die Versuche zu einem Neuverständnis des Traditionsbegriffs wie auch ein Großteil des Bemühens der modernen Exegese verurteilt worden; die Belastung, die daraus der katholischen Theologie für ihren Weg in die Zukunft erwachsen mußte, war nicht abzusehen – sie wäre vermutlich noch gravierender gewesen als die Schwierigkeiten, die sich aus der Einseitigkeit der antimodernistischen Verurteilungen ergaben." Ratzinger, 1967, 500.

102 „Thomas Aquinas, in the first question of the Summa Theologiae, offers an influ-

November 1962 zur Debatte vorgelegten Entwurf aus. Dann wurde es dramatisch: Am 20. November 1962 gab es eine Abstimmung über eine verwirrend formuliert Frage.

> „Es wurde nicht gefragt, wie es normal gewesen wäre, ob der Text das grundsätzliche Placet der Vater finde oder nicht, sondern ob sie für oder gegen eine Unterbrechung der Diskussion seien. Nun mußte mit Ja stimmen, wer gegen das Schema war, mit Nein, wer sich dafür einsetzen wollte. Ob das allen Abstimmenden klar wurde, muß dahingestellt bleiben. Wichtiger war, daß auf diese Weise die Rechtsbasis für die Frage der Annahme umgekehrt wurde: Hätte man das Schema der Placet-Frage unterworfen, so hätte es, um gerettet zu sein, zwei Drittel aller Stimmen benötigt; nun aber, bei der umgekehrt gestellten Frage, mußten die Verneiner des Textes (...) zwei Drittel aufbringen. Das gelang nicht: 1368 Väter stimmten für, 822 gegen die Unterbrechung, 19 Stimmen waren ungültig. Durch die Umkehrung der Prozedur war es dahin gekommen, daß ein gutes Drittel genügte, um den Text zur Annahme zu führen. Der Unmut und die Befürchtungen für das weitere Schicksal des Konzils, die aus diesem Vorgang resultierten, legten sich, als am 21.11. der Generalsekretär des Konzils (...) mitteilte, der Papst habe den Text von der Tagesordnung abgesetzt und die Neubearbeitung einer eignes dafür geschaffenen Gemischten Kommission übertragen, mit deren Vorsitz er die Kardinäle Ottaviani und Bea betraute.“[103]

War die verdrehte Prozedur am 20. November eine Ungeschicklichkeit oder ein Trick der traditionellen Gruppe, ihre Auffassung durchzusetzen? Jedenfalls fand Papst Johannes XXIII. eine Lösung: Der Entwurf war ja von ihm in Auftrag gegeben worden. Also zog er ihn zurück und setzte eine neue Kommission ein, die halb aus Vertretern der einen Meinung, halb aus Vertretern der anderen zusammengesetzt war. So wurde eine inhaltliche Auseinandersetzung in Gang gesetzt. Sie zog sich durch alle Sitzungen des Konzils hindurch. Als der neue Text, mit dem Titel *Dei Verbum* (Gottes Wort), schließlich fertig war, wurde er am 18. November 1965 mit fast 100 Prozent der Stimmen angenommen.

Nichts Entscheidendes an der katholischen Überzeugung, dass die

---

ential description of organized Christian learning and teaching (sacra doctrina) – what we would call theology – as an Aristotelian science: it follows the rules of logic to draw its conclusions, but its principles are based on a limited share of God's own knowledge of himself and creation, communicated to humanity in the ‚data' of revelation and shared most fully by the saints in heaven.“ Daley, 2012, 334f.

103 Ratzinger, 1967, 501.

Bibel das grundlegende und wahre Zeugnis der göttlichen Offenbarung ist, war aufgegeben. Andererseits war einer wissenschaftlichen Bibelforschung freier Raum gegeben.[104] Die Bibel ist gemäß *Dei Verbum* nicht Offenbarung über Gott, sondern in ihr offenbart Gott sich selbst: „Gott hat in seiner Güte und Weisheit beschlossen, sich selbst zu offenbaren und das Geheimnis seines Willens kundzutun" (Dei Verbum 2). Die Offenbarung Gottes ist ein lebendiges Geschehen zwischen Gott und Menschen in Tat und Wort. Dabei liegt die Bedeutung in dem, was das Konzil nicht oder nicht mehr sagt oder was es in einen neuen Kontext zu bringen sucht. Nicht mehr ist die Rede von der „Lehre Christi", sondern von Christus selbst als Wort Gottes in geschichtlicher Erscheinung und dem Zeugnis über ihn im Lebensvollzug der Glaubensgemeinschaft.[105] Damit war in der katholischen Kirche die Auseinandersetzung um das Recht der Bibelwissenschaft beendet.[106] In diesen turbulenten Jahren war Odilo Kaiser Assistent am Lehrstuhl für Neues Testament in Freiburg i. Br.

Odilo Kaiser OP (Taufname Anton, geboren 1930 in Freiburg i. Br.) hat am 14. September 1952 nach dem Noviziat in München die einfache Profess abgelegt und von 1952 bis 1959 in Walberberg studiert, wo er mit dem Lektorat abschloss. Von 1960 bis 1964 war Pater Odilo Assistent bei Professor Anton Vögtle (1910–1996), einem der führenden katholischen Neutestamentler. Vögtle war von 1951 bis 1979 Professor für neutestamentliche Exegese in Freiburg i. Br. und Wegbereiter einer Anerkennung der historisch-kritischen Exegese in der katholischen Theologie. Da er sich den Texten annäherte, um herauszufinden, mit welchem Ziel und für wen die einzelnen Texte im Urchristentum geschrieben wurden, erfuhr er in der Zeit des katholischen Ringens um ein personales Offenbarungsverständnis Anfeindung von jenen, für die das ganze NT Lehre Christi sein soll. Vögtle fragte dagegen nach den echten Worten Jesu und betrachtete die Evangelien im Kontext ihrer Entstehungszeit.[107]

---

104 Lohfink 2013.

105 Reikerstorfer 2012.

106 Das Anliegen einer zeitgemäßen Schriftauslegung wurde 1993 im Dokument der Päpstlichen Bibelkommission über die Interpretation der Bibel in der Kirche weitergeführt. Im Nachsynodalen Apostolischen Schreiben *Verbum Domini* über das Wort Gottes im Leben und in der Sendung der Kirche (2010) hat Papst Benedikt XVI. als Frucht der Bischofssynode von 2008 ausdrücklich empfohlen, „die biblische Pastoral nicht neben anderen Formen der Pastoral, sondern als Seele der ganzen Pastoral zu fördern" (Verbum Domini 73).

107 Vgl. Lorenz Oberlinner, Art. „Vögtle, Anton", LThK^3, Zehnter Band, 2001, 841.

Die Freiburger Dominikaner gründeten

„1958 (...) eine neue Institution, die ‚Gesprächskreise im Dominikanerkloster'. Viele Fragen wurden an die Kirche gestellt, eine neue Aufbruchsstimmung regte sich, das Konzil weckte Erwartungen und Hoffnungen. Die Dominikaner wollten ihrer alten Ordenstradition gerecht werden und (...) Rede und Antwort stehen über den Glauben und die Religion. Sie wollten (...) auf die Fragen, die Nöte, die Ratlosigkeiten und die Vorwürfe der Christen und auch Nichtchristen hören und versuchen, ein neues, den neuen und veränderten Verhältnissen (...) angemessenes, religiöses Orientierungsmuster zu entfalten. (...) Drei Standbeine hat diese Arbeit: die thematischen Predigtreihen in der Klosterkirche, die Arbeitskreise für verschiedene Interessen- und Zielgruppen, die Vortragsreihen über theologische Themenkomplexe."[108]

Abb. 6: Kapelle des Dominikanerkonvents St. Albert in Freiburg im Breisgau, in dem in den fünfziger bis neunziger Jahren die Gesprächskreise im Dominikanerkloster stattfanden (Foto: Archiv des Dominikanerkonvents St. Albert, Freiburg i. Br.).

108 Mayr, 2002, 123.

Pater Odilo hat an den Predigtreihen in der Kapelle und den Arbeitskreisen mitgewirkt. Aus seiner Feder stammen vier Bücher in der Reihe *Christ in der Welt*[109] sowie einige Aufsätze in Sammelbänden.[110]

Dominikaner studieren das Judentum

1945 kam der ganze Schrecken der Judenvernichtung durch die Nazis ans Licht. Zusammen mit der Gründung des Staates Israel im Jahre 1948 führte das Christen aller Konfessionen schrittweise dazu, ihr Denken, Lehren und Beten über Juden und Judentum zu hinterfragen.[111] Dominikaner suchten in der Nachkriegszeit das Gespräch mit Juden und begannen das Judentum zu studieren. Zu dieser Generation gehörte in Deutschland Willehard Paul (Gerhard Maria) Eckert (1926–2004). Nach dem Noviziat und den üblichen Studien in Walberberg wurde er zur Promotion nach München geschickt. Diese Jahre vertieften sein Interesse für das Judentum durch Begegnungen mit Martin Buber und Schalom Ben Chorin. Die Offenlegung und Bekämpfung des christlichen Anti-Judaismus waren ihm ein zentrales Anliegen.

In Jerusalem gründete der in Kairo geborene Bruno Hussar (Taufname André, 1911–1999) zusammen mit Jacques Fontaine 1959 das Haus Saint-Isaïe in der Rehov Agron 20 als Dominikanergemeinschaft hebräischer Sprache, die am 25. März 1960 offiziell errichtet wurde. Als Experte für das Judentum hat er an *Nostra Aetate* mitgearbeitet.[112] Der französische

---

109 *Die ersten drei Evangelien: Einführung in ihre literarische und theologische Gestalt* (Das Buch der Bücher 8b/c), Aschaffenburg: Pattloch, 1970; *Mensch und Gottes-Dienst* (Die Liturgie der Kirche 2), Aschaffenburg: Pattloch, 1971; *In der Wahrheit leben: Perspektiven des Johannesevangeliums; kritisch-theologisch-meditativ*, Aschaffenburg: Pattloch, 1975; *Dynamik und Struktur des Christlichen: die Agape-Liebe als individuale und soziale Gestaltungskraft in Christentum und Welt*, Aschaffenburg: Pattloch 1977.

110 „Menschensohn, Menschensohnforschung und praktische Verkündigung. Überlegungen zur Dialektik von Autonomie und Finalisierung neutestamentlicher Wissenschaft“, in: R. Pesch u. R. Schnackenburg (Hg.), *Jesus und der Menschensohn. Festschrift für A. Vögtle* (Zur Vollendung des 65. Lebensjahres am 17. Dez. 1975 von Freunden und Kollegen gewidmet), Freiburg i. Br.: Herder, 1975, 435–488; zusammen mit Rudolph Pesch, „Augsteins Pseudo-Wissenschaftlichkeit: Aufklärung über einen Aufklärer“, in: R. Pesch u. G. Stachel (Hg.), *Augsteins Jesus: Eine Dokumentation*, Einsiedeln / Köln: Benziger: 1973, 80–100.

111 Vgl. Viviano, 2012, 310.

112 1970 gründete Bruno Hussar Neve Shalom *Wahat as Salam* („Oase des Friedens“), ein israelisches Dorf, in dem israelische Juden und arabische Muslime zusammenleben, um zu zeigen, dass Frieden möglich ist. Jacques Fontaine arbeitete mit Abraham Shmue-

Dominikaner Marcel-Jacques Dubois (1920–2007) gilt als eine der Hauptfiguren der jüdisch-christlichen Annäherung. 1962 ging er ins Haus Saint-Isaïe. Als Fachmann für die Philosophie des Thomas von Aquin wurde er Professor an der Hebräischen Universität in Jerusalem.

1966 bestätigte Papst Paul Vl. das Einheitssekretariat als permanente Einrichtung des Heiligen Stuhles. Kardinal Bea blieb dessen Präsident bis zum seinem Tod im Jahre 1968. Am 22. Oktober 1974 errichtete Papst Paul VI. eine Kommission für die religiösen Beziehungen mit den Juden als ein eigenes Amt, das mit dem Einheitsrat eng verbunden ist. Denn der Kardinalpräsident des Einheitsrates ist zugleich Präsident der Kommission für die religiösen Beziehungen mit den Juden; der Sekretär des Einheitsrates ist gleichzeitig deren Vizepräsident.[113] Das Judentum ist also für den Vatikan ein Teil der Ökumene.

Manfred Kniewasser OP (geboren in Peggau 1943, gestorben in Wien 1989) ist der erste Dominikaner der süddeutsch-österreichischen Provinz, der sich jüdischen Studien zugewandt hat. 1979 erlangte er mit der Dissertation *Die Kenntnis der nachbiblischen jüdischen Literatur und ihre Rolle für die Polemik bei den lateinischen Autoren vom 9. bis zum 13. Jahrhundert* an der Universität Wien (katholisch-theologische Fakultät) den Doktorgrad der Theologie. Verdienste für die österreichische Kirche erwarb er sich durch seine Arbeit für das Österreichische Hospiz in der Altstadt von Jerusalem. Nach 1948 hatte die jordanische Armee dort ein Lazarett eingerichtet, später wurde es als Spital verwendet. Erst im Dezember 1985 wurde das Gebäude dem Eigentümer, der Erzdiözese Wien, zurückgegeben. Manfred Kniewasser überwachte die Renovierung. Am 19. März 1988 wurde es wieder als Pilgerhospiz eröffnet. Manfred Kniewasser war ab 1979 bis zu seinem Tode Mitglied im Koordinierungsausschuss für christlich-jüdische Zusammenarbeit unter der Leitung des Professors für Judaistik Kurt Schubert. Seit

lof (1913–1994), einem melkitischen Priester jüdischer Herkunft zusammen, der im Haus Saint-Isaïe wohnte und die Lesung der hebräischen Bibel im Stile des Synagogenvortrags mit einem Kassettenrekorder aufnahm. Die Aufnahme ist inzwischen digitalisiert und als CD bei einem Karmel in Frankreich zu erwerben. Auf der Webseite Altes Testament der Universität Luzern kann man Audiodateien anklicken und die Lesung durch Abraham Shmuelof anhören.

113 Mit der Apostolischen Konstitution *Pastor Bonus* vom 28. Juni 1988 wandelte Papst Johannes Paul II. den Namen des Einheitssekretariates in Päpstlicher Rat zur Förderung der Einheit der Christen (Einheitsrat) um. Diese Änderung trat mit Wirkung vom 1. März 1989 in Kraft.

2011 wohnt ein Dominikaner im Wiener Konvent, der Rabbinisches Judentum studiert hat.

Benedict Viviano OP (Thomas, geboren am 22. Januar 1940 in St. Louis, Missouri) stammt aus einer italienischen Familie mit sizilianischen Wurzeln. 1959 trat er in die Provinz des Heiligen Albert in den USA (Provinzialssitz Chicago) ein, studierte am Rabbiner-Seminar in Cincinnati, an den Universitäten in Tübingen, Harvard, Jerusalem und Wien. 1976 erhielt er den Ph.D. (*Bible*) von der Duke University, Durham, North Carolina, für eine Arbeit, die 1978 unter dem Titel *Study as worship: Aboth and the New Testament* in der Reihe *Studies in Judaism in Late Antiquity* (Band 26) bei E. J. Brill in Leiden herauskam. Darin setzte er den rabbinischen Traktat *Aboth* in Beziehung zum NT. Seine Karriere als akademischer Lehrer begann im amerikanischen Hochschulsystem, in dem man Stufe für Stufe zum Professor aufsteigt. Von 1972 bis 1976 war er *Instructor in New Testament*, Aquinas Institute of Theology, Dubuque, Iowa, von 1976 bis 1978 *Assistant Professor of New Testament* ebendort, von 1978 bis 1981 *Professor of New Testament* ebendort, 1981–1984 dasselbe im Aquinas Institute, St. Louis, Missouri. Dann folgte der Wechsel ins Heilige Land. Er war von 1984 bis 1995 Professor für Neues Testament an der *Ecole Biblique* in Jerusalem und wirkte schließlich von 1995 bis 2008 als Professor für NT an der Universität von Freiburg i. Ue. US-Bürger mit italienischen Wurzeln fühlen sich von irischstämmigen Katholiken ausgebootet, weil diese die meisten Bischofsstühle in den USA besetzten. Daher bewunderte der junge Benedict Thomas die von deutschen Einwanderen gegründeten Benediktinerabteien im Mittleren Westen der USA, in denen deutschstämmige Katholiken eine religiöse Heimat außerhalb der Bistümer fanden. Das rief bei ihm Interesse an der deutschen Geistesgeschichte und Liebe zu Wien hervor. So zog er nach der Emeritierung 2009 und Verhandlungen mit dem Albertinum in Freiburg i. Ue., seinem Konvent bis dahin, und dem Provinzial in Chicago 2011 in den Dominikanerkonvent zu Wien und bereichert seitdem die Dominikanerstudenten mit seinem Wissen über die Universitätsgeschichte in Deutschland, England und Amerika.[114]

---

114 Weitere Veröffentlichungen zum Judentum umfassen: *What Catholics Should Know About Jews*, mit Rabbi Edward Zerin, Priory Press, 1966; *Le Judaïsme, L'anti-judaïsme, le Christianisme*, St-Maurice, Schweiz: Editions St-Augustin, 1999; „Hillel and Jesus on Prayer", in: Hillel and Jesus, ed. J. H. Charlesworth. Minneapolis: Fortress, 1994; Article „1 Q Mess ar" = Messianic Aramaic text from Qumran, for Anchor Bible Dictionary;

Sprach- und Kulturwissenschaft beeinflussen die Bibelwissenschaft

Nachdem *Dei Verbum* die historisch-kritische Exegese für katholische Bibelwissenschaftler statthaft gemacht hatte, stürzten diese sich auf die Arbeiten ihrer evangelischen Kollegen, um zu lernen, teils zu übernehmen, teils zu widersprechen. In Jerusalem kam nach dem Sechstagekrieg (5. bis 10. Juni 1967) eine politische Aufbruchstimmung hinzu. Die Heilige Stadt war ganz in israelischer Hand, die arabische Bevölkerung erhielt das Angebot, sich in das vereinte Jerusalem integrieren zu lassen. Den Dominikanern an der *Ecole Biblique*, die bis dahin im jordanischen Sektor der Stadt gelegen hatte, stand nun der Zugang zur Hebräischen Universität offen. So stieg François Langlamet OP (Taufname Robert, 1931–2005) zum Scopus Berg hinauf, um an den Seminaren von Isaak Leo Seeligmann (1907–1982) teilzunehmen, der seit 1950 am *Bible Departement* der Hebräischen Universität Professor war. Seeligmann interessierte sich für die Phasen der Geschichtsschreibung in der Bibel, über die er auch auf Deutsch veröffentlichte.[115] Das Interesse an den Geschichtsbüchern der Bibel sprang auf François Langlamet über, der sich der Darstellung Jonatans, Davids und Salomos in den Samuel- und Königsbüchern widmete.[116] In seinem Forschungsüber-

„Sadducees, Angels, and Resurrection (Acts 23:8–9)“, Journal of Biblical Literature 111 (1992) 505–507; „Beatitudes Found Among Dead Sea Scrolls“, Biblical Archaeology Review 18.6 (1992) 53–55, 66; „Eight Beatitudes from Qumran“, The Bible Today 31.4 (July 1993) 219–224; „Eight Beatitudes at Qumran and in Matthew? A New Publication from Cave Four“, Svensk Exegetisk Årsbok 58 (1993) 71–84; „Catholic Perceptions of the Jewish People Since the Second World War,“ in: R.S. Wistrich (Hg.), Terms of Survival: The Jewish World Since 1945 (London / N.Y.: Routledge, 1995) 349–367; „From Sabbath to Sunday,“ Mishkan 22 (1995) 90–93; „Jewish Feasts and Prayer in the Work of Michael Maher and his Circle,“ Proceedings of the Irish Biblical Association 32 (2009) 74–90.

115 Hebräische Erzählung und biblische Geschichtsschreibung (1962); Von historischer Wirklichkeit zu historiosophischer Konzeption in der Hebräischen Bibel (1971); Die Auffassung von der Prophetie in der deuteronomistischen und chronistischen Geschichtsschreibung (1977).

116 Le cadre alphabétique du „Livre de Jonathan“ (1 Sam 16:14–2 Sam 1:27), in: Texts, Temples, and Traditions (ed. by Haran Menahem), Winona Lake: Eisenbrauns, 1996, 163–186; „David – Jonathan – Saül“ ou le „Livre de Jonathan“ 1 Sam 16,14–2 Sam 1,27, Revue biblique 101 (1994) 326–354; De „David, fils de Jessé“ au „Livre de Jonathan“: Deux éditions divergentes de l'„Ascension de David“ en 1 Sam 16–2 Sam 1?, Revue biblique 100 (1993) 321–357; David, fils de Jessé: Une édition prédeutéronomiste de l'„Histoire de la Succession“, Revue biblique 89 (1982) 321–379; Pour où contre Salomon? La rédaction prosalomonienne de I Rois, I–II, Revue biblique 83 (1976) 321–379.

blick aus dem Jahre 1970 *Les récits de l'institution de la royauté (I Sam., VII–XII): De Wellhausen aux travaux récents* in der *Revue biblique* Band 77, 161–200, nennt er Wellhausen, der für eine Schule evangelischer Bibelwissenschaftler Vorbild ist, die an der Universität Göttingen ausgebildet wurden. Zu dieser Göttinger Schule gehörte auch Timo Veijola (1947–2005), den ein Foto aus dem Mai 1978 zusammen mit seinem Freund François Langlamet im Garten der Ecole Biblique zeigt. Timo Veijola war 1970 in der Lutherischen Kirche Finnlands als Pfarrer ordiniert worden, unternahm Zusatzstudien in Göttingen bei Rudolf Smend und Walther Zimmerli und verteidigte seine Doktorarbeit 1975 an der Universität Helsinki. 1980 wurde er dort Assoziierter Professor, 1985 mit 38 Jahren Ordentlicher Professor. Langlamet und Veijola teilen mit dem Verfasser das Forschungsinteresse am Deuteronomium und den Büchern Josua bis Könige, der so genannten deuteronomistischen Literatur. Pater Langlamet hätte gerne gewollt, dass der Verfasser nach seinem Aufenthalt als Gastprofessor an der Ecole Biblique 1994/95 seine Nachfolge in Forschung und Lehre über diesen Teil der Bibel übernähme. Doch das Provinzkonsil der süddeutsch-österreichischen Provinz lehnte 1995 ein Gesuch der *Ecole Biblique* ab, den Verfasser nach Jerusalem ziehen zu lassen, und bot diesem statt dessen an, sich im deutschsprachigen Raum zu habilitieren. Da wurde Timo Veijola erneut wichtig, denn dessen Untersuchung zu Psalm 89 *Verheissung in der Krise* von 1982 lieferte den Gesprächspartner für die Arbeit an der Habilitationsschrift über diesem Psalm. Während Timo Veijoa Psalm 89 als Volksklagelied aus der Zeit des babylonischen Exils sah, in dem das Ende des Königtums betrauert wird, filtert der Verfasser im Psalm literarkritisch als älteste Stufe einen Bestattungsgesang für die verstorbenen Könige von Jerusalem heraus. Die unterschiedliche Datierung zeigt die Schwierigkeit der historisch-kritischen Arbeit. Man erkennt die Brüche im Text, aber wie die Schichten zu datieren sind, darüber scheiden sich die Geister.

Da die historisch-kritische Arbeitsweise also kaum zu übereinstimmenden Ansichten führt, verloren katholische Bibelwissenschaftler ihre Begeisterung dafür. Tatsächlich hat man die Bedeutung eines Texts noch nicht verstanden, wenn man sich eine Vorstellung davon gemacht hat, wann der Text entstanden ist. Die historische Fragestellung blickt auf den Verfasser des Textes und dessen Lebensumstände. Doch man kann auch nach den Strukturen im Text fragen, die seine Bedeutung festlegen. Solch eine Werkinterpretation ist verbunden mit einem Interesse an der Sprachwissenschaft,

Abb. 7: François Langlamet OP (rechts) und Timo Veijola im Garten des Konvents Saint-Étienne und der Ecole Biblique in Jerusalem im Mai 1978 (Foto: privat).

dem *linguistic turn*. Grundlegend dafür war der linguistische Strukturalismus von Ferdinand de Saussure (1857–1913), der in der Semiotik, das ist die Lehre von der Bedeutung der Zeichen, z. B. von Juri Michailowitsch Lotman (1922–1993) aufgegriffen wurde. Mein Doktorvater, der Wiener Benediktiner Georg Braulik, berief sich in der Einleitung seiner bibelwissenschaftlichen Doktorarbeit auf Lotmans Buch *Die Struktur des künstlerischen Textes*, um das Arbeitsprogramm einer Bibelauslegung als Werkinterpretation anzuzeigen. „Von entscheidender Bedeutung ist dabei die ‚Struktur' als Gesamtsumme verschiedenster Relationen, die im Text linguistischen Ausdruck gefunden haben."[117] Damit steht Saussures Suche nach den Zeichen und dessen Beziehungen zu anderen Zeichen im Blickpunkt.

Doch auch die Wirklichkeit als Ganzes kann als ein System von Zeichenbeziehungen gesehen werden. So entsteht ein semiotischer Kulturbegriff. Kulturen funktionieren als Zeichensysteme, die Bedeutungen hervorbringen.[118] Religionen gehören zu den kulturellen Symbolsystemen. Kultur als Text zu verstehen, bildet die Grundlage für den *cultural turn* und die Entstehung der Kulturwissenschaft als Forschungszweig an den Universitäten. Einer ihrer Vorläufer war die Kulturgeschichte, der sich Vin-

117 Braulik, 1978, 5, vgl. ebd. Anm. 21.
118 Vgl. Gruber, 2012, 99–105.

cenz Zapletal verschrieben hatte. Nicht nur Religionsgeschichte, sondern auch Kulturwissenschaft scheinen in Titeln von Reihen durch, die in den siebziger Jahren gegründet wurden und kulturelle Räume des Alten Orients zusammenbinden. 1971 gründete Othmar Keel in Freiburg i. Ue. die Reihe *Orbis Biblicus et Orientalis*; 1979 gründete Manfred Görg die Reihe *Ägypten und Altes Testament. Studien zu Geschichte, Kultur und Religion Ägyptens und des Alten Testaments*. In ersterer Reihe erschien 1995 als Band 145 die Dissertation des Verfassers unter dem Titel *Deuteronomium 28 und die adê zur Thronfolgeregelung Asarhaddons: Segen und Fluch im Alten Orient und in Israel*. In letztgenannter Reihe erschien 2006 als Band 65 die Doktorarbeit von Martin Staszak unter dem Titel *Die Asylstädte im Alten Testament: Realität und Fiktivität eines Rechtsinstituts*.

Martin Staszak OP (geboren in Berlin am 21. September 1959) trat nach dem Abitur 1978 in das Noviziat der Provinz Teutonia in Warburg in Westfalen ein. Von 1979 bis 1985 studierte er in Freiburg i. Ue. Es schlossen sich Spezialstudien an, 1986 bis 87 an der *Ecole Biblique*, 1987 bis 1988 an der Johns Hopkins University in Baltimore USA (*Departement of Near Eastern Studies*). 1988 erwarb er das Biblische Lizentiat vor der Päpstlichen Bibelkommission. Von 1990 bis 1991 war er Dozent an der Theologischen Hochschule Chur. 2004 erhielt er den Doktortitel, betreut durch Manfred Görg in München. Ab Dezember 2003 arbeitete er als Hochschulseelsorger in Freiburg i. Br., seit 2010 ist er Hochschulpfarrer. Aus seiner Feder stammen bibelwissenschaftliche Aufsätze.[119] 2012 hat er begonnen, semesterweise an der *Ecole Biblique* zu unterrichten.

Da man die Habilitationsschrift über einen anderen Bereich des Alten Testaments und mit einer anderen Methode verfassen soll, wandte sich der Verfasser vom Kulturvergleich zur strukturalen Literaturwissenschaft und damit dem *linguistic turn* zu. Doch der *cultural turn* ließ ihn nicht los, denn Erich Zenger an der Universität Münster, unter dessen Leitung er das Habilitationsprojekt betrieb, führte ihn als Forscher im Sonderforschungsbereich 493 „Funktionen von Religion in antiken Gesellschaften des Vorderen Orients". In dem von Erich Zenger als Fachmann für Psalmen

119 Zu einer Lesart und dem historischen Hintergrund des Fragments B der Stele von Dan, in: Biblische Notizen 142 (2009), 67–77; „Vielleicht" im Alten Testament …, in: Kristinn Ólason (Hg.), Alttestamentliche und epigraphische Textinterpretationen. Symposion in Skálholt, 1.–3. Juni 2009 (Arbeiten zu Text und Sprache im Alten Testament 94), St. Ottilien: EOS Verl. 2011, 201–220.

geleiteten Teilprojekt „Religiöse Dichtung als Konstituierung von Gegenwelten" ging es um die Konstruktion von Bedeutung in religiösen Symbolsystemen. So entstand die Habilitationsschrift *Psalm 89 und der Davidbund: eine strukturale und redaktionsgeschichtliche Untersuchung*, in Wien 2003 eingereicht und 2005 gedruckt.

Vorläufer der Kulturwissenschaften war auch der Philosoph Ernst Cassirer.[120] Die von dessen Freund Erwin Panofsky ausgearbeitete Vorgehensweise zur Bilddeutung in der Ikonographie lieferte das Rüstzeug für den Forschungsschwerpunkt von Othmar Keel, der die Bibel zusammen mit altorientalischer und ägyptischer Bildkunst betrachtet. Das verlangt Kenntnis der altorientalischen Kunstgeschichte, in die sich der Verfasser einzuarbeiten hatte, als er den Lehrstuhl von Othmar Keel 2004 als Assoziierter Professor übernahm. Seit 2013 ist er Ordentlicher Professor. Das Studium der orientalischen Archäologie in Wien hatte ihn mit der formalen Bilduntersuchung vertraut gemacht, die ein Bildnis stilistisch beschreibt und datiert. Ikonographie jedoch ist einerseits anspruchsvoller, denn sie verlangt neben dem typologischen Vergleich mit anderen Bildern zur Identifikation aller auf dem Bildnis gezeigten Figuren und Objekte eine Einordnung in den kulturellen Kontext, aus dem das Bildnis stammt. Andererseits ist sie wagemutiger, denn sie verbindet das Bild im Idealfall mit Mythen, Heldenliedern und biblischen Motiven, ohne die Verbindung beweisen zu können, solange keine Beischrift auf einem Monument die Identifizierung eindeutig macht. Inzwischen hat der Verfasser zu diesem Forschungsbereich veröffentlicht.[121]

---

120 Vgl. Böhme, Matussek, Müller, 2007, 66–80; Ferretti, 1989.

121 „Gewalt in Wort und Bild: Löwe und Jagd, Kind und Krieg in phönizischer Kunst und im biblischen Fluch", in: Irmtraud Fischer (Hg.), *Macht – Gewalt – Krieg im Alten Testament: Gesellschaftliche Problematik und das Problem ihrer Repräsentation* (Quaestiones disputatae 254), Freiburg i. Br.: Herder, 2013, 225–285. *Gilgamesch – Ikonographie eines Helden. Gilgamesh – Epic Iconography* (OBO 245), Freiburg / Schweiz: Universitätsverlag, Göttingen: Vandenhoeck & Ruprecht, 2010. „Münzen aus dem perserzeitlichen Sidon mit dem Motiv des neuassyrischen Königssiegels. Eine ikonographische Untersuchung zweier Silbermünzen der Sammlung Bibel + Orient", in: *Jerusalem und die Länder. Ikonographie – Topographie – Theologie. Festschrift für Max Küchler zum 65. Geburtstag* (hg. von Gerd Theißen u. a.; NTOA 70; Göttingen: Vandenhoeck & Ruprecht, 2009) 13–38. „Harry Potter's Preservation and Horus' Protective Power: The Semiotic of the Horus-Stelae and the Semantic of Psalm 91:13", in: *Psalms and Mythology* (hg. von Dirk J. Human, Liberary of Hebrew Bible / Old Testament Studies 462; New York, London: T&T Clark, 2007) 126–146.

Zwei Neutestamentler aus Asien und Afrika

Auf dem Generalkapitel von Bologna wurde 1998 dafür geworben, Dominikanerstudenten zu unterstützen. So rief man in der süddeutsch-österreichischen Provinz Stipendien für Mitbrüder aus Indien, Vietnam, Kolumbien und Nigeria ins Leben, die an einer staatlichen theologischen Fakultät auf dem Provinzgebiet den Doktortitel erwerben wollen. Die ausländischen Mitbrüder werden von den Ausbildungsleitern begleitet, so dass Studienabschluss und Rückkehr in die Heimat sichergestellt sind. Damit soll der Erfahrung abgeholfen werden, dass sich Empfänger von Stipendien in einem Dissertationsprojekt verzetteln, niemals abschließen und angesichts des Fehlschlags nicht nach Hause zurückkehren wollen. Der erste Stipendiat kam aus Indien und schrieb seine Doktorarbeit im Neuen Testament.

Dominic Mendonca OP zog 1999 in den Konvent zu Augsburg ein und begann sein Doktoratsstudium an der Universität München bei Hans-Josef Klauck, der von 1997 bis 2001 Professor für Neues Testament an der Katholisch-Theologischen Fakultät war. Auch nach seinem Wechsel zur *University of Chicago Divinity School* betreute er Pater Dominic weiter, so dass dieser 2004 seine Dissertation mit dem Titel *Shipwreck and providence: The mission programme of acts 27–28* einreichen konnte. Nach dem Erwerb des Doktorgrads kehrte Dominik Mendonca im September 2004 nach Indien in seine Heimatprovinz zurück und wurde noch im selben Jahr zum Provinzial gewählt. Er übte das Amt bis 2008 aus. Von 2009 bis 2012 war er Rektor des *St. Charles Seminary* in Nagpur. Es ist geplant, dass er ab 2014 zur *Ecole Biblique* in Jerusalem wechseln soll. Von dem erfolgreichen Abschluss der Studien durch Dominic Mendonca ermutigt, nahm auch der Konvent in Wien einen Stipendiaten auf, der im Neuen Testament promovieren wollte.

Augustine Agwulonu OP kam am 1. September 2001 aus Nigeria in Wien an. Er schrieb seine Doktorarbeit bei dem Wiener Neutestamentler Roman Kühschelm und reichte sie 2006 unter dem Titel *A sinner's encounter with Jesus: A study of Jesus' relevance in Luke 7:36–50; with a contextual application* ein. Nach abgeschlossenem Doktorat war Augustine die Rückkehr nach Nigeria verwehrt. Statt seine Kenntnisse am *Dominican Institute* in Ibadan fruchtbar zu machen, hatte er Geld für die Heimatprovinz zu verdienen. Der Erzbischof von Wien setzte ihn zwischen 2007 und 2009 als Pfarrer in Pressbaum ein, von 2009 bis 2011 in Lanzenkirchen. Beide Pfarren liegen in Niederösterreich. 2011 durfte Augustine Agwulonu end-

lich in die Heimatprovinz und unterrichtet seit Oktober jenes Jahres am Institut für Philosophie und Theologie der Dominikaner in Ibadan. Zur Zeit gibt er Vorlesungen in den Fächern *Introduction to the Scriptures*, *New Testament Theology* und Homiletik. Er fühlt sich beim Lehren wohl. Es macht im Freude.

Schluss

Bibelwissenschaften nahmen und nehmen unzweifelhaft einen gewichtigen Platz im akademischen Profil der Dominikaner des süddeutschen und österreichischen Raums ein. Ihr Studieren und Lehren strahlt international aus, nach Freiburg in der Schweiz, nach Jerusalem, durch die Stipendiaten sogar nach Indien und Nigeria. Was die Gesamtkirche anbelangt, ging es den Bibelwissenschaften sicherlich seit den Tagen des Heiligen Hieronymus nicht mehr so gut wie heute.

Das Verständnis von Offenbarung als Selbstmitteilung Gottes erlaubt vielgestaltige Vorgehensweisen, um das Glaubenszeugnis der Bibel darüber zu erforschen. Das Studium der Bibel beschränkt sich nicht auf den Verstand, es ruft in ein Leben vor Gottes Angesicht (Psalm 16,8). Für die Leitung in Orden und Bistümern stellt sich die Wahl, ob sie Priester zum Weiterstudium zulassen soll oder ob der Priestermangel sie zwingt, alle Kräfte in die Seelsorge zu stellen. Wer sich durch Begabung für Fremdsprachen und Interesse für das Bibelstudium eignet, sollte die Möglichkeit erhalten, sich zu qualifizieren.

Als mich der Alttestamentler Hans-Winfried Jüngling SJ durch das Bibelinstitut in Rom führte, wunderte ich mich darüber, dass Bibelwissenschaftler aller Konfessionen trotz Meinungsverschiedenheiten im Ringen um den Bibeltext ein Zusammengehörigkeitsgefühl ausstrahlen. Er antwortete: „Die Beschäftigung mit dem heiligen Buch formt den Menschen."

Anhang: Rektoratsrede von Vinzenz Zapletal 1910

Über einige Aufgaben
der
katholischen alttestamentlichen Exegese

Rektoratsrede

gehalten am 15. November 1910
zur
feierlichen Eröffnung des Studienjahres
1910–1911
von
Prof. Dr. Vinzenz Zapletal O.P.
Freiburg (Schweiz): St. Paulus-Druckerei, 1910.[122]

HOCHANSEHNLICHE VERSAMMLUNG!
Es ist Sitte, bei der feierlichen Übernahme dieser Würde als Gegenstand der Festrede das Fach zu wählen, welches der Rektor als akademischer Lehrer zu vertreten hat. Man pflegt seine Stellung im Organismus der Universität zu charakterisieren und seine Aufgaben zu bestimmen, oder eine Übersicht über die jüngste Entwickelung dieser Wissenschaft zu geben, oder doch eine Frage von allgemeiner Bedeutung aus diesem Gebiete zu behandeln. Ich werde daher in einer kurzen Übersicht versuchen, einige Aufgaben der katholischen alttestamentlichen Exegese zu schildern.

Das Studium des Alten Testamentes, der semitischen Sprachen und Literaturen hat in den letzten Dezennien einen solchen Aufschwung gefun-

122 Die originalen Seitenzahlen sind in kleinen Kästchen in den Text eingefügt. Die Seitenzählung beginnt im Original mit Seite 6. Die am Ende der Rede geforderte Einleitung ins Alte Testament ist tatsächlich von katholischer Seite geliefert worden: Erich Zenger [et al.], Einleitung in das Alte Testament von (Kohlhammer-Studienbücher Theologie 1,1), 8., vollst. überarb. Aufl., hrsg. von Christian Frevel, Stuttgart: Kohlhammer, 2012. Es gibt auf evangelischer Seite nichts Ebenbürtiges. Die Kommentare werden heute zumeist ökumenisch geschrieben, so dass manche Bände von jüdischen, manche von evangelischen und manche von katholischen Exegetinnen und Exegeten stammen. Die Aufgaben der alttestamentlichen Exegese stellen sich heute noch weitgehend ebenso dar wie 1910.

den wie noch niemals. Wohl weist das 13. Jahrhundert diesbezüglich auch ein grosses Streben auf. Der Dominikanerorden hat nämlich auf dem Generalkapitel im J. 1250 beschlossen, [6] dass an seinen Lehranstalten neben dem Griechischen auch das Hebräische und Arabische gelehrt werde, und Papst Clemens V. hat dann auf dem Konzil von Vienne (1311) diese Vorschrift auf die übrigen Universitäten ausgedehnt, indem er bestimmte, dass an den Universitäten von Rom, Paris, Salamanca, Oxford und Bologna Lehrstühle für orientalische Sprachen errichtet werden. Der Zweck dieser Bestimmungen war zwar ursprünglich nur die Förderung von Missionen unter Juden und Mohammedanern, aber auch das Bibelstudium zog daraus grossen Nutzen, indem man von da an neben dem Vulgatatext auch das hebräische Original mehr berücksichtigte und aus dem Talmud und andern jüdischen Schriften Stellen zur Bestätigung und Illustration der katholischen Erklärung des Alten Testamentes beibrachte, wie wir es namentlich in den nicht genug zu schätzenden, selbst heute noch wertvollen Schriften des berühmten Dominikaners Raymund Martini sehen.

Seit jener Zeit waren die theologischen Fakultäten eifrige und vielfach die einzigen Pflegestätten der semitischen Sprachen und Literaturen, insofern als die Professoren der alttestamentlichen [7] Exegese die Pflicht hatten, semitische Sprachen, namentlich Hebräisch, Aramäisch, Syrisch und Arabisch zu dozieren. Dass im Laufe der Jahrhunderte und besonders in letzter Zeit auch an den philosophischen Fakultäten Lehrstühle für orientalische Sprachen errichtet wurden, ist mit Freude zu begrüssen.

Einen früher nie geahnten Aufschwung fand das Studium des Alten Testamentes in den letzten Dezennien, nachdem der Boden des Orients uns die Jahrtausende lang mit Schutt überdeckten literarischen Schätze wieder eröffnet, die vielen assyrisch – babylonischen, phönizischen, altarabischen und andere Inschriften zu Tage fördernd. Diese bieten uns nämlich Parallelen und Illustrationen zum Alten Testamente, daneben freilich auch Angaben, deren Verhältnis zum biblischen Bericht Schwierigkeiten bereitet.

Dazu kam die vergleichende Religionsgeschichte, welche die israelitische Religion nur für das Resultat einer längeren natürlichen Entwicklung erklärte. Animismus, Fetischismus, Totemismus, Polydämonismus seien die ersten Religionsformen der alten Hebräer gewesen, von denen sie sich zum Polytheismus und nachher [8] durch den Henotheismus zum Monotheismus durchgerungen hätten. Das Alte Testament, das seither von vielen einfach für eine orientalische Literatur gehalten wird, erhalte noch Spuren all der niedrigen Religionsformen.

Zu diesen hochwichtigen Fragen kam dann noch eine Anzahl textkritischer und literarischer Probleme, die alle die Aufmerksamkeit der Gebildeten, ja selbst der weitesten Kreise fesseln mussten.

Welche Stellung muss nun der katholische Exeget zu diesen Fragen einnehmen, wie soll seine Arbeit beschaffen sein, und welches Ziel soll er anstreben? Soll er ruhig und bequem daheim sitzen bleiben, fern von jedem Schlachtgetöse über die schlechten Zeiten jammernd, oder soll er vielleicht hinaus aufs Schlachtfeld, um für die Sache der Wahrheit mutig zu kämpfen? Und wählt er das letztere, wie soll er dazu ausgerüstet sein? Soll er eine Schleuder gebrauchen, oder Schwert und Lanze schwingen, oder sollte er vielleicht, nicht bloss um nicht mitleidsvoll belächelt zu werden, sondern um überhaupt am Kampfe teilnehmen, um wenigstens gewisse Hiebe parieren zu können, zeitgemässe, moderne Waffen wählen? [9] Es scheint, das letztere sei doch vorzuziehen; denn gegen moderne Waffen werden Schleudern, Lanzen, Schwerter und Schilder wenig ausrichten können.

Ein katholischer Exeget ist sich dessen bewusst, dass er Bücher zu erklären hat, die, vor Jahrtausenden in den damaligen Sprachen verfasst, von Juden und Christen für heilig angesehen werden, weil sie von Gott ihren verschiedenen Verfassern inspiriert wurden. Für einen katholischen Exegeten ist die Inspiration eine Tatsache, die er von der Kirche als eine Glaubenswahrheit annimmt und dem gemäss die Kirche nicht bloss als die Bewahrerin dieser heiligen Urkunden anerkennt, sondern auch als solche, die den von Gott intendierten Sinn authentisch zu erklären hat. Weil aber diese Bücher in menschlicher Sprache verfasst sind, muss der Exeget bei aller Anerkennung der kirchlichen Autorität, die er hochschätzt und von der er in seiner Argumentation Gebrauch macht, auch solche Argumente vorbringen, die der Wissenschaft entnommen sind und von den Gegnern, mit denen er es zu tun hat, anerkannt werden. In einer Person vereinigt er das Wissenschaftliche zugleich mit der [10] Bereitwilligkeit, der Kirche zu folgen. Und je mehr er die Kirche liebt, umso wissenschaftlicher wird er vorgehen, weil er auf diese Weise seiner Aufgabe besser gewachsen ist und die kirchliche Erklärung der heiligen Schrift erfolgreicher verteidigen kann.

Der alttestamentliche Exeget muss sich daher gewisse allgemeine und spezielle Kenntnisse aneignen, er muss die Textkritik, die literarische und die historische Kritik beherrschen und gewissenhaft ausüben.

I. Die wissenschaftliche Ausrüstung.

Der Exeget wird sich zunächst mit all den Kenntnissen ausrüsten, die zum Verständnis des Alten Testamentes notwendig sind. Neben einer gediegenen philosophischen Bildung, die ihm das richtige Denken ermöglicht, neben einer gründlichen theologischen Schulung, die ihn mit dem Glaubensinhalt genauer bekannt macht, und der allgemeinen wissenschaftlichen Bildung, die zu einem modernen wissenschaftlichen Betrieb not-[11]wendig ist, muss er orientalische Sprachen erlernen, genügende Kenntnisse aus der Religionsgeschichte sich aneignen und dazu die Geschichte des alten Orients, die biblische Archäologie und Geographie beherrschen.

Was die Sprachen anbelangt, so muss ihm namentlich das Hebräische wie zu einer zweiten Muttersprache werden. Er soll es so gut beherrschen, dass er selbst die schwierigsten Partieen des Alten Testamentes leicht lesen kann. Durch das Studium der ältesten Stücke, wie des Deboraliedes, des davidischen Klageliedes über Saul und Jonathan, des Segens Jakobs, der Bücher Isaias, Osee, Amos wird er zur Kenntnis des ältesten Hebräisch gelangen und dadurch leichter über die später verfassten Teile des Alten Testamentes sich ein Urteil bilden.

Weil jedoch nicht der ganze hebräische Sprachschatz erhalten ist und viele Ausdrücke des Alten Testamentes dunkel sind, wird ein gewissenhafter Exeget so weit als möglich auch die assyrisch-babylonische und die äthiopische Sprache berücksichtigen, weil sie vielfach dieselben Wörter und Wortbildungen mit denselben Bedeutungen wie das Hebräische enthalten, so [12] dass der Exeget sich dort mehr als einmal holen wird.

Wegen der aramäischen Partieen des Alten Testamentes und der Aramaismen in den hebräisch geschriebenen Büchern wird der Exeget auch das Aramäische studieren.

Durch das Arabische kann er zum vollen Verständnis der hebräischen Grammatik gelangen, und das Syrische kann ihm neben dem Koptischen in der Textkritik von Nutzen sein.

Die allgemeine Religionsgeschichte muss der Exeget wenigstens so weit kennen, dass er die verschiedenen niedrigen Religionsformen nicht verwechselt. Aber möglichst genau soll er die Religionen der alten Araber, der Babylonier sowie der Ägypter studieren, weil sie in die religiösen Vorstellungen der Hebräer oft hinein spielen:

Die Israeliten lebten im Zentrum der damals bekannten Welt, sie kamen in freundschaftliche und noch öfters in feindliche Berührung mit ih-

ren Nachbarvölkern und liessen sich von ihnen in religiöser und kultureller Hinsicht beeinflussen. Von den Kriegen, die sie geführt, berichtet das Alte Testament, aber auch die Assyrer, Babyionier, Moabiter und Ägypter liessen über diese Gescheh-[13] nisse Berichte zurück. Deshalb müssen die Exegeten die Geschichte des alten Orients studieren, und zwar so, dass sie sich nicht bloss mit den Schlachten, sondern ganz besonders mit der Kultur der Nachbarvölker Israels beschäftigen, um jede im Alten Testament erzählte Begebenheit in das richtige Milieu zu stellen. Nur im Zusammenhange mit der Geschichte des Orients versteht man voll und ganz die Geschichte des Volkes Israels, sein Denken und Sehnen, sein Tun und Lassen.

Dass die Archäologie und die Geographie dieses Verständnis erleichtern, darüber brauche ich keine Worte zu verlieren. Ein längerer Aufenthalt in Palästina und einige Reisen mit Beduinen durch die Wüste ersparen uns vieles Nachdenken, und mancher, der vielleicht den Kopf schüttelte über Dinge, die in der Bibel erzählt werden, wird dadurch eines Besseren belehrt.

Aus dem Dargelegten geht hervor, dass zur Ausrüstung eines alttestamentlichen Exegeten viel, sehr viel gehört. Und da er diese Ausrüstung nicht anders als durch langes, ernstes Studium und Forschen erwerben kann, muss er viel [14] arbeiten, um sich dieselbe anzueignen, ja sein ganzes Leben lang muss er mit eisernem Fleiss daran schmieden, ohne sich jemals sagen zu können, dass er ganz fertig ist. Denn das eben geschilderte Ideal eines alttestamentlichen Exegeten ist so erhaben, es übersteigt so sehr die Kräfte eines einzigen Menschen, dass kaum einer behaupten kann, es in Wirklichkeit erreicht zu haben. Wenn mehrere mit vereinten Kräften zusammen arbeiten, können sie dem Ideale näher kommen, das zu erstrebende Ziel viel leichter erreichen.

II. Die Textkritik.

Tritt nun der so wohl vorbereitete Exeget an den Text heran, so wird er sich zunächst die Frage stellen, ob der Text auch gut erhalten sei: denn die Inspiration schliesst keineswegs aus, dass er durch Abschreiber und Glossatoren Änderungen erlitten hat. Bevor er nämlich von den Masoreten fixiert worden ist, ist er durch sehr viele Abschreiberhände gegangen, so dass es zum voraus unmöglich ist anzunehmen, er sei überall so [15] rein erhalten, wie ihn die Verfasser aufgezeichnet haben. Und was auf diese Weise a priori

behauptet wird, findet in den Varianten der Codices und durch andere Anhaltspunkte seine volle Bestätigung.

Der uns überlieferte Text enthält verhältnismässig viele verdorbene Stellen.

1. Einige kommen daher, dass die hebräische Schrift mangelhaft war:

a) dies führte zu zahlreichen Verwechslungen von Buchstaben; dabei ist die althebräische, die mittlere und die Quadratschrift ins Auge zu fassen.

Wie die althebräische Schrift aussah, können wir an der Siloeinschrift beobachten, die aus der Mitte oder aus der zweiten Hälfte des 8. Jahrhunderts v. Chr. stammt. Diese Schrift hat grosse Ähnlichkeit mit der altphönizischen und mit der moabitischen der Mesasäule, die bekanntlich dem 9. Jahrhundert angehört. In dieser Schrift wurden die ältesten Bücher des Alten Testamentes niedergeschrieben.

Neben der Steinschrift entstand beim Schreiben auf weichere Stoffe, wie Tierhäute und Papyrus, gewöhnlich ein jüngerer, z. T. abgerundeter Schrifttypus. So entstand auch bei den Hebräern [16] die sogenannte mittlere Schrift, die teilweise von der aramäischen abhängig gewesen sein mag und wahrscheinlich mit der alten samaritanischen Schrift identisch ist.

In der Zeit vor dem Exil konstatiert man nämlich den Einfluss des Aramäischen auf das Hebräische. Aramaismen werden immer häufiger. Im Exil kommen dann die Juden in einen viel regeren Verkehr mit den Aramäern und nehmen allmählich ihre Sprache an. Bei dieser Sachlage ist es jedenfalls nicht ausgeschlossen, dass die Israeliten auch den Schrifttypus von den Aramäern annahmen, und dieser findet sich in der alten samaritanischen Schrift, die eine Mittelstellung zwischen der archaischen und der Quadratschrift einnahm. Nach dem Talmud (Sanh. 21^{b} 22^{a}) überliessen die Juden den Samaritern mit der Thora zugleich auch die althebräische Schrift, was wohl nichts anderes bedeutet, als dass die Samariter sie von nun an übernahmen, falls sie dieselbe noch nicht hatten.

Wann diese mittlere Schrift von der sogenannten Quadratschrift, die jetzt noch gebraucht wird und die in viel stärkerem Masse auf aramäischen Einfluss zurückgeht, abgelöst wurde, [17] ist nicht leicht zu bestimmen. Wahrscheinlich geschah es allmählich, aber so, dass zur Zeit Christi die Quadratschrift schon im allgemeinen Gebrauch war. Wenn die jüdische Überlieferung berichtet, dass Esra diese Schrift aus Babylon mitgebracht, so mag es insoweit richtig sein, als sie den Juden in der Gefangenschaft zuerst bekannt und von den Exulanten nach Palästina gebracht wurde, ohne jedoch von Anfang an allgemein gebraucht worden zu sein.

Die Varianten der sogenannten Septuaginta, der ältesten und verbreitetsten griechischen Übersetzung, beruhen teils auf dem älteren und mittleren Schrifttypus, teils auf der Quadratschrift. Auf alle Fälle wurden die meisten alttestamentlichen Bücher in die Quadratschrift überschrieben und man kann wohl annehmen, dass dies nicht ohne Fehler, insonderheit nicht ohne Verwechslung von Buchstaben vor sich gegangen ist.

Wie die Septuaginta zeigt, wurden in der alten und mittleren Schrift verwechselt: א und ד, ז und ת, ת und ל, ם und ע, ה und י, ג und ת, ד und כ, פ und כ. In der Quadratschrift verwechselte man besonders י und ז, ב und ם, ר und ד, ה, ח und מ. Diese Verwechslungen [18] fanden namentlich dann statt, wenn die Schrift des Originals unleserlich, verwischt oder erloschen war. Leider muss ich es mir versagen, Beispiele anzuführen; ich kann jedoch nicht umhin zu merken, dass das, was ich hier in Bezug auf die Textkritik bemerke, eine von allen Exegeten anerkannte Tatsache ist. Das meiste gilt ja für jede Textkritik, das übrige lehrt die semitische Epigraphik.

b) Die mangelhafte Schrift führte auch zu verschiedenen Trennungen der Wörter.

Die Mesasäule und die Siloeinschrift trennen zwar die einzelnen Wörter durch einen Punkt und dieses Trennungszeichen mag auch in den ältesten Handschriften angewendet worden sein. Aber dieser Brauch bestand nicht immer. Viele hebräische Handschriften reihen die Wörter einander ohne jedes Trennungszeichen. Je nachdem, wie die Buchstaben getrennt werden, ist auch der Sinn ein anderer.

c) Viel nachteiliger war der Umstand, dass die althebräische Schrift nur die Konsonanten ohne die Vokalzeichen bot, was selbstverständlich zu den verschiedensten Lesungen desselben Wortes Anlass gab. Nicht einmal die sogenannten Matres [19] lectionis, die Zeichen א, ז, י, ה, die nur in den seltensten Fällen den Vokal, und dies auch nur unbestimmt, andeuteten, wurden allgemein verwendet. Die Inschrift des Königs Mesa und die Siloeinschrift wenden sie nur in seltenen Fällen an.

Jedem, der diese Schreibweise kennt, leuchtet es gleich ein, wie leicht sie zur ungenügenden Erhaltung des Textes Anlass gab und zu welchen Unterschieden in der Deutung sie führte.

2. Damit das Abschreiben schneller vor sich gehe, las einer den Text vor und andere schrieben das Gelesene nach. Das führte zu Hörfehlern, d. h. zur Verwechslung von ähnlich lautenden Buchstaben.

3. Eine dritte Klasse von Fehlern hat ihren Grund in der Nachlässigkeit der Abschreiber; dazu gehören vor allem Dittographieen und ihr Gegenteil, Haplographieen.

a) Dittographie, doppelte Schreibung desselben Buchstabens, ja ganzer Wörter und Sätze, kam sehr oft vor. Um das Manuskript nicht zu entwerten, unterliess es der Schreiber selbst dann, wenn er seinen Fehler nachträglich entdeckt hatte, das Überflüssige zu tilgen.

b) Ebenso häufig sind Lücken im Text zu [20] entdecken, indem der Schreiber durch irgendeinen Umstand einen Buchstaben, ein Wort, ja ganze Sätze übersah. Grund der Auslassung einer Reihe von Wörtern ist meistens das sogenannte Homoioteleuton, d. h. Abirren des Schreibers auf ein gleiches oder ähnliches Wort, das erst später folgt. Dies wird hauptsächlich in poetischen Stücken konstatiert, wenn anfangs eines Verses dasselbe Wort vorkam, mit dem der vorhergehende Vers anfängt.

c) Auch Versetzungen von Buchstaben kamen vor. Es geschah dies besonders dann, wenn der Abschreiber den Text flüchtig las, ohne dem Sinn eine besondere Aufmerksamkeit zu widmen.

d) Es gab auch Abschreiber, welche dem Gedächtnis folgten, und wenn dieses nicht treu genug war, wurden Wörter und ganze Sätze versetzt oder ausgelassen oder nach Parallelstellen verändert.

4. Eine vierte Klasse von Fehlern beruht auf willkürlicher Änderung. Diese kam besonders bei den Wörtern ב ע ל (Herr) und מ ל ך (König) vor, bei dunklen Wörtern, die durch bekanntere ersetzt wurden, und bei gewissen scharfen Aus-[21]drücken, zu denen die Abschreiber mildere hinzusetzten.

5. Dazu kommt noch eine Reihe von Fehlern, die teils auf Nachlässigkeit der Abschreiber, teils auf absichtlicher Änderung beruhen.

a) Es gab Leser des Alten Testamentes, die am Rande ihres Exemplars Parallelstellen und Erklärungen aufzeichneten. Benützte man dann ein solches Exemplar zur Abschrift, so kam es vor, dass diese Randnotizen hier und da in den Text eingesetzt wurden.

b) Manchmal standen jedoch am Rande auch solche Wörter, die zum Text gehörten, aber von einem Abschreiber vergessen und nachträglich von ihm selbst oder von einem andern am Rande notiert wurden. Wurde dieses Exemplar zu Abschriften benutzt, so geschah es, dass die Wörter vom Rande zwar in den Text, aber nicht immer an ihre ursprüngliche Stelle eingesetzt wurden.

c) Die Abschreiber benützten auch Abkürzungen, die von ihren Nachfolgern vielfach unrichtig aufgelöst wurden.

d) Schliesslich gibt es noch Stellen, die uns zeigen, dass man einen verdorbenen Text korrigierte, um einen Sinn herauszubekommen. 22

Das Vorgehen eines Exegeten, der diese Grundsätze kennt und nach ihnen handelt, mag Uneingeweihten willkürlich erscheinen; aber das alles lehren uns schon die Kirchenväter. Sie sprachen mit dem heiligen Augustinus[123] von „codices mendosi", mit Origenes[124] und dem heiligen Hieronymus[125] von „schläfrigen Abschreibern", von „unbesonnenen Verbesserern", von „vermessenen Kopisten, welche Randnotizen in den Text einsetzten".

Die Exegeten dürfen auch nicht willkürlich vorgehen; sie sollen nur dann Textverderbnisse annehmen, wenn sie dafür zwingende Gründe haben, wenn nämlich der Text unklar ist, ja so, wie er lautet, im Widerspruch mit andern steht, wenn die alten Übersetzungen einen andern Sinn enthalten, wenn Parallelstellen einen Wink geben, wenn die Masoreten durch einen senkrechten Strich, der Paseq heisst, andeuten, dass der Text mangelhaft ist, oder schliesslich, in den poetischen Stücken, wenn die Metrik und Strophik uns dazu eine Handhabe geben. 23

Im Grossen und Ganzen kennen wir jetzt die Regeln der hebräischen Metrik. Finden sich nun Gedichte, in welchen diese Regeln beobachtet werden, und bemerkt man, dass z. B. 20 Verse ganz richtig gemacht, während zwei oder drei fehlerhaft sind, so wird man nicht den Verfasser für diese Fehler verantwortlich machen, sondern die Abschreiber.

Man hat alte Nachbildungen des Laokon gefunden, denen zu entnehmen ist, dass die Restauration der Gruppe durch Bernini falsch ist, weil sie mit den alten Nachbildungen nicht übereinstimmt. So haben auch Sammler und Abschreiber die herrlichen Säulen und Statuen des grossartigen Tempels, welcher das Alte Testament ist, nicht immer richtig zusammengestellt, davon ganz abgesehen, dass sich im Laufe der Jahrtausende an die mächtigen Quadern und Säulen, Kapitaler und Statuen auch Staub angesetzt, und dass das eine oder das andere Ornament durch Ungunst der Zeiten gelitten hat.

Wenn wir all das Gesagte zusammenfassen, kommen wie zu dem Resultate, dass zwar etwas Wesentliches nicht geändert wurde, dass aber Einzelheiten, die man als nebensächliche be- 24 zeichnen kann, durch Ab-

---

123 Epist. 82 ad Hieron.

124 In Matth, tom. XV, 4.

125 Ad Damasum praef. in Evang.; ad Sunn. ep. 106, 46.

schreiber gelitten haben. Gelingt es jedoch der Exegese, die ursprüngliche Form des alttestamentlichen Textes herauszufinden, so erscheint der Inhalt viel ausdrucksvoller und erglänzt in seiner ganzen Erhabenheit.

III. Die literarische Kritik.

Die Textkritik gibt einem alttestamentlichen Exegeten viel zu schaffen; doch das ist noch nicht alles. Unvergleichlich schwieriger wird seine Arbeit, wenn er an die literarische Kritik herantritt.

1. Weil bekanntlich jeder Autor ein Kind seiner Zeit ist und für seine Zeitgenossen schreibt, ist es bei jedem Buche wichtig zu erfahren, wen es zum Verfasser hat oder wenigstens, welcher Zeit es angehört. Dasselbe gilt nach allgemeiner Ansicht auch von den inspirierten Werken, weil ja die Inspiration kein Diktieren ist, sondern eine motio des Schriftstellers durch Gott, wobei der Schriftsteller nach seiner Veranlagung, nach seinem Temperament das schreibt, wozu ihn [25] Gott bewegt. Deshalb spricht man von der Schreibweise eines Isaias, eines Jeremias, eines heiligen Paulus und anderer mehr.

In Bezug auf das Alte Testament muss leider anerkannt werden, dass die Verfasser vieler Schriften unbekannt sind. In jener alten Zeit fragte man wenig nach dem Autor, das ganze Gewicht legte man auf den Inhalt. Selbst die Kirchenväter kümmerten sich noch wenig darum. So sagt Gregor der Grosse,[126] es sei eine unnütze Frage (valde supervacue quaeritur), wer das Buch Job geschrieben, wenn nur geglaubt wird, dass es vom heiligen Geist verfasst ist, und Theodoret[127] sagt mit Bezug auf das Buch der Psalmen, es komme nicht viel darauf an, ob alle Psalmen von David seien oder nicht, da es sicher sei, dass sie alle vom heiligen Geist inspiriert seien.

So kam es, dass uns die Namen der Verfasser mehrerer Schriften des Alten Testamentes nicht überliefert wurden, weshalb sich der Exeget damit begnügen muss, annähernd die Zeit ihrer Entstehung zu eruiren.

2. Nun, entsteht aber gleich eine andere [26] Frage: Können wir in einem und demselben Buche mehrere Quellen annehmen, oder müssen wir immer die ganze Schrift einem einzigen Verfasser zuweisen?

So viel ist sicher, dass die Kirchenlehrer und die Exegeten der ersten Jahrhunderte und des Mittelalters in einigen alttestamentlichen Schriften

126 Moralium libri, Praefatio c. 1, n. I, 2.
127 Migne, P. G., LXXX, p. 861.

mehrere Quellen annahmen. So glaubte Dorotheus von Tyrus,[128] dass der Inhalt des Buches der Richter von heiligen Schreibern, die an der Bundeslade angestellt waren, aufgezeichnet wurde, während der berühmte Dominikanerexeget Kardinal Hugo a S. Caro behauptete, dass jeder Richter seine Taten niedergeschrieben und der König Ezechias die einzelnen Teile in einem Bande vereinigt habe.

Ähnliches wird von den Büchern Samuels und der Könige behauptet, in denen die konservativste Exegese die Arbeit mehrerer Propheten annimmt.

Steht nun dieser Grundsatz fest, so darf er, wenn schwerwiegende Gründe vorhanden sind, auch auf andere Bücher angewendet werden. [27]

Ja, es darf uns nicht wundernehmen, wenn manchmal in einem und demselben Kapitel ein Mosaik von Stellen aus verschiedenen Quellen gefunden wird. Der Orientale schreibt nämlich ganz anders Geschichte als unsere Historiker; er legt eine Quelle zu Grunde, die er wörtlich anführt, und dazu trägt er aus anderen Quellen Wörter und Sätze ein. Er ändert nicht den Text der Quelle, denn er ist der Ansicht, dass das einmal gut Geschriebene ohne Änderung übernommen werden soll. Gewöhnlich nennt er auch nicht den Verfasser der Quelle; literarisches Eigentumsrecht und Plagiat waren damals meistens unbekannte Begriffe.

Ich habe anfangs meiner Rede den berühmten Orientalisten Raymund Martini aus dem 13. Jahrhundert erwähnt. Als ich vor mehreren Jahren sein Werk „Pugio Fidei“ studierte, fiel mir im ersten Teile seines hochwichtigen Foliobandes die grosse Ähnlichkeit mit der „Summa contra gentes“ und der „Summa theologica“ des heiligen Thomas auf. Ich traute meinen Augen nicht: ich konstatierte eine wörtliche Übereinstimmung. Woher kam sie? Hat der heilige Thomas aus Raymund Martini geschöpft, oder war es umge-[28]kehrt, oder hatten vielleicht beide eine gemeinsame Quelle? Als ich alles erwogen hatte, kam ich zu dem Schluss, dass Raymund Martini diesen Teil den Werken des heiligen Thomas, seines Zeitgenossen, entnommen, ohne den grossen Lehrer zu nennen. Er nahm das Gute, wo er es fand, und wir täten ihm Unrecht, wenn wir ihn einen Plagiator nennen würden. Zufällig konnte man leicht diese Entdeckung machen, weil die Werke des heiligen Thomas bekannt sind.

Nicht so leicht ist es, die Quellen der alttestamentlichen Schriftsteller immer zu entdecken; denn sie haben sich nicht selbständig erhalten. Aber

---

128 De Prophet. (Bibliotheca max. Patr. lII, 424).

sie können da sein, auch wenn sie oder ihre Verfasser gar nicht genannt werden.

Freilich kommen da viele mit dem Einwand, dass dies eines inspirierten Buches unwürdig sei. Aber das ist eine aprioristische Voraussetzung, die sich im Grund gegen den katholischen Begriff der Inspiration verfehlt. Denn die motio Dei geschieht bekanntlich – das ist jedenfalls die Lehre des heiligen Thomas von Aquin – nach der Veranlagung und Beschaffenheit dessen, der bewegt wird. Und so hat Gott einen Orientalen inspiriert, dass er als Orientale, nicht als ein [29] abendländischer Schriftsteller des 20. Jahrhunderts schreibe.

Wenn demnach anfangs der Genesis – was schon im 16. Jahrhundert der Kardinal Cajetan bemerkt hat – zwei verschiedene Schöpfungsberichte zu lesen sind, deren Inhalt und Sprache von einander abweichen, und von denen jeder von ganz andern Voraussetzungen ausgeht, so darf man annehmen, dass sie zwei verschiedenen Quellen entstammen; dies um so mehr, als der erste Bericht durchgehend in zweihebigen Stichen verfasst ist, während der folgende zweite Bericht dieses Metrum nicht aufweist.

3. Und noch etwas sehr Wichtiges! Gewisse Schriftsteller haben ihre Werke, um mich modern auszudrücken, nicht selbst herausgegeben, sondern andere haben die Ausgabe besorgt. Der Prophet Isaias z. B. hielt oft Reden an das Volk, die als eine Art Proklamation besonders aufgeschrieben und verbreitet wurden. Als man die verschiedenen Teile nachher sammelte, geschah es, dass Zusammengehöriges vielfach getrennt und Verschiedenartiges zusammengestellt wurde. So erklärt es sich, dass Isaias, dieser Fürst unter den Propheten, seine Berufung zum Propheten erst im 6. Kapitel seines [30] Buches erzählt, nachdem mehrere prophetische Reden von ihm angeführt worden, die er sicher erst nach seiner Berufung zur Prophetenwürde gehalten hat.

Wer sich die Mühe nimmt, nur einige Kapitel des Buches Isaias allseitig, also auch metrisch zu analysieren, dem wird das Gesagte ganz klar sein. Diesem Umstande ist das Mosaikartige seines Buches und auch einiger anderer Schriften des Alten Testamentes zuzuschreiben, weshalb der Exeget immer die Herkunft einer jeden Rede, eines jeden Stückes genau untersuchen wird.

Viele, die von diesem Sachverhalte keine Ahnung haben, werfen uns freilich vor, dass wir hierin der modernen protestantischen Kritik Zugeständnisse machen. Nein, nostra sunt! Wir folgen den Begründern der literarischen Kritik, und diese waren bekanntlich Katholiken. Wenn im 19. Jahrhundert hauptsächlich Protestanten nach den Quellen forschten, so ist die

Annahme von Quellen deshalb noch nicht akatholisch. Das Studium des Alten Testamentes wurde im vorigen Jahrhundert, fast bis gegen das Ende desselben, von den Katholiken vernachlässigt; man braucht nur die Programme gewisser theologischer Lehr- [31] anstalten aus der damaligen Zeit und die von katholischen Exegeten veröffentlichten Schriften ins Auge zu fassen, und man wird sich vieles erklären können. In den letzten Jahren hat sich aber die Sachlage geändert. Hervorragende Kräfte arbeiten an der Lösung der Schwierigkeiten, die nicht wegzuleugnen sind, und ganze Institute, die biblische Akademie, die biblische Kommission und das biblische Institut sind zu dem Zwecke ins Leben getreten. Mit Freude wurde in den exegetischen Kreisen auch die Vorschrift aufgenommen, welche Pius X. erlassen hatte, dass die Theologiestudierenden jetzt jedes Jahr exegetische Vorlesungen anzuhören haben. Da sie nicht gezwungen werden können, dieselben Vorlesungen nochmals anzuhören, so müssen die Professoren der Exegese ihren Stoff jedenfalls auf vier Jahre ausdehnen, wodurch sie in die Lage kommen, wenigstens die wichtigsten Schwierigkeiten berühren zu können.

4. Der Vollständigkeit halber muss noch ein Einwand erwähnt werden, welchen man den jetzigen Exegeten macht. Wenn sie von unbekannten Verfassern sprechen und nach den Quellen forschen, müssen sie oft den bitteren [32] Vorwurf hören, dass sie gegen die heilige Schrift selbst vorgehen, die bei jedem Buche seinen Verfasser erwähne. So sei die Rede von den Büchern Samuels, vom Buche Job usw.

Ist dem wirklich so, oder ist auf diese Weise nicht vielmehr der Inhalt des Buches bezeichnet? Das Buch der Richter führt doch diesen Namen, weil es ihre Taten behandelt; das Buch Job heisst so, weil es die Geschichte dieses Mannes, der in dem Buche in jeder Hinsicht als die Hauptperson erscheint, schildert, und dasselbe ist von vielen andern Büchertiteln zu sagen.

Ausserdem ist zu beachten, dass in den letzten Jahrhunderten vor Christus bei den Juden eine literarische Form im Gebrauch war, wonach der Verfasser die Person eines berühmten Vorgängers annahm. Wir begegnen ihr in den sogenannten Psalmen Salomos, im Buche der Jubiläen, im Buche Henoch, in der Himmelfahrt des Moses, in den Testamenten der zwölf Patriarchen usf. Diese literarische Form drang auch in die kanonischen Bücher ein; so tritt der Verfasser des Buches der Weisheit und der sogenannte Ecclesiastes-Kohelet als Salomo auf, obgleich es ausser allem Zweifel steht, dass die beiden Bücher [33] nicht vor 200 v. Chr. entstanden sind. Weil diese Tatsache früher nicht allgemein bekannt war, gab es Männer, welche die beiden Bücher dem Salomo zuschrieben.

IV. Die historische Kritik.

Hochansehnliche Versammlung! Sie glauben vielleicht, dass ich mit den Aufgaben eines alttestamentlichen Exegeten fertig bin. Das ist leider noch nicht der Fall, aber ich will mich in dem Folgenden so kurz fassen, als es nur möglich ist, um sie nicht zu ermüden. Ich muss noch die historische Kritik erwähnen, das, was man früher einfach die objektive Wahrheit des Erzählten nannte.

Ist das, was das Alte Testament erzählt, auch wirklich wahr, oder enthält es naturgeschichtliche Ungereimtheiten und falsche historische Angaben? Früher hiess es, die Aufgabe eines Exegeten gehe nicht weiter als zur Eruierung und Darlegung der hermeneutischen Wahrheit, d. h. der Exeget brauchte nur zu sagen, was die heilige Schrift lehrt. Damit hatte er seine Pflicht getan, denn an [34] der Wahrheit des Erzählten zweifelte man nicht. Heute kann der Exeget nicht umhin, auch die Wahrheit des Erzählten in Schutz zu nehmen.

1. In Bezug auf die Naturwissenschaften besteht kaum eine nennenswerte Schwierigkeit. Alle geben jetzt zu, dass die Bibel kein Handbuch der Naturwissenschaften sein will und dass sie sich bei diesen Dingen der volkstümlichen Ausdrucksweise bedient. Man gelangte zu diesem Resultate hauptsächlich durch das Studium der biblischen Kosmogonie. Sie kennen den Inhalt des 1. Kapitels der Genesis. Zuerst schafft Gott das Licht, dann das Firmament, durch welches er die Wasser über dem Firmament von denen scheidet, die sich unten befinden; am dritten Tage trennt er die Erde von den unteren Wassern, und die Erde bringt die Pflanzen hervor. An den drei letzten Schöpfungstagen bekommen die geschaffenen Regionen ihr Heer, ihre Bewohner. Oben am Firmament werden die Gestirne erschaffen, in der Luft die Flugtiere, im Wasser die Fische, auf Erden die übrigen Tiere, und zuletzt erscheint der Mensch als Krone der ganzen Schöpfung.

Müssen wir nun annehmen, dass die Schöpfung in dieser Reihenfolge vor sich ge-[35]gangen? Die heilige Schrift gibt uns selbst einen Anhaltspunkt, dass dies nicht der Fall ist. In dem gleich darauf im 2. Kapitel folgenden Bericht ist ja die Ordnung eine ganz andere. Hier ist die Erde zuerst trocken; dann wird das Wasser erwähnt, worauf Adam entsteht, dann Bäume, nachher Tiere und zuletzt Eva. Die heilige Schrift scheint demnach anzudeuten, dass die Ordnung der Schöpfungen im 1. Kapitel nicht chronologisch sein muss. Religiöse Wahrheiten wollte der Verfasser den Israeliten einschärfen, hauptsächlich die eine grosse Wahrheit, gegen die sie sich oft

verfehlten: Gott allein sollst du anbeten, denn er hat alles erschaffen. Auf die Art und Weise nun, wie die Israeliten es zu tun pflegten, zählte er die geschaffenen Dinge auf, und zwar so vollständig, dass für sie keine Lücke blieb. Alles, aber auch alles ohne Ausnahme, hat Gott der Herr ins Dasein gerufen.

2. Viel schwieriger ist es, in jedem Punkte die Wahrheit der im Alten Testamente erzählten Geschichte darzutun. Diesbezüglich sind die Untersuchungen bei weitem noch nicht abgeschlossen. Viele Schwierigkeiten werden ihre Lösung dadurch finden, dass man verschiedene [36] Arten der Geschichte im Alten Testamente unterscheiden wird. Neben geschichtlichen Erzählungen im strengsten Sinne des Wortes mag es auch erbauliche Geschichte geben, wie z. B. in den Büchern Tobias, Esther und Judith. Damit soll gesagt sein, dass die Elemente der Erzählung der Geschichte entnommen sind, dass aber ihre Aneinanderreihungen ein Werk des inspirierten Schriftstellers sein dürfte.

* * *

Bei diesen verschiedenartigen, mühevollen Untersuchungen wird der Exeget an die Worte denken, welche in dem Briefe Pius' X. an Bischof Le Camus vom 11. Jänner 1906 zu lesen sind:

> „In derselben Weise, in der Tat, wie man die Verwegenheit derjenigen verurteilen muss, die sich verleiten lassen, viel mehr dem Geschmacke der Neuheit zu folgen als der Unterweisung der Kirche, und nicht zaudern, auf kritische Prozesse von einer ausschweifenden Freiheit zu rekurrieren, geziemt es sich ebenso, die Stellung derjenigen zu missbilligen, die auf keine Weise wagen, mit der bis vor kurzem herrschenden Schriftexegese zu brechen, auch wenn unter Wahrung der Unver-[37]sehrtheit des Glaubens der weise Fortschritt der Studien sie einlädt, es mutig [‚corragiosamente'] zu tun".

* * *

Doch wir befanden uns bis jetzt gewissermassen nur in den Vorhallen der alttestamentlichen Exegese. Wohl sind sie gross und erhaben, aber es sind immerhin nur Vorhallen zu dem eigentlichen Tempel, der das Allerheiligste birgt. Erst in diesem wird die ganze Pracht offenbar, und mit Ehrfurcht tritt der Hohepriester in dasselbe, um darin den Herrn anzubeten und ihm Opfer darzubringen. Wohl dachte der Exeget bisher bei seinem wissenschaftlichen Streben an den Herrn, aber umso mehr denkt er an ihn, sobald er die

erhabenen Wahrheiten ins Auge fasst, welche das Alte Testament enthält. Wie sich der alttestamentliche Hohepriester durch Reinigungen auf den Eintritt in das Allerheiligste vorbereitete und in aller Demut vor den Herrn trat, so neigt sich der Exeget vor dem Herrn und der ihn umgehenden Schar, der Kirche, bereitwilligst vollführt er die ihm gebotenen Opfer und ruft mit den Seraphim beim Propheten Isaias aus: „Heilig, [38] heilig, heilig ist der Herr der Heerscharen", indem er mit einer kleinen Änderung des Folgenden hinzufügt: „Und voll ist das Alte Testament seiner Herrlichkeit!"

* * *

Ich muss schliessen. Fragt man uns Exegeten, welche Einleitung ins Alte Testament zu benützen wäre, so kommen wir in Verlegenheit. Will man eine kritische Ausgabe des hebräischen Textes haben, ein gutes hebräisches Wörterbuch, die beste hebräische Grammatik, so müssen wir Werke nennen, die nicht von Katholiken verfasst sind. Und so ist auch noch manches andere Gebiet der alttestamentlichen Exegese von Katholiken in letzter Zeit nicht genügend durchforscht worden.

Womöglich sollte bald folgender Plan verwirklicht werden: Es sollte ein vollständiger, mit dem ganzen wissenschaftlichen Apparat versehener Kommentar zum Alten Testamente für den Klerus in lateinischer Sprache herausgegeben werden, wobei eine neue, gute lateinische Übersetzung die Krone der mühevollen Arbeit sein müsste. Darnach sollte – für weitere Kreise – [39] eine genaue Übersetzung in moderne Sprachen, mit wenigen Fussnoten versehen, angefertigt werden. Eine kritische und metrische Ausgabe des hebräischen Textes, ein gediegenes Wörterbuch, eine allen Anforderungen der heutigen Zeit entsprechende Grammatik der hebräischen Sprache und eine gründliche Einleitung ins Alte Testament würden sich dann wie von selbst ergeben.

Literaturverzeichnis

Avneri, Zwi (Hans Lichtenstein), 1978, Artikel „Bavaria“, in: Encyklopaedia Judaica 4 (8. Aufl.), 343–345.

Barthélemy, Dominique, Idéologie et fondation (Etudes et documents sur l'histoire de l'Université de Fribourg / Suisse. Etudes 1), Freiburg (Schweiz): Ed. universitaires, 1991 (Fribourg: Impr. Saint-Paul).

Barwasser, Carsten, „Edward Schillebeeckx OP (* 1914)“, in: Eggensperger, Thomas [et al.] (Hg.), 2007, 231–264.

Beumer, Johannes, Art. „Lamentabili“, LThK², Sechster Band, 1961, 765.

Böhme, Hartmut; Matussek, Peter; Müller, Lothar, Orientierung Kulturwissenschaft: Was sie kann, was sie will (Rowohlts Enzyklopädie 55608), Reinbek bei Hamburg: Rowohlt Taschenbuch Verl., 2007.

Bongardt, Michael, Einführung in die Theologie der Offenbarung (Einführung Theologie), Darmstadt: Wissenschaftliche Buchgesellschaft, 2005.

Braulik, Georg, Die Mittel deuteronomischer Rhetorik: Erhoben aus Deuteronomium 4, 1–40 (Analecta Biblica 68), Rom: Biblical institute press, 1978.

Breviarium juxta ritum Sacri Ordinis Praedicatorum auctoritate Apostolica approbatum et reverendissimi Patris Fr. Andreae Frühwirth ejusdem ordinis Generalis Magistri praemissu, 2 Bände, Mecheln: H. Dessain, 1893.

Bühler, Karl, Sprachtheorie. Die Darstellungsfunktion der Sprache. G. Fischer, Jena 1934; 2., unveränd. Aufl. mit einem Geleitwort von Friedrich Kainz, G. Fischer, Stuttgart 1965; 3. Aufl., G. Fischer, Stuttgart [u. a.] 1999 (UTB für Wissenschaft; 1159).

Chenu, Marie-Dominique, Le Saulchoir: Eine Schule der Theologie (Collection Chenu 2), Berlin: Morus, 2003.

Conway, Micheal A., „Maurice Blondel and Ressourcement, in: Flynn, Gabriel [et al.] (Hg.), 2012, 65–82.

Cormier, Hyacinthe-Marie, L'instruction des novices à l'usage des Frères Prêcheurs: ouvrage pouvant également servir aux novices des autres ordres, aux élèves ecclésiastiques et aux personnes pieuses, Paris: Poussielgue, 2. Aufl. 1905.

Daley, Brian E., „Knowing God in History and in the Church: Dei Verbum and ‚Nouvelle Théologie‘“, in: Flynn, Gabriel [et al.] (Hg.), 2012, 333–354.

Eggensperger, Thomas [et al.] (Hg.), „Mutig in die Zukunft“: dominikanische Beiträge zum Vatikanum II (Dominikanische Quellen und Zeugnisse 10), Leipzig: Benno-Verl., 2007.

Ferretti, Silvia, Cassirer, Panofsky, and Warburg: Symbol, art, and history, New Haven; London: Yale University Press, 1989.

Figl, Johann; Fürlinger, Ernst, „Nostra aetate – Grundsatzerklärung über die Beziehungen der Kirche zu den Religionen, in: Tück, Jan-Heiner (Hg.), Erinnerung an die Zukunft: Das zweite vatikanische Konzil, Freiburg / Basel: Herder, 2012, 405–419.

Flynn, Gabriel [et al.] (Hg.), Ressourcement: A movement for renewal in Twentieth-Century Catholic theology, Oxford: Oxford University Press, 2012.

Gruber, Judith, Theologie Interkulturell: Eine fundamentaltheologische Studie nach dem Cultural Turn (Dissertation zur Erlangung des Doktorgrades der Katholisch-Theologischen Fakultät der Paris-Lodron Universität Salzburg), Salzburg, 2012.

Höpfl, Hildebrand, Art. „Bibelkommission", LThK[1], Zweiter Band, 1931.

Hoyer, Wolfram: „‚… aber der Jude war ihm geblieben'. Ludwig Adler OP (1837–1907)" in: Füllenbach, Elias H.; Miletto, Gianfranco (Hg.), Dominikaner und Juden (Quellen und Forschungen zur Geschichte des Dominikanerordens. Neue Folge) (im Druck).

Jüngel, Eberhard, Art. „Karl Barth", TRE V, 1980.

Kestenberg-Gladstein, Ruth, Art. „Familitants Laws", in: Encyklopaedia Judaica 6 (8. Aufl.), 1978, 1162–1164.

Lohfink, Norbert, Fastenpredigt Vaticanum II, Dei Verbum, Kriftel, St. Vitus, 24.2.2013.

Loughlin, Gerard, „Nouvelle Théologie: A Return to Modernism?", in: Flynn, Gabriel [et al.] (Hg.), 2012, 36–50.

LThK[1], Hg. Buchberger, M., 10 Bde., Freiburg: Herder, 1930–38.

LThK[2], Hg. Höfer, J.; Rahner, K., 11 Bde., Freiburg: Herder, 1957–1967.

LThK[3], Hg. Kasper, W. u. a., 11 Bde., Freiburg: Herder, 1993–2001.

Mayr, Peter H., „Dominikaner Freiburg", in: Hogg, Theodor; Kremer, Bernhard Mathias (Hg.), Wo Gott die Mitte ist: Ordensgemeinschaften in der Erzdiözese Freiburg in Geschichte und Gegenwart. Lindenberg: Kunstverl. Fink, 2002, 122f.

Mettepenningen, Jürgen, „Nouvelle Théologie: Four Historical Stages of Theological Reform towards Ressourcement", in Flynn, Gabriel [et al.] (Hg.), 2012, 172–184.

Meyer, Michael A., Anfänge des Modernen Judentums. Jüdische Identität in Deutschland 1749–1824 (Beck'sche Reihe 1955), München: C. H. Beck, 2011.

Montagnes, Bernard, Marie-Joseph Lagrange: une biographie critique, Paris: Ed. du Cerf, 2004.

Mörsdorf, Klaus, Art. „Kardinalskongregationen", LThK[2], Fünfter Band, 1960.

Mühling-Schlapkohl, Markus, Art. „Ebner, Ferdinand", RGG 2, 1999.

Oberlinner, Lorenz, Art. „Vögtle, Anton", LThK[3], Zehnter Band, 2001.

Oesterreicher, Johannes M., Erklärung über das Verhältnis der Kirche zu den nichtchristlichen Religionen, kommentierende Einleitung, in: Brechter, Heinrich Suso u. a. (Hg.), Das Zweite Vatikanische Konzil: Konstitutionen, Dekrete und Erklärungen, Teil II (Lexikon für Theologie und Kirche), Freiburg u. a.: Herder, 1967, 406–478.

Pesch, Otto Hermann, „Mannes Dominikus Koster OP (1901–1981)", in: Eggensperger, Thomas [et al.] (Hg.), 2007, 191–230.

Pilz, Johannes Chr., Art. „Antimodernisteneid", LThK Erster Band, 1957.

Petráček, Tomáš, Le père Vincent Zapletal O.P. (1867–1938): Portrait d'un exégète catholique (Studia Friburgensia 102. Series historica 6) Fribourg (Suisse): Academic Press, 2007.

Ratzinger, Joseph, Dogmatische Konstitution über die göttliche Offenbarung, Einleitung und Kommentar zum I. Kapitel, in: Heinrich Suso Brechter u. a. (Hg.), Das Zweite Vatikanische Konzil: Konstitutionen, Dekrete und Erklärungen, Teil II (Lexikon für Theologie und Kirche), Freiburg u. a.: Herder, 1967, 497–515.

Reikerstorfer, Johann, „Der Wandel im Offenbarungsverständnis. Vatikanum I – Vatikanum II – weiterführende Perspektiven, in: Tück, Jan-Heiner (Hg.), Erinnerung an die Zukunft: Das zweite vatikanische Konzil, Freiburg / Basel: Herder, 2012, 477–490.

Religion in Geschichte und Gegenwart (RGG), 8 Bde., Tübingen: Mohr Siebeck, 1998–2007.

Schößler, Franziska, Literaturwissenschaft als Kulturwissenschaft: Eine Einführung (UTB 2765), Tübingen: A. Franke, 2006.

Riedele, Martin Benno: Die Wiederkunft Christi nach den katholischen Briefen. (1921) XVII, 180 Bl. Diss.1020. https://fedora.phaidra.univie.ac.at/fedora/get/o:15315/bdef .../download, Zugriff am 27.11.2013.

Schütz, Christian, Art. „Martin Buber", TRE VII, 1981.

Smend, Rudolf, Deutsche Alttestamentler in drei Jahrhunderten, Göttingen: Vandenhoeck & Ruprecht, 1989.

Theologische Realenzyklopädie (TRE), 36 Bde., Berlin / New York: de Gruyter, 1977–2007.

Tück, Jan Heiner (Hg.), Erinnerung an die Zukunft: Das zweite vatikanische Konzil, Freiburg; Basel: Herder, 2012.

Viviano, Benedict T., „The Renewal of Biblical Studies in France 1934–1954 as an Element in Theological Ressourcement, in: Flynn, Gabriel [et al.] (Hg.), 2012, 305–317.

Walz, Angelus, Andreas Kardinal Frühwirth (1845–1933): Ein Zeit- und Lebensbild, Wien: Herder,1950.

Walz, Angelus, Dominikaner und Dominikanerinnen in Süddeutschland (1225–1966), Meitingen [etc.]: Kyrios-Verl., 1967.

Wohlmuth, Josef (Hg.), Dekrete der ökumenischen Konzilien = Conciliorum oecumenicorum decreta / besorgt von Giuseppe Alberigo ... [et al.]; in Zusammenarb. mit Hubert Jedin ; hrsg. vom Istituto per le scienze religiose, Bologna. Bd. 3, Konzilien der Neuzeit: Konzil von Trient (1545–1563), Erstes Vatikanisches Konzil (1869/70), Zweites Vatikanisches Konzil (1962–1965), Indices, im Auftrag der Görres-Gesellschaft, Paderborn; Zürich [etc.]: F. Schöningh, 2002.

Erinnerungen an die Taiwan-Mission in den Jahren 1959–2004

Paul Heribert Welte OP

1. Wie ich die Taiwan-Mission erlebte (1959–2004)

Im Zuge der Vorbereitung der 800-Jahr-Feier unseres Ordens wurde ich vom Provinzial der Teutonia, P. Dr. Johannes Bunnenberg OP, eingeladen, von meinen Erfahrungen in der Taiwan-Mission zu berichten. Erwartet wurde von mir keine Chronik[1] der Mission in Taiwan, keine letztgültige Darstellung, sondern schlicht Erinnerungen von einem, der dabei war. Zu Anfang wurde ich bisweilen gefragt:

Wie bist Du überhaupt nach Taiwan und China gekommen?
Das fragten mich in Deutschland und Amerika, Taiwan und China nicht nur andere, sondern manchmal fragte ich mich das selbst, zum Beispiel, als ich in der Nähe von Peking die Große Mauer, im Hafen von Fuchow die Schleppschiffe und bei einer Vorlesung über dem Seminar von Shanghai die Flagge des kommunistischen Chinas wehen sah.

Mein Interesse an der Missionsarbeit
Nun, der Missionsgedanke faszinierte mich schon sehr früh. In den eigentlich verbotenen katholischen Jugendgruppen wurden während des Dritten Reiches alte Hefte des „Scheideweg" aufbewahrt und gelesen. Darin wurde die Geschichte des Christentums in Korea beschrieben. Die Bauern, bei denen ich in den Nachkriegsjahren oft zur Erntehilfe war, hatten alte Hefte der von den Steyler Missionaren herausgegebenen „Stadt Gottes". In den letzten Schuljahren las ich gerne die Zeitschrift „Die Katholischen Missionen". All dies trug dazu bei, dass ich selber Missionar werden wollte.

Als ich im Verlauf von Exerzitien in Beuron mit einem Benediktiner darüber sprach, riet er mir, in einen der alten großen Orden einzutreten,

1 Ein Visitator rügte einmal, dass wir schon länger keine Chronik führten. In der Tat, ein Versäumnis.

die Missionen haben. Wegen der Predigten von P. Diego Goetz waren in Freiburg die Dominikaner bekannt. Bevor ich jedoch mit dem Orden Kontakt aufnahm, erkundigte ich mich bei dem Redaktor der „Katholischen Missionen", ob die Dominikaner eine Mission hätten. Die Antwort des Jesuiten kam prompt: Ja, die Dominikaner hätten eine Mission in China in der Provinz Fukien. Als ich noch vor dem Ordenseintritt den damaligen Provinzial der süddeutschen Provinz P. Marianus Vetter aufsuchte, sprach ich von meinem Interesse an der Mission. Er wies darauf hin, dass die Chinamission eigentlich Sache der norddeutschen Provinz Teutonia sei, dass aber auch ein Mitbruder der süddeutschen Provinz (P. Richard Krupicka) in diese Mission entsandt worden sei.[2] So stand von Anfang an der Missionsgedanke über meinem Leben im Dominikanerorden.

Wie kam ich nach Taiwan?

Nach dem Sieg der Kommunisten und der Gründung der sogenannten „Chinesischen Volksrepublik" wurden unsere deutschen Mitbrüder, wie andere ausländische Missionare, „für ewig aus dem Reich der Mitte" ausgewiesen. Doch bald danach übernahm die Teutonia 1954 eine Mission im südlichsten Landkreis Taiwans. Damals nannte man Taiwan oft noch (mit einem auf die Portugiesen zurückgehendem Namen) *Formosa* (= „Schöne Insel"). So konnten nach einem kurzen Aufenthalt in Europa einige der ‚alten' Missionare in dem nicht von den Kommunisten eroberten (National-)China auf der Insel Taiwan ihre Missionsarbeit im chinesischen Volk fortsetzen. Natürlich brauchten sie neue Mitarbeiter. Während früher manche Mitbrüder auch einfach in die Mission geschickt wurden, suchten nun die Oberen und die ‚alten' Missionare nach Freiwilligen für die neu übernommene Mission in Taiwan.

Da man in den frühen fünfziger Jahren immer wieder von Verfolgung der Kirche und Ausweisungen von Missionaren hörte und Berichte der eigenen Mitbrüder erhielt, war bei mir der Wunsch, Missionar zu werden, etwas zurückgetreten. Darum galt ich sogar nicht einmal als ein an der Mission Interessierter, zumal ich zur süddeutschen Provinz gehöre, die damals auch zahlenmäßig schwächer war als die für die Mission zuständige Teutonia. So wusste ich nichts von einem Treffen von (sechs?) an der Mis-

2 Als ich etwa fünf Jahre später in die Taiwan-Mission gehen wollte, erinnerte ich den Provinzial an dieses Gespräch.

sion interessierten Mitbrüdern[3] mit den ‚alten' Missionaren. Doch sprach mich einmal im Kreuzgang von Walberberg der erste Vicarius Provincialis der Taiwan-Mission, P. Albin Cramer, an, in die Mission nach Taiwan zu kommen.

Ende 1955 schrieb ich dem damaligen Provinzial P. Marianus Vetter, dass ich in die Taiwan-Mission gehen wolle. Obwohl er andere Pläne für mich hatte und obgleich unsere Provinz nicht mit Berufen gesegnet war, gab er sein Placet zu meinem Plan, mit P. Theodor im folgenden Jahr zur Vorbereitung für die Mission zuerst nach Kalifornien zu gehen, um das Studium abzuschließen und Englisch zu lernen. Auf Drängen des damaligen Regens des Studienhauses in Walberberg (P. Adolf Hoffmann) gab er mir den Auftrag, das Lektorat in Kalifornien zu machen.

Langwierige Vorbereitung

In Kalifornien

Sechs Wochen nach der Priesterweihe in Walberberg und der Primiz im Freiburger Münster war ich zusammen mit P. Theodor Kucznierz im Studienhaus der Dominikaner in Oakland in der Nähe von San Francisco und Berkeley. Dieser Aufenthalt in Amerika war für uns sehr wertvoll: Wir lernten Englisch, was wir in Taiwan im Verkehr mit anderen Missionaren und den Behörden sowie in der Sprachschule dringend brauchten. Wir lernten einen anderen Stil des Christ- und Dominikaner-Seins kennen und schätzen. Ein Mitbruder half uns, den Führerschein zu machen.[4] Da P. Theodor in allem (Geburt, Ordenseintritt, Studium, Priesterweihe) mir ein Jahr voraus ist, blieb er nur für ein Jahr in Kalifornien und machte sich schon 1957 auf den Seeweg über Japan nach Taiwan. Nach einem weiteren Jahr des Studiums bis zum Lektorat und einem Besuch in Cincinnati[5] machte ich mich Ende 1958 per Frachtschiff auf den Weg über den Pazifik und Japan auf den Weg nach Taiwan, wo ich im Januar 1959 zum ersten Mal (national-)chinesischen Boden betrat.

---

3 Doch nur einer dieser Gruppe – P. Theodor Kucznierz – kam schließlich nach Taiwan.

4 Als bei ihrem ersten Versuch, den Führerschein zu machen, P. Theodor und ein Spanier durchgefallen waren, hatte sich das im Nu im Konvent durchgesprochen und führte zu wohlwollender Heiterkeit sogar beim lateinischen Chorgebet.

5 Bei P. Agilolf Piepenbreier, der während des Krieges von Amerika aus die Mission unterstützte, und Katherine Landwehr, einer Kusine von P. Gordian Landwehr, die nach dem Krieg den Wiederaufbau der Teutonia tatkräftig förderte.

Sprachstudium

Damals waren schon zwei ‚neue' Mitbrüder (P. Matthias Grewe und P. Theodor Kucznierz) etwa ein Jahr zuvor nach Taiwan gekommen und bemühten sich, mit Hilfe von Grundschullehrern Mandarin-Chinesisch zu lernen. Vielleicht haben es die damaligen Oberen (richtig!) gesehen, dass ich auf diese Weise die Sprache nie lernen könnte. So wurden P. Theodor und ich zu der von den Jesuiten im Norden Taiwans geführten Sprachschule geschickt, um Mandarin-Chinesisch zu lernen.

Doch schon bevor man das erste Wort lernt, muss die Frage entschieden werden: Mit welcher Sprache fängt man an? In Taiwan werden nämlich nicht nur 14 (unter sich sehr verschiedene) Sprachen der Ureinwohner, sondern auch drei verschiedene chinesische Sprachen gesprochen: nämlich Taiwanesisch (Amoy Dialekt),[6] Hakka (die Sprache einer im Süden Chinas, Taiwan, Singapur und Malaysia verbreiteten chinesischen Volksgruppe) und Mandarin (das sowohl in Festlandchina wie in Taiwan die offizielle Umgangssprache ist). Zwar nennt man Taiwanesisch und Hakka oft „Dialekte", doch sind sie eigentlich (wie Deutsch und Schwedisch) verschiedene Sprachen. Wenn man eine gelernt hat, kann man die andere nicht verstehen, aber leichter lernen. Bei der Entscheidung der Frage „Welche Sprache sollten neue Missionare (zuerst) lernen?" gingen die Orden verschiedene Wege: Die spanischen Dominikaner und die amerikanischen Maryknoll Missionare lernten meistens zuerst einen der „Dialekte"; die Jesuiten und wir deutsche Dominikaner hingegen lernten zuerst Mandarin. Alles hat Vor- und Nachteile. Wer einen Dialekt lernt, steht den Einheimischen näher, wirkt aber auf viele Menschen in Taiwan wie ein Afrikaner in Deutschland, der nur Plattdeutsch oder Schweizerdeutsch gelernt hat. Wer Mandarin lernt, dem stehen bessere Lehrmittel zur Verfügung und der kann sich leichter überall im Riesenreich China mit den Menschen verständigen, wirkt aber in Taiwan wie ein nur Hochdeutsch sprechender Deutscher in der Schweiz.

Im Hinblick auf meine spätere Aufgabe, an die damals keiner dachte, war es gut, dass ich zwei Jahre an der Sprachschule Mandarin lernen konnte. In Taiwan war ich der erste Dominikaner, der volle zwei Jahre zur Sprachschule gehen konnte. Bei durchschnittlicher Begabung sind zwei Jahre das Minimum für ein Studium der chinesischen Sprache. Wenn ich

6 Diesem Dialekt verdanken wir das Wort „Tee", das mit dem Getränk nach Europa kam.

später gefragt wurde: „Wie lange braucht man, um Chinesisch zu lernen?“, gab ich oft die Antwort: „Mindestens zwei Jahre an der Sprachschule und den Rest des Lebens.“ Zu jener Zeit aber war bei uns deutschen Dominikanern ein zweijähriges Sprachstudium nicht selbstverständlich, und in meinem Fall schon gar nicht. Ich hatte ja nicht wie die Kursgenossen im September 1958, sondern erst im Februar 1959 mit dem Studium begonnen; nach einiger Zeit und mit viel Mühe hatte ich auch den Kurs erreicht, der im Sommer 1960 eigentlich endete. Trotz gewisser Ungeduld von Seiten anderer Mitbrüder aber sagte der damalige Vicarius Provincialis P. Richard Krupicka zu mir: „Wenn Du zwei volle Jahre willst, kannst Du sie haben“. Und ich sagte: „Ich will“ und blieb dann noch bis Weihnachten 1960 an der Sprachschule.

Tätigkeiten in Taiwan

Das Missionsgebiet, das die Teutonia ein paar Jahre zuvor übernommen hatte, war ein Teil der (erst später offiziell errichteten) Diözese Kaohsiung. Als ich nach Taiwan kam, bestanden in unserem Distrikt (im Landkreis Pingtung) schon etwa fünf Missionsstationen, an denen kleine Gemeinden entstanden waren. P. Walter Lödding (und später auch P. Mattias Grewe) gab(en) Deutschunterricht am Medical College in Kaohsiung. Doch betrachteten alle Missionare die Arbeit auf den Missionsstationen als ihre Hauptaufgabe, die auch die ‚neuen‘ Missionare einmal übernehmen sollten.

In der Missionsstation Tungkang

In diesem Sinne kam ich Anfang 1961 nach Tungkang, wo P. Franz Späth schon seit einigen Jahren gewirkt hatte. Wie der Name andeutet („Osthafen“), ist der Ort eine Hafen- und Fischerstadt. Obwohl er an der Westküste Taiwans liegt, wird er *Ost*hafen genannt, denn für die in der Straße von Formosa arbeitenden Fischer liegt er eben im Osten. Mit ihren kleinen Schiffen fahren sie oft weit hinaus aufs Meer, zu den Philippinen, ja bis in die Nähe von Neuseeland und Australien. Dabei sind sie vielen Gefahren wie Taifunen und Seeräubern ausgesetzt. In diesen Nöten nehmen sie oft Zuflucht zu ihrer traditionellen Religion, die in der Zeit nach dem Krieg eine Renaissance erlebte. Die kleine Stadt hatte eine Vielzahl von teils aufwendig restaurierten Tempeln. Alle drei Jahre findet ein mehrtägiges Tempelfest mit vielen Riten und Prozessionen statt. Als ich einmal zusehen

wollte, wie die Träger der Statuen von Göttern und Geistern über glühende Kohlen gehen, merkte ich, dass mir meine kleine Brieftasche gestohlen worden war. Es müssen ‚gute' Diebe gewesen sein, die es nur auf mein Geld (200 NT = etwa 20 DM) abgesehen hatten, mir aber sonst nicht schaden wollten. Darum warfen sie die Brieftasche, in der auch mein Führerschein war, in einen Postkasten. Schon am folgenden Tag, einem Sonntag, wurde sie mir von der Post ins Haus gebracht. Ein Zeitungsbericht über das Tempelfest berichtete mit einem unübersetzbarem Wortspiel[7] von diesem kleinen Zwischenfall: „Ein Dieb (dao) ist tugendhaft (dao), so berichtet (dao) der Missionar."

In dieser Stadt von ca. 30 000 Einwohnern bekam ich einen kleinen Eindruck von der Bedeutung der Religionssoziologie: Für Leute, die tief in die Gesellschaft verwoben sind, ist es äußerst schwierig, Christ zu werden. Das bekam P. Franz zu spüren. Er hatte einmal in einem Fischerdistrikt eine kleine ‚Station' eröffnet. Doch bald musste er sie schließen, weil nur wenige sich dafür interessierten. Dabei spielte die Furcht vor den bislang verehrten Geistern eine Rolle: Wenn Unglück, Krankheit, Misserfolg Christen trifft, sehen die Nachbarn darin eine Strafe der Geister. Die Mutter einer aus dem Ort stammenden Ordensschwester wagte nicht, auch nur den Hof der Kirche zu betreten. Ein Apotheker für chinesische Arzneien, dessen Tochter katholisch wurde und einer sehr konservativen Gemeinschaft beigetreten ist, war Präses der von P. Theodor gegründeten Caritas-Gruppe, doch wurden er und andere Mitglieder dieser Caritas Gruppe nicht Christen. Sie wären in dieser von der traditionellen Religion bestimmten Stadt zu Außenseitern geworden. So sind in der Stadt Tungkang nur wenige eigentlich einheimische Menschen Christen geworden.

Mehr Anklang fand die Mission unter den mit Chiang Kai Shek vor den Kommunisten geflüchteten (sogenannten) ‚Festländern'. In Tungkang, der kleinen Fischerstadt, bestand damals eine Akademie der Luftwaffe. Die Lehrer (Offiziere) und ihre Familien lebten in eigenen Siedlungen und hatten auch eigene Schulen für ihre Kinder. Aus ihrer Heimat geflohen und in Taiwan nicht integriert, waren sie nicht so sehr dem Druck der einheimischen Religion ausgesetzt und darum zugänglicher für das Christentum als die ‚Taiwanesen'. Überdies war unter diesen Leuten eine Katholikin aus Shanghai, mit deren Hilfe P. Franz guten Kontakt

7 Der für uns scheinbar gleiche Laut „dao" wird im Chinesischen in verschiedenen Tönen gesprochen und mit verschiedenen Zeichen geschrieben.

zu Familien fand. So wurden im Laufe der Zeit mehrere Familien, meistens mit 4–6 Kindern, getauft. Bei ihnen und auch bei der jüngeren Generation konnte ich das in der Sprachschule gelernte Mandarin gebrauchen und einüben.

In den fünfziger und sechziger Jahren des vergangenen Jahrhunderts kamen zahlreiche Missionare, die vom kommunistischen Regime „für ewig aus dem Reich der Mitte verbannt" worden waren, nach Taiwan und gründeten Gemeinden und bauten Kirchen in Gebieten, in denen man bislang die katholische Kirche nicht kannte. Die in Peking von amerikanischen Benediktinern gegründete, später von den Steyler Missionaren geführte, nach ihrer Machtergreifung aber von den Kommunisten geschlossene Katholische Universität entstand in Taiwan von neuem. Ein Bischof gründete ein Priesterseminar für Spätberufene. Die Jesuiten planten die Verlegung ihrer (in Shanghai gegründeten und später in den Philippinen weitergeführten) Theologischen Fakultät nach Taiwan. Schwesterngemeinschaften nahmen einheimische Novizinnen auf. Auch die mit uns (schon in China) arbeitenden Ilanzer Dominikanerinnen eröffneten ein Noviziat.

Diese Entwicklung beeinflusste auch unsere Einstellung zu unserer Aufgabe und unsere Planungen. Bei einer Visitation (1965) durch den Provinzial P. Friedrich Quatmann kam es zu einem gewissen Wandel im Verständnis unserer Aufgabe in Taiwan: Wir sollten uns nicht wie bisher ausschließlich auf die missionarische und pastorale Arbeit in den Stationen und Pfarreien beschränken, sondern einen Beitrag leisten zum Auf- und Ausbau der Lokalkirche Taiwans durch Förderung der Caritasarbeit und Ausbildung des einheimischen Priesternachwuchses. Und wir planten, chinesische Kandidaten in den Orden aufzunehmen und – wie die Jesuiten – an der Mission interessierte deutsche Mitbrüder nach Taiwan zu holen, sie dort die Sprache lernen und in Taiwan ihr theologisches Studium machen zu lassen. Dafür wurde in der Nähe der Universität ein Haus gebaut, für die an der Universität und an der Theologischen Fakultät studierenden Dominikaner. Diese Entwicklung wirkte sich darin aus, dass ich nicht (wie es ursprünglich auch von mir gemeint war) nach einem Jahr an der Sprachschule für Taiwanesisch wieder in die Arbeit auf einer Missionsstation zurückkehrte, sondern im Priesterseminar für Spätberufene Dozent wurde.[8]

8 P. Marianus Vetter, der mich beauftragt hatte, in Amerika das Lektorat zu machen, schrieb mir damals: „So hat Ihr Lektorat doch seinen Sinn gefunden".

Dozent in einem Priesterseminar für Spätberufene
Manche der Seminaristen waren älter als ich, stammten vom Festland aus katholischen Familien und wollten schon früher Priester werden. Doch im Lauf des Bürgerkrieges zwischen Nationalisten und Kommunisten kamen sie in die Armee Chiang Kai Sheks und mit ihr nach Taiwan. Nach Beendigung des Wehrdienstes wollten sie ihren Weg zum Priestertum wieder aufnehmen. Natürlich fehlte ihnen vieles in der schulischen Ausbildung. Um ihnen eine Möglichkeit zu geben, Priester zu werden, gründete der spätere Erzbischof von Taipei dieses Seminar für Spätberufene, das auch andere Kandidaten[9] fürs Priestertum vorbereiten sollte. Natürlich konnten in diesem Seminar (anders als früher in den chinesischen Seminaren) die Vorlesungen nicht auf Latein, sondern mussten in Mandarin-Chinesisch gegeben werden. So wurde ich (meines Wissens) der erste, der Dogmatik in Chinesisch gab.

Von manchen – besonders von spanischen – Mitbrüdern wurde ich gelegentlich gefragt, ob es überhaupt möglich sei, in chinesischer Sprache Theologie zu lehren. Gewiss, leicht war es damals besonders für einen Ausländer nicht.[10] Doch war die Notwendigkeit, in Chinesisch zu unterrichten, eine fruchtbare Herausforderung, den christlichen Glauben zu überdenken und ohne manche der bei uns geläufigen und scheinbar selbstverständlichen, jedoch oft unverständlichen Begriffen und Klischees, darzustellen.[11]

Drei Jahre (1965–1968) blieb ich in diesem Seminar und gab Vorlesungen über Fundamentaltheologie und Dogmatik. Vieles davon war gewiss sehr unvollkommen, aber doch nicht wertlos, denn in diesen Jahren gab es überhaupt keine andere theologische Ausbildungsstätte in Taiwan und kein Lehrmaterial in Chinesisch. Dem Mangel an theologischer Literatur versuchte ich abzuhelfen durch die Mitarbeit an der Übersetzung des

9 Solche, die aus irgendeinem Grund kein Abitur gemacht oder die zentrale Aufnahmeprüfung für die Universität nicht geschafft hatten.

10 Seither hat sich die Situation wesentlich gebessert: Eine von der theologischen Fakultät der Fujen Universität herausgegebene Reihe theologischer Studien zählt schon über 50 Bände. Es wurden verschiedene Nachschlagewerke geschaffen oder übersetzt.

11 Diese Erfahrung fand ihren (zugegeben etwas boshaften) Ausdruck in dem „guten Rat" für die europäische Theologie: Neben jedem europäischen theologischem Autor sollte ein gut Deutsch sprechender sich auf den Lehrdienst vorbereitender Chinese sitzen und immer wieder dazwischen fragen: „Was meinen Sie damit? Wenn ich das übersetzen will, wie könnte man das anders sagen? Unsere chinesischen Theologen verstehen ja kein Theologen-Chinesisch."

Lehrbuchs „Grundriss der Dogmatik“ von Ludwig Ott. In dieser Zeit entstanden mit Hilfe von Studenten meine ersten chinesischen Büchlein: Kommentare zur Offenbarungskonstitution und zum Dekret über das Laienapostolat. Diese Kommentare wurden von in Rom studierenden Chinesen und in Taiwan von einem bekannten Priester gerne in Schulungskursen benutzt. Bis heute sind sie die einzigen in chinesischer Sprache verfassten Kommentare der Konzilsdokumente.

An der Theologischen Fakultät in Taipei

Aufgrund solcher Schriften kannten mich die Jesuiten, die ihre theologische Fakultät 1967 nach Taiwan brachten und in der Nähe der Universität gleichsam neu gründeten. Im ersten Jahr gaben sie zwar (hauptsächlich für ihre eigenen Studenten) die Vorlesungen noch in Latein und Englisch. Ein Jahr später jedoch nahmen sie Priesterkandidaten der Diözesen, Mitglieder anderer Orden und Schwesterngemeinschaften als Studenten und Studentinnen auf und machten an dieser von Rom anerkannten Theologischen Fakultät Chinesisch zur Unterrichtssprache.[12] Da man wusste, dass wir in der Nähe der Universität ein Haus bauten und dass ich nach Taipei kommen würde, wurde ich vom Provinzial der Jesuiten eingeladen, an dieser Fakultät zu unterrichten. Mittlerweile hatten ja die ersten chinesischen Ordenskandidaten ihr Noviziat gemacht; deutsche Mitbrüder hatten mit dem Sprachstudium begonnen; der Bau des Hauses bei der Universität wurde in Angriff genommen. So brach ich meine Tätigkeit im Spätberufenenseminar im Süden Taiwans ab, siedelte in den Norden Taiwans über und nahm Kurse an der Theologischen Fakultät auf. Für die Jesuiten war meine erste Tätigkeit (1968–1970) vermutlich nicht nur eine befristete Aushilfe, sondern auch eine Zeit des ‚Ausprobierens‘ meiner Eignung und meines Interesses. Da ich weiterhin bei dieser Arbeit bleiben wollte und die Mitbrüder und Oberen – trotz vieler Arbeit in den Missionsstationen – keinen unüberwindlichen Widerstand leisteten, wollte und konnte ich nochmals Theologie studieren und an der Graduate Theological Union in Berkeley (Kalifornien) das Doktorat (Th. D) erwerben.

Danach (1974) nahm ich wieder meine ‚alte‘ Arbeit auf: Vorlesungen über Erbsünde, Soteriologie, Gnadenlehre, Mariologie und über die Sakra-

---

12 Dies verlangte natürlich die Ausarbeitung einer chinesischen theologischen Terminologie. Daran beteiligte sich später P. Erwin Schawe bei der Abfassung eines englisch-chinesischen Wörterbuchs.

mente der Eucharistie, der Versöhnung und der Krankensalbung. Mit Hilfe von Studentinnen konnte ich Bücher über die (im chinesischen Kulturraum brisante) Frage der Erbsünde, über Erlösungs- und Gnadenlehre, über die Eucharistie und die Krankensalbung und über den ersten Teil der Fundamentaltheologie veröffentlichen. Diese Bücher enthalten gewiss nicht der theologischen Weisheit allerletzten Schluss, doch offensichtlich erwiesen sie sich als hilfreich im chinesischen Sprachraum (Festlandchina, Taiwan, Hongkong, Singapur und in Teilen von Malaysia). So wurden trotz des kleinen Marktes für theologische Literatur fast alle meine Bücher mindestens zweimal aufgelegt. Und man wird – leider – vermutlich noch längere Zeit auf sie angewiesen bleiben.

In Festlandchina

Erster Besuch in China

In den ersten (über 25) Jahren seit meiner Ankunft in Taiwan (1959) war es undenkbar, dass ich jemals das chinesische Festland betreten würde.[13] Festlandchina betrachtete Taiwan als eine abtrünnige Provinz. Die nationalchinesische Regierung auf der kleinen Insel Taiwan beanspruchte, die einzige rechtmäßige Regierung des ganzen riesigen Chinas zu sein. Jede Seite versprach der anderen „Befreiung" und drohte mit militärischer Gewalt. Zur Zeit der auch für treue Kommunisten schrecklichen „Großen Kulturrevolution" (1966–1976) fügten die NachrichtensprecherInnen im taiwanischen Fernsehen den Namen der führenden Leute auf dem Festland oftmals den Titel „Bandit" bei. Erst mit dem Aufstieg von Deng Xiaoping kam es auf Seiten Chinas zu einer gewissen Liberalisierung im Innern, zu einer vorsichtigen Öffnung nach Außen, zu einer langsamen Entspannung des Verhältnisses zu Taiwan.

Damit wurden – anfangs nur über Hongkong und offiziell ‚geheime' – Besuche von Leuten aus Taiwan aufs chinesische Festland zu ihren Verwandten möglich. P. Simon Hsü, der ursprünglich zur Teutonia gehörte, konnte so nach Jahrzehnten in seiner Heimat seine Schwester wieder sehen. Und als es noch ein wenig den Reiz des Verbotenen hatte, kam ich im Anschluss an eine Konferenz in Hongkong im Jahr 1984 zum ersten

13 Nur einmal (vermutlich war es 1970) brachte mich von Hongkong P. Romanus Zeller an die Grenze, wo man von einem Hügel aus einen kleinen Blick ins damals verschlossene Reich der Mitte werfen konnte.

Mal als Tourist nach China. Vom Holy Spirit Study Center in Hongkong, welches schon damals die Beziehung zur chinesischen Kirche pflegte, hatte ich einige Adressen erhalten. So besuchte ich eine kleine Kirche und die Kathedrale in Canton, ein erst ein Jahr früher eröffnetes Seminar in Chengdu, die Kathedrale in Shanghai und das sich damals organisierende Nationale Seminar in Peking. Als ich in Shanghai den späteren Bischof von Shanghai zu erreichen suchte, sagte mir zu meiner großen Freude eine Frau: „Ich kenne Ihre Bücher." Als ich im Nationalen Seminar in Peking mit dem leitenden Bischof und einigen Lehrern sprach, wussten sie schon von meinem Buch über die Erbsünde und die Kontroverse darum. Die Erfahrung dieses Besuchs in China verstärkte bei mir die Überzeugung von der Wichtigkeit, theologisches Lehrmaterial für die chinesische Kirche zu schaffen. Nach Taiwan zurückgekehrt, konnte ich in den folgenden Jahren mit Hilfe von Studentinnen dazu einen Beitrag leisten: durch meine Bücher über Eucharistie und Krankensalbung, Erlösungs- und Gnadenlehre und über den ersten Teil der Fundamentaltheologie. Doch bald bot sich eine neue Möglichkeit, der chinesischen Kirche einen Dienst zu leisten.

Gastdozent in Chinesischen Priesterseminaren

Nach langem hartnäckigen Bemühen erlangte der Bischof von Shanghai von den Behörden die Erlaubnis, für zeitlich befristete Kurse im Seminar bei Shanghai Dozenten aus Hongkong, Taiwan und Übersee einzuladen. So gaben im Jahr 1989 der Liturgiker von Hongkong, der spätere Bischof von Hongkong Kardinal Zen, und drei Jesuiten philosophische und theologische Kurse im damals größten Seminar in China. Im selben Jahr erhielt ich völlig überraschend vom damaligen Direktor des Holy Spirit Center, dem heutigen Bischof von Hongkong, Dr. John Tong, einen Brief mit der Anfrage, ob ich im kommenden Jahr (1990) zu Vorlesungen im Seminar von Shanghai gehen könne. Er drängte mich, diese Möglichkeit wahrzunehmen. Nach telefonischer Rücksprache mit P. Theodor sagte ich nach Hongkong zu. Ein paar Tage später lag in meinem Fach ein Brief des Bischofs von Shanghai. Nach den vielen Jahren, in denen es keinerlei Postverbindung zwischen dem Festland und Taiwan gab, zeigte sich darin eine große Wende für Taiwan und für mich.

So kam ich im September 1990 zum ersten Mal (nicht mehr als Tourist, sondern als ‚Missionar') nach China. Meine Tätigkeit war zugleich illegal und legal: Sie war illegal, weil ich für eine derartige Tätigkeit eigent-

lich die Einladung einer Universität brauchte.[14] Sie war aber auch legal, denn die zuständige Behörde, das Büro für Religionsangelegenheiten in Shanghai (und später in Xi An und Wuhan), wusste Bescheid und hatte grünes Licht gegeben. Gleich am Tag nach meiner ersten Ankunft im Seminar von Shanghai kamen drei Herren dieses Büros und gaben mir ein paar Anweisungen: Ich könne ruhig dem Papst treu sein, doch habe der in China nichts zu sagen. Ich solle zu den Studenten nur die gewöhnliche Lehrer-Schüler Beziehung haben.[15] Ich könne nur deshalb im Seminar unterrichten, weil ich ein Freund des Bischofs sei. Diese Erlaubnis sei aber nur ein Experiment.

Zu gleicher Zeit war als Gastdozent im Seminar der Salesianer P. Josef Zen tätig, der später Weihbischof, danach Bischof von Hongkong und schließlich Kardinal wurde. Mit ihm ging ich oft nach den Mahlzeiten im Hof des Seminars in Sichtweite der Seminaristen spazieren. Wir plauderten, diskutierten und wurden gute Freunde. Vielleicht war es für die Studenten wichtiger als unsere Vorlesungen zu hören, immer wieder zu sehen, dass hier ein Chinese und ein Ausländer, ein Salesianer und ein Dominikaner gute Freunde waren. Offensichtlich waren auch die Behörden mit uns zufrieden, denn nach zwei oder drei Jahren konnten auch andere Seminare Leute aus Hongkong, Taiwan und Übersee als Gastdozenten einladen. So war ich insgesamt fünfmal in Shanghai, viermal in Xi An, wo seit ca. 2 200 Jahren die Terrakottaarmee das Grab des ersten Kaisers von China bewacht, und einmal in Wuhan, wo Mao Tse Tung mit seinem Schwimmen im Yangtse seine Fitness demonstrierte.

Anfangs war dieser Einsatz in den chinesischen Priesterseminaren nicht unumstritten. Diese Seminare waren ja der Patriotischen Vereinigung Chinesischer Katholiken, dem Büro für Religionsangelegenheiten und der Einheitsfront unterstellt. 1990 lebte im Seminar von Shanghai ein „Berater“ der Religionsbehörde. Die Studenten bekamen politischen Unterricht. Ihre Lehrer (auch Priester) mussten manchmal zu Schulungskursen gehen. So ist es begreiflich, dass manche Leute, die selbst die (‚Befreiung‘ genannte) Machtergreifung der Kommunisten und die Gründung

---

14 Das erfuhr ich, als mit dieser Begründung mir ein Visum von der Quasi-Botschaft Chinas in Hongkong verweigert wurde. Ein Touristenbüro besorgte mir dann aber doch ohne weiteres ein Touristenvisum.

15 Vermutlich bedeutete dies: Ich solle nicht versuchen, sie zum Anschluss an die Untergrundkirche zu bewegen.

der (von den Kommunisten geförderten und in ihren Statuten den Papst nicht anerkennenden) Patriotischen Vereinigung erlebten, Bedenken hatten, dieser Kirche zu helfen. Doch die Mehrzahl der Leute, die davon hörten, freuten sich darüber, dass wir auf diese Weise der Kirche Chinas einen Dienst erweisen konnten. Einmal bekam ich sogar einen kleinen Brief vom Generalmeister des Ordens P. Damian Byrne, in dem er diesen Einsatz als wertvoll anerkannte. Und auch manche Mitbrüder, denen bislang meine Arbeit nicht als „eigentliche" Missionsaufgabe galt, konnten sie nun leichter als sinnvoll anerkennen. Für mich jedoch war diese Aufgabe trotz mancher Schwierigkeiten wie die Erfüllung des Traums, der mich seit langem in verschiedener Deutlichkeit begleitete, bis er schließlich in dieser völlig unerwarteten Gestalt Wirklichkeit wurde. Und so frage ich mich heute: War es vielleicht eine besondere Fügung, dass ich genau am 40. Jahrestag meiner Einkleidung meine erste Vorlesung im Priesterseminar von Shanghai hielt?

Kontakt mit der alten Mission

In unsere ‚alte', vor dem ersten Weltkrieg übernommene Mission im Süden der Provinz Fukien kam ich nie. Da sie die Heimat von P. Simon Hsü ist, hat er sie nach der erwähnten Entspannung öfters „zum letzten Mal" besucht.[16] Zusammen mit P. Damian Meyer konnte sogar der einstmals „für immer aus dem Reich der Mitte ausgewiesene" P. Franz Späth die alte Mission besuchen. Besonders bewegend für ihn war es wohl, als sich eine Frau im Großmutter-Alter als eines der ausgesetzten Mädchen vorstellte, die von den Ilanzer Schwestern aufgenommen und so gerettet wurden; unter den Schwestern, die diese Arbeit leisteten, war auch eine leibliche Schwester von P. Franz gewesen.

Doch kam ich selbst zwei Mal nach Fuchow, d. h. in die Hauptstadt der Provinz Fukien, welche den Dominikanern als Missionsgebiet zugewiesen war. In ihr wirkten bis zur Machtergreifung der Kommunisten spanische, amerikanische und deutsche Dominikaner. Ein chinesischer Jesuit, der einmal am Fest des hl. Dominikus bei den dortigen Priestern war, erinnerte sie an ihre Dankespflicht gegenüber den Dominikanern. Natürlich wurde ich auch bei diesem Besuch von den Behörden beobachtet. Am Flughafen wurde ich gleich von der damaligen Chefin des Büros für Reli-

16 Vermutlich aufgrund traumatischer Erfahrungen wollte P. Albert Wei seine Heimat nicht wieder sehen.

gionsangelegenheiten begrüßt. Im Bischofshaus war eine alte ehemalige Ordensschwester, vor der man mich warnte. Auf den Fahrten in die Umgebung wurden wir „begleitet“.

Fuchow war Missionsgebiet der (spanischen) Rosenkranzprovinz. In dieser Stadt war das Regionalseminar, in dem P. Hilarius Albers Rektor war und in dem (mit spanischen Mitbrüdern) P. Romanus Zeller und P. Agilolf Piepenbreier Priesterkandidaten aus der ganzen Provinz theologisch ausbilden sollten. Während meiner kurzen Aufenthalte in Fuchow konnte ich von außen das ehemalige Gebäude dieses Seminars sehen und den von Pater Hilarius Albers für das Seminar gebauten Wasserturm fotografieren. Er soll der erste der (jetzt Millionen-)Stadt Fuchow gewesen sein.

Den Kontakt mit der alten Mission in Fukien pflegten wir später auch auf folgende Weise: Das Seminar in Shanghai ist ein Seminar für die Mammutstadt Shanghai und fünf Provinzen, darunter auch die Provinz Fukien. Um unserer Verbundenheit mit der alten Mission Ausdruck zu geben, bezahlten wir (natürlich mit Wissen und Hilfe der Missionsprokur unter P. Adolf Weber) in den Jahren 1992–2004 das Studium aller aus Fukien kommenden in Shanghai studierenden Seminaristen. Dies war eine Entlastung sowohl der Bischöfe in Fukien, wie auch eine kleine Unterstützung des Seminars in Shanghai. Die Seminaristen wussten offensichtlich davon, denn einmal kamen einige auf mich zu und dankten für diese Hilfe.

Zeuge tiefgreifender Veränderungen im Leben Taiwans

Verkehrswesen

Als ich Anfang 1959 nach Taiwan kam, war in Taipei die Fahrradrikscha ein wichtiges Verkehrsmittel. In unserem Gebiet im Süden waren viele Straßen schmal und nicht asphaltiert. Die Fahrt vom Süden nach Taipei dauerte mit dem besten Zug oder mit dem Motorrad oder Auto 6–7 Stunden. – Später verschwanden die Rikschas. Nun wimmelt es in Taipei (mit seiner 2,3 Mio.-Bevölkerung) von Taxen und Privatwagen. Autobahnen durchziehen die Insel. Mehrere Fluggesellschaften konkurrieren um Passagiere für die nur kurzen (ca. 40 Minuten) Binnenflüge. Heute kann man in knapp zwei Stunden per Zug von Nord nach Süd kommen.

Produktion und Export

Als ich nach Taiwan kam, erregte eine importierte Vespa Aufsehen und Neugierde. Lichtbildervorträge lockten zahlreiche Menschen an. Damals produzierte und exportierte Taiwan Bananen und Pilze, Textilien, Schirme und Ventilatoren. – Im Laufe der Jahre jedoch wurde das kleine Taiwan zu einem der großen Produzenten und Exporteur von Kühlschränken, Fernsehgeräten und Computern.

Familienstruktur

Als ich in den Jahren 1961–1964 in der Stadt Tungkang in der Jugendarbeit tätig war, kamen die Schüler meistens aus Familien mit 4–6 Kindern. – Jetzt hat aus jener Altersgruppe meines Wissens nur eine einzige damalige Schülerin[17] mehr als zwei Kinder.

Beziehung Taiwans zum kommunistischen China

Im Januar 1959 kam ich per Schiff von Kalifornien nach Taiwan. Im Jahr zuvor 1958 startete die chinesische Regierung auf dem Festland die Kampagne des Großen Sprunges, die zu einer der größten Hungersnöte der Menschheit führte. Zur gleichen Zeit beschoss China die vor dem Festland liegenden Inseln Quemoy und Matsu, welche von den Kommunisten nicht erobert werden konnten. Zwar war zur Zeit meiner Ankunft in Taiwan die sogenannte Quemoy-Krise in etwa beendigt, doch wegen der anhaltenden Spannungen nahm das Schiff, mit dem ich von Amerika kam, nicht die kürzere Route durch die Straße von Formosa, sondern umfuhr die Südspitze, um die Hafenstadt Kaohsiung zu erreichen. In Form von Drohungen einer militärischen Invasion hielten die Spannungen noch lange Zeit an. – Doch auch diese schwierige Beziehung erfuhr eine langsame Veränderung. Während Taiwan früher jeden Kontakt mit dem Festland ablehnte, kam es später zu ‚inoffiziellen' Kontakten, Gesprächen und Besuchen von beiden Seiten der Wasserstraße. Seit neuer Zeit gibt es direkten Flugverkehr zwischen Taiwan und den Handelsmetropolen Canton und Shanghai.

17 Inzwischen ist sie glückliche Oma geworden.

Politische Struktur

Als ich nach Taiwan kam, stand die Insel seit 1949 unter Kriegsrecht („martial law"). Die eigentliche Macht lag in Händen des mit Chiang Kai Shek vom Festland nach Taiwan geflohenen Militärs. Die nationalistische Partei (Kuomintang) beherrschte das Land. Keine Oppositionsparteien waren zugelassen. Pro-kommunistische oder separatistische Regimegegner wurden verhaftet. – Im Gefolge einer rasanten wirtschaftlichen Entwicklung in den sechziger und siebziger Jahren kam es in den achtziger Jahren zu einer langsamen Liberalisierung der politischen Struktur: Das Kriegsrecht wurde 1987 aufgehoben, politische Parteien wurden zugelassen. Im Jahr 2000 wurde zum ersten Mal ein Präsident gewählt, der nicht der Kuomintang angehörte. Acht Jahre später kam es nochmals zu einem Regierungswechsel, als wieder ein Kandidat der Kuomintang zum Präsidenten gewählt wurde.

Ortskirche

Bis zum Ende des Zweiten Weltkrieges arbeiteten nur spanische Dominikaner und einige wenige einheimische Diözesanpriester als Missionare in Taiwan. Erst nach ihrer Ausweisung aus dem kommunistisch gewordenen China kamen verschiedene Orden und Gemeinschaften dorthin. Als ich 1959 nach Taiwan kam, war Taipei eine Erzdiözese mit einem chinesischen Erzbischof, in der Mitte Taiwans gab es eine Diözese mit einem chinesischen Bischof, im Süden eine Apostolische Präfektur, der ein spanischer Dominikaner vorstand. – Doch schon wenige Jahre später entstanden durch Abtrennung und Aufwertung sieben Diözesen. So standen (mit einer einzigen Ausnahme, die mir wie ein Anachronismus erschien) allen Diözesen chinesische Bischöfe vor. Unter den Orden und Missionsgesellschaften förderten vor allem die Jesuiten die „Sinisierung", sodass an der Spitze ihrer wichtigen Institutionen meistens chinesische Obere standen.[18]

Dominikanerorden

Wie schon gesagt waren bis nach dem Ende des Zweiten Weltkrieges die spanischen Mitbrüder der Rosenkranzprovinz die ersten und einzigen Missionare in Taiwan. Unter manchmal großen Schwierigkeiten waren kleine Gemeinden entstanden. Während der Zeit der Annexion Taiwans durch

18 Auf Grund des Mangels an Nachwuchs mussten jedoch etwa seit dem Jahr 2000 wieder einige Ausländer wichtige Ämter übernehmen.

Japan (1895–1945) hatten die Dominikaner in Taipei unter Mitarbeit einer Kongregation von Dominikanerinnen eine (wahrscheinlich die erste) höhere Mädchenschule gegründet, die bis heute besteht und gutes Ansehen genießt.

Nach der Ausweisung aus ihrer Mission auf dem Festland übernahmen die deutschen Mitbrüder ein Gebiet in der Präfektur Kaohsiung, die damals von einem spanischen Dominikaner geleitet wurde. Die spanischen Mitbrüder sprachen kein Deutsch und kaum Englisch und Mandarin. Wir Deutsche aber verstanden kaum Spanisch und kaum Taiwanesisch. So war schon auf Grund der Sprache die Kommunikation unter den Mitbrüdern schwach. Jede Gruppe hatte ihre Selbständigkeit und ihren eigenen Ordensoberen.

In den siebziger Jahren erreichten die zur spanischen Provinz gehörigen chinesischen Mitbrüder die Errichtung eines eigenen Provinzvikariates. Somit hatten wir Dominikaner in Taiwan drei Gruppen: das spanische und das chinesische Vikariat der Rosenkranzprovinz und das Vikariat der Teutonia.

Dies erregte einmal Heiterkeit bei anderen und Verlegenheit bei uns, als bei einer Versammlung der höheren Oberen gesagt wurde, dass es wegen den Dominikanern in Taiwan mehr höhere Ordensobere als Orden gebe. Es widersprach auch dem damaligen Trend. Damals hatten die Jesuiten ihre aus verschiedenen Ordensprovinzen und Nationen kommenden Mitbrüder zu einer einzigen chinesischen Provinz zusammengefasst. Ähnliches hatten auch die Franziskaner und die Vinzentiner getan oder planten es. So wurde zu dieser Zeit die Frage gestellt: Wie soll die Zukunft des Ordens in Taiwan gestaltet werden?

Natürlich gab es darüber verschiedene Ansichten. Manche dachten an die Vereinigung der drei Entitäten in einer Vizeprovinz oder in einer Kongregation. Andere hingegen widersprachen mit Hinweis auf unsere Struktur und unser Wahlrecht derartigen Vorstellungen. Sie machten geltend, dass dann die Ausländer stets die chinesischen Mitbrüder überstimmen könnten, dass durch eine Zusammenlegung der verschiedenen Gruppen die chinesischen Mitbrüder nicht richtig zum Zug kommen würden und auch versucht wären, sich auf die Ausländer und ihre Finanzen zu verlassen. Die Anhänger dieser Meinung befürworteten darum die Gründung eines Generalvikariates für die chinesischen Mitbrüder, das nicht einer ausländischen Provinz, sondern nur dem Generalmeister und dem Generalkapitel unterstellt war. Das würde zwar nicht die Dreiheit der do-

minikanischen Gruppen beseitigen, wohl aber die Selbständigkeit und Eigenverantwortung der chinesischen Mitbrüder fördern und die Grundlage für eine genuin chinesische Provinz schaffen.

Trotz mancher Bedenken wurde dieser letztere Weg eingeschlagen. Er gestaltete sich schwierig: Im Verlauf des ersten Versuchs trat der mit der Etablierung des Generalvikariates Beauftragte zurück und verließ Taiwan und später auch den Orden. Andere wurden Diözesanpriester oder laisiert. Die Gefahr bestand, dass es überhaupt nicht zur Gründung einer eigenen chinesischen Gemeinschaft kommen würde. Schließlich aber setzten sich doch einige Mitbrüder (darunter auch der damals zur Teutonia gehörige P. Simon Hsü) für die Gründung des chinesischen Generalvikariates ein. Dieses wurde offiziell am 29. Juni 1978 in einer Zeremonie in der Dominikusschule in Kaohsiung errichtet. Während der Zeremonie unterzeichnete der erste Generalvikar die notwendigen Dokumente. Vertreter der Rosenkranzprovinz und der Teutonia übergaben die Grundstückspapiere der von der Rosenkranzprovinz gegründeten Dominikusschule bzw. des von der Teutonia gebauten Studienhauses in Taipei, sodass seither das Generalvikariat kirchen- und ordensrechtlicher Eigentümer dieser Häuser und Institutionen ist. Mit der Gründung dieses Generalvikariates war die Hoffnung verbunden, dass aus ihm einmal eine eigenständige chinesische Ordensprovinz werden würde.

Nach der Gründung des chinesischen Generalvikariates (1978) bestanden also die Provinzvikariate der Rosenkranzprovinz und der Teutonia weiter. Doch gab es vielerlei Kontakte, ja vielleicht mehr als zuvor: Die Oberen hielten regelmäßige Treffen. Das Fest des hl. Dominikus wurde gemeinsam gefeiert. Für Exerzitien holte man gerne Mitbrüder aus der anderen Gemeinschaft.

Meiner Meinung nach erwies sich diese Neuordnung als fruchtbar. Die Errichtung des Generalvikariates bezweckte ja weder eine Art Rassentrennung noch war sie Ergebnis einer Revolution, sondern sie diente der Eigenständigkeit der chinesischen Mitbrüder. Auf sich gestellt, mussten sich die chinesischen Mitbrüder zusammenfinden und die Verantwortung für den Orden und sein Apostolat in Taiwan und China übernehmen. Dies geschah in den neunziger Jahren, als ein Neuanfang des Chinaapostolats des Ordens möglich schien. Zunächst wurden damals verschiedene andere Modelle erwogen und zeitweise auch erprobt. Schließlich aber wurde das Apostolat des Ordens in China ganz dem Generalvikariat anvertraut. Die gewünschte Beteiligung des Gesamtordens an der Evangeli-

sation im Reich der Mitte soll in Zukunft dadurch geschehen, dass Mitbrüder aus anderen Provinzen entweder dem Generalvikariat beitreten oder in es assigniert werden.

2. Wandel in der Missionskonzeption

Als ich im März 2010 eingeladen wurde, Erinnerungen an meine Zeit in der Taiwan-Mission schriftlich festzuhalten, wurde ich mit den Worten: „Was war die Perspektive am Anfang? Wie hat sie sich evtl. im Laufe der Zeit verschoben?“ nach einem möglichen Wandel in der Missionskonzeption gefragt.

Anfangs machte ich mir über die grundsätzliche Frage nach Sinn und Ziel der Mission wenig Gedanken. Man kannte ja den Missionsbefehl Jesu im Neuen Testament, die Hochschätzung der Missionsarbeit im Lauf der Geschichte des Ordens.[19] Die damals gültigen Konstitutionen erklärten ausdrücklich, dass unser Gehorsamsgelübde die Bereitschaft einschließe, sogar bei Lebensgefahr in die Mission zu gehen und dass jede Ordensprovinz eine Mission haben sollte.[20] Und nach der Ankunft in Taiwan ging es zunächst darum, die Sprache zu lernen und sich von den ‚alten‘ Missionaren in die konkreten Aufgaben einführen zu lassen. Da trat die Frage nach einer Missionskonzeption in den Hintergrund. Doch auf die Dauer ließ sich diese Frage nicht umgehen, sondern sie gewann mit der Zeit an Schärfe und Dringlichkeit in der nur scheinbar einfachen Form: „Was wollen wir eigentlich“?

Unbefriedigende Anschauungen

Mission zur Rettung vom ewigen Verderben

Nie habe ich die Meinung vertreten, dass alle Nicht-Christen vom ewigen Heil ausgeschlossen wären. Und ich denke mit Grauen daran, dass einmal

---

19 Vgl. den Brief des Generalmeisters des Ordens Humbert von Romans († 1277) vom Generalkapitel in Mailand (1255) in: Proprium des Predigerordens. III: Feier des Stundengebetes. Proprium der Heiligen. Ausgabe in deutscher Sprache. Köln 1991, S. 514–516.

20 Constitutiones Fratrum S. Ordinis Praedicatorum. Romae 1932, S. 205, N. 544–545.

bei einer theologischen Studienwoche für Deutschsprechende ein Teilnehmer (kein Dominikaner) von sich (etwa sinngemäß) sagte, dass immer, wenn er sehe oder höre, dass jemand zu Grabe getragen würde, er sich Vorwürfe mache, dass er ihm nicht zur Rettung verholfen habe.[21] Nein, eine derartige Missionskonzeption kann nicht Grundlage für die Verkündigung des „Evangelium von Gottes Gnade“ (Apg 20,24) sein.

Mission soll den Anteil der Christen an der Bevölkerung erhöhen

Auch mit dieser Auffassung konnte ich mich nicht befreunden. Denn wenn der Anteil der Christen an der heutigen Bevölkerung Taiwans (ca. 23 Mio.) jedes Jahr auch nur um ein einziges Prozent wachsen sollte, dann müssten jedes Jahr etwa 230 000 Menschen in die Kirche aufgenommen werden. Und im heutigen China mit seiner 1,3 Mrd.-Bevölkerung müssten jedes Jahr 13 Millionen Menschen zum christlichen Glauben und zur Kirche finden.[22]

Elemente einer theologisch fundierten Missionskonzeption

Da ich die genannten Auffassungen ablehnte, musste ich solche Elemente finden, die ich zwar damals nicht zusammen fügte, die mich aber beeinflussten.

Auftrag der Jünger Jesu, „Salz der Erde“ und „Licht der Welt“ (Mt 5, 13–16) zu sein

Dieser Auftrag geht auf die Bergpredigt zurück. Die Jünger sollen aber nicht die Erde versalzen oder sie zu einer Salzwüste machen. Und als Licht der Welt sollen sie nicht versuchen, Menschen in Brand zu stecken und zu brennenden Fackeln zu machen. Als Salz der Erde sollen sie ‚nur‘ die Welt, das Leben vor Fäulnis und Verderbnis bewahren, es würzig und schmackhaft machen. Und als Licht der Welt sollten sie ‚nur‘ anderen Menschen wie Leuchttürme Orientierung geben und sichere Fahrt ermöglichen.

---

21 Ähnliche Gedanken finden sich in einem Brief des hl. Franz Xaver an den hl. Ignatius v. Loyola. Lektionar zum Stundenbuch I/1, S. 197–198.

22 Diesen Gedanken verdanke ich P. Elmar J. Bohmann.

Theologisches Nachdenken über die Gnadenlehre[23]

Dieses führt zu einer ähnlichen Sicht. Wenn man zu Chinesen sprechen will, muss man sich vor Augen halten, dass viele Chinesen um die lange Geschichte ihres Volkes und seine hohe Kultur wissen. Wenn da von Gnade und Heil (durch Christus, die Kirche und Taufe) die Rede ist, denken viele Hörer an das Heil ihrer Eltern und Vorfahren, Weisen und Großen ihres Volkes, die nichts von Jesus Christus und Kirche und Sakramenten hörten und wussten. Natürlich (und sehr zu Recht) fragen dann nachdenkliche Menschen: Wie steht es um Gnade und Heil dieser Menschen? Aufs erste lässt sich diese Frage im Hinblick auf die Lehre des Zweiten Vatikanum leicht in positiver und optimistischer Weise beantworten. Doch entsteht sofort die Frage: Welchen Sinn hat dann die Missionsarbeit und das Christ-Sein? In der chinesischen Geisteswelt steht diese Frage gleichsam immer im Raum. Das zeigte sich deutlich, als Hans Küng einmal in Taipei vor einem großen Auditorium von der positiven Bedeutung der nichtchristlichen Religionen sprach. Während der folgenden Aussprache stellte ich ausdrücklich die Frage nach dem Sinn der Mission und des Christ-Seins. Andere Zuhörer sagten mir nachher, dass auch sie genau diese Frage stellen wollten.

Wenn wir im Einklang mit der Heiligen Schrift (z. B. 1 Tim 2,4) und der Lehre des Zweiten Vatikanischen Konzils (z. B. Lumen Gentium 16) glauben, dass Gott allen Menschen, gleichgültig, ob sie vor oder nach Christus lebten, ob sie Jesus Christus kannten oder (in den meisten Fällen) gar nicht kennen konnten, die Gnade des ewigen Heiles anbietet, müssen wir unterscheiden zwischen der allen Menschen angebotenen Heilsgnade und der Gnade des ‚Christ-Seins'. Letztere wird nur den Hörern der Frohbotschaft angeboten und geht über die ‚Heilsgnade' hinaus im Sinne des Wortes, das Jesus an seine Jünger richtet: „Selig sind die, deren Augen sehen, was ihr seht. Ich sage euch: Viele Propheten und Könige wollten sehen, was ihr seht, und haben es nicht gesehen, und wollten hören, was ihr hört, und haben es nicht gehört." (Lk 10,23–24; vgl. Mt 13,16–17) Es ist ja ein großer Unterschied, ob wir als „Dasein zum Tode" mit Konfuzius (sehr zu Recht!) sagen: „Ich verstehe nicht das Leben, wie

23 Obwohl in den vergangenen vier Jahrhunderten Dominikaner und Jesuiten oft und heftig über die Gnadenlehre stritten, wurde bei der Verteilung der theologischen Traktate mir, dem damals einzigen Dominikaner an der von Jesuiten geleiteten Fakultät, der alte Zankapfel gern und bedingungslos überlassen.

könnte ich etwas über den Tod wissen?", oder ob wir im Glauben an Jesus Christus bekennen: „Ich glaube an die Auferstehung der Toten." Und das Leben, das sich immer wieder als ins Böse verstrickt erfährt, kann sehr verschieden sein, je nachdem, ob man mit dem großen Weisen Chinas sagt: „Wenn du den Himmel beleidigt hast, gibt es nichts, wohin du dich wenden kannst" oder ob man das Gleichnis vom verlorenen Sohn kennt und ernst nimmt und im Blick auf Jesus Christus bekennt: „Ich glaube an die Vergebung der Sünden". Zugleich ist das Angebot der Gnade des Christ-Seins eine „Berufung zum Apostolat", denn genau dies lehrt das Zweite Vatikanische Konzil im Dekret über das Laienapostolat (Nr. 2) mit den Worten: „Die christliche Berufung ist ihrer Natur nach auch Berufung zum Apostolat."

Sinn der Missionsarbeit[24]
Auf der Grundlage der dargelegten Überlegungen versuche ich nun, den Sinn der Missionsarbeit zu umschreiben. Im Hinblick auf die Lehre der Schrift und besonders des Zweiten Vatikanischen Konzils über den universalen Heilswillen Gottes und die Bedeutung der nichtchristlichen Religionen können wir sagen:

Der Sinn der Mission besteht nicht darin, den Menschen die Heilsmöglichkeit und die Heilsgnade zu vermitteln, als ob erst durch die christliche Verkündigung, durch Kirche und Sakramente die den Menschen zugedachte, sie heiligende, rechtfertigende und zum ewigen Leben berufende Gnade Gottes ihnen begegnen und ihnen angeboten würde und von ihnen angenommen werden könnte.

Wohl aber ist es Sinn der Missionsarbeit,
- das Licht des Evangeliums, seine Orientierung und Hoffnung vermittelnde Kraft, in den Lebensraum jener Menschen zu bringen, wo das Licht des Evangeliums gleichsam noch nicht installiert wurde. Sie bringt

---

24 Als ich selbst zur Mission gehörte, habe ich die hier vertretene Sicht nicht ausführlich entwickelt. Doch hat sie unausdrücklich mein Befinden und Tun bestimmt. Ja, ich meine, dass auch Missionare, die meine Sicht als falsch und schädlich ablehnen, sich von ihr bestimmen lassen. Denn: Wenn wir glauben würden, dass alle Nichtgetauften in die Hölle fahren, wie könnten wir dann an den „Gott aller Gnade" (1 Petr 5,10) glauben und uns guten Gewissens erholen und in Urlaub fahren?

also das *Angebot der Gnade des Christ-Seins zu Menschen*, die *diesem* Angebot ‚noch' nicht begegnen konnten. Sie lässt die immer schon angebotene und vielleicht schon angenommene Heilsgnade wie einen bislang im Acker des Lebens verborgenen Schatz entdecken und ergreifen (vgl. Mt 13, 44) und so das Leben der Menschen bereichern.

Und den Menschen, welche die Gnade des Christ-Seins annehmen, überbringt Missionsarbeit

– *die Berufung zum Apostolat* und die Einladung, „Arbeiter für die Ernte des Herrn" (vgl. Lk 10,2) und den Menschen „Helfer zur Freude" (vgl. 2 Kor 1, 24) zu sein.

Diese Sicht leugnet keineswegs die Wichtigkeit der traditionellen Missionsarbeit, der Aufnahme von Menschen in die Kirche und der Gründung von christlichen Gemeinden. Denn wenn Menschen den Wert ihres Glaubens und Christ-Seins erkennen, wollen sie andere Menschen daran Anteil geben. Es sind ja vor allem *gläubige Menschen und Gemeinden*, die an verschiedenen Orten das Licht Christi aufnehmen, es in ihrem Leben leuchten lassen und es so gleichsam in ihrer Welt installieren, sodass es anderen (auch nicht-christlichen Menschen) sein Licht spenden kann. Das Salz, das die Welt von der Fäulnis der Hoffnungslosigkeit bewahren kann, muss durch Menschen und Gemeinden, die das Salz nicht nur haben, sondern *sind*, verbreitet und wirksam werden.

Konsequenzen der hier vertretenen Sicht

Bevorzugte Orte der Missionsarbeit

Wenn wir glauben, dass Gott *allen* Menschen die Heilsgnade anbietet, können wir das (immer begrenzte) Personal und die (knappen) finanziellen Mittel ohne Sorge um das ewige Heil vieler Menschen an den ‚Orten' einsetzen, wo nach menschlichem Ermessen Menschen zugänglicher sind für die Aufnahme des Evangeliums. Wenn wir dies tun, folgen wir eigentlich nur dem Beispiel des Apostels Paulus. Dieser wandte sich meistens an die jüdischen Gemeinden und an die schon aus den damaligen Religionen herausgelösten Gottesfürchtigen sowie an Menschen in den Zentren des Lebens, wo sie verschiedenen Kulturen und Religionen begegneten und nicht so sehr dem Druck einer bestimmten Religion unterworfen waren.

Prioritäten in der Missionsarbeit

Die hier vertretene Sicht berechtigt zur Kritik mancher (wenigstens früher befürworteten) Auffassungen über die vornehmlichen Aufgaben der Missionare. Als P. Elmar Bohmann sich hauptsächlich der sozial-caritativen Tätigkeit zuwandte und als ich von der Stationsarbeit in die theologische Lehrtätigkeit überwechselte, mochte dies manchen Missionaren wie ein Luxus erscheinen, den man sich eigentlich nicht leisten konnte. Damals kursierte ja eine Missionskonzeption, nach welcher die Gründung von Missionsstationen in allen Kleinstädten und die Arbeit in den Missionsstationen als ‚eigentliche Mission' oder als ‚erste Stufe' der Mission, Sozial- und Caritasarbeit und theologische Lehrtätigkeit hingegen als ‚nicht eigentliche Missionsarbeit' oder als ‚zweite Stufe der Mission' betrachtet wurden.

Diese Auffassung widerspricht der Lehre des Apostolischen Schreibens „Evangelii nuntiandi" von Papst Paul VI. über die Evangelisierung in der Welt von heute vom 8. Dezember 1975. In ihm (Nr. 18–19) sagt der Papst über den Sinn der Missionsarbeit:

> „Evangelisieren besagt für die Kirche, die Frohbotschaft in alle Bereiche der Menschheit zu tragen und sie durch deren Einfluss von innen her umzuwandeln und die Menschheit selbst zu erneuern: ‚Seht, ich mache alles neu!'. Es gibt aber keine neue Menschheit, wenn es nicht zuerst neue Menschen gibt durch die Erneuerung aus der Taufe und ein Leben nach dem Evangelium. Das Ziel der Evangelisierung ist also die innere Umwandlung. *Wenn man es mit einem Wort ausdrücken müsste, so wäre es wohl am richtigsten zu sagen: die Kirche evangelisiert, wenn sie sich bemüht, durch die göttliche Kraft der Botschaft, die sie verkündet, zugleich das persönliche und kollektive Bewusstsein der Menschen, die Tätigkeit, in der sie sich engagieren, ihr konkretes Leben und jeweiliges Milieu umzuwandeln. (...)* Für die Kirche geht es nicht nur darum, immer weitere Landstriche oder immer größere Volksgruppen durch die Predigt des Evangeliums zu erfassen, sondern zu erreichen, dass *durch die Kraft des Evangeliums die Urteilskriterien, die bestimmenden Werte, die Interessenpunkte, die Denkgewohnheiten, die Quellen der Inspiration und die Lebensmodelle der Menschheit, die zum Wort Gottes und zum Heilsplan im Gegensatz stehen, umgewandelt werden.*"

Abgesehen von dem hier mit Absicht klein gedruckten Satz, der wie ein Einsprengsel wirkt und die bleibende Wichtigkeit der traditionellen Missionsarbeit (Aufnahme von Menschen in die Kirche und der Gründung von christlichen Gemeinden) hervorheben soll, betrachtet das Apostolische Schreiben als Ziel der Evangelisation vor allem die Umwandlung des per-

sönlichen und kollektiven Bewusstseins der Menschen, der Urteilskriterien, der bestimmenden Werte, der Interessenpunkte, der Denkgewohnheiten, der Quellen der Inspiration und der Lebensmodelle der Menschen, die zum Wort Gottes und zum Heilsplan im Gegensatz stehen. Die hier von mir vertretene Missionskonzeption entspricht also der Lehre dieses päpstlichen Schreibens und verlangt immer wieder eine Prüfung der Prioritäten. Dann können, ja müssen wir sagen: Auch wenn sie nicht die Zahl der Taufen und der Christen vermehren, sind Einsatz für Gerechtigkeit, Frieden und Bewahrung der Schöpfung, Förderung des Dialogs mit religiösen und weltanschaulichen Strömungen und ihrer führenden Persönlichkeiten und Stellungnahmen zu den die Menschen bewegenden Fragen vollwertige Aufgaben der Evangelisation. Und: Auch wenn manche Missionsstationen nicht gegründet oder nicht mehr mit einem Priester besetzt werden können, so sollten, ja müssen dafür begabte Missionare die Möglichkeit haben, sich ganz den genannten Aufgaben zu widmen.

RÜCKBLICK

Die Provinz des hl. Albertus Magnus in Süddeutschland und Österreich 1939–2014

Wolfram Hoyer OP *

2. Februar 1939 – die Errichtung einer neuen Ordensprovinz

> „Die Provinzgründungsfeier fand an Mariä Lichtmess 1939 in Wien statt. Es hatten sich P. Vetter, der Provinzial der Teutonia P. Siemer und der Provinzial der Hungaria P. Badalik sowie Kardinal Erzbischof Innitzer eingefunden. Im Kapitelsaal des Wiener Konvents wurde vor der versammelten Gemeinschaft und den geladenen Gästen durch P. Well, Prior von Graz, die Urkunde verlesen, durch die der Ordensmeister P. Martin Stanislaus Gillet die oberdeutsche Provinz errichtete und als ihren ersten Provinzial P. Marianus Vetter ernannt wurde. Im Auftrag des Ordensmeisters nahm P. Siemer den Amtseid des neuen Provinzials entgegen. P. Well sprach namens der Hausoberen die Ergebenheit aus. Er zeichnete Verdienste, Werke und Stand zumal des österreichischen Teils des neuen Verwaltungszweiges. Der neue Provinzial sprach Worte des Dankes und des Vertrauens Gott gegenüber, der Verehrung Mariens an ihrem Fest und St. Alberts. Ihn hat der Ordensmeister der neuen Provinz als Patron gegeben. Im Siegelbild der Provinz erscheint St. Albert. Der Segen des hl. Vaters Dominikus und des Papstes, von P. General und P. Sozius Kuhlmann übersandt, wurde übermittelt. Kardinal Innitzer hob die Verbundenheit Wiens mit den Dominikanern und den Mut des Ordens, in so schwerer Zeit zu einer Neugründung zu schreiten, hervor. Bei Tisch sprachen P. Badalik und P. Siemer mit nachbarlichen Gefühlen für den neuen Verwaltungsbezirk."

Soweit ein Bericht von Angelus Walz über die Errichtungsfeier der dominikanischen Ordensprovinz des hl. Albertus Magnus in Süddeutschland und Österreich am 2. Februar 1939, auf deren 75-jähriges Bestehen wir 2014 zurückblicken.[1] Bevor wir uns aber ihrer Geschichte widmen können, sind zwei Fragen zu klären: Was war hier entstanden? Und wie war es dazu gekommen?

---

* Dieser Beitrag sei in dankbarer Erinnerung P. Max Svoboda gewidmet.

1 Walz: *Dominikaner*, S. 132–133. Wohl ebenfalls aus dessen Feder stammt ein zweiter, etwas ausführlicherer Bericht darüber in *ASOP* (1939) S. 95–99, in dem außerdem ein dem Festakt vorangegangenes levitiertes Hochamt erwähnt und auf die bei der Feier gehaltenen Reden näher eingegangen wird.

Walz spricht von einem neuen Verwaltungsbezirk des Predigerordens. Diesen Orden zeichnen seit seiner päpstlichen Bestätigung im Jahr 1216 zwei Eigentümlichkeiten aus, nämlich sein Charakter als ortsunabhängiger Personalverband und seine zentrale Gesamtleitung. Ausdruck findet beides in der Profess – dem Gelübde des Lebens nach den Ordenssatzungen –, nämlich durch ihre Ablegung auf die Person des Ordensmeisters, womit dieser zum Oberen aller Dominikaner wird und den Predigerorden als Gesamtgemeinschaft repräsentiert. Diese Betonung der Gesamtgemeinschaft bedeutet aber für den jeweiligen einzelnen Ordensbruder auch einen Verzicht auf die Möglichkeit, sein Leben nur in einem einzigen Kloster, an einem einzigen Ort führen zu dürfen, da der Ordensmeister jeden Dominikaner innerhalb der Gesamtgemeinschaft – theoretisch also weltweit – einsetzen kann. Natürlich findet das konkrete Leben des Einzelnen trotzdem immer lokal statt, in einem bestimmten Kloster, ebenso wie die von ihm geleistete praktische Seelsorge oder seine anderen Tätigkeiten. Aufgrund des raschen Wachstums der Mitglieder- und Niederlassungszahlen wurde es dem Ordensmeister schon in den ersten Jahren nach 1216 unmöglich, diese lokalen Aktivitäten seiner Brüder zu verwalten. Daher entwickelte das dominikanische Verfassungs- und Verwaltungssystem bald eine Struktur aus drei übereinander liegenden Ebenen: Konvent, Provinz und Gesamtorden. Den Konvent bildet die örtliche Kommunität der in einem Klostergebäude und unter einem gemeinsamen Hausoberen, dem Prior, wohnenden Predigerbrüder. Ein regionaler Zusammenschluss mehrerer Konvente, ebenfalls ausgestattet mit einem eigenen, höheren Oberen, dem Provinzial, wird Provinz genannt. Die weltweite Gesamtebene wird durch den höchsten Oberen aller Dominikaner, den Ordensmeister, dargestellt, dessen eigentlicher Titel deswegen auch „Meister der Predigerbrüder" lautet. Diese Oberen werden auf Versammlungen der jeweiligen Ebene gewählt, einem sogenannten Kapitel: Das Hauskapitel, die Versammlung der Konventualen, wählt den Konventsprior, das Provinzkapitel als Versammlung von Stellvertretern der jeweiligen Konvente einer Provinz den Provinzial und das Generalkapitel als Versammlung der Vertreter der Provinzen den Ordensmeister. Diesen Kapitelsversammlungen kommen außerdem je nach ihrer Ebene weitere gesetzgebende und kontrollierende Vollmachten zu, worauf wir aber hier nicht weiter eingehen können.

Bedingt durch die schon genannte schnelle Ausbreitung der Predigerbrüder über das ganze christliche Abendland und das Aufblühen ihrer Konvente verschob sich der Schwerpunkt der Ordensverwaltung bis zum

Ende der 1220er Jahre auf die Provinzebene. Die oberste Gewalt in Exekutive, Judikative und Legislative verblieb immer beim Ordensmeister und beim Generalkapitel, aber üblicherweise bildete nun die Provinz den Lebensrahmen eines Dominikaners, zu der er gehörte, in deren Konventen er heranwuchs, ausgebildet und eingesetzt wurde. Versetzungen zu Aufgaben, die einen Bruder außerhalb der eigenen Provinz führten, kamen und kommen vor – etwa für die Mission, zu Studienzwecken oder wegen spezieller individueller Fähigkeiten, z. B. als Lehrer – aber die alltäglichen Aktivitäten im Ordenslebens des Einzelnen enden üblicherweise an den Provinzgrenzen.

Bereits dieser kurze Blick auf die Verfassungsstruktur des Predigerordens beantwortet die erste unserer beiden Fragen: Durch die Gründung einer neuen Ordensprovinz wurde ein neuer regionaler Zusammenschluss von Dominikanerkonventen in Süddeutschland und Österreich errichtet, und die dazu gehörenden Brüder kamen unter die Obhut eines neuen gemeinsamen Oberen, Provinzial Marianus Vetter. Diese neue Verwaltungseinheit bildete aber gleichzeitig auch eine neue Herausforderung für die von ihr betroffenen Dominikaner, einen neuen gemeinsamen Lebensrahmen zu schaffen und den Gesamtorden in diesem Gebiet authentisch zu repräsentieren.

Wie war es dazu gekommen? Um das zu beantworten, müssen wir ein bisschen weiter ausholen.

Die Vorgeschichte

Die Ausbreitung der Dominikaner im deutschen Sprachraum

Tatsächlich war die neue Provinz nicht die erste dominikanische Verwaltungseinheit im süddeutsch-österreichischen Raum. Es hatte schon zwei Jahrhunderte zuvor bereits eine sogenannte oberdeutsche Provinz gegeben. Die Provinz des hl. Albert bildete demnach nur eine weitere Phase in der Geschichte des Predigerordens in der Region, die sehr lang und äußerst wechselhaft verlaufen war.[2]

2 Wo nicht anders ausgewiesen beruht der folgende Überblick auf Hoyer: *Provinzen und Kongregationen*; Lohrum: *Wiederanfänge*, S. 1–22 und Groothuis: *Im Dienste*, S. 35–45.

Begonnen hatte sie noch zu Lebzeiten des Ordensgründers Dominikus: Schon vor dessen Tod im Jahre 1221 hatten Brüder im deutschsprachigen Gebiet erste Niederlassungen gegründet – konkret in Friesach in Kärnten und in Köln am Rhein. Auf dem Generalkapitel von 1226 wurde der erste Provinzial der deutschen Ordensprovinz Teutonia eingesetzt, der auch im selben Jahr das erste Provinzkapitel abhielt. Im Laufe der folgenden Jahrzehnte breiteten die Dominikaner die Zahl ihrer Niederlassungen und damit die Teutonia im ganzen Gebiet des Heiligen Römischen Reiches und darüber hinaus aus. Da die Provinz damit zu riesig wurde und kaum mehr zu verwalten war, nahm man 1303 die Konvente im Norden und Osten des Reiches aus der Teutonia heraus und schloss diese unter dem Namen Provincia Saxoniae zu einer selbständigen Verwaltungseinheit zusammen. Die Menge an Konventsgründungen wuchs auch danach weiter, allerdings langsamer. Daher konnte 1460 aus der Saxonia noch eine Provinz für die niederländisch-flämischen Konvente herausgeschnitten werden, die Provincia Germaniae Inferioris. Die protestantische Reformation des 16. Jahrhunderts beendete nicht nur abrupt dieses dominikanische Wachstumsstreben – der einsetzende Klostersturm führte zum Verlust aller europäischen Konvente der Germania Inferior und beinahe aller Niederlassungen der Saxonia. Deren letzte vier Häuser wurden 1608 zur Teutonia geschlagen; die Saxonia war damit aufgelöst. Auch die Teutonia hatte viele ihrer Niederlassungen verloren. Dennoch gelang ihr nicht nur das Überleben, sondern sie kam im 17. Jahrhundert sogar zu einer neuerlichen Blüte, sodass aus ihrem Klosterbestand wiederum mehrere selbständige Verwaltungsbezirke gebildet werden konnten: 1690 wurden die Häuser im Elsass zu einer eigenen sogenannten elsässischen Kongregation zusammengefasst, 1702 trennten sich die österreichisch-ungarischen Konvente als Provincia (Austro-)Hungarica ab und 1709 formten die Niederlassungen in Süddeutschland die Provincia Germaniae Superioris. Diese barocke Provinzenvielfalt fand ihr Ende mit den Klosteraufhebungen der französischen Revolution und der deutschen Mediatisierung und Säkularisation: 1825 wurde der letzte Dominikanerkonvent auf deutschem Boden geschlossen. Die Provincia Austro-Hungarica bestand zu diesem Zeitpunkt noch, stark reduziert.

Die kirchenpolitische Lage in Deutschland und in der Habsburgermonarchie erlaubte dem Predigerorden erst einige Jahrzehnte später, diese erbärmliche Situation zu ändern. 1856 schloss Ordensmeister Vincent Alexandre Jandel die sechs Dominikanerkonvente in Österreich und Ungarn

mit den sieben noch existierenden Konventen der böhmischen Provinz zusammen und konstituierte sie 1857 zu einer neuen Provinz, Provincia Imperii oder Reichsprovinz genannt. Diese Maßnahme sollte zum einen der gegenseitigen Hilfe und Unterstützung der Niederlassungen im Habsburgerreich dienen (worauf auch der Name der Provinz anspielte) und zum anderen zur Grundlage der Wiedereinführung des Ordens in Deutschland werden. Ein erster zaghafter Versuch mit einer Niederlassung in Materborn bei Kleve 1856 war bald als gescheitert abzuschreiben. 1860 gelang eine Klostergründung in Düsseldorf, 1867 eine weitere in Berlin-Moabit. Im Zusammenhang des Kulturkampfes wurden beide Häuser 1875 von der preußischen Regierung jedoch wieder geschlossen und die Brüder mussten ins Ausland flüchten. Sie errichteten 1879 in Venlo in den Niederlanden einen Konvent. Erst 1887 durften sie nach Düsseldorf und 1889 nach Berlin zurückkehren. Nun kam es endlich zu dem erhofften Aufschwung; 1895 erfolgte die Wiedererrichtung der Provinz Teutonia. Weitere Niederlassungen wurden 1898 in Köln, 1899 in Meckinghoven, 1901 in Warburg, 1902 in Vechta, 1925 in Worms, 1926 in Walberberg bei Bonn und 1930 in Leipzig geschaffen.

Anfang der 1930er Jahre gelang der Teutonia der Sprung nach Süddeutschland: Schon 1927 hatte man seitens des Provinzialates begonnen, sich für die Übernahme der Wallfahrtskirche Heilig Kreuz in Augsburg zu bewerben. Diese war ursprünglich eine Stiftskirche der Augustinerchorherren gewesen, die nach der Säkularisation unter die Obhut von Weltpriestern gelangt war. Außerdem barg sie mit dem sogenannten Wunderbarlichen Gut – einer aus dem Mittelalter stammenden eucharistischen Reliquie – eines der Stadtheiligtümer der Augsburger Katholiken. Das Interesse an Heilig Kreuz war mutig, denn die Seelsorge dort blühte und gedieh; die Kirche galt als eine der meistbesuchten und schönsten der Stadt und war damit etwas, was die Diözese so leicht nicht aus der Hand geben wollte. Nach langwierigen Verhandlungen einigten sich Bistum und Provinz auf ein Doppelpaket: Die Teutonia sollte Heilig Kreuz bekommen, wenn sie auch eine neuzugründende Pfarrei in der Spickelvorstadt übernehmen würde. Im Sommer 1931 trafen die ersten beiden Dominikaner, P. Matthias Bigge und Br. Johannes Rummel, im Spickel ein. Am 19. Juli 1931 wurde dort im Saal einer Gaststätte die erste hl. Messe gefeiert. Im September errichtete Br. Jordan Reith eine provisorische Holzkirche. Knapp zwei Jahre später war der Bau der neuen Pfarrkirche vollendet, die am 30. September 1934 dem hl. Wolfgang geweiht wurde. Das Pfarrhaus

wurde am 6. August 1935 fertig und eingeweiht. Mit Dekret vom 7. Februar 1932 setzte die Bistumsleitung rückwirkend zum 1. Februar P. Pankratius Koch zum Kustos, zum Kirchenrektor von Heilig Kreuz ein. Dieser bezog zusammen mit Br. Innozenz Neumann eine Wohnung im zur Kirche gehörenden sogenannten Benefiziatenhaus. Damit war der Grundstein für eine Klostereröffnung der Dominikaner in Augsburg gelegt. In den folgenden Monaten verstärkte die Teutonia ihre Präsenz an beiden Augsburger Standorten. Mit Dekret vom 1. Januar 1935 übergab Bischof Joseph Kumpfmüller Heilig Kreuz dem Predigerorden. Am 12. November 1936 erhob die Provinz Teutonia ihre Augsburger Gemeinschaft in den Rang einer *domus formata*, also eines selbständigen Klosters des Ordens, das aber auf-

Abb. 1: Die Wallfahrtskirche Heilig Kreuz in Augsburg, aufgenommen zwischen 1913 und 1944 (Archiv des Augsburger Dominikanerkonvents, Fotosammlung).

Abb. 2: Augsburg Heilig Kreuz: Reliquiar für das „Wunderbarliche Gut" (Archiv des Augsburger Konvents, Fotosammlung).

grund mangelnder Mitgliederzahlen noch nicht den Rang und die Rechte eines Konvents genoss – dazu war unter anderem eine Besetzung mit mindestens acht Ordenspriestern notwendig, von denen mindestens fünf das volle Stimmrecht im Orden innehaben mussten.[3]

3 Zur Gründung in Augsburg: Hoyer: *Heilig Kreuz*, S. 629–654; siehe auch: Groothuis: *Im Dienste*, S. 191–194; speziell zu St. Wolfgang: Groll: Mutterpfarrei, S. 1328–1352.

Abb. 3: Augsburg Heilig Kreuz: das Benefiziatenhaus im Otmarsgäßchen hinter der Kreuzkirche (Foto aus: Chronik der Dominikaner bei Heilig Kreuz 1935–1962, fol. 18v).

Angeregt durch die Heiligsprechung Alberts des Großen am 16. Dezember 1931, an welcher der deutsche Episkopat maßgebenden Anteil gehabt hatte, lud der Erzbischof von München und Freising, Michael Kardinal Faulhaber, die Dominikaner ein, in München-Freimann eine Pfarrei unter dem Schutz des „neuen" Heiligen zu übernehmen. Im Mai 1932 reiste der erste Dominikaner, P. Burkhard Zimmermann, nach München. Innerhalb von elf Monaten, ab dem ersten Spatenstich am 17. August 1932 bis zur feierlichen Konsekration am 16. Juli 1933, war die neue St.-Albert-Kirche errichtet. 1934 war auch das Pfarr- und Klostergebäude fertig; die Gemeinschaft hatte den Rang einer *domus*. Da es in München nie zuvor eine dominikanische Niederlassung gegeben hatte, war hier eine echte Neugründung erfolgt.[4]

Zum Unterschied zwischen *domus formata* und *conventus* siehe: *Constitutiones 1932*, S. 95–96, Nrn. 258–262; zur nötigen Besetzung mit Priestern mit Stimmrecht: Nr. 260.

4 Zur Gründung in München: Groothuis: *Im Dienste*, S. 194; Walz: *Dominikaner*, S. 131–132 sowie *ASOP* (1933) S. 255.

Noch schneller erfolgte die Gründung in Freiburg im Breisgau – nicht nur wegen des Interesses der Provinzleitung der Teutonia, sondern auch wegen des persönlichen Engagements von Erzbischof Conrad Gröber, der selbst einmal mit dem Eintritt bei den Dominikanern geliebäugelt hatte. In den Fokus für eine Niederlassung geriet eine Villa am Fuß des Schlossbergs in Freiburg, die bis dahin als katholisches Studentenwohnheim genutzt wurde. Am 6. März 1934 traf sich der Provinzial mit dem Erzbischof und nach einigen zähen Verhandlungen über die Höhe des Kaufpreises konnte eine Einigung erzielt werden. Bereits am 7. Oktober 1934 konnte die Villa bezogen werden. Auch dieses Kloster unter seinem ersten Oberen P. Hugo Vogt wurde dem hl. Albert dem Großen geweiht und stand im Rang einer *domus.*[5]

Damit war der Provinz Teutonia zwischen dem Ende des ersten Weltkrieges und dem Beginn des zweiten die Errichtung von insgesamt sechs neuen Niederlassungen in Worms, Walberberg, Leipzig, Augsburg, München und Freiburg geglückt. Berücksichtigt man die angespannte wirtschaftliche und politische Situation der Zeit, so muss man darin einen sehr schönen Erfolg sehen.

Die Geschicke der Reichsprovinz verliefen hingegen weniger glücklich. Auch sie konnte ein personelles Wachstum verzeichnen – 1858 hatte sie 90 Dominikaner gezählt, 1905 waren es 240[6] – aber es war ihr nur die Gründung dreier neuer Niederlassungen gelungen: 1857 war sie mit den bestehenden Konventen in Wien und Retz in Niederösterreich, in Prag, Leitmeritz, Aussig und Eger in Böhmen, Olmütz, Znaim und Ungarisch Brod in Mähren, sowie in Ungarn in Steinamanger, Ödenburg, Kaschau und einer Residenz in Eisenburg errichtet worden. In Graz in der Steiermark hatte Ordensmeister Jandel 1856 das Predigerkloster wiederbesiedeln lassen; dieses verblieb aber unter der direkten Jurisdiktion des Ordensmeisters. Der Grazer Konvent befand sich somit zwar auf dem Gebiet der Reichsprovinz, aber deren Provinzial hatte keinen Zugriff auf ihn. Erst 1891 übergab Ordensmeister Frühwirth dieses Kloster in die Jurisdiktion

---

5 Zur Gründung in Freiburg: Walz: *Dominikaner*, S. 132; Groothuis: *Im Dienste*, S. 194–196 sowie *ASOP* (1934) S. 624.

6 Zahlen laut: *Schematismus patrum et fratrum ordinis Praedicatorum ad provinciam Imperii, quae e conventibus Bohemiae, Moraviae, Austriae et Hungariae coaluit, pertinentium pro anno 1858*. S. l., s. a., S. 13 und *Schematismus patrum et fratrum sacri ordinis Praedicatorum ad provinciam Imperii (Austriaco-Hungarici) pertinentium anno Domini 1905*. Viennae 1904, S. 36.

der Provinz.[7] Weitere rechtlich selbständige Häuser kamen keine mehr hinzu, nur kleine, unselbständige Niederlassungen: 1881 eine *domus* in Eppan in Südtirol als Filialhaus von Graz, 1889 eine *domus* in Friesach in Kärnten als Filialhaus von Wien und 1903 eine *domus* in Budapest.[8] Das Personalwachstum der Provincia Imperii wirkte sich also kaum auf die Ausbreitung der Dominikaner in ihrem riesigen Provinzgebiet aus, sondern hauptsächlich als Stärkung der vorhandenen Niederlassungen. Zusammen mit den zur selben Zeit immer mächtiger werdenden nationalistischen Tendenzen in der Donaumonarchie förderte dies dominikanische Separationstendenzen in den habsburgischen Kronländern. Das Provinzkapitel der Reichsprovinz des Jahres 1900 stellte beim Ordensmeister den Antrag auf Wiederherstellung der böhmischen Provinz.[9] Ordensmeister Hyacinth Marie Cormier trennte am 14. September 1905 den böhmisch-mährischen vom österreichisch-ungarischen Provinzteil und entließ beide in die Selbständigkeit, wobei die Konvente in Eger und Aussig, obwohl in Böhmen liegend und nominell zur Bohemia gehörend, unter der Jurisdiktion des österreichisch-ungarischen Provinzials verblieben; außerdem wurde der Grazer Konvent endgültig der neuen Provincia Austro-Hungarica zugeschlagen.[10] Damit hatte die Reichsprovinz zu Bestehen aufgehört.

Probleme in Österreich nach dem ersten Weltkrieg

Bei dieser Teilung blieb es jedoch nicht. Schon vor dem ersten Weltkrieg wurden in der österreichisch-ungarischen Provinz Stimmen laut, die eine Unabhängigkeit der Konvente in Ungarn forderten. Die ungarischen Brüder

7 Für die Dauer seiner Amtszeit als Ordensoberhaupt inkorporierte Ordensmeister Andreas Frühwirth mit Brief vom 15. November 1891 den Grazer Konvent der Jurisdiktion des Provinzials der Reichsprovinz (*ASOP* (1892 / 93) 23). Diese Amtszeit dauerte bis zur Wahl seines Nachfolgers, Hyacinth Marie Cormier, am 21. Mai 1904 (Datum laut: ACG 1904, denunciacio I, S. 1).

8 Daten laut: *Schematismus patrum et fratrum sacri ordinis Praedicatorum ad provinciam Austriaco-Hungaricam pertinentium anno Domini 1906*. Viennae 1905, S. 10–11, 17–18 und 23.

9 *Acta congregationis intermediae provinciae Imperii ordinis fratrum Praedicatorum Pragae in conventu ad s. Aegydium abbatis diebus 8–9 Maii 1900 celebrati*. Viennae 1900, S. 7.

10 In ACG 1906, S. 9, Nrn. 19 und 29 finden sich die entsprechenden Anträge der Provinz beim Ordensmeister. Ebd., S. 19–37 sind abgedruckt: das Restitutionsedikt der beiden Provinzen vom 14.9.1905, das Jurisdiktionsdekret für Eger und Aussig vom 17.9.1905 und das Inkorporationsdekret für Graz vom 27.9.1905.

fühlten sich von den Österreichern unterdrückt, ihre Nation würde nicht respektiert und ihr Nachwuchs müsste außerhalb ihres Vaterlandes in Graz ausgebildet werden, was als Benachteiligung empfunden wurde – so gab Provinzial Raymund Glund in einem Bericht an den Ordensmeister am 26. April 1914 die Klagepunkte wieder.[11] Nach Meinung Glunds hatte der ungarische Provinzteil aber nicht genügend Mitbrüder und zu geringen Rückhalt, als dass man ihn zu einer eigenen Provinz hätte machen können. Nach der Niederlage des ersten Weltkrieges wurden die Forderungen der Ungarn immer lauter, denn die Folgen des Krieges waren für die österreichisch-ungarische Provinz katastrophal: Die staatspolitische Einheit zwischen ihren Teilen war zerbrochen; die Niederlassungen der Provinz lagen nun in vier souveränen Staaten und in jedem von diesen herrschten schwierigste Verhältnisse. Die österreichischen Häuser wurden durch wirtschaftliche Probleme stark bedrückt, in die sie teils aus eigenem Verschulden, teils aufgrund der Inflation geraten waren. Die ungarischen Brüder hatten Gefahr für Leib und Leben auszustehen, als sich in Ungarn für ein halbes Jahr eine Räterepublik hatte etablieren können. Aus Kaschau sollten die ungarischen Dominikaner vertrieben werden, da der starke Nationalismus in der Tschechoslowakei keine Ungarn mehr duldete – ähnliche, wenn auch nicht gewalttätige Konflikte gab es in Eger und Aussig, wo die deutschsprachigen Brüder hinausgeworfen werden sollten. Die italienische Regierung untersagte jeglichen wirtschaftlichen Kontakt mit dem Haus in Eppan; selbst der Briefverkehr wurde dort unterdrückt, und letztlich sollten die deutschsprachigen Dominikaner auch von dort vertrieben werden.[12]

Angesichts dieser Probleme rief Ordensmeister Ludwig Theissling, so schnell, wie es das Kriegsende zuließ, den österreichisch-ungarischen Provinzial Alexander Horváth und zwei weitere Provinzvertreter für den 19. Dezember 1918 zu einem Treffen in die neutrale Schweiz nach Zürich, um über das weitere Vorgehen zu beraten. Hauptpunkte dieser Konferenz

11 AGOP XIII 76 130: Relatio administrationis provincialis provinciae Austriaco-Hungaricae ab anno 1910–1914 vom 26.4.1914, v.a. Nr. 1.

12 Zusammenfassung laut AGOP XIII 76 130: Relatio de administratione officii provincialatus a die 23.4.1918–8.5.1922 et de statu provinciae Austro-Hungaricae provincialatus A[lexandri] Horváth vom 8.5.1922 und Relatio de administratione officii provinciali 9.5.1922–26.6.1926 et de statu provinciae Austro Hungaricae in fine officii Raimundi Glund; siehe auch: Chronologia provinciae Austriaco-Hungaricae ab anno 1915–1920, in: *ASOP* (1921) S. 39–43, 108–113, 314–317 (wo allerdings nur die Ereignisse in Ungarn beschrieben werden).

waren die mögliche Trennung der Provinzteile und die Gefahr der Aufhebung mancher Niederlassungen. Die Provinzleitung wollte aber am weiteren Zusammenbleiben festhalten: Es sei zwar „seitens der Ungarn der Wunsch einer Trennung wenigstens latent vorhanden und vereinzelt auch geäußert" worden, jedoch „seitens der Österreicher direkt keine Äußerung auf Trennung erfolgt." Abgesehen davon seien „die Personalverhältnisse in der Provinz doch so, dass jetzt eine Trennung nicht ratsam sei", daher setzte Theissling „gemäß den Umständen" für Ungarn einen eigenen Generalvikar ein. Auch wurde für die Ungarn die Errichtung eines eigenen Noviziats geplant; die Ausbildung der Studenten sollte aber weiterhin gemeinsam in Graz erfolgen.[13]

Wie die weitere Entwicklung zeigte, irrte sich der Provinzial über den Willen zum Zusammenbleiben seiner Provinz. Es kam bald zu schweren Auseinandersetzungen darüber, aus denen Horváth sich zurückzog, weil er sich nicht mehr durchsetzen konnte.[14] Die Vertreter der Konvente und Häuser, die sich auf dem Provinzkapitel 1922 trafen, beantragten einstimmig beim Ordensmeister die Teilung nach Nationen und deren jeweilige Erhebung zu selbständigen Provinzen.[15] Nun gab auch der Ordensmeister die

---

13 Zu diesem Züricher Treffen und als Quelle der Zitate siehe AGOP XIII 76 123: Protokoll der Konferenz in Zürich vom 19.12.1918, besonders Nrn. 1–3.

14 Vielsagend ist der persönliche Brief Horváths an Theissling vom 17. April 1922 (AGOP XIII 76 120, Reg. fol. 39, Nr. 743), in dem Horváth resignierend über die Provinzteilung schreibt: „Ich wollte nur meine Pflicht bis zum letzten Augenblick erfüllen und von der Provinz jenes Unglück abwenden. … Mir persönlich macht es gewiss nichts, was am [sc. Provinz-]Kapitel vor sich gehen wird, da ich ohnehin die Absicht habe, mich von demselben gänzlich fern zu halten. Ich verhehle es nicht, dass ich die Aktion, diese Frage dem Pöbel der Provinz vorgelegt zu haben, für ein Verbrechen halte, da wie Ew. Paternität es sehen, die Patres Provinciae [sc. die Provinzleitung] diese Frage mit Ihnen und eventuell mit dem Diffinitorium [sc. dem Leitungsgremium] des Kapitels ganz gut hätte ordnen können, ohne dass eine Kluft in den Herzen hätte entstehen müssen. Nur dies wollte ich verhindern! Ich habe meinerseits alles getan um die weitere Ausbreitung der Aktion zu verhindern. Jetzt glaube ich, dass an eine weitere Vereinigung der Provinz nicht mehr gedacht werden kann. Wird durch die Verhandlung des Kapitels die Sache in Ungarn bekannt, so ist die Entfremdung der Herzen unvermeidlich und das Leben in einer innerlich geteilten Provinz könnte nur mehr höllisch sein."

15 Die Akten dieses Provinzkapitels, das vom 9.–11. Mai 1922 stattfand, wurden zusammen mit denen des Intermediums von 1924 gedruckt: *Acta capituli provincialis provinciae Austriaco-Hungaricae ordinis Praedicatorum 1922 et acta congregationis intermediae provinciae Austriaco-Hungaricae 1924 celebratae*. Egrae 1924. Der Teilungsantrag findet sich dort S. 12, Nr. 37. Ein Auszug der Akten von 1922, einschließlich des Antrags, steht auch in *ASOP* (1923) S. 200.

Provinzeinheit grundsätzlich auf. In einem Schreiben vom 10. Juni 1923 schlug Theissling dem Provinzkonsil der Austro-Hungarica einen praktischen Weg zur Selbständigwerdung des ungarischen Provinzteiles vor: Bis es in Ungarn genügend Mitbrüder für die Errichtung einer eigenständigen Provinz gäbe und dort auch die religiöse und wissenschaftliche Ausbildung des Ordensnachwuchses gewährleistet sei, sollten beide Provinzteile zusammen bleiben. Ausdrücklich erwähnte der Ordensmeister seine Hoffnung, dass die Trennung bald geschehen möge; zur Zeit sei dies aber nicht möglich.[16]

Abb. 4: Ordensmeister P. Ludwig Theissling (PA, Fotosammlung).

Durch die höchste Ordensleitung wurde auch das Problem der außerhalb des Provinzgebietes liegenden Niederlassungen gelöst: Theissling zog am 29. September 1923 das Haus in Eppan und den Konvent in Kaschau unter die direkte Jurisdiktion des Ordensmeisters, wobei er in Eppan den dortigen Superior und für Kaschau den österreichisch-ungarischen Provinzial als Generalvikare einsetzte.[17] Dasselbe geschah für die Konvente in Eger und Aussig, mit dem böhmischen Provinzial als Generalvikar.[18] Schließlich übertrug Theisslings Nachfolger, Ordensmeister Bonaventura de Paredes, mit Dekret vom 26. Februar 1927 Eger, Aussig und Kaschau in die volle Jurisdiktion der böhmischen Provinz.[19] Auf Druck der italienischen Regierung und der lombardischen Provinz, in deren Territorium Eppan lag, schickte de Paredes' Nachfolger, Ordensmeister Martin Stanislaus Gillet, die österrei-

16 Siehe das Schreiben Theisslings vom 10.6.1923 an das Provinzkonsil der Provincia Austro-Hungarica (AGOP XIII 76 120).

17 Siehe *ASOP* (1923) S. 228, sowie den Auszug aus den Akten des Provinzkapitels der Austro-Hungarica von 1924, S. 66.

18 So laut Notiz in *ASOP* (1924) S. 492, wobei hier leider kein Datum angegeben wird.

19 Siehe *Acta capituli provincialis provinciae Bohemiae diebus 14. mensis Septembris anni 1926 et sequenti in conventu s. Aegydii abbatis Pragae celebrati.* Pragae 1927, S. 10–11.

Abb. 5: Dominikanerkloster St. Josef in Eppan bei Bozen, Postkarte (PA, Fotosammlung).

chischen Dominikaner 1932 zurück in ihre Heimat und besetzte das Haus mit Dominikanern italienischer Nationalität, obwohl das Gebäude selbst weiter im Besitz der Austro-Hungarica verblieb.[20]

Haupthindernis der Verselbständigung der Ungarn war der Mangel an formalrechtlichen Konventen und die Personalschwäche. Um beidem abzuhelfen, wurde zunächst die Ordenspräsenz in Budapest verstärkt, sodass de Paredes 1928 die Niederlassung in der Hauptstadt zum Konvent erheben konnte.[21] 1929 wurde in Steinamanger ein eigenes Noviziat für die ungarische Nation eingerichtet, das 1930 mit immerhin elf Kandidaten seine Arbeit aufnahm; die *domus* wurde 1933 zum Konvent erhoben.[22]

In einem Bericht an den Ordensmeister vom 12. Mai 1934 hielt der aus seinem Amt scheidende Provinzial Sadok Szabó die Errichtung einer selbständigen ungarischen Ordensprovinz inzwischen für durchführbar, da es dort nun genügend Konvente gäbe. Nur wäre jetzt, im Gegensatz zu 1923,

20 So laut Brief des Ordensmeisters Gillet an den österreichisch-ungarischen Provinzial Sadok Szabó vom 22.12.1932 (AGOP XIII 76 158).

21 Siehe Bericht darüber in: *ASOP* (1929) S. 56.

22 Daten der Noviziatseinrichtung und der Konventserhebung laut *Catalogus conventuum et fratrum provinciae Austriaco-Hungaricae ordinis Praedicatorum simul et cœnobiorum monialium ac sororum ibi existentium ineunte anno 1938*. Budapest s.a., S. 14; Meldung über Kandidaten: *ASOP* (1930) S. 754.

in Österreich der Personalstand für eine eigene Verwaltungseinheit nicht mehr ausreichend. Sorgen machten Szabó in diesem Zusammenhang auch die politisch instabile Situation in Mitteleuropa und die Machtergreifung der Nationalsozialisten in Deutschland, die die Eigenstaatlichkeit Österreichs gefährdeten. Szabó brachte deshalb den Gedanken der Gründung einer neuen Provinz aus den süddeutschen und österreichischen Häusern auf – dies ist die erste aktenkundige Erwähnung der Idee der Errichtung einer süddeutsch-österreichischen Provinz.[23] Das Provinzkapitel von 1934 hatte so etwas nicht im Sinn, sondern plante weiter an einer eigenen österreichischen Verwaltungseinheit. Dankbar nahm es die Schützenhilfe an, die ihm das österreichische Konkordat vom 5. Juni 1933 geliefert hatte: Der Heilige Stuhl wurde darin aufgefordert, dafür zu sorgen, dass die Grenzen der österreichischen Ordensprovinzen mit denen der Republik Österreich übereinstimmten. Entsprechend beauftragte das Provinzkapitel den neugewählten Provinzial Bartholomäus Badalik, die Teilung der Provinz nach Maßgabe der Ordenskonstitutionen vorzubereiten.[24] Im Februar 1936 reiste Ordensmeister Martin Stanislaus Gillet nach Wien, Budapest und Prag.[25] In einer Sitzung des Provinzkonsils der Austro-Hungarica unter seinem Vorsitz wurde die letzte Phase der Vorbereitung zur Trennung eingeleitet.[26]

Durch die Machtübernahme der Nationalsozialisten und den Anschluss Österreichs an das Deutsche Reich im März 1938 trat genau die von Szabó vier Jahre zuvor befürchtete Situation ein. In Reaktion darauf erneuerte das Provinzkonsil der österreichisch-ungarischen Provinz am 28. April 1938 beim Ordensmeister den Antrag, auf dem für den kommenden Herbst vorgesehenen Generalkapitel die ungarische Provinz wiederherzustellen und den österreichischen Provinzteil als neue „Provincia Austriaca" zu errichten.[27] Provinzial Badalik fuhr Anfang Mai nach Rom, um die

23 Szabó schrieb: „Si ‚Anschluss' evenerit, conventus Austriaci uniri possent domibus in München et Augsburg erectis et cum illis formare provinciam novam ‚Germaniae superioris' seu potius ‚Süddeutschland'" (Appendix zu AGOP XIII 76 130: Relatio redanda R.P. magistro ordinis de statu provinciae Austro-Hungaricae 1930–1934 vom 12.5.1934).

24 Siehe *Acta capituli provincialis provinciae Austriaco-Hungaricae ordinis fratrum Praedicatorum Viennae in conventu ad basilicam ss. rosarii diebus 15.–19. Maii 1934 celebrati*. Viennae 1934, S. 25, commissio I (dort auch der Verweis auf das Konkordat).

25 Siehe *ASOP* (1936) S. 401.

26 So laut Brief des Provinzials Badalik an den Sozius des Ordensmeisters Bernard Kuhlmann vom 1.3.1936 (AGOP XIII 76 158).

27 AGOP 76 158: Petitio consilii provinciae Austro-Hungaricae ut restituatur antiqua provincia Hungaricae et erigatur in Austria nova provincia Austriaca, vom 28.4.1938,

Verhandlungen mit dem Ordensmeister zu führen.[28] Tatsächlich wartete Ordensmeister Gillet das Generalkapitel nicht ab, sondern errichtete bereits mit Dekret vom 8. Mai 1938 die Provincia Hungariae in den damaligen Grenzen des ungarischen Staates.[29] Das Generalkapitel, das sich vom 25.–28. September 1938 in Rom traf, bestätigte dieses Vorgehen nachträglich.[30] Auch wenn der Anschluss Österreichs in den römischen Quellen zur Restauration der Hungaria nicht genannt wird, so ist er wohl dennoch als Grund für die plötzliche Schnelligkeit des Verhaltens der Ordensleitung anzunehmen, die die nicht einmal mehr vier Monate bis zur Einberufung des Generalkapitels abwarten konnte oder wollte. Allerdings war diese Trennung schon über viele Jahre in Vorbereitung gewesen. Anders gesagt: Die Einverleibung Österreichs ins Deutsche Reich war nicht der Auslöser für das Ende der österreichisch-ungarischen Provinz gewesen, hatte aber als Katalysator dafür gedient.

Der Weg zur süddeutschen Provinz

Was sollte nun aber mit den österreichischen Dominikanerklöstern geschehen? In seinem Teilungsantrag vom April 1938 hatte das Provinzkonsil der Austro-Hungarica ausdrücklich um die Konstituierung der vier Niederlassungen als selbständiger Entität gebeten.[31] Von einem Wunsch, der Pro-

---

Nr. 5. Dieser Bitte voraus ging ein mehrseitiger geschichtlicher Abriss, der die ganze Entwicklung von 1221 bis 1938 schilderte. Dann wurden vier Gründe für die Bitte angegeben: Erstens seien die Sprachen und Nationalitäten zu verschieden, als dass eine gemeinsame Regierung weiter möglich sei. Zweitens sei die kirchliche Verwaltung in beiden Teilen zu unterschiedlich (v.a. durch die unterschiedlichen Konkordate). Drittens mache die politische Lage eine Trennung wünschenswert und viertens seien jetzt alle Bedingungen, die die Konstitutionen für eine Provinzneugründung erforderten, in beiden Teilen erfüllt bzw. durch kleinere Änderungen sofort erfüllbar (nämlich durch die Erhebung der *domus* Retz und der *domus* Ödenburg zu formalrechtlichen Konventen). Hingewiesen wurde außerdem darauf, dass seit 1914 die wirtschaftliche Verwaltung in beiden Provinzteilen getrennt geführt würde, sodass verwaltungsmäßig hier ebenfalls keine Hindernisse im Weg stünden.

28 Siehe dazu AGOP XIII 76 158: Brief Badaliks an den Ordensmeister vom 22.4.1938.

29 Text dieses Dekrets: *ASOP* (1939) S. 15–17.

30 ACG 1938, S. 56, denuntiatio 12.

31 „Omnes congregati … petierunt, ut quattuor domus Austriacae adunaretur in uno corpore, sive provincia sive congregatione, proprio." (AGOP 76 158: Petitio consilii provinciae Austro-Hungaricae ut restituatur antiqua provincia Hungaricae et erigatur in Austria nova provincia Austriaca, vom 28.4.1938, Nr. 5).

vinz Teutonia zugeschlagen zu werden, war nicht die Rede.[32] Zu einer Provinz konnte man die Österreicher nicht ohne weiteres machen: Die Restrukturierungsmaßnahmen der Austro-Hungarica seit dem ersten Weltkrieg hatten sich auf die Verstärkung ihres ungarischen Provinzteils beschränkt. Die Ordenssatzungen forderten als Bedingungen für eine selbständige Provinz die Zugehörigkeit von mindestens 30 vollrechtlichen Dominikanern, die in mehreren Niederlassungen lebten, von denen mindestens drei formalrechtliche Konvente zu sein hatten.[33] Die Mitbrüderzahl war in Österreich zwar vorhanden, allerdings sah es mit dem Nachwuchs schlecht aus.[34] Von den vier Niederlassungen waren gerade einmal zwei rechtliche Konvente, Wien und Graz, während Retz und Friesach nur den Rang einer *domus* hatten. Anders als bei den Ungarn setzte Ordensmeister Gillet daher auf Zeit; er machte aus den österreichischen Häusern ein Vikariat und setzte P. Alfons Well aus dem Grazer Konvent als Vikar ein. Anscheinend hatten Gillet und andere dabei bereits als mögliche Zukunft die Gründung einer weiteren Provinz im Blick.[35]

Well nahm mit dem Provinzial der Teutonia, Laurentius Siemer, Kontakt auf und fuhr zu ihm nach Köln. Im Gepäck hatte er einen Brief Gillets mit dem Vorschlag, die österreichischen Häuser mit den süddeutschen in einem Vikariat zu vereinen.[36] Ergebnis der Gespräche war ein gemeinsamer Brief vom 13. Juni 1938 an den Ordensmeister, in dem die beiden folgendes

---

32 Groothuis: *Im Dienste*, S. 194 hingegen postuliert einen Anschlusswunsch an die Teutonia.

33 Zu den Bedingungen für eine Provinz siehe: *Constitutiones 1932*, S. 101, Nr. 280.

34 1936 waren für den österreichischen Provinzteil in Graz vier Kleriker- und zwei Konversennovizen eingetreten, 1937 ebenfalls vier Kleriker- aber nur ein Konversennovize und 1938 nur mehr ein Klerikernovize (siehe *Catalogus conventuum et fratrum provinciae Austriaco-Hungaricae ordinis Praedicatorum simul et cœnobiorum sororum ibi existentium ineunte anno 1936*. Vác s.a., S. 8–9; *Catalogus conventuum et fratrum provinciae Austriaco-Hungaricae ordinis Praedicatorum simul et cœnobiorum sororum ibi existentium ineunte anno 1937*. Budapest s.a., S. 11 und *Catalogus conventuum et fratrum provinciae Austriaco-Hungaricae ordinis Praedicatorum simul et cœnobiorum monialium ac sororum ibi existentium ineunte anno 1938*. Budapest s.a., S. 11).

35 Zu Wells Einsetzung ließ sich leider kein entsprechendes Dokument finden; diese, wie auch die Idee des Zusammenschlusses mit süddeutschen Klöstern, ergibt sich aber aus dem Zusammenhang späterer Quellen, die im Folgenden zitiert werden; siehe dazu Walz: *Dominikaner*, S. 132.

36 So Groothuis: *Im Dienste*, S. 199, der auf Siemers Erinnerungen Bd. 2, S. 361 verweist. Dabei handelt es sich laut Groothuis: *Im Dienste*, S. 583 um ein zweibändiges Typoskript im Provinzarchiv der Teutonia in Köln.

Abb. 6: P. Laurentius Siemer (PA, Fotosammlung).

vorschlugen: Für die kommenden zwei Jahre sollte über die österreichischen Häuser ein provisorischer Status verhängt werden, währenddessen das Vikariat dem Provinzial der Teutonia untergeben sein sollte. Danach könne man an die Gründung einer neuen Provinz denken. Die Regierung des Vikariats sollte in Übereinstimmung mit dem Ordensmeister erfolgen. Ausgenommen war davon ausdrücklich die Frage der finanziellen Abgaben an die Ordenskurie, die der Provinzial selber regeln durfte. Der Ordensmeister sollte einen Provinzialsvikar über das Vikariat einsetzen, der im Auftrag des Provinzials die Geschäfte führen sollte. Das Ordensstudium in Graz sollte provisorisch an das Generalstudium der Teutonia angeschlossen und die Grazer Studenten nach Walberberg zur Ausbildung geschickt werden.[37]

In einem persönlichen, vertraulichen Schreiben an Gillet, das er dem gemeinsamen Brief am nächsten Tag, dem 14. Juni, folgen ließ, machte Provinzial Siemer allerdings seine eigene Meinung zu diesem Vorhaben deutlich, die sich durchaus unterschied: Er hob darin die geringe Anzahl an Brüdern in den Niederlassungen des Vikariats, deren vorgerücktes Alter und den geringen Nachwuchs besonders hervor. Daraus folge für ihn nicht, dass es sich bei der geplanten Provinz um eine aufstrebende handele, sondern eher um eine absteigende.[38] Das wichtigste, was das Vikariat brauche, sei eine Regeneration des Ordenslebens. Diese sei aber nur durch eine

37 AGOP XIII 73 100: Brief von Provinzial Siemer und Vikar Well an den Ordensmeister vom 12.6.1928.

38 „Voilà qui est bien regrettable, d'autant plus qu'il ne s'agit pas d'une province naissante, mais d'une province qui semble bien être en décadence." (AGOP XIII 73 100: Brief Siemers an den Ordensmeister vom 14.6.1938, S. 1). Es wird wohl kein Zufall gewesen sein, dass Siemer Französisch für seine Ausführungen wählte, die Muttersprache Gillets.

Radikalkur möglich, denn jede andere Art von Bemühung in dieser Richtung würde durch die starke Opposition der österreichischen Brüder abgeblockt werden. Die Entsendung von Brüdern aus der Teutonia in das Vikariat könnte die Wiederherstellung ordentlicher Zustände dort erbringen und sei daher genauso notwendig wie der Zusammenschluss der bayerischen Häuser mit den österreichischen. Aber es stehe zu befürchten, dass diese deutschen Mitbrüder sich von der verweichlichenden Atmosphäre in Österreich anstecken lassen würden. Überdem könnten das ausgezeichnete Apostolat und die gesunde wirtschaftliche Lage der bayerischen Häuser leiden.[39] Aus diesen Gründen schlug Siemer eine schärfere Gangart gegenüber den österreichischen Brüdern vor: Der Status quo sollte für einige Monate andauern. Er wolle selber nach Wien und Graz reisen, um die österreichischen Brüder persönlich kennenzulernen. Durch die Entsendung von drei oder vier deutschen Mitbrüdern nach Graz und die Entfernung aller derjenigen, die sich verweigerten, sollte der Konvent in Graz reformiert werden. Nach zwei Jahren solle man mit Wien ebenso vorgehen. Die Häuser in Friesach und Retz sollten zunächst ungeschoren bleiben. Drei Jahre später könne man dann die drei bayrischen Häuser anschließen und eine oberdeutsche Provinz gründen.[40] Zu diesen Maßnahmen war Siemer ganz im eigenen Namen bereit. Er hoffte auf Gillets Hilfe und versprach ein Vorgehen in Sanftmut, ohne jemanden zu verletzen.[41]

---

39 „Je sais bien qu'il faut envoyer des Pères en Autriche et j'y consens volontiers. De même, il me semble que l'incorporation des couvents bavarois dans une province dite ‚Germania superior' est, objectivement, une nécessité indiscutable. Mais je crains de deux choses l'une: ou bien ce zèle des Pères envoyés la-bàs s'y heurtera à des obstacles insurmontables ou bien eux-mêmes se laisseront gagner par l'atmosphère plus ou moins amollissante qui règne là-bas. De même, je redoute que nos couvents de Bavière, dont l'état économique est parfaitement saint et le travail apostolique, au dire des Évêques, excellent, n'aient à souffrir de l'influence des couvents d'Autriche." (ebd.).

40 „Je me permets donc de proposer ce qui suit: 1. Le statut quo pendant quelques mois. Je me rendrai à Vienne et à Graz pour y faire une visite d'amitié et faire connaissance avec les Pères. 2. Un couvent serait choisi comme base de la réforme – je pense à Graz – et l'on éloignerait ceux qui n'y auraient pas leur place. Les autres y resteraient et seraient aidés par trois ou quatre Pères de notre province. 3. Après deux ans, on procéderait de la mème manière à Vienne. … 4. Les deux petites maisons de Friesach et de Retz seraient pas pour le moment touchées par notre action. 5. Après trois ans, la province ‚Germania superior' serait constituée et les trois couvents de Bavière y seraient adjoints." (ebd., S. 2).

41 „Je me garderai, Rév. Père, d'agir en mon nom personnel, sans votre consentement. Je compte beaucoup sur votre aide. Je veux procéder avec douceur et ne heurter personne." (ebd., S. 3).

Abb. 7: Ordensmeister P. Martin Stanislaus Gillet (PA, Fotosammlung).

Der Sozius des Ordensmeisters, P. Hieronymus Wilms, nahm am 20. September 1938 zu den Plänen Siemers schriftlich Stellung: Die Vorschläge des Provinzials der Teutonia seien recht detailliert, aber besser nicht im Alleingang, sondern mit den zuständigen Gremien auszumachen. Wilms riet der Ordensleitung, die ehemalige, in der Säkularisation untergegangene Provincia Germaniae superioris wiederzuerrichten, mit Österreich, Bayern (ohne Rheinpfalz), Württemberg und Südbaden als Territorium und den Konventen in Wien und Graz sowie den Häusern in Retz, Friesach, Augsburg, Augsburg-Spickel, München und Freiburg im Breisgau. Da die Niederlassungen in München und Freiburg schon jetzt alle Bedingungen erfüllten, könnte man sie zu Konventen erheben. Dazugehören sollten alle diejenigen Mitglieder der Ex-Austro-Hungarica, die nicht bereits Mitglieder der neuen ungarischen Provinz waren, sowie aus der Teutonia alle diejenigen, die in Bayern, Südbaden und Württemberg geboren seien, ausgenommen jene, deren Anhänglichkeit an die Teutonia stärker war.[42]

Dieser Ratschlag überschnitt sich zeitlich mit einem Bericht von Laurentius Siemer, den dieser am 16. September 1938 an den Ordensmeister schickte. Der Provinzial der Teutonia hatte, wie angekündigt, die österreichischen Dominikanerklöster tatsächlich bereist und legte Gillet nun seine Beobachtungen vor. Dieser Besuch hatte Siemers Meinung über die Vorgehensweise im Süden geändert: Nun wollte er „aus Österreich lieber sofort eine eigene Provinz machen" und bot die süddeutschen Häuser dafür an.[43]

42 AGOP XIII 76 100 (1938), Nr. 7–38: Quaestio Austriaca, consilium (Stellungnahme des P. Hieronymus Wilms vom 20.9.1938).

43 Groothuis: *Im Dienste*, S. 199–200; dort auch die Auswertung von Siemers Schreiben vom 16.9.1938 an Gillet (AGOP XIII 71 124), das ich nicht gesehen habe.

Nach diesem strategischen Rückzug Siemers orientierte sich Gillet am Rat seines Sozius: Nach Erhalt des dafür notwendigen Reskripts der Religiosenkongregation vom 24. November 1938 verband er mit Dekret vom 19. Dezember 1938 die österreichischen Predigerklöster mit denen in Süddeutschland, die er von der Teutonia abtrennte, und ordnete zum 2. Februar 1939 die Errichtung einer neuen Provinz an, der er den Namen „Provincia Germaniae superioris" – also „oberdeutsche" oder „süddeutsche Provinz" – gab. Der Text dieser Gründungsurkunde lautet in deutscher Übersetzung wie folgt:

> „Wir, Fr. Martin Stanislaus Gillet, Professor der Theologie und Ordensmeister und demütiger Diener des gesamten Predigerordens.
>
> Da der ungarische Teil der ehemaligen österreichisch-ungarischen Provinz aufgrund der veränderten politischen Lage und der äußerst schwierigen Zeitumstände von dieser Provinz abgetrennt worden war, mußten wir nun auch für den österreichischen Teil dieser Provinz Vorsorge treffen. Was zunächst Kummer verursacht hat, trägt durch Gottes Hilfe aber auch Trost in sich; denn wir haben dadurch die günstige Gelegenheit erhalten, um für den österreichischen Teil besser Vorsorge treffen zu können. So konnten wir nämlich die Wiedererrichtung der Provinz anstreben, die früher den Namen Oberdeutsche Provinz (Germania superior) trug. Wir müssen uns an diejenigen erinnern, die uns bei der Durchführung dieser schwierigen Angelegenheit geholfen haben. Unter all jenen aber muß man vor allem unserer lieben Provinz Teutonia gedenken, die für die Errichtung jener neuen Provinz einen großen Teil ihres Gebietes, verschiedene Häuser und viele Brüder mit deren Zustimmung großmütig abgetreten hat, so daß die neue Provinz nun mit allem ausgestattet ist, wodurch sie mit Gottes Gnade und unter Aufbietung aller Kräfte in Zukunft gedeihen und völlig unabhängig bestehen können möge, dem Orden zur Zier und den Seelen zum Heil.
>
> Daher errichten wir gemäß dem Erlaß Nr. 7713/38 der Kongregation für die Ordensleute vom 24. November 1938, in dem uns die Erlaubnis zur Errichtung einer neuen Provinz erteilt wird, kraft unseres Amtes die Oberdeutsche Provinz und erklären sie vom 2. Februar 1939 an mit all den Rechten und Befugnissen, die unseren Provinzen aufgrund des kanonischen Rechts und des Eigenrechts unseres Ordens bzw. aufgrund des Gewohnheitsrechts zukommen, für errichtet. Die Grenzen dieser Provinz entsprechen den politischen Grenzen der Gebiete Österreich, Bayern, Württemberg und Baden, mit Ausnahme des Gebietes der alten Pfalz. Die Häuser, die zur Zeit zur Provinz gehören, sind folgende: der Wiener Konvent, der Grazer Konvent, das Haus in München, das Haus in Friesach, das Haus in Retz, das Augsburger Haus, das Haus in Freiburg (im Breisgau) und das Haus in Augsburg-Spickel. Zur Oberdeutschen Provinz werden mit wenigen Ausnahmen alle Brüder deutscher Muttersprache gehören, die vorher zur österreichisch-ungarischen Provinz gehört haben, sowie die Brüder

der Provinz Teutonia, die im Gebiet der neu errichteten Provinz geboren sind oder die sich trotz ihrer Zugehörigkeit zur Teutonia damit einverstanden erklärt haben, in die neue Provinz überzutreten. In einem eigenen Dokument, das sich an dieses anschließt, werden alle Brüder aufgezählt, die dieser Provinz vom Tag ihrer Errichtung an transfiliiert sind. Als Provinzial dieser neu errichteten Provinz haben wir den hochwürdigen Pater Marianus Vetter eingesetzt und erklären ihn hiermit vom 2. Februar 1939 an für eingesetzt, wie aus der hier angeschlossenen Urkunde hervorgeht. Zum Provinzkonsil der neuen Provinz werden als Patres Provinciae jene Patres gehören, die schon von Rechts wegen Patres Provinciae sind, sowie die hochwürdigen Patres Alfons Well, Leo Schölzhorn, Ulrich Kaiser und Suso Geiselhart.
Damit alle wichtigeren Angelegenheiten der Provinz gleich von Anfang an in der in unserem Orden üblichen Weise gehandhabt werden, tragen wir dem hochwürdigen P. Provinzial auf, bald ein Provinzkapitel einzuberufen und sich mit uns über diesen Neubeginn zu beraten; diesem Kapitel sind mit Ausnahme der Wahl des Provinzials alle anderen Wahlen vorbehalten, und als Diffinitoren dieses Kapitels haben wir die hochwürdigen Patres Alfons Well, Leo Schölzhorn, Ulrich Kaiser und Suso Geiselhart eingesetzt. An diesem Provinzkapitel können alle teilnehmen, die von Rechts wegen Sitz und Stimme im Provinzkapitel haben. Von den Häusern, die keine Konvente sind, und den übrigen Brüdern, die das Recht haben, einen Deputierten zu wählen, wird noch ein Deputierter gewählt werden können. Unter den Fragen, die auf diesem Kapitel zu behandeln sind, nennen wir die Errichtung eines oder zweier Konvente, damit die Provinz möglichst bald zumindest drei Konvente hat.
Die Novizen dieser Provinz werden in den ersten Jahren ihr Noviziat in dem der Provinz Teutonia verbringen und sich nach ihrer Profeß im Studium generale derselben Provinz ihren Studien widmen, bis die neue Provinz selbst dafür sorgen kann. Damit keine Verwirrung entsteht: Bis alle nötigen Veränderungen durchgeführt sind, wird der hochwürdige Pater Marianus Vetter die Gebiete, Häuser und Brüder, die zu dieser neu zu errichtenden Provinz gehören, vom 25. Dezember 1938 bis zum 2. Februar 1939 als unser Generalvikar führen und die Angelegenheiten, die beide Provinzen betreffen, mit dem hochwürdigen P. Provinzial der Teutonia besprechen.

Im Namen des Vaters und des Sohnes und des Hl. Geistes. Amen.

Gegeben zu Rom in unserer Generalkurie unter dem Siegel unserer Kanzlei am 19. Dezember 1938.

Fr. Martin Stanislaus Gillet OP, Ordensmeister
Fr. Bernhard Kuhlmann OP, Socius des Ordensmeisters“[44]

44 Volltext des Errichtungsdekrets Gillets vom 19.12.1938 in Latein in: *ASOP* (1939) S. 177–178 und in den APKap 1939, S. 3–5; obige deutsche Übersetzung von Sonja Reisner in: *Dominikus* 1–1999, S. 10–11.

Wie man sieht, hatte Gillet sich dabei genau an das gehalten, was ihm Wilms geraten hatte, nur dass das Territorium der neuen Provinz nun nicht nur Südbaden, sondern ganz Baden enthalten sollte. Eine der ersten Amtshandlungen des neuen Provinzials, P. Marianus Vetter, bestand am 26. Januar 1939 darin, den Ordensmeister um den hl. Albert den Großen als Patron der Germaniae Superioris zu bitten.[45]

Die Feuertaufe der ersten Jahre (1939–1945)

Die Ausgangslage

Mit der ersten Sitzung des Provinzkonsils am 3. Februar 1939 in Wien begann die Arbeit der neuen Provinz zum ersten Mal aktenkundig zu werden.[46] Eine Gemeinschaft von 143 Dominikanern musste verwaltet werden. Wie der erste Provinzkatalog – ein zu einem Stichdatum erscheinendes Personalstandsverzeichnis – angibt, waren 84 davon Priester, 44 Laienbrüder, 13 Klerikerstudenten und je einer war Kleriker- bzw. Laienbrudernovize.[47] Was die Herkunft dieser Brüder anging, so zeigt dieser Katalog, dass ihre Heimatgebiete weit über die Grenzen der Provinz hinausgingen: Etwa 42 Prozent stammten aus dem Deutschen Reich (vor 1938), 18 Prozent aus Österreich (vor 1938), 16 Prozent aus anderen Gebieten der Donaumonarchie (sie hatten zum österreichischen Provinzteil der ehemaligen Austro-Hungarica gehört) – und 24 Prozent, also beinahe ein Viertel, kamen aus der Schweiz. Einige dieser Schweizer Brüder waren Mitglieder der österreichisch-ungarischen Provinz gewesen, einzelne waren sogar noch in die Provincia Imperii eingetreten, aber die meisten von ihnen wechselten aus der Teutonia nach Süddeutschland. Sie bildeten v. a. in Freiburg, aber auch in Augsburg und München einen Großteil der Klosterbesatzungen.

---

45 PA, Provinzialsregestenbuch 1 (1939–1966), Eintrag vom 26.1.1939, S. 6, Nr. 17.

46 Siehe PA, Liber consiliorum provinciae, Sitzung vom 3.2.1939, S. 3–4 und *ASOP* (1939) S. 98–99.

47 Die Angaben des Mitgliedersummariums im PKat 1939, S. 25 (dort: 85 Priester und 12 Kleriker) sind falsch, was man erkennt, wenn man die unter den Konventen und Häusern usw. aufgeführten Namen zählt. Ähnliche Fehler finden sich auch in vielen der Konventssummarien dieses Katalogs, wie auch der Kataloge der folgenden Jahre. Ich habe für diesen Beitrag jene Angaben stillschweigend korrigiert.

So unterschiedlich die Herkunft aller Brüder war, so verschieden waren auch Charakter und Tätigkeitsfelder der Niederlassungen der Provinz: Die ursprünglich teutonischen Häuser in Süddeutschland waren sehr neu und frisch aufgebaut, die österreichischen hingegen blickten auf eine lange Tradition, die teilweise bis zu den Gründungsjahren des Ordens selbst zurückreichte. In Wien stand in der Seelsorge neben einer dem Konvent seit dem 18. Jahrhundert anvertrauten Innenstadtpfarrei die geistliche Betreuung mehrerer Schwesterngemeinschaften im Vordergrund. Zu diesem Konvent gehörten zwölf Ordenspriester und neun Laienbrüder, außerdem nahm hier der neue Provinzial seine Residenz. Vom domus Friesach aus wurden ebenfalls Schwestern betreut; abgesehen davon bestand die Seelsorge der kleinen Gemeinschaft von vier Priestern und zwei Laienbrüdern aus der Sakramentenpastoral an der Klosterkirche. Ähnlich war es in Retz: Auch hier stand die Klosterkirche im Mittelpunkt, wobei ein Mitbruder als Kaplan und ein anderer als Katechet an der Stadtpfarrei angestellt war; hier lebten fünf Priester und fünf Laienbrüder. Diese drei Klöster waren in ihrem Lebensalltag kaum von der Provinzneugründung betroffen worden. Ganz anders stand es in Graz: Mit der Verlegung der Ausbildung des Nachwuchses in die Teutonia hatte dieser Konvent zwei seiner Standbeine verloren, das Generalstudium und das Noviziat. Nur ein Laienbrudernovize durfte 1939 sein Probejahr noch in Graz fertig machen. Vom Verlust seiner Rolle als Generalstudium erholte sich der Grazer Konvent niemals wieder. Übrig blieben hier vor allem die große Pfarrei und die sakramentale Betreuung der Pfarr- und Klosterkirche. In Graz-Wetzelsdorf betrieb der Konvent außerdem noch ein Juvenat, also ein Internat für Gymnasialschüler, als eine Art Nachwuchsschmiede. Im Grazer Kloster lebten elf Priester, acht Laienbrüder und ein Laienbrudernovize. In Augsburg war aufgrund der doppelten Niederlassung des Konvents an Heilig Kreuz und an St. Wolfgang die Pastoral ebenfalls zweigeteilt: Beicht- und Messseelsorge in der Innenstadt und Pfarrseelsorge in der Vorstadt. Dazu kam an Heilig Kreuz noch die Aufgabe der Gefängnisseelsorge. Zu Augsburg gehörten zehn Priester und sieben Laienbrüder. Die Aufgabe der Brüder in Freiburg im Breisgau bestand hauptsächlich in Schwestern- und Studentenseelsorge. Hier wohnten neun Priester und fünf Laienbrüder. Naturgemäß stand auch in München-Freimann die Pfarrseelsorge im Vordergrund, wobei die Brüder ebenfalls mehrere Schwesterngemeinschaften geistlich betreuten. Im *domus* von München / St. Albert wohnten fünf Priester und drei Laienbrüder. An allen sechs Niederlassungen waren Gruppen des Dritten Ordens angesiedelt oder wurden von dort aus betreut.

Abb. 8: Die Leitung der neugegründeten Provinz im Februar 1939.
Von links: P. Leo Schölzhorn, P. Alfons Well, P. Provinzial Marianus Vetter, P. Ulrich Kaiser, P. Suso Geiselhart, P. Angelikus Töffler
(Foto aus: Chronik der Dominikaner bei Heilig Kreuz 1935–1962, fol. 58v).

Rechnet man diese Zahlen der Bewohner der Klöster der Provinz zusammen, kommt man auf insgesamt 96. Anders gesagt: In der Provinz selbst lebten nur etwa zwei Drittel ihrer Mitglieder. Abgesehen von einem Priester, der als Seelsorger bei den Dominikanerinnen in Schlehdorf wohnte, hatte dies mit der Anordnung des Ordensmeisters zu tun, wonach der Nachwuchs nicht in der Provinz ausgebildet wurde: Im Generalstudium der Teutonia in Walberberg wirkten zwei Provinzmitglieder als Dozenten, acht Priester und elf Kleriker studierten und zwei Laienbrüder arbeiteten dort – insgesamt 23 Brüder aus der Germania superior, was Walberberg sozusagen zum größten Kloster der süddeutschen Provinz machte. Ein süddeutscher Klerikernovize machte sein Probejahr im Noviziatskonvent der Teutonia in Warburg in Westfalen. Weitere 24 Provinzmitglieder wirkten und lebten an der Kurie des Ordens in Rom und an der dortigen Ordenshochschule „Angelicum" (fünf Priester, drei Laienbrüder und ein Kleriker), an den beiden dominikanischen Niederlassungen und der Universität in Freiburg in der Schweiz (sechs Priester und ein Kleriker), zwei Priester arbeiteten im Konvent der böhmischen Provinz in Znaim und drei Priester betreuten jeweils Schweizer Dominikanerinnenklöster.

Zu dem vom Provinzkonsil festgelegten Termin, dem 3. Mai 1939, trafen die Vertreter der Konvente und Häuser in Wien ein, um dort das erste Provinzkapitel der Germania superior abzuhalten, das bis zum 6. Mai dauerte. In einem lateinischsprachigen Brief an den ungarischen Provinzial wurde dankbar der guten Zusammenarbeit mit den ungarischen Mitbrüdern gedacht. Ein weiterer Brief an den Provinzial der Teutonia – auf Deutsch – hob dessen persönliche Bemühungen als für die Errichtung der Provinz von grundlegender Bedeutung hervor. Zum Sitz des Provinzialats wurde Wien bestimmt. Die notwendigen Ämter wurden besetzt und die Aufgaben verteilt. Darüber hinaus fällt die Ermahnung des Kapitels auf, die Laienbrüder der Provinz zur aktiven Teilnahme an der Liturgie besser auszubilden und zu fördern und ihnen zu ihrer Unterstützung die liturgischen Bücher des Ordens in deutscher Übersetzung in die Hand zu geben. Zum Ausbildungszentrum für künftige Katecheten und Pfarrseelsorger wurde das Haus in München-Freimann bestimmt, da dort die geeignetsten Verhältnisse dafür herrschten.[48] Besonders wichtig war den Kapitelsvätern die Verbesserung der Studiensituation in der Provinz: Sie beauftragten daher den Provinzial, so bald als möglich für die Errichtung eines eigenen Ordensstudiums zu sorgen und dafür auch Mitbrüder für Spezialstudien freizugeben. Um die seitens der Konstitutionen für eine Provinz notwendige Konventszahl zu erreichen, wurde der Ordensmeister gebeten, die *domus formatae* Freiburg im Breisgau / St. Albert und Augsburg / Heilig Kreuz zu formalrechtlichen Konventen zu erheben. Anschließend wurde als Termin für das nächste Provinzkapitel die Woche vor Pfingsten 1943 und als Tagungsort Wien festgelegt.[49]

Ordensmeister Gillet folgte der Bitte des Provinzkapitels und erhob die *domus* an Heilig Kreuz in Augsburg am 11. Juni 1939 zum Konvent. Der Provinzial setzte P. Ulrich Kaiser zum ersten Prior ein.[50] Am 4. August 1939 folgte die Erhebung der *domus* St. Albert in Freiburg in Breisgau; hier wurde P. Meinrad Schumpp zum ersten Prior.[51] Der ordentliche Beginn der Provinzverwaltung schien damit geregelt. Aber anstatt sich um ihren weiteren Aufbau kümmern zu können, sah sich die Provinz vier Wochen spä-

---

48 Zum Ausbau eines solchen pastoralen Ausbildungsganges kam es in Freimann jedoch nie. Erst 17 Jahre später wurde in Augsburg der Versuch dazu unternommen.

49 Zu alle dem siehe: APKap 1939.

50 PA, Provinzialsregestenbuch 1 (1939–1966), Eintrag vom 11.6.1939, S. 10, Nr. 53.

51 PA, Provinzialsregestenbuch 1 (1939–1966), Eintrag vom 14.8.1939, S. 12, Nr. 65.

ter ganz anderen Sorgen gegenüber: Am 1. September überfiel die deutsche Wehrmacht Polen. Der zweite Weltkrieg hatte begonnen.

Einberufungen und Einquartierungen

Die ersten Auswirkungen dieses Ereignisses trafen die Provinz bald: Bis zum 1. Oktober 1939 wurden drei Kleriker und vier Laienbrüder zum Militär eingezogen. Ab Juli 1940 waren es 14 Priester, acht Kleriker und 15 Laienbrüder. Der Höhepunkt der Einziehungen von insgesamt 46 Mitbrüdern (18 Priester, sechs Kleriker und 22 Laienbrüder) war im Februar 1942 erreicht. Sie wurden auf praktisch alle Kriegsfronten verteilt.[52] Abgesehen von den Auswirkungen auf die Seelsorge wurde durch die Einberufungen das klösterliche Leben deutlich erschwert, weil ab Mitte 1940 beinahe alle Laienbrüder unter 60 Jahren in den Konventen fehlten. Die älteren und teilweise kranken Laienbrüder, die zurückgeblieben waren, müssen ein ungeheures Arbeitspensum zu leisten gehabt haben, „das sie jedoch bereitwillig tragen“, wie der Provinzial immer wieder betonte.[53] Trotz dieser großen Anstrengungen mussten verschiedene Dienste nun durch Kräfte von außen versehen werden. So wurde Anfang 1940 die Küche in fast allen Häusern „außer Klausur gesetzt“, wie es hieß, damit Ordensschwestern, Tertiarinnen bzw. Angestellte die anfallenden Arbeiten übernehmen konnten.[54]

Außerdem mussten Ausländer das Staatsgebiet des Deutschen Reiches verlassen, was dazu führte, dass den Mitbrüdern schweizerischer Herkunft in den süddeutschen Häusern entweder die Aufenthaltserlaubnis ganz entzogen wurde oder ihnen nur mehr ein Kurzaufenthalt gewährt war. Das brachte weitere schwere personelle Einbußen mit sich, vor allem in Freiburg im Breisgau.[55] Die meisten dieser exilierten Brüder übernahmen Seelsorgsposten an verschiedenen Dominikanerinnenklöstern der Eidgenossenschaft oder gingen in die *domus* S. Hyacinthe in Freiburg in der Schweiz. Auch zur Mannschaft der im September 1941 in Luzern neugegründeten *domus* gehörten Mitglieder der Germania superior. Damit unterstützte diese staatliche Zwangsmaßnahme letztlich die von Ordensmeis-

52 Siehe PA, Provinzrundbrief vom 29.1.1940, vom 3.7.1940 und vom 2.2.1942, sowie die PKat 1939, 1941 und 1943.

53 PA, Provinzrundbrief vom 10.2.1941, S. 4, vom 2.2.1942, S. 6 und öfter.

54 PA, Provinzrundbrief vom 29.1.1940, S. 5 und vom 10.2.1941, S. 1.

55 PA, Provinzrundbrief vom 29.9.1939.

ter Gillet 1937 begonnene Schaffung einer eigenen Schweizer Provinz, die nach dem Krieg erfolgte.[56]

Die Regierung suchte sofort nach Kriegsausbruch die Möglichkeit, unliebsame Prediger außer Gefecht zu setzen. Der Grazer P. Gundisalv Sommer wurde Mitte Oktober 1940 in der Steiermark inhaftiert, musste Österreich verlassen und verbrachte die Kriegsjahre im Konvent der böhmischen Provinz in Znaim.[57] P. Diego Hanns Goetz aus dem Wiener Konvent wurde aufgrund seiner Predigttätigkeit im Rahmen der Studentenseelsorge und der Betreuung von Künstlern „aus der Ostmark ausgewiesen", ging zunächst nach München und dann nach Freiburg im Breisgau.[58] Nach Predigten gegen die Unterdrückungs- und Verfolgungsmaßnahmen der Nationalsozialisten im Wiener Stephansdom am 25., 28. und 29. Oktober 1943 wurde Provinzial Marianus Vetter für seine „defätistischen" Worte schärfstens verwarnt, erhielt Redeverbot für das gesamte Reichsgebiet und musste ein „Sicherungsgeld" von 3000 Reichsmark zahlen.[59] Vetter – als Domprediger in Berlin, Bamberg und Wien weithin bekannt – war in seinen Ansprachen und Predigten schon seit 1933 als Gegner der Nationalsozialisten, insbesondere Alfred Rosenbergs, aufgetreten und hatte bereits mehrere Rügen und Verwarnungen erhalten.[60] P. Karl Stumpf, obwohl gebürtig aus Speyer und Mitglied der österreichisch-ungarischen Provinz, hatte vor der Gründung der Germania superior zum Wiener Konvent gehört. Nach der Provinzgründung verschwand er fast völlig aus den Provinzkatalogen und den Rundbriefen des Provinzials, obwohl er sicher weiter zur süddeutschen Provinz gehörte, denn einmal wird er im Provinzkatalog von 1943 genannt.[61] Erst nach dem Krieg taucht Stumpf wieder auf, als er 1946 nach München / St. Albert assigniert wurde.[62] Was Stumpf in den Jahren zwischen 1938 und 1946 widerfahren war, schildert ein Nachruf auf ihn: Demnach wirkte er

56 Siehe dazu allgemein: Hodel, Bedouelle, Müller: *Die Schweizer Dominikanerprovinz*, S. 167–169, die PKat 1939, 1941 und 1943, sowie die Provinzrundbriefe von 1939 bis 1941 (PA).

57 PA, Provinzrundbrief vom 29.1.1940, S. 5 und die PKat 1939–1946.

58 PA, Provinzrundbrief vom 2.2.1942, S. 3.

59 Groothuis: *Im Dienste*, S. 268.

60 Dazu in detaillierter Deutlichkeit: ebd., S. 260–269.

61 PKat 1943, S. 21 – nämlich in der Liste der Provinzmitglieder nach Professalter.

62 PA, Provinzialsregestenbuch 1 (1939–1966), Eintrag vom 25.1.1946, S. 32, Nr. 17.

> „in Wien, wo er vor allem unmittelbar vor der Naziherrschaft gegen die Irrlehre des Nationalismus in den Predigten Stellung nahm. 1938 flüchtete er über Ungarn nach Jugoslawien, hielt sich im Dominikanerkloster in Agram auf und hielt dort Vorträge gegen die Irrlehre des Nationalismus, und um sich zu tarnen, nahm er den Namen Dragodin Müller an. …
> Als die Deutschen in Jugoslawien einrückten, flüchtete P. Karl von Agram zuerst nach Split, dann nach Dubrovnik und wollte über die Türkei nach Amerika, hatte aber keine genügende Mittel und als die Italiener, die Dubrovnik besetzthielten, von den deutschen Truppen gefangen wurden, wurde auch P. Karl verhaftet und in die Festung von Belgrad gebracht. Es war beschlossen worden, daß die Engländer an einem bestimmten Tag die Festung mit Bomben belegen werden und die Partisanen hatten für alle Gefangenen schon Reservekleider gerichtet, damit sie flüchten können. Einen Tag vor dem Fliegerangriff der Engländer wurde die Sache verraten und alle Gefangenen ins Reich gebracht, so auch P. Karl Stumpf, der in Dachau landete, wo er beim Einmarsch der Amerikaner befreit wurde.“[63]

Der Vollständigkeit halber seien noch zwei weitere Fälle erwähnt, die sich aber vor der Gründung der süddeutschen Provinz zutrugen: P. Matthias Bigge, Pfarrseelsorger an St. Wolfgang in Augsburg-Spickel, wurde im Juni 1934 wegen einer Pfingstpredigt gegen falsche Propheten und Neuheidentum verwarnt. Weitere Folgen sind nicht aktenkundig. P. Ulrich Kaiser, der als Pfarrer in St. Paulus in Berlin-Moabit einen evangelisch konvertierten Juden mit einer Katholikin verheiratet hatte, wurde am 12. Juli 1937 wegen Vergehen gegen das Personalstandsgesetz („Rassenschande“) zu drei Monaten Gefängnis verurteilt. Nach eingelegter Berufung wurde das Verfahren zwar wegen des Amnestiegesetzes vom 30. April 1938 eingestellt, aber Kaiser galt nun als vorbestraft und hatte Unterrichtsverbot.[64]

Ebenfalls schon in den ersten Kriegswochen mussten die Dominikanerklöster in Süddeutschland und Österreich eine weitere Schikane hinnehmen: Beschlagnahmungen und Einquartierungen. In Friesach zog 1939 die Heeresverwaltung in einen Großteil der Räume ein,[65] später befand sich da-

---

63 So laut des anonymen (vielleicht von P. Gottfried Prischink stammenden) handschriftlichen Nachrufes über Stumpf; vier Blätter Xeroxkopie, betitelt „P. Karl Stumpf † 1951, 4. August i. Speyer“ (Beilage in PA, Chronik für das Noviziat der oberdeutschen Dominikanerprovinz), Zitat S. 1 und 4.

64 Groothuis: *Im Dienste*, S. 242 (Bigge) und S. 433–437 (Kaiser). Groothuis bezeichnet Kaisers als typischen Fall des Widerstands im Alltag (ebd., S. 437.)

65 PA, Provinzrundbriefe vom 29.9.1939 (zum Zeitpunkt) und vom 2.2.1942 (zur Heeresverwaltung).

rin die Arbeitsfront mit einem Umschulungskurs.[66] Am 14. September 1940 wurden die Klostergebäude in Retz „für volksdeutsche Rückwanderer aus Bessarabien in Anspruch genommen und mussten sofort geräumt werden."[67] Zur Aufrechterhaltung der Seelsorge an der Klosterkirche und der Stadtpfarrei verblieben den Dominikanern nur die Wohnräume für drei Priester und einen Laienbruder. Der Grazer Konvent musste im Herbst 1940 „einen beträchtlichen Teil seines Hauses an den Reichsnährstand vermieten und sein früheres Noviziat für ein Rückwandererlager freigeben."[68] Etwa ein Jahr später änderte sich die Belegschaft: Am 1. November 1941 mietete der Gau Steiermark einen Großteil der Räume im Kloster, zwecks Einrichtung eines Schülerinnenheims. Darunter fielen auch das Refektorium und die Bibliothek, die geräumt werden mussten.[69] Den Dominikanern verblieben das Erdgeschoß im Kreuzgang und im ersten Stock die beiden an die Kirche anlehnenden Flügel.[70] Das Schülerinnenheim zog Anfang 1943 ein.[71] In Wien wurden seit dem 1. Januar 1941 der Thomassaal und der Gästetrakt durch Einquartierungen des Militärs belegt.[72] Zu Jahresbeginn 1942 folgte die Beschlagnahmung des sogenannten Priestergangs im zweiten Stock, einschließlich des Provinzialats.[73] Die Brüder des Freiburger Konvents, der in Grenznähe und damit im militärischen Operationsgebiet lag, befürchteten anfangs ihre Evakuierung und die Beschlagnahme ihres Klosters, was sich nicht erfüllte. Mit dem Einzug einer Lazarettverwaltung am 17. November 1941 verloren sie aber mit neun Zimmern im ersten und zweiten Stock einen Großteil ihrer Wohnräume.[74] Die Lazarettverwaltung zog 1943 aus, dafür der Stab des weiblichen Arbeitsdienstes ein.[75] Im Kloster an Heilig Kreuz in Augsburg wurden Ende Januar 1942 in mehreren Räumen im ersten Stock zwei Militärbeamte einquartiert.[76] Obwohl auch im Pfarrhaus von St. Wolfgang im Spickel am 21. Juni 1941 eine ganze Reihe von Zimmern von der

66 PA, Bericht des Provinzials zum Provinzkapitel 6.11.1946 (Provinzrundbrief), S. 1.
67 PA, Provinzrundbrief vom 10.2.1941, S. 4.
68 PA, Provinzrundbrief vom 29.1.1940, S. 3.
69 PA, Provinzrundbrief vom 2.2.1942, S. 5.
70 PA, Provinzrundbrief vom 2.10.1942.
71 PA, Provinzrundbrief vom 3.3.1943.
72 PA, Provinzrundbrief vom 10.2.1941, S. 2.
73 PA, Provinzrundbrief vom 2.2.1942, S. 4.
74 PA, Provinzrundbriefe vom 29.1.1940, S. 2 und vom 2.2.1942, S. 4.
75 PA, Provinzrundbrief vom 6.9.1943.
76 Hoyer: *Heilig Kreuz*, S. 665–668.

Stadt sozusagen vorausschauend beschlagnahmt wurden, wurden diese in der Folge nicht in Anspruch genommen.[77] In München-Freimann verloren nicht die Brüder selbst Räume, sondern ihre Seelsorgearbeit, da sich die Polizei in das Pfarrheim einquartierte.[78] Neben der Raumnot hatten diese Beschlagnahmungen auch eine politische Folge: Die Brüder waren nun in den eigenen Häusern engem Kontakt zu nationalsozialistischen Organisationen oder dem Militär ausgesetzt und mussten sich in ihrem Verhalten sehr in Acht nehmen.

Seelsorge und klösterliches Leben

Trotz des Krieges hielt der Provinzial im November und Dezember 1939 eine erste kanonische Visitation aller Niederlassungen der Provinz ab.[79] Wichtigstes Anliegen seiner Besuche war für Vetter die Observanz: „Die harte Kriegszeit, in der unser Volk steht, fordert auch von uns, dass wir im Geiste unseres hl. Albert unser Ordensideal mit besonderem Ernst erfassen. So dienen wir auf unsere Weise unserem Volk und unserer hl. Kirche."[80] Vetter zeigte sich von seinen Mitbrüdern zufrieden: „Die Visitation hat ergeben, dass alle Häuser sich Mühe geben, ihre Ordensverpflichtungen nach jeder Richtung gut durchzuführen."[81] Selbst die noch vom Ordensmeister beauftragte Errichtung einer eigenen Ausbildungsstätte für Ordenskandidaten nahm Vetter in Angriff: Am 30. April 1940 erbaten Provinzial und Provinzkonsil beim Ordensmeister die kanonische Errichtung eines Noviziats im Konvent von Wien, was auch geschah.[82] Wegen der Beschlagnahmung der dafür vorgesehenen Räume in Wien verlegte Vetter am 12. Februar 1941 das Noviziat nach Freiburg im Breisgau.[83] Praktische Folgen hatte dies jedoch keine, da es keine Novizen gab.

Auch vom Oktober 1940 bis zum Februar 1941 gelang es Vetter noch einmal, eine kanonische Visitation durchzuführen.[84] Dabei wurde ihm „ersichtlich, wie die einzelnen Konvente einen schweren Stand haben, trotz des

77 PA, Provinzrundbrief vom 2.2.1942, S. 4.

78 PA, Bericht des Provinzials zum Provinzkapitel 6.11.1946 (Provinzrundbrief), S. 1.

79 PA, Provinzialsregestenbuch 1 (1939–1966), S. 14.

80 PA, Provinzrundbrief vom 12.11.1939.

81 PA, Provinzrundbrief vom 29.1.1940, S. 6.

82 PA, Provinzialsregestenbuch 1 (1939–1966), Eintrag vom 30.4.1940, S. 16, Nr. 13.

83 Ebd., Eintrag vom 12.2.1941, S. 20, Nr. 11.

84 Ebd., S. 18 und 21.

Ausfalls der jungen Seelsorgskräfte und der vielen Laienbrüder ihren Aufgaben gewachsen zu sein. … Alle Häuser und Konvente der Provinz haben ihr Möglichstes getan, um das innere Konventsleben und das apostolische Arbeiten voll aufrecht zu erhalten. Das Chorgebet und die sonstigen Ordensverpflichtungen werden überall treu gehalten. Nur in Retz und München ist wegen der besonderen Umstände ein ständiges Chorgebet zur Zeit nicht möglich. Wir sind uns bewusst, dass gerade die Schwere der Zeit von uns eine besondere Treue im innerlichen Leben und Beten fordert."[85]

In seinen Rundbriefen an die Provinz beschrieb Vetter die Seelsorge an den verschiedenen Standorten der Brüder zu dieser Zeit: In Augsburg lag die Arbeit an Heilig Kreuz, wie schon vor dem Krieg, hauptsächlich auf der Eucharistiefeier und dem stark frequentierten Beichtstuhl – Vetter nennt den Konvent einmal „sozusagen die Großpönitentiarie für Stadt und Land von Augsburg";[86] an St. Wolfgang bestand sie in der Pfarr- und Schulseelsorge. Durch die Aufhebung der theologischen Fakultät der Universität München und den Ausfall der Laienbrüder wurde die Lage in St. Albert in Freimann für die Dominikaner hingegen schwer: Hatten vorher eine ganze Reihe von Doktoranden, die als Gäste im Kloster gewohnt hatten, in der Seelsorge mitgeholfen und dadurch manche Möglichkeiten wie Gastpredigten und Volksmissionen eröffnet, so fand man sich nun den Anforderungen der Pfarrei kaum mehr gewachsen. In Graz waren die Brüder mit der großen Münzgrabenpfarrei vollauf beschäftigt; das Juvenat in Wetzelsdorf war geschlossen und an die Schwestern der Caritas Socialis als Altersheim vermietet worden,[87] wobei ein Pater dort weiter die Stellung hielt.[88] In Freiburg im Breisgau wirkte die räumlich wie personell sehr stark eingeschränkte Mannschaft hauptsächlich als Aushilfsgeistliche für Predigt und Beichtstuhl, womit sie der Erzdiözese Freiburg sehr entgegenkamen, da dort ein großer Teil des Weltklerus zum Militär eingezogen war und der Erzbischof diese Hilfe dringend benötigte. In Retz und Friesach bestand die Aufgabe in der Pastoral an den örtlichen Pfarrkirchen, denn in beiden Häusern war durch die Einquartierungen keine andere Seelsorgsarbeit mehr möglich.[89]

---

85 PA, Provinzrundbrief vom 10.2.1941, S. 2.

86 In: PA, Provinzrundbrief vom 29.1.1940, S. 1.

87 Wann genau dies geschah, ist unklar. Vetter gibt nur „in der Nazizeit" an (PA, Bericht des Provinzials zum Provinzkapitel 6.11.1946 (Provinzrundbrief), S. 2.

88 Siehe die PKat 1939, 1941, 1943 und 1946, jeweils unter Graz.

89 Die obige Zusammenfassung ist aus den Angaben der Provinzrundbriefe vom

Auch was die satzungsgemäße Verwaltung der Provinz anging, hinterließen die Umstände der Kriegszeit ihre Spuren: Das Priorat von P. Schumpp in Freiburg im Breisgau lief im Juli 1942 aus. Hier war wegen der zu geringen Besetzung des Konvents eine Priorenwahl nicht mehr möglich. Der Ordensmeister setzte deshalb Schumpp noch einmal zum Prior ein.[90] Ein paar Monate später, im Frühjahr 1943, endete auch die Amtszeit von P. Marianus Vetter als Provinzial. Das ursprünglich vorgesehene Provinzkapitel konnte in der derzeitigen Situation jedoch nicht abgehalten werden. Auf Antrag der Prioren und des Provinzkonsils wurde es „bis nach dem Krieg verschoben" und das Provinzialat Vetters bis dahin verlängert.[91] Dies geschah wohl in Analogie zu der Regelung des Heiligen Stuhles, der die Einberufung des für September 1941 in Rom geplanten Generalkapitels und die Wahl des Ordensmeisters auf unbestimmte Zeit aussetzte.[92] Am 10. Oktober 1944 beantragte Vetter über die Apostolische Nuntiatur die Verlängerung aller aktuellen Priorate bis zum nach dem Krieg abzuhaltenden Provinzkapitel.[93]

Sterben an der Front und Bombenkrieg

Erst in der zweiten Kriegshälfte musste die Provinz schwerste Schäden und Einbußen hinnehmen. Noch im Juli 1942 – im dritten Kriegsjahr – konnte der Provinzial schreiben: „Aus dem Felde habe ich, Gott sei Dank, von allen Mitbrüdern gute Nachricht. In Russland und Norwegen, im Süden und an der Westküste und auch im Dienst des Heimatheeres sind alle noch wohlauf."[94] Im Oktober 1942 meldete er: „In den Konventen hat sich nichts Besonderes ereignet. Die Arbeiten gehen auch mit stark verminderten Kräften ihren Gang."[95] Im November 1942 fügte Vetter hinzu: „Zuweilen lässt sich auch ein Fronturlauber blicken."[96] Im Provinzrundbrief vom 1. April 1943

29.1.1940, S. 2–4, vom 10.2.1941, S. 2–4 und vom 2.2.1942, S. 4–6 zu den einzelnen Häusern gewonnen.

90 PA, Provinzrundbrief vom 20.7.1942 und Provinzialsregestenbuch 1 (1939–1966), Eintrag vom 15.8.1942, S. 22, Nr. 7.

91 PA, Provinzrundbrief vom 4.5.1943.

92 Siehe Reskript der Religiosenkongregation vom 30.9.1941 in: *ASOP* (1941) S. 85 und 86.

93 PA, Provinzialsregestenbuch 1 (1939–1966), Eintrag vom 10.10.1944, S. 26, Nr. 13.

94 PA, Provinzrundbrief vom 20.7.1942.

95 PA, Provinzrundbrief vom 2.10.1942.

96 PA, Provinzrundbrief vom 11.11.1942.

musste der Provinzial jedoch die Liste der Kriegsopfer beginnen: Am 16. Februar 1943 fiel Laienbruder Ignaz Fenzl / Augsburg „bei den Abwehrkämpfen zwischen Wolchow und Ladogasee“, im Alter von 25 Jahren.[97] Ihm folgte in Russland am 18. August 1943 der einundzwanzigjährige Laienbruder Karl Göstl aus dem Grazer Konvent.[98] Am 20. November 1943 fiel P. Roland Zaversnik westlich der ukrainischen Stadt Krementschuk im Alter von 30 Jahren.[99]

Zum fünften Jahrestag der Provinzgründung, dem 2. Februar 1944, analysierte der Provinzial die Lage:

> „Wir haben vor allem zu danken für den Schutz Gottes. Unsere Kirchen und Konvente sind noch unversehrt, wenngleich uns die Kriegsverhältnisse überall Einschränkung auferlegen. Wir haben auch noch reiche apostolische Arbeitsmöglichkeit, wenngleich sich der Mangel an aktiven Kräften stark fühlbar macht. Dieser Mangel kommt zum Teil schon von der eigenartigen Zusammensetzung unserer Provinz, wonach ein großer Teil bester Kräfte auswärts wirkt, nämlich 17 Patres in der Schweiz, 4 Patres und 2 Brüder in Rom, 2 Patres im Sudetengau. In den Heimatdiözesen sind auf Seelsorgsposten [sc. außerhalb der Klöster] 7 Patres. ... Beim Militär stehen zur Zeit 14 Patres, 5 Kleriker und 20 Brüder. ... Die Mitbrüder im Felde stehen in ständiger Verbindung mit mir. Wir sind in der Heimat immer froh, wenn ein Lebenszeichen von den Frontkameraden kommt. Ich bitte alle Mitbrüder dringend, unsere Frontkämpfer mit ihren täglichen Gebeten besonders im hl. [sc. Mess-]Opfer und beim Rosenkranz zu begleiten. Unsere Frontsoldaten verlassen sich darauf, während uns die heimatliche stille Arbeit gewährleistet ist. Der Entwicklung der nächsten Zukunft sehen wir mit Vertrauen entgegen. Wir wissen wohl, dass dieses laufende Jahr ein besonderes Maß von zuversichtlicher innerer Ruhe fordert. Vielleicht wird es eine Zeit der seelischen Bewährung, in der uns Gott prüft, ob er uns aufbewahren kann für den kommenden großen Einsatz im Friedensbau des Gottesreiches. Dem Ordensmann, der an eine neue Blüte des Gottesreiches glaubt, wächst auch die persönliche Verantwortung. Nach dem Zeugnis der Kirchengeschichte ist ja das Aufblühen des religiösen Lebens immer ganz innig verknüpft mit Blütezeiten religiöser Orden. Umgekehrt war auch der Verfall von Ordensgeist und Ordenszucht immer wieder der Schrittmacher für eine religiöse Verfallszeit. So liegt auf uns die große Verantwortung, dass wir im Strudel der Zeit nicht in eine geistige Säkularisierung hinein-

97 PA, Provinzrundbrief vom 1.4.1943.

98 PA, Provinzrundbrief vom 6.9.1943, S. 2, Nachtrag.

99 PA, Provinzrundbrief vom 15.12.1943. Zaversnik war als noch studierender Pater aus dem Konvent Walberberg eingezogen worden und hatte zuletzt zum Augsburger Konvent gehört (PA, Provinzrundbrief vom 2.2.1944).

gerissen werden, in eine Verweltlichung, die unsere innersten Kräftequellen verschüttet, sodass wir ungeeignet werden für unsere besondere Aufgabe im Organismus der Kirche und im Dienste am Heil der Welt. Der Ernst der Zeit, der den Soldaten-Mitbruder zu treuester Pflichterfüllung drängt, ruft uns zum treuen Gehorsam gegen die Lebensaufgabe und Lebensordnung, für die wir uns vor Gott verpflichtet haben. …“[100]

Mit der Betonung der Notwendigkeit eines besonderen Maßes an zuversichtlicher innerer Ruhe für das Jahr 1944 hatte Vetter völlig recht. Drei Wochen, nachdem er sie heraufbeschworen hatte, brach der Bombenkrieg über die Klöster der Provinz herein. Vetter berichtet anschaulich über die Geschehnisse in Augsburg, wo er selber Augenzeuge war:

„Die beiden schweren Luftangriffe auf die alte Kulturstadt Augsburg in der Nacht vom 25. zum 26. Februar [sc. 1944] haben auch unsere Niederlassungen hart betroffen. Das Dach von Heilig Kreuz erhielt mehrere Brandbomben und brannte an vielen Stellen zugleich. Die brennende Kuppel über dem Hochaltar setzte im Einstürzen den ganzen Chor in Brand. Der Tabernakel mitsamt dem ‚Wunderbarlichen Gut‘ konnte aus dem Feuerbereich herausgetragen werden. Die große Sakristei und die Kapelle der Schmerzhaften Mutter wurden gerettet. Der Turm ist völlig ausgebrannt. Die große Glocke ist geschmolzen. Die brennende Kuppel des Turmes bot ein grausig-schönes Bild. Das Gewölbe über dem Schiff hat starke Risse und Brandlöcher. Aber es hat den Mittelraum der Kirche geschützt. Die Orgel ist total abgebrannt. Das Haus von Heilig Kreuz erhielt mehrere Brandbomben. Die Dachbrände konnten gelöscht werden. Besondere Schwierigkeiten bot der Phosphor in der Decke der Hauskapelle. Die Decke musste teilweise eingestoßen werden. Sehr gefährdet war das Haus durch das radikal niederbrennende evangelische [sc. benachbarte] Hedwigstift. Die Flammen, die in unsere Zimmer herüberschlugen, konnten nur mit äußerster Anstrengung abgewehrt werden. Unser ganzes Haus bot den Anblick eines Gräuels der Verwüstung. Fast sämtliche Fenster waren zerstört und die Türen zerschlagen.
Im Spickel hatte P. Richard Kolter mit seinen wenigen Hilfskräften einen schweren Stand. Das Löschen der Brandbomben im Kirchendachboden musste bis in den nächsten Vormittag fortgesetzt werden. Im Pfarramtszimmer lag ein Phosphorkanister, der auch den benachbarten Raum unrettbar in Brand setzte. Die rückwärtigen Zimmer konnten gerettet werden, haben aber auch keine heilen Fenster und Türen mehr. Im Garten lagen mehrere Blindgänger. Zwischen den Bänken der Kirche lag eine Bombe schwersten Kalibers, deren Hülle allein 6 Zentner wog. Sonderbarerweise war die Hülle leer. Wenn dieser Volltreffer gefüllt gewesen wäre, stünde von Kirche und Haus kein Stein mehr

100 PA, Provinzrundbrief vom 2.2.1944, S. 1.

> auf dem anderen. Durch Sprengbomben wurden mehrere Häuser gegenüber der Kirche fast ganz niedergerissen. Die Toten, die aus den Trümmern geborgen wurden, hat man in unsere Kirche getragen.
> Anfang der folgenden Woche begannen langsam die Wiederherstellungsarbeiten. Im Spickel hat sich P. Richard durch die Säuberung der Albertuskapelle einen brauchbaren gottesdienstlichen Raum geschaffen. In Heilig Kreuz … [konnte] in der großen Sakristei der Gottesdienst wieder eröffnet werden. …"[101]

Die Decke der Sakristei von Heilig Kreuz war aber doch zu beschädigt und einsturzgefährdet:

> „Vorläufig haben wir den Gottesdienst in den Konvent verlegt. Wir haben im ersten Stock die Wand vom früheren Priorat zum früheren Rekreationszimmer durchgebrochen und dadurch einen guten Raum für den Gottesdienst gewonnen, allerdings sehr behelfsmäßig."[102]

In München und Wien blieben die Konvente und Klosterkirchen trotz Luftangriffen auf diese Städte in den ersten Monaten des Jahres 1944 von größeren Schäden verschont; nur in Graz gingen einige Fensterscheiben zu Bruch.[103] Zwischen Juni 1944 und Mai 1945 wurde die Provinz jedoch von einem Schlag nach dem anderen getroffen: Beim Tagesangriff auf München am 9. Juni 1944 „explodierte eine 40-Zentner-Bombe am mittleren Südausgang unserer Kirche in Freimann, zwischen Kirche und Gartenzaun. Kirche und Haus stehen noch. Jedoch sind Türen, Fenster und Dächer demoliert."[104]

Ab Juni 1944 wurde P. Adalhard Knorr bei Napadowka vermisst (32 Jahre alt).[105] Am 13. Juni 1944 wurde beim Tagesangriff auf München P. Pirmin Ziegelmüller getötet (39 Jahre alt).[106] Bruder Wendelin Schöllhorn erlag im Alter von 47 Jahren am 22. Juni 1944 infolge eines Dienstunfalls bei einem Zugunglück in Lichtenwald / Untersteier tödlichen Verletzungen.[107] Seit Juni 1944 kamen alle Briefe an Br. Krispin Sauter (38 Jahre) zurück; ebenso wurde ab Oktober 1944 P. Fulgentius Weimer (45 Jahre) „im Osten" vermisst.[108]

---

101 PA, Provinzrundbrief vom 8.3.1944.

102 PA, Provinzrundbrief vom 3.5.1944. Bei diesen Räumlichkeiten handelte es sich übrigens um die für Militärbeamte beschlagnahmten Zimmer.

103 Ebd.

104 PA, Provinzrundbrief vom 14.6.1944.

105 PA, Provinzrundbrief vom 9.6.1944. Ich gebe oben nur diejenigen Vermissten an, deren Schicksal auch nach Kriegsende ungeklärt blieb und die später daher für tot erklärt wurden.

106 PA, Provinzrundbrief vom 14.6.1944.

107 PA, Provinzrundbrief vom 1.8.1944.

108 PA, Provinzrundbrief vom 2.10.1944.

Im November 1944 trafen Bomben die Dominikanerklöster in Graz und Wien. Vetter berichtet:

> „An Allerheiligen [sc. 1.11.1944] wurde im Luftangriff auf Graz unsere Münzgrabenkirche völlig zerstört. Es steht buchstäblich kein Stein mehr auf dem anderen. Der Konvent ist bewohnbar, hat aber starke Luftdruckschäden. Die Mitbrüder haben alles gut überstanden und sind – wie ich mich persönlich überzeugen konnte – voll Eifer an der Arbeit, um die Schäden am Bau zu beheben. Bibliothek und Vestiarie [sc. Wäschekammer] liegen unter den Trümmern und werden aus dem Schutt geborgen. Für den Sonntagsgottesdienst hat der Heimleiter des Schülerinnenheims unser großes Refektorium zur Verfügung gestellt, das eine sehr brauchbare Notkirche geworden ist. Die Haltung der Patres und Brüder ist vorbildlich einmütig und zuversichtlich. Am Sonntag, den 5. November, fielen beim Großangriff auf Wien ganze Serien von Bomben rings um unseren Konvent in unmittelbarster Nähe. Eine Bombe explodierte am Seitenausgang unserer Rosenkranzbasilika in der Predigergasse und richtete in dieser Gasse schweres Unheil an. Die Mauern unserer Kirche haben standgehalten. Die Kirchenfenster sind alle eingedrückt und die Seitenaltäre an der Predigergasse in Fensterhöhe geköpft. Im Konvent sind viele Schäden an Fenstern und Türen und besonders empfindliche Dachschäden über Kirche und Haus. Ein Zeitzünder fiel in das große [sc. angrenzende] Mietshaus und zwar gerade in den Trakt Postgasse 2, der dem Konvent gehört. Er explodierte am nächstfolgenden Abend und richtete große Zerstörungen an: neun Wohnungen sind völlig zerstört und zwei Menschenleben zu beklagen. Ein weiterer Zeitzünder fiel unmittelbar vor den Dominikanerkeller an der Vorderseite des Hochhauses. Er explodierte gleichfalls am Montagabend und richtete starke Verwüstung an. Auch im Wiener Konvent helfen alle zusammen, um der Schäden Herr zu werden. … Infolge der Frontnähe und der Luftgefahr haben wir einige Mitbrüder [sc. aus Wien und Graz] in ruhigeren Gegenden untergebracht.“[109]

Die Dach- und Fensterschäden an der Wiener Kirche machten sie in der kalten Jahreszeit unbrauchbar, daher wurde der Gottesdienst in die sogenannte Sommerchorkapelle verlegt.[110]

Auch das Freiburger Kloster kam im November 1944 zu Schaden: „In Freiburg hat der Angriff vom 27. November, der fast die ganze Altstadt in ein Trümmerfeld verwandelte, auch unser Haus samt der Kapelle schwer beschädigt. Der Luftdruck hat nicht bloß Dach, Fenster und Türen zerstört, sondern auch mehrere Zwischenwände im Haus eingerissen, sodass

109 PA, Provinzrundbrief vom 27.11.1944.

110 PA, Provinzrundbrief vom 2.2.1945, S. 1.

unsere Mitbrüder nur einige kleine Räume notdürftig wiederherstellen konnten. Die Kapelle ist wieder benutzbar."[111] Wenige Wochen vor Kriegsende schrieb Vetter an seine Mitbrüder:

> „Bevor der Postverkehr aus Wien eingestellt wird, möchte ich Ihnen noch einen Gruß schicken. Wien ist Frontstadt geworden. Wenn es bis zum Äußersten verteidigt wird, kann es sehr hart werden. Wir sind uns darüber klar. Aber wir wollen nicht fliehen, sondern treu aushalten an der Stätte, an der unser Orden seit sieben Jahrhunderten wirkt. Möge der Herr das Opfer – wenn er es will, auch das Opfer des Lebens – fruchtbar werden lassen, damit daraus neues, wirklich echtes dominikanisches Leben entspringe, getragen von einer tiefen, heiligen Liebe zum Orden und zum Apostolat des Gottesreiches in einer neuen Zeit. In der nächsten Zeit werden wir äußerlich voneinander ganz getrennt sein. Dafür wollen wir umso treuer füreinander vor Gott einstehen, bis er uns nach seinem heiligen Willen ein gutes Wiedersehen schenkt, auf das ich mit aller Zuversicht hoffe."[112]

„Wiederhergestellte Städte und neugebaute Ordnungen"

Die Lage, in der sich die süddeutsche Provinz nach Kriegsende wiederfand, teilte sie mit allen ihren Nachbarprovinzen in Europa: Von vielen Konventen und Kirchen standen nicht einmal mehr die Mauern. Die Anzahl der Mitbrüder, vorwiegend der jüngeren, war erschreckend dezimiert: Die Lücken, die Tod, Gefangenschaft und auch Flucht in die Reihen der Dominikaner gerissen hatten, waren kaum durch neue Professen aufgefüllt worden, denn während der Kriegszeit hatten die Noviziate beinahe keine Aspiranten aufnehmen dürfen. Die Studien hatten nur unzureichend oder gar nicht aufrechterhalten werden können. Neben diesen materiellen und personellen Auswirkungen hatte sich durch den Krieg aber auch noch eine weitere Veränderung auf das Ordensleben ergeben: Die Männer, die aus dem Militärdienst zurückkamen, hatten in den Schützengräben und Kriegsgefangenenlagern Erfahrungen gemacht, die sie klösterliche Bräuche und Traditionen hinterfragen ließen. Etwaige Folgen, die sich daraus für die Provinz und den Gesamtorden ergaben, waren noch nicht abzusehen. Hier gab es etwas zu tun, das sahen Ordensmeister und Generalkonsil sehr

111 Ebd., S. 2.
112 PA, Provinzrundbrief vom 4.4.1945.

deutlich. Im September 1946 wollte man alles Anstehende auf einem Generalkapitel besprechen.[113]

Erst im September 1945, vier Monate nach Einstellungen der Kampfhandlungen in Europa, erhielt man im süddeutschen Provinzteil erste Kenntnisse über das Schicksal der österreichischen Mitbrüder und des Provinzials. Durch Zeitung und Radio hatten sich wilde Gerüchte über den Tod Vetters verbreitet: Vetter sei in Wien von der SS ermordet worden, man habe ihn am Karfreitag gekreuzigt. Vetter sei an Typhus gestorben. Vetter sei von den Russen durch Genickschuss erledigt worden. Der Apostolische Nuntius in Deutschland hatte dem Provinzial der Teutonia Siemer ähnliches übermitteln lassen, nämlich dass Vetter kurz vor dem Einmarsch der Roten Armee von der Gestapo getötet worden sei. Siemer war vom Wahrheitsgehalt dieser Nachrichten überzeugt und zelebrierte für Vetter in Walberberg ein feierliches Requiem.[114] Danach fuhr Siemer nach Süddeutschland „und erklärte in München, dass er die Konvente wieder heimhole. Der einmütige Einsatz aller süddeutschen Mitbrüder für die Einheit unserer Provinz hat ihn jedoch von weiteren Schritten abgehalten."[115]

Da die Grenzen der Besatzungszonen sowohl auf deutschem wie auf österreichischem Gebiet fast undurchlässig geworden waren, konnte Marianus Vetter erst im Dezember 1945 wieder nach Süddeutschland reisen.[116] Solange der Grenzübertritt so erschwert war, war eine zentrale Verwaltung der Provinz unmöglich, sodass man gezwungen war, die bisher eine Provinz in einen süddeutschen und einen österreichischen Teil aufzuspalten, mit jeweils eigener Besetzung der Wirtschafts- und Verwaltungsämter und der Provinzkonsilien.[117] Nur noch das Provinzkapitel und natürlich die

---

113 Zum Zustand des Ordens nach dem Krieg und Vorstellungen Gillets vgl. das Schreiben zur Einberufung des Generalkapitels 1946 in: *ASOP* (1945) S. 79–88.

114 Groothuis: *Im Dienste*, S. 268–269 (dort auch die Quellenangaben zu den Gerüchten); PA, Bericht des Provinzials zum Provinzkapitel 6.11.1946 (Provinzrundbrief), S.4; Archiv des Augsburger Dominikanerkonvents: Konventschronik Augsburg, fol. 71r, Eintrag vom 10.9.1945.

115 PA, Bericht des Provinzials zum Provinzkapitel 6.11.1946 (Provinzrundbrief), S. 4, auch: Groothuis: *Im Dienste*, S. 393–395.

116 Archiv des Augsburger Dominikanerkonvents: Konventschronik Augsburg, fol. 71v, Eintrag vom 10.12.1945.

117 Siehe dazu: PA, Bericht des Provinzials zum Provinzkapitel 6.11.1946 (Provinzrundbrief), S. 2; Provinzkonsilsbuch des österreichischen Provinzteils, Eintrag vom 18.9.1945, S. 15 und Eintrag vom 24.10.1945, S. 16 sowie Archiv des Augsburger Dominikanerkonvents: Konventschronik Augsburg, fol. 75r, Eintrag vom 22.4.1948.

Person und das Amt des Provinzials blieben für beide Teile gemeinsam. Die jeweils unterschiedlichen staatspolitischen und ökonomischen Entwicklungen in Deutschland und Österreich verstärkten in den kommenden Jahren diese Teilung der Provinz, sodass diese eigentlich als Provisorium gedachte Verwaltungslösung sich institutionalisierte und weiter bestand.

Glücklich war Provinzial Vetter darüber nicht. Aber er sah in den Kriegsfolgen nicht nur die furchtbaren Zerstörungen des Alten, sondern auch die Möglichkeit, besseres Neues zu errichten:

> „Immer, wenn die Menschen ihre Erde zum Trümmerfeld gemacht haben, schenkt die Erbarmung Gottes Zeit und Möglichkeit zum neuen Aufbau. … Die Ruinen der Städte sind ja nur ein Spiegelbild vom innerlichen Gräuel der Verwüstung unter den Völkern. Zerbrochen sind die heiligsten Ordnungen, verschüttet sind die höchsten Werte, und wie ein Feuersturm der Hölle wütet über den Trümmern die Verwirrung der Geister und die Glut der Triebe. So ist es die Sehnsucht unserer Zeitenstunde, dass die Erde ein neues Gesicht bekomme: nicht bloß wiederhergestellte und neugebaute Ordnungen, sondern vor allem erneuerte Menschen.“[118]

Zonengrenzen, Reisebeschränkungen, Provinzeinheit

Auf dem Generalkapitel im September 1946 in Rom wurde P. Emmanuel Suárez zum Nachfolger von Martin Stanislaus Gillet als Ordensmeister gewählt. Suárez war Kanonist am „Angelicum“ und hatte sich „als Lehrer und Begutachter einen bedeutenden Namen erworben. … Er war der gegebene Anwärter für das Ordensmeisteramt auf Grund seiner Rechts- und Geschäftskenntnisse, seiner Beziehungen und – nach dem Krieg – als Spanier.“[119] Die Akten dieses Generalkapitels lassen nicht erkennen, dass der Orden die Erfahrungen der vergangenen sieben Jahre als Anregung zu Veränderungen wahrnahm; stattdessen zeigen sie auf jeder Seite das angestrengte Bemühen dort weiterzumachen, wo man durch den Krieg unterbrochen worden war. Der neue Ordensmeister beschwor in seinem ersten Schreiben seine Dominikaner gerade wegen der Verwüstungen des Krieges zur Rückkehr zu disziplinarischer, moralischer und dogmatischer Strenge. Er rief sie auf, sich trotz der Kriegsgegensätze als Brüder zu begegnen, als Soldaten Christi. Grundsätzliche Neuerungen im Leben des Ordens seien nicht durch Einzelne oder durch Provinzen einzuführen, sondern dem Ge-

---

118 VETTER: *Erlöste Menschlichkeit*, S. 5.
119 WALZ: *Wahrheitskünder*, S. 155.

neralkapitel vorbehalten. Dementsprechend sollten die Provinzen etwaige Änderungsvorschläge bei der Ordenskurie einreichen, die sie dann für das nächste Generalkapitel vorbereiten würde.[120]

Abb. 9: P. Marianus Vetter (PA, Fotosammlung).

Ganz ähnlich sahen das auch die Vertreter der Provinz, die sich vom 7. bis 10. November 1946 zum Provinzkapitel trafen. Da Reisebeschränkungen über die Besatzungszonen noch griffen, konnte das Kapitel, wie ursprünglich 1939 vorgesehen, nicht in Wien stattfinden. Mit Dispens des Ordensmeisters wurde es in eine von Kampfhandlungen weniger betroffene Gegend Österreichs, nach Vorarlberg ins Dominikanerinnenkloster von Altenstadt verlegt, das außerdem leichter von allen Standorten der Provinz aus erreichbar war.[121]

Provinzial Marianus Vetter war noch im Juni 1945 nach Graz in die russische Besatzungszone gereist, um nach den dortigen Brüdern zu sehen. Der Übertritt über die russisch-englische Zonengrenze wurde ihm verwehrt, sodass er nicht nach Friesach kam, wie er es vorgehabt hatte.[122] Ende August fuhr er nach Retz, wo er das Kloster vollständig von den Russen besetzt vorfand; der Prior hauste in der Sakristei und die Brüder wohnten verteilt in der Stadt.[123] Ende Oktober gelang ihm ein Besuch in Friesach, wo er den Konvent und die Brüder in gutem Zustand vorfand.[124] Die Grenze zwischen Österreich und Deutschland wurde von den vier Alliierten ganz besonders gut behütet. Dennoch gelang es dem Provinzial, von

---

120 ACG 1946, S.11–14.

121 Zur Verlegung siehe: PA, Provinzkonsilsbuch des österreichischen Provinzteils, Eintrag vom 28.5.1946, S. 17 und APKap 1946, S. 3, Nr. 1. Abgesehen davon sagt der volle Titel dieser Provinzkapitelsakten dazu bereits alles.

122 PA, Provinzialsregestenbuch 1 (1939–1966), Einträge vom 19.–21.6. und 22.6.1945, S. 28, Nr. 2.

123 Ebd., Eintrag S. 28–29, o. D., o. Nr.

124 Ebd., Eintrag vom 26.–30.10.1945, S. 29, Nr. 9.

allen Besatzungsmächten eine Passiererlaubnis zu erhalten, sodass er ab dem 7. Dezember die Häuser in Deutschland aufsuchen konnte. Im Dezember 1945 und im Januar 1946 visitierte er die Brüder in München, Augsburg und Freiburg und einige der Schwesternklöster.[125] Auch gelang ihm die Teilnahme am Generalkapitel in Rom, zusammen mit Diffinitor Alfons Well.[126]

Ansonsten war der Grenzübertritt zwischen den beiden Teilen der Provinz beinahe unmöglich. Deshalb beantragte das Provinzkonsil am 18. September 1945 beim Apostolischen Stuhl und beim Ordensmeister die Erlaubnis, in Graz ein zweites Noviziat einrichten zu dürfen.[127] Dies geschah am 24. Oktober.[128] Das Noviziat für die deutschen Kandidaten lag zu dieser Zeit theoretisch noch in Freiburg im Breisgau. Allerdings war das Kloster durch den Krieg so stark beschädigt worden, dass man dort die Personalstärke hatte verringern müssen, sodass die Niederlassung nicht mehr die Erfordernisse für einen formalen Konvent erfüllte.[129] Damit musste Freiburg als *domus* behandelt werden und fiel als Sitz eines Noviziates aus. Das Provinzkonsil hatte in einer Sitzung am 28. Dezember 1945 deshalb beschlossen, das Noviziat nach München-Freimann verlegen und die dortige *domus* in einen formalrechtlichen Konvent erheben zu lassen.[130] Der Ordensmeister bewilligte dies im Frühjahr 1946 und am 24. Juni 1946 wurde P. Magnus Beck zu dessen erstem Prior eingesetzt.[131]

Zur Vorbereitung der Teilnehmer des Provinzkapitels fasste Vetter seine Beobachtungen über die Lage der Provinz in einem ausführlichen Bericht zusammen: Ein kurzer Überblick über die Schicksale der einzelnen

---

125 Ebd., Eintrag S. 30, o. D., o. Nr.

126 Ebd., Eintrag vom 9.–30.9.1946, S. 36, o. Nr. und ACG 1946, S. 6 und 8 (Teilnehmerliste).

127 PA, Liber consiliorum, Eintrag zum 18.9.1945, S. 15.

128 PA, Provinzialsregestenbuch 1 (1939–1945), Eintrag vom 24.10.1945, S. 29, Nr. 7.

129 Nämlich sechs Priester und sechs Laienbrüder, von denen einer in Luzern wohnte und ein anderer noch in Kriegsgefangenschaft war (PKat 1946, S. 12–13). Ebd., S. 12 auch die Begründung der Personalreduzierung. Zu den Bedingungen für ein Noviziat: *Constitutiones 1932,* S. 45–47, Nrn. 97–104.

130 PA, Liber consiliorum, Sitzung in Wien vom 28.12.1945, S. 16.

131 Leider nennen die vorliegenden Quellen nur den Erhalt eines diesbezüglichen Dekrets des Ordensmeisters (PA, Provinzialsregestenbuch 1 (1939–1966), Einträge vom 24.6.1946 über verschiedene Assignationen nach München und die Einsetzung Becks zum Prior, S. 34, Nrn. 36–39), aber geben das genaue Datum der Konventserhebung oder des Dekrets nicht an.

Klöster während des Krieges leitete ihn ein. Dann folgte eine Beschreibung der Auswirkungen der Jahre 1939 bis 1945 auf den Personalstand der Provinz (dazu später im Detail). Was den Nachwuchs betraf, so hatte der Provinzial Gründe zu Zuversicht:

> „In München befinden sich 5 Klerikernovizen, in Graz 4 … Der Wiederbeginn des Juvenates in Wetzelsdorf ist erst möglich, wenn das Haus von einer genügenden Anzahl besetzt werden kann, weil sonst die Gefahr der Beschlagnahmung durch Wohnungsamt oder Besatzungsmacht gegeben ist. Der Ansatz zu einem Juvenat ist dadurch gemacht, dass im freigegebenen Trakt des Grazer Konventes einige Studenten Aufnahme und Betreuung finden. P. Raymund Lang ist zur Zeit mit der geistlichen Leitung betraut."

Was die Errichtung eines provinzeigenen Studienhauses anging, stand die Germania superior noch vor einem Anfang:

> „Das Studentat kann zur Zeit nicht eröffnet werden, da die dazu nötige Anzahl von Klerikern erst wachsen muss. Beim letzten Generalkapitel wurden in den italienischen Provinzen alle Studentate vereinigt. Bei dieser Tendenz haben wir erst dann eine Möglichkeit zum eigenen Studium, wenn wir die nötigen Professoren und Studenten haben. Die Ausbildung von Lektoren für ihre Spezialdisziplinen ist im Rahmen des Möglichen im Auge behalten worden und muss weiterhin sorgsam (trotz äußerstem Personalmangel) betreut werden, wenn wir der Provinz ein geistiges Zentrum im kommenden Aufbau des Studiums schaffen wollen. Vorläufig müssen unsere Studenten aus dem süddeutschen Teil wie aus dem österreichischen Teil im Generalstudium in Walberberg studieren oder teilweise ins Ausland geschickt werden (Paris, Fribourg, Rom)."

Die Frage nach der Strenge des Ordenslebens sah Vetter realistisch:

> „Über die regulare Observanz der Konvente lässt sich sagen, dass die durch die letzten Kriegsjahre notwendig gelockerte Klausur allmählich wieder zu ihrem normalen Zustand zurückgeführt werden konnte und dass die Tendenz bestehen muss, mit dem Fortschreiten der Freigabe unserer Klosterräume auch die Klausur wieder im alten Umfang herzustellen. Das Chorgebet ist in allen Konventen und Häusern wieder in Ordnung. Nur in Retz ist es zur Zeit noch nicht möglich … Die klaustrale Atmosphäre unserer Konvente, das Stillschweigen und die ungestörte Arbeitsruhe in den Zellen muss auch erst allmählich wieder in einzelnen Konventen aufgefrischt werden. Das capitulum culparum [sc. das Schuldkapitel] und die geistliche Ansprache der Prioren sind auch in den Kriegsverhältnissen etwas zu stark aus dem Konventsleben verschwunden. Sie sind aber undispensierbare Mittel zum regularen Aufbau der Konvente."

Auch bezüglich der Seelsorge war der Provinzial zufrieden: „Das apostolische Leben unserer Konvente beginnt sich wieder lebhafter zu entfalten. Es scheint mir aber Sorge getragen werden zu müssen, dass die eigenen Ordenskirchen in Predigt und Beichtstuhl gut betreut werden. Jedoch muss auch eine regere Beteiligung an den Volksmissionen im Auge behalten werden.“ Daran schloss Vetter den eigentümlich verwickelten Satz an: „In der Aussprache des Generalkapitels wurde der Grundsatz aufgestellt, dass Apostolate, die sich mit einer Teilnahme am regulären Konventsleben grundsätzlich nicht vereinbaren lassen, außerhalb unseres Ordens liegen“. Dies war wohl als Hinweis darauf gedacht, dass solche Seelsorgsposten nicht zu übernehmen waren. Je eigene Abschnitte widmete Vetter den drei Personengruppen, die von je her durch Dominikaner betreut wurden:

> „Die Schwesternklöster sind durch das Generalkapitel besonders der Betreuung durch unsere Patres empfohlen. Es fehlt in der Provinz an der Auswahl geeigneter Exerzitienleiter für unsere Schwestern. Diesem Übelstand muss nach Möglichkeit dadurch abgeholfen werden, dass auch jüngere Patres allmählich in die Exerzitienarbeit eingearbeitet werden. Der Dritte Orden leidet im Bereich unserer Provinz daran, dass er meist nach Art einer Bruderschaft aufgebaut ist und überwiegend aus alten Frauen bestand. Ich kann mich auf keine einzige Ortsgruppe erinnern (etwa mit Ausnahme der ehemaligen Gruppe von Stuttgart), die ein spezifisch apostolisches Betätigungsfeld sich zu eigen gemacht hätte. Unser gesamter Dritter Orden schreit nach einem Neubau. Die Rosenkranzbruderschaft stellt einen wesentlichen Teil des dominikanischen Apostolats dar. Durch den hervorragenden Eifer unseres Rosenkranzapostels P. Paulus Gunz sind in seinem Wirkungsbereich zahlreiche Bruderschaften errichtet worden. … Das Rosenkranzapostolat muss weiterhin ausgebaut werden.“

Vor dem Hintergrund der Besatzungszonengrenzen und der Trennung Österreichs von Deutschland lag Vetter eine Frage besonders auf dem Herzen:

> „Mir scheint die geschlossene Einheit der Provinz unbedingt nötig zu sein, wenn sowohl Österreich wie auch Süddeutschland ein dominikanisches Eigenleben aufbauen wollen. Wir sind aufeinander angewiesen, wenn wir in absehbarer Zeit an ein eigenes Studium denken wollen, das ja als geistiges Zentrum der Provinz unerlässlich ist. Es muss nur vermieden werden, dass sowohl der österreichische wie auch der süddeutsche Teil sich in dieser kommenden Entwicklung irgendwie benachteiligt fühlen kann. Darum müsste auch beim Aufbau des Noviziates wie des Studentates der Gesamtbereich der Provinz berücksichtigt werden, etwa so, dass München das Noviziat erhält, Graz das Philosophiestudium und Wien die Theologie, während der vorgeschriebene Predigerkurs für die ‚materiales‘ wiederum in München

> oder Augsburg sein sollte. Das sind gewiss jetzt noch Zukunftsbilder. Aber sie können in entfernter Vorarbeit (z. B. bezüglich der Bibliothek) im Auge behalten werden. Wir müssen die Einheit der Provinz auch von unten her aufbauen: durch gemeinsame Erziehung unseres Nachwuchses und der Studenten."

Mit dem Verweis auf die Verehrung des hl. Alberts als gemeinsamen Patron der Provinz schloss Vetter seine Ausführungen.[132]

Die Provinzialswahl in Altenstadt endete mit der Wiederwahl von P. Marianus Vetter. Offensichtlich war man mit seiner Leitungstätigkeit zufrieden.[133] Auch in den Besetzungen der restlichen Provinzämter tauchten die Namen derjenigen auf, die schon vor dem Krieg diese Aufgaben inne gehabt hatten, wobei manche Verwaltungsaufgaben nun doppelt besetzt wurden, für jeden Provinzteil eigens.[134] Zwar betonten die Kapitularen in einer eigens hervorgehobenen Erklärung ihren Willen zur einmütigen Erhaltung der Einheit der Provinz,[135] dennoch förderten sie durch die Ämterdoppelungen die Zementierung der faktischen Teilung in zwei Hälften, die über Jahrzehnte anhalten würde.

„Neugebaute Ordnungen"?

Neben diesen verwaltungstechnischen Fragen wurden auf dem Provinzkapitel aber auch die menschlichen und geistlichen Erfahrungen thematisiert, die man während der vergangenen sieben Jahre gemacht hatte. Gewisse Observanzen, auf die man vor dem Krieg großen Wert gelegt hatte, hatten sich als unpraktisch erwiesen. Nun war der Ausnahmezustand vorbei – aber wie sollte es weitergehen? Die Provinzkapitelsakten machen die Ziele und Vorstellungen der Kapitularen klar: Man wollte wieder zur alten Ordnung zurückkehren – eine andere Ordnung kannte man ja auch nicht –, aber man wollte den im Krieg gemachten Erfahrungen der Brüder ebenso Rechnung tragen. Letztlich zwang diese Haltung zu einem Spagat: Die alten Observanzen wurden wieder eingeschärft, aber manche davon in

---

132 Die obigen Zitate aus: PA, Bericht des Provinzials zum Provinzkapitel 6.11.1946 (Provinzrundbrief), S. 2–4.

133 APKap 1946, S. 4, Nr. 6.

134 Siehe APKap 1946, S. 4–5, Nrn. 7–20 und S. 8–9, Nrn. 40–42 bzw. vgl. PKat 1939, S. 7–8 mit PKat 1946, S. 6–7.

135 APKap 1946, S. 6, Nr. 22.

der Ausführung abgemildert. So sollten die Oberen grundsätzlich darauf achten, ihre Gemeinschaften wieder zu einem vollkommen nach den Satzungen geführten klösterlichen Leben zurückzuführen. Dazu wurde ausdrücklich auf das regelmäßig abzuhaltende Schuldkapitel und auf das Tragen des Ordenshabits hingewiesen. Nur auf längeren Reisen sollten Priesterkragen bzw. das weltpriesterliche Gewand genügen, keinesfalls aber zivile Kleider. Zum äußeren Erscheinungsbild der Brüder gehörte auch die Haartracht: Die Oberen sollten auf eine möglichst einfache Frisur ihrer Untergebenen achten. In einem eigenen Abschnitt wurde ausdrücklich die Regel in Erinnerung gerufen, dass keiner ohne vorherige Inspektion durch den Oberen Briefe entgegennehmen oder absenden dürfe. Den Oberen wurde außerdem die Sorge für die Förderung der Laienbrüder im Geist des Ordens ins Gewissen gerufen. Ein Pater wurde beauftragt, die für die Laienbrüder relevanten Teile der Konstitutionen ins Deutsche zu übersetzen. Bezüglich der liturgischen Observanzen riefen die Kapitularen allen Konventen die Zelebration eines feierlichen Hochamtes ins Gedächtnis, an dem alle Brüder teilnehmen sollten und für das Choralgesang empfohlen wurde, bei dem auch die anwesenden Gläubigen teilhaben sollten. Die Förderung von Ordensberufen wurde allen Brüdern ans Herz gelegt: Dem gemeinsamen Rosenkranz sollte dazu täglich eine Litanei angeschlossen werden, und die Patres sollten in ihren Predigten die evangelischen Räte thematisieren. Die Prioren von Graz und Freiburg im Breisgau sollten für die Aufnahme von Ordenskandidaten Vorsorge leisten. Außerdem wurde je ein süddeutscher und ein österreichischer Pater mit dem Aufbau und der Unterstützung des sogenannten Dominikuswerkes betraut – eines Vereins, der bereits 1933 in Österreich gegründet worden war mit dem Ziel, „durch geistliche und materielle Unterstützung zur Heranbildung von Dominikanerordenspriestern … beizutragen.“[136] Der Dritte Orden sollte ebenfalls neu aufgebaut werden, allerdings erließ das Provinzkapitel keine konkreten Anweisungen dazu, abgesehen von dem Auftrag, irgendeine Zeitschrift für den Dritten Orden herauszugeben. Was wirtschaftliche Fragen anging, so wurde – nach den Provinzteilen getrennt – ein Finanzrahmen für die Konvente und Häuser festgelegt und den Niederlassungen empfohlen, sich bei Einnahmen und Ausgaben an den Absichten des Ordensgründers, des hl. Dominikus, zu orientieren, also beides zu reduzieren. Abschließend

136 *Statuten des Vereines St.-Dominikus-Werk*. Albertinum [sc. Graz-Wetzelsdorf] 1933, §§ 1–2.

wurde als Tagungsort des nächsten Provinzkapitels im Jahr 1950 der Konvent in München-Freimann bestimmt.[137]

Für diese Maßnahmen bekam das Provinzkapitel von Ordensmeister Suárez ein großes Lob gespendet.[138] Sie drückten die Haltung aus, die dieser schätzte: keine Experimente, wenn auch Erleichterungen in unwesentlichen Dingen. Suárez war Zeit seines Amtes mit der Germania superior sehr zufrieden: Als er die Provinz Anfang Dezember 1949 visitierte, nannte er sie eine „provincia optima".[139] Auch später lobte er den eingeschlagenen Weg zurück zur Strenge des Ordenslebens.[140]

An diesem Weg der weniger neuerbauten als vielmehr restaurierten alten Ordnung hielt auch das folgende Provinzkapitel fest, das vom 2. bis 5. Mai 1950 in München / St. Albert tagte. Wieder blieb die Provinzleitung im Großen und Ganzen die alte; auch P. Vetter wurde wieder in das Amt des Provinzials gewählt.[141] Hauptanliegen war die Vertiefung des Klosterlebens. In den Kapitelsakten finden sich daher Anordnungen zur Klausur, zum Fasten, zu Exerzitien. Wiederum betonte das Provinzkapitel die Bedeutung der Förderung von Ordensberufen sehr stark: Die Exerzitien- und Volksmissionsprediger sollten diese Frage immer vor Augen haben. Der Provinzial wurde beauftragt zu überprüfen, ob das Grazer Juvenat nicht etwa besser nach Vorarlberg verlegt werden sollte und wo man in Süddeutschland ein solches Juvenat errichten könnte. Den Prioren wurde die gute Ausbildung der ihnen anvertrauten jungen Laienbrüder ins Gedächtnis gerufen. Unter den verschiedenen Danksagungen des Kapitels

---

137 APKap 1946, S. 6–8, Nrn. 22–44, wenn nicht anders ausgewiesen. Der Punkt über die Anpassungen der Klosterfinanzen an die Absichten des hl. Dominikus – Nr. 39 der Akten – würde in Graz noch sehr wichtig werden; siehe Anm. 157.

138 „Non possumus quin vos debitis laudibus prosequamur ob bonum spiritum qui ex actis capituli apparet, dum regulas tradere curatis ut post difficultates ex bello ortas, regularis observantia ad pristinum statum restituatur." (Bestätigungsdekret vom 20.11.1946 für die APKap 1946, innere hintere Umschlagseite).

139 PA, Chronik für das Noviziat der oberdeutschen Dominikanerprovinz, Eintrag vom 15.12.1949, S. 145.

140 Ein Zitat möge hier genügen: „Nunc vero placet ad vos has litteras dirigere, imprimis ut iterum vobis gratulationes nostras porrigamus, quia post tot aerumnas perdurante bello passas, religiosam vitam renovato vigore iterum incœpistis; deinde autem, ut vos hortemur, ut per incœptam viam ad ulteriora procedatis." (Brief des Ordensmeisters Suárez vom 15.2.1940 zum Abschluss seiner kanonischen Visitation der oberdeutschen Provinz, in: APKap 1950, S. 6–7, Nr. 25).

141 Zur Besetzung der Provinzämter siehe: APKap 1950, S. 4–6, Nrn. 5–24; Veränderungen gab es nur aufgrund von Todesfällen.

ragt besonders die an die Provinz Teutonia hervor, für das Ausleihen von Patres an die oberdeutsche Provinz, durch die man mehrere Seelsorgsstellen hatte besetzen können.[142]

Abb. 10: Monatlicher Fahrradausflug des Noviziats (Zeichnung aus PA: Chronik für das Noviziat der oberdeutschen Dominikanerprovinz, S. 154).

Tatsächlich entsprach die Germania superior mit dieser Haltung des „Zurück zum strengen Klosterleben" genau dem Zeitgeist. Wie stark selbst die unbedeutendsten Angelegenheiten mit einzelnen Observanzvorstellungen zusammenstoßen konnten, illustriert ein Ereignis, das Ende 1950 / Anfang 1951 Wellen schlug: In einem Brief vom 23. Januar 1951 setzte Ordensmeister Emmanuel Suárez den Provinzial Marianus Vetter davon in Kenntnis, dass die oberdeutsche Provinz direkt beim Heiligen Stuhl verklagt worden sei, weil angeblich einige Provinzmitglieder außerhalb ihres Klosters ohne Notwendigkeit nicht ihren Habit, sondern Laienkleidung getragen hätten. Wie sich herausstellte, hatte der Novizenmeister von München / St. Albert mit seinen Novizen einen Fahrradausflug nach Altötting gemacht. Dabei hatten alle Hemden und Hosen getragen und erst vor der Wallfahrtskirche hatte die Gruppe zum Gottesdienst den Ordenshabit übergezogen. P. Vetter wehrte sich gegen diese Anschuldigung, indem er auf die diesbezügliche Anweisung des Provinzkapitels von 1946 hinwies und etwaige Vorkommnisse dieser Art als Tat einzelner, nicht aber als Provinzbrauch darstellte. Um einem angedrohten scharfen Verweis des Ordensmeisters zuvorzukommen, gab er allerdings eine eidesstattliche Erklärung heraus, die alle Patres der Provinz unterschreiben mussten und mit der jeder erklärte, völlige Kenntnis über das Verbot zu haben, die Klöster in rein laikaler Kleidung zu verlassen. Damit wollte Vetter seine Provinz davor bewahren, in

142 APKap 1950, S. 7–9, Nrn. 30–45.

einen schlechten Ruf zu kommen, was ihm anscheinend auch gelang, denn weitere Folgen sind nicht aktenkundig.[143] – Ein lächerlicher Vorfall, der aber immerhin die gesamte Verwaltung der katholischen Kirche, angefangen bei der päpstlichen Kurie über die Ordenskurie und den Provinzial bis hinunter zu jedem Priester der Provinz beschäftigte und der als Zeichen seiner Zeit eine deutliche Sprache spricht. In diesen Zusammenhang gehörten auch die von der Religiosenkongregation angeregten und vom Ordensmeister weitergeleiteten Verhandlungen des Provinzkonsils vom 28. September 1951 über das Tabakrauchen. Das Provinzkonsil stellte fest, dass in der Provinz die Gewohnheit des moderaten Tabakgebrauchs bestand, allerdings nur in der jeweils eigenen Zelle und bei der Rekreation der Konventsgemeinschaft. Ansonsten ermahnte es die Brüder nicht zu vergessen, dass sie auch beim Rauchen der Ordensarmut, dem Abtötungsgeist und der Erbauung Außenstehender verpflichtet waren.[144]

„Wiederhergestellte Städte" – rege Bautätigkeit

Um eine möglichst rasche Wiederaufnahme des klösterlichen und seelsorglichen Lebens verwirklichen zu können, mussten zuerst einmal die Gebäude wieder instand gesetzt werden. Die Reparatur der großen Schäden an den Kirchen und Klöstern zog sich an allen Standorten der Provinz wegen der Unsicherheit der politischen und wirtschaftlichen Lage, der Währungsschwankungen, des Mangels an Baumaterial, Bauarbeitern und Energie in den Jahren nach dem Krieg lange hin, trotz aller Kraft, die die Brüder dafür investierten.

Keine Schäden hatte der Krieg in Friesach hinterlassen. Daher beschränkten sich die Bauarbeiten hier Anfang der 1950er Jahre auf notwendig gewordene Reparaturen, v. a. an den riesigen Dachflächen von Kirche und Kloster. In der Kirche wurden 1957 die Pietà, die elektrischen Leitun-

---

143 Siehe PA, Provinzrundbrief vom 1.2.1951 mit Zitat des Briefs des Ordensmeisters an Vetter vom 23.1.1951. Diesem Provinzrundbrief sind im PA die eidesstattlichen Erklärungen aller Patres der Konvente von München, Wien, Freiburg, Graz und Friesach beigeheftet; in München, Augsburg und Retz hatte Vetter selbst für die Durchführung dieser Anweisung gesorgt (laut handschriftl. Notiz: „München, Augsburg, Retz persönlich erledigt. M.V." des Provinzials). Auf meine Frage an einen der damaligen Novizen wurde mir erklärt, die Anklage sei von einem Kapuzinerpater ausgegangen, der sich über das Verhalten der Dominikaner geärgert habe.

144 PA, Liber consiliorum, Sitzung in Wien am 28.9.1951, S. 35.

gen und die Kirchenbeleuchtung renoviert, außerdem wurde die Orgel in Stand gesetzt und erhielt ein elektrisches Gebläse. Große Investitionen wurden in die Sanierung und den Ausbau der Wirtschaftsgebäude des Konvents und des landwirtschaftlichen Maschinenparks gesteckt.[145]

Aus der Stadt Retz hatten sich die letzten Einheiten der Roten Armee am 2. Juni 1946[146] zurückgezogen und damit auch das Dominikanerkloster verlassen, das sie seit Mai 1945 besetzt gehalten hatten. Die Klostergebäude waren schon nach deren Verwendung als Umsiedlerlager nicht mehr in gutem Zustand gewesen und die Sowjetsoldaten hatten das nicht verbessert. Die Reparaturen zogen sich ein Jahrzehnt hin, weil die bescheidenen finanziellen Möglichkeiten des Konvents nur ein schrittweises Vorgehen ermöglichten. Einen Abschluss dieser Arbeiten stellte die Einweihung der „radikal renovierten" Kirchenorgel dar, die am 8. Dezember 1956 unter großer Beteiligung der Bevölkerung feierlich begangen werden konnte.[147]

An Kloster und Kirche in Wien waren zwar im Vergleich zu den anderen Niederlassungen der Provinz relativ wenige Bombenschäden entstanden, aber man nutzte die Gelegenheit der notwendigen Bauvorhaben zu Umstrukturierungen der Pfarrräumlichkeiten und zu einer grundlegenden Renovierung der Rosenkranzbasilika. 1950 wurde die Pfarrkanzlei vom 1. Stock über dem Südarm des Kreuzganges in das Erdgeschoß des Westtraktes an der Postgasse verlegt. Die Zimmer des Gangs darüber (1. Stock über dem Westarm des Kreuzgangs) wurden zu Jugend- und anderen Räumen für die Pfarrei umgewidmet. In 1200 Arbeitsstunden räumte die Pfarrjugend auf dem Kirchen- und Klosterdachboden den Schutt weg, der sich noch seit den Bombenangriffen dort befunden hatte. Auch die Schäden an der Kirchenverglasung an der Predigergasse konnten erst jetzt behoben werden. 1954 begann man mit der Renovierung der beiden Kirchtürme, wobei ein Turmhelm fast ganz erneuert und beide Türme neu mit Kupferblech gedeckt wurden. Im Folgejahr wurden das ganze Kirchendach, die Außenseite und die Hauptfassade der Kirche samt beiden großen Stein-

145 PA, Provinzrundbriefe von „Ende Januar 1952" (Bericht des Provinzials über das Jahr 1951), S. 5, vom „Januar 1955" (Bericht des Provinzials über das Jahr 1954), S. 5, vom 2.2.1957, S. 5 und vom 2.2.1958, S. 4–5.

146 Datum laut: Resch: *Retzer Heimatbuch*. 2. Band, S. 556.

147 PA, Provinzrundbriefe vom 2.2.1951 (Bericht des Provinzials über das Jahr 1950), S. 6, von „Ende Januar 1952" (Bericht des Provinzials über das Jahr 1951), S. 6, vom 2.2.1953 (Bericht des Provinzials über das Jahr 1952), S. 7, vom „Januar 1955" (Bericht des Provinzials über das Jahr 1954), S. 6, vom 2.2.1957, S. 5 und vom 2.2.1958, S. 5.

statuen repariert; die Kuppel wurde gegen drohenden Einsturz gesichert. 1956 begann man mit der Sanierung des Kircheninnenraums: Der Stuck wurde gereinigt, das Schiff neu ausgemalt, die Brüstungen der Oratorien und Emporen und das Orgelgehäuse farblich neu gefasst. Die 104 Fresken, das Kuppelbild und acht Ölbilder im Kuppelraum wurden gereinigt, teilweise von einer Übermalung befreit und in ihren ursprünglichen Zustand zurückgeführt. Auch die Kirchenelektrik wurde ersetzt und neue Luster im barocken Stil aufgehängt. 1956 wurden die beiden großen Seitenaltäre überholt, 1957 folgten die Ausbesserung der Kapellen des Kirchenschiffes und des Bodenpflasters. 1958 sanierte man das Presbyterium und den Hochaltar. Provinzial Vetter vermerkte in seinen Rundbriefen mehrmals, dass die hohen Kosten dieser Tätigkeiten schuldenfrei getragen werden konnten. Zum Abschluss der Renovierung im Rahmen der Neuweihe des Hochaltares durch Kardinalerzbischof Franz König am 7. Dezember 1958 erschien ein bebilderter Kirchenführer.[148] 1964 wurde die Gruft unter der Kirche als Begräbnisstätte für die Wiener Dominikaner umgebaut und wiedereröffnet; sie erhielt 1965 einen Altar aus Margaretner Sandstein.[149]

Kloster und Fatimakirche in Graz

Ein ganz anderes Problem bot sich in Graz: Dort standen die Brüder vor einem Schutthaufen, den die vollständige Zerstörung ihrer Annenkirche durch den Bombenangriff vom 1. November 1944 hinterlassen hatte. Diese Kirche war aber nicht nur Kloster-, sondern auch Pfarrkirche gewesen, und zwar die einer großen und weiter wachsenden Pfarrei. Der Behelfsgottesdienstraum, der im großen Refektorium des Konvents (dem nachmaligen Albertussaal) als Notkirche eingerichtet worden war, reichte bei weitem nicht aus und erlaubte nicht einmal einen „günstigen Beichtstuhlbetrieb“, weil „das Gedränge überhaupt sehr hinderlich“ war[150] und die Gläubigen daher vermehrt auf die umliegenden Pfarrkirchen auswichen. Ein Wiederaufbau der Annenkirche an ihrem ursprünglichen Ort entlang der Münz-

---

148 PA, Provinzrundbriefe vom 2.2.1951 (Bericht des Provinzials über das Jahr 1950), S. 1 und 2, vom „Januar 1955“ (Bericht des Provinzials über das Jahr 1954), S. 2, vom 2.2.1957, S. 2, vom 2.2.1958, S. 2 und vom 11.3.1959, S. 1.

149 PA, Provinzrundbrief vom 12.3.1965, S. 1 und vom 15.3.1966, S. 1.

150 PA, Provinzrundbrief vom 2.2.1951 (Bericht des Provinzials über das Jahr 1950), S. 3.

Abb. 11: Darstellung der Zerstörung der Grazer Annenkirche durch Bombeneinschlag; Relief an der Fatimakirche Graz (PA, Fotosammlung).

Abb. 12: Graz, Annenkirche: Blick Richtung Hochaltar (PA, Fotosammlung).

grabenstrasse hätte das Platzproblem aber nicht gelöst, denn diese war zwar „zierlich, aber klein, sie hatte kaum 100 Sitzplätze."[151] Deshalb wurde als

151 PA, Kirchenbauchronik der Münzgrabenkirche, fol. 80.

Abb. 13: Die Notkirche im Grazer Dominikanerkloster – nachmaliger Albertussaal (Foto aus: PA, Kirchenbauchronik der Münzgrabenkirche, fol. 1).

Bauplatz eine Stelle am südlichen Ende des Klosterkomplexes vorgesehen. Inwieweit der ebenfalls geplante Wechsel des Patroziniums der neuen Kirche auf das Unbefleckte Herz Mariens der Frömmigkeit des Hauptbetreibers des Bauprojekts, des Grazer Priors Leo Schölzhorn, geschuldet war, ließ sich nicht mehr ermitteln.[152] Jedenfalls konnte Schölzhorn auf einer Audienz am 7. Dezember 1946 den Grazer Fürstbischof Ferdinand Pawlikowski von seinen Ideen überzeugen.[153] Zwei Tage später richtete er ein Kirchenbaufondskonto ein und begann zuversichtlich mit der Spendenkampagne.[154]

Zunächst aber mussten die Ruinen der Annenkirche abgetragen und der daran anliegende, ebenso zerstörte Westtrakt des Klostergebäudes wiederhergestellt werden. Die Kostenschätzung eines Baumeisters über dieses Projekt am 16. Dezember 1946 belief sich auf 371.134 öS, eine im ersten Nachkriegsjahr sehr große Summe.[155] Prior Leo Schölzhorn holte Erkundigungen über den möglichen Wert der Liegenschaften des Konvents ein.

152 Provinzial Vetter hob die tragende Rolle Schölzhorns immer wieder hervor, z. B. im Provinzrundbrief vom 2.2.1953 (Bericht des Provinzials über das Jahr 1952), S. 5.

153 PA, Kirchenbauchronik der Münzgrabenkirche, fol. 3. Das Provinzkonsil stimmte dem neuen Patrozinium ebenfalls zu (PA, Liber consiliorum, Sitzung in Wien vom 4.9.1946, S. 19).

154 PA, Kirchenbauchronik der Münzgrabenkirche, fol. 4.

155 Ebd.

Abb. 14: Dominikanerkloster Graz: der zerstörte Westtrakt (Foto aus: PA, Kirchenbauchronik der Münzgrabenkirche, fol. 2).

Diese wurde auf etwa 200.000 öS beziffert – was zusammen mit dem Vorhandensein von Baumaterialien durch den Abbruch der Ruinen wenigstens etwa den Rohbau des neuen Westtraktes ermöglicht hätte.[156] Danach legte er dem Konsil und dem Kapitel seines Konvents zwei Fragen vor: 1. Sollte man mit dem nötigen Bau trotz der widrigen Zeitumstände warten? 2. Waren die Brüder grundsätzlich bereit, „jeglichen Grundbesitz (mit Ausnahme dessen, der für Konvent und Kirche unmittelbar notwendig ist) aufzugeben und die Lebenshaltung der fernen Zukunft … einzig auf die Seelsorgserträge und die Vorsehung Gottes aufzubauen?“[157] Das Konventskonsil

156 Ebd., fol. 6.

157 Ebd., zu fol. 6: Einberufung des Konventskapitels für 3.1.1947. Hervorhebenswert sind ebd. Schölzhorns Gründe für die Veräußerung des Klosterbesitzes: „Es hat dies die Vorsehung mit dem Bombenwurf vom 1.11.1945 schon entschieden: dieser Bau kann kaum anders finanziert werden. Bei der geringen Zahl der Provinzangehörigen ist die Ausübung des Nebenberufs eines Landwirts eine unerträgliche, auf Kosten des Hauptberufes gehende Last. De facto bewies sich, dass Geldspekulationen … und Güterverwaltungen … sei es durch unrationelle Bewirtschaftung (wir sind ja nicht Landwirte), sei es durch Fügung der Vorsehung nicht die erstrebten Ziele, wohl aber viele Lasten brachten. Der Herr wollte von seinen Predigern Armut (verbunden mit Nichtsorge ums Zeitliche) und ebenso S. Dominikus. Getreide und Wein werden auch für uns wachsen, wenn auch nicht auf eigenen Gütern, wenn wir wirklich unsere eigenen Ziele erfüllen (und umgekehrt werden wir diesen umso hingebungsvoller dienen, wenn wir keine falsche irdische

stimmte am 31. Dezember 1946 einstimmig für den baldigen Baubeginn und für die Veräußerung des Klosterbesitzes, wenn auch unter Beibehaltung einer kleinen Liegenschaft in Haseldorfberg, zu Erholungszwecken.[158] Dieselbe Zustimmung gewährte auch das Konventskapitel am 3. Januar 1947.[159] Damit war der Weg frei für die Planung des Westtraktbaus – und für die Suche nach einer „kreditfähigen" Baufirma.[160]

Dem Provinzkonsil hingegen wurde das Ausmaß der geplanten Grundstücksverkäufe unheimlich. Auf der Sitzung am 13. Mai 1948 kam durch Stimmenpatt keine Entscheidung darüber zustande. Provinzial Vetter, dem der Wiederaufbau des ruinierten Klostertraktes ein großes Anliegen war, da der Grazer Konvent ja ein Juvenat beherbergen sollte, wandte sich am 14. Mai 1948 deshalb an die Ordensleitung in Rom. Die Ordenskurie gab mit Brief vom 6. Juni 1948 ihre Erlaubnis, ihr folgte der Heilige Stuhl am 19. Juni 1948.[161] Damit war der Weg frei, die Güter des Grazer Konvents nach Maßgabe des Punktes 39 der Akten des Provinzkapitels von 1946 zu behandeln. Am 18. Oktober 1947 wurden die ersten Liegenschaften des Konvents verkauft.[162]

Lebenssicherung hinter uns haben). Das Provinzkapitel legt es uns in Punkt 39 nahe. Daher scheint es so dem Herzen der Unbefleckten zu gefallen."

158 Ebd., fol. 7.

159 Ebd., fol. 8. Das Provinzkonsil stimmte dem Verkauf der Güter für die Klosterreparatur zu (PA, Liber consiliorum, Sitzung in Wien am 1.5.1947, S. 19–20. In seiner nächsten Sitzung am 23.5. wurden Einzelheiten des Liegenschaftsverkaufs behandelt; Widerstand dagegen ging nur von einem Konsilsmitglied aus, das überstimmt wurde (ebd., Sitzung in Wien am 23.5.1947, S. 20–22). Auch in folgenden Sitzungen wurde immer wieder über den Verkauf bestimmter Grazer Liegenschaft gehandelt.

160 PA, Kirchenbauchronik der Münzgrabenkirche, fol. 8.

161 Dazu: PA, Liber consiliorum, S. 25–29, samt Beilage 29a.

162 PA, Kirchenbauchronik der Münzgrabenkirche, fol. 26. In diesem Zusammenhang wurde auch die seit dem Ende des ersten Weltkrieges schwebende Frage nach dem Schicksal Wetzelsdorfs und Eppans gelöst: Beide Liegenschaften gehörten noch immer dem Grazer Konvent. 1947 wurden Haus und Grund in Wetzelsdorf verkauft (PA, Liber consiliorum provinciae, Sitzung vom 20.9.1947, S. 22). Schon 1939 hatten Teile der Eppaner Besitzungen an Privatleute verkauft werden können (ebd., Sitzung vom 5.5.1939, S. 6). 1948 trat Prior Schölzhorn mit dem Provinzial der norditalienischen Provinz, Henrico Brianza, in Verhandlungen, der für Kirche und Klostergebäude und den Rest des Eppaner Besitzes 2,5 Millionen Schilling bot. Das Provinzkonsil billigte diesen Handel, obzwar die faktische Zahlung des Kaufpreises einige Jahre auf sich warten ließ (ebd., Sitzung in Wien vom 7.5.1948, S. 24–25, Sitzung in Wien vom 23.7.1949, S. 25 und Sitzung in Graz vom 28.5.1952, S. 37).

Abb. 15: Dominikanerkloster Graz: der 1947–1949 neu errichtete Westtrakt an der Münzgrabenstraße (PA, Fotosammlung).

Im August 1947 wurden die Bauarbeiten am Westtrakt begonnen; ausgeführt wurden sie durch eine Gruppe Strafgefangener, die das Arbeitsamt vermittelt hatte, was die Lohnkosten niedriger hielt. Die lang anhaltende gute Witterung erlaubte es, dass bereits am 26. April 1948 die Gleichenfeier für den neuen Trakt abgehalten werden konnte.[163] Grundstücksverkäufe an die Stadt Graz zur Verbreiterung der Münzgrabenstraße ermöglichten die Fertigstellung des Westtraktes und Sanierungen und Reparaturen im restlichen Kloster, die durch die Verlegung der Pfarrräumlichkeiten ins Parterre des Westtraktes und des Südflügels des Kreuzganges sowie die Verlegung der Bibliothek in den zweiten Stock des sogenannten Ziegelbaus notwendig geworden waren.[164] Ende Dezember 1949 waren schließlich die Bücher der Bibliothek an ihre neue Stelle im zweiten Stock des Ziegelbaus übertragen und das Kloster und die Räume des Juvenats baulich fertig gestellt.[165]

163 PA, Kirchenbauchronik der Münzgrabenkirche, fol. 15, 19, 22, 23, 25, 30, 32, 33 und 35 mit Beilagen.

164 Ebd., fol. 48–50.

165 Ebd., fol. 50–54, 108–109 mit Beilagen.

Abb. 16: Modell einer zukünftigen Pfarr- und Klosterkirche in Graz; Architekt unbekannt (PA, Fotosammlung).

Währenddessen gingen die Planungen und Vorbereitungen am neuen Kirchenbau weiter. Ende Februar 1947 schrieb Schölzhorn drei Grazer und drei Wiener Architekten an und bat sie in der Art eines Wettbewerbs um Projektvorschläge. Als Maßgaben legte der Prior nicht nur die inzwischen vom Konvent erarbeiteten Wünsche und Vorstellungen zur Innen- und Außeneinrichtung der neuen Kirche bei, mit sehr detaillierter Darlegung ihrer Raumaufteilung, sondern auch umfangreiche Übersetzungen aus dem Caeremoniale des Predigerordens über Kirchenbau und -ausstattung.[166] Bis zum 6. Juni 1947 lagen die sechs Entwürfe vor; keiner befriedigte ganz.[167] Anfang September beschloss der Konvent, „unter Verringerung der zuvor vorgesehenen Größe der Kirche (Fassungsraum)" einstimmig, den Architekten Georg Lippert (Wien) in Arbeitsgemeinschaft mit Ing. Max Ehrenberger (Graz) und Dr. Hans Petermair (Wien) „je zu einer neuen Planverfassung heranzuziehen".[168] Am 2. Juni 1948 lagen die Pläne und Modelle Lipperts und Petermairs der Begutachtung des Konvents vor. Für Lipperts Entwurf sprach vor allem sein Vorschlag der Aufstellung der geplanten Fatima-Statue in einem „Rosarium" genannten Wandelgang mit Kapelle nördlich der Kirche, der Prozessionen und Bitt-

166 Ebd., fol. 13 mit 15 Seiten Beilagen.
167 Ebd., fol. 18.
168 Ebd., fol. 23.

Abb. 17: Zeichnung des Innenraumeindrucks einer zukünftigen Pfarr- und Klosterkirche in Graz; Zeichner unbekannt (PA, Fotosammlung).

Abb. 18: Modell einer zukünftigen Pfarr- und Klosterkirche in Graz; Hans Petermair (PA, Fotosammlung).

Abb. 19: Modell einer zukünftigen Pfarr- und Klosterkirche in Graz; Georg Lippert (FA, Fotosammlung).

Abb. 20: Modell des Altarraums einer zukünftigen Pfarr- und Klosterkirche in Graz; Georg Lippert (PA, Fotosammlung).

gänge ermöglichte.[169] Seine Pläne wurden auch von mehreren Mitgliedern des Landesbauamts besichtigt, die sie vorbehaltslos lobten (die Gliederung des Kirchenbaues sei „wunderbar", „ein Kabinettstück").[170] Nachdem sich Provinzial Marianus Vetter ebenfalls mit den Lippertschen Plänen einverstanden erklärt hatte und am 15. Juni 1948 auch die Erlaubnis des Generalkonsils aus Rom zum Verkauf der restlichen Klostergüter vorlag, beauftragte das Konventskonsil mit seiner Sitzung am 18. Juni 1948 die Arbeitsgemeinschaft Lippert-Ehrenberger als Kirchenarchitekten.[171]

Alle bisherigen Bauarbeiten am Kloster waren ausschließlich durch Verkäufe von Konventsgütern finanziert worden.[172] Diese Mittel waren nun fast erschöpft und trotz der angestrengten Bemühungen des Priors war keine Unterstützung der Kirchenbaufinanzierung von anderer Seite in

169 Ebd., fol. 18 und 38–39.
170 Ebd., fol. 39.
171 Ebd., fol. 41–42 sowie dreiseitige Beilage zu fol. 42.
172 Ebd., fol. 56: „einzig aus der Veräußerung aller Werte, die der Konvent … besaß".

Sicht.[173] Um das Interesse der Öffentlichkeit zu wecken und dadurch eine wirkungsvolle Spendenaktion in Gang setzen zu können, inszenierte Schölzhorn die feierliche Grundsteinlegung der zukünftigen Kirche zum Unbefleckten Herzen, die der Grazer Weihbischof Leo Pietsch am 1. November 1950 vornahm, unter reger Beteiligung des Klerus, der Landes- und Stadtregierung und einer großen Volksmenge.[174] Mit Tatendrang widmete sich P. Prior nun der Herbeischaffung von Geldmitteln. Auch die festliche Übertragung der vom Bischof von Leiria in Portugal gestifteten Kopie der Originalstatue von Fatima in die Notkirche der Grazer Dominikaner am 7. Oktober 1951 wurde von ihm so öffentlichkeitswirksam wie möglich zelebriert. Am 20. Dezember 1951 beschloss das Konventskonsil die Gründung eines Kirchenbauvereins, die am 3. Februar 1952 vorgenommen wurde.[175] Im Januar 1952 übernahm ein Baukomitee die Spendensammlung; dieses hatte sich in den letzten Monaten des Vorjahres gebildet und bestand aus mehreren Persönlichkeiten des öffentlichen Lebens unter der Leitung von Prof. Dr. Ferdinand Wultsch. Immerhin waren acht bis zehn Millionen Schilling aufzutreiben – so hoch wurden die Kosten des anstehenden Baus beziffert.[176] Wieder genehmigte das Konventskonsil den Verkauf weiterer Liegenschaften, dieses Mal für den Kirchenbau.[177] Am 11. März 1952 langte endlich die erste öffentliche Subvention durch die Stadt Graz ein.[178] Zusammen mit weiteren Privatspenden standen nun die Mittel zur Verfügung, den ersten Bauabschnitt (konkret des Kirchenschiffes) zu beginnen, was am 15. April 1952 geschah.[179]

Die „Kirchenbauchronik" Schölzhorns dokumentiert bis ins kleinste Detail auf der einen Seite die angestrengte Spendensammlungstätigkeit, aber auf der anderen Seite auch, dass der Kirchenbau finanziell von der Hand in den Mund lebte. Gerettet wurde der erste Bauabschnitt durch den Entschluss der Stadt Graz Mitte November, große Teile des Klostergartens als Baugründe aufzukaufen. So konnte am 21. November 1952 die

173 Ebd., fol. 55–60 mit Beilagen.

174 Ebd., fol. 65–1 mit Beilagen.

175 Ebd., fol. 73–86 mit Beilagen und fol. 88.

176 Zum Komitee: PA, Provinzrundbrief von „Ende Januar 1952" (Bericht des Provinzials über das Jahr 1951), S. 4 und Kirchenbauchronik der Münzgrabenkirche, fol. 85 ff.; zur Kostenschätzung ebd., fol. 87.

177 PA, Kirchenbauchronik der Münzgrabenkirche, fol. 88 und 89.

178 Ebd., fol. 90.

179 Ebd., fol. 91f. mit Beilagen.

Gleichenfeier des Kirchenschiffs und der Vorhalle stattfinden.[180] Am 10. Februar 1953 begann man mit dem Erdaushub des Presbyteriums.[181] Bis Ende Mai waren die Mauern dort hochgezogen. Bezahlen konnte man diese Arbeiten nicht; der Baumeister erhielt lediglich 100.000 Schilling und einen „Verdienstausweis“ über 500.000 öS.[182] Mit der ihm eigenen Zuversicht beauftragte der Prior dennoch mehrere Künstler mit Entwürfen zu Statuen und Fresken der zukünftigen Inneneinrichtung.[183] Am 17. Juni 1953 tagte das Baukomitee über die Frage der notwendigen Einstellung der Bauarbeiten „nach Erreichung der Dachdeckung des Presbyteriums. Begründung: ein zu erwartender Schuldenstand von ca. 600.000 Schilling erlaubt nicht die Weiterführung.“[184]

Auftrieb erhielt das Bauprojekt durch Liturgiefeiern: Schon am 7. Juni 1953 war die Fronleichnamsprozession im Rohbau des Kirchenschiffes beendet worden, als erste gottesdienstliche Handlung dort.[185] Über Vermittlung des Wiener Erzbischof Theodor Kardinal Innitzer, der sich von Schölzhorns Begeisterung für die neue Kirche hatte anstecken lassen, zelebrierte der Graz-Seckauer Fürstbischof Ferdinand Pawlikowski am 9. August 1953 im Rohbau eine Pontifikalmesse als Feier des „Dominikus-Sonntages für die Rosenkranzvereine“, bei der Provinzial Vetter predigte. Zu diesem Zeitpunkt war das Presbyterium noch voller Gerüste und besaß keinen Boden. Als Innitzer selbst zwei Wochen später, am 23. August, zu einer Pontifikalmesse kam, war der Innenraum des Presbyteriums so weit fertiggestellt, dass es benutzt werden konnte. In seiner Predigt zeigte der Kardinal sich von der Kirche beeindruckt: Er sei „von der schönen Formgebung und der Größe des Gotteshauses überrascht“, wünschte „dem Bau die Unterstützung ganz Österreichs“ und brachte zum Ausdruck, „dass er gerne und in Bälde das vollendete Gotteshaus besichtigen“ wolle.[186]

Wohl nicht zuletzt aufgrund Innitzers Einsatzes erklärte sich Landeshauptmann Josef Krainer am 23. September bereit, dem Baukomitee als Präsident vorzustehen und Professor Wultsch zu ersetzen. Krainer brachte

---

180 Ebd., fol. 100; zur Gleichenfeier fol. 100–102 mit Beilagen.
181 Ebd., fol. 105. Das Provinzkonsil hatte in seiner Sitzung in Wien am 14.3.1953 dem Beginn dieses Bauabschnittes zugestimmt (PA, Liber consiliorum, S. 39).
182 PA, Kirchenbauchronik der Münzgrabenkirche, fol. 107.
183 Ebd., fol. 106–107.
184 Ebd., fol. 108.
185 Ebd., fol. 108.
186 Ebd., fol. 110–111 mit Beilagen.

sogar den im Rahmen der Eröffnung der Herbstmesse in Graz weilenden Bundeskanzler Julius Raab dazu, am 26. September 1953 den Rohbau zu besichtigen.[187] Dies änderte allerdings nichts an den Geldproblemen; weiterhin gingen ausschließlich Privatspenden ein, die hauptsächlich über Straßensammlungen in Graz zusammengebracht wurden. Diese liefen immerhin insoweit gut, dass Anfang Januar 1954 nur mehr 190.000 öS Schulden zu verzeichnen waren[188] und man weitere Arbeiten (z. B. die Elektrifizierung des Rohbaus, den Abbruch und die Angleichung des südlichen Abschlusses des Klostergebäudes an die neue Kirche) fortführen konnte. Weitere finanzielle Vereinbarungen mit der Diözese Graz-Seckau, die Anfang Oktober 1954 zustande kamen, retteten das Fortführen des Bauprojekts.[189]

Nun wurde fieberhaft an der Kirche gearbeitet, sogar nachts. Rosarium und Fatimakapelle konnten zwar nicht mehr begonnen werden, aber am 31. Oktober 1954 schritt Diözesanbischof Schoiswohl zur Benediktion der neuen Kirche.[190] Am 6. Dezember kamen dann die vom Ordinariat bewilligten Gelder an – zur großen Beruhigung aller am Bau beteiligten Handwerker.[191] Dennoch stand das Bauprojekt Anfang Januar 1955 mit mindestens 700.000 öS in der Kreide.[192] Das Baukomitee organisierte daraufhin eine Landessammlung in der ganzen Steiermark, mit der im April 1955 begonnen wurde – „Motto: Jeder Steirer gebe wenigstens 2 S für den Weiterbau des Fatima-Heiligtums".[193] Die Landessammlung erfüllte die in sie gesetzten Erwartungen nicht.[194] Zur Unterstützung alle diese Spendenaufrufe und -aktionen durch Druckschriften baute Prior Schölzhorn einen klostereigenen Verlag auf.[195] Am 26. Juli 1955 erfolgte die Einweihung der neuen Annenkapelle, am 25. September die Einweihung der Maria-Goretti-Kapelle, beides Nebenkapellen der Hauptkirche.[196]

187 Ebd., fol. 111.
188 Ebd., fol. 115.
189 Ebd., fol. 121.
190 Ebd., fol. 122–124 mit Beilagen.
191 Ebd., fol. 124.
192 Ebd., fol. 127.
193 Ebd., fol. 129.
194 Ebd., fol. 131. Bis Anfang Oktober 1955 hatte die Landessammlung etwa 150.000 öS erbracht (ebd., S. 134).
195 Siehe ebd., fol. 136. u. ö. Dieser hieß ursprünglich „Rosenkranzverlag" und wurde am 16. November 1957 in „Fatima-Verlag" umgetauft (ebd., S. 148).
196 Ebd., fol. 131 und 132.

Abb. 21: Fatimakirche in Graz: der erste Gottesdienst im Rohbau anlässlich der Fronleichnamsfeier am 7. Juni 1953 (Foto aus: PA, Kirchenbauchronik der Münzgrabenkirche, Beilage zu fol. 119/4).

Am 2. Oktober war auch die Kapelle am Fuß des Kirchturms fertig, wo die Fatimastatue aufgestellt wurde. Damit konnte die Notkirche endlich aufgegeben werden.[197] Am 16. Dezember 1956 erfolgte die Weihe der Orgel durch Diözesanbischof Schoiswohl.[198] Ende Mai 1957 wurden weitere Schulden aufgenommen, was den Abschluss des Kirchturmbaus und seine Gleichenfeier am 12. Dezember 1957 ermöglichte.[199]

Auch im Jahre 1958 wurde die Finanzlage nicht besser. Die einlangenden Spendenmittel gingen insgesamt zurück.[200] Trotzdem legte Prior Schölzhorn dem Konventskonsil am 13. März 1958 die Frage zur Abstim-

197 Ebd., fol. 134. Im Juli 1958 wurde sie zum Festsaal umgewidmet und das Refektorium in den ersten Stock des Klosters verlegt; der bis dahin als Speisesaal genutzte kleine Saal im Erdgeschoß sollte als Raum für Exerzitien, Einkehrtage u. Ä. dienen (ebd., fol. 154).

198 Ebd., fol. 140.

199 Ebd., fol. 143 und 148.

200 So laut Interimsabschluss über den Kirchenbau vom 5.11.1958 (PA, Kirchenbauchronik der Münzgrabenkirche, fol. 155).

Abb. 22: Die Fatimakirche in Graz 1964 (PA, Fotosammlung).

Abb. 23: Fatimakirche in Graz: Blick in den Altarraum (aufgenommen ca. 1965; PA, Fotosammlung).

Abb. 24: Fatimakirche in Graz: Blick ins Kirchenschiff (aufgenommen ca. 1965; PA. Fotosammlung).

Abb. 25: Fatimakirche in Graz: Rosarium mit Fatimakapelle (aufgenommen ca. 1965; PA, Fotosammlung).

mung vor, „ob Fatimakapelle und Rosarium heuer im Rohbau errichtet werden“ sollten – was das Konsil mit sechs von sieben Stimmen bejahte.[201] Am 14. April tagte das Provinzkonsil in Wien über dasselbe Problem. Nicht alle Konsilsväter zeigten sich von Schölzhorns Antrag begeistert, dennoch ging er mit Mehrheitsbeschluß durch, aber mit der Einschränkung, dass „zuerst die ganze Vollendung der Kirche angestrebt werden“ sollte und zwar so, „dass das Geld für die restlichen Anliegen nicht nur in spe, sondern in re vorhanden sei.“[202] Bei Landeshauptmann Krainer sprach Schölzhorn am 29. April um eine Sondersubvention des Landes zum Verputz der Kirche vor; Krainer versprach Hilfe, wies aber darauf hin, dass diese nicht vor November erwartet werden konnte.[203] Durch diese Zusage beflügelt, nahm das Konventskonsil Anfang Juni den Entwurf Josef Troyers für das große Fresko an der Ostwand des Presbyteriums an; leider erwies sich der

201 Ebd., fol. 151.

202 Ebd., fol. 153. Dazu: PA, Liber consiliorum, Sitzung des Provinzkonsils in Wien am 14.4.1958, S. 47.

203 PA, Kirchenbauchronik der Münzgrabenkirche, fol. 153.

Abb. 26: Fatimakirche in Graz: Altarfresko von Josef Troyer (Abb. aus: PA, Kirchenbauchronik der Münzgrabenkirche, Beilage zu fol. 162/2).

Putz an den Seitenwänden des Presbyteriums als so mangelhaft, dass das ganze Presbyterium neu verputzt werden musste, bevor Troyer mit der Freskierung beginnen konnte.[204] Anfang Oktober langte die Nachricht von Bischof Schoiswohl ein, dass die Diözese in den Jahren 1959 und 1960 jeweils 200.000 öS zu geben bereit war. Mit diesen Zusagen von Geldmitteln im Rücken beschloss das Grazer Konventskonsil am 7. Februar 1959 den Bau der Fatimakapelle und des Rosariums.[205] Am 9. März 1959 begann die Außenverputzung des Turms. Die Arbeiten am Rosariums begannen am 13. April.[206]

Mitte Juni 1959 war Josef Troyer mit seinem Fresko fertig.[207] Nicht nur wegen der extensiven Werbetätigkeit des Fatima-Verlages gab es darauf ein großes Medienecho, auch die durchaus kontroversen Inhalte des 10 auf 13 Meter großen Werkes führten zu lauten Diskussionen. Schölzhorn erklärte die sieben aufeinander bezogenen Großbilder, aus denen es bestand, in einer seiner Publikationen unter dem Titel „Zwischen Gott und Satan". Das Fresko zeige „den Ursprung des Bösen, seinen Eintritt in die Welt der Menschen und seine auf Vernichtung bedachte Wirksamkeit in ihr", aber auch „die Großtaten … die Gott wirkte, um uns den Folgen und Einflüssen der Sünde zu entziehen und uns zu befähigen, das Heil zu erlangen. So stellt es allen in hohem Ernste unablässig vor Augen, dass jeder, zwischen Gott und Satan gestellt, in allen seinen freien Willensentscheidungen letzten Endes immer zwischen diesen beiden zu entscheiden hat."[208]

Der Rest des Jahres wurde mit dem Weiterbau am Rosarium verbracht, dessen Dach im November gedeckt werden konnte.[209] 1960 folgte die weitere figurale und freskantische Ausgestaltung von Kirche und Rosarium, die Aufstellung der Seitenaltäre und die Installation der Turmuhr sowie die Fertigstellung der Fatimakapelle. Am 31. Oktober 1960 konnte die Fatimakapelle durch Provinzial Gierlich benediziert werden und am 1. November weihte Diözesanbischof Schoiswohl die Kirche und konsekrierte den Hochaltar (als Herz-Jesu-Altar) und die beiden Seitenaltäre, den Jo-

204 Ebd., fol. 154–155.
205 Ebd., fol. 158.
206 Ebd., fol. 160.
207 Ebd., fol. 161.
208 Zitate und Beschreibung laut: ebd., Beilage zu fol. 162 / 2.
209 Ebd., fol. 163.

Abb. 27: Fatimakirche in Graz: „Triumph der beiden heiligsten Herzen Jesu und Mariä"; Mosaik von Josef Troyer an der Außenwand der Fatimakapelle (aufgenommen ca. 1964; PA, Fotosammlung).

sephs- und den Rosenkranzaltar.[210] Auch war es gelungen, viele Darlehen zu tilgen.[211] Am 19. März 1961 folgte die Weihe der sieben neuen Kirchenglocken, die von Johann Graßmayr in Innsbruck gegossen worden waren, durch Bischof Schoiswohl.[212] Am 8. Dezember 1961 weihte Münzgrabenpfarrer P. Michael Lenz das Turmrelief.[213] Ende Juni 1963 wurde an der Außenwand der Fatimakapelle das Mosaik „Triumph der beiden heiligsten Herzen" aufgezogen, das ebenfalls durch Josef Troyer erstellt worden war.[214] Mit der durch Prior Seraphicus Weber am 24. November 1963 vollzogenen

210 Zu alle dem: ebd., fol. 164–175 mit zahlreichen Beilagen.
211 Ebd., fol. 175.
212 Ebd., fol. 176–180 mit Beilagen.
213 Ebd., fol. 184.
214 Ebd., fol. 194.

Weihe der letzten Kunstwerke war in den Augen Schölzhorns „praktisch die Hauptsache des Kirchenbaus vollendet".[215] Schölzhorn selbst beging den Bauabschluss dankbar mit einer Fußwallfahrt nach Maria Zell.[216] 1965 wurden die Annenkapelle und das Presbyterium der Kirche noch den Anforderungen an die neue Liturgie – nicht ohne kontroverse Diskussion zwischen den jüngeren und den älteren Mitbrüdern des Konvents – angepasst.[217] Damit war das teuerste Bauprojekt der Provinz zum Abschluss gekommen.

Kirchen- und Klosterbau in Augsburg

Ähnlich große Anstrengungen mussten in Augsburg für den Wiederaufbau der Heilig-Kreuz-Kirche unternommen werden.[218] Die Wallfahrtskirche war beim Bombenangriff im Februar 1944 schwer beschädigt worden. Die Gauleitung der NSDAP in Schwaben verweigerte trotz Intervention des Denkmalamtes und der Diözese Augsburg jegliche Hilfe zur Rettung und zum Schutz des übriggebliebenen Bestandes. Anscheinend sah man dort die Zerstörung von Heilig Kreuz als stadtplanerisch günstige Chance zur Erweiterung des hinter der Kirche liegenden Ottmarsgäßchens und damit zur Schaffung einer weiteren Verkehrsverbindung ins Stadtzentrum. Daher wurden von öffentlicher Seite weder Baumaterial noch Arbeiter für Heilig Kreuz zur Verfügung gestellt. Die Augsburger Dominikaner mussten deshalb jedes Brett und jeden Baumstamm in den Pfarreien des Umlandes zusammenbetteln, weswegen erst Mitte Juli 1944 die große Sakristei von Heilig Kreuz mit einem Notdach versehen und das Klostergebäude im Ottmarsgäßchen repariert werden konnte. Mit Hilfe der Waisenkinder des benachbarten städtischen Waisenhauses wurde bis September 1944 auch der Bombenschutt beiseite geräumt. Danach gelang es mit Unterstützung durch die städtische Feuerwehr, auch auf das Kirchenschiff eine Notbedachung aufzulegen. Diese war immerhin so stabil, dass sie am 15. Januar 1945 einem weiteren Luftangriff standhielt. Die Sakristei war Anfang De-

215 Ebd., fol. 195.

216 Ebd., fol. 197.

217 Ebd., fol. 199–207 mit Beilagen. Das Provinzkonsil sprach in seiner Sitzung in Graz am 22.3.1965 die Erlaubnis dafür aus (PA, Liber consiliorum, S. 58).

218 Da der Wiederaufbau der Kreuzkirche und der Bau des Klosters in Augsburg an anderer Stelle detailliert beschrieben wurden, wird hier nur eine kurze Überblicksdarstellung geboten. Diese folgt: Hoyer: *Heilig Kreuz*, S. 685–706 – wenn nicht anders ausgewiesen.

zember 1945 soweit wiederhergestellt, dass sie als Gottesdienstraum verwendet werden konnte. Inzwischen aber hatte die Witterung in der Kirche zerstört, was die Bomben an Mauern, Pfeilern und Gewölben übriggelassen hatten:

> „Die Massivgewölbe des Langhauses gingen nach und nach durch das ungehinderte Eindringen von Regen und Schnee verloren. An den Gewölben der Seitenschiffe, die anfangs die geringsten Schäden aufwiesen, zeigten sich in zunehmendem Maße Löcher und Risse, sodass sie abgetragen werden mussten. Einige der überschlanken Säulen (Sandsteintrommeln) gerieten hierdurch aus dem Lot. Ihr dicker barocker Stuckmantel war allenthalben abgefallen. Die massiven Gewölbe der im ersten Langhausjoch liegenden Orgelempore hatten samt ihrem Rippennetzwerk standgehalten. Erhalten blieben ferner die Gewölbe in den unteren Kapellen und Sakristeiräumen zu Seiten des Chores. Die der darüber angeordneten Oratorien waren hingegen weitgehend zerstört. Der starke, teilweise romanische Glockenturm war völlig ausgebrannt. Die barocke reiche Innenausstattung war vernichtet.“[219]

Letztlich mussten im Frühjahr 1946 alle Gewölbereste und die Nordwand der Kirche abgerissen werden. Die Arbeiten an der Wiederherstellung des Mauerkranzes waren am 24. Juni 1947 abgeschlossen. Dann wurde darauf ein eiserner Dachstuhl aufgesetzt, der am 13. Februar 1948 fertig wurde. Am 5. April 1948 wurde in Anwesenheit des Augsburger Bischofs Joseph Kumpfmüller der Hebauf gefeiert. Ursprünglich war die Wiederherstellung des gewohnten Außeneindrucks von Heilig Kreuz geplant gewesen, also auch der Wiederaufbau der barocken Kuppel über dem Chor. Aber nicht nur der Mangel an Geldern und Baumaterial verhinderte diese Idee: „Die Zerstörung der barocken Überarbeitung war eine so vollständige und das wieder deutlich gewordene gotische Raumbild erwies sich als so überzeugend, dass über den einzuschlagenden Weg nicht lange Unklarheit bestand.“[220] Denkmalamt und Dominikanerkonvent waren sich bald über eine Regotisierung der Kirche einig. Allerdings konnte auch diese Idee nicht konsequent durchgeführt werden: Statische Gründe und das Fehlen von entsprechend ausgebildeten Gewölbemaurern verhinderten sowohl das Aufsetzen einer Holzflachdecke, als auch den Aufbau eines gemauerten Netzgewölbes im gotischen Stil. Daher wurde eine Gußbetonschale in Kreuzgratgewölbeform aufgesetzt. Die Arbeiten daran begannen im Juli

219 Bertram: Wiederinstandsetzung, S. 123–124.
220 Ebd., 124.

Abb. 28: Kirche Heilig Kreuz in Augsburg: Blick zum Hochaltar, aufgenommen zwischen 1949 und 1962 (Archiv des Augsburger Dominikanerkonvents, Fotosammlung).

1949 und waren im November desselben Jahres vollendet. Am 26. November 1949 war Heilig Kreuz wieder sozusagen liturgisch betriebsbereit. An die Stelle des reich ausgestatteten Rokokogotteshauses war eine nüchterne, dem finanziellen Mangel und dem Nachkriegszeitgeist entsprechende Kirche getreten.

Allerdings hatte der Bombenangriff vom Februar 1944 durch die völlige Vernichtung des neben der Kirche liegenden ehemaligen Augustinerchorherrenstiftes auch eine neue Perspektive aufgetan, nämlich die Möglichkeit, ein großes Klostergebäude für den Konvent errichten zu können. Provinzial Marianus Vetter traf sich am 25. November 1954 mit Diözesanbischof Josef Freundorfer, dem Nachfolger Kumpfmüllers, und legte diesem einen Klosterbauplan vor. Gedacht war an ein teilweise vierstöckiges Gebäude mit immerhin 17.000 Kubikmetern umbauten Rauminhalts, entworfen durch Professor Michael Kurz. Das neue Kloster war deshalb so groß geplant, weil es nicht nur den Konvent, sondern auch das Noviziat, das Provinzialat und wenigstens Teile des seit 1939 erträumten Provinzstudienhauses aufnehmen sollte. Wie in Graz bestand das Hauptproblem beim Augsburger Projekt in der Finanzierung: Professor Kurz schätzte die

Abb. 29: Kirche Heilig Kreuz in Augsburg: Blick ins Kirchenschiff, aufgenommen zwischen 1949 und 1962 (Archiv des Augsburger Dominikanerkonvents, Fotosammlung).

Abb. 30: Br. Klaus Limacher, einer der am Kirchen- und Klosterbau in Augsburg werktätigen Brüder, mit einer von ihm gefertigten Wappenschnitzerei (Archiv des Augsburger Dominikanerkonvents, Fotosammlung).

Abb. 31: Dominikanerkloster an Heilig Kreuz, Augsburg: Fassade zur Heilig-Kreuz-Straße, aufgenommen vor 1960 (Archiv des Augsburger Dominikanerkonvents, Fotosammlung).

Abb. 32: Dominikanerkloster an Heilig Kreuz, Augsburg: Blick in den Kreuzganggarten, aufgenommen vor 1960 (Archiv des Augsburger Dominikanerkonvents, Fotosammlung).

Abb. 33: Dominikanerkloster an Heilig Kreuz, Augsburg: Blick ins große Treppenhaus (Archiv des Augsburger Dominikanerkonvents, Fotosammlung).

Kosten des Klosterbaus auf 800.000 bis 900.000 DM. Der Orden wandte sich daher an den Bischof und den Diözesansteuerausschuss um einen Zuschuss und ein Darlehen, um mit dem Bau beginnen zu können. Erleichtert wurden diese Verhandlungen des Provinzials durch die Tatsache, dass das Benefiziatenhaus im Ottmarsgäßchen nach dem Neubau nicht mehr benötigt werden würde und in die Hände des Diözesansteuerausschusses für andere Verwendungszwecke übergehen konnte. Ein weiteres Darlehen einer Bank lag im Februar 1956 vor.

Mit Einsetzen der besseren Witterung begannen die Bauarbeiten, die so zügig vorangingen, dass der Rohbau innerhalb weniger Monate stand. Am 15. August 1957 konnten die Brüder in ihr neues Kloster in der Heilig-Kreuz-Straße einziehen, wobei zunächst nur das Parterre und der erste Stock möbliert waren. Am Albertusfest, dem 15. November 1957 – dreizehn Jahre nach dem Bombenangriff – war der Wiederaufbau von Kirche und Kloster in Augsburg abgeschlossen und die Klosterchronik meldete: „Heute wurde durch unseren hochwürdigsten Herrn Bischof Dr. Josef

Abb. 34: Dominikanerkloster an Heilig Kreuz, Augsburg: Blick in den Gang vor dem Refektorium im Erdgeschoß, aufgenommen vor 1960
(Archiv des Augsburger Dominikanerkonvents, Fotosammlung).

Abb. 35: Dominikanerkloster an Heilig Kreuz, Augsburg: Refektorium
(Archiv des Augsburger Dominikanerkonvents, Fotosammlung).

Abb. 36: Dominikanerkloster an Heilig Kreuz, Augsburg: Kapitelsaal
(Archiv des Augsburger Dominikanerkonvents, Fotosammlung).

Abb. 37: Dominikanerkloster an Heilig Kreuz, Augsburg: Gang im ersten Stock mit den Klosterzellen der Brüder (Archiv des Augsburger Dominikanerkonvents, Fotosammlung).

Freundorfer die Konsekration des Hauptaltares vollzogen. Mitkonsekratoren waren für den Marienaltar der hochwürdige Herr Abt Johannes Ruhland OSB und für den Albertusaltar der hochwürdige Herr Prälat und Generalvikar Dr. Albert Vierbach. Anschließend fand die Weihe des Klosters statt, die der hochwürdigste Herr Bischof vollzog."[221]

Bemerkenswert ist der Augsburger Bau deshalb, weil mit ihm das erste Kloster in Süddeutschland entstand, das sich der Predigerorden selbst gebaut

221 Archiv des Augsburger Dominikanerkonvents: Chronik der Dominikaner bei Hl. Kreuz (1935–1962), fol. 80r.

Abb. 38: Dominikanerkloster an Heilig Kreuz, Augsburg: eine der Klosterzellen im ersten Stock mit ihrem Bewohner, P. Emmanuel Kairys (Archiv des Augsburger Dominikanerkonvents, Fotosammlung).

hat. Bis dahin hatten die Dominikaner in für ihre Zwecke mehr oder weniger funktionalen Provisorien leben müssen – in Freiburg / St. Albert in einer Villa, in Augsburg-Spickel und München / St. Albert in Pfarrhöfen, an Augsburg / Hl. Kreuz in einem Nebengebäude. Zwar präsentiert der Neubau an der Heilig-Kreuz-Straße zwischen der Heilig-Kreuz-Kirche und der Intendantur des Augsburger Stadttheaters eine geschlossene, vierstöckige Fassade, verziert mit einem Flacherker, aber dahinter liegt kein geschlossener Baublock, sondern ein mehrflügeliger Gebäudekomplex um zwei Innenhöfe. Diese Anlage ist der länglichen Form des Grundstücks an der Südwand der

Kirche und eng benachbarten Nebengebäuden des Stadttheaters geschuldet: Als breiter und hoher Rahmen flankieren das mächtige Kulissenlager und seine Werkstätten im Westen und die Proberäumlichkeiten der Musiker im Süden das Kloster. Dieses selbst besteht aus einem vierstöckigen Haus, das mit drei Flügeln einen trapezförmigen Innenhof umschließt; die vierte Hofseite schließen der Turm und die Apsis der Heilig-Kreuz-Kirche ab. Im Erdgeschoß an der Heilig-Kreuz-Straße liegt der Eingangsbereich mit Pforte und Sprechzimmern, im Erdgeschoß des Südflügels befinden sich das große Refektorium, der Kapitelsaal und die Bibliothek. Hinter seinem Westflügel liegt an der Südwand der Kirche entlang ein weiterer, kleinerer, längsrechteckiger Hof, auf allen vier Seiten umgeben von einem nur zweistöckigen Gebäude, mit einem Wandelgang als Kreuzgang im Erdgeschoß. Wie die Kreuzkirche, so macht auch das Kloster an Heilig Kreuz einen nüchternen Eindruck: Nichts war darin zu Repräsentationszwecken errichtet worden, sondern alles folgte rein funktionellen Aufgaben. Entsprechend fehlt ihm jegliche Eleganz und – bis auf den schon genannten Flacherker – architektonischer Schmuck. Die Gänge des Eingangsbereichs, der Gemeinschaftsräume im Erdgeschoß, das Stiegenhaus und der Kreuzgang waren mit Kalkstein ausgelegt, alles andere mit Linoleum. Alle Wände und Decken wurden weiß gestrichen. Das hatte nicht nur mit dem Mangel an Geldmitteln zu tun, sondern mit einem ausdrücklichen Gestaltungswillen – schließlich hatte der Wohnort eines Bettelordenskonvents auch entsprechend auszusehen. Die Satzungen des Ordens schrieben zum Beispiel für die Zellen, also die Zimmer der Brüder vor, dass sie ärmlich zu sein hatten, ohne Ornamente oder Bilderschmuck. Erlaubt waren nur ein Kreuz, ein Marienbild und eine Darstellung des hl. Dominikus.[222] Das neue Augsburger Dominikanerkloster entsprach diesem Formwillen sehr genau.

Ausbau der Präsenz in München-Freimann und Übernahme von St. Kajetan

Ganz anders bauten die Brüder in München nach dem Krieg aus: Sie erweiterten nämlich ihre Präsenz in der Stadt. Haupteinsatzgebiet der Brüder war die rasch wachsende Pfarrei von St. Albert in München-Freimann, deren Mitgliederzahl der Provinzial Anfang 1951 auf etwa 6000 schätzte, Anfang 1952 auf circa 8000. Dieser Zuzug war nicht zuletzt der Ankunft vieler Vertriebener bedingt, für die auf dem Pfarrgebiet ein neues Wohnviertel eingerichtet wur-

222 *Constitutiones 1932*, S. 226, Nr. 610 § 1.

Abb. 39: Dominikanerkloster und -kirche St. Albert in München-Freimann (Zeichnung aus PA: Chronik für das Noviziat der oberdeutschen Dominikanerprovinz, S. 165).

de. Für sie weihte man am 16. Dezember 1951 eine Notkirche auf das Patrozinium der hl. Katharina von Siena ein, die von St. Albert aus betreut wurde. 1955 gab Vetter die Zahl von 5000 Gläubigen an St. Albert und 3000 an St. Katharina an. Ein weiterer Mitbruder kümmerte sich um die Sonn- und Feiertagsgottesdienste in der Pfarrfiliale in Eching-Dietersheim mit etwa 450 Seelen.[223] Als Pfarrer bzw. Pfarradministratoren wirkten an St. Albert die Dominikaner Burkhard Zimmermann (1934–1946), Alfred Willebrand (1946–1949), Matthäus Weiß (1949–1951), Rainer Kessler (1951–1956), Berthold Kaiser (1956–1963), Johannes Oderich Edelbauer (1963–1978), Clemens Wehrle (1978–1984) und Adalbert von Papius (1984–1990).

Trotz dieser starken seelsorgerlichen Belastung und des Noviziates, das seit 1946 an St. Albert bestand und das ebenfalls Kräfte band, ergriff der Konvent eine große Chance, als ihm 1953 als weitere Seelsorgestätte die ehe-

223 Angaben laut: PA, Provinzrundbriefe vom 2.2.1951, S. 8, von „Ende Januar 1952", S. 10 und „im Januar 1955", S. 10.

Abb. 40: Dominikanerkloster St. Albert in München-Freimann: Blick vom Kirchturm auf den Kreuzgang (PA, Fotosammlung).

Abb. 41: Dominikanerkloster und -kirche St. Albert in München-Freimann: Blick auf den Hochaltar (aufgenommen vor 1966; PA, Fotosammlung).

malige Theatinerkirche St. Kajetan im Stadtzentrum angeboten wurde. Das Provinzkonsil befasste sich am 16. September 1953 mit der Frage, ob eine solche Übernahme durch die vorhandenen Kräfte überhaupt möglich war, und beauftragte den Augsburger Konventualen P. Suso Geiselhart mit der Aufnahme der Verhandlungen mit dem erzbischöflichen Ordinariat der Erzdiözese München und Freising[224] – wohl, weil Geiselhart schon bei der Gründung des Konvents an Heilig Kreuz erfolgreich vermittelt hatte. Alles ging sehr schnell: Anfang Dezember 1953 hatte Provinzial Vetter den entsprechenden Vertrag vorbereitet und schon am 4. Februar 1954 war die Vereinbarung zwischen Erzbistum und Provinz unter Dach und Fach.[225]

Zum 1. Januar 1954 wurde P. Magnus Beck zum Rektor dieses bedeutenden Gotteshauses eingesetzt. Mit ihm zusammen zogen drei weitere Dominikanerpriester und ein Laienbruder in das Mesnerhaus hinter der Kirche. Provinzial Vetter beschrieb ihre Aufgaben so:

> „Gottesdienstordnung: an Sonn- und Feiertagen sind 5 hl. Messen, davon 4 mit Predigt. Zahl der Kirchenbesucher: ca. 900. Werktags 4 hl. Messen, täglich [um] 5 Uhr Rosenkranz. Beichtgelegenheit: täglich während der hl. Messen, außerdem Freitag von 17–18.30 Uhr, Samstag von 16–18.30 Uhr und ab 19 Uhr. Der Rektor der Kirche hat wöchentlich 6 Stunden Religionsunterricht an einer Handelsschule zu erteilen. An die Kirche ist die altehrwürdige Allerseelenbruderschaft angeschlossen, die auf Kurfürst Maximilian zurückgeht. Die Mitgliederzahl beträgt 2500. Täglich wird für diese Bruderschaft der Rosenkranz gebetet, außerdem sind das Jahr über 6 Konvente [sc. Zusammenkünfte] mit Predigten und Andacht und 5 großen Gedächtnisgottesdiensten. Ferner wird in St. Cajetan die Drittordensgruppe betreut, die ihre Versammlungen am 3. Sonntag im Monat hält. Einer der Patres von St. Cajetan versieht das Amt des Dompredigers. Sein Dienst umfasst in der Dompfarrei an Vorabenden von Sonn- und Feiertagen Beichtgelegenheit und an Sonn- und Feiertagen selbst dreimalige Predigt, sowie 8 Stunden wöchentlich Religionsunterricht.“[226]

Bereits im Laufe eines Jahres verdreifachte sich die Zahl der Beichtenden; Marianus Vetter schätzte sie Anfang 1957 auf „ca. 17.500“.[227] Damit erhielt die neue Niederlassung an St. Kajetan ein ähnliches Pastoralprofil wie Hei-

224 PA, Liber consilii provincialis, Sitzung vom 16.9.1953 in Augsburg.

225 PA, Liber consilii provincialis, Sitzungen vom 9.12.1953 in Augsburg und vom 4.2.1954 in Augsburg.

226 PA, Provinzrundbrief „im Januar“ 1955, S. 10.

227 PA, Provinzrundbrief vom 2.2.1957, S. 8.

lig Kreuz in Augsburg, als zentrale Beichtkirche für die bayerische Landeshauptstadt.

1956 waren Renovierung und Umbau des Mesnerhauses „auf die Bedürfnisse des Klosters“ vollendet; es bestand nun aus vier Zellen und der Pforte mit drei Sprechzimmern,[228] dazu gehörten noch einige Zimmer über der Sakristei. Diese Niederlassung war also nur für eine kleine Gemeinschaft geeignet, die ordensrechtlich einen unselbständiger Ableger des Konvents von St. Albert darstellte – wenn auch durch Erlaubnis des Ordensmeisters der Prior des Konvents in der Person von P. Theophil Tschipke an St. Kajetan wohnte.[229] Durch den Bau des neuen Gebäudes für das bayerische Kultusminsterium auf dem Gelände des ehemaligen Theatinerklosters neben der Stiftskirche änderte sich auch die Raumsituation für die Dominikaner. Ab dem Juni 1970 zog der größere Teil der Patres in eine Wohnung in der Pacellistraße, die ihnen vom erzbischöflichen Ordinariat zur Verfügung gestellt worden war. Im Innenhof des Ministeriums wurde im Anschluss an das Mesnerhaus auch das Kloster neu erstellt, das deutlich mehr Zimmer umfasste. Die neuen Wohnräume wurden am 9. September 1973 eingeweiht.[230]

Mit dem Abzug des Noviziats aus St. Albert 1958 (siehe dazu unten) fiel die dominikanische Arbeit in Freimann ganz auf die Pfarrseelsorge zurück, was einen Umbau der Infrastruktur der dominikanischen Präsenz in München zur Folge hatte. Das Provinzkonsil beriet am 16. Mai 1959 über die Verlegung der Konventsrechte von St. Albert nach St. Kajetan.[231] Am 20. Juni 1959 bat Provinzial Augustinus Gierlich Kardinalerzbischof Joseph Wendel um die Erlaubnis, in München ein zweites, selbständiges Haus des Ordens errichten zu dürfen.[232] Nachdem auch seitens der Ordenskurie und der Religiosenkongregation das nötige Einverständnis eingeholt worden war, erhob Gierlich zum 18. Februar 1960 das bisherige Filialhaus an St. Kajetan zur eigenständigen *domus*. Erster Superior der neuen Niederlassung wurde Theophil Tschipke. Nach St. Kajetan wurden acht Priester und zwei Laienbrüder assigniert.[233] Am selben Tag wurde der bisherige

---

228 PA, Provinzrundbrief vom 2.2.1957, S. 8.

229 PA, Provinzialsregestenbuch 1 (1939–1966), Eintrag vom 7.7.1955, Nr. 2, S. 69.

230 *Ewige Weisheit* (1974) Nr. 1–2, eingeheftetes Beiblatt zwischen den S. 21 und 22.

231 PA, Liber consilii provincialis, Sitzung vom 16.5.1959.

232 PA, Provinzialsregestenbuch 1 (1939–1966), Eintrag vom 20.6.1959, Nr. 48, S. 97.

233 PA, Provinzialsregestenbuch 1 (1939–1966), Einträge vom 18.2.1960, S. 107–108, Nr. 88 (mit Erwähnung des Reskripts der Religiosenkongregation vom 14.1.1960,

Konvent von St. Albert in Freimann auf den Status einer *domus* reduziert, mit P. Oderich Edelbauer als Superior. Nach St. Albert assignierte der Provinzial fünf Patres und einen Laienbruder.[234] Der nächste Schritt – den das Provinzkonsil noch im Januar 1960 vorbereitete[235] – bestand in der Erhebung der Niederlassung an St. Kajetan zum formalrechtlichen Konvent. In seiner Sitzung vom 29. Mai 1961 beschloss das Provinzkonsil einstimmig einen entsprechenden Antrag beim Ordensmeister.[236] Dieser antwortete mit Schreiben vom 16. Juni 1961 positiv.[237] So konnte am 4. August 1961, dem Festtag des Ordensgründers, des hl. Dominikus, die *domus* an St. Kajetan feierlich zum formalrechtlichen Konvent erhoben werden.[238]

„Erneuerte Menschen" – Nachwuchsgewinnung und Nachwuchsbetreuung

Nach der Gründung der Niederlassung an St. Kajetan konnte sich die Provinz für längere Zeit keine weiteren neuen Niederlassungen mehr leisten – und das nicht nur aus finanziellen Gründen. Hauptproblem war der unsichere Personalpool.[239] Der Krieg hatte nicht nur die Kloster- und Kirchengebäude, sondern auch die personelle Situation der Germania superior empfindlich geschädigt. Bei ihrer Gründung hatte die Provinz aus 143 Brüdern bestanden (84 Priestern, 44 Laienbrüdern, 13 Klerikern und jeweils einem

---

Nr. 16293 / 60 und des Reskripts der Ordenskurie vom 26.1.1960, Nr. 3 / 60) und Nr. 89, S. 109, Nr. 95 und vom 23.2.1960, S. 109, Nr. 96.

234 PA, Provinzialsregestenbuch 1 (1939–1966), Einträge vom 18.2.1960 mit Verweis auf das Reskript der Ordenskurie zur Reduktion vom 26.1.1960, Prot. Nr. 4 / 60), S. 107, Nr. 86 und 87, sowie S. 109, Nr. 94.

235 Siehe PA, Liber consilii provincialis, Sitzung vom 22. Januar 1960 in Augsburg.

236 PA, Liber consilii provincialis, Sitzung vom 29.5.1961 und Provinzialsregestenbuch 1 (1939–1966), Eintrag vom 29.5.1961, Nr. 168, S. 128–129.

237 PA, Provinzialsregestenbuch 1 (1939–1966), Eintrag vom 21.6.1961, Nr. 171, S. 129 mit Bezug auf das Schreiben des Ordensmeisters vom 16.6.1961, Prot. Nr. 3 / 60–61.

238 Ebd., Eintrag vom 4.8.1961, Nr. 179, S. 132.

239 So lehnte das Provinzkonsil 1950 die angebotene Übernahme von Kloster und Schule in Tegernsee wegen der seinerzeitigen unsicheren politischen Lage, des Mangels an Ordenspriestern und wegen finanzieller Schwierigkeiten ab (PA, Liber consilii provincialis, Sitzung in Augsburg am 28.4.1950). Aus denselben Gründen wurde vom Provinzkonsil 1960 auch der Vorschlag, am Standort der Dominikanerinnen in Bludenz ein Provinzinternat zu errichten, nicht weiterverfolgt (PA, Liber consiliorum provinciae, Sitzung in Wien am 4.5.1960).

Kleriker- und einem Laienbrudernovizen); 1946 waren es 122 (81 Priester, 33 Laienbrüder, ein Kleriker, ein eingekleideter Tertiar und sechs Klerikernovizen).[240] Die Heimkehr der kriegsgefangenen Mitbrüder geschah nur langsam; fünf von ihnen blieben verschollen. Diese fünf wurden 1956 für tot erklärt.[241] Zwölf Provinzmitglieder hatten den Orden – mit oder ohne Dispens – verlassen.[242] Etwa ein Drittel des gesamten Personalbestandes, nämlich 26 Patres und drei Laienbrüder, war mit Kriegsausbruch in ihre Heimat in die Schweiz exiliert worden. Durch den erschwerten Grenzverkehr konnten diese nicht so leicht in die Provinz zurückkommen. Manche wollten das auch nicht: Während des Krieges waren die Vorbereitungen des Ordens, in der Schweiz eine eigene Provinz zu errichten, sehr weit gediehen. Sechs Patres und drei Laienbrüder wurden auf eigenen Wunsch Anfang 1952 in das Schweizer Vikariat assigniert.[243] Gerade diese sechs Priester hatten weiterführende akademische Studien abgeschlossen und waren ursprünglich für das Eröffnen eines provinzeigenen Studienhauses vorgesehen gewesen. Provinzial Vetter reagierte darauf diplomatisch: „Wenn wir auch den Abgang dieser Mitbrüder aus der Provinz schmerzlich empfinden, so wollen wir uns doch ehrlich freuen, dass der Orden in der Schweiz zu einer neuen Blüte ansetzt. Wir freuen uns aber ebenso, dass die zahlreichen anderen Mitbrüder Schweizer Nationalität der Provinz des hl. Albert weiterhin die Treue bewahren."[244] Mit Dekret vom 24. Juni 1953 errichtete Ordensmeister Emmanuel Suárez die Provincia Annuntiationis beatae Mariae virginis in Helvetia.[245] In der Germania superior fehlten außerdem die ebenfalls sehr gut ausgebildeten Mitbrüder, die an den Universitäten des Ordens in Rom und in Freiburg in der Schweiz tätig waren; auch die Kleriker waren nicht auf dem Provinzgebiet, sondern studierten in Walberberg in der Teutonia. Im Übrigen waren zwischen 1939 und 1945 zwanzig Mitbrüder verstorben, aber erst 1946 kamen einfache Professen nach. Nachwuchs tat also dringend not.

---

240 Diese Zahlenangaben wurden aus dem PKat 1939 und dem PKat 1946 gewonnen – unter Korrektur der dortigen Summarien durch Vergleich mit dem tatsächlichen Mitgliederbestand.

241 PA, Liber consilii provincialis, Sitzung in Augsburg vom 14. Juni 1956, Punkt 5.

242 PA, Bericht des Provinzials zum Provinzkapitel (Provinzrundbrief vom 6.11.1946), S. 2.

243 PA, Liber consilii provincialis, Sitzung in Augsburg am 21.1.1952.

244 PA, Provinzrundbrief vom 2.2.1953.

245 Datum laut: Hodel, Bedouelle, Müller: *Die Schweizer Dominikanerprovinz*, S. 167.

Juvenate in Freiburg und Graz

Eine Möglichkeit, unter der Jugend auf den Orden aufmerksam zu machen, bestand in der Errichtung eines sogenannten Juvenats – also eines Internats oder Konvikts, das Jugendlichen den Besuch einer höheren Schule ermöglichte. Die Einrichtung des Juvenats in Graz-Wetzelsdorf zum Beispiel hatte sich in den 1930er Jahren für die Nachwuchsgewinnung der österreichisch-ungarischen Provinz als sehr nützlich erwiesen. Dasselbe galt für die Teutonia mit dem Kolleg St. Josef in Vechta.[246] Daher lag es nahe, sich dieses Mittels wieder zu bedienen. Das Provinzkapitel von 1946 der Germania superior beauftragte die Prioren von Freiburg im Breisgau und Graz, in ihren Klöstern jeweils ein solches Juvenat aufzubauen.[247]

In Freiburg hatte diese Einrichtung keinen guten Start. Grund dafür waren die sehr beengten räumlichen Verhältnisse dort. Erst 1951 waren die letzten Kriegsschäden an der Villa beseitigt. Durch weitere Umbauten am Haus gelang es, das obere Stockwerk freizubekommen, sodass das Provinzkonsil am 6. Oktober 1952 das Juvenat gründen konnte.[248] Der Betrieb wurde unter der Leitung von Superior Ulrich Kaiser Ostern 1953 mit zwölf Zöglingen aufgenommen, die ein staatliches Gymnasium besuchten. Mehr Aufnahmen waren platzbedingt nicht möglich. Das Freiburger Juvenat hatte daher von Anfang an einen eher provisorischen Charakter. Durch den Verlust von Wohnräumen war auch der Konvent sehr in seinen Ausbreitungsmöglichkeiten eingeengt. Provinzial Vetter hoffte deshalb auf eine bessere Lösung, die aber nie gefunden wurde. 1960 wurde das Freiburger Juvenat daher geschlossen.[249]

Das ehemalige Juvenatsgebäude in Graz-Wetzelsdorf beherbergte inzwischen ein von Schwestern geführtes Altenheim. Da direkt nach dem Krieg die Gefahr bestand, dass Teile des Grazer Klosters durch Besatzungsmacht oder Wohnungsamt beschlagnahmt werden würden, richtete man an der Münzgrabenstraße einige Räume als Studentenwohnheim her, das unter der Lei-

246 Groothuis: *Im Dienste*, S. 88–97.
247 APKap 1946, S. 7, Nr. 32.
248 Errichtungsdatum laut: PA, Liber consilii provincialis, Sitzung in Augsburg vom 6.10.1952.
249 PA, Provinzrundbriefe vom 2.2.1953 (Bericht des Provinzials über das Jahr 1952), S. 12, vom „Januar“ 1955 (Bericht über das Jahr 1954), S. 12 und vom 2.2.1958, S. 9.

Abb. 42: Das „Albertinum" genannte Juvenat der österr.-ungar. Provinz in Graz-Wetzelsdorf (PA, Fotosammlung).

tung von P. Raimund Lang stand.[250] Zum Schuljahresbeginn 1948 konnte unter der Leitung von P. Innozenz Varga das Juvenat des sel. Jordan von Sachsen mit zehn Zöglingen eröffnet werden.[251] Mit Fertigstellung des Westtrakts des Grazer Klosters 1949/1950 bezog das Juvenat dort seinen Sitz. Nach Vargas Wahl zum Prior des Wiener Konvents 1959 wurde ad interim Seraphicus Weber auf ein Jahr zum Direktor bestellt.[252] Vom 16. Januar 1960 bis zu seiner Versetzung 1965 nach München war Adalbert von Papius Direktor,[253] ihm folgten mit Einsetzung vom 7. September 1965 Anselm Henssler[254] und mit

250 PA, Provinzrundbrief vom 6.11.1946 (Bericht des Provinzials zum Provinzkapitel), S. 2.

251 PKat 1949, S. 15.; *St. Dominikuswerk* (1959), S. 3.

252 PKat 1959, S. 18.

253 PA, Provinzialsregestenbuch 1 (1939–1966), Einträge vom 16.1.1960, Nr. 77, S. 104 und vom 20.8.1965, Nr. 403, S. 182.

254 Datum laut: PKat 1966, S. 20.

Einsetzung vom 6. Januar 1967 Benedikt Füssinger.[255] Die Anzahl der betreuten Schüler stieg bis 1957 auf 31 an, was zu Platzproblemen und zur kurzzeitigen Diskussion über die Verlegung des Juvenats nach Bludenz in Vorarlberg führte.[256] Bald darauf nahm die Zahl der Belegschaft aber wieder ab; Anfang der 1960er Jahre lag sie bei zehn.[257] Diese schlechte Nachfrage brachte die Provinz zum Überdenken ihres Angebots. Der Grazer Konvent schlug dem Provinzkonsil im August 1963 die Schließung des Juvenates vor, aber das Provinzkonsil vertagte eine Entscheidung.[258] Fünf weitere Jahre wurde darüber diskutiert; neben Bludenz wurde auch das Dominikanerinnenkloster in Bregenz-Thalbach als möglicher Standort eines Juvenats ins Auge gefasst. Erst im Sommer 1968 raffte sich das Provinzkonsil zu der Entscheidung auf, das Grazer Juvenat zu schließen.[259]

Das „St. Dominikus-Werk"

Zur finanziellen Unterstützung beider Juvenate hatte das Provinzkapitel 1946 die Patres Bernhard Braun für Österreich und Magnus Beck für Süddeutschland mit dem Aufbau des „Dominikus-Werkes" beauftragt.[260] In Deutschland wurde mit Eröffnung des Juvenats der Sitz des Vereins nach Freiburg im Breisgau verlegt. Dort stand ihm von 1953 bis 1960 Ulrich Kaiser und von 1961 bis 1981 Donatus Leicher vor.[261] Bedingt durch die Schließung des Freiburger Juvenats hatte aber das Interesse der Bevölkerung an diesem Finanzierungsverein immer stärker abgenommen. Anders lag die Sache in Österreich: Das Dominikuswerk war in Graz, wo man den

---

255 PA, Provinzialsregestenbuch 2 (1966–2010), Eintrag vom 16.9.1966, Nr. 17.

256 PA, Liber consilii provincialis, Sitzung in Augsburg am 14.6.1956.

257 PA, Provinzrundbriefe vom 2.2.1957, S. 4: 31 Grazer Juvenisten; vom 2.2.1958, S. 4: 28 Juvenisten; vom 11.3.1959, S. 2: 16 Juvenisten; vom 17.3.1962: acht Juvenisten; vom 18.3.1963, S. 5: zehn Juvenisten.

258 PA, Liber consiliorum provinciae, Sitzung in Graz am 17.8.1963.

259 Die Diskussion über das Juvenat taucht häufig in den Provinzkonsilsprotokollen dieser Jahre auf; siehe besonders PA, Liber consiliorum provinciae, Sitzung vom 14.5.1965, S. 158–159 und Sitzung vom 22.3.1966, S. 166. Zum Schließungsbeschluss siehe Sitzung vom 7.6.1968, S. 72: „Es war die Meinung des Konsils, das Juvenat in Graz aufzulösen. Grund: Seit zehn Jahren kein Eintritt von dort und man habe auch keinen geeigneten Juvenatsdirektor."

260 APKap 1946, S. 7, Nr. 33.

261 Siehe Angaben der Provinzkataloge zu diesen beiden Patres im Zeitraum 1953–1981.

Abb. 43: Titelbild der ersten Ausgabe des Jahresberichts St. Dominikuswerk, Heft 1952.

Verein 1933 gegründet hatte, stärker verwurzelt. Braun hatte schon vor dem Krieg das Juvenat in Graz Wetzelsdorf und das Dominikuswerk geleitet. Dieser ursprüngliche Verein war in den Jahren des Nationalsozialismus zwar eingeschlafen,[262] aber Brauns Nachfolger als Direktor des Vereins, Innozenz Varga, der am 28. Februar 1951 vom Provinzial zum Direktor des Dominikuswerks eingesetzt wurde, gründete ihn am 7. März 1951 neu.[263] Varga engagierte sich sehr stark für seine Ausbreitung in Österreich. Neben vielen Aktionstagen zur Ordensberufung in Schulen und dem persönlichen Anwerben von Mitgliedern veröffentlichte er ab 1952 unter dem Titel „St. Dominikuswerk" eine jährlich erscheinende, zwischen acht und zehn Seiten umfassende, bebilderte Broschüre als Dank- und Jahresgabe für Mitglieder und Unterstützer des Vereins und seiner Anliegen. Darin berichtete er nicht nur über das Juvenat, sondern auch über Ereignisse in der Provinz und im Orden. Die Publikation dieses Heftes mit Erscheinungsort Graz setzte Varga auch nach seinem Ausscheiden aus dem Juvenatsbetrieb fort;[264] insgesamt erschien es bis ins Jahr 2000 siebenundvierzigmal und fand großen Anklang unter der Bevölkerung.

---

262 Ein Aufhebungs- oder Gleichschaltungsakt ließ sich aus dem Material des Provinzarchivs nicht erheben.

263 Datum laut: *St. Dominikuswerk* (1952) 6.

264 Mit Vargas Umzug nach Wien im Januar 1959 wurde auch der Sitz des Dominikuswerkes von Graz nach Wien verlegt (PA, Provinzrundbrief vom 11.3.1959, S. 1).

Das Noviziat zwischen 1939 und 1971

Dem Dekret des Ordensmeisters Gillet zur Errichtung der Provinz folgend hatte der erste Novize der Germania superior – Fr. Gabriel Saur – zur Ausbildung in den Noviziatskonvent der Provinz Teutonia, nach Warburg geschickt werden müssen. Da die Wehrmacht im Warburger Kloster aber ein Lazarett einrichtete, mussten die Novizen weichen; im April 1940 beschloss das Provinzkonsil daher die Einrichtung eines provinzeigenen Noviziates unter der Leitung von Theophil Tschipke im Wiener Konvent.[265] Wegen der Einquartierungen konnte es aber auch dort nicht lange bleiben: Mit einstimmiger Entscheidung des Provinzkonsils vom 8. Januar 1941 wurde es nach Freiburg im Breisgau verlegt; Novizenmeister Tschipke wurde ebenfalls dorthin versetzt.[266] Inwieweit er dort auch als solcher arbeiten konnte, ist unklar: Laut der Provinzkataloge von 1941 und 1943 gehörten zum Freiburger Konvent zwar in diesen Jahren jeweils zwei Klerikernovizen, diese dienten aber als Soldaten an der Front. Tschipke selbst lebte 1943 an einer Seelsorgsstelle außerhalb des Klosters.[267] Die Einquartierungen im Haus und der damit einhergehende Zimmerverlust sprechen ebenfalls gegen einen geregelten Noviziatsbetrieb – ganz zu schweigen davon, dass die Wehrmeldeämter keine Ordenseintritte der männlichen Jugend mehr zuließen.

Nach dem Krieg verhinderten die Besatzungszonengrenzen, dass Kandidaten aus Österreich in Freiburg ihr Noviziat antreten konnten. Das Provinzkonsil bat daher den Ordensmeister um die Einrichtung eines zweiten Noviziates für den österreichischen Provinzteil, in Graz.[268] Dieses nahm am 24. Oktober 1945 unter der Leitung von Novizenmeister Fidelis Gallati

265 PA, Liber consiliorum provinciae, Sitzung vom 22.4.1940, S. 9. Provinzial Vetter bat Ordensmeister Gillet mit Brief vom 30.4.1940, dies in die Wege zu leiten (PA, Provinzialsregestenbuch 1 (1939–1966), Eintrag vom 30.4.1940, Nr. 13, S. 16). Zu Warburg siehe: Groothuis: *Im Dienste*, S. 145–153; dort konnten erst 1947 wieder Novizen aufgenommen werden.

266 PA, Liber consiliorum provinciae, Sitzung vom 8.1.1941, S. 11; Provinzialsregestenbuch 1 (1939–1966), Einträge vom 28.1.1941, S. 19, Nr. 2 und vom 12.2.1941, S. 20, Nr. 11.

267 Siehe PKat 1941, S. 12–13 und PKat 1943, S. 8–9. Der Vollständigkeit halber sei noch erwähnt, dass in beiden Katalogen auch zwei Laienbrudernovizen in Graz aufgeführt werden, die aber ebenfalls eingezogen waren (ebd., S. 15 bzw. 11).

268 PA, Liber consiliorum provinciae, Sitzung vom 18.9.1945, S. 15 und Sitzung in Graz vom 24.10.1945, S. 16.

seine Tätigkeit auf.[269] Die rege Bautätigkeit, die in Graz wenige Jahre später einsetzte, störte aber in den Augen des Provinzials die notwendige Ruhe für die Novizenausbildung. Auf seinen Vorschlag hin sprach sich das Provinzkonsil für eine Verlegung „ad tempus“ des Noviziats nach Wien aus, bis in Graz wieder geeignetere Umstände dafür herrschen würden.[270] Mit Erlaubnis des Heiligen Stuhls kam das Noviziat am 23. März 1948 nach Wien;[271] Als Pro-Magister der Novizen diente zunächst Andreas Martis, am 11. Januar 1950 folgte ihm Maximilian Göbel als Novizenmeister.[272] Diese Interimslösung dauerte immerhin bis 1956; erst dann sah Provinzial Vetter die Lage im Grazer Kloster wieder als genügend stabilisiert und ruhig für Novizen an. Dementsprechend wurde am 7. März 1956 das Noviziat neuerlich in die Steiermark verlegt und Gallati wurde wieder Novizenmeister.[273] Dieses Hin und Her täuscht bezüglich der Größe und Bedeutung des Noviziats des österreichischen Provinzteils: Die Provinzkataloge dieser Jahre zeigen, dass 1946 in Graz nur drei Klerikernovizen wohnten, 1948 ein Laienbrudernovize in Graz und 1949 zwei Laienbrudernovizen in Wien, sowie 1957 ein Laienbruder- und ein Klerikernovize in Graz. Zwar notieren die Provinzkataloge bei Fidelis Gallati bis einschließlich 1967 den Titel eines Novizenmeisters, aber dies hatte keine praktischen Auswirkungen mehr und ist wohl eher als Erinnerungszeichen dafür zu sehen, dass eine Ordensprovinz einen Novizenmeister haben sollte, auch wenn die Ausbildung der Novizen außerhalb ihres Gebietes stattfand.

Auch im süddeutschen Provinzteil musste das Noviziat wandern: Wegen der Kriegszerstörungen des Freiburger Klosters entschied das Provinzkonsil am 28. Dezember 1945, das Noviziat nach München zu verlegen. Rechtlich und baulich war das Freimanner Pfarrkloster dafür zunächst ungeeignet, daher wurde die *domus* von St. Albert in den Rang eines Konvents erhoben[274] und Prior Magnus Beck ließ 1948 im Kirchengarten, der dafür

---

269 PA, Provinzialsregestenbuch 1 (1939–1966) Einträge vom 19.9.1945, Nr. 6, S. 29 und vom 24.10.1945, S. 29, Nr. 7.

270 PA, Liber consiliorum provinciae, Sitzung in Wien vom 26.2.1948, S. 23.

271 PA, Provinzialsregestenbuch 1 (1939–1966), Eintrag vom 23.3.1948, Nr. 4, S. 41.

272 Zu Martis: PA, Liber consiliorum provinciae, Sitzung in Wien vom 26.2.1948, S. 23; Datum der Einsetzung Göbels laut: PKat 1953, S. 9.

273 Siehe PA, Liber consiliorum provinciae, Sitzung vom 6.1.1956, S. 45 und Provinzialsregestenbuch 1 (1939–1966), Einträge vom 6.1.1956, S. 73 Nrn. 2 und 3 und vom 7.3.1956, S. 74 Nrn. 7 und 8.

274 PA, Liber consiliorum provinciae, Sitzung in Wien vom 28.12.1945, S. 16.

von der Pfarrei erworben wurde, ein neues Noviziatsgebäude errichten[275] – und zwar praktischerweise gleich von den Novizen selbst. Da man gleichzeitig am möglichst monastischen Konzept eines Noviziates festhielt, ergab sich für die Novizen der Jahrgänge 1947, 1948 und 1949 bis zur Fertigstellung des Baus eine starke Belastung.[276] Im Rahmen seiner Provinzvisitation besuchte Ordensmeister Emanuel Suárez vom 4. bis 9. Dezember 1949 auch das Noviziat in St. Albert. Er zeigte sich von der dort herrschenden Armut sehr beeindruckt.[277]

Ein für die Novizen wichtiger Vorteil des provinzeigenen Noviziats ergab sich durch die vielen Besuche, die das Noviziat vom Provinzial und anderen Mitbrüdern erhielt. So wurden sie häufiger über die Vorgänge im Orden und in der Provinz informiert, lernten die Mitbrüder besser kennen und wuchsen leichter in ihr zukünftiges Umfeld hinein.[278] Als Novizenmeister fungierte wieder Theophil Tschipke, der dafür am 24. Juni 1946 von Freiburg nach München versetzt wurde.[279] Tschipke bat Ende Januar 1951 um die Befreiung von diesem Amt; sein Nachfolger wurde Oderich Edelbauer, zunächst als Promagister und mit dem 20. April 1951 als Magister.[280] Ihm folgte am 6. März 1952 Erwin Röhr als Promagister und mit dem 20. April 1952 als Novizenmeister. Wenige Monate später wurde Röhr, der aus der Teutonia sozusagen ausgeliehen worden war, wieder in seine Heimatprovinz zurückgerufen.[281] Daraufhin wurde Prior Magnus Beck durch spezielles Mandat des Ordensmeisters am 25. September 1952 zum Novizenmeister eingesetzt. Er behielt dieses Amt laut den Provinzkatalogen

---

275 PA, Liber consilii provincialis, Sitzung in Augsburg am 28.4.1950 und Sitzung in Augsburg am 23.1.1951.

276 Siehe PA, Chronik für das Noviziat der oberdeutschen Dominikanerprovinz, S. 98: Eintrag vom 15.8.1947 und S. 124: Einträge vom 22.3.1949 und vom 23.4.1949.

277 PA, Chronik für das Noviziat der oberdeutschen Provinz, S. 140–145: Eintrag vom 7. / 8.12.1949 und Eintrag vom 15.12.1949. Zur Datierung der Visitation: APKap 1950, S. 6, Nr. 25.

278 Siehe z. B. PA, Chronik für das Noviziat der oberdeutschen Provinz, S. 49: Eintrag vom 16.6.1939, S. 165–169: Einträge von 1947–1951, v.a. die Beschreibung der Tagung des Provinzkapitels 1950 in München u. ö.

279 PA, Provinzialsregestenbuch 1 (1939–1966), Eintrag vom 24.6.1946, S. 34, Nr. 36: Assignation und Einsetzung als Novizenmeister am selben Tag.

280 PA, Liber consilii provincialis, Sitzung in Augsburg am 31.1.1951 und Sitzung in Augsburg am 20.4.1951.

281 PA, Provinzialsregestenbuch 1 (1939–1966), Einträge vom 6.3.1952, S. 55, Nr. 6 und vom 20.4.1952, S. 56, Nr. 10.

der folgenden Jahre sogar, als er 1955 ins Mesnerhaus von St. Kajetan zog, obwohl dort keinerlei räumliche Möglichkeiten für ein Noviziat vorhanden waren – möglich war dies nur, weil die Novizen sich inzwischen woanders aufhielten: Obwohl sich zahlenmäßig der Nachwuchs im süddeutschen Provinzteil zunächst recht erfreulich entwickelt hatte – laut Provinzkatalogen waren 1946 in St. Albert drei Klerikernovizen im Noviziat, 1948 sieben Klerikernovizen und ein Laienbrudernovize, 1949 fünf Kleriker- und zwei Laienbrüdernovizen, 1951 fünf Kleriker- und zwei Laienbrudernovizen und 1952 sechs Kleriker- und zwei Laienbrudernovizen – schickte man die sechs Klerikernovizen des Jahrgangs 1954/1955 in den Noviziatskonvent der Teutonia nach Warburg.[282] Als Grund dafür ist wohl die Übernahme von St. Kajetan zu sehen, die viele Kräfte des Münchner Konvents band, aber als Chance zu wichtig war, um sie nicht zu ergreifen. Letztlich beendete dies für lange Zeit das provinzeigene Noviziat: Zwar hatte die Provinz den Bau des Klosters in Augsburg deswegen so großzügig angelegt, um darin auch endgültig die Novizen in geeigneter Weise unterbringen zu können – der vierte Stock des Klosterflügels an der Heilig-Kreuz-Straße war für das Noviziat vorgesehen gewesen – und nach entsprechendem Antrag des Provinzkonsils verlegte Ordensmeister Michael Browne zum 25. Mai 1958 das Noviziat nach Augsburg, unter Einsetzung von Egino Holzhauser als Novizenmeister,[283] aber die Einrichtung des sogenannten Predigerkurses veränderte auch an Heilig Kreuz die Konventsperspektive. Abgesehen davon nahm der Zustrom von Kandidaten nun deutlich ab, weshalb man wohl nach Abzug des Predigerkurses auf eine Wiederaufnahme eines provinzeigenen Noviziatsbetriebes in Augsburg verzichtete.[284] 1968 dis-

282 Es gab 1955 außerdem noch einen Klerikernovizen der Provinz in Angers in Frankreich.

283 PA, Provinzialsregestenbuch 1 (1939–1966), Eintrag vom 25.5.1958, Nrn. 8 und 9. Siehe auch Liber consilii provincialis, Sitzung in Augsburg am 12.5.1958. Holzhauser behielt, ähnlich wie Gallati, laut den Provinzkatalogen den Titel des Novizenmeisters bis einschließlich 1962.

284 Die Provinzkataloge nennen 1956 in Warburg drei Kleriker- und einen Laienbrudernovizen, 1957 vier Klerikernovizen in Warburg und je einen Kleriker- und einen Laienbrudernovizen in Graz, 1958 zwei Klerikernovizen in Warburg, 1959 einen Laienbrudernovizen in Augsburg und fünf Klerikernovizen in Warburg und 1959 fünf Kleriker- und einen Laienbrudernovizen, 1960 drei Klerikernovizen, 1961 fünf Klerikernovizen, 1962 zwei Klerikernovizen, 1964 vier Kleriker- und einen Laienbrudernovizen, 1965, 1966 und 1967 je zwei Klerikernovizen, 1969 vier Kleriker- und einen Laienbrudernovizen – alle in Warburg.

kutierte die Teutonia die Verlegung ihres Provinznoviziates von Warburg nach Walberberg, um gegebenenfalls Warburg schließen zu können. Dieser Idee stand das Provinzkonsil der süddeutsch-österreichischen Provinz skeptisch gegenüber.[285] Wieder kam das Projekt eines provinzeigenen Noviziates auf. Das Provinzkapitel 1970 in Augsburg stellte fest: „Die Provinz beabsichtigt, ihre Novizen in der eigenen Provinz auszubilden. Im Hinblick auf die politische Teilung der Provinz sollen sie je ein halbes Jahr in unserem Kloster in Augsburg und ein halbes Jahr in unserem Kloster in Wien diese Ausbildung erhalten." Das Provinzkonsil wurde beauftragt, ein Statut für die Noviziatsausbildung zu erarbeiten.[286] Mit dem 1. Oktober 1970 begannen die beiden Novizen dieses Jahrgangs unter der Leitung von Raphael Börger ihr Noviziat in Augsburg; am 2. Mai 1971 gingen sie dann nach Wien, wo Heinrich Suso Rüsch ihr Novizenmeister war.[287] Allerdings machte der letzte dieser Novizen im Herbst 1971 Profess und für einige Jahre kam keiner mehr nach. Dadurch erlosch auch dieser zweite provinzeigene Noviziatsversuch.

Die Ausbildung der Studenten zwischen 1939 und 1977

Auch ihre Studenten hatte die Germania superior ab 1939 in die entsprechende Einrichtung der Teutonia, ins Studienhaus von Walberberg bei Bonn geschickt. Mit Kriegsausbruch begannen hier ernste Schwierigkeiten: Immer mehr Studenten wurden zum Heeresdienst eingezogen. Für sie wurden verkürzte und verknappte Vorlesungen gehalten, um wenigstens schon begonnene Fächer abschließen zu können. Die übrigbleibenden mussten Sanitätsdienste leisten, als das Walberberger Kloster im September 1939 zum Lazarett erklärt und ein Großteil der dortigen Räume für diesen Zweck verwendet wurde. Der dadurch entstandenen Doppelbelastung wurde durch eine Verminderung des Vorlesungsbetriebes Rechnung getragen. 1941 wurde das Kloster zum ersten Mal gänzlich von der Gestapo be-

285 PA, Liber consiliorum provinciae, Sitzung in Wien am 7.6.1968, S. 72.

286 APKap 1970, S. 14, Nr. 33.

287 Zum Noviziatsstatut und zur Einsetzung von Börger und Rüsch siehe: PA, Liber consiliorum provinciae, Sitzung vom 6. und 6.8.1970, S. 76. Laut den Provinzkatalogen galt Börger bis einschließlich 1977 als Novizenmeister, ohne nach 1972 als solcher zu fungieren. Auch Rüsch wird bis 1977 in diesem Amt genannt. Als dessen Nachfolger wurde 1979 Martin Gyöngyös eingesetzt (PA, Liber consilii provincialis, Sitzung in Augsburg vom 4.1.1977 und Sitzung in Augsburg vom 5.6.1979).

schlagnahmt. Provinzial Laurentius Siemer gelang es aber, diese Maßnahme rückgängig machen zu lassen, da der Lazerettbetrieb auf den Schultern der Dominikanerstudenten ruhte. Eine neuerliche Beschlagnahmung 1942 war aber nicht abzuwenden. Ein kleiner Teil der Studenten zog daraufhin nach Bonn, um an der dortigen Universität die Studien fortzusetzen. Die religiöse und dominikanische Ausbildung dieser Fratres versuchte man dadurch zu garantieren, dass der Studienleiter – der Ordenstitel für ihn lautete Studienregens – sie in Bonn zwei- bis dreimal die Woche besuchte und Vorträge religiösen Inhalts und Vorlesungen über die Lehre des Aquinaten hielt. An den Sonn- und Feiertagen kamen auch die wenigen Lektoren, die in Walberberg verblieben waren, um Vorlesungen zu halten. Selbst Prüfungen wurden regulär durchgeführt. Mit der Besetzung Walberbergs durch die Amerikaner 1945 durften die Studenten zurückkehren und man nahm, soweit es ging, den Vorlesungsbetrieb wieder auf. Die Besatzungsmacht benutzte einen Teil der Klostergebäude für ihre Zwecke; die Bücher der Bibliothek, die man während des Krieges an verschiedenen Orten ausgelagert hatte, kamen nur schwer, teilweise zerstört oder gar nicht zurück. Viele Studenten waren in Kriegsgefangenschaft, manche für viele Jahre. Für diejenigen, denen eine Heimkehr gelang, richtete man Repetitorien ein, damit sie den vor dem Krieg gelernten Stoff wiederholen konnten. An finanzieller und materieller Unterstützung mangelte es an allen Ecken und Enden.[288]

In Süddeutschland oder Österreich existierten zu dieser Zeit noch nicht einmal ruinierte Strukturen zur Eröffnung eines provinzeigenen Studienhauses. Die Wiederaufbausituation der Klöster der Germania superior behinderte bereits die Errichtung eigener Noviziate. Dementsprechend kehrten die Kleriker der Germania superior nach dem Krieg nach Walberberg zurück, wo sie bis 1975 blieben. Einzelne kamen an die Hochschulen des Ordens wie das Angelicum in Rom, Freiburg in der Schweiz oder Le Saulchoir in Étiolles bei Paris.[289]

Einen kleinen Beitrag zum Lehrbetrieb in Walberberg leistete die Germania superior, in dem sie Lektoren und Professoren zur Verfügung

---

288 Zur Beschreibung der oben genannten Verhältnisse während des Kriegs in Walberberg siehe: PA, Relatio de studiis in provincia Teutonia peractis durante bello et tempore immediate subsequente, i.e. ab anno 1939 ad annum 1947, Typoskr., S. 1–4 und Groothuis: *Im Dienste*, S. 167–176.

289 Siehe Angaben der Provinzkataloge der Jahre 1946–1977.

stellte – meist aber nur wenige. Der Hauptteil der Brüder, die eine akademische Lehrtätigkeit inne hatten, tat dies in Rom oder in Freiburg in der Schweiz: Anselm Rohner (1953 transfiliiert ins Schweizer Vikariat) und Angelus Walz (bis 1967) am Angelicum, Gallus Manser (bis 1942), Anton Rohner (bis 1948), Meinrad Morard (bis 1949), Gallus Häfele (bis 1952), Heinrich Lüthi (bis zu seinem Tod 1968), Fulko Groner (bis 1975) und Arthur Fridolin Utz (bis 1977) in Freiburg / CH.[290] Schon die Provincia Imperii und die Provincia Austro-Hungarica hatten Brüder für diese Hochschulen freigestellt. Diese Tradition wurde weitergepflegt – gerade im Hinblick auf die Hoffnung, vielleicht doch eines Tages ein eigenes Studienhaus aufmachen zu können. Spezial- oder Aufbaustudien waren den Brüdern immer ermöglicht worden.

Die Mitgliederzahlen der Klerikerjahrgänge der Provinz hielt sich in Grenzen: 1951 und 1952 waren es zwanzig, danach ging die Klerikerzahl Jahr für Jahr zurück: 1960 und 1961 waren es elf. Ein neuer Höhepunkt wurde 1964, 1965 und 1966 mit jeweils 16 erreicht, aber danach machten immer weniger Novizen Profess: 1969 waren es noch neun Studenten in Walberberg. Die drei Studenten der Stichjahre 1971 und 1973 wohnten in Wien und Augsburg, der eine Student des Jahres 1977 in Wien.[291]

Der Pastoral- oder Predigerkurs in Augsburg (1958–1966)

Das Studium im Walberberg der 1950er und 1960er Jahre gliederte sich in zwei Teile: Philosophiestudium und Theologiestudium. Bereits im Noviziat hatte der Kleriker Einführungen in Spiritualität, Liturgie, Ordensgeschichte u. ä. gehört. In den auf die Profess folgenden drei Jahren wurden ihm die philosophischen Fächer Logik, Erkenntnislehre, Naturphilosophie, philosophische Psychologie, Metaphysik, Ethik, Philosophiegeschichte und Religionsphilosophie vorgetragen. Daneben begann aber auch eine Einführung in die Theologie im Rahmen einer Ringvorlesung, in der alle theologischen Fächer kurz vorgestellt und wo auf ihren Zusammenhang hingewiesen wurde. Außerdem gab es Lehrveranstaltungen zur Fundamentaltheologie, Einführung in die Heilige Schrift, biblische Zeitgeschichte, Griechisch, Hebräisch, Kirchengeschichte und Spiritualität. Danach kamen die vier Jahre des eigentlichen Theologiestudiums mit Exegese, Dogmatik, Moraltheologie,

290 Siehe Angaben der Provinzkataloge der Jahre 1939–1989.

291 Siehe Angaben der Provinzkataloge der Jahre 1946–1977.

Kirchenrecht, Liturgie und Theologie der Predigt. Nach dem zweiten theologischen Studienjahr wurde normalerweise die Priesterweihe erteilt. Dann gab es auch eine rhetorische Ausbildung mit Stimmbildung und Predigtübungen. Ergänzend zu den Pflichtvorlesungen wurden auch Spezialvorlesungen oder Seminare angeboten, die zur Vertiefung oder Fortführung einzelner Themen dienen sollten.[292]

Mit der Fertigstellung des Klosterbaus in Augsburg im Sommer 1957 stellte sich die Frage nach der Errichtung eines Studienhauses auf dem Gebiet der Germania superior. Die Hoffnung darauf hatte die Provinz seit dem Krieg gepflegt.[293] Nun boten die neuen Räumlichkeiten in Augsburg die Möglichkeiten, diesen Wunsch wenigstens teilweise zu verwirklichen – konkret, die Predigtausbildung nach Süddeutschland zu holen. Provinzial Vetter trat in Verhandlungen mit der Leitung des Generalstudiums in Walberberg.[294] Dazu wurde P. Philipp Seidl als Homiletiklehrer aus Walberberg nach Augsburg versetzt[295] und zum 1. November 1958 begann unter dessen Leitung dort der sogenannte Predigerkurs, mit zwei Patres aus der Germania superior, zwei Patres aus der Schweizer Provinz und einem Pater aus der Teutonia als Studenten.[296]

Das Generalkapitel des Ordens kam im September 1958 den Augsburger Plänen entgegen. Es führte für die Zeit nach dem akademischen Grundstudium ein für alle Ordenspriester in Ausbildung verpflichtendes sogenanntes Pastoraljahr ein, mit insgesamt einhundert Vorlesungstagen, mit drei Vorlesungsstunden pro Tag (zwölf Stunden wöchentlich bzw. 300 Stunden insgesamt) und einem Abschlussexamen. Als Inhalte dieser Lehrveranstaltungen waren vorgesehen: Pastoraltheologie, Homiletik, Mystik und Spiritualität, sowie eine Ausbildung zur Leitung von Drittordensgruppen und Gruppen der Katholischen Aktion. Weitere psychologische, pastorale oder auch ökonomische Veranstaltungen konnten eingebaut werden. Dieses Ausbildungsjahr musste nicht notwendigerweise in einem förmlich

292 Zu dieser Zusammenfassung des Walberberger Studienplanes siehe PA, Relatio de studiis in provincia Teutonia peractis und *St. Dominikuswerk* (1966) S. 8–9.

293 Entsprechende Äußerungen finden sich z. B. in: APKap 1946, S. 8, Nr. 42 und APKap 1950, S. 8, Nr. 35.

294 Daher sprach Provinzial Gierlich 1959 auch über das von seinem verehrten Vorgänger im Amt des Provinzials begründeten Pastoralseminar in Augsburg (PA, Provinzrundbrief vom 11.12.1959, S. 1).

295 PA, Provinzialsregestenbuch 1 (1939–1966), Eintrag vom 25.11.1957, S. 81, Nr. 28.

296 PA, Provinzrundbrief vom 2.2.1958, S. 7.

Abb. 44: Der Konvent der Dominikaner an Heilig Kreuz, aufgenommen während des Besuchs von Ordensmeister Michael Browne am 2. Juni 1959. Vordere Reihe, sitzend (von links): P. Egino Holzhauser, P. Burkhard Zimmermann, P. Prior Thomas Aquinas Dillis, P. Provinzial der Teutonia Hilarius Albers, P. Provinzial der oberdeutschen Provinz Augustinus Gierlich, Ordensmeister P. Michael Browne, Socius P. Chrysostomus Vijverberg, P. Marianus Vetter, P. Subprior Barnabas Birx, P. Suso Geiselhart. Hintere Reihe, stehend (von links): P. Eckehart Mayer, P. Lukas Saffraniak, P. Emmanuel Kairys, Br. Ludwig Glöckler, Br. Leo Hecker, P. Hermenegild Braun, P. Theodulph Knodt, P. Gregor Ruf, , Br. Meinrad Kreuz, P. Philipp Seidl, Br. Haimo May, P. Jordan Gebhard, Br. Titus Schrall, P. Alfred Willebrandt, Br. Hyacinth Grom, P. Raphael Börger (Foto aus: Chronik der Dominikaner bei Heilig Kreuz 1935–1962, fol. 83r).

errichteten Studienhaus des Ordens stattfinden; außerdem wies das Generalkapitel ausdrücklich auf die Möglichkeit der Zusammenarbeit mehrerer Provinzen bezüglich dieses Lehrgangs hin.[297]

Dementsprechend wurde der Augsburger Predigerkurs am 21. September 1959 als Pastoralseminar neu konstituiert und ausgebaut:[298] Zum Leiter wurde der Prior, Thomas Aquinas Dillis, als „lector primarius cursus pastoralis“ bestimmt, ihm folgten für die Kurse 1962/63 und 1963/64 Jordan Gebhard und für die Kurse 1964/65 und 1966/67 Gregor Ruf. Als

297 ACG 1958, S. 79–80, Nr. 174.

298 PA, Provinzialsregestenbuch 1 (1939–1966), Einträge vom 21.9.1959, S. 100, Nr. 63 und vom 29.9.1959, S. 101, Nr. 64. Diese Neukonstituierung ist auch erwähnt in: APKap 1958, S. 6, Nr. 25.

Fächer wurden unterrichtet: Seelsorgsmethoden für Volksmissionen (Dillis, 1959–1967), Pastoralpsychologie (Dillis, 1961–1966), Katechetik (1959–1962: Egino Holzhauser, 1962–1964: Jordan Gebhard, 1964–1966: Sturmius Nowowiejski), Homiletik (Philipp Seidl, 1959–1966), Kirchenrecht und praktische Moraltheologie (Gregor Ruf, 1959–1966), sowie Darlegung ausgewählter pastoraler Fragen (Ambrosius Ruf, 1961–1966) und Liturgie (Amadeus Schmalhofer, 1964–1966).[299] Auch Seminarübungen, Hospitierstunden im Schulunterricht und Lehrübungen in verschiedenen Schularten gehörten dazu.[300]

Die Anpassungen an die Bestimmungen des Generalkapitels dauerten bis Anfang Oktober 1960.[301] Insgesamt schienen die gemachten Erfahrungen dem Experiment „Predigerkurs Augsburg“ recht zu geben. Sowohl die Germania superior als auch die Teutonia waren daher bereit, ihre Zusammenarbeit stärker zu institutionalisieren. Dazu traf man sich in Augsburg am 23. Juni 1964 zu einer Konferenz.[302] Das dabei erarbeitete Statut für ein gemeinsames oder interprovinzielles Studium Germania superior-Teutonia approbierte das süddeutsche Provinzkonsil am 1.3.1965.[303] Laut dieses Statuts sah man den Zweck dieses gemeinsamen Studium Generale darin, „a) die schon bestehende Zusammenarbeit zu vertiefen und rechtlich zu begründen; b) die wissenschaftliche Begabung beider Provinzen durch Koordination der Planung zu fördern“. Es bestand aus dem philosophischen und theologischen Kurs in Walberberg und dem pastoralen Kurs in Augsburg, wobei in Walberberg der „regens studii“ und in Augsburg der „lector primarius“ saßen. Beide Provinzen verpflichteten sich, „normalerweise ihre Studenten in das gemeinsame Studium zu schicken, das ist für die Philosophie und Theologie nach Walberberg und für das Pastoraljahr nach Augs-

---

299 Siehe Angaben der Provinzkataloge der Jahre 1959–1966 zum Augsburger Konvent. Die für das Studienjahr 1966 / 67 vorgesehene Lehrveranstaltung Theophil Tschipkes über Pastoraltheologie fiel aus (s.u.).

300 So z. B. laut PA, Provinzrundbrief vom 17.3.1962, S. 2 u. ö. Die Kurse dauerten jeweils von Oktober bis April (siehe die Provinzrundbriefe 1959–1966). Vom 25.4. bis 15.7. 1960 wurde außerdem ein „Pastoralsonderkurs“ für sieben Pallotinerpatres veranstaltet (Provinzrundbrief vom 1.3.1961, S. 2).

301 Siehe entsprechende Anmerkung des Provinzials in: PA, Provinzrundbrief vom 11.3.1960, S. 2.

302 PA, Provinzialsregestenbuch 1 (1939–1966), Eintrag vom 23.6.1964, S. 175, Nr. 366).

303 PA, Liber consilii provincialis, Sitzung in Augsburg am 1.3.1965 und Provinzialsregestenbuch 1 (1939–1966), Eintrag vom 1.3.1965, S. 179, Nr. 390.

burg." Ordensmeister Aniceto Fernandez approbierte das Statut am 29. Mai 1965 auf fünf Jahre „ad experimentum", nachdem er das „gemeinsame Generalstudium für die Provinzen deutscher Zunge" am 3. Mai 1965 errichtet hatte.[304]

Die rechtliche Grundlage für einen Kurs bildete dieses Statut aber nur 1965/66. Im Studienjahr 1966/67 fiel er aus und wurde auch später nicht wieder aufgenommen; Philipp Seidl wurde im September 1966 nach Wien assigniert und im November in die Teutonia zurückgerufen.[305] Der Augsburger Pastoralkurs und mit ihm der süddeutsche Beitrag zum interprovinziellen Generalstudium war beendet. Betrachtet man die Teilnehmerzahlen, so kam dies nicht unbedingt überraschend:

1958/59: sechs Teilnehmer = drei Dominikaner (Teutonia), drei Missionare von Mariannhill;[306]

1959/60: sechs Teilnehmer = drei Dominikaner (Teutonia), drei Mariannhiller;[307]

1960/61: elf Teilnehmer = sechs Dominikaner (drei Teutonia, drei Germ. sup.), zwei Mariannhiller, zwei Missionare der hl. Familie, ein Missionar von La Salette;[308]

1961/62: sechs Teilnehmer = zwei Dominikaner (1 Germ. sup., 1 Helvetia), ein Mariannhiller, ein Zisterzienser, ein Missionar der hl. Familie, ein Missionar von La Salette;[309]

1962/63: zwölf Teilnehmer = sieben Dominikaner (3 Teutonia, 3 Germ. sup., 1 Helvetia), zwei Karmeliten, drei Mariannhiller;[310]

---

304 Volltextabdruck beider Texte, des Errichtungsdekrets wie des Statuts in: *ASOP* (1965) 229–231; daraus auch die obigen Zitate. Das Generalkapitel von Bogotá 1965 approbierte die Errichtung ebenfalls (siehe: ACG 1965, S. 31, Nr. 30.

305 Zu Seidl: PA, Provinzialsregestenbuch 2 (1966–2010), Einträge vom 20.9.1966, Nr. 19 und vom 9.11.1966, Nr. 28.

306 PA, Provinzrundbrief vom 11.12.1959, S. 1. Für die zwei Predigtkurse der beiden vorhergehenden Studienjahre fehlen leider Teilnehmerangaben.

307 PA, Provinzrundbrief vom 11.3.1960, S. 2.

308 Für 1960 / 61 divergieren die Angaben der Quellen: Laut PA, Provinzialsregestenbuch 1 (1939–1966), Eintrag vom 5.10.1960 zur Inauguration des Kurses, S. 117, Nr. 123 begannen elf Teilnehmer den Kurs (Zusammensetzung wie oben) und schlossen ihn am 23.3.1961 ab (Eintrag vom 23.3.1961, S. 124, Nr. 148). Laut Provinzrundbrief vom 1.3.1961, S. 2 waren es nur zehn Teilnehmer, davon nur zwei Dominikaner der Teutonia. Die Provinzialsregesten haben als Quelle aber das größere Gewicht.

309 PA, Provinzrundbrief vom 17.3.1962, S. 2.

310 PA, Provinzrundbrief vom 18.3.1962, S. 2.

1963/64: zwölf Teilnehmer = drei Dominikaner (Teutonia), vier Mariannhiller, zwei Karmeliten, ein Missionar der hl. Familie, ein Missionar von La Salette;[311]
1964/65: acht Teilnehmer = drei Karmeliten, vier Mariannhiller, ein Arnsteiner Pater;[312]
1965/66: sieben Teilnehmer = drei Karmeliten, vier Mariannhiller.[313]

Anders gesagt: Ab dem Studienjahr 1964/65 nahm kein Dominikaner mehr am Pastoralkurs teil, der gleichzeitig aber mindestens fünf Dozenten beschäftigte. Damit war die Sinnhaftigkeit dieser aufwändigen Fortbildungsveranstaltung grundsätzlich in Frage gestellt. Provinzial Innozenz Varga stellte dazu abschließend fest:

> „Der Pastoralkurs in Augsburg ist für das Schuljahr 1966/67 ausgefallen. Dazu die folgende Erklärung: Durch die Errichtung des Studium Interprovinciale erhielt der Cursus Pastoralis in Augsburg seinen rechtlich gesicherten Bestand. Bei der Übernahme meines Amtes [sc. Juli 1966] war dieser bereits illusorisch geworden. Die Gründe für diese unvorhergesehene Entwicklung sind:
>
> 1. Die Befreiung vom Pastoralkurs wurde sehr großzügig gehandhabt. Bei den Studenten war die Abneigung gegen dieses Ergänzungsjahr weit verbreitet. Die Zuweisung zum Pastoralkurs wurde vielfach als Strafmaßnahme empfunden.
>
> 2. Aus verschiedenen Gründen sah sich die Walberberger Studienleitung genötigt, katechetisch-pastorale Vorlesungen und Übungen in die dortige Ausbildung einzubauen. Dadurch aber wurde der Augsburger Pastoralkurs auch grundsätzlich in Frage gestellt. Im Hinblick auf die Pläne einer weitgehenden Studienreform des Walberberger Studium Commune kann zur Zeit diese Angelegenheit nicht grundsätzlich bereinigt werden.
>
> 3. Die erwähnte Abneigung bei den Studenten – durch die Walberberger katechetischen und pastoralen Übungen einigermaßen begründet – führten dazu, dass für das Studienjahr 1966/67 die Teutonia keinen Pater studens zur weiteren Ausbildung nach Augsburg zu schicken für nötig ansah. Von dieser Sachlage ausgehend sah ich mich berechtigt, auch unsere zwei in Frage kommenden jungen Mitbrüder zu dispensieren, da es ein zu großer Aufwand wäre, für zwei Hörer allein den Kurs halten zu lassen."[314]

Mit dem Pastoralkurs gestorben war auch der Traum eines eigenen Provinzstudiums. Es sollte keinen weiteren Versuch mehr geben, ein solches

311 PA, Provinzrundbrief vom 3.3.1964, S. 2.
312 PA, Provinzrundbrief vom 11.12.1964, S. 2.
313 PA, Provinzrundbrief vom 12.3.1965, S. 2.
314 PA, Provinzrundbrief „am vierten Adventssonntag" 1966, S. 2.

in der Germania superior zu errichten. Da nun auch die Noviziatsausbildung in der Teutonia stattfand, standen im Augsburger Kloster nun viele Zimmer leer. Mit eigenen Mitbrüdern oder Projekten waren diese nicht zu füllen. Daher vermietete der Konvent zunächst Räumlichkeiten an die 1970 neugegründete Universität Augsburg; später zogen Teile der Diözesanverwaltung ein.

Projekte und Pastoral (1950–1965)

Die Rundbriefe, die die Provinziäle Marianus Vetter und Augustinus Gierlich an die Konvente und Brüder versandten und in denen sie Neuigkeiten mitteilten und die bei ihnen eingelangten Arbeitsberichte aus den Klöstern zusammenfassten, geben zahlreiche Details über die Pastoral der Dominikaner in Süddeutschland und Österreich wieder. Vetter legte dabei großen Wert auf die Verobjektivierung der Tätigkeit der Konvente in Zahlen, bei Gierlich ließ diese Tendenz nach – vielleicht, weil sich die Berichte der Konvente entsprechend geändert hatten. Manche dieser Zahlenangaben dürften auf Schätzungen beruhen bzw. auf Hochrechnungen: Die Kommunikantenzahlen konnte vergleichsweise sicher über den Hostienverbrauch an einer Kirche ermittelt werden; die Beichtzahlen beruhen wohl auf Hochrechnungen, ausgehend von der Auflage der Osterbeichtbildchen u. ä. Überprüfbar sind alle diese Daten heute ohnehin kaum mehr. Aufgrund dieser Quellenlage ist es schwer, ein übersichtliches Bild von den Aktivitäten der einzelnen Niederlassungen zu zeichnen, ohne sich in zu vielen Details zu verlieren. Dennoch kann auf ihrer Grundlage ein Tätigkeitsprofil des jeweiligen Dominikanerklosters deutlich werden.[315]

315 Die folgenden Angaben zur Seelsorge aller Niederlassungen in diesem Kapitel stammen aus: PA, Provinzrundbriefe vom 2.2.1951, von „Ende Januar“ 1952, vom 2.2.1953, „im Januar“ 1955, vom 2.2.1957, vom 2.2.1958, vom 11.3.1959, vom 1.3.1961, vom 17.3.1962, vom 18.3.1963, vom 3.3.1964, vom 12.3.1965 und vom 15.3.1966. Diese Rundbriefe waren jeweils Berichte über das abgelaufene Kalenderjahr (so stellt z. B. der Rundbrief vom 2.2.1951 die Aktivitäten des Jahres 1950 dar). Keine Berichte gibt es über die Arbeitsjahre 1953, 1955 und 1959.

Wien: Pfarrei, spirituelle und religiöse Weiterbildung

Zwischen 1949 und 1965 bestand der Wiener Konvent aus 16 bis 20 Personen; durchschnittlich waren es zwölf Priester und sechs Laienbrüder.[316] Darunter fiel auch der Provinzial – sowohl Vetter als auch Gierlich hatten in Wien ihre Residenz aufgeschlagen –, der aber rechtlich betrachtet nicht zum Wiener Konvent gehörte und wegen seiner Amtsverpflichtungen nur unregelmäßig zur Seelsorge beitragen konnte. Von den Konventspriestern war einer, Dalmatius Hruschka, schwer erkrankt und fiel daher für die Seelsorge völlig aus; ebenso von der regelmäßigen Konventspastoral abzuziehen waren 1961 bis 1963 P. Amandus Suárez aus der spanischen Provinz, der zwar im Wiener Konvent assigniert war, aber außerhalb, bei Ursulinen wohnte, der ab 1963 in Wien assignierte P. Franz Schmölz, der an der Universität in Salzburg unterrichtete und auch dort lebte, und ab 1964 P. Isnard Frank, der einer Lehrtätigkeit in Walberberg nachging und während des Studienbetriebes dort wohnte.

In der Klosterkirche Maria Rotunda fanden werktags täglich fünf bis sechs Messen statt. An Sonn- und Feiertagen waren es sieben, wobei in vier davon gepredigt wurde – darunter in der Pfarrmesse und in einer Messe für Künstler und Akademiker. Gepredigt wurde darüber hinaus allabendlich im Mai und während der Festoktav zu Maria Königin im Oktober, sowie zu den Roratemessen im Advent und während einer Allerseelennovene (1.–9. November), die bis 1957 bestand. Alltäglich wurde vor ausgesetztem Allerheiligsten der Rosenkranz als Segensandacht gebetet. Mit Einführung der neuen Liturgie am 7. März 1965 gab es sonn- und feiertags fünf Messfeiern, in denen allen Ansprachen bzw. Predigten gehalten wurden. Am 1. September 1965 wurde in der Kirche zwischen Kanzel und Nepomukaltar ein provisorischer Volksaltar errichtet, auf dem die seit 1957 wieder erlaubten werktäglichen Abendmessen zelebriert wurden, ebenfalls mit kurzen Ansprachen, die es auch in der 7-Uhr-Messe an Werktagen gab. Weitere Predigten gab es regelmäßig an Marien- oder hohen Ordensfesten, sowie im Marianischen Jahr 1953/54. Als Zahl der Kommunionen in der

---

316 Laut der Provinzkataloge der Jahre 1949–1965 gliederte sich der Wiener Konvent summarisch wie folgt: 1949: zwölf Priester (P.), sechs Laienbrüder (L.), zwei Laienbrüdernovizen; 1951: 11 P., 6 L., 1952: 11 P., 6 L., 1953: 10 P., 6 L., 1955–1957: 11 P., 6 L., 1958: 13 P., 6 L.; 1959: 14 P., 6 L.; 1960–1961: 13 P., 6 L.; 1962: 14 P., 6 L.; 1964: 14 P., 4 L.; und 1965: 15 P., 4 L.

Abb. 45: Die Rosenkranzbasilika St. Maria Rotunda der Dominikaner in Wien: Fassade (Postkarte; PA, Fotosammlung).

Kloster- und Pfarrkirche werden angegeben: für 1950 48.000, für 1951 43.350, für 1952 52.000, für 1954 35.050, für 1956 28.660, für 1957 30.800, für 1960 32.253, für 1963 und 1964 30.000. Beichtgelegenheit wurde täglich von 6.30–8.30 Uhr und abends um 18 Uhr sowie während der Gottesdienste angeboten.

Vom Konvent wurde auch der Dritte Orden betreut: in Wien selbst eine Männergruppe (ursprünglich aus 30 Mitgliedern bestehend; diese Zahl nahm 1959 auf 20 und 1963 auf 15 ab) und eine Frauengruppe (ursprünglich aus 250 Mitgliedern bestehend; diese Zahl schrumpfte bis 1957

Abb. 46: Die Rosenkranzbasilika St. Maria Rotunda der Dominikaner in Wien: Blick auf den Hochaltar (PA, Fotosammlung).

auf 160, nahm dann aber bis 1963 wieder auf 220 zu), ab 1951 eine weitere in Hinterbrühl im Bezirk Mödling (1951 werden 20 Mitglieder angegeben, danach fehlen die Mitgliederzahlen; es ist zu vermuten, dass diese Gruppe klein blieb). Für alle Gruppen wurde jeweils einmal im Monat eine Generalkommunion mit Konferenz abgehalten. In Hinterbrühl bestand die Seelsorge der Gruppe in der Betreuung eines Altersheimes und von Feriengästen durch Vorträge und Beichthören. Die beiden Wiener Gruppen arbeiteten in der Krankenfürsorge und der Caritas. Außerdem halfen sie aktiv beim St.-Dominikuswerk mit, dessen Sitz 1960 nach Wien verlegt und dessen Mitgliederstand bis dahin auf 14.000 angewachsen war – konkret unterstützten sie P. Varga bei der Erstellung und Verschickung der jährlich erscheinenden Broschüre und eines Weihnachtsgrußes und bei der Spendenverwaltung.

Maria Rotunda diente auch als Kirche für die dem Orden anvertraute Innenstadtpfarrei. Als Pfarrer fungierte seit 1938 bis zu seinem Tod 1946 P. Willibald Funk. Ihm folgten von 1946 bis 1980 Gottfried Prischink, vom 1980 bis 1986 Fulko Hilgefort, von 1986 bis 2001 Martin Gyöngyös, von 2001 bis 2008 Johannes Maria Schyma und seit 2008 wieder Martin Gyöngyös.[317] Je nach personeller Möglichkeit stellte der Konvent außerdem einen oder mehrere Kapläne. Die Pfarrei zählte zwischen 3000 und 3500 Katholiken. Zunächst monatlich mit 1400 Exemplaren, ab 1958 zweimonatlich mit 1500 Exemplaren erschien ein Pfarrblatt. Pfarrer Prischink baute im Laufe der Jahre drei Pfadfindergruppen, drei Pfarrjugendgruppen (Jungschar) und eine Frauen- und Müttergruppe auf; die Männergruppe wurde 1957 an St. Stefan angeschlossen. Zu erwähnen sind noch die Pfarrwallfahrt und eine dreiwöchige Ferienaktion für Jugendliche, die jährlich stattfanden.

Sehr aktiv waren die Wiener Dominikaner im Bereich der Schwesternseelsorge: Zwischen 1949 und 1957 stellte der Konvent auf acht Posten ordentliche oder außerordentliche Beichtväter bei den Dominikanerinnen in Wien-Hacking, den Ursulinen, den Niederlassungen der Schwestern vom Armen Kinde Jesu in Döbling und Stadlau und den Klöstern der Töchter der göttlichen Liebe. 1962 waren es neun Posten als ordentliche und sechs als außerordentliche (hinzugekommen waren u. a. Niederlassungen der Schwestern vom Guten Hirten und die Dominikanerinnen in Kemmelbach). Dazu kam noch die Bestellung eines Beichtvaters für die Barmherzigen Brüder in der Taborstraße. Zu diesen Posten gehörte auch das

317 Angaben laut der Provinzkataloge ab 1949 unter Wien.

Halten eines Vortrags einmal im Monat in der jeweiligen Gemeinschaft. Zahlenmäßig lässt sich diese Arbeit nur schwer fassen. Provinzial Vetter meldet einmal für 1957 das Hören von etwa 5.000 Beichten in Maria Rotunda, aber circa 10.000 Beichten in anderen Kirchen und Klöstern. Unter letzteres fiel auch der von zwei Patres abwechselnd ab 1962 im Stefansdom täglich geleistete dreistündige Beichtdienst. Für die Schwesternbeichten war Maximilian Göbel praktisch freigestellt; er wurde aber von drei bis vier weiteren Patres darin unterstützt. Auch was das Exerzitienangebot des Dominikanerkonvents betraf, bildeten Ordensleute, v. a. Schwestern, die Hauptzielgruppe.[318]

Darüber hinaus gehörte zur Arbeit der Patres auch die Abhaltung von Volksmissionen,[319] zahlreicher Einkehrtage für verschiedene Stände (Priester, Erwachsene, Jugend),[320] religiöser Wochen, Vorträge und andere Bildungsveranstaltungen, Fasten- und Maipredigten in anderen Kirchen u. ä., das aufzuzählen den Rahmen sprengen würde. Hervorzuheben ist außerdem die Lehrtätigkeit einzelner Brüder auf den verschiedensten Gebieten: So hielt Alfons Well an der Wiener Katholischen Akademie und am „Theologischen Laienkurs" des Seelsorgeinstituts Österreichs Vorlesungen über

---

318 Dieses Angebot des Konvents war zahlenmäßig sehr schwankend: 1950 fanden zwölf Kurse für Ordensleute (441 Teilnehmer) und Laien (754 Teilnehmer) statt, 1951 17 Kurse für Ordensleute (696 Teilnehmer, ein Kurs für Priester (30 Teilnehmer), neun Kurse für Laien (470 Teilnehmer), 1952 neun Kurse für Ordensleute (440 Teilnehmer), ein Kurs für Laien (50 Teilnehmer), 1954 acht Kurse für Ordensleute (450 Teilnehmer), ein Kurs für Studenten (30 Teilnehmer – danach fehlen leider die Teilnehmerangaben), 1956 zehn Kurse für Ordensleute, 1957 neun Kurse für Ordensleute, zwei Kurse für Priester und zwei für Studenten, 1958 elf Kurse für Ordensfrauen, einer für Alumnen, 1959 elf Kurse für Ordensfrauen, sechs für Priester, 13 für die Jugend, 1960 15 Kurse für Ordensfrauen, drei für Ordensmänner, einer für Priester, zwei für die Jugend, 1961 elf für Ordensfrauen, einer für Priester, sechs für die Jugend, 1962 fünf Kurse für Ordensmänner, 17 für Ordensfrauen, je einer für Männer, Burschen, Mädchen und ein Knabenseminar, 1963 18 Kurse für Ordensfrauen, einer für Ordensmänner, einer für den Dritten Orden, zwei für Mädchen, einer für Burschen, 1964 fünf Kurse für Ordensfrauen, zwei für die Jugend, einer für Männer und 1965 vier Kurse für Ordensfrauen, zwei für Priester und zwei für die Jugend.

319 1950 waren es sechs Missionen (mit 12.700 Teilnehmern), 1951 drei (mit 5000 Teilnehmern, danach darüber keine Angaben mehr), 1952 zwei, 1958 fünf, 1959 sieben, 1960 neun, 1961 13, 1962 neun, 1963 acht, 1964 sechs und 1965 sechs.

320 1950 waren es 29 Einkehrtage (878 Teilnehmer), 1951 17 (1030 Teilnehmer), 1952 sechs (200 Teilnehmer), 1954 zehn (465 Teilnehmer – danach fehlen die Teilnehmerzahlen), 1956 drei, 1957 sieben, 1959 13, 1960 zehn, 1961 neun, 1962 neun, 1963 drei und 1964 neun.

Philosophie. Diego Hanns Götz unterrichtete Ethik am Max-Reinhardt-Seminar – über seine Radio- und Fernsehansprachen und seine Publikationen war Götz ein in Süddeutschland und Österreich weit bekannter Prediger und religiöser Redner – und ab 1956 hielt Johannes Czerny zunächst die Dozentur für Dogmatik, dann die für Fundamentaltheologie an der Hauslehranstalt der Augustinerchorherren in Klosterneuburg. Norbert Rieth und ab 1957 Angelik Pekarek gaben Religionsunterricht am „Neuland"-Realgymnasium in Döbling und an den Schulen der Dominikanerinnen in Hacking (Frauen-Berufsschule, Mittel- und Hauptschule).

Graz: Pfarr- und Marienapostolat

In den Jahren 1949 bis 1965 bestand der Grazer Konvent aus 17 bis 22 Mitgliedern; im Durchschnitt waren es 20, nämlich 14 Priester, fünf Laienbrüder und ein Kleriker.[321] Für die Seelsorge in Graz fiel ein im Grazer Konvent assignierter Priester völlig aus, Gundisalv Sommer, der erkrankt in Gnas in der Steiermark bei seinen Verwandten lebte, wo er auch 1958 verstarb. Ein weiterer assignierter, schon älterer Pater, Otmar Posch, wohnte 1953–1956 als Spiritual bei den Dominikanerinnen in Altenhohenau in Bayern, 1959–1961 als Religionslehrer in Rohrbach an der Gölsen in Niederösterreich und 1962 in Hinterbrühl. Ebenso beteiligten sich die 1963 formal nach Graz assignierten Patres Friedrich Gegenbauer und Odilo Mehl nicht an der dortigen Seelsorge: Gegenbauer wohnte in seiner Schweizer Heimat, 1963 im Pfarramt Schönenwerd / Kanton Solothurn und übernahm 1964 die Mitarbeit am Schweizer katholischen Sonntagblatt, wofür er nach Wil / Kanton St. Gallen zog. Mehl hatte 1963 den Übertritt in die Erzdiözese München-Freising beantragt und wohnte an verschiedenen Orten des Diözesangebiets. Nur eingeschränkt seelsorglich verwendbar waren die Senioren unter den Priestern des Konvents, Benedikt Bertignol († 1952), Edmund Prantner († 1952) und

321 Summarisch gliederte sich der Konvent laut den Provinzkatalogen 1949–1965 wie folgt: 1949: 14 Priester (P.), drei Laienbrüder (L.); 1951: 15 P., 3 L.; 1952: 15 P., 3 L.; 1953: 14 P., 4 L., 1 Kleriker (K.), 1955: 15 P., 4 L., 1 K.; 1956: 15 P., 4 L., 1 K.; 1957: 15 P., 4 L., 1 K., 1 Klerikernovize, 1 Laienbrudernovize; 1958: 14 P., 5 L., 1 K.; 1959: 13 P., 5 L., 1 K.; 1960: 15 P., 5 L., 1 K., 1 Tertiar (T.); 1961: 14 P., 4 L., 1 K., 1 T.; 1962: 13 P., 4 L., 1 K., 1 T.; 1964: 13 P., 4 L., 1 K., 1 T. und 1965: 14 P., 4 L., 1 K.; 1 T. Der Kleriker mit ewiger Profess lebte für die Dauer einer schweren Erkrankung in Graz in Pflege. Der Tertiar taucht schon vor 1960 unter Graz namentlich in den Provinzkatalogen auf, wird aber erst 1960 unter den Laienbrüdern des Konvents geführt.

Leander Klotz († 1969). Ein weiterer Pater, Reginald Ladner, war durch eine Kriegsverletzung erblindet und kümmerte sich besonders um die Blindenseelsorge in Österreich.

In der Notkirche und dann in der neuen Fatimakirche wurden täglich fünf Messen und abends ein sakramentaler Segen mit Rosenkranzgebet gefeiert. Sonntags fanden acht Gottesdienste statt. Abendmessen wurden an allen Marienfesten und an allen Tagen im Mai und Oktober zelebriert. Predigten gab es zunächst sonntäglich in vier, ab 1956 in sechs Messen, außerdem Ansprachen am Herz-Jesu-Freitag, Herz-Mariä-Samstag (erster Freitag und erster Samstag im Monat), an allen Marienfesten und an allen Festen der Ordensheiligen. Ab 1952 kamen noch Predigten an jedem Monatsdreizehnten zu Ehren Unserer Lieben Frau von Fatima hinzu. Monatlich wurde vor jedem Herz-Mariä-Samstag eine sogenannte Sühne-Anbetungsnacht gehalten, mit Ansprache und Betrachtung zu jeder Betstunde, sowie mitternächtlichem Chorgebet des Konvents (Matutin und Laudes). Beichtmöglichkeiten wurden während der Gottesdienstzeiten angeboten – in der Notkirche an zwei Beichtstühlen und in der Maria-Schutz-Kapelle, mit Benediktion des neugebauten Kirchenschiffs 1954 dort und in einem Beichtzimmer an der Klosterpforte. Die Notkirche fasste im Hauptraum etwa 200 Personen, im Notfall im Chorraum weitere 200. Etwa 1300 Gläubige besuchten sie durchschnittlich am Sonntag. Mit Benediktion des neugebauten Kirchenschiffs nahm der Gläubigenbesuch zu; als die Fatimakirche fertig war, besuchten sie etwa 30 Prozent der Pfarrangehörigen. Die Kommunionzahlen im Gotteshaus der Grazer Dominikaner betrugen 1951 71.000, 1952 64.000, 1956 73.000, 1957–1959 70.000, 1960 65.000, 1961 62.000, 1962–1964 60.000 und 1965 68.000. Ab 1965 zelebrierten die Dominikaner auch täglich in der zur Pfarrei gehörenden Sacré-Cœur-Kirche.

In Graz bestand eine Drittordensgruppe für Männer (1951: 18 Mitglieder, 1957 und später: 20 Mitglieder) und eine für Frauen (1951: 142 Mitglieder, 1957 und später 130 Mitglieder);[322] diese wurden durch eine vierzehntägige Glaubensstunde, monatliche Generalkommunion mit Konferenz und einen jährlichen Exerzitienkurs betreut. Der Konvent kümmerte sich ab 1954 auch um eine Gruppe in Gleisdorf (20 Mitglieder) mit monat-

322 Die Unterscheidung der Provinzrundbriefe 1950–1952 zwischen den beiden Grazer Ortsgruppen und der von Graz als Sitz des Provinzpromotors für den Dritten Orden ebenfalls betreuten, etwa 140 zählenden Provinzmitglieder hat wahrscheinlich damit zu tun, dass mit den 140 die Drittordensmitglieder in Vorarlberg gemeint waren.

Abb. 47: Fatimakirche in Graz: Fatimakapelle im Rosarium (aufgenommen ca. 1970); PA, Fotosammlung).

licher Generalkommunion und Konferenz, sowie um etwa einhundert in Vorarlberg lebende Drittordensmitglieder, mit einer vierteljährlich angebotenen Konferenz.

Wichtigstes seelsorgliches Standbein des Grazer Dominikanerklosters war die ihm anvertraute Pfarrei. Zu dieser gehörten 1951 10.000 Gläubige; 1958 waren es 12.000. Als Pfarrer amtierte von 1934 bis 1965 Michael Lenz; seine Nachfolger waren Bonaventura Neuberger (1965–1980), Vinzenz Paller (1980–1992), Günter Reitzi (1992–1998), Paul Schäferskúpper (1998–2001) und Max Svoboda (2001–2012). In den Jahren 1950 bis 1965 standen dem Pfarrer zwei weitere Priester des Konvents als Kapläne und einer als Aushilfskaplan zur Seite. Abgesehen von einer ausgebreiteten Pfarrcaritas und einer Volksbibliothek bestand ein wesentliches Merkmal der Münzgrabenpfarrei in ihrer Jugendarbeit: 1950 gab es eine Ministrantengruppe, 1954 waren es zwei, 1956 drei und 1965 vier. Die Zahl der Jugendgruppen wuchs ebenfalls über die Jahre, bis es 1965 zwei Buben- und drei Mädchengruppen der Jungschar, sowie zwei Buben- und drei Mädchengruppen der Katholischen Arbeiterjugend gab. Dazu kamen seit 1958 Gruppen der katholischen Männer- und Frauenbewegung und eine Aktivistenrunde der Katholischen Arbeiterbewegung. Für alle diese Gruppen wurde mindestens monatlich eine Messe mit Zusammenkunft abgehalten; die Kinder- und Jugendgruppen trafen sich wöchentlich. Ferner wurden ein Lehrlingsheim und das Schülerheim Josefinum von der Pfarrei mit Vorträgen und Gottesdiensten betreut.

Als schwere Aufgabe erwies sich der den beiden Kaplänen anvertraute Religionsunterricht an den Volks- und Hauptschulen im Pfarrgebiet. 1950 unterrichteten sie zwölf Klassen der Mädchenvolksschule und 14 Klassen der Mädchenhauptschule mit insgesamt 52 Wochenstunden. Dazu kamen jährlich viermal Schulkommunionen mit Beichte, sowie die reguläre Vorbereitung der Pfarrkinder für Erstbeichte, Erstkommunion und Firmung. 1954 wurden die Unterrichtslasten auf vier Dominikanerkatecheten verteilt. Ihre Lehrverpflichtungen wuchsen weiter an: 1956 hielten vier Patres an den Volks- und Hauptschulen je 14, 12, 16 und 14 Wochenstunden, ein weiterer Pater 17 Wochenstunden an der Handelsakademie. 1959 war der Höhepunkt mit 70 Wochenstunden für vier Patres erreicht. Danach gingen die Lehrverpflichtungen zurück, bis sie 1965 bei 38 Wochenstunden an Volks- und Hauptschulen lagen.

Auch in Graz waren die Patres in der Seelsorge für Ordensfrauen tätig: 1950 hatten sie sechs Posten als ordentliche und zwei Posten als außer-

ordentliche Schwesternbeichtväter inne. Bis 1962 reduzierte sich diese Tätigkeit aber auf drei ordentliche (je bei den Dominikanerinnen in Gleisdorf, St. Ruprecht an der Raab und Thondorf) und vier außerordentliche Stellen (je bei den Dominikanerinnen in Gleisdorf, St. Ruprecht an der Raab, Thondorf, Nestelbach und bei den Schwestern vom Guten Hirten in Graz). Dieses Engagement für die Schwestern schlug sich auch in der Exerzitientätigkeit des Konvents nieder; die meisten der Kurse waren für Ordensfrauen.[323]

Volksmissionen fielen demgegenüber weniger ins Gewicht.[324] Die Zahl der Einkehrtage war sehr unterschiedlich, was wohl auf das Engagement einzelner Konventualen zurückging. Hier scheint sich die Seelsorge Ladners für Blinde auszudrücken, wobei die Provinzrundbriefe bei ihren summarischen Angaben nur selten spezifizieren.[325] Auffallend sind die sehr zahlreichen Aushilfen zu Gottesdiensten mit Predigt und Beichtstuhl, die der Konvent vor allem bis 1959 in auswärtigen Pfarreien leistete. In deren Hintergrund mag vielleicht auch die Bitte um finanzielle Unterstützung des Kloster- und Kirchenbau gelegen haben.[326] Hierzu gehören wohl auch die außerhalb der eigenen Kirche abgehaltenen Predigtzyklen.[327]

Sein ganz besonderes Profil erhielt der Grazer Konvent durch sein Marien- und Rosenkranzapostolat. Zum Druck und Vertrieb von haupt-

323 1950: drei Kurse für Ordensleute, sechs für Laien; 1951: sieben für Ordensleute, vier für Laien; 1952: 12 für Ordensfrauen, je einer für Ordensmänner, für Pfarrhaushälterinnen und für Blinde; 1956: sieben für Ordensfrauen, acht für verschiedene Stände; 1957: zehn für Ordensfrauen, elf für verschiedene Stände, 1962: zwölf für Ordensfrauen, je einer für Ordenskandidatinnen und für Ordensmänner; 1963: 16 für Ordensfrauen, einer für ein Säkularinstitut; 1964: zehn für Ordensfrauen, je einer für Mädchen und für den Dritten Orden und 1965: 18 für Ordensschwestern, je zwei für Kandidatinnen und Ordenspriester, je einer für ein Säkularinstitut und für Tertiarinnen. Die Angaben zu den anderen Jahren sind nur summarisch.

324 1950: drei Missionen, eine Nachmission, zwei kroatische Missionen; 1951: sechs Missionen, eine kroatische Mission; 1952: fünf Missionen, 1954: eine Nachmission, 1957: zwei Missionen; 1960: neun Missionen; 1961: sechs Missionen und 1963 und 1965 je eine Mission.

325 1950: sieben Einkehrtage, 1951: sechs; 1952: zwölf; 1954: sieben; 1956: fünfzehn; 1957 und 1959: dreiundzwanzig; 1960: acht; 1961: zwölf; 1962: sechzehn (davon vier für Blinde); 1963: vier; 1964: elf (davon drei für Blinde) und 1965: sechs (je einer für Blinde, für die Legio Mariae, für Mädchen und für Burschen, sowie zwei für Frauen).

326 1950: 95 Aushilfen; 1951: 80; 1952: 171 [!], 1954: 79–80; 1956: 44; 1957: 61; 1959: 59; 1960: 39; 1961: 46; 1962: 30; 1963: 25; 1964: 8.

327 1954: 58 [!] Zyklen; 1956: 4; 1957: 2; 1959: 4; 1961: 18 und 1965: 1 Zyklus von 32 Maipredigten.

Abb. 48: Fatimakirche in Graz: „Maria – Schutzfrau Österreichs"; Relief an der Kirchenaußenwand; der links von Maria kniende Dominikaner mit Kirchenmodell trägt die Gesichtszüge von P. Leo Schölzhorn (PA, Fotosammlung).

sächlich marianisch geprägten Kleinschriften, der monatlich erscheinenden „Rosenkranzbriefe", die später „Mit Maria" hießen, und des jährlich publizierten Kalenders „Bote unserer Lieben Frau", der später „Bote unserer Lieben Frau von Fatima" hieß – die Druckleitung für diese beiden Periodika lag bei P. Amandus Baronig –, baute Prior Schölzhorn den „Rosenkranzverlag" aus, den er 1957 in „Fatima-Verlag" umtaufte. Da der Promotor für den Rosenkranz für den österreichischen Provinzteil im Grazer Kloster seinen Sitz hatte, wurden vom Konvent aus auch die Rosenkranzbruderschaften in Österreich betreut, wiederbelebt oder neu gegründet.[328] 1950 gründete die

328 Leider sind die diesbezüglichen Angaben der Provinzrundbriefe nicht nur sehr summarisch – sie betreffen auch nur den Zeitraum 1950–1957, um danach lakonisch als betreut zusammengefasst zu werden. Wiederbelebung oder Neuerrichtung einer Bruderschaft: 1950: fünf neue Bruderschaften, 1951: an elf Orten der Steiermark, des Burgenlands und Vorarlbergs, 1952: an 25 Orten; 1954: an 65 Orten; 1956: in 38 Pfarreien der Steiermark und 1957: in 24 Pfarreien der Steiermark, vier in Vorarlberg und zwei in Oberösterreich.

Legio Mariä ein Präsidium in Graz und hielt ihren wöchentlichen Dienste im Dominikanerkloster und in der Münzgrabenpfarrei. 1951 folgte die Gründung eines zweiten Präsidiums, weshalb in Graz eine Curia errichtet wurde, die ihren Sitz im Kloster nahm. 1956 kam ein Jugendpräsidium hinzu. Die Legionäre wurden im Rahmen eines wöchentlichen Legions- und eines monatlichen Curientreffens von Dominikanern betreut. 1957 übersiedelte ein Präsidium in die Grazer Pfarrei von St. Andrä; die beiden anderen blieben am Münzgraben. Schölzhorn errichtete und betreute außerdem 1962 ein Sekretariat des Fatima-Weltapostolats, das zunächst „Blaue Armee Mariens" hieß. Dieses hatte 1963 2.090 Mitglieder.

Zu erwähnen ist abschließend noch die langjährige, von 1949 bis 1976 dauernde Lehrtätigkeit von P. Fidelis Gallati an der katholisch-theologischen Fakultät der Universität Graz, die bis 1960 sechs und danach vier Wochenstunden und inhaltlich philosophisch-thomistische Themen umfasste.

Friesach: Klosterkirche und Pfarrseelsorge mit Steigeisen

Zwischen 1949 und 1965 bestand die *domus* in Friesach in Kärnten zumeist aus vier Priestern und zwei Laienbrüdern.[329] Für die Seelsorge fielen aus Alters- und Krankheitsgründen in diesen Jahren aus: Ludwig Haab, der 1953 starb und Hugo Reiter in seinem letzten Lebensjahr vor seinem Tod 1960. Die finanziellen Einnahmen des Klosters ruhten großteils auf der landwirtschaftlichen Bewirtschaftung der eigenen Liegenschaften, besonders des großen Klostergartens. Am 1. April 1961 wurde die Landwirtschaft in Pacht gegeben.[330] Bis 1956 wurden in der Klosterkirche täglich zwei Messen zelebriert, dann werktags nur mehr eine Messe um 6 Uhr früh. Sonn- und feiertags wurde nur in einer der beiden Messen gepredigt; ab 1960 wurde dieses Angebot auf eine Messe um 8 Uhr morgens reduziert. Täglich gab es abends um ein öffentliches Rosenkranzgebet, das im Mai und Oktober mit einer Segensandacht verbunden war. Dazu kam jeden ersten Monatssonntag eine kurze Rosenkranzpredigt mit Prozession. Die Gottesdienstzeiten an der Klosterkirche hingen von den Wünschen des Friesacher Stadtpfarrers ab.[331] Der Mess-

329 Summarische Gliederung des Friesacher Klosters aufgrund der Provinzkataloge 1949–1965: 1949–1951: fünf Priester (P.), zwei Laienbrüder (L.); 1952: 6 P., 4 L.; 1953: 5 P., 2 L.; 1956–1960: 4 P., 2 L.; 1961: 3 P., 2 L.; 1962–1965: 4 P., 2 L.

330 Datum laut PA, Provinzrundbrief vom 17.3.1962, S. 4.

331 Siehe dazu PA, Provinzrundbrief vom 18.3.1963, S. 5.

Abb. 49: Dominikanerkirche St. Nikolaus in Friesach (PA, Fotosammlung).

Abb. 50: Dominikanerkirche St. Nikolaus in Friesach: Astkreuz (PA, Fotosammlung).

besuch war – bedingt durch die Lage des Klosters am Stadtrand und das Messangebot in den weiteren Kirchen Friesachs – nicht sonderlich gut: Die Provinzrundbriefe zwischen 1950 und 1954 geben durchschnittlich 15 Besucher der Werktags- und zwischen durchschnittlich 150 und 180 Besuchern der Sonntagsmessen an. Letztere Zahl schrumpfte bis 1965 auf 65 bis maximal 90. Dementsprechend verhielt sich auch die Zahl der Kommunionen: Ausgehend von etwa 5.000 im Jahre 1950 stieg sie bis 1954 auf 8.000 an und pendelte in den Jahren 1956 und 1963 zwischen 6.000 und 7.000; 1964 waren es 5.100, 1965 2.500. Ähnlich verhielt

Abb. 51: Dominikanerkirche St. Nikolaus in Friesach: Madonna mit Jesuskind (PA, Fotosammlung).

sich auch die Zahl der an der Klosterkirche gehörten Beichten, die die Provinzrundbriefe 1950 mit ca. 2.600 angaben. Bis 1957 wuchs sie auf bzw. hielt sie sich bei etwa 3.500, um danach stetig abzunehmen; 1965 lag sie bei 2.050.

Ein Priester des Konvents betreute als Rektor auch die Kapelle des benachbarten St.-Josefsklosters der Dominikanerinnen. Er hielt dort täglich eine Messe für die Schwestern, zu der sonntags weitere 35 Gläubige erschienen, werktags etwa 25. Zu seinen Aufgaben gehörte auch die seelsorgliche Betreuung der Schülerinnen der Schule der Schwestern, mit einmal wöchentlichem Schulgottesdienst, Beichte und acht Wochenstunden Religionsunterricht. Die Patres stellten für den Dominikanerinnenkonvent außerdem den ordentlichen und den außerordentlichen Beichtvater – ebenso den außerordentlichen Beichtvater für die Friesacher Deutsch-Ordens-Schwestern.

Seit 1946 betreute ein Konventspriester auch die Pfarrei St. Georg am Friesach benachbarten, 1153 Meter hohen Gaisberg mit der Filialkirche St. Thomas in Höfl. Diese Gemeinde war mit etwa 280 Mitgliedern sehr klein. Um dort den einen Sonntagsgottesdienst mit Ansprache halten zu können, war ein eineinhalbstündiger Fußmarsch vom Kloster nötig – Provinzial Vetter wies einmal darauf hin, dass P. Hugo Reiter „oft Steigeisen braucht, um seine Pfarrkirche zu erreichen".[332] Reiter war dort von 1946 bis 1959 Pfarrprovisor; ihm folgten Raymund Lang (1959–1976), Fidelis Gallati (1976–1984), Jordan Gebhard (1984–1986) und Fulko Hilgefort (seit 1986).

1956 übernahm der Konvent eine Kaplansstelle an der Stadtpfarrei Friesach, mit der zwischen 15 und 18 Wochenstunden Religionsunterricht

332 PA, Provinzrundbrief vom 2.2.1951, S. 5.

an der Stadtschule und Jugend- und Pfadfinderbetreuung verbunden waren. Kaplan P. Bonaventura Neuberger übernahm 1962–1964 auch einige wenige Stunden Religionsunterricht an einer Berufsschule. Sein Nachfolger Heinrich Stumpf-Seregely unterrichtete 1964 nur acht Stunden an der Stadtschule; dessen Nachfolger Jakob Schattovich übernahm dann wieder 14 Wochenstunden dort, plus eine an der Berufsschule. In den weiteren Bereich der Pfarrseelsorge gehörte auch das Amt des sogenannten Exhortators, das ein Pater des Konvents inne hatte. Dessen Aufgabe bestand im regelmäßigen Abhalten von Vorträgen bei den monatlichen Priesterkonferenzen des Dekanats.

In Friesach bestand auch eine kleine Drittordensgruppe mit ursprünglich 20 Mitgliedern. Diese Zahl wuchs bis 1952 auf 29 an, um danach stetig zu schrumpfen: 1965 waren es noch 16 (zwei Weltpriester, 13 Frauen, ein Mann). Besser entwickelte sich die 1951 mit 140 Mitgliedern gegründete Werkgruppe des St.-Dominikuswerkes: Deren Mitgliederzahl stieg bis 1954 auf 340, um sich danach auf 330 einzupendeln; 1965 waren es 318.

Kaum ins Gewicht fielen Volksmissionen (für 1950 werden zwei, für 1951 drei genannt, danach keine mehr) oder Exerzitien (1950 waren es drei Kurse und 1951 und 1952 sechs Kurse, danach werden keine mehr genannt). Einkehrtage wurden nur einzeln veranstaltet, die alle im Zusammenhang mit der Seelsorge an der Dominikanerinnenschule standen. Wichtiger waren die Aushilfsleistungen, die der Friesacher Konvent für die Pfarreien der Umgebung erbrachte. So wirkte ein Pater z. B. 1952 für dreieinhalb Monate als Vertretung in einer anderen Pfarrei, 1954 einer für eineinhalb Monate und 1956 ein dreiviertel Jahr in zwei Pfarreien. Dazu kamen je nach Möglichkeit Mess-, Predigt- und Beichtaushilfen, so 1954 20 Sonn- und Feiertagsaushilfen, 1959 68 oder 1963 25 Aushilfen.

Retz: vier Kirchen und Kapellen für vier Patres

Sehr arm war auch das kleine Dominikanerkloster in Retz, dessen Besatzung zwischen 1949 und 1965 durchschnittlich aus vier Priestern und zwei Laienbrüdern bestand.[333] Finanziell hing das Kloster von den Einkünften aus der Landwirtschaft des nur geringen Grundbesitzes ab. Die großen

---

333 Laut der Provinzkataloge der Jahre 1949–1965 waren es 1949 drei Priester (P.) und zwei Laienbrüder (L.); 1951 4 P., 2 L.; 1952 3 P., 2 L.; 1953–1956 4 P., 2 L.; 1957 und 1958 5 P., 2 L.; 1959–1961 4 P., 2 L.; 1962 4 P., 1 L.; 1964 4 P., 2 L.; und 1965 3 P., 2 L.

Ausgaben für die Renovierung der großzügigen Klostergebäude stellten für das Haus eine starke Belastung dar, weshalb sich die Reparaturen über ein Jahrzehnt hinzogen. Ein weiteres Problem war der hohe Altersdurchschnitt der Gemeinschaft; Provinzial Vetter meinte 1955, „dass unser Kloster in Retz fast den Charakter eines Altenheimes der Provinz hat; denn die vier dort assignierten Patres stehen im Alter von 81, 68, 63 und 62 Jahren."[334] Besonders die Patres Pius Schreiner († 1958) und Bonaventura Cottier († 1961) konnten aus Altersgründen nur mehr wenig oder gar nichts mehr zur Seelsorge beitragen. Erst gegen 1960 schickte die Provinz jüngere Kräfte. In noch stärkerem Maße als Friesach genoss der Retzer Konvent eine gewisse regionale Bedeutung, da es das einzige Männerkloster im weiten nordöstlichen Umkreis Niederösterreichs war. Dadurch wurde das Dominikanerkloster zur Anlaufstelle für viele Priesterbeichten. Auch die monatliche Priesterkonferenz des Dekanats Retz mit jährlichem Einkehrtag fand bei den Dominikanern statt, wobei ein Pater die Ansprache (Exhortation) hielt.

Die Seelsorge der Dominikaner war stark in die pastoralen Notwendigkeiten der Stadtpfarrei Retz und der Nachbarorte eingebunden. Der Konvent wirkte durchaus als spirituelles Zentrum für die Stadt, aber weniger als Ort, zu dem die Gläubigen hinströmten, sondern mehr als Wohnstätte der Patres, von wo aus sie selbst ins Umland gingen. Dies zeigte sich deutlich beim Gottesdienstangebot an der Klosterkirche, das von den außerklösterlichen Verpflichtungen der wenigen Ordenspriester abhängig war: Anfangs der 1950er Jahre gab es in der Klosterkirche drei tägliche Messen und jeden Abend eine Segensandacht; in einer der drei Sonntagsmessen wurde gepredigt, eine zweite war als Kindermesse gestaltet. In den Marienmonaten Mai und Oktober gab es Abendandachten mit Predigten und Volksgesang und an jedem ersten Sonntag eines jeden Monats Rosenkranzpredigten. 1954 wurde eine der Messen an Sonn- und Feiertagen mit Predigt in der Stadtpfarrkirche übernommen und die Zahl der Sonntagsmessen in der Klosterkirche auf zwei reduziert. Die Übernahme der Kaplansstelle an der Stadtpfarrei – in der Stadtpfarrkirche waren täglich eine Messe und sonntags zwei mit Predigt zu halten – und der Seelsorge an der Expositur in Klein-Riedenthal, ebenfalls mit Sonntagsmesse und Predigt, brachte ab 1960 weitere Veränderungen im Liturgieangebot an der Klosterkirche. Entsprechend stark schwankte die Zahl der Kommunionen in der

334 PA, Provinzrundbrief „im Januar" 1955, S. 6.

Abb. 52: Retz in Niederösterreich (Postkarte): links im Vordergrund die Gebäude des Dominikanerklosters mit -kirche Mariä Himmelfahrt (PA, Fotosammlung).

Klosterkirche: 1950 waren es 9.000, 1951 circa 7.000. Bis 1957 stiegen sie auf 12.000 an, um sich bis 1965 auf etwa 7.600 einzupendeln. Die Zahl der Beichten in der Klosterkirche, die 1950 bei 4.000 lagen, nahmen bis 1956 auf 2.000 ab und bewegten sich in den Jahren danach zwischen 2.200 und 2.500 – auch hier wirkte sich die Übernahme anderer Seelsorgsstellen mit deren Beichtangebot aus.

Zu den übernommenen Verpflichtungen gehörte die Seelsorge des Bezirksaltenheims Retz, wo ab 1950 ein Pater Rektor der Heimkapelle war. Abgesehen von Beichten und Versehgängen zelebrierte dieser zunächst eine Messe in der Woche und eine Messe mit Predigt an Sonn- und Feiertagen; ab 1962 wurde dort täglich eine Messe gefeiert. Außerdem besetzte er auch den Posten des ordentlichen Beichtvaters für die Schwestern der Kongregation des göttlichen Erlösers (Niederbronner Schwestern), die das Heim leiteten. Ab 1951 übernahm ein Pater auch die seelsorgliche Betreuung des Caritas-Bubenheimes Turmhof; dieses Heim entwickelte sich bis 1962 zum größten Caritasheim der Erzdiözese Wien. Als Rektor der Heimkapelle zelebrierte er während der Woche eine Messe und an Sonn- und Feiertagen eine Messe mit Predigt, hörte die Beichten (ursprünglich monatlich, ab 1956 wöchentlich), hielt an den Feiertagen und den Sonntagen im Mai und Oktober Abendandachten mit Ansprache und in der Fasten-

Abb. 53: Blick auf die Apsis der Dominikanerkirche Retz von der Klostergasse aus (PA, Fotosammlung).

zeit Kreuzwegandachten und kümmerte sich um Erstbeicht- und Erstkommunionunterricht. Mit diesen beiden Heimen, der Expositur Klein-Riedenthal und ihrer eigenen Klosterkirche waren die vier Patres des Konvents also Rektoren in vier Kirchen.

Dazu kam noch der 1952 übernommene Religionsunterricht an der landwirtschaftlichen Fortbildungsschule, der gewerblichen Fortbildungsschule und verschiedenen Volks- und Hauptschulen von Retz, Klein-Riedenthal und Klein-Höflein. Diese Tätigkeit wuchs bis 1962 auf insgesamt 36 Wochenstunden an.

Die Zahl der Aushilfen für abwesende Pfarrgeistliche, die 1951–1956 jährlich zwischen 20 und 30 lag, nahm nach der Übernahme der Stadtkaplansstelle stark ab. Exerzitienkurse, Einkehrtage und Volksmissionen wurden vom Retzer Konvent nur vereinzelt gehalten. Zu erwähnen ist noch, dass der Konvent auch den Posten des außerordentlichen Beichtvaters bei den Borromäerinnen im erzbischöflichen Knabenseminar in Hollabrunn stellte.

Augsburg: ein breites Spektrum von Sakramenten-, Pfarr- und Kategorialpastoral

Auch in Süddeutschland konnten sich die Dominikaner nicht über mangelnde Arbeitsbelastung beklagen. Der Augsburger Konvent, der bis zu seinem Umzug in das neue Klostergebäude an der Heilig-Kreuz-Straße 15 bis 17 Mitglieder zählte, wurde nach 1957 zum größten der Provinz, was auch mit den dort assignierten Priestern zu tun hatte, die den Pastoralkurs besuchten: 1961 und 1964 zählte er 31 Mitglieder, 1965 waren es 26. Unter diesen Personalstand fiel auch die Dependance in St. Wolfgang in Augsburg-Spickel, die mit drei Dominikanern besetzt war.[335] Von 1951 bis 1962 lebte einer der Patres als Seelsorger bei den Dominikanerinnen in Diessen und ab 1962 einer als Seelsorger der Dominikanerinnen von Bad Wörishofen; in einzelnen Jahren stellte der Konvent auch Seelsorger für weitere Dominikanerinnenklöster. Ab 1960 lebte der erkrankte P. Suso Geiselhart in Schruns in Vorarlberg. Freigestellt von der Seelsorge in Augsburg war zwischen 1950 und 1954 auch der aus der ungarischen Provinz stammende P. Bonaventura Neuberger, dessen Aufgabe in der Betreuung der ungarischen Auslandsdeutschen in der Diözese Rottenburg bestand.

Die meisten Augsburger Dominikaner arbeiteten zunächst in der Sakramentenseelsorge an Heilig Kreuz: Mit der Wiederaufnahme der Gottesdienste in der neuerstandenen Kirche nahm ab Dezember 1949 der Kirchbesuch stetig zu. Täglich wurden dort vier bis fünf Messen angeboten, abhängig davon, ob auch Schulmessen zu zelebrieren waren. An Sonn- und Feiertagen waren es fünf bis sechs Messen, davon eine als feierliches Hochamt. In den Sommermonaten Mai bis Ende September gab es an Sonn- und Feiertagen zunächst sogar eine Messe für Wanderer um 4 Uhr früh, die sehr gut besucht war; später wurde dieser Gottesdienst am Bahnhof für alle Ausflügler gefeiert. Täglich wurde abends der Rosenkranz mit Segensandacht gebetet. An den Samstagen folgte danach eine gesungene Komplet mit Salve-Regina-Prozession. Die Zahl der Sonntagsmessbesucher

---

335 Laut den Provinzkatalogen der Jahre 1949–1965 setzte sich der Konvent wie folgt zusammen: 1949: zehn Priester (P.), vier Laienbrüder (L.), ein Tertiar; 1951: 10 P., 5 L.; 1952: 10 P., 6 L.; 1953: 9 P., 5 L., 1 Kleriker; 1955: 11 P., 6 L.; 1956: 10 P., 6 L.; 1957: 10 P., 6 L.; 1958: 18 P., 6 L.; 1959: 19 P., 5 L., 1 Laienbrudernovize; 1960: 19 P., 6 L.; 1961: 24 P., 7 L.; 1962: 22 P., 7 L.; 1964: 24 P., 7 L. und 1965 19 P., 7 L. Davon wohnten in dieser Zeit im Spickel 2 P. und 1 L. (als Mesner) – mit Ausnahme der Jahre 1951 und 1955 (jeweils nur 1 P., 1 L.).

wurde für 1950 auf 2.000 geschätzt. Sie stieg bis 1954 auf etwa 2.700 an, um über die Jahre danach abzunehmen: 1960 lag sie bei etwa 2.000, 1965 wurden an den Pflichtzählsonntagen 1.132 bzw. 1.243 Messbesucher gezählt. Die Kommunionzahl kann über das Hostienbüchlein relativ sicher angegeben werden: Sie lag 1950 bei 110.000, fiel 1951 auf 96.000 ab und stieg bis 1962 kontinuierlich auf 127.500 an. 1964 lag sie bei 114.000. Für 1965 geben die Provinzrundbriefe einen Hostienverbrauch von 4.350 großen und 112.000 kleinen Hostien an, wobei erstere Zahl insofern von Interesse ist, als sie im Zeitalter vor dem Üblichwerden der Priesterkonzelebration bedeutet, dass in Kirche und Kloster von Heilig Kreuz in einem Jahr über 4.300 Messen gefeiert wurden. Eigene regelmäßige Messen wurden während der Schulzeit unter der Woche auch für das Maria-Theresia-Gymnasium, für das Realgymnasium (seit 1965 Peutingergymnasium) und für das Jakob-Fugger-Gymnasium zelebriert, sowie zunächst einmal im Monat, später wöchentlich eine Abendmesse mit Ansprache für die Pax-Christi-Gemeinschaft. Zur Einführung der Liturgiereform am 7. März 1965 wurde ein von Laienbruder Titus Schrall geschreinerter Volksaltar auf einem eigenen Treppenaufsatz vor dem steinernen Hochaltar aufgestellt, in dem das Altarsakrament und die Reliquie des „Wunderbarlichen Gutes“ aufbewahrt blieben. Auf diesem Volksaltar wurde nach den neuen Liturgievorgaben *versus populum* zelebriert; der Wortgottesdienst wurde auf einem ebenfalls von Schrall verfertigten Lesepult abgehalten. Diese räumliche Vorverlegung des Zelebrationsortes in Richtung Kirchenschiff änderte auch die Art des Kommunionempfanges – die Gläubigen knieten nicht mehr am Kommuniongitter, sondern kamen in Zweierreihen nach vorne, um stehend zu kommunizieren. Auch die Gottesdienstzeiten in Heilig Kreuz wurden 1965 etwas verschoben: Die Eucharistiefeiern an Sonn- und Feiertagen fanden nun um 6, 7, 7.30, 10.15 und 11.30 Uhr statt (in letzteren vier mit Ansprache), an Werktagen um 6, 6.40, 7.15, 8 und 9 Uhr, jeden Dienstag dazu um 19.30 Uhr mit Ansprache (am ersten Dienstag jeden Monats als Pax-Christi-Gottesdienst). Die drei Schulmessen blieben erhalten.

Die zweite große Aufgabe an Heilig Kreuz bestand in der Beichtseelsorge. Beichtgelegenheit wurde in der Kirche vormittags täglich von 6 bis 10 Uhr angeboten, sowie unter der Woche ganztägig am Hausbeichtstuhl des Klosters. 1965 war Beichtgelegenheit in der Kirche werktags von 6 bis 9.30 Uhr, samstags und vor Feiertagen von 16–18.30 Uhr und ab 19.30 Uhr, sowie sonn- und feiertags von 6–8.30 Uhr. Das ganztägige Wochentagsangebot des Hausbeichtstuhls blieb unverändert erhalten. Diese Menge an

Beichtangebot entsprach der großen Nachfrage danach: Die Zahl der Beichtenden, die 1950 auf 18–19.000 im Jahr geschätzt wurden, stieg explosionsartig an. 1957 wurden 33–34.000 Beichtende im Jahr geschätzt. Danach waren keine Jahresschätzungen mehr möglich, dafür konnten die Provinziäle in ihren Rundbriefen auf die vergleichsweise sicheren Zahlen der während der Osterbeichten verteilten Beichtzettelchen zurückgreifen. Diese hatten 1954 bei über 6.000 gelegen. Ab 1959 waren es regelmäßig 13.000.

Die Bruderschaften waren die dritte Seelsorgsaufgabe an Heilig Kreuz. Schon bevor die Dominikaner diese Kirche übernommen hatten, waren zahlreiche Bruderschaften und geistliche Vereinigungen dort angesiedelt gewesen. Ihre Betreuung bestand aus mindestens einer Versammlung im Monat, bestehend aus einer Messe und einer Konferenz; gegebenenfalls kamen weitere Messfeiern, Andachten oder Einkehrtage hinzu. Manche der Provinzrundbriefe von 1950 bis 1965 geben Mitgliedszahlen an. Diese sind nicht mehr überprüfbar. Dennoch seien sie hier wiedergegeben, weil die Daten der Provinzrundbriefe meist die einzigen sind, die sich von diesen Bruderschaften aus den besagten Jahren erhalten haben:

Marianische Männerkongregation: 1950: 1.363 Sodalen; 1951: 1.428; 1952: 1.520; 1954: 1.560; 1956: 1.144; 1957: 1.332; 1958: 1.158; 1959: 1.222; 1962: ca. 1.300; 1964: 2.394); ihr Präses betreute auch zahlreiche sogenannte Außenkonvente; zu dieser Kongregation gehörte ein großer Messbund: 1951: 4.300 Mitglieder; 1952: 4.700; 1954: 4.754; 1956: 3.275; 1957: 3.076; 1962: ca. 3.800;

Marianische Frauenkongregation: 1950: 500 Sodalinnen; 1951: 525; 1952: 520; 1954: 535; 1956: 350; 1957: 345; 1958 357; 1959: 357; 1962: ca. 250;

Gut-Tod-Bruderschaft: 1950: 388 Mitglieder; 1951: 384; 1952: 393; 1954: 410; 1956: 57; 1957: 44 (diese beiden Angaben sind wohl Tippfehler); 1958: 294; 1959: 294; 1964: 194;

Liebesbund zu Ehren des Wunderbarlichen Gutes: 1950: 1.967 Mitglieder; 1951: 2.436; 1952: 2.458; 1954: 2.510; 1956: 2.400; 1957: 1.836; 1958: 2.817; 1959: 2.817; 1962: ca. 2.908);

Namen-Jesu-Bruderschaft: 1950: 104 Mitglieder; 1951: 104; 1952: 133; 1954: 133; 1956: 136; 1957: 128; 1958: 211; 1959: 229; 1962: ca. 220;

St. Thomas-Gürtelbruderschaft: 1950: 58 Mitglieder; 1951: 58; 1952: 71; 1954: 71; 1956: 74; 1957: 70; 1958: 117; 1959: 135 (diese Bruderschaft wird ab 1960 nicht mehr erwähnt);

Rosenkranzbruderschaft: 1950: 1.278 Mitglieder; 1951: 1.278; 1952: 1.458; 1954: 1.510; 1956: 1.714; 1957: 1.745; 1958: 1.850; 1959: 2.096; 1962: ca. 2.100;

Dominikanischer Dritter Orden: 1950: 60 Mitglieder; 1951: 63; 1952: 63; 1954: 65; 1956: 115; 1957: 118; 1958: 58; 1959: 58; 1962: 55; 1964: 64.

Dazu kamen ab 1958 noch der sogenannte Freundeskreis von Heilig Kreuz und ein St.-Albertuskreis, jeweils ebenfalls mit monatlich stattfindenden Vorträgen, Konzerten oder anderen Bildungsveranstaltungen. Als Kirchenrektoren von Heilig Kreuz wirkten die Dominikaner Pankratius Koch (1932–1936), Suso Geiselhart (1936–1939, Ulrich Kaiser (1939–1946), wieder Suso Geiselhart (1946–1950), Thomas Aquinas Dillis (1950–1960), Gregor Ruf (1960–1966), Hermann Weber (1966–1982), Raphael Börger (1983–2004), Dominikus Jakob (2005–2010) und seit 2010 Thomas Schuster.

Auch außerhalb der Mauern von Heilig Kreuz fand Sakramentenpastoral durch Dominikaner statt. Ab 1952 zelebrierten die Patres täglich eine Messe, sonntags mit Ansprache, in der Klinik der Borromäerinnen in Haunstetten. Dazu kam ab 1960 auch eine tägliche Messe im Wöchnerinnenheim in Göggingen. Der Konvent stellte für verschiedene Schwesterngemeinschaften ab 1950 drei Posten als ordentliche und sieben bis zehn als außerordentliche Beichtväter; ab 1959 waren es fünf oder sechs ordentliche und ebenso viele außerordentliche Posten. Neben den wöchentlichen Beichten waren auch hier mindestens monatliche Konferenzen anzubieten. In den Zusammenhang der Sakramentenseelsorge gehört auch die Gefängnisseelsorge, die der Konvent schon 1939 übernommen hatte[336] – ursprünglich im „Fronfeste" genannten Landesgerichtsgefängnis in der Karmelitergasse und in dessen Nebenstelle „Am Katzenstadel", An der blauen Kappe. Letztere wurde beim Luftangriff 1944 ausgebombt; nach Kriegsende wurde im Arresttrakt der Prinz-Karl-Kaserne eine Jugendstrafanstalt errichtet. Beide Gefängnisse waren laut Provinzrundbriefen durchschnittlich mit 200–300 Insassen katholischen Bekenntnisses belegt. Deren Betreuung bestand an Sonn- und Feiertagen jeweils abwechselnd mit einem protestantischen Gottesdienst aus einer Messe mit Ansprache, sowie Beicht- und Aussprachegelegenheit. Ab 1957 wurde eine regelmäßig alle Sonntage stattfindende Messe daraus. Als Gefängnisseelsorger fungierten laut der Pro-

336 Siehe dazu ausführlich: Hoyer: *Heilig Kreuz*, S. 681–685.

vinzkataloge: Dalmatius Hruschka (1939–1944), Winfried Strunk (1944–1946), Sebald Brückner (1946–1950), Suso Geiselhart (1950–1959), Barnabas Birx (1959–1964), Hermann Weber (1964–1978) und Raphael Börger (1978–2003).

Ein Augsburger Pater, Egino Holzhauser, war ab 1950 der hauptamtliche Katechet des Konvents. Er unterrichtete zunächst 19 Wochenstunden Religionsunterricht an der Berufsschule für Mädchen und sieben bis neun Klassen an der städtischen Gewerbeschule, um sich ab 1956 ganz der Mädchenberufsschule zu widmen, zuerst mit 30, ab 1960 mit durchschnittlich 24 Wochenstunden.

Schon vor dem Krieg hatten die Augsburger Dominikaner Volksmissionen, Exerzitienkurse u. ä. angeboten. So geben die Provinzrundbriefe zwischen 1950 und 1954 fünf bis zehn jährliche Volksmissionen an, zwischen 1956 und 1959 drei. 1960 waren in Zusammenarbeit mit dem ganzen süddeutschen Provinzteil 16, 1961 acht, 1962 neun, 1963 14 und danach sechs bis acht Gebietsmissionen, alle in Kooperation mit der Gebietsmission der Diözese. Religiöse Wochen wurden 1950 bis 1965 durchschnittlich acht pro Jahr abgehalten. Das Exerzitienangebot des Konvents schwankte in dieser Zeit stark: Die Spitzenjahre waren 1950 mit 49 Kursen (davon 31 für Ordensschwestern), 1951 mit 30 (davon 23 für Ordensschwestern) und 1962 mit 21 Kursen (unspezifiziert). Sonst waren es durchschnittlich zwischen elf und 19. 1965 bot der Konvent fünf Kurse für Priester, vier für Ordensschwestern, vier für Laien und einen für Ordensbrüder an. Auch die Zahl der jährlich angebotenen Einkehrtage – die für die Bruderschaften nicht eingeschlossen – schwankte: 1963 waren es 17, 1962 und 1965 23; sonst bewegten sie sich zwischen sechs und 14.

Die Zahl der Pfarr- und Predigtaushilfen war immer sehr groß, was mit der Bautätigkeit der Augsburger Dominikaner an ihrer Kirche und dem Erbetteln von Baumaterial und sonstiger Unterstützung zu tun hatte. Mit dem Anwachsen des Konvents nach 1958 nahmen die Aushilfen noch zu. So wurden 1950 bis 1965 durchschnittlich fünf bis zehn Fasten- und Maipredigtzyklen in Pfarrkirchen gehalten. Dazu kamen an Aushilfen mit Predigt und Beichtstuhl: 1935: 37, 1951: 29, 1952: 35, 1954: 27, 1956: 55, 1959: 67, 1960: 84, 1961: 169, 1962: 141, 1963: 135 und 1965: 77. Wichtig waren diese Leistungen auch deshalb, um das noch immer vergleichsweise neue Dominikanerkloster in der Stadt und im Umland bekannt zu machen – was sich dann wieder in erhöhtem Mess- und Beichtbesuch an Heilig Kreuz ausdrückte.

Abb. 54: Autobahnkirche Maria – Schutz der Reisenden an der Bundesautobahn 8 bei Adelsried (Archiv des Augsburger Dominikanerkonvents, Fotosammlung).

Das Kloster an Heilig Kreuz diente auch als Vortragszentrum, Treffpunkt für monatliche Priesterkonferenzen, die Zusammenkünfte einer Sühnegemeinschaft, des Heliandbundes und dominikanischer und anderer Seminare und Tagungen. Einzelne Patres übernahmen weitere Ämter oder Posten, so war z. B. P. Eckehart Mayer ab 1962 in der Leitung des Sozialseminars der Diözese Augsburg tätig.

Mit der Übernahme der Autobahnkapelle „Maria – Schutz der Reisenden“ im Oktober 1958 bekam der Dominikanerkonvent ein ganz neues Seelsorgeprojekt übertragen. Um in der Art eines traditionellen Wegkreuzes oder Bildstockes die Kraftfahrer auf der Bundesautobahn 8 an Gott zu erinnern, hatte das Augsburger Ehepaar Georg und Marie Luise Haindl an der Strecke zwischen Augsburg und Ulm, konkret an der Ausfahrt Adelsried, eine große Kapelle gestiftet, die am 12. Oktober 1958 vom Augsburger Diözesanbischof Josef Freundorfer eingeweiht worden war. Aber bereits vor der Kirchweihe hatten die Gläubigen gezeigt, dass sie mehr wollten als nur ein Denkmal, das sie beim Vorbeifahren an Gott erinnerte: Sie wollten einen Ort, an dem sie ihre Fahrt zum Gebet und zur stillen Einkehr unterbrechen konnten. Amtskirchlicherseits sah man in der Kapelle zunächst nur eine Möglichkeit, den Kraftfahrern die Gelegenheit zur Erledigung ihrer Sonntagspflicht, also zum Messbesuch zu geben. Da sich der Pfarrer des Ortes Adelsried, Benedikt Sternegger, der die Stiftung und den Bau der Kapelle sehr unterstützt hatte, aufgrund seiner beruflichen Verpflichtungen nicht in der Lage sah, auch noch dieses neue Gotteshaus zu betreuen, fragte die Diözese im Augsburger Dominikanerkonvent an. Hier war gerade P. Gregor Ruf zurückgekehrt, nachdem er im Juli desselben Jahres seine Studien in Rom abgeschlossen hatte. Ruf sah in

Abb. 55: Autobahnkirche Maria – Schutz der Reisenden: Altar mit Kruzifix (Archiv des Augsburger Dominikanerkonvents, Fotosammlung).

der Autobahnkapelle nicht nur eine Kirche für Sonntagsgottesdienste – immerhin drei an der Zahl, um 8, 10 und 18 Uhr – sondern er nahm auch die neuen Seelsorgsperspektiven wahr, die sich dort eröffnet hatten: Beichten, Aussprachen und Begegnungen mit allen Arten von Menschen, die auf der Autobahn reisten, Katholiken, Mitgliedern anderer Konfessionen oder Religionen und selbst Atheisten, denen dieses Gotteshaus vierundzwanzig

Stunden am Tag, sieben Tage die Woche offen stand. Mit der finanziellen Hilfe der Familie Haindl sorgte Ruf dafür, dass der Parkplatz an der Kapelle erweitert und für andere Notwendigkeiten gesorgt wurde. Dieses Angebot wurden im Laufe der Jahre sehr dankbar angenommen. Seit 1968 konnte sich die Autobahnkapelle aus den Erträgen ihres Opferstocks und aus Spenden selbst tragen. Der große Erfolg dieses neuen Adelsrieder Projekts regte schon bald zur Nachahmung an. 1959 wurde in Exter in Westfalen an der A 2 die dortige evangelische Gemeindekirche zur Autobahnkirche umgewidmet und als solche tagsüber von 8 bis 20 Uhr geöffnet. Heute, 2013, gibt es insgesamt 40 katholische, evangelische oder ökumenische Autobahnkirchen in Deutschland.[337] Nachfolger Rufs an der Kirche bei Adelsried wurden Dietmar Schon (1998–2006) und Wolfram Hoyer (seit 2007).

In St. Wolfgang in Augsburg-Spickel waren erst 1955 mit der Reparatur der hölzernen Kirchendecke alle Kriegsschäden endgültig beseitigt. Mit dem 1. November 1950 wurde die bisherige Expositur zur Stadtpfarrei erhoben; 1955 wurde von der Diözese an St. Wolfgang eine Kaplansstelle formal eingerichtet, die ebenfalls mit einem Dominikaner besetzt wurde. Die Angaben der Provinzrundbriefe über die Katholikenzahl zwischen 1950 und 1965 verzeichnen sehr deutliche Sprünge zwischen manchen Jahren: 1950: ca. 2.600, 1951 und 1952: 1.993, 1954: 2.300, 1956: 2.209, 1957: 2.260, 1959: 3.240, 1960: 3.600, 1964: 2.300 und 1965: 1.600. Anzunehmen ist, dass die Angabe für 1950 auf einer sehr groben Schätzung beruht. Der Zuwachs bis 1960 hatte mit dem Wohnungsausbau im an den Spickel angrenzenden und zur Expositur bzw. zur Pfarrei von St. Wolfgang gehörenden Augsburger Stadtteil Herrenbachviertel zu tun. Dort wurde 1961 eine neue Pfarrei unter dem Patrozinium von Don Bosco und unter der Leitung der Salesianer errichtet, unter Beschneidung des Pfarrgebietes und damit der Katholikenzahl von St. Wolfgang. Bedingt durch die Abwanderung junger Ehepaare ging die Zahl der St. Wolfganger Pfarrangehörigen bis 1965 noch weiter zurück.

1951 wurden an der Pfarrkirche an Sonn- und Feiertagen zwei Messen mit Predigt angeboten; werktags waren es ein bis zwei, je nach An- bzw. Abwesenheit eines der beiden an St. Wolfgang wohnenden Ordenspriester. Mit der Einrichtung der Kaplansstelle 1955 wurde das Gottesdienstangebot angehoben: Ab 1956 waren es werktags zwei und sonn- und feiertags drei

---

337 Zur Geschichte der Autobahnkirche Adelsried und der dortigen Seelsorge siehe: Hoyer: *Autobahnkirche*, S. 8–11.

Abb. 56: Pfarrkirche St. Wolfgang in Augsburg-Spickel; im Vordergrund das Pfarrhaus (Foto: Florian Lettl, Augsburg).

Messen, letztere drei mit Ansprache. Alle diese Gottesdienste waren anscheinend überdurchschnittlich gut besucht. Die Kommunionzahlen lagen laut der Provinzrundbriefe 1950 bei 15.000, 1951: 15.200, 1952: 15.100, 1954: 13.500, 1956: 20.000, 1957 sogar bei 20–22.000, 1959: 17.000, 1960: 18.400 und 1965 bei 14.804.

Neben den in der Pfarrarbeit üblichen Gruppenstunden für die Pfarrjugend (jeweils werktags) und dem Religionsunterricht, den der Pfarrer und später auch der Kaplan zu halten hatte (an der Volksschule durchschnittlich sechs bis acht Wochenstunden des Pfarrers, zwischen 1956 und 1960 zwischen sechs bis 15 Wochenstunden des Kaplans an einer kaufmännischen Berufsschule) leistete die kleine Dominikanergemeinschaft auch ordensspezifische Seelsorge, so z. B. anfangs der 1950er Jahre Exerzitienkurse (1951: sechs für Ordensleute, vier für Laien; 1952: 16 für Ordensleute, drei für Laien und 1954: 21 meist für Ordensschwestern). Dieses Engagement verschob sich danach mehr in Richtung von Einkehrtagen,

Abb. 57: Pfarrkirche St. Wolfgang in Augsburg-Spickel: Blick in den Altarraum (Foto: Florian Lettl, Augsburg).

Aushilfen durch Fastenpredigtzyklen und v a eine reiche Vortragstätigkeit für Ordensleute, Jugendliche, kaufmännische Angestellte oder auch die Meistervereinigung der M. A.N.

Dominikanische Expositi bzw. Pfarrvikare waren an St. Wolfgang: Mathias Bigge (1931–1942), Richard Kolter (1942–1946), Burkhard Zimmermann (1946–1963), Matthäus Weiß (1963–1964), Sturmius Nowowiejski (1964–1971), Eckehart Mayer (1972–2000) und Dominkus Jakob (2000–2004).[338]

Soweit die Berichte über die Tätigkeiten der Priester des Augsburger Konvents. Was die Laienbrüder angeht, so nennen die Provinzrundbriefe gewöhnlich nur sehr allgemein deren treue Mitarbeit. Selbst die Provinzkataloge melden erst ab 1981 Informationen über deren Offizien oder Ämter.

338 Diese Angaben aus Groll: Mutterpfarrei, S. 1328–1352; dort auch die Aufzählung der anderen an St. Wolfgang lebenden Dominikaner und Berichte über die Geschichte der Pfarrei.

Aus diesem Rahmen fällt nur eine einzige Notiz, die einen Blick auf die interne Arbeitssituation in einem Dominikanerkloster der Provinz bietet – konkret über den Konvent an Heilig Kreuz im Jahre 1964: „Durchschnittsalter der *fratres cooperatores* [sc. der Laienbrüder]: 60 Jahre. Angestellt sind vier weibliche Kräfte, die Küche, Wäscherei und bestimmte Hausputzarbeiten versorgen; halbtags hilft ein Rentner an der Pforte aus. ... Außer den gewöhnlichen Aufgaben in Kirche und Konvent leisteten die ehrwürdigen Brüder als Provinzschneider- und Schreinermeister zusätzliche Arbeiten. Die Gärtnereiarbeit in zwei Quadren [sc. Innenhöfen] und im großen Kreuzhof wurde ebenfalls von unseren Brüdern versorgt. Der Schriftenstand in unserer Kirche ist einer der besten der Augsburger Kirchen."[339]

München: Pfarreien, Bildung und eine Stiftskirche

Die Personalstand des Münchner Konvents war starken Schwankungen unterworfen, bedingt durch den Wandel, den die Gemeinschaft gerade in den Jahren 1950 bis 1965 durchmachte: Während der Zeit, in der er als Noviziatskloster diente, 1946 bis 1954, bestand der Konvent von St. Albert in München-Freimann aus durchschnittlich zwanzig Mitgliedern – acht bis zehn Priestern, vier bis sechs Laienbrüdern und einer Anzahl von Kleriker- und Laienbrüdernovizen. Einer der Patres lebte allerdings meist als Seelsorger bei den Dominikanerinnen in Bad Wörishofen. Mit der Übernahme der Stiftskirche St. Kajetan nahm die Zahl der Priester des Konvents sogar zu, auf durchschnittlich 13; Laienbrüder waren es durchschnittlich drei. Aber dieser Anstieg bezog sich nur auf die rechtliche Zugehörigkeit in den Konvent: Ein Pater, Josef Rottenecker, lebte seit 1958 ständig *extra conventum*, als Religionslehrer bei den Dominikanerinnen in Schlehdorf, später in derselben Funktion in Villingen im Schwarzwald. Münchner Patres betreuten auch weiterhin die Dominikanerinnen in Bad Wörishofen. Dazu übernahmen sie die Posten eines Spirituals bei den Dominikanerinnen in Lohhof bei Mindelheim und anderen Schwesterngemeinschaften; 1959/60 war einer von ihnen Präfekt im Knabenseminar in Kaufbeuren. Insgesamt arbeiteten also zwei bis drei dieser 13 Patres nicht in München. Zudem war die Konventsgemeinschaft ab 1954 auf zwei Orte verteilt, denn an St. Kajetan lebten und arbeiteten 1954 bis 1960 vier Priester und meist zwei Laienbrüder. In Freimann blieben also effektiv nur durchschnittlich sechs Pries-

339 PA, Provinzrundbrief vom 12.3.1965, S. 2 und S. 3.

ter für die Seelsorge zurück. Diese Zahl behielt St. Albert auch nach der Reduktion auf den Status einer *domus formata* 1960; dazu kam noch ein Laienbruder.[340]

In Freimann lag einer der beiden Arbeitsschwerpunkte der Dominikaner auf der Betreuung der Pfarrei St. Albert. Zu ihr gehörten Anfang der 1950er Jahre etwa 5.000 Katholiken, wobei diese Zahl bis 1959 auf ungefähr 6.700 anwuchs.[341] Nach dem Krieg hatte die amerikanische Militärverwaltung ein Durchgangslager in der ehemaligen Funkkaserne und das Lager Neu-Freimann für Flüchtlinge und Heimatvertriebene eingerichtet, das 1949 geschlossen wurde. Die Flüchtlinge wurden an der Ingolstädter Straße angesiedelt. Ab 1948 entstand nördlich der Heidemannstraße auf einem ehemaligen Truppenübungsplatz eine weitere neue Siedlung für Heimatvertriebene. Pfarrlich gehörten diese ebenfalls zu St. Albert und wurden von den Dominikanern betreut. Da die katholische Bevölkerung der neuen Siedlungen aber stark anwuchs – 1950 lebten dort etwa 700 Katholiken, 1952 und 1954 waren es bereits etwa 3.000, nach 1957 pendelte sich die Zahl auf etwa 2.500 ein –, reichten die Kapazitäten an der Albertuskirche nicht mehr aus. Für dieses neue Siedlungsgebiet wurde innerhalb der Pfarrei eine Notkirche errichtet, die am 16. Dezember 1951 der hl. Katharina von Siena geweiht wurde. Dazu kam als dritte Kirche noch die Pfarrfiliale von Eching-Dietersheim mit etwa 450 Katholiken, die von 1950 bis 1957 ebenfalls von den Dominikanern betreut wurde. Damit waren drei Patres des Konvents (ein Pfarrvikar und zwei Kapläne) vollauf mit der Pfarrseelsorge beschäftigt.

In der Albertuskirche gab es 1950 täglich vier fixe Messen, an Sonn- und Feiertagen waren es sieben Messen, bei denen in sechs gepredigt wurde. Nach Einweihung der Katharinenkirche verteilte sich das Messangebot der Pfarrei auf vier Messen sonntags und zwei Messen in der Woche an

340 Laut der Provinzkataloge 1949–1965 gehörten zu München / St. Albert 1949: neun Priester (P.), sechs Laienbrüder (L.), ein Kleriker, fünf Klerikernovizen (KN.), zwei Laienbrüdernovizen (LN.); 1951: 11 P., 4 L., 1 Kleriker, 5 KN., 2 LN.; 1952: 8 P., 4 L., 6 KN., 2 LN.; 1953: 8 P., 4 L., 2 KN., 2 LN.; 1955: 10 P., 2 L.; 1956: 11 P., 2 L.; 1957: 11 P., 4 L.; 1958: 13 P., 3 L.; 1959: 13 P., 3 L.; 1960: 15 P., 3 L.; 1961 und 1962: 6 P., 1 L.; 1964 und 1965: 7 P., 1 L. An St. Kajetan wohnten 1954–1956 4 P., 1 L. und 1957–1960 4 P., 2 L.

341 Laut den Provinzrundbriefe waren es 1950: 6.000, 1951: ca. 8.000; 1952 und 1954: ca. 5.000; 1956: ca. 6.500 und 1957–1959: ca. 6.700; danach fehlen Angaben zur Pfarrgröße. Die Gründe für das Wachstum auf 8.000 und der schlagartige Abfall auf 5.000 1952 sind unklar, aber vielleicht von der Insassenzahl von Flüchtlingslagern gewonnen.

St. Albert und eine Sonntagsmesse mit Predigt plus eine Wochentagsmesse an St. Katharina. Dazu kam an St. Albert allabendlich eine Segensandacht mit Rosenkranzgebet. Dieses liturgische Angebot wurde auch wahrgenommen: Die Provinzrundbriefe melden für die gesamte Pfarrei 1950 ca. 42.000 Kommunionen, 1951 ca. 28.000, 1952 und 1954 etwa 31.000 und nach 1956 26.000. Die Zahl der Osterbeichten geben sie 1952 bis 1957 mit zwischen 2.030 und 2.800 an. Die Pfarrei hatte zwischen sechs und 14 Jugend- und Pfarrgruppen, davon drei an St. Katharina. Die Pfarrgeistlichkeit hatte 1952 bis 1963 zwischen 26 und 38 Wochenstunden Religionsunterricht an der Volksschule zu geben; durchschnittlich waren es 28 Wochenstunden. Pfarrer bzw. Pfarrvikare an St. Albert waren: Burkhard Zimmermann (1934–1946), Alfred Willebrandt (1946–1949), Matthäus Weiß (1949–1951), Rainer Kessler (1951–1956), Berthold Kaiser (1956–1963), Oderich Johannes Edelbauer (1963–1978) und Clemens Wehrle (1978–1984). Nach Wehrle übernahm der Kurat von St. Katharina, Adalbert von Papius von 1984 bis 1990 auch die Leitung der Pfarrei St. Albert; danach ging diese in andere Hände über.

Die Dominikanerpfarrer sorgten auch dafür, dass die ganz großen kirchlichen Ereignisse dieser Zeit ihren Eindruck in St. Albert hinterließen. So stand die Arbeit des Konvents 1960 und 1961 ganz im Zeichen des Eucharistischen Weltkongresses. Dafür wurde nicht nur jeder Donnerstag als Tag der hl. Eucharistie begangen, mit eucharistischer Anbetung nach der zweiten Vormittagsmesse bis zur Rosenkranzandacht abends, mit Aussetzung des Ziboriums und verschiedenen anderen liturgischen Akzenten, sondern auch einer deutlich aufwändigeren Ausbildung der Erstkommunionkinder. 1962 wurde die Pfarrkirche St. Albert einer Innenrenovierung unterzogen. P. Lukas Saffraniak gestaltete ein Mosaik für die neugeschaffene Taufkapelle. Bei dieser Gelegenheit erhielt auch St. Katharina ein neues Altarbild und Fensterbilder von ihm.[342] Zur Vertiefung und Umsetzung der Anregungen des zweiten vatikanischen Konzils wurde 1966 der Marienaltar in St. Albert zu einem Sakramentsaltar umgebaut. Auf den Stufen des Presbyteriums wurde ein provisorischer Zelebrationsaltar errichtet. Dem Hochaltar verblieb die Funktion eines Expositionsthrones.

Die anderen Priester des Konvents leisteten in der Pfarrei Mitarbeit auf der Kanzel und im Beichtstuhl. Deren Hauptaugenmerk lag aber auf einer ausgebreiteten Bildungspastoral, die den zweiten Schwerpunkt der

342 Dazu: PA, Provinzrundbrief vom 17.3.1962, S. 4.

Arbeit der Dominikaner an St. Albert bis zur Übernahme von St. Kajetan ausmachte. Konkret bestand dieser aus regelmäßigen Konferenzen für Jugendliche, den Dritten Orden, theologischen Vorträgen für die Schulung und religiöse Fortbildung von Laien und die Betreuung von Akademikern und des Quickborn. Die Provinzrundbriefe geben sehr detaillierte summarische Jahresberichte dazu, aber um das Ausmaß dieser Arbeit zu illustrieren, muss hier der Hinweis genügen, dass ein Pater allein 1957 300 Vorträge und Predigten meldete. In Zusammenarbeit mit den Klöstern in Augsburg und Freiburg wurden 1950 bis 1952 auch Volksmissionen unternommen (1950: zwei; 1951: fünf und sechs Nachmissionen; 1954: vier und drei Nachmissionen), Exerzitienkurse angeboten[343] und Fasten- und Maipredigtzyklen auswärts gepredigt.[344] Dazu kamen zahlreiche religiöse Wochen, Predigttriduen, Einkehrtage, Rundfunkvorträge u. ä. Diese Aktivitäten nahmen mit der Übernahme von St. Kajetan ab bzw. verlagerten sich dorthin. Anders als die anderen großen Konvente der Provinz stellten die Münchner Dominikaner nur sehr wenige Posten als ständige Beichtväter bei Schwestern: Ab 1960 nahm einer die Aufgabe eines ordentlichen und ein weiterer die eines außerordentlichen Beichtvaters wahr.

Mit der Erhebung der Niederlassung an St. Kajetan 1960 zur *domus formata* und 1961 zum Konvent verschob sich das Zentrum der dominikanischen Aktivitäten in München in die Innenstadt. Bis 1960 wohnten an St. Kajetan meist vier Priester und zwei Laienbrüder, danach waren es zwischen zehn und zwölf Priester und zwei Laienbrüder.[345] Meist zwei der Priester wohnten als Schwesternseelsorger oder Religionslehrer im Lohhof bei Mindelheim, in Schlehdorf oder in Bad Wörishofen. Eine Besonderheit der Gemeinschaft an St. Kajetan war auch die Tatsache, dass vergleichsweise viele der dort assignierten Patres – manchmal bis zur Hälfte – aus anderen Ordensprovinzen stammte und an der Münchner Universität studierten.

---

343 1950: 24 Kurse für Ordensschwestern, je vier für Priester und für Laien; 1951: 22 Kurse, hauptsächlich für Ordensleute; 1952: neun für Ordensschwestern und vier für Ordensmänner; 1954: vier für Ordensmänner und zwei für Kleriker; 1956 neun für Schwestern, je einen für Kleriker und für Laien; 1957: sieben für Schwestern, je einen für Ordensleute und für Laien; 1958: insgesamt neun Kurse und 1959: zwei für Priester.

344 1950 waren es vier Fasten- (F.) und fünf Marienpredigtzyklen (M.), 1951: drei F. und zwei M.; 1952: drei F.; 1954: acht F., ein M.; 1956: zehn F., neun M.; 1957: neun F., drei M.; 1958: zehn F., drei M.; 1959: sechs F., sieben M. und 1963: zwei F.

345 Laut Provinzkatalogen waren es summarisch 1961: zwölf Priester (P.), zwei Laienbrüder (L.); 1962 10 P., 2 L.; 1964 11 P., 2 L. und 1965 12 P., 2 L.

Abb. 58: Die ehemalige Theatiner- und Stiftskirche St. Kajetan in München (aufgenommen am 20.9.2009; PA, Fotosammlung).

Die Zahl der in St. Kajetan angebotenen Messen stieg 1957 auf sechs sonn- und feiertags, wobei in vier davon gepredigt wurde (eine war als Abendmesse mit Predigt gestaltet). Werktags waren es vier Messen täglich. Dazu kam der Tagesbeichtstuhl von morgens 6.30 bis 17.30 Uhr, unterbrochen lediglich durch zwei Stunden Mittagspause. Leider sprechen die Provinzrundbriefe nicht über die Kommunionzahlen; erwähnt wird nur einmal, dass die Zahl der Gottesdienstbesucher an den Zählsonntagen 1962 zwischen 1.800 und 2.200 lag. Auch für die Zahl der Beichten haben wir nur die Angaben, dass sie 1956 bei circa 17.500 und 1957 bei 22.000 lag.

Die Betreuung des Dritten Ordens in München war ebenfalls von Freimann nach St. Kajetan gewandert. Die Provinzrundbriefe melden für die Jahre 1956 bis 1960, dass sich die Münchner Ortsgruppe am dritten Sonntag jeden Monates dort für eine Konferenz traf. Außerdem erhielten die in Süddeutschland wohnenden Mitglieder des Dritten Ordens viermal im Jahr einen Rundbrief. Weiter betreuten die Patres an St. Kajetan zwei Gruppen ehemaliger Handelsschülerinnen, eine Gruppe von einer Dolmetscherschule und eine Gruppe des Neudeutschland-Jugendbundes; 1960

Abb. 59: Die ehemalige Theatiner- und Stiftskirche St. Kajetan in München: Blick zum Hocha tar (aufgenommen am 20.9.2009; PA, Fotosammlung).

Abb. 60: Das Dominikanerkloster an St. Kajetan in München hinter der Apsis der Kirche: Blick auf das ehemalige Mesnerhaus und auf das rechts anschließende Gebäude des Bayerischen Kultusministeriums (aufgenommen am 20.9.2009; PA, Fotosammlung).

kam eine Heliand-Gruppe hinzu. Mit allen diesen Gruppen verbunden waren ebenfalls monatliche Messen und Konferenzen.

Der Konvent von St. Kajetan stellte mit P. Theophil Tschipke auch den Domprediger. Tschipke wurde in diesem Amt 1966 von P. Pirmin Mattes abgelöst. Zu den Pflichten dieses Amtes gehörte neben der Sonn- und Feiertagspredigt im Liebfrauendom auch der Religionsunterricht im Ausmaß von acht Wochenstunden an einer privaten Handelsschule; der Kirchenrektor von St. Kajetan hatte ebenfalls sechs Wochenstunden Religionsunterricht zu leisten.

Auch von St. Kajetan aus versuchten die Brüder, in der Bildungsseelsorge mitzuwirken, was ihnen in ihren ersten Jahren dort auch gelang.[346]

346 So melden die Provinzrundbriefe für 1963: Fastenpredigten in München-Solln, in St. Georg und im Dom zu Eichstätt, Maipredigten in St. Bonifaz, Mitarbeit in zwei Volksmissionen, zwei Triduen, acht Einkehrtage, zwei Exerzitienkurse, 25 Einzelpredigten und Ansprachen bei verschiedenen Anlässen, zehn Vorträge zur religiösen Weiterbildung von Katechetinnen, 38 Schwesternvorträge, 25 Referate, acht Vorträge für den Freundeskreis, sechs Rundfunkansprachen; für 1964: Mitarbeit an einer Volksmission, drei Fasten- und drei Maipredigtzyklen, verschiedene Einzelpredigten, einen Exerzitienkurs, eine Rund-

Dieses Engagement in freier Bildungstätigkeit mußte jedoch im Laufe weniger Jahre den wachsenden Verpflichtungen in der Sakramentenpastoral an St. Kajetan weichen. Erster dominikanischer Kirchenrektor von St. Kajetan war Magnus Beck (1954–1990); ihm folgten Klaus Obermeier (1990–2012) und Johannes Weise (seit 2012).

Freiburg: Aushilfen, Studenten, Gesprächskreise für Laien

Das Kloster St. Albert in Freiburg im Breisgau zählte von 1949 bis 1965 durchschnittlich elf Mitglieder (zwischen sechs und zehn Priester und zwei bis vier Laienbrüder).[347] Aber diese summarischen Zahlen geben die Situation der Gemeinschaft zu Füßen des Schlossbergs nicht korrekt wieder: Schon 1942 hatten im Kloster in Freiburg im Breisgau keine Priorwahlen mehr stattfinden können, weil durch die Vertreibung der Schweizer Mitbrüder nicht mehr genügend voll stimmberechtigte Priester vorhanden waren. Dadurch verlor das Kloster seinen Stand als formalrechtlicher Konvent und wurde zur *domus formata* zurückgestuft – in der während des Krieges und in den Nachkriegsjahren hauptsächlich ältere Brüder wohnten.[348] Der personelle Wiederaufbau des Hauses hatte für Provinzial Vetter zwar Priorität, war aber schwierig, da der Provinz zunächst kaum jüngere Priester zur Verfügung standen und im Haus selbst wegen des Juvenats Wohnräume mangelten. So konnte Vetter erst Mitte der 1950er Jahre nach und nach eine kleine Gruppe jüngerer Patres dorthin assignieren. Den meisten von diesen fehlte aber zunächst das von den Ordenssatzungen geforderte Stimmrecht.[349] Erst 1960 waren alle Bedingungen soweit erfüllt, dass die Freiburger Brüder wieder einen eigenen Prior wählen durften, wo-

funkansprache, 46 Schwesternvorträge, acht Vorträge religiöser und kultureller Art und für 1965: ein Triduum, zehn Vorträge religiöser und kultureller Art, 42 Schwesternvorträge und zwei Rundfunkvorträge.

347 Laut Provinzkatalogen zählte Freiburg 1949 sechs Priester (P.), vier Laienbrüder (L.) und einen Kleriker; 1951: 7 P., 4 L.; 1952: 6 P., 3 L.; 1953: 7 P., 4 L., 1 Kleriker; 1955: 7 P., 4 L.; 1956: 7 P., 3 L.; 1957: 8 P., 3 L.; 1958: 7 P., 3 L.; 1959: 8 P., 4 L.; 1960: 9 P., 3 L.; 1961: 8 P., 3 L.; 1962: 8 P., 3 L.; 1964: 10 P., 2 L. und 1965: 10 P., 2 L.

348 Aufgrund dieser Situation war die Zahl der *extra conventum* lebenden Klosterangehörigen gering: Konkret handelte es sich dabei um den von 1953 bis zu seinem Tod 1960 in Savognin in der Schweiz wohnenden P. Gallus Häfele und ab 1964 um einen älteren Pater in Karlsruhe und einen Pater im Ruhestand in Neusatzeck.

349 Voll stimmberechtigt waren nämlich nur Ordenspriester mit einem Professalter von neun Jahren, gezählt seit der einfachen Profess (*Constitutiones 1932*, S. 111, Nr. 305 § 1 3°).

Abb. 61: Das Dominikanerkloster St. Albert in Freiburg im Breisgau (PA, Fotosammlung).

mit die Konventsrechte für St. Albert wieder auflebten. Was sich formalrechtlich einerseits als Hindernis darstellte, wirkte sich andererseits aber pastoral als Chance aus: Die jüngeren Patres entwickelten neue seelsorgliche Perspektiven, durch die sie die eher traditionellen Aktivitäten der älteren Brüder ersetzten.

Obzwar die Klosterkapelle nur klein war, boten die Dominikaner 1950 dort täglich drei Messen an. Sonntags wurde in einer der Messen gepredigt; außerdem fand alle 14 Tage eine Abendpredigt statt. Dazu kamen täglich ein Abendrosenkranz mit Segen, sowie im Advent, in der Fastenzeit und in den Marienmonaten Mai und Oktober sonntags weitere Abendpredigten. 1956 wurde das Gottesdienstangebot auf zwei Messen unter der Woche reduziert; sonn- und feiertags gab es weiterhin drei Messen um 6.30, 7.30 und 8.30 Uhr, bei denen zunächst in zwei, ab 1957 in allen dreien gepredigt wurde. Ab 1961 waren es sonntags sogar vier Messen, davon eine am Abend, jede mit Predigt. Der Besuch dieser Gottesdienste war sehr gut, was sich in den Kommunikantenzahlen niederschlug: 1950 waren es 24.000, 1951: ca. 20.000; 1952: 22.000; 1954: etwa 20.000; 1956: 18.000;

1957: 18.000; 1959: 20.000; 1960: ca. 22.000; 1961: 22.800 und 1962: 23.000. Auch zur Beichte wurde das Freiburger Dominikanerkloster gut in Anspruch genommen. Leider machen die Provinzrundbriefe hierzu keine sinnvoll auszuwertenden Zahlenangaben, jedoch deutet die dokumentierte reichlich bemessene Beichtbereitschaft der Patres im Kapellenbeichtstuhl während der Gottesdienste und im Hausbeichtstuhl zwischen 6 und 12 und zwischen 14 bis 20.30 Uhr darauf hin.

Deutlich umfangreicher waren die Beicht-, Mess- und Predigtaushilfen, die die Patres auswärts in Freiburg und im Umland hielten – eine Tätigkeit, die sie schon während des Krieges aufgenommen hatten. Die Provinzrundbriefe geben für die erste Hälfte der 1950er Jahre jährlich etwa 60 derartige Aushilfen an. Von 1956 bis 1962 lagen sie jährlich zwischen 120 und 160, nach 1963 gingen sie auf etwa 50 jährlich zurück. Dazu kamen immer auswärts gepredigte Fasten- und Maizyklen, Missionssonntage und Ferienvertretungen in Pfarreien. Über die Jahre verschob sich der Akzent der auswärtigen Tätigkeit hin zu Einzelpredigten, Vorträgen und Ähnlichem.[350] Diese Verschiebung der Aktivitäten in Richtung Vortrags- und Bildungspastoral spiegelt sich auch bei den von Freiburger Dominikanern organisierten Volksmissionen, religiösen Wochen, Einkehrtagen und Exerzitien wieder, deren Zahl nach 1960 jeweils abnahm.[351]

Gebündelt wurden diese Bildungs- und Fortbildungsanstrengungen der Freiburger Patres 1958 in einem neuen Entwurf. Laut Provinzial Gierlich führten „die Mitbrüder des Hauses P. Thomas Hegglin, P. Ambrosius

350 So werden 1960 103 Einzelvorträge zusätzlich zu den obigen Aushilfen angegeben, 1961 53 Einzelpredigten und 24 Einzelvorträge, 1962 97 Einzelpredigten, 1963 zwar nur drei Einzelpredigten, dafür aber zehn Rundfunkansprachen, 32 Einführungen in die Sonntagsliturgie für Studenten sowie verschiedene andere Vorträge, 1964 124 Einzelpredigten, 32 Einführungen in die Sonntagsliturgie, 45 Einzelvorträge und vier Müttererholungskurse (mit jeweils vier Vorträgen) und 1965 vier Rundfunkansprachen, 94 Einzelpredigten, sechs Müttererholungstage und 33 Einzelvorträge.

351 Volksmissionen: 1950: 14, 1951: 18 (z. T. in Gemeinschaft mit anderen Konventen), 1952: 23 Volks- und sechs Nachmissionen, in den folgenden Jahren bis 1965 nur mehr zwei bis fünf pro Jahr; religiöse Wochen: 1950 und 1951: drei, 1952: elf, 1954: sieben, 1958: zwölf, in den folgenden Jahren bis 1965 zwei bis fünf pro Jahr; Einkehrtage: 1950: vier, 1951: 19, 1952: drei, 1954: zwei, 1956: fünf, 1957 und 1958: sechs, 1959: 22, 1960: 13, 1961: achtzehn, 1962: neun, 1963: einer, 1964: sechs und 1965: acht; Exerzitienkurse: 1950: fünfzehn, 1951: 24, 1954: 18, 1956: 15, 1957: zehn, 1958: 20, 1959 und 1960 zwölf, 1961: acht, 1962: neun, 1963: zwei, 1964: fünf und eine Woche Abendexerzitien sowie 1965: zwei.

Ruf, P. Cornelius Paulus und ein Mitbruder aus dem Strassburger Konvent, P. Reginald Dorland, […] ein besonderes apostolisches Werk durch: ‚Gesprächskreise für akademisch gebildete Laien', in Vortragsreihen, Einkehrtagen und Diskussionsabenden."[352] Die Gesprächskreise, die durch Arbeitskreise ergänzt wurden, erfreuten sich steigender Beliebtheit. 1959 leisteten die Dominikaner 91 Vorträge in Gesprächskreisen und 20 Arbeitskreissitzungen, 1960 waren es 49 Vorträge in Gesprächskreisen, 39 Arbeitskreissitzungen und 123 Diskussionsabende. Gierlich meldete für 1962 mit Stolz:

> „Die Vorträge bei den ‚Gesprächskreisen für Laien' waren auch in diesem Jahr wieder gut besucht und blieben wie bisher ein fester Bestandteil unserer apostolischen Arbeit. Die Abende werden auch von Andersgläubigen oft und gerne besucht und erfreuen sich einer immer größeren Beliebtheit. Die Besucherzahl schwankt je nach Thema zwischen 25 und 100 Teilnehmern und setzt sich aus allen Schichten zusammen. Hauptsächlich sind es aber Studenten der Universität, der pädagogischen Hochschule und des Wohlfahrtshelferseminars. Die Einzelvorträge und Vortragsreihen behandeln aktuelle Fragen unserer Zeit. […] Die Besinnungstage wollen zu einer religiösen Vertiefung mithelfen und werden gut besucht. Ein weiterer Ausbau wäre möglich, wenn wir mit anderer Arbeit nicht so überfüllt wären. Die wissenschaftlichen Arbeitskreise, an denen Universitätsprofessoren teilnehmen, dienen der Klärung von Zeitproblemen. Die Ergebnisse dieser Arbeitskreise werden von anerkannten Wissenschaftlern, auch außerhalb von Freiburg, dankbar angenommen und in ihr eigenes Forschen eingebaut. Unser Wirken unter den Akademikern und v. a. unter der akademischen Jugend erfreut sich der besonderen Wertschätzung unseres hochwürdigen Herrn Erzbischofs Dr. Hermann Schäufele und auch seines Weihbischofs Karl Gnädinger."[353]

Ab 1963 fanden jeden Donnerstagabend von 20 bis 23 Uhr Arbeitskreissitzungen statt, dazu kamen die Gesprächskreise und weitere Diskussionsabende.

Unterstützt wurde diese neue, ihrer Zeit entsprechende Seelsorgeform, die die Freiburger Brüder über Jahrzehnte anboten und erst nach 2003 langsam auslaufen ließen, durch die Tatsache, dass P. Ambrosius Ruf 1961 zum zweiten Studentenpfarrer für die Hochschulen Freiburgs ernannt wurde. Ruf übernahm am 1. September 1961 die Leitung der im Mai eingeweihten Thomas-Morus-Burse in der Kapplerstraße, wo er auch seinen Wohnsitz aufschlug.

---

352 PA, Provinzrundbrief vom 11.3.1959, S. 3.
353 PA, Provinzrundbrief vom 18.3.1963, S. 3.

Vom Freiburger Dominikanerkloster aus wurden außerdem mehrere Schwesternkonvente betreut, so die Dominikanerinnen in Neusatzeck und Freiburg-Stegen, die Schwestern vom Guten Hirten in Rastatt, die Freiburger Franziskanerinnen und die Elisabethschwestern. Die Brüder hatten dort teilweise den Posten des ordentlichen oder außerordentlichen Beichtvaters inne, mit dem wöchentliche Beichten verbunden waren (zwischen 1950 und 1965 waren es meist jeweils zwei offizielle Posten); in den anderen Fällen besuchten sie diese Klöster vierteljährlich. Auch bei den Barmherzigen Brüdern in Freiburg / St. Urban hörten sie die Beichten.

Große Aufmerksamkeit schenkten die Brüder auch dem Dritten Orden. Sie kümmerten sich den Gruppen in Freiburg und Karlsruhe, um die 1952 hinzugekommene Gruppe in Ettlingen und ab 1954 auch um eine Gruppe in Stuttgart. Ab 1962 erwähnen die Provinzrundbriefe eine weitere Gruppe in Böblingen. 1962 war dem Konvent an allen diesen Orten eine monatliche Konferenz möglich. Danach konnten sie dies nur mehr in Freiburg selbst aufrechterhalten; die anderen Gruppen wurden zweimonatlich oder gar nur mehr vierteljährlich besucht. Mit der Hilfe eines aus der polnischen Provinz stammenden Dominikaners, P. Matthäus Schutter, der von 1962 bis 1970 als Seelsorger bei den Dominikanerinnen in Karlsruhe wohnte, gelang es aber wieder, alle Gruppen monatlich zu betreuen.

Die Heiligsprechung Heinrich Seuses und zwei Zeitschriften „Die ewige Weisheit“

Der Freiburger Konvent war von 1954 bis 1963 auch Sitz des Herausgebers und Erscheinungsort der Zeitschrift „Die ewige Weisheit“. Hintergrund dieser Publikation waren Anstrengungen zur Heiligsprechung des Dominikanermystikers Heinrich Seuse († 1366). Dessen Verehrung als Seliger war unter Papst Gregor XVI. mit Dekret vom 22. April 1831 erlaubt worden.[354] Allerdings galt diese Erlaubnis – wie bei allen Seligen – nur für bestimmte Kirchen, Gegenden oder kirchliche Gemeinschaften, z. B. Orden. Um eine allgemeinkirchliche Empfehlung zur liturgischen Verehrung zu erreichen, war ein Kanonisationsprozess, ein kirchenrechtliches Heiligsprechungsverfahren nötig. Um ein solches voranzubringen, brauchte es eine Vertiefung und Ausbreitung der Bekanntheit eines Seligen unter den Gläubigen. Da Seuse selbst im südwestdeutschen Raum gelebt und gewirkt hatte, bestand

354 Datum laut: Venchi: *Catalogus hagiographicus*, S. 59.

in der Provincia Germaniae superioris ein besonderes Interesse, seine Kanonisation zu erreichen.

Nach Kriegsende scheinen die Vorzeichen dafür günstig zu sein. Provinzial Marianus Vetter berichtete am 22. April 1948 seinem Provinzkonsil, dass der Generalprokurator des Ordens Papst Pius XII. eine Petition zur Heiligsprechung Seuses zugestellt hatte.[355] Damit hatte der kanonische Prozess die höchste kirchliche Ebene erreicht. Mit der Einsetzung von P. Friedrich Gegenbauer in das Amt des sogenannten Promotors für die Selig- und Heiligsprechungen fand das Provinzkapitel von 1950 einen Mann, der sich dieses Anliegens annahm.[356] „Promotor" bedeutet „Förderer" – ein Begriff, der aus sich selbst heraus den Inhalt dieses Amtes erklärt. Das Provinzkapitel konnte solche Promotoren für verschiedene Aufgabenbereiche einsetzen. Die Ordenssatzungen schrieben eingesetzte Provinzpromotoren für die Mission, die Bruderschaften und den Dritten Orden vor. Darüber hinaus gab es in der Germania superior Zeit ihres Bestehens aber auch immer Promotoren für die Belange der Nonnen und Schwestern des Ordens und eben auch für Selig- und Heiligsprechungen. In späteren Jahrzehnten kamen noch die Bereiche der Öffentlichkeitsarbeit und für Gerechtigkeit und Frieden hinzu. Wieviel Wirksamkeit ein solcher „Förderer" in seinem Auftragsgebiet entwickelte, hing sehr stark von dessen persönlichem Engagement ab und natürlich von dem Echo, das dessen Bemühungen fanden.

Im Falle Gegenbauers traf beides in bester Weise zusammen. Gegenbauer, ein gebürtiger Schweizer aus Wil / Kanton St. Gallen, lebte seit 1946 im Freiburger Dominikanerkonvent.[357] Im Januar 1954 brachte er die erste Ausgabe seiner neuen Zeitschrift „Die ewige Weisheit" heraus. In deren Geleitwort gab Gegenbauer alle Informationen zu Zustandekommen und Ziel dieses Druckwerkes an:

> „Die Katholiken Badens, des Schwabenlandes und der Schweiz erstreben mit neuem Bemühen die längst ersehnte Heiligsprechung des seligen Heinrich Suso. Die Verehrer des Seligen begrüßen darum von Herzen die Idee einer Zeitschrift, die über Leben und Werk des Seligen Kunde in alle Lande hinausträgt. Besonderer Dank gebührt dem Initianten dieser Zeitschrift, Herrn Verleger Konrad Baier in Weingarten / Württemberg. Möge sie dazu beitragen, die Liebe und Andacht zu unserem seligen Heinrich Suso zu mehren und, falls es Gottes Wille ist, die Wege zu bereiten zu seiner Heiligsprechung. Was seine

355 PA, Liber consilii provincialis, Sitzung in Augsburg am 22.4.1958.

356 APKap 1950, S. 6 Nr. 23.

357 PA, Provinzialsregestenbuch 1 (1939–1966), Eintrag vom 28.6.1946, S. 34, Nr. 41.

Heiligsprechung voraussetzt, sind noch zwei einwandfreie wunderbare Heilungen auf seine Fürbitte hin. Dass der selige Heinrich Suso durch seine Fürsprache bei Gott viel vermag, das steht einwandfrei fest. Darum wollen wir mit den allgemeinen Zielen des Marianischen Jahres [sc. 1954] auch das Sonderziel: Heiligsprechung des seligen Heinrich Suso, mit anstreben …“[358]

Die Ewige Weisheit

UND IHR DIENER, DER SELIGE HEINRICH SUSO O.P.

AUS DEM INHALT:

P. Friedr. Gegenbauer O.P.
Zum Geleit

Albert Krautheimer
Vom seligen Heinrich Suso

Das Büchlein der Ewigen Weisheit

M. Regina Mager O.P.
Der selige Heinrich Suso als Sohn seiner Heimat

Die weinende Madonna von Syrakus

15 Jahre Pius XII. im Marianischen Jahr

Dank dem seligen Heinrich Suso für belohntes Vertrauen

Aus Kirche und Welt

Einzelnummer 40 Pfg.

Sel. Heinrich Suso (Original von Frau Gertrudis Endres O.P. †)

Seliger Heinrich Suso, bitte für uns!

BEHARRE AUF NICHTS, DAS NICHT GOTT IST

1. Jahrgang — Januar–März 1954 — Heft 1

Abb. 62: Titelblatt der ersten Ausgabe von Die ewige Weisheit, Heft 1, 1954.

Der Impuls zur Zeitschriftgründung war also nicht von Gegenbauer, sondern vom Buchhändler und Verleger Baier ausgegangen. Sie erschien vierteljährlich, laut Impressum zum Preis von 40 Pfennig pro Einzelheft, und war über Baier und die Prokuratur des Freiburger Dominikanerklosters zu beziehen. Insgesamt wurden von 1954 bis 1963 zehn Jahrgänge veröffentlicht. Bis zur insgesamt fünften Ausgabe, Nr. 2 des Jahres 1955, lautete ihr vollständiger Titel „Die ewige Weisheit und ihr Diener, der selige Heinrich Suso OP“. Die restlichen 35 Ausgaben bis Nr. 4 des Jahres 1963 trugen „Blätter für Gottesfreunde“ als Untertitel. Die ersten vier Nummern, der Jahrgang 1954, wurde von Konrad Baier in Weingarten verlegt und in Ravensburg gedruckt. Danach erfolgten Druck und Verlag durch das Schweizerische Katholische Sonntagsblatt in Wil / Sankt Gallen. Ab der Nr. 2 von 1958 wird im Impressum als Bezugsort nicht mehr die Prokuratur des Freiburger Konvents genannt, sondern ein Verlag „Die Ewige Weisheit“ mit Adresse des Klosters – Gegenbauer hatte also das Verlagsgeschäft selbst in die Hand genommen. Leider fehlen zu diesem Verlag weitere Quellen; er taucht nur immer wieder in den Werbeanzeigen für Bücher und Kleinschriften auf, mit denen sich die Zeitschrift von Anfang an mitfinanzierte.

358 *Die ewige Weisheit* (1954) Nr. 1, S. 2.

Umfasste die erste Ausgabe der „Ewigen Weisheit" nur 16 Seiten, so wuchs die Zeitschrift schon in der nächsten Ausgabe auf 22 Seiten an; später konnten es bis zu 32 Seiten werden. Der Fokus des Inhalts galt immer Heinrich Seuse: Gegenbauer leuchtete dessen historische Person und ihren Hintergrund, Werke, Andachtsformen, Lebensratschläge oder Bedeutung als Mystiker und Seliger in den 40 Heften in alle Richtungen aus und zitierte dabei nicht nur Seuses Schriften, sondern auch die Gedanken vieler andere Schriftstellerinnen und Schriftsteller, Theologen oder Dichter zu Seuse, einschließlich Nachrichten über Gebetserhörungen, die auf die Fürbitte Seuses zurückgeführt wurden. Dazu traten bereits in der zweiten Ausgabe größere Artikel oder kleine Beitragssammlungen zu anderen Heiligen oder Seligen, so etwa in der Nr. 2 von 1954 zur Heiligsprechung Pius X., in der Nr. 3 von 1954 zu Bruder Klaus von der Flüe, in der Nr. 3 von 1955 zu Vinzenz Ferrer, in der Nr. 4 von 1956 zu Albertus Magnus usw. Auch Berichte über das Leben und die Geschichte der Dominikaner und Dominikanerinnen fanden Aufnahme, ebenso seitenlange Sammlungen von Nachrichten aus dem Predigerorden und der Weltkirche, so z. B. ausführliche Dokumentationen über das zweite vatikanische Konzil. Regelmäßig trugen Autoren wie Hieronymus Wilms oder Angelus Walz Texte bei. Abgerundet wurde jede Ausgabe mit oft mehreren Seiten mit Besprechungen von Büchern religiösen oder kirchlichen Inhalts.

Als letzte Ausgabe erschien die Nr. 4 des Jahres 1963. Innerhalb des 28 Seiten langen Heftes findet sich kein Hinweis oder Kommentar, warum Gegenbauer „Die ewige Weisheit" danach einstellte. Tatsächlich war er am 2. Februar 1963 nach Graz versetzt worden.[359] Die beiden letzten Nummern (3 und 4 von 1963) gab er laut deren Impressum von dort aus heraus. Warum Gegenbauer die Zeitschrift aufgab, bleibt unklar. 1964 zog er sich in die Schweiz zurück, wo er bis zu seinem Tod 1975 als Mitherausgeber des Schweizerischen Katholischen Sonntagsblattes in seinem Heimatort Wil arbeitete.[360]

Wenn auch „Die ewige Weisheit" die Bekanntheit Seuses im deutschsprachigen Raum sicher verbreitete – das Ziel seiner Heiligsprechung wurde nicht erreicht; sein Kanonisationsprozess dauert noch an. Das Provinzkapitel der Germania superior von 1962 bat den Ordensmeister, sich beim Heiligen Stuhl für Seuses Heiligsprechung einzusetzen;[361] ein

359 PA, Provinzialsregestenbuch 1 (1939–1966), Eintrag vom 2.2.1963, S. 153, Nr. 271.
360 So laut den Provinzkatalogen 1964–1977.
361 APKap 1962, S. 9, Nr. 52.

Wunsch, den das Kapitel von 1966 wiederholte.[362] Das Provinzkonsil beantragte 1972 bei der Ordenskurie die Erlaubnis, seinen Gedenktag als *memoria obligatoria* begehen zu dürfen, was auch gewährt wurde.[363]

In diesem Jahr 1972 erschien neuerlich ein Periodikum namens „Ewige Weisheit", untertitelt als „Zeitschrift für Schwestern, Brüder und Freunde des Predigerordens". In seinem Geleitwort zur ersten Ausgabe (Nr. 1 des Jahres 1972) gab Provinzial Innozenz Varga als dreifaches Ziel dieser neuen Veröffentlichung an, sie solle „die Verbundenheit unter Brüdern und Schwestern des Dominikanerordens im deutschen Sprachraum durch Austausch von Gedanken und Nachrichten stärken, das geistige Erbe unseres Ordens sowie das Andenken an seine Heiligen und Seligen pflegen und die Dominikanermystik eines Meister Eckhart, Tauler und Seuse lebendig erhalten."[364] Anders als Gegenbauers Publikation, die aus einer Privatinitiative erwachsen war, stand hinter der neuen „Ewigen Weisheit" ein direkter Auftrag des Provinzials an P. Hilarius Barth als Redakteur, dem ein Redaktionsrat zur Seite stand, bestehend aus P. Magnus Beck (München), P. Reginald Ladner (Graz), P. Theophil Tschipke (München), Sr. Roswitha Schneider (Niederviehbach), Sr. Paula Wascher (Wien-Hacking) und Sr. Johanna Gessner (Regensburg).[365] Auch diese Zeitschrift erschien vierteljährlich, im Umfang von 40 bis 48 Seiten, in Regensburg, dem Wohnort Barths, zum Preis von 1 bzw. 1,50 DM.

Gegenbauers ältere Publikation wurde in der neuen Zeitschrift nirgendwo genannt, sondern nur auf die Anspielung auf Heinrich Seuse verwiesen, die sich im Titel „Ewige Weisheit" ausdrückte.[366] Dennoch darf man davon ausgehen, dass Gegenbauers neun Jahre zuvor eingestelltes Vorbild weiterwirkte. Barth hatte große Pläne mit diesem neuen Projekt:

> „Aus dem Zweck, den sich die neue Zeitschrift gesetzt hat, ergibt sich, dass es nicht darum geht, das im Überfluss vorhandene bedruckte Material um eine weitere, belanglose Variation zu bereichern. Vielmehr muss man eingestehen: es gibt im deutschen Sprachraum zur Zeit keine Zeitschrift mit vergleichbarer Zielsetzung. Wir glauben daher umso eher eine Lücke zu füllen, als in der gegenwärtigen Epoche selbst die sichersten Maßstäbe des geistlichen und reli-

362 APKap 1966, S. 9, Nr. 26.
363 PA, Liber consiliorum provinciae, Sitzung vom 13.9.1972, S. 80.
364 *Ewige Weisheit* (1972) Nr. 1, S. 1.
365 So laut Angabe auf den inneren vorderen oder hinteren Umschlagseiten beinahe aller Ausgaben.
366 Siehe *Ewige Weisheit* (1972) Nr. 1, S. 2–3.

giösen Lebens zu wanken beginnen, und der gegenseitige Dienst der Ermunterung, der Weisung und der geistlichen Tröstung doppelt nötig ist. Der Plan zu vorliegendem Werk entsprang Gesprächen, die der verantwortliche Redakteur mit mehreren Schwesternklöstern in Süddeutschland und Österreich geführt hat. ... Doch möchte unsere Zeitschrift, je nach dem Echo, das sie findet, Mitteilungen allgemeineren Interesses aus dem ganzen deutschen Sprachraum in ihre Spalten aufnehmen. Weitgehend hängt das von der Bereitschaft der Brüder und Schwestern ab, der Zeitschrift ihre Mitarbeit zu schenken, um die wir höflich ersuchen, und uns ihre Nachrichten zuzusenden."[367]

Abb. 63: Umschlag der ersten Ausgabe der Zeitschrift Ewige Weisheit, Heft 1/I 1972.

Wichtig war ihm, dass die „die geistige Linie der ‚Ewigen Weisheit' stets eindeutig bleiben und klar umrissen" sein würde, nämlich „Treue zur Lehre der Kirche und zur großen Überlieferung unseres Ordens", wobei „als Schwerpunkt die geistliche Ausrichtung der Zeitschrift bestimmend" war.[368] Ihren Inhalt stellte er sich so vor: „Allen zugängliche, leicht verständliche Aufsätze werden mit theologischen Abhandlungen abwechseln, die zu längerem Verweilen einladen; Beiträge zur Geschichte stehen neben besonnenen Ausblicken auf Gegenwart und Zukunft; Gedichte und Gebete würzen das Ganze."[369] Dieser Ankündigung entsprach auch der Inhalt des ersten Heftes, der in der Hauptsache aus zwei Artikeln Barths bestand – einer Analyse zur Lage der Kirche unter dem Titel „Ein Anfang im Winter" mit Aufrufen zur Aufrechterhaltung der Traditionen und einer programmatischen Darlegung der Absichten des Ordensgründers, überschrieben mit „Der Einklang von Wahrheit und Leben beim hl. Dominikus". Dazu kamen verschiedene Nachrichten, Nachrufe

367 *Ewige Weisheit* (1972) Nr. 1, S. 3.
368 *Ewige Weisheit* (1972) Nr. 1, S. 4–5.
369 *Ewige Weisheit* (1972) Nr. 1, S. 5.

und kleinere Texte. Am Schluss stand der erste Teil eines Beitrags des niederländischen Dominikaners Valentin Walgrave über die „Allgemeine Lage des Ordens in Bezug auf die gegenwärtigen Strömungen", der in den folgenden Heften weitergeführt und abgeschlossen wurde.

Das erste Heft war bald vergriffen und es meldeten sich rund 500 Abonnenten. Barth ging in der zweiten Ausgabe ausführlich auf das gemischte Echo ein, das er mit reichlichen Zitaten dokumentierte. Da sein Adressatenkreis – nämlich die Angehörigen der verschiedenen Zweige des Ordens – enger war als der Gegenbauers, waren auch die Inhalte eher auf die Selbstreflexion der verschiedenen Bereiche des Ordenslebens (Gebet, Liturgie, Observanzen) ausgerichtet. Dennoch gelang es Barth in den ersten Jahren des Erscheinens der „Ewigen Weisheit", neben thematischen Artikeln auch ein breites Spektrum an Nachrichten über Ordensmitglieder und Ereignisse aus dem Orden zusammenzutragen. In diesen Punkten erfüllte er die in der ersten Ausgabe geweckten Erwartungen. Nicht in jedem Jahr erschienen wirklich vier Ausgaben: 1973 wurden die Nummern 3 und 4 zu einem Sonderheft zum Thema „Geistliche Erneuerung" zusammengefasst, 1974 die Nummern 1 und 2 zu einem Sonderheft zu „Thomas von Aquin 1274–1974". 1977 erschienen nur mehr drei Hefte; danach wurde die Zeitschrift eingestellt, sodass die ganze Reihe auf insgesamt 21 Ausgaben kam. Auch hier liefert das letzte Heft keinen Hinweis auf die Gründe für das Ende der Publikation. Eine gewisse Tendenz lässt sich aber nach 1974 erkennen: Die auf mehrere Ausgaben verteilten längeren Beiträge nahmen zu, ebenso wurden immer häufiger ältere Artikel gebracht, die schon in anderen Medien veröffentlicht worden waren. Gleichzeitig nahm die Zahl der Beitragenden ab, ebenso die Menge der Personal- und anderer Neuigkeiten aus dem Orden – was wohl als Zeichen zu werten ist, dass Barth in seiner Redaktionsarbeit immer mehr allein gelassen wurde. In diese Richtung deutet auch die Tatsache, daß der Provinzial keinen Nachfolger für ihn als verantwortlichen Schriftleiter einsetzte, trotz des großen Redaktionsrats. Barth selbst verließ im September 1977 Regensburg und nahm in München eine Stelle als Spiritual am Priesterseminar an. Dieser Schritt würde erklären, warum keine Winterausgabe 1977, also kein viertes Heft der „Ewigen Weisheit" mehr herauskam.

Rosenkranzapostolat

Als wichtiger Bestandteil des spirituellen Profils des Predigerordens galt die Pflege des Rosenkranzgebets. Die Konstitutionen der Dominikaner sahen vor, dass die Brüder täglich gemeinsam ein sogenanntes Drittel des Rosenkranzes, also 15 Gesätze, beten sollten; dieses Gebet ersetzte sogar eine der zwei vorgeschriebenen halben Stunden täglicher Meditation. Falls einer am gemeinsamen Gebet verhindert war, hatte er das tägliche Rosenkranzgebet privat zu verrichten.[370] Zur Verbreitung dieser Andachtsform unter den Gläubigen waren alle Brüder aufgerufen.[371] Die Satzungen verpflichteten den Provinzial aber auch, zur Förderung und Betreuung der dem Orden angeschlossenen Bruderschaften einen Bruder als sogenannten Promotor einzusetzen.[372] Dazu gehörten auch die Rosenkranzbruderschaften. Der Teilung der Germania Superior entsprechend setzten die Provinzkapitel für jeden Provinzteil einen eigenen Rosenkranzpromotor ein. Dieser war nach Möglichkeit seines Assignationsklosters für diese Arbeit freizustellen. Die Provinzrundbriefe geben für die Jahre 1950 bis 1965 auch Hinweise darauf, wie man sich die seelsorgliche Tätigkeit dieser Rosenkranzpromotoren praktisch vorstellen darf.

Das Provinzkapitel von 1946 ernannte P. Karl Stumpf zum Rosenkranzpromotor im süddeutschen Provinzteil.[373] Stumpf hatte seinen Sitz im Konvent von St. Albert in München.

Leider meldet nur ein Provinzrundbrief, der Arbeitsbericht über 1950, etwas über dessen Tätigkeit:

> „Im Einzelnen sind folgende Arbeiten zu vermerken: 9 religiöse Wochen über den Rosenkranz, 3 Rosenkranz-Triduen, 1 Kurs marianischer Lehrerinnenexerzitien, 5 wissenschaftliche Vorträge, 4 Lichtbildervorträge, Gesamtsumme 161 Predigten und Vorträge in 8 verschiedenen Diözesen. Zahl der von den Vorträgen erfassten Personen: 7.900. Zahl der Neuaufnahmen in die Rosenkranzbruderschaft: 3247. Zahl der gehörten Beichten: 3500. Zahl der neu errichteten Bruderschaften: 8. 19 Diplome für den Lebendigen Rosenkranz wurden ausgestellt. Eine Neuauflage der Rosenblätter (15.000) wurde besorgt.

---

370 *Constitutiones 1932*, S. 219 Nr. 588 § 1 und 589.

371 So z. B. ausdrücklich in den APKap 1954, S. 8, Nr. 36 oder den APKap 1958, S. 8 Nr. 41.

372 *Constitutiones 1932*, S. 290 Nr. 815.

373 APKap 1946, S. 5 Nr. 18.

> Desgleichen Mitgliederlisten mit praktischer Anweisung für Förderer, sowie ein Mitgliedsbüchlein mit Ablässen."[374]

Stumpf verstarb 1951. Nach seinem Tod übernahm P. Hermenegild Braun diese Aufgabe, allerdings von seinem Assignationskonvent Freiburg im Breisgau aus. Braun widmete sich mit Feuereifer dieser Sache; er hielt von Freiburg aus Rosenkranzwochen (1951: vier, 1954: 13, 1957: fünf), Rosenkranztriduen (1951: sechs, 1952: 23, 1954: 35), Rosenkranzsonntage (1950: drei, 1954: vier, 1957: einen), Rosenkranzmissionen und dem Rosenkranz gewidmete religiöse Wochen (1956 und 1957 je eine Mission, aber 1956 16 religiöse Wochen). Ebenso gründete er neue Rosenkranzbruderschaften (1954: sechs, 1956: 15, 1957: elf) und Gebetsgemeinschaften des Lebendigen Rosenkranzes (1956 z. B. 24). 1957 zog Braun in den Konvent von Augsburg um. Allein zwischen September und Dezember 1957 hielt er von dort aus eine Rosenkranzmission, drei Rosenkranzwochen, zehn Rosenkranztriduen und einen Rosenkranztag. In diesem Kalenderjahr hatte er 21 neue Rosenkranzbruderschaften und 29 Vereine vom Lebendigen Rosenkranz errichtet. Auf sein Wirken ist wohl auch das deutliche Wachstum der Augsburger Rosenkranzbruderschaft zurückzuführen – trotz des Konkurrenzdrucks, sozusagen, durch die anderen Bruderschaften und Vereinigungen. Für 1963 melden die Provinzrundbriefe, dass insgesamt 1.446 Pfarreien in das Rosenkranzapostolat aufgenommen waren; 1965 waren es 1.458. Braun betreute diese Aufgabe bis zu seinem Tod 1977. Das Provinzkapitel von 1962 stellte ihm in der Person von P. Dominikus Kirchmaier einen Assistenten zur Seite.[375]

In Österreich bildete der Konvent in Graz das Zentrum für dieses Apostolat – nicht nur wegen der marianischen Ausrichtung der dortigen Seelsorge allgemein, sondern auch, weil Graz schon von Zeiten der österreichisch-ungarischen Provinz her Sitz der schon genannten Periodika „Rosenkranzbriefe" / „Mit Maria" und „Bote Unserer Lieben Frau" / „Bote unserer Lieben Frau von Fatima" war. Die Redaktion beider Druckschriften führte P. Amandus Baronig bis zu seinem Tod 1972. Die Sicherstellung des monatlichen Erscheinens der „Rosenkranzbriefe" war für ihn nicht einfach, insbesondere wegen des Erstellens der notwendigen Artikel. Daher verwundert es nicht, wenn das Provinzkapitel 1954 die ganze Provinz dazu aufrief,

---

374 PA, Provinzrundbrief vom 2.2.1951, S. 8.
375 APKap 1962, S. 9 Nr. 53.

ihm bei dieser Arbeit zu helfen,[376] und das Provinzkapitel von 1958 an den Provinzial appellierte, mit den Provinziälen der Teutonia und der Schweiz in Verbindung zu treten, um u. a. über eine gemeinsame Rosenkranzzeitschrift für die deutschsprachigen Länder zu beraten,[377] zu der es aber nicht kam. Die Arbeit der Rosenkranzpromotoren Paul Gunz (1946 bis 1958) und Seraphicus Weber (1958 bis 1966) gestaltete sich ähnlich wie die von Braun, wobei die Provinzrundbriefe leider kaum Details darüber berichten. Im August 1963 wurde Weber ebenfalls mit einem Assistenten ausgestattet, Friedrich Gegenbauer,[378] der aber in dieser Sache kaum tätig wurde, weil er wenige Monate später in die Schweiz zog.

Nach 1965 findet das Rosenkranzapostolat in den Provinzrundbriefen kaum mehr Erwähnung, allerdings deshalb, weil die Provinziäle in ihnen keine Arbeitsberichte der Konvente mehr publizierten.

Mitarbeit in der China- und Taiwanmission

Die Provincia Germaniae superioris beschäftigte sich nur wenig mit Missionsarbeit. Ein erstes, wenn auch indirektes Engagement in diese Richtung gab es während des Krieges: Einer der von den Nazis aus Süddeutschland vertriebenen Schweizer Mitbrüder, P. Suso Geiselhart, kam im September 1939 als Seelsorger zur Kongregation der Missionsdominikanerinnen nach Ilanz im Kanton Graubünden. Dort übernahm er auch die sogenannte Missionsprokuratur, also die Spendenverwaltung und Förderung der Missionstätigkeit dieser Schwestern, v. a. durch Druckschriften.[379] 1914 waren die ersten Dominikanermissionare der Provinz Teutonia in den Bezirk Tingchou der Provinz Fukien (heute Provinz Fujian, sozusagen der Insel Taiwan gegenüber) im Südosten Chinas gekommen. 1922 kamen Dominikanerinnen der Ilanzer Kongregation dazu; im folgenden Jahr konnte das Missionsgebiet zur Apostolischen Präfektur erhoben werden, mit P. Egbert Pelzer OP († 1945) als erstem Präfekten. Zwischen 1928 und 1933 wurde die dominikanische Arbeit dort zum ersten Mal empfindlich durch kom-

376 APKap 1954, S. 8 Nr. 37.
377 APKap 1958, S. 8 Nr. 39.
378 PA, Provinzialsregestenbuch 1 (1939–1966), Eintrag vom 18.8.1963, S. 164, Nr. 319.
379 PA, Provinzialsregestenbuch 1 (1939–1966), Eintrag vom 30.9.1939, S. 13, Nr. 72, sowie die Provinzkataloge der Jahre 1941 und 1943.

munistische Eingriffe gestört. Nach Ausbruch des zweiten Weltkrieges sollten die deutschsprachigen Brüder und Schwestern aus China ausgewiesen werden, was aber durch den Einsatz des nachmaligen Kardinals Paul Yü-Pin verhindert werden konnte. Im Mai 1946 wurde Tingchou zur Diözese erhoben, mit P. Werner Lesinski († 1963) als erstem Bischof. Am 1. Februar 1948 wurde P. Richard Krupitschka als erster echter Missionar der Germania superior nach Fukien entsandt.[380] Zu diesem Zeitpunkt bestand das dominikanische Personal der Diözese aus einem Bischof, 21 Patres, fünf Brüdern, 26 europäischen und zwei chinesischen Dominikanerinnen; dazu kam noch ein Weltpriester. 1949 kamen die Kommunisten zum zweiten Mal in das Gebiet; bis 1954 waren alle ausländischen Schwestern und Geistlichen aus Tingchou ausgewiesen oder vertrieben.

Im Juli 1954 gingen drei Dominikaner, darunter P. Krupitschka,[381] auf die Insel Taiwan. Dorthin folgten ihnen bald die meisten der Patres und Schwestern, die in Tingchou eingesetzt gewesen waren. Zwar war ihre jahrzehntelange Arbeit in Festlandchina zunichte gemacht worden, aber ihre ebenso lange Erfahrung mit den Menschen dieses Kulturraumes half diesen Dominikanern beim Neuaufbau ihres Werkes im Süden der Insel, wo zwölf neue Missionsstationen entstanden. Krupitschka arbeitete laut Auskunft der Provinzkataloge bis 1969 in Chaochow-Pingtung, von 1971 bis 1973 in Taipeh-Hsien und danach bis zu seinem Tod wieder in Chaochow-Pingtung. Er verstarb 1990 während eines Heimaturlaubs in Wien.[382] 1958 kam P. Paul Heribert Welte, der zweite Chinamissionar der Germanias superior, nach Taiwan. Er arbeitete zunächst auf den Missionsstationen in Hsinchau, 1961 bis 1963 in Chaochow und 1964 bis 1965 in Tungkang-Pingtung. Danach übernahm er eine Lehrtätigkeit am Priesterseminar in Tainan, um ab 1969 bis zu seiner Emeritierung 2003 in Taipeh an der katholischen theologischen Fakultät der Fujen-Universität Dogmatik zu unterrichten.[383] Welte kehrte 2004 für den Ruhestand in die Provinz zurück und wurde in den Augsburger Konvent assigniert.[384]

---

380 PA, Provinzialsregestenbuch 1 (1939–1966), Eintrag vom 1.2.1948, S. 41, Nr. 2; *ASOP* (1949) S. 43.

381 PA, Provinzialsregestenbuch 1 (1939–1966), Eintrag vom 6.4.1954, S. 65, Nr. 8.

382 PA, Provinzialsregestenbuch 2 (1966–2010), Eintrag vom 2.1.1990, Nr. 5.

383 So laut den Provinzkatalogen der Jahre 1958–2004.

384 PA, Provinzialsregestenbuch 2 (1966–2010), Eintrag vom 18.7.2004, Nr. 30.

Ziel dieser dominikanischen Missionsarbeit war der Aufbau einer einheimischen Ortskirche. In gewisser Weise war diese Absicht erreicht, als die Anstrengungen des Ordens 1978 in die Gründung eines eigenständigen chinesischen Generalvikariates münden konnten.[385] Danach wurde die deutschsprachige Präsenz auf der Insel schrittweise abgebaut.[386]

Kapitel, Konzil, Konstitutionen, Krisen

Provinzkapitel und Provinziäle 1954 bis 1966

Das Provinzkapitel, das sich vom 18. bis 21. Mai 1954 in Graz traf, lief auf den Gleisen, die 1946 und 1950 gelegt und bestätigt worden waren: Innovationen gingen nicht von ihm aus. Manifest wurde dies v. a. in der Wiederwahl von Marianus Vetter zum Provinzial. Aber auch für die anderen zu besetzenden Provinzposten griffen die Kapitularen hauptsächlich auf die Brüder zurück, die diese schon vorher inne gehabt hatte. Abgesehen von den Besetzungen von Ämtern und Kommissionen und den oben unter Rosenkranzapostolat genannten Beschlüssen konzentrierte sich das Kapitel auf Fragen der Regulardisziplin: Die Oberen wurden ermahnt, sich nicht nur als Vorsteher von Untergebenen, sondern als gute Hirten zu betrachten und sich um das geistliche wie das leibliche Wohl der ihnen Anvertrauten anzunehmen. Allen Brüdern wurde das Vorbild Jesu ins Gedächtnis gerufen, der zu dienen gekommen sei, nicht um bedient zu werden (vgl. Mt 20,28) und immer das Wohl der Gemeinschaft und das Wachstum des Ordens im Blick zu haben. Obzwar ein kritisches Urteil nicht generell abgelehnt wurde, wurden die Brüder ermahnt, ihre Diskussionen nicht zum Schaden von Personen oder Sachen beitragen zu lassen. Im Übrigen wurde den Prioren und Pfarrern aufgetragen, dass sie die Schwierigkeiten, die aus ihren Ämtern erwuchsen, durch die Liebe des Ordens, auf den sie Profess gemacht hätten, und bewegt durch den Eifer für die Seelsorge lösen sollten.[387] Die ersteren Bestimmungen erklären sich von selbst – sie waren ge-

385 Zur Entstehung des Generalvikariates siehe: Hoyer: *Provinzen und Kongregationen*, Teil 3, S. 203–204.
386 Zur Geschichte der China-Mission der Teutonia siehe: PA, Provinzrundbrief 2–1993, S. 26–29.
387 APKap 1954, S. 6, Nr. 25–28.

gen etwaige Tyrannei von Oberen, gegen Wichtigtuerei Einzelner und gegen klerikalen Klatsch gerichtet. Die letzte Bestimmung ist ein wenig kryptisch; vielleicht deutet sie auf Überforderung Einzelner bei der Ausübung eines anvertrauten Amtes hin. Ausdrücklich wurde der Provinz Teutonia für ihre Bereitschaft gedankt, der Germania superior, die unter Personalmangel litt, einige Mitbrüder zur Hilfe zu schicken (dazu später).

Das folgende Provinzkapitel, das vom 21. bis 24. Oktober 1958 in Wien stattfand, brachte eine wesentliche Veränderung: Zum ersten Mal stand P. Vetter nicht mehr als Provinzial zur Verfügung. Eine Ära ging zu Ende: Über 19 Jahre, seit der Gründung der Provinz, hatte Vetter ihr als höherer Oberer vorgestanden. Seine neuerliche Wiederwahl erlaubten weder die Ordenssatzungen noch seine stark angegriffene Gesundheit – Vetter litt an der Parkinson'schen Krankheit. Er setzte sich im Konvent von Augsburg zur Ruhe. Sein Zustand verschlechterte sich dahingehend, dass er schließlich an den Rollstuhl gefesselt war. Bis 1967 nahm er dennoch rege am Konventsleben, an der gemeinsamen Eucharistiefeier und am Chorgebet teil. Im Alter von 76 Jahren verstarb er, am 24. April 1968.[388] In ihren Dankesworten an Vetter hoben die Akten des Provinzkapitels von 1958 hervor, dass er als Provinzial in seiner fast zwanzigjährigen Amtszeit trotz allerschwerster Umstände, unter einem antikatholischen und nationalistischen Regime, während einer ungeheuren Kriegs- und Wiederaufbauzeit keine Mühe gescheut und keine Rücksicht auf seine eigene Gesundheit genommen habe.[389] An seiner Stelle wurde ein Mitbruder aus der Provinz Teutonia zum Provinzial gewählt: P. Augustinus Gierlich. Gierlich, aus Meckenheim im Rheinland gebürtig, war 1934 zum Studium in den Konvent von Freiburg im Breisgau geschickt worden und hatte dort 1938 im Fach Neutestamentliche Exegese promoviert. Von 1939 bis 1946 war er Prior des Konvents von Walberberg gewesen und hatte am dortigen Ordensstudium unterrichtet. 1946 war er als Nachfolger von Laurentius Siemer zum Provinzial der Teutonia gewählt worden. Nach Ablauf seiner Amtszeit 1950 kehrte er nach Walberberg zu seiner Lehrtätigkeit zurück. 1954 bis 1958 wirkte er als Prior des Wormser Konvents, von wo aus er weiterhin Unterricht am Ordensstudium hielt.[390]

388 Zu Vetter: *St. Dominikuswerk* (1969), S. 9 und PA, Provinzrundbrief vom „dritten Adventssonntag" 1967, S. 3.

389 APKap 1958, S. 9, Nr. 51.

390 PA, Provinzrundbrief vom 27.7.1984, S. 6 (Nachruf auf Gierlich).

Abb. 64: P. Augustinus Gierlich (PA, Fotosammlung).

Ansonsten erbringen die Akten des Provinzkapitels von 1958 inhaltlich wenig Aufregendes: Die Brüder wurden mit einem Bibelzitat vor modernem Aktivismus und fortschreitendem Materialismus gewarnt: „Wir aber wollen beim Gebet und beim Dienst am Wort bleiben." (Apg 6,4). Die in Süddeutschland begonnene Weise der Abhaltung der vorgeschriebenen Exerzitien – nämlich dass dreimal im Jahr in einem der Konvente ein Kurs stattfand, der allen süddeutschen Brüdern offen stand – wurde für den österreichischen Provinzteil empfohlen. Die Brüder wurden ermahnt, sich nicht zu Duzen. Die Bestimmungen des Provinzkapitels von 1946 über das Habittragen wurden in Erinnerung gerufen. Zur Fürbitte für mehr Ordensberufungen wurde den Klöstern die tägliche Rezitation der Antiphon „O spem miram" anbefohlen. Dem Provinzial wurde aufgetragen, so bald als möglich dafür zu sorgen, dass die Novizen und Studenten wenigstens bis zu ihrer feierlichen Profess auf dem Provinzgebiet ausgebildet werden konnten. Außerdem wurde er mit der Gründung einer Ordensniederlassung an St. Peter in Bludenz in Vorarlberg beauftragt, als Filiale des Konvents Graz. Übrigens melden die Akten auch, dass Paul Gunz der ihm vom Provinzkapitel 1946 übertragenen Aufgabe nachgekommen war und seine Übersetzung der für die Laienbrüder relevanten Teile der Ordenssatzungen nun vorlag.[391]

Inhaltlich mehr oder weniger austauschbar mit den Akten des Kapitels von 1958 waren die des Provinzkapitels, das vom 13. bis 16. November 1962 im Konvent an Heilig Kreuz in Augsburg stattfand. Selbst die Provinzämter und -aufgaben wurden größtenteils noch immer mit Brüdern besetzt, die noch vor dem Krieg in den Orden eingetreten waren – einzige Ausnahmen waren Jordan Gebhard als Diffinitor, Raphael Börger als Archivar des süddeutschen Provinzteiles und Isnard Frank als Korrespondent

391 APKap 1958, S. 6–9, Nrn. 24, 29–32, 35 und 48–49.

für die „Analecta", sozusagen das Amtsblatt des Ordens. Jüngere Brüder wurden auch nachrangige Mitglieder von Gremien wie der Kommission zur Organisation von Volksmissionen oder der für die Erteilung der kirchlichen Druckerlaubnis; die Schlüsselpositionen blieben in den Händen der Älteren. Auch die Person des Provinzials blieb mit Augustinus Gierlich dieselbe. Selbst wenn man bedenkt, wie eingeschränkt die gesetzgebenden Kompetenzen eines Provinzkapitels grundsätzlich sind und dass in der Provincia Germaniae superioris nie die Tendenz bestand, alle vier Jahre das Rad neu zu erfinden und umfangreiche Provinzkapitelsakten zu produzieren, so fällt doch auf, wie allgemein die Anweisungen von 1962 gehalten sind: Da jegliche Konkretheit fehlt, sind Ermahnungen wie jene, dass die Brüder sich immer vor Augen halten sollten, dass das Wesen des Ordensgehorsams darin bestehe, mit gutem Willen alles zu erfüllen, was die Ordenssatzungen und die Oberen ihnen auferlegten, eher als Gemeinplätze zu interpretieren, denn als Reaktion auf eine Krise oder ein bestimmtes Problem. Auch die Ermahnung an alle wegen des herrschenden Personalmangels zur Bereitschaft zur Übernahme eines Amtes zeigt in diese Richtung und ist nicht als Zeichen eines allgemeinen Desinteresses zu interpretieren. Dasselbe gilt für die Ermahnung, trotz seelsorglicher Belastung regelmäßig am Chorgebet teilzunehmen oder die Anweisung, laikale Kleidung nur mit Erlaubnis der Oberen zu tragen. Die einzige Sorge, die aus den Akten sichtbar wird, ist die nach der Gewinnung von Ordensberufungen: in der schon genannten Ermahnung zur Amtsübernahme, in der Anweisung, dass jede Niederlassung der Provinz einmal im Jahr in Zusammenarbeit mit den Berufungspromotoren einen Tag der Förderung von Ordensberufungen abhalten solle, im Hinweis auf das täglichen Betens der Antiphon „O spem miram" oder eines anderen Gebets (auch auf Deutsch) für Berufungen oder in den Ermahnungen, dass die Echtheit des eigenen Lebensbeispieles das erste Mittel zur Berufungsförderung sei und die Prediger bei Volksmissionen, Exerzitienkursen oder Konferenzen die Vortrefflichkeit des Priester- und Ordenslebens verstärkt zur Sprache bringen sollten. Den Brüdern, die das Dominikuswerk verwalteten und unterstützten, wurde ausdrücklich gedankt. In den Zusammenhang der Pflege der bereits erhaltenen Berufungen gehört der einzige auffälligere Punkt der Akten, nämlich die Ermahnung der Oberen, in eigener oder durch eine andere geeignete Person dafür zu sorgen, den jüngeren Brüdern Beistand in ihren Seelsorgeaufgaben zu gewähren und ihnen gegenüber sanftmütig aufzutreten. Auch hier verbietet die Allgemeinheit der Formulierung

einen Rückschluss auf einen etwaig auftretenden Generationenkonflikt in der Provinz, allerdings schließt sie diese Konsequenz ebensowenig aus. Drei Aufträge gingen speziell an den Provinzial: die Bereitstellung von Assistenten für die Rosenkranzpromotoren, die Bestimmung eines Beauftragten für die Berufungsförderung in jeder Niederlassung und die Erhebung eines der beiden österreichischen Häuser Retz oder Friesach zum Konvent.[392] Von der Gründung einer weiteren Niederlassung in Vorarlberg war übrigens nicht mehr die Rede.

Erst die Akten des Provinzkapitels, das vom 4. bis 8. Juli 1966 in Graz begangen wurde, zeigten signifikante Änderungen. Das lag zum einen an der Sprache: Zum ersten Mal waren die Akten nicht mehr auf Latein, sondern auf Deutsch verfaßt. Zum anderen hatte sich der Titel der Provinz geändert: Das Generalkapitel von Toulouse hatte den Namen der Provincia Germaniae superioris mit „et Austriae" erweitert, also aus ihr eine „Provinz Süd- [oder Ober-]deutschland und Österreich" gemacht.[393] Zum dritten hatte sich, was die Beschickung des Kapitels mit Vertretern aus den Konventen betraf, ein Generationswechsel vollzogen: Die meisten der teilnehmenden Prioren und Socii waren nach dem Krieg in den Orden eingetreten. Dies spiegelte sich nicht im Inhalt der Akten, der weiterhin nicht innovativ zu nennen ist. Allerdings wird in den Bestimmungen dieses Provinzkapitels zum ersten Mal ein Problembewusstsein ausdrücklich formuliert, das die Akten früherer Kapitel bestenfalls andeuteten:

> „Die neuen Richtungen, die sich in der Seelsorge abzeichnen, stellen das klösterliche Leben vor bisher unbekannte Fragen. Die Schwierigkeiten haben ihre Ursache: in der vom zweiten vatikanischen Konzil geforderten Zusammenarbeit mit den Ortsbischöfen und in der Spezialisierung der heutigen Seelsorge. Neue Auffassungen über die soziale, wirtschaftliche und politische Struktur unserer Gesellschaft bringen, besonders bei jüngeren Mitbrüdern, Gedankengänge mit sich, die mit dem Leben in der Gemeinschaft nur schwer zu vereinbaren sind. Um auf diese schwierigen Fragen eine Antwort zu geben, verweisen wir auf die Grundlage und den Sinn klösterlichen Lebens, die im wesentlichen unveränderlich sind, nämlich auf die Liebe Christi: Er hat uns zu einer Einheit gesammelt, damit wir einander so lieben, wie auch er uns geliebt hat. Zeugnis dieser Liebe sind unsere Gebete. Deshalb ermahnen wir unsere Mitbrüder, dass sie nach Möglichkeit beim Chorgebet anwesend seien; dass täglich die Betrachtung zu gemeinsamer Zeit gehalten

392 APKap 1962, S. 7–9, Nrn. 29–40, 46 und 53–55.
393 ACG 1962, S. 71, Nr. 90.

> werde; dass jeder Mitbruder dem persönlichen Gebet genügend Zeit widmen möge.“[394]

Die konkreten Bestimmungen, die diesem Aufruf folgten, waren ein wenig umfangreicher als vordem üblich, erinnerten aber in vielem an die Anweisungen älterer Provinzkapitel: Die Brüder sollten Fernsehapparate, Rundfunkgeräte und Zeitungen in kluger Weise nutzen, damit das religiöse Leben keinen Schaden erlitte. Vor der Gemeinschaft sollten die Hausoberen einmal im Monat eine geistliche Ansprache halten; vor dem Einzelnen sollten sie sich als gute Hirten erweisen. Wieder wurde bestimmt, dass die Brüder entweder das Ordensgewand oder klerikale Kleidung tragen und diesbezüglich die Anordnungen der Ortsbischöfe genau befolgt werden sollten. Die tägliche Messfeier aller Ordenspriester wurde eingeschärft, aber dafür die Gebete, die frühere Provinzkapitel für verschiedene Anliegen auferlegt hatten, abgeschafft. Einzige Ausnahme war die Dauersorge der Provinz, die Förderung von Ordensberufungen: Hier wurde den Brüdern, wie immer, die Bedeutung des eigenen Lebensbeispiels zur Mehrung der Zahl an Ordensberufungen vor Augen gehalten. Alle Brüder wurden eindringlich gebeten, auf jede kluge Weise Berufungen zu fördern. Einer allgemeinkirchlichen Empfehlung folgend bestimmte das Provinzkapitel, dass der zweite Sonntag nach Ostern besonders der Förderung religiöser Berufe zu widmen war. Zur Berufungsförderung sollte die Antiphon „O lumen“ nach der Komplet gebetet werden. Bezüglich der Studien legten die Akten fest, dass alle Brüder sich mit Eifer um eine Fortbildung in jenen Wissensgebieten sorgen sollten, die zum Bereich des Ordens gehören – diese sehr offene Formulierung war wohl bewusst gewählt, um so wenige Fortbildungsgebiete auszuschließen wie möglich. Beabsichtigt war damit die Beteiligung von Brüdern an von der Provinz veranstalteten Fortbildungsveranstaltungen, Kursen oder Akademien; Universitätsstudiengänge wurden nicht genannt, allerdings waren diese durch die Ordenssatzungen und die Ordensausbildungsprogramme (die sogenannte „Ratio formationis“ des Ordens und die „Ratio formationis particularis“ der Provinz) bereits eigens geregelt. In Erinnerung gerufen wurde die Anordnung des Provinzkapitels von 1962 über die Pflicht zur Rechenschaftsberichtslegung für alle Universitätsstudenten.[395] Bezüglich der Seelsorge erging sich das Kapitel in Ermahnungen:

394 APKap 1966, S. 9–10, Nr. 27.
395 Ebd., S. 10–11, Nr. 28–40.

„Unsere Mitbrüder sollen daran denken, dass sie Diener des Wortes Gottes sind. Deshalb sollen sie in der Verkündigung des Wortes die Gläubigen durch eine gesunde Lehre erbauen und sie nicht durch theologisch ungewisse Meinungen verwirren. In den einzelnen Häusern soll jeden Monat eine Seelsorgskonferenz abgehalten werden, in der auch Überlegungen angestellt werden mögen, wie in der Seelsorge vorzugehen sei. Die Oberen sollen dafür sorgen, dass die Arbeit in den uns anvertrauten Kirchen und die von uns fest übernommenen Seelsorgsarbeiten keinen Schaden leiden. Mit Gelegenheitsaushilfen sollen die Mitbrüder nicht zu sehr belastet werden."[396]

Dazu traten noch drei Einzelpunkte, nämlich die Aufforderung, den Reichtum des Rosenkranzgebets der heutigen Zeit zu eröffnen, zusammen mit den Drittordensmitgliedern nach neuen Wegen des geistlichen und apostolischen Lebens der Laien zu suchen und den Nonnen und Schwestern des Ordens zu helfen, sich die sie betreffenden Dekrete des zweiten vatikanischen Konzils zu eigen zu machen.[397] An den Provinzial ergingen die speziellen Aufträge, über die Studenten der Provinz in Walberberg zu wachen und sorgfältig die aus dem „Studium commune" erwachsenen Rechte zu wahren, mit besonderer Achtung der Fächer der Pastoral. Weiter sollte er Erkundigungen über die Art und Weise einer Krankenversicherung einholen und dafür sorgen, dass in den Niederlassungen das 750-jährige Jubiläum der Ordensgründung würdig gefeiert wurde.[398]

Außerdem wurde P. Augustinus Gierlich für die zwei Amtszeiten gedankt, in denen er als Provinzial die Provinz geführt hatte. Gierlich zog sich zu den Dominikanerinnen nach Neusatzeck zurück, wo er bis 1974 als Spiritual wirkte. Er verstarb nach langer Krankheit 1984 in Köln.[399] Zu seinem Nachfolger als Provinzial der süddeutsch-österreichischen Provinz wählte das Provinzkapitel von 1966 P. Innozenz Varga.[400] Varga unterschied sich in einem wesentlichen Punkt von seinen beiden Amtsvorgängern Vetter und Gierlich: Er war nur kurze Zeit vor der Provinzgründung in den Orden eingetreten – er hatte 1936 Profess in der österreichisch-ungarischen Provinz gemacht –, war also in und mit der Provinz aufgewachsen. Bereits für den Polenfeldzug war er Anfang September 1939 zum Wehrdienst eingezogen worden. Nach Beendigung seiner philosophisch-theologischen

396 Ebd., S. 11–12, Nrn. 41–43.
397 Ebd., S. 12, Nrn. 44–46.
398 Ebd., S. 13, Nrn. 50–53.
399 PA, Provinzrundbrief vom 27.7.1984, S. 6 und *St. Dominikuswerk* (1985), S. 10.
400 APKap 1966, S. 6, Nr. 6.

Studien und der Priesterweihe 1947 wirkte er 1949 bis 1959 als Direktor des Juvenats in Graz und hatte 1951 das St.-Dominikuswerk neu gegründet. Von 1959 bis 1966 war er als Prior dem Wiener Dominikanerkonvent vorgestanden. Insgesamt würde Varga genauso lange wie Vetter als Provinzial amtieren, zwanzig Jahre. Und ebenso wie Vetter würde er Schwierigkeiten zu meistern haben, die die Provinz in ihren Grundfesten erschüttern würden: Vetter hatte mit Faschismus, Zerstörung und Wiederaufbau zu kämpfen gehabt – Varga sah sich in seiner Amtszeit den Phänomenen gegenüber, die die Akten des Provinzkapitels von 1966 andeuteten: einer allgemeinen Krise, die das Ordensleben nach dem Konzil durchlebte, einer gesteigerten Personalnot, neuen seelsorglichen Aufgabenstellungen, die mit den alten pastoralen Angeboten nicht mehr zu leisten waren, und einem sich immer deutlicher ausdrückende Zug zum Individualismus, der die Klostergemeinschaften an der Wurzel bedrohte.

Legislative Auswirkungen des Konzils:
Die Konstitutionen des Generalkapitels von River Forest 1968

„Liebe Mitbrüder! Nun kann ich Ihnen die Akten unseres letzten Provinzkapitels überreichen. Das Heft ist zwar nicht umfangreich, doch versuchten wir, darin auf das Wesentliche einer zeitgemäßen Erneuerung des Ordenslebens hinzuweisen. Die Erreichung des in den Akten gesetzten Zieles hängt ab vom täglichen Bemühen aller Mitbrüder und vom Mut zu wirklichen Opfern." – So lauteten die ersten Zeilen des ersten Rundbriefs des neuen Provinzials vom 7. Oktober 1966.[401] Stolze Worte für die Bestimmungen des Provinzkapitels von 1966, die wir oben zitiert bzw. skizziert haben. Welchen Abschnitt der Akten bezeichnete Varga als Hinweis auf das Wesentliche einer zeitgenäßen Erneuerung des Ordenslebens? Wahrscheinlich den Verweis „auf die Grundlage und den Sinn klösterlichen Lebens, die im Wesentlichen unveränderlich sind, nämlich auf die Liebe Christi: Er hat uns zu einer Einheit gesammelt, damit wir einander so lieben, wie auch er uns geliebt hat." Der Ausdruck der „zeitgemäßen Erneuerung des Ordenslebens" stammte aus den Konzilstexten: Am 28. Oktober 1965 hatte Papst Paul VI. das „Decretum de accomodata renovatione vitae religiosae" unterzeichnet, das nach seinem Incipit unter dem Namen „Perfectae caritatis" bekannt wurde. Tatsächlich war die deutsche Übersetzung des Dekrettitels

401 PA, Provinzrundbrief „am Rosenkranzfest" 1966, S. 1.

selbst bereits Interpretation: „Accomodata renovatio" bedeutet nur „angepasste Erneuerung". Der Dekrettext verwies aber als Maßstab dafür auf eine „ständige Rückkehr zu den Quellen jeglichen christlichen Lebens und zum Geist des Ursprungs der einzelnen [sc. Ordens-] Institute, zugleich aber deren Anpassung an die veränderten Zeitverhältnisse", konkret auf die Nachfolge Christi als letzte Norm, sowie als weitere Prinzipien auf die Bewahrung der Eigenart des Instituts durch Rückkehr zum Geist des Gründers und die Pflege gesunder Überlieferungen, die Teilnahme an der allgemeinen kirchlichen Erneuerung in Liturgie, Pastoral, Mission usw. und den Erwerb von Kenntnissen über die gesellschaftlichen und menschlichen Verhältnisse in der modernen Welt, aufbauend nicht nur auf eine äußerliche Erneuerung, sondern auf einer geistlichen Reform".[402] Aus dieser und den anderen Darlegungen des Dekrets ergab sich demnach eine angepasste Erneuerung des Ordenslebens in zwei Zeitrichtungen: die Vergangenheit, verkörpert im Geist der Gründung des jeweiligen Ordens, und die Gegenwart, die Anforderungen der modernen Welt. Anders gesagt: Das zweite vatikanische Konzil verpflichtete die Orden beim geforderten Neuentwurf ihres Lebenskonzepts auf einen Spagat.

Die Frage nach notwendigen Veränderungen hatte die Dominikaner nicht erst mit „Perfectae caritatis" beschäftigt. 1963 hatte der Orden seinen liturgischen Eigenritus reformiert und versucht, ihn an die Vorstellung der sogenannten Liturgischen Erneuerung anzupassen. Er blieb aber beim Eigenritus.[403] Im Juli 1965, auf dem Generalkapitel von Bogotá, versuchte man eine Korrektur der Satzungen an die Erfordernisse des 20. Jahrhunderts. In der für die Reform der Konstitutionen zuständigen Kapitelskommission saß auch Innozenz Varga. Die Satzungsänderungen nahmen den größten Teil der Kapitelsakten ein (S. 35–109). Sehr viele Einzelheiten wurden geändert, wobei auch vor der Abschaffung ältester Bräuche des Ordens nicht zurückgeschreckt wurde – so fiel z. B. die äußerliche Trennung der Laienbrüder von den Dominikanerklerikern im Ordenshabit durch die Abschaffung des schwarzen Skapuliers und der schwarzen Kapuze der Brü-

---

402 Für diesen Konzilstext wird hier die zweisprachige, lateinisch-deutsche Ausgabe von „Perfectae caritatis" benutzt aus: *Lexikon für Theologie und Kirche*. Ergänzungsband 2, S. 266–307; wörtliches Zitat: Nr. 2, S. 269, die restlichen Punkte ebenfalls Nr. 2, S. 269–273.

403 Vgl. die diesbezüglichen Anordnungen: „Diversae variationes in missae rubricis" in: *ASOP* (1963) S. 173–180.

der.[404] Weitere Änderungen betrafen die Observanzen und andere Rechtsfragen (S. 110–121), liturgische Punkte (S. 122–129), Fragen des Studiums (S. 130–136) und Fragen der Seelsorge, besonders der Verkündigung (S. 137–144). Die grundsätzlichen Leitungsprinzipien und traditionellen Strukturen blieben unangetastet. Die Bestimmungen von Bogotá[405] hätten ein Höhepunkt dominikanischer Legislative werden können – tatsächlich waren sie etwa dreizehn Monate nach Beginn ihrer Geltung obsolet.

Mit der Arbeit des Generalkapitels von Bogotá wurde eine kurze, aber bedeutende Ära der dominikanischen Eigenrechtsgeschichte abgeschlossen. Diese hatte 1917 mit der Kodifikation des katholischen Kirchenrechtes in der Ausgabe des ersten allgemeinen kirchlichen Gesetzbuches, des sogenannten Codex Juris Canonici, begonnen. An dieses Gesetzbuch hatten alle Orden ihr Eigenrecht anzupassen – eine Aufgabe, die die Generalkapitel von Corias in Asturien (1920), Rom (1924), Ocaña (1926) und Rom (1929) für die Dominikaner übernahmen. Am Ende stand eine völlig neue Ausgabe der Ordenskonstitutionen, erlassen durch das Generalkapitel von Le Saulchoir 1932. Man nannte sie auch Gillet-Konstitutionen, weil Ordensmeister Martin Stanislaus Gillet ihre Druckausgabe in Auftrag gegeben hatte.[406] Im auffallenden Unterschied zu den vor 1917 geltenden Satzungen, die sich in Aufbau, Struktur und Inhalt immer direkt auf die im 13. Jahrhundert begonnene und durch die folgenden Jahrhunderte gewachsene dominikanische Eigenrechtstradition bezogen hatten, orientierten sich die Gillet-Konstitutionen nun ganz am Codex Juris Canonici. Um es mit einem Bild auszudrücken: An der Stelle eines alleinstehenden Baumes mit einem mächtigen Stamm und vielen Zweigen, der im Nährboden der kirchlichen (Rechts-)Lehre wuchs, stand nun ein Spaliergewächs, befestigt am Rankgerüst des allgemeinen Kirchenrechts. Faschismus und Weltkrieg behinderten noch dazu die Pflege dieser neuen Pflanze. Dies erklärt auch die hauptsächlich restaurativen Bemühungen von Ordensmeister Emmanuel Suárez und der Generalkapitel nach 1945, da der Orden erst jetzt die Bemühungen fortsetzen konnte, seine Rechtstraditionen in die Gillet-

---

404 Zur Änderung des Laienbrüderhabits siehe: ACG 1965, S. 99, Nr. 198. Laut PA, Liber consiliorum provinciae, Sitzung in Wien am 7.6.1966, S. 63 beschloss das Provinzkonsil der süddeutsch-österreichischen Provinz übrigens, dass die Laienbrüder der Provinz am Rosenkranzfest, dem 7.10.1966, den Habit zu wechseln hatten.

405 Publiziert als: *Collectio inchoationum, declarationum et ordinationum.* Roma 1966, auf 133 Seiten.

406 *Constitutiones 1932.*

Konstitutionen einzuarbeiten. Von allen Nachkriegsgeneralkapiteln war das von Bogotá 1965 dasjenige, das sich am innovativsten und umfangreichsten mit der Pflege des Spalierbäumchens beschäftigte und, angeregt durch die Impulse des zweiten vatikanischen Konzils, versuchte, die neueren Entwicklungen in Kirche, Gesellschaft und Orden in die Satzungen einzuarbeiten. – Diese Hintergrundinformationen, soweit entfernt sie auch von der Geschichte der süddeutsch-österreichischen Provinz zu sein scheinen, sind wichtig, um die Tiefe des Einschnitts der folgenden Entwicklung zu verstehen.

Am 6. August 1966 erließ Papst Paul VI. das Motu Proprio „Ecclesiae sanctae“ zur praktischen Durchführung von „Perfectae caritatis“. „Ecclesiae sanctae“ schrieb vor, dass alle Ordensmitglieder bei der Erneuerung ihrer Gemeinschaft, ihrer Gesetze und Normen mitzuarbeiten hatten. Dazu sollte innerhalb der folgenden zwei oder drei Jahre in jedem Orden ein Sondergeneralkapitel zusammentreten. Zur Vorbereitung dieses Sondergeneralkapitels sollte der Generalrat umfangreiche Vorbereitungen treffen, die Meinung der Provinzen, Konvente und Brüder hören und ihnen eine Reihe von relevanten Fragen stellen. Das Sondergeneralkapitel selbst sollte alles Recht haben, die geltenden Ordensgesetze zu ändern. Selbst Experimente gegen das allgemeine Recht (experimenta contra jus commune), die allerdings klug vorzunehmen wären, würden bei dieser Gelegenheit vom Heiligen Stuhl gerne (libenter) erlaubt. Diese Experimente sollten dann bis zum nächsten gewöhnlichen Generalkapitel ausprobiert werden können, um danach gegebenenfalls bestätigt oder wieder abgeschafft zu werden, aber nicht über dieses nächste Generalkapitel hinaus.[407] „Ecclesiae sanctae“ machte die bisherigen Anpassungen des dominikanischen Eigenrechtes – und damit auch die Bestimmungen von Bogotá – obsolet. Die Anpassungsarbeit musste von neuem begonnen werden.

Die dominikanische Ordenskurie erstellte einen umfangreichen Fragebogen, der über die jeweiligen Provinziäle jedem Mitbruder auf der ganzen Welt zur Einsichtnahme und Kommentierung zugestellt wurde. Provinzial Varga versandte die deutsche Übersetzung dieses Fragebogens im Provinzrundbrief vom 25. Januar 1967 an die Brüder in Süddeutschland und Österreich mit der Erklärung: „[Es] wird im September diesen Jahres

407 Für diese Arbeit lag nur der Auszug der Nrn. 2–6 von „Ecclesiae sanctae“ vor, den Ordensmeister Aniceto Fernandez in seinem Schreiben an den Orden vom 1.11.1968 wörtlich zitiert; siehe: *LCO 1969*, S. v–xvii, Zitat auf S. vii–ix.

ein für vier Wochen anberaumter Kongress der Provinziäle stattfinden, bei dem die beantworteten Fragen behandelt werden. Zu diesem Kongress soll den Provinzial ein *peritus* [sc. ein Fachmann] begleiten. Unser Provinzkonsil bestimmte P. Isnard Frank für diese Aufgabe. … Der Fragebogen hat hinweisenden Charakter. Die Mitbrüder können auch bezüglich anderer Fragen ihre Wünsche und Ratschläge vorbringen. Der Provinzial kann die Befragung in seinem Bereich frei ordnen, z. B. bezüglich der Hinzuziehung der Hauskonsilien oder anderer Gremien.“[408] Die Antworten der Brüder sollten bis zum 7. April 1967 im Wiener Konvent angelangt sein, damit das Provinzkonsil auf seiner Tagung vom 11. April diese behandeln und bis zum 1. Mai an die Generalkurie nach Rom schicken konnte.[409] Insgesamt waren es 64 Hauptfragen. Allesamt betrafen sie keine Kleinigkeiten, sondern reichten tief in ganze Gebiete hinein. So lauteten z. B. die Fragen nach den Grundlagen des Ordens:

> „A. Worin besteht der besondere Charakter des Geistes und des Lebens unseres hl. Vaters Dominikus? Was war sein eigentliches Anliegen bei der Gründung des Ordens? B. Wenn wir auf das Beispiel der Kirche schauen, die sich selbst auf eine neue Art sieht, welche Selbstvorstellung muss der Orden nach Absicht der Dokumente des 2. vatikanischen Konzils, besonders der Dokumente ‚Lumen gentium‘ (Kap. 5 und 6) und ‚Perfectae caritatis‘ für sich herausbilden? C. Angesichts der Menschen unserer Zeit, denen wir das Wort Gottes verkünden müssen: welche Fragen ergeben sich für uns aus den Konzilsdokumenten, besonders aus ‚Gaudium et spes'? Gemäß dem oben Gesagten: D. Wie ist die heutige Zielsetzung des Ordens zu definieren? Wie sind heute die wesentlichen Mittel, die mit diesem Ziel verbunden sind, praktisch durchzuführen? …“[410]

Gefragt wurde auch nach möglichen Veränderungen im Bereich des Noviziats, des Studiums und generell der Ausbildung, nach einer erforderlichen engeren Einbindung der Laienbrüder in die Leitungsstruktur durch Erhalt des aktiven und passiven Wahlrechts, nach dem Sinn und der praktischen Ausführung der evangelischen Räte und der klösterlichen Observanzen in der heutigen Zeit, nach der Rolle des Konventskapitels und der anderen Leitungsgremien des Ordens usw.

---

408 PA, Provinzrundbrief vom 25.1.1967, S. 1–2.

409 So laut Blatt 1 „Praktische Hinweise“ des dem Provinzrundbrief vom 25.1.1967 beigelegten Fragebogens.

410 So ebd., „Fragebogen“, Blatt 2.

Mit dem Ergebnis der Fragebogenaktion in seiner Provinz zeigte Varga sich zufrieden und so schrieb er seinen Brüdern kurz vor seiner Abreise zum Provinziälekongress: „Nicht nur das Provinzkonsil, sondern auch sehr viele Mitbrüder unserer Provinz haben den von Rom zugesandten Fragebogen beantwortet und sich dabei viel Mühe gegeben. Diese Antworten sind eine wertvolle Hilfe für die Entscheidungen des Kongresses."[411] Aus den 2.500 Antwortschreiben der Provinzen und Brüder aus dem gesamten Orden destillierte eine dreißigköpfige Kommission 6.556 Sätze und fügte sie zu einem Basistext zusammen. Dieser wurde dann auf dem angekündigten, den ganzen Monat September dauernden Kongress im „Angelicum" in Rom behandelt. Die Provinziäle und Fachleute konkretisierten 389 Schlussfolgerungen daraus, die für eine Redaktion des Satzungstextes des Ordens als Normen zu berücksichtigen waren.[412] Der Bericht, den P. Isnard Frank seinen Mitbrüdern in der Provinz über diesen Kongress vorlegte, ist sehr beachtenswert, weil Frank ihn in die gesamte Erneuerungsbemühung des Ordens einordnete, die er durchaus kritisch sah:

> „Alle bedeutenderen Ordensgemeinschaften haben in den letzten Jahren die vom Konzil vorgezeichneten Wege zur Erneuerung eingeschlagen und dabei manchmal beachtliche Initiativen entwickelt. Unser Orden hat sich diesen Bemühungen ziemlich spät angeschlossen. Erst der römische Kongress wurde zum Forum, auf dem sich der gesamte Orden nicht nur Rechenschaft über die veränderte Situation zu geben versuchte, sondern auch die Anweisung erhielt, präzise Direktionen für die Umarbeitung der Konstitutionen vorzulegen. Man könnte diese verspätete Aktivität (die natürlich auch ihre Vorteile hat) zum Anlass nehmen und fragen, ob die Ordensleitung und mit ihr ein Teil des ganzen Ordens sich zu einem solchen Schritt überhaupt nur herbeigelassen hat, weil eindeutige konziliare Richtlinien dafür vorliegen und es jetzt nur darum geht, alle im Orden aufgebrochenen Initiativen wieder auf eine gemäßigte und möglichst wenig ‚modernistische' Linie zu bringen. Die Ansprache des Generalmeisters zu Beginn der Arbeit kann man in einem solchen Sinn deuten; ganz sicher aber sieht eine breite vor allem in Italien, Spanien, Südamerika und Irland vertretene Gruppe das Erneuerungswerk

---

411 PA, Provinzrundbrief vom 30.8.1967. Im Protokoll des Povinzkonsils wird die Besprechung der Fragebögen verständlicherweise nur summarisch erwähnt (PA, Liber consiliorum provinciae, Sitzung in Wien vom 11.–13.4.1967, S. 67). Demnach wurden dort die erhaltenen Antworten zu einer Stellungnahme der Provinz zusammengefasst und nach Rom geschickt.

412 So laut Brief des Ordensmeisters Aniceto Fernandez vom 1.11.1968 (in: *LCO 1969*, S. ix–x).

schon dadurch geleistet, dass man in diesem oder jenem Fall einige Abstriche macht und im Übrigen mit viel konziliaren Ausdrücken die alte und wohlbewährte Gestalt des Ordens möglichst weitgehend schont. Bei jeder Diskussion um eine wichtigere Sache wurde diese Intention sichtbar. In einem anderen Sinn dagegen verstand die um die Franzosen gesammelte Gruppe die nötige Ordenserneuerung. Hier ging es überhaupt um ein neues Konzept, das in einer gewandelten Zeit die ursprüngliche Zielsetzung des Ordens adäquat auszudrücken vermag. Die französischen Dominikaner waren auch auf dem Kongress gut vertreten. Mehr oder weniger eng schloss sich ihrem Programm die ganze Region Nord an, die englische und kanadische Provinz, sowie die amerikanischen Provinzen von St. Joseph und St. Albert. …

Über die grundsätzliche Gestalt des Ordens wurde keine tiefgehende Diskussion geführt; … Gegenstand heftiger Kontroversen war nur die Frage, wie das in seinem Grundbestand evangelische Programm des im 13. Jahrhundert entstandenen und von jener Gesellschaft geprägten Ordens der heutigen Aufgabe entsprechende Strukturen finden könne; mit anderen Worten: Welche konkreten Lebensformen und Vorstellungen behindern heute die echte und lebendige Verwirklichung des alten und evangelischen Ordenszieles. … Neben den eigentlichen und überall gleich verbindlichen Konstitutionen wird es ein Direktorium geben, das wieder in ein solches für den ganzen Orden und eines für die Provinz beziehungsweise für eine Region geteilt sein wird. … Die Idee, die hinter diesem Aufbau steht, ist der Gedanke einer weitreichenden Dezentralisation der Verfassung und vor allem der Verwaltung, die mehr als bisher – und ohne das Dispensprinzip strapazieren zu müssen – den Gegebenheiten und Erfordernissen eines Landes besser Rechnung zu tragen vermag.

Der andere vorherrschende Gedanke ist die Demokratisierung. Das Wort selber vermag vielleicht nicht richtig wiederzugeben, worum es dabei geht. Natürlich ist der Orden nicht in allem mit einer parlamentarischen Demokratie zu vergleichen. Für die ‚evangelische Ordnung' des Gemeinschaftslebens bedarf es aber Strukturen, die die Verantwortlichkeit eines jeden einzelnen für die Gemeinschaft möglich machen. Die ganze Verfassung des Ordens soll ein Appell an diese Verantwortlichkeit werden. Darum ist in jedem Konvent das Konventskapitel gedacht als Ort der brüderlichen Beratung und Meinungsbildung über die konkrete Gestalt der Lebensweise und der apostolischen Arbeit. Von diesem Kapitel, in dem auch die Fratres cooperatores [sc. die Laienbrüder] Stimmrecht haben sollen, werden auch die Mitglieder des Hauskonsils gewählt. Im Dienst der Verantwortlichkeit steht auch jener hart umstrittene und nur mit knapper Mehrheit verabschiedete Gedanke, dass es in Zukunft nur noch gewählte Vertreter für jede Art von Verwaltung und Gesetzgebung auf Haus-, Provinz- und Gesamtordensebene geben wird. …

> [An] der Notwendigkeit des Gebets, der Sammlung eines ‚religiösen Lebensstils' wurde überhaupt nicht gerüttelt. Sehr wohl aber stand zur Diskussion, ob die bisherige Form unseres gemeinsamen [sc. Chor-]Gebetes wirklich sinnvoll ist; ob sie echtes Gebet nicht eher verhindere als ermögliche und ob unsere Art der Persolvierung überhaupt modernes Gebetsethos unterbiete. … Dem Generalkapitel von Chicago wird also in diesem hart umkämpften Bereich noch eine schwierige Aufgabe bevorstehen. …
>
> Ausführlich wurde auch über die Studienordnung gesprochen. Man kann aber konstatieren, dass hier Dinge zur Sprache kamen, die z. B. für unsere deutschen Provinzen schon des längeren zur Selbstverständlichkeit geworden sind. Sehr heikle Probleme allerdings – wie etwa der Sinn des Angelicums – wurden zwar ausgiebig besprochen, aber nicht geklärt. Andere kamen gar nicht zur Sprache, z. B. wo am besten das Noviziat (an dessen Berechtigung man nicht zweifelt) in der Ausbildung seinen Ort haben müsse. Über solche Dinge lässt sich wohl auch in Zukunft kein Konsens erreichen. Dies aber mit Bedauern zur Kenntnis zu nehmen, wäre wohl nicht am Platze. Denn sehr viele Dinge, die bisher als für den ganzen Orden in gleicher Weise verbindlich angesehen wurden, dürften in Zukunft in den Zuständigkeitsbereich der einzelnen Provinzen fallen. Diese also sind in einem viel höheren Maß als bisher zu der Verantwortlichkeit dem Orden gegenüber aufgerufen; eine Verantwortlichkeit, die sich mit Überwachung und Administration natürlich nicht erfassen lässt, sondern die einer genauen Kenntnis der Situation eines Landes und seiner Bedürfnisse, der psychischen Verfasstheit potentieller Kandidaten bedarf und gepaart sein müsste mit der Fähigkeit, Initiativen zu entwickeln …“[413]

Franks Beobachtungen über die allgemeine dominikanische zeitgemäße Anpassung des Lebens des gesamten Ordens sind direkt auf die Meinungslage in der süddeutsch-österreichischen Provinz übertragbar: Wie unser Blick in die Provinzkapitelsakten von 1962 oder 1966 (und auch ältere Akten) gezeigt hat, herrschte auch hier eine eher beharrende Haltung vor. Außerdem nennt Frank alle wesentlichen Elemente der Veränderung, die der Predigerorden in seinen Satzungen vornahm: 1. der Versuch der konkreten Fassung des Ordensideals beziehungsweise des Ordenszieles; 2. die weitreichende Dezentralisierung der Ordensstruktur von der Ebene der Gesamtordensleitung auf die Provinzebene (man könnte auch von einer Provinzialisierung des Ordens sprechen, gerade weil dieser Begriff eine doppelte Bedeutung trägt); 3. die Aufwertung des Konventskapitels als leitungs-

413 PA, „Bericht über den römischen Provinzialkongress (2. –28. September 1967) von P. Isnard Frank, Anhang zum Provinzrundbrief „am dritten Adventssonntag“ 1967, S. 7–10.

berechtigte Versammlung aller Konventualen, auch der bisher stimmrechtslosen Laienbrüder und 4. die Institutionalisierung der Verwaltungsgremien durch Wahl ihrer Mitglieder (die bisher meistens Versammlungen bestimmter Amtsträger und traditionell privilegierter Einzelner bestanden).

Die 389 Schlussfolgerungen des Kongresses wurden vom Ordensmeister einer Zentralkommission vorgelegt, die sie in sechsmonatiger Arbeit mit den aus der Fragebogenaktion gewonnenen Erkenntnissen zu einem Textvorschlag der zukünftigen Gestalt der Ordenssatzungen zusammenstellte, der auf dem Generalkapitel von River Forest bei Chicago besprochen wurde.[414] Eigentlich hatte das Generalkapitel von Bogotá ja Jerusalem als Tagungsort des nächsten Generalkapitels vorgesehen,[415] aber das dortige Dominikanerkloster St. Stephan erwies sich als viel zu klein für die Zahl der Provinziäle, *periti* und anderen Teilnehmer, die für die Erledigung der anstehenden Aufgaben notwendig waren. Stattdessen wurde als Tagungsort das Generalstudienhaus der Provinz des hl. Albert in den USA in River Forest / Illinois, einem Vorort von Chicago ausgewählt, wo die Kapitularen zwei Monate, vom 30. August bis zum 24. Oktober 1968, tagten. Die süddeutsch-österreichische Provinz war durch ihren Provinzial, Innozenz Varga und seinen *peritus*, Isnard Frank vertreten. Varga saß in der Kommission „de vita regulari“, über das Ordensleben, Frank in der Kommission „de regimine“, über die Leitung.

Abb. 65: P. Innozenz Varga (aufgenommen 1988; PA, Fotosammlung)

Ergebnis der Beratungen war ein neues Satzungsbuch, „Liber constitutionum et ordinationum“.[416] Ordensmeister Fernandez hob in seiner Einführung dazu besonders eine Innovation hervor: Dem Satzungstext war eine sogenannte Fundamentalkonstitution vorgeschaltet worden, in der versucht worden war, das Ordensziel in Worte zu fassen. Die

414 So laut *LCO 1969*, S. xii.
415 ACG 1965, S. 34, Nr. 43.
416 *LCO 1969*.

Satzungen waren in der neuen Ausgabe in thematische Kapitel gegliedert: über das Ordensleben, über Gebet und Liturgie, über die Ausbildung / Studien, über den Dienst am Wort / die Seelsorge usw. Perfekt seien die neuen bzw. neuformulierten Satzungen noch nicht, meinte Fernandez, was aber kein großes Problem darstelle, weil ja die Möglichkeit bestand, sie nach Art des Ordens durch die Generalkapitel zu verbessern.[417]

Provinzial Varga sah die Lage in seinem ausführlichen Bericht an die Provinz über das Generalkapitel von River Forest differenzierter:

> „Die neuen Konstitutionen sind sicherlich kein Meisterwerk. … Obwohl die Anregungen der Mitbrüder (die Antworten auf die Befragungen) aufgegriffen und beim Kapitel in eine fassliche Gestalt gebracht wurden, wird unser Werk von River Forest trotzdem vielen Enttäuschung bereiten. Enttäuscht werden jene Mitbrüder sein, die hofften, unsere Lebensordnung werde in einem neuen Verfassungwerk endlich in einer anderen als in der juristischen Sprache unserer alten Konstitutionen zum Ausdruck gebracht werden; das neue Verfassungswerk werde eine erleuchtete Handreichung sein, mit welcher der Orden aus verfahrenem Konservatismus herausgebracht und den fälligen radikalen Änderungen zugeführt werde. Enttäuscht werden aber auch jene Mitbrüder sein, die in den neuen Konstitutionen viele Anzeichen finden, die sie in ihrer Meinung bestätigen, dass das Generalkapitel den seit Jahren vorhandenen Trend verstärkte: abzuschaffen, aufzulösen, der willkürlichen Lebensform Tür und Tor zu öffnen. Vielleicht werden sich diese enttäuschten Mitbrüder sogar fragen, ob eigentlich dieser Ordo Praedicatorum noch jene Gemeinschaft ist, auf die sie einmal Profess ablegten, der sie ein Leben lang in Treue zu dienen versuchten; kurz gesagt: eine Enttäuschung, weil dieser Orden jetzt ein anderer geworden ist."

Diese Feststellung Vargas erwies sich im Hinblick auf die Personalkrise, die noch kommen würde, geradezu als prophetisch. Wie der Ordensmeister, so verwies auch Varga auf die Möglichkeit, ja die Notwendigkeit, die neuen Satzungen im Laufe der kommenden Generalkapitel zu verbessern, sowie auf ein die neuen Konstitutionen leitendes Grundprinzip:

> „So wie jeder von uns konkret den Orden vor allem in seiner eigenen Gemeinschaft erfährt, so ist der Orden vor allem von dem conventus fratrum, der einzelnen Gemeinschaft her zu begreifen, die ein Zentrum der Seelsorge, der Studien und des geistlichen Lebens sein soll. Von dieser Lebensform und Aufgabe her hat die Ordensgesetzgebung ihr Maß zu nehmen. Es ist nicht so, dass das Erste, das, was immer und überall und ohne Abstriche zu gelten

417 Siehe Brief des Ordensmeisters Aniceto Fernandez vom 1.11.1968 (*LCO 1969*, S. xi–xvii).

hätte, das abstrakte Gesetz, die Konstitutionen, sind. Nicht einem Gesetz als heiligem und unveränderlichem Buchstaben binden wir uns in der Profess; das Verfassungswerk, der abstrakte Ordensverband ist nicht Selbstzweck; er steht in der Funktion der Existenz und Aufgabe des conventus fratrum. … Daher die Betonung des capitulum conventus … daher auch die neu gefassten Vorschriften über die Wahl der höheren Oberen, bei der grundsätzlich gilt, dass nur gewählte Vertreter und nicht irgendwelche Titulare beteiligt sein sollen. In diesem Zusammenhang muss auch die beschlossene Dezentralisierung gesehen werden: bei sehr vielen Einzelheiten verzichtet die Gesetzgebung auf eine genauere Angabe; sie sieht vielmehr vor, dass von den einzelnen Provinzen, je nach Bedürfnissen, dies so oder so gemacht werden kann."

Bezüglich der weiterhin sehr trockenen, juristischen Sprache der Satzungen führte Varga aus:

„Unsere Konstitutionen sind – wie schon erwähnt – nicht einen ganz neuen Weg gegangen. Wir haben uns in River Forest nicht von der Regel der Brüder von Taizé inspirieren lassen wie andere Orden, die weniger ein Handbuch des praktischen Lebens als vielmehr ein Handbuch des spirituellen Lebens zu schaffen versuchten. Wir wollten kein reines Erbauungsbuch schaffen. In der allgemeinen Befragung und in den Antworten darauf war zwar oft die Forderung nach einer biblischen, einer erbaulichen Sprache; aber beim Provinzialkongress vergangenen Jahres in Rom zeichnete sich ab, dass dieser Weg nicht gangbar ist und zudem ein Gemisch von beidem keinem nützen kann. River Forest hatte darüber schon gar nicht mehr debattiert. Es ist eine der Funktion der Verfassung angemessene Sprache: Vorschriften, Anweisungen, genaue Umschreibungen dort, wo solche gegeben werden können und erwartet werden müssen. … Man darf hier noch anfügen, dass es nie Aufgabe unserer Konstitutionen war, die spirituellen Grundlagen unseres gemeinsamen Lebens darzustellen. Diese bilden die Heilige Schrift, die geistlichen Traditionen der Kirche und für uns noch die in der Regula Augustini verdichtete Vita-Apostolica-Bewegung des 12. und 13. Jahrhunderts und die im Orden selber dann ausgebildeten und von seiner Theologie befruchteten Formen des geistlichen Lebens. … Gesetzgebung aber war und soll auch heute jener Rahmen einer ‚Hausordnung' sein, die bei aller spiritueller Akzentsetzung unsere äußere Einheit noch zu garantieren vermag."

Insgesamt wertete Varga die Neuausgabe aber als ein „sehr flexibles und ein sehr von der Verantwortung der Brüder, die den Orden der Fratrum Praedicatorum ausmachen, getragenes Verfassungswerk" und betonte in diesem Zusammenhang abschließend:

> „Diese Verantwortung freilich kann das neue Gesetzeswerk nicht wecken. Es setzt sie voraus und glaubt sich in dieser Annahme durch die Antworten der Befragung, die darauf so großes Gewicht legten, bestätigt. Darin liegt heute unsere Hoffnung, wo sich andererseits bereits die Interesselosigkeit am Gesamtorden verbreitet, die sich in der Resignation und Mutlosigkeit vieler Mitbrüder zeigt und die sehr verschiedene Ursachen hat. Mit dieser Interesselosigkeit aber ist weder der Buchstabe, noch weniger der Geist der neuen Gesetzgebung in unserer Provinz lebendig zu machen. Gerade in der kommenden Zeit, wenn es darum geht, den Übergang und den Anschluss an die neue vorgesehene Lebensform zu finden, sind wir alle auf unsere gutwillige und auch mutige Mitarbeit angewiesen. Wir müssen uns über viele Einzelheiten der neuen Konstitutionen gemeinsam klar werden."[418]

Das Provinzstatut von 1970

Dieses Klarwerden bezog sich nicht nur auf einen Bewusstwerdungsprozess, sondern auch auf eine konkrete Aufgabe: Das Generalkapitel von River Forest hatte alle Provinzen auf die Erstellung eines sogenannten Provinzstatuts verpflichtet – das, was Frank in seinem Bericht über den römischen Kongress als „Direktorium" bezeichnet hatte.[419] Die neuen Konstitutionen traten mit 1. Januar 1969 in Kraft, aber erst im Februar 1969 hatten alle süddeutsch-österreichischen Häuser den Text erhalten. Provinzial Varga lud für den 15. April unter Einbeziehung aller Hausoberen und des *peritus* Frank zum erweiterten Provinzkonsil in den Augsburger Konvent ein. Haupttagesordnungspunkte waren die „Erstellung des ‚Statuts der Provinz' unter möglicher Beteiligung aller interessierten Mitbrüder" und die Vorbereitung des nächsten Provinzkapitels.[420] In der Provinz waren die legislativen Anpassungsanstrengungen des Ordens mit geteiltem Interesse verfolgt worden. Nicht nur die Fragebogenaktion, sondern auch das für River Forest vorbereitete Textschema wurde auf dem Provinzkonsil in mehreren Sitzungen diskutiert.[421] Da das nächste Provinzkapitel ohnehin im kommenden Jahr abgehalten werden sollte, beschränkte sich das Pro-

---

418 Alle Zitate Vargas stammen aus: PA, Provinzrundbrief vom 15.12.1968, S. 1–4.
419 ACG 1968, S. 63–64, Nrn. 100–103.
420 PA, Provinzrundbrief vom „1. Passionssonntag" 1969, S. 1.
421 PA, Liber consiliorum provinciae, S. 70–72: Sitzung vom 12.2.1968, Sitzung vom 9.5.1958 und Sitzung vom 7.6.1968. Leider sind die Protokolle dieser Besprechungen hauptsächlich nur summarisch.

vinzkonsil am 15. April 1969 mit der Besetzung von vier dieses Provinzkapitel vorbereitenden Kommissionen: einer für die Verwaltung, einer für das gemeinschaftliche Leben und das Apostolat, einer für die Formung des Nachwuchses und für das Studium und einer für die finanziellen Angelegenheiten; letztere wurde doppelt besetzt, eine für den süddeutschen und eine für den österreichischen Provinzteil. Allen Kommissionsmitgliedern wurden genau die Nummern der von ihnen zu bearbeitenden Konstitutionen bekanntgegeben.[422] Allerdings wurden alle Mitbrüder der Provinz „gebeten, ihre Vorschläge den zuständigen Kommissionen bis Mitte Oktober zukommen zu lassen (jeweils an den Präses). Die Kommissionen werden diese Vorschläge bearbeiten und ihr Elaborat bis Weihnachten allen Mitbrüdern bekannt geben. Dann kann dazu noch Stellung genommen werden. Das Provinzkapitel, das Ende April 1970 gehalten wird, wird dann über die Vorschläge der einzelnen Kommissionen die Entscheidung treffen und ein Statut für unsere Provinz erarbeiten und in Kraft setzen."[423] Diese vorbereitende Arbeit ging eher zäh, fast widerwillig vor sich. Anfang Oktober 1969 meldete der Provinzial im Provinzrundbrief: „Die Präsides klagen, dass sie bis jetzt keine Vorschläge erhalten haben. Vielleicht haben die Ferienmonate mein Ersuchen in Vergessenheit gebracht. Deshalb möchte ich Ihnen mit diesem Schreiben das Anliegen des Provinzkapitels nochmals sehr ans Herz legen."[424] Anscheinend half dieser Appell, denn im Provinzrundbrief vom 2. Februar 1970 konnte Varga allen Brüdern die Ergebnisse der Kommissionsarbeiten ausführlich vorstellen, verbunden mit dem Hinweis, dass weitere schriftliche Verbesserungen und Vorschläge noch bis zum 20. März Berücksichtigung finden würden.

Vom 20. bis 28. April 1970 tagte das Provinzkapitel in Augsburg, auf dem P. Innozenz Varga zum Provinzial wiedergewählt wurde. In einer „Grundbestimmung" äußerten sich die Kapitularen zu ihren Absichten:

> „Da wir das Buch der Konstitutionen unseres Ordens zur Hand haben, das den Geist des hl. Ordensstifters und den Charakter des Ordens bestens wiederspiegelt und durch praktische Anordnungen unser Leben bestens regelt, nehmen wir das Buch mit großer Freude auf. Das Ziel dieses Provinz-

422 PA, Liber consilii provincialis, Sitzung in Augsburg vom 15.4.1969. Übrigens wurde bei dieser Gelegenheit die Erhebung der *domus formata* Retz zum Konvent mehrheitlich abgelehnt, womit der diesbezügliche Auftrag des Provinzkapitels von 1962 gescheitert war.

423 PA, Provinzrundbrief vom 21. Mai 1969, S. 2.

424 PA, Provinzrundbrief vom „Rosenkranzfest" 1969, S. 1.

> kapitels haben wir vor allem darin gesehen, dieses Buch der Konstitutionen unseres Ordens uns zu eigen zu machen. Um überflüssige Wiederholungen zu vermeiden, sind unsere Akten kurz. Mit großer Aufmerksamkeit aber haben wir das Provinzstatut, durch welches die Rechtsgrundsätze der Konstitutionen unseren Bedürfnissen angeglichen werden, ausgearbeitet."[425]

Die Akten waren tatsächlich sehr kurz: 13 von insgesamt 27 DIN-A-5-Druckseiten waren Personalfragen und Ämterbesetzungen gewidmet. Etwas über zwei Seiten behandelten die Möglichkeit, das Tischgebet sowohl auf Deutsch wie auf Latein zu verrichten (wenn es sich um einen vom Provinzial und dem Provinzkonsil approbierten Text handelte), die Betonung der Bedeutung der an den jeweiligen Konventen und Pfarreien eingegangenen pastoralen Verpflichtungen, die Absicht, die Noviziatsausbildung in die Provinz zurückzuholen, die Sorge um die Betreuung der Dominikanerinnenklöster in der Provinz, die Sorge um die Gewinnung von Berufungen und weitere kleinere Bestimmungen. Ein Auftrag an den Provinzial verdient hervorgehoben zu werden: „P. Provinzial wird beauftragt, mit dem polnischen P. Provinzial in Verhandlung zu treten zwecks einer Besetzung des Konvents zu Retz mit Hilfe von polnischen Mitbrüdern (und einer eventuellen späteren Mitarbeit in unserem Kloster zu Friesach)."[426] Dies würde später noch wichtig werden.

Das Provinzstatut selbst fand auf den S. 18–27 Platz – nach Abzug des Titelblatts und der Unterschriftenliste füllte es etwas über acht Druckseiten. Ein erster Passus definierte den Zweck des Statuts: „Das Statut der Provinz ist die Sammlung der Anordnungen über das Leben und die Leitung der Konvente und der Provinz, vor allem in den Fragen, die von den einzelnen Provinzen im Sinne unserer Gesetze noch zu bestimmen bleiben."[427] Damit war auch die Gestalt des Statuts beschrieben: Es war kein aus sich selbst heraus verständlicher, fließender Text, der Begründungen oder Erklärungen lieferte, sondern es bestand nur aus einzelnen Abschnitten mit den zu regelnden Punkten, die in vier Kapitel gegliedert waren. Anders gesagt: Die Abschnitte füllten nur die Lücken aus, die die jeweiligen Konstitutionen gelassen hatten. Im ersten Kapitel „Das Leben im Konvent" wurde dargelegt, dass das in der Regel monatlich zu haltende Konventskapitel die Bereiche des gemeinsamen Lebens, der Arbeit und der Finanzen regelte und

---

425 APKap 1970, S. 13, Nr. 30.

426 Ebd., S. 16, Nr. 41.

427 Ebd., S. 18.

dass seine Beschlüsse grundsätzlich bindende Kraft hätten. Dem Konventskonsil wurde nur die Aufgabe übertragen, über persönliche Fragen vertraulicher Art zu entscheiden, die ihm vom Prior vorgebracht wurden. Die Amtsdauer der vom Prior eingesetzten Amtsträger wurde auf drei Jahre festgelegt. Das Stillschweigen, als Voraussetzung des religiösen und apostolischen Lebens, sollte besonders in den Morgen- und Abendstunden beobachtet und Fernsehen, Radio und Schallplatten so benützt werden, dass das notwendige Recht auf Stille jedem Mitbruder garantiert war. Die Art des Fastens wurde jedem einzelnen Mitbruder selbst überlassen; entscheidend sei der Opfergeist, der sich in der brüderlichen Liebe und in der bereitwilligen Mitarbeit im Apostolat auswirken sollte. Neue Formen der Buße sollten von den jeweiligen Hauskapiteln festgelegt werden. Hingewiesen wurde auf die Verpflichtung jedes Mitbruders zum Rosenkranzgebet. Außerdem wurde jedem Mitbruder eine angemessene Handbibliothek zur persönlichen apostolischen Tätigkeit, zum Studium und zur Weiterbildung zugestanden, die er bei Versetzung auch mitnehmen durfte. Im zweiten Kapitel „Die Provinz" wurden Formalia zu den Provinzkapiteln geregelt. Das dritte Kapitel „Ausbildung und Studien" war mit sechs Zeilen das kürzeste: Es ging um die Errichtung eines Ausbildungsrates zur Beratung des Provinzials in Ausbildungsfragen und um die Festlegung, die Ausbildung eines Studenten von Fall zu Fall zu regeln. Das längste Kapitel war Nr. 4 „Wirtschaftsverwaltung". Wichtigste Punkte waren hier zum ersten die Grundsätze: „Hauptquelle unseres Lebensunterhaltes ist unsere Arbeit. Jedes Mitglied ist daher verpflichtet, den Möglichkeiten entsprechend und den Kräften angemessen, zu einer Mitarbeit, welche die Sicherung des Lebensunterhaltes garantiert. Unsere Armut äußert sich in der Möglichkeit ausgedehnter Mitverantwortung für die Güter der Gemeinschaft."[428] Zum zweiten wurde „auf Grund der geographischen, politischen und wirtschaftlichen Gegebenheiten" beiden Provinzteilen, Süddeutschland und Österreich, „vollständige ökonomische Selbständigkeit unter Ausschluss gegenseitiger Haftung" zugesichert. Drittens wurden das Recht jedes Hauses oder Konvents „auf Selbstverwaltung seiner finanziellen und wirtschaftlichen Angelegenheiten" bestätigt und weitere Verwaltungsfragen auf Haus- und Provinzebene geregelt. Viertens wurde je ein Wirtschaftsrat für die beiden Provinzteile eingesetzt, bestehend aus dem Provinzial sowie dem jeweiligen Provinzsyndikus und den amtierenden Prokuratoren der Niederlas-

428 Ebd., S. 23.

sungen. Ein letzter, umfangreicherer Passus regelte die Fragen der Sach-, Unfall- und Krankenversicherung sowie die Altersvorsorge der Brüder.

Ebenso wie die neuen Konstitutionen war das Provinzstatut nur ein Regelwerk, eine Hausordnung. Das Provinzkapitel hatte damit genau die konkreten, rechtlich offenen Fragen beantwortet. Die Kürze des Textes erklärt sich auch damit, dass die Provinz keine Missionsvikariate, Schulen und andere Ausbildungshäuser oder ein größeres pastorales Werk unterhielt. Diesbezügliche Lücken der Konstitutionen waren in Süddeutschland und Österreich nicht zu füllen. Die Provinz hatte sich damit im Rahmen ihrer Kompetenz auf ihren Weg begeben und musste nun das, was die Satzungen und sie selbst neuerlich festgelegt hatten, in der Praxis erproben.

Nachwuchsmangel und Austritte: Die Personalkrise (1966–1983)

Nach dem Provinzstatut gab es noch ein weiteres Statut, das vom Provinzkonsil im Auftrag des Provinzkapitels konzipiert werden musste, ein Noviziatsstatut.[429] Doch nach dem ersten Noviziatsjahrgang, für den dieses in Geltung war, kamen keine Novizen mehr nach, und so erlosch die Wirkung dieses Statuts. Inzwischen war die Provinz in einer ernsten Personalkrise angelangt.

Laut Auskunft der Provinzkataloge hatte sich die Zahl der Dominikaner in Süddeutschland und Österreich nach dem Krieg recht erfreulich entwickelt: 1955 zählte die Provinz 125 Mitglieder, konkret 73 Priester (P.), 26 Laienbrüder (L.), 19 Kleriker (K.) und sieben Klerikernovizen. 1960 waren es 138 Mitglieder (96 P., 27 L., elf K., drei KN., ein Tertiar) und 1965 141 Mitglieder (98 P., 24 L., 16 K., zwei KN., ein Laienbrudernovize). 1966 war mit 145 Mitgliedern der personelle Höchststand erreicht (102 P., 24 L., 16 K., zwei KN., ein Tertiar) – das einzige Jahr, in dem der Ausgangspersonalstand von 1939 (143 Mitglieder) sogar übertroffen wurde. Danach ging es allerdings rapide abwärts: 1971 wurden 120 Mitglieder gezählt (92 P., 21 L., drei K., zwei KN., zwei Tertiaren), 1977 103 Mitglieder (78 P., 18 L., ein K., drei KN., drei Tertiaren), 1981 90 Mitglieder (65 P., 15 L., drei K., sechs KN., ein Laienbrudernovize) und 1984 nur mehr 82 Mitglieder (61 P., 13 L., fünf K., zwei KN., ein Laienbrudernovize). Relativ formuliert: 1984 waren nur mehr 56 Prozent des Mitgliederstandes von 1966 übrig.

---

429 Dazu: Ebd., S. 14, Nr. 33; PA, Liber consiliorum provinciae, Sitzung vom 5. / 6.8.1970, S. 76, Sitzung vom 23.8.1970, S. 77 und Provinzrundbrief vom 28.8.1970, S. 8.

Die versiegenden Neueintritte waren aber nur ein Grund für diese negative Entwicklung. Das sie entscheidend beeinflussende Moment waren die stark angestiegenen Austrittszahlen. Dieses Phänomen war an sich nichts Neues: Schon während und nach dem Krieg hatte es eine signifikante Anzahl von Austritten gegeben – wie erinnerlich hatten in dieser Zeit zwölf Dominikaner die Provinz und den Orden mit oder ohne Dispens verlassen. Auch in den 1950er und zu Anfang der 1960er Jahre waren einzelne Austritte immer wieder vorgekommen. Nach dem Generalkapitel von River Forest wurde daraus aber eine echte Austrittswelle, die bis etwa ins Jahr 1983 anhielt: Zwischen 1968 und 1983 verließen 25 Provinzmitglieder den Orden – eine Entbindung von den feierlichen Gelübden, zehn Säkularisierungen (Übertritte ins Weltpriestertum), neun Laisierungen und fünf sogenannte Apostasien (eigenmächtige Austritte ohne Erlaubnis, durch standesamtliche Heirat).[430] Dazu kam noch die Zahl der einfachen Professen, die ihre Ordensgelübde nicht verlängerten und dadurch ebenfalls aus Orden und Provinz ausschieden.

Da aber zwischen 1968 und 1983 auch 43 Todesfälle zu verzeichnen waren, verlor die süddeutsch-österreichische Provinz innerhalb dieser 15 Jahre insgesamt 68 Mitglieder, deren Verlust durch die neun Mitbrüder, die zwischen 1969 und 1982 Profess machten und blieben, nicht aufgefangen werden konnte.

Die von Austritten betroffene Gruppe war die der Patres. Die Laienbrüder hingegen litten vor allem unter den fehlenden Eintritten. Dies war ein weltweites Phänomen: Die Lebensform des Laienbruders geriet in den 1970er Jahren in eine schwere Krise, von der sie sich nicht mehr erholte. Zwischen 1965 und 1989 traten zwei Kandidaten als Laienbrüder in die Provinz ein, von denen einer später in den Priesterstand überwechselte. Von den 24 Laienbrüdern des Jahres 1969 in Süddeutschland und Österreich waren bis 1989 14 verstorben.

Worin bestanden die Motive für den Austritt? Diese Frage ist aus zwei Gründen schwer zu beantworten. Zum einen – und am mit Abstand wichtigsten – unterliegen die im Provinzarchiv diesbezüglich enthaltenen

430 Diese Zahlen wurden aus den Angaben der folgenden Provinzrundbriefe im PA zusammengefasst: vom 15.12.1968, S. 2, vom 9.4.1970, vom 15.12.1970, vom 16.12.1971, S. 3 und 8, vom 12.12.1974, S. 1, vom 18.3.1975, S. 1, vom 1.10.1975, S. 2a, vom 14.12.1976, S. 2, vom 1.9.1977, vom 23.1.1978, S. 2, vom 8.9.1978, vom 10.12.1980, S. 4b, vom 2.8.1982, vom 20.4.1983, S. 6 und vom 18.5.1985.

Akten nach 1962 dem Archiv- und deren Angaben dem Datenschutz. Zum anderen waren die Austrittsmotive nur schwer fassbar. Allgemein lässt sich sagen, dass die praktischen Nachwirkungen des Konzils und die Art der Erneuerung der Konstitutionen für viele wirklich enttäuschend waren – wie Provinzial Varga es im oben zitierten Provinzrundbrief vom 15. Dezember 1968 ja ausgedrückt hatte: Den einen gingen die Reformen zu weit, den anderen nicht weit genug. Ein zitierbares Zeugnis eines austretenden Paters kann zur Dokumentation genügen: „Meine Gründe sind theologischer, kirchenpolitischer sowie ordensrechtlicher Art und ergeben sich aus der gegenwärtigen Verfassung der katholischen Kirche."[431] Viele gaben persönliche Gründe für ihren Austritt an, die sich meist auf individuelle Schwierigkeiten mit einzelnen Gelübden bezogen. Dies lässt sich zumindest – ohne Datenschutzbestimmungen zu verletzen – aus der baldigen Heirat mancher nach ihrem erlaubten oder durch ihren durch standesamtliche Trauung erzwungenen Austritt so interpretieren. Auch hier muss ein allgemeines Zeugnis reichen: Ein Pater begründete seinen Austritt damit, „dass mir die Lebensform zu einer Belastung geworden ist, die ich nicht mehr ertragen konnte."[432]

Das Hinterfragen der klösterlichen Lebensform lässt sich für die Provinz sogar statistisch nachweisen, denn immerhin bestanden zehn von 25 Austritten aus Übertritten in den Weltklerus. Dies beweist, dass es bei dieser Krise zwar auch um Schwierigkeiten mit dem Priesterberuf als solchem ging, aber mehr noch um Schwierigkeiten mit dem Leben als Ordenspriester. In diese Richtung lassen sich auch die gleichzeitig fehlenden Neueintritte interpretieren.

Über die fehlenden Eintritts- und wachsenden Austrittszahlen hinaus wurde die Personalkrise in der Provinz aber noch durch ein weiteres Phänomen verschärft, nämlich die Zahl der Brüder, die *extra conventum* lebten. Jeder Dominikaner gehörte rechtlich zu einem Konvent, einer Gemeinschaft, der er zugewiesen – assigniert – war. Aber nicht alle Dominikaner lebten dort, wo diese Gemeinschaft ihren Sitz hatte. Manche Seelsorgsposten lagen zu weit von einem Predigerkloster entfernt, so dass ihre Inhaber auch dort wohnen mussten. Dies war meist bei jenen Brüdern der Fall, die als Seelsorger an Schwesternklöstern abgestellt waren, betraf aber auch Fälle von kategorialer Pastoral, Pfarrseelsorge oder Lehrtätigkeit.

---

431 PA, Provinzrundbrief vom „Rosenkranzfest" 1969, S. 2a.

432 PA, Provinzrundbrief vom 2.8.1982, S. 5.

Manchmal brachte die Ausbildung, das Studium, einen Dominikaner an einen Ort, wo es kein Dominikanerkloster gab, ebenso die notwendige Pflege in einem Altersheim. In diesen oder ähnlichen Fällen lebte ein Bruder außerhalb seines Konvents, *extra conventum*.

Wie wir bei der Beschreibung der pastoralen Aktivitäten der Niederlassungen der Provinz bereits erwähnt hatten, kamen solche Fälle zu allen Zeiten und an allen Konventen und Häusern vor. Ab 1966 verzeichnen die Provinzkataloge aber eine klare Veränderung: 1966 lebten 14 Brüder *extra conventum*, bis 1973 stieg deren Zahl auf 25 an, 1977 waren es 21, 1979 22 und 1981 20, um 1981 auf zwölf abzufallen. Die meisten dieser Brüder betreuten keine Schwesterngemeinschaften und gingen auch nicht in Altenheime, sondern sie übernahmen – wohlgemerkt mit Genehmigung der Oberen – Seelsorgsposten, die ihnen ein Leben außerhalb eines Klosters ermöglichten. In vielen Fällen bildete dies den ersten Schritt der Vorbereitung eines Austrittes.

Alle drei Faktoren, fehlende Eintritte, Brüder *extra conventum* und Austritte, führten dazu, dass die im Predigerorden übliche Fluktuation des Personals in den Konventen zurückging: Es gab immer weniger Mitbrüder, die seelsorglich eingesetzt werden konnten bzw. deren Stelle man mit einem anderen hätte besetzen können. Dieser Rückgang der Versetzungen erbrachte in der Provinz eine für Dominikaner eigentlich irreguläre Stabilität in der Besetzung der Klöster. Einzelne Mitbrüder lebten manchmal für viele Jahrzehnte in dem Konvent, in den sie nach ihrem Studium versetzt worden waren. Da sie nicht versetzt werden konnten oder wollten, fielen sie als Kandidaten für bestimmte Provinzämter oder als wählbare Obere in anderen Konventen weg. Dadurch entstand ein für die süddeutsch-österreichische Provinz nach 1970 charakteristisches Merkmal, nämlich die Herausbildung von Kerngemeinschaften in ihren Niederlassungen: Eine klar umgrenzte Personengruppe, deren Mitglieder aus verschiedensten Gründen nie versetzt wurden und zu der mangels Personal auch kaum neue Mitglieder hinzustießen, bildeten das Gesicht des jeweiligen Dominikanerklosters in der lokalen Öffentlichkeit, weil sie die Amtsträger der wichtigsten Seelsorgeaufgaben darstellten, die der jeweilige Konvent übernommen hatte. Man muss dies aber auch positiv sehen: Es waren die Brüder dieser Kerngemeinschaften, die nicht austraten, im Orden blieben und manchmal noch mehr Arbeit schulterten, damit ihre Klöster lebendig blieben und weiter funktionierten. Eine negative Konsequenz brachten diese Kerngemeinschaften aber für die Provinz: Sie förderten die Desintegration der ohnehin durch die Teilung in eine süddeutsche und

eine österreichische Hälfte angegriffenen Provinzeinheit. Über die folgenden Jahre kam es zu einer Art Inselbildung; die Ebene der Ordensidentität verschob sich von der Provinz weg auf die Klöster.

In den Zusammenhang der Analyse des Personalbestandes der Provinz zwischen 1966 und 1983 gehört noch eine letzte Beobachtung. Ein kleiner Teil der Provinzmitglieder arbeiteten *extra provinciam*, außerhalb der Provinzgrenzen, etwa als Professoren oder Missionare. Diese Gruppe reduzierte sich in der uns interessierenden Zeit auf einige wenige Einzelpersonen und kann daher vernachlässigt werden. Gleichzeitig wirkten aber auch Brüder aus anderen Provinzen in Süddeutschland und Österreich. Diese gehörten in den hier relevanten Jahren alle zu Konventen oder Häusern der Provinz, waren also Teil der oben genannten Mitgliedszahlen. Angesichts der Personalkrise ist daher die Frage nach ihrem Einfluss auf die Provinzaktivitäten interessant. Von ihrem Arbeitsfeld her, soweit dies sich aus den Provinzkatalogen erheben lässt, kann man diese Brüder in drei Gruppen einteilen.

Da war zum einen die Gruppe der aus der norddeutschen Provinz Teutonia stammenden Dominikaner. Die Teutonia hatte zur Gründung der Provincia Germaniae superioris einen großen Teil ihrer Mitglieder und ihres Territoriums geopfert. Ihre Noviziats- und Studieneinrichtungen erlaubten die Ausbildung der süddeutsch-österreichischen Brüder. Besonders in den Jahren nach dem Krieg half die Teutonia ihrer Nachbarin im Süden großzügig mit Priestern aus: Waren 1949 zwei norddeutsche Dominikaner in der Germania superior tätig, so waren es 1951 acht und in den folgenden Jahren bis 1959 durchschnittlich sieben pro Jahr. Dies stellte eine echte Unterstützung dar, da es sich bei diesen sozusagen ausgeliehenen Mitbrüdern um ausgebildete und voll arbeitsfähige Patres handelte, die im Süden sofort wichtige Aufgaben übernehmen und aufgrund der dort sehr kurzen Personaldecke klaffende Lücken schlossen. Die Provinzkapitel der Germania superior brachten ihren Dank dafür regelmäßig zum Ausdruck. Die Zahl der „Teutonen" wuchs 1960 bis 1966 auf durchschnittlich zehn an. Dies lag im Augsburger Predigerkurs begründet, da viele der norddeutschen Teilnehmer für dieses Ausbildungsjahr im Augsburger Konvent assigniert waren und weil ein Teutone dort unterrichtete. 1967 ging die Zahl der norddeutschen Dominikaner in der süddeutsch-österreichischen Provinz auf vier zurück, 1969 waren es drei und 1973 nur mehr zwei. Grund dafür war nicht nur das Ende des Predigerkurses, sondern die norddeutschen Mitbrüder hatten einen beträchtlichen Teil der Besatzung

von St. Albert in München-Freimann gestellt. Mit der Verschiebung der Konventsrechte auf St. Kajetan und der Reduktion von St. Albert auf den Status einer *domus formata* fiel in Freimann die Notwendigkeit weiterer personeller Hilfe weg. In den Jahren 1977 bis 1981 wirkten wieder vier bis fünf Teutonen in Süddeutschland und Österreich – wiederum als Helfer in der dort immer schlimmer werdenden Personalkrise.

Eine zweite Gruppe bildeten die Mitbrüder aus den osteuropäischen Nachbarprovinzen, die vor dem kommunistischen Regime flohen. Bereits der Provinzkatalog von 1949 nennt zwei solche Patres aus der böhmischen Provinz, die bis zu ihrem Tod in der süddeutsch-österreichischen Provinz blieben. Auch aus der Ungarischen Volksrepublik kamen Mitbrüder: 1951 und 1952 werden drei Patres der Provincia Hungariae in den Provinzkatalogen genannt. Von diesen blieb nur einer; 1964 kam ein zweiter hinzu. Von 1964 bis 1969 lebte ein aus der polnischen Provinz stammender Pater in Karlsruhe, der in dieser Zeit zum Freiburger Konvent gehörte. Ab 1973 arbeiteten zwei andere polnische Patres in Österreich, als Mitglieder des Grazer Konvents bzw. des Friesacher Hauses. Die Anwesenheit dieser beiden hatte einen anderen Hintergrund; mit ihnen begann die vom Provinzkapitel 1970 dem Provinzial zu erlangen aufgetragene personelle Unterstützung durch die polnische Provinz.

Eine dritte Gruppe bestand aus Gästen aus anderen Provinzen, die sich für Studienzwecke in der süddeutsch-österreichischen Provinz aufhielten – etwa zwischen 1958 und 1966 ein oder zwei Schweizer Mitbrüder, die am Augsburger Predigerkurs teilnahmen, 1965, 1966 und 1981 jeweils ein Bruder aus den USA in St. Kajetan zum Studium in München, 1958 bis 1962 und 1966 bis 1971 ein oder zwei Mitbrüder aus Spanien, 1964 einer aus den Niederlanden, 1965 einer aus der englischen und 1971 bis 1973 einer aus der irischen Provinz und 1966 bis 1973 einer aus der Provinz Francia. Alle diese Mitbrüder waren zwar seelsorglich nicht einsetzbar, weil ihr Aufenthalt anderen Zwecken diente, aber durch ihre Anwesenheit entstanden Kontakte ins nähere und fernere dominikanische Umfeld, die zum Teil über Jahrzehnte hielten.

Resignation und Pessimismus (1969–1979)

Der wachsende Mangel an Seelsorgekräften war die augenfälligste Konsequenz der Personalkrise in der süddeutsch-österreichischen Provinz. Ihre Hauptkonsequenz reichte aber tiefer, denn sie betraf das Verständnis

des Ordenslebens an seiner Wurzel: Sie wurde auch zur Krise für das noch vorhandene Personal. Schließlich traten ja keine Feinde und Gegner aus der Provinz aus, sondern Mitbrüder. Und sie taten dies nicht mit einem Paukenschlag, in einem einzigen Akt, sondern zwischen 1970 und 1974 waren es durchschnittlich pro Jahr zwei, 1975 waren es sechs und danach bis 1983 zwei bis vier jährlich. Dazu kamen noch immer mehr Brüder, die ihre Gemeinschaft verließen und außerhalb ihrer Klöster Posten übernahmen. Die Austritte und Weggänge waren am Körper der Provinz wie eine sich nicht schließen wollende Wunde, die mal mehr, mal weniger, aber stetig blutete. Wir haben keine Zeugnisse darüber, wie die einzelnen Dominikaner, die blieben, persönlich mit der Krise umgingen. Die Mitteilungen des Provinzials sind jedoch sehr deutlich.

Varga hielt mit seiner Meinung nicht hinter dem Berg. Seine direkteste und umfassendste Analyse der Lage richtete er nicht an einen kleinen Kreis von Auserwählten, sondern an die Freunde und Unterstützer des Ordens, im Publikationsorgan der Provinz mit der weitesten Verbreitung, dem Jahresheft des St. Dominikuswerkes für 1968:

> „Wir erleben heute eine Krisenzeit in der Kirche. Innerhalb und außerhalb der Kirche spricht man von ‚Krise der Erneuerung' – ‚Krise vor dem Untergang'. Unser P. Congar spricht von einer Psychologie der Unruhe. Diese Unruhe ist heute kennzeichnend für die Glaubenssituation. Vielleicht beunruhigt viele von Ihnen die Feststellung, dass es auch in unseren Reihen, sowohl in den Studienhäusern wie auch in den Klöstern, heute für manchen Mitbruder schwer ist, sein Ordensleben täglich neu zu bejahen, sich täglich neu zu entscheiden, in der Welt und doch nicht ‚von der Welt' zu sein.
> Diese Krise, die letztlich eine Krise des Glaubens ist, erkennt man an verschiedenen Symptomen. Die einen sind sich unschlüssig in der Entscheidung (Entscheidungsschwäche), andere sehen ihre Probleme in den evangelischen Räten, in Armut und Reichtum, Gehorsam und Autorität, Verzicht und Freiheit; wieder andere haben es mit Lebensangst, Vereinsamung und Verbitterung zu tun; andere leiden an Unlust, können nicht mehr richtig beten, sind ständig auf der Suche nach neuen Wegen und vergessen dabei oft das Ziel. Wieder andere können nicht genug tun in Neuerungssucht, andere dagegen hängen fest und unbeweglich an überholten Ideen, Dingen oder Traditionen. …
> Lebendiger Glaube darf nicht statisch ruhend sein, sondern dynamisch fortschreitende Antwort des Menschen auf das Wort Gottes. Echter Glaube ist darum auch immer notwendig ‚in der Krise'. Krise heißt nicht nur, dass etwas gefährdet ist oder schon zerfällt. Das Wort besagt in seiner eigentlichen Bedeutung so viel wie ‚Scheidung, Entscheidung'. Der Glaube in der

Entscheidung. Tag für Tag muss die Entscheidung neu vollzogen werden, für den Priester und Ordensmann, genauso wie für den Laien."[433]

In ähnlicher Weise richtete Varga sich auch an seine Mitbrüder. Sein Ende 1967 verfasster Provinzrundbrief liest sich wie ein Mahnschreiben:

> „[Unsere] Ordensfamilie wird auf Dauer ihren Dienst am Worte Gottes und an seiner Liebe nicht ausüben können, wenn sie immer kleiner wird. In den letzten Jahren haben einige Glieder unserer Familie den Orden verlassen, einige sich sogar vom Priestertum losgesagt und nur wenige sind an ihre Stelle gerückt. Zur Zeit haben wir keinen Novizen. Sollte uns diese Tatsache nicht zu einer Selbstkritik veranlassen, ob wir wohl noch ein echtes dominikanisches Leben führen? Die Berufe zum Priester- und Ordensstand nehmen nach der Lehre des hl. Thomas von Seiten Gottes nicht ab. Er versagt sie seiner Kirche nicht. Wohl kann der Mangel an Berufen zurückgeführt werden auf das Schwinden des Glaubensgeistes und das Vordringen des materialistischen Geistes und eines ausschließlich innerweltlichen Humanismus. Aber liegt nicht auch auf unserer Seite die Schuld? Geben wir immer das Beispiel eines frohen und wahren Ordenslebens? Und ist die Sorge um Berufe zum Orden auch wirklich die Sorge aller Mitbrüder?"[434]

Aber zu diesem Zeitpunkt betrachtete Varga nur die fehlenden Novizen als Grund des Personalproblems. Im Laufe der folgenden Jahre, in denen die Austrittszahlen zunahmen, wurden Vargas Mahnungen immer dringender: „Dies muss uns alle mit großer und bedrückender Sorge erfüllen. Deshalb wollen wir alles tun, um auf jede kluge Weise die Berufungen zu fördern. Das Geheimnis der Berufungen steht bei Gott; an uns liegt es aber, uns der Berufungen würdig zu erweisen durch ein echt dominikanisches Leben."[435] Immer noch stand das Nachwuchsproblem im Vordergrund. Dies änderte sich spätestens mit dem Provinzrundbrief vom 12. Dezember 1974. Hier thematisierte Varga zum ersten Mal in diesem Medium das Problem der wachsenden Zahl der Brüder *extra conventum*:

> „Es gibt Mitbrüder in der Provinz, die sich selbst von den Gemeinschaften der Provinz abgesondert haben oder absondern wollen. … Niemand von uns darf sich der Resignation hingeben! Ein jeder möge auf den anderen zugehen, damit wir Gemeinschaften schaffen, in denen die Menschwerdung Christi immer neu stattfinden kann."[436]

433 *St. Dominikuswerk* (1968), S. 2–3.
434 PA, Provinzrundbrief vom „dritten Adventssonntag" 1967, S. 1.
435 PA, Provinzrundbrief vom 15. Juni 1971, S. 1.
436 PA, Provinzrundbrief vom 12.12.1974, S. 1.

1975 wandte P. Varga sich in einem sehr offenen Bekenntnis seiner Sorgen an alle Provinzmitglieder. Dieses zeigte, wie weit und wie tiefgehend eine depressive Stimmung in der Provinz Platz gegriffen hatte:

> „Auch wenn viele von Ihnen mit Arbeiten überlastet sind, bitte ich Sie dennoch, sich die Zeit zu nehmen und diese Zeilen zu lesen und über sie nachzudenken. … Hat unsere Provinz noch eine Zukunft? Man kann die Veränderungen in der heutigen Gesellschaft, die rein diesseits ausgerichtet ist, für den Mangel an Berufen verantwortlich machen. Aber es gibt Länder, in denen Ordensberufe gedeihen. … Deshalb möchte ich eine Frage an unser Gewissen stellen: Inwieweit sind wir, jeder einzelne als auch die Gemeinschaften schuldig, dass wir keine Berufe haben? … Wie steht es mit dem Beispiel unseres Lebens? Die Menschen erwarten heute von uns besonders Frömmigkeit, Männlichkeit, Weltoffenheit, Dialogbereitschaft, Redlichkeit in der eigenen Glaubensüberzeugung und das Eingeständnis der eigenen Schwäche und Schwierigkeiten.“[437]

Zu jedem der angesprochenen Punkte führte der Provinzial genau aus, wo er Mängel in der Provinz sah oder Schwächen, und forderte die Brüder zum Nachdenken auf.

Und wirklich brachte dieser Brief eine Diskussion in der Provinz in Gang. Im Provinzialat trafen Antworten von den Brüdern ein, die sehr unterschiedlich ausfielen, je nachdem, ob sich einer angesprochen oder angegriffen fühlte. Varga zitierte einige davon in seinem Rundbrief vom 28. April 1975: „Ihr Rundschreiben hat vieles aufgezeigt, was bisher im allgemeinen mit Schweigen geduldet wurde. Würde dies alles nun richtig gestellt, dann kämen wir wohl einige Schritte voran.“ „Wir haben deshalb keinen Nachwuchs, weil wir kein deutliches Zeugnis dafür ablegen, dass unsere Provinz treu zum Papst und zum unverkürzten Vaticanum II steht. Man kann niemandem raten einzutreten, wenn man ihm nicht sagen kann, dass diesbezüglich alle eines Sinnes sind.“ „Keiner ist ein richtiger Dominikaner, der auch nur ein katholisches Dogma leugnet.“ „Ihre aneifernden Worte haben mich tief gerührt. Es ist sicher zu einem großen Teil auch unsere Schuld, dass wir nicht mehr Berufe haben. Denn die jungen Leute sind nicht so materialistisch eingestellt, wie es immer gesagt wird. Wenn ihnen unser Ordensleben lebendig vorgestellt wird, wenn wir über die Gestaltung unseres Ordens nicht nur diskutieren, sondern stramm an den gegebenen

437 PA, Provinzrundbrief vom 18.3.1975, S. 1. Leider ist es nicht möglich, das ganze vierseitige Schreiben Vargas hier wiederzugeben.

Konstitutionen festhalten und sie mit Geist erfüllen, vor allem wenn wir die theologischen Studien unserer Tradition vertiefen, dann bekommen wir Berufe. Es gibt so viele junge Leute, die darauf ohne Hemmungen und ohne Zaudern positiv reagieren würden."[438] u. v. m. Auch mit Kritik an Vargas Brief wurde nicht gespart. Varga fiel auf, dass es in den Antworten um Observanz, Konstitutionen, Konzil und Lehre der Kirche ging, dass aber „die Themen: Weltoffenheit, Dialogbereitschaft, Eingeständnis der eigenen Schwäche und Schwierigkeiten" nicht vorkamen.[439] Am Austrittsphänomen selbst änderte sich durch diese Diskussion freilich nichts, aber sie trug zur Gewissensbildung bei und bereitete durch ihre Offenheit und Ehrlichkeit den Boden für die Zeit nach der Krise.

Ende des Jahres 1975 empfand dann auch der Provinzial kaum mehr Hoffnung: „Die Gegenwart, in der wir leben, ist dunkel und schwierig, fast aussichtslos … In der Provinz selbst sieht es nicht rosig aus. … Wie soll es weitergehen? Das ist die brennende Frage."[440]

Aufgaben und Aufgeben: Wege aus der Krise

‚Business as usual' oder ‚the show must go on'

Ausgerechnet in diese so von Sorgen und Nöten überschatteten Jahre fielen eine ganze Reihe von Ordens- oder Provinzjubiläen, die alle festlich begangen sein wollten: Den Reigen dieser Feiern eröffnete 1966 das 750-jährige Jubiläum der päpstlichen Anerkennung des Predigerordens, das in allen Konventen und Häusern mit Triduen und Festakademien gewürdigt und auch von Presse, Funk und Fernsehen mitverfolgt wurde.[441] Ein Jahr später gab es ein Provinzjubiläum: Das älteste Dominikanerkloster auf deutschsprachigem Boden, Friesach, feierte 1967 sein 750-jähriges Bestehen mit Gedenkveranstaltungen und einem Pontifikalgottesdienst.[442] 1971 wurde

---

438 Alle Zitate aus: PA, Provinzrundbrief vom 28.4.1975, S. 1. Auch in den folgenden Rundbriefen zitierte Varga weitere Meldungen.

439 PA, Provinzrundbrief vom 28.4.1975, S. 1.

440 PA, Provinzrundbrief vom 19.12.1975, S. 1.

441 Siehe dazu: PA, Provinzrundbrief vom „vierten Adventssonntag" 1966, sowie die Broschüre „750 Jahre Dominikanerorden", die P. Varga zu diesem Anlass herausgab.

442 Siehe dazu: PA, Provinzrundbrief vom 6.8.1967 und *St. Dominikuswerk* (1968), S. 7, wo diese Feiern ausführlich beschrieben werden.

als „Dominikusjahr“ begangen – gefeiert wurde der 750. Todestag des Ordensgründers.[443] Beendet wurde die Reihe der Jubeljahre 1974 mit einem „Thomasjubiläum“, zum 700. Geburtstag des Aquinaten.[444]

Mitte der 1970er Jahre wurde das Personalloch in der Provinz akut spürbar. Vergleicht man die Angaben bezüglich des Personalstandes der Niederlassungen des Provinzkataloges des Jahres 1969 mit dem des Jahres 1979, so erkennt man die schleichende Reduktion: Wien schrumpfte nur leicht, von 23 auf 20 Mitbrüder, ebenso Freiburg (von 13 auf 11) und München / St. Kajetan (von elf auf acht). München / St. Albert blieb gleich (sieben). Deutlich waren davon betroffen Augsburg (von 21 auf 16) und Graz (von 22 auf 16). In Friesach reduzierte sich der Personalstand nur wenig (von sechs auf fünf), dafür halbierte er sich in Retz (von sechs auf drei).

Zur *domus formata* Retz, die vom Provinzkapitel 1962 noch als Kandidat zur Erhebung zum formalrechtlichen Konvent betrachtet worden war, hatten im Frühjahr 1969 noch vier Priester und zwei Laienbrüder gehört. Ein Priester starb im Sommer 1969, ein weiterer im Januar 1970.[445] Damit war für das Provinzkonsil, das sich am 23. August 1970 traf, klar: „Die domus formata von Retz kann als solche nicht mehr gehalten werden. Sie wird zur domus filialis von Wien erklärt. … Das Ordinariat von Wien soll in Kenntnis gesetzt werden, dass wir Retz nicht mehr halten können und es spätestens im Sommer 1971 aufgeben wollen.“[446] Einer der zwei Retzer Priester wurde im September 1970 auf eigenen Wunsch nach Graz versetzt, um dort als Kaplan in der Pfarrei eine dringende Lücke zu füllen.[447] Der letzte verbliebene wurde zum Vikar des Wiener Priors eingesetzt. Allerdings führte man diesen Schließungsbeschluss nicht aus; Retz blieb Filiale von Wien.

Nachdem die Nachbarprovinz Teutonia ähnliche personelle Schwierigkeiten durchzustehen und der süddeutsch-österreichischen Provinz bereits Mitbrüder zur Hilfe gesandt hatte, war von dort keine weitere Personalaufstockung mehr zu erwarten. Daher fuhr P. Varga in Begleitung zweier Mitbrüder nach Krakau, Warschau und Breslau. „Mit dem pol-

---

443 Siehe dazu: *St. Dominikuswerk* (1970) S. 4f., (1971), S. 2 und (1972), S. 3–7.

444 Das Heft *St. Dominikuswerk* (1974) wurde ganz diesem Anlass gewidmet; dazu auch: PA, Provinzrundbriefe vom „Advent“ 1973 und vom 5.7.1974.

445 PKat 1971, S. 27.

446 PA, Liber consiliorum provinciae, Sitzung vom 23.8.1970, S. 77.

447 PA, Liber consiliorum provinciae, Sitzung vom 23.8.1970, S. 77 und Provinzialsregestenbuch 2 (1966–2010), Eintrag vom 25.9.1970, Nr. 15.

nischen Provinzial wurden Verhandlungen zwecks einer Assignation von Patres nach Österreich geführt."[448] Und mit Erfolg: Am 1. Dezember 1970 kamen zwei polnische Mitbrüder nach Wien. „Sie studieren jetzt die deutsche Sprache und werden zur gegebenen Zeit in der Seelsorge in unserer Provinz eingesetzt werden."[449] Konkret kam einer nach Friesach, der andere nach Graz.[450]

Zu einer kleinen Aufmunterung der Stimmung in der Provinz trug die Visitation des Ordensmeisters Aniceto Fernandez bei, die er zusammen mit seinem Socius vom 14. bis 26. Oktober 1972 hielt. Der Provinzial lieferte über diesen Besuch einen mehrseitigen Bericht Ende 1972 im Provinzrundbrief: „P. General meinte, … dass Zeichen vorhanden seien, die berechtigten anzunehmen, dass die Krise in der Kirche und im Orden den tiefsten Punkt überschritten hätte und es bereits wieder aufwärts ginge. Es gibt Provinzen …, wo die Berufungen stark zunehmen. … P. General ist überzeugt, dass wir nicht nur überleben werden, sondern dass der Orden eine große Zukunft haben wird."[451] In einem Interview mit der Zeitung „Die Presse" verlautete Fernandez, dass er mit den Mitbrüdern in der Provinz „höchst zufrieden sei. Nicht nur, dass der Einsatz der Patres an allen ‚Fronten' überdurchschnittlich gut funktioniert – auch Probleme, ausgelöst durch die Spannungen zwischen ‚konservativem' und ‚progressivem' Flügel" seien „hierzulande kaum mit Unfreundlichkeiten gekoppelt. Dass es Verschiedenheiten gibt, sieht der Obere sogar positiv."[452]

Von Krise also keine Spur? Die süddeutsch-österreichische Provinz setzte jedenfalls auf das Motto ‚Weitermachen wie bisher'. Dies wird sehr deutlich, wenn man sich die Akten des Provinzkapitels von 1975 ansieht. Wegen einer Terminüberschneidung mit einem Generalkapitel musste das eigentlich für Mai 1974 vorgesehene Provinzkapitel verschoben werden, und so trafen sich die Kapitularen mit Erlaubnis des Ordensmeisters vom 2. bis 4. Januar 1975 in Augsburg.[453] Was diese Teilnehmer und auch die Ämterbesetzungen angeht, hatte sich inzwischen ein Generationswechsel

448 PA, Provinzrundbrief vom 28.8.1970, S. 2.
449 PA, Provinzrundbrief vom 15.12.1970, S. 2.
450 Siehe: PKat 1973, S. 18 und 20.
451 PA, Provinzrundbrief „im Advent" 1972, S. 4.
452 Dieses Interview erschien laut PA, Provinzrundbrief „im Advent" 1972, S. 7 in der Wochenendausgabe der Tageszeitung „Die Presse" vom 28. / 29.10.1972. Zitate laut Provinzrundbrief wie angegeben.
453 APKap 1975, S. 5, Nr. 1.

vollzogen: Die weit überwiegende Mehrheit der anwesenden wie eingesetzten Brüder war nach dem Krieg eingetreten – aber dies war nicht Ergebnis einer bewussten Entscheidung, sondern eine schlichte biologische Konsequenz, da die Mitglieder der Vorkriegsgeneration nun zu alt oder sogar verstorben waren. Die wichtigste Personalentscheidung betraf die Wiederwahl von P. Innozenz Varga zum Provinzial. Er begann am 21. Januar 1975 seine dritte Amtszeit.[454]

Die inhaltlichen Bestimmungen wurden nun in ein einziges Kapitel zusammengefasst, überschrieben mit „Anordnungen, Ermahnungen, Erklärungen und Aufträge“. Seine 19 Punkte brachten wenig Neues.[455] Die meisten lesen sich als Hinweise. Allerdings kam das von der neuen Rechtslage her, die im Orden seit 1968 herrschte, da die Konstitutionen von River Forest die Konventskapitel so deutlich aufgewertet und diesen Gremien Entscheidungskompetenzen zugeschoben hatte, die sie vorher nicht gehabt hatten. Dementsprechend konnte das Provinzkapitel in verschiedenen Punkten die Konventskapitel nur auf notwendige Beschlüsse aufmerksam machen. So wurde angeordnet, dass das Fest des sel. Heinrich Seuse und das Fest des hl. Jakob von Ulm als verpflichtende Gedenktage zu feiern waren und die Feier weiterer nicht verpflichtender Ordensheiligenfeste in die Hände der Konvente gelegt wurde (Nr. 28). Die Hauskapitel wurden aufgefordert, genauere Anweisungen bezüglich der Feierlichkeit der Liturgie und dem gemeinsamen Gebet zu treffen (Nr. 29). Bei Tisch sollte nicht leichtfertig vom Silentium dispensiert werden; bei der Auswahl der Tischlesung sollten die Konstitutionen und die Augustinusregel bevorzugt werden (Nr. 30). Bezüglich des Fastens sollten die Mitbrüder sich den Fastenordnungen der Diözesen anschließen (Nr. 31). Die Mitbrüder wurden gebeten, die gemeinschaftsfördernden Mittel, nämlich den gemeinsamen Tisch, die Rekreation und das Kapitel, hochzuschätzen (Nr. 35). Nur in zwei Bereichen traf das Provinzkapitel klare Maßnahmen: Für jedes Dienstverhältnis, das einen Bruder *extra conventum* führte, wurde eine zeitliche Befristung von fünf Jahren festgelegt; danach war es neu zu prüfen bzw. zu regeln (Nr. 32). Grundsätzlich hatten diese Brüder jährlich eine angemessene Zeit in ihrem Assignationskonvent zu leben (Nr. 33). Ebenso waren ihre finanziellen Beiträge jährlich zu überprüfen und zu adaptieren (Nr. 34). Der zweite Bereich betraf das Bemühen um Ordensnachwuchs.

---

454 Ebd., S. 6–7, Nr. 9.
455 Ebd., S. 9–12, Nrn. 27–45.

Hier wurden die Mitbrüder neuerlich an ihre Verantwortung erinnert und die Konvente um Propagation von diesbezüglichen Druckschriften aufgefordert (Nr. 36). Der Provinzial wurde beauftragt, den Akten des Provinzkapitels ein Gebet um Ordensnachwuchs beizufügen (Nr. 37) – welches in den gedruckten Akten allerdings fehlt. Ausdrücklich wurde darauf hingewiesen, dass jungen Leuten, die Interesse am Ordensleben zeigten, die Möglichkeit geboten werden sollte, am Konventsleben teilzunehmen (Nr. 38). Daneben gab es noch weitere Einzel- und Verwaltungsbestimmungen. Mit dem Dank an den Ordensmeister für seinen Besuch, an die Provinziäle der Teutonia und der Polonia für die zur Unterstützung überlassenen Mitbrüder und an P. Hilarius Barth für die Herausgabe der Zeitschrift „Ewige Weisheit" schlossen die Akten, die bis auf den Hinweis auf die Notwendigkeit von Ordensberufen nicht erkennen lassen, dass sich die Provinz in irgendeiner Notsituation befand.

Das Jahr 1975, das so schwer verlief, brachte vom 13. bis 15. Dezember wichtigen Besuch: Der neue Ordensmeister Vincent de Couesnongle und sein Socius Mark De Caluwe verbrachten einige Tage im Wiener Konvent, um einen ersten Kontakt mit der Provinz aufzunehmen. In seinen Gesprächen mit den Brüdern legte de Couesnongle seine Ansichten über die Probleme dar, deren er sich als Ordensoberer stellen wollte: die Studien als gesamtmenschliche Prägung des Dominikaners, die Präsenz des Ordens in der Welt und das gemeinschaftliche und private Gebet. Die Mitbrüder der Provinz fühlten sich von ihrem Ordensmeister verstanden: „Der Besuch des Generalmeisters hat uns das Gefühl gegeben, dass wir in unserer Arbeit und unseren Problemen nicht allein stehen, sondern dass hinter uns die helfende Bereitschaft besteht, zu einer gemeinsamen Lösung der Schwierigkeiten zu kommen. Denn in unseren Gesprächen war nicht davon die Rede, durch ein Dirigieren von oben her einzugreifen, sondern von Zusammenarbeit, die auf die jeweils besondere Lange der Konvente bzw. Provinzen eingeht."[456] Um auf diese Weise mit der Provinz zusammenzuarbeiten, kündigte Sozius De Caluwe für das kommende Frühjahr seinen längeren Besuch an, um gemeinsam mit den Brüdern der Provinz „die Ziele des Ordens, so wie sie sich heute in ihrer Dringlichkeit darstellen, besser zum Tragen zu bringen."[457] Tatsächlich begann mit diesen drei Tagen im Winter in Wien für die Provinz eine Zeit, in der Hoffnung wieder möglich wurde.

---

456 PA, Provinzrundbrief vom 19.12.1975, S. 4.
457 Ebd.

Der Wendepunkt: der Besuch Mark de Caluwes 1976

Wie versprochen kam P. De Caluwe am 18. März 1976 in die Provinz und blieb bis zum 6. April. Der Socius des Ordensmeisters fühlte sich hier sehr wohl und bereiste intensiv das Provinzgebiet, um in jedem Haus gewesen zu sein. In einem Brief an die Provinz zog er ein Fazit: Besonders beeindruckte ihn die große Aktivität der Mitbrüder bis ins hohe Alter. Lobenswert fand er, „wie sehr die Mitbrüder einander wirklich als Mitbrüder zu begegnen versuchen". De Caluwe war kritisch genug, auch vor drei Dingen zu warnen: Zum einen dürfe die Provinz bei der institutionalisierten, innerkirchlichen Seelsorge, etwa durch die Übernahme von Pfarreien, nicht stehen bleiben, sondern es müssten auch andere, der apostolischen Berufung des Dominikaners gemäße Formen gefunden werden. Zum anderen spürte er zwar beim gemeinsamen Gebet, „wie in fast jedem Konvent versucht wird, diesem Gebet Ruhe und Würde zu geben", aber es würden bei weitem nicht alle liturgischen Möglichkeiten ausgenützt und außerdem sei es die Frage, ob die bestehenden Formen des Gemeinschaftsgebets „von den Jüngeren wirklich als eine befreiende Offenheit für Gott erfahren werden können". Hier hielt der Socius „eine weitere Information über das, was in anderen Konventen des deutschen Sprachgebietes geschieht oder über das, was andere Orden machen" für „inspirativ". Schließlich sprach er noch das Problem der Staatsgrenze an, die sich durch die Provinz zog; De Caluwe erkannte, dass diese äußerliche Trennung auch zu einer innerlichen führte: „In dieser Provinz habe ich eine Situation kennengelernt, die ich in anderen Provinzen niemals erlebt hatte, nämlich dass eine Provinz sich über zwei Staatsterritorien erstreckt. Dies bringt auch Unterschiede in der Pastoral mit sich. Vielleicht wäre es möglich, dass die Mitbrüder beider Teile oder auch die Mitbrüder eines Teiles einander öfters begegnen könnten." Nach dem Vorbild anderer Provinzen schlug De Caluwe jährliche Tagungen und andere Kontaktmöglichkeiten vor.[458]

Insgesamt machte De Caluwes Besuch den Brüdern neuen Mut. Die Talsohle der Depression schien endgültig durchschritten zu sein, als der Provinzial seinen Mitbrüdern verkünden konnte, „nach langer Zeit wieder Novizen zu haben".[459] Das Postulat hatten die drei Kandidaten im Konvent St. Hyacinthe in der Schweiz gemacht, wo sie auch ihr Noviziatsjahr absol-

458 PA, Provinzrundbrief vom 26.5.1976, S. 1–2.
459 PA, Provinzrundbrief vom14.12.1976, S. 2.

vierten.[460] Nach diesem Jahrgang 1976/77 meldeten sich auch für 1977/78 Kandidaten. Provinzial Varga gab unumwunden zu: „Wenn es auch nur wenige sind: sie sind für uns alle eine tröstende und ermunternde, eine leibhaftige Demonstration der Lebendigkeit und der dynamisch in die Zukunft voranschreitenden Kirche und der Orden.“[461] Auch in den folgenden Jahren gab es nun immer wieder Eintritte.

Ermutigt durch diese neue Situation ging man auf der Ebene des Provinzkonsils daran, De Caluwes Ratschläge in die Tat umzusetzen. Provinzial Varga wurde Anfang Januar 1977 beauftragt, „die Umstrukturierung der bisher rein klerikalen Pfarrseelsorge (speziell Freimann und Graz) zur partnerschaftlichen Mitarbeit der Laien anzuregen“.[462] Außerdem wurde vom 22. bis 27. August eine Provinztagung im Kloster der Dominikanerinnen in Wettenhausen zum Thema Sakramentenpastoral geplant, zu der alle Mitbrüder eingeladen werden sollten. Zwölf Mitbrüder kamen und waren „im Allgemeinen zufriedengestellt – und das ist bei einer Zusammenkunft von Mitbrüdern nicht unbedingt selbstverständlich“. Man ging danach wieder auseinander mit dem Gefühl, dass sich Zeit und Ort bewährt hatten und man die letzte Augustwoche und Wettenhausen für kommende Tagungen beibehalten sollte. Abgesehen vom Erfahrungs- und Wissensaustausch über die Eucharistie und das Bußsakrament wurde als wichtig empfunden, dass „die Mitbrüder miteinander ins Gespräch kamen; wie überhaupt die Zufriedenheit darüber, sich zu treffen und (besser) kennenzulernen, groß war. Das Bewusstsein, das wir uns etwas zu sagen haben, kann uns sicher weiter bringen als allgemeine Lamentation über uns selber, unsere Konvente und die Provinz.“[463] Die nächste Tagung war für die Zeit vom 22. bis 26. August 1978 zum Thema „Frage nach den Normen und der Normenfindung heute“ vorgesehen; seitens des Provinzials erging „an alle Mitbrüder und Hausoberen die Bitte, sich den fraglichen Termin freizuhalten“.[464]

460 Obwohl das Provinzkonsil sich ursprünglich für Warburg entschieden hatte; siehe PA, Liber consiliorum provinciae Sitzung vom 5.8.1976, S. 89 und Provinzrundbrief vom 14.12.1976, S. 2.

461 *St. Dominikuswerk* (1978) S. 1.

462 PA, Liber consilii provincialis, Sitzung vom 4.1.1977 in Augsburg, Nr. 6.

463 PA, Provinzrundbrief vom 1.9.1977, S. 4.

464 PA, Provinzrundbrief vom 23.1.1979, S. 3.

1979: ein neuer Aufbruch

Vom 2. bis 4. Januar 1979 traf man sich im Augsburger Konvent zu einem Provinzkapitel. Viel, v. a. Ermutigendes war seit 1975 geschehen, das aufgearbeitet werden musste. Zunächst einmal drückte die Provinz P. Varga ihren Dank aus, indem sie ihn neuerlich zum Provinzial postulierte – was Ordensmeister de Couesnongle bestätigte. Dann ging es an die Verbesserung des Provinzstatuts, da sich durch die vorangegangenen Generalkapitel einige Konstitutionen geändert hatten. In den Anordnungen für die Provinz hielt sich das Kapitel streng an die Ratschläge De Caluwes: Neben der Betonung der Bedeutung der täglichen Konventsmesse für das Gemeinschaftsleben wurden alle Konvente darauf angewiesen, das deutschsprachige Stundengebet einzuführen und dabei den Gläubigen eine aktive Teilnahme zu ermöglichen. Der Erfahrungsaustausch innerhalb der Gemeinschaften sollte durch regelmäßige Gespräche angeregt werden. Ausdrücklich wurde den Brüdern die Teilnahme an der Provinztagung in Wettenhausen anempfohlen. Ins Gedächtnis gerufen wurden Gebet und Sorge für den Nachwuchs, sowohl für den vorhandenen als auch für den zu erhoffenden.[465]

Abschließend wandten sich die Kapitelsväter in einem Brief an die Brüder – ein bis dahin einmaliger Schritt des höchsten Leitungsgremiums der Provinz:

> „Alle Kapitularen danken allen Mitbrüdern für die Arbeit, die sie in unseren Konventen und Häusern leisten. Was uns aber Sorge macht, ist der Geist und das Interesse, das der Einzelne für das Ganze des Ordens hat. Der Individualismus hat sich bis hin zu einigen egoistischen Zügen gesteigert. Man behauptet sich in seiner Arbeit und verschließt sich dem anderen Mitbruder …
> Das Mitmenschliche, von dem heute so viel geredet wird, ist auch in unseren Gemeinschaften durch Kontaktarmut und negative Kritik stark belastet. Ohne Rücksicht auf unsere wirkliche personale Situation werden Forderungen an das Leben der Gemeinschaft gestellt, die einfach nicht erfüllt werden können. Es wird Kritik am Mitbruder, besonders den Oberen laut, die ihnen Amt, Verantwortung und Initiative erschwert und schwer macht, einen Mitbruder für das Amt eines Oberen zu bewegen. Ohne Verständnis und Mitarbeit am Ganzen, auch unter persönlichen Opfern, ist ein Gemeinschaftsleben gefährdet, versinkt in Resignation und Müdigkeit. Die Erfahrung aber lehrt, dass die Atmosphäre im Haus, das Wohlwollen untereinander und die persönliche Anerkennung im

465 APKap 1979, S. 18–21, Nrn. 30–32, 34, 36 und 40–41.

> offenen Kontakt miteinander unverzichtbare Voraussetzung für das Leben miteinander sind.
> Wir predigen den Gläubigen mit Verantwortung und Auftrag das große Gebot der Liebe. Umso glaubwürdiger und wirkungsvoller wird diese Botschaft, wenn sie in unseren Häusern gelebt wird. ... Darum bitten wir jeden Mitbruder, das Seinige zu einem echten Wohlwollen und brüderlichem Zusammenleben beizutragen."[466]

Dieser in Inhalt und Form deutliche Appell war sicher dem Engagement P. Vargas für einen Prozess der Gewissensbildung zu verdanken, der durch die Anstrengungen des Ordensmeisters und seines Socius verstärkt worden war. Zum ersten Mal hatte ein Provinzkapitel nicht nur auf die Einhaltung der formalen Elemente des Ordenslebens gedrängt, sondern hatte versucht, die mitmenschliche Dimension innerhalb der Gemeinschaften zu thematisieren, was seit 1939 nie geschehen war. Am Ende der Krise stand also ein Lernprozess mit dem Ergebnis, dass es nicht nur darum ging, die Klöster für Außenstehende (etwaige Kandidaten) attraktiv zu machen, sondern auch für diejenigen, die in ihnen lebten. In dieser Richtung wurde nach 1979 weitergearbeitet.

Für den Herbst 1979 hatte sich Ordensmeister de Couesnongle zu einer kanonischen Visitation angesagt. Diese gehörte sicher zu den am besten vorbereiteten Visitationen seit Provinzgründung. Die Besuche de Couesnongles und seines Socius hatten der Ordenskurie schon ein gewisses Bild über die Provinz ermöglicht. Im Februar 1979 wurde Provinzial Varga zu einer außerordentlichen Sitzung des Generalkonsils nach Rom geladen, in der er einen „Situationsbericht über die Provinz" abgeben sollte.[467] Der Ordensmeister visitierte vom 23. bis 25. Oktober 1979.

In einem ausführlichen Bericht, der allen Brüdern als Rundbrief zuging,[468] legte de Couesnongle seine Eindrücke dar:

> „Die allgemeine Atmosphäre ist eine der Ruhe. Es gibt keine starken Oppositionen und keine tiefgreifenden Kontraste: man nimmt einander an, man schätzt sich gegenseitig und lässt jeden sich in seiner Arbeit entfalten. Dies alles ist unbedingt wertvoll. Jedoch könnte man sich ein dominikanisches Leben denken, wo die Kreativität und die Lebenskraft ab und zu einige Spannungen erzeugen würden. Solche Spannungen sind heilsam."

466 Ebd., S. 31–32.

467 PA, Provinzrundbrief vom 4.4.1979, S. 1.

468 PA, Brief des Ordensmeisters Vincent de Couesnongle an Provinzial Innozenz Varga und die Mitbrüder der Provinz, Rom, 26.11.1979.

Individualismus sei zwar eine dominikanische Schwäche, führe aber zur Interesselosigkeit an der Arbeit der anderen Konvente. Man mache sich nicht mehr die Mühe, die großen Entfernungen zwischen den Häusern zu überwinden, und die *stabilitas loci* blühe, wie in anderen Provinzen selten. Aber diese seltenen Veränderungen innerhalb der Personalstruktur der Häuser führten auch zur Förderung der Tendenz, Ämter immer mit denselben Brüdern zu besetzen. Zur Unterstützung der Einheit innerhalb der Provinz habe man zwar Provinztagungen eingerichtet, diese sollten aber stärker und öfter von den Brüdern besucht werden. Auch das Provinzkonsil sollte sich öfter zu gemeinsamen, provinzteilüberschreitenden Sitzungen zusammenfinden: „Ein wirklicher Lebensaustausch … wird uns dazu bringen, uns miteinander zu konfrontieren und so immer wieder neu voneinander zu lernen."

Ähnliches gelte auch für die einzelnen Hausgemeinschaften: „Es scheint mir, dass das gemeinsame Leben in den Gemeinschaften gut ist. Durch den angenehmen und familialen Charakter kann sich jeder zu Hause fühlen. Ich war froh zu sehen, dass ohne Ausnahme alles, was durch die Arbeit erworben wird, wirklich in die Gemeinschaft geht." Aber trotz der erfreulichen Abwesenheit einer *vita privata* sei auch hier der Individualismus spürbar, auf den das Provinzkapitel aufmerksam gemacht habe. Mehr Austausch und Kontakt sei nötig.

Ein besonderes Problem bilde das Chorgebet: „In jedem Konvent betet man gemeinsam. Bisweilen aber nimmt man sich wenig Zeit für dieses Beten. Es scheint nicht immer ein reiches Gebet zu sein. Manchmal gibt dieses Gebet einen formalen Eindruck: man betet das, was die Rubriken vorschreiben." Ein Hinweis auf diese Haltung sei die Tatsache, dass trotz der Anordnung des Provinzkapitels das gemeinsame Gebet noch immer nicht auf Deutsch gebetet würde: „Würde man wirklich im liturgischen Geist des Konzils leben, so scheint mir, würde man gerne in der Muttersprache beten." Hier müsse man auch auf die Neueintretenden Rücksicht nehmen, die vorher fast nie auf Latein gebetet hätten.

Auch über die in der Provinz geleistete Arbeit machte sich der Ordensmeister Gedanken: „Ohne Zweifel wird in der Provinz viel und gut gearbeitet. Ich meine sogar, dass man bisweilen zu viel arbeitet." Das Apostolat der Provinz sei zu sehr innerkirchlich ausgerichtet: „Die Entwicklung nach dem II. vatikanischen Konzil und die Lage Ihrer Länder und der Provinz haben Sie dazu geführt, sich immer mehr in die Arbeitsstrukturen der Diözesen einzugliedern. … Ich frage mich, inwiefern die Arbeit in den

Pfarreien wirklich das spezifische Antlitz des Ordens sehen lässt." Eine Auswahl bei der Übernahme von Arbeiten auf der Grundlage einer theologischen Weiterbildung mit typisch dominikanischen Akzenten würde auch hier ein stärker dominikanisches Zeugnis ablegen.

Auf diesem Weg sei auch das Nachwuchsproblem anzugehen: „Leben und arbeiten wir so, dass junge Menschen dazu angezogen werden, mit uns in einer gleichen Inspiration mitzuleben? Heutzutage begnügen sich die Jugendlichen nicht mehr mit der Lebensgeschichte des hl. Dominikus. Sie möchten kommen und sehen." Der konkrete Vorschlag de Couesnongles lautete: „In diesem Zusammenhang frage ich mich, ob die Provinz nicht versuchen müsste, wenigstens ein Haus zu haben, das durch die Auswahl seiner Arbeit und durch seinen Lebensstil diese Rolle erfüllen könnte." Das Leben in diesem Haus sollte wesentlich getragen werden von gegenseitigem Austausch, kreativer Liturgiefeier, dominikanischer Arbeit und von Mitbrüdern, die „sich anstrengen müssten, den Werten, die wir alle zu leben versuchen, eine neue Form und größere Tiefe und Konturen zu geben." Für die Errichtung eines solchen Modellkonventes sollte der Provinzial eine Kommission einsetzen, um alles Nötige zu besprechen und zu organisieren. In diesen Reflexionsprozess sollten auch die Studenten der Provinz eingebunden werden.

Diese Visitation bedeutete für die Provinz eine Zäsur: Sie beendete die schweren Jahre der Krise und setzte durch ihre lobende Tendenz und ihre positiven Vorschläge neue Hoffnungen. Jahrelang hatte die Provinzplanung hauptsächlich darin bestanden, aufbrechende Löcher zu stopfen. Nun waren neue Zukunftsperspektiven gegeben. Das vom Ordensmeister vorgeschlagene Projekt eines Modellkonvents war in der Ordensgeschichte nichts Neues. Immer wieder hatte die höchste Ordensleitung sogenannte Observanzkonvente eingerichtet, als Heilmittel zur Gesundung und zum Wiederaufbau von Provinzen – im deutschen Sprachraum zuletzt 1857 in Graz, von wo aus die Provincia Imperii revitalisiert werden sollte. De Couesnongles Idee hatte einen wesentlichen Unterschied: Er zwang der Provinz keine Maßnahmen von oben auf, sondern regte sie an, einen eigenen Weg zu gehen.

1979 bis 1982: Weichenstellungen

Diese Art der Planung der Zukunft der Provinz durfte sich aber nicht nur auf die traditionelle Therapie von Äußerlichkeiten beschränken, sondern musste von jedem einzelnen Mitbruder nach Kräften getragen werden. Dazu war

eine Rückbesinnung jeder Gemeinschaft und jedes Bruders nötig auf das, was Provinzial Varga die „Gnade der dominikanischen Berufung" nannte:

> „Niemand von uns kann sich aus der Verantwortung für seine Mitbrüder, seine Mitmenschen und seine Mitwelt wegstehlen. ... Es kommt vor, dass ältere und jüngere Generation sich einfach nicht mehr verstehen, weil die Auffassungen vom Ordensleben und seinen Fragen zu sehr auseinandergehen – und sie sich gegenseitig den Stuhl vor die Tür setzen! Manche Mitbrüder schlagen sich die Türe zum echten Ordensleben zu, weil sie nur ihre Gedanken und Vorstellungen gelten lassen, dabei aber die Ordenssatzungen missachten, indem sie das Gemeinschaftsleben vernachlässigen, die hl. Eucharistie nicht mehr regelmäßig feiern und an der Tischgemeinschaft nicht teilnehmen. Die Folge: Rechthaberei statt Gerechtigkeit und Liebe, Trennung statt Treue, hemmungsloser Fortschritt statt verantworteter Sorge um die Zukunft, Wissenschaftsgläubigkeit statt Vertrauen in den Menschen und seine Fähigkeiten."[469]

Wie die Provinzrundbriefe zeigen, die Varga in seiner vierten Periode im Amt des Provinzials, von 1979 bis 1982 herausgab, widmete er sich mit starkem persönlichem Einsatz der Arbeit an dieser Rückbesinnung und gegen Egoismus, Resignation und formalisierte Liturgie. Dabei ging es ihm um die dominikanische Eigenart, die für den Orden charakteristische Lebensweise, die er vor der Gefahr, abzuflachen, bewahren wollte, sowie um ein gut funktionierendes Gemeinschaftsleben, das getragen sein sollte von Ehrlichkeit und Interesse füreinander.

Auf seiner Sitzung vom 3. Januar 1980 arbeitete das Provinzkonsil die Ergebnisse der Visitation des Ordensmeisters auf. Besonders machte man sich über die „Errichtung eines Hauses" Gedanken, „in dem die Ordensobservanz in besonderer Weise beachtet und befolgt werden kann".[470] Das Konsil setzte dafür eine Kommission unter Vorsitz des Provinzials ein, deren Mitglieder aus beiden Provinzteilen stammten. Ihre Aufgabe war die Beantwortung der Fragen, „wo, wie und mit wem eine Kommunität" errichtet werden könne, „die im vollen Umfang die Konstitutionen lebt und die exemplarisch und anziehend wirkt hinsichtlich des Ordenslebens und des Apostolats."[471] An so einer Kommunität interessierte Mitbrüder sollten sich bei der Kommission melden. Außerdem sollte bei der Planung der Kontakt mit den Ortsbischöfen aufgenommen werden, da „die Existenz ei-

469 PA, Provinzrundbrief vom 10.12.1980, S. 1.
470 PA, Liber consilii provincialis, Sitzung in Augsburg vom 3.1.1980.
471 PA, Provinzrundbrief vom 10.3.1980, S. 4.

nes observanten Konventes … auf jeden Fall auch wirtschaftlich gesichert werden“ musste; „dazu sei unbedingt die Verbindung mit den Ortsbischöfen nötig.“[472] Abgesehen vom Problem, dass ja eigentlich in allen Niederlassungen des Ordens die Ordenssatzungen in vollem Umfang befolgt werden sollten: Entsprach ein solcher Observanzkonvent wirklich dem „anziehenden Modellkonvent“, der de Couesnongle vorgeschwebt war? Der Vorschlag des Rückgriffs auf die Ortsbischöfe zur finanziellen Absicherung einer solchen Gemeinschaft, also eine neuerliche Übernahme innerkirchlichen Apostolats, tat dies sicher nicht.

Die Kommission tagte am 10. April und 27. Mai 1980. Es hatten sich immerhin so viele am Projekt interessierte Brüder gefunden, dass sogar eine Unterkommission gebildet werden musste, die sich am 31. Juli traf.[473] Auf seiner Sitzung am 29. August 1980 trug das Provinzkonsil die Ergebnisse dieser Gremien zusammen: „Aus Personalgründen dürfte für diesen Reformkonvent praktisch nur München in Frage kommen. Damit ist die zweite Frage gestellt: St. Kajetan oder München-St. Albert. Für beide Konvente ergeben sich seelsorgliche und personelle Schwierigkeiten.“ Gewichtiger waren die räumlichen Probleme, denn an beiden Orten fehlte die Zimmerzahl für eine Vergrößerung der Gemeinschaft. Sowohl der auf dem Konsil vorgeschlagene Ausbau des Mesnerhauses, als auch die Erweiterung des Klosters in Freimann hätten beachtlicher Investitionen bedurft, damit „ein Reformkonvent auf ordenseigenem Besitz errichtet werden“ konnte. Deshalb wurde auch der Augsburger Konvent „als Ausweiche“ in den Blick genommen. In jedem Fall wurde die Notwendigkeit der Verhandlung mit den Ortsbischöfen betont; „ebenfalls wurde die finanzielle Auswirkung auf die Provinz und ihre Konvente ventiliert, die ein solcher ‚Zuschusskonvent‘ bringen würde.“[474] Aus dem ursprünglich vorgeschlagenen „attraktiven Modellkonvent“ war über einen „Observanzkonvent“ nun also ein „Reformkonvent“ geworden. Dabei blieben die Planungsarbeiten zunächst einmal stehen.

Auf einem anderen Feld gab es Innovationen: Im Herbst 1976 waren die ersten Postulanten, die die Provinz seit Jahren hatte, im Konvent St. Hyacinthe in Freiburg in der Schweiz angekommen und am 8. Dezember eingekleidet worden. Das unter einem Schweizer Magister zusammen mit

472 PA, Liber consilii provincialis, Sitzung in Augsburg vom 3.1.1980.
473 PA, Provinzrundbrief vom 10.12.1980, S. 3.
474 PA, Liber consilii provincialis, Sitzung in Wettenhausen vom 29.8.1980, Nr. 1.

den Novizen der Schweizer Provinz gehaltene Noviziatsprogramm unterschied sich wesentlich von dem, was in den 1960er Jahren in Warburg durchgeführt worden war, vor allem dadurch, dass St. Hyacinthe ein hauptsächlich französischsprachiger Konvent war und bestimmte Lehrveranstaltungen der Universität über die Heilige Schrift und die Liturgie in den Unterricht eingebaut waren. Insgesamt bildeten die Novizen keine abgeschlossene, von den anderen Brüdern getrennte und streng kontemplativ lebende Sondergruppe mehr, wie vor River Forest, sondern wurden in die ganze Hausgemeinschaft eingebunden, zu der in St. Hyacinthe auch viele Studenten gehörten.[475] Nach ihrer Profess verblieben diese Fratres, wie auch die kommenden Jahrgänge, zum Studium in Freiburg in der Schweiz. Um diese neuen Mitbrüder auch in die eigene Provinz einzubinden, sollten sie die vorlesungsfreie Zeit in verschiedenen Konventen in Österreich verbringen. Dass dies nur eine Übergangslösung sein durfte, war allen bewusst.[476] Trotz der Kürze ihres Ferienaufenthaltes in der Heimat brachten die Studenten gewissermaßen einen frischen Wind in die Konvente, z. B. durch das von ihnen getragene Angebot an Jugendliche und junge Erwachsene, die Kar- und Ostertage im Konvent von Wien zu feiern, was Interessenten die Möglichkeit bot, unverbindlich das Klosterleben kennenzulernen.[477]

Als einigermaßen gesichert schien, dass Kandidaten nicht mehr ausbleiben würden, diskutierte das Provinzkonsil über die Errichtung eines Noviziates in der Provinz. Schwierigkeiten bereitete das Finden eines zum Novizenmeister geeigneten Mitbruders und eines Konventes, der bereit war, Novizen aufzunehmen – und seinen bisherigen Lebensstil, den Liturgieablauf usw. für das Noviziat zu ändern. Der Provinzial wurde beauftragt, einen geeigneten Mann und einen geeigneten Ort ausfindig zu machen.[478] Im Herbst war es dann soweit: Vom Provinzkonsil wurde am 16. September 1981 der Konvent Graz zum Noviziatskonvent kanonisch errichtet. Mit P. Hilarius Barth hatte man auch einen Bruder gefunden, der bereit war, die Aufgabe des Novizenmeisters zu übernehmen.[479] Zum 1. Juli 1982 sollte

475 *St. Dominikuswerk* (1977) S. 7–8.
476 PA, Liber consilii provincialis, Sitzung in Augsburg vom 2.1.1981, Nr. 3.
477 *St. Dominikuswerk* (1982) S. 6–7.
478 PA, Liber consilii provincialis, Sitzung in Augsburg vom 2.1.1981, Nr. 3 und Provinzrundbrief vom 1.12.1981, S. 2.
479 PA, Liber consilii provincialis, Sitzung in Augsburg vom 7.9.1981, Nr. 2.

das provinzeigene Noviziat seine Arbeit in Graz aufnehmen, wobei die beiden Novizen des Jahrganges 1981/82 ihr Probejahr in der Schweiz vollendeten.[480]

War noch das 750. Jubiläum des Bestehens des Wiener Konvents 1976 in einer schwierigen Zeit gefeiert worden,[481] so wurde das Albertus-Magnus-Gedenkjahr 1980 in allen Häusern der Provinz und auch in den Albert-Gedenkorten Lauingen und Regensburg, die auf dem Provinzgebiet lagen, sehr festlich und sehr öffentlichkeitswirksam begangen.[482] In dasselbe Jahr fiel auch die Feier des 600. Todestages der hl. Katharina von Siena – ebenfalls Anlass von Festveranstaltungen.[483] Von besonderer Bedeutung war die Seligsprechung der Mystikerin Margaretha Ebner († 1351) am 24. Februar 1979, da sie als Dominikanerin im Kloster Maria Medingen auf dem Provinzgebiet gelebt und gewirkt hatte.[484] Dazu kamen drei Provinzjubiläen: 1981 das 30-jährige Bestehen der Kuratie St. Katharina in München-Freimann,[485] 1983 der 200. Jahrestag des Bestehens der Münzgrabenpfarrei in Graz[486] und 1984 der 350. Jahrestag der Weihe der Basilika S. Maria Rotunda in Wien.[487]

Auch mit den Provinztagungen ging es, zwar ein wenig zäh, voran. Vom 25. bis 30. August 1979 traf man sich in Friesach zum Thema „Die dominikanische Berufung nach Albert dem Großen und Katharina von Siena". Ihr Organisator, Christoph von Schönborn, meinte dazu: „Die Teilnahme war zwar zahlenmäßig nicht überwältigend, aber umso intensiver und, wie mir scheint, für alle wirklich bereichernd."[488] Deutlich größer war die Teilnehmerzahl an der Tagung vom 25. bis 29. August 1980 in Wet-

---

480 PA, Provinzrundbriefe vom 1.12.1981, S. 2 und vom 2.8.1982, S. 4.

481 Siehe dazu *St. Dominikuswerk* (1976), das fast ganz diesem Anlass gewidmet ist.

482 Siehe dazu ausführlich: PA, Provinzrundbriefe vom 10.3.1980, S. 4 und vom 10.12.1980, S. 2 sowie *St. Dominikuswerk* (1981) S. 10.

483 Siehe dazu: PA, Provinzrundbrief vom 10.12.1980, S. 3 und *St. Dominikuswerk* (1981) S. 10f.

484 Venchi: *Catalogus hagiographicus*, S. 140–141.

485 Siehe dazu: PA, Provinzrundbrief vom 9.1.1982.

486 Siehe PA, Provinzrundbrief vom 14.12.1983, S. 14, *St. Dominikuswerk* (1983) S. 3–5 und die sehr informative *Festschrift 200 Jahre Pfarre Münzgraben*. Graz 1983.

487 Siehe *St. Dominikuswerk* (1985) S. 3–8 und *Die Dominikaner in Wien. Zur Geschichte der Wiener Dominikaner und ihrer Kirche. Festschrift, herausgegeben aus Anlaß des 350. Jahrestages der Weihe der Basilika S. Maria Rotunda 1634–1984*. Hg. vom Dominikanerkonvent Wien. Graz o.J.

488 PA, Provinzrundbrief vom 10.3.1980, S. 2.

tenhausen über „Vita activa – vita contemplativa bei Thomas von Aquin“.[489]

Selbst die Lage eines Sorgenkindes der Provinz hatte sich inzwischen stabilisiert: Das Kloster in Retz, das man Anfang der 1970er Jahre noch hatte schließen wollen, hatte in der Kleinstbesetzung von drei Mann überlebt. Es gab verschiedene Projekte für eine Revitalisierung von Kirche und Kloster. Neben dem Vorschlag der Errichtung eines Gästehauses brachte ein Architekt und Lehrbeauftragter an der Wiener Akademie für angewandte Kunst die Idee ein, sich mit seinen Studenten in den Gebäuden einzumieten und dort Werkstätten für Keramik, Weberei und Architektur einzurichten.[490] Das Provinzkonsil gewährte dem Provinzial diesbezüglich Handlungsfreiheit.[491] Auf der Sitzung des Provinzkonsils vom 7. September 1981 kristallisierte sich die mögliche Zukunft für Retz heraus: „Es bestünde nach gewissen baulichen Veränderungen [die Möglichkeit], das Haus für Exerzitien und Einkehrtage, Begegnungen zu verwenden.“[492] Jedenfalls wurden 1980 das Archiv des Retzer Klosters der Stadt Retz leihweise überlassen und in das Stadtarchiv überführt[493] und der Filialverband der Niederlassung mit Wien gelöst; Retz war wieder selbständige *domus formata* mit P. Augustinus Deutsch als Superior.[494]

Das Provinzkapitel von 1982

Im Hinblick auf das bevorstehende Generalkapitel wurde das eigentlich für die erste Januarwoche 1983 geplante Provinzkapitel vorverlegt:[495] Es fand vom 1. bis 5. Juni 1982 im Augsburger Konvent statt. Drei große Tagesordnungspunkte standen auf seinem Programm: die Anpassung des Provinzstatuts, eine Bilanz der Entwicklung seit 1979 und die Wahl eines neuen Provinzials. P. Innozenz Varga hatte dieses Amt 16 Jahre innegehabt und

489 PA, Provinzrundbrief vom 10.12.1980, S. 4.

490 PA, Liber consiliorum provinciae, Sitzung in Wien vom 6.3.1980, S. 94 und Sitzung in Wien vom 9.6.1981, S. 95–96.

491 PA, Liber consilii provincialis, Sitzung in Augsburg vom 29.8.1980, Nr. 3.

492 PA, Liber consilii provincialis, Sitzung in Augsburg vom 7.9.1981, Nr. 4.

493 PA, Liber consiliorum provinciae, Sitzung in Wien am 6.3.1980, Nr. 2, S. 94 und Sitzung in Wien vom 1.4.1980, Nr. 1, S. 95.

494 PA, Provinzialsregestenbuch 2 (1966–2010), Eintrag vom 7.12.1980, Nr. 25.

495 APKap 1979, S. 17, Nr. 26 und PA, Liber consilii provincialis; Sitzung vom 7.9.1981 in Augsburg, Nr. 1.

Abb. 66: P. Dominikus Kirchmaier (aufgenommen 2004; PA, Fotosammlung).

kam dafür nicht mehr in Frage, weil die Ordenskurie seiner neuerlichen Postulation nicht zugestimmt hätte. Die Wahl der Kapitelsväter fiel auf den Prior des Augsburger Konvents, Dominikus Kirchmaier. P. Kirchmaier war seit 1970 für zwei Pfarreien im Augsburger Raum verantwortlich, eine Arbeit, die er nicht aufgeben wollte und mit der Unterstützung seiner Augsburger Mitbrüder auch als Provinzial nicht aufgeben musste. Dies hatte eine Neuerung zur Folge: Nun wurde Augsburg zum Hauptsitz des Provinzialats und Wien zum Zweitsitz.[496] P. Exprovinzial Varga wurde zum Socius des Provinzials ernannt. Varga ging zunächst als Superior nach Friesach, wurde aber 1983 vom Wiener Konvent zum Prior gewählt, von wo aus er P. Kirchmaier effektiver unterstützen konnte.[497]

Abgesehen von dieser Personalveränderung widmete sich das Provinzkapitel inhaltlich vor allem der Aufgabe, klare Entscheidungen für die Zukunft zu fällen. Dazu gehörten neben der Erinnerung an die liturgischen Verpflichtungen des Einzelnen und der Häuser seitens der Konstitutionen auch die Richtlinien, die das Generalkapitel von Quezon City 1974 zur Klärung gottesdienstlicher Fragen erlassen hatte, die sich aus der Aufgabe des dominikanischen Eigenritus‘ und der Übernahme der römischen Liturgie ergeben hatten. Diese ausführlichen „Hinweise für die liturgischen Feiern im Predigerorden“ wurden, versehen mit einem ebenso ausführlichen Vorwort ihres Übersetzers, Hilarius Barth, als 15-seitiger Anhang den Kapitelsakten beigegeben. Bezüglich der Pastoral in der Provinz meinte das Kapitel, dass Pfarreien „vom Orden nur betreut werden“ sollten, „wenn für die dort arbeitenden Mitbrüder die Teilnahme am Konventsleben gesichert ist.“

496 PA, Provinzrundbrief vom 2.8.1982, S. 3.

497 PA, Provinzialsregestenbuch 2 (1966–2010), Einträge vom 15.7.1982, Nr. 8 und vom 10.2.1983, Nr. 3.

Auch sollten „in Zukunft jenen Gestellungsverträgen der Vorzug gegeben werden, durch die eine gemeinsame Arbeit und ein intensives Gemeinschaftsleben ermöglicht und gesichert" wurden. In diesem Zusammenhang wurde der Provinzial gebeten, „zu prüfen, ob die Pfarrei St. Wolfgang in Augsburg / Spickel unter den gegenwärtigen Umständen weiterhin vom Orden versorgt werden" könne. Weiterhin wurde dem Provinzial aufgetragen, „den Status der Mitbrüder, die außerhalb der Gemeinschaft leben, sofort zu überprüfen und sie – je nach den Umständen – in die Gemeinschaft zurückzuführen." Was den Nachwuchs anging, so empfahl das Kapitel, „dass die Fratres nach Ausbildungsabschluss nach Möglichkeit nicht einzeln zum Einsatz kommen" sollten. In einem weiteren Schritt wurde gefordert, „dass das Studentat grundsätzlich in die Provinz zurückverlegt werden sollte. Für diese Rückführung des Studentates in die Provinz soll der Provinzial mit dem Ausbildungsrat die notwendigen Bedingungen schaffen." Dazu war ordensrechtlich ein provinzeigenes Ausbildungsprogramm, eine sogenannte *Ratio formationis particularis* notwendig. Dieses zu erstellen fiel ebenfalls in die Kompetenz des Ausbildungsrats. Die Teilnahme an den Provinztagungen zur Weiterbildung und zum brüderlichen Austausch wurde den Mitbrüdern dringend ans Herz gelegt. Mit der Anpassung des Provinzstatus an die geltenden Normen schloss das Kapitel.[498]

Ordensmeister de Couesnongle war zufrieden: „Ich sehe in den Akten in erster Linie eine positive Antwort auf meinen Brief, den ich nach der Visitation der Provinz im Oktober 1979 an euch gerichtet habe. Denn zahlreiche Bestimmungen stehen mit meiner Ansicht, die ich im erwähnten Brief geäußert habe, in engstem Zusammenhang."[499]

Damit war die Provinz in ihrem Bemühen, einen neuen Aufstieg zu wagen, einen Schritt weitergekommen.

Ausführungsarbeiten: 1982 bis 1986

Provinzial Kirchmaier nahm die Planungen auf, die seit 1979 in der Provinz liefen, und machte sie seiner Politik zu eigen. Das wichtigste Werk, das er in Angriff nahm, war der Aufbau von Noviziat und Studentat.

Um den Kontakt zur Heimatprovinz zu gewährleisten, kamen die süddeutsch-österreichischen Studenten für das Studienjahr 1979/80 nach

498 APKap 1982; zitiert wurden oben S. 14–16 die Nrn. 40, 42–45, 48, 49 und 53.
499 APKap 1982, S. 5.

Wien. Aufgrund der guten Erfahrungen, die man dabei machte, wurde ein solcher Aufenthalt für das Studienjahr 1983/84 wiederholt. Prior Varga schlug daraufhin vor, den Wiener Konvent zu dem vom Provinzkapitel gewünschten provinzeigenen Studentatskonvent zu machen und dabei gleichzeitig dort den „Konvent zu bilden, der den Wünschen des P. Generals nach einem ‚attraktiven Konvent' entspricht."[500] Diese Idee wurde positiv aufgenommen, denn durch diese Lösung waren sowohl das Projekt des „Modellkonvents" als auch das des Studentatskonvents zum Abschluss zu bringen. Man verwies die Sache an den Ausbildungsrat, der grünes Licht gab. Das Provinzkonsil beschloss in seiner Sitzung am 8. Juni 1983 offiziell, „den Wiener Konvent als Studentatsort zu bestimmen". Die Studenten der Provinz, die eigentlich nur in Wien ihr Freisemester hatten machen sollen, blieben dort, und neue Studenten sollten ab Herbst 1984 ihr Studium an der Wiener Universität beginnen. Nur die Besetzung des Amtes des Studentenmagisters bereitete noch Schwierigkeiten, da der Kandidat, P. Clemens Wehrle, zwar gerne dazu bereit war, aber sein Posten als Pfarrer in München / St. Albert nachzubesetzen war.[501] Nachdem am 1. August 1984 der Pfarrvikar von St. Katharina-Freimann, P. Adalbert von Papius, auch die Pfarrei von St. Albert mit übernahm, wurde Wehrle am 15. September 1984 zum Studentenmagister ernannt und nach Wien versetzt.[502]

Der Novizenjahrgang 1983/84 war der erste, der sein Noviziat in Graz begann.[503] Die Provinz hatte damit zwei eigene Nachwuchszentren, Graz und Wien. Eine Zusammenlegung von Noviziat und Studentat in Wien wurde vom Provinzkonsil am 19. Juni 1984 abgelehnt.[504] Die Wichtigkeit des eigenen Noviziates stand nun außer Frage; selbst in Ausnahmefällen wollte man kein Noviziat außerhalb der Provinzgrenzen mehr zulassen.[505] Nach einiger Zeit revidierte das Provinzkonsil aber seine Entscheidung über den Ort des Noviziatskonvents wieder. Diesmal fiel ein neuerlicher Antrag des Ausbildungsrates, das Noviziat von Graz nach Wien zu verlegen, auf fruchtbaren Boden; er wurde vom Provinzkonsil am 25. Juni 1986 angenommen: „Für Wien sprechen: die zentralere Lage (besser als

500 PA, Provinzrundbrief vom 20.4.1983, S. 4.

501 PA, Provinzrundbrief vom 4.8.1983, S. 3.

502 PA, Provinzialsregestenbuch 2 (1966–2010), Einträge vom 1.8.1984, Nr. 19 und vom 15.9.1984, Nr. 23.

503 PA, Provinzrundbrief vom 14.12.1983, S. 14.

504 PA, Provinzrundbrief vom 27.7.1984, S. 4.

505 PA, Provinzrundbrief vom 18.5.1985, S. 2.

Graz), die Möglichkeit der Universität, die Tatsache, dass das Studentat bereits gut integriert ist, die räumlichen Möglichkeiten.“[506] Am 30. Juli 1986 gab Ordensmeister Damian Byrne die Erlaubnis zu dieser Verlegung,[507] sodass, nach vier Jahren Noviziatsaufenthalt in Graz, sich die Provinz nun in Wien ihr Nachwuchszentrum errichtet hatte.

Weniger erfolgreich verlief die Geschichte der Provinztagungen. Diese waren immer schlechter besucht und daher 1983 mit der jährlichen Tagung der Oberinnen der deutschsprachigen Dominikanerinnen in Augsburg-Leitershofen zusammengelegt worden.[508] Thema war „Der neue Codex und seine Bedeutung für das Ordensleben“. Die Anmeldungen der Brüder blieben gering. Provinzial Kirchmaier mahnte daraufhin dringend im Provinzrundbrief: „Die Studenten bzw. alle Fratres müssen die Tagung als ‚Provinztagung‘ mitmachen. Alle Mitbrüder sind wenigstens für den letzten Tag herzlich eingeladen.“[509] Trotz weiterer Bitten des Provinzials war auch bei der Tagung des Jahres 1984 über die „Nachfolge des armen Jesus“ das Interesse der Brüder nicht größer.[510] Die Tagung des Jahres 1985 über „Dominikanische Mystik im Umgang mit der Welt“ fand besseren Anklang,[511] ebenso nahmen an der Tagung von 1986 in Leitershofen über „20 Jahre nach dem Vaticanum II: Was haben wir verwirklicht? Was können wir besser machen?“ wieder einige Patres und Studenten aus der süddeutsch-österreichischen Provinz und der Teutonia teil.[512] Das Provinzkapitel vom November 1986 befand, dass die Provinz-Studientage „von der jährlichen Tagung der Schwestern … losgelöst werden“ sollten. „Wie früher“ sollten sie „einmal jährlich stattfinden und der Weiterbildung der Mitbrüder dienen“. Den Mitbrüdern sollte dennoch der Besuch der Dominikanerinnentagung in Leitershofen „zur Förderung der Dominikanischen Familie ein Anliegen sein.“[513] Dementsprechend wurde 1987 neben der Leitershofer Tagung wieder ein eigener Provinzstudientag veranstaltet, im Konvent von Freiburg im Breisgau, den das Provinzkapitel von 1986 zum Zentrum der Weiterbildung der Provinz bestimmt hatte. Thema war „Die

---

506 PA, Provinzrundbrief vom 18.7.1986, S. 3.
507 Datum laut PA, Provinzrundbrief vom 7.11.1986, S. 2.
508 PA, Provinzrundbrief vom 20.4.1983, S. 4.
509 PA, Provinzrundbrief vom 14.12.1983, S. 16.
510 PA, Provinzrundbrief vom 10.12.1984, S. 2.
511 PA, Provinzrundbrief vom 12.12.1985, S. 5.
512 PA, Provinzrundbrief vom 7.11.1986, S. 2.
513 APKap 1986, S. 14, Nr. 37.

Weltanschauung aus der Sicht des hl. Thomas von Aquin". Das Echo war dürftig. Neben den Freiburger Mitbrüdern selbst kamen nur einige der Studenten mit ihrem Magister und der Provinzial.[514] Für den September 1988 widmete sich die Studienwoche in Freiburg dem Thema: „New Age und Esoterik".[515] 1989 beschäftigte sich die Tagung im März in Wien mit dem 50-jährigen Provinzjubiläum und dem Thema: „50 Jahre danach. Unsere Spiritualität und unser Apostolat im Lichte gegenwärtiger, innerkirchlicher Bewegungen", wozu noch aus den meisten Konventen Mitbrüder erschienen.[516] Im April 1990, bei der Tagung über „Christentum und moderne Gesellschaft" in Graz kamen nur mehr Grazer und Wiener Mitbrüder.[517] Damit schlief das Projekt „Studientage" ein. Der Aufwand an Organisation und an Einladung von Referenten war zu groß für das geringe Echo.

Das Provinzkapitel von 1986 und das Provinzjubiläum 1989

Aufgrund einer Terminkollision mit dem bevorstehenden Generalkapitel bat das Provinzkonsil den Ordensmeister am 5. Januar 1985, das ursprünglich für die Woche nach Pfingsten 1986 geplante Provinzkapitel in die letzte Novemberwoche verschieben zu dürfen.[518] Dementsprechend trat das Provinzkapitel vom 24. bis 28. November 1986 in Augsburg zusammen. Es war ein Wahlkapitel – und die Kapitelsväter wählten wieder P. Innozenz Varga in das Amt des Provinzials. Es war seine fünfte Amtsperiode und der Gewählte war bereits 73 Jahre alt. Diese Wiederwahl war nicht unumstritten, wie Varga in den ersten Zeilen seines ersten Provinzrundbrief als neuer Provinzoberer schilderte: „Pater General hat meine Wahl zum Provinzial bestätigt. Nach langem und hartem Ringen habe ich mich entschlossen, die Wahl anzunehmen. Ich habe Verständnis, wenn manche Mitbrüder über die Wahl und meine Annahme enttäuscht sind. Haben sie doch (und ich schließe mich dabei nicht aus) vom Provinzkapitel eine Wende erwartet, die vor allem in der Person eines neuen Provinzials kommen sollte. Ob hinter dieser Erwartung nicht Illusionen und kaum zu realisierende Vor-

514 PA, Provinzrundbrief vom 22.12.1987, S. 3.
515 Ebd., S. 4.
516 PA, Provinzrundbrief vom 2.7.1989, S. 4.
517 PA, Provinzrundbrief vom 20.7.1990, S. 2.
518 APKap 1982, S. 13, Nr. 27, PA, Provinzrundbriefe „zum Osterfest" 1986, S. 4 (über Provinzkonsilssitzung in Augsburg am 5.1.1986) und vom 5.7.1986, S. 1.

stellungen stehen oder standen? – Das Provinzkapitel hat nun anders entschieden. Ich bitte Sie alle, die Entscheidungen des Kapitels zu respektieren." Und Varga machte deutlich, wohin er die Provinz führen wollte: „Die gegenwärtige Stunde fordert von uns lebendige und wirkkräftige Ordensgesinnung. Erneuerung und fruchtbare Selbstdarstellung müssen bei uns, bei jedem einzelnen beginnen. Sehen wir zu, dass wir wahrhaftige, also dem Sein und der Berufung entsprechende Söhne des hl. Vaters Dominikus seien!"[519]

Seinem Amtsvorgänger sprach das Kapitel einen ausdrücklichen Dank „für seine aufopfernde Tätigkeit als Provinzial zum Wohle unserer Mitbrüder und des Ordens" aus.[520] P. Kirchmaier kehrte zu seiner Pfarrseelsorge zurück.

Die Anordnungen des Kapitels waren nicht umfangreich. Abgesehen von der Ämterbesetzung, Verwaltungsregelungen, dem schon zitierten Beschluss über die Provinzstudientage und Bestimmungen über das Haus St. Albert in München-Freimann (zu diesen später) kümmerten sich die Kapitularen hauptsächlich um den Zusammenhalt der Zweige der Dominikanischen Familie in der Provinz: Der Provinzpromotor der dominikanischen Laiengemeinschaften wurde zusammen mit den Promotoren für die Ordensschwestern und -nonnen aufgefordert, zu prüfen, „ob und in welcher Weise ein Provinzrat der Dominikanischen Familie gebildet werden" könne und solle. Zur Intensivierung der Betreuung der Schwestern und Nonnen vor allem in Westösterreich sollte der Schwesternpromotor „die Bedürfnisse der einzelnen Schwesternklöster" erfragen, „sodass eine planmäßigere und mehr koordinierte Betreuung möglich" wurde. Auch die Frage nach der Situation der Laienbrüder wurde gestellt: „Allen Mitbrüdern empfehlen wir die Gestalt des Frater Cooperator, wie er in unseren erneuerten Konstitutionen gesehen wird, zu bedenken und daraus neue Impulse für den Beruf des Frater Cooperator zu schöpfen." Ein Laienbruder wurde gebeten, „eine Kurzinformation über Berufung und Stellung des Frater Cooperator zu erstellen."

Dies leitete über zum zweiten Inhaltspunkt des Provinzkapitels, den Regelungen zu Ausbildung und Weiterbildung: Das Kloster in Wien wurde zum Konvent der Provinz für die Grundausbildung (in der Sprache der Konstitutionen zum *centrum studiorum institutionalium*) bestimmt, der Freibur-

---

519 PA, Provinzrundbrief vom 14.12.1986.
520 APKap 1986, S. 20, Nr. 70.

ger Konvent zum Provinzkonvent für die Fortbildung (*centrum formationis permanentis*). Der Ausbildungsrat wurde in diesem Zusammenhang dringend aufgefordert, so bald als möglich das provinzeigene Ausbildungsprogramm auszuarbeiten. Die Konventslektoren – die Verantwortlichen in jedem Kloster für die Fortbildung der Mitbrüder –, Offizialen, die bis dato noch nie in den Provinzkapitelsakten vorgekommen waren, wurden angewiesen, an der jährlichen Studientagung der Provinz teilzunehmen. Außerdem sollten sie sich um die Anschaffung aktueller Literatur für die Konventsbibliotheken kümmern, wofür die Konvente in ihrem Jahreshaushalt ein Budget bereitzustellen hatten. Für die Studenten der Provinz wurde während ihres regulären Studiums „in der Regel ein Studienjahr in einer fremdsprachigen Provinz oder in einem fremdsprachigen Studienkonvent vorgesehen". Zu guter Letzt wurde das „Experiment ‚Sommerkloster Bronnbach'" vom Provinzkapitel erlaubt (auch dazu später).[521]

Ordensmeister Damian Byrne fand in seinem Bestätigungschreiben einige lobende Worte für die Akten. Er wies aber ausdrücklich darauf hin, dass das provinzeigene Ausbildungsprogramm „wenn nötig und möglich ergänzende Studiengänge, etwa in thomasischer Philosophie und Theologie" vorsehen möge: „Ähnliches gälte für die Fächer Ordensgeschichte und Geschichte der dominikanischen Spiritualität. Es wäre bedauerlich, wenn die Kenntnis der geistigen und geistlichen Traditionen unseres Ordens nur noch wenigen Spezialisten vorbehalten bliebe, während sie doch zum Allgemeingut des Ordens und daher aller Ordensmitglieder gehört." Zwei Kritikpunkte hob Byrne ausdrücklich hervor: Erstens vermisste er „ein näheres Eingehen auf die Frage der Gewinnung von Ordensberufen. Wahrscheinlich ist darüber während des Kapitels gesprochen worden, aber diese Gespräche haben offensichtlich noch keine Auswirkungen auf die Beschlüsse des Kapitels gehabt." Byrne empfahl konkrete Anfänge etwa „durch die Gestaltung von Informationstagungen für interessierte junge Menschen, die Erarbeitung von Informationsmaterial für diese Gruppe und ähnliches mehr". Zweitens betonte er die Bedeutung der Erstellung eines pastoralen Konzepts für die Zukunft: „Es wäre zwar wenig sinnvoll, sich angesichts der angespannten Personallage in der Provinz mit utopischen pastoralen Projekten beschäftigen zu wollen", andererseits könnte eine konkrete und realistische Reflexion darüber „besonders den jüngeren Mitbrüdern Perspektiven für ihre zukünftige pastorale Tätigkeit eröff-

521 Ebd., S. 14–17, Nrn. 35, 40, 41, 46, 48–52 und 54.

nen. ... Die Zukunftsperspektiven einer Provinz sind weitgehend identisch mit den pastoralen Perspektiven, die erarbeitet werden; auch wenn sich diese Perspektiven angesichts des zeitbedingten Personalmangels in einem eher bescheideneren Rahmen artikulieren.“[522]

Eine Sache, über die sich das Provinzkapitel noch Gedanken gemacht hatte, war das für 1989 anstehende 50-jährige Jubiläum der Gründung der Provinz: „Aus diesem Anlass möge entweder das Dominikus-Werk-Heft 1989 in erweiterter Form oder eine eigene Festschrift geplant werden. Neben der Selbstdarstellung der Vergangenheit sollten vor allem die Standortbestimmung in der Gegenwart und die Diskussion über die Zukunft breiten Raum einnehmen.“[523]

Zu einer Festschrift kam es nicht – es war ja noch nicht einmal ein Mitbruder mit ihrer Herausgabe betraut worden.[524] Zur Standortbestimmung und Zukunftsdiskussion diente die im April 1989 in Wien stattfindende Studientagung, die ja der spirituellen und pastoralen Nutzanwendung des Provinzjubiläums gewidmet war. „Aus fast allen Konventen waren Mitbrüder da, die über die Arbeiten und das Leben der jeweiligen Gemeinschaft“ berichteten.[525] Der Direktor des St.-Dominikuswerkes, P. Innozenz Varga, widmete, wie aufgetragen, das Heft für das Jahr 1989 eben diesem Anlass. In seinem Grußwort an die Freunde und Wohltäter des Ordens gab Varga einen gerafften Überblick über die Ereignisse in der Provinz zwischen 1939 und etwa 1966. Von besonderem Wert waren die darauf folgenden Stellungnahmen von vier Mitbrüdern, die die Provinzgründung noch persönlich miterlebt hatten, nämlich von P. Gottfried Prischink (der 1989 87 Jahre alt war), P. Maximilian Göbel, P. Seraphikus Weber und P. Magnus Beck – die letzteren drei waren 86 Jahre alt. Jeder von ihnen lieferte einen eigenen Blickwinkel auf das damalige Geschehen. Auch der Provinzial der Teutonia, P. Karl Meyer, würdigte in einem Schreiben den sozusagen runden Provinzgeburtstag: „Da das Goldene Jubiläum einer Provinz, anders als andere Goldene Jubiläen, nicht schon das Ende vorankündigt, sondern gleichsam eine Jugendzeit anschaut und von dort in die Vollkraft der Jahre aufbricht“ wünschte er dem Provinzial und den Mit-

522 Ebd., S. 6–7.

523 Ebd., S. 14, Nr. 38.

524 Dafür wurde im *Dominikus* 1–1999, S. 2–10 dem 60-jährigen Provinzjubiläum mit einem kurzen Artikel über die Provinzgründung gedacht.

525 PA, Provinzrundbrief vom 2.7.1989, S. 4.

brüdern Gottes reichen Segen: „Nach schwierigen Jahren, die wir alle erleben, möge sich die Provinz zu neuem und kräftigem Leben erheben. Mögen sich immer wieder viele Mitglieder mit geistlicher Freude und Phantasie dem so notwendigen Dienst am Wort widmen.“[526]

Eile und Unentschlossenheit: das Provinzkapitel von 1990

Die Provinzkapitel der 1980er Jahre waren eher administrative als zukunftsweisende Versammlungen gewesen. In noch viel größerem Maße traf dies auf das Provinzkapitel zu, das vom 31. Juli bis 5. August 1990 in Augsburg / Heilig-Kreuz zusammentrat: Ämterbesetzungen und wirtschaftliche Bestimmungen dominierten seine Akten. Zum Thema des Gemeinschaftslebens wurden nur allgemeine Ordensanregungen und ältere Beschlüsse über die Bedeutung der Konventsmesse und der jährlichen Exerzitien wiederholt. Bezüglich der seelsorglichen Perspektiven sollte alles beim Alten bleiben: „Das Kapitel weist mit Nachdruck darauf hin, dass Sorge getragen werden muss für die Weiterführung der bestehenden Aufgaben der einzelnen Konvente“. Wie diese Weiterführung unter den gegebenen personellen Umständen aussehen sollte, wurde nicht angedacht. Stattdessen delegierte man diese Frage an eine Planungskommission, die innerhalb der nächsten zwei Jahre ein Konzept vorlegen sollte, „welche pastoralen Schwerpunkte angesichts der konkreten Situation unserer Provinz beachtet werden sollen“. Hervorgehoben wurde nur, dass die Lage des Augsburger Konvents die Kapitularen „mit besonderer Sorge“ erfüllte und deshalb möglichst bald jüngere Mitbrüder dorthin assigniert werden sollten. Im Zusammenhang mit der Fortbildung der Brüder wurde den inzwischen eingeschlafenen Studienwochen in Wettenhausen nachgeweint. Stärkeres Interesse galt der Dominikanischen Familie, also den Beziehungen zwischen Brüdern, Schwestern, Nonnen und den Mitgliedern der dominikanischen Laiengemeinschaften in der Provinz: Zur Förderung des Zusammenhaltes wurde ein jährlich abzuhaltender „regionaler dominikanischer Tag“ für „Gebet, Glaubensvertiefung und Gespräch“ angeregt, ebenso wie ein zweimal jährlich erscheinender „Provinzbrief der dominikanischen Familie“.[527]

Ordensmeister Damian Byrne approbierte diese Akten zwar – weil er musste –, war aber nicht glücklich damit:

526 Ebd., S. 3.

527 APKap 1990, S. 15–19, Nrn. 31–34, 45 und 51.

> „Ihre Provinz steht an einem kritischen Punkt ihrer Geschichte. Die Entscheidungen, die Sie jetzt fällen, bestimmen ihre Zukunft. Obwohl es mir weh tut, habe ich das Gefühl, Ihnen sagen zu müssen, dass die Akten Ihres Kapitels Zeichen von Eile und Unentschlossenheit zeigen."

In sehr deutlichen Worten hob er das Versagen der Kapitularen hervor, die sich vor seiner Ansicht nach wesentlichen Entscheidungen gedrückt hatten:

> „Wenn die Zahl der Mitbrüder abnimmt, wird es für eine Provinz immer schwieriger, ihren apostolischen Verpflichtungen nachzukommen. Provinzen, die sich diesem Problem stellen und ihre Verpflichtungen neu organisieren, sind in einer sehr viel gesünderen Situation als solche, die das nicht tun. Das Aufschieben einer notwendigen Reorganisation vergrößert nur die Probleme, mit denen man sich schließlich doch befassen muss. Mit großer Sorge bemerke ich, dass das Kapitel Entscheidungen aufgeschoben hat, die für die Zukunft Ihrer Provinz wesentlich sind. Sie stellen fest, ‚dass Sorge getragen werden muss für die Zukunft der bestehenden Aufgaben der einzelnen Konvente'. Ist es nicht an der Zeit, Ihr Apostolat kritischer zu prüfen und Prioritäten zu setzen?"

In dieselbe Richtung ging auch seine Anweisung zum Umgang mit dem Ordensnachwuchs: „Sie müssen sich genau im Klaren darüber sein, warum Sie Berufungen haben und wie Sie sie ausbilden wollen", denn man dürfe „die jungen Mitbrüder nicht als bloßen Ersatz für sich selbst, die eigene Arbeit und die Institutionen, die wir betreuen, ansehen. Freilich können sie die Arbeiten fortsetzen, die wir bisher getan haben, aber wir dürfen Berufungen nicht nur als Lückenbüßer für uns selbst betrachten". Deshalb forderte Byrne „eine große Klarheit über die verschiedenen Ausbildungsstadien und das Ziel der einzelnen Ausbildungsschritte". Er betonte die Wichtigkeit eines geordneten Pränoviziates und die Gestaltung der Noviziatszeit als vor allem geistliches Jahr. Nach den Auszubildenden wandte er sich schließlich an die Ausgebildeten, d. h. an die Brüder der Provinz: „… ich möchte gerne die Verbindung zwischen unserem Gemeinschaftsleben, dem Studium und der Predigt hervorheben. Ohne eine ernsthafte Bindung an das Leben der Gemeinschaft sind wir unserer Berufung nicht treu. Wenn die Predigt die höchste Priorität besitzt, dann ist das sichtbare Zeugnis eines Lebens in Gemeinschaft nach dem Evangelium eine Form der Predigt."[528]

Nie zuvor hatte sich ein Provinzkapitel der süddeutsch-österreichischen Provinz so harsche und berechtigte Kritik gefallen lassen müssen.

---

528 Ebd., S. 5–9.

Abb. 67: P. Gregor Ruf (aufgenommen ca. 1987; Archiv des Augsburger Dominikanerkonvents, Fotosammlung).

Der neue Provinzial übernahm diese Worte des Ordensmeisters nicht nur als eine schwere Bürde, sondern auch als Auftrag. Tatsächlich war den Kapitularen ein innovativer Schritt geglückt: Als Nachfolger für Innozenz Varga hatten sie Gregor Ruf zum Provinzoberhaupt gewählt. Dadurch wurde ein echter Wachwechsel vollzogen, denn Ruf brachte Qualifikationen mit, die bisher keiner seiner Povinzialsvorgänger besessen hatten – er hatte 1959 an der Ordensuniversität „Angelicum" in Rom im Fach Kirchenrecht promoviert, war im selben Jahr in den Konvent an Heilig Kreuz in seiner Heimatstadt assigniert worden und hatte sich in der Diözese Augsburg neben seiner Tätigkeit als Kurat der Autobahnkirche bei Adelsried vor allem durch seine Arbeit in der Ausbildung von Gemeinde- und Pastoralassistenten einen Namen gemacht, als Leiter des Instituts für theologisch-pastorale Fortbildung hauptberuflich pastoraler Laiendienste, als Lehrer an der bischöflichen Fachakademie für Gemeindepastoral in Neuburg an der Donau und als Mitarbeiter bei der Erwachsenenbildung an Volkshochschulen, an der katholischen Akademie und im religionspädagogischen Seminar.[529] Darüber hinaus hatte er seit dem 1. Januar 1963 als Syndikus des deutschen Provinzteils fungiert, war also seit 27 Jahren in die Abläufe und Probleme der Provinz eingearbeitet[530] und hatte damit dieses Amt länger bekleidet als Innozenz Varga das des Provinzials (20 Jahre). Dies garantierte den Brüdern eine gewisse Kontinuität in der Provinzleitung, die Ruf auch dadurch unterstrich, dass er Varga zu seinem Socius und zum Vikar für den österreichischen Provinzteil bestimmte. Dennoch brachten Rufs juristische Ausbildung, sein Verständnis der Kirchen- und Ordensstrukturen und seine Erfahrungen als Lehrer von Gemeindeseelsorgern einen neuen Wind in die Provinz. Auch wenn er kein ausdrückliches

529 *St. Dominikuswerk* (1991), S. 3.
530 Datum laut: PKat 1965, S. 14.

Programm für sein Provinzialat formulierte, so machte er sich doch die von Byrne kritisierten Punkte zu eigen. Dadurch wurden Byrnes Worte von 1990 zu einer ebenso wichtigen Anregung für die Entwicklungen in der Provinz, wie es die de Couesnongles von 1979 gewesen waren.

Rufs Ziele

Die erste Änderung nahm Ruf sehr schnell vor: Da er die Autobahnkirche als Seelsorgsaufgabe nicht aufgeben wollte, verlegte er den Sitz des Provinzialats nach Augsburg in den Konvent Heilig Kreuz – wo der Amtssitz seither auch geblieben ist. Danach ließ Ruf sich aber Zeit: In den folgenden Monaten besuchte er alle Niederlassungen, um sich mit jeder Gemeinschaft zu treffen und jeden einzelnen Mitbruder persönlich zu sprechen. Im November 1991 begann er mit einer zweiten Rundreise durch die Provinz, diesmal im Rahmen der ihm als Oberen aufgetragenen kanonischen Visitationen, die Anfang Februar 1993 abgeschlossen war.[531] Das Ergebnis seiner Beobachtungen fasste er in folgende Worte:

> „[Wir werden], sollen die kommenden Jahrzehnte gelingen, einiges überdenken müssen, was unser Leben im Orden angeht. Unser Streben und Trachten muss sich an zwei wichtigen Zielen orientieren. Das erste ist die Fähigkeit, Selbstverantwortung für das Leben als Dominikaner zu übernehmen. Wir haben zwar die Regel und die Konstitutionen, die den großen Rahmen abstecken. Wie aber jeder einzelne von uns konkret sein Leben gestaltet, ist weitgehend ihm selbst überlassen. Welche Schwerpunkte er setzt im Apostolat, im Studium oder im Konvent, wie er mit seinen Kräften und Fähigkeiten umgeht, ob er sie brach liegen lässt oder mit ihnen wuchert, damit sie für Gottes Herrschaft Frucht bringen, wird jeder Mitbruder selbst planen und verantworten müssen. Über diese Freiheit sind wir froh. Und damit wir bei dieser Freizügigkeit der Versuchung zum Individualismus oder gar zum Egoismus nicht erliegen, richten wir uns am zweiten, gleich wichtigen Ziel aus.
> Es ist der große Eifer und der unermüdliche Einsatz für das Gemeinsame, für die Kirche, den Orden, die Provinz, den Konvent, das Haus. Alle persönlichen Planungen prüfen wir mit der Frage: ‚Nützt das, was ich will, der Gemeinschaft?' Wir fördern diese unsere Verpflichtung der ‚res publica' gegenüber dadurch, dass wir bei allen wichtigen Entscheidungen mitwirken. Dazu haben wir die verschiedenen Kommissionen und Räte, schließlich die

531 Siehe dazu PA, Provinzialsregestenbuch 2 (1966–2010), Einträge beginnend mit 8.8.1990, Nr. 1 bis 2.2.1993, Nr. 6.

> Konsilien und Kapitel. Sie ordnen unser gemeinsames Bemühen und sollen verhindern, dass ein Mitbruder als ‚frater privatus', ein der gemeinsamen Sache Beraubter, unter uns lebt.
> Wenn ich eine Bitte als derzeitiger Moderator der Gespräche unter den Mitbrüdern in unserer Provinz äußern darf, dann ist es die, dass wir alle gerade dieses zweite Ziel sehr ernsthaft verfolgen. Von ihm hängt der unverwechselbare Charakter unserer Provinz ab."[532]

Der Ermöglichung dieser beiden Ziele widmete sich Ruf in den kommenden Jahren. Leider ist es an dieser Stelle noch nicht möglich, die Verwirklichung des ersten Zieles nachzuzeichnen: Die Beschreibung der letzten zwei Jahrzehnte der Provinzgeschichte stößt hier an die wichtigen Grenzen des Daten- und Aktenschutzes. Auch was das zweite Ziel angeht, sind noch zu viele Projekte im Fluss, als dass darüber abschließende Beobachtungen angestellt werden könnten. Vom Standpunkt des Historikers aus wäre es daher wahrscheinlich sinnvoller, nur die ersten fünfzig Jahre der Provinzgeschichte zu beschreiben und mit dem Jahr 1990 zu schließen. Gleichzeitig kam in diesen letzten Jahrzehnten einiges von dem zum Abschluss, was das Provinzgeschehen bisher stark geprägt hatte. Darüber hinaus wurden neue Gelegenheiten wahrgenommen, an denen ebenfalls nicht einfach vorübergegangen werden darf. Unter den gegebenen Umständen der historischen Quellen – und mit einem Mut zur Lücke – lässt sich zwar keine echte Geschichte der Provinz zwischen 1990 und 2013 schildern, wohl aber lassen sich einzelne Themen aus dieser Geschichte abhandeln.

Suchbewegungen und Meilensteine auf dem Weg in die Zukunft: Die Provinzkapitel 1994 bis 2011

Leitlinien für die Ausbildung: das Provinzkapitel von 1994

Auch wenn der Name des Ordensmeisters Damian Byrne und seine schneidende Kritik nicht in den Akten des Provinzkapitels auftauchten, das sich vom 25. bis 30. Juli 1994 in Augsburg traf, so standen dessen Inhalte ganz im Zeichen seiner Anregungen und entsprachen den Absichten Rufs, der bei dieser Gelegenheit als Provinzials wiedergewählt wurde. Die Akten waren mit 34 Seiten umfangreicher als die der früheren Provinzkapitel. Zum

532 PA, Provinzrundbrief 1–1993, S. 1–2.

ersten Mal fassten die Kapitularen ihre Bestimmungen in einen langen systematischen Text, aus dem sie ihre Anordnungen ableiteten.[533]

Gleich die Überschrift dieses auf die Ämterbesetzungen folgenden Textes machte klar, worum es ging: „Die Sorge um die Berufungen und um die Bewahrung unserer Berufungen“; sie wurde als „der zentrale Gegenstand der inhaltlichen Arbeit dieses Provinzkapitels“ bezeichnet (Nr. 33). In einem ersten Kapitel wurden verschiedene Beobachtungen über den Erstkontakt von Interessenten mit dem Orden zusammengetragen: die Wichtigkeit der Begegnung eines Interessenten mit einem einzelnen Dominikaner und einer dominikanischen Gemeinschaft als konkrete Darstellung der realen Lebensform des Ordens, die Bedeutung der Profess – nicht als Vertrag zwischen Orden und Bruder, sondern als Bindung des Einzelnen an Gott, die aus der Profess folgende Einbindung des Bruders in die Kirche und besonders in ihren Gebets- und Gottesdienst (Nrn. 34–39) – insgesamt die Beschreibung des Ordenslebens als Antwort auf eine Berufung durch Gott, also als persönliche und individuelle Grundentscheidung. Diese „personale Grundlegung … inkarniert sich im brüderlichen Leben“ (Nr. 40) und muss durch die Gemeinschaft begleitet und überprüft werden (Nr. 41). Um diese generelle Anforderung zu konkretisieren, müsse daher die jeweilige Gemeinschaft bereits dem Ordensinteressenten (im sogenannten Postulat oder Pränoviziat) einen bestimmten Mitbruder als Ansprechpartner und Begleiter zur Verfügung stellen (Nr. 41–42). Im Noviziat übernimmt diese Aufgabe der Novizenmeister (Nr. 43). Die folgenden Schritte im Ausbildungsprozess eines Dominikaners (Studium, Erstassignation und Fortbildung) werfen neue Fragen nach der Berufung und Aufgaben für die Begleitung des Bruders auf, da „die dominikanische Berufung“ in diesem Lebensabschnitt „besonders der Gefahr der Erosion ausgesetzt“ sei: Überforderung und Mutlosigkeit, einseitige Betonung des geistlichen Lebens oder der Studien, aber auch Unterforderung und Verdruss (Nr. 44). Um dieser Erosion entgegenzuwirken und eine individuellere Betreuung des Einzelnen zu gewährleisten, schuf das Provinzkapitel neben den von den Ordenssatzungen vorgesehenen Oberenämtern des Studentenmagisters und des Studienregens eine weitere Funktion, die des Tutors:

533 APKap 1994, S. 14–29, Nrn. 33–96. Zur Entlastung des Anmerkungsapparates werden in diesem Kapitel des Beitrags für die Zitate dieser und der folgenden Provinzkapitelsakten die Seitenzahlen oder Abschnittsnummern in Klammern direkt im Text zitiert.

> „Das geistliche, intellektuelle und theologische Wachstum in der Studienzeit soll von dem Magister, dem Regens und einem Tutor begleitet werden. Der Tutor, Mitbruder eines Konventes unserer Provinz, wird dem *frater studens* als Dialogpartner zur Verfügung stehen. Jeder Konvent unserer Provinz kann *fratres studentes* in dieser Ausbildungsphase aufnehmen. Magister und Regens halten zusammen mit dem Tutor den institutionellen Charakter der Ausbildung aufrecht, wobei der *frater studens* … seinen Tutor selbst wählen kann“ (Nr. 45).

Damit war ein neues Ausbildungsmodell mit dialogalem Charakter gefunden: Zugunsten einer besseren individuellen Betreuung wurde das übliche Konzept eines einzigen Studentatskonventes, nach dem die Provinz so lange gesucht hatte, aufgegeben und die bisherigen Ausbildungsstrukturen markant erweitert.

Im Folgenden regelte der Text administrative und disziplinarische Fragen, die dieses neue Tutorenmodell zur Folge hatte, um es in die Regelungen der Ordenssatzungen einzupassen, und widmete sich dann einer grundsätzlichen Beobachtung, der Bedeutung der Beheimatung des Ordenslebens: „Unsere Berufungen werden sicher gewahrt, wenn wir den Mitbrüdern das vermitteln, was man ‚Heimat‘ nennt. Heimat ist für uns der Orden, die Provinz, der Konvent. … Sollen unsere Ordensverbände Heimat für die Mitbrüder bieten, sind einige Forderungen zu erfüllen“ – genannt werden „ein gewisser Grad an Wohnlichkeit“ der Klöster und die Sicherung der Kranken- und Altenfürsorge, aber auch die Traditionen des Ordens, „sei es in den Gepflogenheiten der Gemeinschaft, sei es in den liturgischen Formen“: Die „Lebensordnung im heimatlichen Kloster“ müsse „eine Atmosphäre gemeinschaftlicher Identität bilden, in der trotz verschiedener Meinungen der Wille vorherrscht, beieinander zu bleiben und den Konvent als ein Haus der Predigt … anzusehen“ (Nrn. 52–54).

Zur praktischen Durchführung des neuen Modells ordnete das Kapitel in dreizehn Punkten konkrete Maßnahmen an, die an die verschiedenen Amtsträger in der Ausbildung gingen (Nrn. 55–68) und deren wichtigste darin bestand, dass der Ausbildungsrat (das Versammlungsgremium dieser Ausbildungsamtsträger) „eine Liste der Mitbrüder erstellt, die als Tutoren zur Begleitung der *fratres studentes* zur Verfügung stehen. Aus dieser Liste sollen die künftigen Studenten gegen Ende ihrer Noviziatszeit ihren Tutor wählen und ihren Vorschlag an den Regens senden“ (Nr. 60).

Das zweite Kapitel mit dem Titel „Berufung leben in unserer Provinz“ befasste sich zuerst mit dem Versuch einer Selbstdefinition: „Die Provinz des hl. Albertus Magnus Germaniae superioris et Austriae versteht sich als

eine Gemeinschaft von Brüdern, die ein klassisch-traditionelles Ordensleben führen", mit den in der Fundamentalkonstitution der Ordenssatzungen aufgeführten Grundelementen wie etwa Predigt des Gotteswortes in armen und klösterlichen Gemeinschaften, religiöse Lebensform zum eigenen Heil und zum Heil der Menschheit, aber auch Hinhören auf die Menschen und Offenheit gegenüber den Erfordernissen der Zeit (Nr. 69): „Das Provinzkapitel ist sich darin einig, dass diese Elemente nicht ständig zur Disposition gestellt und auch nicht grundlegend verändert werden können, soll nicht die Grundlage ins Wanken kommen, auf der unser Leben und Wirken sowie die Sinnhaftigkeit unserer Existenz aufbaut" (Nr. 71).

In diesem Zusammenhang wurde auch die pastorale Arbeit der Niederlassungen und Brüder betrachtet. Hier gingen die Kapitelsväter auf die Analysen der 1990 angeregten Planungskommission ein und bemerkten ausdrücklich:

> „Das Kapitel kommt zu dem Ergebnis, dass es schädlich wäre, bewährte und auch heute dringend erforderliche Arbeitsgebiete zu verlassen und krampfhaft nach neuen Wegen zu suchen. Unter den gegebenen Umständen sieht das Provinzkapitel keine Berechtigung, bestehende Häuser zu schließen, da diese immer noch eine unverzichtbare Funktion im Leben der Ortskirche ausüben" (Nr. 77 und 78).

Stattdessen – und in Folgerichtigkeit zu dem im ersten Abschnitt über die Berufung Gesagten – wandte sich das Provinzkapitel Beobachtungen über die spirituellen Herausforderungen zu, denen es die Brüder ausgesetzt sah:

> „Das 2. Vatikanische Konzil hat dem Ordensstand neue Impulse gegeben. … An die Stelle eines abstrakten Ideals der Vollkommenheit trat ein neues Verständnis von konkreter Nachfolge. Diese tiefere Theologie will innerlich angeeignet und ihr Reichtum verspürt werden, damit die humanen und religiösen Wurzelkräfte einer Gemeinschaft nicht verdorren. Der Zeitgeist, der sagt: ‚Ich bin, was ich leiste!', bedroht das Ordensleben und das religiöse Leben der Kirche überhaupt. Der Säkularismus dringt durch alle Ritzen in unsere Klöster ein. Unser geistliches Leben, das aus Gottes Berufung erwächst, läuft Gefahr, zu verbürgerlichen. Wenn das Gebet nichts mehr gilt, Aktivität alles wird, das Anspruchsdenken in den Vordergrund rückt, dann verliert das Leben die Mitte in Gott und in Jesus Christus" (Nrn. 79 und 80).

Entsprechend forderte das Provinzkapitel die Brüder zu einer Pflege ihres geistlichen Lebens und zu vertieftem persönlichem wie liturgischem Gebet auf und ermahnte sie, aktiv am Leben ihrer Gemeinschaften mitzuwirken und das Privatinteresse dem allgemeinen Wohl unterzuordnen (Nr. 84).

Besonders betont wurden die regelmäßige Abhaltung der Hauskapitel und die Teilnahme daran (Nr. 85). Außerdem erging die Anordnung, dass im Falle, dass in einem Haus aus einem rechtmäßigen Grund das ganze Stundengebet nicht regelmäßig gefeiert werden könne, „dieser Grund vom Provinzial mit seinem Konsil anerkannt werden“ müsse (Nr. 86).

Das dritte Kapitel dieses Textes handelte über „die gemeinsame apostolische Berufung der Dominikanischen Familie“. Für die Brüder, Nonnen, Schwestern, Mitglieder von Säkularinstituten, Bruderschaften von Priestern und Laien sowie Gruppen mit weniger verbindlichen Strukturen, die sich dem Charisma und der Gestalt des hl. Dominikus verbunden fühlten, sei ein wesentlicher verbindender Grundzug „die gemeinsame dominikanische Berufung“, durch die die einzelnen Zweige sich ergänzten und in der sie zusammenarbeiteten (Nr. 88). Da diese gemeinsame Berufung ein Geschenk Gottes sei und nicht Frucht einer etwaigen eigenen Initiative, könnten sich die verschiedenen Gemeinschaften in ihrer Autonomie und besonderen Ausprägung gegenseitig annehmen, „ohne dass eine Gruppe von der anderen beherrscht würde“ (ebd.). Im Folgenden bedachte das Provinzkapitel jeden dieser Zweige mit einem eigenen Aktenabschnitt, wodurch zum ersten Mal auf dieser höchsten Ebene der Provinz der Versuch unternommen wurde, die Gesamtheit der Dominikanischen Familie Süddeutschlands und Österreichs nicht nur zu beschreiben, sondern als eine Gemeinschaft aufzufassen (Nrn. 89–94). Für die Pflege dieser Gemeinschaft setzte das Provinzkapitel einen Mitbruder in das neu geschaffene Offizium des Promotors für die Öffentlichkeitsarbeit ein und beauftragte ihn, aufbauend auf den bereits erscheinenden Periodika der Provinz, mit der Erarbeitung eines Konzeptes für eine Publikation zur Förderung des Zusammenhaltes der Zweige (Nr. 95). Die beiden Promotoren für die dominikanischen Laiengemeinschaften bekamen zur Aufgabe, innerhalb von zehn Monaten einen schriftlichen Überblick über den Ist-Zustand der Laiengemeinschaften in der Provinz vorzulegen und auf die Einhaltung von Regeln und des in der Provinz gültigen Direktoriums für diese Gemeinschaften sorgfältig zu achten (Nrn. 96–97).

Mit recht detaillierten wirtschaftlichen Bestimmungen und Anpassungen des Provinzstatuts an das neue Tutorenmodell schlossen die Akten dieses Provinzkapitels, das wirklich Eigeninitiative entwickelt hatte und von der Ordenskurie in Rom mit lobenden Worten bedacht wurde. Die Betonung der Verantwortung des Einzelnen für seine persönliche Berufung wie für seine Gemeinschaft, die darin zum Ausdruck kam, ist wohl Rufs

Abb. 68: P. Hans Ulrich Steymans (aufgenommen 2013; PA, Fotosammlung).

Beobachtungen zu verdanken, die er schon 1993 formuliert hatte (siehe oben). Letztlich reagierten diese Ausführungen von 1994 auf die Anregung, die Ordensmeister Byrne der Provinz 1990 gegeben hatte: „Sie müssen sich genau im Klaren sein, warum Sie Berufungen haben und wie sie ausbilden wollen."[534]

Diese zweite Amtszeit Gregor Rufs als Provinzial war überschattet von einer schweren und überraschenden Erkrankung. Rufs Gesundheitszustand machte eine Fortführung seines Provinzialats unmöglich. Mit seinem Einverständnis berief der Socius des Provinzials, Innozenz Varga, für den 22. Oktober 1997 ein Provinzkonsil ein, das den Rücktritt Rufs der Ordenskurie meldete. Mit Schreiben vom 12. November 1997 erklärte Ordensmeister Timothy Radcliffe Rufs Amtszeit für beendet und ernannte Varga zum Vikar des Ordensmeisters für die Provinz – verbunden mit dem Auftrag, ein außerordentliches Provinzkapitel zur Wahl eines neuen Provinzials einzuberufen. Dieses Kapitel trat am 26. Januar 1998 zusammen und wählte P. Hans Ulrich Steymans in dieses Amt.[535] P. Gregor Ruf verstarb wenige Monate später, am 3. Mai 1998.[536] Steymans war mit 37 Jahren der bisher jüngste Provinzial der süddeutsch-österreichischen Dominikaner. Er hatte 1982 Profess abgelegt, in alttestamentlicher Bibelwissenschaft an der Universität Wien promoviert und war 1997 zum Prior des Augsburger Konvents gewählt worden.

534 APKap 1990, S. 6.
535 PA, Provinzrundbriefe 1–1997, S. 1 und 1–1998, S. 1.
536 PA, Provinzrundbrief 2–1998, S. 11–13.

Leitlinien für die Struktur und die Pastoral der Provinz: das Provinzkapitel von 1998

Nachdem die Provinzialswahl schon vorweggenommen worden war, hatten sich die Brüder, die vom 30. August bis zum 5. September 1998 in Augsburg zum Provinzkapitel zusammenkamen, nur mehr um die inhaltlichen Aspekte zu kümmern. Noch nie hatte ein Provinzkapitel der süddeutsch-österreichischen Provinz so lange getagt und nie zuvor hatte diese Versammlung so umfangreiche Akten produziert: Auf 14 Seiten wurde zunächst der Visitationsbrief des Ordensmeisters Timothy Radcliffe vom 8. Juli 1998 wiedergegeben (S. IV–XVII), dann kamen die zwei Seiten des Bestätigungsschreibens des Ordensmeisters (S. XX–XXI), danach folgten auf 61 Seiten die in 184 Abschnitte aufgeteilten Analysen, Ermahnungen und Bestimmungen des Provinzkapitels.

Dass ein Visitationsschreiben des Ordensmeisters die Akten einleitete, war Absicht: Radcliffe hatte mit seinem Socius Diethard Zils im Juni die Provinz kanonisch visitiert und mit allen Mitbrüdern gesprochen. Wie sein Visitationsbrief vom 8. Juli deutlich machte, hatte er dabei besonders zwei Punkte im Blick gehabt, nämlich die seit seinem Vorgänger Byrne angemahnte mangelhafte pastorale Planung und das neu eingeführte Tutorialsystem. Die Kapitularen machten sich Radcliffes diesbezügliche Beobachtungen und Anmerkungen zu eigen und stellten sie daher in der Art eines Vorworts ihren Akten voran.[537]

Radcliffes Darlegungen waren sehr umfangreich und berührten viele Themenkreise. Besonders wirkten im Provinzkapitel seine Analysen über die Personalsituation in der Provinz nach:

> „Wenn es weniger Brüder gibt, die mehr arbeiten – welche Schritte sollten unternommen werden? Das ist eine Frage, die ihr auf dem nächsten Provinzkapitel behandeln müsst. Es könnte auch wichtig sein, einmal zu fragen, welche Gemeinschaften es sind, die die Provinz zu Zentren des Lebens und der Sendung ausbauen sollte. Es ist unmöglich, alle Gemeinschaften der Provinz so aufzubauen, aber einige, in denen es ein starkes dominikanisches Leben und eine Sendung gibt, die sich auf unser Charisma bezieht, könnten zu Stützpfeilern werden. Das sind auch die Gemeinschaften, in die ihr die Jungen schicken könnt, im Vertrauen, dass sie dort die Unterstützung finden, die sie für das Wachstum in ihrer Berufung brauchen.“

---

537 APKap 1998, S. iv–xxi.

Als Beispiele dafür führte Radcliffe die Konvente in Wien und München / St. Kajetan an und stellte dann die Frage: „Wo könnte ein drittes Lebenszentrum liegen? Augsburg oder Graz? Muss es an einem Ort liegen, an dem wir schon präsent sind?" (S. IX–X).

Im Gegenzug zum Ausbau von bestimmten Niederlassungen diskutierte der Ordensmeister auch die Frage nach dem Aufgeben anderer Häuser:

> „Die Provinz wird in der nächsten Zukunft genauso vor der schwierigen Entscheidung stehen, einige Gemeinschaften zu schließen. Es wäre gut, das als Teil einer gemeinsamen Vision über die Entwicklung der Sendung der Provinz zu tun, als eher passive Antwort auf die schrumpfenden Zahlen. … Aber dass wir einen Ort verlassen und woanders hinziehen, ist oft auch ein Zeichen dafür, dass wir unsere Arbeit gut gemacht haben. Manchmal müssen wir Orte verlassen, die schon lange in Verbindung mit der Geschichte des Ordens stehen. Das ist nicht nur traurig, sondern fühlt sich an wie Verrat. Trotzdem müssen wir den Mut haben, es zu tun. Die Tradition hat solange keine Zukunft, solange wir nicht solche harten Entscheidungen zu fällen wagen. Unserer Tradition zentral ist die Wanderschaft, und wir entsprechen treu unserer Tradition, wenn wir unsere Koffer packen und gehen" (S. X).

Die Ausbildung der jungen Mitbrüder bezeichnete Radcliffe als „eine der größten Sorgen in der Provinz" und forderte daher dazu auf, sie zum Thema auf dem Provinzkapitel zu machen. Er stellte eine Reihe von Beobachtungen über die guten und die schlechten Seiten des neuen Tutorialsystems dar und meinte dann:

> „Jede Provinz hat heute Schwierigkeiten, Ausbilder zu finden, die denen, die in den Orden eintreten, die notwendige sensible Begleitung in diesem tiefen persönlichen Umwandlungsprozess anbieten können. Viele Mitbrüder drückten die, wie ich finde, gerechtfertigte Sorge aus, ob das Tutorialsystem diese Begleitung wirklich leisten kann. … Für eine Provinz ist es schon schwer, eine solche Gemeinschaft zu bilden, geschweige denn drei oder vier. … Wenn es auch wahr ist, dass das gegenwärtige System ‚wirklichkeitsnah' ist und die Studenten sehen, wie das Leben in einer normalen Gemeinschaft ist – ist Realismus immer eine gute Sache? … Die jungen Mitbrüder sollen sich nicht damit abfinden, dass die Provinz dieselbe bleibt. Wenn sie zusammen sind, dann können die jungen Mitbrüder den Traum einer verwandelten Provinz aufrechterhalten. Das trägt natürlich das Risiko eines Generationenkonflikts in sich. Die Alternative dazu besteht wahrscheinlich in Stagnation und Pessimismus" (S. XIII).

Abschließend wies der Ordensmeister noch auf den Grundgedanken dominikanischen Gemeinschaftslebens hin: „Ein Konvent ist per definitionem ein Ort des ‚Zusammenkommens', ein ‚conventus'." Daher sei die Begegnung der Brüder im Konvent, das Gespräch miteinander und das gegenseitige Vertrauen umso wichtiger, um aus den Konventen „Orte der Unterstützung" zu machen, also Orte, aus denen das geistliche Leben des einzelnen Bruders und seine Seelsorgstätigkeit Kraft, Ermutigung und Anregung schöpfen könnten: „Daher möchte ich empfehlen, dass jede Gemeinschaft sich trifft, um zu überlegen, wie sie ihr Leben in Richtung auf einen Ort der Begegnung erneuern möchte: Begegnung mit Gott durch Gebet und Stille, Begegnung miteinander in Kapiteln und einem untereinander geteilten Glauben, Begegnung mit der heutigen Welt mit ihren Fragen und ihren Bedürfnissen." Hier hob Radcliffe die Bedeutung der Kontaktaufnahme mit den Nachbarprovinzen, dem weltweiten Orden, aber auch mit den Niederlassungen und Gruppen der Zweige der dominikanischen Familie innerhalb der Provinz hervor (S. XIV–XVI).

Die Kapitularen reagierten auf diese Anregungen mit einer Grundsatzantwort, die die Seiten 10–51 und die Abschnitte Nr. 29–184 der Akten einnahm. Sie trug weder Titel noch Überschrift und befasste sich inhaltlich mit der Gestalt der „dominikanischen Sendung" in der Provinz. Den Begriff der „dominikanischen Sendung" hatte das Provinzkapitel vom Generalkapitel übernommen, das wenige Wochen zuvor, Ende Juli bis Anfang August 1998, in Bologna getagt hatte. Unter dem traditionell lateinischsprachigen Titel „De missione ordinis" hatte das Generalkapitel in Englisch eine Betrachtung über den Verkündigungsauftrag angestellt, der von Gott generell an die Mitglieder der Kirche gerichtet sei und den die Dominikaner speziell durch ihre Ordensprofess übernommen hätten,[538] und sich dann der Frage nach der Verwirklichung dieses Auftrags innerhalb der dominikanischen Familie, in verschiedenen Gebieten der Erde und in mehreren intellektuellen Ordenseinrichtungen zugewandt. Dieser Hintergrund der lateinisch-englischen Begriffsgeschichte erklärt den im Deutschen ein wenig eigenwillig klingenden Ausdruck „dominikanische Sendung" des Provinzkapitels, der nichts anderes als eine zu wortgetreue Übersetzung von „missio" bzw. „mission" darstellte. Inhaltlich hätten den Ausführun-

538 „The mission of the Order receives its freedom from the vow of obedience which makes us available and responsive to confront together new challenges." (ACG 1998, S. 21, Nr. 33). Der ganze Text „de missione ordinis": ebd., S. 21–41, Nr. 33–83.

gen des Provinzkapitels eher „Profil", „Proprium" oder „Aufgabe" entsprochen, denn es ging um die bereits erreichten oder noch anzustrebenden Wirkungen des spezifisch dominikanischen Ordenslebens in der Provinz. Dieses zu beschreiben wurde in fünf Kapiteln versucht.

Das erste Kapitel trug den Titel „Die dominikanische Sendung (‚mission') in unserer Provinz". Mit Verweis auf die Aussagen der Fundamentalkonstitution über das spezifische Profil der dominikanischen Sendung, auf das Bemühen des Provinzkapitels von 1994, ein spirituelles Profil der Provinz zu erstellen, und mit Berufung auf den Visitationsbrief Radcliffes (Nrn. 29–31) leiteten sie in einer Präambel die Folgen ab, die sich aus der Profess für den einzelnen Bruder (Nrn. 32–34) und für das Leben in Gemeinschaft, im Konvent ergaben (Nrn. 35–43), um sich dann „Impulsen zur Erneuerung der dominikanischen Sendung" in der Provinz zuzuwenden. Diese wurde von der Erkenntnis eingeleitet: „Die gemeinsame dominikanische Sendung bedarf nicht nur auf Konvents-, sondern auch auf Provinzebene eines klaren Profils. Dieses Profil entwickelt sich aus Prioritäten, auf die wir unsere Kräfte konzentrieren" (Nr. 48). Erste Priorität sei die Verkündigung, die in den Häusern und der Provinz auf unterschiedlichste und vielfältige Weise bereits stattfinde: „Wir sehen keinen Anlass, bewährte und auch heute dringend erforderliche Arbeitsgebiete zu verlassen … Es bedarf jedoch auch auf Provinzebene der Prüfung, ob die derzeitigen Gewichtungen unserer Verkündigungstätigkeit noch den Erfordernissen der Zeit und den spirituellen Bedürfnissen der Menschen entsprechen" (Nr. 49). Leitlinien dieser Überprüfung sei die in der Tradition seit Dominikus dem Orden entsprechende Mobilität („Unterwegs sein"; Nr. 51) sowie das Problem der mangelnden Präsenz des Ordens im Gesamtgebiet der Provinz:

> „Wenn wir unsere Präsenz nur an der geographischen Verteilung der Konvente messen, gleicht sie eher Inseln im Meer als einer Wahrnehmung des ganzen Provinzgebiets. Selbstverständlich müssen wir unsere begrenzten Kräfte überlegt einsetzen. Wenn die Bereitschaft der Mitbrüder zum ‚Unterwegs sein' ermutigt wird und wächst, wäre es jedoch durchaus möglich, an einigen Schwerpunkten im Provinzgebiet präsent zu werden, an denen kein Konvent besteht. Ausgangspunkt könnten günstig gelegene Schwesternkonvente oder diözesane Einrichtungen sein. Koordinierte Beiträge von Mitbrüdern verschiedener Konvente könnten dort eine dominikanische Präsenz herstellen, ohne dass die betreffenden Mitbrüder ihren Konventen ‚verloren gehen'. Als geeignete Standorte erscheinen z. B. Regensburg, Bamberg oder Salzburg" (Nr. 52).

Daraus ergebe sich auch für die bestehenden Niederlassungen der Provinz die von Radcliffe angeregte „Bildung von Schwerpunkten“:

> „Eine solche Konzentration ist notwendig, weil unsere personelle Situation nicht zulässt, alle Konvente und Häuser der Provinz gleichermaßen in die Entwicklung der ganzen Provinz einzubeziehen. ... Um Missverständnissen entgegenzuwirken betonen wir nachdrücklich, dass ‚Zentrenbildung‘ keineswegs eine Konzentration aller Kräfte, ein Präjudiz für künftige Assignationen oder ähnliches nach sich zieht. Dies vorausgesetzt, soll im österreichischen Provinzteil Wien ein solcher Schwerpunkt sein. Im süddeutschen Provinzteil wäre München der sich anbietende Schwerpunkt, doch sind die räumlichen Möglichkeiten in St. Kajetan begrenzt und unsere Präsenz zudem auf mehrere Standorte in der Stadt München verteilt. ... Deshalb sollen – zumindest auf absehbare Zeit – die Konvente von München und Augsburg ein gemeinsames Zentrum im süddeutschen Provinzteil bilden“ (Nr. 54).

Dies würde auch die Zusammenarbeit beider Konvente verstärken. Dennoch machte Konzentration auf Zentren den Abzug von Kräften an anderer Stelle notwendig. Das Provinzkapitel fasste daher den Beschluss, das Kloster in Retz zu schließen:

> „Die Provinz sieht sich vor die schwierige Entscheidung gestellt, aus personellen, finanziellen und pastoralen Notwendigkeiten nicht alle derzeitigen Strandorte aufrechterhalten zu können. ... Das Provinzkapitel von 1994 hat auf der Basis mehrjähriger umfangreicher Vorarbeiten einer speziellen Kommission Beschlüsse bezüglich des Hauses in Retz gefasst. Das Konzept ..., mit einer kleinen Gemeinschaft die dominikanische Präsenz in Retz wiederzubeleben, lässt sich nicht verwirklichen. Nunmehr sehen wir keine andere Möglichkeit, als uns aus Retz zurückzuziehen und die Zukunft des traditionsreichen Hauses dort in Zusammenarbeit mit der slowakischen Vizeprovinz und der Erzdiözese Wien oder aber in Zusammenarbeit mit dem Land Niederösterreich, der Stadt Retz und der Erzdiözese Wien neu zu regeln“ (Nr. 55).

Konkret wurde angeordnet, „dass unsere Niederlassung in Retz, die *domus filialis* des Konventes Wien, bis spätestens zum 30.6.2000 aufgehoben wird“ (Nr. 78.1) und dass für eine künftige Nutzung der Klostergebäude in Retz „die Übergabe an die slowakische Vizeprovinz Priorität erhält“ (Nr. 78.2). Der Ordensmeister wurde gebeten, diesen Schließungsbeschluss durchzuführen (Nr. 184).

In den folgenden Abschnitten handelten die Kapitelsväter über den Ausbau der bestehenden bzw. über die mögliche Aufnahme neuer Kontakte mit dem weltweiten Orden, konkret mit der Provinz Teutonia, der Vize-

provinz der Slowakei (Nrn. 57–60) und mit der Provinz von Indien (Nr. 60). Eine Anfrage des polnischen Provinzials, der auf dem Gebiet der Provinz eine weitere Niederlassung errichten wollte, lehnte das Provinzkapitel ab: „Es gibt in unserer Provinz bereits ein solches Haus der polnischen Dominikanerprovinz, St. Albert in Freimann. Die Gründung eines weiteren derartigen Hauses halten wir nicht für opportun. Wir befürworten allerdings die Gründung eines interprovinziellen Konvents" (Nr. 61) – zu dem es allerdings nicht kam. Angeregt durch eine Initiative des Generalkapitels, das wenige Wochen zuvor in Bologna getagt hatte, verwies das Provinzkapitel auch auf die Möglichkeit der Übernahme befristeter Lehraufträge an dominikanischen Hochschulen im Ausland (als Beispiele wurden das Dominican Institute in Ibadan / Nigeria und das Dominican College in Port Moresby / Papua-Neuguinea genannt), als Gelegenheiten der Kontaktaufnahme mit Einrichtungen des internationalen Ordens (Nr. 62).

Das zweite Kapitel mit der Überschrift „Unsere gemeinsame dominikanische Sendung als Priesterbrüder und Kooperatoren" (Nrn. 80–91) beschäftigte sich vor allem mit einem Thema, das bisher nur sehr selten von Provinzkapiteln behandelt worden war und über das v. a. das Provinzkapitel von 1994 geschwiegen hatte, nämlich mit dem Verhältnis zwischen den Priester- und den Laienbrüdern in der Provinz. Nach einer allgemeinen Darstellung der Rolle der Laienbrüder im dominikanischen Ordensleben (Nrn. 80–87) – ohne jedoch auf die traditionellen Tätigkeitsfelder der Laienbrüder, also Pforte, Küche, Sakristei etc. positiv einzugehen – kamen die Kapitularen zu der Schlussfolgerung:

> „Immer unter der Voraussetzung, dass alle Brüder gleich und ihre Beiträge zu unserer dominikanischen Sendung gleich wertvoll sind, sollte der Grundsatz gelten: Je apostolischer, desto besser. Das heißt, dass eine direkte Teilnahme der Kooperatoren am Verkündigungsauftrag bzw. die Ausbildung dazu nicht behindert werden darf, nur weil eine Begrenzung auf eine indirekte Teilnahme vordergründige Probleme in unseren Konventen zu lösen scheint. Umgekehrt sollen Brüder, die ihre Ordensberufung durch indirekte Teilnahme an unserer gemeinsamen dominikanischen Sendung leben (wollen) nicht entmutigt werden; dies wäre zu befürchten, wenn die Priesterbrüder die Kooperatoren mit einer Erwartung auf effiziente Entlastung bedrängen oder aber die Chance, neue Tätigkeitsfelder zu erschließen, als ‚exotisch' empfinden würden" (Nr. 88).

Als praktische Konsequenz forderte das Provinzkapitel die Einfügung der Laienbrüder in den Ausbildungsplan der Provinz (Nrn. 89–90).

Das dritte Kapitel handelte über „Die gemeinsame Sendung der dominikanischen Familie“ (Nrn. 92–124). Zunächst wurde die gemeinsame Berufung der verschiedenen Zweige des Ordens allgemein als Chance und Aufgabe beschrieben (Nrn. 92–98). Dann ging es um die Beziehungen der Brüder zu den Nonnen und Schwestern des Ordens (Nrn. 99–104) und um die zu den Laiengemeinschaften und Bruderschaften (Nrn. 105–113). Die daraus resultierenden praktischen Anordnungen (Nrn. 114–124) bezogen sich im Wesentlichen auf eine Intensivierung des Kontaktes der Brüder zu den anderen Zweigen des Ordens und auf eine Verbesserung der Kommunikation und des Informationsflusses untereinander.

In den beiden folgenden Kapiteln kamen die Akten dem Auftrag Radcliffes nach, die Frage nach der Berufungsfindung und nach der Ausbildung der jungen Mitbrüder zu klären. Unter der Überschrift „Zugänge zur dominikanischen Sendung öffnen – Wege einer aktiven Berufungspastoral unserer Provinz“ (Nrn. 125–148) nahmen die Kapitelsväter den Faden des Provinzkapitels von 1994 noch einmal auf, mit Feststellungen über den Wert und neue Möglichkeiten der Berufungswerbung (Nrn. 125–130), mit Verweisen auf entsprechende Projekte der indischen und der süditalienischen Provinzen (Nrn. 131–137) und mit der Erarbeitung von „Grundelementen einer aktiven Berufungspastoral.“ Konkret wurde auf die Wichtigkeit des stärkeren Bekanntwerdens des Ordens im Provinzgebiet durch Multiplikatoren, gedrucktes Informationsmaterial und durch die Einbindung der Möglichkeiten des Internets hingewiesen (Nrn. 138–140). Auch wurde die Erstellung eines „Direktoriums für die Berufungspastoral“ (Nr. 142) – also eine Art Fahrplan dafür – und eine erhöhte Vernetzung der Zweige der dominikanischen Familie in der Berufungsfindung angeregt, unter Einbindung des Internets (Nr. 144 und 147). Dann folgte unter „Die Ausbildung zu unserer gemeinsamen dominikanischen Sendung“ (Nrn. 149–164) die Evaluierung des 1994 erneuerten Ausbildungssystems der Provinz, unter der Anpassung der *ratio formationis particularis*, des Provinzausbildungsplans, auf der Basis der bisher gemachten Erfahrungen. Abgesehen von einer Erweiterung – der Einrichtung eines vom Provinzial bestimmten Postulatsbegleiters in jedem Ausbildungskonvent – kam es hier zu Einschränkungen. Die Zahl der möglichen Ausbildungskonvente wurde auf drei reduziert: Wien, München / St. Kajetan und Augsburg (Freiburg im Breisgau und Graz fielen weg), die Zahl der für einen Mitbruder in Ausbildung wählbaren Tutoren in diesen Ausbildungskonventen wurde auf zwei beschränkt (Nr. 154.2), und das Provinz-

kapitel gab eine Liste dieser möglichen Tutoren vor (Nr. 159). Die weiteren Abschnitte zum Ausbildungsthema bezogen sich auf die Abstimmungen zwischen den Ämterinhabern in den verschiedenen Ausbildungsstadien.

Nach diesen umfassenden Ausführungen über die „dominikanische Sendung" wandte das Provinzkapitel sich noch zwei weiteren Themen zu: Die notwendig gewordenen Anpassungen des Provinzstatuts waren schnell abgehandelt (Nrn. 165–168). Weitaus mehr Raum nahmen die zu regelnden juristischen und wirtschaftlichen Angelegenheiten in den Akten ein (Nrn. 169–182). Aufruhend auf den noch unter Provinzial Ruf ausgeführten Vorarbeiten traf das Provinzkapitel mehrere Grundsatzentscheidungen zur Struktur und zu Einrichtungen der Provinz. Hintergrund dafür waren der Wunsch einer näheren Anpassung der juristischen Gestalt der Niederlassungen an das staatliche Recht Deutschlands bzw. Österreichs und die Bemühung um Angleichung der Ordenseinrichtungen in den beiden Provinzteilen unter stärkerer Berücksichtigung der in den Ordenssatzungen niedergelegten Bedingungen – die Satzungen wurden vom Kapitel der Einfachheit halber unter der im Orden üblichen Abkürzung „LCO" für „Liber constitutionum et ordinationum fratrum ordinis Praedicatorum" genannt. Das zu behandelnde Problem bestand darin, dass in Österreich der Staat die Dominikanerklöster in einer eigenen Rechtsform behandelte, der deutsche Staat eine solche aber nicht kannte:

> „Im österreichischen Provinzteil gibt es eine ununterbrochene dominikanische Tradition. Sie ist äußerlich sichtbar an historisch bedeutsamen Kirchen, Konventsgebäuden, Bibliotheken und Kunstgegenständen, die einen großen Wert und zugleich eine große finanzielle Belastung darstellen. Sie drückt sich weiterhin in einem bestimmten Rechtsstatus des Provinzteils und der Konvente aus, die der österreichische Staat Ordensgemeinschaften mit kontinuierlicher Präsenz verliehen hat. Deshalb konnte gewissermaßen automatisch das Leitbild des LCO erreicht werden, Ordensrecht und staatliches Recht in Einklang zu bringen.
>
> Im süddeutschen Provinzteil hat die Säkularisierung den Fortbestand aller Konvente und damit die Tätigkeit im Sinn unserer dominikanischen Sendung für rund 120 Jahre beendet. Die für die Wiedergründung unserer Konvente maßgeblichen Bedingungen wirken bis heute fort; dazu gehört, dass in Deutschland der Status als öffentlich-rechtliche Körperschaft nicht erreichbar ist, sondern die Anerkennung als Rechtsperson in der zivilrechtlichen Form des eingetragenen Vereins gesucht werden muss. Bis vor kurzem gab es nur eine solche Einrichtung, den ‚Süddeutsche Provinz des Dominikanerordens e. V.' Damit war der Forderung des LCO nur teilweise Rechnung getragen, ordensrechtlichen Entitäten Anerkennung vor dem staat-

> lichen Recht zu verschaffen, da die Autonomie der Konvente in rechtlicher und wirtschaftlicher Hinsicht ohne staatliches ‚Gegenstück' blieb. In mehrjähriger Arbeit wurde in enger Zusammenarbeit zwischen der Provinzsyndikatur und den Konventen eine Lösung entwickelt und vom Provinzial mit seinem Konsil am 16. April 1997 approbiert. Nunmehr besteht auch im süddeutschen Provinzteil Übereinstimmung zwischen LCO und dem staatlichen Recht. Zugleich wurde ein struktureller Unterschied zum österreichischen Provinzteil abgebaut" (Nr. 170).

Warum die Akten die auf der Provinzkonsilssitzung vom 16. April 1997 gefundene Lösung nicht konkret benennen – nämlich die Gründung jeweils eines eingetragenen Vereins für jede der süddeutschen Niederlassungen als vor dem deutschen Recht anerkannte Rechtsform – ist unklar. Wahrscheinlich lag es daran, dass dieser Schritt schon vor dem Provinzkapitel durchgeführt worden war und daher nur von der höchsten Provinzinstanz noch einmal bestätigt zu werden brauchte.

Außerdem sollte etwas, das es im österreichischen Provinzteil schon lange gab, nun auch im süddeutschen Provinzteil eingeführt werden: Nach dem Vorbild des als vom Orden autonom und nach einer eigenen Satzung geführten „Dominikuswerk e. V." und auf denselben Zweck, die wirtschaftliche Förderung dominikanischer Tätigkeiten, ausgerichtet, wurde im süddeutschen Provinzteil „in einer flexibleren und zeitgemäßeren Form" die „Capa – Gemeinnützige Gesellschaft zur Förderung dominikanischer Ordenstätigkeit mbH" gegründet und ebenfalls auf dem Provinzkonsil vom 16. April 1997 approbiert (Nr. 171). Auch hier reagierte das Provinzkapitel nur auf die schon erfolgte Gründung und stimmte diesem Schritt zu (Nr. 182). Gleichzeitig forderte es eine Anpassung des Dominikuswerks an die veränderten Aufgaben und Probleme, für die im österreichischen Provinzteil wirtschaftliche Vorsorge getroffen werden musste, v. a. wegen der Altersvorsorge der in Österreich lebenden Brüder (Nr. 173) und wegen der mit den dortigen historischen Klosterbauten verbundenen hohen Kostenlast (Nr. 174). Diese beiden Phänomene hatten sich inzwischen zu den finanziellen Hauptsorgen in Österreich entwickelt, waren aber vom Zweck, zu dem das Dominikuswerk gegründet worden war, nämlich der Nachwuchsförderung, nicht abgedeckt. Dementsprechend ordnete das Provinzkapitel bezüglich des Dominikuswerkes „eine Überprüfung der derzeitigen Rechtsform und der Bandbreite seiner dominikanischen Zweckbestimmungen (insbesondere Ausweitung auf eine subsidiäre Altersvorsorge und Unterstützung zur Erhaltung der Konvente)" an, die sehr tief greifen sollte: „Im Fall,

dass rechtliche oder wirtschaftliche Vorteile eine andere Rechtsform nahelegen, ist der jetzige e. V. entsprechend umzuformen oder aber aufzulösen und in anderer Form neu zu gründen", allerdings unter Beibehaltung der bisher gewohnten und von den Ordenssatzungen gewünschten rechtlichen Autonomie (Nr. 180). Letzterer Wunsch und die deutlich rückläufige Mitgliederzahl des St. Dominikuswerkes führten dazu, daß der Verein mit Beschluß des Provinzkonsils vom 5. Dezember 2000 am 15. Februar 2001 aufgelöst wurde. Die Anliegen des Vereins konnten nach der staatlichen Anerkennung der Rechtspersönlichkeit der süddeutsch-österreichischen Provinz durch das österreichische Bundesministerium für Unterricht und kulturelle Angelegenheiten am 14. Dezember 1999 auch durch den Provinzial und die ihm unterstehenden Organe fortgeführt werden.[539]

Diese beiden Schritte, die juristische Neuaufstellung der Niederlassungen in Deutschland und die Schaffung eines Förderungswerkes in jedem Provinzteil, hatten nicht nur zur Folge, dass die Einrichtungen der Provinz nun besser den Ansprüchen des Staats-, Kirchen- und Ordensrechts entsprachen, sondern sie führten auch provinzintern zu einer deutlich größeren Einheit: Nach dem Ende des zweiten Weltkrieges hatten zunächst die Grenzen der alliierten Besatzungszonen zu einer Teilung der Provinz geführt. Diese Teilung war durch die unterschiedlichen Wege, die die souveränen Staaten der Bundesrepublik Deutschland und der Republik Österreich und ihre Rechtssysteme nahmen, zementiert worden. Hinter diesen Gegebenheiten hatten die beiden Provinzteile sich im Laufe der Jahrzehnte auch gerne versteckt, um eine gewisse v. a. wirtschaftliche Unabhängigkeit voneinander zu behaupten. Die von den Ordensmeistern seit de Couesnongle beklagte „Inselbildungstendenz" der Konvente hatte die Trennung noch verstärkt. Dem Provinzkapitel von 1998 war nun aber die Überwindung eines der größten Hemmnisse gelungen: Die Struktur und die Einrichtungen des Ordens waren in beiden Provinzteilen rechtlich einander angeglichen worden. Damit fielen zwar die immer noch bestehenden juristischen Unterschiede zwischen Deutschland und Österreich nicht weg, aber es wurde eine verbesserte interne Homogenität erreicht. Einen weiteren Ausdruck fand diese beginnende Rückführung der Provinzeinheit in der Tatsache, dass zum ersten Mal seit 1946 die Provinzämter, v. a. die der Promotoren, nicht mehr doppelt besetzt wurden – abgesehen von den Provinzsyndici, den Wirtschaftsverwaltern der Provinzteile. Dies hing wohl auch mit dem inzwischen stark

539 *Dominikus* (2001), S. 5–6.

geschrumpften Personalpool der Provinz zusammen; dennoch hätten sich sicher Träger für eine doppelte Besetzung der Ämter gefunden, wenn die Trennung der Provinzteile weiterhin wichtig gewesen wäre.

Das Bestätigungsschreiben des Ordenskurie vom 16. Oktober 1998 war kurz (S. XX–XXI) und voll des Lobes: „Es ist beeindruckend zu sehen, wie ihr eure Aufmerksamkeit auf einige wesentliche Punkte unseres dominikanischen Ordenslebens konzentriert habt, darunter unsere gemeinsame Sendung sowohl auf der Ebene der Konvente wie der Provinz, eine Neubewertung der Rolle der Fratres Cooperatores, eine kreative Sicht der Dominikanischen Familie und ein aktives Pastoralprojekt in der Suche nach Berufungen." Besonders hervorgehoben wurden auch die eingeforderte Verstärkung der internationalen Beziehungen zu anderen Provinzen des Ordens und die Verbesserungen am Tutorenmodell. Auf die wirtschaftlich-rechtlichen Schritte des Provinzkapitels ging der Approbationsbrief kaum ein. Seine einzige Bemerkung dazu ist interessant, weil die Ordenskurie die provinzinternen Folgen dieser Maßnahmen offensichtlich erkannt hatte, ohne dass diese Konsequenzen in den Akten ausdrücklich thematisiert worden waren: Es wurde zugesichert, „dass eure Anstrengungen im finanziellen Bereich die Sendung [der] Provinz unterstützen werden, da sie zu einer Stärkung der Einheit innerhalb der Provinz führen, deren Territorium sich über zwei Länder erstreckt" (S. XXI).

Profilierung der Niederlassungen: das Provinzkapitel von 2002

Das nächste Provinzkapitel tagte vom 26. bis 31. August in Augsburg. Nicht nur seine Dauer, sondern auch seine Akten waren mit 44 Seiten kürzer als die von 1998 – was nicht nur daran lag, dass das Provinzkapitel von 1998 eine Ausnahmeanstrengung gewesen war, sondern auch daran, dass man auf dieser Anstrengung aufbauen konnte. Die Pastoralplanung war bisher eher wenig konkret geblieben. Dies wollte das Provinzkapitel von 2002 nun ändern.

Der Titel des diesbezüglichen Kapitels der Akten (S. 9–23; Nrn. 25–101): „‚Der Mensch ist der Weg der Kirche' – Akzente unserer dominikanischen Verkündigung am Beginn des 21. Jahrhunderts" fiel weniger klar aus als sein Inhalt. Er spielte auf eine Grundidee der Enzyklika „Redemptor hominis" Papst Johannes Pauls II. an, die auch in wenigen Zeilen als eine Art Motto zitiert wurde (Nr. 25). Die folgenden, allgemein gehaltenen Ausführungen zur religiösen Lage der Menschen heute und der diesbezügli-

chen Aufgaben der Kirche und des Ordens (Nrn. 26–31) dienten als Einleitung zu einer durchaus kritischen Analyse der an den Niederlassungen der Provinz stattfindenden oder von diesen ausgehenden Pastoral (Nrn. 32–35). Neben der lobenden Aufzählung der Aktivitäten wurden vier Defizite festgestellt: Zum einen wurden größere Gruppen junger Menschen von der Seelsorge der Provinz nur an wenigen Standorten und zu seltenen Gelegenheiten erreicht und bei den Erreichten „handelt es sich in der Regel nur um solche junge Menschen, die ‚von selbst' zu uns finden. Wir tun uns schwer, den Weg zu jungen Menschen zu finden, die kirchlich nicht gebunden sind" (Nr. 34). Zum zweiten: „Neuevangelisierung beschäftigt uns weniger als andere Fragen." Zum dritten: „Obwohl fast ein Drittel unserer Mitbrüder promoviert oder habilitiert ist und einige eine Lehrtätigkeit ausüben, sind wir im akademischen Bereich wenig seelsorglich präsent." Zum vierten belegten zwar die Rechenschaftsberichte der Amtsträger der Provinz, „dass die Anordnungen des Provinzkapitels von 1998 in hohem Maß angenommen und umgesetzt worden" waren, allerdings nicht die Bitte um Evaluierung der apostolischen Tätigkeiten und die Anregungen über die Einrichtung einer Berufungspastoral – letztere „wohl vor allem deshalb, weil nicht klar ist, wie und wo wir junge Menschen erreichen können" (Nr. 35). Daher nahm das Provinzkapitel diese Evaluierung selbst vor, und zwar in zwei Schritten, in einer Setzung von anvisierten Schwerpunkten der seelsorglichen Aktivität und in Vorschlägen von entsprechender Profilierung der Tätigkeiten an den Niederlassungen.

An den Beginn der Schwerpunktsetzung (Nrn. 36–51) stellten die Kapitulare das ausdrückliche Bekenntnis: „Auch wenn unsere Zahl sinkt, haben wir die feste Absicht, unseren Status als Provinz in Österreich und Süddeutschland zu halten. Ebenso wollen wir die bestehenden Standorte in unserer Provinz erhalten und erneuern. Dazu ist es nötig, für jeden Standort ein klares Profil an Tätigkeiten zu erarbeiten. Diese Kapitelsakten wollen dazu einen Beitrag leisten" (Nr. 36). Das gemeinsame Profil der Arbeit der Provinz und der Häuser sollte von drei Punkten geprägt werden: 1. Bildungsapostolat (Nrn. 38–40): „Unter Bildungsapostolat verstehen wir in einem sehr weiten Sinn jede Tätigkeit im geistlichen und intellektuellen Bereich, von geistlicher Begleitung über verschiedenste Vortragstätigkeit bis hin zu wissenschaftlicher Lehre und Forschung. Wir erkennen bei vielen Menschen eine große Sehnsucht nach Spiritualität, aber auch oft große Unkenntnis oder Unsicherheit in religiösen Fragen" (Nr. 38). Dieser Herausforderung sollte verstärkt durch Vortrags-, Lehr- und andere entspre-

chende Tätigkeiten begegnet werden. 2. City- und Großstadtpastoral (Nrn. 41–45), aufbauend auf der Beobachtung: „Unsere Häuser liegen fast ausschließlich in großen Städten unserer Provinz. Auch wenn ihr Tätigkeitsprofil sehr unterschiedlich ist, sind alle gleichermaßen von der heutigen Großstadtatmosphäre betroffen“ (Nr. 42). Der City- und Großstadtpastoral wollte sich die Provinz „in den kommenden Jahren verstärkt theoretisch und praktisch widmen. Auf Provinzebene sollen Arbeitskreise zu diesem Thema eingerichtet werden“ (Nr. 43). Angeregt wurden weiter diesbezügliche Treffen und Tagungen (Nr. 44). 3. Vernetzung, Kooperation und Kommunikation (Nrn. 46–51), die wegen der erforderlichen Mobilität und Flexibilität, der geringen eigenen Kräfte und aus Gründen der Profilierung gegenüber anderen Ordensgemeinschaften geboten schienen.

Daraus leitete das Provinzkapitel seine Vorschläge an die Niederlassungen ab (Nrn. 52–90) – *Vorschläge* und nicht Anordnungen oder Befehle: „Es kann nicht Aufgabe eines Provinzkapitels sein, den einzelnen Kommunitäten bis ins Detail vorzuschreiben, was sie zu tun haben. Solche Versuche einer ‚Pastoralplanung von oben‘ sind in der Vergangenheit schon oft fehlgeschlagen, haben sich als undurchführbar erwiesen oder wurden einfach ignoriert. Es kann aber auch nicht sinnvoll sein, alles einfach ‚unten‘ unkoordiniert laufen zu lassen. Wir versuchen einen mittleren Weg. Wir treffen zu den einzelnen Standorten Feststellungen, machen darauf basierende Vorschläge und bitten die Angesprochenen, die Vorschläge zu überdenken, Konzepte zu erarbeiten, zu verbessern oder fortzusetzen und diese uns mitzuteilen. So soll eine Pastoralplanung von oben und unten, eben in Kommunikation, entstehen“ (Nrn. 52 und 53).

Bezüglich des Konvents in Wien (Nrn. 55–59) wurde die ununterbrochene Tradition des Ordens in diesem Kloster seit dem 13. Jahrhundert betont, aber auch auf die Fülle von anderen Ordensgemeinschaften und kirchlichen Einrichtungen in dieser Stadt hingewiesen, die eine pastorale Profilierung vor Ort trotz großer Anstrengungen der Mitbrüder erschwerte. Als weiteres Problem wurde die große finanzielle Last zum Erhalt der Konventsgebäude, der Kirche und des historischen Inventars genannt, die die konventseigenen Mittel überfordere. „Wir schlagen vor, dass die Gemeinschaft einen Schwerpunkt auf das Bildungsapostolat legt … Aufgrund des konkreten Umfelds erscheint ein Engagement in Richtung Citypastoral nicht unbedingt als wegweisend. Die Kompetenz der Mitbrüder, die etwa als Theologen, Exerzitienleiter, Spiritual am Priesterseminar und in anderen Bereichen tätig sind, erlaubt es jedoch, sich in der spirituellen und theologi-

schen Bildung zu engagieren. Auch die Funktion als Ausbildungskonvent unserer Provinz ist mit einzuplanen. Im Zusammenhang mit dieser Schwerpunktbildung wäre die Position der Pfarre zu überdenken“ (Nr. 57).

In Augsburg (Nrn. 60–63) habe der Konvent seine pastoralen Tätigkeiten evaluiert und durch die Teilnahme am City-Pastoral-Projekt der Diözese neue Akzente gesetzt, mit dem Ergebnis: „Heute werden die Dominikaner als Gemeinschaft in Augsburg weit besser und als profilierter wahrgenommen“ (Nr. 60). Augsburg sei außerdem der zweite Ausbildungskonvent der Provinz und trage die Seelsorgsdienste am „Dominikanischen Zentrum“ in Regensburg (dazu unten). Das Provinzkapitel bat um die Fortführung dieser Tätigkeiten. Bezüglich der Pfarrei von St. Wolfgang in Augsburg-Spickel stellte man zwar die kürzlich erfolgte Nachbesetzung der Pfarrstelle fest, aber „die mittelfristige Fortführung dieser Tätigkeit“ müsse „mit den Erfordernissen des Konvents abgestimmt werden“ (Nr. 64).

Die Gemeinschaft in Freiburg (Nrn. 65–68) hatte sich inzwischen zu einem Sorgenkind der Provinz entwickelt:

> „Der Konvent St. Albert hat sein Profil erhalten, als in den 60er Jahren eine Gruppe jüngerer Mitbrüder nach Freiburg assigniert wurde und dort Gesprächskreise aufbaute … Diese Gesprächskreise bestehen z. T. noch heute. Sie ziehen jedoch inzwischen wenig neue Teilnehmer an. Dadurch haben sie sich zu Treffen von Multiplikatoren gewandelt. Andere Tätigkeiten mussten entsprechend der Altersstruktur aufgegeben oder reduziert werden. St. Albert ist der einzige Konvent der Provinz, in dem kein Mitbruder unter 60 Jahren lebt und arbeitet; das Durchschnittsalter liegt bei 71 Jahren. … Dabei ist der Standort Freiburg in vieler Hinsicht von großem Interesse für die Provinz: Freiburg ist durch die Anziehungskraft als Universitäts- und Wirtschaftsstandort eine der ‚jüngsten‘ Städte in Deutschland; die theologische und die philosophische Fakultät [gehören] zu den anerkannt besten im Land. Die Präsenz anderer Männerorden ist in Freiburg stark rückläufig“ (Nrn. 65–66).

Das Provinzkapitel bat daher, in Zukunft „die personelle und pastorale Erneuerung in Freiburg als vordringlich zu behandeln“ (Nr. 67).

Auch in Graz sei die Überalterung der Brüder ein Problem, da von den sieben im dortigen Kloster assignierten und wohnenden Mitbrüdern fünf das übliche Pensionsalter bereits überschritten hätten. „Unter dieser Hinsicht muss die Hauptaufgabe des Konvents gesehen werden: die Betreuung der Pfarre Graz-Münzgraben mit 11.000 Menschen“ (Nr. 69). Auf dem Pfarrgebiet befänden sich aber der Großteil der technischen Universität Graz und drei große Studentenheime. Ehedem seien deshalb auch Brüder

in der Hochschulseelsorge tätig gewesen, dies sei derzeit jedoch nicht möglich: „Studentenseelsorge in Graz bleibt aber weiter eine Option der Provinz, weil am Standort Graz Hochschulseelsorge nicht extra conventum ausgeübt werden muss und sich die Möglichkeit einer Vernetzung mit der Pfarre ergibt …“ (Nr. 70). Konvent und Kirche waren nach 1945 als Zentrum der Marienverehrung geplant: „Freilich sind die Besucherzahlen drastisch zurückgegangen. Dies liegt einerseits an einem allgemeinen Rückgang der Marienverehrung, andererseits sind in den letzten Jahren viele neue marianische und andere geistliche Bewegungen entstanden, die z. T. zueinander und zu bestehenden in Konkurrenz treten“ (Nr. 71). Das Kapitel bat daher darum, dass der Konvent die Münzgrabenpfarrei als Hauptaufgabe mit den Mitteln einer modernen Großstadtpastoral weiterbetreue und die Provinz die Studentenseelsorge dort als Option im Auge behalte (Nr. 74). Zu überlegen sei auch eine längerfristige Sicherung der gefährdeten materiellen Grundlage des Konvents (Nr. 76).

Bezüglich Friesach (Nrn. 77–80) stellte das Kapitel fest: „Die materielle Situation ist gesichert. Die derzeitige personelle Besetzung ist ausreichend“ (Nr. 77). Nach der Aufgabe von Retz sei Friesach die einzige Niederlassung der Provinz in ländlicher Umgebung:

> „Die regionalen Tätigkeiten und die ländliche Lage eröffnen folgende Möglichkeit: Friesach ist als Lebensort für (ältere) Mitbrüder interessant, die nicht (mehr) in einem Groß- oder Stadtkonvent leben, aber dennoch in einer dominikanischen Niederlassung seelsorglich tätig sein wollen. Zudem könnte Friesach ein Ort für einzelne Mitbrüder sein, die in einem ordenseigenen Haus vorübergehend Ruhe und Erholung suchen. Zu diesem Zweck müssten ein oder zwei Gästezimmer im Kloster zur Verfügung gestellt werden. Die Frage nach der Verpflegung der Gäste wäre zu lösen. Dieser Vorschlag hat ausschließlich Mitbrüder als mögliche Gäste im Blick“ (Nr. 79).

Den Konvent St. Kajetan / München (Nrn. 81–85) beschrieb das Kapitel als „unsere einzige Großstadtkirche in markanter, zentraler Lage“, von der aus „ein sehr großer Personenkreis erreicht“ würde (Nr. 81). Es schlug daher vor, „das bestehende Seelsorgskonzept an St. Kajetan im Sinn einer projektbezogenen Citypastoral zu erweitern“ (Nr. 84).

An St. Katharina / München (Nrn. 86–90) gäbe es die jüngste Pfarrei der Provinz: „Die stark wachsende Gemeinde ist geprägt durch junge Familien, Kinder und Jugendliche, kirchenferne Menschen und Ausländer. Damit reicht die pastorale Verantwortung für die Pfarrei in ein nicht kirchlich geprägtes Milieu hinein“ (Nr. 86). Das Kapitel schlug vor, die Nieder-

lassung zu einer kleinen Gemeinschaft auszubauen, vielleicht mit Hilfe von Brüdern anderer Provinzen, die in München studieren wollten und in der Pfarrarbeit mithelfen konnten. St. Katharina käme auch als Ort für pastorale Praktika für Mitbrüder in Ausbildung in Frage.

Auch ein neues Projekt konnte analysiert werden, das sogenannte „Dominikanische Zentrum“ in Regensburg, das 2001 hatte eingeweiht werden können (Nrn. 91–95). Es handelte sich dabei um einen „Predigtstützpunkt“, an dem dominikanische Seelsorge geleistet werden konnte, ohne dass eine Niederlassung oder Gemeinschaft am Ort bestand (Nr. 91). In den Räumen des Zentrums wurden Veranstaltungen wie Vortragsreihen, geistliche Begleitung u. ä. angeboten; darüber hinaus wurden von dort aus Messfeiern mit Predigt in der ehemaligen Dominikanerkirche St. Blasius, in St. Emmeram und Mitarbeit an der Regensburger Hochschulseelsorge abgehalten (Nrn. 92–93). Die Kapitelsväter stellten das positive Echo fest, das diese Aktionen in der Stadt und der Diözese Regensburg gefunden hatten, sowie eine weitere erfreuliche Folge: „Unsere Präsenz vor Ort hat bereits mehrere Ordensinteressenten in engeren Kontakt mit uns gebracht und Klärungsprozesse ermöglicht. Im Hinblick auf Berufungspastoral erweist sich das Dominikanische Zentrum als bedeutsamer Faktor“ (Nr. 94). Dementsprechend erging die Bitte, die seelsorgliche Präsenz in Regensburg fortzusetzen und auszubauen, nicht nur durch den Konvent von Augsburg, sondern auch durch die Mithilfe anderer Konvente.

Erwähnt wurden außerdem die positiven Erfahrungen, die die Provinz bisher mit dem Internet als „neuartiger Möglichkeit dominikanischer Präsenz und Seelsorge“ gemacht hatte und die einen weiteren Ausbau sinnvoll erscheinen ließen (Nrn. 96–101).

An diese Bewertung der Standorte und äußeren Tätigkeiten der Provinz und ihrer Mitglieder schlossen die Akten ein in der Provinzgeschichte bisher einmaliges Kapitel an, nämlich eine Evaluation des geistlichen Lebens der Brüder. Bereits zur Vorbereitung dieses Textes hatte es eine Neuerung gegeben, denn zum ersten Mal waren vier Schwestern aus dem Orden als *peritae* – Fachfrauen – zur Teilnahme an einer Kommission „Spiritualität“ gebeten worden. Inhaltlich schlossen sich die Ausführungen an die in der allgemeinen Analyse der Situation der Menschen von heute festgestellte Beobachtung des „geistlichen Hungers“ und der Suche nach Spiritualität und Gott an. Um die Menschen gut und sinnvoll betreuen und ihre geistlichen Bedürfnisse stillen zu können, bestünde „die grundlegende Voraussetzung darin, dass wir selbst neu lernen, Jesus Christus als den Weg, die

Wahrheit und das Leben (vgl. Joh 14,6) anzunehmen. Glaubenserneuerung und Glaubensvertiefung sind notwendig, um andere auf dem Glaubensweg begleiten zu können“ (Nr. 27).

Die darauf aufbauenden Aussagen des Provinzkapitels über „Kontemplation und spirituelle Kompetenz“ (S. 24–27, Nrn. 102–113) stellen wohl die tiefsten Aussagen dar, die jemals auf dieser höchsten Ebene in der Provinz verlautbart wurden, und es ist zu bedauern, dass eine vollständige Wiedergabe als Zitat den Rahmen dieser Geschichtsdarstellung sprengen würde. Das Provinzkapitel stellte einleitend fest: „Wenn Menschen voll solcher [sc. spiritueller] Sehnsucht einem Dominikaner begegnen, ist er als Ordensmann und Geistlicher gefragt. … Sich Kompetenz zum Antworten zu erwerben, gehört zu den Pflichten apostolischen Wirkens“ (Nr. 103). Diese Kompetenz könne „nur aus einer inneren geistlichen Haltung erwachsen, die täglich geübt werden muss“, entsprechend der auf den hl. Dominikus zurückgehenden dominikanischen Tradition (Nr. 104): „Das gemeinsame Stundengebet, das Studium, das Verweilen vor dem Gekreuzigten und die Eucharistiefeier waren für ihn Mittel, sich auf Gott auszurichten und mit Christus zu verbinden. Hier sind zwei Zielrichtungen zu unterscheiden, eine theozentrische und eine christozentrische“ (Nr. 105), die das Kapitel mit Beispielen aus der dominikanischen Spiritualitätsgeschichte anschaulich beschrieb (Nrn. 106–109).

Als praktische Konsequenz aus dieser dominikanischen Spiritualität forderte das Kapitel zum einen die Ehrlichkeit in der täglichen Suche, Gott wahrzunehmen und sich als von Gott Wahrgenommener bewusst zu werden: „Seine Gegenwart befreit dazu, den Mut aufzubringen, sich selbst auf den Grund zu gehen. … Ehrlich und wahrhaftig bis auf den eigenen Grund zu sehen, ist eine schwere Aufgabe.“ Hilfreich sei hierzu v. a. das eigene geistlich Begleitet-Sein und der Empfang des Sakraments der Buße (Nr. 110). Zum zweiten sei Konzentration und Einfachheit notwendig:

> „Die gemeinschaftliche Lebensform der Dominikaner ist wesentlich darauf ausgerichtet, den Brüdern die äußeren Bedingungen zur Kontemplation zu bieten. Studium und Betrachtung, grundlegende Elemente einer kontemplativen Lebenshaltung, werden gefördert durch den Raum, in dem der Bruder lebt. Der Raum soll arm sein im Sinne von einfach, ordentlich, sauber. … Stille sollte ein selbstverständliches Element des Gemeinschaftslebens sein, die diesem seine Ausstrahlung gibt. Es ist nützlich, wenn in den Konventen darüber gesprochen wird, wie dies ermöglicht werden kann“ (Nr. 111).

Zum Erwerb der erforderlichen Kompetenz sei außerdem nötig, „dass der Dominikaner die Werke der spirituellen Autoren seines Ordens kennt. Jeder Bruder sollte die Hauptwerke dieser Autoren selbst gelesen haben, nicht nur zum eigenen Nutzen, sondern auch, um Menschen in spirituellen Fragen Rede und Antwort stehen zu können. Eine intensive Lektüre dieser Werke und eine gründliche Auseinandersetzung mit ihnen sollte schon in der Ausbildungszeit beginnen“ (Nr. 112). Hingewiesen wurde auch darauf, dass sich die dominikanische Spiritualität auch weiterentwickeln und ihre Geschichte im 21. Jahrhundert fortgeschrieben werden müsse, um „nicht nur Altes und Bewährtes zu wiederholen, sondern auch Neues zu integrieren“ (Nr. 113).

Das folgende Kapitel der Akten handelte über „die Ausbildung zu unserer dominikanischen Sendung“ (Nrn. 114–139). Hier ging es darum, die Beobachtungen und Analysen des Pastoralplanungskapitels und des Spiritualitätskapitels in die lebenslange Ausbildung der Brüder einfließen zu lassen: „Diese Elemente unserer Lebensweise zu einer Einheit zusammenzuführen, muss erlernt werden. Dabei handelt es sich um einen lebenslangen Prozess, der die stufenweise Eingliederung in den Orden umfasst, mit der feierlichen Profess jedoch nicht endet“ (Nr. 114). Festgestellt wurde, dass sich die Ausbildungsordnung der Provinz in der Praxis bewährt habe; veränderte Gegebenheiten bedingten jedoch weitere Anpassungen, u. a. weil viele der Ordensinteressenten bereits mit abgeschlossenem Theologiestudium oder anderen Ausbildungsabschlüssen kämen (Nr. 115). Dazu gehörte aber auch die Umstrukturierung, die die Provinz im Noviziat vorgenommen hatte. Dieses fand inzwischen zusammen mit der Provinz Teutonia in deren Noviziatskonvent in Worms statt, womit man positive Erfahrungen gemacht habe: „Die Zusammenarbeit beider Provinzen soll fortgesetzt werden“ (Nr. 117). Ungeachtet dessen hielt das Provinzkapitel aber am Fortbestand von Wien als Noviziatskonvent der Provinz und an der Besetzung des Postens eines Novizenmeisters fest: „Ein zusätzliches eigenes Noviziat erlaubt, dass das gemeinsame Noviziat einen Teil dieser Ausbildungsphase in Wien verbringt“ (Nr. 119). Für das Grundstudium stünden „im Provinzgebiet derzeit die Ausbildungskonvente Wien und Augsburg zur Verfügung. Die Studienmöglichkeiten an diesen Standorten sind gut; die notwendige Begleitung der Auszubildenden ist befriedigend gelöst“; weitere Möglichkeiten böten die Einrichtungen der Teutonia und der Schweizer Provinz (Nr. 122). Neu war die Betrachtung der Frage der Qualifikation von Brüdern zur Übernahme von Ämtern in der Provinz und in den Konventen: „Wahlen zu Lei-

Abb. 69: P. Dietmar Thomas Schon (PA, Fotosammlung).

tungsämtern gestalten sich in unseren Konventen schwierig. Das liegt auch daran, dass wir der Frage einer Ausbildung für die verschiedenen Aufgaben in der Vergangenheit weniger Aufmerksamkeit geschenkt haben als der wissenschaftlichen Qualifikation oder dem pastoralen Einsatz der Mitbrüder. Aus diesem Grund fühlen sich Brüder, die zur Übernahme eines solchen Amtes in Frage kommen, oft unvorbereitet und überfordert" (Nr. 126). Deshalb sollte die Teilnahme an Kursen über Gruppendynamik oder Supervision, auch nach der Erstassignation, zum Bestandteil des Ausbildungswegs gemacht werden; Ähnliches gelte für die Ausbildung zu den Verwaltungs- und Wirtschaftsämtern (Nrn. 126–127). Besonders sei der Mangel an Ausbildnern in der Provinz spürbar, daher gelte es als Ziel, mehr Formatoren auszubilden (Nr. 128).

Bei den abschließenden wirtschaftlichen Bestimmungen (Nrn. 147–161) handelte es sich im Wesentlichen um Vollzugsmeldungen der Anordnungen des Provinzkapitels von 1998.

Ordensmeister Carlos Azpiroz Costa bestätigte die Akten mit Worten des Lobes und der Ermutigung (S. VI–VIII) – ebenso die Wahl eines neuen Provinzials: Nach Ablauf seiner Amtszeit kehrte P. Hans Ulrich Steymans zu seiner wissenschaftlichen Tätigkeit zurück; bis 2004 wirkte er noch in Augsburg als Prior des Konvents Heilig Kreuz, um dann eine Professur für Altes Testament am Departement für biblische Studien an der theologischen Fakultät der Universität in Freiburg in der Schweiz anzunehmen. Zu seinem Nachfolger wählte das Provinzkapitel P. Dietmar Thomas Schon. Schon war mit der Ausbildung als Rechtsassessor in den Orden eingetreten und hatte 1989 Profess abgelegt. Nach seiner Priesterweihe war er als Beicht- und Gesprächsseelsorger an Heilig Kreuz in Augsburg und als Rektor der Autobahnkirche tätig gewesen. 2001 war er zum Prior des Augsburger Konvents gewählt worden. Darüber hinaus hatte er seit 1994 das Amt des Syndikus des süddeutschen Provinzteils innegehabt.

Analyse des Erreichten: das Provinzkapitel von 2006

Dass Provinzkapitel in der Geschichte der Provinz nicht nur innovative oder regulierende Rollen spielten, sondern auch manchmal nur als Wegmarkierungen dienten, wurde an dem Provinzkapitel deutlich, das vom 21. bis 26. August 2006 im Augsburger Konvent zusammentrat. Abgesehen von der Wiederwahl von P. Schon in das Amt des Provinzials liegt in seinen 48 Seiten langen und 248 Nummern umfassenden Akten ein durchgehendes Interesse im Mittelpunkt: die Betrachtung und Analyse des seit 1998 Erreichten. Dementsprechend verfassten die Kapitularen auch keinen längeren systematischen Text mehr, sondern betrachteten die Ergebnisse von sieben thematischen Aspekten, die in den letzten zwölf Jahren umfassend behandelt worden waren.

Das erste dieser Themen war das Apostolat (Nrn. 25–51). Die 2006 getroffenen Aussagen über die Gemeinschaftlichkeit dominikanischen Apostolats (Nrn. 25–36) gingen nicht über das hinaus, was frühere Provinzkapitel schon gesagt hatten – mit einer Ausnahme, nämlich der Medienarbeit, insbesondere der Einbindung des Internet als Plattform für die Erstbegegnung mit dem Orden: „Immer mehr Menschen informieren sich via Internet über unsere Angebote. So ist es besonders förderlich, wenn es darum geht, einen ersten Kontakt herzustellen. Dabei geht es aus Sicht des Internetnutzers um eine Vorabinformation, die ansprechend und aktuell auf Angebote hinweist; der Informationssuchende fühlt sich anonym, die ‚Schwelle' ist sehr niedrig. Auch kirchlich gebundene Personen nutzen immer häufiger diese Art der Informationsbeschaffung. Es gilt also, den Erstkontakt durch das Internet zu optimieren und auch weitere Angebote, bis hin zu Informationen über unseren Orden und unsere Ziele selbst, anzubieten" (Nr. 37). Zwar böte das Internet auch Möglichkeiten für Apostolat, aber „eine direkte Pastoral über das Internet ist zur Zeit zu aufwendig. Gerade in Glaubensfragen ist das persönliche Gespräch unerlässlich" (Nr. 40). Entgegen dem sonst bezüglich Internetpräsentationen üblichen Trend zur corporate identity, also zur Gleichförmigkeit des Auftritts von mehreren zusammengehörenden Institutionen, hielt das Provinzkapitel fest: „Unsere Internetseiten sind so verschieden wie unsere Konvente. Deshalb entspricht eine allzu starke Vereinheitlichung unserer Internetpräsenz nicht der Realität. Um die Zusammengehörigkeit der einzelnen Häuser zur Provinz deutlich zu machen, käme allenfalls ein gemeinsames Design des Banners oder Logos mit Schriftzug des einzelnen Hauses in Frage. Auch im Internet soll

sowohl die Verschiedenheit als auch die Einheit deutlich werden können" (Nr. 41). Gewünscht wurde aber eine Koordination und Optimierung der Internetpräsenz (Nr. 42) und eine stärkere Publikation von Predigten, Vorträgen und Ähnlichem, um ein größeres Publikum zu erreichen (Nr. 44). Weiter sollten aber auch die Möglichkeiten der Printmedien nicht außer Acht gelassen werden (Nr. 45). Insgesamt traf das Provinzkapitel strengere Regeln bezüglich Publikationen: „Informationen über den Orden und die Provinz sind mit dem Provinzialat abzustimmen, solche über Konvente mit dem jeweiligen Prior" (Nr. 46). „Mitbrüder, die sich wissenschaftlich qualifiziert haben, bedürfen für Publikationen (Bücher, Monographien, Beiträge) keiner Erlaubnis" (Nr. 49). „Mitbrüder, die sich (noch) nicht wissenschaftlich qualifiziert haben, bedürfen für Publikationen der Zustimmung des Provinzials und des Studienregens. Dies gilt für alle Publikationen, die den Glauben oder die Pastoral, die Kirche oder den Orden betreffen" (Nr. 51).

Unter der Überschrift „Strukturen, Profil und Entwicklung der Provinz des hl. Albert" wandte sich das Kapitel dem zweiten Thema zu, der Analyse der gemeinschaftlichen Pastoral (Nrn. 52–104), in Rückbindung auf das Provinzkapitel von 2002 und dessen diesbezüglicher Impulse: „Seither sind die Einsichten in unsere Stärken und Schwächen gewachsen. Wir sehen es als Aufgabe dieses Provinzkapitels, weitere Schlussfolgerungen zu ziehen" (Nr. 53). Als generelle Ziele hielten die Akten fest, „die Provinz des hl. Albert in Süddeutschland und Österreich als selbständige Einheit im Dominikanerorden zu konsolidieren und fortzuführen" (Nr. 55) und das Bewusstsein um die Einheit der Provinz weiter zu stärken: „Dies ist trotz regionaler Notwendigkeiten und ohne Vermehrung von Institutionen möglich, wenn Brüder in bestimmten Aufgaben ‚quer' über die Provinzteile und Regionen miteinander ins Gespräch kommen, insbesondere die Ausbildungsverantwortlichen, die Provinzsyndici und die Promotoren" (Nr. 56). Bezüglich der Niederlassungen stellte das Provinzkapitel eine Art Hierarchie auf: Als Ausbildungs- und Provinzialatskonvente stellten die Konvente Freiburg, Augsburg und Wien die institutionellen Schwerpunkte der Provinz dar. Ziel sei es daher, „diese Standorte zu entwickeln und zu stärken, weil sie trotz personeller Engpässe die Mindesterfordernisse als Provinz und unsere Präsenz im Provinzgebiet garantieren" (Nr. 57). Demgegenüber sollten die Gemeinschaften in Graz und St. Kajetan / München mindestens als *domus formatae* aufrechterhalten werden, da die dortigen dominikanischen Arbeitsmöglichkeiten hervorragend seien: „Konventsstatus ist zu einer

Wahrnehmung der örtlichen Chancen wünschenswert, aber nicht unbedingt notwendig. Wesentlich ist hingegen die Bildung örtlicher Seelsorgeteams“ (Nr. 58). Friesach, St. Katharina / München und Regensburg sollten als dominikanische Seelsorgsstellen wahrgenommen werden: „Ein Status als *domus* ist zur Nutzung der örtlichen Chancen nicht notwendig … Diese Seelsorgestellen sehen wir als ‚pastorale Zukunftsoptionen'“ (Nr. 59).

In der folgenden Betrachtung der Veränderungen, die sich an manchen Standorten der Provinz inzwischen ergeben hatten, stand der Konvent Freiburg im Breisgau an erster Stelle – das Provinzkapitel von 2002 hatte ja um vordringliche Behandlung der dortigen Probleme gebeten. In Freiburg war eine neue Initiative entwickelt und die dominikanische Präsenz durch die Eröffnung einer weiteren kleineren Gemeinschaft verstärkt worden. Diese in der Erwinstraße beheimatete Gruppe gehörte rechtlich als zweiter Standort zum Konvent St. Albert. Auch wenn die Akten dies nicht so ausdrückten, so bildete die neue Gemeinschaft sozusagen den Fuß in der Tür zu einem größeren Ziel: Provinzial Schon war mit dem Erzbischof und anderen Vertretern der Bistumsleitung in Gespräche über die etwaige Übernahme einer Innenstadtkirche und die Nutzung der mit dieser verbundenen Wohn- und Arbeitsräumlichkeiten getreten (Nr. 64). Beabsichtigt waren eine Änderung der pastoralen Aufgaben der Provinz in Freiburg, langfristig eine Zusammenlegung beider Konventsstandorte (Nrn. 66–67) und der Ausbau der Freiburger Niederlassung als Ausbildungsplatz: „Die Provinzkapitel 1994, 1998 und 2002 haben beschlossen bzw. bestätigt, dass es mehr als einen Ausbildungsstandort in der Provinz geben soll, um die Integration der Brüder in eine grenzüberschreitende Provinz und die Qualität der Ausbildung zu fördern. Mit Blick auf deutliche Rückschritte in der Studienqualität und -intensität der Augsburger theologischen Fakultät hat das Provinzkonsil vom 2. Februar 2004 die Verlegung des süddeutschen Ausbildungskonvents von Augsburg nach Freiburg beschlossen, wo eine hervorragende theologische Ausbildung gewährleistet ist“ (Nr. 69). Dieser Provinzkonsilsbeschluss wurde vom Provinzkapitel ausdrücklich bestätigt (Nr. 70).

Auch was den Augsburger Konvent anging, waren Änderungen erfolgt; die seit 1932 bestehende Situation des einen Konvents an zwei Standorten wurde beendet: „Die Pfarrei St. Wolfgang wurde an die Diözese zurückgegeben. Das Filialhaus St. Wolfgang besteht somit nur noch auf dem Papier“ (Nr. 74). Daher ordnete das Provinzkapitel an, die *domus filialis* aufzuheben, und bat den Ordensmeister um das entsprechende Dekret (Nr. 75).

Genauso sollte mit St. Katharina / München vorgegangen werden: Der Versuch, mit einem ausländischen Mitbruder, der in München studierte, aus dem dortigen Einzelposten eine kleine Gemeinschaft zu konstruieren, war nach erfolgter Promotion des Stipendiaten beendet. Die Personalknappheit der Provinz verhinderte einen Ausbau mit eigenen Brüdern. Das Provinzkapitel stellte fest: „Die dauerhafte Präsenz eines einzelnen Mitbruders und der rechtliche Status als *domus filialis* widersprechen sich. Deshalb sollen die rechtlichen Verhältnisse den tatsächlichen angepasst werden" (Nr. 80). Es ordnete an, „mit der Erzdiözese Gespräche über die Situation zu führen und nach erlangter kirchenrechtlicher Zustimmung die *domus filialis* St. Katharina spätestens zum 1. Oktober 2008 zu beenden", verbunden mit der Bitte eines entsprechenden Aufhebungsdekrets des Ordensmeisters (Nr. 81).

Das Dominikanische Zentrum in Regensburg hatte sich hingegen seit seiner Eröffnung zu einer in die Innenstadtpastoral integrierten Seelsorgsstelle entwickelt, die mit einem Mitbruder besetzt war (Nr. 82). Dabei konnte es nach Meinung des Provinzkapitels bleiben: „Die Verstärkung des Dominikanischen Zentrums zu einer domus filialis ist auf absehbare Zeit personell nicht möglich und deshalb nicht intendiert" (Nr. 86).

Was den ehemaligen Standort in Retz anging, so waren nach Schließung des Klosters als *domus* die Eigentumsrechte an Klosteranlage und Grundbesitz an die Körperschaft öffentlichen Rechts des österreichischen Provinzteils übergegangen. Der Erhalt dieses Eigentums war aufgrund der drückenden Baulast aber nicht mehr zu finanzieren (Nr. 89). Das Provinzkapitel bestimmte daher: „Das Eigentum der Provinz an der Klosteranlage Retz soll baldmöglichst, spätestens aber bis 1. Juni 2008 beendet werden. Dies kann geschehen durch Vereinbarung mit einem kirchlichen Träger, durch Ausgliederung der wesentlichen Teile in eine Stiftung oder auf eine andere Weise, die zur selben Entlastung der Provinz von ihrer (Kosten-)Verantwortung führt" (Nr. 90).

In Friesach gab es diese wirtschaftlichen Probleme zwar nicht, dafür herrschte hier eine andere Sorge: Falls dem bisherigen Verwalter etwas zustoßen würde, „wäre die Körperschaft ‚Dominikanerkloster Friesach' handlungsunfähig. Der Grazer Konvent hat erklärt, selbst bei Notfällen dieses Problem seiner *domus filialis* nicht lösen zu können. Wir halten [es] in dieser Lage für geboten, es nicht auf Notfall-Lösungen ankommen zu lassen, sondern jetzt eine Weichenstellung für die Zukunft vorzunehmen …" (Nr. 96) – nämlich das gesamte Eigentum des Dominikanerklosters St. Nikolaus in

Friesach auf die Körperschaft des österreichischen Provinzteils zu überschreiben (Nr. 97) und die *domus filialis* in Friesach zu schließen (Nr. 100).

Die Gemeinschaft im Kloster in Graz war seit 2002 auf fünf Mitbrüder geschrumpft. Eine dauerhafte personelle Verstärkung auf Konventsstärke schien nicht möglich. Auch hier hielt es das Provinzkapitel für geboten, den rechtlichen Status den tatsächlichen Verhältnissen anzupassen (Nr. 101) und ordnete die Reduktion des Konvents Graz zur *domus formata* an (Nr. 102).

Auf die Analyse der Niederlassungen folgte die der Dienste, Ämter und administrativen Strukturen der Provinz, der Aufgaben des Provinzials und der Prioren, der Provinz- und Konventsverwalter, der Ausbildungsamtsträger und der verschiedenen Promotoren (Nrn. 105–134). Die Ergebnisse dieser Evaluierung blieben im Allgemeinen verhaftet, ebenso die sich anschließende Analyse der Herausforderungen, denen das Provinzkapitel die Klostergemeinschaften der Provinz ausgesetzt sah (Nrn. 135–150). Als provinzspezifisch formulierten die Kapitelsväter die Beobachtungen, dass kleiner werdende Gemeinschaften mehr als in früheren Jahren das Verantwortungsbewusstsein des Einzelnen für die Gemeinschaft (Nr. 139) und eine gesteigerte Vorbildfunktion der älteren für die jüngeren Mitbrüder erfordere (Nr. 140). Abgesehen davon stellten sie „hinsichtlich der Anzahl und der Thematik der Konventskapitel … in einigen Konventen Defizite fest" und mahnten häufiger abgehaltene, dafür kürzere Kapitel ein (Nr. 147), wie auch regelmäßige gemeinsame Rekreationen (Nr. 148) und gemeinschaftliche Einkehr- oder Studientage (Nr. 150).

Ähnlich unkonkret erwies sich auch die Analyse der Kommunikation in der Provinz (Nrn. 151–177). Neben einigen diesbezüglichen Stärken (Nrn. 152–160) hoben die Kapitularen auch Schwächen hervor, darunter „schwelende, oft unausgesprochene Konflikte" im Umgang der Brüder untereinander, die zur Sprache gebracht werden sollten (Nr. 162), das Schrumpfen der Gemeinschaften und ihre teilweise Überalterung (Nr. 163), die Behinderung der Kommunikation zwischen den Häusern durch die Ausdehnung des Provinzgebiets und durch die Staatsgrenze, die die Provinz faktisch teilte (Nr. 164), oder der angerissene Mangel an Versetzungen und Versetzbarkeit der Brüder (Nr. 165). Das Provinzkapitel gab zwar einige Empfehlungen zur Verbesserung ab, hütete sich aber davor, klare Maßnahmen – etwa Versetzungen – anzuberaumen.

Die Analyse der Beziehungen zu den Zweigen der dominikanischen Familie (Nrn. 178–206) brachte konkrete Ergebnisse, v. a. was die Laien-

gemeinschaften betraf. Hier stellten die Kapitelsväter fest, dass in manchen anderen Ordensprovinzen die Laiengemeinschaften apostolisch tätig seien: „Die Realitäten in unserer Provinz sprechen meist eine andere Sprache. Hier treffen sich in den Gruppen oft Menschen, die den regelmäßigen Gruppenbesuch als eine Art persönlicher Seelsorgeplattform nutzen, um mit den Problemen ihres Alltags oder ihres Glaubens besser zurecht zu kommen. Das ist menschlich und pastoral verständlich. An eine gemeinsame Ausrichtung auf eine Form des Apostolates ist aber unter diesen Voraussetzungen noch nicht zu denken" (Nr. 196). Wie bei den Nonnen und Schwestern sei ein gemeinsamer Austausch wichtig und zu verstärken (Nrn. 198–199). „Ein grundlegendes Problem im deutschen Sprachraum dürfte das Fehlen der einschlägigen Texte zu den Dominikanischen Laiengemeinschaften auf Deutsch sein. Hier ist Abhilfe zu schaffen …" (Nr. 203), weshalb ein Mitbruder gebeten wurde, sein begonnenes Projekt einer Herausgabe der einschlägigen Texte zügig voranzutreiben (Nr. 204).

Sehr viel bedeutender war das letzte der analysierten Themen, nämlich die rechtlichen und administrativen Strukturen der Provinz (Nrn. 207–243). Absicht dieses Abschnittes der Akten war das Zusammentragen und die Beschreibung des erreichten Ist-Zustandes der unter Gregor Ruf begonnenen profanjuristischen Umstrukturierung der Provinzinstitutionen. Entsprechend der staatlichen Teilung der Provinz waren die Provinzteile vor den Rechtssystemen Österreichs und Deutschlands nun in zwar unterschiedlichen, aber effektiv einander ähnlichen Formen organisiert, die auch dem Ordens- und allgemeinen Kirchenrecht entsprachen: „Der süddeutsche Provinzteil ist als eingetragener Verein organisiert und damit Rechtsperson sowie staatlich anerkannt. Die Aufgaben und Zuständigkeiten sind in einer approbierten Satzung niedergelegt" (Nr. 207). „Die Buchhaltung und die Bilanzerstellung werden von einer Steuerberatungsgesellschaft nach den gesetzlichen Vorschriften wahrgenommen. … Alle drei Jahre findet eine Gemeinnützigkeitsprüfung durch das Finanzamt statt, die sich auf den gesamten Tätigkeits-, Mittelverwendungs- und Rechtsbereich erstreckt" (Nr. 208). „Die Konvente im süddeutschen Provinzteil sind ebenfalls als eingetragene und gemeinnützige Vereine organisiert. … Alle drei Jahre werden sie vom Finanzamt einer Gemeinnützigkeitsprüfung unterzogen" (Nr. 210). Für St. Katharina / München und den neuen Standort in Freiburg war dies aus rechtlichen Gründen nicht möglich, weshalb diese in der Wirtschaftsverwaltung dem süddeutschen „Provinz e. V." zuge-

ordnet wurden (ebd.). „Der österreichische Provinzteil ist als Körperschaft öffentlichen Rechts anerkannt. Dasselbe gilt für die Konvente Wien und Graz sowie derzeit für die *domus filialis* in Friesach" (Nr. 211). Sehr ausführlich wurden Aufbau und Zielsetzung der „Capa – Gemeinnützige Gesellschaft zur Förderung dominikanischer Ordenstätigkeit mbH" abgehandelt (Nrn. 212–216). Abschließend wurde festgehalten: „Die administrativen Strukturen im Wirtschaftsbereich entsprechen dem Ordensrecht und dem jeweiligen staatlichen Recht. Durch erfolgreiche Zusammenarbeit mit Fachleuten hat die Wirtschaftsverwaltung in unserer Provinz [einen] sehr hohen Standard. Die nach LCO und zusätzlich nach staatlichem Recht vorgesehenen Kontrollinstanzen funktionieren. Die Beteiligung vereidigter Wirtschaftsprüfer erleichtert den ordensinternen Kontrollgremien ihre Aufgabe. Die nötige Transparenz ist vorhanden. Wir sehen keinen Änderungs- oder Verbesserungsbedarf" (Nrn. 217 und 218). Vor dem Hintergrund der Tatsache, dass die Provinz im Wesentlichen von der Arbeit der Brüder lebte, diözesane Gestellungsverträge dabei eine wichtige Rolle spielten (Nr. 225), die Zahl der arbeitsfähigen Brüder aber am Zurückgehen war, hielten die Kapitelsväter warnend fest: „Wir gehen davon aus, dass sich die finanzielle Lage der Häuser und der Provinz, zumindest mittelfristig, eher verschlechtern wird. Deshalb halten wir auf allen Ebenen Überlegungen für notwendig, wo sinnvolle Einsparungen vorgenommen, die Einnahmen verbessert oder mindestens stabil gehalten werden können" (Nr. 223).

Im Bestätigungsschreiben des Ordensmeisters Carlos Azpiroz Costa vom 25. Oktober 2006 (S. V–VII) ernteten diese Akten großes Lob. Den einzigen Kritikpunkt bildete der Hinweis bezüglich der neuen Gemeinschaft in Freiburg, „dass Brüder in Ausbildung das Recht haben, in einem vollständig errichteten Konvent zu leben, um die Fülle des dominikanischen Gemeinschaftslebens erfahren zu können. Daher ermutigen wir euch, weitere Schritte zu unternehmen, eine Gemeinschaft zur Ausbildungsgemeinschaft im Sinne des LCO zu formen" (S. VI).

Teambildung und Konsolidierung: das Provinzkapitel von 2011

Das Provinzkapitel, das sich vom 11. bis 19. Januar 2011 im Konvent an Heilig Kreuz in Augsburg traf, postulierte P. Christophe Holzer zum Provinzial der süddeutsch-österreichischen Provinz. Dieser hatte 1995 Profess gemacht und war in Wien und in St. Kajetan / München Prior gewesen.

Seit dem 1. April 2006 fungierte er an der Ordenskurie in Rom als Sekretär des Ordensmeisters.[540] Als solcher konnte er nicht einfach in ein anderes Amt gewählt werden, sondern musste vom Ordensoberhaupt dafür freigegeben werden. Ordensmeister Bruno Cadoré bestätigte allerdings die Bitte und den Wunsch des Provinzkapitels, und so konnte Holzer die Nachfolge P. Schons als Leiter der Provinz antreten.

In den Akten des Provinzkapitels – 42 Seiten, 173 Nummern – waren noch immer die Nachwirkungen der Anstrengungen der letzten zwei Jahrzehnte zu spüren. Dementsprechend wurde inhaltlich manches wiederholt und in Erinnerung gerufen. Wie schon 2006, so wurden auch diesesmal mehrere Themen gesondert behandelt. Vor allem die Frage nach der Weiterführung mancher Niederlassungen kam nun zu einem Abschluss.

Im ersten großen Thema, dem Gemeinschaftsleben (Nrn. 25–54) ragten vor allem zwei Inhalte besonders hervor: Zum einen wurde der Blick ausdrücklich auf die Situation der alten Mitbrüder gerichtet, von denen „viele noch vorbildlich apostolisch tätig“ seien bzw. „zuweilen jenseits aller Aktivität … lebendige Zeichen für Wesentliches unseres Ordenslebens“ böten (Nr. 43). Daher stellten die Kapitularen fest:

> „Aufgrund dieser Erfahrungen ist es uns wichtig, dass die alten Brüder so lange wie möglich in unseren Gemeinschaften leben. Die Einrichtung von speziellen Konventen für ältere Brüder, in die sie an ihrem Lebensabend versetzt werden, halten wir nicht für sinnvoll, weil sie allen anderen Konventen etwas sehr wertvolles entzieht und die alten Brüder in eine Umgebung versetzt, die sie häufig nicht mehr für lebenswert halten“ (Nr. 44).

Bei Betreuungsbedarf stellte das Kapitel die Richtlinien auf:

> „1. Solange es möglich ist, sollen unsere alten Brüder im Konvent leben und tätig sein können. 2. Wenn Pflege nötig wird, soll diese, solange es möglich ist, im Konvent geschehen und der alte Bruder in der Gemeinschaft der Mitbrüder bleiben. 3. Ist eine Pflege im Konvent nicht mehr möglich, muss sie außerhalb in einer anderen Pflegeeinrichtung gesucht werden. Die Auswahl und Entscheidung über den Ort soll durch den Betroffenen, die zuständigen Oberen unter Beiziehung brüderlicher Vertrauenspersonen oder der gesamten Gemeinschaft und medizinisch-fachlicher Beratung getroffen werden“ (Nr. 45).

Zum zweiten sind die Ausführungen des Kapitels über die Bedeutung der Versöhnung interessant – leider wurden sie in den Akten getroffen, ohne

540 Datum laut: PA, ProvinzZeitung 4–2006, S. 3.

dass klar ist, ob es sich um eine Reaktion auf konkrete (Streit)Fälle oder nur um eine allgemeine Ermahnung handelt:

> „Unser Gemeinschaftsleben ist immer auch geprägt von Versagen, Schuld und Sünde. Persönliche Verletzungen führen zu dauerhaften Brüchen und Blockaden in unseren Gemeinschaften. Hierin sind von allen Beteiligten der Geist und die Bereitschaft zur Versöhnung erforderlich. … Der Wille zur Versöhnung beinhaltet auch die Bereitschaft, eigene Schwächen und Fehler anzuerkennen und zuzugeben. Diese Bereitschaft kann in regelmäßigen Kapiteln und Revisionen zum Ausdruck gebracht werden. Sie soll aber jederzeit das informelle Zusammenleben der Brüder prägen. Solche Bereitschaft vorausgesetzt kann eine liebevolle und diskrete *correctio fraterna* viel zu einer gesunden Gemeinschaftsatmosphäre beitragen. Gelingende Versöhnung in unseren Gemeinschaften ist ein wichtiges Zeichen des Evangeliums in einer Welt, die häufig nur von Ahndung, Ausgrenzung, Bestrafung und Rache geprägt ist“ (Nrn. 52–54).

In der Behandlung des zweiten großen Themas, des Apostolats (Nrn. 55–86), konzentrierte das Provinzkapitel seine Bemühungen auf einen Appell zur Teambildung. Ausgehend von der Beobachtung, „dass die apostolische Sendung zuerst der Gemeinschaft und nicht den einzelnen Brüdern anvertraut“ sei (Nr. 56), seien „die Gemeinschaften unserer Provinz … unter anderem dadurch geprägt, dass sie alle an einer Kirche und in einem daran angeschlossenen Haus leben und tätig sind. … Ein Kloster als reine Wohngemeinschaft gibt es bei uns nicht. Deshalb soll die Tätigkeit an Kirche und Kloster als Aufgabe der ganzen Gemeinschaft und nicht nur einzelner Mitbrüder verstanden werden“ (Nr. 57). Dies bedeute jedoch nicht, „dass alle Mitbrüder in gleicher Intensität daran mitarbeiten können, sollen und müssen. … Die Gründe für ein eher geringes Engagement am gemeinsamen Pastoralprojekt können vielfältig sein. Sie reichen von gesundheitlicher Beeinträchtigung über unterschiedliche Auffassungen und Ziele bis zu fast ausschließlicher Tätigkeit außerhalb der Gemeinschaft“ (Nr. 58). Zusammenfassend gesagt: Die Seelsorge an Kloster und Kirche sollte, soweit möglich, im Team von der Gemeinschaft getragen werden. Solche Arbeitsgruppen existierten längst, denn „ein weiteres Merkmal des Apostolats an unseren Häusern ist die Tatsache, dass nicht ausschließlich unsere Brüder darin tätig sind. In vielfältiger Weise sind andere Organisationen und Institutionen (Pfarrei, Laiengemeinschaften, kategoriale Gemeinden etc.) oder Einzelpersonen (haupt- und ehrenamtliche MitarbeiterInnen in Pastoral oder Verwaltung) an den Aktivitäten unserer Gemeinschaften beteiligt und in sie eingebunden …“ (Nr. 59).

Zur Entfaltung der Möglichkeiten der Teambildung gab das Provinzkapitel im Folgenden „einige Anregungen zu den vier Grundfunktionen kirchlicher Gemeinschaften" (Nr. 61) in den theologischen, aus der Tradition der griechischen Kirchenväter stammenden Begriffen der „martyria" (Zeugnisabgabe hier verstanden als Verkündigung; Nrn. 62–64), „leiturgia" (die Bedeutung der verschiedenen Formen des Gottesdienstes; Nrn. 65–71), „diakonia" (verstanden als die sozial-caritative Dimension der dominikanischen Sendung; Nrn. 72–75) und „koinonia" (verstanden als von der dominikanischen Seelsorge ausgehende Gemeinde- und Gemeinschaftsbildung; Nrn. 76–79). Als praktische Konsequenz dieses Appells zur Teambildung sah das Provinzkapitel eine bessere Einbindung der sozusagen nichtdominikanischen Kräfte in die gemeinsame Pastoral an Kirche und Kloster durch die Bildung von Koordinationsgruppen aus drei bis sieben Personen vor, nämlich jenen, „die das Apostolat vor Ort hauptsächlich tragen" (Nr. 81). Teambildung sei „auch auf Provinzebene ein Gebot der Stunde. Viele Aufgaben, die früher einem einzelnen Mitbruder anvertraut wurden, können heute nur noch im Team und unter Beiziehung externer Experten erfüllt werden. Solche Teambildungen haben wir auf diesem Kapitel in folgenden Bereichen angeregt bzw. durchgeführt: Provinzsyndikatur, Öffentlichkeitsarbeit und Medien, Dominikanische Laiengemeinschaften" (Nr. 85).

Abgesehen von der genannten Bildung eines Teams von mehreren Assistenten für die Öffentlichkeitsarbeit unter der Leitung des Promotors für die Öffentlichkeitsarbeit, um die diesbezüglichen Aufgaben aufzuteilen oder an weitere Mitarbeiter delegieren zu können (Nr. 104), bestand eine Neuerung bezüglich des dritten großen Themas – Öffentlichkeitsarbeit und Medien (Nr. 87–107) – in der Hinwendung des Provinzkapitels zum Phänomen der sozialen Netzwerke im Internet. Die hier getroffenen Beobachtungen und Regelungen sind deshalb interessant, weil sie keine nachträglichen Reaktionen, sondern Präventivmaßnahmen darstellten:

> „Soziale Netzwerke im Internet wie Facebook prägen zunehmend die Kommunikation unter den Menschen. Nicht alle können oder wollen daran teilnehmen. Wir begrüßen alle bestehenden Initiativen, diese neuen Foren für Kommunikation und Verkündigung zu nützen. Auf Provinzebene ist dies eine Entscheidung des Provinzials, des Provinzkonsils oder des Teams für Öffentlichkeitsarbeit. Diese Instanzen entscheiden, ob und wie die Provinz auf diesen Plattformen auftritt. Kein anderer Bruder oder keine andere Organisationseinheit hat das Recht, im Namen der Provinz aufzutreten. Allen Mitbrüdern ist es gestattet, im eigenen Namen und auf eigene Verantwortung

> in diesen Medien und Plattformen aufzutreten. Im Falle von Auftritten und Äußerungen, die dem Geist der Kirche und des Ordens widersprechen, haben sie sich, wie in allen anderen Verkündigungssituationen auch, vor den kirchlichen und ordensinternen Instanzen zu verantworten. In diesem Zusammenhang weisen wir nachdrücklich auf die Einhaltung des Datenschutzes hin. Jeder Bruder kann selbst entscheiden, welche eigenen persönlichen Daten er im Internet bekannt gibt. Es ist verboten, Daten von Brüdern oder vertrauliche Daten der Provinz bzw. des Ordens (Kapitelsgeheimnis und ähnliches) zu publizieren“ (Nrn. 97–100).

Im Bereich der Ausbildung (Nr. 108–134), dem vierten Thema, wurden verschiedene Maßnahmen getroffen, um trotz der angespannten Personalsituation wenigstens eine Errungenschaft der früheren Versuche in diesem Bereich zu erhalten: „Aufgrund der gegenwärtig geringen Studentenzahlen unserer Provinz sollen die Mitbrüder in Grundausbildung in einem Konvent zusammengefasst werden. Dies soll in der kommenden Zeit der Wiener Konvent sein. Gleichzeitig soll das Ausbildungskonzept an zwei Standorten (Wien und Freiburg) beibehalten werden und so Freiburg als Option für den Ausbildungsort gewahrt bleiben“ (Nr. 119). In Freiburg hatten sich inzwischen entscheidende Veränderungen ergeben, die diese Regelung ermöglicht hatten (siehe unten). Angefordert wurde außerdem für die Grundausbildung die Erstellung eines Homiletikcurriculums mit regelmäßigen Übungen (Nr. 122). Näher betrachtet wurde auch die Phase der sogenannten Erstassignation (Nrn. 126–132), also der ersten Jahre nach der Priesterweihe, in der besonders eine notwendige Heranführung an zukünftige Leitungsaufgaben (Nr. 127) und eine gute Einführung in das Beichtehören (Nr. 128) betont wurde. Zwischen der Priesterweihe und dem Beginn weiterführender Studien wurde eine Mindestwartezeit von zwei Jahren beschlossen (Nr. 131).

Bezüglich der „familia dominicana“, Thema Nummer fünf (Nrn. 135–145), legte das Kapitel fest, dass der Promotor für die Nonnen des Ordens die vier Nonnenklöster der Provinz in seiner vierjährigen Amtszeit nach Möglichkeit je zweimal besuchen sollte und zur Teilnahme an der jährlichen Tagung der Nonnenpriorinnen verpflichtet war (Nr. 136). Bei den auf dem Provinzgebiet weit zahlreicheren Schwesternklöstern war eine häufige Besuchsfrequenz für den Schwesternpromotor unmöglich. Dieser sollte jedoch nach Möglichkeit Kontakte knüpfen und an der Jahrestagung der Dominikanerinnenoberinnen teilnehmen (Nr. 137–138). Auch für die Betreuung der Laiengemeinschaften regte das Kapitel Teambildung

an; konkret sollte es für die ganze Provinz ein Leitungsteam für alle Laiengemeinschaften geben, bestehend aus dem Promotor und vier vom Provinzial nach Vorschlag des Promotors als Mitglieder zu ernennenden Laien. Diese Gruppe sollte die Gemeinschaften koordinieren, als ihre Vertretung nach oben (internationale Ordensebene) und außen (Provinznachbarschaft etc.) dienen, das Direktorium der Laiengemeinschaften überarbeiten, einen Provinzkatalog der Laiengemeinschaften mit allen Gruppen und Mitgliedern erstellen und Studien- und Einkehrtage vorbereiten (Nr. 140). Weiter sollte der Provinzpromotor für die Laiengemeinschaften für seine Aufgabe teilweise freigestellt werden (Nr. 141).

Das letzte Thema handelte über „Recht und Wirtschaft" (Nrn. 146–170). Hier ging es v. a. um das Schicksal ehemaliger oder (noch) bestehender Niederlassungen: Die Akten meldeten die inzwischen vorgenommene Überführung der Gebäude und bestimmter Liegenschaften des ehemaligen Klosters Retz in eine Stiftung und die Übertragung des Verkaufspreises anderer Liegenschaften in das Vermögen des österreichischen Provinzteils (Nr. 148), was ebenso mit den Besitztümern und Liegenschaften des am 9. Juli 2010 aufgehobenen Klosters in Friesach geschehen war (Nr. 149). Die Anordnung des Provinzkapitels von 2006 über die Schließung von St. Katharina / München hatte „wegen verschiedener Umstände seitens der Erzdiözese München-Freising noch nicht umgesetzt werden" können, allerdings wurde der Provinzial mit dem Vollzug dieses Beschlusses beauftragt (Nr. 150). Aber es wurde nicht nur geschlossen: Inzwischen hatte auch der Plan, die Präsenz in Freiburg weiter auszubauen, zu Ergebnissen geführt und der Provinz war die Innenstadtkirche St. Martin mit einem geräumigen Pfarrhaus übertragen worden. Daher wurde der Provinzial um die Einleitung der nötigen Schritte zur Erhebung der neuen Niederlassung zu vollen Konventsrechten gebeten (Nr. 152); gleichzeitig sollte das Kloster St. Albert in Freiburg zur *domus filialis* von St. Martin reduziert werden (Nr. 153). Von den weiteren Feststellungen ragte noch eine heraus, die hier zitiert werden soll:

> „Im Zusammenhang mit den Missbrauchsfällen in der Kirche in Deutschland und Österreich stellen wir fest: In unserer Provinz wurden bisher keine Anschuldigungen in dieser Richtung erhoben. Dennoch rufen wir die für solche Fälle getroffenen Bestimmungen in Erinnerung. Für Deutschland gelten die Richtlinien der Deutschen Ordensoberenkonferenz. Für Österreich gilt die Vereinbarung zwischen der österreichischen Bischofskonferenz und der Superiorenkonferenz der männlichen Orden Österreichs" (Nr. 162).

Abgeschlossen wurden die Akten durch den Abdruck des überarbeiteten Provinzstatuts (S. 40–42). In seinem Bestätigungsschreiben vom 2. März 2011 lobte der Ordensmeister die Beschlüsse des Provinzkapitels und hob vor allem die bezüglich der Maßnahmen um Teambildung unter Einbindung der Laien, bezüglich der Versorgung der alten Brüder und über die Ausbildung hervor (S. VI–IX).

Nachrichtenorgane der Provinz nach 1990

Neben den Provinzkapitelsakten stellen auch die verschiedenen von der Provinz herausgegebenen Publikationen für die Zeit nach 1990 die historiographisch verwendbaren Quellen dar. Hier ist an erster Stelle der Provinzrundbrief zu nennen. Von 1939 bis einschließlich Dezember 1991 bestand dieser aus Mitteilungen in der Form eines offenen Briefes des Provinzials an seine Mitbrüder, die das Provinzoberhaupt zusammentippte und in unregelmäßiger Folge – oft mehrmals, manchmal nur einmal im Jahr – an die Konvente und Brüder versandte. Bis 1966 enthielten diese Rundschreiben auch die Jahresarbeitsberichte der Niederlassungen. Diese fielen dann weg, dafür kamen Nachrichten aus dem weltweiten Orden hinzu. Adressaten der Rundschreiben waren die Brüder; einige wenige, meist die inhaltlich eher allgemein gehaltenen, wurden auch an die Dominikanerinnenklöster verschickt.

Das Provinzkapitel von 1990 hatte eine Erweiterung des Adressatenkreises dieser Mitteilungen angeregt und gewünscht, „dass zweimal jährlich ein Provinzbrief der dominikanischen Familie“ erscheinen sollte.[541] Dieses Anliegen wurde im Sommer 1992 umgesetzt: Unter Beibehaltung des Namens „Provinzrundbrief“ erstellte nun ein Redaktionsteam ein halbjährlich erscheinendes Heft im Umfang zwischen 24 und 40 Seiten, mit einem Grußwort des Provinzials, hauptsächlich bestehend aus Nachrichten aus den Schwestern- und Laiengemeinschaften der Provinz und dem gesamten Orden. Dieser Rundbrief neuen Typs besaß eher den Charakter einer Zeitung; da sein Inhalt aber für einen breiteren Personenkreis bestimmt war, fielen die provinzinternen Informationen – etwa die Protokolle der Provinzkonsilssitzungen – nun aus, auch wenn immer noch über wichtige Entscheidungen berichtet wurde. Aufgrund eines häufigen Wechsels in der

541 APKap 1990, S. 18, Nr. 51.

Leitung des Redaktionsteams – bedingt durch andere Arbeitsaufgaben für die jeweils zuständigen Brüder – ließ sich der ursprünglich vorgesehene Herausgaberhythmus des „Provinzrundbriefs" nicht immer durchhalten. In den Jahren 1992 bis einschließlich 1999 kamen insgesamt dreizehn Ausgaben heraus.[542] Durch diese Umstellung des Rundbriefs gelang tatsächlich eine Verbesserung des Informationsflusses zwischen den Konventen und den verschiedenen Zweigen des Ordens in der Provinz. Dem trugen die beiden letzten Ausgaben (für 1999) durch den Versuch einer Professionalisierung Rechnung: Bisher war der Rundbrief im Format DIN-A-4 einfach fotokopiert und geklammert worden, nun wurde im Format von 240 x 170 mm gedruckt. Die beiden Hefte hatten einen Umfang von 32 Seiten; ihre Umschlagseiten wurden farbig gestaltet und anstatt „Provinzrundbrief der Dominikanerprovinz des hl. Albert in Süddeutschland und Österreich" hieß sie nun „Dominikus. Mitteilungen der Dominikanischen Familie in Süddeutschland und Österreich".

Die beiden Ausgaben des „Dominikus" von 1999 fanden einen sehr großen Anklang. Dieses gute Echo machte klar, dass ein für eine weitere, über die Belange der Dominikanischen Familie reichende Öffentlichkeit gedachtes Mitteilungsblatt im Interesse der Provinz lag – unter anderem auch, weil das Heft des Dominikuswerkes im Jahr 2000 seine letzte Ausgabe erlebte und damit als Möglichkeit zur Spendengewinnung wegfiel. Gleichzeitig bestand aber das Problem des mit der Herausgabe einer interessanten und vielseitigen Publikation verbundenen Aufwandes an Mühe und Zeit, da der herausgebende Bruder hauptberuflich in ganz anderen Bereichen tätig war. Daher wurde die Idee eines häufiger im Jahr publizierten Rundbriefs aufgegeben und der Weg ausgewählt, den das Heft des Dominikuswerkes so erfolgreich beschritten hatte: Aus dem „Dominikus" wurde ein Jahrbuch, das von 2000 bis 2010 regelmäßig erschien, jeweils zwischen 42 und 56 Seiten stark und reich bebildert. Mit dem Heft für 2005 wurde der Untertitel verändert; die Publikation hieß nun „Dominikus. Aus Leben und Wirken der Dominikanischen Familie in Süddeutschland und Österreich" – dies deutete das Profil an, welches die „Dominikus"-Jahr-

---

542 Konkret erschienen die von P. Philippe-André Holzer besorgten fünf Nummern 1–1992 bis 1–1994 wirklich halbjährlich; die Ausgabe 2–1994 erschien nicht. P. Dietmar Thomas Schon besorgte zwei Ausgaben für das Jahr 1995. 1996 erschien kein „Provinzrundbrief" wegen schwerer Erkrankung des Provinzials. P. Wolfram Hoyer brachte für 1997 eine Ausgabe heraus, 1998 drei und 1999 mit Veränderungen (siehe oben) zwei.

Abb. 70: Umschlag der ersten Ausgabe des Jahrbuchs Dominikus, 2000.

bücher von Anfang an hatten: Der private, wenn man so will, intimere Charakter der alten Rundbriefe war nun völlig durch ein Mitteilungsblatt ersetzt worden.

Parallel zur Umgestaltung des Provinzrundbriefs kam es im österreichischen Provinzteil zu einer eigenen publizistischen Initiative: Als Ergebnis einer Begegnung der Dominikanischen Familie im Frühjahr 1991 im Wiener Konvent fasste ein kleines Team unter der Leitung von P. Max Svoboda den Beschluss, ein halbjährlich erscheinendes Informations- und Kommunikationsblatt herauszugeben, das zunächst nur zur Weitergabe von Terminen und Veranstaltungen für die Brüder, Schwestern und Laien im Wiener Raum gedacht war, aber bald an die Klöster und Gruppen des Ordens in ganz Österreich versandt wurde.[543] Unter dem Titel „Der Funke. Informationsblatt für Mitglieder und Freunde der Dominikanischen Familie" erschienen, beginnend im Herbst 1992 bis zum Sommer 1998, insgesamt elf einfach gestaltete Hefte. Das erste bestand nur aus einem fotokopierten Doppelblatt; in ihm wurden nach einem Grußwort nur Veranstaltungstermine weitergegeben. Bereits die folgenden Ausgaben besaßen einen Umfang von zwanzig Seiten und beinhalteten darüber hinaus Text- und Artikelsammlungen zu Themen, die für die verschiedenen Zweige des Ordens von Interesse waren.[544] Diese Initiative endete leider, als P. Svo-

543 Siehe *Der Funke* (Herbst 1992) S. 2 und (Frühjahr 1994) S. 10; zur Zielsetzung auch: PA, Provinzrundbrief 2–1993, S. 32–33.

544 So wurde z. B. in der Ausgabe von *Der Funke* im Frühjahr 1994, S. 6–10 das Direktorium der Laiengemeinschaften des Dominikanerordens in der Provinz des hl. Albert in Süddeutschland und Österreich abgedruckt; in der Herbstausgabe 1994 wurden Vita und Schriften Heinrich Seuses vorgestellt, das Herbstheft 1995 war dem evangelischen Rat der Armut gewidmet; die beiden Hefte des Jahres 1998 waren dem 4. Treffen der Landesverantwortlichen der dominikanischen Laiengemeinschaften gewidmet, das in Wien statt-

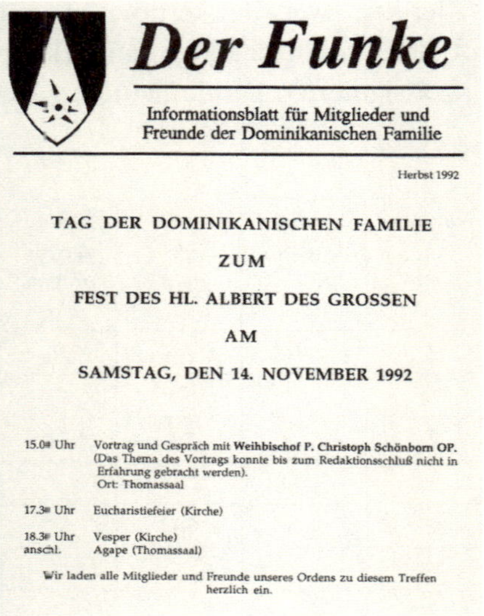

Der Funke

Informationsblatt für Mitglieder und Freunde der Dominikanischen Familie

Herbst 1992

TAG DER DOMINIKANISCHEN FAMILIE

ZUM

FEST DES HL. ALBERT DES GROSSEN

AM

SAMSTAG, DEN 14. NOVEMBER 1992

15.00 Uhr	Vortrag und Gespräch mit **Weihbischof P. Christoph Schönborn OP.** (Das Thema des Vortrags konnte bis zum Redaktionsschluß nicht in Erfahrung gebracht werden). Ort: Thomassaal
17.30 Uhr	Eucharistiefeier (Kirche)
18.30 Uhr	Vesper (Kirche)
anschl.	Agape (Thomassaal)

Wir laden alle Mitglieder und Freunde unseres Ordens zu diesem Treffen herzlich ein.

Abb. 71: Titelblatt der ersten Ausgabe des Bulletins Der Funke, Herbst 1992.

bodas Arbeitsfelder sich änderten, allerdings gelang es dem „Funken“ mit einfachsten Mitteln, eine Lücke in den Kommunikationsabläufen in der Provinz zu füllen, an die das „Dominikus“-Jahrbuch wegen seiner völlig anderen Konzeption nicht herankam. Anders gesagt: Ein Medium zur aktuellen und kurzfristigen Information fehlte.

Abhilfe sollte durch ein neues Projekt geschaffen werden: Ab dem Jahr 2004 veröffentlichte das Provinzialat eine „ProvinzZeitung“. Diese erschien bis 2009 monatlich, 2010 zweimonatlich. Ihre meist 12 bis 14 Seiten starken Hefte im Vierfarbdruck wandten sich nicht mehr nur an die Mitbrüder und -schwestern, sondern waren für alle am Predigerorden Interessierten gedacht, weswegen alle Ausgaben auch im PDF-Format auf der Homepage der Provinz im Internet einsehbar waren. Aus Gründen des finanziellen und des Arbeitsaufwandes wurde der Druck der ProvinzZeitung Ende 2010 aufgegeben. Seit August 2012 erscheint sie im Abstand von zwei bis drei Monaten nur mehr in elektronischer Form, als über Email verschicktes PDF-Dokument.

Die Personalentwicklung 1984 bis 2013

Die Zahlen

Die Achillesferse aller Planungen und Unternehmungen der Provinz blieb die Personalentwicklung. Wir haben oben bereits festgestellt, dass die Zahl der in der Provinz tätigen Dominikaner bis 1984 auf 82 zurückgegangen

---

fand. Darüber hinaus wurden auch regelmäßig Dominikanerinnenklöster oder Laiengemeinschaften vorgestellt.

war (61 Priester, 13 Laienbrüder, fünf Kleriker, zwei Klerikernovizen und ein Laienbrudernovize). Laut Auskunft der Provinzkataloge entwickelte sich der Personalstand der in der Provinz assignierten Dominikaner in absoluten Zahlen wie folgt:

Katalog	*Priester*	*Laien-brüder*	*Kleriker*	*Novizen*	*ständiger Diakon*	*Gesamt-summe*	*Summe der filii provin-ciae*
1987	59	11	5	2		77	70
1989	62	10	5	2		79	71
1991	56	9	6	2		73	66
1994	51	8	5	3		67	60
1997	48	8	2	2		60	57
1999	45	7	3	3		58	54
2000	47	9	3	3		62	58
2003	45	3	4	3	1	56	48
2004	47	2	7	2	1	59	52
2005	43	1	6	3	1	54	49
2006	44	1	8	2	1	56	50
2007	43	1	9		1	54	50
2008	42	1	8	2	1	54	50
2009	42	1	8		1	52	48
2010	45	1	8	3	1	58	53
2011	50	2	3	1	1	57	53
2013	49	2	5	2	1	59	50

Zur Interpretation dieser Zahlen ist der Hinweis wichtig, dass das vorhandene Datenmaterial ungleichmäßig auf der Zeitachse verteilt ist: In den 13 Jahren von 1987 (dem Stichjahr für den auf 1984 folgenden Provinzkatalog) bis 2003 kamen insgesamt acht Provinzkataloge heraus; in den neun Jahren von 2004 bis 2013 hingegen neun (was in der Tabelle durch die Leerzeilen ausgedrückt wird).[545]

Zu fast allen obigen Stichjahren verzeichnen die Provinzkataloge Novizen; die Provinz hatte also Nachwuchs – konkret hauptsächlich die Priesterbrüder, die Laienbrüder kaum. Allerdings genügt es nicht, nur die absolute Gesamtsumme aller assignierten Dominikaner zu betrachten: Wie schon seit Beginn der Provinz gehörten zu ihren Konventen als Vollmitglieder mit allen Rechten auch Mitbrüder, die nicht aus der Germania superior et Austria stammten. Zieht man die zu anderen Provinzen gehörenden Dominikaner vom absoluten Personalstand ab, erhält man die Zahl der sogenannten *filii provinciae*, also der über die Provinz in den Orden eingetretenen Brüder.[546] Die obige Entwicklung dieser *filii*-Zahl macht deutlich, dass der Personalrückgang, den die Provinz seit den 1960er Jahren verzeichnete, danach zwar nicht vollends aufgehört hatte, aber seit 1984 mehrfach erfolgreich ausgebremst worden war. Wie stark sich der Nachwuchs wirklich in die Personalentwicklung der letzten Jahrzehnte einbrachte, wird durch die Untersuchung des Professalters der *filii provinciae* deutlich. Hierzu genügt ein Blick in den Provinzkatalog von 2013. Von den dort genannten 50 Provinzmitgliedern hatten 48 Profess gemacht (zwei waren noch Novizen, also ohne Profess), nämlich:

Profess vor 1950:	5
Profess zwischen 1950 und 1959:	9
Profess zwischen 1960 und 1969:	5
Profess zwischen 1970 und 1979:	3
Profess zwischen 1980 und 1989:	7
Profess zwischen 1990 und 1999:	4
Profess zwischen 2000 und 2009:	12
Profess nach 2010:	3

545 Hinzuweisen ist auch darauf, dass die oben genannten Provinzkataloge nicht zum gleichen Stichtag erschienen. Dieses Problem kann aber für den Zweck eines Überblicks vernachlässigt werden.

546 Dominikaner können auch vom Ordensmeister aus einer Provinz in eine andere transfiliiert werden. Abgesehen von Provinzneugründungen handelt es sich dabei aber um einzelne Ausnahmefälle; im Fragezeitraum waren es zwei.

Erkennbar ist der Ausfall einer ganzen Generation: Aus der Zeit der Personal- und Nachwuchskrise der 1960er und 1970er Jahre waren 2013 in der Provinz weniger Mitbrüder übrig (acht) als selbst aus den Jahren vor 1959 (14). Über die Hälfte (26) der *filii provinciae* waren hingegen in den letzten dreißig Jahren eingetreten.

Dieser Befund macht die Art der Reaktion bzw. des Fehlens einer solchen auf die Krisenlage in den Provinzkapitelsakten der 1980er Jahre verständlich: Die Provinz wurde bis etwa 1990 hauptsächlich auf den Schultern der Brüder getragen, die vor 1960 in den Orden eingetreten waren. In den 1980er Jahren liefen die Eintrittszahlen nur ganz langsam wieder an; bedingt durch die lange Studien- und Ausbildungszeit bis zur Priesterweihe konnten die jüngeren Kräfte erst zu Beginn der 1990er Jahre aktiv an der Seelsorge teilhaben. Wenn auch die absolute Personalzahl der *filii provinciae* 2013 mit 50 Dominikanern für sich selbst nicht gerade beeindruckend ist, so zeigt die Verteilung des Professalters die Provinz als gesund strukturiert. Die kleine *filii*-Gesamtzahl erklärt auch die im selben Zeitraum 1984 bis 2013 vorgenommenen Schließungen von Niederlassungen.

Aber kehren wir zurück zur Gesamtzahl der assignierten Dominikaner. Hier ist noch ein weiterer Trend zu erwähnen, nämlich der Rückgang der *extra conventum* wohnenden und arbeitenden Brüder. Laut Auskunft der Provinzkataloge pendelte von 1984 bis 1994 deren Zahl zwischen elf und sechs; von 1997 bis 2003 waren es sechs, danach zwischen zwei und vier. Noch in den 1980er Jahren gab es also das schon vorher beobachtbare Phänomen, dass ein größerer Teil der Provinzmitglieder (1987 immerhin etwa ein Siebtel der Gesamtzahl) nicht im jeweiligen Assignationskloster wohnte. In den 1990er Jahren lag der Grund dafür meist in ihrem Umzug in den Ruhestand, in ein Schwesternkloster oder in ein Altenheim; nur mehr einige wenige *extra conventum* lebende Brüder gingen Lehr- und Seelsorgsaufträgen nach.[547]

Auch stellte die Provinz weiterhin Brüder für den Dienst für den weltweiten Orden, außerhalb ihres Gebiets, *extra provinciam*, zur Verfügung. Zwar melden die Provinzkataloge hier zum Teil sehr hohe Zahlen – so waren es zwischen 1984 und 2000 fünf bis sieben, 2003 sogar neun, um danach wieder zwischen drei und sieben zu pendeln – aber dies hatte haupt-

547 Der PKat 2013 zählt zwar wieder sechs Brüder *extra conventum* auf, was aber mit einer durch die Schließung der Klöster in Friesach und Graz notwendigen Umstrukturierung zu tun hatte.

sächlich damit zu tun, dass Studenten der Provinz für ein oder mehrere Ausbildungsjahre an ausländische Hochschulen geschickt wurden bzw. die Novizen ihr Noviziatsjahr in der Teutonia in Worms machten. Wirklich permanent außerhalb der Provinz wirkte in diesem Zeitraum nur eine kleine Gruppe von drei bis vier Brüdern.

Deutlich größer war hingegen die Unterstützung, die die Klöster der Provinz vom weltweiten Orden erhielten, also durch *filii* anderer Provinzen, die in die Niederlassungen der Provinz assigniert waren. Deren absolute Zahlen pendelten von 1984 bis 2013 zwischen vier und neun – ihr genauer Zahlenverlauf lässt sich aus der obigen Tabelle leicht als Unterschied zwischen der Gesamtsumme des Provinzpersonals und der *filii provinciae* ablesen. Dabei handelte es sich zum einen um Nachbarschaftshilfe aus der Teutonia und der slowakischen (Vize-)Provinz, ab 2003 waren es aber auch Brüder aus der indischen und der nigerianischen Provinz, sowie seit 2011 aus den Provinzen von Kolumbien und Vietnam. Gerade die Zusammenarbeit mit der indischen Provinz, die 1997 begonnen worden war, erwies sich für Süddeutschland und Österreich als besonders fruchtbar.[548] Die meisten dieser Brüder aus anderen Entitäten des weltweiten Ordens kamen zu Studienzwecken nach Süddeutschland und Österreich, leisteten darüber hinaus aber wesentliche seelsorgliche Beiträge und übernahmen Provinzämter. Nicht zu unterschätzen waren die positiven Impulse für das Klosterleben, die diese Internationalisierung in den letzten zwanzig Jahren für die Konvente brachte: Die meisten der in den 1970er Jahren entstandenen „Kerngemeinschaften“ in den Niederlassungen nahmen dadurch im eigenen Haus von außen kommende Anregungen auf und wurden so automatisch dazu gebracht, wieder über den eigenen Tellerrand hinauszublicken.

Ab 1987 melden die Provinzkataloge ein neues Phänomen, nämlich Dominikaner anderer Provinzen, die zwar in Süddeutschland oder Österreich lebten und arbeiteten, aber nicht in die Niederlassungen der Provinz assigniert waren. Deren Zahl wuchs kontinuierlich, von sieben (1987) auf 15 (1997) und pendelte danach zwischen 13 und 20 pro Jahr. Manche dieser nicht assignierten Brüder lebten für längere Zeit als Gäste in Häusern der Germania superior et Austria, gingen kategorialen Seelsorgsaufgaben nach oder betreuten Dominikanerinnenklöster. Der Anstieg ihrer Zahl nach 1994 verdankte sich der Übernahme des Hauses St. Albert in Mün-

548 Siehe dazu: PA, Provinzrundbrief 3–1998, S. 10–11 und *St. Dominikuswerk* (2000) S. 5–6.

chen-Freimann und der Pfarrei St. Gertrud durch die polnische Provinz sowie der Übernahme des Klosters in Retz durch die slowakische Provinz.

Noviziat und Studentat

Mit dem Umzug des Noviziats 1986 von Graz nach Wien hatte sich die Provinz für ihre Novizen und Studenten ein Ausbildungszentrum geschaffen. Dies wurde vom Provinzkonsil mit einem Beschluss vom 11. November 1987 unterstrichen, dementsprechend „alle Mitbrüder, die in der Ausbildung stehen, in den Wiener Konvent assigniert werden" sollten.[549]

1981 hatten die Studenten im Wiener Konvent, die zu dieser Zeit ja selber noch Gäste dort waren, für Interessierte die Möglichkeit eröffnet, während der Kar- und Ostertage im Kloster mitzuleben und an der Liturgie teilzunehmen. Dies fand Anklang – nicht nur bei einzelnen Teilnehmern, die über diese unverbindliche Kontaktaufnahme mit dem Orden den Weg in das Noviziat fanden, sondern auch bei der Klostergemeinschaft, die sich durch die Anwesenheit einer größeren Gruppe junger Menschen bei diesem Hauptfest bereichert fand. Darüber hinaus hielt Novizenmeister Hilarius Barth auch immer wieder Besinnungs- und Einkehrtage oder -wochenenden ab, die inner- oder außerhalb Wiens stattfanden. Ab 1985 konzentrierte er diese Bemühungen im Kloster Bronnbach bei Wertheim im Main-Tauber-Kreis. Da Barth für diesen Ort weiterreichende Perspektiven sah, bat er 1990 um seine Entpflichtung als Novizenmeister, um in Bronnbach eine Seelsorgsstelle aufzubauen.[550] Sein Nachfolger wurde P. Max Svoboda, zunächst als Pro-Magister, ab Sommer 1990 als Novizenmeister.

Anfang Januar 1990 ergab sich eine weitere Veränderung im Wiener Noviziat: Die ungarische Provinz hatte sich nach dem Fall des Kommunismus neu konstituiert.[551] Sie besaß zwar noch keine Klöster, aber Brüder, die zum Teil viele Jahre als Dominikaner im Untergrund gelebt hatten, außerdem inzwischen auch einen Novizen. Daher bat sie darum, dass dieser sein Noviziat in Wien weitermachen und vollenden durfte. Außerdem schickte sie zusätzlich einen als Novizenmeister vorgesehenen Pater mit, der zwar schon seit vielen Jahren Priester und Ordensmann war, aber sich Anregun-

549 PA, Provinzrundbrief vom 22.12.1987, S. 4, mit Bezug auf die Provinzkonsilssitzung in Augsburg vom 11.11.1987.

550 PA, Provinzialsregestenbuch 1 (1966–2010), Eintrag vom 1.1.1990, Nr. 1.

551 Siehe dazu auch: PA, Provinzrundbrief vom 2.7.1989, S. 1–2.

gen für seine zukünftige Tätigkeit erhoffte, nachdem sein eigenes Noviziat unter schwierigsten und unzulänglichen Bedingungen abgelaufen war. Beide Mitbrüder mussten zunächst erst Deutsch erlernen.[552] Die guten Erfahrungen, die beide Provinzen mit dem gemeinsamen Noviziatsprojekt machten, führten zu seiner Wiederholung, so dass 1990/91 zwei weitere Ungarn in Wien ihr Noviziat begannen.[553] Im Noviziatsjahr 1991/92 besaß die ungarische Provinz sieben Novizen – zu viele, als dass sie in Wien hätten Unterkunft finden können. Die süddeutsch-österreichische Provinz bot daher die Übernahme eines Stockwerks im Grazer Kloster an, wohin dieser Noviziatsjahrgang zusammen mit seinem ungarischen Novizenmeister zog.[554] Fünf der Novizen machten Profess. Der eine ungarische Novize des Jahrgangs 1992/93 konnte in der eigenen Provinz untergebracht werden,[555] aber für 1993/94 kehrte das ungarische Noviziat, bestehend aus Novizenmeister, Submagister und zwei Novizen, noch einmal nach Graz zurück.[556] Erst im Mai 1995 war der Ausbau des von den Dominikanern betreuten Pfarrhauses in Budapest fertig, sodass die Noviziatsausbildung dort ohne Hilfe aus Österreich stattfinden konnte.[557] Offiziell wurde das ungarische Noviziat in Graz aber erst am 19. April 1996 für beendet erklärt.[558]

In gewisser Weise war die Gastfreundschaft für die ungarischen Novizen Frucht einer jahrzehntelangen Unterstützung der während der sozialistischen Jahre in Ungarn im Untergrund lebenden Dominikaner gewesen. Vor allem P. Innozenz Varga hatte während seiner Amtszeit als Provinzial die Kontakte nach Ungarn, Jugoslawien, Polen und der Tschechoslowakei aufrecht erhalten und den dortigen Mitbrüdern Spenden und andere Hilfe zukommen lassen. Da dies im Geheimen stattfinden musste, fehlen naturgemäß zitierbare Akten, und aus den wenigen Andeutungen der vorhandenen Quellen lässt sich diese Untergrundhilfe leider nicht näher beschreiben. Allerdings ist die freundschaftliche Bereitwilligkeit, mit der die Brüder aus den nach 1989 neu entstandenen östlichen Nachbarprovinzen die süddeutsch-österreichischen Dominikaner unterstützten, ein deutlicher Hinweis auf diese Hilfeleistung der 1960er bis 1980er Jahre.

552 PA, Provinzrundbrief vom 2.2.1990, S. 5.
553 PA, Provinzrundbrief vom 1.12.1990, S. 3.
554 PA, Provinzrundbrief vom „Dezember" 1991, S. 3 und 6.
555 PA, Provinzrundbrief 2–1992, S. 4.
556 *St. Dominikuswerk* (1994) S. 11.
557 *St. Dominikuswerk* (1995) S. 9.
558 PA, Provinzialsregestenbuch 2 (1966–2010), Eintrag vom 19.4.1996, Nr. 13.

Da P. Wehrle 1990 aus gesundheitlichen Gründen als Studentenmeister ausschied, übernahm Svoboda interimsmäßig auch die Aufgaben eines Pro-Studentenmeisters.[559] Das Provinzkapitel vom Sommer 1990 setzte ihn dann auch in dieses Amt ein.[560] Für die folgenden Jahre herrschte damit die ziemlich bemerkenswerte Situation, dass es nicht nur ein Ausbildungszentrum in der Provinz gab, sondern auch beide Zweige, Noviziat und Studentat, von derselben Person geleitet wurden. Dies änderte sich erst durch das Provinzkapitel von 1994, das P. Martin Staszak zum Studentenmagister einsetzte.[561]

Dasselbe Provinzkapitel führte das schon angesprochene Tutorenmodell in die Ausbildung ein. Dadurch ergaben sich zwei wesentliche Veränderungen: Zum einen war Wien nun nicht mehr das einzige Ausbildungshaus der Provinz, sondern theoretisch kamen alle formalrechtlichen Konvente als Wohnstätten der Studenten in Frage, neben Wien also auch Graz, St. Kajetan in München, Augsburg und Freiburg. Tatsächlich wurden in den folgenden Jahren Studenten nach Wien, Graz, St. Kajetan und Augsburg assigniert. Zum zweiten änderte sich die Rolle des Studentenmagisters, weg vom Erstzuständigen für die geistliche und disziplinarische Formung jedes Studenten, wie es die Ordenssatzungen vorsahen,[562] hin zu „Begleitung und Koordination der Ausbildung in den verschiedenen Konventen, in denen Studenten mit ihren Tutoren leben", sowie zum Organisator des Diakonatskurses.[563] Nicht der Magister benannte die möglichen Tutoren, sondern der Ausbildungsrat; nicht der Magister bestimmte den Tutor für den einzelnen Studenten, sondern der Student wählte selbst seinen Betreuer.[564] Damit kam dem Studentenmagister eher eine Verwaltungsaufgabe auf Provinzebene zu – abgesehen natürlich von dem Fall, in dem Studenten, die im Assignationskonvent des Magisters wohnten, ihn zu ihrem Tutor erbaten. Entsprechend dieses Tutorenmodells wurde auch die *Ratio formationis particularis*, der provinzeigene Ausbildungsplan gestaltet, den die römische Ordenskurie am 9. Januar 1996 approbierte.[565]

---

559 Ebd., Eintrag vom 1.3.1990, Nr. 12.
560 APKap 1990, S. 17, Nr. 40.
561 APKap 1994, S. 22, Nr. 65.
562 LCO 2010, S. 90, Nr. 159.
563 APKap 1994, S. 21, Nr. 58.
564 Ebd., S. 21, Nr. 60.
565 Datum laut: PA, Ratio formationis particularis der Dominikanerprovinz des hl. Albert des Großen in Süddeutschland und Österreich vom 9. Januar 1996. Geändert durch das Provinzkapitel von 1998 und das Provinzkapitel von 2002. Stand: 15. Juli 2003, S. 3.

Ausgerechnet nach Einführung des neuen Modells nahm die Zahl der Novizen in der Provinz jedoch wieder ab, was in der Praxis zur Vereinzelung der Studenten in den Konventen führte. Das Provinzkapitel von 1998 suchte daher nach einem „Mittelweg zwischen der sehr uniformen alten und der sehr individuellen neuen Form der Ausbildung“[566] und reduzierte die Zahl der möglichen Ausbildungskonvente auf drei – Wien, St. Kajetan und Augsburg – sowie die Zahl der möglichen Tutoren in diesen Konventen auf zwei. Außerdem regte das Provinzkapitel notwendige genaue Bestimmungen zur praktischen Durchführung des Modells und zur Kompetenzbeschreibung der Funktionsträger in der *Ratio formationis particularis* an: Seinen Ausbildungsort durfte der Auszubildende dem Provinzial, bei dem das Assignationsrecht lag, nach Absprache mit dem Studienregens und dem Studentenmeister vorschlagen. Die Kompetenzen des Tutors im spirituellen, praktisch-apostolischen und gemeinschaftlichen Bereich sollten näher definiert werden, wobei der Tutor hier dem Studentenmagister verantwortlich und weisungsgebunden blieb. Für alle Mitbrüder in Ausbildung hatte der Studentenmagister Praktika, Exerzitien und gemeinsame Ausbildungseinheiten zu organisieren. Er hatte die Auszubildenden und ihre Tutoren mehrmals im Semester zu besuchen und Gespräche mit ihnen zu führen. Der Studienregens war ausschließlich für die (Universitäts-)Studien der Auszubildenden zuständig; auch er sollte die Studenten im Semester besuchen und sich ihrer Studienfortschritte vergewissern. Außerdem sollte er ordensinterne Studienveranstaltungen für die vorlesungsfreie Zeit organisieren. Auf die möglichst klare Aufgabentrennung zwischen Regens und Magister legte das Provinzkapitel großen Wert. Für die Festlegung des Diakonatskurses, dessen Organisation und die Begleitung des Diakons blieb weiterhin der Studentenmagister zuständig. Als Mittel zur Verstärkung einer Gemeinschaftsbildung innerhalb des auf mehrere Konvente verstreuten Studentats verwies das Provinzkapitel auf die gemeinsamen Ausbildungszeiten in den vorlesungsfreien Zeiträumen.[567]

Trotz dieser Feinabstimmungen hatte das Tutorenmodell nur mehr kurze Zeit Bestand. Das Provinzkapitel von 2002 nahm es nicht wieder auf. Stattdessen beschränkte es die Zahl der Ausbildungskonvente auf Augsburg und Wien und setzte als Studentenmagister P. Dominic Mendonca in Augs-

566 APKap 1998, S. 48, Nr. 153.
567 Ebd., S. 49, Nrn. 154.2, 154.3 und 155.

burg und als Submagister in Wien P. Christophe Holzer ein.[568] Von Tutoren war nicht mehr die Rede. Daraus ergab sich, dem offiziellen Sprachgebrauch der Provinz folgend, „eine faktische Suspension der Regeln über die Tutorenwahl, die Tutorenliste sowie ihre Ergänzungen" in der Ausbildungsordnung.[569] Das Faktum bestand allerdings wohl eher in der geringen Zahl der vorhandenen Studenten, von denen die meisten noch dazu im Studienjahr 2002/03 außerhalb des Provinzgebiets studierten.[570] Nach deren Rückkehr in die Provinz und nach der Professablegung des starken Noviziatsjahrganges 2002/03 hätte sich durchaus die Möglichkeit zur Weiterführung des Tutorensystems ergeben. Andererseits wurde das 1994 eingeführte System auch nicht restlos abgeschafft: Als positive Errungenschaft blieb die Möglichkeit mehrerer Ausbildungskonvente in der Provinz bestehen. Dies ermöglichte einen flexibleren Umgang mit Brüdern mit einfacher Profess, die vor ihrem Noviziat schon ein Theologiestudium abgeschlossen hatten bzw. eine andere Ausbildung machen oder beenden wollten, was in der Praxis ein besseres Eingehen auf die persönlichen Bedürfnisse des einzelnen Mitbruders erlaubte – also in den Worten des Provinzkapitels von 1998 einen Mittelweg zwischen der sehr uniformen alten Ausbildungsweise und der sehr individuellen neuen Form des Tutorenmodells.[571]

Am 2. Februar 2004 verlegte das Provinzkonsil den Sitz des süddeutschen Ausbildungskonvents von Augsburg nach Freiburg. Hintergrund dieser Maßnahme waren schon länger schwelende Gerüchte über eine etwaige Reduzierung der katholisch-theologischen Fakultät der Universität Augsburg sowie die nur mehr provisorisch nachbesetzten freigewordenen Professorenposten und andere Lehraufträge.[572] Zu dieser Reduktion kam es zwar nicht, aber das Provinzkapitel von 2006 bestätigte diese Verlegung des Ausbildungskonvents.[573] Durch die Assignation einiger Studenten

568 APKap 2002, S. 6, Nr. 16 und S. 29, Nr. 122.

569 PA, Ratio formationis particularis der Dominikanerprovinz des hl. Albert des Großen in Süddeutschland und Österreich vom 9. Januar 1996. Geändert durch das Provinzkapitel von 1998 und das Provinzkapitel von 2002. Stand: 15. Juli 2003, S. 6, Vorbemerkung.

570 Siehe PKat 2003, S. 33.

571 So machten z. B. – laut der Provinzkataloge für 2006, 2007, 2009 und 2010 – trotz der Festlegung von Wien und Freiburg als Ausbildungskonvente einzelne Mitbrüder Teile ihrer Ausbildung weiterhin in Augsburg.

572 PA, ProvinzZeitung 2–2004, S. 2–3 und APKap 2006, S. 17, Nr. 69.

573 APKap 2006, S. 18, Nr. 70.

nach Freiburg konnte über die Frage der Universitätsqualität hinaus noch ein weiteres Problem angegangen werden, nämlich die schwierige personelle Lage des Konvents in Freiburg. So verbrachte ab 2004 eine kleine Gruppe von Studenten zusammen mit dem Studentenmagister P. Martin Staszak bis 2009 fünf Jahre in einer Wohnung in der Erwinstraße in Freiburg. Für Wien bestimmte das Provinzkapitel von 2006 für ein Jahr P. Martin Gyöngyös zum Submagister und ab 1. September 2007 P. Viliam Doci.[574] Mangels Studentenzahlen wurden 2012 die Mitbrüder in Grundausbildung alle in Wien konzentriert und ab dem 1. September 2012 P. Thomas Gabriel Brogl zum Studentenmeister eingesetzt[575] – unter Beibehaltung der Option mit Freiburg als zweitem Ausbildungskonvent.

Einen weiteren Grund für die Aufgabe des Tutorenmodells hatte Ordensmeister Timothy Radcliffe schon in seinem Visitationsbericht 1998 genannt: Durch die immer kürzer werdende Personaldecke fiel es der Provinz schwerer, geeignete Mitbrüder für die Rolle des Ausbilders zu finden. Dies hatte sich bereits 1990 in der Notwendigkeit gezeigt, einen einzigen Bruder sowohl mit der Aufgabe des Novizen-, als auch mit der des Studentenmeisters zu beauftragen. P. Svoboda amtierte als Novizenmeister bis zum 30. Juni 2000, dann folgten ihm P. Rupert Johannes Mayer und ab 2002 P. Martin Gyöngyös in diesem Amt nach.[576] Allerdings war der Noviziatsjahrgang 1999/2000 der letzte, der sein Probejahr in Wien machte. Ab dem nachfolgenden Jahrgang gingen die Novizen der süddeutsch-österreichischen Provinz nach Worms, in den Noviziatskonvent der Teutonia. Schon vorher hatten die Postulanten und Novizen beider Provinzen gemeinsame Ausbildungszeiten durchgeführt. Die guten Erfahrungen damit – und der Personalmangel – veranlassten die Leiter und die Ausbildungsverantwortlichen der zwei deutschen Provinzen, die Zusammenarbeit nicht nur fortzusetzen, sondern noch zu verstärken. Am 16. Dezember 2002 schlossen die Teutonia und die Germania superior et Austria eine interprovinzielle Vereinbarung, laut der das Noviziat und Teile des Postulats in den Einrichtungen der Teutonia stattfanden.[577] Trotzdem ließ die

574 Ebd., S. 7, Nr. 16.
575 APKap 2011, S. 7, Nr. 16.
576 APKap 1998, S. 6, Nr. 13 und APKap 2002, S. 6, Nr. 15.
577 Text dieser Vereinbarung in: PA, Ratio formationis particularis der Dominikanerprovinz des hl. Albert des Großen in Süddeutschland und Österreich vom 9. Januar 1996. Geändert durch das Provinzkapitel von 1998 und das Provinzkapitel von 2002. Stand: 15.

süddeutsch-österreichische Provinz Wien als Noviziatskonvent fortbestehen und bestimmte auch weiterhin einen ihrer dortigen Mitbrüder zum Novizenmeister. Dies ermöglichte kirchenrechtlich nämlich, dass das gemeinsame Noviziat beider Provinzen auch Teile seiner Ausbildung in Wien durchführen konnte, ohne dass dadurch das kanonisch vorgeschriebene Noviziatsjahr unterbrochen und für die Novizen verlängert werden musste.[578]

Die Niederlassungen der Provinz 1984 bis 2013

Die Entwicklungen der Krisenzeit ließen keine der Niederlassungen der Provinz ungeschoren; es gab allerorts Veränderungen, bis hin zur Schließung mancher der Klöster. Auch gingen Häuser in andere Hände über. Allerdings gab es auch Neugründungsversuche.

„Sommerkloster" und Seelsorgsstelle Bronnbach

Wie schon erwähnt, spielte die ehemalige Zisterzienserabtei Bronnbach bei Wertheim im Main-Tauber-Kreis Ende der 1980er Jahre eine Rolle in der Noviziats- und Studentatsausbildung der Provinz. Die Güter dieses 1803 im Rahmen der Säkularisation aufgehobenen Klosters waren an die Fürsten Löwenstein-Wertheim-Rosenberg gekommen, die sie 1986 an den Landkreis Main-Tauber verkauften. Von 1921 bis 1931 hatte es dort einen Wiederbesiedelungsversuch durch Zisterzienser und von 1931 bis 1958 durch Kapuziner gegeben.[579] Zu den Dominikanern unterhielt die Fürstenfamilie alte und gute Kontakte: Der seinerzeitige Chef des Hauses, Fürst Karl Heinrich († 1921), war 1907 unter dem Ordensnamen Raimund in die Teutonia eingetreten und hatte seine letzten Lebensjahre als Predigerbruder verbracht.[580] In den Quellen der süddeutsch-österreichischen Provinz tauchte Bronnbach 1985 zum ersten Mal auf: Ein aus dem benachbarten Wertheim

---

Juli 2003, S. 38–42 (Anhang I); zur Vorgeschichte: ebd., S. 38, Präambel sowie *Dominikus* (2005) S. 24–27.

578 APKap 2002, S. 28, Nr. 119.

579 Daten laut: *Klosterführer aller Zisterzienserklöster im deutschsprachigen Raum*, S. 60.

580 Dazu: Siebertz: *Karl Fürst zu Löwenstein*, S. 513–568.

stammender Mitbruder hatte dort im Juli einen Dankgottesdienst zur Nachprimiz gefeiert.[581]

Bereits wenige Wochen später, im September 1985, war das Noviziat aus Wien mit seinem Novizenmeister einen Monat als Gäste des Fürsten in Bronnbach: „Der Aufenthalt diente als Noviziatspraktikum. Es sollte eine gesunde Mischung des dominikanischen Lebens von Kontemplation und apostolischem Wirken erprobt werden und Ordensinteressenten aus dem süddeutschen Raum eine Anlaufstelle geboten werden, wo sie unsere Art des Betens und Arbeitens miterleben und mittragen können. Der Versuch hat ein solch günstiges Echo gefunden, dass er 1986 auf breiterer Basis wiederholt werden soll." – was das Provinzkonsil auch erlaubte.[582]

Die „Sommerkloster Bronnbach" genannte und von Mitte Juli bis Ende September 1986 laufende Veranstaltung war mehr als ein bloßes Feriencamp: Die Brüder des Noviziats und des Studentats nahmen zusammen mit ihren Magistern daran teil, unterstützt von zwei Dominikanerinnen. Darüber hinaus gab es „für interessierte Leute die Möglichkeit, in dieser klösterlichen Gemeinschaft als Gast aktiv mitzuleben, mitzubeten und mitzuarbeiten. Insgesamt waren es wohl mehr als zwei Dutzend Personen, vorwiegend junge Studenten, die von Deutschland und Österreich her anreisten, um mehrere Tage oder auch Wochen in Bronnbach zu verbringen. Ein wichtiger Beweggrund für den Sommeraufenthalt war der Wunsch, jungen Leuten geistliches Leben erfahrbar zu machen …"[583] Für die Gläubigen in der näheren und ferneren Nachbarschaft wurde die von den Dominikanern sehr feierlich gestaltete Liturgie in der Abteikirche zu einem besonderen Anziehungspunkt. Dadurch erhielten die Sommerklosterinsassen aus der Umgebung große Unterstützung für ihr Leben in den alten und zum Teil sehr renovierungsbedürftigen Mauern.[584] Durch diese positiven Erfahrungen wurde das Interesse sowohl des Landrats der Main-Tauber-Kreises, als auch der Erzdiözese Freiburg an einem weiteren Verbleib der Dominikaner in Bronnbach geweckt. Die Erzdiözese wollte „sehr gerne eine Dauerlösung für Bronnbach begrüßen (zwei Mitbrüder für Daueraufgaben)."[585] Das

---

581 PA, Provinzrundbrief vom 25.9.1985, S. 4.

582 PA, Provinzrundbriefe „zum Osterfest" 1986: Zitat S. 5 (Beiblatt) und vom 18.7.1986, S. 3 mit Verweis auf die Erlaubnis des Provinzkonsils vom 25.6.1986.

583 *St. Dominikuswerk* (1987) S. 7.

584 Ebd.

585 So laut PA, Provinzrundbrief vom 22.6.1987, S. 3 (über die Provinzkonsilssitzung vom 20.5.1987 in Augsburg).

„Sommerkloster" wurde von Mitte Juli bis Mitte September 1987 ein weiteres Mal wiederholt. Laut Provinzial „wurde sichtbar, in Gesprächen mit den für dieses Haus Verantwortlichen, dass der Zeitpunkt für eine Entscheidung heranreifen muss, ob unsere Provinz dort eine Neugründung wagen oder sich wieder zurückziehen will."[586] P. Barth zeigte sich zur Übernahme einer Aufgabe in Bronnbach bereit, „allerdings in Zusammenarbeit mit Mitbrüdern, die daran Interesse haben (eventuell auch aus anderen Provinzen)."[587]

Diese Idee war in der Provinz umstritten – nicht nur vor dem Hintergrund der kurzen Personaldecke, die die Neugründung einer Niederlassung unklug erschienen ließ. Gerade die Studenten distanzierten sich in einem fünfseitigen Schreiben vom 28. Januar 1988 ausdrücklich davon: „Bronnbach war nie und ist nicht unser Projekt. Daher bitten wir, für eine Zukunftsplanung bezüglich Bronnbach nicht auf die Mitglieder des jetzigen Studentats zurückzugreifen." Als geeigneteren Ort für eine etwaige Neugründung schlugen sie stattdessen Nürnberg vor.[588]

Die Provinzleitung wollte aber einer Wiederbelebung von Bronnbach nicht im Wege stehen. Daher beschloss das Provinzkonsil am 18. Oktober 1988:

> „Die Provinz übernimmt die Seelsorgsstelle in Bronnbach ab 1. Juli 1990 und stellt dafür einen Priester zur Verfügung. Vorgesehen ist P. Hilarius Barth. Im Falle seiner zeitweisen oder dauernden Verhinderung benennt die Provinz einen anderen Priester, der in Bronnbach die Seelsorge ausübt. Bis zu diesem Zeitpunkt führt die Provinz die Seelsorge in Bronnbach in der bisherigen Form weiter (Weihnachten, Ostern und Sommer). Weiterhin bemüht sich die Provinz, bis zum Jahre 1992 zwei weitere Ordensmitglieder nach Bronnbach zu schicken, damit dort eine Ordensniederlassung gegründet werden kann."[589]

Zur Errichtung einer offiziellen Niederlassung des Ordens war aber mehr als ein Bruder notwendig. Das Provinzkapitel von 1990 bestätigte diesen

586 PA, Provinzrundbrief vom 22.12.1987, S. 2.
587 So laut PA, Provinzrundbrief vom 22.12.1987, S. 4 (über die Provinzkonsilssitzung vom 11.11.1987 in Augsburg).
588 PA, Provinzrundbrief vom 12.12.1988: fünfseitige Beilage des Briefs der Wiener Studenten an die Mitbrüder der Provinz, datiert Wien, 28.1.1988 (Zitat S. 3, der Vorschlag in Nürnberg: S. 4–5).
589 PA, Provinzrundbrief vom 22.12.1988, S. 3 (über die Provinzkonsilssitzung vom 18.10.1988).

Beschluss des Konsils, fügte aber hinzu: „Wenn bis zum 31.12.1992 keine drei Mitbrüder zur Verfügung stehen und deshalb das Haus nicht errichtet werden kann, dann soll die Provinz nach einer Übergangszeit von zwei Jahren ihre Verpflichtung in Bronnbach am 31.12.1994 beenden, es sei denn, das nächste Provinzkapitel würde etwas anderes beschließen." Es distanzierte sich auch „von der Benennung ‚Dominikaner-Kloster Bronnbach'. Im Zusammenhang mit dem ‚Projekt Bronnbach' darf diese Benennung noch nicht verwendet werden."[590]

Im Oktober 1990 traf sich Provinzial Ruf zu Gesprächen mit dem Freiburger Weihbischof Wolfgang Kirchgässner und dem Generalvikar der Erzdiözese Otto Bechtold zur Klärung der Bedingungen der Übernahme eines Seelsorgsposten in Bronnbach durch P. Barth. Dieser konnte am 11. November 1990 die Eröffnung der Seelsorgsstelle mit einem Hochamt in der Abteikirche feiern.[591]

Ein Jahr später war die dominikanische Präsenz in Bronnbach auf drei Patres angewachsen. Nach einem Besuch Ende Mai 1992 berichtete Ruf der Provinz über den Fortschritt in Bronnbach:

> „Die Gebäude werden jetzt etwas großzügiger renoviert. Sie gehören dem Main-Tauber-Kreis; das Erzbistum Freiburg hat mit dieser Behörde einen Nutzungsvertrag für das Klostergebäude abgeschlossen und stellt die Räume unserer Provinz für eine Ordensniederlassung zur Verfügung. Die Verträge wurden am 27. Januar 1992 in Freiburg abgeschlossen. Wenn wir uns dort niederlassen, können wir 25 Jahre mietfrei wohnen. Ob wir ein Haus gründen werden, hängt von einem Verfahren ab, das ich mit den dortigen Mitbrüdern eingeleitet habe. Ziel dieses Vorgangs ist, ein Kloster zu gründen, das nicht als eine Randerscheinung angesehen wird, sondern von der ganzen Provinz maximale Annahme erfährt. Deshalb sollen die Pastoralplanung, die Liturgiegestaltung, die wirtschaftlichen Belange und die Ordnung des Lebens im Kloster von den Mitbrüdern durchdacht und erprobt werden, damit gegen Ende des Jahres, wenn der Termin für den Auftrag einer Gründung abläuft, eine überlegte Entscheidung getroffen werden kann. Selbstverständliche Voraussetzung für die Gründung ist die Zusage von drei Mitbrüdern, dass sie ihren Aufenthalt … für die nächsten Jahre im Kloster Bronnbach nehmen werden."[592]

---

590 APKap 1990, S. 16, Nr. 35.
591 PA, Provinzrundbrief vom 1.12.1990, S. 4 und 5.
592 PA, Provinzrundbrief 1–1992, S. 3.

Aber genau daran haperte es, weil einer der drei sich für Bronnbach interessierenden Brüder zuerst seine Dissertation fertigstellen wollte, ohne dafür aber in Bronnbach wohnen zu können. Daher verschob das Provinzkonsil die Entscheidung über die Gründung einer Niederlassung um ein Jahr, auf den 31. Dezember 1993.[593] In der Zwischenzeit wurde die Renovierung des Klostertraktes in Bronnbach auf Kosten des Landes Baden-Württemberg, der Erzdiözese Freiburg und des Landkreises Main-Tauber fertiggestellt, die mit Wohn- und Gemeinschaftsräumen für acht Ordensleute und einer Ausbaumöglichkeit für weitere fünf Ordensleute sehr großzügig bemessen war.[594] Am 28. Mai 1994 wurden diese Gebäude offiziell der Erzdiözese Freiburg übergeben.[595] Dennoch errichtete die Provinz dort keine Niederlassung, da sich letztlich doch keine zwei weiteren Brüder fanden, die sich in Bronnbach niederlassen wollten. Provinzial Gregor Ruf meldete daher im Provinzrundbrief: „Im Februar 1995 habe ich einen Konsilsbeschluss durchgeführt und in vollem Einverständnis mit der Erzdiözese Freiburg das Experiment ‚Bronnbach' geschlossen. Es war nichts aufzuheben, weil eine Ordensniederlassung zu keiner Zeit bestanden hatte."[596] Auch P. Barth wurde abgezogen und andernorts eingesetzt. Im Jahre 2000 übernahm die Kongregation der Missionare der hl. Familie die Seelsorgsstelle.

Wien

Mehr oder weniger unbeschadet überlebte der Wiener Konvent die Krisenzeit. Laut Auskunft der Provinzkataloge fluktuierte der Stand des assignierten Personals im Kloster nach 1965 sehr, bedingt durch seine Rolle als Ausbildungskonvent:[597]

---

593 So laut PA, Provinzrundbrief 2–1992, S. 6 (über die Provinzkonsilssitzung vom 21.10.1992).

594 PA, Provinzrundbrief 2–1993, S. 20.

595 PA, Provinzrundbrief 1–1994, S. 9.

596 PA, Provinzrundbrief 1–1997, S. 1.

597 Die folgende Tabelle stellt den Stammpersonalstand des Wiener Konvents dar, also ohne die Brüder des Retzer Klosters in der Zeit, in der Retz Filialhaus von Wien war. Auf die Darstellung durch Leerzeilen derjenigen Jahre, in denen Provinzkataloge fehlen, wurde aus Platzgründen verzichtet. Gerade deshalb gilt auch hier der Hinweis auf die ungleichmäßige Datenverteilung auf der Zeitachse.

Katalog	*Priester*	*Laienbrüder*	*Studenten*	*Novizen*	*Gesamtzahl*
1965	15	4			19
1966	18	4			22
1967	16	3			19
1969	19	3	1		23
1971	23	3			26
1973	20	3	1		24
1977	18	3	1		22
1979	16	3	1		20
1981	13	3	1		17
1984	12	2	2		16
1987	13	2	5	2	22
1989	16	2	5	2	25
1991	16	2	6	2	26
1994	14	2	5	3	24
1997	11	1		2	14
1999	11		2	3	17
2000	12	1	2	3	18
2003	9		1		10
2004	10		4		14
2005	9		4		13
2006	10		5		15
2007	9		7		16
2008	9		5		14
2009	9		3		12
2010	9		5		14
2011	10		3		13
2013	12		5		17

Deutlich werden aus diesem tabellarischen Überblick die große Bedeutung, die die Verlegung des Studentats und Noviziats nach Wien für den Personalstand des Konvents bekam bzw. die Auswirkungen, die der Abzug der Novizen nach 2000 für Wien hatte. Die klosterinternen Dienste der Laienbrüder mussten mit deren allmählichen Übertritt in den Ruhestand durch Angestellte ersetzt werden. Was die Tabelle nicht ausdrückt, ist die

Zahl der wirklich am Konvent seelsorglich aktiven Priester. Bis zu seinem Tod 1973 fiel einer von ihnen wegen schwerer Erkrankung aus. Von 1965 bis 1969 lebten und arbeiteten drei Priester außerhalb des Konvents, 1971 bis 1973 waren es fünf, danach durchschnittlich drei. Ab 2003 bis 2011 lebte tatsächlich keiner der Wiener Priester *extra conventum*, mit der Ausnahme des letzten Paters in Retz, der dort seinen Lebensabend verbrachte. Seit 2011 lebt ein Priester als Seelsorger außerhalb. Weiter betreute zwischen 1965 und 1977 ein Priester dauerhaft die Dominikanerinnen in Wien-Hacking. Nicht alle der oben genannten Priester oder Studenten waren *filii* der süddeutsch-österreichischen Provinz: So stammte von 1966 bis 1986 ein Priester aus der Teutonia in Wien, von 1969 bis 1976 ein Priester aus der Provinz Francia, 1999 und ab 2005 ein bis zwei Priester aus der slowakischen Vizeprovinz bzw. Provinz sowie von 2003 bis 2006 ein Priester aus der nigerianischen Provinz. Seit 2012 ist ein Priester aus der Provinz des hl. Albert in den USA dort assigniert.

Leider hören die Provinzrundbriefe ab Mitte der 1960er Jahre auf, die in den Konventen stattfindende Seelsorgsarbeit zu beschreiben. Die Provinzkataloge geben bei den einzelnen Brüdern nur deren Tätigkeitsfelder wieder; Auskünfte über die Details intellektueller oder spiritueller Bildungstätigkeit wie Vorträge, Einkehrtage usw. fehlen. Pastorales Zentrum des Wiener Konvents blieben die Klosterkirche und die daran angeschlossene Pfarrei, an der zwei Brüder – als Pfarrer und Kaplan – tätig waren. Den zweiten Arbeitsschwerpunkt des Konvents bildete auch nach 1965 die Beichtseelsorge: So wirkten Ende der 1960er Jahre fünf bis sieben Patres des Wiener Konvents als ordentliche oder außerordentliche Beichtväter in mehreren Schwesternklöstern unterschiedlicher Orden und bei den Barmherzigen Brüdern, davon zwei hauptberuflich. Nach dem Abschluss des zweiten vatikanischen Konzils fiel für die Schwesternklöster die Notwendigkeit weg, konkrete Priester für diese Aufgabe zu bestimmen, daher geben die Provinzkataloge ab 1969 die einzelnen Beichtväterposten nicht mehr an. Dennoch gehen Priester des Konvents dieser Aufgabe bis heute nach. Seit 1965 betreut der Konvent auch permanent einen Beichtstuhl im Stephansdom. Die regelmäßige Abhaltung von Volksmissionen endete 1969; danach wird bei keinem Pater mehr die Tätigkeit als Volksmissionar genannt.

Insgesamt verschob sich das Gewicht der Aktivität des Konvents nach 1965 auf Lehr- und Unterrichtstätigkeit sowie auf Schul- und Hochschulseelsorge: P. Alfons Well unterrichtete bis 1969 Philosophie an der Wiener Katholischen Akademie und am „Theologischen Laienkurs“ des Seelsor-

geinstituts Österreichs. P. Johannes Czerny dozierte bis 1969 Fundamentaltheologie an der theologischen Hauslehranstalt in Klosterneuburg, danach – laut den Provinzkatalogen von 1977 bis 1994 – Philosophie an der Hauslehranstalt des Stiftes Heiligenkreuz. Die Provinzkataloge von 1971 bis 1977 melden die Lehrtätigkeit in Kirchengeschichte von P. Isnard Frank am Generalstudium des Dominikanerordens in Walberberg, an der philosophisch-theologischen Hochschule der Steyler Missionare an St. Gabriel in Mödling und bei den theologischen Fernkursen für Laien in Wien sowie für 1979 an der katholisch-theologischen Fakultät der Universität Wien. Die Kataloge von 1991 und 1994 nennen P. Hans Ulrich Steymans als Vortragenden bei den Wiener theologischen Kursen am Stephansplatz, ab 1994 außerdem als Hochschulassistenten am Institut für alttestamentliche Bibelwissenschaft der katholisch-theologischen Fakultät der Universität Wien. 1998 und 1999 wirkte P. Wolfram Hoyer als Vertragsassistent am Institut für Dogmatik und Dogmengeschichte derselben Fakultät. Seit 2002 unterrichtet P. Rupert Johannes Mayer am Internationalen Theologischen Institut Gaming / Trumau. Bis 1977 waren und seit 1984 sind mehrere Patres des Konvents als Religionslehrer und Schulseelsorger an verschiedenen Schulen in Wien tätig. Von 1969 bis 1971 waren P. Fulko Hilgefort und P. Helmut Oberguggenberger als Studentenseelsorger an der Universität Wien aktiv; ihnen folgte von 1994 bis 1997 P. Rupert Johannes Mayer in dieser Aufgabe. 1987 übernahm P. Hilarius Barth das Rektorat der Kirche St. Ursula in Wien, die dem Institut für kirchenmusikalische Werkpraxis der Hochschule (heute Universität) für Musik und darstellende Kunst gehörte. Mit diesem Rektorat verbunden war auch die Studentenseelsorge an diesem Institut bzw. dieser Hochschule, außerdem Rundfunkarbeit, durch die Live-Übertragung von sechs bis acht Gottesdiensten pro Jahr im ORF-Radio. Barth wirkte an St. Ursula bis 1988, seine Nachfolger waren P. Innozenz Varga (1988–1997), P. Wolfram Hoyer (1997–2000), P. Rupert Johannes Mayer (2000–2012) und seit 2012 P. Jörg Wegscheider.[598] In das Gebiet der Studentenseelsorge gehört auch die Tätigkeit von P. Max Svoboda als Verbindungsseelsorger des KÖHV Nordgau von 1991 bis 2001 in Wien.

Dazu kamen weitere Seelsorgsaufgaben, denen einzelnen Brüdern des Konvents nachgingen: Von 1969 bis 1976 betreute P. Louis Deltombe aus der Provinz Francia die französische Nationalgemeinde in Wien. Von 1969 bis 1973 erwähnen die Provinzkataloge die Mitarbeit von P. Heinrich Suso

598 Zur Arbeit in St. Ursula: PA, Provinzrundbrief 3–1998, S. 18.

Abb. 72: Erzbischof Christoph Kardinal Schönborn (aufgenommen 2004; PA, Fotosammlung).

Rüsch und P. Martin Gyöngyös an den „Religiösen Schulwochen". P. Gyöngyös wirkte von 1975 bis 1986 und 2003 bis 2005 als Spiritual des Burgenländischen Priesterseminars in Wien. Von 1976 bis 1982 wirkte P. Heinrich Suso Rüsch als Vikariatsjugendseelsorger des Vikariats Wien-Stadt. P. Manfred Kniewasser leitete von 1984 bis 1987 die Pressestelle der Caritas Wien; außerdem war er von 1984 bis 1989 Leitungsmitglied der österreichischen Kommission Justitia et Pax, Vorstandsmitglied des internationalen Kulturzentrums Wien und der Koordinierungsstelle für christlich-jüdische Zusammenarbeit. P. Clemens Wehrle wirkt seit 1994 hauptamtlich als Exerzitienbegleiter.

Am 29. September 1991 durften die Wiener Dominikaner ein besonderes Ereignis mitfeiern: die Bischofskonsekration von P. Christoph Schönborn, den Papst Johannes Paul II. zum Weihbischof der Erzdiözese Wien (mit dem Titularbistum Sutri-Nepi) bestimmt hatte.[599] Schönborn hatte 1964 für die süddeutsch-österreichische Provinz Profess abgelegt. Nach Studien in Walberberg und Le Saulchoir in Étiolles-sur-Seine war er 1972/73 im Wiener Konvent assigniert gewesen, hatte aber während dieser Zeit zur Promotion *extra conventum* in Regensburg gelebt. 1974 hatte er am Institut Catholique in Paris promoviert. Von 1973 bis 1976 wirkte er im Grazer Konvent als Mitarbeiter in der Studentenseelsorge. Ab 1975 unterrichtete er das Fach Dogmatik an der katholisch-theologischen Fakultät der Universität Freiburg in der Schweiz, zunächst als außerordentlicher, später als ordentlicher Professor. Deshalb assignierte der Ordensmeister ihn im Oktober 1976 in den Konvent Albertinum in dieser Stadt, dessen Mitglied er bis zu seiner Bischofsweihe blieb. Obwohl er damit *extra provinciam* lebte, hielt er den Kontakt zu seiner Heimatprovinz regelmäßig aufrecht. So vertrat er die Provinz z. B. als Diffinitor auf dem Generalkapitel von 1977 in Quezon City und betreute ab 1982 die Studenten als

599 PA, Provinzrundbrief vom „Dezember" 1991, S. 1.

Studienregens.[600] 1980 wurde Schönborn zum Mitglied der Internationalen Theologenkommission des Heiligen Stuhl berufen; 1987 wurde er zum Redaktionssekretär des sogenannten Weltkatechismus ernannt.[601] Dieses Projekt hatte 1985 begonnen, als die Bischofssynode anlässlich des 20. Jahrestages des Abschlusses des zweiten vatikanischen Konzils den Papst um ein Kompendium der Lehre der Kirche gebeten hatte, das weltweit als Grundlage bei der Erstellung örtlicher Katechismen dienen sollte. Dazu hatte Papst Johannes Paul II. zur Vorbereitung eine Bischofs- und eine Kardinalskommission gebildet, die von einem Redaktionskomitee unterstützt wurde, dessen Sekretär Schönborn war. Dieses Komitee hatte ein gewaltiges Arbeitspensum zu bewältigen: Während der verschiedenen Stadien der Textentwicklung wurde von 1986 bis 1992 der Entwurf an jeden Bischof weltweit, alle Bischofskonferenzen und 40 ausgewählte Expertinnen und Experten mit der Bitte um Stellungnahme versandt. Über 900 Antworten mit etwa 24.000 Änderungs- und Ergänzungsvorschlägen gingen ein und wollten berücksichtigt werden. Zur Unterstützung bat Schönborn 1989 das Provinzkonsil um Freistellung eines Mitbruders, P. Philippe-André Holzer, der ihm bis September 1990 dafür zur Verfügung gestellt wurde. Da Holzer im Herbst 1990 nach Wien assigniert wurde, um dort das Amt des Studienregens zu übernehmen, fand die letzte Redaktionsphase des „Weltkatechismus“ im dortigen Konvent statt, wo er einige Hilfe bei dieser Arbeit fand. Im November 1992 konnte der „Katechismus der katholischen Kirche“, wie das Werk nun offiziell hieß, in französischer Sprache erscheinen.[602] Am 10. Dezember 1992 wurde Holzer mit den Vorbereitungsarbeiten für die deutschsprachige Ausgabe betraut,[603] die – wiederum mit Hilfe von Wiener Brüdern – 1993 erscheinen konnte. Schönborn wurde am 13. April 1995 zum Koadjutor des Wiener Erzbischofs Hans Hermann Kardinal Groër ernannt und übernahm am 14. September desselben Jahres als Erzbischof die Leitung des Erzbistums. Am 29. Juni 1996 überreichte ihm

600 Daten laut der Provinzkataloge der fraglichen Jahre; zur Assignation nach Freiburg in der Schweiz: PA, Provinzialsregestenbuch 2 (1966–2010), Eintrag vom 12.10.1976, Nr. 53; siehe auch: *St. Dominikuswerk* (1992) S. 3–4.

601 Daten laut: http://de.wikipedia.org/wiki: Christoph Schönborn (Zugriff am 13.12.2013).

602 Angaben laut Schönborns Bericht im Provinzrundbrief 1–1993, S. 33–34; zur Freistellung Holzers: Provinzrundbrief vom 2.7.1989, S. 7 (über die Provinzkonsilssitzung am 30.3.1989).

603 PA, Provinzrundbrief 2–1992, S. 8.

Abb. 73: Die Aufführung eines Nô-Theaterstücks vor dem japanischen Botschafter anlässlich des Abschlusses der Renovierung des Refektoriums im Wiener Dominikanerkloster 1991 (PA, Fotosammlung).

Papst Johannes Paul II. das Pallium; im Konsistorium vom 21. Februar 1998 wurde er zum Kardinal kreiert und übernahm als Kardinalpriester die Titelkirche Gesù Divin Lavoratore im 15. römischen Stadbezirk, dem „quartiere Marconi".[604]

Abgesehen von den personellen Umbauten, die der Wiener Konvent als Ausbildungszentrum der Provinz seit den 1980er Jahren erlebte, prägten auch echte bauliche Unternehmungen die letzten Jahrzehnte. So konnten 1989 sowohl die Schaffung eines zweiten Bibliotheksraumes als auch die Erneuerung des Thomassaales abgeschlossen werden.[605] 1991 erfolgten die Renovierung des Refektoriums, deren Abschluss mit der Aufführung eines Nô-Theaterstücks durch Brüder des Konvents in Anwesenheit des japa-

604 Daten laut: http://de.wikipedia.org/wiki: Christoph Schönborn (Zugriff am 13.12. 2013).

605 PA, Provinzrundbriefe vom 22.6.1987, S. 4 (mit Verweis auf die Provinzkonsilssitzung vom 20.5.1987 in Augsburg) und vom 2.7.1989, S. 8 und 9.

Abb. 74: Dominikanerkloster Wien: Bei der Renovierung des Kreuzgangs 1994–1998 aufgefundener gotischer Doppelfensterbogen aus dem 13. Jahrhundert (Foto: Adam Rokosz, Wien). Eine Darstellung dieses Funds bildet auch die Umschlaggraphik dieser Festschrift.

nischen Botschafters eingeweiht wurde, sowie im selben Jahr die Wiederherstellung der historischen romantischen Orgel in der Klosterkirche, zu der sich 1992 noch eine Chororgel gesellte.[606] Von 1994 bis 1998 wurde der Kreuzgang unter Entdeckung und Freilegung mittelalterlicher Bauteile und Fresken restauriert und der Innenhof neu gestaltet.[607] 2008 bis 2010 folgte die Renovierung der Kirchen- und Konventsfassaden.[608]

1996 belebte der Konvent den früheren Brauch einer Festakademie zum Thomasfest neu, bestehend aus einem feierlichen Hochamt, einem Vortrag

606 Zum Nô-Theaterstück: PA, Provinzrundbrief vom „Dezember“ 1991, S. 6; zu den Orgeln: ebd., S. 5 und Provinzrundbrief 2–1992, S. 8.
607 PA, Provinzrundbrief 3–1998, S. 15–17 und *Dominikus* 1–1999, S. 14.
608 *Dominikus* (2008 / 09) S. 38 und (2009 / 10) S. 29–31.

Abb. 75: Rosenkranzbasilika St. Maria Rotunda der Dominikaner in Wien: die 2010 renovierte Ostfassade (PA, Fotosammlung).

scholastisch-thomasischen Inhalts und einem nachfolgenden geselligen Beisammensein. Inauguriert wurde diese Veranstaltung am 29. Januar 1996 mit einem Vortrag Josef Piepers über „Ist Thomas von Aquin noch aktuell?“ 1997 sprach P. Paulus Engelhardt OP über „Die Heilsgewissheit des Thomas von Aquin als ökumenische Herausforderung“, 1998 P. Augustinus Wucherer-Huldenfeld OPraem über „Gibt es einen Grundgedanken der Gottesbeweise bei Thomas von Aquin?“ Diesen Vorbildern folgten thematisch auch die anderen Vortragenden der bis heute stattfindenden Festakademie.[609]

609 PA, Provinzrundbrief 1–1997, S. 7–8 und S. 11–12 sowie 2–1998, S. 35–40; siehe auch *Dominikus* (2004) S. 20–22 und (2007 / 08) S. 18–19.

Als medienhistorisches Detail sei erwähnt, dass der Wiener Konvent der erste in der Provinz war, der sich 1998 eine Emailadresse besorgte und sich seit 1999 mit einer Homepage im Internet präsentiert.[610] Mit Hilfe des Webmasters der Kurie des Ordens, P. Martin Badenhorst, folgten dann die anderen Konvente mit ihren Seiten, der Internetauftritt der Provinz und der Capa.[611]

Einen Höhepunkt in der Geschichte des Ordens stellte auch das 4. Europa-Treffen der Landesverantwortlichen der Dominikanischen Laiengemeinschaften dar, das vom 2. bis 8. März 1998 in Wien-Lainz abgehalten und von der Wiener Laiengemeinschaft unter der Leitung von P. Clemens Wehrle organisiert worden war. Inhaltlich ging es dabei um die Leitfragen: „Wir verstehen wir unsere dominikanische Sendung am Ende des zweiten Jahrtausends? Wie umschreiben wir sie? Und vor allem: Wie können wir einander helfen, sie zu leben?“[612] Im Hintergrund stand die praktische Ausführung der Regel von Montreal für die Laiengemeinschaften im Orden des hl. Dominikus, die Ordensmeister Damian Byrne am 16. Februar 1987 approbiert hatte. Mit dieser Regel von Montreal kam ein Anpassungsprozess der Statuten für die Laiendominikaner zum Abschluss, der 1923 begonnen hatte, als Ordensmeister Ludwig Theissling die sogenannte Drittordensregel des Ordensmeisters Munio von Zamora aus dem 13. Jahrhundert den Bestimmungen des Codex Juris Canonici angeglichen hatte. Weitere Veränderungen waren 1964 und 1968 vorgenommen worden. Ziel der Regel von Montreal war, „das Selbstverständnis, das Leben und die Sendung der Laien, die sich in den dominikanischen Laiengemeinschaften zusammengeschlossen haben und die Mitglieder des Ordens sind, zu umreißen“.[613] Eine wesentliche Forderung der Regel war die Erstellung von Rahmenordnungen in jeder Provinz für Formalia wie die Zulassungsbedingungen, die Dauer der Probezeit und der Zulassung, die Häufigkeit der Treffen der Gruppen, die Art und Weise der Errichtung und ihrer Ämter und Aufgaben usw.[614] Diese Rahmenordnung für die Laiengemeinschaften in der süddeutsch-österreichischen Provinz – hier „Di-

---

610 PA, Provinzrundbrief 2–1998, S. 40.

611 *Dominikus* (2000) S. 17–19.

612 PA, Provinzrundbrief 2–1998, S. 22; ebd. S. 18–34 detaillierte Programm- und Ablaufbeschreibungen, Pressemitteilungen etc.

613 PA, Provinzrundbrief 2–1998, S. 21; Text der Regel von Montreal ebd., S. 18–20, Text der „allgemeinen Erklärungen des Ordensmeisters zur Regel“ ebd., S. 20–21.

614 Siehe „Allgemeine Bedingungen des Ordensmeisters zur Regel von Montreal“, in: PA, Provinzrundbrief 2–1998, S. 21.

rektorium" genannt – hatten Provinzial Gregor Ruf und P. Dietmar Schon 1992 fertiggestellt. Wie beim Provinzstatut war ein hauptsächlich nach praktischen Gesichtspunkten entworfenes Dokument entstanden:

> „Mit dem neuerschienenen Direktorium liegt die Anwendung der Regel von 1987 für die dominikanischen Laien unserer Provinz vor. Damit wird versucht, den bestehenden Gruppen neue Impulse zu geben und für zukünftige Gruppen Leitlinien zu schaffen. Im Vergleich zum Direktorium der Nachbarprovinz Teutonia fällt die Kürze auf. Nicht Spiritualität sollte geregelt werden; der Text beschränkt sich vielmehr auf den organisatorischen Rahmen und auf ergänzende Hinweise zu den Quellen des dominikanischen Lebens. Dadurch soll den Gruppen die Möglichkeit gegeben werden, ihr jeweiliges spirituelles Profil selbst zu entwickeln. Sie können darüber hinaus eigenständig entscheiden, wie sie die vorgesehenen organisatorischen Spielräume nutzen wollen ... Regel und Direktorium fassen die gemeinsamen Grundlagen der dominikanischen Familie für den Gebrauch der Laien und Laiengruppen zusammen; beide Texte wurden deshalb in einem handlichen Heft zusammengestellt."[615]

Nach der Renovierung der romantischen Orgel war die Wiener Dominikanerkirche auch wieder verstärkt Schauplatz des Kulturlebens in der österreichischen Hauptstadt. Seit 1997 fand im Herbst alljährlich ein Konzert-Zyklus „Romantische Orgel" statt. Im Oktober und November 2000 war Maria Rotunda auch Veranstaltungsort des renommierten Konzertfestivals „Wien Modern". Bereits im April und dann wieder im November 2000 hatte der Schauspieler und Rezitator Max Müller Passagen der Johannesapokalypse vorgetragen, untermalt durch die von Florian Pagitsch gespielte Orgel und unterstützt durch Licht- und Beleuchtungseffekte von Cécile Nordegg und Jonathan Berkh. Diese Veranstaltung hinterließ bei allen Teilnehmern einen bleibenden Eindruck und führte zu einer Kooperation von Nordegg und Berkh mit Prior P. Max Svoboda bei einem ehrgeizigen Projekt: Die Künstler schufen zum Thema der sieben letzten Worte Jesu am Kreuz sieben Fastentücher, die in der Fastenzeit 2001 den Hochaltar und sechs Seitenkapellen der Dominikanerkirche verhüllten.[616] Auch hierzu gab es ein positives Echo; das Tuch für den Hochaltar verblieb bei den Dominikanern. Darüber hinaus gab es auch 2001 drei Rezitationsabende, zur Apokalypse, zum Buch Hiob und zum Hohelied Salomos.[617] Nach seinem Umzug nach Graz

---

615 PA, Provinzrundbrief 2–1992, S. 16.
616 Dokumentiert in: *In deine Hände lege ich meinen Geist. Die sieben Worte Jesu am Kreuz.* Hg. v. Max Svoboda, Cécile Nordegg, Jonathan Berkh. Wien 2001.
617 *Dominikus* (2000) S. 29–31 und (2001) S. 7–11.

Abb. 76: Rosenkranzbasilika St. Maria Rotunda der Dominikaner in Wien: Fastentuch für den Hochaltar, gestaltet 2001 von Cécile Nordegg und Jonathan Berkh (aus: In deine Hände lege ich meinen Geist. Die sieben Worte Jesu am Kreuz. Hg. v. Max Svoboda, Cécile Nordegg, Jonathan Berkh. Wien 2001, S. 1).

Abb. 77: P. Christophe Holzer gratuliert P. Innozenz Varga beim Festgottesdienst anlässlich dessen 100. Geburtstag
(aufgenommen am 1. Juli 2013; Foto: Adam Rokosz, Wien).

2001 und die Übernahme der Münzgrabenpfarrei engagierte sich Svoboda auch dort zusammen mit Nordegg und Berkh. 2003 wurde in Graz der Hauptaltarraum ebenfalls durch ein neues Fastentuch verhüllt.[618]

Den 100. Geburtstag von Exprovinzial P. Innozenz Varga am 1. Juli 2013 gestaltete der Wiener Konvent zu einem großen Fest. Dazu durften sie zwei Erzbischöfe, Kardinäle und Mitbrüder willkommen heißen, nämlich Dominik Duka aus Prag und Christoph Schönborn aus Wien, die zusammen mit den Provinziälen Johannes Bunnenberg von der Teutonia und Christophe Holzer von der süddeutsch-österreichischen Provinz, mit zahlreichen Dominikanern und Dominikanerinnen und v. a. mit P. Varga selbst die Dankmesse zelebrieren. Die Anwesenheit vieler Familienmitglieder, Freunde und Landsleute Vargas machte aus diesem Fest eine doppelte Familienfeier.[619] P. Innozenz Varga verstarb wenige Monate später, am 8. September 2013.

618 Dokumentiert in: Cécile Nordegg / Jonathan Berkh: *Stabat Mater.* Hg. von der r. k. Pfarrei Graz-Münzgraben. Graz / Wien 2003.
619 PA, ProvinzZeitung Juni-Juli 2013, S. 15–18.

Retz

Mit dem Wiener Konvent verbunden ist die Geschichte des Klosters in Retz. Zwar war der Schließungsbeschluss des Provinzkonsils vom 23. August 1970 nicht durchgeführt worden, der Verbund als Filialhaus des Konvents von Wien durch die Einsetzung eines eigenen Superiors im Dezember wieder gelöst und Retz wieder selbständige *domus formata*, aber dennoch blieb der Personalstand dort sehr klein: 1980 waren dort nur P. Augustinus Deutsch und die Laienbrüder Jakob Koosz und Wolfgang Burtscher assigniert. 1985 wurde ein weiterer Priester nach Retz versetzt; da dieser aber bis 1988 *extra conventum* arbeitete, blieb diese Personalverstärkung zunächst Papier. In der Folge konzentrierte sich die pastorale Arbeit, die vom Kloster aus geleistet werden konnte, auf die Betreuung der Klosterkirche und des Altenheimes Retz sowie auf Aushilfe in der Stadtpfarrei.

Trotz dieser prekären Lage bildete das Kloster noch immer einen wesentlichen Fixpunkt im Leben von Retz. So fand der große Festgottesdienst anlässlich des 700. Jahrestags der Gründung der Stadt, in Anwesenheit des Bundespräsidenten Rudolf Kirchschläger, am 17. Juni 1979 in der Klosterkirche statt, mit Provinzial Varga als Haupt- und mit zwei weiteren Brüdern als Konzelebranten.[620] Die 1980 bis 1985 durchgeführte Außenrenovierung von Kirche und Klostergebäuden wurde durch das österreichische Bundesdenkmalamt, die niederösterreichische Landesregierung, die Stadtgemeinde Retz und durch Spendenaufrufe finanziert, die eine Retzer Jugendkulturgruppe für das Kloster durchführte.[621] Aus dieser Jugendgruppe entwickelte sich später der „Freundeskreis des Klosters Retz". Leider zerschlug sich der Plan, die niederösterreichische Landesausstellung des Jahres 1985 im Dominikanerkloster Retz stattfinden zu lassen – das Bundesland hätte bei dieser Gelegenheit wesentliche Innenrenovierungen durchführen lassen.[622] Dennoch konnte die Fassade des großen Innenhofs noch 1985 mit lokaler Hilfe restauriert werden.[623]

Von den beiden Projekten zur Nutzung der weitgehend leerstehenden Klostergebäude hatte sich inzwischen eines verwirklicht, nämlich die Ver-

620 PA, Provinzrundbrief vom 20.7.1979, S. 3.

621 PA, Provinzrundbrief vom 10.3.1980, S. 3 und vom 10.12.1980, S. 4.

622 PA, Provinzrundbrief vom 20.4.1983, S. 4 (über die Provinzkonsilssitzung vom 9.3.1983 in Augsburg).

623 PA, Provinzrundbrief vom 25.9.1985, S. 5.

wendung des Südtraktes des Hauses mit neun Zimmern im Obergeschoß, mit dem sogenannten Winterrefektorium und weiteren Räumlichkeiten als Gästehaus für kleine Gruppen, Exerzitien u. ä. unter der Leitung des „Freundeskreises Retz“.[624]

Br. Jakob Koosz verstarb 1989, Br. Wolfgang Burtscher 1991. Da die Wirtschaftsverwaltung zuletzt in deren Händen gelegen hatte und das Problem der Baulasten immer dringender wurde, setzte das Provinzkonsil am 21. Oktober 1992 auf Antrag des Provinzials für die pastoralen und finanziellen Fragen eine Kommission ein, um „die bestehenden Pachtverträge zu prüfen und, wenn möglich, zu verbessern, weiterhin die Nutzung eines Teils des Klosters durch den Freundeskreis Retz vertraglich zu regeln.“[625] Durch diese Arbeit vorbereitet gab das Provinzkapitel von 1994 die Zustimmung zur Weiterführung des Gästehauses im Eigenbetrieb des Klosters unter der Leitung eines Angestellten. Zur Verwaltung der Liegenschaften und der *domus* setzte das Provinzkapitel eine ständige, aus dem Provinzial und zwei weiteren Brüdern bestehende Kommission ein, der insbesondere alle Bau-, Renovierungs- und Wirtschaftsmaßnahmen vorzulegen waren.[626] Wegen einer Änderung in den Ordenssatzungen durch das Generalkapitel von Calaruega 1995, nach denen für ein selbständiges Haus nun mindestens vier dort assignierte Brüder erforderlich waren,[627] wurde Retz vom Provinzkonsil am 25. Oktober 1995 neuerlich zum Filialhaus des Konvents Wien erklärt. Da damit die Wiener Ordensinstitutionen die Verwaltung von Retz übernahmen, endete auch die Zuständigkeit der „Retzkommission“ des Provinzkapitels von 1994; sie wurde aufgelöst.[628]

Vom Wiener Konvent aus wurden Anstrengungen zur Fortführung der Renovierungsarbeiten unternommen; ein Wiederbelebungsversuch der dominikanischen Präsenz gelang jedoch nicht. Letztlich erwies sich der Erhalt der Kloster- und Kirchenanlage als finanzielles Fass ohne Boden – seit dem Ende des zweiten Weltkrieges waren die Erneuerungsarbeiten nie abgeschlossen gewesen. Das Provinzkapitel von 1998 fasste daher den schon zitierten Beschluss, das Kloster Retz als Niederlassung der

---

624 Siehe Projektbeschreibung in: Liber consilii provincialis, Sitzung des Provinzkonsils in Augsburg am 7.9.1981, Beilage von P. Christoph Schönborn.

625 Datum der Kommissionseinsetzung: PA, Provinzrundbrief 2–1992, S. 7; Zitat: Provinzrundbrief 1–1993, S. 3.

626 APKap 1994, S. 30–32, Nr. 100.

627 ACG 1995, S. 93; Änderung LCO Nr. 331 – bis.

628 PA, Provinzrundbrief 2–1995, S. 8 (über die Provinzkonsilssitzung am 25.10.1995).

Abb. 78: Dominikanerkloster Retz: Statue des hl. Dominikus im Innenhof des Kreuzgangs (PA, Fotosammlung).

süddeutsch-österreichischen Provinz bis spätestens 30. Juni 2000 zu schließen.[629] Da die slowakische Vizeprovinz Interesse an einer Übernahme von Retz zeigte, ordnete das Provinzkapitel an, dass

„bezüglich der künftigen Nutzung des Klosters Retz die Übergabe an die slowakische Vizeprovinz Priorität erhält. Die rechtlichen, finanziellen, pasto-

629 APKap 1998, S. 20, Nr. 55 und S. 25, Nr. 78.1.

> ralen und dominikanischen Aspekte sind in einem mehrseitigen Vertrag zu regeln, der nach österreichischem Zivilrecht Geltung besitzt. Dabei ist eine Lösung zu entwickeln, wie das Eigentum an den Klostergebäuden und den von ihnen überbauten Grundstücken durch einen Rechtsträger des österreichischen Provinzteils fortgeführt werden kann."

Für den Fall, dass sich eine solche Lösung nicht finden ließ, befahl das Provinzkapitel,

> „dass das Eigentum am Kloster Retz unter Beachtung der kirchenrechtlichen Vorschriften durch Schenkung oder Verkauf an die Erzdiözese Wien, das Land Niederösterreich und / oder die Stadt Retz oder anderweitig zu beenden ist ... Eine solche Lösung muss endgültig sein, d. h. der Tatsache Rechnung tragen, dass die Provinz weder personell noch finanziell in der Lage ist, die Verantwortung für das Kloster Retz fortzuführen."[630]

Das „Eigentum an den nicht vom Kloster überbauten Grundstücken und von dem nicht in die Schenkung / den Verkauf einbezogenen Inventar" wurde auf die Provinz, konkret den österreichischen Provinzteil, übertragen.[631] Mit Dekret vom 5. September 2000 schloss der Ordensmeister Retz als *domus* der süddeutsch-österreichischen Provinz. 2001 zogen Mitbrüder des Konvents von Bratislava dort ein, die die dominikanische Präsenz im alten Kloster seither fortführen.[632] Auf seiner Sitzung vom 2. Februar 2004 gab das süddeutsch-österreichische Provinzkonsil die Erlaubnis zur Erhebung der slowakischen Niederlassung zur selbständigen *domus formata*.[633] Nichtsdestotrotz standen Kloster und Kirche – und damit die Baulast – nach wie vor im Eigentum des österreichischen Provinzteils. Daher urgierte das Provinzkapitel von 2006 die Beendigung des Eigentums der Provinz an der Klosteranlage durch Ausgliederung in eine Stiftung bis zum 1. Juni 2008.[634] Die diesbezüglichen Verhandlungen verliefen schwierig.[635] Endlich konnten am 27. Juni 2007 die notariellen Urkunden unterzeichnet werden, durch die das Erzbistum Wien, unter Federführung der Mensalgut-Stiftung, die Privatstiftung „Dominikanerkloster in Retz" errichtete, zum

630 Ebd., S. 25, Nrn. 78.2 und 78.5.

631 Ebd., S. 25, Nr. 78.6.

632 Beide Daten laut: PKat 2003, S. 38; zur Übergabe von Retz an die slowakische Provinz: *Dominikus* 2–1999, S. 18–19.

633 PA, ProvinzZeitung 2–2004, S. 3.

634 APKap 2006, S. 20, Nr. 90.

635 Siehe PA, ProvinzZeitung 1–2–2006, S. 2, 3–2006, S. 2 und 3–2007, S. 2.

Zweck der Erhaltung des Klosterkomplexes in seiner geistlichen und dominikanischen Tradition.[636]

Graz

Abgesehen von der Zeit, in der das Grazer Kloster Ordensnachwuchs beherbergte, kannte der dortige Personalstand in den letzten Jahrzehnten nur eine Tendenz: abnehmend. Bestand der Konvent 1969 noch aus 22 Mitgliedern (15 Priestern, vier Laienbrüder, einem Kleriker und zwei Tertiaren), so waren es 1979 16 Mitglieder (zehn Priester, drei Laienbrüder, zwei Kleriker und ein Tertiar), 1989 elf Mitglieder (neun Priester und zwei Laienbrüder), 1999 neun Mitglieder (sieben Priester und zwei Laienbrüder) und 2009 nur mehr fünf (die alle Priester waren). Zu dieser Stammbesatzung gehörten mehrere Patres aus anderen Provinzen: von 1969 bis 1997 zwei Priester aus Ungarn, bis 1973 ein Priester aus der böhmischen Provinz, von 1972 bis 2000 ein Priester aus Polen und ab 2009 ein Priester aus der indischen Provinz. Von den Patres lebten und arbeiteten 1969 drei *extra conventum*, 1971 zwei und 1973 einer, 1994 nochmals drei und 1997 nur noch einer. Zwar gab es auch in den Jahren dazwischen und danach immer wieder einzelne Brüder, die nicht in ihrem Assignationskonvent lebten, aber dies deshalb, weil sie in Alten- und Pflegeheime gingen.

Das pastorale Hauptaugenmerk der Gemeinschaft lag nach 1965 immer auf der Münzgrabenpfarrei, bedingt durch deren schiere Größe und die zurückgehenden Personalressourcen des Klosters. So stellte der Konvent neben dem Pfarrer bis 1973 vier, bis 1987 drei und ab 2000 zwei Kapläne. Von 2003 bis 2008 nennen die Provinzkataloge keinen Kaplan; 2009 bis 2012 wurde der Pfarrer wieder durch einen Mitbruder als Kaplan unterstützt. Mit dem Kaplansjob war ursprünglich auch der Religionsunterricht an verschiedenen Schulen verbunden gewesen; diese Arbeit teilten sich die Kapläne auch mit anderen Mitbrüdern. So waren bis 1977 drei Dominikaner Religionslehrer und Katecheten, 1979 nur mehr einer; danach wird keiner mehr in dieser Funktion genannt. Von 1953 bis 1973 unterrichtete P. Fidelis Gallati an der katholisch-theologischen Fakultät der Universität Graz – leider melden die Provinzkataloge nicht, in welchem Fach.

Mit der Assignation von P. Jordan Gebhard 1964 nach Graz übernahmen die Mitbrüder ein neues Arbeitsfeld: die Studentenseelsorge.

636 PA, ProvinzZeitung 7–2007, S. 1–3.

Gebhard wird bis einschließlich des Katalogs von 1981 als Seelsorger der Studenten der Universität genannt, Wolfgang Keil in dieser Funktion im Katalog von 1969, Manfred Kellner im Katalog von 1979, Christoph Schönborn von 1973 bis 1976, Hilarius Barth im Katalog von 1984, Dominikus Jakob in den Katalogen von 1989 und 1991. Gebhard wirkte außerdem als Kurat ab 1965 bis 1983 bei mehreren Studentenverbindungen und bei der „Overseas Students Coordination", Max Svoboda ab 2009 als Seelsorger der katholischen österreichischen Studentenverbindung Traungau-Graz.

Einzelne Brüder steuerten darüber hinaus zum pastoralen Profil des Klosters eigene Beiträge bei: So wirkte P. Reginald Ladner von 1965 bis zu seinem Tod 1984 als Seelsorger beim steirischen Blindenapostolat. P. Richard Kurecki, ein Mitbruder, der zur Unterstützung des Konvents 1972 aus der polnischen Provinz nach Graz gekommen war, arbeitete von 1977 bis 2000 als Seelsorger am Landeskrankenhaus Graz und betreute die polnische Gemeinde. Von 1984 bis zu seinem Tod 1996 fungierte P. Bonaventura Neuberger als Ehebandverteidiger am Diözesangericht des Bistums Graz-Seckau. P. Wolfgang Rexeisen wird in den Katalogen von 1987 bis 1991 als hauptberuflicher Jugendseelsorger genannt, zuletzt als Jugendseelsorger der Stadt Graz, Bundesseelsorger der katholischen Jugend, gesetzlicher Assistent der Arbeitsgemeinschaft Katholische Jugend Österreich, Rektor des katholischen Jugendwerks und Mitglied der Pastoralkommission der österreichischen Bischofskonferenz. Von 1997 bis 2013 arbeitete P. Miroslav Mlčoch hauptsächlich als Seelsorger an vier Alten- und Pflegeheimen im Gebiet der benachbarten Pfarrei St. Leonhard.

Mit steigendem Lebensdurchschnittsalter zogen sich die Brüder zwar von Gestellungen zurück, nicht aber von der Betreuung der vielen Gruppen und Verbände, die über die Pfarrei am Kloster angesiedelt waren. Auch die Schwesternbeichte – 1969 noch durch sieben Posten als ordentliche oder außerordentliche Beichtväter gewährleistet – blieb immer Bestandteil der vom Grazer Konvent ausgehenden Pastoral. Das für das Kloster spezifische marianische Pastoralprofil blieb ebenfalls lange Zeit erhalten. Mit dem Tod von P. Amandus Baronig endete zwar 1972 die Herausgabetätigkeit des „Rosenkranzkalenders", aber P. Leo Schölzhorn blieb bis 1989 Schriftleiter der Zeitschrift „Mit Maria" und Seelsorger der österreichischen Zweigstelle des Fatima-Weltapostolats. In der Betreuung der Grazer „Legio Mariae" wurde er 1977 bis 1984 durch Bonaventura Neuberger unterstützt.

Abb. 79: Dominikanerkloster Graz: Ansicht des Innenhofes um den Kreuzgang, des ab 1970 als Studentenwohnheim vermieteten Gebäudebereichs (PA, Fotosammlung).

Eine Folge des schrumpfenden Personalstandes wurde allerdings schon sehr bald spürbar: Nach dem Verkauf der Liegenschaften für die Klosterrenovierung und den Kirchenbau in den 1950er und 1960er Jahren besaß der Grazer Konvent als finanzielle Einnahmequellen nur mehr die Gehälter der Brüder. Mit Abnahme der arbeitsfähigen Brüderzahl gingen diese natürlich ebenfalls zurück. Schon auf seiner Sitzung vom 3. Juli 1968 musste das Provinzkonsil feststellen: „Der Grazer Konvent kann von seinen bisherigen Einkünften nicht mehr leben."[637] Daher stimmte es dem Vorschlag der Grazer Brüder zu, ein Drittel des Klostergebäudes – konkret den aus der Barockzeit stammenden Teil um den Kreuzgang – an die katholische Hochschulgemeinde Graz als Studentenwohnheim zu vermieten. Ein entsprechender Vertrag des Grazer Konvents mit dem Studentenrat der Diözese Graz-Seckau wurde am 9. August 1968 unterzeichnet.[638] Die Umbauten und Anpassungen der vermieteten Klostertrakte waren innerhalb

637 PA, Liber consiliorum provinciae, Sitzung vom 3.7.1968, S. 73.
638 PA, Liber consiliorum provinciae, Sitzung vom 14.9.1968, S. 73.

eines Jahres abgeschlossen, sodass das Studentenwohnheim 1970 seinen Betrieb aufnehmen konnte.[639] Der Kontakt des Konvents mit dem Wohnheim blieb nur sehr locker, da dieses in vom Kloster autonomer Trägerschaft geführt wurde; die Brüder hatten mit der Betreuung der Studenten kaum etwas zu tun. 2007 zog sich die Katholische Hochschulgemeinde aus dem Gebäude zurück, das inzwischen abgewohnt war und den baupolizeilichen Vorschriften nicht mehr entsprach, weil sie sich nicht in der Lage sah, die Gelder für eine Renovierung aufzubringen. Auch die Grazer Dominikaner konnten sich dies nicht leisten, daher wurde der gesamte Komplex am 19. September 2007 an das Stift Admont verkauft, welches die Räume renovieren ließ. Als Betreiber dieses neuen Studentenwohnheims fand sich die Akademikerhilfe.[640]

Durch die Beherbergung des Noviziates unter seinem Dach 1981 bis 1986 rückte der Grazer Konvent wieder etwas stärker in den Fokus der Aufmerksamkeit der Provinz; ebenso brachten die ungarischen Gäste 1991/92 bzw. 1993/94 frischen Wind in die Gemeinschaft. Nachdem die ungarische Provinz ihre Novizen aber in eigenen Häusern unterbringen konnte, stand der Grazer Konvent wieder mit vielen leeren Zimmern da. Diese Situation erwies sich bald als Möglichkeit für die überraschende Lösung eines Problems innerhalb der dominikanischen Familie:

> „Am 31. Dezember 1996 zogen 10 Schwestern aus dem Kloster Gleisdorf in das Klostergebäude der Mitbrüder in Graz um; mit 1. Januar 1997 begann damit am Münzgraben eine neue Zeit mit zwei Klostergemeinschaften unter einem Dach. Für die Schwestern waren die Verwaltung und die Besorgung ihres großen Hauses in Gleisdorf schon in den letzten Jahren zu mühsam geworden. … Die Pflege der alten Mitschwestern hatte keine andere äußere Tätigkeit mehr zugelassen. So lag der Gedanke schon länger nahe, Gleisdorf zu verlassen. Da aber keine der anderen Gemeinschaften der Union der Dominikanerinnen in Österreich, zu der Gleisdorf gehört, in der Lage gewesen wäre, die ganze Gemeinschaft aufzunehmen, die Schwestern aber kein Mitglied ihrer Gemeinschaft in ein Pflegeheim geben wollten, entstand der Plan, im großen Gebäude des Konventes der Mitbrüder in Graz einen Stock zu mieten und diesen für ihre Zwecke baulich zu adaptieren. Aber auch hier war nicht Raum genug, um alle [sc. 13 Schwestern] unterzubringen. So zogen drei Schwestern in das Kloster der Union nach Kramsach / Hilariberg. Ausschlaggebend für den Umzug nach Graz war vor allem die opti-

---

639 Dieses Datum wurde rückgerechnet vom Datum der Zehnjahresfeier des Bestehens am 6.5.1980 (darüber: PA, Provinzrundbrief vom 10.12.1980, S. 3).
640 PA, ProvinzZeitung 10–2007, S. 5 und *Dominikus* (2008 / 09) S. 25.

Abb. 80: Fatimakirche in Graz: Innenansicht nach der Renovierung 2010 (Foto: Suresh Christian, Graz).

> male religiöse Betreuung, die im Münzgraben für den größeren Teil der Gemeinschaft möglich ist."[641]

Die Schwestern bauten sich das zweite Stockwerk des Hauses für ihre Zwecke um. Durch ihren Einzug war kein Doppelkloster an der Münzgrabenstraße entstanden, sondern zwei selbständige Gemeinschaften teilten sich gemeinsam ein sehr weitläufiges Gebäude.

Auch nach 1965 waren immer wieder Bau- und Renovierungsmaßnahmen am Kloster nötig – unter anderem wegen des Einzugs des Studentenwohnheims oder der Schwestern. 1997 wurde auch die Fatimakirche verändert: sie erhielt neue, von Gunter Damisch und Fritz Panzer bemalte Glasfenster, die am 21. September der Öffentlichkeit vorgestellt werden konnten. Sie waren „der Versuch, aus Licht und Farben auf das zentrale Fenster hinzuführen und eine freudige Stimmung in den Altarraum zu bringen. Das zentrale Fenster musste zum Apokalypse-Fresko

641 PA, Provinzrundbrief 1–1997, S. 11; zur Geschichte von Kloster Gleisdorf und zum Umzugsbeschluss nach Graz siehe: *Der Funke* (Frühjahr / Sommer 1997) S. 14–15.

passen. Das ist der Grund, warum in dieses Fenster eine Art Mandorla aufgemalt wurde, die beim richtigen Licht und von der richtigen Betrachtungsposition aus wie ein Glorienschein die davor hängende Madonna mit einem Strahlenkranz aus Licht umgibt."[642] Von April bis Oktober 2010 erfolgte eine groß angelegte Innenrenovierung der Münzgrabenkirche. Nicht nur die Elektroanlagen, die Heizung, die Lautsprecher und die Leuchtkörper wurden komplett erneuert, die Malereien und Glasfenster gereinigt und die Wände gestrichen, sondern der ganze liturgische Raumbereich wurde neu gestaltet: Nach einem Entwurf des Architekten Ferdinand Certov wurde die sehr große, ursprünglich für einen Hochaltar gebaute Plattform an der Apsis flächenmäßig verkleinert und durch Glaswände als Ort für Wochentagsmessen und Taufen vom Kirchenschiff getrennt. Die beiden Glaswände rechts und links wurden mit einer Weihnachtspredigt des Dominikaner Johannes Tauler beschrieben. Ein neuer Zelebrationsaltar und ein Ambo wurden ins Kirchenschiff, vor die Stufen zur ehemaligen Hochaltarplattform, gestellt. Diözesanbischof Egon Kapellari nahm die Weihe dieses neuen Zelebrationsaltares am 31. Oktober 2010 vor.[643]

Bereits am 1. September 2010 wurde die Pfarrei Münzgraben mit der Nachbarpfarrei St. Josef in einem Pfarrverband zusammengelegt. Dadurch stieg die Zahl der zu betreuenden Katholiken deutlich an. Zur Unterstützung des Pfarrers P. Max Svoboda gelang es dem Provinzial, im Januar 2009 einen Mitbruder aus der indischen Provinz als Kaplan in den Grazer Konvent zu assignieren.[644] Die sich sehr gut entwickelnde Zusammenarbeit beider endete plötzlich durch einen tragischen Autounfall, bei dem Svoboda am 17. Februar 2012 ums Leben kam. Nach intensiven Beratungen entschied das Provinzkonsil Anfang Mai 2012, dass die Provinz die Pfarrerstelle aus eigenen Kräften nicht nachbesetzen und auch eine weitere Unterstützung der betagten Grazer Mitbrüder nicht gewährleisten konnte. Da über diese Krise hinaus das permanente Problem der Baulast an Kirche und Kloster bestand, das durch Gehälter nicht zu stemmen war, wurde entschieden, den Grazer Konvent zu schließen. Ordensmeister Bruno Cadoré

642 PA, Provinzrundbrief 1–1998, S. 7–8.

643 Angaben laut: http://www.kleinezeitung.at/steiermark/graz/graz/2535215/strahlt-neuem-glanz.story (Zugriff am 6.12.2013); zu den Planungen 2008 / 09: PA, ProvinzZeitung 12–2008, S. 1–2; zum Beginn: ProvinzZeitung 4–2010, S. 11.

644 PA, ProvinzZeitung 11–2008, S. 5.

Abb. 81: Fatimakirche und Dominikanerkloster in Graz: Ansicht von Osten (aufgenommen ca. 1980; PA, Fotosammlung).

stellte am 31. August 2013 das entsprechende Dekret aus.[645] Die Pfarrei ging bereits am 1. September 2012 in die Obhut eines Weltpriesters der Diözese Graz-Seckau über; die Klostergebäude wurden an das Stift Admont verkauft.[646] Am 4. August 2013 verließ der letzte Dominikaner das Münzgrabenkloster.[647]

Friesach

Betrachtet man die Zahl der in Friesach nach 1965 assignierten Dominikaner, so stellt man fest, dass der dort seit 1949 übliche Personalstand von durchschnittlich sechs Brüdern bis 1981 erhalten blieb, um erst 1984 auf fünf, zwischen 1987 und 1994 auf drei und ab 1997 auf zwei Dominikaner zurückzugehen. Allerdings ist dieser vergleichsweise stabil anmutende Stand

645 PA, Provinzialsakten.

646 Daten laut: http://mj.graz-seckau.at/muenzgraben/pfarrgeschichte# (Zugriff am 6.12.2013).

647 PA, ProvinzZeitung Juni-Juli 2013, S. 20–21.

nur das Ergebnis einer sozusagen kreativen Buchführung der Provinziäle, die versuchten, dem Haus seine Rechte als *domus formata* zu erhalten. Die Zahl der wirklich im Friesacher Kloster wohnenden Insassen sah anders aus: Bis 1966 lebten und arbeiteten im Konvent vier Priester, 1967 waren es sogar fünf. Diese wirkten auf den schon traditionellen Arbeitsfeldern der Friesacher Predigerbrüder: in der Betreuung der Pfarrei Gaisberg, als „Exhortator" der Priester des Dekanats, als Kirchenrektor der Kirche der Friesacher Dominikanerinnen, als Religionslehrer und als Kaplan an der Propsteikirche Friesach. Auch betreuten sie weiterhin als Beichtväter die Dominikanerinnen und die Schwestern des Deutschen Ordens. P. Paulus Gunz unternahm bis zu seinem Tod 1968 Volksmissionen. 1968 jedoch wurde einer der Friesacher Patres in ein anderes Kloster der Provinz versetzt; ein zweiter zog ins Burgenland, um dort eine Pfarrei zu übernehmen – letzterer blieb aber bis 1985 in Friesach assigniert. Realiter lebten also ab 1968 nur mehr drei Patres in Friesach selbst. Im Mai 1968 diskutierte daher das Provinzkonsil die Frage, ob Friesach als *domus formata* gehalten werden konnte, allerdings ohne in der Folge an der rechtlichen Selbständigkeit des Hauses etwas zu ändern.[648] Aus eigener Kraft war eine Aufstockung des Personalstands nicht zu leisten. Das Provinzkapitel von 1970 beauftragte daher den Provinzial, die polnische Provinz um Hilfe zu bitten.[649] Tatsächlich wurde 1972 ein Pater aus der polnischen Provinz nach Friesach versetzt.[650]

Im selben Jahr verstarb der Laienbruder Anton Lipták im Alter von 76 Jahren. Lipták hatte bis dahin zusammen mit dem zweiten Laienbruder des Konvents, Johannes Pfundner, noch den großen Klostergarten bewirtschaftet. Die anderen Liegenschaften des Klosters waren verpachtet. Da Pfundner inzwischen ebenfalls schon 75 Jahre alt war, war ihm der Gartenbau allein nicht mehr möglich. Große Teile des Klostergartens wurden daher 1974 an die Stadt Friesach vermietet.[651]

Im April 1975 verstarb P. Albert Häller, im November P. Raimund Lang. Im Januar 1976 wurde daher P. Fidelis Gallati von Graz nach Friesach assigniert.[652] Der polnische Mitbruder suchte 1977 um Übertritt in den

648 PA, Liber consiliorum provinciae, Sitzung vom 27.5.1968, S. 71.

649 APKap 1970, S. 16, Nr. 41.

650 PA, Provinzialsregestenbuch 2 (1966–2010), Eintrag vom 20.8.1972, Nr. 51.

651 PA, Liber consiliorum provinciae, Sitzung vom 21.3.1974, S. 83 und vom 7.8.1974, S. 84.

652 PA, Provinzialsregestenbuch 2 (1966–2010), Eintrag vom 21.1.1976, Nr. 40.

Weltklerus an und lebte bis dahin *extra conventum*. Das reduzierte die Zahl der im Kloster wohnenden Priester auf zwei: P. Gallati betreute die Pfarrei Gaisberg, P. Heinrich Stumpf arbeitete als Kaplan an der Propsteikirche und als Kurat der Pfarrei Zeltschach; dazu kam noch als Mesner Br. Johannes Pfundner. Für diese drei Mitbrüder war das Klostergebäude viel zu groß. Daher wurde nun auch der Trakt des Kreuzgangs mit dem Refektorium, das zwischenzeitlich als Maschinenfabrik in Verwendung gewesen war, 1977 an die Stadt Friesach vermietet, die den Klostertrakt renovierte und den alten Speisesaal zum Festsaal umgestalten ließ. Der Kärntner Landeshauptmann Leopold Wagner eröffnete den neuen Festsaal am 23. April 1977.[653] Auch andere Teile des Klosters waren an Wirtschaftsbetriebe verpachtet, sodass der Klostergemeinschaft nur der Südtrakt verblieb – was aber immer noch sehr viel Raum darstellte.

1980 wurde der inzwischen emeritierte P. Arthur Fridolin Utz vom Ordensmeister in die Provinz und vom Provinzial nach Friesach assigniert;[654] Utz wurde dadurch bis zu seinem Tod 2001 das wohl berühmteste Mitglied des Friesacher Konvents der Neuzeit. Allerdings blieb er an seinem Altersruhesitz in der Schweiz wohnhaft. Durch diesen juristischen Kunstgriff entstand die eigenartige Situation einer halbierten Kommunität: zwei Patres und ein Laienbruder im Kloster und drei Patres außerhalb. Im Juli 1982, nach Ablauf seines Provinzialats, wurde P. Innozenz Varga nach Friesach assigniert, allerdings wählten ihn schon im Februar 1983 die Wiener Brüder zu ihrem Prior.[655] Für Varga ging im März 1983 P. Jordan Gebhard nach Friesach.[656]

Danach reduzierte sich die Konventualenzahl schnell: P. Stumpf verstarb 1983, P. Gallati 1984. Im April 1986 wurde Gebhard zum Prior von St. Kajetan-München gewählt und zog dorthin. Im Mai desselben Jahres verstarb Laienbruder Johannes Pfundner, wodurch die *domus* nur mehr aus dem *extra conventum* lebenden P. Utz bestand. Um diese unhaltbare Lage zu retten, erklärte P. Fulko Hilgefort sich bereit, nach Friesach zu gehen. Da Hilgefort aber Pfarrer der Pfarrei am Wiener Konvent war, konnte er erst im November umziehen. In der Zwischenzeit übernahmen Patres aus Graz und

---

653 PA, Provinzrundbrief vom 23.4.1977, S. 2.

654 PA, Provinzialsregestenbuch 2 (1966–2010), Eintrag vom 3.3.1980, Nr. 10.

655 PA, Provinzialsregestenbuch 2 (1966–2010), Einträge vom 15.7.1982, Nr. 8 und vom 20.2.1983, Nr. 3.

656 PA, Provinzialsregestenbuch 2 (1966–2010), Eintrag vom 1.3. / 6.3.1983, Nr. 10.

Wien sozusagen ambulant die Seelsorge an der Friesacher Ordenskirche, bei den Dominikanerinnen und in der Pfarrei Gaisberg.[657] Über die folgenden Jahre hinweg arbeitete Hilgefort allein an der Klosterkirche, der Pfarrei Gaisberg und als Beichtvater bei den Dominikanerinnen, den Deutschordensschwestern und beim Benediktinerstift St. Lambrecht. Erst 1998 zog mit P. Adalbert von Papius ein weiterer Mitbruder ins Kloster ein.[658]

Noch unter Varga waren 1982 die Konventszimmer im Südtrakt des Klosters renoviert worden.[659] Inzwischen wurden aber umfassendere Erneuerungs- und Reparaturarbeiten an der ganzen Anlage notwendig. Im Juli 1983 beschloss das Provinzkonsil den Beginn eines ersten Bauabschnitts, die Entfeuchtung der Kirche und eines Teils des Kreuzgangs, dessen Kosten vom Friesacher Konvent selbst, von der Stadt Friesach, von der Diözese Gurk-Klagenfurt, vom Land Kärnten und von den anderen Häusern der Provinz getragen wurde.[660] Die Entfeuchtung war im März 1984 abgeschlossen.[661] Der zweite Bauabschnitt bestand in der Renovierung der Kirche. Von den zwei dafür eingeholten Restaurierungsentwürfen entschied sich das Provinzkonsil für den des Grazer Architekten Reinhard Schöpf.[662] Problematisch war die Finanzierung, da die von der Diözese, dem Land Kärnten und dem Denkmalamt zugesicherten Zuschüsse das Kostenvolumen bei weitem nicht trugen; daher appellierte der Provinzial an alle Klöster des Ordens und alle Mitglieder der dominikanischen Familie im deutschsprachigen Raum für Spenden.[663] Immerhin war durch Eigenmittel des Konvents und die Zuschusszusagen eine Summe von etwa 1,8 Millionen öS für die Malerarbeiten vorhanden.[664] Für den fehlenden Rest von 370.000 DM übernahm das Provinzkonsil eine Bürgschaft.[665] Ins-

657 PA, Provinzrundbrief vom 18.7.1986, S. 2.

658 Der Vollständigkeit halber sei erwähnt, dass 1997 / 98 für kurze Zeit ein in Deutschland arbeitender Pater ebenfalls *extra conventum* zu Friesach gehörte.

659 PA, Provinzrundbrief vom 12.11.1982, S. 4.

660 PA, Provinzrundbrief vom 4.8.1983, S. 5 (über die Sitzung des Provinzkonsils vom 18.7.1983 in Friesach).

661 PA, Provinzrundbrief vom 12.4.1984, S. 2.

662 PA, Provinzrundbrief vom 12.4.1984, S. 2 (über die Sitzung des Provinzkonsils am 13.3.1984) und Liber consiliorum provinciae, S. 4, Sitzung des Provinzkonsils in Wien am 22.3.1984.

663 PA, Provinzrundbrief vom 27.7.1984, S. 2.

664 Ebd, S. 3 (über Sitzung des Provinzkonsils in Augsburg am 19.6.1984).

665 PA, Provinzrundbrief „im Dezember“ 1984, S. 3 (über Sitzung des Provinzkonsils in Augsburg am 6.11.1984).

Abb. 82: Dominikanerkirche St. Nikolaus in Friesach: Innenansicht nach der Renovierung 1985 (PA, Fotosammlung).

gesamt machte die Renovierung gute Fortschritte, sodass Diözesanbischof Egon Kapellari am 6. Oktober 1985 den neuen Zelebrationsaltar weihen konnte.[666] Danach stand noch eine Restschuld von etwa einer Million öS bzw. 150.000 DM offen, die durch Spenden und Ratenzahlungen abgetragen werden konnte.[667] Besonders verdient um die Finanzierung machte sich ein im Frühjahr 1983 aus Kartellbrüdern des CV, KV, KÖL und MKV gegründetes Kuratorium durch Spendenaufrufe und tätige Mitarbeit.[668] Im April 1993 wurden mit der Restaurierung der Dominikuskapelle die Arbeiten abgeschlossen.[669]

Zusammen mit Retz wurden auch die pastoralen und wirtschaftlichen Fragen des Friesacher Hauses der vom Provinzkonsil auf seiner Sitzung am 21. Oktober 1992 eingesetzten Kommission unterstellt.[670] Das Provinzkapitel von 1994 befand – anders als in Retz – die wirtschaftliche Lage Friesachs als gesund; nur die Personallage machte Sorgen.[671] Die Arbeit der Kommission endete aus dem gleichen Grund wie in Retz: Aufgrund der Nichterfüllbarkeit der geänderten Ordenssatzungen über die Bedingungen des Personalstands für ein selbständiges Haus – vier assignierte Dominikaner – erklärte das Provinzkonsil am 25. Oktober 1995 das Friesacher Kloster zur *domus filialis* des Konvents Graz.[672] In der Praxis änderte sich dadurch an den Abläufen in Friesach nichts. Auch die Idee des Provinzkapitels von 2002, Friesach zum Urlaubskloster der Provinz zu machen, wurde nicht umgesetzt.[673] Allerdings hielt noch das Provinzkapitel von 2006 an Friesach als Seelsorgsstelle bzw. „pastorale Zukunftsoption" der Provinz fest.[674] Nur war durch die Überalterung der Friesacher Brüder und das Unvermögen der Provinz, diese zu ersetzen, inzwischen auf der zivilrechtlichen Seite ein großes Problem entstanden, da die Körperschaft öffentlichen Rechts „Dominikanerkloster Friesach" bei Ausfall von P. Hilgefort handlungsunfähig werden konnte. Um eine solche Krise gar nicht erst aufkommen zu las-

---

666 PA, Provinzrundbrief vom 12.12.1985, S. 2.
667 PA, Provinzrundbrief „zum Osterfest" 1986, S. 3.
668 *St. Dominikuswerk* (1986), S. 9–10.
669 PA, Provinzrundbrief 1–1993, S. 7.
670 PA, Provinzrundbrief 2–1992, S. 7 (über die Provinzkonsilssitzung am 21.10.1992).
671 APKap 1994, S. 30, Nr. 109.
672 PA, Provinzrundbrief 2–1995, S. 8 (über die Provinzkonsilssitzung in Augsburg am 25.10.1995).
673 APKap 2002, S. 19, Nrn. 77–80.
674 APKap 2006, S. 15, Nr. 59.

sen, beauftragte das Provinzkapitel den Provinzial, das Eigentum des Friesacher Klosters auf die Körperschaft des österreichischen Provinzteils überschreiben zu lassen und den Ordensmeister zu bitten, die *domus filialis* Friesach zu schließen.[675] Mit Dekret vom 9. Juli 2010 hob Ordensmeister Carlos Azpiroz Costa Friesach als Kloster auf.[676]

München

Waren im Konvent an St. Kajetan laut Angaben der Provinzkataloge 1965 noch 14 Dominikaner assigniert (zwölf Priester, zwei Laienbrüder) und 1971 noch zwölf (zehn Priester, zwei Laienbrüder), so nahm diese Zahl danach ab: Zwischen 1973 und 1999 waren es durchschnittlich pro Jahr zwischen sieben und neun. Im Jahr 2000 – bedingt durch das Tutorenmodell, in dem St. Kajetan ebenfalls Ausbildungskonvent war – stieg der Personalstand wieder auf zehn (sechs Priester, ein Laienbruder, drei Kleriker). Nachdem Bruder Benedikt Kern bereits 1994 verstorben war, starb mit Benno Hermann 2002 der letzte Laienbruder des Klosters. Danach waren nur mehr Patres an St. Kajetan assigniert: zwischen 2003 und 2005 sechs, zwischen 2007 und 2009 vier, 2010 und 2011 fünf und seit 2013 sieben. Diese Assignationszahlen geben aber nicht die Zahl des wirklich im Haus vorhandenen Personalstandes wieder: 1965 bis 1971 lebten drei Patres *extra conventum* auf Seelsorgsstellen, 1973 bis 1977 und 2003 bis 2005 zwei. Dass der Personalstand des Klosters dennoch lange vergleichsweise stabil blieb, war nicht nur den Kräften der süddeutsch-österreichischen Provinz zu verdanken. Wegen seines zentralen Standorts neben der Münchner Universität war St. Kajetan auch für Brüder aus anderen Provinzen attraktiv, die dort studieren wollten. So kamen 1965 bis 1966 zwei Patres aus der Schweiz, 1965 zwei und 1966 einer aus den USA, in denselben Jahren einer aus der Teutonia, einer aus der Provinz Francia, 1969 bis 1971 einer aus der Provinz Hispania und 1971 bis 1973 einer aus Irland. Auch in den folgenden Jahrzehnten wohnten immer wieder einzelne ausländische Dominikaner für ein oder mehrere Jahre zu Studienzwecken an St. Kajetan. Darüber hinaus nahm der zur Teutonia gehörende P. Ulrich Horst als Inhaber des Lehrstuhls für die Geschichte der Theologie seit dem Ausgang der Väterzeit an der Ludwig-Maximilian-Universität und als Vorstand des Grabmann-

675 Ebd., S. 21, Nrn. 96–100.
676 Datum laut APKap 2011, S. 31, Nr. 149 und PA, ProvinzZeitung 6–2010, S. 8.

Abb. 83: Der Konvent an S. Kajetan-München anlässlich der Visitation der Provinz durch Ordensmeister Damian Byrne im Juni/Juli 1988. Von links: P. Amadeus Schmalhofer, P. Ulrich Horst, Br. Benedikt Kern, P. Prior Jordan Gebhard, P. Henri Lecapitaine, Ordensmeister P. Damian Byrne, P. Richard Aquinas Schenk, P. Magnus Beck, P. Klaus Obermeier, P. Subprior Wolfram Drühe, P. Provinzial Innozenz Varga (PA, Fotosammlung).

Instituts laut den Provinzkatalogen von 1986 bis 2000 an St. Kajetan seinen Wohnsitz, ohne dort assigniert zu sein. Ebenso war P. Richard Aquinas Schenk von 1977 bis 1994 Gast an St. Kajetan, zunächst als Doktorand, später als wissenschaftlicher Mitarbeiter an der Universität München und an der Bayerischen Akademie der Wissenschaften.

Die Kerngemeinschaft des Konvents, die sich ab 1979 herauskristallisiert hatte, blieb klein: Laienbruder Benedikt Kern war bis 1994 Pförtner des Klosters, Laienbruder Benno Hermann bis zu seinem Tod Mesner an St. Kajetan. P. Magnus Beck verstarb 1994; er war bis 1990 Kirchenrektor von St. Kajetan gewesen. P. Amadeus Schmalhofer hatte bis 2007 als Organist und Leiter der Vokalkapelle an St. Kajetan amtiert;[677] er verstarb 2012. P. Klaus Obermeier gehört seit 1972 zum Konvent; er arbeitete laut den Provinzkatalogen von 1977 bis 2007 als Religionslehrer und Schulseelsorger und übernahm von 1990 bis 2012 außerdem die Aufgabe des Kirchenrektors von St. Kajetan. Der aus der Teutonia stammende P. Wolfram Drühe,

677 PA, ProvinzZeitung 11–2007, S. 6.

der schon von 1964 bis 1966 als Religionslehrer zum Konvent gehört hatte, war von 1974 bis 1995 Seelsorger an St. Kajetan. Da seitens der süddeutsch-österreichischen Provinz keine Verstärkung zu erhoffen war, entwickelte der Konvent eine eigene Taktik zur Personalaufstockung, die darin bestand, Mitbrüder aus anderen Konventen und Provinzen zum Prior zu wählen, was oft auch gelang. Erst Anfang der 1990er Jahre konnten die durch Todesfälle im Konvent entstandenen Lücken wieder mit provinzeigenen Brüdern gefüllt werden. Weitere Assignationen nach St. Kajetan erfolgten nach 2010.

Die Seelsorgstätigkeit des Konvents konzentrierte sich mit Schrumpfen der Gemeinschaft auf die Sakramentenpastoral in der Kirche St. Kajetan. Dennoch nahmen die Brüder auch andere Aufgaben wahr, die meist im Zusammenhang mit Lehrtätigkeit standen, etwa als Religionslehrer an Schulen oder an Hochschulen und Universitäten; so wirkte seit 1997 P. Wolfgang Müller als Professor für Dogmatik der katholisch-theologischen Fakultät Luzern oder P. Paul Hellmeier seit 2009 als Dozent für Philosophie an der Hochschule der Jesuiten in München. Die Betreuung von Schwestern spielte für den Konvent in den letzten Jahrzehnten keine Rolle mehr. Dafür stellten Brüder Spirituale an Priesterseminaren, so von 1979 bis 1981 P. Hilarius Barth am erzbischöflichen Priesterseminar und 2001 bis 2002 P. Paul Schäfersküpper am Herzoglichen Georgianum. Schäfersküpper nahm danach eine Stelle der Erzdiözese München-Freising als Tourismus-, Zirkus- und Schaustellerseelsorger wahr.[678]

Hilfreich war, dass die Stiftskirche von St. Kajetan dem Freistaat Bayern gehört – wodurch die umfangreiche Innenrenovierung, die 1998 begonnen wurde und erst 2008 im Wesentlichen abgeschlossen war, nicht auf Kosten des Dominikanerkonvents ging.[679]

In der *domus* St. Albert in Freimann waren von 1961 bis 1977 zwischen sechs und acht Dominikaner assigniert, ein Laienbruder und fünf bis sechs Patres. Laienbruder Kilian Recher starb 1980. Danach bestand die Gemeinschaft bis 1989 meist aus fünf (1987 aus vier) Priestern. Zunächst hatten noch Mitbrüder aus anderen Provinzen wesentlich zum Personalstand beigetragen: 1964 wohnte dort ein Pater aus der niederländischen Provinz; von 1961 bis 1964 stammten zwei der Patres aus der

---

678 Dazu: *Dominikus* (2008 / 09) S. 33–37.

679 Dazu: PA, Provinzrundbrief 3–1998, S. 20–21; *Dominikus* 1–1999, S. 14; Provinz-Zeitung 2–2004, S. 6 und 8–9–2005, S. 4.

Teutonia, 1964 bis 1966 drei. P. Johannes Oderich Edelbauer, ebenfalls *filius* der Teutonia, war schon seit 1950 in St. Albert assigniert und trat 1970 in die süddeutsch-österreichische Provinz über. Ab 1964 war jedoch ein verhältnismäßig großer Teil der assignierten Patres *extra conventum* tätig: von 1964 bis 1967 zwei, 1969 bis 1977 meist drei (1973 vier). Ab 1978 lebten zwei der assignierten Priester in Pflegeheimen, die sie auch seelsorglich betreuten. Die Kerngemeinschaft im Kloster war dementsprechend kleiner: Sie bestand aus den für Pfarrseelsorge in Freimann von der Erzdiözese München-Freising angestellten Brüdern, dem Pfarrer, dem bis 1977 zwei Patres als Kapläne zur Seite standen. Einer davon, P. Adalbert von Papius, war ab 1977 für die Betreuung der Kuratie von St. Katharina zuständig.

Im Rahmen der Diskussionen über den Vorschlag von Ordensmeister de Couesnongle bezüglich der Errichtung eines Modellkonvents Anfang der 1980er Jahre hatte auch St. Albert kurzfristig eine Rolle als möglicher Standort gespielt;[680] da es aber nie zur Bildung eines solchen Konvents kam, blieb St. Albert Pfarrkloster. 1980 wurde das Klostergebäude innen und außen renoviert; die Hauptlast der Kosten trug die Erzdiözese.[681] In der Pfarrkirche war schon 1977 eine neue Orgel aufgestellt und eingeweiht worden;[682] 1981 und 1982 folgte die Renovierung des Gotteshauses selbst, die am 19. Dezember 1982 mit der Weihe des neuen Zelebrationsaltars durch Weihbischof Ernst Tewes abgeschlossen werden konnte.[683] Der Beschluss, dass P. Clemens Wehrle St. Albert verlassen und als Studentenmagister nach Wien gehen sollte, wirbelte die Pfarrmitglieder auf; durch eine Unterschriftenaktion und schriftliche Proteste versuchten sie, ein Bleiben von P. Wehrle zu erreichen – die Provinz blieb bei jedoch ihrem Entschluss.[684] Unverständlich war der Protest nicht: Die Pfarrei hatte den Schrumpfungsprozess des Personalstands des Klosters in den vorausgehenden Jahren hautnah miterlebt und der Priestermangel in der Provinz war kein Geheimnis. Mit der Übernahme des Pfarreramtes durch P. von Papius rückte der Sitz des Pfarrers von St. Albert weg auf die Kuratie St. Katharina.

680 Siehe PA, Liber consilii provincialis, Provinzkonsilssitzung in Augsburg vom 3.1.1980.

681 PA, Provinzrundbrief vom 10.12.1980, S. 4.

682 PA, Provinzrundbrief vom 23.1.1978, S. 2.

683 PA, Provinzrundbrief vom 20.4.1983, S. 2.

684 Siehe PA, Provinzrundbriefe vom 27.7.1984, S. 4 (über die Sitzung des Provinzkonsils in Augsburg am 19.6.1984) und vom 25.9.1985 (über die Provinzkonsilssitzung in Augsburg am 26.7.1985).

Allerdings war sich auch die Leitung der süddeutsch-österreichischen Provinz der Lage bewusst. Provinzial Varga trat deshalb 1986 in Kontakt mit der polnischen Provinz, die ja schon in den 1970er Jahren in Österreich ausgeholfen hatte.[685] Am 20. Mai 1987 konnte er dem Provinzkonsil mitteilen, „dass im Herbst ein polnischer Mitbruder nach Freimann kommen werde und im Herbst 1988 zwei weitere nachkommen würden"[686]. Am 15. November 1987 wurde P. Lucjan Puzon Kaplan an St. Albert begrüßt, am 1. Oktober 1988 außerdem P. Józef Zboržil.[687] Die guten Erfahrungen, die man mit beiden Mitbrüdern machte, brachten das Provinzkonsil zu dem Beschluss: „In München Freimann soll neben der bestehenden *domus formata* unserer Provinz eine andere *domus formata* der polnischen Provinz errichtet werden. Dies ist auch das Ergebnis des Gespräches mit dem polnischen Provinzial vom 15./16. April [sc. 1989] in München Freimann."[688] Wie das konkret aussah, berichtete P. Varga seinen Mitbrüdern im Provinzrundbrief:

> „Beim Provinzkonsil am 15. November [sc. 1989] wurde der Vertragsentwurf zur Übernahme von St. Albert-Freimann durch die polnische Provinz besprochen. Der Vertrag zwischen der polnischen Provinz und unserer Provinz wurde mit Wirkung vom 1. Januar 1990 am 4. Januar geschlossen. Laut Vertrag verlegt unsere Provinz mit Datum vom 31. Dezember 1989 unsere *domus formata* von der Situlistraße 81, D-8000 München 45 nach der Kuratie St. Katharina von Siena, Pferggasse 4, D-8000 München 45. Mit Einverständnis des Provinzkonsils errichtete P. General mit 1. Januar 1990 eine *domus religiosa* der polnischen Provinz in der Situlistraße 81. St. Albert untersteht damit dem polnischen Provinzial. Der Vertrag kann von jeder Seite mit Frist von einem Jahr gekündigt werden, jeweils zu Beginn eines Quartals. Mit dem gleichen Datum wurde ein Vertrag zwischen dem Ordinariat München und der polnischen Provinz geschlossen."[689]

Die Erzdiözese München-Freising übergab den polnischen Dominikanern die Pfarrei St. Albert am 1. Februar 1990.[690] Das Kloster ist seither mit einem Pfarrer und drei Kaplänen bzw. priesterlichen Seelsorgemitarbeitern

685 PA, Provinzrundbrief „zum Osterfest" 1986, S. 3 (über Provinzkonsilssitzung vom 5.1.1986 in Augsburg).
686 PA, Provinzrundbrief vom 22.6.1987, S. 3 (über die Provinzkonsilssitzung in Augsburg am 20.5.1987).
687 PA, Provinzrundbriefe vom 22.12.1987, S. 4 und vom 12.12.1988, S. 5.
688 PA, Provinzrundbrief vom 2.7.1989, S. 7 (über die Provinzkonsilssitzung in Augsburg am 21.6.1989).
689 PA, Provinzrundbrief vom 2.2.1990, S. 4.
690 Ebd., S. 8.

Abb. 84: Pfarrkirche St. Katharina von Siena in München-Freimann (PA, Fotosammlung).

besetzt. Im September 2000 übernahmen die polnischen Mitbrüder auch die Seelsorge in der benachbarten Pfarrei St. Gertrud, die sie ebenfalls mit einem Pfarrer und zwei Kaplänen bzw. priesterlichen Seelsorgemitarbeitern ausstatteten. Im Juli 2008 wurde in der zur Pfarrei St. Gertrud gehörenden Neubausiedlung Nordheide das Dominikuszentrum eingeweiht.[691] Dieses von Professor Andreas Meck entworfene Gebäude beherbergt das Pfarr-

691 Laut: http://www.erzbistum-muenchen.de/Pfarrei/Page011413.aspx (Zugriff am 9.12.2013); dazu: PA, ProvinzZeitung 12–2006, S. 3.

heim mit Kapelle, eine Kindertagesstätte, eine katholische Jugendstelle und ein Caritaszentrum.[692]

Dass die Rechte einer *domus formata* überhaupt auf St. Katharina überhaupt übertragen werden konnten, war dem Anwachsen der Bevölkerung der dortigen Pfarrkuratie und dem damit einhergehenden Ausbau der Gebäude zu verdanken, die auch größere Wohnmöglichkeiten für die Seelsorger mit einbezogen. Anfang der 1990er Jahre waren 2000 der 3000 geplanten und geförderten neuen Wohnungen fertiggestellt; die Pfarrei St. Katharina sollte damit etwa zehntausend Menschen umfassen.[693] Die ursprüngliche Barackenkirche war zu Beginn der 1970 Jahre einem „Mehrzweckbau" gewichen, „der Räume sowohl für die gottesdienstliche Versammlung als auch für die Begegnung der verschiedenen Gemeindegruppen zur Verfügung" stellte; dieser Bau hatte am 27. Oktober 1973 eingeweiht werden können.[694] Am 3. Dezember 1989 legte Weihbischof Engelbert Siebler den Grundstein für ein neues Pfarr- und Caritaszentrum.[695] Der Mehrzweckbau wurde durch eine neue Kirche ersetzt, die Kardinalerzbischof Friedrich Wetter am 23. Juni 1991 einweihte.[696] Bedingt durch den Auszug aus St. Albert begann der Personalstand in der *domus* St. Katharina 1990 mit vier Priestern – von denen drei allerdings nicht dort lebten; P. Hilarius Barth gehörte während seines Aufenthaltes in Bronnbach bis 1995 dazu, ebenso die beiden älteren, in Seniorenheimen wohnenden P. Johannes Edelbauer († 1991) und P. Joseph Rottenecker († 1992). Ein weiterer *extra conventum* lebender Bruder wurde ab 2003 nach St. Katharina assigniert. Die *domus* wurde somit immer von der Präsenz des Pfarrers von St. Katharina getragen: bis 1998 von P. Adalbert von Papius und nach dessen Rückzug in den Ruhestand von P. Günter Reitzi. Anfang der 1990er Jahre beherbergte die *domus* aber noch einen Mitbruder aus den USA und einen aus der Teutonia, die sich zu Studienzwecken in München aufhielten, aber nicht an St. Katharina assigniert waren. Von 2003 bis 2006 wurde außerdem ein Mitbruder aus der indischen Provinz in die *domus* assigniert, der neben seiner Promotion an der Universität auch in der Seelsorge in der Pfarrei mithalf. Aufgrund dieser unbefriedigenden per-

---

692 Angaben laut: http://architektur.mapolismagazin.com/meck-architekten-dominikuszentrum-muenchen-muenchen (Zugriff am 9.12.2013).

693 Angaben laut: PA, Provinzrundbriefe vom „Dezember" 1991, S. 2 und 1–1993, S. 22.

694 PA, Provinzrundbrief vom 9.1.1982.

695 PA, Provinzrundbrief vom 2.2.1990, S. 8.

696 PA, Provinzrundbrief vom „Dezember" 1991, S. 2 und 7.

sonellen Situation wurde die *domus formata* 1995 zur *domus filialis* des Konvents an St. Kajetan erklärt.[697]

Da der Personalmangel eine Behebung der Lage nicht zuließ, entschied das Provinzkapitel 2006, die *domus* an St. Katharina bis spätestens zum 1. Oktober 2008 zu schließen.[698] Dieser Termin ließ sich aber nicht halten. Daher beauftragte das Provinzkapitel von 2011 den Provinzial neuerlich, den Schließungsbeschluss durchzuführen.[699] Ordensmeister Bruno Cadoré hob mit Dekret vom 31. August 2013 die Niederlassung auf.[700]

Augsburg – Regensburg

Nach dem Ende des Predigerkurses 1966 fluktuierte der Personalstand des Konvents an Heilig Kreuz in Augsburg stark. Die Zahl der dort assignierten Brüder blieb bis zum Beginn der 1980er Jahre erfreulich hoch, nicht aber die Zahl der wirklich im Kloster lebenden Brüder.

Katalog	*Priester*	*Laien-brüder*	*Novizen – Studenten*	*ständiger Diakon*	*Gesamt-zahl*	*davon extra conventum*
1967	15	7			22	3 P.
1966	14	7			21	4 P.
1971	17	5	2 Nov.		24	5 P
1973	17	6	2 S.		25	7 P., 1 L., 1 S.
1977	16	4			20	7 P.
1979	13	3			16	6 P.
1981	12	3			15	5 P.
1984	9	2			11	3 P.
1987	8	2			10	2 P.
1989	7	1			8	1 P.
1991	6	1			7	1 P.
1994	5	1			6	1 P.

697 PA, Provinzrundbrief 2–1995, S. 8 (über die Provinzkonsilssitzung vom 25.10.1995).
698 APKap 2006, S. 19, Nr. 81.
699 APKap 2011, S. 31, Nr. 150.
700 PA, Provinzialsakten.

Katalog	*Priester*	*Laien-brüder*	*Novizen – Studenten*	*ständiger Diakon*	*Gesamt-zahl*	*davon extra conventum*
1997	7	1			8	
1999	6	2	1 S.		9	
2000	9	1	1 S.		11	1 P.
2003	10			1	11	1 P.
2004	9			1	10	1 P.
2005	6			1	7	*Regens-burg*
2006	7		1 S.	1	9	1 P.
2007	7		1 S.	1	9	1 P.
2008	7			1	8	1 P.
2009	7		3 S.	1	11	3 P.
2010	8		1 S.	1	10	3 P.
2011	12			1	13	3 P.
2013	10			1	11	3 P.

Bezüglich der Dominikanerpräsenz im Kloster an Heilig Kreuz sind außerdem zwei weitere Dinge zu berücksichtigen: Zum einen besaß der Augsburger Konvent zwei Standorte: Die Mitbrüder, die an St. Wolfgang in Augsburg-Spickel wohnten, lebten daher zwar nicht *extra conventum*, aber auch nicht an Heilig Kreuz. Allerdings wohnten an St. Wolfgang von 1967 bis 1978 nur ein Pater und ein Laienbruder, danach nur mehr ein Pater. Zum zweiten endete mit dem Predigerkurs auch zunächst die sozusagen internationale Besetzung des Konvents. Von 1967 bis 1971 stammten von den im Konvent assignierten Patres zwei aus der Teutonia, von 1973 bis 1981 war es nur noch einer. Ab 1982 gehörte auch ein aus der kroatischen Provinz stammender Mitbruder zum Konvent, der 2000 in die süddeutsch-österreichische Provinz übertrat. Zu einer stärkeren Internationalisierung des Hauses kam es nach 1999: Von 1999 bis 2004 gehörte ein Mitbruder aus der indischen Provinz dazu, von 2000 bis 2003 einer aus der slowakischen Provinz und von 2002 bis 2004 einer aus dem baltischen Vikariat des Ordens. Die Präsenz im Dominikanischen Zentrum im Regensburg, wo ein Pater des Augsburger Konvents seit 2006 seinen festen Wohnsitz hatte, wurde ab 2009 mit einem Mitbruder aus der indischen und einem Mitbruder aus der kolumbianischen Provinz verstärkt.

Werden beide Punkte bei der Interpretation der obigen Tabelle einberechnet, lässt sich die Personalentwicklung des Augsburger Konvents in den letzten vier Jahrzehnten in drei Phasen gliedern: Die erste Phase dauerte von 1967 bis 1994. Sie war seit Anfang der 1970er Jahre gekennzeichnet durch einen Personalabbau im Kloster, der deutlich wird, wenn man die *extra conventum* und in St. Wolfgang lebenden Brüder von der Gesamtzahl der Assignierten abzieht. 1967 lebten im Kloster an der Heilig-Kreuz-Straße 15 Dominikaner, 1977 waren es elf, 1987 sieben und 1994 noch vier. Es ist kein Wunder, dass „die Situation des Augsburger Konvents" das Provinzkapitel von 1990 „mit besonderer Sorge" erfüllte.[701] Die Einführung des Tutorenmodells erlaubte es aber, auch Brüder mit einfacher Profess nach Augsburg zu assignieren, was eine zweite Phase einläutete, die von 1995 bis 1999/2000 dauerte. Zwar war diese Phase nur sehr kurz, jedoch rettete die Versetzung jüngerer Mitbrüder nach Augsburg den Bestand des Klosters, dessen Zahlenbestand durch Todesfälle inzwischen sehr geschwächt war. Augsburg blieb selbst nach dem Ende des Tutorenmodells und der Verlegung des süddeutschen Ausbildungskonvents nach Freiburg Wohnort von Brüdern mit einfacher Profess. Um diesen Brüdern ein vernünftiges Klosterleben bieten zu können, wurde der Augsburger Personalstand durch Dominikaner anderer Provinzen aufgefüllt, die diese zur Hilfe und Unterstützung zur Verfügung stellten. So begann 1999 die dritte Phase der Personalstandsentwicklung, die in einer Internationalisierung des Augsburger Konvents bestand, wobei diese sich ab 2009 im Dominikanischen Zentrum in Regensburg konkretisierte, um dort eine Zukunftsperspektive herausbilden zu können.

Das von den Augsburger Dominikanern nach 1967 ausgehende Pastoralangebot, das vorher so reichhaltig und vielfältig gewesen war, schrumpfte mit dem Personalstand – oder besser ausgedrückt, es konzentrierte sich auf die Kerngemeinschaft, die sich herausbildete. Fokus blieb dabei die mit der Heilig-Kreuz-Kirche zusammenhängende Sakramentenpastoral. Sehr lange waren bzw. sind an dieser Kirche tätig: P. Hermann Weber (von 1964 bis 1967 als Benefiziat und von 1967 bis zu seinem Tod 1982 als Kirchenrektor), P. Raphael Börger (von 1960 bis 1983 als Benefiziat, danach bis 2004 als Kirchenrektor), P. Egino Holzhauser (bis 1969 Lehrer an einer Berufsschule, danach bis zu seinem Tod 1987 als Benefiziat) und P. Mirko Šarič (seit 1982 als Benefiziat). Viele weitere Mitglieder des Konvents wirkten ebenfalls als Ge-

701 APKap 1990, S. 16. Nr. 34.

sprächsseelsorger an Heilig Kreuz; die Betreuung dieses Gotteshauses und der Autobahnkirche bildet heute die Hauptaufgaben des Konvents. Von 2000 bis 2005 kümmerten sich nacheinander zwei Mitbrüder aus der slowakischen Provinz um die Seelsorge für Spätaussiedler aus Russland und Kasachstan.[702] 2004 wurde nach langen Jahren die Gefangenenseelsorge aufgegeben.[703] 2013 ging P. Dominikus Kirchmaier als Pfarrer in den Ruhestand, nachdem er sich bis 1987 um die Pfarreien in Batzenhofen, Hirblingen und Heretsried sowie um die Pfarreien Aulzhausen, Gebenhofen und Mühlhausen gekümmert hatte. Hinzu kamen von 2005 bis 2011 Mitarbeiten an der Augsburger Hochschulseelsorge und seit 2007 am Projekt „Moritzpunkt" in der Citypastoral.[704]

Im Rahmen der Personalkrise musste der Konvent auch seinen zweiten Standort, St. Wolfgang, aufgeben. Schon das Provinzkapitel von 1982 hatte den Provinzial gebeten, „zu prüfen, ob die Pfarrei St. Wolfgang in Augsburg / Spickel unter den gegebenen Umständen weiterhin vom Orden versorgt werden" könne.[705] Auf Wunsch des dortigen Mitbruders, P. Eckehart Mayer, der seine Arbeit als Pfarrer nicht aufgeben wollte, blieb der Standort jedoch bestehen.[706] Im Jahre 2000 trat Mayer in den Ruhestand; als Pfarrer folgte ihm P. Dominikus Jakob nach.[707] Jakob wurde im Oktober 2004 zum Prior des Konvents gewählt. Da P. Raphael Börger inzwischen das 80. Lebensjahr erreicht hatte und sich als Kirchenrektor von Heilig Kreuz zur Ruhe setzen wollte, tat sich dort eine Lücke auf, die von den im Konvent verbliebenen Mitbrüdern nicht zu füllen war. Deshalb wurde die Pfarrei St. Wolfgang aufgegeben und P. Jakob ging als Kirchenrektor nach Heilig Kreuz. Am 1. Januar 2005 vereinte die Diözese die Pfarrei St. Wolfgang mit der Nachbarpfarrei St. Don Bosco; sie wird seither von Salesianerpatres betreut.[708]

---

702 *Dominikus* (2000) S. 25–27.

703 PA, ProvinzZeitung 1–2004, S. 5.

704 Zur Mitarbeit in der Studentenseelsorge: *Dominikus* (2005 / 06) S. 22–23; zur Teilnahme am Projekt „Moritzpunkt": *Dominikus* (2005) S. 16–18.

705 APKap 1982, S. 15, Nr. 44.

706 PA, Provinzrundbriefe vom 27.7.1984, S. 3 (über die Provinzkonsilssitzung in Augsburg am 19.6.1984) und „im Dezember" 1984, S. 3 (über die Provinzkonsilssitzung in Augsburg am 6.11.1984).

707 *Dominikus* (2000) S. 25.

708 Hoyer: *Heilig Kreuz*, S. 754 und Groll: Mutterpfarrei, S. 1351–1352.

Abb. 85: Kirche Heilig Kreuz in Augsburg: Skulptur „Der Triumph des Kreuzes" von Hans Ladner in der Apsis (Postkarte; PA, Fotosammlung).

Mitte der 1970er Jahre wurde eine groß anlegte Renovierung von Heilig Kreuz nötig, die zu einer Neugestaltung der Apsis der Kirche führte: Der Hochaltar und der nach der Liturgiereform provisorisch errichtete Volksaltar wurden durch einen neuen Zelebrationsaltar aus weißem Marmor er-

Abb. 86: Kirche Heilig Kreuz in Augsburg: Aufsetzen der neuen Turmzwiebel am 27. Oktober 1989 (Archiv des Augsburger Dominikanerkonvents, Fotosammlung).

setzt, der näher am Kirchenschiff, im Westende der Apsis aufgestellt wurde. Der Tabernakel, groß genug, um die Monstranz mit dem „Wunderbarlichen Gut“ aussetzen zu können, kam an das Ende des ersten Drittels der Apsis, flankiert von zwei marmornen Leuchterbänken, die die letzten zwei Drittel optisch abgrenzten. Dadurch entstand im Rest der Apsis ein eigener Bereich für das Chorgebet der Brüder. Abgeschlossen wurde die Apsis an ihrem Ostende durch eine neue Skulptur von der Hand des Münchner Bildhauers Hans Ladner, die den Triumph des Kreuzes Christi, umgeben von den Leidenswerkzeugen der Passion Jesu darstellte, in die Ladner auch die beiden aus der Barockzeit stammenden Holzfiguren des Kaisers Heraklius und der Kaiserin Helena integrierte. Auch die Neugestaltung der Apsisfenster durch den Maler Hubert Distler aus Wildenroth an der Amper bezog sich auf das Kreuz: In dunklen Farben wurde im unteren Bereich der Fenster die Sünde und die Schuld der Menschen zum Ausdruck gebracht, die den Erlösungstod Christi nötig gemacht hatten; hinter Ladners Holzkreuz hingegen stieg, angedeutet durch eine goldene Sonne, das Osterereignis empor.[709] Diözesanbischof Josef Stimpfle weihte am 19. De-

709 Zur Renovierung: Hoyer: *Heilig Kreuz*, S. 727–743.

Abb. 87: Kirche Heilig Kreuz in Augsburg: Der durch Hans Ladner neugestaltete Aussetzungstabernakel mit der Monstranz der Reliquie des „Wunderbarlichen Guts" (Archiv des Dominikanerkonvents Augsburg, Fotosammlung).

Abb. 88: Dominikanerkonvent an Heilig Kreuz in Augsburg: Blick auf den neuen Altar in der Hauskapelle (Archiv des Dominikanerkonvents Augsburg, Fotosammlung).

zember 1982 den neuen Zelebrationsaltar.[710] 1987/88 wurde der Kirchturm von außen saniert. In diesem Zusammenhang kam die Idee auf, statt des nach dem Weltkrieg aufgesetzten flachen Daches den Turm wieder mit einer Zwiebelhaube zu bekrönen. Am 27. Oktober 1989 setzte ein riesiger Kran die neue Turmzwiebel auf.[711] 1990 und 1991 wurden das Klostergebäude, die Heizung, Dächer und Fassaden umfangreich saniert.[712] Von 1991 bis 1993 folgte die Renovierung der Kirchenfassade und des Kirchendaches.[713] Einen besonderen Höhepunkt im Leben des Konvents stellte das 800-Jahr-Jubiläum des „Wunderbarlichen Gutes" dar, das in einer Festoktav vom 9. bis 16. Mai 1999 feierlich begangen werden konnte.[714] Am 28. Januar 2008 wurde mit der Konsekration des Zelebrationsaltars die neue Hauskapelle im Erdgeschoss des Klosters eingeweiht. Bedingt durch

710 PA, Provinzrundbrief vom 20.4.1983, S. 2.
711 Hoyer: *Heilig Kreuz*, S. 758–759.
712 PA, Provinzrundbrief vom „Dezember" 1991, S. 3–4.
713 PA, Provinzrundbrief 2–1993, S. 19.
714 *Dominikus* 1–1999, S. 15–16.

Umbauarbeiten im Wohnbereich des Konvents hatten die Brüder ihre frühere Hauskapelle im ersten Stock aufgegeben. Praktische Gründe, v. a. die Notwendigkeit, auch außerhalb der großen Heilig-Kreuz-Kirche Gottesdienste für kleinere Gruppen feiern zu können, hatten aber die Idee einer Hauskapelle nie verschwinden lassen. Ein länger nicht mehr genutzter Meditationsraum im Erdgeschoss bot sich dafür an. Zur Erstellung des dafür nötigen Altars wurden Teile (Säulen, eine Wappenschnitzerei und die marmorne Altarplatte) des Altars verwendet, den Weihbischof Franz Xaver Eberle 1933 für die Hauskapelle des Dominikanerklosters im Otmarsgäßchen konsekriert hatte. Damit knüpfte die neue Kapelle an die Wiedergründungszeit der Dominikaner in Augsburg an.[715]

1999 dehnte die Provinz ihre Präsenz nach Regensburg aus. Die alte Reichsstadt an der Donau war bis zum Beginn des 19. Jahrhunderts Sitz eines bedeutenden Dominikanerkonvents gewesen; das dortige Dominikanerinnennonnenkloster hatte die Säkularisation überlebt. Von 1973 bis 1977 hatte mit P. Hilarius Barth schon einmal ein Mitbruder der süddeutsch-österreichischen Provinz seinen Wohnsitz in Regensburg gehabt und sich für die Übernahme des Rektorats der ehemaligen Dominikanerkirche St. Blasius interessiert, was aber nicht gelungen war. Inzwischen hatten sich die Zeiten allerdings geändert. Das Provinzkapitel von 1998 hatte Regensburg – zusammen mit Bamberg oder Salzburg – als möglichen Ort für einen Stützpunkt für sozusagen ambulante dominikanische Seelsorge in den Blick genommen.[716] Treibende Kräfte hinter der Auswahl des Standorts Regensburg waren Augsburger Mitbrüder, besonders P. Dietmar Schon, die sich bereits bestehende Kontakte mit den Nonnen, einer Gemeinschaft seelsorglich tätiger Dominikanerinnen und mehreren Gruppen dominikanischer Laien vor Ort nutzbar machten. Die ersten Schritte des Fußfassens in Regensburg 1998 beschrieb Schon so:

> „Unsere Angebote in Regensburg bestehen aus sogenannten ‚Dienstagsgesprächen in Heilig Kreuz‘, einem Zyklus von Vorträgen zu spirituellen Themen mit anschließender Gesprächsmöglichkeit. Am 1. Dezember 1999 hat ein zweiter Zyklus mit meditativen Impulsen unter dem Titel ‚Zeit für Gott‘ begonnen. Eine dritte ‚Säule‘ bildet das Jahresprogramm der Laiengemeinschaften. Diese verschiedenen Programme zusammengenommen bedeuten zwei bis drei Angebote im Monat und sollen sich zu einer seelsorglichen dominikanischen

---

715 *Dominikus* (2009 / 10) S. 26–27.

716 APKap 1998, S. 18–19, Nr. 52.

> Präsenz ergänzen. Wir hoffen, dass diese Angebote auf das Interesse der Menschen stoßen, die ihren Glauben erneuern, vertiefen oder wieder entdecken wollen. … Regensburg wurde auch deshalb gewählt, weil unsere Provinz [St.] Albertus Magnus eine besondere Beziehung zu der Stadt hat. Albert war hier von 1260 bis 1262 Bischof. Die ehemalige Dominikanerkirche steht dieser Zeit durch Alter und Stil vergleichsweise nahe. … Dennoch sind historische Gebäude und auch die Wirkungsstätte großer Heiliger nicht der letzte Maßstab für die Auswahl der Standorte unserer seelsorglichen Tätigkeit. Entscheidend sind die Menschen, zu denen wir heute gesandt sind. Angesichts der derzeitigen Personalstärke der Provinz gibt es zwar kein Wiedergründungsprojekt in Regensburg, aber einen gezielten Ausbau unserer seelsorglichen Präsenz. Dass junge Menschen die dominikanische Sendung als ihr eigenes Charisma und ihren persönlichen Auftrag entdecken mögen, ist ein naheliegender Wunsch, den wir in unser Gebet einschließen wollen."[717]

Dieses Seelsorgsangebot wurde gut aufgenommen, wie das Provinzkapitel von 2002 feststellen durfte:

> „Gerade weil es keine feste Niederlassung in Regensburg gibt, waren die am Projekt beteiligten Brüder von vornherein auf Zusammenarbeit mit verschiedenen Institutionen, Gruppen und Personen angewiesen. Die seelsorglichen Beiträge im Zentrum sind mit der Diözese und den Pfarreien abgesprochen. Sie füllen bestehende pastorale Lücken und vermeiden den Aufbau paralleler Strukturen. Hinzu kommt eine Reihe von Aktivitäten außerhalb des Zentrums", nämlich „einmal im Monat eine Messe mit Predigt in der Dominikanerkirche St. Blasius, ein Vortragszyklus über den Hl. Albertus Magnus im Rahmen der Ausstellung im Kreuzgang des ehemaligen Konventsgebäudes. In Vorbereitung ist die Übernahme des Fastenpredigtzyklus 2003 in St. Emmeram, eine Predigt im Hochschulgottesdienst und ein Vortrag im Zusammenhang mit der Hochschulseelsorge."[718]

Daher bat das Provinzkapitel, „die seelsorgliche Präsenz in Regensburg fortzusetzen und nach Möglichkeit weiter zu entwickeln"[719]. Kurz zuvor hatte die Provinz ein Gebäude gegenüber der Blasius-Kirche gekauft, das am 10. September 2001 als sogenanntes Dominikanisches Zentrum eingeweiht werden konnte, weil es doch sinnvoll erschien, einen räumlichen Anknüpfungspunkt für das Pastoralangebot zu bieten.[720] 2006 erklärte das Provinzkapitel Regensburg zur dominikanischen Seelsorgsstelle, im Sinne

717 *St. Dominikuswerk* (2000), S. 9.
718 APKap 2002, S. 21, Nrn. 91 und 93.
719 Ebd., S. 22, Nr. 95.
720 Zur Einweihung: *Dominikus* (2002) S. 42.

einer „pastoralen Zukunftsoption“, an der mit P. Schon auch ein Augsburger Dominikaner nun seinen festen Wohnsitz nahm. Am 1. April 2009 wurde ihm auch das Kirchenrektorat von St. Blasius übertragen.[721] Im selben Jahr wurde diese Präsenz durch zwei ausländische Mitbrüder zu einer kleinen Gemeinschaft ausgebaut.[722]

Freiburg

Das Phänomen der Herausbildung einer Kerngemeinschaft hatte sich im Freiburger Konvent früher als in den anderen Niederlassungen der Provinz entwickelt. Zählte Freiburg-St. Albert bis 1969 noch zwölf Mitbrüder (zehn Priester, zwei Laienbrüder), so waren es 1971 bis 1973 acht, 1977 bis 1987 elf, 1989 acht und danach bis 2003 noch sechs (fünf Priester, ein Laienbruder). Da von 1965 bis 1969 drei der Priester *extra conventum* lebten,[723] 1971 zwei, 1973 einer, von 1977 bis 1987 zwei Priester und ein Laienbruder und 1989 zwei Priester, bestand die im Kloster lebende Gemeinschaft aus entsprechend weniger Mitgliedern.

Relativ dazu konzentrierte der Konvent auch sein Pastoralangebot: Die Provinzkataloge melden bis einschließlich 1967 noch drei Patres als hauptamtliche Volksmissionare; im Katalog von 1969 war davon nicht mehr die Rede, ebensowenig wie von Beichtväterposten, obwohl die Dominikanerinnen von Neusatzeck und anderen Klöstern noch jahrzehntelang von Freiburger Brüdern seelsorgerlich betreut wurden. Bis zum Katalog von 1973 wird auch die Studentenseelsorge noch genannt: P. Ambrosius Ruf, der 1961 die Leitung der Thomas-Morus-Burse übernommen hatte und zum Studentenpfarrer für die Hochschulen Freiburgs ernannt worden war, übernahm 1967 das Amt des Priors des Konvents von Walberberg und schied daher aus der Freiburger Hochschulseelsorge aus. Sein Nachfolger wurde P. Anselm Henssler, der bis Anfang der 1970er Jahre als Seelsorger der Studenten der Pädagogischen Hochschule Freiburg wirkte.[724] Nach seinem Weggang konnte der Konvent die Stelle nicht nachbesetzen.

---

721 PA, ProvinzZeitung 3–4–2009, S. 3.

722 PKat 2013, S. 29.

723 Von diesen stammte einer aus der polnischen Provinz und arbeitete bis 1969 als Hausgeistlicher bei den Dominikanerinnen in Karlsruhe.

724 Leider kam nach dem Provinzkatalog von 1973 erst 1977 wieder ein Katalog heraus,

Abb. 89: Titelblatt des Programmhefts für die „Gesprächskreise" des Freiburger Dominikanerkonvents St. Albert im Wintersemester 2005/06.

Zur Säule der Pastoral der Freiburger Dominikaner hatten sich längst die „Gesprächskreise für Laien" und die Arbeitskreise entwickelt. 1983 konnten die Brüder auf 25 Jahre des Bestehens dieses Projekts zurückblicken:

„Der Versuch, sich in Gesprächskreisen für Laien in einen vertieften Dialog über religiöse und theologische Fragen mit all jenen, die sich dafür interessierten, einzulassen, hat sich gelohnt. Die Absicht, über kontinuierliche, thematisch durchgliederte Vortragsreihen, Diskussionen, intensive Gruppengespräche (dieser Arbeit zugeordnete Predigtreihen in unserer Klosterkirche) Grundfragen des Gott-Welt-Verhältnisses zu erarbeiten, Theologie und Zeitgeschichte, Religion und modernes Leben zueinander in Beziehung zu setzen, religiöses Lebensverständnis und heutiges Weiterleben und Lebensgefühl miteinander in Verbindung zu bringen, hat in diesen zweieinhalb Jahrzehnten bei zahlreichen Gruppen ein unvermindertes und nachhaltiges Echo gefunden. Viele Menschen haben zu uns Kontakt gefunden und mit uns Verbindung gehalten. In einer reichen Sprechzimmertätigkeit konnten wir Menschen persönlich helfen, ihre Lebensprobleme (aufgrund dieser öffentlich vorgetragenen Gott-Welt-Theorie) zu lösen, ihnen helfen, wenigstens ihre Problemlast besser zu verstehen und tapferer zu (er-)tragen. Mut hat uns immer wieder die Anerkennung und der Dank für diese ‚Aufklärung' von Seiten der Menschen gemacht, die sich auf diese Zusammenarbeit eingelassen haben. …
Mit Freude können wir rückblickend feststellen, dass unsere Veranstaltungen nichts von ihrem Anfangselan, ihrer Aktualität und Lebendigkeit verloren haben. Wir haben nicht das Gefühl, dass wir in diesen 25 Jahren in der Routine erstickt sind, eher, dass wir noch am Anfang stehen: Die Probleme unserer Epoche, die Last der Entwicklung in unserer immer größer und zugleich kleiner werdenden Welt, immer fortschrittlicher und gleichzeitig gefährlicher werdenden Zeit, unserer Nöte und unserer Hoffnung auf Leben sind nicht geringer geworden."[725]

---

daher ist das Ende von Hensslers Studentenseelsorge in Freiburg mit diesem Hilfsmittel nicht klar datierbar; 1977 hatte er ein anderes Amt inne.

725 PA, Provinzrundbrief vom 14.12.1983, S. 16 (Zitat aus dem Programmheft der Gesprächskreise für Laien für das Jahr 1983 / 84). Zum thematischen Programm und zur

Abb. 90: Kirche und Kloster St. Martin in Freiburg (Foto: Sebastian Tönnesen, Freiburg im Breisgau).

Allerdings waren mit den Gesprächskreisen keine regelmäßigen Einkünfte verbunden. Um diese Säule tragen zu können, übernahmen mehrere Brüder des Konvents Stellen als Lehrer an Schulen verschiedenen Typs. Dadurch ermöglichten sie es anderen, für die „Gesprächskreise" sozusagen freigestellt zu sein und halfen selbst ebenfalls bei den Gesprächs- und Arbeitskreisen mit. P. Cornelius Paulus leitete die Gesprächs- und Arbeitskreise bis zu seinem Tod 2012. Die Provinzkataloge nennen als sozusagen hauptamtliche Mitarbeiter P. Odilo Kaiser und P. Hyazinth Mayr († 2008). Gleichzeitig bedeutete diese Konzentration nicht den Ausschluss anderer Betätigungsfelder. So wirkte P. Franz Gero Thimm von 1977 bis 1987 als wissenschaftlicher Mitarbeiter und Dozent am Physiologischen Institut der Universität Freiburg, als Assistent an der Sporthochschule Köln, in der Arbeitsgruppe für Suchtforschung am Institut für Neuropsychopharmakologie der Freien Universität Berlin und als wissenschaftlicher Leiter der Abteilung für Verhaltenspharmakologie in einem Forschungsunterneh-

Geschichte siehe auch: Cornelius Paulus: „40 Jahre Gesprächskreise im Dominikanerkloster Freiburg", in: Provinzrundbrief 2–1998, S. 6–9.

Abb. 91: Weihe des Altars der neuen Hauskapelle in St. Martin am 11. April 2013; von links: P. Markus Fischer, P. Martin Grandinger, P. Peter Huynh Thuc Quan Cau, Br. Klaus Limacher, P. Odilo Kaiser, Provinzial P. Christophe Holzer, Erzbischof Robert Zollitsch (PA, Fotosammlung).

men in Reutlingen. P. Donatus Leicher war Lehrer an der Gewerbeschule Freiburg im Fachbereich des Steinmetz-, Stein- und Holzbildhauerhandwerks, Mitglied des Kulturausschusses im Zentralverband des deutschen Handwerks in Bonn als Fachberater des wissenschaftlichen Beirats des Bundesinnungsverbandes des deutschen Steinmetz-, Stein- und Holzbildhauerhandwerks und geistlicher Betreuer der Jungmeistergruppen desselben Verbandes sowie Beiratsmitglied der Arbeitsgemeinschaft Friedhof und Denkmal in Kassel (AFD).

Ab 1991 bestand der Konvent nur mehr aus sieben Brüdern (sechs Priestern, einem Laienbruder). Zum Zeitpunkt des Provinzkapitels von 2002 lag das Durchschnittsalter der Gemeinschaft bei 71 Jahren. Die Provinzleitung wollte das Kloster aber nicht einfach abschreiben und aussterben lassen – umso mehr, da sich in dieser Zeit die Frage nach der Sinnhaftigkeit der Beibehaltung von Augsburg als Ausbildungskonvent stellte, die katholisch-theologische Fakultät der Freiburger Universität aber einen sehr guten Ruf besaß. Daher sollte ein „Erneuerungsprozess" des Freibur-

ger Konvents „auf breiter Basis" in Angriff genommen werden.[726] Dies geschah durch die Eröffnung einer zweiten Niederlassung in der Erwinstraße in Freiburg am 29. März 2004, deren Mitglieder zum Konvent von St. Albert gehörten.[727] Im Studienhaus Erwinstraße lebten zunächst zwei Priester und zwei Studenten; bis 2010 wuchs die Zahl auf fünf Priester und zwei Studenten an. Durch die Assignation 2006 von einem und 2008 eines zweiten Priesters (die allerdings beide *extra conventum* lebten) nach St. Albert stieg auch dort die Personalstärke, sodass 2011 insgesamt wieder 14 Dominikaner (zwölf Priester und zwei Laienbrüder) zum Freiburger Kloster gehörten. Möglich war dies auch durch die Unterstützung aus anderen Provinzen: Von 2004 bis 2007 gehörte ein Mitbruder aus der indischen Provinz dazu, von 2008 bis 2010 einer aus der polnischen Provinz und seit 2011 einer aus der Provinz von Kolumbien. Vom Studienhaus aus konnten die Dominikaner auch wieder Hochschulseelsorgsaufgaben übernehmen, so ab 2005 die Mitarbeit der katholischen Hochschulgemeinde an der KFH und der PH Freiburg und am geistlichen Mentorat. 2008 bis 2010 kam außerdem die Hochschulseelsorge in Offenburg-Kehl hinzu.[728] Darüber hinaus ist seit 2005 auch ein Dominikaner Mitarbeiter am sogenannten „c-punkt" des Stadtdekanats, also an der Freiburger Citypastoral. 2008 wirkte ein Bruder auch als Vikar an der Innenstadtkirche St. Martin. Diese Kirche übergab die Erzdiözese Freiburg 2009 den Dominikanern.[729] Noch während des Umbaus der dortigen Wohnraummöglichkeiten zogen die Brüder im Herbst 2011 aus der Erwinstraße nach St. Martin um. Das Studienhaus wurde als Standort geschlossen. Am 10. Februar 2012 übertrug Ordensmeister Bruno Cadoré, der sich im Rahmen seiner Visitationsreise in der Provinz selbst in Freiburg aufhielt, die Konventsrechte des Konvents von St. Albert auf St. Martin. Erster Prior des neuen Konvents wurde am 11. Februar 2012 P. Sebastian Tönnesen. Am selben Tag wurde die Niederlassung an St. Albert zur *domus filialis* von St. Martin reduziert.[730]

---

726 APKap 2002, S. 17–18, Nrn. 65–68; Zitat S. 18, Nr. 67.

727 Zur Eröffnung: PA, ProvinzZeitung 4–2004, S. 3 und *Dominikus* (2004) S. 30–33.

728 *Dominikus* (2008 / 09) S. 15–18 und PA, ProvinzZeitung 6–2010, S. 12–13.

729 PA, ProvinzZeitung 10–2008, S. 1.

730 Daten laut: PKat 2013, S. 30; siehe auch: PA, ProvinzZeitung 4–2008, S. 8.

Zusammenfassung

Nach diesem Überblick über die letzten 75 Jahre der Geschichte einer Ordensprovinz der Dominikaner in Süddeutschland und Österreich stellt sich die Frage: Was bleibt festzuhalten?

Zunächst einmal das, was diese Darstellung nicht oder viel zu wenig berücksichtigen konnte: Erstens kam Gott darin kaum vor. Als Ordensgemeinschaft der katholischen Kirche verstehen die Predigerbrüder aber den Gottesdienst in Verkündigung, Liturgie und Gebet als den Zweck und die Aufgabe ihrer Existenz. Diese Punkte fanden zwar Erwähnung, aber nur in Hinsicht auf ihre äußerliche Organisation. Ihre Bedeutung, die sie als Antriebskräfte für die Dominikaner der süddeutsch-österreichischen Provinz zwischen 1939 und 2014 hatten und haben, musste vorausgesetzt werden. Jedoch war diese Lücke Absicht: Eine inhaltliche Beschreibung des Gebetslebens und der Theologie dieser Menschen in dieser Zeit hätten jeglichen Rahmen gesprengt – eines Rahmens, der erst durch die historiographische Arbeit geschaffen werden musste, die das Ziel dieser Darstellung war. Zweitens wären diese Inhalte nur über die Lebensgeschichte und Äußerungen der beteiligten Brüder darzustellen gewesen, denn eine sozusagen einzige Verkündigung, einzige Liturgie und ein einziges Gebetsleben gab und gibt es in der Provinz nicht. Gerade die Analyse der Provinzkapitelsakten und anderer offizieller Dokumente hat deutlich gezeigt, dass die Provinzleitung immer nur versucht hat, die theologischen und pastoralen Felder abzustecken, die dann von jedem Mitbruder selbst auf seine Weise zu beackern waren, nicht aber, diese Felder genau zu beschreiben. Abgesehen davon wäre schon die Idee, für diese Festschrift zu jedem Mitglied der Provinz eine historisch einwandfreie Biographie abzufassen, illusorisch. Auch hier musste sich dieser Überblick der Notwendigkeit beugen, zuerst zu versuchen, ein Fundament zu setzen, auf dem Detailstudien aufgebaut werden können.

Nach dieser Rechtfertigung dessen, was fehlt, kommen wir zu dem, was dargestellt werden konnte.

Bedingt durch das Auseinanderbrechen der österreichisch-ungarischen Provinz und die Verselbständigung ihres ungarischen Provinzteils am 8. Mai 1938 waren die Brüder in Österreich alleine nicht mehr in der Lage, eine eigenständige Entität im Dominikanerorden zu bilden. Anstatt den sich aus politischen Gründen nahelegenden Schritt wählen und die österreichischen Klöster an die deutsche Provinz Teutonia anzuschließen – wie ja die Repu-

blik Österreich inzwischen an das Deutsche Reich „angeschlossen" worden war – entschied Ordensmeister Martin Stanislaus Gillet sich dazu, mit Dekret vom 19. Dezember 1938 die Klöster und Brüder in Süddeutschland aus der Teutonia herauszunehmen und mit den österreichischen in einer neuen Provinz unter dem Namen Provincia Germaniae superioris (süd- oder oberdeutsche Provinz) und unter dem Patronat des hl. Alberts des Großen zu vereinen. 1962 wurde der Provinzname auf Provincia Germaniae superioris et Austriae (süddeutsch-österreichische Provinz) erweitert. Zum von Gillet bestimmten Errichtungsdatum, dem 2. Februar 1939, bestand die Provinz aus 143 Brüdern und den Niederlassungen in Freiburg im Breisgau, Augsburg, München, Graz, Friesach, Wien und Retz.

Wenige Monate nach Provinzerrichtung brach im September 1939 der zweite Weltkrieg aus, der nicht nur während seiner Dauer katastrophale Auswirkungen auf die Provinz hatte, sondern dessen Spätfolgen das Leben der Dominikaner in Süddeutschland und Österreich bis weit in die 1960er Jahre hinein prägten: Der Wiederaufbau der durch den Bombenkrieg schwer beschädigten Kloster- und Kirchengebäude band die wenigen finanziellen Mittel und viele personelle Energien. Ersteres zwang die Brüder, bezahlte Anstellungen finden zu müssen, um nach Abbau der Schutthügel auch die Schuldenberge abtragen zu können. Dies führte dazu, dass sich nach 1950 die seelsorgliche Aktivität der süddeutsch-österreichischen Predigerbrüder häufig in den engen Grenzen des Schul- und Diözesandienstes bewegte und sich nur wenige eigene Projekte entwickeln konnten. Dennoch kamen solche Eigenprojekte zustande, z. B. die „Gesprächskreise" am Freiburger Konvent. Zweiteres, die Bindung personeller Energien durch den Wiederaufbau, drückte sich auch als Konzentration auf die Wiederherstellung des Ordenslebens aus, wie es vor dem Krieg Tradition gewesen war. Zur Einführung von Innovationen durch die von den einzelnen Brüdern unter Diktatur und Frontenkampf gewonnenen Erfahrungen konnte sich die süddeutsch-österreichische Provinz nicht aufschwingen – was im Übrigen der Haltung des weltweiten Dominikanerordens zu dieser Zeit entsprach. Erst als die ganze katholische Kirche durch das zweite vatikanische Konzil neue Impulse für sich nutzbar machte, gab es auch bei den Dominikanern größere Veränderungen, die in der Folge auch in der Provinz eingeführt wurden. Der Weltkrieg hatte außerdem ein großes Loch in die Personaldecke der Provinz gerissen; 1946 bestand sie aus 122 Brüdern, von denen einige noch in Kriegsgefangenschaft saßen und eine andere, größere Gruppe bei der Errichtung der Schweizer Provinz 1953 dorthin sozusagen

verloren ging. Gleichzeitig hatten zwischen 1939 und 1945 nur sehr wenige Brüder in den Orden eintreten dürfen. Die Ausbildung und das Studium von Ordensinteressenten zum in der Seelsorge einsetzbaren Dominikaner dauerten jedoch fünf bis sechs Jahre. Nachwuchs tat nach 1945 dringend Not. Für die süddeutsch-österreichische Provinz spezifisch wurde eine weitere Spätfolge des Weltkrieges: Der Aufbau einer Gemeinschaftsidentität war in den wenigen Monaten vor dem Krieg gerade erst in den Gang gekommen. Die kriegsbedingten Einschränkungen, die Zonengrenzen der Nachkriegszeit, vor allem aber die Staatsgrenze, die nach der Wiedergründung der Republik Österreich die Provinz in zwei Teile durchschnitt, waren für die innere Einheit der Provinz hinderlich und machten eine Verdoppelung von Verwaltungsämtern und Ordensstrukturen notwendig. Der ohnehin durch den Wiederaufbau der beschädigten Klöster und Kirchen vorhandene Hang zur Konzentration der Identität, weg von der Provinzebene hin zur lokalen Ebene der einzelnen Niederlassung, wurde dadurch noch verstärkt.

Die 1966 beginnende Welle der Austritte aus dem Orden und die parallel in dieser Zeit fehlenden Neueintritte kürzten die Personaldecke der Provinz drastisch: 1966 bestand die Provinz aus 145 Mitgliedern, 1984 nur mehr aus 82. Diese Personalkrise erschütterte die Provinz nachhaltig; der Weggang von Brüdern, mit denen man lange Jahre zusammengelebt und -gearbeitet hatte, und das anscheinend offensichtliche Desinteresse der jungen Generation am Orden hinterfragte bei denen, die blieben, das Verständnis ihrer Lebensweise. Auch die sich durch Konzil und Generalkapitel in der Provinz angebahnten Veränderungen in den Ordenssatzungen und -strukturen brachten nur eine größere Verunsicherung. Aus ihrer daraus resultierenden Depression wurde die Provinz durch Impulse von außen gerissen, konkret ab 1979 durch den Ordensmeister und seine Kurie. Ebenso von außen, aus benachbarten wie aus weiter entfernt liegenden Provinzen, wie der Teutonia, aus Polen, der Slowakei und besonders aus Indien, wurde der süddeutsch-österreichischen Provinz ab den 1990er Jahren Hilfe zuteil. Gerade in dieser Krise, die tiefer einschnitt als selbst der Weltkrieg und seine Folgen, erwies es sich als segensreich, einem weltweit agierenden und verbreiteten Personalverband anzugehören, nicht nur, weil ausländische Mitbrüder Dienste übernahmen, für die die Provinz selbst kein Personal mehr hatte, sondern vor allem durch die Weitung der Perspektiven auf das Ordensleben, die die geschrumpften und gealterten Gemeinschaften in ihren Klöstern in Süddeutschland und Österreich erfuhren.

Die Provinz nutzte diese Impulse von außen zu einem längst nötigen Selbstfindungsprozess und zu einer Verstärkung der Einheit ihrer Brüder und Klöster untereinander. Dieser Prozess fand seinen Niederschlag auf den Provinzkapiteln nach 1994. Auch dieser Weg wurde – durchaus kritisch – von den Ordensmeistern und ihrer Kurie begleitet. Besonderes Interesse wurde den Leitlinien für die Ausbildung der jungen Brüder gewidmet, außerdem wurden die Verwaltungsstruktur der Provinz und ihre Organe neu geordnet, für die einzelnen Niederlassungen wurde ein Pastoralprofil erstellt und die Standorte wurden evaluiert. Nicht nur der Personalmangel, sondern auch das Problem der mit einzelnen Häusern verbundenen erdrückenden Baulast führten dazu, dass sich die Provinz aus manchen ihrer bisherigen Klöster zurückzog. Andererseits ermöglichten diese Planungen auch die Niederlassung an anderen Standorten und neue Perspektiven für die Mitbrüder. Heute, 2013, leben die 59 zur Dominikanerprovinz des hl. Alberts des Großen in Süddeutschland und Österreich gehörenden Predigerbrüder in den Klöstern St. Martin und St. Albert in Freiburg im Breisgau, Hl. Kreuz in Augsburg, St. Kajetan in München und St. Maria Rotunda in Wien.

Gott loben, segnen und verkünden war in den vergangenen 75 Jahren für die Predigerbrüder nicht immer einfach. Dennoch ist es bisher gelungen. Wenn es vom Herrn ist, wird es bleiben (vgl. Apg 5, 39).

Abkürzungsverzeichnis

ACG	Acta capituli generalis ... [mit Angabe des Tagungsjahres; siehe Literaturverzeichnis]
AGOP	Archivio Generalizio dell'Ordine dei Predicatori, Rom.
APKap	Akten des Provinzkapitels der süddt.-österr. Dominikanerprovinz ... [mit Angabe des Tagungsjahres; siehe Literaturverzeichnis]
ASOP	Analecta sacri ordinis Praedicatorum. Romae 1893–.
	Constitutiones 1932 *Constitutiones fratrum sacri ordinis Praedicatorum reverendissimi P. Fr. Martini Stanislai Gillet, eiusdem ordinis magistri generalis, iussu editae*. Romae 1932.
LCO 1969	*Liber constitutionum et ordinationum ordinis fratrum Praedicatorum iussu Aniceti Fernandez magistri ordinis editus*. Romae 1969.
LCO 2010	*Liber constitutionum et ordinationum fratrum ordinis Praedicatorum iussu Fr. Carlos A. Azpiroz Costa magistri ordinis editus*. Romae 2010,
PA	Provinzarchiv der süddt.-österr. Dominikanerprovinz, Augsburg.
PKat	Provinzkatalog der süddt.-österr. Dominikanerprovinz ... [mit Angabe des Ausgabejahres; siehe Literaturverzeichnis]

Archivalienverzeichnis

Augsburg, Archiv des Dominikanerkonvents an Heilig Kreuz:

Chronik der Dominikaner bei Hl. Kreuz (1935–1962):

Mss. 245 x 190 mm. Brauner Ledereinband, innen mit braun meliertem Papier beklebt, daraus auch Vor- und Nachsatzblatt. Buchdeckel innen und außen ohne Vermerke. Buchblock: 98 Blatt cremefarbiges Papier mit Goldrand; moderne Bleistiftfoliierung, beschrieben fol. 1r-87v, Rest leer. Titelvermerk fol. 1r: „Chronik der Dominikaner bei Hl. Kreuz in Augsburg" (neben Zeichnung eines Kreuzes mit Lilienwappen); abgesehen von Text auch Fotos und andere Beilagen. Umfasst inhaltlich die von mehreren Autoren verfasste Chronik der Dominikaner an Heilig Kreuz in Augsburg vom 1.1.1935 bis Januar 1962. Sprache: Deutsch. Zitiert nach Folii.

Augsburg, Provinzarchiv der süddt.-österr. Dominikanerprovinz:

Chroniken:

Chronik für das Noviziat der oberdeutschen Dominikanerprovinz:

Mss. 330 x 215 mm. Schwarzer Kartoneinband, Rücken und Ecken durch weißen Stoff verstärkt, Buchdeckelinnenseiten mit weißem Papier überklebt; auf Vorderdeckel außen Papierschildchen mit Titelvermerk: „Chronik für das Noviziat der oberdeutschen Dominikanerprovinz", Buchdeckel sonst innen und außen leer, vor fol. 1 ein Pergamentblatt und ein kleinformatigeres Blatt eingeklebt (letzteres be-

malt mit IHS-Monogramm, umgeben von ornamentalem Rahmen). Buchblock: 130 Blatt grauliniertes Papier; gestempelte fehlerhafte Paginierung, beginnend mit p. 2 = fol. 2v (die Paginierung springt zwischen fol. 3v und fol. 4r von S. 4 auf S. 25 (kein Textverlust, kein Blattverlust erkennbar). Textbeginn fol. 1r: „Chronik des Noviziates der oberdeutschen Dominikanerprovinz“ (in der Mitte Zeichnung des Lilienwappens mit Umschrift: Laudare, Benedicere, Praedicare); fol. 1v leer, ab fol. 2r bis fol. 91r = S. 209 beschrieben, Rest leer; auf den Seiten zahlreiche Zeichnungen, gezeichnete Kapitalien und Beilagen, darüber hinaus zahlreiche Loseblattbeilagen. Umfasst die Berichte der Novizen der Provincia Germaniae superioris über ihre Erfahrungen und Aktivitäten vom 2.2.1939 bis September 1951. Sprache: Deutsch. Zitiert nach Paginierung.

Kirchenbauchronik der Münzgrabenkirche:

Autor: Leo Schölzhorn (so laut Unterschrift unter Postskriptum fol. 207r, datiert 14.11.1967). Typoskript. 310 x 210 mm. Drei jeweils mit Paketschnur zusammengeheftete umfangreiche Loseblattsammlungen zwischen je eigenen Kartondeckeln, als vorderer und hinterer Deckel für die ganze Sammlung dienen zwei außen mit grauem, innen mit gelbem Papier beklebte, dazu zweitverwertete Aktenkartone; auf dem vorderen Karton außen Papierschildchen mit Aufschrift: „Kirchenbauchronik“, darunter Stempel. Die Blätter sind unterschiedlicher Größe und bestehen aus verschiedenem Papier- und Kartonmaterial; sie sind teilweise foliiert (fol. 1–207), andere als Beilagen zu bestimmten Folii ausgewiesen, andere nicht markiert. Heft 1: Titel auf vorderem Deckel: „Kirchenbau-Chronik I. Teil: 1944(6). 1953“; 207 Blätter (fol. 1–114). Heft 2: Titel auf vorderem Deckel: „Kirchenbau-Chronik II. Teil: 1954–1961“; 182 Blätter (fol. 115–184). Heft 3: Titel auf vorderem Deckel: „Kirchenbauchronik III. Teil ab 1962“; 59 Blätter (fol. 185–207). Umfasst inhaltlich einen in tagebuchartigem Stil gehaltenen, sehr detaillierten Bericht über die gesamte Bauunternehmung in Graz nach dem zweiten Weltkrieg (Konventsbau und Kirchenbau, Renovierungen und Gebäudeanpassungen, Planungen und Finanzierungen). Dieser Bericht wird illustriert und verdeutlicht durch die Beigabe zahlreicher Fotos, Zeitungsartikel, Broschüren, Einladungskarten u. ä. Sprache: Deutsch. Zitiert nach Folio (da nur einseitig beschrieben, kann die Unterscheidung in recto und verso entfallen).

Provinzialsregesten:

Provinzialsregestenbuch 1 (1939–1966):

Mss. 240 x 190 mm. Roter, geriffelter Plastikeinband, vorne und hinten ohne Vermerke, vorderer und hinterer Innendeckel sowie Vorsatzblatt bedruckt mit grauem Papier mit Ringmuster, ebenfalls ohne Vermerke. Titelvermerk auf S. 1: „Acta prioris provincialis provinciae Germaniae superioris sacri ordinis Praedicatorum“, darunter Stempelabdruck. Buchblock: 94 Blatt blauliniertes Papier; beschrieben fol. 1r-94r; zeitgenössische Tintenpaginierung fol. 1r = pag. 1 – fol. 83r= pag. 85, danach modern mit Bleistift weitergeführt bis Textende. Umfasst inhaltlich die Regesten der Amtszeiten der Provinziäle M. Vetter und A. Gierlich (Februar 1939 – Juni

1956). Sprache: Latein. Zitiert nach Seite, Eintragsdatum und Protokollnummer.
Provinzialsregestenbuch 2 (1966–2010):
Mss. 295 x 210 mm. Einband aus hellrotem kartoniertem Papier. Titelvermerk auf Papierschildchen auf vorderem Einbanddeckel außen: „Regestenbuch des Provinzials d. süddt. österr. Provinz St. Albert ab 1966", Einband sonst innen und außen leer. Buchblock: 90 Blatt blauliniertes Papier ohne Foliierung oder Paginierung; fol. 1r als Titelvermerk: „Regestenbuch des Provinzials", darunter Stempelabdruck; fol. 1v unbeschrieben; 2r–89r beschrieben; 89v–90v leer. Umfasst inhaltlich die Regesten der Amtszeiten der Provinziäle I. Varga, D. Kirchmaier, G. Ruf, H.-U. Steymans und D. Schon (4./8. Juli 1966–23.8.2010). Sprache: Deutsch. Zitiert nach Eintragsdatum und Protokollnummer.

Provinzkonsilsprotokolle:
Liber consiliorum provinciae:
Mss. 350 x 210 mm. Mit grünem Stoff überzogener Kartoneinband, Deckel innen mit hellgrünem Papier beklebt; vordere und hintere Innenseite: Bindung mit aufgeklebtem grauem Stoffstreifen verstärkt; Deckel außen und innen ohne Vermerke; Vorsatzblatt trägt rechts oben den aufgestempelten Vermerk „261C-120-E41" (wohl Warenkennziffer), sonst Vorsatz- und Nachsatzblatt leer. Titelvermerk S. 1: „Liber consiliorum provinciae Germaniae superioris ordinis Praedicatorum ab anno Domini 1939", darunter Stempelabdruck. Buchblock: 120 blauliniierte Blätter, fol. 1r-49v zeitgenössisch paginiert; Paginierung modern S. 99 bis Textende S. 107 fortgeführt; fol. 1r-54r beschrieben (p. 1–107; 3.2.1939–27.11.1991). Sprachen: Latein und Deutsch. Zitiert nach Seite und Sitzungsdatum.
Liber consilii provincialis:
Mss. 325 x 210 mm. Schwarz und grau melierter Kartoneinband, Rücken und Einbandecken mit schwarzem Stoff verstärkt, Innenseiten des Buchdeckels mit weißem Papier überklebt, weißes Vor- und Nachsatzblatt; Titelvermerk auf Papierschildchen auf Vorderdeckel außen: „Liber Consilii Provincialis Provinciae Germaniae Superioris O.P. 1948–1982" (1982 ergänzt durch andere Hand), Deckel und Vorsatz- und Nachsatzblatt sonst leer. Buchblock: 48 graulinierte Blätter, keine Foliierung oder Paginierung; fol. 1 leer; beschrieben fol. 2r–47v, fol. 48 leer (22.4.1948–22.9.1982). Sprachen: Latein und Deutsch. Zitiert nach Sitzungsdatum und -ort.

Serie Provinzrundbriefe:
Typoskripte beginnend am 29.9.1939 bis 1.5.1982; Xeroxkopien vom 2.8.1982 bis 1998 (Nummerierung der Ausgaben von 1–1992 bis 3–1998 unter dem Titel: „Provinzrundbrief der Dominikanerprovinz des hl. Albert in Süddeutschland und Österreich"); Druck 1991 unter dem Titel: „Dominikus. Mitteilungen der Dominikanischen Familie in Süddeutschland und Österreich" (2 Nrn.); ab 2004 unter dem Titel: „ProvinzZeitung für die Dominikaner-Provinz des Hl. Albert in Süddeutschland und Österreich", ab 2010 unter dem Titel: „ProvinzZeitung der Dominikanerprovinz des Hl. Albertus Magnus in Süddeutschland und Österreich".

Einzelne Dokumente:

Relatio de studiis in provincia Teutonia peractis durante bello et tempore immediate subsequente, i. e. ab anno 1939 ad annum 1947. Typoskript.

Brief des Ordensmeisters Vincent de Couesnongle an Provinzial Innozenz Varga und die Mitbrüder der Provinz, Rom, 26.11.1979. Typoskript.

Ratio formationis particularis der Dominikanerprovinz des hl. Albert des Großen in Süddeutschland und Österreich vom 9. Januar 1996. Geändert durch das Provinzkapitel von 1998 und das Provinzkapitel von 2002. Stand: 15. Juli 2003.

Rom, Archivio Generalizio dell'Ordine dei Predicatori:

Serie XIII, Bestände 73 100, 73 100, 76 100, 76 120, 76 123, 76 130 und 76 158.

Gedruckte Quellen

Provinzkataloge (Personalschematismen)

Provincia Imperii:

Schematismus patrum et fratrum ordinis Praedicatorum ad provinciam Imperii, quae e conventibus Bohemiae, Moraviae, Austriae et Hungariae coaluit, pertinentium pro anno 1858. S. l., s. a.

Schematismus patrum et fratrum sacri ordinis Praedicatorum ad provinciam Imperii (Austriaco-Hungarici) pertinentium anno Domini 1905. Viennae 1904.

Schematismus patrum et fratrum sacri ordinis Praedicatorum ad provinciam Austriaco-Hungaricam pertinentium anno Domini 1906. Viennae 1905.

Provincia Austriaco-Hungaricae:

Catalogus conventuum et fratrum provinciae Austriaco-Hungaricae ordinis Praedicatorum simul et coenobiorum sororum ibi existentium ineunte anno 1936. Vác s. a.

Catalogus conventuum et fratrum provinciae Austriaco-Hungaricae ordinis Praedicatorum simul et coenobiorum monialium ac sororum ibi existentium ineunte anno 1938. Budapest s. a.

Provincia Germaniae superioris et Austriae (zitiert: PKat mit Ausgabejahr):

Catalogus provinciae sancti Alberti Magni Germaniae superioris sacri ordinis Praedicatorum (restauratae die 2. Februarii 1939) 1939–1940. Status 1. Octobris 1939. Viennae s. a.

Catalogus provinciae sancti Alberti Magni Germaniae superioris sacri ordinis Praedicatorum (restauratae die 2. Februarii 1939) 1941. Status 1. Aprilis 1941. Viennae s. a.

Catalogus provinciae Germaniae superioris ordinis Praedicatorum 1943. Status 1. Mai[i] 1943. Viennae s. a.

Catalogus provinciae Germaniae superioris sacri ordinis Praedicatorum sub patronatu sancti Alberti Magni 1946. Status 1. Augusti 1946. Viennae (Austria) s. a.

Catalogus provinciae sancti Alberti Magni Germaniae superioris 1948. Status 1. Martii 1948. Viennae (Austria) s. a.

Catalogus provinciae sancti Alberti Magni Germaniae superioris 1949. Status 30. Aprilis 1949. Viennae (Austria) s. a.

Catalogus provinciae sancti Alberti Magni Germaniae superioris 1950–1951. Status 2. Februarii 1951. Vindobonae (Viennae in Austria) s. a.

Catalogus provinciae sancti Alberti Magni Germaniae superioris 1952. Status 7. Martii 1952. Vindobonae (Viennae in Austria) s. a.

Catalogus provinciae sancti Alberti Magni Germaniae superioris 1953. Status 7. Martii. Vindobonae (Viennae in Austria) s. a.

Catalogus provinciae sancti Alberti Magni Germaniae superioris 1955. Status 1. Januarii. Vindobonae (Viennae in Austria) s. a.

Catalogus provinciae sancti Alberti Magni Germaniae superioris 1956. Status 2. Februarii. Vindobonae (Viennae in Austria) s. a.

Catalogus provinciae sancti Alberti Magni Germaniae superioris ordinis Praedicatorum 1957. Status 1. Januarii. Vindobonae (Viennae in Austria) s. a.

Catalogus provinciae sancti Alberti Magni Germaniae Magni superioris ordinis Praedicatorum 1958. Status 1. Januarii. Vindobonae (Viennae in Austria) s. a.

Catalogus provinciae sancti Alberti Magni Germaniae superioris ordinis Praedicatorum 1959. Status 2. Februarii. Vindobonae (Viennae in Austria) s. a.

Catalogus provinciae sancti Alberti Magni Germaniae superioris ordinis Praedicatorum 1960. Status 2. Februarii. Vindobonae (Viennae in Austria) s. a.

Catalogus provinciae sancti Alberti Magni Germaniae superioris ordinis Praedicatorum 1961. Status 2. Februarii. Vindobonae (Viennae in Austria) s. a.

Catalogus provinciae sancti Alberti Magni Germaniae superioris ordinis Praedicatorum 1962. Status 2. Februarii. Vindobonae (Viennae in Austria) s. a.

Catalogus provinciae sancti Alberti Magni Germaniae superioris ordinis Praedicatorum 1964. Status 2. Februarii. Vindobonae (Viennae in Austria) s. a.

Catalogus provinciae sancti Alberti Magni Germaniae superioris et Austriae ordinis Praedicatorum 1965. Status 2. Februarii. Vindobonae (Viennae in Austria) s. a.

Catalogus provinciae sancti Alberti Magni Germaniae superioris et Austriae ordinis Praedicatorum 1966. Status 2. Februarii. Vindobonae (Viennae in Austria) s. a.

Catalogus provinciae sancti Alberti Magni Germaniae superioris et Austriae ordinis Praedicatorum 1967. Status 2. Februarii. Vindobonae (Viennae in Austria) s. a.

Catalogus provinciae sancti Alberti Magni Germaniae superioris et Austriae ordinis Praedicatorum 1969. Status 2. Februarii. Vindobonae (Viennae in Austria) s. a.

Catalogus provinciae sancti Alberti Magni Germaniae superioris et Austriae ordinis Praedicatorum 1971. Status 2. Februarii. Vindobonae (Viennae in Austria) s. a.

Catalogus provinciae sancti Alberti Magni Germaniae superioris et Austriae ordinis Praedicatorum 1973. Status 2. Februarii. Vindobonae (Viennae in Austria) s. a.

Catalogus provinciae sancti Alberti Magni Germaniae superioris et Austriae ordinis Praedicatorum 1977. Status 2. Februarii. Vindobonae (Viennae in Austria) s. a.

Catalogus provinciae sancti Alberti Magni Germaniae superioris et Austriae ordinis Praedicatorum 1979. Status 2. Februarii. Vindobonae (Viennae in Austria) s. a.

Catalogus provinciae sancti Alberti Magni Germaniae superioris et Austriae ordinis Praedicatorum 1981. Status 2. Februarii. Vindobonae (Viennae in Austria) s. a.

Catalogus provinciae sancti Alberti Magni Germaniae superioris et Austriae ordinis Praedicatorum 1984. Status 2. Februarii. Graz 1984.

Catalogus provinciae sancti Alberti Magni Germaniae superioris et Austriae ordinis Praedicatorum 1987. Status 2. Februarii. Graz 1987.

Catalogus provinciae sancti Alberti Magni Germaniae superioris et Austriae ordinis Praedicatorum 1989. Status 2. Februarii. Graz 1989.

Catalogus provinciae sancti Alberti Magni Germaniae superioris et Austriae ordinis Praedicatorum 1991. Status 2. Februarii. Graz 1991.

Catalogus provinciae sancti Alberti Magni Germaniae superioris et Austriae ordinis Praedicatorum 1994. Status 2. Februarii. Graz 1994.

Catalogus provinciae sancti Alberti Magni Germaniae superioris et Austriae ordinis fratrum Praedicatorum 1997. Status 2. Februarii. Graz 1997.

Catalogus provinciae sancti Alberti Magni Germaniae superioris et Austriae ordinis fratrum Praedicatorum 1999. Status 1. Martii. Wien s. a.

Catalogus provinciae sancti Alberti Magni Germaniae Superioris et Austriae ordinis fratrum Praedicatorum 2000. Status 1. Februarii. S.l., s. a.

Provinzkatalog. Dominikaner-Provinz des Hl. Albert in Süddeutschland und Österreich 2003. Status 1. Mai. O.O., o.J.

Provinzkatalog. Dominikaner-Provinz des Hl. Albert in Süddeutschland und Österreich 2004. Status 1. Mai. O.O., o.J.

Provinzkatalog. Dominikaner-Provinz des hl. Albert in Süddeutschland und Österreich 2005. Status 1. Mai. O.O., o.J.

Provinzkatalog. Dominikaner-Provinz des hl. Albert in Süddeutschland und Österreich. Sonderausgabe mit den Änderungen des Provinzkapitels 2006. O.O., o.J.

Provinzkatalog. Dominikaner-Provinz des hl. Albert in Süddeutschland und Österreich 2007. Status 1. April. O.O., o.J.

Provinzkatalog. Dominikanerprovinz des hl. Albert in Süddeutschland und Österreich 2008. Stand 1. Mai. O.O., o.J.

Provinzkatalog. Dominikanerprovinz des hl. Albert in Süddeutschland und Österreich 2009. Stand 1. Mai. O.O., o.J.

Provinzkatalog. Dominikanerprovinz des hl. Albert in Süddeutschland und Österreich 2010. Stand 1. Mai. O.O., o.J.

Provinzkatalog. Dominikanerprovinz des hl. Albert in Süddeutschland und Österreich 2011. Stand 18. Juni. O.O., o.J.

Provinzkatalog. Dominikanerprovinz des hl. Albert in Süddeutschland und Österreich 2011. Stand Dezember. O.O., o.J.

Provinzkatalog. Dominikanerprovinz des hl. Albert in Süddeutschland und Österreich 2013. Stand Juni. O.O., o.J.

Generalkapitelsakten

(zitiert: ACG mit Tagungsjahr)

Acta capituli generalis ordinis Praedicatorum Viterbii in conventu s. Mariae ad Quercum celebrati in festo Pentecostes a die 21. ad diem 28. Maii 1904. Romae 1904.

Acta capituli generalis diffinitorum sacri ordinis Praedicatorum Viterbii in conventu s. Mariae ad Quercum celebrati in festo Pentecostes a die 18 ad diem 27 Maii 1907. Romae 1907.

Acta capituli generalis diffinitorum sacri ordinis Praedicatorum Romae in conventu s. Sabinae celebrati a die 25 ad diem 28 Septembris anno Domini 1938. Romae 1938.

Acta capituli generalis electivi sacri ordinis fratrum Praedicatorum in conventu ss. Dominici et Xysti ad ‚Angelicum' a die 21. ad diem 30. Septembris 1946. Romae 1946.

Acta capituli generalis diffinitorum sacri ordinis fratrum Praedicatorum Calarogae in conventu sancti patris Dominici a die 24. ad diem 30. Septembris 1958. Romae 1958.

Acta capituli generalis electivi sacri ordinis fratrum Praedicatorum Tolosae in conventu sancti Thomae Aquinatis a die 22. ad diem 29. Julii 1962. Romae 1962.

Acta capituli generalis diffinitorum sacri ordinis fratrum Praedicatorum Bogotae in conventu sancti patris Dominici a die 15. ad diem 23. Julii 1965. Romae 1965.

Acta capituli generalis provincialium ordinis fratrum Praedicatorum River Forest in conventu sancti Thomae de Aquino a die 30. Augusti ad diem 24. Octobris 1968. Romae 1968.

Acta capituli generalis diffinitorum ordinis fratrum Praedicatorum Calarogae in conventu sancti Dominici a die 17 mensis Julii ad diem 8 mensis Augusti 1995. Romae 1995.

Acta capituli generalis priorum provincialium Bononiae in conventu patriarcali sancti patris Dominici a die 13. mensis Julii ad diem 4. mensis Augusti 1998. Romae 1998.

Provinzkapitelsakten

Acta congregationis intermediae provinciae Imperii ordinis fratrum Praedicatorum Pragae in conventu ad s. Aegydium abbatis diebus 8.-9. Maii 1900 celebrati. Viennae 1900.

Acta capituli provincialis provinciae Austriaco-Hungaricae ordinis fratrum Praedicatorum Viennae in conventu s. Mariae Rotundae diebus 1.–3. Maii 1906 celebrati. Viennae 1906.

Acta capituli provincialis provinciae Austriaco-Hungaricae ordinis Praedicatorum 1922 et acta congregationis intermediae provinciae Austriaco-Hungaricae 1924 celebratae. Egrae 1924.

Acta capituli provincialis provinciae Bohemiae diebus 14. mensis Septembris anni 1926 et sequenti in conventu s. Aegydii abbatis Pragae celebrati. Pragae 1927.

Acta capituli provincialis provinciae Austriaco-Hungaricae ordinis fratrum Praedicatorum Viennae in conventu ad basilicam ss. rosarii diebus 15.–19. Maii 1934 celebrati. Viennae 1934

der süddt.-österr. Provinz (zitiert: APKap mit Tagungsjahr):

Acta capituli provincialis provinciae Germaniae superioris (s. Alberti Magni) ordinis fratrum Praedicatorum Viennae in conventu ad basilicam ss. rosarii diebus 3–6. Maii 1939 celebrati. Viennae 1939.

Acta capituli provincialis provinciae Germaniae superioris ordinis fratrum Praedicatorum Viennae in conventu ad basilicam ss. rosarii assignati, sed propter temporum difficultates in vico Altenstadt apud ecclesiam monialium ordinis nostri ‚Ad salutationem angelicam' diebus 7.–10. Novembris 1946 celebrati. Viennae 1946.

Acta capituli provincialis provinciae s. Alberti Magni Germaniae superioris s. ordinis Praedicatorum 1950. Vindobonae 1950.

Acta capituli provincialis 1954 provinciae sancti Alberti Magni Germaniae superioris sacri ordinis Praedicatorum. Viennae s. a.

Acta capituli provincialis provinciae Germaniae superioris sacri ordinis Praedicatorum 1958. Vindobonae s. a.

Acta capituli provincialis provinciae sancti Alberti Magni Germaniae superioris sacri ordinis Praedicatorum 1962. Viennae s. a.

Akten des Provinzkapitels der Provinz des hl. Albert in Süddeutschland und Österreich sacri ordinis Praedicatorum 1966. Graz o.J.

Akten des Provinzkapitels der Dominikanerprovinz des hl. Albert in Süddeutschland und Österreich 1970 und das Provinzstatut. Wien o.J.

Akten des Provinzkapitels der Provinz des hl. Albert des Großen in Süddeutschland und Österreich sacri ordinis Praedicatorum 1975. Graz o.J.

Akten des Provinzkapitels der Provinz des hl. Albert des Großen in Süddeutschland und Österreich sacri ordinis Praedicatorum 1979. O.o., o.J.

Akten des Provinzkapitels der Dominikanerprovinz des hl. Albert des Großen in Süddeutschland und Österreich 1982 und das Provinzstatut. Graz 1982. Als Beilage in eigener Broschüre: *Hinweise für die liturgischen Feiern im Predigerorden (Anhang zu den Akten des Provinzkapitels 1982, Nr. 35)*. Graz 1982.

Akten des Provinzkapitels der Dominikanerprovinz des hl. Albert des Großen in Süddeutschland und Österreich 1986. Graz 1987.

Akten des Provinzkapitels der Dominikanerprovinz des hl. Albert in Süddeutschland und Österreich 1990. Graz o.J.

Akten des Provinzkapitels der Dominikanerprovinz des hl. Albert des Großen in Süddeutschland und Österreich 1994. O.O., o.J.

Dominikaner. Die süddeutsch-österreichische Ordensprovinz. Visitationsbrief und Provinzkapitel 1998. Augsburg o.J.

Dominikaner-Provinz des hl. Albert in Süddeutschland und Österreich. Provinzkapitel 2002 und Provinzstatut. Augsburg o.J.

Dominikaner-Provinz des hl. Albert in Süddeutschland und Österreich. Akten des Provinzkapitels 2006. O.O., o.J.

Dominikaner-Provinz des hl. Albert in Süddeutschland und Österreich. Provinzkapitel 2011. Provinzstatut. O.O., o.J.

Periodika

Analecta sacri ordinis Praedicatorum. Romae 1893–.

Der Funke. Wien 1992–1998.

Die ewige Weisheit. Freiburg im Breisgau 1954–1963.

Ewige Weisheit. Regensburg 1972–1977.

St. Dominikuswerk. Wien-Graz 1952–2000.

Dominikus. Mitteilungen der dominikanischen Familie in Süddeutschland und Österreich. Augsburg 2000–2004. *Dominikus. Aus Leben und Wirken der dominikanischen Familie in Süddeutschland und Österreich*. Augsburg 2005–2008. *Dominikus. Leben und Wirken der dominikanischen Familie in Süddeutschland und Österreich*. Augsburg 2009.

Literatur

750 Jahre Dominikanerorden. Wien 1966.

Bertram, Walther: Die Wiederinstandsetzung dreier Augsburger Kirchen, in: *Zeitschrift des historischen Vereins für Schwaben* 58 (1961), 113–126.

Collectio inchoationum, declarationum et ordinationum. Romae 1966

Constitutiones fratrum sacri ordinis Praedicatorum reverendissimi P. Fr. Martini Stanislai Gillet, eiusdem ordinis magistri generalis, iussu editae. Romae 1932.

Dekret über die zeitgemäße Erneuerung des Ordenslebens, in: *Lexikon für Theologie und Kirche*. Zweite, völlig neu bearbeitete Auflage. Ergänzungsband 2: *Das zweite vatikanische Konzil. Konstitutionen, Dekrete und Erläuterungen*. Freiburg-Basel-Wien 1967, S. 250–307.

Groll, Thomas: St. Ulrich und Afra als Mutterpfarrei von St. Anton, St. Canisius und St. Wolfgang, in: *Benediktinerabtei St. Ulrich und Afra in Augsburg (1012–2012). Geschichte, Kunst, Wirtschaft und Kultur einer ehem. Reichsabtei. Festschrift zum tausendjährigen Jubiläum*. (Jahrbuch des Vereins für Augsburger Bistumsgeschichte, 45. Jahrgang, 2011) Textband. Augsburg 2011, S. 1296–1356.

Groothuis, Rainer Maria: *Im Dienste einer überstaatlichen Macht. Die deutschen Dominikaner unter der NS-Diktatur*. Münster 2002.

Hodel, Bernard / Bedouelle, Guy / Müller, Franz E.: Die Schweizer Dominikanerprovinz (seit 1953), in: *Die Dominikaner und Dominikanerinnen in der Schweiz*. Hrsg. vom Kuratorium der Helvetia Sacra. (Helvetia Sacra, Abteilung IV, Bd. 5) Basel 1999. 1. Teil, 167–172.

Hoyer, Wolfram: Achtzig Jahre Dominikaner an Augsburg / Heilig Kreuz (1932–2012), in: *Jahrbuch des Vereins für Augsburger Bistumsgeschichte*. 47. Jahrgang. 2013. Augsburg 2013, S. 625–761.

Ders.: Das erste halbe Jahrhundert der Geschichte der Autobahnkirche ‚Maria –

Schutz der Reisenden', in: *50 Jahre Maria – Schutz der Reisenden Adelsried*. Hg. v. Wolfram Hoyer. Augsburg (im Selbstverlag) 2008.

Ders: Die Provinzen und Kongregationen des Dominikanerordens in: *Dominican History Newsletter* (Roma), Teil 1 in Nr. 10 (2001) S. 248–288, Teil 2 in Nr. 11 (2002) 265–295 und Teil 3 in Nr. 12 (2003) S. 187–209.

In deine Hände lege ich meinen Geist. Die sieben Worte Jesu am Kreuz. Hg. v. Max Svoboda, Cécile Nordegg, Jonathan Berkh. Wien 2001.

Klosterführer aller Zisterzienserklöster im deutschsprachigen Raum. Hg. v. Peter Pfister. Strasbourg 1997.

Liber constitutionum et ordinationum ordinis fratrum Praedicatorum iussu Aniceti Fernandez magistri ordinis editus. Romae 1969.

Liber constitutionum et ordinationum fratrum ordinis Praedicatorum iussu Fr. Carlos A. Azpiroz Costa magistri ordinis editus. Romae 2010.

Lohrum, Meinolf: *Die Wiederanfänge des Dominikanerordens in Deutschland nach der Säkularisation 1856–1875*. (Walberberger Studien, Theologische Reihe 8) Mainz 1971.

Nordegg, Cécile / Berkh, Jonathan: *Stabat Mater*. Hg. von der r.k. Pfarrei Graz-Münzgraben. Graz-Wien 2003.

Resch, Rudolf: *Retzer Heimatbuch*. 1. Band: Neuauflage (Reproduktion) Retz 1984. 2. Band: Retz 1951.

Siebertz, Paul: *Karl Fürst zu Löwenstein. Ein Bild seines Lebens und Wirkens nach Briefen, Akten und Dokumenten*. München-Kempten 1924.

Statuten des Vereines St.-Dominikus-Werk. Albertinum [sc. Graz-Wetzelsdorf] 1933.

Venchi, Innocentius: *Catalogus hagiographicus ordinis Praedicatorum*. Editio altera, revisa et aucta. Romae 2001.

Vetter, Marianus: *Erlöste Menschlichkeit. Die Frucht des Geistes*. Wien 1947.

Walz, Angelus: *Dominikaner und Dominikanerinnen in Süddeutschland (1225–1966)*. Freising 1967.

Ders.: *Wahrheitskünder. Die Dominikaner in Geschichte und Gegenwart 1206–1960*. Essen 1960.

Verzeichnis der Autorinnen und Autoren

Johannes Bunnenberg OP, Dr. theol., Provinzial der Dominikanerprovinz Teutonia, Köln.

Bruno Cadoré OP, Dr. med. Dr. theol., Meister des Ordens der Predigerbrüder, Rom.

Michael Carragher OP STL, Dr. theol., DCL, Dip. Lett. Lat., Professor für Kirchenrecht an der päpstlichen Universität des hl. Thomas von Aquin „Angelicum" in Rom.

Manfred Entrich OP, Dr. theol., Geschäftsführer des Instituts für Pastoralhomiletik (IPH), Düsseldorf.

Sr. M. Dominika Geyder OP, Kloster Hl. Keuz, Regensburg.

Paul Dominikus Hellmeier OP, Dr. phil. Mag. theol., Dozent an der Hochschule für Philosophie in München.

Benedikta Hintersberger OP, Dr. theol., Priorin der Dominikanerinnen von St. Ursula, Augsburg.

Christophe Holzer OP, Lic. theol. Lic. jur. can., Provinzial der Dominikanerprovinz des hl. Albert in Süddeutschland und Österreich, München.

Philippe André Holzer OP, Dr. phil. Lic. theol., Professor für Philosophie an der Päpstlichen Universität des hl. Thomas von Aquin „Angelicum" in Rom.

Wolfram Hoyer MAS OP, Dr. theol., Dominikanerkonvent an Heilig Kreuz, Augsburg.

Erich Leitenberger, Prof., Chefredakteur der „kathpress", Pressesprecher der österreichischen Bischofskonferenz und von Erzbischof Christoph Kardinal Schönborn, Wien.

Rupert Johannes Mayer OP, Dr. theol. Dipl. Ing. Univ., Professor am Internationalen Theologischen Institut in Trumau/Niederösterreich.

Wolfgang Müller OP, Dr. theol. Dr. theol. habil., Professor für Dogmatik an der Universität Luzern.

Gabriele Neu-Yilik, Dr. rer. nat., Privatdozentin für Molekulare Medizin an der Universität Heidelberg, Einzelmitglied im Laienzweig des Dominikanerordens.

Paul Schäferskuüpper OP, Dr. phil. Mag. theol., Prior des Dominikanerkonvents an Heilig Kreuz, Augsburg.

Christoph Kardinal Schönborn OP, Dr. theol., Erzbischof der Erzdiözese Wien.

Aurelia Spendel OP, Dr. theol., Dominikanerin von St. Ursula, Augsburg.

Wolfgang Hariolf Spindler OP, Dipl.-Jur., Dr. theol., Professor für Politische Philosophie und Sozialethik an der Philosophisch-Theologischen Hochschule in St. Pölten.

Martin Staszak OP, Dr. theol. Sacr. Script. Lic., Hochschulpfarrer der KHG Edith Stein der Universität Freiburg im Breisgau.

Hans Ulrich Steymans OP, Prof. Dr. theol., Mag. phil., Professor für Altes Testament am Departement für Biblische Studien der theologischen Fakultät der Universität Freiburg in der Schweiz.

Franz Gero Thimm OP, Dr. rer. nat. habil., Lect. theol., Privatdozent an der Universität Freiburg im Breisgau.

Benedict Thomas Viviano OP, Dr. phil., Mag. theol., SSL (Rom), Mag. art., em. Professor für Neues Testament der Universität Freiburg in der Schweiz.

Paul Heribert Welte OP, Dr. theol., em. Professor der theologischen Fakultät der Fujen-Universität in Taipei.

Jochen Wolffgramm, Dr. rer. nat., em. Professor für biologische Suchtforschung der Universität Tübingen.